Volume 2 • 2008

WHAT DO
I READ
NEXT?

A Reader's Guide to Current Genre Fiction

- Fantasy
- Popular Fiction
- Romance
- Horror
- Mystery
- Science Fiction
- Historical
- Inspirational
- Western

ISSN 1052-2212

Volume 2 • 2008

WHAT DO I READ NEXT?

A Reader's Guide
to Current
Genre Fiction

- Fantasy
- Popular Fiction
- Romance
- Horror
- Mystery
- Science Fiction
- Historical
- Inspirational
- Western

DANIEL S. BURT
DON D'AMMASSA
NATALIE DANFORD
STEFAN DZIEMIANOWICZ
JIM HUANG
MELISSA HUDAK
KRISTIN RAMSDELL
CLAY REYNOLDS

GALE
CENGAGE Learning

Detroit • New York • San Francisco • New Haven, Conn • Waterville, Maine • London

What Do I Read Next 2008, Volume 2

Project Editor: Marie Toft

Editorial: Dana Ferguson, Jaclyn Hermesmeyer

Editorial Support Services: Tom Potts

Composition and Electronic Prepress: Gary Leach, Evi Seoud

Product Design: John Watkins

Manufacturing: Rita Wimberley

For product information and technology assistance, contact us at **Gale Customer Support, 1-800-877-4253.**
For permission to use material from this text or product, submit all requests online at **www.cengage.com/permissions.**
Further permissions questions can be emailed to **permissionrequest@cengage.com**

Gale
27500 Drake Rd.
Farmington Hills, MI, 48331-3535

LIBRARY OF CONGRESS CONTROL NUMBER 82-15700

ISBN-13: 978-1-4144-0019-8
ISBN-10: 1-4144-0019-5

ISSN: 1052-2212

Printed in the United States of America
1 2 3 4 5 6 7 12 11 10 09 08

Contents

Introduction

Thousands of books are published each year intended for devoted fans of genre fiction. Dragons, outlaws, lovers, murderers, monsters, and aliens abound on our own world or on other worlds, throughout time—all featured in the pages of fantasy, western, romance, mystery, horror, science fiction, historical, inspirational, and popular fiction. Given the huge variety of titles available each year, added to the numbers from previous years, readers can be forgiven if they're stumped by the question "What do I read next?" And that's where this book comes in.

Designed as a tool to assist in the exploration of genre fiction, *What Do I Read Next?* guides the reader to both current and classic recommendations in nine widely read genres: Mystery, Romance, Western, Fantasy, Horror, Science Fiction, Historical, Inspirational, and Popular Fiction. *What Do I Read Next?* allows readers quick and easy access to specific data on recent titles in these popular genres. Plus, each entry provides alternate reading selections, thus coming to the rescue of librarians and booksellers, who are often unfamiliar with a genre, yet must answer the question frequently posed by their patrons and customers, "What do I read next?"

Details on Titles

Volume 2 of this year's edition of *What Do I Read Next?* contains entries for titles published primarily in the last half of 2008. These entries are divided into sections for Mystery, Romance, Western, Fantasy, Horror, Science Fiction, Historical, Inspirational, and Popular Fiction. Experts in each field compile the entries for their respective genres. The experts also discuss topics relevant to their genres in essays that appear at the beginning of each section.

The criteria for inclusion of specific titles vary somewhat from genre to genre. In genres such as Romance and Mystery, where large numbers of titles are published each year, the inclusion criteria are more selective, with the experts attempting to select the recently published books that they consider best. In genres such as Horror and Western, where the amount of new material is relatively small, a broader range of titles is represented, including many titles published by small or independent houses and some young adult books.

The entries are listed alphabetically by main author in each genre section. Most provide the following information:

- **Author or editor's** name and real name if a pseudonym is used. Co-authors, co-editors, and illustrators are also listed where applicable.
- **Book title.**
- **Date and place of publication; name of publisher.**
- **Series name.**
- **Story type:** Specific categories within each genre, identified by the compiling expert. Definitions of these types are listed in the "Key to Genre Terms" section.
- **Subject(s):** Gives the subject matter covered by the title.
- **Major character(s):** Names and brief descriptions of up to three characters featured in the title.
- **Time period(s):** Tells when the story takes place.
- **Locale(s):** Tells where the story takes place.
- **What the book is about:** A brief plot summary.
- **Where it's reviewed:** Citations to reviews of the book, including the source of the review, date of the source, and the page on which the review appears. Reviews are included from genre-specific sources such as *Locus* and *Affaire de Coeur*, as well as more general reviewing sources such as *Booklist* and *Publishers* Weekly.
- **Other books by the author:** Titles and publication dates of other books the author has written, useful for those wanting to read more by a particular author.
- **Other books you might like:** Titles by other authors written on a similar theme or in a similar style. These titles further the reader's exploration of the genre.

Indexes Answer Readers' Questions

The nine indexes in *What Do I Read Next?* used separately or in conjunction with each other, create many pathways to the featured titles, answering general questions or locating specific titles. For example:

"Are there any new Maisie Dobbs books?"

The SERIES INDEX lists entries by the name of the series of which they are a part.

"I like Regency Romances. Can you recommend any new ones?"

The GENRE INDEX breaks each genre into story types or more specialized areas. In the Romance genre for example, there is a story type heading "Regency." For the definitions of story types, see the "Key to Genre Terms."

"I'm looking for a story set in Paris."

The GEOGRAPHIC INDEX lists titles by their locale. This can help readers pinpoint an area in which they may have a particular interest, such as their home town, another country, or even Cyberspace.

"Do you know of any science fiction stories set during the 22nd century?"

The TIME PERIOD INDEX is a chronological listing of the time settings in which the main entry titles take place.

"What books are available that feature teachers?"

The CHARACTER DESCRIPTION INDEX identifies the major characters by occupation (e.g. Accountant, Editor, Librarian) or persona (e.g. Cyborg, Noble woman, Stowaway).

"Has anyone written any new books with Sherlock Holmes in them?"

The CHARACTER NAME INDEX lists the major characters named in the entries. This can help readers who remember some information about a book, but not an author or title.

"What has Laurell K. Hamilton written recently?"

The AUTHOR INDEX contains the names of all authors featured in the entries and those listed under "Other books you might like."

The TITLE INDEX includes all main entry titles and all titles recommended under "Other books by the author" and "Other books you might like" in one alphabetical listing. Thus a reader can find a specific title, new or old, then go to that entry to find out what new titles are similar.

"I'm interested in books that depict military life."

The SUBJECT INDEX is an alphabetical listing of all the subjects covered by the main entry titles.

The indexes can also be used together to narrow down or broaden choices. A reader interested in Mysteries set in New York during the 19th century would consult the TIME PERIOD INDEX and GEOGRAPHIC INDEX to see which titles appear in both. Time Travel is a common theme in Science Fiction but occasionally appears in other genres such as Fantasy and Romance. Searching for this theme in other genres would enable a reader to cross over into previously unknown realms of reading experiences. And with the AUTHOR and TITLE indexes, which include all books listed under "Other books by the author" and "Other books you might like," it is easy to compile an extensive list of recommended reading, beginning with a recently published title or a classic from the past.

Also Available Online

The entries in this book can also be found online in Gale's new *Books & Authors* database. This electronic product encompasses over 130,000 books, including genre fiction, mainstream fiction, and nonfiction. All the books included in the online version are recommended by librarians or other experts, award winners, or appear on bestseller lists. The user-friendly functionality allows users to refine their searching by using several criteria, while making it easy to identify similar titles for further research and reading. *Books & Authors* is updated with new information several times a year. For more information about *Books & Authors*, please visit Gale online at gale.cengage.com.

Suggestions Are Welcome

The editors welcome any comments and suggestions for enhancing and improving *What Do I Read Next?* Please address correspondence to the Editor, *What Do I Read Next?*, at the following address:

Gale, Cengage Learning

27500 Drake Rd.

Farmington Hills, MI 48331-3535

Phone: 248-699-GALE

Toll-free: 800-347-GALE

Fax: 248-699-8054

About the Genre Experts

Daniel S. Burt (Historical Fiction) Burt is a writer and college professor who teaches undergraduate courses at Trinity College and graduate literature courses at Wesleyan University, where he was a dean for nine years. He is the author of *The Chronology of American Literature* (Houghton Mifflin, 2004), *What Historical Novel Do I Read Next?* Volumes 1-3 (Gale, 1997-2003), *The Novel 100* (Facts on File, 2003), *The Literary 100* (Facts on File, 2001), *The Biography Book* (Greenwood/Oryx, 2001). His latest book is *Drama 100* (Facts on File, 2007). He is the academic director for an annual series of educationally-based workshops held in Ireland (www.discoverytours.ws). When not teaching and traveling to Ireland, he lives with his wife on Cape Cod, Massachusetts.

Don D'Ammassa (Science Fiction, Horror, and Fantasy) D'Ammassa was the book reviewer for *Science Fiction Chronicle* for almost thirty years. He has had fiction published in fantastic magazines and anthologies and has contributed essays to a variety of reference books dealing with fantastic literature. D'Ammassa is the author of the novels *Blood Beast* (Windsor, 1988), *Servants of Chaos* (Leisure, 2002), *Scarab* (Five Star, 2004), *Haven* (Five Star, 2004), *Narcissus* (Five Star, 2007), and the nonfiction works *Encyclopedia of Science Fiction* (Facts on File, 2005), the *Encyclopedia of Fantasy and Horror* (Facts on File, 2006), and the *Encyclopedia of Adventure Fiction* (Facts on File, 2008).

Natalie Danford (Popular Fiction) Danford is the author of *Inheritance*, a novel published by St. Martin's Press. She is also coeditor of the annual *Best New American Voices* anthology series, which introduces emerging writers. An experienced freelance writer and book critic, Natalie has published articles and reviews in *People, The Los Angeles Times, Salon,* and many other publications.

Stefan Dziemianowicz (Horror Fiction) Dziemianowicz is a medical editor for a New York-based law book publisher. He authored the definitive study, *The Annotated Guide to Unknown and Unknown Worlds* (Starmont House, 1991) and is also the author of *Bloody Mary and Other Tales for a Dark Night* (Barnes and Noble, 2000). He has co-edited numerous horror and mystery anthologies,

among them the Bram Stoker Award-winning *Horrors! 365 Scary Stories* (Barnes and Noble, 1998). Dziemianowicz also writes features on horror fiction for *Publishers Weekly.*

Jim Huang (Mystery Fiction) Huang has sold mystery books for 20 years, including stints in Boston, Kalamazoo, Michigan, and now Carmel, Indiana, where he and his wife own The Mystery Company, a bookstore devoted to the genre. From 1982 through 2005, Huang edited and published The Drood Review, a mystery book review newsletter. He has edited reference books for mystery lovers, including *100 Favorite Mysteries of the Century* (winner of the Anthony and Agatha Awards for best nonfiction of 2000), *They Died in Vain: Overlooked, Underappreciated and Forgotten Mystery Novels* (winner of the Agatha, Anthony and Macavity Awards for best nonfiction of 2002) and *Mystery Muses: 100 Classics That Inspire Today's Mystery Writers* (a nominee for the Agatha Award for best nonfiction of 2006), the latter co-edited with Austin Lugar. Since 2000, he has volunteered as the Program Director for Magna Cum Murder, a festival for mystery lovers that takes place each October in Muncie, Indiana. He is the co-chair of the 2009 Boucheron, the World Mystery Convention scheduled for Indianapolis in October 2009. In 2006, Huang was elected to the board of Sisters in Crime, an international organization devoted to combating discrimination against women in the mystery genre; he is the first "brother" to serve on the board in this organization's 20 year history. Huang lives with his wife, Jennie Jacobson, and their two daughters in Carmel.

Melissa Hudak (Inspirational Fiction) Hudak is a medical librarian for Methodist Medical Center in Peoria, Illinois. She was previously employed in public libraries and wrote a column on inspirational literature for *Library Journal.*

Kristin Ramsdell (Romance Fiction) Ramsdell is a librarian at California State University, East Bay and is a nationally known speaker and consultant on the subject of romance fiction. Besides writing articles about the romance genre, she writes a romance review column for *Library Journal* and is the author of *Romance Fiction: A Guide to the Genre* (Libraries Unlimited, 1999) and its predecessor,

Happily Ever After: A Guide to Reading Interests in Romance Fiction (Libraries Unlimited, 1987). She was named Librarian of the Year by Romance Writers of America in 1996 and received in 2007 the Melinda Helfer Fairy Godmother Award from *Romantic Times* Magazine.

Clay Reynolds   (Western Fiction) Native Texan novelist and scholar, Clay Reynolds has penned more than eight hundred publications ranging from short fiction, poems, essays, reviews and twelve published volumes. He holds academic degrees from the University of Texas at Austin, Trinity University, and the University of Tulsa. His novels include *The Vigil, Franklin's Crossing*, and *The Tent-maker*. His most recent books are *Ars Poetica* and *Threading the Needle*. His nonfiction books include *Taking Stock: A Larry McMurtry Casebook, A Hundred Years of Heroes: A Centennial History of the Southwestern Exposition and Livestock Show*, and *The Plays of Jack London*. His work has won numerous awards, and he is a National Endowment for the Arts Fellow. He is a member of the Texas Institute of Letters and serves as professor of Arts and Humanities at the University of Texas at Dallas. His most recent work includes a collection of essays, *Of Snakes and Sex and Playing in the Rain*, and a collection of short fiction, *Sandhill County Lines*. Reynolds lives in Lowry Crossing, a community near McKinney, Texas, with his wife Judy, a Medical Technologist.

Contributors

John Charles   (Romance Fiction) Charles, a reference librarian and retrospective fiction selector for the Scottsdale Public Library, was named 2002 Librarian of the Year by the Romance Writers of America. Charles reviews books for *Library Journal, Booklist*, the *Chicago Tribune*, and *VOYA(Voice of Youth Advocates)* and co-authors VOYA's annual "Clueless: Adult Mysteries with Young Adult Appeal" column. John Charles is co-author of *The Mystery Readers' Advisory: The Librarian's Clues to Murder and Mayhem* (ALA, 2001). Along with co-author Shelley Mosley, Charles has twice been the recipient of the Romance Writers of America's Veritas Award.

Shelley Mosley   (Romance Fiction) Retired library manager Shelley Mosley has co-authored several nonfiction books: The Suffragists in Literature for Youth; Romance Today: An A-to-Z Guide to Contemporary American Romance Writers; The Complete Idiot's Guide to the Ultimate Reading List;and Crash Course in Library Supervision. With John Charles, she has won two Romance Writers of America's Veritas awards. Mosley, Romance Writers of America's 2001 Librarian of the Year, reviews books for both Booklist and Library Journal. She also writes romantic comedies with Deborah Mazoyer under the pen name Deborah Shelley. Their novels have been published by Kensington and, most recently, Avalon Books.

Key to Genre Terms

The following is a list of terms used to classify the story type of each novel included in What Do I Read Next? along with brief definitions of the terms. To find books that fall under a particular story type heading, see the Genre Index.

Action/Adventure ❚ Minimal detection; not usually espionage, but can contain rogue police or out of control spies.

Adult ❚ Fiction dealing with adult characters and mature, developed ideas.

Adventure ❚ The character(s) must face a series of obstacles, which may include monsters, conflict with other travelers, war, interference by supernatural elements, interference by nature, and so on.

Alternate History ❚ A story dealing with how society might have evolved if a specific historical event had happened differently, e.g., if the South had won the American Civil War.

Alternate Intelligence ❚ Story featuring an entity with a sense of identity and able to self-determine goals and actions. The natural or manufactured entity results from a synergy, generally unpredictable, of individual elements. This subgenre frequently involves a computer-type intelligence.

Alternate Universe ❚ More accurately, in most cases, alternate history, in which the South won the Civil War, the Nazis triumphed, etc. The idea is a venerable one in SF.

Alternate World ❚ The story starts out in the everyday world, but the main character is transported to an alternate/parallel world by supernatural means.

Amateur Detective ❚ Detective work is performed by a non-professional rather than by police or a private detective.

Americana ❚ A romance set in the present that features themes that are particularly American; often focuses on small-town life.

Ancient Evil Unleashed ❚ The evils may take familiar forms, like vampires undead for centuries, or malevolent ancient gods released from bondage by careless humans, or ancient prophecies wreaking havoc on today's world. The so-called *Cthulhu Mythos* originated by H.P. Lovecraft, in which *Cthulhu* is prominent among a pantheon of ancient evil gods, is a specific variation of this.

Anthology ❚ A collection of short stories by different authors, usually sharing a common theme.

Apocalyptic Horror ❚ Traditionally, horrors that signal or presage the end of the world, or the world of the characters, and the establishment of a new, possibly very sinister order.

Arts ❚ Fiction that incorporates some aspect of the arts, whether it be music, painting, drama, etc.

Biblical Fiction ❚ Novels that take their plots or characters from the Bible.

Black Magic ❚ Magic directed toward malevolent ends, as distinct from white magic, which is directed toward benevolent ends. Witchcraft is commonly thought of as a black art. Voodoo consists of mysterious rites and practices, including sorcery, magic and conjuration, and often has evil goals.

Carnival-Circus Horror ❚ Derived from its setting, especially the freakish world of the sideshow, in which the distorted or horrific is the norm and is sometimes used as a distorting mirror to reveal hidden selves.

Chase ❚ A traditional Western in which the action of the plot is based on some form of pursuit.

Child-in-Peril ❚ The innocence of childhood is often used to heighten the intensity and unpredictability of evil.

Collection ❚ A book of short stories by a single author.

Coming-of-Age ❚ A story in which the primary character is a young person, usually a teenager. The growth of maturity is chronicled.

Contemporary ❚ A story set in the present.

Contemporary/Exotic ❚ Set in the present but with an especially unusual or exotic setting, e.g., the tent of a desert sheik or a boat on the Amazon.

Contemporary/Fantasy ❚ A contemporary story that makes use of fantasy or supernatural elements.

Contemporary/Innocent ❚ Story set in the present that contains little or no sex.

Contemporary/Mainstream ❚ A story set in the present that would be more properly categorized as general fiction rather than a work in a specific genre.

Contemporary Realism ❚ An accurate representation of characters, settings, ideas, themes in the present day. Not idealistic in nature.

Curse ❚ Words said when someone wishes evil or harm on someone or something, such as a witch's or prophet's curse.

Cyberpunk ❚ Usually applied to the stories by a group of writers who became prominent in the mid-1980s, such as

William Gibson and his *Necromancer* (1984). The "cyber" is derived from cybernetics, nominally the study of control and communications in machines. These books also feature a downbeat, punk sensibility reminiscent of the hardboiled school of detective fiction writers.

Disaster ▌ A tale recounting some event or events seriously disruptive of the social fabric but not as serious as a holocaust.

Domestic ▌ Fiction relating to household and family matters. Concerned with psychological and emotional needs of family members.

Doppelganger ▌ A double or alter ego, popularized in the works of E.T.A. Hoffmann, Edgar Allan Poe, and Robert Louis Stevenson.

Dystopian ▌ The antonym of utopian, sometimes called anti-utopian, in which traditionally positive utopian themes are treated satirically or ironically and the mood is downbeat or satiric.

End of the World ▌ A story that concerns the last events following some sort of disaster.

Erotic Horror ▌ Sexuality and horror are often argued to be inextricably linked, as in Bram Stoker's *Dracula* and Sheridan Le Fanu's "Carmilla," although others have argued that they are antithetical. Sexuality became increasingly explicit in the 1980s, sometimes verging on the pornographic, as in Brett Easton Ellis' *American Psycho*.

Espionage ▌ Involving the CIA, KGB, or other organizations whose main focus is the collection of information from the other side. Can be either violent or quiet.

Espionage Thriller ▌ Plot contains a high level of action and suspense relating to espionage.

Ethnic ▌ A work in which the ethnic background of the characters is integral to the story. Usually the focus is on an American ethnic minority group (e.g., African American, Asian American, Native American, Latino) and the two main characters are members of this group.

Evil Children ▌ The presumed innocence of a child is replaced with adult-like malevolence and cunning, contradicting the reader's usual expectations.

Family Saga ▌ Stories focusing on the problems or concerns of a family; estrangement and reunion are common themes.

Fantasy ▌ A story that contains some fantasy or supernatural elements.

Femme Fatale ▌ A seductress for whom men abandon careers, families, and responsibilities and who feels no pity or compunction in return; a common figure in history and literature.

First Contact ▌ Any story about the initial meeting or communication of humans with extraterrestrials or aliens. The term may take its name from the eponymous 1945 story by Murray Leinster.

Future Shock ▌ A journalistic term derived from Alvin Toffler's 1970 book and which refers to the alleged disorientation resulting from rapid technological change.

Futuristic ▌ A story with a science fiction setting. Often these stories are set on other planets, aboard spaceships or space stations, or on Earth in an imaginary future or, in some cases, past.

Gay/Lesbian Fiction ▌ Stories portraying homosexual characters or themes.

Generation Starship ▌ If pseudoscientific explanations involving faster-than-light drives are rejected, then the time required for interstellar travel will encompass many human generations.

Genetic Manipulation ▌ Sometimes called genetic engineering, this assumes that the knowledge exists to shape creatures, human or otherwise, using genetic means, as in *Brave New World* (1932).

Ghost Story ▌ The spirits of the dead, who can be benevolent, as in Charles Dickens, or malevolent, as in the tales of M.R. James.

Gothic ▌ A story with a strong mystery suspense plot that emphasizes mood, atmosphere, and/or supernatural or paranormal elements. Unexplained events, ancient family secrets, and a general feeling of impending doom often characterize these tales. These stories are most often set in the past.

Gothic Family Chronicle ▌ A story often covering several generations of a family, many of whose members are typically evil, perverted, or loathsome, and in which family violence is common. The family may live in a decaying mansion suggestive of those in 18th century Gothic novels.

Hard Science Fiction ▌ Stories in which the author adheres with varying degrees of rigor to scientific principles believed to be true at the time of writing, principles derived from hard (physical, biological) rather than soft (social) sciences.

Haunted House ▌ Literally, a house visited by ghosts, usually with evil intentions in horror fiction, but sometimes the subject of comedy.

Historical ▌ Set in an earlier time frame than the present.

Historical/American Civil War ▌ Set during the American Civil War, 1861-1865.

Historical/American Revolution ▌ Set during the American Revolutionary period.

Historical/American West ▌ Set in the Western portion of the United States, usually during the second half of the 19th century. Stories often involve the hardships of pioneer life (Indian raids, range wars, climatic disasters, etc.) and the main characters (most often the hero) can be of Native American extraction.

Historical/American West Coast ▌ Set in the American Far West (California, Oregon, Washington, or Alaska). Stories often focus on the Gold Rush and the tension between Spanish Land Grant families and immigrants from the Pacific Rim, usually China.

Historical/Americana ▌ A story dealing with themes unique to the American experience.

Historical/Ancient Egypt ▌ A novel set during the time of the pharaohs from the fourth century B.C. to the first century A.D. and the absorption of Egypt into the Roman Empire.

Historical/Ancient Greece ▌ Set during the flowering of the ancient Greek civilization, particularly during the age of Pericles in the 5th century B.C.

Historical/Ancient Rome ▌ Covering the history of Rome from its founding and the Roman Republic before Augustus through the decline and fall of the Roman Empire in the fifth century.

Historical/Antebellum American South ▌ Set in the American Old South (prior to the Civil War).

Historical/Canadian West ▌ Set in the western or frontier portions of Canada, usually during the 19th century. Stories most often revolve around the hardships of frontier life.

Historical/Colonial America ▌ Set in America before the American Revolution, 1620-1775. Stories featuring the Jamestown Colony, the Salem Witch Trials, and the French and Indian Wars are especially popular.

Historical/Depression Era ▌ Set mainly in America during the period of economic hardship brought on by the 1929 Stock Market Crash that continued throughout the 1930s.

Historical/Edwardian ▌ Set during the reign of Edward VII of England, 1901-1910.

Historical/Eighteenth Century ▌ A work of fiction set during the eighteenth century.

Historical/Elizabethan ▌ A novel set during the reign of Elizabeth I of England (1558-1603). There is some overlap with the last part of the Historical Renaissance category but the emphasis is British.

Historical/Exotic ▌ Setting is an unusual or exotic place.

Historical/Fantasy ▌ A historical work that makes use of fantasy or supernatural elements.

Historical/French Revolution ▌ Set during the French Revolution, 1789-1795.

Historical/Georgian ▌ Set during the reigns of the first three "Georges" of England. Roughly corresponds to the 18th century. Stories often focus on the Jacobite Rebellions and the escapades of Bonnie Prince Charlie.

Historical/Mainstream ▌ Historical fiction that would be more properly categorized as fiction rather than a specific genre.

Historical/Medieval ▌ Set during the Middle Ages, approximately the fifth through the fifteenth centuries. Stories feature battles, raids, crusades, and court intrigues; plot-lines associated with the Battle of Hastings (1066) are especially popular.

Historical/Napoleonic Wars ▌ Set between 1803-1815 during the wars waged by and against France under Napoleon Bonaparte.

Historical/Post-American Civil War ▌ Set in the years following the Civil War/War Between the States, generally from 1865 into the 1870s.

Historical/Post-American Revolution ▌ Set in the years immediately following the Civil War, 1865-1870s.

Historical/Post-French Revolution ▌ Set during the years immediately following the French Revolution; stories usually take place in France or England.

Historical/Pre-History ▌ Set in the years before the Middle Ages.

Historical/Regency ▌ A novel that is set during the Regency period (1811-1820).

Historical/Renaissance ▌ Novel set in the years of the Renaissance in Europe, generally lasting from the 14th through the 17th centuries.

Historical/Roaring Twenties ▌ Usually has an American setting and takes place in the 1920s.

Historical/Russian Revolution ▌ These stories are set around and during the 1917 Russian Revolution.

Historical/Seventeenth Century ▌ A work of fiction set during the 17th century. Stories of this type often center around the clashes between the Royalists and the Cromwellians and the Restoration.

Historical/Tudor Period ▌ A novel set during the Tudor dynasty in England (1485-1603). Roughly corresponds to the Renaissance, but the emphasis is British. Overlaps with the Elizabethan period, which is marked by the reign of Elizabeth Tudor.

Historical/Victorian ▌ Set during the reign of Queen Victoria, 1837-1901. This designation does not include works with a predominately American setting.

Historical/Victorian America ▌ Set in America, usually the Eastern part, during the Victorian Period, 1837-1901.

Historical/War of 1812 ▌ Set during the British-U.S. conflict which lasted from 1812 to 1814.

Historical/World War I ▌ Set during the First World War, 1914-1918.

Historical/World War II ▌ Set in the years of the Second World War, 1939-1945.

Holiday Themes ▌ Fiction that focuses on or is set during a particular holiday or holiday season (e.g., Christmas, Valentine's Day, Mardi Gras).

Horror ▌ Refers to stories in which interest in the events, the intellectual puzzle characteristic of much of SF, is subordinated to a feeling of terror or horror by the reader, which could result from a variety of causes, including a disaster or an invasion of earth.

Humor ▌ Story with an amusing story line.

Immortality ▌ Usually includes extreme longevity, resulting from fountains of youth, elixirs, or something with a pseudoscientific basis.

Indian Culture ▌ These novels center on the lives, customs, and cultures of characters who are American Indians or who lived among the Indians.

Indian Wars ▌ Often traditional Westerns, these stories are set during the period of the Indian wars and rely on this warfare for plots, characters, and themes.

Inspirational ▌ A novel with an uplifting, often Christian theme, and usually considered "innocent."

Invasion of Earth ▌ An extremely common theme, often paralleling historical events and reflecting fears of the time. Most invasions are depicted as malign, only occasionally benign.

Legal ▌ Main focus is on a lawyer, though it does not always involve courtroom action.

Legend ❚ A story based on a legend, myth, or fairy tale that has been rewritten.

Lesbian/Contemporary ❚ A story with lesbian protagonists set in the present.

Lesbian/Historical ❚ Historical fiction with lesbian protagonists.

Light Fantasy ❚ There is a great deal of humor throughout the story and it is almost guaranteed to have a happy ending.

Literary ❚ Relates to the nature and knowledge of literature; can be applied to setting or characters.

Lost Colony ❚ Stories centering around a colony on another world that loses contact with or is abandoned by its parent civilization and the type of society that evolves under those conditions. Conflict usually arises when contact is re-established between the colony and its home world.

Magic Conflict ❚ The main conflict of the story stems from magical interference. Protagonists may be caught in the middle of a conflict between sorcerers or may themselves be engaged in conflict with other sorcerers.

Magic Realism ❚ A style of prose fiction writing in which the author blends the realism of describing ordinary places and incidents with fantastic, dreamlike, or mythical events and does not differentiate between the real and the magical.

Man Alone ❚ A lone man, alienated from the society that would normally support him, faces overwhelming dangers.

Medical ❚ Stories in which medical themes are dominant.

Military ❚ Stories have a military theme; may deal with life in the armed forces or military battles.

Modern ❚ Reflection of the present time period.

Mountain Man ❚ Any story in which the principal characters are mountain men and women, living in mountain areas remote from civilization and depending upon their own resourcefulness for survival.

Multicultural ❚ A romance in which the ethnic background of the characters is integral to the story.

Mystery ❚ Usually a story where a crime occurs or a puzzle must be solved.

Mystical ❚ Fiction dealing with spiritual elements. Miraculous or supernatural characteristics of events, characters, settings, and themes.

Nature in Revolt ❚ Tales in which normally docile plants or animals suddenly turn against humankind, sometimes transformed (giant crabs resulting from radioactivity, predatory rats, plagues, blobs that threaten London or Miami, etc.).

Occult ❚ An adjective suggesting fiction based on a mystical or secret doctrine, but sometimes referring to supernatural fiction generally. Implies that there is a reality beyond the perceived world that only adepts can penetrate.

Paranormal ❚ Novel contains supernatural elements. Story may include ghosts, UFOs, aliens, demons, and haunted houses among other unexplained phenomenon.

Parody ❚ A narrative that follows the form of the original but usually changes its sense to nonsense, thus making fun of the original or its ideas.

Police Procedural ❚ A story in which the action is centered around a police officer.

Political ❚ The novel deals with political issues that are skewed by the use and presence of fantastic elements.

Possession ❚ Domination, usually of humans, by evil spirits, demons, aliens, or other agencies in which one's own volition is replaced by an outside force.

Post-Disaster ❚ Story set in a much degraded environment, frequently involving a reduction in population and the resulting loss of access to processes, resources, technology, etc.

Post-Holocaust ❚ The events following a world-wide disaster, often the result of human folly rather than natural events (collision with a meteor, etc.).

Post-Nuclear Holocaust ❚ The events following a world-wide nuclear disaster.

Private Detective ❚ Usually detection, involving a professional for hire.

Psychic Powers ❚ Parapsychological or paranormal powers.

Psychological ❚ Fiction dealing with mental or emotional responses.

Psychological Suspense ❚ Tales in which the psychological exploration and quirks of characters generate suspense and plot.

Quest ❚ The central characters are on a journey filled with dangers to reach some worthwhile goal.

Ranch Life ❚ The basic cowboy story, in which the plot and characters are inextricably bound up in the workings of a ranch.

Reanimated Dead ❚ These can take many forms, such as mummies and zombies (often the result of Voodoo).

Regency ❚ A light romance involving the British upper classes, set during the Regency Period, 1811-1820. During this time, the Prince of Wales acted as Prince Regent because of the incapacity of his father, George III. In 1820, "Prinny" became George IV. These stories, in the style of Jane Austen, are essentially comedies of manners and the emphasis is on language, wit, and style. Georgette Heyer set the standard for the modern version of this genre. This designation is also given to stories of similar type that may not fit precisely within the Regency time period.

Reincarnation ❚ A tale in which the horror arises in connection with the reincarnation of one of the characters.

Religious ❚ Religion of any sort plays a primary role in the plot.

Revenge ❚ A character who has suffered an unjust loss returns to take vengeance. This is one of the most common traditional themes.

Robot Fiction ❚ From the Jewish Golem to the traditional clanking bucket of bolts to the human-like android, robots in various guises have been among us for centuries. The term comes from Karl Capek's play, *R.U.R.*, which stands for Rossum's Universal Robots. Robots are often surrogates for humans and may be treated seriously or comically.

Romance ▌ Stories involving love affairs and love stories; deals with the emotional attachments of the characters.

Romantic Suspense ▌ Romance with a strong mystery suspense plot. This is a broad category including works in the tradition of Mary Stewart, as well as the newer women-in-jeopardy tales by writers such as Mary Higgins Clark. These stories usually have contemporary settings but some are also set in the past.

Saga ▌ A multi-generational story that usually centers around one particular family and its trials, tribulations, successes, and loves.

Satanism ▌ Suggests worship of evil rather than benevolent gods, the antithesis of conventional theism, whether Christianity or other religions. Evil demons are Satan writ small and usually lack the awful majesty of their parent.

Satire ▌ Fiction written in a sarcastic and ironic way to ridicule human vices or follies; usually using an exaggeration of characteristics to stress a point.

Science Fantasy ▌ A somewhat vague term in which there are "rational" elements from SF and "magical" or "fanciful" elements from fantasy, which hopefully cohere in a plausible story.

Science Fiction ▌ Although the story has been classified in another genre, there are strong elements of science fiction.

Serial Killer ▌ A multiple murderer, going back to Bluebeard and up to Ed Gein, who inspired Robert Bloch's *Psycho*.

Series ▌ A number of books united either by continuing characters and situations or by a common theme. Series books may appear under a single author's name or each book in the series may be by a different author.

Small Town Horror ▌ The coziness and intimacy of a small community is disrupted by some sort of horrific happening, suggesting an unjustified placidity and complacency on the part of the citizens.

Space Colony ▌ A permanent space station, usually orbiting Earth but in principal located in deep space or near other planets or stars.

Space Opera ▌ Intergalactic adventures; westerns in space; a specialized form of the genre type Adventure.

Supernatural Vengeance ▌ Punishment inflicted by God or a godlike creature, whether justly or capriciously.

Sword and Sorcery ▌ Often a muscle-bound swordsman, who is innocent of thought and common sense, up against evil sorcerers and sorceresses, who naturally lose in the end because they are evil.

Techno-Horror ▌ Suggests a catastrophe with horrific elements resulting from a scientific miscalculation or technological hubris; Victor Frankenstein's unnamed monster or a plague resulting from a laboratory mishap.

Techno-Thriller ▌ Stories in which a technological development, such as an invention, is linked to a series of suspenseful (thrilling) events.

Theological ▌ Stories in which religion or religious belief plays an important role.

Time Travel ▌ A story in which characters from one time are transported either literally or in spirit to another time period. The time shifts are usually between the present and another historical period.

Traditional ▌ Traditional stories may deal with virtually any time period or situation, but they are related by shared conventions of setting and characterization.

Trail Drive ▌ Any story in which a cattle drive (or, more rarely, a drive of sheep or horses) is a major plot component.

UFO ▌ Unidentified Flying Objects, literally, although sometimes used more generally to refer to any object of mysterious origin or intent.

Urban ▌ Stories set in large cities; usually the tone of the novel is gritty and realistic and may involve issues such as drugs and gangs.

Utopia ▌ A large, often influential, story type that takes its name from Thomas More's 1516 book. Usually refers to a society considered better by the author, even if not perfect. Aldous Huxley's *Island* (1962) is a utopia, whereas his more famous *Brave New World* (1932) is a dark twin, a dystopia.

Vampire Story ▌ Based on mythical bloodsucking creatures possessing supernatural powers and various forms, both animal and human. The concept can be traced far back in history, long before Bram Stoker's famous novel, *Dracula*.

Wagon Train ▌ A book that deals with wagon trains traveling across the American West.

Werewolf Story ▌ Were is Old English for man, suggesting the ancient lineage of a creature that once dominated a world in which witches and sorcerers were equally feared. Sometimes used to refer to any shape shifter, whether wolves or other animals.

Wild Talents ▌ The phrase comes from Charles Fort's writings and usually refers to parapsychological powers such a telepathy, psychokinesis, and precognition, collectively called psychic or psi phenomena.

Witchcraft ▌ Characters either profess to be or are stigmatized as witches or warlocks, and practitioners of magic associated with witchcraft. This can include black magic or white magic (e.g., Wicca).

Young Adult ▌ A marketing term for publishers; one or more of the central characters is a teenager often testing his or her skills against adversity to achieve a greater degree of maturity and self-awareness. A category used by librarians to shelve books of likely appeal to teenage readers.

Young Readers ▌ A novel with characters, plot, and vocabulary primarily aimed at juveniles.

Award Winners

Mystery Awards
by Jim Huang

The Agatha Awarded on April 26, 2008 at the Malice Domestic convention for work published in 2007. Nominations and voting by the membership. Books must be traditional mysteries that do not rely on excessive violence. The award is a teapot and is named, of course, for Agatha Christie.

Best Novel: *A Fatal Grace* by Louise Penny

Best First Novel: *Prime Time* by Hank Phillippi Ryan

Best Nonfiction: *Arthur Conan Doyle: A Life in Letters* by Jon Lellenberg, Daniel Stashower and Charles Foley

The Edgar Nominations and final voting by committees composed of active members of The Mystery Writers of America. The awards for books published in 2007 were announced at the MWA annual banquet in New York City on May 1, 2008. The award is a statue of Edgar Allan Poe.

Best Novel: *Down River* by John Hart

Best First Novel: *In the Woods* by Tana French

Best Paperback Original: *Queenpin* by Megan Abbott

Best Critical/Biographical: *Arthur Conan Doyle: A Life in Letters* by Jon Lellenberg, Daniel Stashower and Charles Foley

Mary Higgins Clark Award: *Wild Indigo* by Sandi Ault

The Dilys Named for Dilys Winn, the founder of Murder Ink, the world's first brick and mortar mystery bookstore, this award is voted upon by members of the Independent Mystery Booksellers Association and given to the book they "most enjoyed" selling in 2007. The winner was announced on March 8, 2008 during the Left Coast Crime convention in Denver, Colorado.

The Winner: *Thunder Bay* by William Kent Kruger

The Thriller Administered by a committee of the International Thriller Writers organization. The awards for books that were published in 2007 were announced on July 12, 2008 during ThrillerFest in New York City.

Best Novel: *The Ghost* by Robert Harris

Best First Novel: *Heart-Shaped Box* by Joe Hill

Best Paperback Original: *The Midnight Road* by Tom Piccirilli

Romance Awards
by Kristin Ramsdell

As romance fiction has attained increased recognition as a legitimate literary genre, various publications, organizations, and groups have developed to support the interests of its writers and readers. As part of this mission, a number of these offer awards to recognize the accomplishments of the practitioners. Some awards are juried and are presented for excellence in quality and style of writing; others are based on popularity and are selected by the readers. Usually awards are given for a particular work by a particular writer; however, some awards are presented for a body of work produced over a number of years (a type of career award) and others are given for various types of contributions to romance fiction in general. The included categories may change over time to reflect the changing nature of the genre. The Romance Writers of America and the *Romantic Times* are the sponsors of most of the awards listed below.

Romance Writers of America Awards

These awards for excellence in romance fiction writing are presented by the Romance Writers of America at the annual RWA conference in July. The following awards were presented at the 2008 conference in San Francisco, California.

RITA Awards for Published Novels These awards are presented by the Romance Writers of America for the best romance novel published during 2007. Named for Rita Clay Estrada, RWA's first president, RITAs for published works are given in a number of categories, some of which have changed over the years. This year's winners are as follows:

First Book: *Dead Girls Are Easy* by Terri Garey

Contemporary Series Romance: *Snowbound* by Janice Kay Johnson

Contemporary Series Romance (Suspense/Adventure): *Treasure* by Helen Brenna

Young Adult Romance: *Wicked Lovely* by Melissa Marr

Historical Romance: *Lessons of Desire* by Madeline Hunter

Regency Historical Romance: *The Secret Diaries of Miss Miranda Cheever* by Julia Quinn

Paranormal Romance: *Lover Revealed* by J.R. Ward

Romantic Suspense: *Ice Blue* by Anne Stuart

Contemporary Single Title: *Catch of the Day* by Kristan Higgins

Inspirational: *A Touch of Grace* by Linda Goodnight

Novella: "Born in My Heart" by Jennifer Greene (Included in the anthology *Like Mother, Like Daughter*.)

Novel with Strong Romantic Elements: *Silent in the Grave* by Deanna Raybourn

Golden Heart Awards Presented by the Romance Writers of America for the best romance novel manuscript by an unpublished writer. Golden Hearts are given in a number of categories, some of which have changed over the years. The 2008 awards are as follows:

Contemporary Series Romance: "Under a Harvest Moon" by Joleen Wieser

Contemporary Series Romance: Suspense/Adventure: "The Midnight Effect" by Pamela Fryer

Historical Romance: "Wanting Finian" by Kris Kennedy

Regency Historical Romance: *Mistaken by Moonlight* by Susan Gee Heino

Paranormal: "Soul Provider" by Annette McCleave

Romantic Suspense "Sweet Deceit" by Julie Stevens

Contemporary Single Title Romance: "Money, Honey" by Susan Seyfarth

Inspirational Romance: "Running from Trouble" by Kit Wilkinson

Young Adult Romance: "The Cinderella Society" by Kay Cassidy

Novel with Strong Romantic Elements: "The Devil You Know" by Christa Selnick

Borders Awards Presented by Borders and Waldenbooks for the best-selling romances of the previous year. The following awards were for 2007 and were presented at the 2008 RWA Annual conference.

Historical Romance : *Beware a Scot's Revenge* by Sabrina Jeffries

Contemporary Romance: *Dockside* by Susan Wiggs

Hardcover Romance: *Shadow Music* by Julie Garwood

Debut Author, Trilogy: *The Prey, The Hunt, The Kill* by Allison Brennan

Multicultural Romance: *Midnight Dreams* by Kayla Perrin

Paranormal Romance: *Silver Master* by Jayne Castle

Debut Author: *Kiss of Midnight* by Lara Adrian

Romantic Suspense: *Up Close and Dangerous* by Linda Howard

Romantic Comedy: *Natural Born Charmer* by Susan Elizabeth Phillips

Greatest Sales Growth: Linda Lael Miller for the McKettrick series

Romantic Times Bookclub Awards

Romantic Times Bookclub Reviewer's Choice Awards Presented by *Romantic Times Bookclub Magazine* for outstanding romances published in the previous year. Selection is done by the *RT* romance reviewers. Categories may vary from year to year. The awards for books published in 2007 and announced at the *Romantic Times* Booklovers Convention in Pittsburgh, Pennsylvania, at the Awards Luncheon on April 18, 2008.

Best First Series Romance: *The Secret Dreams of Emily Porter* by Judith Raxten

Best Continuity Novel: *Line of Sight* by Rachel Caine (Silhouette's Athena Force series)

Best Harlequin American: *The Texas Ranger* by Jan Hudson

Best Harlequin Blaze: *Stripped* by Julie Leto

Best Harlequin Everlasting Love: *The House on Briar Hill Road* by Holly Jacobs

Best Harlequin Intrigue: *Wolf Moon* by Patricia Rosemoor

Best Harlequin Next: *Prime Time* by Hank Phillippi Ryan

Best Harlequin Presents: *The Tycoon's Princess Bride* by Natasha Oakley

Best Harlequin Romance: *Rescued: Mother-To-Be* by Trish Wylie

Best Harlequin Superromance: *Baby Makes Three* by Molly O'Keefe

Best Kimani Romance: *Just About Sex* by Ann Christopher

Best Silhouette Nocturne: *Raintree: Sanctuary* by Beverly Barton

Best Silhouette Desire: *Stranded with the Tempting Stranger* by Brenda Jackson

Best Silhouette Romantic Suspense: *Seducing the Mercenary* by Loreth Anne White

Best Silhouette Special Edition: *His Brother's Gift* by Mary J. Forbes

Best Steeple Hill Love Inspired: *The Heart of Grace* by Linda Goodnight

Best Steeple Hill Love Inspired Suspense: *Dangerous Secrets* by Lyn Cote

Best Inspirational Romance: *Chasing Fireflies* by Charles Martin

Historical Romance of the Year: *Mine Till Midnight* by Lisa Kleypas

Best First Historical Romance: *Claiming the Courtesan* by Anna Campbell

Best Innovative Historical Romance: *The Hourglass* by Barbara Metzger

Best Historical Love & Laughter: *Bedding the Heiress* by Cathy Maxwell

Best American-Set Historical Romance: *A Reason to Believe* by Maureen McKade

Best British Isles-Set Historical Romance: *Just Wicked Enough* by Lorraine Heath

Best Regency-Set Historical Romance: *A Dangerous Beauty* by Sophia Nash

Best Scotland-Set Historical Romance: *Beware a Scot's Revenge* by Sabrina Jeffries

Best Historical Paranormal: *The Twilight Lord* by Bertrice Small

Best Historical Romantic Adventure: *Her Secret Fantasy* by Gaelen Foley

Best Sensual Historical Romance: *Sinful Between the Sheets* by Barbara Pierce

Best Historical Fiction: *A Week from Sunday* by Dorothy Garlock

Best Historical Biography: *Privilege and Scandal* by Janet Gleeson

Best Historical K.I.S.S. Hero: Zhi-Gang from *Tempted Tigress* by Jade Lee

Best Historical Gothic: *Dark Prince* by Eve Silver

Best Erotic Romance: *Juicy* by Noelle Mack

Best Erotic Fiction: *House of Dark Delights* by Louisa Burton

Best Futuristic Erotic Romance: *Damnation* by Nathalie Gray

Best Futuristic Romance: *Driven* by Eve Kenin

Best Science Fiction Novel: *The Last Colony* by John Scalzi

Best Fantasy Novel: *A Companion to Wolves* by Sarah Monette and Elizabeth Bear

Best Urban Fantasy Novel: *Halfway to the Grave* by Jeaniene Frost

Best Urban Fantasy Protagonist: Rachel Morgan in *For a Few Demons More* by Kim Harrison

Best Epic Fantasy Novel: *The Name of the Wind* by Patrick Rothfuss

Best Contemporary Romance: *All About Evie* by Beth Ciotta

Best Romantic Suspense: *Die for Me* by Karen Rose

Best Romantic Intrigue: *No Regrets* by Shannon K. Butcher

Best Vampire Romance: *Lover Unbound* by J.R. Ward

Best Contemporary Shapeshifter Romance: *Holy Smokes* by Katie MacAlister

Best Paranormal Romance: *Touch of Madness* by C.T. Adams and Cathy Clamp

Best Paranormal Action-Adventure Romance: *Caressed by Ice* by Nalini Singh

Best Paranormal Romantic Suspense: *The Survivors* by Dinah McCall

Best African-American Romance: *Not His Type* by Chamein Canton

Best African-American Fiction Novel: *Pleasure Seekers* by Rochelle Alers

Best Small Press Contemporary Paranormal: *Immaculate Deception* by Sherry Morris

Best Small Press Romance: *a Gentle Rain* by Deborah Smith

Best Women's Fiction Novel: *Loving Frank* by Nancy Horan

Best Chick Lit: *Forget About It* by Caprice Crane

Best Young Adult Novel *Marked* by P.C. Cast and Kristin Cast

Best Contemporary Mystery: *I Heard That Song Before* by Mary Higgins Clark

Best P.I./Procedural Novel: *The Ever-Running Man* by Marcia Muller

Best Historical Mystery: *Why Mermaids Sing* by C.S. Harris

Best First Mystery: *Silent in the Grave* by Deanna Raybourn

Best Suspense Novel: *The Alibi Man* by Tami Hoag

Best Amateur Sleuth Novel: *Bowled Over* by Kasey Michaels

Romantic Times Bookclub Career Achievement Awards Presented by *Romantic Times Bookclub Magazine* for outstanding career achievement. Awards announced at the *Romantic Times* Booklovers Convention in Pittsburgh, Pennsylvania, on April 18, 2008, are listed below.

Historical Romance: Nicole Jordan

Historical Storyteller of the Year: Jennifer Blake

Innovative Historical Romance: Elizabeth Boyle

Series Romance: Jessica Bird

Series Romantic Suspense: Aimee Thurlo

Series Romantic Adventure: Patricia Rosemoor

Series Romance Love & Laughter: Liz Fielding

Series Storyteller of the Year: Cara Summers

Contemporary Romance: Kimberly Cates

Paranormal Romance: Angela Knight

Urban Fantasy: Jim Butcher

Women's Fiction: Dorothea Benton Frank

Romantic Suspense: Lisa Jackson

Mystery Series: Lee Child

Female Sleuth Series: Edna Buchanan

Suspense: Wendy Corsi Staub

Inspirational Romance: Tracie Peterson

African-American Romance: Anita Bunkley

Awards information courtesy of the Romance Writers of America and the Romantic Times Publishing Group.

Western Awards
by Clay Reynolds

The Spur Awards Spur awards are named for the statue that is presented to winners as a symbol of their award. Although announced in advance, the formal presentation of Spur Awards takes place at the annual Awards Banquet held in conjunction with the yearly convention of the Western Writers of America. Awards are open to both members and non-members of the WWA. The 2008 awards for works published in 2007 were presented in Scottsdale, Arizona in June, 2008.

Categories for Spur fiction awards have fluctuated over the past several years, and they are frequently adjusted to reflect both length of published book, first book by a single author, historical or contemporary, and paperback or cloth binding. Notable on this year's list is a change from the previous category, "Best Original Paperback Novel" to "Best Original Mass Market Paperback," a bow to the growing inclination among several publishers to issue volumes in trade paper editions as opposed to cloth bound editions, but still distinct from the traditional paperback formats.

In addition to these categories, the category, "Best Western Short Fiction Story" was significant this year because all three winners' works appeared in anthologies or collections. WWA also recognizes with a Spur award authors of western nonfiction, juvenile and children's fiction, short fiction, short nonfiction, cover art, motion picture and television scripts, poetry, as well as the Medicine Pipe Bearer Award to the Best First Western Novel and the Owen Wister Award for Lifetime Achievement in Western writing.

Best Western Long Novel: *The God of Animals* by Sandra Dallas

Finalists: *The Night Birds* by Thomas Maltman, *Stormy Weather* by Paulette Jiles

Best Western Short Novel: *Tallgrass* by Sandra Dallas

Finalists: *The Canyon of Bones* by Richard S. Wheeler, *Northfield* by Johnny D. Boggs

Best Original Mass Market Paperback: *Hellfire Canyon* by Max McCoy

Finalists: *Lake of Fire* by Linda Jacobs, *Raven Spring*, by John D. Nesbitt

Best First Novel: *The Night Birds* by Tomas Maltman

Finalists: *California* by R. Joe King, *Shadows in the Rain: A Tale of Old Klamath, Turpentine* by Spring Warren

Best Western Short Fiction Story: "Crucifixion River" in the anthology *Crucifixion River*, edited by Marcia Muller and Bill Prozini

Finalists: "The Cody War" in the anthology, *Lost Trails*, edited by Johnny D. Boggs, "The Wild-Eyed Witness" in the anthology, *Lost Trails*, edited by Lori Van Pelt

Texas Institute of Letters Awards The Texas Institute of Letters annually awards book prizes in a variety of categories. Fiction categories include The Jesse H. Jones Award for the Best Work of Fiction, The Steve Turner Award for the Best First Work of Fiction, and the Kay Cattarula Award for the Best Short Story. This year's awards were presented at the annuial Awards Banquet in Dallas, Texas, held in April.

Jesse H. Jones Award for the Best Work of Fiction: *Run in the Fam'ly* by John J. McLaughlin.

Finalists: *Dmitir Esterhaats* by Russell Hardin, *Fire Ants* by Gerald Duff

Steve Turner Award for the Best First Work of Fiction: *Run in the Fam'ly* by John J. McLaughliln

Finalist: *And Silent Left the Place* by Elizabeth Bruce

Western Heritage Awards The Western Heritage Awards, more commonly called "Wranglers" because winners receive a replica of the Charles Russell bronze statue by that name, are awarded by the National Cowboy Hall of Fame to entries in western literature, music, film, and television that best represent subjects and themes reflecting the American West. They give one fiction award each year. The 2008 Wrangler Award for fiction has not been announced at this writing.

Violet Crown Awards The Violet Crown Awards are presented each autumn by the Writers' League of Texas and are given only to members in good standing of the League. They are given in poetry, prose nonfiction and prose fiction. The 2006 Violet Crown Awards included western authors. The 2007 Violet Crown Awards will be announced in September, 2008.

Fantastic Fiction Awards
by Don D'Ammassa

Awards for science fiction, fantasy, and horror fiction are presented by several professional and fan organizations, usually on an annual basis, sometimes with open balloting, sometimes confining the final decision to a group of judges. These awards typically cover short fiction of varying lengths, dramatic presentations, and other categories in addition to those involving a specific book. Since these awards are all presented retroactively, the individual titles below will have been covered in earlier editions of *What Do I Read Next?*. The final ballots for some of these are listed below, with the winners to be presented later in the year.

Hugo Awards The Hugo Awards, named in honor of Hugo Gernsback for his pioneering work in creating science fiction magazines, are presented at the World Science Fic-

tion convention which takes place on Labor Day Weekend each year. This year's convention will take place in Denver, Colorado. This is the fantastic fiction's oldest award originating in 1953. Anyone who purchases a membership is entitled to nominate and vote. The Hugo Awards for work appearing in 2007 includes the following:

Best Novel: *The Yiddish Policemen's Union* by Michael Chabon

Finalists: *Brasyl* by Ian McDonald, *Rollback* by Robert J. Sawyer, *The Last Colony* by John Scalzi, and *Halting State* by Charles Stross.

Best Related Book: *Brave New Words: The Oxford Dictionary of Science Fiction* by Jeff Prucher

Finalists: *The Arrival* by Shaun Tani, *Breakfast in the Ruins: Science Fiction in the Last Millennium* by Barry Malzberg, *The Company They Keep: C.S. Lewis and J.R.R. Tolkien as Writers in Community* by Diana Glyer, *Emshwiller: Infinity x Two* by Luis Ortiz

Nebula Awards The Nebula Awards are presented by the Science Fiction and Fantasy Writers of America at their annual meeting. Only full members are entitled to vote for the final selection. The award has been presented annually since 1965. The nominees for 2007 are as follows:

Best Novel: *The Accidental Time Machine* by Joe Haldeman, *The New Moon's Arms* by Nalo Hopkinson, *Odyssey* by Jack McDevitt, *Ragamuffin* by Tobias Buckell, *The Yiddish Policemen's Union* by Michael Chabon

Bram Stoker Awards This award is presented by the Horror Writers of America at their annual meeting. All members can nominate but only full members can vote on the final ballot. The award is named after the author of *Dracula* and has been presented since 1987.

Best Novel Nominees: *Dead Man's Song* by Jonathan Maberry, *The Dust of Wonderland* by Lee Thomas, *Generation Loss* by Elizabeth Hand, *Ghoul* by Brian Keene, *The Guardener's Tale* by Bruce Boston, *Mr. Hands* by Gary Braunbeck, *The Heart Shaped Box* by Joe Hill, *The Midnight Road* by Tom Piccirilli, *The Missing* by Sarah Langan, *The Terror* by Dan Simmons

Best First Novel: *Dying to Live* by Kim Paffenroth, *The Heart Shaped Box* by Joe Hill, *The Hollower* by Mary SanGiovanni, *I Will Rise* by Michael Cavillo, *The Memory Tree* by John R. Little, *Roses of Blood on Barbwire Vines* by D.L. Snell, *Vacation* by Jeremy Shipp

Best Collection: *Darker Loves* by James Dorr, *5 Stories* by Peter Straub, *Defining Moments* by David Niall Wilson, *The Imago Sequence* by Laird Barron, *Needles and Sins* by James Everson, *No Further Messages* by Brett Alexander Savoury, *Proverbs for Monsters* by Michael A. Arnzen, *Sparks and Shadows* by Lucy Snyder, *Voyeurs of Death* by Shaun Jeffrey, *When It Rains and Other Wreckage* by Christopher Fulbright

Best Anthology: *Astounding Hero Tales* edited by James Lowder, *Dark Delicacies 2* edited by Del Howi-

son and Jeff Gelb, *Five Strokes to Midnight* edited by Gary Braunbeck and Hank Schwaeble, *Gratia Placenti* edited by Jason Sizemore and Gill Ainsworth, *High Seas Cthulhu* edited by William Jones, *History Is Dead* edited by Kim Paffenroth, *Horror Library Volume 2* edited by R.J. Cavender and Vincent VanAllen, *Horrors Beyond 2* edited by William Jones, *Inferno* edited by Ellen Datlow, *Midnight Premiere* edited by Tom Piccirilli

Best Non-Fiction: *The Cryptopedia: A Dictionary of the Weird, Strange, & Downright Bizarre* by Jonathan Maberry and David F. Kramer, *Encyclopedia Horrifica* by Joshua Gee, *The Portable Obituary: How the Famous, Rich, and Powerful Really Died* by Michael Largo, *The Science of Stephen King* by Lois Gresh and Robert Weinberg

Additional ballots and awards will be announced later in the year from the International Horror Guild, the World Fantasy Awards, and the Locus Poll.

Inspirational Fiction Awards
by Melissa Hudak

The Christy Awards In 1999 several Christian publishers launched an award to recognize the good work being published in the area of Christian fiction. The Christy Award is named in honor of the most famous novel of Catherine Marshall, one of the pioneers of Christian fiction. Publishers submit novels they feel are most deserving of the honor of an award. Those novels are then judged by a panel of seven judges. There are currently nine categories for submission, including one for young adult novels.

Contemporary (Stand Alone): *Chasing Fireflies* by Charles Martin

Finalists: *In High Places* by Tom Morrisey; *Quaker Summer* by Lisa Samson

Contemporary (Series, Sequels and Novellas): *Home to Holly Springs* by Jan Karon

Finalists: *A Time to Mend* by Sally John and Gary Smalley; *What Lies Within* by Karen Ball

Historical: *A Proper Pursuit* by Lynn Austin

Finalists: *Lady of Milkweed Manor* by Julie Klassen; *Tendering in the Storm* by Jane Kirkpatrick

Lits: *Hallie's Heart* by Shelly Beach

Finalists: *Doesn't She Look Natural* by Angela Hunt; *Let Them Eat Cake* by Sandra Byrd; *Trophy Wives Club* by Kristin Billerbeck

Romance: *Remembered* by Tamera Alexander

Finalists: *Lightning and Lace* by DiAnn Mills; *Remember to Forget* by Deborah Raney

Suspense: *The Cure* by Athol Dickson

Finalists: *My Hands Came Away Red* by Lisa McKay; *The Pawn* by Steven James

Visionary: *Scarlet* by Stephen R. Lawhead

Finalists: *Auralia's Colors* by Jeffrey Overstreet; *The Restorer* by Sharon Hinck

First Novel: *The Stones Cry Out* by Sibella Giorello

Finalists: *Auralia's Colors* by Jeffrey Overstreet; *Demon: A Memoir* by Tosca Lee

Young Adult: *Hollywood Nobody* by Lisa Samson

Finalists: *In Between* by Jenny B. Jones; *Maggie Come Lately* by Michelle Buckman

ECPA Christian Book Awards The Evangelical Christian Publishers Association revised its Gold Medallion Book Awards in 2006, eliminating several categories. They retained the fiction awards. The awards are now known as the ECPA Christian Book Awards.

Winner: *In Search of Eden* by Linda Nichols

Finalists: *Between Sundays* by Karen Kingsbury; *Chasing Fireflies* by Charles Martin; *Deception* by Randy Alcorn; *Quaker Summer* by Lisa Samson; *Summer of Light* by W. Dale Cramer

Popular Fiction Awards
by Natalie Danford

Book Sense of the Year Award The American Booksellers Association, a non-profit trade association, gives this award annually for the book of adult fiction their members most enjoyed selling.

2008 Winner: *A Thousand Splendid Suns* by Khaled Hosseini

Finalists: *Away* by Amy Bloom, *Bridge of Sighs* by Richard Russo, *Run* by Ann Patchett, *The Yiddish Policemen's Union* by Michael Chabon

National Book Critics Circle Award Each year this award is given by the National Book Critics Circle, an organization of approximately 700 book reviewers, to the best work of fiction for the previous year.

2007 Winner: *The Brief Wondrous Life of Oscar Wao* by Junot Diaz

Finalists: *The Gravedigger's Daughter* by Joyce Carol Oates, *In the Country of Men* by Hisham Matar, *Sacred Games* by Vikram Chandra, *The Shadow Catcher* by Marianne Wiggins

The Pen/Faulkner Award for Fiction This award is given annually to a distinguished work of fiction by a contemporary American author.

2008 Winner: *The Great Man* by Kate Christensen

Finalists: *Chemistry and Other Stories* by Ron Rash, *The Gateway* by T.M. McNally, *The Indian Clerk* by David Leavitt, *The Maytrees* by Annie Dillard

Pulitzer Prize for Fiction Established in 1917, this award is given annually to an American author for a work of fiction about American life.

2008 Winner: *The Brief Wondrous Life of Oscar Wao* by Junot Diaz

Finalists: *Shakespeare's Kitchen* by Lore Segal, *Tree of Smoke* by Denis Johnson

The Mystery Genre in 2008
by
Jim Huang

A just published first novel has four endorsements on the back cover. One describes the book as a "mystery." Another uses the word "thriller." The third and fourth call it simply a "story" and a "novel." The plot involves a serial killer and the intrepid professional who investigates the deaths and ultimately exposes the murderer. A book that we can describe in this way unquestionably belongs in our genre, but it also raises a question about the nature of the genre. What's the difference between a mystery and a thriller, and does the difference matter?

This spring, I spent two days in New York as part of a Sisters in Crime board delegation charged with assessing the state of the genre and reporting back to our membership. We visited with editors and publicists at several major publishing companies, with the mystery buyer at one of the big chain bookstores, and with folks at two important literary agencies. Our conversations touched on a wide range of topics—you can find complete coverage on the Sisters in Crime blog at http://sisters-in-crime-sinc.blogspot.com/2008/05/sisters-in-crime-publishers-su and three subsequent posts—but one theme dominated: "thrillers are hot, hot, hot" while mysteries are not.

We didn't have to go to New York to hear this. The mystery/thriller split is being played out in a variety of arenas, most notably in the high profile efforts of the new International Thriller Writers organization to establish itself as a counterweight to the Mystery Writers of America. Over the past few years, ITW has hosted splashy conferences, created its own set of thriller awards, published an anthology entitled *Thriller*, and created a variety of marketing programs to promote thrillers. There's no question that the ITW has created visibility and buzz for itself. Is this all just sound and fury, or does it signify something? Are mysteries really being muscled aside by thrillers? At heart, is there really a difference between mysteries and thrillers?

The answer to the last question—probably the only one that really matters to readers, instead of just to insiders—is at one level quite simple. It's easy to find ways

to describe some key differences between mysteries and thrillers. Mysteries are about who done it while thrillers are about how perpetrators will be caught. In other words, mysteries are about detection. Thrillers are about pursuit. In a mystery, the perpetrators are unknown and the detective must reveal their identities. In a thriller, readers might know exactly who the bad guys are. The novel then becomes a cat and mouse game between the good guys and the bad guys. Some definitions of thrillers emphasize the urgency of the ongoing contest between good and bad guys by suggesting that mysteries are about crimes that have already taken place, and therefore need to be solved, while thrillers are about crimes that are going to take place, and therefore need to be stopped.

These distinctions make sense to most readers, even as we can think of countless exceptions to a strict mystery/thriller dichotomy. Great thrillers often involve plenty of good old-fashioned ratiocination, while great mysteries often borrow elements of thrillers, especially as detective story protagonists close in on their prey. Still, the labels are meaningful, especially in helping readers know what kind of book they're getting themselves into.

Some segments of the industry—led by the ITW and some of the agents and publishers that Sisters in Crime visited—see an interest in and have had some success in promoting thrillers. This creates a temptation to overextend the thriller label, making it harder for readers. Accurate labels are useful to readers. Labels create specific expectations; writers suffer when their books don't meet readers' expectations. The labels help determine not only what we choose to read, but also define what we think we're getting.

I began this essay by describing a current title that's blurbed as both a mystery and a thriller. I'm not going to identify this book, in part because I want to talk about its ending, and it's a strict rule of writing about mysteries that endings may not be revealed. I also don't want to cast aspersions on a book that I genuinely enjoyed and successfully recommend.

As a mystery novel, this book has a serious flaw: there aren't enough viable suspects to make for a truly satisfying mystery. Most readers will soon realize that there are only two possibilities for the killer. Midway through the book, the protagonist begins to suspect one of these two people. Veteran mystery readers will immediately realize that at this stage of the book, that makes this suspect a red herring. Therefore, the only other possible suspect must be the killer. In a mystery, deducing the identity of the murderer long before the protagonist figures it out is a big problem. In a mystery, the payoff is in the resolution. It's the author's job to keep us in the dark right up to the end. But in a thriller, we're okay with knowing who the bad guy must be because the pleasure is in the chase, which this author handles well.

We've all heard a variation of the line that "every story is a mystery," but genre readers reject that as fuzzy, imprecise thinking. We like the specificity of appropriate labels; it's part of the order that we seek as readers and that we like to see in the fiction that we read. Is *Hamlet* a mystery? You can make a case: at one point, Hamlet decides "to put an antic disposition on" in order to investigate his father's ghost's claim of murder. That makes Hamlet sound like the protagonist of any amateur detective story. It's certainly possible to turn the elements of *Hamlet* into a great thriller, as Alan Gordon demonstrates in his brilliant 2005 novel, *An Antic Disposition*. But Shakespeare, curiously unaware of the conventions of either mysteries or thrillers, fails to live up to genre expectations. Gordon plays up the cat and mouse contest between his Hamlet and Claudius characters. Shakespeare's concerns lie elsewhere.

Even as we agree on ways to differentiate mysteries and thrillers, and both genres from literary fiction, we can also agree on some of the common elements of mysteries and thrillers. In the genres, we still believe in the restoration of order (in mysteries) and/or the preservation of order (in thrillers). There's a sense in which Hamlet restores order at the end of the play; the murderous usurper is punished, after all. But that isn't necessarily what motivates Hamlet, whereas order is central to genre protagonists, who also usually survive to enjoy the fruits of their labors. There aren't a lot of mysteries or thrillers that end with the hero's death.

Indeed, even in the chaotic world of 2008, the search for order remains a relevant concern. Characters in the best books of the year to date strive to understand the world, to find a way to take charge of their environments, and to re-create or preserve the society they value—just as the heroes and heroines of mysteries and thrillers have always done.

There's no question about Anni Koskinen's commitment to justice. A veteran Chicago police officer, she was unable to remain silent when she witnessed an incident of misconduct. Her fellow officers forced her to leave the force. At the opening of Barbara Fister's powerful novel *In the Wind*, Anni is down on her luck, trying to rebuild her home and her life. A priest in her neighborhood asks Anni to give a woman a ride. The woman turns out to be a suspect in the 30-year-old death of FBI Agent Arne Tilquist, father of the man who served as Anni's mentor.

In the Wind is a twisted and complicated story that sends Anni into the past, up against local and federal law enforcement, and on the trail of more than one group of radicals. Billed as "a mystery," the novel offers Fister a big canvas that she uses to paint parallels between the government's Vietnam era treatment of radical groups and the restrictions on civil liberties that we are facing in today's post-9/11 climate. In other words, the "order" that this novel is concerned with leads us to consider some of the biggest issues in today's political discourse. There's no doubt about Anni's—or Fister's—stand, steadfastly opposed to the government's abuses. But Anni is no whiner, and every page of the book is informed by the clarity of her vision. Because Fister's characters wear only black hats and white hats, she's unlikely to change anyone's politics, but Fister's twisty plot builds to a resolution that should satisfy all mystery readers, regardless of where they stand on the larger issues.

Leighton Gage's canvas is also a broad one, and his novel also explores the biggest political and social issues of its setting. *Blood of the Wicked*, Gage's first novel, opens with the assassination of a bishop in a town in a remote region of Brazil. Chief Inspector Mario Silva arrives to direct an investigation on behalf of Brazil's Federal Police. Silva's nephew, Hector Costa, is also a federal police officer, and Silva calls on him for assistance. It doesn't take Silva and Costa long to see that Emerson Ferraz, the local police commander, is thoroughly corrupt and in the pocket of local landowners. Indeed, Ferraz is a landowner himself—something that should not be possible on his salary.

Like Fister, Gage's characters wear either white or black hats, but in the context of Brazilian society, white and black mean different things. Silva is a good man and a good police officer, but Gage also describes Silva's quest for vengeance against the thugs who killed his parents. Indeed, this quest provided the motivation for Silva to join the force in the first place. Interestingly enough, when Silva finally finds and kills the man who shot his father and raped his mother, Silva learns that revenge isn't all that satisfying and does not provide a sense of closure. It's just not that simple.

The same can be said for the larger issues that Gage tackles. In Brazil, the gap between haves and have-nots is a wide, deep chasm, and the conflict between them is thoroughly politicized, extending even into the church and an outlawed doctrine called liberation theology. Gage has skillfully constructed a mystery novel—identified as a mystery on its jacket flap—that lays bare the division and corruption that is today's Brazil. Silva is a warrior, tarnished and yet noble, who still seeks some measure of order, such as it is in this troubled country.

Dan Fesperman also uses his novel to introduce readers to a troubled corner of our world. *The Amateur Spy*

takes place largely in Jordan, where Freeman Lockhart (a great name for this character) is spying on an old friend and colleague, Omar al-Baroody. Freeman has been pressured into this assignment by three masked men, who believe that al-Baroody's new non-governmental organization, the Bakaa Refugee Health Project, is not just raising money to build a hospital but is also funneling money into terrorism. The masked men threaten to expose a secret from Freeman's past as an aid worker in Africa if he refuses to cooperate.

The Amateur Spy is billed as a novel, but the book is squarely in the grand tradition established by the early masters of the thriller, John Buchan, Graham Greene and Eric Ambler. In Lockhart, Fesperman offers a great portrait of a lifelong humanitarian aid worker whose travels have taken him to the most destitute corners of the earth. He's a man of the world who is nevertheless still idealistic enough to be surprised by what he sees on this posting. Like Brazil, Jordan is a mess, a hotbed of radicals who oppose Israel and the West.

Fesperman also shows that radicalism isn't restricted to the Middle East, nor to the obvious suspects whom Lockhart encounters in Amman. In a parallel plot thread based in Washington, D.C., Abbas Rahim's wife is concerned that her husband is distracted and withdrawn. The couple's daughter died a year ago while she traveling abroad. Rahim, a Palestinian immigrant, blames post-9/11 profiling for putting their daughter in danger. Rahim's efforts provide a typical thriller's ticking bomb. His story intersects with Lockhart's in a resolution that defuses the threat and maintains order, but just as in Fister's and Gage's books, it is an uneasy order that leaves us with a lot to think about.

Readers in this genre expect that books set in places like Jordan and Brazil will address the issues of those locales. It's part of what attracts mystery readers to these books. Oddly enough, Julie Hyzy upends expectations with a book set at the White House that's essentially apolitical. *State of the Onion* is packaged as a cozy mystery, complete with recipes for a presidential meal. Politics are not part of the formula for paperback original cozy mysteries, so in that sense Hyzy delivers what readers will expect from this packaging.

But in many other respects, *State of the Onion* is not what we might expect. Though clearly labeled across the top of the front cover as "First in the new White House Chef Mystery series," the story is structured much more as a thriller than a mystery. In the opening pages, chef Olivia Paras stops an intruder by knocking him out with a frying pan. Throughout the novel, Ollie and the Secret Service know who the bad guy is. They just don't know what disguise he's adopted and when he intends to strike. When a plot can be described in these terms, it's pretty clearly a thriller rather than a mystery.

Still, *State of the Onion* will satisfy readers who are attracted by the "White House Chef Mystery series" tagline. Ollie Paras fits the cozy mystery protagonist mold of the intrepid young, single professional strug-

gling to balance a career and a relationship. Cozy fans will also enjoy Hyzy's descriptions of the food, a staple of so many traditional mysteries. I certainly can't think of any other thriller that devotes this much attention to menus. The food turns out to be utterly fascinating, especially in the complex diplomacy of cooking for foreign dignitaries. Indeed, there's as much suspense in learning what will be on the menu as there is in anticipating how the bad guy will be stopped.

As an archaeologist, Faye Longchamp is used to putting pieces together, creating order out of chaos. In *Findings*, Mary Anna Evans offers an intricate, skillfully constructed story that asks Longchamp to solve a murder in the present day and a historical mystery that dates back to the Civil War. Unabashedly published as a mystery by the Poisoned Pen Press, whose motto of "Publishing Excellence in Mystery" appears on the book's back cover, *Findings* offers up everything a mystery lover might look for in a novel.

Evans's story reminds us that we don't have to go far to find mysteries worth investigating. Longchamp's archaeological work centers on her own ancestral home, located on Joyeuse Island off the coast of Florida. The Civil War thread takes us into the workings and finances of the Confederate government, an aspect of our nation's history that is unlikely to be familiar to most readers. Evans takes us effortlessly through both past and present, with more than enough twists and clues and red herrings to keep us on our toes. She adds in a pair of suitors who vie for Longchamp's affections, and sets her story against a vividly portrayed backdrop. *Findings* is an old-fashioned, traditional mystery novel, a thoroughly satisfying reading experience that delivers on everything it promises.

Some reviews of Louise Ure's remarkable second novel *The Fault Tree* have faulted Ure for the way in which the novel shifts gears; Publishers Weekly says that she destroys tension two-thirds of the way through. I believe that the problem lies in the way the book is presented. The book is billed as "A Mystery," an appropriate label for Ure's careful—and fascinating—descriptions of investigative and forensic work that follow from a simple beginning. Auto mechanic Cadence Moran is on the way home from work when robbers burst out of her neighbor's house. Having killed the neighbor, the bandits jump into their car; Cadence just barely escapes being run over.

The twist is that Cadence is blind. The bad guys don't realize that she's blind, and fear that she can identify them to the police. The good guys—police detectives August Dupree and Richard Nellis—don't know what to make of Cadence. Initially, Nellis believes she's worthless as a witness. Dupree is more willing to listen, and begins to appreciate what Cadence is able to testify to based on her other senses. The person who most needs to be convinced about Cadence's ability to be helpful is Cadence herself, not so much because of her blindness—which she works with every day on the job—but because

of her guilt over an incident that we learn about over the course of the novel.

It's a potent mix, and Ure handles all of the elements beautifully. It's a dazzling performance, fresh, original and exciting. But because Ure reveals the identities of the killers long before the ending, the mystery reader might feel shortchanged. Generally in a mystery, the identity of the killer is part of the resolution, not an intermediate plot point. *The Fault Tree* is in fact a great thriller. From the beginning, the novel is a three-sided cat and mouse game involving the two police officers, two murderous thugs and one woman who must find the strength and conviction to be able to help.

Kirkus describes the novel as "by turns an accomplished procedural, an acute study of a fiercely independent heroine and a nail-biting suspenser," accurately capturing the fact that in *The Fault Tree*, Ure is doing more than one thing. Like Evans, Ure also delivers on everything she promises; it's just harder to see at the outset what it is she is promising. For a publishing industry that sees the landscape in simple either/or terms, a multi-faceted work such as *The Fault Tree* poses a challenge, but it's one that the business needs to address because more and more, the best writers are blurring the boundaries and delivering novels that are hard to pigeonhole.

Fortunately, in the mystery genre, we're dealing with smart, devoted readers who will give writers plenty of latitude on the way to a satisfying resolution. We know that the world is chaotic, and that there may be countless pieces to the puzzles that we face. But at the end of the day, as long as writers can find at least some measure of order, then they've done what we ask of them, regardless of how the book is labeled.

Recommended Titles

The Amateur Spy by Dan Fesperman

The Black Dove by Steve Hockensmith

Blood of the Wicked by Leighton Gage

The Fault Tree by Louise Ure

Fiddle Game by Richard Thompson

Findings by Mary Anna Evans

Frames by Loren Estleman

In the Wind by Barbara Fister

The Moneylender of Toulouse by Alan Gordon

State of the Onion by Julie Hyzy

***

I would like to acknowledge the assistance of Robin Agnew, Miriam Guidero, Joella & Ed Hultgren, Austin Lugar, Katie Nakanishi and Nikki Phipps in the preparation of the entries that follow.

Mystery Titles

1

JEFF ABBOTT

Collision

(New York: Dutton, 2008)

Story type: Espionage Thriller
Subject(s): Crime and Criminals; Identity
Major character(s): Benjamin Forsberg, Consultant, Widow(er); Randall Choate, Criminal; Joanna Vochek, Government Official
Time period(s): 2000s; 1990s
Locale(s): Austin, Texas; New Orleans, Louisiana; Jakarta, Indonesia

Summary: Two years ago, Ben Forsberg's wife Emily was killed on their honeymoon. Today, Ben is working as a consultant for a security contracting company, Hector Global, the same company Emily was working for when she died. Irish assassin Nicky Lynch is killed while trying to carry out an assignment in Austin, Texas. Police find Ben's business card in Nicky's pocket. This leads Homeland Security to take Ben into custody, accusing him of having ties to terrorists. Ben assumes that someone must have stolen his identity, and his suspicions are confirmed when an assassin named Pilgrim breaks into the facility where Ben is being held. Ben goes on the run with Pilgrim to discover who set them up.

Where it's reviewed:
Booklist, May 1, 2008, page 24
Library Journal, April 15, 2008, page 70
Mystery Scene, June/July 2008, page 11
Publishers Weekly, May 12, 2008, page 36

Other books by the same author:
Fear, 2006
Panic, 2005
Cut and Run, 2003
Black Jack Point, 2002
A Kiss Gone Bad, 2001

Other books you might like:
Lawrence Block, *Hit and Run*, 2008
Harlan Coben, *Tell No One*, 2001
Barry Eisler, *The Last Assassin*, 2006
David Rosenfelt, *Don't Tell a Soul*, 2008

2

PETER ABRAHAMS

Delusion

(New York: Morrow, 2008)

Story type: Domestic
Subject(s): Crime and Criminals; Family
Major character(s): Nell Jarreau, Museum Curator, Assistant; Clay Jarreau, Police Officer; Alvin DuPree, Convict
Time period(s): 2000s; 1980s
Locale(s): Little Parrot Cay, Bahamas; Belle Ville, Louisiana; New Orleans, Louisiana

Summary: Twenty years ago, college student Nell was standing next to her boyfriend, geology major Johnny Blanton, when a mugger plunged a knife into Johnny's body. Nell's eyewitness testimony helped put Alvin DuPree behind bars. After new evidence in the case is discovered, giving him an alibi for the night of the Blanton murder, DuPree is set free. Now Nell Jarreau, wife of Chief of Police Clay Jarreau, is consumed with guilt. Worried that her testimony was responsible for sending an innocent man to prison, Nell searches for answers to the decades-old murder as her life spins out of control.

Where it's reviewed:
Booklist, February 1, 2008, page 5
Library Journal, April 15, 2008, page 70
Mystery Scene, Spring 2008, page 62
Publishers Weekly, February 18, 2008, page 136

Other books by the same author:
Nerve Damage, 2007
Behind the Curtain, 2006
End of Story, 2006
Down the Rabbit Hole, 2005
Oblivion, 2005

Other books you might like:
Mary Higgins Clark, *Daddy's Little Girl*, 2002
Harlan Coben, *Just One Look*, 2004
Patricia MacDonald, *Stolen in the Night*, 2007
Rick Riordan, *Cold Springs*, 2003

3

ALINA ADAMS

Skate Crime

(New York: Berkley, 2007)

Story type: Amateur Detective
Series: Rebecca Levy. Book 5
Subject(s): Sports/Ice Skating
Major character(s): Rebecca Levy, Researcher, Detective—Amateur
Time period(s): 2000s
Locale(s): Colorado Springs, Colorado

Summary: Rebecca "Bex" Levy is a figure skating researcher for a television network. Bex would like to eventually become a producer of her own show, so when her boss offers her an assignment in Colorado Springs, she eagerly accepts. She is in charge of a tribute to Lucian Pryce, both a famous coach and figure skater. As Bex prepares to shoot the first segment, she and her crew witness a serious fall that deals a deadly blow to Lucian's head. The police assume the incident is an unfortunate accident, but Bex automatically thinks murder and begins putting her research skills to good use. The world of figure skating is ruthless and there seems to be no end to the list of suspects.

Other books by the same author:
Axel of Evil, 2006
Death Drop, 2006
On Thin Ice, 2004
Murder on Ice, 2003

Other books you might like:
John Feinstein, *Winter Games*, 1995
Clyde Linsley, *Death Spiral*, 2000
Meredith Phillips, *Death Spiral*, 1984
Julie Robitaille, *Iced*, 1994

4

BORIS AKUNIN (Pseudonym of Grigory Chkhartishvili)

Sister Pelagia and the Black Monk

(New York: Random House, 2008)

Story type: Historical
Series: Sister Pelagia. Book 2
Subject(s): Religion; Ghosts
Major character(s): Sister Pelagia, Religious; Bishop Mishenka Mitrofanii, Religious (bishop of Zavolzhsk); Donat Savvich Korovin, Doctor
Time period(s): 19th century
Locale(s): Zavolzhsk, Russia; New Ararat, Russia

Summary: In the Russian town of Zavolzhsk, Bishop Mitrofanii is visited in the dead of night by a monk from the island Hermitage at New Ararat with a disturbing message. The apparition of a monk dressed in black has been haunting the monastery. Worried and curious about the mysterious sightings, Mitrofanii sends three emissaries to the island to investigate. Each of the three men suffers a horrible fate: insanity and death. Mitrofanii's strong-willed assistant, Sister Pelagia, begs the bishop's permission to visit the island herself, but female novices are not allowed. Defying his orders, Pelagia goes undercover to New Ararat to investigate who or what is haunting the island.

Where it's reviewed:
Entertainment Weekly, May 16, 2008, page 70
Publishers Weekly, March 24, 2008, page 57

Other books by the same author:
Special Assignments, 2008
Sister Pelagia and the White Bulldog, 2007
The Death of Achilles, 2006
The Turkish Gambit, 2005
Murder on the Leviathan, 2004

Other books you might like:
Ronan Bennett, *Zugzwang*, 2007
Tom Bradby, *The White Russian*, 2003
Alexander McCall Smith, *The No. 1 Ladies' Detective Agency Series*, 2002 -
R.N. Morris, *The Gentle Axe*, 2007

5

BORIS AKUNIN (Pseudonym of Grigory Chkhartishvili)

Special Assignments

(New York: Random House, 2008)

Story type: Historical; Collection
Series: Erast Fandorin. Book 5
Subject(s): Detection; Russians
Major character(s): Erast Fandorin, Detective—Police, Diplomat; Anisii Tulipov, Clerk, Government Official; Mitenka Savvin, Criminal
Time period(s): 1880s
Locale(s): Moscow, Russia

Summary: In the two novellas collected together in this volume, Erast Fandorin faces two cunning criminals. Fandorin, the deputy for special assignments to His Excellency the Governor-General of Moscow, works together with Anisii, Tulipov, his hapless clerk, to investigate these two very different cases. In "The Jack of Spades," Fandorin is asked to track down a con man who has swindled thousands of rubles from citizens of Moscow using clever tricks and disguises. The second novella, "The Decorator," is darker. As Fandorin investigates a series of murders, he notices a disturbing similarity to the murders in London, England, committed by the notorious murderer Jack the Ripper. Fandorin fears that the Ripper is now in Moscow.

Where it's reviewed:
Entertainment Weekly, February 15, 2008, page 69
Library Journal, January 15, 2008, page 68
Publishers Weekly, December 3, 2007, page 52

Other books by the same author:
Sister Pelagia and the Black Monk, 2008
Sister Pelagia and the White Bulldog, 2007
The Death of Achilles, 2006
The Turkish Gambit, 2006
Murder on the Leviathan, 2005

Other books you might like:
Tom Bradby, *The White Russian*, 2003
Michael Gregorio, *Critique of Criminal Reason*, 2006
Marie Belloc Lowndes, *The Lodger*, 1914
R.N. Morris, *The Gentle Axe*, 2007

6

TASHA ALEXANDER

A Fatal Waltz

(New York: Morrow, 2008)

Story type: Historical/Victorian
Series: Emily Ashton. Book 3
Subject(s): Espionage
Major character(s): Emily Ashton, Noblewoman,
  Widow(er); Colin Hargreaves, Spy, Diplomat; Kristi-
  ana von Lange, Spy, Noblewoman
Time period(s): 1890s
Locale(s): Yorkshire, England; London, England; Vienna,
  Austria-Hungary

Summary: While attending a hunting party at a Yorkshire
estate, Lady Emily Ashton meets an Austrian countess,
Kristiana von Lange. Emily learns that Kristiana is not
only a diplomatic colleague of her fiance, Colin Hargreaves, but also his former lover. When the host of the
party, Lord Basil Fortescue, is found dead, his protege
Robert Brandon is accused of murder and arrested. Ivy,
Robert's wife and a friend of Emily's, begs Emily to
clear her husband's name. With the only clue to the
murder a letter about a political assassination, Emily
travels to Vienna, Austria, in search of answers. Needing
help, Emily is forced to ally herself with Kristiana to
gain the answers she needs.

Where it's reviewed:
Library Journal, April 1, 2008, page 67
Publishers Weekly, April 7, 2008, page 42

Other books by the same author:
A Poisoned Season, 2007
And Only to Deceive, 2005

Other books you might like:
David Dickinson, *Death on the Nevskii Prospekt*, 2006
C.S. Harris, *Why Mermaids Sing*, 2007
Anne Perry, *Seven Dials*, 2003
Will Thomas, *To Kingdom Come*, 2005

7

MADELYN ALT

Hex Marks the Spot

(New York: Berkley, 2007)

Story type: Amateur Detective
Series: Maggie O'Neill. Book 3
Subject(s): Witches and Witchcraft
Major character(s): Maggie O'Neill, Empath, Detective—
  Amateur; Tom Fielding, Police Officer; Marcus
  Quinn, Artisan
Time period(s): 2000s

Locale(s): Stony Mill, Indiana

Summary: Maggie O'Neill works at a shop in Stony Mill,
Indiana, called Enchantments that specializes in witchcraft odds and ends. Maggie has recently discovered that
she is an empath, a person who can feel other people's
emotions as she would her own. Sometimes she can even
tell the reasons behind the emotions. While visiting a local craft fair with her boss, Maggie meets an Amish man
who has crafted a beautiful armoire. Later, the man is
found dead and there is a strange mark that suggests he
may have been hexed. After the murder, Maggie experiences a spiritual disturbance and has some interesting
dreams that may prove useful in the murder investigation.

Other books by the same author:
A Charmed Death, 2006
The Trouble with Magic, 2006

Other books you might like:
Shirley Damsgaard, *Witch Hunt*, 2007
Rosemary Edghill, *Book of Moons*, 1995
Yasmine Galenorn, *Ghost of a Chance*, 2003
Victoria Laurie, *Better Read than Dead*, 2005

8

STEPHEN ANABLE

The Fisher Boy

(Scottsdale, Arizona: Poisoned Pen, 2008)

Story type: Amateur Detective
Subject(s): Comedians
Major character(s): Mark Winslow, Actor, Entertainer;
  Roberto Schreiber, Actor; Edward Babineaux, Cult
  Member
Time period(s): 2000s
Locale(s): Provincetown, Massachusetts; Gloucester, Mas-
  sachusetts; Truro, Massachusetts

Summary: Bostonian Mark Winslow is in Provincetown,
Massachusetts, hoping to book a few club dates for his
comedic improv troupe. At a party given by philanthropist Arthur Hilliard to kick off the summer season, Winslow gets into an argument with Ian Drummond, a former
prep school friend. When Drummond is discovered on
the beach with his throat slashed open, Winslow fears he
may be a suspect in the murder, especially since he was
one of the last people to see Drummond alive. Starting
his own investigation into the murder, Winslow discovers a startling link between Drummond and himself.

Where it's reviewed:
Booklist, March 1, 2008, page 52
Publishers Weekly, March 3, 2008, page 31

Other books you might like:
Nathan Aldyne, *Cobalt*, 1982
Susan Rogers Cooper, *Funny as a Dead Comic*, 1993
Paul Kemprecos, *Bluefin Blues*, 1997
David Stukas, *Going Down for the Count*, 2002

9

SUZANNE ARRUDA

The Serpent's Daughter

(New York: Obsidian, 2008)

Story type: Historical/Roaring Twenties
Series: Jade del Cameron. Book 3
Subject(s): Africa; Kidnapping
Major character(s): Jade del Cameron, Photojournalist; Inez Maria Isabelle de Vincente; Olivia Worthy, Gentlewoman
Time period(s): 1920s
Locale(s): Tangier, Morocco

Summary: Jade del Cameron is meeting her mother, Inez, in the port city of Tangier for a hopefully uncomplicated reunion. Things don't go as planned. Inez disapproves of Jade, and the two argue. Then Inez is kidnapped. When Jade searches the tunnels under the city she finds a dead man instead of her mother. French authorities think Jade is the guilty party, and Jade goes into the mountains to avoid being detained by the police. She ends up in Marrakech, searching for both her mother and the true killer. Along the way she encounters the unfriendly mother of her dead boyfriend.

Where it's reviewed:
Booklist, November 15, 2007, page 22
Mystery News, December/January 2008, page 10
Publishers Weekly, October 29, 2007, page 34

Other books by the same author:
Stalking Ivory, 2007
Mark of the Lion, 2006

Other books you might like:
Agatha Christie, *Death Comes as the End*, 1944
Barbara Cleverly, *The Tomb of Zeus*, 2007
Dianne Day, *Emperor Norton's Ghost*, 1998
Elizabeth Peters, *The Deeds of the Disturber*, 1988

10

NANCY ATHERTON

Aunt Dimity: Vampire Hunter

(New York: Viking, 2008)

Story type: Paranormal
Series: Aunt Dimity. Book 13
Subject(s): Vampires; Ghosts
Major character(s): Lori Shepherd, Housewife; Christopher Smith, Equestrian; Dimity Westwood, Disembodied Personality, Spirit
Time period(s): 2000s
Locale(s): Finch, England; Upper Deeping, England

Summary: Ever since Lori Shepherd's five-year-old twins, Will and Rob, started school in the small English village of Upper Deeping, Lori has spent her time worrying about their health and safety. When the twins report that they saw a vampire in the woods while riding horses, Lori is skeptical at first, but then begins to believe them. Enlisting the aid of her friend Kit Smith, Lori's hunt for the mysterious, cloaked figure leads her to Aldercot Hall,

an old, ancestral home shrouded in rumors. Consulting almost daily with the spirit of Aunt Dimity through a blue leather journal, Lori pieces together the truth about the mysterious figure in the woods.

Where it's reviewed:
Publishers Weekly, November 26, 2007, page 32

Other books by the same author:
Aunt Dimity Goes West, 2007
Aunt Dimity and the Deep Blue Sea, 2006
Aunt Dimity and the Next of Kin, 2005
Aunt Dimity Snowbound, 2004
Aunt Dimity Takes a Holiday, 2003

Other books you might like:
Mignon F. Ballard, *Final Curtain*, 1992
M.C. Beaton, *Agatha Raisin and the Haunted House*, 2003
Patricia Harwin, *Arson & Old Lace*, 2004
Alice Kimberly, *The Ghost and Mrs. McClure*, 2004

11

SANDI AULT

Wild Inferno

(New York: Berkley, 2008)

Story type: Indian Culture
Series: Jamaica Wild. Book 2
Subject(s): Environment; Indians of North America
Major character(s): Jamaica Wild, Ranger; Rob Crane, FBI Agent; Kerry Reed, Ranger
Time period(s): 2000s
Locale(s): Southern Ute Reservation, Colorado; Chimney Rock, Colorado

Summary: Bureau of Land Management Agent Jamaica Wild goes up against a wildfire that is erupting on the Colorado/New Mexico border and in the Chimney Rock Archaeological Area. She races into the inferno searching for a Ute man named Grampa Ned. She finds a badly burned firefighter who is about to lose consciousness. Before going under, he tells Jamaica "save the grandmother." She continues to search for Grampa Ned and to uncover the meaning of the firefighter's cryptic message, as she also struggles to save a group of Pueblo people who refuse to leave the area where they are celebrating a sacred celestial phenomenon.

Where it's reviewed:
Library Journal, January 15, 2008, page 66
Publishers Weekly, December 10, 2007, page 38

Other books by the same author:
Wild Indigo, 2007

Other books you might like:
Nevada Barr, *Firestorm*, 1996
Tony Hillerman, *Sacred Clowns*, 1993
Kirk Mitchell, *High Desert Malice*, 1995
Judith Van Gieson, *The Wolf Path*, 1992

12

DEB BAKER

Murder Talks Turkey

(Woodbury, Minnesota: Midnight Ink, 2008)

Story type: Amateur Detective
Series: Yooper Mystery. Book 3
Subject(s): Robbers and Outlaws
Major character(s): Gertie Johnson, Aged Person; Blaze Johnson, Police Officer; Angie Gates, Office Worker
Time period(s): 2000s
Locale(s): Stonely, Michigan; Trenary, Michigan; Gladstone, Michigan

Summary: Gertie Johnson is one of several witnesses when a masked man attempts to rob the credit union in Stonely, Michigan. Gertie, Cora Mae, and Kitty are partners in Trouble Busters Investigative Company. When the would-be robber is shot, police deputy Dickey Snell opens the man's loot bag and finds Monopoly money. Since Gertie and Cora Mae witnessed the robbery and shooting, they decide to investigate the mystery themselves. From the orange high top shoes the robber was wearing, to the odd behavior of the credit union manager and his wife, Gertie discovers that the answers to the robbery and the murders lie with the new teller at the credit union, Angie Gates.

Where it's reviewed:
Mystery News, April/May 2008, page 12

Other books by the same author:
Dolly Departed, 2008
Goodbye Dolly, 2007
Murder Grins and Bears It, 2007
Dolled Up for Murder, 2006
Murder Passes the Buck, 2006

Other books you might like:
G.M. Ford, *Blown Away*, 2006
Sara Sue Hoklotubbe, *Deception on All Counts*, 2003
Henry Kisor, *Season's Revenge*, 2003
Suzann Ledbetter, *East of Peculiar*, 2000

13

JONATHAN BARNES

The Somnambulist

(New York: Morrow, 2008)

Story type: Historical/Fantasy; Historical/Victorian
Subject(s): Magicians
Major character(s): Edward Moon, Magician, Detective—Private; Somnambulist, Assistant, Sidekick; Thomas Cribb, Time Traveler
Time period(s): 1900s
Locale(s): London, England

Summary: Edward Moon, stage magician and detective, has solved some of London's most baffling crimes. Working with his assistant, a strange mute giant known only as the Somnambulist, Moon begins an investigation into a strange religious cult. Several recent murders have been connected to this organization, known as The Church of the Summer Kingdom. In the course of his investigation, Moon encounters Thomas Cribb, a man who claims to have knowledge of future events because he is living his life in reverse. When Moon's sister, Charlotte, goes to work undercover at the church, Moon discovers that this shadowy organization is working to overthrow the government.

Where it's reviewed:
Booklist, November 15, 2007, page 31
Library Journal, February 1, 2008, page 59
Publishers Weekly, November 19, 2007, page 34

Other books you might like:
Martin Bedford, *The Houdini Girl*, 1999
Christopher Fowler, *Ten Second Staircase*, 2006
Neil Gaiman, *Neverwhere*, 1997
Robert Rankin, *The Antipope*, 1992

14

NEVADA BARR

Winter Study

(New York: Putnam, 2008)

Story type: Mystery
Series: Anna Pigeon. Book 14
Subject(s): Animals/Wolves; Wildlife Conservation
Major character(s): Anna Pigeon, Ranger; Robin Adair, Researcher; Bob Menechinn, Government Official
Time period(s): 2000s
Locale(s): Isle Royale, Michigan

Summary: Anna Pigeon is called back to Isle Royale in the month of January with a group of researchers and a man from the Department of Homeland Security, Bob Menechinn. Anna is there to observe how wolves interact with moose, their prey, and determine if the wolves are a threat to park visitors. Homeland Security is there to determine the feasibility of keeping the isolated park open year round. The wolves begin to act atypically and one of the scientists disappears. Anna begins to investigate what's really going on. Because of the extreme isolation of the setting, she faces what is essentially a locked room mystery.

Where it's reviewed:
Booklist, February 15, 2008, page 5
Mystery Scene, Spring 2008, page 67
Publishers Weekly, February 25, 2008, page 57

Other books by the same author:
High Country, 2004
Hunting Season, 2002
Endangered Species, 1997
A Superior Death, 1994
Track of the Cat, 1993

Other books you might like:
Peter Bowen, *Wolf, No Wolf*, 1996
C.J. Box, *Free Fire*, 2008
Jessica Speart, *A Killing Season*, 2002
Dana Stabenow, *Breakup*, 1997

15

LORNA BARRETT

Murder Is Binding

(New York: Berkley, 2008)

Story type: Amateur Detective
Subject(s): Books and Reading; Real Estate
Major character(s): Tricia Miles, Store Owner
  (bookseller), Detective—Amateur; Wendy Adams,
  Police Officer; Angelica Prescott, Relative (sister of
  Tricia)
Time period(s): 2000s
Locale(s): Stoneham, New Hampshire

Summary: Stoneham, New Hampshire's dying downtown
is undergoing a makeover modeled on Hay-on-Wye.
Among the new bookstores is Haven't Got a Clue, Tricia
Miles' mystery bookstore. Tricia is delighted to be a part
of a downtown full of bookstores, but her neighbor, Doris
Gleason, proprietor of a cookbook store, isn't as happy
with Bob Kelly, who as a realtor and president of the
Chamber of Commerce conceived of and implemented
the town's transformation. Tricia finds Gleason murdered
in her store. Sheriff Wendy Adams immediately suspects
Tricia. As Tricia launches her own investigation into
Gleason's murder, she also copes with the unexpected
and unexplained arrival of her sister in town and with a
mysterious leaflete er who's leaving nudist tracts in
books in her store.

Where it's reviewed:
Deadly Pleasures, Spring 2008, page 40
Publishers Weekly, March 10, 2008, page 64

Other books you might like:
Jane K. Cleland, *Consigned to Death*, 2006
John Dunning, *Booked to Die*, 1992
Carolyn Hart, *Death on Demand*, 1987
Joan Hess, *Strangled Prose*, 1986

16

STEPHANIE BARRON (Pseudonym of Francine Mathews)

A Flaw in the Blood

(New York: Bantam, 2008)

Story type: Historical/Victorian
Subject(s): Secrets; Family
Major character(s): Patrick Fitzgerald, Lawyer; Georgiana
  Armistead, Doctor, Ward; Wolfgang von Stuhlen,
  Nobleman
Time period(s): 1860s
Locale(s): London, England; Cannes, France; Coburg,
  Germany

Summary: In 1861, on the evening that Prince Albert,
beloved consort to Queen Victoria, passes away, Irish
barrister Patrick Fitzgerald, who defended a would-be
assassin of the queen 20 years ago, is summoned to
Windsor Castle. Shortly after Patrick and his ward, Georgiana Armistead, leave they are nearly killed when the
royal coach in which they are traveling is overturned.
When Patrick's law office is ransacked and his partner

murdered, Patrick and Georgiana flee London. Patrick is
certain that he and Georgiana, a formally trained doctor
and niece of the late Dr. Snow who attended Her Majesty
during childbirth, are being targeted. While both Patrick
and Georgiana unknowingly carry a royal secret, they
have to discover who wants to see them both dead.

Where it's reviewed:
Booklist, February 1, 2008, page 31
Publishers Weekly, January 21, 2008, page 158

Other books by the same author:
Jane and the Barque of Frailty, 2006
Jane and His Lordship's Legacy, 2005
Jane and the Ghosts of Netley, 2003
Jane and the Prisoner of Wool House, 2001
Jane and the Stillroom Maid, 2000

Other books you might like:
Tasha Alexander, *A Fatal Waltz*, 2008
David Dickinson, *Goodnight Sweet Prince*, 2002
Will Thomas, *Some Danger Involved*, 2004
Barbara Vine, *The Blood Doctor*, 2002

17

WILLIAM BERNHARDT

Capitol Conspiracy

(New York: Ballantine, 2008)

Story type: Political
Series: Ben Kincaid. Book 16
Subject(s): Government; Terrorism
Major character(s): Ben Kincaid, Political Figure, Lawyer;
  Christina McCall, Government Official, Spouse; Nic-
  hole Muldoon, Government Official
Time period(s): 2000s
Locale(s): Washington, District of Columbia; Oklahoma
  City, Oklahoma; Baltimore, Maryland

Summary: During a memorial ceremony ten years after
the bombing of the federal building in Oklahoma City,
Senator Ben Kincaid is present as President Franklin
Blake's speech is cut short by a terrorist attack. While
both Kincaid and the president escape unharmed, First
Lady Emily Blake is killed and Kincaid's best friend,
Tulsa homicide investigator Mike Morelli, slips into a
coma from his injuries. In the aftermath of the tragedy,
President Blake calls for a constitutional amendment
severely limiting civil rights, and he wants Kincaid to
help him push it through the Senate. Kincaid's new wife
and chief of staff, Christina McCall, strongly disagrees
with the amendment and decides to look into the events
of that fateful day herself.

Where it's reviewed:
Booklist, January 1, 2008, page 47
Publishers Weekly, October 29, 2007, page 32

Other books by the same author:
Capitol Threat, 2007
Capitol Murder, 2006
Dark Eye, 2005
Hate Crime, 2004
Death Row, 2003

Other books you might like:
Barbara Fister, *In the Wind*, 2008
William Kent Krueger, *The Devil's Bed*, 2003
Mike Lawson, *The Inside Ring*, 2005
John Lescroart, *Betrayal*, 2008

18

BENJAMIN BLACK (Pseudonym of John Banville)

The Silver Swan

(New York: Henry Holt, 2008)

Story type: Amateur Detective
Series: Quirke. Book 2
Subject(s): Detection; Murder
Major character(s): Quirke, Doctor, Consultant; Billy
  Hunt, Businessman, Friend; Leslie White, Business-
  man, Addict
Time period(s): 1950s
Locale(s): Dublin, Ireland

Summary: Dublin pathologist Quirke is trying to establish
a new relationship with his daughter, Phoebe. Having
thought that Quirke was her uncle all her life, Phoebe
recently discovered that she was adopted by Quirke's
sister-in-law and husband. During this time, Quirke
receives a call from an old acquaintance, Billy Hunt.
Billy's wife Deirdre has apparently committed suicide
by drowning. When Billy pleads with Quirke not to
perform an autopsy on his wife, Quirke's suspicions are
raised. As he looks into Deirdre's death, Quirke discovers that Deirdre's connection to her business partner Leslie White wasn't all business. Quirke becomes worried,
however, when he spots Leslie White with a new lady
on his arm: his own daughter Phoebe.

Where it's reviewed:
Booklist, February 1, 2008, page 32
Library Journal, February 1, 2008, page 51
Mystery Scene, Spring 2008, page 71
Publishers Weekly, January 7, 2008, page 36

Other books by the same author:
Christine Falls, 2007

Other books you might like:
John Brady, *The Good Life*, 1995
Terence Faherty, *Orion Rising*, 1999
Declan Hughes, *The Wrong Kind of Blood*, 2006
Julie Parsons, *The Courtship Gift*, 2000

19

CARA BLACK

Murder in the Rue de Paradis

(New York: Soho, 2008)

Story type: Private Detective
Series: Aimee Leduc. Book 8
Subject(s): Terrorism; Journalism
Major character(s): Aimee Leduc, Detective—Private; Na-
  dira Abouz, Terrorist
Time period(s): 1990s (1995)

Locale(s): Paris, France

Summary: Aimee Leduc's on-again, off-again boyfriend,
Yves Robert, an investigative journalist, shows up in her
life unexpectedly. This time, he says, it's for keeps, and
he proposes to her. She happily says yes, but the next
morning when she wakes up, he is gone. Later, she finds
herself identifying his body at the morgue. Angry at the
police, she decides to track down his killer herself. What
story was he working on that could have gotten him
murdered? Meanwhile, in a comfortable French family, a
quiet, well-spoken child's nanny is not what she seems
to be. A sleeper in a jihad cell, Nadira is told to target a
prominent Kurdish woman for assassination. Aimee's
investigation into Yves' death converges with Nadira's
plans in a violent confrontation.

Where it's reviewed:
Booklist, October 1, 2007, page 36
Deadly Pleasures, Spring 2008, page 41
Library Journal, November 1, 2007, page 46
Mystery Scene, June/July 2008, page 18
Publishers Weekly, November 26, 2007, page 31

Other books by the same author:
Murder on the Ile Saint-Louis, 2007
Murder in Montmarte, 2006
Murder in Clichy, 2005
Murder in the Bastille, 2003
Murder in the Sentier, 2002

Other books you might like:
Michael Genelin, *Siren of the Waters*, 2008
Jean-Christophe Grange, *The Empire of Wolves*, 2005
Jake Lamar, *Ghosts of Saint-Michel*, 2006
Fred Vargas, *Seeking Whom He May Devour*, 2006

20

ANNA BLUNDY

The Bad News Bible

(New York: Felony & Mayhem, 2008)

Story type: Political
Series: Faith Zanetti. Book 1
Subject(s): Middle East; Journalism
Major character(s): Faith Zanetti, Journalist (foreign cor-
  respondent); Don McCaughrean, Photojournalist
Time period(s): 2000s
Locale(s): Jerusalem, Israel

Summary: Faith Zanetti is enjoying her work as a foreign
correspondent. She gets to live in nice hotels and
embrace an element of danger. She is currently located
in the middle of Jerusalem. She becomes very upset
when her best friend and drinking buddy, Shiv, is
murdered. Faith can tell there is a story behind this death
so she continues the investigation Shiv started. The trail
leads to a child-trafficking ring that may be connected to
a possible mole in Israeli intelligence. Faith struggles to
investigate while living in the midst of tensions between
Israelis and Palestinians.

Where it's reviewed:
Booklist, May 1, 2008, page 17

Other books by the same author:
Vodka Neat, 2008

Other books you might like:
Dan Fesperman, *The Amateur Spy*, 2008
Matt Beynon Rees, *The Collaborator of Bethlehem*, 2007
Daniel Silva, *The Messenger*, 2006
Minette Walters, *The Devil's Feather*, 2006

21

ANNA BLUNDY

Vodka Neat

(New York: St. Martin's, 2008)

Story type: Political
Series: Faith Zanetti. Book 3
Subject(s): Journalism; Marriage
Major character(s): Faith Zanetti, Journalist (foreign correspondent); Dimitri Sakhnov, Criminal
Time period(s): 2000s
Locale(s): Moscow, Russia

Summary: Foreign correspondent Faith Zanetti returns to Russia to work for a leading newspaper there. Upon arrival, she is arrested for the murders of her old neighbors. The killings took place 15 years ago, when Faith was last in Moscow. At the time, at age 19, she was married to Dimitri Sakhnov, a black marketer. Originally, Dimitri confessed to the murders, but after years in prison he fingers Faith. So the search is on to find out what really happened 15 years ago and to also find Dimitri, who has gone missing. Unfortunately, Faith can't rely on her own memory of the night of the murders; she was too drunk to remember what happened.

Where it's reviewed:
Booklist, May 1, 2008, page 43
Kirkus Reviews, March 15, 2008
Mystery News, June/July 2008, page 15
Mystery Scene, Summer 2008, page 76
Publishers Weekly, March 24, 2008, page 54

Other books by the same author:
The Bad News Bible, 2008

Other books you might like:
Jan Brogan, *A Confidential Source*, 2005
Brent Ghelfi, *Volk's Game*, 2007
Denise Mina, *The Dead Hour*, 2006
Boris Starling, *Vodka*, 2005

22

STEPHEN BOOTH

Scared to Live

(New York: Bantam, 2008)

Story type: Police Procedural
Series: Ben Cooper & Diane Fry. Book 7
Subject(s): Family
Major character(s): Ben Cooper, Detective—Police; Diane Fry, Detective—Police; Brian Mullen, Spouse, Survivor
Time period(s): 2000s
Locale(s): Derbyshire, England

Summary: A wife and two of her three children are killed in a house fire, which turns out have been arson. A reclusive woman is shot to death in her bedroom. Detective Sergeant Diane Fry and Detective Constable Ben Cooper and the rest of the police force in Edendale, Derbyshire, are hard at work trying to solve the crimes. The Mullen family seemed to be happy and close. They had just adopted a baby. Why would anyone try to kill them? Rose Shepherd lived quietly by herself in a small village and was thought to be a retired schoolteacher. Why would someone assassinate her at three in the morning? As Fry and Cooper research the lives of the victims, surprising links begin to turn up.

Where it's reviewed:
Publishers Weekly, March 3, 2008, page 30

Other books by the same author:
The Dead Place, 2007
One Last Breath, 2006
Blind to the Bones, 2003
Blood on the Tongue, 2002
Dancing with the Virgins, 2001

Other books you might like:
Reginald Hill, *Dialogues of the Dead*, 2001
P.D. James, *The Murder Room*, 2003
Peter Lovesey, *The Last Detective*, 1991
Barry Maitland, *No Trace*, 2006

23

RHYS BOWEN

A Royal Pain

(New York: Berkley, 2008)

Story type: Amateur Detective; Historical
Series: Lady Georgiana Rannoch. Book 2
Subject(s): Identity, Concealed; Satire
Major character(s): Victoria G. C. Eugenie Rannoch, Noblewoman; Darcy O'Mara, Nobleman; Princess Hannelore, Royalty
Time period(s): 1930s (1932)
Locale(s): London, England

Summary: Lady Georgiana, aka Georgie, is trying to stay solvent when the Queen calls her with a "job." In a desperate attempt to wrest the Prince of Wales from the alluring grasp of Mrs. Simpson, Her Majesty has invited Princess Hannelore of Bavaria to visit, in the hopes that her son will fall for her. One always obeys the Queen, so Georgie takes on Hanni, her maid, and her chaperone, with the help of her retired policeman grandfather and his neighbor, who act as butler and cook. Nothing goes as planned. The Prince shows no interest in Hanni, but Hanni is quite enthusiastic about other British men, including Darcy O'Mara, the Irish cad Georgie has fallen for despite herself. Then there is the dead body of the Communist sympathizer Hanni finds in a used bookshop.

Where it's reviewed:
Publishers Weekly, May 12, 2008, page 39

Other books by the same author:
Tell Me, Pretty Maiden, 2008
Her Royal Spyness, 2007
In Dublin's Fair City, 2007
Evanly Bodies, 2006
Evan Blessed, 2005

Other books you might like:
James Anderson, *The Affair of the 39 Cufflinks*, 2003
Jill Churchill, *Love for Sale*, 2003
Barbara Cleverly, *The Tomb of Zeus*, 2007
Carola Dunn, *The Bloody Tower*, 2007

24

RHYS BOWEN
Tell Me, Pretty Maiden
(New York: St. Martin's, 2008)

Story type: Historical/Victorian America
Series: Molly Murphy. Book 7
Subject(s): Irish Americans; Actors and Actresses
Major character(s): Molly Murphy, Immigrant (Irish), Detective—Private; Daniel Sullivan, Detective—Police (suspended)
Time period(s): 1900s (1902)
Locale(s): New York, New York

Summary: During the winter of 1902, private detective Molly Murphy is swamped with too many cases. A famous Broadway actress has hired Molly to investigate the spooky troubles that may prevent her new show from opening. A rich matron wants to investigate her nephew to see if he has vanished because he's suspected in a murder. Yet the case that Molly and Daniel Sullivan, her recently suspended police detective beau, are interested in the most is the discovery of a beautiful young woman lying unconscious in a snowdrift in the middle of Central Park. The woman wakes up confused and unable to speak.

Where it's reviewed:
Booklist, March 1, 2008, page 55
Publishers Weekly, January 21, 2008, page 158

Other books by the same author:
In Dublin's Fair City, 2007
O Danny Boy, 2006
In Like Flynn, 2005
Death of Riley, 2002

Other books you might like:
Karen Rose Cercone, *Steel Ashes*, 1997
Kathryn Miller Haines, *The War Against Miss Winter*, 2007
Troy Soos, *The Gilded Cage*, 2002
Victoria Thompson, *The Sarah Brandt Series*, 1999-

25

C.J. BOX
Blood Trail
(New York: Putnam, 2008)

Story type: Police Procedural
Series: Joe Pickett. Book 8

Subject(s): Revenge; Hunting
Major character(s): Joe Pickett, Game Warden; Nate Romanowski, Fugitive; Klamath Moore, Activist
Time period(s): 2000s
Locale(s): Saddlestring, Wyoming

Summary: As a special agent of the governor of Wyoming, Joe Pickett is ordered to help investigate the murder of a hunter. The man has been left hanging from a tree, dressed out like a game animal. The only clue is a poker chip found underneath the body. Joe discovers that two other men have been killed, also with poker chips left on the bodies. Under pressure, the Governor shuts down hunting season. Meanwhile, nationally known anti-hunting activist Klamath Moore has arrived in town and stirs things up. Is the killer someone in his group? When the professional tracker the State hired to find the killer is accidentally killed, Joe asks that falconer Nate Romanowski be released from prison to help him.

Where it's reviewed:
Booklist, February 15, 2008, page 4
Library Journal, April 1, 2008, page 63
Mystery News, June/July 2008, page 19
Publishers Weekly, March 17, 2008, page 46

Other books by the same author:
Blue Heaven, 2008
Free Fire, 2007
In Plain Sight, 2006
Out of Range, 2005
Trophy Hunt, 2004

Other books you might like:
Nevada Barr, *Winter Study*, 2008
Joseph Heywood, *Ice Hunter*, 2001
Craig Johnson, *Death without Company*, 2006
Clinton McKinzie, *The Edge of Justice*, 2002

26

C.J. BOX
Blue Heaven
(New York: St. Martin's, 2008)

Story type: Action/Adventure
Subject(s): Crime and Criminals
Major character(s): Annie Taylor, Child; William Taylor, Child; Jess Rawlins, Rancher
Time period(s): 2000s
Locale(s): Kootenai Bay, Idaho

Summary: While fishing in a creek, Annie Taylor and her brother William witness an execution carried out by four men. The sight sends them running through the woods of northern Idaho, inclined to distrust anyone they meet. The four men, who are retired corrupt police officers, set out to silence the two young witnesses. A search is soon underway for the missing kids and the killers offer their help to the town sheriff, who gladly accepts. When Annie and William find a barn to hide in for the night, they meet rancher Jess Rawlins, the only trustworthy person willing to help them.

Where it's reviewed:
Booklist, October 1, 2007, page 5
Crimespree, January/February 2008, page 63
Mystery News, February/March 2008, page 16
Publishers Weekly, October 15, 2007, page 37

Other books by the same author:
Free Fire, 2007
In Plain Sight, 2006
Winterkill, 2003
Savage Run, 2002
Open Season, 2001

Other books you might like:
Craig Johnson, *The Cold Dish*, 2004
Kris Nelscott, *A Dangerous Road*, 2000
Thomas Perry, *Dance for the Dead*, 1996
Rick Riordan, *Cold Springs*, 2003

27

GYLES BRANDRETH

Oscar Wilde and a Death of No Importance

(New York: Touchstone, 2007)

Story type: Historical/Victorian
Series: Oscar Wilde. Book 1
Subject(s): Writing
Major character(s): Oscar Wilde, Writer, Historical Figure; Robert Sherard, Historical Figure, Writer; Aidan Fraser, Detective—Police
Time period(s): 1880s; 1930s (1939)
Locale(s): London, England; Broadstairs, England; Paris, France

Summary: In the fall of 1889, poet and playwright Oscar Wilde discovers the bloody body of Billy Wood in a house of questionable reputation in London. When Wilde returns to the scene of the crime with his friends, Robert Sherard and Arthur Conan Doyle, Wood's body is gone. Although Doyle is returning to Edinburgh, he gives Wilde the name of a Scotland Yard detective who might be of some use, Aidan Fraser. When Fraser seems uninterested in the case, Wilde decides to conduct his own investigation. Looking at several suspects, including Wood's violent and abusive uncle, the case is taken more seriously when Billy Wood's head arrives at the Wilde household.

Where it's reviewed:
Booklist, November 1, 2007, page 29
Library Journal, November 1, 2007, page 46
Mystery News, December/January 2008, page 26
Mystery Scene, Winter 2008, page 78
Publishers Weekly, October 8, 2007, page 38

Other books you might like:
William J. Palmer, *The Dons and Mr. Dickens*, 2000
Roberta Rogow, *The Problem of the Evil Editor*, 2000
Walter Satterthwait, *Wilde West*, 1991
Donald Thomas, *Sherlock Holmes and the Voice of the Crypt and Other Tales*, 2002

28

GERRI BRIGHTWELL

The Dark Lantern

(New York: Crown, 2008)

Story type: Historical/Victorian
Subject(s): Identity; Secrets
Major character(s): Jane Wilbred, Servant; Mina Bentley, Spouse; Robert Bentley, Scientist
Time period(s): 1890s (1893); 1900s (1901)
Locale(s): London, England; Torquay, England

Summary: Sixteen-year-old Jane Wilbred has arrived in London to work as a maid in the Bentley home. An orphan from the Devon countryside, Jane is hoping to hide the fact that her late mother was a convicted murderess. Jane isn't the only one in the Bentley household with secrets. The servants are stealing from the Bentley family, and Mina, wife of Robert Bentley and the new lady of the house, is terrified that her former husband will find her in London. There is also a strange woman who appears at the Bentley house claiming to be the widow of Robert's brother Henry, recently lost at sea.

Where it's reviewed:
Booklist, February 1, 2008, page 26
Publishers Weekly, December 17, 2007, page 29

Other books you might like:
Ann Granger, *The Companion*, 2007
Robin Paige, *Death at Bishop's Keep*, 1994
Kate Ross, *A Broken Vessel*, 1994
Sarah Waters, *Fingersmith*, 2005

29

ANDREW BRITTON

The Invisible

(New York: Kensington, 2008)

Story type: Espionage
Series: Ryan Kealey. Book 3
Subject(s): Terrorism; Kidnapping
Major character(s): Ryan Kealey, Spy; Jonathan Harper, Government Official, Spy; Naomi Kharmai, Spy
Time period(s): 2000s
Locale(s): Islamabad, Pakistan; Washington, District of Columbia; Madrid, Spain

Summary: Former CIA operative Ryan Kealey has been wandering the world for four months now, ever since his girlfriend and colleague, Naomi Kharmai, left him. Jonathan Harper, Kealey's CIA handler, approaches Kealey in Iceland and asks him to return to his job. Several tourists were kidnapped in Pakistan, and Harper wants Kealey to retrieve them. As an incentive, Harper promises Kealey that he'll be working with Naomi. Kealey's job changes, however, when Brynn Fitzgerald, the Secretary of State, is kidnapped while in Pakistan. Authorities suspect Amari Saifi, the same terrorist who is believed to have kidnapped the missing tourists.

Where it's reviewed:
Booklist, March 1, 2008, page 54
Publishers Weekly, January 7, 2008, page 37

Other books by the same author:
The Assassin, 2007
The American, 2006

Other books you might like:
Cheryl Benard, *Moghul Buffet*, 1998
Vince Flynn, *Consent to Kill*, 2005
Jack Higgins, *The President's Daughter*, 1997
Francine Mathews, *The Secret Agent*, 2002

30

GRACE BROPHY

A Deadly Paradise

(New York: Soho Crime, 2008)

Story type: Police Procedural
Series: Alessandro Cenni. Book 2
Subject(s): Blackmail
Major character(s): Alessandro Cenni, Detective—
 Homicide; Elena Ottaviani, Police Officer; Anita Tan-
 gassi, Landlord
Time period(s): 2000s (2007); 1940s (1945)
Locale(s): Perugia, Italy; Paradiso, Italy; Venice, Italy

Summary: When the disfigured body of Jarvinia Baudler,
a former German cultural attache, is found in the small
Italian village of Paradiso, Commissario Alessandro
Cenni is called in to investigate. Among Cenni's suspects
is German diplomat Dieter Reimann who had an affair
with Baudler. Baudler used their affair to blackmail Reimann, using him to falsify passports. Another suspect is
the mysterious African woman with whom the bisexual
Baudler also had a relationship. As Cenni pursues various leads with the help of Inspector Elena Ottaviani,
Cenni discovers a link to an unsolved murder in Paradiso in 1978 involving Baudler's landlord, Anita Tangassi,
who was nine-years-old when she discovered the bodies
of a playmate and her mother.

Where it's reviewed:
Booklist, March 1, 2008, page 52
Library Journal, April 1, 2008, page 64
Publishers Weekly, March 3, 2008, page 32

Other books by the same author:
The Last Enemy, 2007

Other books you might like:
Michael Dibdin, *Dead Lagoon*, 1994
David Hewson, *The Villa of Mysteries*, 2005
Donna Leon, *Acqua Alta*, 1996
Magdalen Nabb, *The Marshal and the Madwoman*,
 1988

31

RITA MAE BROWN
SNEAKY PIE BROWN , Co-Author

The Purrfect Murder

(New York: Bantam, 2008)

Story type: Amateur Detective
Series: Mrs. Murphy. Book 16
Subject(s): Animals/Cats; Abortion
Major character(s): Mary Minor Haristeen, Postal Worker;
 Pharamond Haristeen, Veterinarian, Spouse; Tazio
 Chappers, Architect
Time period(s): 2000s
Locale(s): Crozet, Virginia

Summary: Mary Minor "Harry" Haristeen's cozy home
town of Crozet, Virginia, is being threatened once again.
Two murders have taken place. The first victim is Dr.
William Wylde, a controversial ob-gyn known for his
willingness to perform abortions. Wylde is shot dead by
an anti-abortion activist who surrenders to the police.
The other victim is Carla Paulson, a socialite who was
determined to make her mark in Crozet. She is found
stabbed to death and architect Tazio Chappers, a friend
of Harry's, is holding the knife. Harry knows that Tazio
couldn't be the murderer, but the rest of the town thinks
otherwise. With the help of her intelligent cats, Harry
discovers a connection between these seemingly unrelated cases.

Where it's reviewed:
Publishers Weekly, December 10, 2007, page 38

Other books by the same author:
Puss 'n Cahoots, 2007
Cat's Eyewitness, 2006
Sour Puss, 2006
The Hounds and the Fury, 2006

Other books you might like:
Lilian Jackson Braun, *The Cat Who Blew the Whistle*,
 1995
Elizabeth Brundage, *The Doctor's Wife*, 2004
Carole Nelson Douglas, *Catnap*, 1992
Shirley Rousseau Murphy, *Cat Spitting Mad*, 2001

32

DON BRUNS

St. Barts Breakdown

(Ipswich, Massachusetts: Oceanview, 2008)

Story type: Amateur Detective
Series: Mick Sever. Book 4
Subject(s): Music and Musicians; Journalism
Major character(s): Mick Sever, Journalist; Danny Murtz,
 Musician, Murderer; Michelle Kirkendall, Detec-
 tive—Police
Time period(s): 2000s
Locale(s): Chicago, Illinois; St. Barts, Caribbean

Summary: Chicago music journalist Mick Sever is assigned to interview legendary composer and music

producer Danny Murtz. Murtz is known to have a drug problem and at least two women he dated have disappeared. Sever's editor at the Chicago Tribune wants Sever to fly to St. Bart, where Murtz is staying, and ask him about the missing women. Just after Sever receives the assignment, a car tries to run him over on a Chicago sidewalk. Then, after his arrival on St. Bart, his rental car blows up. Sever begins to wonder if the events are a coincidence, or if Murtz is trying to get rid of him just as he got rid of those women.

Where it's reviewed:
Booklist, November 15, 2007, page 23
Deadly Pleasures, Spring 2008, page 61
Library Journal, January 15, 2008, page 67
Mystery Scene, Spring 2008, page 56
Publishers Weekly, December 24, 2007, page 31

Other books by the same author:
Stuff to Die For, 2007
South Beach Shakedown, 2006
Barbados Heat, 2003
Jamaica Blue, 2002

Other books you might like:
Ace Atkins, *Dark End of the Street*, 2002
Paul Charles, *I Love the Sound of Breaking Glass*, 2004
Elmore Leonard, *Be Cool*, 1999
J.R. Ripley, *Murder in St. Barts*, 2003

33

JEFF BUICK

Delicate Chaos

(New York: Leisure, 2008)

Story type: Action/Adventure
Subject(s): Business; Suspense
Major character(s): Leona Hewitt, Banker, Restaurateur; Mike Anderson, Businessman
Time period(s): 2000s
Locale(s): Washington, District of Columbia; Morgantown, West Virginia; Marsabit, Kenya

Summary: Recently promoted to vice president of a Washington, D.C., bank, Leona Hewitt is given a high profile corporate client, Coal-Balt, which is undergoing a business conversion. Just as Leona and her team begin to investigate Coal-Balt and its financial status, two people connected to the company suddenly die: the CEO of Coal-Balt and a senator who was proposing legislation that would have cost Coal-Balt millions. Leona rejects Coal-Balt's proposal and is soon targeted by a murderer. Meanwhile, Leona's business associate Mike Anderson, who distributes the money raised by her foundation Save Them, a nonprofit organization dedicated to saving African elephants, is kidnapped while on business in Nairobi.

Where it's reviewed:
Mystery News, June/July 2008, page 28

Other books by the same author:
Shell Game, 2007
African Ice, 2006
Bloodline, 2005
Lethal Dose, 2005

Other books you might like:
Suzanne Arruda, *Stalking Ivory*, 2007
John Billheimer, *Drybone Hollow*, 2003
Stephen Frey, *The Takeover*, 1995
Brad Meltzer, *The Milionaires*, 2002

34

MEG CABOT

Big Boned

(New York: Avon, 2007)

Story type: Amateur Detective
Series: Heather Wells. Book 3
Subject(s): College Life
Major character(s): Heather Wells, Administrator
Time period(s): 2000s
Locale(s): New York

Summary: Heather Wells is a plus-size ex-pop star turned Assistant Dormitory Director at New York College. The place where she works has been nicknamed the "Death Dorm" due to the number of murders that have occurred there throughout its existence. The name will stick: the dorm's interim director is found dead. The college suspects graduate student activist Sebastian Blumenthal. Sebastian gives Heather a clue that makes her believe he is innocent, so she decides to solve the case. She also has to deal with casually dating her math professor while she yearns for Cooper Cartwright, her private investigator neighbor.

Where it's reviewed:
Booklist, November 15, 2007, page 20
Publishers Weekly, September 17, 2007, page 39

Other books by the same author:
Size 14 Is Not Fat Either, 2007
Size 12 Is Not Fat, 2006

Other books you might like:
Maggie Barbieri, *Extracurricular Activities*, 2007
Sue Anne Jaffarian, *The Curse of the Holy Pail*, 2007
Harley Jane Kozak, *Dating Dead Men*, 2004
Laura Levine, *Shoes to Die For*, 2005

35

TOM CAIN

The Accident Man

(New York: Viking, 2008)

Story type: Alternate History
Series: Samuel Carver. Book 1
Subject(s): Conspiracies; Murder
Major character(s): Samuel Carver, Criminal; Alexandra Petrova, Criminal, Spy; Grigori Kursk, Criminal
Time period(s): 1990s (1997)
Locale(s): Paris, France; London, England; Geneva, Switzerland

Summary: A former Royal Marine, assassin Samuel Carver makes accidents happen. One August night in 1997, Carver is ordered to create an auto accident under a

bridge in Paris. The supposed victim is a Pakistani playboy and known terrorist. That night as Carver carries out his job, things suddenly go terribly wrong and Carver is targeted by Russian thug Grigori Kursk. As news of the car accident reaches the media, Carver learns that the occupants of the car he caused to crash were the Princess of Wales and her boyfriend. As Carver is now considered a loose end, Carver's mysterious handler, Max, has ordered Carver's death. Now the people Carver works for are out to eliminate him. At the same time, Carver goes after the people who set him up.

Where it's reviewed:
Booklist, December 1, 2007, page 24
Library Journal, February 15, 2008, page 89
Mystery Scene, Winter 2008, page 66
Publishers Weekly, November 12, 2007, page 33

Other books you might like:
Barry Eisler, *Requiem for an Assassin*, 2007
Gary Hardwick, *The Executioner's Game*, 2005
Stephen Hunter, *Point of Impact*, 1993
David L. Robbins, *The Assassins Gallery*, 2006

36

DOROTHY CANNELL

Goodbye, Ms. Chips
(New York: St. Martin's, 2007)

Story type: Amateur Detective
Series: Ellie Haskell. Book 13
Subject(s): Academia
Major character(s): Ellie Haskell, Interior Decorator, Detective—Amateur; Dorcas Critchley, Teacher; Mrs. Battle, Principal
Time period(s): 2000s (2008)
Locale(s): England

Summary: Ellie Haskell, mother of three and interior decorator, gets a call from her old friend Dorcas Critchley, now games mistress at their old boarding school, St. Roberta's. The headmistress has heard of Ellie's detecting skills and wants her to look into the theft of the Loverly Lacrosse Cup. Ellie can't say no to an old friend. When the retired lacrosse coach, Marilyn Chips, is murdered, Ellie looks into both the theft and the murder with the help of a student, Ariel Hopkins.

Where it's reviewed:
Booklist, April 1, 2008, page 30
Deadly Pleasures, Spring 2008, page 39
Mystery News, June/July 2008, page 30
Mystery Scene, Spring 2008, page 64
Publishers Weekly, February 18, 2008, page 139

Other books by the same author:
Withering Heights, 2007
The Trouble with Harriet, 1999
Femmes Fatal, 1992
Mum's the Word, 1990
The Thin Woman, 1984

Other books you might like:
Ruth Dudley Edwards, *Matricide at St. Martha's*, 1994
Kate Flora, *An Educated Death*, 1997
Denise Swanson, *Murder of a Sleeping Beauty*, 2002
Josephine Tey, *Miss Pym Disposes*, 1946

37

ALEX CARR　(Pseudonym of Jenny Siler)

The Prince of Bagram Prison
(New York: Random House, 2008)

Story type: Espionage
Subject(s): Military Bases; Prisoners and Prisons
Major character(s): Katherine Caldwell, Military Personnel, Teacher; Jamal, Fugitive; Harry Comfort, Spy, Aged Person
Time period(s): 2000s; 1970s
Locale(s): Madrid, Spain; Casablanca, Morocco; Saigon, Vietnam

Summary: In Madrid, 18-year-old Jamal is on the run from the CIA. As a CIA informant, Jamal fabricated a sighting of a well-known terrorist, but unfortunately his misinformation has caused Jamal to be the target of agents who want to protect certain secrets and identities. Desperate for help, Jamal contacts his former CIA handler, Harry Comfort. Meanwhile, Arabic specialist Kat Caldwell is called away from her teaching position and ordered to find Jamal. Kat first met the young Moroccan boy when she was an Army interrogator at the Bagram Airbase in Afghanistan. Having earned Jamal's trust once, Kat is now supposed to use that trust to convince Jamal to come out of hiding.

Where it's reviewed:
Booklist, February 1, 2008 page 32
Library Journal, February 15, 2008, page 90
Mystery Scene, Winter 2008, page 76
Publishers Weekly, January 7, 2008, page 36

Other books by the same author:
An Accidental American, 2005

Other books you might like:
Alex Berenson, *The Ghost War*, 2008
Dan Fesperman, *The Prisoner of Guantanamo*, 2006
Stella Rimington, *Secret Asset*, 2007
Greg Rucka, *A Gentleman's Game*, 2004

38

MEGAN CHANCE

The Spiritualist
(New York: Three Rivers, 2008)

Story type: Historical/Victorian America
Subject(s): Spiritualism
Major character(s): Evelyn Atherton, Widow(er); Michel Jourdain, Psychic; Benjamin Rampling, Lawyer
Time period(s): 1850s (1857)
Locale(s): New York, New York

Summary: Evelyn Atherton attends a spirit circle with her husband Peter. She has no idea that it will be the last time she will see her husband alive. Several days later, the police inform Evelyn that Peter's body has been discovered in the river. Peter's family believes Evelyn married Peter for his money. They pressure the police into arresting her for his murder. Evelyn finds shelter at the home of Dorothy Bennett, a wealthy widow who has been using the services of Michel Jourdain, a charismatic medium, to contact her dead sons. It was at Dorothy's house that Evelyn last saw Peter. Believing that Jourdain had something to do with Peter's death, Evelyn investigates the medium under the watchful eye of Peter's law partner, Benjamin Rampling.

Where it's reviewed:
Publishers Weekly, March 17, 2008, page 48

Other books by the same author:
An Inconvenient Wife, 2004
Susannah Morrow, 2002
The Fatal Key, 2002
Seven Roads to Hell, 2000
A Season in Eden, 1999

Other books you might like:
Rhys Bowen, *In Like Flynn*, 2005
Joseph Gangemi, *Inamorata*, 2004
Roy Johansen, *Beyond Belief*, 2001
Roberta Rogow, *The Problem of the Spiteful Spiritualist*, 1999

39

LAURA CHILDS

The Silver Needle Murder

(New York: Berkley, 2008)

Story type: Amateur Detective
Series: Theodosia Browning. Book 9
Subject(s): Movie Industry
Major character(s): Theodosia Browning, Businesswoman, Detective—Amateur; Drayton Conneley, Assistant, Caterer; Burt Tidwell, Detective—Homicide
Time period(s): 2000s
Locale(s): Charleston, South Carolina

Summary: Theodosia Browning, owner of the Indigo Tea Shop, and her staff are busy with the arrival of the Charleston Film Festival. At the opening night party, well-known film director Jordan Cole is shot. Theo, standing nearby, sees the murderer fleeing the scene, but can't quite make out who it is. The festival's organizer, local historian Timothy Neville, asks Theo to clear his granddaughter, Isabelle, as a possible murder suspect in the investigation. Isabelle Neville also works in the film industry, and was one of Cole's many spurned lovers. Theo's own life may be in danger when she receives several warnings to stop her investigation.

Where it's reviewed:
Mystery News, April/May 2008, page 13
Publishers Weekly, January 28, 2008, page 44

Other books by the same author:
Dragonwell Dead, 2007
Blood Orange Brewing, 2006
Motif for Murder, 2006
Chamomile Mourning, 2005
Bound for Murder, 2004

Other books you might like:
Susan Wittig Albert, *Chile Death*, 1998
Donna Andrews, *Revenge of the Wrought-Iron Flamingos*, 2001
Rita Mae Brown, *Whisker of Evil*, 2004
Jill Churchill, *War and Peas*, 1996

40

BLAIZE CLEMENT

Even Cat Sitters Get the Blues

(New York: St. Martin's, 2008)

Story type: Amateur Detective
Series: Dixie Hemingway. Book 3
Subject(s): Pets; Murder
Major character(s): Dixie Hemingway, Detective—Police (former); Ken Kurtz, Scientist
Time period(s): 2000s
Locale(s): Siesta Key, Florida

Summary: Still recovering from the death of her husband and daughter, Dixie Hemingway has given up police work and has opened a pet sitting business. She receives a strange call from a man who wants her to take care of his iguana. Out on a bike ride, Dixie gets caught in the rain and pedals to the gatehouse of a mansion for shelter. When she gets there the guard inside has been shot. Not wanting anything to do with murder she immediately leaves the scene. Whether she likes it or not, however, Dixie is now involved in the case. When she finally leaves to take care of the iguana, she discovers that her appointment is in the same mansion. The man who lives there, a strange and sickly scientist, claims to have never called her.

Where it's reviewed:
Library Journal, December 15, 2007, page 91
Mystery Scene, Winter 2008, page 71
Publishers Weekly, November 12, 2007, page 39

Other books by the same author:
Duplicity Dogged the Dachshund, 2007
Curiosity Killed the Cat Sitter, 2006

Other books you might like:
Lydia Adamson, *A Cat with a Fiddle*, 1993
Liz Evans, *Sick as a Parrot*, 2004
Linda O. Johnston, *Fright of the Iguana*, 2007
Claire Matturro, *Skinny-Dipping*, 2004

41

HARLAN COBEN

Hold Tight

(New York: Dutton, 2008)

Story type: Family Saga; Child-in-Peril
Subject(s): Computers; Suicide

Major character(s): Adam Baye, Teenager; Mike Baye, Doctor, Parent; Tia Baye, Lawyer, Parent
Time period(s): 2000s
Locale(s): Glen Rock, New Jersey; New York, New York

Summary: Mike and Tia Baye are so worried about their teenage son Adam, who hasn't been the same since the death of his best friend Spencer, that they decide to put spyware on his computer. They plan to follow his trail through the electronic world in real time. When Adam disappears, Mike follows him to a terrible neighborhood in New York City, where Mike is beaten to within an inch of his life. The two parents are separated by work and other circumstances as they try desperately to find Adam, who is working through the many issues relating to his best friend's suicide.

Where it's reviewed:
Booklist, March 1, 2008, page 29
Entertainment Weekly, April 18, 2008, page 67
Mystery News, June/July 2008, page 28
Mystery Scene, Spring 2008, page 67
Publishers Weekly, February 18, 2008, page 136

Other books by the same author:
The Woods, 2007
Promise Me, 2006
The Innocent, 2005
Just One Look, 2004
No Second Chance, 2003

Other books you might like:
Michael Connelly, *The Poet*, 1995
Robert Crais, *Hostage*, 2001
Jeffery Deaver, *A Maiden's Grave*, 1995
Marcus Sakey, *The Blade Itself*, 2007

42

TOM COFFEY

Blood Alley

(New Milford, Connecticut: Toby, 2008)

Story type: Historical
Subject(s): Newspapers; Law Enforcement
Major character(s): Patrick Grimes, Journalist, Veteran; Sylvia Price, Socialite; McCracken, Editor
Time period(s): 1940s (1946)
Locale(s): New York, New York; Woodside, New York

Summary: A phone call in the middle of the night summons reporter and World War II veteran Patrick Grimes to a crime scene. The body of Amanda Price, eldest daughter of businessman Harrington Price, was discovered in an alley in a seedy part of New York City. William Anderson, the night watchman who found the body, is taken into custody and he is later arrested for her murder. Grimes is convinced of William's innocence, even after Anderson confesses. Beginning his own investigation into Amanda's murder, Grimes befriends Amanda's socialite sister, Sylvia, to gain some knowledge of who might want to kill her sister.

Where it's reviewed:
Mystery Scene, Summer 2008, page 69
Publishers Weekly, March 24, 2008, page 53

Other books by the same author:
Miami Twilight, 2001
The Serpent Club, 1999

Other books you might like:
Michael Blaine, *The Midnight Band of Mercy*, 2004
Loren D. Estleman, *Gas City*, 2008
Brent Monahan, *The Manhattan Island Clubs*, 2003
Andrew Vachss, *Two Trains Running*, 2005

43

NANCY J. COHEN

Killer Knots

(New York: Kensington, 2007)

Story type: Amateur Detective
Series: Marla Shore. Book 9
Subject(s): Art; Cruise Ships
Major character(s): Marla Shore, Hairdresser, Detective—Amateur; Dalton Vail, Detective—Police; Oliver Smernoff, Museum Curator
Time period(s): 2000s
Locale(s): At Sea

Summary: Beautician and salon owner Marla Shore is excited to be on a cruise with her fiance, Dalton Vail. Marla is even looking forward to spending some time with Dalton's parents and his teenage daughter, Brianna, who are also onboard the ship. After arriving at their room, Marla receives a threatening letter addressed to a Martha Shore. When another name-related mix-up causes Marla and Dalton to be seated with several museum employees during dinner, Marla begins to wonder if the misunderstanding was intentional or an accident. When the museum employees begin having mysterious accidents, Marla can't help but investigate, especially since the museum has a tragic connection to an artist Marla knew personally.

Where it's reviewed:
Publishers Weekly, September 10, 2007, page 43

Other books by the same author:
Perish by Pedicure, 2006
Dead Roots, 2005
Died Blonde, 2004
Highlights to Heaven, 2003
Body Wave, 2002

Other books you might like:
Shelley Freydont, *High Seas Murder*, 2000
Maddy Hunter, *Hula Done It?*, 2005
Hailey Lind, *Feint of Art*, 2006
Grant Michaels, *Dead on Your Feet*, 1993

44

REED FARREL COLEMAN

Empty Ever After

(Madison, Wisconsin: Bleak House, 2008)

Story type: Private Detective; Family Saga
Series: Moe Prager. Book 5

Subject(s): Secrets; Cemeteries
Major character(s): Moe Prager, Detective—Private; Katy Maloney, Divorced Person
Time period(s): 2000s
Locale(s): New York, New York; Dayton, Ohio

Summary: Katy Maloney comes back into ex-NYPD officer Moe Prager's life years after she divorced him. Their marriage was destroyed when she discovered the secrets that Moe had been keeping about her dead brother Patrick. Now Patrick's gravesite has been desecrated and his bones stolen. Then another graveyard is disturbed in Ohio, with connections to Patrick and Moe. Moe has to confront his past to figure out who is trying to send him a message. To do so he needs to look into all of his own cases in order to find the saboteur, and to find the man who belongs in the vacant grave.

Where it's reviewed:
Booklist, May 1, 2008, page 44
Deadly Pleasures, Spring 2008, page 35
Publishers Weekly, January 21, 2008, page 157

Other books by the same author:
Soul Patch, 2006
The James Deans, 2005
Redemption Street, 2004
Walking the Perfect Square, 2002
They Don't Play Stickball in Milwaukee, 1997

Other books you might like:
Raymond Chandler, *The Long Goodbye*, 1954
Michael Connelly, *Angels Flight*, 1999
Michael Koryta, *Sorrow's Anthem*, 2006
S.J. Rozan, *Concourse*, 1995

45

KATE COLLINS

A Rose from the Dead

(New York: Obsidian, 2007)

Story type: Amateur Detective
Series: Abby Knight. Book 6
Subject(s): Murder
Major character(s): Abby Knight, Store Owner (florist), Detective—Amateur; Marco Salvare, Businessman (former); Delilah Dove, Undertaker
Time period(s): 2000s
Locale(s): Midwest

Summary: Abby Knight owns Bloomers, a flower shop in New Chapel, Indiana. In order to increase her business she decides to share a booth with her funeral director friends at the Midwestern Funeral Directors Association convention. Sybil Blount, the organizer of the convention, isn't particularly well-liked. She is found dead, locked in a casket. Abby, who was tricked into being locked into a display coffin earlier by two pranksters, assumes that Sybil's death is another prank gone seriously wrong. The police, however, look to Abby's friend Delilah as a suspect. Abby is determined more than ever to prove the police wrong and asks her boyfriend, Marco, to help. As they investigate, they find that Sybil had made many strange enemies in the funeral business.

Where it's reviewed:
Mystery News, February/March 2008, page 27

Other books by the same author:
Acts of Violets, 2007
Snipped in the Bud, 2006
Dearly Depotted, 2005
Slay It with Flowers, 2005
Mum's the Word, 2004

Other books you might like:
Sandra Balzo, *Grounds for Murder*, 2007
Mark de Castrique, *Foolish Undertaking*, 2006
Janis Harrison, *Lilies That Fester*, 2001
Julie Wray Herman, *Three Dirty Women and the Bitter Brew*, 2001

46

MARSHALL COOK

Obsessions

(Madison, Wisconsin: Bleak House, 2008)

Story type: Amateur Detective
Series: Monona Quinn. Book 4
Subject(s): Writing
Major character(s): Monona Quinn, Editor; Douglas Stennett, Accountant; Lloyd Odoms, Mentally Ill Person
Time period(s): 2000s
Locale(s): Shepherdstown, Wisconsin

Summary: As a gift, newspaper editor Monona Quinn's husband Doug enrolls her in a writer's workshop. Doug and Monona are enjoying their visit to the quiet northwoods town of Shepherdstown, Wisconsin until Doug stumbles over the body of bestselling mystery writer Fletcher Downs. Downs was the writer-in-residence for the conference and was teaching the mystery writing class that Monona is taking. There are many suspects, including Monona's fellow students, the women Downs slept with, and residents of Shepherdstown, which holds its own secrets and is the site of two other recent murders.

Where it's reviewed:
Booklist, May 1, 2008, page 39
Publishers Weekly, April 28, 2008, page 116

Other books by the same author:
Twin Killing, 2007
Murder at Midnight, 2005
Murder Over Easy, 2003

Other books you might like:
Michael Craft, *Body Language*, 1999
Mary Daheim, *The Alpine Escape*, 1995
Dean James, *Faked to Death*, 2003
Joyce Lamb, *Caught in the Act*, 2004

47

THOMAS H. COOK

Master of the Delta

(New York: Harcourt, 2008)

Story type: Psychological Suspense
Subject(s): Small Town Life; Secrets
Major character(s): Jack Branch, Teacher; Eddie Miller, Student—High School
Time period(s): 1950s (1954)
Locale(s): Lakeland, Mississippi

Summary: Jack Branch, the son of a prominent family in Lakeland, Mississippi, takes a job as a teacher at the local high school out of a sense of duty. Deeply interested in evil and its many incarnations, he becomes fascinated when he discovers that one of his students, Eddie Miller, is the son of the famous "Coed Killer," who killed a girl when Eddie was five-years-old. He encourages Eddie to write a paper about his father. As Eddie delves into his research, he uncovers more secrets about the town than is comfortable for anyone, including Jack Branch.

Where it's reviewed:
Booklist, March 1, 2008, page 53
Publishers Weekly, April 14, 2008, page 38

Other books by the same author:
The Cloud of Unknowning, 2006
Red Leaves, 2005
Into the Web, 2004
Peril, 2004
The Chatham School Affair, 1996

Other books you might like:
Patricia Highsmith, *The Talented Mr. Ripley*, 1955
Ruth Rendell, *A Judgement in Stone*, 1977
Peter Robinson, *Caedmon's Song*, 1990
Minette Walters, *Disordered Minds*, 2003

48

PHILIP R. CRAIG

Vineyard Chill

(New York: Scribner, 2008)

Story type: Amateur Detective
Series: Martha's Vineyard. Book 19
Subject(s): Drugs; Boatbuilding
Major character(s): J.W. Jackson, Police Officer (retired); Zee Jackson, Nurse; Clay Stockton, Friend
Time period(s): 2000s
Locale(s): Martha's Vineyard, Massachusetts

Summary: It's winter on the Vineyard in this last book of the series. (Author Philip Craig died in 2007.) J.W. has nothing more on his mind than getting seaweed mulch for his garden when an old friend, Clay Stockton, visits. Clay ends up staying, working on building a boat. Then two rather nasty-looking men come knocking on J.W. and Zee's front door, looking for Clay. Turns out Clay got involved in a marijuana business, tried to leave it, and is running from someone who doesn't like that decision. At the same time, J.W.'s friend Bonzo finds an old robin's nest with some human hair in it, hair that could belong to a young woman who disappeared the spring before. Between helping the local police try to find the girl and keeping Clay safe, J.W. has his hands full.

Where it's reviewed:
Publishers Weekly, April 7, 2008, page 45

Other books by the same author:
Vineyard Stalker, 2007
Dead in Vineyard Sand, 2006
Vineyard Prey, 2005
Murder at a Vineyard Mansion, 2004
A Vineyard Killing, 2003

Other books you might like:
Archer Mayor, *The Ragman's Memory*, 1996
Cynthia Riggs, *Shooting Star*, 2007
Sarah R. Shaber, *Simon Said*, 1997
William G. Tapply, *Out Cold*, 2006

49

LAURA CRUM

Chasing Cans

(McKinleyville, California: Perseverance, 2008)

Story type: Amateur Detective
Series: Gail McCarthy. Book 10
Subject(s): Animals/Horses; Veterinarians
Major character(s): Gail McCarthy, Veterinarian, Detective—Amateur; Jeri Ward, Detective—Police; Rita Hanson, Technician, Murderer
Time period(s): 2000s
Locale(s): Santa Cruz, California

Summary: Horse veterinarian Gail McCarthy is slowly adjusting to motherhood. When neighbor Lindee Stone claims the field between her training barn and Gail's land, Gail storms over to Lindee's. Shortly after her arrival, Gail witnesses Lindee barrel racing a particularly difficult horse. When the horse begins to balk, Lindee yanks on the reins and pulls the horse back on top of her, killing herself instantly. Gail, standing nearby, believes that Lindee was unconscious before she hit the ground. She shares her suspicions with her friend, Detective Jeri Ward. When a second accident at Lindee's puts a horse trainer in a coma, Gail knows that Lindee's death was not an accident.

Where it's reviewed:
Library Journal, February 1, 2008, page 51
Publishers Weekly, February 11, 2008, page 54

Other books by the same author:
Moonblind, 2006
Forged, 2004
Hayburner, 2003
Breakaway, 2001
Slickrock, 1999

Other books you might like:
Cynthia Baxter, *Lead a Horse to Murder*, 2005
Kit Ehrman, *At Risk*, 2002
Jody Jaffee, *Horse of a Different Killer*, 1995
Lillian M. Roberts, *Riding for a Fall*, 1996

50

RONALD CUTLER

The Secret Scroll

(New York: Beaufort, 2008)

Story type: Theological
Subject(s): Archaeology; Christianity
Major character(s): Josh Cohan, Professor, Archaeologist; Danielle Ben Daniel, Archaeologist; Alexander Paul, Wealthy, Benefactor
Time period(s): 2000s
Locale(s): Jerusalem, Israel; Nazareth, Israel

Summary: While on a sabbatical in Jerusalem, American archaeologist Josh Cohan discovers an ancient jar containing a scroll covered with Aramaic text. Translating part of the scroll, Cohan believes that it was written by Jesus Christ. Turning the scroll over to fellow archaeologist Moshe Ben Daniel, who works for the Israel Antiquities Authority in Jerusalem, Cohan soon discovers that another organization wants the scroll as well. The Guardians are an ancient extremist religious group, and will stop at nothing to recover the scroll. When several of the IAA members who were working on the scroll are kidnapped, including Ben Daniel's daughter, Cohan realizes that the scroll is more controversial than he ever thought.

Where it's reviewed:
Booklist, January 1, 2008, page 50
Publishers Weekly, December 17, 2007, page 34

Other books you might like:
William Dietrich, *The Rosetta Key*, 2008
Daniel Easterman, *The Judas Testament*, 1994
Gregg Loomis, *The Sinai Secret*, 2008
James Rollins, *Map of Bones*, 2005

51

MARY DAHEIM

The Alpine Traitor

(New York: Ballantine, 2008)

Story type: Amateur Detective
Series: Emma Lord. Book 20
Subject(s): Newspapers; Small Town Life
Major character(s): Emma Lord, Publisher, Journalist; Milo Dodge, Police Officer; Kelsey Cavanaugh Platte, Heiress
Time period(s): 2000s
Locale(s): Alpine, Washington

Summary: Emma Lord, publisher of Alpine, Washington's weekly newspaper *The Advocate*, is surprised when a man approaches her about buying her newspaper. Emma's surprise soon turns to shock when she finds out that the *Advocate*'s would-be buyer, Dylan Platte, is representing the heirs of her former lover and fiance, the late Tom Cavanaugh. Shortly after Emma turns down Dylan's offer, his body is discovered at the local motel and Sheriff Milo Dodge orders Emma not to leave town, disrupting a weekend getaway in Seattle. Emma's own investigation into Dylan's death takes a strange turn when one of her employees is shot and another Dylan Platte turns up in Alpine.

Where it's reviewed:
Booklist, March 1, 2008, page 54
Publishers Weekly, January 7, 2008, page 39

Other books by the same author:
The Alpine Scandal, 2007
The Alpine Recluse, 2006
The Alpine Quilt, 2005
The Alpine Pursuit, 2003
The Alpine Obituary, 2002

Other books you might like:
Michael Craft, *Bitch Slap*, 2004
Jerome Doolittle, *Kill Story*, 1995
Cynthia Riggs, *The Paperwhite Narcissus*, 2005
Penny Warner, *Dead Body Language*, 1997

52

JEFFERY DEAVER

The Broken Window

(New York: Simon & Schuster, 2008)

Story type: Police Procedural
Series: Lincoln Rhyme. Book 8
Subject(s): Serial Killers; Identity
Major character(s): Lincoln Rhyme, Criminologist, Handicapped (paraplegic); Amelia Sachs, Detective—Police; Andrew Sterling, Businessman, Computer Expert
Time period(s): 2000s
Locale(s): New York, New York

Summary: While overseeing the conclusion of a manhunt taking place in England, Lincoln Rhyme learns that his cousin, Arthur, has been charged with murder. Rhyme, a paraplegic forensic consultant for the NYPD, agrees to look into Arthur's case after a plea from Arthur's wife Judy. Rhyme and his girlfriend/detective partner Amelia Sachs study the evidence against Arthur, which seems incontrovertible. DNA left at the apartment and an eyewitness all point to Arthur Rhyme both killing Alice Sanderson and stealing a valuable painting she had recently purchased. As Rhyme and Sachs dig into the case, they discover other similar cases as well as connections to a data mining company, Strategic Systems Datacorp.

Where it's reviewed:
Booklist, May 1, 2008, page 22
Library Journal, May 15, 2008, page 90
Mystery News, June/July 2008, page 22
Publishers Weekly, April 14, 2008, page 36

Other books by the same author:
The Cold Moon, 2006
The Twelfth Card, 2005
The Vanished Man, 2003
The Empty Chair, 2002
The Stone Monkey, 2002

Other books you might like:
Harlan Coben, *Hold Tight*, 2008
Sue Grafton, *T Is for Trespass*, 2007
Judith Kelman, *Every Step You Take*, 2003
Thomas Perry, *Death Benefits*, 2001

53

HANNAH DENNISON

A Vicky Hill Exclusive!

(New York: Berkley, 2008)

Story type: Amateur Detective; Humor
Series: Vicky Hill. Book 1
Subject(s): Journalism; Animals/Chickens
Major character(s): Vicky Hill, Journalist; Annabel Lake, Journalist
Time period(s): 2000s
Locale(s): Gipping-on-Plym, England

Summary: Vicky Hill works the funeral beat for The Gipping Gazette. She hates that her job is so dull, but it is about to become interesting. A handsome man crashes a funeral and ends up kissing the widow. And there might be a connection between the gruesome deaths of three chickens and local celebrity Sir Hugh Trewallyn, a hedge-jumping enthusiast. Sir Hugh was found with chicken legs in his mouth. Vicky starts to uncover many secrets in the small English harbor town of Gipping-on-Pym. This could be Vicky's big break if her rival, Annabel Lake, doesn't succeed with her campaign of sabotage against Vicky.

Where it's reviewed:
Mystery News, April/May 2008, page 13

Other books you might like:
Jan Brogan, *A Confidential Source*, 2005
Dorothy Cannell, *The Thin Woman*, 1984
Kit Frazier, *Dead Copy*, 2007
Leslie Meier, *Bake Sale Murder*, 2006

54

JO DERESKE

Index to Murder

(New York: Avon, 2008)

Story type: Amateur Detective
Series: Helma Zukas. Book 11
Subject(s): Libraries; Artists and Art
Major character(s): Helma Zukas, Librarian; Ruth Winthrop, Artist
Time period(s): 2000s
Locale(s): Bellehaven, Washington

Summary: Ruth Winthrop is an avant-garde artist who specializes in painting pictures of an ex-lover who meets an untimely and mysterious end. Two of her paintings are stolen before they can be shown. Ruth turns to her best friend, crime-solving librarian Helma Zukas. Helma uses her orderly—almost OCD—skills to investigate her cases. The trail leads Helma to rival artists, angry ex-

wives and a disruptive group of local tree-huggers. Since no one is asking for a ransom for the paintings, Helma and Ruth figure that someone doesn't want them to be seen.

Other books by the same author:
Catalogue of Death, 2007
Bookmarked to Die, 2006
Miss Zukas Shelves the Evidence, 2000
Miss Zukas in Death's Shadow, 1999
Final Notice, 1998

Other books you might like:
Charlaine Harris, *Poppy Done to Death*, 2003
D.R. Meredith, *Murder by the Book*, 2006
Louise Penny, *Still Life*, 2006
Janice Steinberg, *Death of a Postmodernist*, 1995

55

DAVID DICKINSON

Death on the Holy Mountain

(New York: Soho Constable, 2008)

Story type: Historical/Edwardian
Series: Lord Francis Powerscourt. Book 7
Subject(s): Detection; Art
Major character(s): Lord Francis Powerscourt, Nobleman, Detective—Private; Johnny Fitzgerald, Writer; Richard Butler, Landowner
Time period(s): 1900s (1905)
Locale(s): London, England; Butler's Cross, Ireland; Tuam, Ireland

Summary: Lord Francis Powerscourt is hired to investigate a series of art thefts in Ireland. Paintings, including family portraits in addition to more valuable items, have been stolen from several stately Irish homes. Lord Brandon, the Earl of Lincoln, asks Powerscourt to travel to Ireland to recover his missing paintings. Powerscourt is an Irishman by birth; he brings along his wife Lucy and his friend Johnny Fitzgerald to assist in the investigation. Powerscourt finds Ireland consumed with its struggle for survival and independence. Things become even more difficult when the thieves decide to change their tactics, and instead of taking paintings from Dennis Ormond's home, they kidnap his wife and sister-in-law instead.

Where it's reviewed:
Booklist, March 1, 2008, page 52
Mystery News, April/May 2008, page 23
Mystery Scene, Spring 2008, page 68
Publishers Weekly, January 28, 2008, page 43

Other books by the same author:
Death Called to the Bar, 2006
Death on the Nevskii Prospekt, 2006
Death of a Chancellor, 2004
Death of an Old Master, 2004
Death and the Jubilee, 2002

Other books you might like:
Rhys Bowen, *In Dublin's Fair City*, 2007
Robin Paige, *Death on the Lizard*, 2006
Anne Perry, *Ashworth Hall*, 1997
Peter Watson, *Landscape of Lies*, 1989

56

BRANDT DODSON

White Soul

(Eugene, Oregon: Harvest House, 2008)

Story type: Chase; Religious
Subject(s): Gangs; Morality
Major character(s): Ron Ortega, Police Officer (undercover); Ricardo Estevez, Drug Dealer; Libby Ortega, Spouse
Time period(s): 2000s
Locale(s): Miami, Florida

Summary: Ron Ortega has just received his big break. He's been working undercover as Ron Acuna for some time now, assigned to arrest Michael Santiago. Instead Ortega decides to use Santiago to reach the largest drug lord in Miami, Ricardo Estevez. Ron quickly becomes a member of Estevez's gang and faces temptation. Estevez keeps giving Ron money, but Ron is trying to hold onto his Christian values, never personally committing a crime or allowing one to occur around him. At the same time, he knows he can't get caught. He has a pregnant wife waiting at home for him to come back safely.

Other books by the same author:
The Lost Sheep, 2007
The Root of All Evil, 2007
Original Sin, 2006
Seventy Times Seven, 2006

Other books you might like:
Lee Child, *Persuader*, 2003
George P. Pelecanos, *The Sweet Forever*, 1998
Joseph D. Pistone, *Donnie Brasco: Deep Cover*, 1999
Don Winslow, *The Power of the Dog*, 2005

57

TIM DORSEY

Atomic Lobster

(New York: Morrow, 2008)

Story type: Humor
Series: Serge Storms. Book 10
Subject(s): Cruise Ships; Drugs
Major character(s): Serge Storms, Murderer; Coleman, Sidekick; Johnny Vegas, Friend
Time period(s): 2000s
Locale(s): Tampa, Florida

Summary: Serge Storms—a killer who practices a weird form of justice, killing only evil people—is on the road again with his hard-drinking pal Coleman. The plot loosely hangs on Serge's plan to protect his old friend Jim Davenport, whom he encountered in *Triggerfish Twist* (2002). Jim is being threatened by the McGraw brothers, one of whom Jim helped to put in prison. There's also a matter of a cruise ship that may or may not be transporting drugs. The cruise ship is full of innocent old ladies, who are perhaps less innocent than they appear.

Where it's reviewed:
Booklist, December 1, 2007, page 24
Entertainment Weekly, January 25, 2008, page 75
Mystery Scene, Winter 2008, page 76
Publishers Weekly, December 3, 2007, page 49

Other books by the same author:
Hurricane Punch, 2007
The Big Bamboo, 2006
Torpedo Juice, 2005
Cadillac Beach, 2004
The Stingray Shuffle, 2003

Other books you might like:
Tim Cockey, *The Hearse You Came In On*, 2000
Carl Hiaasen, *Native Tongue*, 1991
Lawrence Shames, *Florida Straits*, 1992
Randy Wayne White, *The Man Who Invented Florida*, 1993

58

JOAN DRUETT

Deadly Shoals

(New York: St. Martin's, 2007)

Story type: Historical
Series: Wiki Coffin. Book 4
Subject(s): Ships; Sea Stories
Major character(s): Wiki Coffin, Linguist
Time period(s): 1830s (1839)
Locale(s): At Sea; Patagonia, Argentina

Summary: Wiki Coffin acts as a translator on a ship that is a part of the U.S. South Seas Naval Exploring Expedition. Angry New England whaler Captain Stackpole says that he's been cheated out of money and his schooner. Wiki must act as a sheriff and detective to investigate. While his ship lies off the coast of Patagonia, Wiki searches for the trader whom Stackpole accused. When Wiki finds the man dead. He must face the infamous South American gauchos along with revolutionaries while he searches for a murderer and a thief.

Where it's reviewed:
Library Journal, August 15, 2007, page 56
Publishers Weekly, October 15, 2007, page 45

Other books by the same author:
Run Afoul, 2006
Shark Island, 2005
A Watery Grave, 2004

Other books you might like:
Stephanie Barron, *Jane and the Prisoner of Wool House*, 2001
David Donachie, *An Element of Chance*, 2002
Jan Needle, *The Wicked Trade*, 2001
Wilder Perkins, *Hoare and the Headless Captains*, 2000

59

BRENDAN DUBOIS

Twilight

(New York: St. Martin's, 2007)

Story type: Futuristic
Subject(s): Terrorism; Civil War
Major character(s): Samuel Simpson, Journalist; Miriam van der Pol, Doctor
Time period(s): 2000s
Locale(s): New York

Summary: In the not too distant future, Canadian journalist Samuel Simpson joins a UN group investigating war crimes in upstate New York. The United States has suffered several massive terrorist attacks that sent it spiraling into a civil war. Simpson agrees to be a record keeper as the UN attempts to keep peace and uncover evidence of wartime atrocities. As Simpson becomes further acquainted with this UN group, he begins to believe that there may be a traitor among them who is attempting to prevent the mission from being successful and is ready to betray the entire team.

Where it's reviewed:
Booklist, October 15, 2007, page 38
Publishers Weekly, October 1, 2007

Other books by the same author:
Buried Dreams, 2004
Betrayed, 2003
Killer Waves, 2002
Resurrection Day, 1999
Shattered Shell, 1999

Other books you might like:
Dan Fesperman, *The Small Boat of Great Sorrows*, 2003
Joseph Kanon, *Alibi*, 2005
Blaine Kerr, *Wrongful Death*, 2002

60

MARTIN EDWARDS

Waterloo Sunset

(Scottsdale, Arizona: Poisoned Pen, 2008)

Story type: Psychological Suspense
Series: Harry Devlin. Book 8
Subject(s): Serial Killers; Legal Thriller
Major character(s): Harry Devlin, Lawyer; Jim Crusoe, Lawyer; Theresa May, Friend
Time period(s): 2000s
Locale(s): Liverpool, England

Summary: Harry Devlin is settling into his new office when he gets a faked newspaper death notice for himself on Midsummer's Eve, a few days away. He's inclined to treat it as a joke but then his business partner is viciously assaulted, and another friend falls prey to a serial killer with the particularly gruesome habit of severing tongues. As the deadline draws near, Harry's complicated life—made more so by the reappearance of a former girlfriend—becomes even more complex as he races against

the deadline to save himself and to investigate his friend's murder.

Where it's reviewed:
Booklist, March 1, 2008, page 54
Kirkus Reviews, February 15, 2008
Library Journal, April 1, 2008, page 63
Mystery Scene, Spring 2008, page 59
Publishers Weekly, December 24, 2008, page 31

Other books by the same author:
The First Cut is the Deepest, 1999
The Devil in Disguise, 1998
Eve of Destruction, 1996
Yesterday's Papers, 1994
I Remember You, 1993

Other books you might like:
Jo Bannister, *No Birds Sing*, 1996
Val McDermid, *The Wire in the Blood*, 1997
Ian Rankin, *Mortal Causes*, 1994
Peter Robinson, *Blood at the Root*, 1997

61

J.F. ENGLERT

A Dog Among Diplomats

(New York: Dell, 2008)

Story type: Amateur Detective
Series: Bull Moose Dog Run. Book 2
Subject(s): Animals/Dogs; Missing Persons
Major character(s): Harry, Artist; Randolph, Animal; Peter Davis, Detective—Police
Time period(s): 2000s
Locale(s): New York, New York

Summary: When Harry, a New York City artist, receives a phone call from Detective Peter Davis, he rushes from his apartment to an old boardinghouse. Davis is leading the investigation into the disappearance of Harry's girlfriend, Imogen. Imogen went missing over a year ago, leaving her beloved Labrador retriever, Randolph, with Harry. An intelligent dog, Randolph reads Proust and has recently learned how to order books online. At the boardinghouse, a murder has recently occurred and the police consider Imogen to be a suspect. Going undercover as a therapy dog, Randolph has the opportunity to work on his detection skills and to find his missing mistress.

Where it's reviewed:
Mystery News, June/July 2008, page 31
Publishers Weekly, March 24, 2008, page 57

Other books by the same author:
A Dog about Town, 2007

Other books you might like:
Leslie O'Kane, *Give the Dog a Bone*, 2002
Carolyn Parkhurst, *The Dogs of Babel*, 2003
Leonie Swann, *Three Bags Full*, 2007

Mystery

62

KJELL ERIKSSON

The Demon of Dakar

(New York: St. Martin's, 2008)

Story type: Police Procedural
Series: Ann Lindell. Book 03
Subject(s): Psychological Thriller
Major character(s): Ann Lindell, Detective—Police; Slobodan Andersson, Restaurateur; Manuel Alvarez, Migrant Worker; Eva Williams, Waiter/Waitress
Time period(s): 2000s
Locale(s): Uppsala, Sweden

Summary: Police Detective Ann Lindell has a difficult homicide case in Uppsala, Sweden. She and her colleagues work to identify a victim found floating in a river and the cause of death. The corpse is identified as Armas, a co-owner of the upscale restaurant Dakar. Lindell visits his partner, Slobodan Andersson, who has shady connections in his past and plenty of enemies. Armas shared his partner's murky reputation. The suspect list is long, including Slobodan and his kitchen crew and staff: recently hired waitress Eva Willman and her two teen boys, meat chef Johnny Kvarnheden, homeless man Konrad Rosenberg, and Mexican peasant Manuel Alavarez, who has traveled to Sweden seeking to free his incarcerated brother, in prison for drug smuggling.

Where it's reviewed:
Booklist, March 15, 2008, page 30
Library Journal, April 1, 2008, page 6
Mystery Scene, Summer 2008, page 75
Publishers Weekly, March 31, 2008, page 43

Other books by the same author:
The Cruel Stars of The Night, 2004
The Princess of Burundi, 2002

Other books you might like:
K.O. Dahl, *The Fourth Man*, 2008
Peter Hoeg, *The Quiet Girl*, 2006
Hakan Nesser, *Borkmann's Point*, 2006
Helen Tursten, *The Glass Devil*, 2007

63

LOREN D. ESTLEMAN

Frames

(New York: Forge, 2008)

Story type: Amateur Detective; Humor
Series: Valentino. Book 1
Subject(s): Movies; College Life
Major character(s): Valentino, Detective—Amateur (film detective); Kyle Broadhead, Professor; Fanta, Student—College
Time period(s): 2000s
Locale(s): Los Angeles, California

Summary: Without proper foresight, Valentino decides to buy an abandoned movie theatre. He doesn't make much money working as a film archivist—or film detective as he likes to call himself—for UCLA, but he makes just enough to buy the place. Once inside, he finds what could be one of the most important discoveries in film history: the lost reels for Erich von Stroheim's *Greed*, which was drastically edited before its release. Unfortunately there' s also a dead body in the theatre. Valentino proceeds to walk the fine line of helping out with the investigation but trying not to let the police take the reels as evidence for fear of damage to the prints.

Where it's reviewed:
Booklist, May 1, 2008, page 33
Library Journal, March 15, 2008, page 62
Mystery Scene, Summer 2008, page 71
Publishers Weekly, February 11, 2008, page 53

Other books by the same author:
Gas City, 2008
American Detective, 2007
Nicotine Kiss, 2006
Retro, 2004

Other books you might like:
Jeffrey Cohen, *Some Like It Hot-Buttered*, 2007
Terence Faherty, *Come Back Dead*, 1997
Ron Goulart, *Groucho Marx, Private Eye*, 1999
Stuart M. Kaminsky, *Bullet for a Star*, 1977

64

LOREN D. ESTLEMAN

Gas City

(New York: Forge, 2008)

Story type: Serial Killer; Police Procedural
Subject(s): Organized Crime; City and Town Life
Major character(s): Francis Russell, Police Officer; Anthony Zeno, Organized Crime Figure
Time period(s): 2000s
Locale(s): Gas City

Summary: In Gas City, the Mafia and police have learned to coexist to their mutual benefit. Police chief Francis Russell maintains a deal with mob boss Anthony Zeno: if the crime stays in one part of the city, the rest of the city stays crime free. It is not until Russell's wife dies that he reconsiders his moral compromise. Meanwhile, a serial killer is at large and Russell must start acting like the police officer he is. As he acts to set things right in this industrial city, the landscape will change just as Russell has.

Where it's reviewed:
Booklist, May 1, 2008, page 56
Entertainment Weekly, January 25, 2008, page 74
Mystery Scene, Winter 2008, page 72
Publishers Weekly, December 17, 2007, page 29

Other books by the same author:
American Detective, 2007
The Adventures of Johnny Vermillion, 2006
Little Black Dress, 2005
Port Hazard, 2005
Black Powder White Smoke, 2002

Other books you might like:
Dashiell Hammett, *Red Harvest*, 1929
Jack Kelly, *Mobtown*, 2002
Richard Price, *Lush Life*, 2008
Ross Thomas, *The Fools in Town Are on Our Side*,
  1970

65

JANET EVANOVICH

Fearless Fourteen

(New York: St. Martin's, 2008)

Story type: Private Detective; Humor
Series: Stephanie Plum. Book 14
Subject(s): Kidnapping; Robbers and Outlaws
Major character(s): Stephanie Plum, Bounty Hunter; Lula,
  Sidekick; Joe Morelli, Detective—Private
Time period(s): 2000s
Locale(s): Trenton, New Jersey

Summary: Joe Morelli's cousin Dom has been released
after being jailed for bank robbery. Dom's sister Loretta
is in jail because she can't afford bail on a liquor store
robbery charge. Stephanie Plum and Morelli are babysit-
ting Loretta's teenaged son, Mario, aka Zook, who may
or may not be Joe's son. Dom goes into hiding when his
former gang members start turning up dead. Odd people
are digging up Morelli's basement and yard when word
gets out that the money might have been hidden in or
near the house before he owned it. Finally out of jail,
Loretta is kidnapped. Find the bank money, says the
kidnapper to Stephanie, or Loretta begins losing body
parts.

Where it's reviewed:
Booklist, May 15, 2008, page 4
Publishers Weekly, May 19, 2008, page 35

Other books by the same author:
Lean Mean Thirteen, 2007
Twelve Sharp, 2006
Eleven on Top, 2005
Ten Big Ones, 2004
To the Nines, 2003

Other books you might like:
Jennifer Crusie, *Tell Me Lies*, 1998
Anne George, *Murder Carries a Torch*, 2000
Chris Grabenstein, *Tilt a Whirl*, 2005
Lisa Lutz, *The Spellman Files*, 2007

66

JIMMIE RUTH EVANS

Bring Your Own Poison

(New York: Berkley, 2008)

Story type: Amateur Detective
Series: Wanda Nell Culpepper. Book 4
Subject(s): Working Mothers; Small Town Life
Major character(s): Wanda Nell Culpepper, Waiter/
Waitress, Detective—Amateur; Miranda Culpepper,
Single Parent; Bill Warren, Detective—Police
Time period(s): 2000s
Locale(s): Tullahome, Mississippi

Summary: In Tullahome, Mississippi, hard working Wanda
Nell Culpepper holds down two jobs: waitress at the
Kountry Kitchen by day, convenience store clerk by
night. It's still tough to pay the bills so she agrees to
waitress at a rowdy bachelor party, though she has
misgivings. The groom-to-be is poisoned. Then the state
police officer called in on the case, Bill Warren, ignores
Wanda's son's partner's legal advice only because he is
gay. Wanda decides to solve the murder on her own. Her
efforts are complicated by the pregnancy of her daughter,
Miranda, who already lives with her and has a young
son to boot.

Where it's reviewed:
Mystery News, April/May 2008, page 13

Other books by the same author:
Best Served Cold, 2007
Murder Over Easy, 2006
Flamingo Fatale, 2005

Other books you might like:
Selma Eichler, *Murder Can Kill Your Social Life*, 1994
Joan Hess, *Malice in Maggody*, 1987
Susan McBride, *Night of the Living Deb*, 2007
Kathleen Taylor, *Sex and Salmonella*, 1996

67

MARY ANNA EVANS

Findings

(Scottsdale, Arizona: Poisoned Pen, 2008)

Story type: Amateur Detective
Series: Faye Longchamp. Book 4
Subject(s): Archaeology; Civil War
Major character(s): Faye Longchamp, Archaeologist,
Detective—Amateur; Joe Wolf Mantooth, Archaeolo-
gist; Mike McKenzie, Police Officer
Time period(s): 2000s
Locale(s): Joyeuse Island, Florida

Summary: Faye Longchamp continues to excavate the
grounds around her family's ancestral home on Joyeuse
Island, just off the coast of Florida, only now she's being
paid for her work by Douglass Everett and his new
Museum of American Slavery. Soon after Faye finds a
fabulous emerald, intruders break into Douglass' home
and beat him to death. Oddly enough, the thieves miss
the emerald, which Douglass has tucked away in a hidden pants pocket. Faye realizes that the only thing taken
from the scene is the notebook that contains field notes
documenting her excavations. Faye believes that the
emerald dates back to he Civil War; her investigation
leads her to letters written by a Confederate government
official that hint of treasure buried on Joyeuse Island.

Where it's reviewed:
Booklist, May 1, 2008, page 34
Library Journal, May 1, 2008, page 43
Publishers Weekly, May 19, 2008, page 39

Other books by the same author:
Effigies, 2007
Relics, 2005
Artifacts, 2003

Other books you might like:
Dana Cameron, *The Emma Fielding Series*, 2002 -
William Rawlings, *The Rutherfold Cipher*, 2004
Sarah R. Shaber, *Simon Said*, 1997
Malcolm Shuman, *The Meriwether Murder*, 1998

68

LINDA FAIRSTEIN
Killer Heat
(New York: Doubleday, 2008)

Story type: Legal
Series: Alex Cooper. Book 10
Subject(s): Serial Killers; Law Enforcement
Major character(s): Alexandra Cooper, Lawyer; Mike Chapman, Detective—Homicide; Troy Rasheed, Criminal, Bouncer
Time period(s): 2000s
Locale(s): New York, New York

Summary: During a particularly hot August in New York City, Assistant District Attorney Alexandra Cooper is preparing to prosecute Floyd Warren, a rapist whose original trial was over 30 years ago. Alex is confident that she will finally find justice for her client, Kerry Hastings, who was one of Warren's victims. While prosecuting this case, Alex receives a call about a corpse found in an abandoned building. Shortly thereafter, a second body is discovered, closely followed by a third. Alex and her colleagues, police detectives Mike Chapman and Mercer Wallace, realize there may be a serial killer in the city.

Where it's reviewed:
Booklist, November 15, 2007, page 5
Entertainment Weekly, March 21, 2008, page 64
Library Journal, February 1, 2008, page 60
Publishers Weekly, January 7, 2008, page 36

Other books by the same author:
Bad Blood, 2007
Death Dance, 2006
Entombed, 2005
The Kills, 2004
The Bone Vault, 2003

Other books you might like:
Alafair Burke, *Judgment Calls*, 2003
Jilliane Hoffman, *Retribution*, 2004
Jonnie Jacobs, *Cold Justice*, 2002
Ellery Queen, *Cat of Many Tails*, 1949

69

DAN FESPERMAN
The Amateur Spy
(New York: Knopf, 2008)

Story type: Espionage
Subject(s): Middle East; Charity

Major character(s): Freeman Lockhart, Civil Servant (aid worker); Omar al-Baroody, Civil Servant (aid worker); Abbas Rahim, Doctor, Zealot
Time period(s): 2000s
Locale(s): Amman, Jordan

Summary: After years of humanitarian aid work, Freeman and Mila Lockhart are looking forward to retirement on a Greek island. Three men accost Freeman and threaten to reveal a secret about his work in Africa unless he agrees to travel to Jordan where he is to spy on an old friend and colleague, Omar al-Baroody. The men are suspicious about Omar's work as director of a new organization, the Bakaa Refuge Health Project; they want Freeman to take an undercover job at the project and report on money moving through the organization. Meanwhile, in Washington, Abbas Rahim's wife is concerned that her husband is distracted and withdrawn. The couple's daughter died a year ago while she traveling abroad. Rahim, a Palestinian immigrant, blames post-9/11 profiling for putting their daughter in danger.

Where it's reviewed:
Booklist, February 1, 2008, page 30
Library Journal, January 15, 2008, page 82
Publishers Weekly, January 7, 2008, page 36

Other books by the same author:
The Prisoner of Guantanamo, 2006
The Warlord's Son, 2004
The Small Boat of Great Sorrows, 2003
Lie in the Dark, 1999

Other books you might like:
Eric Ambler, *A Coffin for Dimitrios*, 1939
John le Carre, *The Little Drummer Girl*, 1983
Robert Littell, *Vicious Circle*, 2006
Matt Beynon Rees, *A Grave in Gaza*, 2008

70

JANE FINNIS
Buried Too Deep
(Scottsdale, Arizona: Poisoned Pen, 2008)

Story type: Historical/Ancient Rome
Series: Aurelia Marcella. Book 3
Subject(s): Roman Empire; Adventure and Adventurers
Major character(s): Aurelia Marcella, Innkeeper; Lucius Aurelius Marcellus, Spy, Innkeeper; Bodvocos, Chieftain
Time period(s): 1st century (98)
Locale(s): Oak Bridges, Roman Empire (Roman Britain)

Summary: In 98 AD, Aurelia Marcella is busy running the Oak Tree inn in the village of Oak Bridges, with her twin brother Lucius Aurelius Marcellus. Also a government investigator, Lucius is away when a severely injured farmer named Belinus is brought to the doctor at Oak Bridges. Belinus, one of Lucius' informers, gives Aurelia an urgent message before he dies: sea raiders led by the barbarian Voltacos have been attacking people along the coast. When returning Belinus's body to his family, Aurelia and Lucius learn of a shipwreck nearby that may have been caused by Voltacos and his pirates. This event adds to the hostilities between the natives of

Britannia and the settlers who distrust any non-Roman citizen.

Where it's reviewed:
Mystery News, June/July 2008, page 27
Mystery Scene, Summer 2008, page 76
Publishers Weekly, April 7, 2008, page 45

Other books by the same author:
A Bitter Chill, 2005
Get Out or Die, 2003

Other books you might like:
Lindsey Davis, *Silver Pigs*, 1989
Ruth Downie, *Medicus*, 2007
Michael Allen Dymmoch, *The Cymry Ring*, 2006
Rosemary Rowe, *Enemies of the Empire*, 2005

71

BARBARA FISTER

In the Wind

(New York: St. Martin's, 2008)

Story type: Private Detective
Subject(s): Political Movements; Indians of North America
Major character(s): Anni Koskinen, Detective—Private; Jim Tilquist, FBI Agent
Time period(s): 2000s
Locale(s): Chicago, Illinois; Minnesota

Summary: Chicago police officer Anni Koskinen's career ended when she testified against a fellow officer in a police brutality case. Now, she's a sometime private investigator. She gets a 6:00 am call from Father Sikora, a neighborhood priest. He asks her to drive a woman who introduces herself as Rosa out of Chicago, to Minnesota. On the way to the highway, Anni stops at an ATM where she's accosted by two men who turn out to be FBI agents. Rosa disappears during the scuffle. The agents tell Anni that Rosa is really Verna Basswood, who's been in hiding for 30 years since she killed FBI agent Arne Tilquist. Jim Tilquist, Arne's son, is also an FBI agent and Anni's mentor. Anni does not believe that Rosa could be a killer; with Jim's blessing, she gets involved in an investigation that stirs passions.

Where it's reviewed:
Mystery Scene, Summer 2008, page 85
Publishers Weekly, April 14, 2008, page 41

Other books by the same author:
On Edge, 2002

Other books you might like:
Barbara D'Amato, *Good Cop, Bad Cop*, 1998
Kate Flora, *Liberty or Death*, 2003
Sara Paretsky, *Blacklist*, 2003
Greg Rucka, *Patriot Acts*, 2007

72

KATE FLORA

Stalking Death

(Carmel, Indiana: The Mystery Company, 2008)

Story type: Amateur Detective
Series: Thea Kozak. Book 8
Subject(s): Academia; Sports/Basketball
Major character(s): Thea Kozak, Troubleshooter, Detective—Amateur; Shondra Jones, Student—Boarding School; Jamison Jones, Student—Boarding School
Time period(s): 2000s
Locale(s): New Hampshire

Summary: Thea Kozak works as a troubleshooter for a small firm that consults for independent private boarding schools. She gets a call from her partner asking her to leave her home and new husband to look into a case of stalking at client school St. Matthews. The school is dismissive of Shondra Jones' claims of being stalked, very possibly because the boy Shondra accuses is the grandson of the school's major donor. When the boy turns up dead, Thea is more determined than ever to find out the truth behind Shondra's accusation. The school is being obstructive and she feels she must work on her own, both to put the school to rights and to find justice for Shondra.

Where it's reviewed:
Booklist, May 1, 2008, page 42
Kirkus Reviews, May 1, 2008, page 458
Library Journal, June 1, 2008, page 77

Other books by the same author:
Liberty or Death, 2003
Death in Paradise, 1998
Steal Away, 1998
An Educated Death, 1997
Death at the Wheel, 1996

Other books you might like:
Linda Barnes, *Heart of the World*, 2006
Harlan Coben, *Fade Away*, 1996
Jane Haddam, *The Headmaster's Wife*, 2005
Sara Paretsky, *Blood Shot*, 1988

73

BILL FLOYD

The Killer's Wife

(New York: St. Martin's, 2008)

Story type: Serial Killer
Subject(s): Murder; Stalking
Major character(s): Nina Mosley, Computer Expert; Randall Mosley, Serial Killer; Carson Beckman, Murderer, Crime Victim
Time period(s): 2000s
Locale(s): Cary, North Carolina; El Ray, California

Summary: Six years after learning that her husband Randall Mosley was a serial killer and testifying at the trial that sentenced him to death, Nina Mosley is working

Mystery

hard to maintain a normal life for herself and her son, Hayden. Charles Pritchett, the father of one of Randy's victims, has employed private investigators to track Nina down. Pritchett's appearance in Nina's life is just the beginning of the nightmare that starts with Nina's true identity being revealed to the community she lives in. When Hayden is kidnapped from his school, Nina knows that the answer to finding her son is with the one person in the world she tried to forget: her ex-husband Randy.

Where it's reviewed:
Crimespree, January/February 2008, page 70
Library Journal, November 15, 2007, page 49
Mystery Scene, Winter 2008, page 66
Publishers Weekly, January 14, 2008, page 41

Other books you might like:
Harlan Coben, *Tell No One*, 2001
Jessie Prichard Hunter, *Blood Music*, 1993
Stan Latreille, *Perjury*, 1998
Denise Mina, *Deception*, 2004

74

JOANNE FLUKE

Carrot Cake Murder

(New York: Kensington, 2008)

Story type: Amateur Detective
Series: Hannah Swensen. Book 10
Subject(s): Cooks and Cooking; Reunions
Major character(s): Hannah Swensen, Baker, Detective—Amateur; Norman Rhodes, Dentist; Mike Kingston, Detective—Police
Time period(s): 2000s
Locale(s): Lake Eden, Minnesota

Summary: Hannah Swensen, owner of The Cookie Jar bakery, is happy to help out her business partner Lisa Beeseman with her family reunion. The Beeseman family is surprised when long-lost family member Gus Klein arrives just in time for the reunion. Bragging about his successes and flashing money around, Gus isn't the person his family remembers. Hannah discovers that someone in Lake Eden isn't thrilled with Gus' return when she finds his dead body only a few days into the reunion. When Lisa's father Jack, who suffers from Alzheimer's, becomes a suspect in Gus death, Hannah works with both of her boyfriends, dentist Norman Rhodes and cop Mike Kingston, to discover the identity of the murderer and to clear Jack's name.

Where it's reviewed:
Booklist, March 15, 2008, page 30
Publishers Weekly, January 28, 2008, page 44

Other books by the same author:
Key Lime Pie Murder, 2007
Cherry Cheesecake Murder, 2006
Peach Cobbler Murder, 2005
Fudge Cupcake Murder, 2004
Sugar Cookie Murder, 2004

Other books you might like:
Mignon F. Ballard, *The Angel Whispered Death*, 2003
Diane Mott Davidson, *The Last Suppers*, 1994
Joan Hess, *Death by the Light of the Moon*, 1992
Toni L.P. Kelner, *Dead Ringer*, 1994

75

JEFFREY FORD

The Shadow Year

(New York: Morrow, 2008)

Story type: Domestic
Subject(s): Brothers and Sisters; City and Town Life

Summary: For three Long Island children in the 1960s, the beginning of a new school year is also the beginning of a series of strange events. First, a prowler is stalking their neighborhood at night. Then a classmate, Charlie Edison, disappears. A strange man in a large white car lurks near the school and several nearby homes. The narrator, his older brother Jim and their younger sister Mary keep track of events in "Botch Town," a cardboard recreation of their town that Jim has built in their basement. When the narrator realizes that another neighbor has gone missing around Halloween, he and his siblings begin to investigate the disappearances.

Where it's reviewed:
Booklist, March 1, 2008, page 49
Library Journal, February 1, 2008, page 62
Publishers Weekly, January 21, 2008, page 153

Other books by the same author:
The Girl in the Glass, 2005
The Portrait of Mrs. Charbuque, 2002
The Physiognomy, 1997

Other books you might like:
Orson Scott Card, *Lost Boys*, 1992
Robert R. McCammon, *Boy's Life*, 1991
Carol O'Connell, *Judas Child*, 1998
Peter Straub, *Lost Boy, Lost Girl*, 2003

76

KARIN FOSSUM

Black Seconds

(Orlando, Florida: Harcourt, 2008)

Story type: Police Procedural
Series: Konrad Sejer. Book 5
Subject(s): Missing Persons
Major character(s): Konrad Sejer, Police Officer; Helga Joner, Parent; Ida Joner, Crime Victim, Child
Time period(s): 2000s
Locale(s): Norway

Summary: Helga Joner is an overly protective mother who lives on her own with her daughter Ida. One night Ida is late getting home. Helga calls her sister Ruth, Helga's husband Anders, and finally the police. Ruth's son Tomme has an accident at almost the same time Ida goes missing, and Tomme's friend Willy helps to mend Tomme's car. Willy is a drug dealer. The search for Ida is unsuccessful until ten days later when her body is found lying on the road side. Ida's corpse is not wearing the clothes she was wearing the day she left home; instead she is wearing a beautiful nightie.

Where it's reviewed:
Booklist, April 1, 2008, page 30
The New York Times Book Review, July 27, 2008, page 26
Publishers Weekly, April 14, 2008, page 40

Other books by the same author:
The Indian Bride, 2005
When the Devil Holds the Candle, 2004
He Who Fears the Wolf, 2003
Don't Look Back, 2002

Other books you might like:
Arnaldur Indridason, *Voices*, 2007
Mari Jungstedt, *Unseen*, 2006
Yrsa Sigurdardottir, *Last Rituals*, 2007
Helene Tursten, *The Torso*, 2006

■ 77 ■

ARIANA FRANKLIN

The Serpent's Tale

(New York: Putnam, 2008)

Story type: Historical/Medieval
Series: Adelia Aguilar. Book 2
Subject(s): Political Thriller; Kings, Queens, Rulers, etc.
Major character(s): Adelia Aguilar, Doctor Henry II, Royalty; Rowley Picot, Religious
Time period(s): 12th century
Locale(s): England

Summary: When Henry II's mistress, Rosamund Clifford, dies of an apparent poisoning, Henry summons Adelia Aguilar out of the countryside, where she is living quietly with her infant daughter. Reluctantly she travels to the scene of the crime, summoning the Bishop of St. Albans, Rowley Picot, to assist her. Picot is her baby's father as well as the king's "fixer." As Adelia investigates Rosamund's home, Queen Eleanor of Aquitaine arrives and takes Adelia and her party hostage. Eleanor is waiting with a band of mercenaries to overthrow Henry. Meanwhile, bodies are piling up and Ariana and Rowley must race against the clock to solve the case.

Where it's reviewed:
Booklist, April 15, 2008, page 63
Entertainment Weekly, February 1, 2008, page 78
Mystery News, April/May 2008, page 19
The New York Times Book Review, February 10, 2008, page 34
Publishers Weekly, November 12, 2007, page 37

Other books by the same author:
Mistress of the Art of Death, 2007
City of Shadows, 2006

Other books you might like:
Alys Clare, *Fortune Like the Moon*, 1999
Roberta Gellis, *A Personal Devil*, 2001
Sharon Kay Penman, *Dragon's Lair*, 2003
Caroline Roe, *Draught for a Dead Man*, 2002

■ 78 ■

BRIAN FREEMAN

Stalked

(New York: St. Martin's, 2008)

Story type: Police Procedural
Series: Jonathan Stride. Book 3
Subject(s): Sexuality; Revenge
Major character(s): Jonathan Stride, Police Officer; Serena Dial, Detective—Private; Maggie Bei, Police Officer
Time period(s): 2000s
Locale(s): Duluth, Minnesota

Summary: Police officer Maggie Bei is dreaming about sex when she's awakened by the sound of a gunshot. She finds her husband shot to death in his home office. Her partner, Lieutenant Jonathan Stride, arrives on the scene and knows immediately that this case will be trouble: there are no footprints in the snow around the house and he can tell that Maggie is lying to him. Because they're partners, the case is turned over to Abel Teitscher, a detective who holds a grudge against Stride. At the same time, Stride's lover, private detective Serena Dial, is hired to deliver blackmail money on behalf of a city official and a killer escapes his captors in Alabama, looking for revenge.

Where it's reviewed:
Booklist, November 1, 2007, page 31
Library Journal, November 1, 2007, page 59
Publishers Weekly, November 5, 2007, page 41

Other books by the same author:
Stripped, 2006
Immoral, 2005

Other books you might like:
Elizabeth Gunn, *Triple Play*, 1997
Theresa Monsour, *Clean Cut*, 2003
John Sandford, *Easy Prey*, 2000
P.J. Tracy, *Snow Blind*, 2006

■ 79 ■

DAVID FULMER

The Blue Door

(New York: Harcourt, 2008)

Story type: Historical
Subject(s): Sports/Boxing; Interracial Dating
Major character(s): Eddie Cero, Sports Figure; Sal Giambroni, Detective—Private; Valerie Pope, Singer
Time period(s): 1960s (1962)
Locale(s): Philadelphia, Pennsylvania

Summary: Eddie Cero stumbles upon Sal Giambroni being mugged in an alley, and saves him. In return, Giambroni offers the aging welterweight a job at his private detective agency. Eddie is reluctant, but agrees. His first case concerns the disappearance of Johnny Pope, lead singer for a washed up rock group. In the course of his investigation he meets Johnny's sister, Valerie, and while she resists his efforts to uncover information about her brother, he becomes attracted to her. The relationship is

complicated because it's 1962, and Eddie is Italian American and Valerie is African American.

Where it's reviewed:
Booklist, October 15, 2007, page 34
Kirkus Reviews, December 1, 2007
Library Journal, December 1, 2007, page 91
Mystery News, February/March 2008, page 10
Publishers Weekly, November 5, 207, page 47

Other books by the same author:
Lost River, 2008
The Dying Crapshooter's Blues, 2007
Rampart Street, 2006
Jass, 2005
Chasing the Devil's Tail, 2001

Other books you might like:
Megan Abbott, *The Song is You*, 2007
Ace Atkins, *White Shadow*, 2006
Mitchell Bartoy, *The Devil's Own Rag Doll*, 2005
David Benz, *The Flip Side of Forever*, 2005

80

ALAN FURST

The Spies of Warsaw

(New York: Random House, 2008)

Story type: Historical/World War II
Subject(s): Espionage; Armed Forces
Major character(s): Jean-Francois Mercier, Military Personnel, Spy; Anna Szarbek, Lawyer; August Voss, Military Personnel
Time period(s): 1930s
Locale(s): Warsaw, Poland; Paris, France; Glogau, Germany

Summary: In 1937, French aristocrat and decorated war hero Jean-Francois Mercier is working in Warsaw, Poland, as a military attache. Part of his assignment is to spy on the German forces and gain insight into their intentions. Edvard Uhl is a German engineer who smuggles manufacturing plans to Mercier. When Uhl is uncovered as a traitor to Germany, Mercier has to work quickly to save Uhl's life. Meanwhile, Mercier finds love with Anna Szarbek, a Polish lawyer who works for the League of Nations. Doing fieldwork himself, Mercier learns of the German army's tank maneuvers and their sinister intentions, which the French government ignores.

Where it's reviewed:
Booklist, March 15, 2008, page 6
Library Journal, April 1, 2008, page 75
Publishers Weekly, April 14, 2008, page 35

Other books by the same author:
The Foreign Correspondent, 2006
Dark Voyage, 2004
Blood of Victory, 2002
Kingdom of Shadows, 2000
Red Gold, 1999

Other books you might like:
Eric Ambler, *Journey into Fear*, 1940
James R. Benn, *The First Wave*, 2007
Emily Grayson, *Night Train to Lisbon*, 2004
Francine Mathews, *The Alibi Club*, 2006

81

LEIGHTON GAGE

Blood of the Wicked

(New York: Soho, 2008)

Story type: Police Procedural
Series: Mario Silva. Book 1
Subject(s): Catholicism; Political Movements
Major character(s): Mario Silva, Detective—Police; Hector Costa, Detective—Police; Orlando Muniz, Landowner, Wealthy
Time period(s): 2000s
Locale(s): Cascatas do Pontal, Brazil; Sao Paulo, Brazil; Brasilia, Brazil

Summary: In the remote Brazilian village of Cascatas do Pontal, a bishop is murdered in front of a large crowd when he arrives to consecrate a new church. The Chief Inspector of Criminal Matters, Mario Silva, is sent to investigate. Working with his nephew Hector Costa, also a federal police officer, Silva finds himself pitted against the corrupt, local government in his search for answers. From information supplied by Father Gaspar Farias, Silva and Costa suspect that the bishop was opposed to the Landless Workers' League, an organization that wants to return land held by the wealthy and powerful to the poor.

Where it's reviewed:
Booklist, November 1, 2007, page 28
Library Journal, December 15, 2007, page 92
Mystery Scene, Winter 2008, page 75
Publishers Weekly, November 5, 2007, page 47

Other books you might like:
Luiz Alfredo Garcia-Roza, *A Widow in Copacabana*, 2005
Michael Gruber, *Night of Jaguar*, 2006
R.M. Koster, *Glass Mountain*, 2001
J.R. Ripley, *The Body from Ipanema*, 2004

82

MICHAEL GENELIN

Siren of the Waters

(New York: Soho, 2008)

Story type: Police Procedural
Subject(s): Organized Crime; Political Movements
Major character(s): Jana Matanova, Detective—Police; Stephan Trokan, Detective—Police; Dmitri Levitin, Detective—Police
Time period(s): 2000s
Locale(s): Slovakia; Ukraine; France

Summary: When six women and one man are killed in a

violent car wreck, Commander Jana Matanova of the Bratislava police gets involved in the investigation. She learns that the male driver had two different passports with two different identities. She suspects a human smuggling ring. She goes to the Ukraine, on the trail of an elusive international criminal named Koba. Summoned to Strasbourg for a special European Union conference on human rights, she finds herself working with a Russian detective, Dmitri Levitin, who is also searching for his sister. At the same time, she meets her American son-in-law and tries desperately to reconnect with her daughter Katka, whom she was able to secretly send out of Slovakia while it was under Communist rule. Katka mistakenly believes that Jana killed her husband, Katka's father.

Where it's reviewed:
Booklist, May 15, 2008, page 26
Library Journal, June 1, 2008, page 77
Mystery Scene, Summer 2008, page 77
Publishers Weekly, April 28, 2008, page 114

Other books you might like:
Donna Leon, *Suffer the Little Children*, 2007
Ian Rankin, *Fleshmarket Alley*, 2005
Josef Skvorecky, *Two Murders in My Double Life*, 2001
Helen Tursten, *The Torso*, 2006

83

ELIZABETH GEORGE

Careless in Red

(New York: Bantam, 2008)

Story type: Police Procedural; Psychological Suspense
Series: Inspector Thomas Lynley. Book 14
Subject(s): Family Saga; Sports/Surfing
Major character(s): Thomas Lynley, Detective—Police, Widow(er); Barbara Havers, Detective—Police; Bea Hannaford, Detective—Police
Time period(s): 2000s
Locale(s): Cornwall, England

Summary: Detective Inspector Thomas Lynley is walking the Cornwall coast alone to assuage his grief over the loss of his wife Helen when he stumbles over a body. He is drawn into the subsequent investigation by the local police force. The victim, a young man named Santo Kerne, had been rock climbing alone when he fell to his death; it turns out not to be an accident but intentional murder. As Lynley helps the local police investigate the crime, his old partner, Barbara Havers, is sent out to Cornwall by New Scotland Yard to help out as well. Sometimes the three officers—Lynley, Havers, and local detective Bea Hannaford—seem to be working at cross purposes but between them they untangle the family secrets that lie at the heart of Santo's death.

Where it's reviewed:
Booklist, October 15, 2007, page 33
Kirkus Reviews, October 1, 2007, page 984
Mystery News, April/May 2008, page 18
Mystery Scene, Summer 2008, page 85
Publishers Weekly, October 2, 2007, page 38

Other books by the same author:
What Came before He Shot Her, 2006
With No One as Witness, 2005
A Traitor to Memory, 2001
In Pursuit of the Proper Sinner, 1999
Deception on His Mind, 1997

Other books you might like:
Deborah Crombie, *Water Like a Stone*, 2006
Caroline Graham, *A Ghost in the Machine*, 2004
Cynthia Harrod-Eagles, *Game Over*, 2008
Jill McGown, *Plots and Errors*, 1999

84

FRIEDRICH GLAUSER

The Chinaman

(New York: Bitter Lemon, 2008)

Story type: Police Procedural
Series: Jakob Studer. Book 4
Subject(s): Social Issues
Major character(s): Jakob Studer, Detective—Police
Time period(s): 1930s
Locale(s): Switzerland

Summary: Sergeant Studer is called to the scene of what appears to be a suicide, until it is noted that the man has been shot through the heart with no trace of a bullet hole in his clothing. Studer recognizes the man as James Farny, or the "Chinaman," a nickname he had given him when they first met a few months earlier. Studer also recalls that Farny mentioned to him that he might be murdered. Farny's body was found lying on the grave of Anna Hungerlott, the wife of the warden of the poorhouse, who had died not long ago from supposed gastric influenza. Studer must venture into his memories of what he knows of the Chinaman and piece together his life in order to find what led to his murder.

Where it's reviewed:
Booklist, December 1, 2007, page 25
Publishers Weekly, November 5, 2007, page 47

Other books by the same author:
Fever, 2006
In Matto's Realm, 2005
Thumbprint, 2005

Other books you might like:
Friedrich Durrenmatt, *The Pledge*, 2000
Doris Gercke, *How Many Miles to Babylon*, 1991
Petra Hammesfahr, *The Sinner*, 2007
Bernhard Schlink, *Self's Deception*, 2007

85

LAWRENCE GOLDSTONE

The Anatomy of Deception

(New York: Delacorte, 2008)

Story type: Historical/Victorian America
Subject(s): Doctors

Major character(s): Ephraim Carroll, Doctor; William Osler, Historical Figure, Doctor; Abigail Benedict, Heiress, Artist

Time period(s): 1880s (1889); 1930s (1933)

Locale(s): Philadelphia, Pennsylvania; Baltimore, Maryland; Seattle, Washington

Summary: In 1889 at the University of Philadelphia Medical School, Dr. Ephraim Carroll is just one of the physicians studying under the leading medical professor of the time, Dr. William Osler. Working with cadavers, Carroll is surprised when Dr. Osler slams down the lid of a coffin containing a beautiful young woman. Attending a dinner party with Dr. Osler, Carroll meets heiress Abigail Benedict. Benedict, a painter, shows Carroll a portrait she painted of her dear friend, Rebecca Lachtmann. Staring at the painting, Carroll believes that Lachtmann is the woman he saw in the coffin just days ago. Sharing his suspicions with Benedict, the young heiress then begs Carroll to find out what happened to her friend.

Where it's reviewed:
Booklist, December 15, 2007, page 27
Deadly Pleasures, Spring 2008, page 53
Entertainment Weekly, February 1, 2008, page 78
Mystery News, February/March 2008, page 17
Publishers Weekly, November 12, 2007, page 33

Other books you might like:
Cordelia Frances Biddle, *The Conjurer*, 2007
Caleb Carr, *The Alienist*, 1994
Tess Gerritsen, *The Bone Garden*, 2007
Mark Graham, *The Black Maria*, 2000

86

PHILIP GOODEN

The Salisbury Manuscript

(New York: Soho Constable, 2008)

Story type: Historical/Victorian
Series: Tom Ansell. Book 1
Subject(s): Clergy; Murder
Major character(s): Thomas Ansell, Lawyer; Helen Scott, Girlfriend, Writer; Eric Selby, Religious
Time period(s): 1870s (1873)
Locale(s): London, England; Salisbury, England

Summary: In 1873, lawyer Thomas Ansell travels from London to the village of Salisbury. Ansell is to meet with client Felix Slater, a canon in the church, to pick up a manuscript. Slater's father George was a friend of some of the romantic poets of his era, including Lord Byron and Percy Shelley. Before he died, George Slater wrote his memoirs, detailing both everyday events and the racy times he had with Byron and Shelley. Felix Slater asks Ansell to take the manuscript back to London for safekeeping. When Slater is found murdered, Ansell is the prime suspect. To clear his name, Ansell and his soon-to-be fiancee Helen Scott try to find out who really killed Felix Slater.

Where it's reviewed:
Publishers Weekly, May 12, 2008, page 39

Other books by the same author:
An Honourable Murder, 2005
Mask of Night, 2004
Alms for Oblivion, 2003
The Pale Companion, 2002
Death of Kings, 2001

Other books you might like:
David Dickinson, *Death of an Old Master*, 2004
Anne Fleming, *Death and Deconstruction*, 1995
Diana Killian, *High Rhymes and Misdemeanors*, 2003
Jane Langton, *The Transcendental Murder*, 1964

87

ALAN GORDON

The Moneylender of Toulouse

(New York: St. Martin's, 2008)

Story type: Historical/Medieval
Series: Fools' Guild. Book 7
Subject(s): Religious Life; Family Relations
Major character(s): Theophilos, Entertainer (jester), Spy; Claudia, Entertainer (jester), Spouse; Helga, Apprentice
Time period(s): 13th century (1204)
Locale(s): Toulouse, France

Summary: Theo and his family—his wife Claudia, their infant child Portia and apprentice fool Helga, who travels as their daughter—are sent to Toulouse to convince the current bishop, Raimon de Rabastens, to retire so the Fools' Guild can install a bishop more sympathetic to their mission. The bishop is heard in a loud argument with moneylender Milon Borsella, who is found murdered the next day. Theo learns that the bishop is in financial hot water. When another murder occurs and a local fool is arrested, Theo and Claudia work extra hard to exonerate one of their own, and also to complete their larger mission.

Where it's reviewed:
Booklist, May 1, 2008, page 37
Mystery News, June/July 2008, page 27
Publishers Weekly, March 24, 2008, page 56

Other books by the same author:
The Lark's Lament, 2007
An Antic Disposition, 2004
The Widow of Jerusalem, 2003
A Death in the Venetian Quarter, 2002
Jester Leaps In, 2000

Other books you might like:
Margaret Frazer, *The Clerk's Tale*, 2002
Sharan Newman, *The Wandering Arm*, 1995
Sharon Kay Penman, *Dragon's Lair*, 2003
Candace Robb, *The Cross-Legged Knight*, 2003

88

SARAH GRAVES

The Book of Old Houses

(New York: Bantam, 2008)

Story type: Amateur Detective
Series: Jacobia Tiptree. Book 11
Subject(s): Murder; Housing
Major character(s): Jacobia Tiptree, Carpenter, Detective—Amateur
Time period(s): 2000s
Locale(s): Eastport, Maine

Summary: Because Jake Tiptree has spent a considerable amount of time renovating her 1823 house, she's become an expert in home repair. She finds what appears to be an extremely old book with a list of names. To her surprise, Jake finds her own name on the list. It looks as if it has been written in blood. Jake decides to consult a rare book expert, who then turns up dead—a result of what the police call a random mugging. Then, a few weeks later, a stranger turns up at her house, claiming to be a friend of the book expert. He is very interested in the book, which has gone missing.

Where it's reviewed:
Booklist, May 1, 2008, page 52
Library Journal, December 15, 2007, page 91
Publishers Weekly, November 12, 2007, page 39

Other books by the same author:
Trap Door, 2007
Nail Biter, 2006
Mallets Aforethought, 2004
Tool and Die, 2004
The Dead Cat Bounce, 1998

Other books you might like:
Mary Kay Andrews, *Hissy Fit*, 2004
Leslie Meier, *Tippy-Toe Murder*, 1994
Katherine Hall Page, *The Body in the Basement*, 1994
Valerie Wolzien, *Murder in the Forecast*, 2001

89

KERRY GREENWOOD

Queen of the Flowers

(Scottsdale, Arizona: Poisoned Pen, 2008)

Story type: Amateur Detective; Historical/Roaring Twenties
Series: Phryne Fisher. Book 14
Subject(s): Circus; Family Relations
Major character(s): Phryne Fisher, Detective—Amateur, Socialite; James Murray, Musician
Time period(s): 1920s
Locale(s): Australia

Summary: It's time for the Flower Festival at St. Kilda's and the Honorable Phryne Fisher has been asked to be the parade's Queen of the Flowers. Four young girls are also picked as Flower Maidens to ride on the float with Phryne: Joannie, Diane, Marie, and Rose. All seem ordinary, except for Rose, who has been seen with some unsavory men keeping late hours at a local restaurant. Then she goes missing. Has she been kidnapped? Has she run away? It turns out that her home life has been anything but homey. To complicate things even more, Phryne's adopted daughter, Ruth, also disappears. The police are brought in, but it is Phryne who ventures forth, searching on a gambling boat and in an upscale house of prostitution—among other locations.

Where it's reviewed:
Booklist, May 1, 2008, page 40
Deadly Pleasures, Spring 2008, page 42
Library Journal, June 1, 2008, page 78
Publishers Weekly, March 31, 2008, page 42

Other books by the same author:
Raisins and Almonds, 2007
The Green Mill Murder, 2007
Cocaine Blues, 2006
Flying Too High, 2006
Murder on the Ballarat Train, 2006

Other books you might like:
Suzanne Arruda, *Mark of the Lion*, 2006
Rhys Bowen, *Her Royal Spyness*, 2007
Barbara Cleverly, *The Last Kashmiri Rose*, 2002
Elizabeth Peters, *Crocodile on the Sandbank*, 1975

90

MICHAEL GREGORIO

Days of Atonement

(New York: St. Martin's, 2008)

Story type: Historical/Napoleonic Wars
Series: Hanno Stiffeniis. Book 2
Subject(s): Anti-Semitism; Children and War
Major character(s): Hanno Stiffeniis, Judge; Serge Lavadrine, Police Officer; Helena Stiffeniis, Spouse
Time period(s): 1800s (1807)
Locale(s): East Prussia, Prussia

Summary: In Prussia under French occupation, Hanno Stiffeniis works as a magistrate. He is called on to investigate the brutal killings of three children in a remote cottage in a bleak Prussian forest. The children's mother is missing, presumed dead. Stiffeniis works with French Colonel Lavadrine, a fellow student of Immanuel Kant, to smooth things over with the French authorities. When Stiffeniis travels to the remote Russian border to tell the children's father of their deaths, he discovers that the father has also been murdered. Stiffeniis and Lavadrine enlist the help of Stiffeniis' wife Helena to solve the crime, using the fledgling science of criminology along with phrenology and forensic psychiatry.

Where it's reviewed:
Booklist, March 15, 2008, page 31
Kirkus Reviews, March 1, 2008
Mystery News, April/May 2008, page 16
Mystery Scene, Spring 2008, page 71
Publishers Weekly, February 18, 2008, page 138

Other books by the same author:
Critique of Criminal Reason, 2006

Other books you might like:
Louis Bayard, *The Black Tower*, 2008
Margaret Frazer, *The Traitor's Tale*, 2007
R.N. Morris, *The Gentle Axe*, 2007
C.J. Sansom, *Dissolution*, 2003

91

ANDREW GROSS

The Dark Tide

(New York: Morrow, 2008)

Story type: Police Procedural
Subject(s): Conspiracies; Money
Major character(s): Karen Friedman, Real Estate Agent, Widow(er); Ty Hauck, Detective—Police; Saul Lennick, Banker
Time period(s): 2000s
Locale(s): Old Greenwich, Connecticut; Stamford, Connecticut; St. Hubert, British Virgin Islands

Summary: When an explosion destroys several train cars in New York's Grand Central Station, Karen Friedman's ideal life is also destroyed. Karen's husband Charles, the manager of a successful hedge fund, was on the train that fateful morning. A year goes by and Karen attempts to create a new life for herself and her two children without Charles. Karen's life is once again turned upside down when two men appear at her home asking questions about Charles' business and inquiring about a large sum of money. Lieutenant Ty Hauck, a Greenwich, Connecticut, police detective, meets Karen when a hit-and-run accident victim has an apparent connection to Charles.

Where it's reviewed:
Booklist, March 1, 2008, page 51
Library Journal, February 1, 2008, page 53
Publishers Weekly, January 21, 2008, page 152

Other books by the same author:
The Blue Zone, 2007

Other books you might like:
David Baldacci, *Total Control*, 1997
Bill Floyd, *The Killer's Wife*, 2008
Howard Roughman, *The Promise of a Lie*, 2004
Eugenia Lovett West, *Without Warning*, 2008

92

JANE HADDAM

Cheating at Solitaire

(New York: St. Martin's, 2008)

Story type: Psychological Suspense
Series: Gregor Demarkian. Book 23
Subject(s): Movie Industry; Psychological Thriller
Major character(s): Gregor Demarkian, Consultant; Kendra Rhode, Socialite; Arrow Normand, Actress
Time period(s): 2000s
Locale(s): Margaret's Harbor, Massachusetts
Summary: Gregor Demarkian is finally set to marry his

long time love, Bennis Hannaford, but he's eager to take a case in far off Margaret's Harbor to escape his own wedding preparations. The isolated Margaret's Harbor has been prey to a group of young celebrities who are filming a movie; they are acting out in all kinds of ways. When one of the most prominent of them, Arrow Normand, staggers through a blizzard, bloody and disheveled, and her boyfriend is found dead in his truck, Arrow is the prime suspect. Gregor is called in to consult and take a look at the case against her.

Where it's reviewed:
Booklist, March 1, 2008, page 52
Deadly Pleasures, Spring 2008, page 49
Entertainment Weekly, April 18, 2008, page 67
Publishers Weekly, January 14, 2008, page 43

Other books by the same author:
Glass Houses, 2007
The Headmaster's Wife, 2005
Skeleton Key, 2000
A Stillness in Bethlehem, 1992
Not a Creature Was Stirring, 1990

Other books you might like:
Jane Dentinger, *Murder on Cue*, 1983
Parnell Hall, *Actor*, 1993
P.D. James, *The Murder Room*, 2003
Ngaio Marsh, *Night at the Vulcan*, 1951

93

PARNELL HALL

The Sudoku Puzzle Murders

(New York: St. Martin's, 2008)

Story type: Amateur Detective; Humor
Series: Puzzle Lady. Book 9
Subject(s): Games; Samurai
Major character(s): Cora Felton, Detective—Amateur; Sherry Felton, Writer (crossword puzzle constructor)
Time period(s): 2000s
Locale(s): Bakerhaven, Connecticut

Summary: Cora Felton is known as the face of the Puzzle Lady, a star crossword puzzle constructor, even though her daughter is the one writing the puzzles. Despite being the Puzzle Lady in public, Cora can't solve a crossword to save her life. She has recently discovered that she's really good at sudoku. A dead body is found with both a crossword and a sudoku at the crime scene. The victim had half of his head cut off by a rare samurai sword. Cora has agreed to write a sudoku book for a Japanese publisher, but she can't remember which of two Japanese publishers in town she signed the deal with. Both publishers are suspected in the murder. This volume includes four sudokus written by Will Shortz.

Where it's reviewed:
Booklist, March 1, 2008, page 54
Kirkus Reviews, February 15, 2008
Library Journal, February 1, 2008, page 49
Publishers Weekly, February 11, 2008, page 54

Other books by the same author:
Hitman, 2007
You Have the Right to Remain Puzzled, 2006
Stalking the Puzzle Lady, 2005
And a Puzzle to Die On, 2004
With This Puzzle I Thee Kill, 2003

Other books you might like:
Nero Blanc, *Two Down*, 2000
Shelley Freydont, *The Sudoku Murder*, 2007
Anne George, *Murder Runs in the Family*, 1997
Kaye Morgan, *Death by Sudoku*, 2007

94

PETRA HAMMESFAHR

The Sinner

(London, England: Bitter Lemon, 2008)

Story type: Psychological Suspense
Subject(s): Family
Major character(s): Cora Bender, Accountant; Rudolf
  Grovian, Police Officer; Georg Frankenberg, Doctor
Time period(s): 2000s
Locale(s): Buchholz, Germany; Cologne, Germany

Summary: As her young son plays nearby on the beach,
Cora Bender takes the small knife she has just used to
slice an apple and stabs a man to death. Witnesses to the
brutal event are shocked, and a young bride is now a
widow. Police chief Rudolf Grovian refuses to accept
Cora's odd behavior and insistence that she did not know
the young man she killed. As Grovian digs deeper into
Cora's past, the investigation undergoes a startling turn
of events when Cora's relationship with her family is
revealed. From a bizarre, controlling mother to a disabled
sister, Cora's reason for killing is eventually uncovered.

Where it's reviewed:
Booklist, December 1, 2007, page 28
Publishers Weekly, December 24, 2007, page 32

Other books you might like:
Karin Alvtegen, *Missing*, 2008
Karin Fossum, *Don't Look Back*, 2004
Camilla Trinchieri, *The Price of Silence*, 2007
Minette Walters, *The Sculptress*, 1993

95

ROSEMARY HARRIS

Pushing Up Daisies

(New York: St. Martin's, 2008)

Story type: Amateur Detective
Subject(s): Gardens and Gardening
Major character(s): Paula Holliday, Gardener; Lucy Ca-
  vanaugh, Television Personality; Mike O'Malley,
  Police Officer
Time period(s): 2000s
Locale(s): Springfield, Connecticut

Summary: Hired by the local historical society to restore
the garden of Halcyon, the old Peacock mansion, Paula
Holliday is shocked to dig up a box containing a mummified baby. Paula continues her work on the garden, but
she is haunted by the baby, and does some other digging,
online and through papers. Were the two Peacock sisters
merely the kindly but distant dowagers of Springfield?
Or is there more to their story? Paula's housekeeper is
attacked, Paula is locked into a greenhouse, and a rival
landscaper is found with a sharp garden tool stuck in his
back. Paula finds herself trying to solve several mysteries, while attempting to keep from being a victim herself.
Police officer Mike O'Malley, attractive but a little on
the tubby side, is determined to keep Paula safe.

Where it's reviewed:
Booklist, December 15, 2007, page 30
Mystery News, April/May 2008, page 27
Publishers Weekly, December 17, 2007, page 31

Other books you might like:
Susan Wittig Albert, *Nightshade*, 2008
Anthony Eglin, *The Water Lily Cross*, 2007
Julie Wray Herman, *Three Dirty Women and the Shady
  Acres*, 2003
Heather Webber, *A Hoe Lot of Trouble*, 2004

96

LIBBY FISCHER HELLMANN

Easy Innocence

(Madison, Wisconsin: Bleak House, 2008)

Story type: Private Detective
Series: Georgia Davis. Book 1
Subject(s): Schools/High Schools; Prostitution
Major character(s): Georgia Davis, Detective—Private;
  Lauren Walcher, Student—High School, Madam;
  Paul Kelly, Lawyer
Time period(s): 2000s
Locale(s): Chicago, Illinois; Winnetka, Illinois; Glencoe,
  Illinois

Summary: When the body of teenager Sara Long is
discovered in a Chicago forest preserve, police arrest a
mentally challenged sex offender, Cameron Jordan.
Certain her brother is innocent of the crime, Ruth Jordan
hires private investigator Georgia Davis to look into the
case. A former cop, Davis is familiar with Newfield, the
posh high school that Sara attended. Recalling a hazing
incident from two years ago that turned violent, Davis
believes some of the students may have revived the
practice. When Davis gets the chance to talk to Lauren
Walcher, a friend of Sara's and a student at Newfield,
she discovers the ugly truth behind the beautiful girl's
death.

Where it's reviewed:
Booklist, March 1, 2008, page 52
Deadly Pleasures, Spring 2008, page 32
Mystery News, June/July 2008, page 10
Publishers Weekly, February 4, 2008, page 41

Other books by the same author:
A Shot to Die For, 2005
A Picture of Guilt, 2003
An Image of Death, 2003
An Eye for Murder, 2002

Other books you might like:
Kate Flora, *Stalking Death*, 2008
Mary Logue, *Maiden Rock*, 2007
Cornelia Read, *The Crazy School*, 2008
Donna Tartt, *The Secret History*, 1992

97

JOAN HESS

Mummy Dearest

(New York: St. Martin's, 2008)

Story type: Amateur Detective
Series: Claire Malloy. Book 17
Subject(s): Espionage
Major character(s): Claire Malloy, Store Owner (bookseller), Detective—Amateur; Peter Rosen, Police Officer; Alexander Bledrock, Banker
Time period(s): 2000s
Locale(s): Luxor, Egypt; Cairo, Egypt

Summary: Having at long last gotten married, Claire Malloy and her new husband Peter Rosen are on their honeymoon in Luxor, Egypt. Accompanying the newlyweds are Caron, Claire's 17-year-old daughter, and Caron's best friend, Inez. This is a working vacation for Peter; he has to spend time meeting with various Egyptian government officials. Claire spends her time shopping and sightseeing with Caron and Inez. Strange events begin to occur when Caron and Inez claim that they are being followed by a mysterious man with a scar. Then a young American woman, Buffy Franz, is kidnapped during a sightseeing trip. Claire is determined to unravel the puzzling events around her. She encounters Lady Amelia Peabody Emerson, a descendant of English archaeologists, along the way.

Where it's reviewed:
Deadly Pleasures, Spring 2008, page 40
Mystery News, June/July 2008, page 11
Publishers Weekly, March 10, 2008, page 63

Other books by the same author:
Damsels in Distress, 2007
The Goodbye Body, 2005
Out on a Limb, 2002
A Conventional Corpse, 2000
A Holly Jolly Murder, 1997

Other books you might like:
Agatha Christie, *Death on the Nile*, 1937
Aaron Elkins, *Dead Men's Hearts*, 1994
Lyn Hamilton, *The African Quest*, 2001
Elizabeth Peters, *Crocodile on the Sandbank*, 1975

98

DAVID HEWSON

The Garden of Evil

(New York: Delacorte, 2008)

Story type: Police Procedural
Series: Nic Costa. Book 6
Subject(s): Art; Cults
Major character(s): Nic Costa, Detective—Homicide, Widow(er); Agata Graziano, Religious; Franco Malaspina, Nobleman, Criminal
Time period(s): 2000s
Locale(s): Rome, Italy

Summary: In a hidden studio in a seedy part of Rome, the police discover two recently murdered bodies. One of the victims was an art expert at the Louvre. Newly promoted detective Nic Costa is sent to investigate the gruesome scene, and ends up chasing a masked figure through the streets to a tragic end. Evidence from the studio leads Costa to Franco Malaspina, a wealthy aristocrat and patron of the arts. Costa's superior, Inspector Leo Falcone, sends Costa to Sister Agata Graziano, a woman who has spent her life studying art, and is familiar with Malaspina. Costa and Sister Agata soon learn that Malaspina is part of a cult known as the Ekstasists, whose sinister intentions involve young immigrant women.

Where it's reviewed:
Booklist, June 1, 2008, page 8
Publishers Weekly, May 26, 2008, page 40

Other books by the same author:
The Seventh Sacrament, 2007
The Lizard's Bite, 2006
The Sacred Cut, 2005
The Villa of Mysteries, 2005
A Season for the Dead, 2004

Other books you might like:
Michael Dibdin, *Cabal*, 1993
Donna Leon, *Doctored Evidence*, 2004
Iain Pears, *The Last Judgment*, 1996
Peter Watson, *Landscape of Lies*, 1989

99

REGINALD HILL

The Roar of the Butterflies

(New York: Harper, 2008)

Story type: Private Detective
Series: Joe Sixsmith. Book 5
Subject(s): Sports/Golf; Conspiracies
Major character(s): Joe Sixsmith, Detective—Private; Christian Porphyry, Heir; Ratcliffe King, Criminal, Businessman
Time period(s): 2000s
Locale(s): Luton, England

Summary: Private investigator Joe Sixsmith is somewhat surprised when handsome young Christian Porphyry comes to him for help. A member of one of Luton, England's upper-class families, Porphyry is being accused of cheating at the golf club his family created, the Royal Hoo Golf Course. Meeting with Porphyry at the Royal Hoo, Sixsmith has never felt more out of place, that is until crime lord Ratcliffe King, also known as "King Rat," hires Sixsmith for an immediate out-of-town job. Joe discovers that there is a conspiracy against Christian Porphyry involving one of the Royal Hoo's members and King Rat.

Other books by the same author:
Singing the Sadness, 1999
Killing the Lawyers, 1997
Born Guilty, 1995
Blood Sympathy, 1994
Recalled to Life, 1993

Other books you might like:
Keith Miles, *Bullet Hole*, 1987
Ruth Rendell, *Adam and Eve and Pinch Me*, 2002
Mike Ripley, *Angel in the House*, 2005

100

KATHLEEN HILLS

The Kingdom Where Nobody Dies

(Scottsdale, Arizona: Poisoned Pen, 2008)

Story type: Historical
Series: John McIntire. Book 4
Subject(s): Internment; Children
Major character(s): John McIntire, Police Officer; Mia Thorsen, Care Giver, Artisan; Joey Hofer, Child
Time period(s): 1950s
Locale(s): St. Adele, Michigan; Baraga, Michigan

Summary: On a hot summer day in the 1950s, young Claire Hofer learns from Township Constable John McIntire that her father has been killed. As McIntire begins his investigation, he discovers that Hofer was not a newcomer to St. Adele, Michigan, as most people thought. During World War II, Hofer was interned in a camp for conscientious objectors, not far from St. Adele. When news of Hofer's death is made public, former acquaintances from the camp turn up, and all of them seem to be looking for something Hofer left behind. McIntire soon realizes that someone in the Hofer family may hold the key to solving the murder.

Where it's reviewed:
Booklist, December 1, 2007, page 27
Mystery News, February/March 2008, page 23
Mystery Scene, Winter 2008, page 65
Publishers Weekly, November 19, 2007, page 41

Other books by the same author:
Witch Cradle, 2006
Hunter's Dance, 2004
Past Imperfect, 2002

Other books you might like:
Ray Bradbury, *Death Is a Lonely Business*, 1985
Michael Collins, *The Resurrectionists*, 2002
Ed Gorman, *Save the Last Dance for Me*, 2002
Henry Kisor, *A Venture into Murder*, 2005

101

STEVE HOCKENSMITH

The Black Dove

(New York: St. Martin's, 2008)

Story type: Amateur Detective; Historical/American West Coast

Series: Holmes on the Range. Book 3
Subject(s): Chinese Americans; Cowboys/Cowgirls
Major character(s): Otto "Big Red" Amlingmeyer, Cowboy, Detective—Amateur; Gustav "Old Red" Amlingmeyer, Cowboy, Detective—Amateur; Diane Corvus, Detective—Private
Time period(s): 1890s (1893)
Locale(s): San Francisco, California (USA)

Summary: Old Red and Big Red are cowboys who go wherever the roads take them. After losing their railroad jobs, they look for work in San Francisco. Once there they find an old friend, Dr. Chan—but only for so long. Dr. Chan is murdered shortly after their reunion. Ever since he heard Big Red read to him his first Sherlock Holmes story, Old Red believes he too can use the powers of deducifying to solve crimes. So the cowboy brothers join up with Diane Corvus, a former railroad detective, to search for answers to Dr. Chan's murder in Chinatown.

Where it's reviewed:
Booklist, December 15, 2007, page 28
Mystery News, February/March 2008, page 15
Mystery Scene, Winter 2008, page 69
Publishers Weekly, November 5, 2007, page 46
Roundup Magazine, April 200, page 26

Other books by the same author:
On the Wrong Track, 2007
Holmes on the Range, 2006

Other books you might like:
Sir Arthur Conan Doyle, *"The Red-Headed League"*, 1891
Oakley Hall, *Ambrose Bierce and the Ace of Shoots*, 2006
Laurie R. King, *Locked Rooms*, 2005
Shirley Tallman, *The Russian Hill Murders*, 2005

102

ANNE HOLT

What Never Happens

(New York: Grand Central, 2008)

Story type: Serial Killer
Series: Adam Stubo and Johanne Vik. Book 2
Subject(s): Family; Murder
Major character(s): Adam Stubo, Detective—Police; Johanne Vik, Spouse, Lawyer; Wencke Berger, Writer, Serial Killer
Time period(s): 2000s
Locale(s): Oslo, Norway; Tasen, Norway; Villefranche, France

Summary: A serial killer is stalking celebrities in Oslo, Norway. First, popular talk show host Fiona Helle is found brutally murdered, her tongue cut out. Then the body of local politician Victoria Heinerback is discovered by her boyfriend, a copy of the Koran stuck between her thighs. When a literary critic is stabbed in the eye, Detective Inspector Adam Stubo enlists his wife Johanne's help in the case. A former profiler, Johanne is startled by the similarities in these recent murders to cases she studied in an FBI program several years ago, especially

since this leads Johanne to believe that she and her family could be the next victims.

Where it's reviewed:
Booklist, December 1, 2007, page 26
Mystery News, April/May 2008, page 14
Mystery Scene, Winter 2008, page 76
Publishers Weekly, November 19, 2007, page 34

Other books by the same author:
What Is Mine, 2006

Other books you might like:
Karin Alvtegen, *Missing*, 2008
K.O. Dahl, *The Fourth Man*, 2008
Karin Fossum, *The Indian Bride*, 2007
Jo Nesbo, *The Redbreast*, 2007

103

DAVID HORWITZ

Murder Bay

(Oak Park, Illinois: Top Five Books, 2008)

Story type: Historical/American Civil War; Police Procedural
Series: Ben Carey. Book 1
Subject(s): Haunted Houses; Civil War
Major character(s): Benjamin Carey, Police Officer; Norman Crawford, Police Officer; Louisa Morrison, Nurse
Time period(s): 1950s (1957); 1860s (1862)
Locale(s): New York, New York; Washington, District of Columbia; Manassas, Virginia

Summary: At the Battle of Manassas during the Civil War, young Mordechai Finkel is wounded and left on the battlefield. When he reawakens, Finkel finds himself in the Washington, D.C., home of Louisa Morrison, who is nursing him and several other wounded soldiers back to life. When Finkel dies unexpectedly, Louisa is heartbroken and doesn't believe that his death was caused by his battle wounds. Over 90 years later, newly promoted Sergeant Ben Carey is the head of a new police planning unit that is stationed in a run-down old mansion. When marital problems force Carey to stay at the old mansion, he begins to hear footsteps and see people who shouldn't be there. Looking into the building's history, Carey learns of Finkel's death and investigates the decades-old crime.

Where it's reviewed:
Publishers Weekly, February 18, 2008, page 140

Other books you might like:
Mary Anna Evans, *Findings*, 2008
Michael Kilian, *Murder at Manassas*, 2000
Jane Langton, *The Deserter*, 2003
Miriam Grace Monfredo, *Children of Cain*, 2002

104

DAVID HOUSEWRIGHT

Madman on a Drum

(New York: St. Martin's, 2008)

Story type: Private Detective
Series: Rushmore McKenzie. Book 5
Subject(s): Kidnapping; Crime and Criminals
Major character(s): Rushmore McKenzie, Wealthy, Detective—Private; Bobby Dunston, Detective—Homicide; Karen Studder, Parole Officer
Time period(s): 2000s
Locale(s): St. Paul, Minnesota; Minneapolis, Minnesota; Orono, Minnesota

Summary: When young Victoria Dunston is kidnapped on her way home from school, former Minnesota cop Rushmore "Mac" McKenzie's world is turned upside down. Victoria is the daughter of Bobby Dunston, a homicide detective and lifelong friend, and also McKenzie's goddaughter. The Dunstons receive a call from the kidnappers demanding a million dollars in ransom. When Dunston replies he doesn't have the money, the kidnapper tells him to get it from McKenzie. This bit of telling information leads both McKenzie and Dunston to realize that Victoria's kidnapper is someone they already know. After recovering Victoria, McKenzie calls the kidnapper by name and sets off a series of events that includes a contract on his life.

Where it's reviewed:
Booklist, May 15, 2008, page 24
Publishers Weekly, April 7, 2008, page 46

Other books by the same author:
Dead Boyfriends, 2007
Pretty Girl Gone, 2006
Tin City, 2005
A Hard Ticket Home, 2004
Dearly Departed, 1999

Other books you might like:
Raymond Chandler, *The Long Goodbye*, 1953
Michael Koryta, *Sorrow's Anthem*, 2006
William Kent Krueger, *Mercy Falls*, 2005
P.J. Tracy, *Monkeewrench*, 2003

105

LIS HOWELL

The Chorister at the Abbey

(New York: Soho Constable, 2008)

Story type: Amateur Detective
Series: Norbridge Chronicles. Book 2
Subject(s): Christmas; Religion
Major character(s): Edwin Armstrong, Musician; Alex Gibson, Secretary, Writer; Suzy Spencer, Producer
Time period(s): 2000s
Locale(s): Norbridge, England; Tarnfield, England; Uplands, England

Summary: The town of Norbridge, England, is preparing

for Christmas. Shortly after choir rehearsal, the body of local shopkeeper Morris Little is discovered outside the music department of Norbridge College by student Tom Firth. Tom's screams draw frumpy secretary Alex Gibson to the scene. When the police arrest the Frost boys, the local troublemakers, for the crime, they obligingly confess. While discussing the murder scene with deputy head of the music department, Edwin Armstrong, Alex and Tom both remember seeing a psalter lying next to Morris' body. When no evidence of the psalter is found by the police, Edwin begins to investigate the crime, along with Alex and his friends, TV producer Suzy Spencer and her boyfriend, writer Robert Clark.

Other books by the same author:
The Flower Arranger at All Saints, 2007

Other books you might like:
Marian Babson, *The Twelve Deaths of Christmas*, 1980
Cyril Hare, *An English Murder*, 1951
Kate Kingsbury, *Slay Bells*, 2006
Jane Langton, *The Shortest Day*, 1995

106

ADRIAN HYLAND

Moonlight Downs
(New York: Soho, 2008)

Story type: Amateur Detective
Subject(s): Australian Aborigines
Major character(s): Emily Tempest, Detective—Amateur; Hazel Flinders Lively, Healer; Blakie Japanangka, Sorcerer
Time period(s): 2000s
Locale(s): Moonlight Downs, Australia; Bluebush, Australia

Summary: Emily Tempest, a half-Aboriginal woman, has returned to her childhood home of Moonlight Downs in the Australian Outback after attending university and spending several years traveling the world. Shortly after Emily's arrival, Moonlight Downs' tribal leader, Lincoln Flinders, is brutally murdered, one of his kidneys ripped from his body. All signs point to Blakie Japanangka, a local sorcerer, as Lincoln's killer. While Emily does some investigating, she also reconnects with her childhood friend Hazel, Lincoln's daughter. As she begins to doubt Blakie's guilt, Emily and police sergeant Tom McGillivray uncover several other suspects, including land owner Earl Marsh.

Where it's reviewed:
Booklist, October 1, 2007, page 36
Deadly Pleasures, Spring 2008, page 32
Library Journal, January 15, 2008, page 69
Mystery Scene, Winter 2008, page 73
Publishers Weekly, October 29, 2007, page 33

Other books you might like:
Caroline Carver, *Blood Junction*, 2002
Jon Cleary, *Pride's Harvest*, 1991
Hannah Nyala, *Leave No Trace*, 2002
Peter Temple, *The Broken Shore*, 2007

107

JULIE HYZY

State of the Onion
(New York: Berkley, 2008)

Story type: Amateur Detective
Series: Olivia Paras. Book 1
Subject(s): Cooks and Cooking
Major character(s): Olivia Paras, Cook, Detective—Amateur
Time period(s): 2000s
Locale(s): Washington, District of Columbia

Summary: Olivia "Ollie" Paras is excited at the idea of becoming executive chef on the White House staff, but she runs into trouble as she tries to snag the position. Ollie stops a man fleeing Secret Service agents on the White House lawn by hitting him over the head with a frying pan. The man says something about warning the president of danger before he's taken away. Before long, Ollie is in over her head. She witnesses a murder and feels compelled to investigate further. Her Secret Service agent boyfriend asks her not to get involved, but she does anyway. Ollie also continues to work for the prestigious job she wants and tries to salvage her relationship. The book includes recipes for a presidential meal.

Where it's reviewed:
Booklist, December 15, 2007, page 30
Crimespree, January/February 2008, page 75
Mystery News, February/March 2008, page 11
Publishers Weekly, November 12, 2007, page 41

Other books by the same author:
Deadly Interest, 2006
Deadly Blessings, 2005
Artistic License, 2004

Other books you might like:
Miranda Bliss, *Cooking Up Trouble*, 2006
Andrew M. Greeley, *The Bishop in the West Wing*, 2002
Phyllis Richman, *The Butter Did It*, 1997
Elliott Roosevelt, *Murder in the East Room*, 1993

108

J.A. JANCE

Hand of Evil
(New York: Touchstone, 2007)

Story type: Amateur Detective
Series: Alison Reynolds. Book 3
Subject(s): Sexual Abuse
Major character(s): Alison Reynolds, Journalist (former), Detective—Amateur; Dave Holman, Detective—Police
Time period(s): 2000s
Locale(s): Sedona, Arizona

Summary: Still dealing with the death of her soon-to-be-ex husband, Alison Reynolds returns to her home in Sedona, Arizona, after losing her job as a newscaster.

Along the San Juan Road, a man is dragged along the road to his death. Meanwhile, an older, wealthy woman gives her diary to Ali and asks for her help in writing a memoir including details about a childhood of sexual abuse. Then the daughter of Dave Holman, a high school friend of Ali's, disappears. Is there some connection between all of these events? In an attempt to help out her friend, Ali finds herself on the trail of a murderer.

Where it's reviewed:
Booklist, October 1, 2007, page 35
Mystery News, April/May 2008, page 21
Publishers Weekly, September 17, 2007, page 35

Other books by the same author:
Web of Evil, 2007
Dead Wrong, 2006
Edge of Evil, 2006
Partner in Crime, 2002
Desert Heat, 1993

Other books you might like:
Susan Wittig Albert, *Bleeding Hearts*, 2006
Robert Barnard, *A Cry from the Dark*, 2004
Lee Martin, *The Day that Dusty Died*, 1993
J.M. Redmann, *The Intersection of Law and Desire*, 1995

109

CRAIG JOHNSON

Another Man's Moccasins

(New York: Viking, 2008)

Story type: Police Procedural; Historical
Series: Walt Longmire. Book 4
Subject(s): Vietnam War; Native Americans
Major character(s): Walt Longmire, Police Officer; Henry Standing Bear, Friend; Tran Van Tuyen, Businessman
Time period(s): 2000s; 1960s
Locale(s): Durant, Wyoming; Vietnam

Summary: Ranchers find the body of a Vietnamese girl by a road in Wyoming. When Sheriff Walt Longmire explores the culvert under the road, he is attacked by a mentally unstable Crow Indian named Virgil White Eagle. Virgil has taken up residence in the culvert. Is he the murderer? Walt isn't sure. The girl's purse contains a photograph of a much younger Walt and a woman he befriended when he served in Vietnam in 1967. Tran Van Tuyen, a Vietnamese businessman from Los Angeles, arrives, claiming to be the victim's grandfather. As he investigates the murder, Walt has flashbacks to his first military case in Vietnam, which involved the woman in the photograph.

Where it's reviewed:
Booklist, May 15, 2008, page 2
Publishers Weekly, April 21 2008, page 1

Other books by the same author:
Kindness Goes Unpunished, 2007
Death without Company, 2006
The Cold Dish, 2005

Other books you might like:
C.J. Box, *Open Season*, 2001
Robert Greer, *The Fourth Perspective*, 2006
Henry Kisor, *Season's Revenge*, 2003
William Kent Krueger, *Boundary Waters*, 1999

110

MORAG JOSS

The Night Following

(New York: Delacorte, 2008)

Story type: Psychological
Subject(s): Accidents; Guilt
Major character(s): Unnamed Character, Spouse; Arthur Mitchell, Aged Person, Widow(er); Ruth Mitchell, Spouse
Time period(s): 2000s
Locale(s): Sailsbury, England

Summary: After discovering that her husband Jeremy is having an affair, the wife of a doctor accidentally runs over a bicyclist in the Wiltshire countryside. The victim of the hit-and-run is Ruth Mitchell, who was on her way to her writing group. Ruth's widowed husband Arthur is devastated at his loss and begins to leave notes to his wife all over the house, looking for some sign that she is still here. Horrified with what she has done, the unnamed narrator becomes obsessed with both the victim and Arthur. She watches over Arthur from outside the house, and knowing that she has something to atone for, begins to fill Ruth's shoes as Arthur's caretaker.

Where it's reviewed:
Booklist, January 1, 2008, page 49
Entertainment Weekly, February 29, 2008, page 64
Mystery News, April/May 2008, page 20
Mystery Scene, Spring 2008, page 68
Publishers Weekly, January 28, 2008, page 42

Other books by the same author:
Puccini's Ghosts, 2006
Fearful Symmetry, 2005
Fruitful Bodies, 2005
Funeral Music, 2005
Half Broken Things, 2005

Other books you might like:
Elizabeth George, *A Traitor to Memory*, 2001
Peter Robinson, *Strange Affair*, 2005
Barbara Vine, *Anna's Book*, 1993
Minette Walters, *The Dark Room*, 1996

111

JONATHAN KELLERMAN

Compulsion

(New York: Ballantine, 2008)

Story type: Psychological Suspense
Series: Alex Delaware. Book 22
Subject(s): Psychology; Serial Killers

Mystery

Major character(s): Alex Delaware, Psychologist; Milo Sturgis, Detective—Police
Time period(s): 2000s
Locale(s): Los Angeles, California; New York, New York
Summary: Once again, LAPD detective Milo Sturgis needs psychologist Alex Delaware's help. A woman disappears along a highway. A retired schoolteacher is stabbed to death. Two women are killed in a beauty parlor. These brutal and violent deaths around Los Angeles have only one thing in common: the killer is always driving a black luxury car. Alex and Milo follow the trail of blood around L.A. then all the way to New York City, looking for a killer who doesn't seem to have any clear motivation for the crimes. On the home front, Alex is once again living with his off-again, on-again girlfriend, Robin.

Where it's reviewed:
Library Journal, February 15, 2008, page 92
Publishers Weekly, February 25, 2008, page 50

Other books by the same author:
Obsession, 2007
Gone, 2006
Rage, 2005
Therapy, 2004
Twisted, 2004

Other books you might like:
Jeffery Deaver, *The Bone Collector*, 1997
Chris Mooney, *Missing*, 2007
John Sandford, *Silent Prey*, 1992
Stephen White, *Missing Persons*, 2005

112

GENE KERRIGAN

Little Criminals

(New York: Europa Editions, 2008)

Story type: Police Procedural
Subject(s): Kidnapping; Crime and Criminals
Major character(s): Frankie Crowe, Criminal; Angela Kennedy, Crime Victim; John Grace, Detective—Police
Time period(s): 2000s
Locale(s): Ireland

Summary: Small-time criminal Frankie Crowe tries to pull off a pub robbery. When that goes awry, he gathers together a gang of like-minded friends and plans an elaborate kidnapping. The problems begin when they discover that the banker they had planned to take is not a banker, but a lawyer. So they decide instead to kidnap his wife, Angela. Thanks to fingerprints left in the stolen getaway car, the police soon identify Frankie, but the gang's whereabouts—and Angela's safety—are still unknown. Frankie's plans begin to unravel as he moves his people from place to place, and Detective Inspector John Grace is hot on his heels.

Where it's reviewed:
Publishers Weekly, March 17, 2008, page 46

Other books by the same author:
The Midnight Choir, 2007

Other books you might like:
Bartholomew Gill, *The Death of an Irish Tinker*, 1997
Bill James, *Protection*, 1992
Stuart MacBride, *Dying Light*, 2006
George P. Pelecanos, *Right as Rain*, 2001

113

ALICE KIMBERLY (Pseudonym of Alice Alfonsi and Marc Cerasini)

The Ghost and the Femme Fatale

(New York: Berkley, 2008)

Story type: Amateur Detective
Series: Haunted Bookshop. Book 4
Subject(s): Actors and Actresses
Major character(s): Penelope Thornton-McClure, Store Owner, Detective—Amateur; Jack Shepard, Spirit, Detective—Private; Maggie Kline, Writer
Time period(s): 2000s; 1940s (1948)
Locale(s): Quindicott, Rhode Island; New York, New York

Summary: The Movie Town Theater in Quindicott, Rhode Island, is holding its first Film Noir Festival. Penelope Thornton-McClure, owner of Buy the Book, is hosting several events at her bookshop including book signings and guest speakers. Unfortunately, the beginning of the festival is marred by an almost fatal incident involving legendary femme fatale Hedda Geist-Middleton, onstage at the movie theater. Penelope's sleuthing instincts are further aroused when others connected to the film festival are killed. When the local police refuse to believe Penelope's theory about the murders, she turns to her resident ghost, private investigator Jack Shepard. Shepard, a private investigator in the 1940s, was murdered in what is now Penelope's bookshop. Oddly enough, Jack remembers Hedda and is the perfect partner for Penelope on this case.

Other books by the same author:
The Ghost and the Dead Man's Library, 2006
The Ghost and the Dead Deb, 2005
The Ghost and Mrs. McClure, 2004

Other books you might like:
Madelyn Alt, *The Trouble with Magic*, 2006
Nancy Atherton, *Aunt Dimity Beats the Devil*, 2000
Lorna Barrett, *Murder Is Binding*, 2008
Jeffrey Cohen, *Some Like It Hot-Buttered*, 2007

114

LAURIE R. KING

Touchstone

(New York: Bantam, 2008)

Story type: Historical/Roaring Twenties
Subject(s): Espionage; Political Movements
Major character(s): Bennett Gray, Gentleman, Veteran; Harris Stuyvesant, Government Official, Investigator; Aldous Carstairs, Government Official

Time period(s): 1920s (1926)
Locale(s): Cornwall, England

Summary: Bennett Gray, who fought in the Great War, has emerged from the experience with an extreme sensitivity to the potential for human violence, making human contact very difficult. The government has studied Gray, but he's gone into seclusion, in particular staying away from Aldous Carstairs, a shadowy official who remains interested in Gray's special "touchstone" qualities. When American agent Harris Stuvyesant arrives in England on the trail of a terrorist, Carstairs sees an opportunity to test Gray. He maneuvers Gray and Stuvyesant into a visit with Lady Laura Hurleigh, part of a family of eccentrics whose servants dress in odd costumes and whose daughter has an open relationship with a man who wants to bring down the government.

Where it's reviewed:
Booklist, November 15, 2007, page 6
Deadly Pleasures, Spring 2008, page 53
Mystery News, February/March 2008, page 17
Publishers Weekly, November 26, 2007, page 29

Other books by the same author:
The Game, 2004
O Jerusalem, 1999
The Moor, 1998
The Beekeeper's Apprentice, 1994

Other books you might like:
Rennie Airth, *River of Darkness*, 1999
Anne Perry, *We Shall Not Sleep*, 2007
Charles Todd, *Legacy of the Dead*, 2000
Jacqueline Winspear, *An Incomplete Revenge*, 2008

115

CHRIS KNOPF

Head Wounds

(Sag Harbor, New York: Permanent, 2008)

Story type: Amateur Detective
Series: Sam Acquillo. Book 3
Subject(s): Construction
Major character(s): Sam Acquillo, Carpenter, Detective—Amateur; Amanda Anselma, Landowner, Businesswoman; Jackie Swaitkowski, Lawyer
Time period(s): 2000s
Locale(s): Southampton, New York; Bridgehampton, New York; Hungerford, New York

Summary: Ex-boxer and former engineer Sam Acquillo now makes a living as a carpenter in Southampton, New York. Brawling outside a restaurant one evening, Acquillo makes an enemy of local builder and bully Robbie Milhouser. When Milhouser's body is discovered at one of his job sites a few days later, Acquillo becomes the prime suspect. The police believe that Acquillo killed Milhouser in retaliation for a mysterious fire that destroyed a house owned by Acquillo's girlfriend, Amanda Anselma. Working with his friend and lawyer, Jackie Swaitkowski, Acquillo tries to clear his own name by discovering who really killed Milhouser.

Where it's reviewed:
Publishers Weekly, March 10, 2008, page 62

Other books by the same author:
Two Time, 2006
The Last Refuge, 2005

Other books you might like:
Steve Hamilton, *Night Work*, 2007
John D. MacDonald, *The Travis McGee series*, 1965-1985
Walter Satterthwait, *Wall of Glass*, 1989
Tom Schreck, *On the Ropes*, 2007

116

J.A. KONRATH

Fuzzy Navel

(New York: Hyperion, 2008)

Story type: Police Procedural
Series: Jack Daniels. Book 5
Subject(s): Kidnapping; Revenge
Major character(s): Jack Daniels, Detective—Police; Herb Benedict, Detective—Police; Harry McGlade, Detective—Private
Time period(s): 2000s
Locale(s): Chicago, Illinois

Summary: Three vigilantes are attacking sexual sinners in Chicago, shooting them with sniper rifles. One of the vigilantes is trigger-happy and starts shooting at Lieutenant Jacqueline "Jack" Daniels and other police officers. After narrowly escaping the shootout, the killers follow Jack back to her home. When she arrives, Jack finds out that Alex Kork (the murderer from *Rusty Nail*, Konrath's third novel), has faked her own death and escaped from prison. Now, Alex wants revenge on Jack and everyone she loves. That means kidnapping them all and torturing them in Jack's apartment. Jack has to rely on her own wits to avoid both Alex's psycho behavior and the vigilantes' seemingly never ending supply of ammunition in order to save the lives of all of her friends and family.

Other books by the same author:
Dirty Martini, 2007
Rusty Nail, 2006
Bloody Mary, 2005
Whiskey Sour, 2004

Other books you might like:
Chelsea Cain, *Heartsick*, 2007
Thomas Harris, *Red Dragon*, 1981
John Sandford, *Shadow Prey*, 1990
Steve Thayer, *The Weatherman*, 1994

117

KEN KUHLKEN

The Vagabond Virgins

(Scottsdale, Arizona: Poisoned Pen, 2008)

Story type: Political; Historical
Series: Tom Hickey. Book 5
Subject(s): Missing Persons; Family

Major character(s): Alvaro Hickey, Detective—Private; Clifford Hickey, Journalist; Lourdes Shuler, Crime Suspect
Time period(s): 1970s (1979)
Locale(s): San Diego, California; Tecate, Mexico; Ensenada, Mexico

Summary: In 1979, shortly before Mexico's elections, law clerk and private investigator Alvaro Hickey is approached by Lourdes Shuler, who wants Hickey's help in finding her missing sister Lupe. Lourdes claims that Lupe is the Holy Virgin that has been appearing to children all over Mexico. The Virgin tells children to deliver a message, that the current and corrupt government, the Partido Revolucionario Institucional, should be voted out of power. Hickey doesn't believe that Lupe is a divine spirit, but agrees to help Lourdes find her missing sister. Calling on his brother Clifford for backup, Hickey knows that Lourdes is hiding something important from him.

Where it's reviewed:
Booklist, December 1, 2007, page 28
Library Journal, December 15, 2007, page 92
Mystery News, February/March 2008, page 19
Publishers Weekly, December 24, 2007, page 32

Other books by the same author:
The Do-Re-Mi, 2006
The Angel Gang, 1994
The Venus Deal, 1993
The Loud Adios, 1991

Other books you might like:
Rolo Diez, *Tequila Blue*, 2005
Ruth Francisco, *Confessions of a Deathmaiden*, 2003
Roger L. Simon, *Wild Turkey*, 1974
Paco Ignacio Taibo II, *Some Clouds*, 1992

118

WILL LAVENDER

Obedience

(New York: Shaye Areheart, 2008)

Story type: Psychological Suspense
Subject(s): College Life; Kidnapping
Major character(s): Mary Butler, Student—College; Brian House, Student—College; Leonard Williams, Professor
Time period(s): 2000s
Locale(s): Indiana

Summary: At Winchester University, a small group of students enroll in Logic and Reasoning 204, a seminar taught by the elusive Professor Leonard Williams. The syllabus is simple: a girl named Polly is missing. In six weeks she will be murdered. Williams tells the students that they must find her in time to prevent the murder. He will provide additional information and new clues each time the seminar meets. Many of the students really get into the fictional case, almost to the point of obsession. Pursuing one of the clues, one of the students, Mary Butler, sees a picture of "Polly" in a real-life situation. This leads her to believe that Professor Williams' assignment might not be a hypothetical scenario.

Where it's reviewed:
Entertainment Weekly, February 29, 2008, page 65
Library Journal, January 1, 2008, page 85
New York Times Book Review, March 9, 2008, page 23
Publishers Weekly, December 24, 2007, page 28
USA Today, March 6, 2008, page 7

Other books you might like:
Peter Abrahams, *Lights Out*, 1994
Paul Auster, *City of Glass*, 1994
Harlan Coben, *Tell No One*, 2001
Guillermo Martinez, *The Oxford Murders*, 2005

119

JOYCE LAVENE
JIM LAVENE , Co-Author

Hooked Up

(Woodbury, Minnesota: Midnight Ink, 2008)

Story type: Amateur Detective
Series: Glad Wycznewski. Book 2
Subject(s): Sports/Auto Racing; Twins
Major character(s): Glad Wycznewski, Detective—Police (Retired); Ruby Wycznewski, Spouse; Phil Paxton, Businessman
Time period(s): 2000s
Locale(s): Dover, Delaware

Summary: Glad and Ruby Wycznewski are on their way to the Monster Mile NASCAR race at the Dover International Speedway when Ruby picks up a hitchhiker, much to Glad's annoyance. Ruby even gives the man Glad's bed and PJs. Once they arrive at the speedway, the hitchhiker, Bill Paxton, falls to his death from a bridge while still wearing Glad's pajamas. Paxton's identical twin, Phil, a powerful casino man, arrives to claim the body. Ruby begins to have her suspicions about him when she hears a rumor that $10,000,000 in cash has gone missing. A private eye with an English accent and a black bowler approaches Glad and Ruby; he believes that the twins were responsible for the robbery.

Where it's reviewed:
Booklist, December 1, 2007, page 26
Mystery Scene, Winter 2008, page 68

Other books by the same author:
Poisoned Petals, 2007
Swapping Paint, 2007
Fruit of the Poisoned Tree, 2006
Pretty Poison, 2005

Other books you might like:
Pamela Britton, *Dangerous Curves*, 2005
Steve Eubanks, *Hot Laps*, 2007
Janet Evanovich, *Metro Girl*, 2004
Judith Skillings, *Driven to Murder*, 2006

120

MIKE LAWSON

House Rules

(New York: Atlantic Monthly, 2008)

Story type: Political
Series: Joe DeMarco. Book 3
Subject(s): Terrorism; Government
Major character(s): Joe DeMarco, Lawyer, Troubleshooter; John Mahoney, Political Figure
Time period(s): 2000s
Locale(s): Baltimore, Maryland; Washington, District of Columbia; Cleveland, Ohio

Summary: Reza Zarif is shot down during an attempt to crash a small plane into the White House. Zarif's brother Hassan comes to Speaker of the House of Representatives John Mahoney and asks for help in discovering why Reza would commit an act that was out of his normal character. Mahoney asks Joe DeMarco to look into the incident. Technically a congressional employee, DeMarco is Mahoney's troubleshooter, doing any investigative work that the Speaker wants done quietly. Zarif's attempted attack is one of three that triggers anti-Muslim legislation supported by junior senator William Broderick.

Where it's reviewed:
Publishers Weekly, April 21, 2008, page 33

Other books by the same author:
The Second Perimeter, 2006
The Inside Ring, 2005

Other books you might like:
William Bernhardt, *Capitol Conspiracy*, 2008
William S. Cohen, *Dragon Fire*, 2006
Jerome Doolittle, *Head Lock*, 1993
Vince Flynn, *Separation of Power*, 2001

121

PETER LEONARD

Quiver

(New York: St. Martin's, 2008)

Story type: Family Saga
Subject(s): Hunting; Kidnapping
Major character(s): Kate McCall, Widow(er); Luke McCall; Jack Curran, Convict
Time period(s): 2000s
Locale(s): Detroit, Michigan

Summary: While hunting, 16-year-old Luke McCall accidentally shoots an arrow through a deer and into his father Owen, a racing car driver. Luke and his mother Kate are hit hard by the loss, which leads Luke to run away from home. A former lover of Kate's, Jack Curran, reenters her life shortly after he is released from jail. He first met Kate when he saved her life during her time with the Peace Corps in Guatemala. Curran may be the only one able to help the McCall family when a group of criminals led by Teddy Hicks kidnaps Luke and demands two million dollars for his safety.

Where it's reviewed:
Booklist, April 1, 2008, page 32
Library Journal, April 15, 2008, page 73
Mystery Scene, Summer 2008, page 86
Publishers Weekly, March 10, 2008, page 57

Other books you might like:
Harlan Coben, *The Innocent*, 2005
Thomas H. Cook, *Red Leaves*, 2005
John Hart, *The King of Lies*, 2006
Elmore Leonard, *La Brava*, 1983

122

ERIC LERNER

Pinkerton's Secret

(New York: Henry Holt, 2008)

Story type: Historical
Subject(s): Espionage; Civil War
Major character(s): Allan Pinkerton, Detective—Private, Historical Figure; Kate Warne, Detective—Private; Abraham Lincoln, Lawyer, Political Figure
Time period(s): 1850s (1856); 1860s
Locale(s): Chicago, Illinois; Washington, District of Columbia; Baltimore, Maryland

Summary: Having fled Scotland with his 15-year-old bride, Allan Pinkerton comes to America and founds the Pinkerton National Detective Agency. In 1856, Pinkerton is surprised when Kate Warne, a beautiful young widow, applies for a position with his agency. Claiming that a woman can gain entry to places that a man cannot, Warne convinces Pinkerton that she will be an asset to his agency. Warne soon proves her sleuthing skills when she helps solve a major case and assists Pinkerton in stopping a secessionist plot. When Pinkerton and Warne are thrown together during an attempt to stop an assassination on President Lincoln, a romance begins.

Where it's reviewed:
Booklist, February 1, 2008, page 28
Publishers Weekly, December 17, 2007, page 29

Other books you might like:
James D. Brewer, *No Justice*, 1996
Kate Bryan, *Murder at Bent Elbow*, 1998
Miriam Grace Monfredo, *The Stalking Horse*, 1998
Richard Moquist, *Eye of the Agency*, 1997

123

DAVID LEVIEN

City of the Sun

(New York: Doubleday, 2008)

Story type: Child-in-Peril
Subject(s): Missing Persons; Children
Major character(s): Frank Behr, Detective—Private; Paul Gabriel, Insurance Agent, Parent (of a missing boy); Oscar Riggi, Criminal, Businessman
Time period(s): 2000s
Locale(s): Indianapolis, Indiana; Ciudad del Sol, Mexico

Summary: Twelve-year-old Jamie Gabriel leaves home just before dawn to deliver newspapers in his Indianapolis neighborhood. When Jamie disappears one morning, his parents, Paul and Carol, are devastated. Fourteen months later, Jamie is still missing and the police have no new information in Jamie's case. When a police officer mentions the name of a private investigator to Paul, the Gabriels decide to take a chance on yet another detective. Frank Behr is a former police officer, and can identify with Paul's pain, having lost his own son, Tim. Behr's investigation leads him to local businessman Oscar Riggi and a criminal operation that involves smuggling stolen children to Mexico.

Where it's reviewed:
Entertainment Weekly, February 29, 2008, page 62
Library Journal, January 1, 2008, page 85
Mystery Scene, Winter 2008, page 78
Publishers Weekly, January 14, 2008, page 40

Other books you might like:
Thomas H. Cook, *Red Leaves*, 2005
Ruth Francisco, *Confessions of a Deathmaiden*, 2003
Scott Frost, *Run the Risk*, 2005
Laura Lippman, *What the Dead Know*, 2005

124

CHUCK LOGAN

South of Shiloh

(New York: Harper Collins, 2008)

Story type: Amateur Detective
Subject(s): Civil War; Revenge
Major character(s): John Rane, Photographer, Writer; Kenny Beeman, Police Officer; Mitchell Lee Nickels, Radio Personality, Murderer
Time period(s): 2000s
Locale(s): Stillwater, Minnesota; Corinth, Mississippi; West Alcorn, Mississippi

Summary: Insurance salesman Paul Edin travels to Corinth, Mississippi with two of his friends to take part in a reenactment of a Civil War battle. When a sniper's bullet kills Edin on the battlefield, the local police call it a tragic accident. The locals of Corinth know better. They know that the bullet that killed Edin was meant for police deputy Kenny Beeman, who was standing next to Edin when he was shot. In Minnesota, Edin's widow Jenny is devastated by the loss. Jenny recently reconnected with her daughter's biological father, award-winning photographer and writer John Rane. She asks Rane to go to Mississippi and find out what really happened to her husband.

Where it's reviewed:
Library Journal, March 1, 2008, page 74
Mystery News, June/July 2008, page 23
Mystery Scene, Spring 2008, page 61
Publishers Weekly, February 4, 2008, page 37

Other books by the same author:
Homefront, 2005
Vapor Trail, 2003
Absolute Zero, 2002
The Big Law, 1998
The Price of Blood, 1997

Other books you might like:
Peter Abrahams, *The Last of the Dixie Heroes*, 2001
K.J. Erickson, *The Dead Survivors*, 2002
Michael Kilian, *The Shiloh Sisters*, 2003
Sarah Stewart Taylor, *Judgment of the Grave*, 2005

125

GREGG LOOMIS

The Sinai Secret

(New York: Leisure, 2008)

Story type: Adventure
Series: Lang Reilly. Book 3
Subject(s): Archaeology; Science
Major character(s): Lang Reilly, Lawyer, Businessman; Alicia Warner, Lawyer; Jacob Annueliwitz, Lawyer
Time period(s): 2000s; 1900s (1904)
Locale(s): Atlanta, Georgia; Brussels, Belgium; Mount Horeb, Egypt (Sinai Peninsula)

Summary: When two research scientists are murdered, one in Bruges, Belgium, and the other in Atlanta, Georgia, the only connection between the two men is lawyer Lang Reilly. Reilly heads up a charitable foundation that distributed funds to the two scientists so that they could research alternatives to fossil fuels. When Reilly travels to Amsterdam in search of answers, he is abducted at the airport. A former CIA agent, Reilly has no problem escaping his would-be captors. Realizing that the dead men's research must be more important than he thought, Reilly travels to Tel Aviv on the trail of a biblical parchment that is connected to the recent deaths.

Other books by the same author:
Gates of Hades, 2007
The Julian Secret, 2006
The Pegasus Secret, 2005
Voodoo Fury, 1991

Other books you might like:
William Dietrich, *The Rosetta Key*, 2008
A.J. Hartley, *The Mask of Atreus*, 2006
Douglas Preston, *Blasphemy*, 2008
James Rollins, *Map of Bones*, 2005

126

PETER LOVESEY

The Headhunters

(New York: Soho, 2008)

Story type: Police Procedural
Series: Henrietta Mallin. Book 2
Subject(s): Satire; City and Town Life
Major character(s): Henrietta Mallin, Detective—Police; Jo Stevens, Detective—Amateur
Time period(s): 2000s
Locale(s): Chichester, England

Summary: In a twist on Patricia Highsmith's classic *Strangers on a Train* scenario, Jo Stevens' friend Gemma jokes that they should form a mutual murder society, so

that they can do away with Gemma's boss, whom she detests. When Jo finds a body on the beach, though, it doesn't seem so funny, and it's even less funny when Gemma's boss disappears. The police, in the form of Chichester CID Inspector Henrietta Mallin and her team, investigate. The story is told through the alternating viewpoints of Hen and Jo.

Where it's reviewed:
Library Journal, April 1, 2008, page 6
Mystery Scene, Spring 2008, page 69
Publishers Weekly, February 4, 2008, page 41

Other books by the same author:
The Circle, 2005
The Reaper, 2000
On the Edge, 1989
Rough Cider, 1986

Other books you might like:
Cynthia Harrod-Eagles, *Death to Go*, 1993
Patricia Highsmith, *Strangers on a Train*, 1950
Jill McGown, *Plots and Errors*, 1999
Ruth Rendell, *Adam and Eve and Pinch Me*, 2001

127

LISA LUTZ

Curse of the Spellmans

(New York: Simon & Schuster, 2008)

Story type: Private Detective
Series: Spellman Family. Book 2
Subject(s): Family Relations
Major character(s): Isabel Spellman, Detective—Private; Rae Spellman, Teenager; Henry Stone, Police Officer
Time period(s): 2000s
Locale(s): San Francisco, California

Summary: Izzy Spellman is back, arrested and released for the fourth time. Her 15-year-old sister Rae runs over Police Inspector Henry Stone during a driving lesson. Izzy has been kicked out of her apartment by the tenant who was subletting to her, so she has to move elsewhere. Her best friend and sister-in-law, Petra, seems to have disappeared; she is not answering e-mails or phone calls. There are acts of vandalism being committed on a neighbor's yard that are very much like ones that Izzy committed in her teens, and a new neighbor has moved next door to her parents, a man who Izzy finds highly suspicious and decides to investigate. Hence, his restraining order on her and her breaking of same, leading to another arrest. Then there is her new client, Mr. Davis, whose wife is missing.

Where it's reviewed:
Booklist, February 1, 2008, page 30
Mystery News, February/March 2008, page 20
Mystery Scene, Spring 2008, page 58
Publishers Weekly, January 14, 2008, page 39

Other books by the same author:
The Spellman Files, 2007

Other books you might like:
Donna Andrews, *The Penguin Who Knew Too Much*, 2007
Jennifer Colt, *The Butcher of Beverly Hills*, 2005
Janet Evanovich, *Lean Mean Thirteen*, 2007
Chris Grabenstein, *Whack a Mole*, 2007

128

PETER MAY

The Killing Room

(New York: St. Martin's, 2008)

Story type: Police Procedural
Series: Li Yan. Book 3
Subject(s): China; Serial Killers
Major character(s): Li Yan, Detective—Police; Margaret Campbell, Scientist; Mei Ling, Detective—Police
Time period(s): 2000s
Locale(s): Beijing, China; Shanghai, China

Summary: When 18 mutilated bodies are discovered in a mass grave in Shanghai, Detective Li Yan is sent from Beijing to see if the bodies in Shanghai tie into a case he's working on in Beijing. He works with American pathologist Margaret Campbell to discover the forensic secrets of the bodies, and they learn that all of them had major organs removed before death. Margaret is returning to China after the death of her father, unsure of her relationship with Li, and facing fierce competition from Li's colleague, Detective Mei-Ling. However, the three of them are able to work together to solve the case.

Where it's reviewed:
Booklist, January 1, 2008, page 48
Deadly Pleasures, Spring 2008, page 46
Kirkus Reviews, December 1, 2007
Mystery News, February/March 2008, page 18
Publishers Weekly, December 10, 2007, page 38

Other books by the same author:
The Critic, 2007
The Fourth Sacrifice, 2007
Extraordinary People, 2006
The Firemaker, 2005
The Noble Path, 1993

Other books you might like:
John Burdett, *Bangkok 8*, 2002
Andy Oakes, *Dragon's Eye*, 2004
David Rotenberg, *The Shanghai Murders*, 1998
Qiu Xiaolong, *A Loyal Character Dancer*, 2002

129

JOHN MCEVOY

Close Call

(Scottsdale, Arizona: Poisoned Pen, 2008)

Story type: Action/Adventure
Series: Jack Doyle. Book 2
Subject(s): Horse Racing

Major character(s): Jack Doyle, Public Relations; Celia McCann, Businesswoman, Heiress; Niall Hanratty, Businessman
Time period(s): 2000s
Locale(s): Chicago, Illinois; Dublin, Ireland; Dun Laoghaire, Ireland

Summary: Ex-boxer Jack Doyle is in need of a job. With the help of Moe Kellman, a local furrier with mob connections, Jack is hired as the new publicity director at Monee Park, a thoroughbred racetrack outside Chicago. Heiress Celia McCann owns Monee Park and is attempting to keep her newly inherited business alive. However, Celia's partner and cousin, Niall Hanratty, has other plans for Monee Park. After Arthur Riley, a shady Chicago lawyer, contacts him in Dublin, Niall believes that they should sell Monee Park to developers. Celia refuses to sell. When two thugs hired by Riley begin to pressure Celia, she and Jack have their hands full.

Where it's reviewed:
Booklist, February 1, 2008, page 30
Publishers Weekly, January 7, 2008, page 39

Other books by the same author:
Riders Down, 2006
Blind Switch, 2004

Other books you might like:
Stephen Dobyns, *Saratoga Longshot*, 1987
Kit Ehrman, *Triple Cross*, 2007
William Murray, *The Getaway Blues*, 1990
Mary Monica Pulver, *Show Stopper*, 1992

130

JOHN MCFETRIDGE

Everybody Knows This Is Nowhere

(Orlando, Florida: Harcourt, 2008)

Story type: Police Procedural
Subject(s): Drugs; Illegal Immigrants
Major character(s): Sharon MacDonald, Drug Dealer; Gord Bergeron, Detective—Police; Armstrong, Detective—Police
Time period(s): 2000s
Locale(s): Toronto, Ontario, Canada

Summary: A mysterious Iranian jumps 25 stories and lands on an SUV, dying in the fall. Ex-stripper Sharon Mac-Donald is worried because she lives in the building from which the Iranian fell. Already under house arrest, she is worried that the police will find the rooms in which she grows marijuana. She is approached by a mysterious figure named Ray who wants to help her. One of the detectives, Gord Bergeron, is suspicious of his partner, Detective Armstrong. Gord also has to deal with a missing ten-year-old girl, an unidentified torso and the possibility of corruption within the Toronto police department. All of this leads him into the seedy worlds of drugs, immigration, and the sex trades.

Where it's reviewed:
Booklist, January 1, 2008, page 48
Publishers Weekly, May 5, 2008, page 48

Other books by the same author:
Dirty Sweet, 2006

Other books you might like:
Ken Bruen, *Calibre*, 2006
Brent Ghelfi, *Volk's Game*, 2007
Bill James, *Lovely Mover*, 1999
Scott Mackay, *Old Scores*, 2003

131

MICHAEL MCGARRITY

Death Song

(New York: Dutton, 2008)

Story type: Police Procedural
Series: Kevin Kerney. Book 11
Subject(s): Drugs
Major character(s): Kevin Kerney, Police Officer (chief); Clayton Istee, Police Officer (sergeant detective); Brian Riley, Teenager
Time period(s): 2000s
Locale(s): Santa Fe, New Mexico

Summary: Due to retire shortly from his position as police chief in Santa Fe, New Mexico, Kevin Kerney can't let the double murder of a deputy and his wife go unsolved. He brings in his own son, Sergeant Clayton Istee, to help him find the missing son of the dead couple. The investigation turns up links to drug trafficking and two more murders in Albuquerque. Complicating matters is the discovery that the dead woman was pregnant, despite the fact that her husband had had a vasectomy.

Where it's reviewed:
Booklist, October 15, 2007, page 35
Mystery Scene, Winter 2008, page 68
Publishers Weekly, November 26, 2007, page 30

Other books by the same author:
Nothing but Trouble, 2005
Everyone Dies, 2003
The Judas Judge, 2000
Serpent's Gate, 1998
Mexican Hat, 1997

Other books you might like:
Margaret Coel, *The Spirit Woman*, 2000
James D. Doss, *Grandmother Spider*, 2001
Tony Hillerman, *Skinwalkers*, 1989
Aimee Thurlo, *Tracking Bear*, 2003
    David Thurlo, co-author

132

PAT MCINTOSH

The Rough Collier

(New York: Soho Constable, 2008)

Story type: Historical/Medieval
Series: Gilbert Cunningham. Book 5
Subject(s): Missing Persons; Murder
Major character(s): Gilbert Cunningham, Lawyer; Alys

Mason Cunningham, Spouse; Beatrice Lithgo, Healer
Time period(s): 15th century
Locale(s): Beltane, Scotland; Thorn, Scotland; Forth, Scotland

Summary: Gilbert Cunningham, the Archbishop's Quaestor, and his new bride, Alys Mason, travel to his family estate outside of Glasgow, Scotland, to visit Gil's mother, Lady Cunningham. Shortly after their arrival, a corpse is discovered in a peat bog, head bashed in and throat cut. Sir David Fleming, the parish priest, accuses local healer Beatrice Lithgo of killing the man with witchcraft. At first it is believed that the body is that of Thomas Murray, Beatrice's brother-in-law, but this corpse has been hidden in the peat longer than Murray has been missing. Gil and Alys attempt to identify the murdered man as well as the murderer in order to clear Beatrice's name.

Where it's reviewed:
Publishers Weekly, February 18, 2008, page 138

Other books by the same author:
St. Mungo's Robin, 2007
The Merchant's Mark, 2006
The Nicholas Feast, 2005
The Harper's Quine, 2004

Other books you might like:
P.F. Chisholm, *A Plague of Angels*, 2000
Margaret Frazer, *The Hunter's Tale*, 2004
Sharan Newman, *Cursed in the Blood*, 1998
Candace Robb, *A Trust Betrayed*, 2001

133

G.A. MCKEVETT (Pseudonym of Sonja Massie)

Poisoned Tarts

(New York: Kensington, 2008)

Story type: Private Detective
Series: Savannah Reid. Book 13
Subject(s): Missing Persons; Teen Relationships
Major character(s): Savannah Reid, Detective—Private; Dirk Coulter, Detective—Police; Tiffany Dante, Socialite, Heiress
Time period(s): 2000s
Locale(s): San Carmelita, California; Hollywood, California

Summary: Head of the Moonlight Magnolia Detective Agency, Savannah Reid is always available to help her former partner, Detective Sergeant Dirk Coulter, with any of his cases. Coulter is trying to find missing teen Daisy O'Neil. Daisy's mother Pam is accusing three of Daisy's friends, socialites Tiffany Dante, Bunny Greenaway, and Kiki Wallace, known as the Skeleton Key Three, of being involved in Daisy's disappearance. When the police recover Daisy's car and find a fingerprint belonging to Tiffany, Savannah and Dirk drag the spoiled teen to the police station for questioning. When Tiffany's father, Andrew, is found murdered, a clue from Savannah's visiting grandmother sends Savannah and Dirk on the trail of a killer.

Where it's reviewed:
Publishers Weekly, March 10, 2008, page 62

Other books by the same author:
Fat Free and Fatal, 2007
Corpse Suzette, 2006
Cereal Killer, 2004
Murder a la Mode, 2004
Death by Chocolate, 2003

Other books you might like:
Kate Flora, *Stalking Death*, 2008
Jane Haddam, *Somebody Else's Music*, 2002
Laura Lippman, *To the Power of Three*, 2005
Mary Logue, *Maiden Rock*, 2007

134

NEIL MCMAHON

Dead Silver

(New York: Harper, 2008)

Story type: Amateur Detective
Series: Hugh Davoren. Book 2
Subject(s): Family Life; Grief
Major character(s): Hugh Davoren, Carpenter, Detective—Amateur; Magdahkee, Carpenter, Indian; Renee Callister, Scientist, Researcher
Time period(s): 2000s
Locale(s): Helena, Montana; Phosphor, Montana; Missoula, Montana

Summary: Carpenter Hugh Davoren is drawn to a decades-old unsolved murder case when Renee Callister returns to Helena, Montana. Renee is the daughter of Professor John Callister, a wildlife biologist who was accused of murdering his second wife, Astrid, found in bed with her lover. Never formally charged with the crime, Callister became a broken man and spent the last years of his life in a nursing home. Renee has come home for her father's funeral and finds clues to Astrid's murder in the walls of her father's home. Renee enlists the help of Davoren and his Blackfoot Indian friend Magdahkee, to clean up the house and to clear her father's name.

Where it's reviewed:
Booklist, May 1, 2008, page 28
Publishers Weekly, April 14, 2008, page 37

Other books by the same author:
Lone Creek, 2007
Revolution No. 9, 2005
To the Bone, 2003
Blood Double, 2002
Twice Dying, 2000

Other books you might like:
Peter Bowen, *Coyote Wind*, 1994
C.J. Box, *Trophy Hunt*, 2004
April Christofferson, *Clinical Trial*, 2000
Jamie Harrison, *An Unfortunate Prairie Occurrence*, 1998

135

AMY PATRICIA MEADE

Shadow Waltz

(Woodbury, Minnesota: Midnight Ink, 2008)

Story type: Private Detective
Series: Marjorie McClelland. Book 3
Subject(s): Weddings
Major character(s): Marjorie McClelland, Writer, Detective—Private; Creighton Ashcroft, Detective—Private; Robert Jameson, Detective—Police
Time period(s): 1930s (1935)
Locale(s): Ridgebury, Connecticut; Hartford, Connecticut; Springfield, Massachusetts

Summary: During the Great Depression, in the small town of Ridgebury, Connecticut, mystery author and private investigator Marjorie McClelland is busy trying to plan her wedding to fellow sleuth Creighton Ashcroft, an Englishman. Marjorie's plans are interrupted when a desperate woman asks for help. Elizabeth Barnwell's husband Michael is missing and the police aren't making any attempts to find him. Marjorie and Creighton agree to look for Michael, but their investigation takes a strange turn when they discover a dismembered body in an abandoned house. When Marjorie's former fiance, police detective Robert Jameson, arrives at the crime scene, he and Creighton wager on who can solve the crime first.

Where it's reviewed:
Booklist, February 15, 2008, page 41
Deadly Pleasures, Spring 2008, page 39
Mystery News, April/May 2008, page 20
Mystery Scene, Spring 2008, page 60
Publishers Weekly, February 25, 2008, page 57

Other books by the same author:
Ghost of a Chance, 2007
Million Dollar Baby, 2006

Other books you might like:
Rhys Bowen, *Her Royal Spyness*, 2007
Jill Churchill, *Someone to Watch over Me*, 2002
Annette Meyers, *Murder Me Now*, 2002
David Roberts, *Sweet Poison*, 2001

136

BILL MOODY

Shades of Blue

(Scottsdale, Arizona: Poisoned Pen, 2008)

Story type: Amateur Detective
Series: Evan Horne. Book 6
Subject(s): Music and Musicians; Family
Major character(s): Evan Horne, Musician, Detective—Amateur; Andie Lawrence, FBI Agent; Cameron Brody, Businessman
Time period(s): 2000s
Locale(s): San Francisco, California; Los Angeles, California; New York, New York

Summary: Shortly after jazz pianist Evan Horne settles into his new home in northern California, he learns that his mentor and friend, fellow pianist Calvin Hughes, has passed away. Much to Horne's surprise, Hughes named Horne as his sole beneficiary. While in Los Angeles, sorting through Hughes' belongings, Horne discovers a letter addressed to himself and a photo of Hughes standing next to a baby carriage, and some sheet music with songs from a famous Miles Davis recording, *Birth of the Cool*. Determined to discover the identity of the child in the photograph and whether Hughes was an uncredited composer on the Miles Davis recordings, Horne travels to Boston and New York.

Where it's reviewed:
Booklist, December 15, 2007, page 30
Library Journal, January 15, 2008, page 68
Mystery Scene, Winter 2008, page 71
Publishers Weekly, December 17, 2007, page 37

Other books by the same author:
Looking for Chet Baker, 2002
Bird Lives!, 1999
The Sound of the Trumpet, 1996
Death of a Tenor Man, 1995
Solo Hand, 1994

Other books you might like:
Ace Atkins, *Crossroad Blues*, 1998
Charlotte Carter, *Rhode Island Red*, 1997
David Corbett, *Done for a Dime*, 2003
Harrison Gradwell Slater, *Night Music*, 2002

137

KATE MORGENROTH

They Did It with Love

(New York: Plume, 2008)

Story type: Amateur Detective
Subject(s): Marriage
Major character(s): Sofie, Housewife, Detective—Amateur; Dean, Businessman, Spouse
Time period(s): 2000s
Locale(s): Greenwich, Connecticut

Summary: After the death of her father, Sofie and her husband Dean decide to leave New York City and move to a suburb in Connecticut. An avid mystery reader, Sofie joins the neighborhood book discussion group where she meets other housewives, including Julia, who is unhappy in the suburbs. When Julia is found dead, hanging from a tree in her yard some say suicide, but others are convinced it's murder. The police are investigating Alex, Julia's husband, as their prime suspect, and everyone else is perfectly willing to believe it's him. Sofie, on the other hand, takes her knowledge of mysteries and begins her own investigation. As she does, she learns that everyone in this seemingly perfect suburb carries secrets, even Dean, the husband she thought she knew.

Where it's reviewed:
Booklist, September 15, 2007, page 41
Crimespree, January/February 2008, page 76
Mystery News, December/January 2008, page 28
Publishers Weekly, October 15, 2007, page 44

Other books by the same author:
Saved, 2002
Kill Me First, 1999

Other books you might like:
Peter Blauner, *The Last Good Day*, 2003
Denisa Hanania, *A Talent to Deceive*, 2007
Jonnie Jacobs, *Murder Among Neighbors*, 1994
Peter Lovesey, *Bloodhounds*, 1996

138

R.N. MORRIS

A Vengeful Longing

(New York: Penguin Press, 2008)

Story type: Historical
Series: Porfiry Petrovich. Book 2
Subject(s): Russians
Major character(s): Porfiry Petrovich, Government Official; Pavel Virginsky, Government Official; Yefimov, Civil Servant
Time period(s): 1860s (1868)
Locale(s): St. Petersburg, Russia; Petergof, Russia

Summary: On a sweltering day in St. Petersburg, Russia, Dr. Martin Meyer brings home a box of chocolates for his wife, just as he does every Saturday. Quickly consuming almost the entire box of sweets before they melt, Meyer's wife, Raisa, and their son, Grisha, are soon dead, having died a violent death by poisoning. Investigating magistrate Porfiry Petrovich is assigned to the case and believes that the obvious answer is usually the correct one. In this case, Dr. Meyer brought home the chocolates, Raisa and Grisha died after eating them, so Dr. Meyer must have poisoned his wife and son. When several unrelated murders occur in the city, Petrovich is forced to consider Meyer's theory of what really happened to his family. This is Morris' second novel featuring Petrovich, a character borrowed from Fyodor Dostoyevski's *Crime and Punishment*.

Where it's reviewed:
Booklist, May 1, 2008, page 43
Entertainment Weekly, June 13, 2008, page 73
Publishers Weekly, April 7, 2008, page 41

Other books by the same author:
The Gentle Axe, 2007

Other books you might like:
Boris Akunin, *The Death of Achilles*, 2006
Ronan Bennett, *Zugzwang*, 2007
Tom Bradby, *The White Russian*, 2003
David Dickinson, *Death on the Nevskii Prospekt*, 2006

139

KATE MORTON

The House at Riverton

(New York: Atria, 2008)

Story type: Historical/Edwardian
Subject(s): Servants; Secrets

Major character(s): Grace Reeves Bradley, Servant, Archaeologist; Hannah Hartford Luxton, Spouse; Emmeline Hartford, Socialite, Actress
Time period(s): 1990s (1999); 1910s
Locale(s): Saffron Green, England; Paris, France; London, England

Summary: In 1914, when Grace Bradley is 14-years-old, she gets a job as a housemaid at the Riverton Manor in England. Grace soon meets the Hartford children, David, Hannah, and Emmeline. The kids are visiting their family at Riverton. Grace's life becomes entangled with the Hartfords', especially Hannah's. During a party at Riverton in the summer of 1924, a young poet and friend of the family commits suicide right in front of Hannah and Emmeline. As the only witnesses to the horrible event, only they, along with Grace, know the truth about what really happened that night. In 1999, Grace is approached by filmmaker Ursula Ryan who is making a movie about the events of that summer. Ursula takes Grace back to Riverton House and reawakens some memories that might best be forgotten.

Where it's reviewed:
Booklist, February 15, 2008, page 34
Publishers Weekly, December 3, 2007, page 46

Other books you might like:
Robert Barnard, *A Cry from the Dark*, 2004
Peter Dickinson, *The Yellow Room Conspiracy*, 1994
Daphne du Maurier, *Rebecca*, 1938
Diane Setterfield, *The Thirteenth Tale*, 2006

140

BEVERLE GRAVES MYERS

The Iron Tongue of Midnight

(Scottsdale, Arizona: Poisoned Pen, 2008)

Story type: Historical
Series: Tito Amato. Book 4
Subject(s): Opera
Major character(s): Tito Amato, Singer (castrato); Augustus Rumbolt, Artist; Gabrielle Fouquet, Singer
Time period(s): 18th Century (1740)
Locale(s): Molina Mori, Italy; Padua, Italy

Summary: In the fall of 1740, singer Tito Amato travels to the Dolfini villa in the Italian countryside with his brother-in-law, artist Gussie Rumbolt, after Tito is offered the lead role in a new opera. Soon after rehearsals begin, a stranger is found murdered in the villa's hallways. The local constable is away on a boar hunt, leaving Tito to pursue his own inquiries, which become even more urgent when more murders occur at the villa. To make things even more complicated, Tito discovers that the mysterious Madame Gabrielle Fouquet, one of the opera's sopranos, is actually his long-lost sister Grisella, who was thought to have perished in a fire in Constantinople.

Where it's reviewed:
Library Journal, February 1, 2008, page 51
Mystery News, February/March 2008, page 24
Publishers Weekly, January 14, 2008, page 43

Other books by the same author:
Cruel Music, 2006
Painted Veil, 2005
Interrupted Aria, 2004

Other books you might like:
Barbara Hambly, *Die Upon a Kiss*, 2001
David Hewson, *Lucifer's Shadow*, 2004
Barbara Paul, *Prima Donna at Large*, 1985
Kate Ross, *The Devil in Music*, 1998

141

MAGDALEN NABB

Vita Nuova

(New York: Soho, 2008)

Story type: Police Procedural
Subject(s): Family Relations; Prostitution
Major character(s): Marshal Guarnaccia, Detective—
Police; Daniela Paoletti, Student—Graduate, Single
Parent; Silvana Paoletti, Relative
Time period(s): 2000s
Locale(s): Florence, Italy

Summary: A wealthy and respectable family in Florence
has been torn apart. Daniela Paoletti, single mother and
graduate student, is found shot to death in her room. Her
sister, Silvana, and mother are totally grief-stricken; her
father is ill in the hospital. Slowly and methodically,
Marshal Guarnaccia works to discover who killed
Daniela and why. Meanwhile, both the prosecutor assigned to the case and his own superior try to deflect
him from the case, and Guarnaccia doesn't understand
why. Through a journalist, he discovers a link to a place
of prostitution. What does this have to do with the Paoletti family and Daniela's murder? Why is the mother
drunk all the time? And who is the father of Daniela's
son, Piero?

Where it's reviewed:
Booklist, March 15, 2008, page 33
Mystery News, June/July 2008, page 21
Mystery Scene, Summer 2008, page 75
Publishers Weekly, April 28, 2008, page 115

Other books by the same author:
The Innocent, 2005
Some Bitter Taste, 2002
Property of Blood, 2001
The Marshal Makes His Report, 1992
The Marshal's Own Case, 1990

Other books you might like:
Craig Johnson, *The Cold Dish*, 2005
Donna Leon, *Uniform Justice*, 2003
Barry Maitland, *No Trace*, 2006
Rebecca Pawel, *The Summer Snow*, 2006

142

HAKAN NESSER

Mind's Eye

(New York: Pantheon, 2008)

Story type: Police Procedural
Series: Inspector Van Veeteren. Book 3
Subject(s): Police Procedural
Major character(s): Van Veeteren, Detective—Homicide;
Janek Mitter, Teacher, Convict; Rolf Ringmar, Twin,
Murderer
Time period(s): 1990s
Locale(s): Maardam, Sweden; Willemsburg, Sweden;
Friesen, Sweden

Summary: When high school teacher Janek Mitter wakes
up from a drunken stupor one morning, he makes his
way to the bathroom, only to find the door locked. Breaking the lock, Mitter discovers the body of his new wife,
Eva. Suffering from amnesia due to the night of heavy
drinking, Mitter believes himself innocent of murdering
his wife, and informs Detective Van Veeteren of this during his interrogation. Despite Mitter's protests of innocence, he is convicted and sent to a mental hospital.
While Van Vetteren had reservations about Mitter's guilt,
they vanish when Mitter is brutally murdered while in
the hospital. As he investigates both murders, Van Veeteren realizes that the killings have a connection that
shocks all involved in the case.

Where it's reviewed:
Library Journal, May 1, 2008, page 45
Publishers Weekly, April 28, 2008, page 115

Other books by the same author:
The Return, 2007
Borkmann's Point, 2006

Other books you might like:
Kjell Eriksson, *The Princess of Burundi*, 2006
Henning Mankell, *Sidetracked*, 1999
Maj Sjowall, *The Laughing Policeman*, 1970
Per Wahloo, co-author
Helen Tursten, *Detective Inspector Huss*, 2003

143

SHARAN NEWMAN

The Shanghai Tunnel

(New York: Forge, 2008)

Story type: Historical/American West Coast
Subject(s): Chinese Americans; Smuggling
Major character(s): Emily Stratton, Widow(er); Tom Eliot,
Religious; Robert Stratton, Teenager
Time period(s): 1860s (1868)
Locale(s): Portland, Oregon

Summary: In Shanghai, Horace Stratton found a fortune
and a bride. In 1868, Horace and Emily are on their way
to Horace's home in Portland, Oregon, when Horace
dies unexpectedly. Emily, the daughter of American missionaries who's spent her whole life in China, is left to
continue on to Portland alone. She's met happily by her

son Robert, who's been studying in Boston, and unhappily by Horace's unscrupulous business partners who want to be sure that the new widow does not look too closely at Horace's affairs. However, Emily is not content to simply live off the proceeds of the business; she insists on taking an active management role—a scandalous proposition even in this rowdy frontier city.

Where it's reviewed:
Booklist, February 15, 2008, page 41
Mystery News, April/May 2008, page 24
Mystery Scene, Winter 2008, page 69
Publishers Weekly, December 17, 2007, page 37

Other books by the same author:
The Witch in the Well, 2004
Heresy, 2002
Cursed in the Blood, 1998
The Wandering Arm, 1995

Other books you might like:
Dianne Day, *The Strange Files of Fremont Jones*, 1995
Gillian Linscott, *The Perfect Daughter*, 2001
Miriam Grace Monfredo, *Must the Maiden Die*, 1999
M.J. Zellnik, *Murder at the Portland Variety*, 2005

144

KATHERINE HALL PAGE

The Body in the Gallery

(New York: Morrow, 2008)

Story type: Amateur Detective
Series: Faith Fairchild. Book 17
Subject(s): Art; Museums
Major character(s): Faith Fairchild, Caterer, Detective—
Amateur; Patsy Avery, Friend; Tom Fairchild, Spouse
Time period(s): 2000s
Locale(s): Aleford, Massachusetts; Boston, Massachusetts

Summary: Faith Fairchild's catering business is suffering thanks to the slow economy, so her friend Patsy suggests she temporarily take over running the cafe at Aleford's Ganley Art Museum. Patsy has also discovered that the Romare Beardon she lent the museum has been switched for a fake, and she wants Faith to investigate. When a corpse is discovered at an art installation, Faith becomes even more enmeshed in the mysteries at the Ganley as well as the ins and outs of the Boston art scene. Meanwhile, her son Ben is suffering through a cyberbullying episode at his middle school.

Where it's reviewed:
Booklist, April 1, 2008, page 29
Library Journal, March 1, 2008, page 65
Mystery News, June/July 2008, page 32
Mystery Scene, Spring 2008, page 65
Publishers Weekly, March 3, 2008, page 32

Other books by the same author:
The Body in the Ivy, 2006
The Body in the Lighthouse, 2003
The Body in the Fjord, 1997
The Body in the Vestibule, 1992
The Body in the Belfry, 1989

Other books you might like:
Diane Mott Davidson, *Sticks and Scones*, 2001
Joanne Fluke, *The Chocolate Chip Cookie Murder*, 2000
Jane Langton, *Murder at the Gardner*, 1988
Sarah Stewart Taylor, *Still as Death*, 2006

145

ELIOT PATTISON

Bone Rattler

(New York: Counterpoint, 2008)

Story type: Historical/Colonial America
Subject(s): French and Indian War; Frontier and Pioneer Life
Major character(s): Duncan McCallum, Prisoner
Time period(s): 1750s (1759)
Locale(s): At Sea; New York, American Colonies

Summary: Duncan McCallum, a laird of Scotland, is now a prisoner on a ship bound for the New World. He is an indentured servant to Lord Ramsey who owns an estate in the untamed woods of New York. While aboard the ship, Duncan witnesses several supposed suicides, which later are determined to be murders. Because of Duncan's medical training, the captain asks him to look into the strange deaths. His curiosity about the motive behind the murders carries on even after they land. He continues his investigation and soon finds himself embroiled in the French and Indian War and the reality of frontier life.

Where it's reviewed:
Booklist, October 15, 2007, page 31
Library Journal, November 15, 2007, page 54
Mystery Scene, Winter 2008, page 74
Publishers Weekly, October 29, 2007, page 33

Other books by the same author:
Prayer of the Dragon, 2007
Beautiful Ghosts, 2004
Bone Mountain, 2002
Water Touching Stone, 2001
The Skull Mantra, 1999

Other books you might like:
Joan Druett, *A Watery Grave*, 2005
Margaret Lawrence, *Hearts and Bones*, 1996
Margaret Miles, *A Wicked Way to Burn*, 1998
Karen Swee, *Life, Liberty and the Pursuit of Murder*, 2004

146

MICHAEL PEARCE

Mark of the Pasha

(Scottsdale, Arizona: Poisoned Pen, 2008)

Story type: Historical
Series: Mamur Zapt. Book 16
Subject(s): Police Procedural
Major character(s): Gareth Owen, Civil Servant, Police

Officer; Zeinab Owen, Office Worker, Spouse; Paul Trevelyan, Government Official

Time period(s): 1910s

Locale(s): Cairo, Egypt

Summary: Gareth Cadwallader Owen is the Mamur Zapt, the head of the khedive's secret police in Cairo. When Georgiades, one of Owen's agents, brings word of an assassination attempt on the khedive, Egypt's ruler, during a procession through the streets of Cairo, Owen and his team divert the parade away from the threat. Owen investigates the would-be bombers and attempts to ward off any further attacks. A break in the investigation comes from an unlikely source, Owen's wife Zeinab. In addition to Owen's investigative duties, Oriental Secretary Paul Trevelyan has asked Owen to oversee the security arrangements for the members of a British commission of inquiry that is arriving in the city.

Where it's reviewed:
Mystery News, April/May 2008, page 20
Mystery Scene, Spring 2008, page 69
Publishers Weekly, March 3, 2008, page 32

Other books by the same author:
The Point in the Market, 2005
The Face in the Cemetery, 2001
A Cold Touch of Ice, 2000
Death of an Effendi, 1999
The Last Cut, 1998

Other books you might like:
Conrad Allen, *Murder on the Marmora*, 2004
Agatha Christie, *Death on the Nile*, 1942
Elizabeth Peters, *The Golden One*, 2002
M.J. Trow, *Lestrade and the Kiss of Horus*, 2001

147

LOUISE PENNY

The Cruelest Month

(New York: St. Martin's Minotaur, 2008)

Story type: Police Procedural

Series: Three Pines. Book 3

Subject(s): Psychic Powers; Haunted Houses

Major character(s): Armand Gamache, Detective—Police; Jean Chavet, Psychic; Yvette Nicol, Detective—Police

Time period(s): 2000s

Locale(s): Three Pines, Quebec, Canada; Montreal, Quebec, Canada

Summary: When a psychic comes to the Quebec village of Three Pines for a vacation, she is talked into giving a seance on Easter at the old Hadley Place, scene of several Three Pines tragedies. Though entering into the seance with some skepticism, the assembled few are quickly subdued by the creepiness of the house. One of them, village resident Madeleine Favreau, is literally scared to death. Chief Inspector Armand Gamache of the Surete in Montreal and his team come to town to resolve matters, bringing a bit of personal baggage along with them.

Where it's reviewed:
Deadly Pleasures, Spring 2008, page 40
Library Journal, January 15, 2008, page 69
Mystery News, February/March 2008, page 19
Mystery Scene, Spring 2008, page 61
Publishers Weekly, January 7, 2008, page 39

Other books by the same author:
A Fatal Grace, 2006
Still Life, 2005

Other books you might like:
Meredith Blevins, *The Hummingbird Wizard*, 2003
Caroline Graham, *Death in Disguise*, 1992
Cynthia Harrod-Eagles, *Shallow Grave*, 1998
Martha Lawrence, *Ashes of Aries*, 2001

148

ANNE PERRY

Buckingham Palace Gardens

(New York: Ballantine, 2008)

Story type: Historical/Victorian

Series: Charlotte and Thomas Pitt. Book 25

Subject(s): Wealth; Servants

Major character(s): Thomas Pitt, Police Officer (inspector), Spouse (of Charlotte); Victor Narraway, Government Official; Cahoon Dunkeld, Adventurer, Businessman

Time period(s): 1890s

Locale(s): London, England

Summary: The Prince of Wales invites four wealthy couples to stay at Buckingham Palace while the men discuss a construction project that would create a railway through Africa. When a prostitute's mutilated body is discovered in a linen closet after a late night stag party at the palace, Thomas Pitt of Special Branch is called in to solve the murder. Pitt and his supervisor, Victor Narraway, decide to place Pitt's own housemaid, Gracie Phipps, in the palace staff to assist in the investigation. Pitt is quickly able to clear the large palace staff of the murder, which unfortunately leaves the prince and his guests as the suspects.

Where it's reviewed:
Booklist, February 15, 2008, page 38
Publishers Weekly, January 28, 2008, page 41

Other books by the same author:
Long Spoon Lane, 2005
Seven Dials, 2003
Southampton Row, 2002
The Whitechapel Conspiracy, 2001
Half Moon Street, 2000

Other books you might like:
David Dickinson, *Goodnight Sweet Prince*, 2002
John MacLachlan Gray, *The Fiend in Human*, 2003
Robin Paige, *Death on the Lizard*, 2006
Kate Ross, *A Broken Vessel*, 1994

149

THOMAS PERRY

Fidelity

(Orlando, Florida: Harcourt, 2008)

Story type: Mystery
Subject(s): Secrets; Widows/Widowers
Major character(s): Jerry Hobart, Criminal; Emily Kramer, Widow(er); Ted Forrest, Wealthy
Time period(s): 2000s
Locale(s): Los Angeles, California

Summary: Private investigator Phil Kramer is murdered on the streets of Los Angeles, leaving his widow Emily with lots of questions. For one thing, he had cleaned out their bank accounts, leaving her virtually penniless. The hit man who killed Phil, Jerry Hobart, now has a contract to kill Emily as well. Hobart has questions of his own. He wonders whether uncovering Phil's secrets himself might lead to a larger payoff. So he begins to investigate the man who hired him in the first place, Ted Forrest, a wealthy man with secrets of his own.

Where it's reviewed:
Booklist, February 1, 2008, page 31
Publishers Weekly, April 7, 2008, page 41

Other books by the same author:
Silence, 2007
Nightlife, 2006
Dead Aim, 2002
Death Benefits, 2001
Pursuit, 2001

Other books you might like:
Lee Child, *The Enemy*, 2004
Michael Connelly, *Void Moon*, 1999
Robert Crais, *The Two Minute Rule*, 2006
Jeffery Deaver, *The Empty Chair*, 2000

150

JASON PINTER

The Guilty

(Don Mills, Ontario: Mira, 2008)

Story type: Serial Killer
Series: Henry Parker. Book 2
Subject(s): Journalism; American West
Major character(s): Henry Parker, Journalist; Amanda Davies, Lawyer; Paulina Cole, Journalist
Time period(s): 2000s
Locale(s): New York, New York; Fort Sumner, New Mexico

Summary: A late night phone call from his editor drags reporter Henry Parker from his bed to a trendy Manhattan night club where socialite and superstar Athena Paradis has just been murdered. When other, similar murders occur in the city, Parker learns about the unique, century-old weapon used in each of the cases from a source in the New York Police Department. Digging into the history of the rifle, Parker finds a startling connection to Wild West legend Billy the Kid. As Parker investigates the case, he tries to stay one step ahead of fellow journalist, Paulina Cole.

Where it's reviewed:
Library Journal, February 1, 2008, page 64
Publishers Weekly, December 24, 2007, page 34

Other books by the same author:
The Mark, 2007

Other books you might like:
Jan Brogan, *A Confidential Source*, 2005
Loren D. Estleman, *Billy Gashade*, 1997
Andrew Klavan, *True Crime*, 1995
Julie Kramer, *Stalking Susan*, 2008

151

R.T. RAICHEV

Assassins at Ospreys

(New York: Soho Constable, 2008)

Story type: Amateur Detective
Series: Antonia Darcy. Book 3
Subject(s): Identity; Writing
Major character(s): Antonia Darcy, Writer, Detective—Amateur; Beatrice Ardleigh, Accident Victim, Bride; Leonard Colville, Landlord
Time period(s): 2000s
Locale(s): Hay-on-Wye, Wales; London, England; Wallingford, England

Summary: While attending a literary festival in Wales, crime writer Antonia Darcy meets Beatrice Ardleigh, a very enthusiastic fan. Antonia learns that Bee and her companion, Ingrid Delmar, were brought together as the result of a tragic car accident 30 years ago. Months later, Antonia and her husband, Hugh Payne, receive an invitation to visit Bee at her home in Oxfordshire. Upon their arrival, Antonia and Hugh learn that Bee has recently married, and that Ingrid has been disguising herself as Bee to visit a dying neighbor at his home, an estate called Ospreys. Antonia and Hugh soon discover that the dying man is Ralph Renshawe, Bee's former fiance and the man who caused the car accident many years ago.

Where it's reviewed:
Booklist, March 1, 2008, page 51
Mystery Scene, Spring 2008, page 69
Publishers Weekly, February 11, 2008, page 54

Other books by the same author:
The Death of Corrine, 2007
The Hunt for Sonya Dufrette, 2006

Other books you might like:
Kate Atkinson, *Case Histories*, 2004
Patricia Carlon, *The Whispering Wall*, 1996
Peggy Darty, *When the Sandpiper Calls*, 2005
Peter Lovesey, *Bloodhounds*, 1996

152

ROBERT J. RANDISI

Luck Be a Lady, Don't Die
(New York: St. Martin's, 2007)

Story type: Amateur Detective
Series: Eddie Gianelli. Book 2
Subject(s): Entertainment; Gangs
Major character(s): Eddie Gianelli, Hotel Worker, Detective—Amateur; Jerry Epstein, Bodyguard; Frank Sinatra, Entertainer, Historical Figure
Time period(s): 1990s; 1960s
Locale(s): Las Vegas, Nevada

Summary: Las Vegas pit boss Eddie Gianelli is no stranger to the celebrities that frequent the city, but he still finds it hard to believe that stars like Dean Martin and Frank Sinatra think of him as a friend, someone they can trust. When Eddie is approached by Dean to help Frank with a problem, he agrees to talk to the entertainer. Frank was supposed to meet a girl, Mary Clarke, in Vegas while in town for the premiere of his new movie, *Ocean's 11*. Now Mary is missing, and Eddie's investigation becomes more complicated when a body is discovered in Mary's hotel room. He learns that Mary is connected to mob boss Sam Giancana.

Where it's reviewed:
Booklist, November 15, 2007, page 22
Library Journal, August 15, 2007, page 56
Publishers Weekly, October 8, 2007, page 39

Other books by the same author:
Everybody Kills Somebody Sometime, 2006
Cold Blooded, 2005
Blood of Angels, 2004
The Offer, 2003
Curtains of Blood, 2002

Other books you might like:
Terence Faherty, *Raise the Devil*, 2000
Charles Fleming, *The Ivory Coast*, 2002
Richard Rayner, *The Devil's Wind*, 2005
Michael Ventura, *The Death of Frank Sinatra*, 1996

153

CORNELIA READ

The Crazy School
(New York: Grand Central, 2008)

Story type: Amateur Detective
Series: Madeline Dare. 2
Subject(s): Schools/Boarding Schools
Major character(s): Madeline Dare, Teacher, Detective—Amateur
Time period(s): 1980s (1989)
Locale(s): Massachusetts

Summary: When Madeline Dare moves to Western Massachusetts with her husband for a job that never comes through, she ends up at the Santangelo Academy. The academy is a boarding school for teenagers who deal with mental illness, violence, and drugs, run by a controlling headmaster intent on punishing both students and teachers for getting out of line. When a student and his pregnant girlfriend die from poison while staying at "the Farm," a confinement dorm used for discipline, Madeline is convinced that the two students were murdered. When Madeline is named a suspect and then poisoned, she accepts the help of several of her more dangerous students in discovering who the murderer is.

Where it's reviewed:
Booklist, October 15, 2007, page 35
Library Journal Review, October 15, 2007, page 61
Mystery Scene, Winter 2008, page 79
Publishers Weekly, October 15, 2007, page 39

Other books by the same author:
A Field of Darkness, 2006

Other books you might like:
Kate Flora, *An Educated Death*, 1999
Joanne Harris, *Gentlemen and Players*, 2006
Judith Kelman, *Fly Away Home*, 1997
Donna Tartt, *The Secret History*, 1992

154

MARY REED
ERIC MAYER , Co-Author

Seven for a Secret
(Scottsdale, Arizona: Poisoned Pen, 2008)

Story type: Historical
Series: John the Eunuch. Book 7
Subject(s): Byzantine Empire
Major character(s): John the Eunach, Government Official; Anatolius, Lawyer; Felix, Military Personnel
Time period(s): 6th century
Locale(s): Constantinople, Byzantine Empire

Summary: John, Lord Chamberlain to Emperor Justinian, spends his days counseling the emperor and his nights staring at a mosaic in his home that depicts a young girl. Carrying on conversations with the girl in the mosaic, whom he has named Zoe, John is shocked when he meets a woman who claims to be the model for Zoe. Making arrangements to meet her again, John arrives to find the woman's strangled body dyed red and lying in a cistern. Seeking answers to the woman's identity and her death, John begins an investigation that will lead him to the artist who created the mosaic and a tax collector named Glykos, whose young daughter Agnes could be the child depicted in John's mosaic.

Where it's reviewed:
Booklist, January 1, 2008, page 50
Library Journal, February 1, 2008, page 50
Mystery News, April/May 2008, page 20
Publishers Weekly, January 7, 2008, page 38

Other books by the same author:
Six for Gold, 2005
Five for Silver, 2004
Four for a Boy, 2003
Three for a Letter, 2001
Two for Joy, 2000

Other books you might like:
Jason Goodwin, *The Janissary Tree*, 2006
Alan Gordon, *The Widow of Jerusalem*, 2003
Tom Harper, *The Mosaic of Shadows*, 2005
Jenny White, *The Sultan's Seal*, 2006

155

MATT BEYNON REES

A Grave in Gaza

(New York: Soho, 2008)

Story type: Amateur Detective
Series: Omar Yussef. Book 2
Subject(s): Religious Conflict; Middle East
Major character(s): Omar Yussef, Teacher, Detective—
    Amateur; Magnus Wallender, Inspector (United Na-
    tions)
Time period(s): 2000s
Locale(s): Gaza Strip, Middle East

Summary: Omar Yussef is called from his duties as a
United Nations school principal in Bethlehem to assist in
inspecting another U.N. school in the Gaza Strip. Accompanied by Magnus Wallender, a Swedish U.N.
inspector, he finds a school in turmoil. Eyad Masharawi,
one of the teachers, has been arrested by Palestinian
security agents—supposedly for collaborating with the
CIA—after he accused university officials of selling
degrees to police officers. Then Wallender is kidnapped
by the Saladin Brigades, a powerful gang of gunmen. As
the violence escalates, the U.N. withdraws its staff from
Gaza leaving Omar alone to save Masharawi and
Wallender.

Where it's reviewed:
Booklist, December 15, 2007, page 29
Deadly Pleasures, Spring 2008, page 19
Publishers Weekly, October 22, 2007, page 38
School Library Journal, March 1, 2008, page 233

Other books by the same author:
The Collaborator of Bethlehem, 2007

Other books you might like:
Dan Fesperman, *The Amateur Spy*, 2008
Batya Gur, *Murder in Jerusalem*, 2006
Robert Littell, *Vicious Circle*, 2006
Robert Rosenberg, *Crimes of the City*, 1991

156

BEN REHDER

Holy Moly

(New York: St. Martin's, 2008)

Story type: Police Procedural; Satire
Series: Blanco Country. Book 6
Subject(s): Evangelism; Television Programs
Major character(s): John Marlin, Game Warden; Peter
    Boothe, Television Personality; Billy Don Craddock,
    Detective—Amateur
Time period(s): 2000s

Locale(s): Blanco County, Texas

Summary: Hollis Farley is operating a backhoe to clear
land for televangelist Peter Boothe's new religious
center. He finds a fossil of an Alamosaurus skull. He
hopes to make a profit from his discovery, even though
it was found on Booth's land, but instead he is found
dead under his backhoe, killed by an arrow. The Blanco
County Sheriff loses no time in summoning his best
friend, Game Warden John Marlin, to assist in the
investigation. Word slowly leaks out about the skull,
which is missing, and Red O'Brien convinces his best
pal, Billy Don Craddock, to befriend Hollis' bereaved
sister, Betty Jean, to find out where the skull is. Betty
Jean doesn't appear to know anything about a skull, but
she sure can cook, and Billy Don is smitten.

Where it's reviewed:
Library Journal, April 1, 2008, page 63
Mystery Scene, Spring 2008, page 62
Publishers Weekly, March 17, 2008, page 52
School Library Journal, June 2008, page 172

Other books by the same author:
Gun Shy, 2007
Guilt Trip, 2005
Flat Crazy, 2004
Bone Dry, 2003
Buck Fever, 2002

Other books you might like:
James D. Doss, *Grandmother Spider*, 2001
Carl Hiaasen, *Nature Girl*, 2006
Steve Hockensmith, *Holmes on the Range*, 2006
Patrick F. McManus, *The Blight Way*, 2006

157

RUTH RENDELL

Not in The Flesh

(New York: Crown, 2008)

Story type: Police Procedural
Series: Chief Inspector Wexford. Book 22
Subject(s): Missing Persons
Major character(s): Reginald Wexford, Detective—
    Homicide; Mike Burden, Detective—Homicide;
    Owen Tredown, Writer
Time period(s): 2000s
Locale(s): Flagford, England; Kingsmarkham, England;
    Sewingbury, England

Summary: When a truffle hunter and his dog uncover a
body in the quiet English village of Flagford, Chief
Inspector Wexford is called in to handle the case.
Discovering that the body is male and has been lying in
the dirt for 11 years, Wexford and his team try to match
the remains to one of the 85 men who went missing 11
years ago. The land where the body was discovered
belongs to elderly John Grimble, a disgruntled man who
was denied permission to build more houses on the land.
When a search of the rundown house on Grimble's land
leads to another dead body, Wexford gains new insight
into this baffling case.

Where it's reviewed:
Booklist, March 15, 2008, page 5
Library Journal, April 15, 2008, page 79

Other books by the same author:
End in Tears, 2007
The Babes in the Wood, 2003
Harm Done, 2000
Road Rage, 1998
Simisola, 1996

Other books you might like:
Tana French, *In the Woods*, 2007
Reginald Hill, *Recalled to Life*, 1992
Peter Robinson, *Close to Home*, 2003
Minette Walters, *The Ice House*, 1992

158

DAVID ROSENFELT

Don't Tell a Soul

(New York: St. Martin's, 2008)

Story type: Chase
Subject(s): Secrets; Murder
Major character(s): Tim Wallace, Businessman; Jonathon Novack, Detective—Police
Time period(s): 2000s
Locale(s): Fort Lee, New Jersey

Summary: One day in May, Tim and Maggie Wallace go out on Tim's motorboat. By the end of the day, the motorboat has exploded and Maggie is dead. Detective Jonathon Novack is convinced that Tim murdered his wife despite the fact that Tim passed a polygraph and there's no hard evidence against him. Months later, Tim is at a New Year's Eve party. A drunken stranger approaches Tim and tells him a secret: the stranger murdered a girl three months ago. He finishes the conversation by saying "This is our secret, okay? Don't tell a soul." Then the stranger disappears. Despite the stranger's instruction, Tim tells Novack about the conversation, and ends up a suspect in the girl's death.

Where it's reviewed:
Booklist, May 1, 2008, page 26
Library Journal, April 15, 2008, page 75
Publishers Weekly, May 19, 2008, page 38

Other books by the same author:
Play Dead, 2007
Dead Center, 2006
Sudden Death, 2005
Bury the Lead, 2004
First Degree, 2003

Other books you might like:
Harlan Coben, *Tell No One*, 2001
Chris Grabenstein, *Mad Mouse*, 2006
Brad Meltzer, *Dead Even*, 1998
James Patterson, *Cat & Mouse*, 1997

159

SARA ROSETT

Getting Away Is Deadly

(New York: Kensington, 2008)

Story type: Amateur Detective
Series: Ellie Avery. Book 3
Subject(s): Military Life; Murder
Major character(s): Ellie Avery, Housewife, Detective—Amateur; Summer Avery, Student—College; Tony Zobart, FBI Agent
Time period(s): 2000s
Locale(s): Washington, District of Columbia

Summary: Accompanying her husband Mitch on a business trip, Air Force wife Ellie Avery looks forward to doing some sightseeing with friends in Washington, DC. After touring the city, Ellie and her group are waiting for a train at a metro station when they see a man fall to his death on the tracks below. When the police declare Jorge Dominguez's death a murder, Ellie's sister-in-law Summer becomes a suspect. Jorge occasionally did some landscaping work for the same couple Summer works for. After he asked her out a few times, Summer began to suspect that Jorge was stalking her. Snooping on Summer's behalf, Ellie puts her own life in danger when she starts to put clues together.

Where it's reviewed:
Publishers Weekly, February 18, 2008, page 139

Other books by the same author:
Staying Home Is a Killer, 2007
Moving Is Murder, 2006

Other books you might like:
Laura Durham, *For Better or Hearse*, 2006
Jonnie Jacobs, *Murder Among Neighbors*, 1994
Leslie Meier, *New Year's Eve Murder*, 2006
Ayelet Waldman, *Death Gets a Time Out*, 2003

160

MARCUS SAKEY

At the City's Edge

(New York: St. Martin's, 2007)

Story type: Mystery
Subject(s): Gangs; Arson
Major character(s): Jason Palmer, Veteran; Billy Palmer, Child; Elena Cruz, Detective—Police
Time period(s): 2000s
Locale(s): Chicago, Illinois; Iraq

Summary: When Jason Palmer is beset by two thugs who want something his brother has, he immediately goes to his brother's bar to tell him about it. His brother blows him off. When the bar is torched later the same night, Jason is left with lots of questions, the loss of his brother, and the care of his young nephew, Billy. The responsibility of taking care of Billy helps him to grow up. A returning Iraq war veteran, Jason has many issues to resolve, but none of them take precedence over his brother's murder. He's plunged into a dangerous world of gangs

and Chicago politics, helped reluctantly by a cop on the outs, Elena Cruz.

Where it's reviewed:
Booklist, November 1, 2007, page 28
Publishers Weekly, October 15, 2007, page 36

Other books by the same author:
Good People, 2008
The Blade Itself, 2007

Other books you might like:
Harlan Coben, *Gone for Good*, 2002
Barbara D'Amato, *Good Cop, Bad Cop*, 1998
G.M. Ford, *Fury*, 2001
Steve Hamilton, *Nightwork*, 2007

161

C.J. SANSOM

Winter in Madrid

(New York: Viking, 2008)

Story type: Historical/World War II
Subject(s): Spies; Prisoners of War
Major character(s): Harry Brett, Spy; Sandy Forsyth, Businessman; Barbara Clare, Nurse
Time period(s): 1940s (1940)
Locale(s): England; Spain

Summary: Three young boys met at Rockwood, a British school, between the wars. It is now 1940, and Hitler is invading Europe. Harry Brett has been asked to spy on his former schoolmate, Sandy Forsyth, a businessman with unknown connections in Franco's Spain. Reluctantly, Brett agrees, and is attached to the British embassy as a cover. Meeting Sandy, he is surprised to find him living with Barbara Clare, the former lover of a third schoolmate, Bernie Piper. Piper fought on the Republican side in the Spanish Civil War and was declared missing, believed dead. The British government wants to find out whether Franco is going to enter the war, and on which side. Barbara finds out that Bernie is still alive, a prisoner in a POW camp. She is determined to rescue him.

Where it's reviewed:
Booklist, December 1, 2007, page 24
Mystery News, December/January 2008, page 15
Mystery Scene, Winter 2008, page 78
Publishers Weekly, September 24, 2007, page 42

Other books by the same author:
Sovereign, 2007
Dark Fire, 2005
Dissolution, 2003

Other books you might like:
Laurie R. King, *Touchstone*, 2008
Rebecca Pawel, *Death of a Nationalist*, 2003
Jacqueline Winspear, *An Incomplete Revenge*, 2008
Carlos Ruiz Zafon, *The Shadow of the Wind*, 2004

162

JONATHAN SANTLOFER , Author/Illustrator

The Murder Notebook

(New York: Morrow, 2008)

Story type: Police Procedural
Series: Nate Rodriguez. Book 2
Subject(s): Scientific Experiments
Major character(s): Nathan Rodriguez, Artist; Terri Russo, Detective—Homicide; Perry Denton, Police Officer
Time period(s): 2000s
Locale(s): New York, New York; Hoboken, New Jersey; Colorado

Summary: Working as a freelance sketch artist for the New York Police Department, Nate Rodriguez is assigned to work on a homicide task force that is investigating several recent and unrelated murders in the city. Rodriguez's girlfriend, Terri Russo, is in charge of the task force and is hoping that Rodriguez's sixth sense and uncanny ability to sketch people in current and future homicide cases will give her some clue to these baffling cases. When Rodriguez begins to investigate the people he's been sketching, he discovers a connection that links the killers to a series of horrifying secret scientific experiments that were conducted several years ago. This novel includes more than 100 sketches by the author.

Where it's reviewed:
Booklist, May 1, 2008, page 38
Publishers Weekly, April 21, 2008, page 34

Other books by the same author:
Anatomy of Fear, 2007
The Killing Art, 2005
Color Blind, 2004
The Death Artist, 2002

Other books you might like:
William Bayer, *The Dream of Broken Horses*, 2002
Dorsey Fiske, *Raptor*, 2000
Kay Hooper, *Touching Evil*, 2001
David Lindsey, *The Face of the Assassin*, 2004

163

MARY SAUMS

Mighty Old Bones

(New York: St. Martin's, 2008)

Story type: Amateur Detective
Series: Thistle & Twigg. Book 2
Subject(s): Archaeology; Native Americans
Major character(s): Phoebe Twistle, Widow(er); Jane Twigg, Widow(er)
Time period(s): 2000s
Locale(s): Tullulah, Alabama

Summary: Working on a Halloween party for the local library in the quiet, isolated town of Tullulah, Alabama, best friends and fellow widows Jane Twigg and Phoebe Twistle have vowed not to get involved in any more criminal investigations. Unfortunately, when a huge

thunderstorm uproots a tree on Jane's property and human remains are discovered, they are again drawn into a mystery. Jane calls in some archaeological experts she met through her extensive travels as a military wife, seeking to prove that the body's resting place is part of an Native American burial site. Tests, however, suggest that Jane is wrong, and point to a more recent death. Meanwhile, a Tullulah resident disappears.

Where it's reviewed:
Booklist, April 1, 2008, page 31
Mystery Scene, Summer 2008, page 72

Other books by the same author:
Thistle and Twigg, 2007
When the Last Magnolia Weeps, 2004
The Valley of Jewels, 2001
Midnight Hour, 2000

Other books you might like:
Jimmie Ruth Evans, *Flamingo Fatale*, 2005
Mary Anna Evans, *Effigies*, 2007
Anne George, *Murder on a Bad Hair Day*, 1996
Margaret Maron, *Rituals of the Season*, 2005

164

BERNHARD SCHLINK

Homecoming

(New York: Pantheon, 2008)

Story type: Family Saga; Amateur Detective
Subject(s): Family; Secrets
Major character(s): Peter Debauer, Editor
Time period(s): 1950s; 1980s
Locale(s): Germany; New York, New York

Summary: In the years after World War II, Peter Debauer was raised by his single mother, though he also visited his grandparents in Switzerland. When he becomes an editor for a publishing company, he comes across a manuscript that he remembers reading at his grandparents' house. The story contains details that seem familiar to him and tells of a soldier returning to his home after the war. Debauer decides to find out as much as possible about the book and suspects that the main character could be his father, who was supposedly lost during the war.

Where it's reviewed:
Library Journal, December 15, 2007, page 102
The New Yorker, March 31, 2008, page 113
Publishers Weekly, October 15, 2007, page 37

Other books by the same author:
Self's Deception, 2006
Self's Punishment, 2005
The Reader, 1997

Other books you might like:
William Brodrick, *The 6th Lamentation*, 2003
Joseph Kanon, *The Prodigal Spy*, 1998
Scott Turow, *Ordinary Heroes*, 2005
Carlos Ruiz Zafon, *The Shadow of the Wind*, 2004

165

TOM SCHRECK

TKO

(Woodbury, Minnesota: Midnight Ink, 2008)

Story type: Amateur Detective
Series: Duffy Dombrowski. Book 2
Subject(s): Sports/Boxing; Psychology
Major character(s): Duffy Dombrowski, Social Worker, Sports Figure; Mike Kelley, Police Officer; Claudia Michelin, Businesswoman
Time period(s): 2000s
Locale(s): Crawford, New York

Summary: Duffy Dombrowski is a social worker in Crawford, New York. His new client, Howard Reinhardt, has been released from jail after serving 25 years for killing four high school classmates. Duffy is developing some sympathy for him until Howard misses an appointment and a high school girl is murdered. His colleagues at the agency believe Howard is beyond help. The police have no doubt that Howard is guilty. Duffy wants to stay out of the investigation; he moonlights as a boxer, and he has an opportunity to realize a dream and fight in Madison Square Garden. As the body count rises, though,Howard keeps telephoning Duffy, first to profess his innocence then, in an odd reversal, to confess.

Where it's reviewed:
Publishers Weekly, April 28, 2008, page 116

Other books by the same author:
On the Ropes, 2007

Other books you might like:
G.M. Ford, *Who in Hell Is Wanda Fuca?*, 1995
Steve Hamilton, *Night Work*, 2007
Michael Koryta, *Tonight I Said Goodbye*, 2004
Jeff Shelby, *Wicked Break*, 2006

166

MARK SCHWEIZER

The Mezzo Wore Mink

(Hopkinsville, Kentucky: St. James Music Press, 2008)

Story type: Amateur Detective
Series: Hayden Konig. Book 6
Subject(s): Small Town Life; Episcopalians
Major character(s): Hayden Konig, Police Officer, Musician (Church organist)
Time period(s): 2000s
Locale(s): St. Germaine, North Carolina

Summary: In St. Germaine, North Carolina, Hayden Konig serves as police chief, and as the choirmaster and organist at St. Barnabas Episcopal Church. But what he really wants to be is a hardboiled detective novelist. Pete Moss wants to remain mayor, but he's facing a challenge from Cynthia Johnson. Pete has lured four new businesses to the downtown, which puts a dent in Cynthia's campaign. But it's an eventful fall anyway. Davis Booth is found hanging in St. Barnabas' bell tower. The folks at the new Christian massage parlor turn out to be nudists. The new

bookstore is run by a clairvoyant, a refugee from a Renaissance Fair. And Blueridge Furs is infested with rats—on purpose. The owner of the local crematorium is found dead.

Other books by the same author:
The Bass Wore Scales, 2007
The Soprano Wore Falsettos, 2006
The Tenor Wore Tapshoes, 2005
The Baritone Wore Chiffon, 2004
The Alto Wore Tweed, 2002

Other books you might like:
John Billheimer, *The Contrary Blues*, 1998
Joan Hess, *Madness in Maggocy*, 1991
Jane Langton, *God in Concord*, 1992
Charlotte MacLeod, *The Family Vault*, 1979

167

MANDA SCOTT

The Crystal Skull

(New York: Delacorte, 2008)

Story type: End of the World
Subject(s): Adventure and Adventurers; Suspense
Major character(s): Stella Cody, Scientist; Kit O'Connor, Scientist; Cedric Owen, Scholar, Doctor
Time period(s): 2000s (2007); 16th century (1550s)
Locale(s): Yorkshire, England; Cambridge, England; Zama, Mexico

Summary: Newlyweds Stella Cody and Kit O'Connor go in search of an ancient crystal skull known as Cedric Owen's blue heart-stone. Owen, a 16th-century Cambridge scholar and physician, was the skull's last keeper, having been one of many generations in his family to care for the skull. Having tracked it to a cave in the Yorkshire Dales, Stella and Kit find the hidden skull, but Kit is severely injured by an unknown assailant who also wants to possess the ancient skull. Researching its origins, Stella and Kit discover that the blue skull is one of 13 that will play a major role in saving the world from an apocalypse, according to an ancient Mayan prediction.

Where it's reviewed:
Library Journal, March 15, 2008, page 61
Publishers Weekly, February 25, 2008, page 52

Other books by the same author:
Dreaming the Hound, 2006
Dreaming the Serpent Spear, 2006
Dreaming the Bull, 2004
Dreaming the Eagle, 2003
No Good Deed, 2002

Other books you might like:
Paul Christopher, *The Aztec Heresy*, 2008
Lyn Hamilton, *The Xibala Murders*, 1997
Stel Pavlou, *Decipher*, 2002
Marella Sands, *Sky Knife*, 1997

168

JAMES SHEEHAN

The Law of Second Chances

(New York: St. Martin's, 2008)

Story type: Legal
Series: Jack Tobin. Book 2
Subject(s): Prisoners and Prisons; Trials
Major character(s): Jack Tobin, Lawyer; Henry Wilson, Convict; Benny Avrile, Thief, Addict
Time period(s): 1990s; 1960s (1965)
Locale(s): New York, New York; Bass Creek, Florida; Miami, Florida

Summary: Former trial lawyer Jack Tobin now makes a living defending men on death row in Florida. Tobin's latest case involves convicted murderer Henry Wilson, who was falsely accused of killing a drug dealer 17 years ago. After finding evidence in Wilson's favor, a new trial is granted and Wilson is freed. Grateful for Tobin's help, Wilson travels to New York to aid Tobin with a murder trial. Small time thief Benny Avrile is on trial for the murder of oil tycoon Carl Robertson. Benny is the son of a childhood friend of Tobin's, Luis Melendez. Having been absent for most of Benny's life, Luis hopes that Tobin can save the son he hardly knows.

Where it's reviewed:
Booklist, February 1, 2008, page 31

Other books by the same author:
The Mayor of Lexington Avenue, 2005

Other books you might like:
William Bernhardt, *Death Row*, 2003
James Grippando, *The Pardon*, 1994
Barbara Parker, *Suspicion of Vengeance*, 2001
Scott Turow, *Reversible Errors*, 2002

169

SHARON SHORT

Tie Dyed and Dead

(New York: Avon, 2008)

Story type: Amateur Detective
Series: Josie Toadfern. Book 6
Subject(s): Small Town Life; Teachers
Major character(s): Josie Toadfern, Businesswoman (stain removal expert); Caleb Loudermilk, Journalist
Time period(s): 2000s
Locale(s): Paradise, Ohio

Summary: The Mayfair Sisters are the biggest thing to ever come out of Paradise, Ohio. They are a singing group from the '60s and they are reuniting to raise money to care for their mother who has Alzheimer's. They hire Josie Toadfern to clean their tie-dyed costumes. It's not long before the Mayfair Sisters' manager is found dead inside Josie's shop and everyone is pointing fingers at Josie. Josie has to solve the case to clear her name, but that isn't easy given the influx of new people and suspects who came to Paradise to see the Mayfair Sisters.

Where it's reviewed:
Mystery News, June/July 2008, page 14

Other books by the same author:
Hung Out to Die, 2006
Death in the Cards, 2005
Death by Deep Dish Pie, 2004
Death of a Domestic Diva, 2003
Murder Unfolds, 1997

Other books you might like:
Laura Childs, *Blood Orange Brewing*, 2006
Mary Daheim, *The Alpine Betrayal*, 1993
Annette Meyers, *These Bones Were Made for Dancing*, 1995
Kathy Hogan Trocheck, *Happy Never After*, 1995

170

SUSAN ARNOUT SMITH

The Timer Game

(New York: St. Martin's, 2008)

Story type: Action/Adventure
Subject(s): Kidnapping; Biotechnology
Major character(s): Grace Descanso, Technician (crime scene); Mac McGuire, Journalist
Time period(s): 2000s
Locale(s): San Diego, California

Summary: Grace Descanso was prepared to become a heart doctor, until a trip to Guatemala changed her life. Without much explanation she gave up her medical aspirations and now works in San Diego as a crime scene technician and takes care of her five-year-old daughter, Katie. While at work, Grace is forced to shoot a raving man who attacks two of her partners. Before dying the man not only calls Grace by name but also gives her a cryptic warning about the "Spikeman." Soon after, Katie is kidnapped and Grace begins receiving clues that she must decipher in a certain amount of time in order to find her. Grace is forced to explore her biomedical past and her relationship with Katie's father in the search for her daughter.

Where it's reviewed:
Booklist, December 1, 2007, page 28
Mystery Scene, Winter 2008, page 70
Publishers Weekly, October 15, 2007, page 38

Other books you might like:
Elizabeth Becka, *Trace Evidence*, 2005
Jeffery Deaver, *A Maiden's Grave*, 1995
Andrew Klavan, *Don't Say a Word*, 1991
Joe Schreiber, *Chasing the Dead*, 2006

171

TOM ROB SMITH

Child 44

(New York: Grand Central, 2008)

Story type: Historical
Subject(s): Social Conditions; Political Movements

Major character(s): Leo Demidov, Detective—Police; Raisa Demidov, Teacher, Spouse
Time period(s): 1930s (1933); 1950s (1953)
Locale(s): Moscow, Russia; The Ural Mountains, Russia

Summary: Leo Demidov is a highly placed officer in Stalin's MGB, the State Security Force. His position has brought him a beautiful wife, a comfortable apartment for himself and a comfortable apartment for his parents. Because in Soviet Russia there is no crime, he's sent to convince a grieving family that their child was killed in a railway accident and not murdered. When he's given his wife's name to investigate as a spy, there seems to be no way out. When he and his wife are exiled to the Urals, they discover a series of similar child killings, as well as a way back to each other, even though the rest of their lives are completely torn apart.

Where it's reviewed:
Entertainment Weekly, April 25, 2008, page 122
Library Journal, March 15, 2008, page 63
Mystery Scene, Spring 2008, page 64
The New York Times Book Review, May 4, 2008, page 26L
Publishers Weekly, March 3, 2008, page 29

Other books you might like:
James Church, *Hidden Moon*, 2007
Arnaldur Indridason, *Jar City*, 2004
John le Carre, *The Russia House*, 1989
Martin Cruz Smith, *Gorky Park*, 1981

172

TROY SOOS

Streets of Fire

(New York: Kensington, 2008)

Story type: Historical
Series: Marshall Webb & Rebecca Davies. Book 4
Subject(s): Strikes and Lockouts
Major character(s): Marshall Webb, Journalist, Writer; Rebecca Davies, Activist; Buck Morehouse, Detective—Police
Time period(s): 1890s (1895)
Locale(s): New York, New York; Brooklyn, New York

Summary: In 1895, Harper's Weekly writer Marshall Webb wants to quit his job with the famous newspaper. Known for writing expose articles that helped bring down the corrupt Tammany Hall organization, Webb now feels that he is just rehashing old news stories. Convinced to do freelance work for the paper, Webb's first assignment is to cover the Brooklyn trolley workers strike that threatens to cripple the city, just as the cities of Brooklyn and New York are about to consolidate. Meanwhile, Webb's girlfriend, Rebecca Davies, is busy running a shelter for woman and helping former madam Vivian O'Connell open a shelter for former prostitutes. When O'Connell is murdered, Davies is determined to find her killer, and enlists the help of her boyfriend Webb.

Other books by the same author:
Burning Bridges, 2004
The Gilded Cage, 2002
Island of Tears, 2001
Hanging Curve, 1999
The Cincinnati Red Stalkings, 1998

Other books you might like:
Rhys Bowen, *Tell Me, Pretty Maiden*, 2008
Karen Rose Cercone, *Steel Ashes*, 1997
Richard E. Crabbe, *Suspension*, 2000
Jeanne M. Dams, *Green Grow the Victims*, 2001

173

JULIA SPENCER-FLEMING

I Shall Not Want

(New York: St. Martin's, 2008)

Story type: Amateur Detective; Serial Killer
Series: Clare Fergusson. Book 6
Subject(s): Illegal Immigrants; Episcopalians
Major character(s): Clare Fergusson, Religious, Detective—Amateur; Russ Van Alstyne, Police Officer; Hadley Knox, Police Officer
Time period(s): 2000s
Locale(s): Miller's Kill, New York

Summary: The Rev. Clare Fergusson and Police Chief Russ Van Alstyne, have been staying away from each other in the wake of the death of Russ' wife. That becomes impossible when Russ hires the church sexton's daughter. Sister Lucille, a friend of Clare's, is in an accident. Her passengers, migrant workers, flee the scene. Russ attempts to sort through the migrants' difficulties. Then the bodies of Hispanic men start to turn up. Clare is drawn into Russ' investigation through her ties to the migrant workers' community. The plight of the workers is complex, but even more complicated are the feelings Clare and Russ have for each other.

Where it's reviewed:
Booklist, May 1, 2008, page 36
Publishers Weekly, March 24, 2008, page 55

Other books by the same author:
All Mortal Flesh, 2006
To Darkness and to Death, 2005
Out of the Deep I Cry, 2004
A Fountain Filled with Blood, 2003
In the Bleak Midwinter, 2002

Other books you might like:
Stephen Greenleaf, *Strawberry Summer*, 1999
Jane Haddam, *Precious Blood*, 1991
Robin Hathaway, *Scarecrow*, 2003
Sarah Stewart Taylor, *O' Artful Death*, 2003

174

PATRICIA SPRINKLE

What Are You Wearing to Die?

(New York: Signet, 2008)

Story type: Amateur Detective
Series: MacLaren Yarborough. Book 10

Subject(s): Small Town Life; Family Relations
Major character(s): MacLaren Yarborough, Judge, Businesswoman; Joe Riddley Yarborough, Businessman
Time period(s): 2000s
Locale(s): Hopemore, Georgia

Summary: After MacLaren Yarbrough's recent brushes with death, her husband Joe Riddley hopes that she will stay out of trouble. Yet trouble has hit Hopemore, Georgia again when Starr Knight, the taxidermist's daughter, is found dead in a truck upended in a kudzu-filled gully. Starr was known for wearing revealing clothing, but when her body was found she was wearing bland clothing. Another body—the taxidermist's assistant—is discovered during the state taxidermy convention, also clad in uncharacteristic fashion. Despite Joe's wishes, MacLaren wants to figure out who is responsible for these deaths before the killer strikes again.

Where it's reviewed:
Booklist, March 15, 2008, page 34
Mystery News, February/March 2008, page 13

Other books by the same author:
Guess Who's Coming to Die?, 2007
Did You Declare the Corpse?, 2006
Who Killed the Queen of Clubs?, 2005
When Will the Dead Lady Sing?, 2004
Who Let That Killer in the House?, 2003

Other books you might like:
Anne George, *Murder Carries a Torch*, 2000
Charlaine Harris, *Shakespeare's Trollop*, 2000
Margaret Maron, *Uncommon Clay*, 2001
Sharon Short, *Murder Unfolds*, 2007

175

MICHAEL STANLEY   (Pseudonym of Michael Sears and Stanley Trollip)

A Carrion Death

(New York: HarperCollins, 2008)

Story type: Police Procedural
Subject(s): Kidnapping; Africa
Major character(s): David Bengu, Detective—Homicide; Bongani Sibisi, Professor; Dianna Hofmeyr, Heiress, Businesswoman
Time period(s): 2000s
Locale(s): Gaborone, Botswana; Letlhakeng, Botswana

Summary: When two men discover human remains in a game reserve in the Kalahari Desert in Africa, Assistant Superintendent David "Kubu" Bengu of the Botswana Police Department is called in to investigate. Traveling to the remote crime site, Kubu learns that the victim's teeth had been removed in a possible attempt to disguise the victim's identity. While at the resort, Kubu interviews Bongani Sibisi, an ecology professor at the University of Botswana, who was one of the men to discover the body. When more bodies are discovered, Kubu discovers a connection to the Botswana Cattle and Mining Company, the largest company in Botswana.

Mystery

Where it's reviewed:
Booklist, February 1, 2008, page 30
Mystery News, April/May 2008, page 12
Publishers Weekly, February 25, 2008, page 56

Other books you might like:
Suzanne Arruda, *Mark of the Lion*, 2006
Richard Kunzmann, *Salamander Cotton*, 2007
James McClure, *The Kramer & Zondi Series*, 1971-1991
Alexander McCall Smith, *The Miracle at Speedy Motors*, 2008

176

JENNIFER STURMAN

The Hunt

(New York: Red Dress Ink, 2007)

Story type: Amateur Detective
Series: Rachel Benjamin. Book 4
Subject(s): Missing Persons; Business
Major character(s): Rachel Benjamin, Banker, Detective—Amateur; Peter Forrest, Fiance(e); Ben Lattimer, FBI Agent
Time period(s): 2000s
Locale(s): San Francisco, California

Summary: Rachel Benjamin is a successful investment banker and a sometimes sleuth. Rachel and her fiance, Peter, take a trip to San Francisco to celebrate their engagement with Peter's family. While at their engagement party, Rachel's friend Hilary, a reporter, disappears. Hilary's latest assignment was to interview Iggie Behrenz, an Internet mogul. Rachel was getting ready to close a deal with Behrenz. Determined to find her friend, Rachel starts an informal investigation and finds that Behrenz may be harboring some secrets that Hilary could have exposed. Meanwhile, Rachel also deals with her own commitment issues and her new in-laws.

Where it's reviewed:
Booklist, November 15, 2007, page 23

Other books by the same author:
The Key, 2006
The Jinx, 2005
The Pact, 2004

Other books you might like:
Meg Cabot, *Size 12 Is Not Fat*, 2005
Margaret Dumas, *How to Succeed in Murder*, 2006
Nancy Fairbanks, *Chocolate Quake*, 2003
Melissa Senate, *Love You to Death*, 2007

177

DENISE SWANSON

Murder of a Chocolate-Covered Cherry

(New York: Signet, 2008)

Story type: Amateur Detective
Series: Skye Denison. Book 10

Subject(s): Small Town Life
Major character(s): Skye Denison, Psychologist (high school); Trixie Frayne, Friend; Wally Boyd, Police Officer
Time period(s): 2000s
Locale(s): Scumble River, Illinois

Summary: School psychologist Skye Dennison has never been the greatest of cooks. Yet thanks to the persistence of her mother, she is now entered in Grandma Sal's Soup-to-Nuts Cooking Challenge. The challenge turns sinister when a saboteur arrives. One of the contestants is found drowned inside a chocolate fountain. To add to her troubles, Skye also has to deal with a potential lawsuit after the school's newspaper publishes an article about a cheerleader. Now the cheerleader and the author of the article have gone missing. Skye's police chief boyfriend, Wally Boyd, keeps mysteriously breaking their dinner dates.

Where it's reviewed:
Mystery News, June/July 2008, page 32

Other books by the same author:
Murder of a Botoxed Blonde, 2007
Murder of a Real Bad Boy, 2006
Murder of a Smart Cookie, 2005
Murder of a Pink Elephant, 2004
Murder of a Barbie and Ken, 2003

Other books you might like:
Sandra Balzo, *Grounds for Murder*, 2007
JoAnna Carl, *The Chocolate Bridal Bash*, 2006
Joanne Fluke, *Strawberry Shortcake Murder*, 2001
Tamar Myers, *Eat, Drink, and Be Wary*, 1998

178

LEANN SWEENEY

Pushing Up Bluebonnets

(New York: Obsidian, 2008)

Story type: Private Detective
Series: Abby Rose. Book 5
Subject(s): Adoption
Major character(s): Abby Rose, Detective—Private; Kate Rose, Psychologist; Jeff Kline, Detective—Police
Time period(s): 2000s
Locale(s): Houston, Texas

Summary: Abby Rose runs a private investigation business devoted to finding the biological families of people who were adopted. When a policeman calls Abby and asks her to identify a woman who survived an attempted murder, Abby is inclined to do some investigating of her own. The woman was in a serious car crash and was carrying Abby's business card with her. Abby is able to find a letter from the woman and discovers that she may have connections to a very wealthy family in Houston. When Abby gets a chance to speak to JoLynn's grandfather, he asks her to sort through JoLynn's past and the lies she may or may not have told.

Where it's reviewed:
Mystery News, February/March 2008, page 13

Other books by the same author:
Shoot from the Lip, 2007
A Wedding to Die For, 2005
Dead Giveaway, 2005
Pick Your Poison, 2004

Other books you might like:
Barbara D'Amato, *White Male Infant*, 2002
Judy Fitzwater, *Dying for a Clue*, 1999
Mark Nykanen, *Search Angel*, 2005
Gillian Roberts, *Whatever Doesn't Kill You*, 2001

179

DUANE SWIERCZYNSKI
DENNIS CALERO , Illustrator

Severance Package

(New York: St. Martin's, 2008)

Story type: Action/Adventure
Subject(s): Work; Espionage
Major character(s): Jamie DeBroux, Employer; Molly Lewis, Spy
Time period(s): 2000s
Locale(s): Philadelphia, Pennsylvania; Portobello, Scotland

Summary: Jamie DeBroux goes to work just like any other day. His boss, David Murphy, calls everyone into the conference room. There David tells the staff that the company is not, in fact, in financial services, but instead is a cover for a branch of the intelligence community. He adds that the company is being shut down. He gives members of the staff the choice of drinking poison or being shot in the head. The whole building is rigged with explosives, and all outbound communication is jammed. Trust becomes an issue when Jamie's co-worker Molly Lewis shoots David in the head and reveals that she is a spy.

Where it's reviewed:
Booklist, September 1, 2007, page 64
Library Journal, May 1, 2008, page 60
Publishers Weekly, March 17, 2008, page 47

Other books by the same author:
The Blonde, 2006
Secret Dead Men, 2005
The Wheelman, 2005

Other books you might like:
Joseph Finder, *Power Play*, 2007
Joseph Garber, *Vertical Run*, 1995
Charlie Huston, *Caught Stealing*, 2004
Donald Westlake, *The Ax*, 1997

180

PARI NOSKIN TAICHERT

The Socorro Blast

(Albuquerque: University of New Mexico, 2008)

Story type: Amateur Detective
Series: Sasha Solomon. Book 3
Subject(s): Family; Small Town Life
Major character(s): Sasha Solomon, Consultant, Public Relations; Vincent Sanchez, Detective—Police; Aaron Wahl, Professor
Time period(s): 2000s
Locale(s): Socorro, New Mexico; Albuquerque, New Mexico; San Antonio, New Mexico

Summary: Public relations expert Sasha Solomon is looking forward to spending some time in Socorro, New Mexico. While part of her trip will be spent meeting with a new client, the San Socorro Foundation, Sasha is also going to visit her niece, Gabi Shofet. Then a pipe bomb destroys Gabi's mailbox, injuring the young graduate student, and Sasha begins to worry about Gabi's safety. Being Jewish with an Iranian last name, it appears that Gabi is the victim of a hate crime. In the process of trying to find out what happened to Gabi, Sasha discovers that the family of her new client, Papi Sanchez, may be involved.

Other books by the same author:
Belen Hitch, 2005
The Clovis Incident, 2004

Other books you might like:
Steven Havill, *Convenient Disposal*, 2004
Michael McGarrity, *The Big Gamble*, 2002
Susan Slater, *Flash Flood*, 2002
Judith Van Gieson, *Ditch Rider*, 1998

181

FRANK TALLIS

Vienna Blood

(New York: Random House, 2008)

Story type: Historical
Series: Max Liebermann. Book 2
Subject(s): Psychology; Serial Killers
Major character(s): Max Liebermann, Psychologist; Oskar Rheinhardt, Detective—Police; Andreas Olbricht, Artist, Serial Killer
Time period(s): 1900s (1902)
Locale(s): Vienna, Austria-Hungary; Spittelberg, Austria-Hungary

Summary: During the winter of 1902, while Viennese detective Oskar Rheinhardt is attempting to find out who killed the emperor's favorite anaconda, he is called in to investigate a serial killer. In a brothel in Spittelberg, four women are found brutally murdered. When more victims are discovered Rheinhardt cannot find a pattern, except for the fact that the crimes are eerily similar to that of Jack the Ripper, who murdered prostitutes in London several years before. Disturbed by the crime, Rheinhardt contacts his close friend, Max Liebermann, a psychologist and follower of Sigmund Freud. Both men are astonished to find that the murderer is killing his victims to mirror the plot of Mozart's opera, *The Magic Flute*.

Where it's reviewed:
Booklist, November 15, 2007, page 23
Mystery Scene, Winter 2008, page 72
Publishers Weekly, November 19, 2007, page 41

Other books by the same author:
Mortal Mischief, 2005
Love Sick, 2004
Sensing Others, 2000
Killing Time, 1999

Other books you might like:
Ronan Bennett, *Zugzwang*, 2007
Batya Gur, *The Saturday Morning Murder*, 1992
Jed Rubenfeld, *The Interpretation of Murder*, 2006
Jody Shields, *The Fig Eater*, 2000

182

RICHARD A. THOMPSON

Fiddle Game

(Scottsdale, Arizona: Poisoned Pen, 2008)

Story type: Adventure
Subject(s): Gypsies; Antiques
Major character(s): Herman Jackson, Bail Bondsman;
  Rosie, Waiter/Waitress, Gypsy
Time period(s): 2000s
Locale(s): St. Paul, Minnesota; Skokie, Illinois

Summary: A woman calling herself Amy Cox leaves a violin with St. Paul, Minnesota, bondsman Herman Jackson as security on bond for her brother. She asks Jackson not only to bail out her brother but also for a temporary loaner violin, saying that she needs one for her work. The woman is murdered outside Jackson's office; the killers take the time to stop and grab the replacement violin. Jackson receives an e-mail offering a handsome reward for return of the violin in his possession, which the woman claimed was a 400-year-old Amati worth $60,000. Jackson visits G.B. Feinstein, an expert on rare instruments, to learn more about the violin. The information Feinstein provides sends Jackson on a trail that involves Gypsies and a waitress named Rosie.

Where it's reviewed:
Booklist, October 1, 2007, page 35
Mystery News, February/March 2008, page 26
Mystery Scene, Winter 2008, page 65
Publishers Weekly, October 1, 2007, page 40

Other books you might like:
Joe Gores, *32 Cadillacs*, 1992
Parnell Hall, *Scam*, 1997
Ross Thomas, *Twilight at Mac's Place*, 2003
Donald Westlake, *God Save the Mark*, 1967

183

CHARLES TODD

A Pale Horse

(New York: Morrow, 2008)

Story type: Historical/World War I
Series: Ian Rutledge. Book 10
Subject(s): World War I; Missing Persons
Major character(s): Ian Rutledge, Detective—Police

Time period(s): 1920s (1920)
Locale(s): Yorkshire, England

Summary: Inspector Ian Rutledge is continuing to struggle with life after experiencing the horrors of the Great War, still haunted by the persistent voice of a fallen comrade. He is called on by the British War Office to investigate a missing persons case. Little can be said about the missing man as his real name and his work during the war are too confidential to reveal to Rutledge. The missing person may be connected with an unidentified body that is discovered in the ruins of a Yorkshire abbey, clad in a gas mask and cloak, with a book on alchemy next to it.

Where it's reviewed:
Booklist, November 1, 2007, page 29
Mystery News, December/January 2008, page 16
Publishers Weekly, October 8, 2007, page 38
School Library Journal, April 1, 2008, page 174

Other books by the same author:
A False Mirror, 2007
A Long Shadow, 2006
A Cold Treachery, 2005
Search the Dark, 1999
Wings of Fire, 1998

Other books you might like:
Rennie Airth, *River of Darkness*, 1999
Barbara Cleverly, *Tug of War*, 2007
C.J. Sansom, *Dissolution*, 2003
Jacqueline Winspear, *Birds of a Feather*, 2004

184

LOUISE URE

The Fault Tree

(New York: St. Martin's, 2008)

Story type: Amateur Detective; Police Procedural
Subject(s): Blindness; Guilt
Major character(s): Cadence Moran, Mechanic,
  Handicapped (Blind); August Dupree, Detective—
  Police
Time period(s): 2000s
Locale(s): Tucson, Arizona

Summary: Cadence Moran struggles with guilt over the accident in which she lost both her sight and her three-year-old niece. The blindness isn't a problem at work. She's an auto mechanic who's learned to listen for problems. But the blindness becomes an issue when killers fleeing the scene of a vicious stabbing run into Cadence. The police discount Cadence's testimony, believing in only what can be seen. The killers don't realize that Cadence is blind, and believe that she saw them and will be able to identify them. Police detective August Dupree isn't sure what to believe. Short on leads, he and his partner struggle with Cadence and her efforts to aid the investigation.

Where it's reviewed:
Booklist, December 1, 2007, page 25
Deadly Pleasures, Spring 2008, page 44
Library Journal, January 15, 2008, page 67
Mystery News, February/March 2008, page 21
Mystery Scene, Winter 2008, page 76

Other books by the same author:
Forcing Amaryllis, 2005

Other books you might like:
Cara Black, *Murder in the Bastille*, 2003
Patricia Carlon, *The Whispering Wall*, 1996
Barbara Seranella, *Unpaid Dues*, 2003
George D. Shuman, *Last Breath*, 2007

185

CHRISTIAN VON DITFURTH

A Paragon of Virtue

(New Milford, Connecticut: Toby, 2008)

Story type: Serial Killer
Subject(s): Children and War; Revenge
Major character(s): Josef Stachelmann, Professor, Historian; Oskar Winter, Police Officer; Leopold Kohn, Murderer
Time period(s): 2000s (2001)
Locale(s): Hamburg, Germany; Lubeck, Germany; Berlin, Germany

Summary: Josef Stachelmann is a history professor in Hamburg, Germany. On his way to the university one morning, Stachelmann can't help but notice the newspaper headlines of yet another murder in the Holler family. In the past three years, three members of Maximilian Holler's family have been murdered, his wife and two of his children. Stachelmann is contacted by an old friend, Oskar Winter, who is now a police commissioner. Winter requests Stachelmann's help in determining if Holler's family history has anything to do with the murders. Stachelmann discovers that Holler's father, Herrmann, was involved in a scheme that forced Jewish families to sell their homes to Nazi party members at deflated prices during World War II.

Where it's reviewed:
Publishers Weekly, January 7, 2008, page 38

Other books you might like:
Joseph Kanon, *The Good German*, 2001
Philip Kerr, *The One from the Other*, 2006
Hans Werner Kettenbach, *Black Ice*, 2006
Bernhard Schlink, *Self's Punishment*, 2005
Walter Popp, co-author

186

MINETTE WALTERS

The Chameleon's Shadow

(New York: Knopf, 2008)

Story type: Psychological Suspense
Subject(s): Violence; Mental Illness
Major character(s): Charles Acland, Military Personnel; Jackson, Doctor; Jen Morley, Prostitute
Time period(s): 2000s
Locale(s): Basra, Iraq; Birmingham, England; London, England

Summary: A roadside bomb kills several British soldiers in Iraq. Lieutenant Charles Acland, the only survivor of the attack, is sent back to England for treatment. Disfigured and possibly suffering from post-traumatic stress disorder, Acland's personality is now aggressive and hostile. Acland withdraws from his family and the outside world, and physically attacks his ex-fiancee, Jen Morley, when she visits him. Finally released from the hospital, Acland moves to London where his rage makes him a suspect in a murder investigation. Acland's only hope of proving himself innocent, and of recovering his former self, is a doctor named Jackson who believes Acland is worth saving.

Where it's reviewed:
Booklist, November 15, 2007, page 5
Mystery News, April/May 2008, page 26
Mystery Scene, Winter 2008, page 75
Publishers Weekly, November 26, 2007, page 28

Other books by the same author:
The Devil's Feather, 2006
Disordered Minds, 2004
Fox Evil, 2003
Acid Row, 2002
The Shape of Snakes, 2001

Other books you might like:
Craig Holden, *The Last Sanctuary*, 1996
Franklin Allen Leib, *The House of Pain*, 1999
Margaret Murphy, *Weaving Shadows*, 2005
Charles Todd, *A Test of Wills*, 1996

187

BETTY WEBB

Desert Cut

(Scottsdale, Arizona: Poisoned Pen, 2008)

Story type: Private Detective
Series: Lena Jones. Book 5
Subject(s): Child Abuse
Major character(s): Lena Jones, Detective—Private; Bill Avery, Police Officer; Nicole Hall, Teenager, Runaway
Time period(s): 2000s
Locale(s): Scottsdale, Arizona; Los Perdidos, Arizona; Los Angeles, California

Summary: While scouting locations for a documentary with her film director boyfriend Warren Quinn, private investigator Lena Jones discovers the body of a young girl. Disturbed by the girl's death, Lena leaves her partner Jimmy Sisiwan in charge of their Scottsdale, Arizona, office and returns to Los Perdidos. She is warned off the case by Sheriff Bill Avery, but Lena, whose own childhood was troubled, can't help but do a little investigating of her own. When two more young girls vanish in Los Perdidos, Lena realizes that it isn't the work of pedophiles, but a more sinister force that is mutilating the young immigrant girls in the town.

Where it's reviewed:
Booklist, December 1, 2007, page 24
Library Journal, December 15, 2007, page 92
Mystery Scene, Winter 2008, page 70
Publishers Weekly, December 3, 2007, page 52

Other books by the same author:
Desert Run, 2006
Desert Shadows, 2004
Desert Wives, 2003
Desert Noir, 2001

Other books you might like:
Ruth Francisco, *Confessions of a Deathmaiden*, 2003
Michael McGarrity, *Nothing but Trouble*, 2005
Jim Sanderson, *La Mordida*, 2002
Judith Van Gieson, *The Other Side of Death*, 1991

188

JOSEPH WEISBERG

An Ordinary Spy

(New York: Bloomsbury, 2008)

Story type: Espionage
Subject(s): Secrets; Identity, Concealed
Major character(s): Mark Ruttenberg, Spy, Teacher; Bobby Goldstein, Spy, Teacher; Daisy, Secretary
Time period(s): 2000s (2002)
Locale(s): Washington, District of Columbia; Chicago, Illinois; Beekridge, New Hampshire

Summary: New to the CIA, agent Mark Ruttenberg is sent overseas for his first tour. By day Ruttenberg works at the American Embassy, and by night he spends his time at parties, mingling with diplomats. Part of his job as a CIA operative is to recruit foreigners as informants. This all changes when Ruttenberg meets Daisy, a secretary at another embassy. While trying to recruit her, a romance begins. When his superiors learn of the affair with Daisy, Ruttenberg is shipped back to the States and fired. An anonymous postcard in the mail leads Ruttenberg to Bobby Goldstein, a former CIA operative who, like Ruttenberg, became too involved in a local's life while on tour.

Where it's reviewed:
Booklist, November 1, 2007, page 30
The New Yorker, January 21, 2008, page 81
Publishers Weekly, October 1, 2007, page 37

Other books you might like:
Claire Berlinski, *Loose Lips*, 2003
John Brady, *Unholy Ground*, 1992
John le Carre, *Absolute Friends*, 2004
Dan Fesperman, *The Amateur Spy*, 2008

189

SHIRLEY WELLS

A Darker Side

(New York: Soho Constable, 2008)

Story type: Police Procedural
Series: Jill Kennedy & Max Trentham. Book 2
Subject(s): Psychological Thriller
Major character(s): Jill Kennedy, Writer; Max Trentham, Detective—Police; Donna Lord, Teacher
Time period(s): 2000s

Locale(s): Kelton Bridge, England; Harrington, England; Liverpool, England

Summary: Forensic psychologist Jill Kennedy resigned her position with the Harrington police force in England and is currently enjoying the quiet solitude of her new writing career in the village of Kelton Bridge. Kennedy's new life is disrupted when Detective Chief Inspector Max Trentham asks for help on a recent missing persons case. Seventeen-year-old Martin Hayden disappeared on his way to school one morning. As Kennedy and Trentham investigate the Hayden family for clues to Martin's whereabouts, they discover that Martin is the result of an affair his mother Josie had with a traveling salesman. When Martin's body is discovered, and then the bodies of Josie and another local teen, Kennedy and Trentham are startled to think that they may be dealing with a serial killer.

Where it's reviewed:
Booklist, May 15, 2008, page 23
Mystery News, June/July 2008, page 25
Mystery Scene, Summer 2008, page 83
Publishers Weekly, April 14, 2008, page 41

Other books by the same author:
Into the Shadows, 2007

Other books you might like:
Jo Bannister, *A Bleeding of Innocents*, 1993
Stephen Booth, *Black Dog*, 2000
Patricia Hall, *Dying Fall*, 1995
R.D. Wingfield, *Hard Frost*, 1995

190

VALERIE WILSON WESLEY

Of Blood and Sorrow

(New York: One World, 2008)

Story type: Private Detective
Series: Tamara Hayle. Book 8
Subject(s): Kidnapping
Major character(s): Tamara Hayle, Detective—Private; Thelma Lee Sweets, Teenager; Edna Sweets, Relative
Time period(s): 2000s
Locale(s): Newark, New Jersey; Jersey City, New Jersey

Summary: Private investigator Tamara Hayle is dismayed when Lilah Love strolls into her Newark, New Jersey, office. Having met Lilah after some shady business dealings in Jamaica, Tamara received $30,000 for her services, no strings attached. Now Lilah is demanding that Tamara recover her kidnapped daughter, Baby Dal, which shouldn't be too difficult considering that Baby Dal is with Lilah's younger sister, Thelma Lee Sweets. Tamara turns Lilah down, but changes her mind when Baby Dal's grandfather, businessman Treyman Barnes II, wants to hire Tamara to find Baby Dal. This custody battle becomes even more tangled when both Lilah and Treyman are murdered.

Where it's reviewed:
Booklist, January 1, 2008, page 49
Library Journal, January 15, 2008, page 68
Publishers Weekly, November 19, 2007, page 42

Other books by the same author:
Dying in the Dark, 2004
The Devil Riding, 2000
Easier to Kill, 1998
No Hiding Place, 1997
Where Evil Sleeps, 1996

Other books you might like:
Eleanor Taylor Bland, *Windy City Dying*, 2002
Grace F. Edwards, *If I Should Die*, 1997
Jill McGown, *Death in the Family*, 2003
Marilyn Wallace, *Lost Angel*, 1996

191

EUGENIA LOVETT WEST

Without Warning

(New York: St. Martin's, 2007)

Story type: Amateur Detective; Action/Adventure
Subject(s): Technology
Major character(s): Emma Streat, Detective—Amateur;
    Andrew Rodale, Nobleman, Consultant
Time period(s): 2000s
Locale(s): London, England; Connecticut

Summary: Emma Streat knows that something is bothering her husband, Lewis, but he absolutely refuses to tell her what it is. After what seems like a stressful trip to London, they return to their Connecticut home, where Lewis soon becomes the victim of a hit-and-run incident. Lewis was the CEO of a company that designs high tech weapons. When Emma discovers that Lewis' death may not have been an accident, she is determined to find out who his killer is and what was troubling him before his death. When she starts to investigate, with some help from a British lord, she learns that Lewis was not the only one to be killed over his company's newest technological weapon. Now the killer wants to silence Emma as well.

Where it's reviewed:
Mystery News, December/January 2008, page 12
Publishers Weekly, September 10, 2007, page 43

Other books you might like:
Janet Bettle, *Unnatural Causes*, 2000
Alex Brett, *Cold Dark Matter*, 2005
April Christofferson, *The Protocol*, 1999
Robert Goddard, *Out of the Sun*, 1997

192

JENNY WHITE

The Abyssinian Proof

(New York: Norton, 2008)

Story type: Historical
Series: Kamil Pasha. Book 2
Subject(s): Archaeology; Smuggling
Major character(s): Kamil Pasha, Government Official
    (magistrate), Detective; Omar Loutfi, Police Officer;
    Magnus Owen, Government Official, Criminal

Time period(s): 5th century (1453); 1880s (1887)
Locale(s): Istanbul, Ottoman Empire

Summary: In the late 1800s, the Ottoman Empire is overwhelmed by thefts of religious antiquities, which later show up for sale in Europe. Magistrate Kamil Pasha is given one week to stop the thefts and to put an end to the smuggling. Kamil's friend Malik, the caretaker of the Kariye Mosque in Istanbul, informs Kamil that an ancient reliquary has been taken from the mosque. This latest theft leads Kamil to investigate the mysterious Abyssinian cult Malik belongs to. Working with Omar Loutfi, a local police chief, Kamil finds himself up against a shadowy opponent who desires the ancient reliquary at any cost.

Where it's reviewed:
Booklist, February 1, 2008, page 29
Crimespree, January/February 2008, page 61
Publishers Weekly, October 1, 2007, page 35

Other books by the same author:
The Sultan's Seal, 2006

Other books you might like:
Boris Akunin, *The Turkish Gambit*, 2005
Aileen Baron, *The Gold of Thrace*, 2007
Alan Gordon, *The Widow of Jerusalem*, 2003
Mary Reed, *Four for a Boy*, 2005
    Eric Mayer, co-author

193

RANDY WAYNE WHITE

Black Widow

(New York: Putnam, 2008)

Story type: Adventure
Series: Doc Ford. Book 15
Subject(s): Blackmail
Major character(s): Marion "Doc" Ford, Scientist; Shay
    Money, Bride
Time period(s): 2000s
Locale(s): Sanibel Island, Florida; St. Arc, Caribbean

Summary: Doc Ford delivers a payment of $109,000 to a blackmailer on behalf of his goddaughter Shay Money. On the eve of her wedding, Shay and three friends traveled to the island of Saint Arc, off the coast of South America, for a wild bachelorette party. Ford gets a videotape in exchange for the cash, but he fears the blackmailer remains a threat. He learns that blackmail is an industry on Saint Arc. Before long, one of Shay's friends attempts suicide and Shay is in the hospital after a car accident. Marine biologist Ford interrupts his research, and calls upon skills he learned as an intelligence operative to keep the blackmailers away from Shay.

Where it's reviewed:
Booklist, February 1, 2008, page 4
Deadly Pleasures, Spring 2008, page 44
Mystery News, June/July 2008, page 12
Publishers Weekly, January 21, 2008, page 151

Other books by the same author:
Dark Light, 2006
Dead of Night, 2005
Tampa Burn, 2004
The Heat Islands, 1992
Sanibel Flats, 1990

Other books you might like:
Parnell Hall, *Blackmail*, 1994
E. Howard Hunt, *Guilty Knowledge*, 1999
John D. MacDonald, *The Quick Red Fox*, 1974
Robert B. Parker, *Hush Money*, 1999

194

STEPHEN WHITE

Dead Time

(New York: Dutton, 2008)

Story type: Psychological Suspense
Series: Alan Gregory. Book 16
Subject(s): Missing Persons; Psychology
Major character(s): Alan Gregory, Psychologist; Merideth Gregory, Journalist; Eric Leffler, Consultant, Political Figure
Time period(s): 2000s
Locale(s): Boulder, Colorado; New York, New York; Los Angeles, California

Summary: Dr. Alan Gregory, a Boulder, Colorado, psychotherapist, is busy learning how to be a father to his newly adopted son Jonas, and helping Jonas deal with the death of his mother. Alan is contacted by his ex-wife Merideth. After several miscarriages, Merideth and her fiance Eric Leffler are using the services of a surrogate mother. Days after the surrogate, Lisa, became pregnant, she disappeared. Merideth is desperate to find Lisa and calls on Alan for help. Alan soon realizes that Lisa's disappearance has something to do with an incident that occurred several years ago during a camping trip to the Grand Canyon involving both Eric and Lisa, and the disappearance of another young woman.

Where it's reviewed:
Booklist, January 1, 2008, page 22
Publishers Weekly, January 28, 2008, page 41

Other books by the same author:
Dry Ice, 2007
Kill Me, 2006
Missing Persons, 2005
Blinded, 2004
The Best Revenge, 2003

Other books you might like:
Sarah Dunant, *Birth Marks*, 1992
Kirk Mitchell, *Cry Dance*, 1999
Sharon Zukowski, *Leap of Faith*, 1994

195

DON WINSLOW

The Dawn Patrol

(New York: Knopf, 2008)

Story type: Private Detective
Subject(s): Missing Persons; Law Enforcement
Major character(s): Boone Daniels, Detective—Private; Petra Hall, Lawyer; Johnny Kodani, Detective—Homicide
Time period(s): 2000s
Locale(s): San Diego, California; Pacific Beach, California; Del Mar, California

Summary: Ex-cop Boone Daniels loves to surf. A member of the Dawn Patrol, a group that hits the waves every morning near San Diego, Boone occasionally works as a private investigator. An ambitious young lawyer, Petra Hall, hires Boone to find a missing stripper, Tammy Roddick, a witness in a possible insurance fraud case. Strip club owner Dan Silver is being investigated for arson after he filed a claim for five million dollars when a warehouse he owned burned to the ground. Tammy was willing to testify that she saw Dan burn down the building himself. Now Tammy is missing, and suddenly Boone finds himself involved in something much bigger than an arson case.

Where it's reviewed:
Booklist, June 1, 2008, page 48
Publishers Weekly, April 28, 2008, page 110

Other books by the same author:
The Winter of Frankie Machine, 2006
The Power of the Dog, 2005
California Fire and Life, 1999
The Death and Life of Bobby Z, 1997
Isle of Joy, 1996

Other books you might like:
Richard Barre, *Bearing Secrets*, 1996
Ross Macdonald, *The Goodbye Look*, 1969
Kem Nunn, *Tijuana Straits*, 2004
Jeff Shelby, *Killer Swell*, 2005

196

JACQUELINE WINSPEAR

An Incomplete Revenge

(New York: Henry Holt, 2008)

Story type: Private Detective; Historical/World War I
Series: Maisie Dobbs. Book 5
Subject(s): Rural Life; Gypsies
Major character(s): Maisie Dobbs, Detective—Private; Billy Beale, Assistant; Webb, Gypsy
Time period(s): 1900s (1931)
Locale(s): Kent, England

Summary: Maisie Dobbs is asked to look into some property her friend, James Compton, wants to buy in rural Kent. It seems that there has been some petty vandalism on the estate, which includes a brickworks.

Maisie sends her assistant, Billy Beale, and his family to the area to do some undercover investigating. Before Maisie has a chance to leave London, Billy calls to tell her that two young boys have been arrested for burglary from the estate. He is pretty sure they are innocent, but the current owner is asking for the maximum penalty. Other local people are blaming nearby gypsies. Maisie also hears that her true love, severely injured in the war, is dying, and his mother, who never approved of her, wants to see her.

Where it's reviewed:
Booklist, December 1, 2007, page 26
Library Journal, January 1, 2008, page 69
Mystery News, February/March 2008, page 20
Publishers Weekly, November 26, 2007, page 31

Other books by the same author:
Messenger of Truth, 2006
Pardonable Lies, 2005
Birds of a Feather, 2004
Maisie Dobbs, 2003

Other books you might like:
Robert Goddard, *In Pale Battalions*, 1988
Laurie R. King, *Touchstone*, 2008
Dorothy L. Sayers, *The Nine Tailors*, 1934
Charles Todd, *A Test of Wills*, 1996

197

INGER WOLFE

The Calling

(Orlando, Florida: Harcourt, 2008)

Story type: Police Procedural
Subject(s): Serial Killers
Major character(s): Hazel Micallef, Detective—Police; James Wingate, Detective—Police; Simon Mallick, Serial Killer
Time period(s): 2000s
Locale(s): Port Dundas, Ontario, Canada; Hoxley, Ontario, Canada

Summary: Serving as the acting detachment commander of the Port Dundas Police Department for six years now, 61-year-old Detective Inspector Hazel Micallef is hampered by a staff shortage, inadequate support from her superiors, her 87-year-old mother and a bad back. When the body of Delia Chandler is discovered, her head cut almost completely from her body, Hazel and her team are baffled. Delia was already dying of cancer. Theories of assisted suicide are discussed until more bodies, with similar situations to Delia's, are discovered in nearby towns. Working with newly assigned Detective Constable James Wingate, Hazel realizes that a serial killer is terrorizing Ontario.

Where it's reviewed:
Booklist, April 1, 2008, page 29
Deadly Pleasures, Spring 2008, page 34
Library Journal, March 15, 2008, page 62
Mystery Scene, Summer 2008, page 78
Publishers Weekly, March 24, 2008, page 55

Other books you might like:
Rosemary Aubert, *Free Reign*, 1997
Giles Blunt, *The Delicate Storm*, 2003
Deborah Crombie, *All Shall Be Well*, 1994
Vicki Delaney, *Burden of Memory*, 2006

198

NINA WRIGHT

Whiskey and Water

(Woodbury, Minnesota: Midnight Ink, 2008)

Story type: Amateur Detective
Series: Whiskey Mattimoe. Book 4
Subject(s): Real Estate; Animals/Dogs
Major character(s): Whiskey Mattimoe, Detective—Amateur, Real Estate Agent; MacArthur, Driver, Real Estate Agent; Judy Jenkins, Police Officer
Time period(s): 2000s
Locale(s): Magnet Springs, Michigan

Summary: Whiskey Mattimoe owns a successful real estate agency in Magnet Springs, Michigan, where she still grieves over the loss of her husband Leo. A handsome Scottish real estate agent named MacArthur catches Whiskey's eye when he informs her that he wants to work for her agency. In addition, Whiskey is currently having problems with a new tenant in one of her rental properties. Twyla Rendel is in violation of her lease agreement and in danger of being evicted for having too many children on her property. Suddenly the children vanish and Twyla's body is discovered on the beach. Police chief Judy Jenkins asks Whiskey to help investigate Twyla's death and find the missing children.

Where it's reviewed:
Publishers Weekly, March 31, 2008, page 43

Other books by the same author:
Whiskey and Tonic, 2007
Whiskey Straight Up, 2006
Whiskey on the Rocks, 2005

Other books you might like:
JoAnna Carl, *The Chocolate Cat Caper*, 2002
Jo Dereske, *Savage Cut*, 1996
Charlaine Harris, *Three Bedrooms, One Corpse*, 1994
Tierney McClellan, *A Killing in Real Estate*, 1996

199

ELIZABETH ZELVIN

Death Will Get You Sober

(New York: St. Martin's, 2008)

Story type: Amateur Detective
Subject(s): Alcoholism
Major character(s): Bruce Kohler, Alcoholic, Detective—Amateur; Godfrey Kettleworth R03, Alcoholic; Jimmy, Computer Expert
Time period(s): 2000s
Locale(s): New York, New York (The Bowery)

Summary: On Christmas Day, Bruce Kohler wakes up on

New York's Bowery in detox next to Godfrey Kettleworth III. Godfrey tells Bruce that he's God and an alcoholic. Bruce is interested enough in Godfrey that he tries to stay sober when Godfrey is killed. Godfrey's is only the first death. A string of homeless alcoholics are also killed. Bruce's former drinking buddy Jimmy and Jimmy's wife Barbara, try and help him solve the case. Working through a network of Alcoholics Anonymous meetings all over the city, Bruce finds AA is a small, interconnected world.

Where it's reviewed:
Booklist, February 15, 2008, page 38
Mystery Scene, Spring 2008, page 70
Publishers Weekly, February 11, 2008, page 54

Other books you might like:
Lawrence Block, *When the Sacred Ginmill Closes*, 1973
Ken Bruen, *The Guards*, 2001
Rob Fox, *Buzzkill*, 2007
Jim Thompson, *The Alcoholics*, 1953

Romance Fiction in Review
by
Kristin Ramsdell

"Romance has been elegantly defined as the offspring of fiction and love."

—Benjamin Disraeli

"There's nothing constant in the world,
All ebb and flow, and every shape that's born
Bears in its womb the seeds of change."

—Ovid

Change—relentless, inevitable, but sometimes surprising—continues to impact the romance genre with increasing vigor in a variety of new ways. Technology, of course, is the driving force behind much of this change, and as each new advance sparks another innovation, the ways in which romances are presented and delivered to readers are evolving along both expected and unexpected lines. Audio books, long commonplace in first tape and then CD formats, recently have been joined by downloadable versions, and it's likely only a matter of time—and format standardization—before downloads become the format of choice for most listeners. E-books, as well, have been gradually gaining a committed following, especially among the more tech savvy readers. However, with Harlequin not only making much of its inventory available in this format, but also launching a new Enriched Edition eBooks in mid-2008, more readers may be drawn in by the enhanced potential of the format. (Note: these Enriched Editions are complete with links to illustrations, photographs, historical detail, and other relevant bonus background information not available in the print version.)

However, as important as it is, technology isn't the only thing that is changing. As is their habit, the stories themselves are evolving, as well. Although what gets published is often based on what has sold previously, this conservative trend is constantly being countered by writers who test the limits of the genre either by putting an unconventional spin on an old idea or venturing into new, more dangerous territory, thereby enriching the genre immeasurably and ensuring that romance, as it has done traditionally, provides a little bit of something for everyone.

A Mid-Year Perspective

Although we're only halfway through the year as of this writing, if the first six months are any indication, 2008 promises to be another good year for the genre. Romances of all varieties are well-represented and a number of trends noted in the past are continuing. Some of these trends, of course, are limited to a particular subgenre; others, however, cut across the genre as a whole. One such trend is the increasing use of paranormal elements in romances. Often these involve characters with psychic abilities of some kind that are important but don't overshadow the other elements of the story. *Silent Fall*, a fast-paced romantic suspense thriller by Barbara Freethy, and Connie Brockway's heartwarming, family-centered contemporary *Skinny Dipping* both feature psychic heroines and are only two of the current examples.

Another cross-genre trend that has been with us for some time is the general rise in sexual explicitness and sensuality. Except for the chaste Inspirationals, romances across the board are ramping up the sizzle levels, and even books on the milder side don't always keep the bedroom door closed as tightly as they once did.

Although there are no longer specific lines dedicated to romantic comedy, humor is still alive and well and can be found adding a sense of fun to romances across the board. Light or dark, subtle or overt, humor has left its mark on all the subgenres to some extent; so far, not one has been immune.

More prevalent among the Contemporaries, are stories that reflect society's various diversities, changing demographics, and social concerns are not limited to that particular subgenre. Older protagonists, sometimes widows or widowers (e.g., Susan Grant's futuristic *Moonstruck*), atypical relationships (e.g., the older heroine/younger hero in Susan Wiggs' *Snowfall at Willow Lake*), death and dying issues (e.g., Susan Kay Law's *The Paper Marriage*), and characters of a wide variety of cultures and backgrounds populate romances of all types.

Yet again, linked books are everywhere! Whether part of a formal trilogy or other series (e.g. Celeste Bradley's Heiress Brides series, Nicole Jordan's Courtship Wars series, Marthe Arends' Silver Dragons series) or simply connected by common characters, writers are furiously producing them (sometimes in consecutive month releases) and avid readers are snapping them up.

Finally, there is the growing fascination with food and all things culinary. Whether it's the sensual appeal and natural affinity of food and romance, the current popularity of cooking shows and homemade gourmet cuisine, or something else entirely, heroines (and sometimes heroes) who cook or bake for business or pleasure (e.g., Deidre Martin's *Just a Taste*, Mary Kay Andrew's *Deep Dish*, Barbara Bretton's *Just Desserts*, *Sweet Talk* by Susan Mallery) are dishing up a surfeit of books that are currently being gobbled up by fans—and there are more in the publishing pipeline to come.

Contemporary Romance continues to reign supreme, accounting for the vast majority of titles published, largely thanks to Harlequin's thriving contemporary series romances. Fans continue to enjoy the various aspects of this most popular subgenre, that for all its here-and-now focus is amazingly diverse. From somewhat serious but totally satisfying, heartwarming tales (e. g., *Mystic Horseman* by Kathleen Eagle, *Snowfall at Willow Lake* by Susan Wiggs, *The Vow* by Rebecca Winters, *Promise Me Tomorrow* by Linda Ingmanson) to funny, upbeat romps (e.g., *The Ex-Debutante* by Linda Francis Lee, *Hot Date* by Amy Garvey, *Tall Tales and Wedding Veils* by Jane Graves, *Fast and Loose* by Elizabeth Bevarly) the genre accommodates a wide variety of tastes. As mentioned above, cooks were everywhere, but so were characters as varied as race car drivers (e.g. *Peak Performance* by Helen Brenna), football and baseball players (e.g. *Game for Anything* by Bella Andre, *Strike Zone* by Kate Angell), and breast cancer survivors (e.g., *This Side of Heaven* by Ann Schmidt, *Time Is a River* by Mary Alice Monroe).

In spite of the persistent rumors of the Historical's imminent demise, this subgenre continues to bounce back and currently is alive and well and thriving, especially in 19th century England. As in past years, the British Regency is by far the period of choice, with the Victorian and Medieval periods playing credible, but distant, second fiddles. Filled with adventure, passion and often enhanced with suspense or paranormal elements (e.g., *The Third Circle* by Amanda Quick), these lively tales are attracting plenty of notice and are currently some of the most popular in the genre.

Paranormals and the rest of the Alternative Reality subgenre remain popular, and according to last year's statistics, their appeal is increasing. Vampires are still well-represented within this year's crop (e.g., *The Accidental Vampire* by Lynsay Sands, *Lover's Bite* by Maggie Benson), as are werewolves and shapeshifters of various types (e.g., *Walk on the Wild Side* by Christine Warren, *Because Your Vampire Said So* by Michelle Bardsley, and the anthology *Shifter*). Stories featuring

witches (*Witch Blood* by Anya Bast, *50 Ways to Hex Your Lover* by Linda Wisdom), demons (e.g., *The Hollow* by Nora Roberts, *Hellbent & Heartfirst* by Kassandra Sims), dragons (e.g., *Queen of Dragons* by Shana Abe, *Playing with Fire* by Katie MacAlister), mythical creatures of all kinds (e.g., *Dark Seduction* by Kathleen Korbel, *The Devil's Daughter* by Laura Drewry), and any combination thereof, are also making their mark, reflecting the increasing diversity and broadening appeal within the subgenre. Laced with humor (*A Friend in Need* by Maureen Child) or dark and angst-ridden (*The Darkest Night* by Gena Showalter, *Lover Enshrined* by J.R. Ward), many of these tales hover between the Romance and Fantasy or Science Fiction genres and are quickly finding fans in all three camps.

As usual, Romantic Suspense continues strong, attracting readers with a wide variety of tales which include everything from darkly sinister thrillers (e.g., Allison Brennan's chilling *Killing Fear*, and *Scream for Me* by Karen Rose) to lively, suspenseful romps that are full of fun (e.g., *Weddings Can Be Murder* by Christie Craig, *Overnight Male* by Elizabeth Bevarly). Although most stories in this subgenre are contemporary, a growing number have historical settings. Stephanie Laurens' Victorian mystery *Where the Heart Lies* (the latest in her Cynster series) and Kimberly Logan's Regency murder mystery *Seduced by Sin* are two examples.

Imprints specifically featuring ethnic characters and cultures, such as Harlequin's Kimani and Kensington's Dafina African American lines, continue to hold their own in the romance area with titles such as Shirley Hailstock's *On My Terms* and Candice Poarch's *Long, Hot Nights*. However, multicultural characters and the varying cultures they represent are not limited to specific lines and are rapidly becoming part of the overall romance landscape as part of most publishing houses general releases. *You Gotta Sin to Get Saved* by J.D. Mason, *The Secret Correspondence* by Annette Mahon, and *Mystic Horseman* by Kathleen Eagle are only two of the many examples. Note: Currently there is much ongoing discussion concerning the pros and cons of marketing romances along ethnic and cultural lines.

In spite of the overall downturn in the broader Christian religious and inspirational market, Inspirational Romances remain popular with their particular readers, with Harlequin's Steeple Hill's various Love Inspired lines and Barbour's Heartsong Presents providing some of the more popular titles in this subgenre.

A Romance Statistical Update

The 2007 figures for romance are in, and once again the genre has had a stellar year. According to the 2007 ROMStat Report from Romance Writers of America [http://www.rwanational.org/cs/the_romance_genre /romance_literature_statistics/industry_statistics], which gathered its data from various publications of the Association of American Publishers, Simba Information, and R.R. Bowker, romance released 8090 titles in 2007

(an amazing increase of nearly 26% over the 6400 titles released in 2006) and out-earned the rest of the consumer fiction market by generating $1.375 billion in sales. Now commanding the "largest share of the consumer book market" by sales, romance is followed by the Religious and Inspirational group, which earned $819 million last year (a steep drop from the year before when it surpassed romance); Science Fiction and Fantasy, which garnered $700 million; Mystery, which accounted for $650 million; and Classic Literary Fiction, which brought up the rear with $466 million in sales. Within the romance genre itself, Contemporary Romances accounted for 47.5% of the titles released (of these approximately 54% were series; the rest were single titles). Historicals came in at 16%, and Romantic Suspense claimed 11.9%, of which single titles accounted for more than 60% with series titles making up the rest. Paranormals, Inspirationals, and Young Adult romances garnered 11.8%, 7.1%, and 2.8%, respectively; the remaining 2.8% was split among chick-lit, erotic romance and women's fiction. The overall U.S. book also did well, and sales were up by over $10 billion from the year before. (Information courtesy of the Romance Writers of America. For more detail, please see the website mentioned above.)

Romance News of Interest

As of this writing the romance world is preparing to meet for the Romance Writers of America's (RWA) annual conference, this year to be held in San Francisco at the end of July. Featured speakers will include writers Victoria Alexander and Connie Brockway, as well as other motivational, literary, and industry expert speakers. Writer Suzanne Brockman is slated to be the M.C. for the Rita Awards Ceremonies.

In conjunction with the conference, the Annual Librarians' and Booksellers' Event will feature a day of presentations and networking. Scheduled to be included are such headliners as Debbie Macomber, Heather Graham (aka Heather Graham Pozzessere), Jo Beverley, Jodi Thomas, and Stephanie Laurens, as well as various editors and librarians. An account of both these events will be forthcoming in the first volume of *What do I Read Next? 2009*.

Since 1995 as one of its awards, RWA has named a Librarian of the Year. This year's award will be presented to Susan Gibberman, Head of Reader Services at Schaumburg Township District Library in Schaumburg, Illinois. The award is scheduled to be presented at the Awards luncheon; Ms. Gibberman will also be honored at the Librarians' and Booksellers' Day Event.

Future Trends

Although the future is always murky at best and there are far too any things that can derail even the best guesses, some of the current trends can give us a few clues as to what might be ahead for the genre.

Technology, of course, is at the top of this trend list, and with the speed at which things are now evolving and the impact that it is already having on publishing and communication, in general, the romance world will not be unaffected. Even though ebooks now account for only a miniscule amount of profit for even the largest romance publishers, with improvements in reading devices and publishers learning how to take better advantage of the formats by adding content, providing links, and generally enriching the reading experience, that situation is likely to change. In addition, the potential is there for all kinds of variations (multiple story paths, directions, endings, visual renditions, etc.), although that—and the holodeck version I'm waiting for—are probably not happening in the immediate future.

Another trend mentioned earlier, and one I believe will continue, is the growing inclusion of diverse characters and cultures in romances of all kinds, not just those targeting a particular racial, ethnic, or cultural group. The discussion as to how to market these books is ongoing, and there are strong opinions on both sides. However things fall out, it is certain that the romances of the future will continue to reflect the increasing diversity of our population.

Then there is the issue of sex. How much is too much? Is there such a thing, and if so, are we there, yet? Hot romance is currently the darling of the trade, and erotica, as well as erotic romance, is thriving. However, trends do go in cycles, and considering the tension between the fact that "sex sells" and some growing rumblings in the readership ranks, it will be interesting to see what happens down the road.

Although they've had a marvelous run and some might say they should be ready for a breather, stories of all things magical, paranormal, and futuristic still seem to have more room to go, especially if the crossover appeal continues.

Contemporary romance should remain dominant and both Historicals and Romantic Suspense will continue to shine. Mystery and suspense elements will continue to influence most of the other subgenres, and we could see more Historical Romantic Suspense—and perhaps a few more Historicals in the classic Gothic tradition (ala Victoria Holt et al).

The trend toward books linked together by theme, character, or place, often published in trilogies, quartets, or series, is firmly entrenched; and barring readers' tiring of them, seems likely to continue indefinitely.

Finally, the slowing economy may be a factor. However, with publishing figures on the rise, and romances more popular than ever, the outlook for the year might not be quite so dire as it seems. In any case, the first half of the year has gone rather well; we'll just keep our fingers crossed for the remainder.

Romance in Review

Romance continues to be regularly reviewed in print and online, in *Booklist* [www.ala.org/ala/booklist/booklist.htm], *Library Journal* [www.libraryjournal.

com], to a lesser extent in *Publishers Weekly* [www. publishersweekly.com], and in various newspapers throughout the country. *Library Journal* publishes a regular bimonthly romance review column, with occasional additional mini-columns; *Booklist* has a separate romance fiction category in each issue; and *Publishers Weekly* includes a limited number of romances in its general mass market or fiction review sections. In addition, many of these journal and newspaper reviews are picked up by various indexing services, such as Ebsco-Host's Academic Search Premier, Gale's InfoTrac Onefile (which provides full text reviews), or bookseller's websites, such as Amazon.com. and Barnes & Noble.

In spite of this increased coverage by mainstream sources, the most comprehensive coverage still is provided by the genre-specific publications, with *Romantic Times Bookclub Magazine* [(www.romantictimes. com)] being one of the most comprehensive. Most of these print publications have a web presence, and reviews, as well as other materials, may also be available online. Strictly online romance reviews sites continue to grow in number, variety, and popularity; and while most of them, like any web source, need to be viewed with a critical eye, they are becoming the go-to resource for many readers and are certainly worth checking out. All About Romance (www.allaboutromance. com), A Romance Review (www.aromancereview.com/ news/index.php), Romance Reviews Today (www. romrevtoday.com), The Romance Reader (www. theromancereader.com), Romance in Color (www. romanceincolor.com), and Speculative Romance Online (www.specromonline.com/) are only several of the many currently available. Although less formal, the online lists may provide review commentary that may prove useful. The most important, and also the oldest, is RRA-L (Romance Readers Anonymous). It has an active group of readers and writers who discuss a wide variety of romance fiction topics and new members are welcome. Log on to http://groups.yahoo.com/group/rra-l to subscribe. Fiction-L is another list of interest to readers and librarians that, while not specifically devoted to romance, does focus on the genre on a regular basis. For more information see their website: (www.webrary.org/ rs/flbklistmenu.html). Blogs, wikis, and individuals webpages are popping up like mushrooms and can also be a source of interesting opinions, if not formal reviews. One site that provides links to a number of authors' blogs is Romancing the Blog [www.romancingtheblog. com/blog/]. Those interested in the academic side of the genre should consider joining the Romance Scholar listserv (mailman.depaul.edu/mailman/listinfo/ romancescholar), as well as exploring the Romance Wiki [www.romancewiki.com], an active site useful to readers, writers, and scholars alike.

Recommendations for Romance

Reading tastes vary greatly. What makes a book appeal to one person may make another reject it. By the same token, two people may like the same book for totally different reasons. Obviously, reading is a highly subjective and personal undertaking. For this reason, the recommended readings attached to each entry have tried to cast as broad a net as was reasonably possible. Suggested titles have been chosen on the basis of similarity to the main entry in one or more of the following areas: historical time period, geographic setting, theme, character types, plot pattern or premise, writing style, or overall mood or "feel." All suggestions may not appeal to the same person, but it is to be hoped that at least one would appeal to most.

Because romance reading tastes do vary so widely and readers (and writers) often apply vastly differing criteria in determining what makes a romance good, bad, or exceptional, I cannot claim that the following list of recommendations consists solely of the "best" romance novels of the year. (In fact many of these received no awards or special recognition at all.) It is simply a selection of books that the romance contributors, John Charles and Shelley Mosley, and I found particularly interesting; perhaps some of these will appeal to you, too.

Between the Sheets by Robin Wells

Blame It on Paris by Jennifer Greene

Dark Seduction by Kathleen Korbel

Deep Dish by Mary Kay Andrews

The Healer by Sharon Sala

His Dark and Dangerous Ways by Edith Layton

The Kiss by Sophia Nash

A Lady's Secret by Jo Beverley

Moonstruck by Susan Grant

The Murder Game by Beverly Barton

Mystic Horseman by Kathleen Eagle

On My Terms by Shirley Hailstock

The Paper Marriage by Susan Kay Law

Pitch Black by Susan Crandall

Private Arrangements by Sherry Thomas

Silent Run by Barbara Freethy

Simply Perfect by Mary Balogh

Skinny Dipping by Connie Brockway

The Third Circle by Amanda Quick

This is How It Happened (Not a Love Story) by Jo Barrett

To Wed a Texan by Georgina Gentry

Twisted Creek by Jodi Thomas

Wild and Hexy by Vicki Lewis Thompson

Wild Jinx by Sandra Hill

Your Scandalous Ways by Loretta Chase

For Further Reference

Publisher Websites and Book Clubs

In addition to going to the general websites of online book suppliers like Amazon.com and traditional bookstores such as Borders and Barnes & Noble, readers can now order books in print and/or e-book, and in some cases downloadable audio formats directly from a number of individual publishers' websites. Many of these websites also feature reviews, information on any subscription book clubs the publisher has, and ways for readers to connect with each other. Several of these, (e. g., Avalon, Five Star) target the library market and have standing order plans available. Services vary from website to website; several of the more popular are listed below.

Publishers

Avalon Books. www.avalonbooks.com

Barbour Publishing (Heartsong Presents). www. barbourbooks.com (See Heartsong Presents book club information below.)

Cerridwen Press. www.cerridwenpress.com

Ellora's Cave. www.ellorascave.com

Five Star. www.galegroup.com/fivestar

HarperCollins/Avon Books. www.harpercollins.com (choose Avon Romance in the Categories menu box)

Dorchester Publishing (Leisure and Love Spell). www. dorchesterpub.com. See website for book club information.

Harlequin Books (Harlequin, Silhouette, Spice, MIRA, Red Dress Ink, Luna, HQN, Steeple Hill, Kimani Press, Worldwide Library). eharlequin.com

Kensington Books (Zebra, Dafina, Brava, Strapless, Aphrodisia, Urban Soul, Pinnacle). www.kensingtonbooks. com.

Medallion Press. www.medallionpress.com

Penguin Group. (Berkley, Putnam, Signet, NAL, Jove, Plume, Dutton, Onyx) us.penguingroup.com (Choose Romance under the Special Interests pull-down menu.)

Red Sage Publishing. www.redsagepub.com

Simon and Schuster (Pocket) www.simonsays.com (Choose Browse All Books and then choose the link for Romance)

Sourcebooks, Inc. (Sourcebooks Casablanca) www. sourcebooks.com (Choose the link for Literature and then Fiction. Romance is not listed separately.)

Tom Doherty Associates. (Tor Paranormal Romance) us. macmillan.com/TorForge.aspx (Choose Books and then Romance on the dropdown menu.)

Selected Book Clubs and Mail Order Services

Dorchester Book Clubs. Provides Love Spell and Leisure romance titles, as well as those of several other fiction genres, on a monthly subscription basis. Check the website for club options and subscription information. http://www.dorchesterpub.com/Dorch/BookClub.cfm

Harlequin Romance Book Clubs. Provides books in the Harlequin and Silhouette series on a monthly subscription basis. Check the website below for series descriptions and price information. http://www.bookclubdeals.com/harlequin-book-clubs.html

Heartsong Presents. Provides contemporary and historical Christian romances, published by Barbour Publishing company on a subscription basis. Check the website for titles, price, and subscription information. http://www.heartsongpresents.com

Rhapsody: The Romance Lover's Book Club. Offered through Booksonline.com, a direct marketer created through a partnership between Doubleday Direct, Inc. and Book-of-the-Month club Holdings LLC, Rhapsody provides romances from a variety of sources on a subscription basis. Check the website, phone, or write for more information. http://www.rhapsodybookclub.com

Conferences

Numerous conferences are held each year for writers and readers of romance fiction. Two of the more important national ones are listed below. For a more complete listing, particularly of regional or local conferences designed primarily for romance writers, consult the *Romance Writers' Report*, a monthly publication of The Romance Writers of America or visit their website [www.rwanational.org].

Annual RT Book Lovers Convention is sponsored by *Romantic Times Book Club Magazine*. The 25th Annual RT Book Lovers Convention was held on April 16-20, 2008, in Pittsburgh, Pennsylvania. (This organization also sponsors a number of romance-related tours for readers and writers.) The 26th Annual Book Lovers Convention is scheduled to be held April 22-26, 2009, in Orlando, Florida.

RWA Annual Conference is sponsored by Romance Writers of America and usually held in July. The 2008 Conference was held July 30-August 2 in San Francisco, California. The 2009 conference is scheduled for July 15-18th in Washington, D.C. This "working" conference is aimed at romance writers, editor, librarians, and other romance professionals, rather than fans and readers.

Romance Titles

200

SHANA ABE

Queen of Dragons
(New York: Bantam, 2008)

Story type: Historical/Fantasy
Series: Drakon. Book 3
Subject(s): Dragons; Magic
Major character(s): Maricara, Mythical Creature (dragon), Royalty (princess); Kimber Langford, Mythical Creature (dragon), Nobleman (Earl of Chasen)
Time period(s): 1780s (1782)
Locale(s): England; Transylvania

Summary: The *drakon* of Darkfrith thought they were the only dragons in the world until Kimber Langford, the Earl of Chasen and Alpha Lord of the Darkfrith *drakons*, discovers another tribe living in the mountains of Transylvania. At first, all of Kimber's efforts to establish diplomatic ties with the Transylvanian *drakons* are politely declined by their ruler, Maricara. Several years later, though, when the bodies of English *drakons* begin turning up in her kingdom, Maricara realizes a dragon hunter has also discovered the dragons, which gives Maricara no choice but to agree to work with Kimber to stop the murders.

Where it's reviewed:
Romantic Times, January 2008, page 45

Other books by the same author:
The Dream Thief, 2006
The Smoke Thief, 2005
The Last Mermaid, 2004
The Secret Swan, 2001
Intimate Enemies, 2000

Other books you might like:
Jo Beverley, *Forbidden Magic*, 1998
Susan Carroll, *The Bride Finder*, 1998
Tracy Fobes, *My Enchanted Enemy*, 2002
Mary Jo Putney, *The Marriage Spell*, 2006
Patricia Rice, *This Magic Moment*, 2002

201

BELLA ANDRE

Game for Anything
(New York: Pocket Books, 2008)

Story type: Contemporary; Humor
Subject(s): Sports/Football; Humor; Self-Awareness
Major character(s): Julie Spencer, Businesswoman (image consultant); Ty Calhoun, Sports Figure (star quarterback, Outlaws)
Time period(s): 2000s
Locale(s): San Francisco, California

Summary: Star quarterback Ty Calhoun's reputation as the bad boy of football goes against everything the new owner stands for. Julie Spencer, an image consultant, is hired to do a makeover of the celebrity playboy that will change the media's—and thus, the public's—view of him. Unfortunately, Ty is the one Julie lost her virginity to in high school, and now that they're together, passion is overriding her good sense.

Other books by the same author:
Red Hot Reunion, 2007
Tempt Me, Taste Me, Touch Me, Take Me, 2007
Take Me, 2005

Other books you might like:
Susan Donovan, *The Kept Woman*, 2006
Michele Dunaway, *Hart's Victory*, 2007
Jane Heller, *An Ex to Grind*, 2005
Susan Elizabeth Phillips, *Heaven, Texas*, 1995
Pat White, *Ring around My Heart*, 2004

202

MARY KAY ANDREWS

Deep Dish
(New York: Harper, 2008)

Story type: Humor; Contemporary
Subject(s): Humor; Cooks and Cooking; Television Programs
Major character(s): Gina Foxton, Television Personality (cooking show, "Fresh Start"), Cook; Tate Moody,

Television Personality (cooking show, "Vittles"), Cook
Time period(s): 2000s
Locale(s): Atlanta, Georgia

Summary: When television cooking celebrity Gina Foxton's producer-boyfriend has an affair with the sponsor's wife, Gina's show, "Fresh Start," is canceled. Now, she's being considered for a national show on the Cooking Channel. It's not a done deal, though. Also in the running is Tate "Kill It and Grill It" Moody, whose show, "Vittles," is as charming as its host. Cook-offs were never so much fun.

Where it's reviewed:
Publishers Weekly, December 12, 2007, page 49

Other books by the same author:
Blue Christmas, 2006
Savannah Breeze, 2006
Hissy Fit, 2004
Little Bitty Lies, 2003
Savannah Blues, 2002

Other books you might like:
Millie Criswell, *The Trouble with Mary*, 2001
Susan Mallery, *Delicious*, 2006
Deirdre Martin, *Just a Taste*, 2008
Nora Roberts, *Waiting for Nick*, 1997
Deborah Shelley, *My Favorite Flavor*, 2000

203

KATE ANGELL (Pseudonym of Roberta Brown)

Strike Zone
(New York: Love Spell, 2008)

Story type: Contemporary; Humor
Subject(s): Sports/Baseball; Humor; Adventure and Adventurers
Major character(s): Taylor Hannah, Businesswoman (adventure guide), Adventurer; Brek Stryker, Sports Figure (baseball pitcher)
Time period(s): 2000s
Locale(s): Richmond, Virginia; La Grave, France

Summary: Taylor Hannah, known for her sense of adventure, fearlessness, and penchant for thrill seeking, suddenly turns chicken on her wedding day and leaves the groom at the altar. Three years later, Taylor feels like she's closer to being able to settle down, so she comes back home to reclaim the love of her life, Brek Stryker. Brek, star pitcher of the Rogues, still has a warm place in his heart for Taylor, but he's afraid if he commits to marriage, she'll just run again. Now Taylor will do anything—anything—to win him back.

Where it's reviewed:
Romantic Times, April 2008, page 93

Other books by the same author:
Curveball, 2007
Squeeze Play, 2006
Crazy for You, 2005
Drive Me Crazy, 2004
Calder's Rose, 2003

Other books you might like:
Lori Foster, *Causing Havoc*, 2007
  SBC Fighters. Book 1
Rachel Gibson, *Not Another Bad Date*, 2008
Deirdre Martin, *Chasing Stanley*, 2007
Susan Elizabeth Phillips, *Natural Born Charmer*, 2008
Pat White, *Love on the Ropes*, 2006

204

AMANDA ASHLEY (Pseudonym of Madeline Baker)

Dead Perfect
(New York: Zebra, 2008)

Story type: Contemporary; Vampire Story
Subject(s): Vampires; Paranormal
Major character(s): Shannah, Impostor, Invalid (dying); Ronan Dark, Vampire, Writer (romance)
Time period(s): 2000s
Locale(s): California

Summary: Dying of a rare blood disease, Shannah follows Ronan for months, thinking he might be a vampire and hoping he can save her life. Without her knowledge, he gives her some of his blood, restoring her health, at least temporarily. Attracted to Shannah, Ronan, a vampire and romance writer who hides his masculinity behind female pseudonyms, convinces her to impersonate him for publicity tours. As they spend more time together, their mutual attraction grows, but so does the dilemma that Ronan faces: should he change Shannah into a vampire in order to save her life, or not?

Where it's reviewed:
Romantic Times, February 2008, page 102

Other books by the same author:
Dead Sexy, 2007
Desire After Dark, 2006
Night's Kiss, 2005
After Sundown, 2003
Midnight Embrace, 2002

Other books you might like:
Christine Feehan, *Dark Secret*, 2005
Christine Feehan, *Dark Symphony*, 2003
Laurell K. Hamilton, *Bite*, 2005
  vampire anthology
Sherrilyn Kenyon, *Fantasy Lover*, 2002
Maggie Shayne, *Twilight Hunter*, 2002

205

JENNIFER ASHLEY

Highlander Ever After
(New York: Leisure, 2008)

Story type: Historical/Fantasy; Historical/Regency
Series: Nvengaria. Book 3
Subject(s): Courtship; Family Relations; Magic
Major character(s): Zarabeth, Royalty (Princess of Nvengaria); Egan MacDonald, Laird

Time period(s): 1820s (1820)
Locale(s): Scotland

Summary: When her ex-husband tried to take over the throne of Nvengaria from her cousin, Princess Zarabeth used her gift for reading other's thoughts to stop the scheme from succeeding. Now in danger from her vengeful ex-husband, Zarabeth flees Nvengaria for Scotland, where she will stay with her old friend Egan MacDonald, who is one person whose thoughts Zarabeth could never read. As Zarabeth tries not only to stay one step ahead of assassins sent by her ex-husband but also help the Mac-Donalds break an old family curse, she realizes that her life would be so much easier if she could just know exactly what Egan is thinking.

Where it's reviewed:
Booklist, March 15, 2008, page 34
Romantic Times, April 2008, page 48

Other books by the same author:
Immortals: The Calling, 2007
Immortals: The Gathering, 2007
The Queen's Handmaiden, 2007
Penelope and Prince Charming, 2006
The Mad, Bad Duke, 2006

Other books you might like:
Shana Abe, *The Smoke Thief*, 2005
Naomi Bellis, *Step into Darkness*, 2006
Margo Maguire, *A Warrior's Taking*, 2007
Susan Spencer Paul, *Touch of Night*, 2005

206

ADELE ASHWORTH (Pseudonym of Adele Budnick)

A Notorious Proposition
(New York: Avon, 2008)

Story type: Historical/Victorian
Subject(s): Identity, Concealed; Secrets
Major character(s): Ivy Wentworth, Noblewoman, Spy;
   Garrett Burke, Nobleman, Spy
Time period(s): 1850s (1850; 1852)
Locale(s): England

Summary: Ivy Wentworth comes to Winter Garden to investigate rumors that the Rothebury estate, the new home of the Marquess of Rye, is haunted. Garrett Burke has also come to Winter Garden to investigate the mysterious disappearance of the estate's previous owner, which Garrett believes is somehow connected to the missing Martello diamonds. WIth their complicated romantic history, the last thing Ivy wants to do is work with Garrett, but since both of their cases seem to be connected, Ivy has no choice but to agree to a partnership with Garrett.

Where it's reviewed:
Romantic Times, May 2008, page 44

Other books by the same author:
The Duke's Indiscretion, 2007
Duke of Scandal, 2006
Duke of Sin, 2004
When It's Perfect, 2002
Someone Irresistible, 2001

Other books you might like:
Christina Dodd, *In My Wildest Dreams*, 2001
Lisa Kleypas, *Lady Sophia's Lover*, 2002
Julianne MacLean, *Surrender to a Scoundrel*, 2007
Melody Thomas, *Sin and Scandal in England*, 2007

207

MARY BALOGH

The Devil's Web
(New York: Dell, 2008)

Story type: Regency
Series: Web. Book 3
Subject(s): Courtship; Scandal; Secrets
Major character(s): Lady Madeline Raine, Noblewoman;
   James Purnell, Nobleman, Businessman (fur trader)
Time period(s): 1810s
Locale(s): England

Summary: Returning to England after an absence of four years after becoming a partner in a Canadian fur trading firm, James Purnell, encounters Lady Madeline Raine, the woman he left but could never forget. Their passion remains, but this issue now is are two so different people able to overcome their backgrounds and personality issues and make their relationship work? This classic romance was first published by Signet in 1990.

Other books by the same author:
Simply Perfect, 2008
Simply Love, 2007
Simply Magic, 2007
The Gilded Web, 2006 (reprint of a 1990 title)
The Web of Love, 2006 (reprint of a 1989 title)

Other books you might like:
Liz Carlyle, *The Devil You Know*, 2003
Eloisa James, *Duchess in Love*, 2002
Sabrina Jeffries, *Only a Duke Will Do*, 2006
Edith Layton, *The Cad*, 1998
Donna Simpson, *Lady Delafont's Dilemma*, 2000

208

MARY BALOGH

Simply Perfect
(New York: Delacorte, 2008)

Story type: Historical/Regency
Series: Miss Martin's School for Girls. Book 4
Subject(s): Courtship; Social Classes; Children
Major character(s): Claudia Martin, Teacher; Joseph
   Fawcitt, Nobleman (Marquess of Attingsborough)
Time period(s): 1810s
Locale(s): England

Summary: When Claudia Martin agrees, somewhat against her better judgment, to allow the attractive Marquess of Attingsborough to escort her and two students to London, she has no idea that this will result in an invitation for Claudia and some of her students to spend the summer at a country estate—and that the Marquess will be part

of it. Well-drawn supporting characters, appealing protagonists, and exceptional writing result in a brilliant conclusion to Balogh's series.

Where it's reviewed:
Booklist, February 15, 2008, page 42
Library Journal, February 15, 2008, page 86
Publishers Weekly, January 21, 2008, page 151
Romantic Times, April 2008, page 39

Other books by the same author:
Simply Magic, 2007 (Miss Martin's School for Girls. Book 3)
Simply Love, 2006 (Miss Martin's School for Girls. Book 2)
Simply Unforgettable, 2005 (Miss Martin's School for Girls. Book 1)
Slightly Dangerous, 2004
Slightly Sinful, 2004

Other books you might like:
Candice Hern, *Once a Gentleman*, 2004
Brenda Hiatt, *Rogue's Honor*, 2001
Sabrina Jeffries, *Let Sleeping Rogues Lie*, 2008
Stephanie Laurens, *A Rake's Vow*, 1998
Johanna Lindsey, *A Loving Scoundrel*, 2004

209

NINA BANGS

One Bite Stand

(New York: Leisure, 2008)

Story type: Paranormal; Humor
Subject(s): Humor; Vampires; Family Relations
Major character(s): Daria, Mythical Creature (Harpy), Hotel Worker (night manager); Declan MacKenzie, Vampire
Time period(s): 2000s
Locale(s): Tartarus, Mythical Place

Summary: Daria is a failure as a harpy—never ugly enough, never nasty enough. She eventually gets a job a the Woo Woo Inn as their night manager, but things aren't always easy for her there, either. For starters, a monster begins snacking on the guests. Even Daria's personal life gets complicated, especially since the man she loves is a vampire.

Where it's reviewed:
Booklist, February 1, 2008, page 34
Romantic Times, January 2008, page 94

Other books by the same author:
Eternal Pleasure, 2008
Wicked Fantasy, 2007
Wicked Pleasure, 2007
The Pleasure Master, 2005
Wicked Nights, 2005

Other books you might like:
Judi McCoy, *Almost a Goddess*, 2006
Stephanie Rowe, *Date Me Baby, One More Time*, 2006
Lynsay Sands, *Vampire, Interrupted*, 2008

Argeneau. Book 9
Vicki Lewis Thompson, *Wild and Hexy*, 2008
Minda Webber, *Bustin'*, 2007

210

L.A. BANKS (Pseudonym of Leslie Esdaile Banks)

Bad Blood

(New York: St. Martin's Paperbacks, 2008)

Story type: Contemporary/Fantasy; Werewolf Story
Series: Crimson Moon. Book 1
Subject(s): Werewolves; Politics; Secrets
Major character(s): Sasha Trudeau, Military Personnel (special ops agent), Werewolf (shadow wolf); Max Hunter, Werewolf (shadow wolf); Shogun, Werewolf
Time period(s): 2000s
Locale(s): Earth

Summary: One of a special team of special ops werewolf hunter agents who have been infected with the werewolf virus, Sasha Trudeau is surprised to be sent on a mission alone. However, as a loyal soldier she heads for Korea and is stunned to learn that normal werewolves are nothing like the rogues she and her team have been hunting and she begins to question what she has been told by her superiors. Once back home, a meeting with sexy Max Hunter, a wolf who tells her she is part of his pack, verifies her suspicions and sends her running for safety. Violence and intrigue are interwoven with Native American mysticism and fantasy lore in this first volume in Banks' urban fantasy series.

Where it's reviewed:
Romantic Times, April 2008, page 108

Other books by the same author:
The Cursed, 2008 (Vampire Huntress Legends)
The Darkness, 2008 (Vampire Huntress Legends)
The Wicked, 2007 (Vampire Huntress Legends)
The Hunted, 2005 (Vampire Huntress Legends)
Minion, 2004 (Vampire Huntress Legends)

Other books you might like:
Christine Feehan, *Shadow Game*, 2003
Kim Harrison, *The Outlaw Demon Wails*, 2008
Liz Maverick, *Crimson City*, 2005
Liz Maverick, *The Shadow Runners*, 2004
Rebecca York, *New Moon*, 2007

211

MICHELE BARDSLEY

Because Your Vampire Said So

(New York: Signet Eclipse, 2008)

Story type: Contemporary/Fantasy; Paranormal
Series: Broken Heart, Oklahoma. Book 3
Subject(s): Demons; Vampires
Major character(s): Patsy Donahue, Vampire, Hairdresser (beauty salon owner); Gabriel, Werewolf
Time period(s): 2000s
Locale(s): Broken Heart, Oklahoma

Summary: Dealing with being a vampire, raising her wild teenage son, and keeping her beauty salon afloat, is just about all Patsy Donahue can handle. Unfortunately, things are about to get worse as an increasing number of supernaturals come to Broken Heart because of an ancient prophecy and evil is threatening the town. Patsy's romantic interest comes in the form of sexy shapeshifter Lycan Gabriel, who is determined that he and Patsy will mate and she will become queen and save the day. Plenty of humor, weird characters and happenings, and steamy sex add to this funny romp.

Where it's reviewed:
Romantic Times, May 2008, page 93

Other books by the same author:
Don't Talk Back to Your Vampire, 2007 (Broken Heart, Oklahoma. Book 2)
Fantasyland, 2007
Cupid, Inc., 2006
I'm the Vampire, That's Why, 2006 (Broken Heart, Oklahoma. Book 1)

Other books you might like:
Dakota Cassidy, *The Accidental Werewolf*, 2008
MaryJanice Davidson, *Dead over Heels*, 2008 collection
Katie MacAlister, *Even Vampires Get the Blues*, 2006
Katie MacAlister, *Playing with Fire*, 2008
Lynsay Sands, *Bite Me If You Can*, 2007

212

JO BARRETT

This Is How It Happened (Not a Love Story)

(New York: Avon, 2008)

Story type: Contemporary; Humor
Subject(s): Revenge; Cheating; Humor
Major character(s): Madeline Piatro, Businesswoman, Public Relations; Nick Montana, Government Official (DEA), Investigator
Time period(s): 2000s
Locale(s): Austin, Texas

Summary: It was her business plan, but Madeline Piatro's scum-bucket fiance, Carlton Connors, stole it, took credit for it, and cheated her out of a fortune. All Madeline can think of is revenge—specifically, how to kill Carlton. Eventually, she hires a deceptively gentle hit man, who's all too eager to do her bidding. The only thing that stands in Madeline's way is DEA agent Nick Montana, and she's beginning to like him a little too much.

Where it's reviewed:
Booklist, February 1, 2008, page 33

Other books by the same author:
The Men's Guide to the Women's Bathroom, 2007

Other books you might like:
Beverly Brandt, *Match Game*, 2006
Jennifer Crusie, *Tell Me Lies*, 1999
Janet Evanovich, *Lean Mean Thirteen*, 2007
Lisa Plumley, *Perfect Together*, 2003
Vicki Lewis Thompson, *My Nerdy Valentine*, 2007

213

BEVERLY BARTON (Pseudonym of Beverly Beaver)

The Murder Game

(New York: Zebra, 2008)

Story type: Contemporary; Romantic Suspense
Subject(s): Murder; Serial Killers; Suspense
Major character(s): Nicole Baxter, FBI Agent; Griffin Powell, Detective—Private; Pudge, Serial Killer (Hunter)
Time period(s): 2000s
Locale(s): South

Summary: A sadistic killer, the cousin and partner of the killer who died in *The Dying Game*, starts another murderous game that draws PI Griffin Powell and FBI Agent Nicole Baxter into his dangerous web. Arrogant and clever, the killer intends Nic as his ultimate victim, unless Griff and Nic can outwit him and beat him at his own game. A chilling thriller.

Where it's reviewed:
Romantic Times, February 2008, page 74

Other books by the same author:
Cold Hearted, 2008
A Time to Die, 2007
The Dying Game, 2007
Close Enough to Kill, 2006
Killing Her Softly, 2005

Other books you might like:
Allison Brennan, *Killing Fear*, 2008
Allison Brennan, *Speak No Evil*, 2007
J.D. Robb, *Conspiracy in Death*, 1999 futuristic
Karen Rose, *Die for Me*, 2008
Karen Rose, *I'm Watching You*, 2004

214

ADRIENNE BASSO

How to Enjoy a Scandal

(New York: Zebra, 2008)

Story type: Historical/Regency
Subject(s): Identity, Concealed; Secrets; Seduction
Major character(s): Gwendolyn Ellingham, Gentlewoman; Jason Barrington, Nobleman
Time period(s): 1810s (1817)
Locale(s): Yorkshire, England

Summary: When Gwendolyn Ellingham discovers her sister Dorothea has come up with a plan to trap Jasper Barrington, Viscount Fairhurst, into marrying her, she sets out to stop Dorothea. Fortunately, Gwen is able to get Dorothea out of the married nobleman's bedroom before anyone except for Jasper spots her. Now in exchange for his silence, Gwen must agree to accompany Jasper to a series of local social events. What Gwen doesn't know is that Jasper is really Jason, Jasper's younger twin brother, and that the more time she spends

with him, the more tempted Gwen is to ruin her own reputation all over again.

Where it's reviewed:
Booklist, April 1, 2008, page 35
Romantic Times, April 2008, page 46

Other books by the same author:
The Christmas Heiress, 2006
The Wedding Deception, 2005
To Tempt a Rogue, 2004
To Protect an Heiress, 2002
To Wed a Viscount, 2001

Other books you might like:
Mary Balogh, *Slightly Married*, 2003
Kathryn Caskie, *Love Is in the Heir*, 2006
Candice Hern, *Once a Scoundrel*, 2003
Stephanie Laurens, *On a Wild Night*, 2002
Sari Robins, *More than a Scandal*, 2005

215

ANYA BAST

Witch Blood

(New York: Berkley Sensation, 2008)

Story type: Contemporary; Paranormal
Series: Elemental Witches. Book 2
Subject(s): Witches and Witchcraft; Magic; Demons
Major character(s): Isabelle Novak, Witch (water witch); Thomas Monahan, Witch (earth witch)
Time period(s): 2000s
Locale(s): Illinois

Summary: On a mission of vengeance after a demon named Boyle killed her sister, water witch Isabelle Novak forsakes the "Harm Ye None" vows of her Coven and almost kills another demon before she is stopped by coven head Thomas Monahan. Both Isabelle and Thomas want to find and stop Boyle, so they join forces, but also find passion and romance along the way. A pair of powerful witches, a demon with a diabolical plan, and plenty of hot passion nicely continue Bast's Elemental Witches series.

Where it's reviewed:
Romantic Times, March 2008, page 104

Other books by the same author:
Witch Fire, 2007 (Elemental Witches. Book 1)
Blood of the Angel, 2005
Water Crystal, 2005
Blood of the Raven, 2005
Blood of the Rose, 2004

Other books you might like:
Meljean Brook, *Demon Moon*, 2007
Yasmine Galenorn, *Darkling*, 2008
Kim Harrison, *The Outlaw Demon Wails*, 2008
Angela Knight, *Master of the Night*, 2004
Noelle Mack, *Wild*, 2008
    historical

216

ZELDA BENJAMIN (Pseudonym of Zelda Piskosz)

Chocolate Secrets

(New York: Avalon, 2008)

Story type: Contemporary
Subject(s): Feuds; Trust; Astrology
Major character(s): Alex Martinelli, Nurse; Mike Simone, Fire Fighter
Time period(s): 2000s
Locale(s): New York, New York

Summary: Nurse Alex Martinelli spends what little spare time she has helping Grandpa Max with his small, candy-making business. During the Atlantic Avenue Fair, Max is severely burned by a cooking fire, and firefighter Mike Simone rescues him. It's love at first sight for Mike and Alex. Unfortunately, the Simones and Martinellis have feuded for decades over a stolen chocolate recipe, and so far as Max is concerned, Alex will date Mike over his dead body.

Other books by the same author:
Brooklyn Ballerina, 2001

Other books you might like:
Julie Carobini, *Chocolate Beach*, 2007
Kyra Davis, *Obsession, Deceit, and Really Dark Chocolate*, 2007
Susan Mallery, *Sweet Success*, 2001
Deborah Shelley, *My Favorite Flavor*, 2000
Lori Wick, *White Chocolate Moments*, 2006

217

SARA BENNETT

A Seduction in Scarlet

(New York: Avon, 2008)

Story type: Historical/Victorian
Subject(s): Seduction; Identity, Concealed
Major character(s): Portia Ellerslie, Noblewoman (Lady Ellerslie), Widow(er); Marcus Worthorne, Nobleman
Time period(s): 1850s
Locale(s): England

Summary: Wanting a bit of passion in her life, Portia, the highly respectable friend and confidant of the proper Queen Victoria, seeks the help of renowned courtesan Aphrodite. Her incognito romantic interlude with Marcus Worthorne is the memorable result, but Marcus wants more—and isn't about to stop until he discovers who she is. Hidden identities, an assassination plot, and sizzling sex keep readers entertained in this hot romantic adventure.

Where it's reviewed:
Romantic Times, January 2008, page 46

Other books by the same author:
Lessons in Seduction, 2005

Other books you might like:
Candice Hern, *In the Thrill of the Night*, 2006
Candice Hern, *Just One of Those Flings*, 2006
Eloisa James, *Duchess by Night*, 2008
Susan Johnson, *Legendary Lover*, 2000
Sophie Jordan, *One Night with You*, 2008

218

RENEE BERNARD

A Rogue's Game

(New York: Pocket, 2008)

Story type: Historical
Series: Mistress Trilogy. Book 3
Subject(s): Gambling; Deception; Identity, Concealed
Major character(s): Eve Reynolds, Gambler (cards), Con Artist; Julian Clay, Nobleman (Earl of Westleigh), Gambler
Time period(s): 19th century
Locale(s): England

Summary: A deceptively innocent-looking heroine plans to use her card playing abilities to win enough money to retire to the country, away from her conman uncle, but she attracts the attention of the Earl of Westleigh, a noted rake who has plans for her of his own. This sexy sizzler completes Bernard's Mistress trilogy.

Where it's reviewed:
Romantic Times, May 2008, page 38

Other books by the same author:
Madame's Deception, 2007 (Mistress Trilogy. Book 2)
A Lady's Pleasure, 2006 (Mistress Trilogy. Book 1)

Other books you might like:
Gayle Callen, *Never Trust a Scoundrel*, 2008
Christina Dodd, *A Well-Pleasured Lady*, 1997
Lisa Kleypas, *Mine Till Midnight*, 2007
Stephanie Laurens, *On a Wild Night*, 2002
Robin Schone, *The Lady's Tutor*, 1999

219

ELIZABETH BEVARLY

Fast and Loose

(New York: Berkley Sensation, 2008)

Story type: Contemporary
Subject(s): Art; Friendship; Horse Racing
Major character(s): Lulu Flannery, Artist; Cole Early, Horse Trainer
Time period(s): 2000s
Locale(s): Kentucky

Summary: It's an easy way to earn some money, and heaven knows Lulu Flannery could use the cash. All Lulu has to do is let her friend Eddie rent out her home during Derby week, but Lulu wants to be certain that the person renting her home will treat her place right. When Lulu discovers that her new house guest is scandalous celebrity trainer Cole Early, she almost cancels the contract, but it turns out to be too late, especially once Cole realizes Lulu is the only woman for him.

Where it's reviewed:
Romantic Times, April 2008, page 93

Other books by the same author:
Married to His Business, 2007
Express Male, 2006
My Only Vice, 2006
Indecent Suggestion, 2005
You've Got Male, 2005

Other books you might like:
Jennifer Crusie, *Anyone but You*, 1996
Jennifer Greene, *Blame It on Chocolate*, 2006
Dorien Kelly, *Hot Nights in Ballymuir*, 2004
Susan Elizabeth Phillips, *Match Me If You Can*, 2005
Deborah Smith, *Charming Grace*, 2004

220

ELIZABETH BEVARLY

Overnight Male

(Don Mills, Ontario: HQN, 2008)

Story type: Romantic Suspense; Humor
Series: OPUS. Book 3
Subject(s): Spies; Espionage; College Life
Major character(s): Lila Moreau, Spy; Joel Faraday, Spy
Time period(s): 2000s
Locale(s): Georgetown, Virginia

Summary: OPUS has given Joel Faraday a new assignment—he has to keep an eye on Lila Moreau, a top agent suspected of rogue activity. Lila's a loner. She doesn't want a partner. Part of her skill as an agent is the ability to remain emotionally detached from any situation. Unfortunately, the longer this mission takes, the less detached Lila is in her feelings for Joel, and she doesn't like it one bit.

Other books by the same author:
Fast and Loose, 2008
Flirting with Trouble, 2008
Destinations South, 2006
Express Male, 2005 (OPUS. Book 2)
You've Got Male, 2005 (OPUS. Book 1)

Other books you might like:
Claire Cross, *Third Time Lucky*, 2005
Kyra Davis, *Passion, Betrayal, and Killer Highlights*, 2007
Suzanne Enoch, *A Touch of Minx*, 2007
Ann Kline, *The Ride to Dinah's Wedding*, 2004
Connie Lane, *Dirty Little Lies*, 2004

221

JO BEVERLEY

A Lady's Secret

(New York: Signet, 2008)

Story type: Historical/Georgian
Subject(s): Identity, Concealed; Secrets

Major character(s): Petra d'Averio, Gentlewoman; Robin Fitzvitry, Nobleman (Earl of Huntersdown)
Time period(s): 1760s (1764)
Locale(s): France; England

Summary: After her widowed mother dies, Petra d'Averio sets out from the convent in Italy where she has lived for many years for England to find her father, whom she believed was dead. While traveling through France disguised as Sister Immaculata, Petra finds herself needing some help escaping from an Italian nobleman who is determined to make her his mistress. When a very bored Robin Fitzvitry, the Earl of Huntersdown, offers to do whatever he can to assist Petra, he quickly finds himself caught up in a dangerous adventure with a lady whose secrets could prove deadly to them both.

Where it's reviewed:
Library Journal, April 15, 2008, page 67
Romantic Times, April 2008, page 39

Other books by the same author:
Lady Beware, 2007
The Rogue's Return, 2006
To Rescue a Rogue, 2006
A Most Unsuitable Man, 2005
Skylark, 2004

Other books you might like:
Elizabeth Boyle, *Brazen Heiress*, 1999
Elizabeth Hoyt, *The Raven Prince*, 2006
Eloisa James, *Desperate Duchesses*, 2007
Patricia Rice, *The Trouble with Magic*, 2003

222

HELEN BIANCHIN

The Martinez Marriage Revenge

(Toronto: Harlequin, 2008)

Story type: Contemporary
Series: Wedlocked!
Subject(s): Marriage; Reunions; Revenge
Major character(s): Shannay Robins Martinez, Pharmacist; Marcello Martinez, Wealthy, Businessman; Nicki Martinez, Child
Time period(s): 2000s
Locale(s): Australia; Madrid, Spain

Summary: After an impulsive marriage to wealthy Marcello Martinez which was being torn apart by his antagonistic family and jealous former lover, Shannay left Spain and headed home to Australia, not realizing she was pregnant. Now, four years later, Marcello has located her and is furious she never told him about his daughter, Nicki. Forcing Shannay and Nicki to accompany him back to Spain, ostensibly to visit the critically ill Martinez family patriarch, Marcello sets about doing what he does best—getting what he wants. What he wants now includes both Nicki and Shannay. This book is one of Harlequin Presents Lovelocked series, stories about couples who are wed but not in love—yet.

Where it's reviewed:
Romantic Times, April 2008, page 114

Other books by the same author:
One-Click Buy, 2008
Purchased: His Perfect Wife, 2008
The Marriage Possession, 2007
The Disobedient Bride, 2005
The Greek's Bought Wife, 2005

Other books you might like:
Catherine George, *The Millionaire's Convenient Bride*, 2008
Lynne Graham, *The Italian Billionaire's Pregnant Bride*, 2008
Kim Lawrence, *The Spaniard's Pregnancy Proposal*, 2008
Anne Mather, *Bedded for the Italian's Pleasure*, 2008
Catherine Spencer, *The Giannakis Bride*, 2008

223

JENNA BLACK

Hungers of the Heart

(New York: Tor Romance, 2008)

Story type: Paranormal
Series: Guardians of the Night. Book 4
Subject(s): Vampires; Murder; Kidnapping
Major character(s): Faith, Vampire, Prostitute (concubine); Drake, Vampire
Time period(s): 2000s
Locale(s): Baltimore, Maryland

Summary: Although Drake is a vampire who actually drinks human blood, he works with the Guardians to keep those who don't deserve to die safe. However, when Gabriel, the new leader of the Baltimore Guardians, is kidnapped and suddenly Drake is dragged into a power struggle that involves murder, seduction, and danger. Reluctant vampire concubine Faith is the romantic interest in this dark, sexy adventure that is fourth in Black's popular Guardians of the Night series.

Where it's reviewed:
Romantic Times, May 2008, page 99

Other books by the same author:
Secrets in the Shadows, 2007 (Guardians of the Night. Book 2)
Shadows on the Soul, 2007 (Guardians of the Night. Book 3)
Watchers in the Night, 2006 (Guardians of the Night. Book 1)

Other books you might like:
Amanda Ashley, *After Sundown*, 2003
Meljean Brook, *Demon Moon*, 2007
  Guardians. Book 4
Alexandra Ivy, *When Darkness Comes*, 2007
  Guardians of Eternity. Book 1
Sherrilyn Kenyon, *Seize the Night*, 2004
Angela Knight, *Master of the Night*, 2004

224

JOANNA BOURNE

The Spymaster's Lady

(New York: Berkley Sensation, 2008)

Story type: Historical/Regency
Subject(s): Espionage
Major character(s): Annique Villiers, Spy ("Fox Cub");
    Robert Grey, Spy
Time period(s): 1800s
Locale(s): France; England

Summary: British spy Robert Grey goes to France searching for the Albion Plans: Napoleon's scheme to invade England. Believing that Annique Villiers, the French spy known as the Fox Cub, is the key to locating the plans, Robert sets out to find Annique. This proves easier than Robert expected when they both end up sharing the same French prison cell. Now their only hope is if Robert and Annique can learn to trust each other long enough for them to escape from France.

Where it's reviewed:
Booklist, March 15, 2008, page 35
Romantic Times, January 2008, page 44

Other books you might like:
Celeste Bradley, *The Spy*, 2004
Sabrina Jeffries, *Beware a Scot's Revenge*, 2007
Lynn Kerstan, *Dangerous Deceptions*, 2004
Mary Jo Putney, *Thunder and Roses*, 1993
Sari Robins, *When Seducing a Spy*, 2007

225

CELESTE BRADLEY

Desperately Seeking a Duke

(New York: St. Martin's Paperbacks, 2008)

Story type: Historical/Regency
Series: Heiress Brides. Book 1
Subject(s): Marriage; Social Issues; Identity, Concealed
Major character(s): Phoebe Millbury, Gentlewoman
    (vicar's daughter); Rafael Marbrook, Nobleman,
    Bastard Son; Calder Marbrook, Nobleman (Duke of
    Brookhaven)
Time period(s): 1810s (1815)
Locale(s): England

Summary: The first of the three cousins to marry a duke will inherit a fortune according to their grandfather's will, so Phoebe, Deirdre, and Sophie are out to do just that. Problems arise when Phoebe mistakenly accepts a proposal from the Duke of Brookhaven and then realizes he is not the right man. This sexy romp is the first in a projected series.

Where it's reviewed:
Romantic Times, March 2008, page 39

Other books by the same author:
One Night with a Spy, 2006
Surrender to a Wicked Spy, 2005
To Wed a Scandalous Spy, 2005
The Rogue, 2005
The Charmer, 2004

Other books you might like:
Karen Hawkins, *The Abduction of Julia*, 2000
Caroline Linden, *What a Woman Needs*, 2005
Cathy Maxwell, *Married in Haste*, 1999
Kasey Michaels, *The Illusion of Love*, 1994
Joan Wolf, *The Arrangement*, 1997

226

CELESTE BRADLEY

Duke Most Wanted

(New York: St. Martin's Paperbacks, 2008)

Story type: Historical/Regency
Series: Heiress Brides. Book 3
Subject(s): Marriage; Inheritance; Change
Major character(s): Sophie Blake, Gentlewoman, Scholar;
    Graham Cavendish, Nobleman (Duke of Edencourt)
Time period(s): 1810s (1815)
Locale(s): England

Summary: Plain, bright, clumsy Sophie Blake thinks she has no chance of marrying a duke and winning the Pickering fortune; nevertheless, she goes to London simply to enjoy a bit of freedom. Her favorite times are spent with Graham Cavendish, the wild youngest son of the Duke of Edencourt who has no worries about ever becoming the duke, and friendship blossoms between them. Then the current duke and his three eldest sons are killed by elephants in Africa and everything changes. Graham needs to marry money, and Sophie decides that she's going to be the one to win his heart. This charmingly sexy conclusion to The Heiress Brides trilogy also includes a dash of subterfuge and danger that adds to the fun.

Where it's reviewed:
Romantic Times, May 2008, page 38

Other books by the same author:
Desperately Seeking a Duke, 2008 (The Heiress Brides.
    Book 1)
The Duke Next Door, 2008 (The Heiress Brides. Book
    2)
One Night with a Spy, 2006
The Rogue, 2005
To Wed a Scandalous Spy, 2005

Other books you might like:
Suzanne Enoch, *Reforming a Rake*, 2000
Jo Goodman, *All I Ever Needed*, 2003
Amelia Grey, *A Little Mischief*, 2003
Eloisa James, *Pleasure for Pleasure*, 2006
Julia Quinn, *The Viscount Who Loved Me*, 2000

227

CELESTE BRADLEY

The Duke Next Door

(New York: St. Martin's Paperbacks, 2008)

Story type: Historical/Regency
Series: Heiress Brides. Book 2

Romance

Subject(s): Marriage; Inheritance; Secrets
Major character(s): Deirdre Cantor, Gentlewoman; Calder Marbrook, Nobleman (Marquis of Brookhaven), Parent
Time period(s): 1810s (1815)
Locale(s): England

Summary: With one cousin safely wed and ostensibly out of the running for her great-grandfather's fortune, Deirdre Cantor decides it's her turn and boldly proposes to Calder Marbrook, the somewhat notorious heir to a dukedom. Surprised when he accepts, they are quickly wed. Then Deirdre learns he has a young, incorrigible daughter, Meggie, that he expects her to turn into a lady, and life takes an entirely new turn. Angry, but reminded of her own reaction to her father's unfortunate remarriage, Deirdre sets out to win her husband's love—and make him pay!

Where it's reviewed:
Romantic Times, May 2008, page 38

Other books by the same author:
Desperately Seeking a Duke, 2008 (The Heiress Brides. Book 1)
Duke Most Wanted, 2008 (The Heiress Brides. Book 3)
One Night with a Spy, 2006
Surrender to a Wicked Spy, 2005
The Rogue, 2005

Other books you might like:
Victoria Alexander, *The Husband List*, 2000
Madeline Hunter, *Secrets of Surrender*, 2008
Eloisa James, *Kiss Me, Annabel*, 2005
    Essex Sisters. Book 2
Eloisa James, *The Taming of the Duke*, 2006
    Essex Sisters. Book 3
Cathy Maxwell, *Married in Haste*, 1999

228

HELEN BRENNA

Peak Performance

(Toronto: Harlequin, 2008)

Story type: Contemporary
Series: NASCAR Secrets and Legends. Book 6
Subject(s): Sports/Auto Racing; Family; Careers
Major character(s): Rachel Murphy, Mechanic (race cars), Designer (car engines); Payton Reese, Journalist (sportscaster), Mountaineer (former)
Time period(s): 2000s
Locale(s): Mooresville, North Carolina

Summary: Rachel Murphy, part of a legendary NASCAR racing family, wants only to be a crew chief and engine builder. Payton Reese, mountain climber turned sportscaster, wants off the NASCAR beat as soon as he can wangle something better, preferably hosting an extreme sports show for a national network. There is no way he'd want to stay in the North Carolina hinterlands where NASCAR was the focus of life. No way, until he met Rachel Murphy and the sparks began to fly in unexpected directions. This lively romance is part of the Secrets and Legends NASCAR 2008 continuity series.

Where it's reviewed:
Library Journal, April 15, 2008, page 67
Romantic Times, May 2008, page 112

Other books by the same author:
Finding Mr. Right, 2008
Dad for Life, 2007
Treasure, 2007

Other books you might like:
Bethany Campbell, *Truth and Consequences*, 2008
    NASCAR Secrets and Legends. Book 4
Marissa Carroll, *Forbidden Attraction*, 2008
    NASCAR Secrets and Legends. Book 1
Abby Gaines, *Fully Engaged*, 2008
    NASCAR Secrets and Legends. Book 3
Anna Schmidt, *Slingshot Moves*, 2008
    NASCAR Secrets and Legends. Book 5
Gina Wilkins, *In High Gear*, 2008
    NASCAR Secrets and Legends. Book 2

229

ALLISON BRENNAN

Killing Fear

(New York: Ballantine, 2008)

Story type: Contemporary; Romantic Suspense
Series: Prison Break. Book 1
Subject(s): Serial Killers; Revenge; Murder
Major character(s): Robin McKenna, Businesswoman (dance club owner), Stripper (former exotic dancer); Will Hooper, Detective—Police; Theodore Glenn, Serial Killer, Lawyer
Time period(s): 2000s
Locale(s): California

Summary: Convicted of a series of murders seven years earlier, sociopath Theodore Glenn has escaped from San Quentin (thanks to an earthquake) and is on a mission to make the people who put him in prison pay—with fear, pain, and death. His prime targets are Detective Will Hooper and former stripper Robin McKenna, and Glenn methodically sets out to inflict as much terror and emotional pain on them as possible before he makes his final move. An unexpected twist adds complexity to this chilling, truly frightening story.

Where it's reviewed:
Romantic Times, February 2008, page 78

Other books by the same author:
Tempting Evil, 2008 (Prison Break. Book 2)
Fear No Evil, 2007
Speak No Evil, 2007
See No Evil, 2007
The Hunt, 2006

Other books you might like:
Beverly Barton, *Close Enough to Kill*, 2006
Beverly Barton, *The Murder Game*, 2008
Lisa Jackson, *Absolute Fear*, 2007
S.K. McClafferty, *Be Very Afraid*, 2004
Karen Rose, *I'm Watching You*, 2004

230

BARBARA BRETTON

Just Desserts

(New York: Jove, 2008)

Story type: Contemporary
Subject(s): Inheritance; Surprises; Family Relations
Major character(s): Hayley Maitland Goldstein, Baker, Store Owner (bakery); Finn Rafferty, Lawyer
Time period(s): 2000s
Locale(s): New York; New Jersey

Summary: Thrilled but somewhat suspicious when Finn Rafferty, a smooth Manhattan lawyer, arrives at her bakery in a small town in South Jersey and hires her to bake a cake for a rock star, Hayley Goldstein reluctantly agrees. Her bakery is having financial problems and this job just might solve them, as well as give her bakery the cache it needs. What she doesn't know, however, is that Finn suspects that rock star Tommy Stiles is actually her father and the cake baking job is merely a ploy to check her out and arrange for Tommy to meet her. The truth, of course, shakes her peaceful life to its core. Laced with humor and warmth, this multi-layered story overflows with likable characters and numerous plot threads.

Where it's reviewed:
Romantic Times, March 2008, page 96

Other books by the same author:
Just Like Heaven, 2007
Someone Like You, 2005
Chances Are, 2004
Girls of Summer, 2003
Shore Lights, 2003

Other books you might like:
Barbara Delinsky, *The Passions of Chelsea Kane*, 1992
Barbara Freethy, *The Sweetest Thing*, 1999
Kristin Hannah, *Summer Island*, 2001
Kathleen Gilles Seidel, *Summer's End*, 1999
Susan Wiggs, *Snowfall at Willow Lake*, 2008

231

TERRI BRISBIN

Surrender to the Highlander

(Toronto: Harlequin, 2008)

Story type: Historical/Medieval
Subject(s): Family; Identity, Concealed; Secrets
Major character(s): Margriet Gunnarsdottir, Noblewoman; Rurik Erengislsson, Knight
Time period(s): 14th century (1356)
Locale(s): Scotland

Summary: After spending the last ten years in exile, Rurik Erengislsson has been give an opportunity to return home and reclaim his rightful inheritance. First, however, Rurik must complete one task: bring Lady Margriet Gunnarsdottir home to her father. Rurik thought that this would be easy until he arrives at the Convent of the Blessed Virgin and discovers Margriet is a nun!

Where it's reviewed:
Romantic Times, February 2008, page 48

Other books by the same author:
The Earl's Secret, 2007
Taming the Highlander, 2006
The Maid of Lorne, 2006
The Duchess's Next Husband, 2005
The King's Mistress, 2005

Other books you might like:
Shari Anton, *The Ideal Husband*, 2003
Madeline Hunter, *By Arrangement*, 2000
Betina Krahn, *The Wife Test*, 2003
Mary Reed McCall, *Beyond Temptation*, 2005
Anne Stuart, *Hidden Honor*, 2004

232

CONNIE BROCKWAY

Skinny Dipping

(New York: Onyx, 2008)

Story type: Contemporary
Subject(s): Family Relations; Psychic Powers; Responsibility
Major character(s): Mignonette "Mimi" Olson, Psychic (second sight); Joe Tierney, Businessman (company field assessor); Prescott Tierney, Teenager
Time period(s): 2000s
Locale(s): Fowl Lake, Minnesota; Minneapolis, Minnesota

Summary: An expert at living an irresponsible life, psychic Mimi Olson is not about to let her large, extended family sell the lakeside estate, Chez Ducky, that has been the family vacation retreat for decades. She has her work cut out for her, however, and as she struggles to deal with the various family members, she befriends a brilliant, but socially challenged, teenaged neighbor and is attracted to his sexy, but super-organized, father. This heartwarming, complex, multi-layered story will resonate with family-oriented readers.

Where it's reviewed:
Library Journal, December 2007, page 94
Romantic Times, January 2008, page 84

Other books by the same author:
Hot Dish, 2006
My Surrender, 2005
My Pleasure, 2004
My Seduction, 2004
Bridal Favors, 2002

Other books you might like:
Jennifer Crusie, *Welcome to Temptation*, 2001
Barbara Delinsky, *Lake News*, 2000
Kristin Hannah, *On Mystic Lake*, 1999
Susan Elizabeth Phillips, *Ain't She Sweet*, 2004
Kathleen Gilles Seidel, *Summer's End*, 1999

233

SHANNON K. BUTCHER

No Control

(New York: Forever, 2008)

Story type: Contemporary; Romantic Suspense
Subject(s): Terrorism
Major character(s): Lana Hancock, Survivor, Activist (charity fundraiser); Caleb Stone, Spy, Military Personnel (Delta Force)
Time period(s): 2000s
Locale(s): Armenia; Columbia, Missouri

Summary: After surviving a kidnapping at the hands of the brutal Swarm terrorist organization, Lana Hancock and Caleb Stone, the undercover agent who rescued her, are once again in the deadly sites of the Swarm. With a new, even more vicious, leader in charge, the terrorists are determined to kill both Lana and the spy who betrayed them, in this gritty thriller filled with passion and non-stop action.

Where it's reviewed:
Library Journal, February 15, 2008, page 87
Romantic Times, February 2008, page 74

Other books by the same author:
No Escape, 2008
No Regrets, 2007

Other books you might like:
Cherry Adair, *The Mercenary*, 2008
Suzanne Brockmann, *The Defiant Hero*, 2001
Suzanne Brockmann, *Flashpoint*, 2004
Suzanne Brockmann, *Over the Edge*, 2001
Merline Lovelace, *Dark Side of Dawn*, 2001

234

NICOLE BYRD (Pseudonym of Cheryl Zach)

Enticing the Earl

(New York: Berkley Sensation, 2008)

Story type: Historical/Regency
Subject(s): Marriage; Conduct of Life
Major character(s): Lauryn Applegate Harris, Widow(er); Marcus Elton, Nobleman (Earl of Sutton)
Time period(s): 19th century
Locale(s): England

Summary: In order to reclaim the estate her father-in-law had lost to the Earl of Sutton in a game of cards, widowed Lauryn Harris presents herself under an assumed name and offers herself to the earl as a courtesan in exchange for the estate. Of course, the earl sees through her subterfuge at once, but he is intrigued and plays along with Lauryn with results that surprise the marriage-wary earl. Passion turns to friendship and then to love in this super sexy romance that involves a mystery, as well.

Where it's reviewed:
Romantic Times, April 2008, page 48

Other books by the same author:
A Lady Betrayed, 2007
A Lady of Scandal, 2007
Seducing Sir Oliver, 2006
Beauty in Black, 2004
Lady in Waiting, 2002

Other books you might like:
Jo Beverley, *A Lady's Secret*, 2008
Celeste Bradley, *Desperately Seeking a Duke*, 2008
Celeste Bradley, *The Duke Next Door*, 2008
Thea Devine, *Tempted by Fire*, 1992
Samantha James, *The Seduction of an Unknown Lady*, 2008

235

MEG CABOT

Queen of Babble Gets Hitched

(New York: William Morrow, 2008)

Story type: Humor; Contemporary
Series: Queen of Babble. Book 3
Subject(s): Infidelity; Weddings; Interpersonal Relations
Major character(s): Lizzie Nichols, Fiance(e), Designer (fashion); Charles "Chaz" Pendergast, Wealthy
Time period(s): 2000s
Locale(s): New York, New York

Summary: Lizzie Nichols has it all—a successful job as a fashion designer, a rich fiance, and an engagement ring with a huge diamond. However, while she and her fiance were on hiatus, Lizzie slept with his best friend, Charles "Chaz" Pendergast. No matter how hard she tries, Lizzie can't forget Chaz, especially since her fiance has a less than stellar record himself. There's humor and angst as Lizzie decides who her Prince Charming really is.

Where it's reviewed:
Booklist, March 15, 2008, page 5
Publishers Weekly, March 10, 2008, page 55

Other books by the same author:
Big Boned, 2007 (Heather Wells. Book 3)
Queen of Babble, 2007 (Queen of Babble. Book 1)
Queen of Babble in the Big City, 2007 (Queen of Babble. Book 2)
Size 14 Is Not Fat Either, 2006 (Heather Wells. Book 2)
Size 12 Is Not Fat, 2005 (Heather Wells. Book 1)

Other books you might like:
Mary Kay Andrews, *Hissy Fit*, 2005
Jane Green, *Mr. Maybe*, 2002
Sophie Kinsella, *Remember Me?*, 2008
Jennifer Weiner, *Certain Girls*, 2008
Lauren Weisberger, *Chasing Harry Winston*, 2008

236

GAYLE CALLEN

Never Trust a Scoundrel

(New York: Avon, 2008)

Story type: Historical/Victorian
Subject(s): Seduction; Gambling; Music and Musicians

Major character(s): Grace Banbury, Gentlewoman; Daniel Throckmorten, Gentleman
Time period(s): 1840s (1845)
Locale(s): England

Summary: Furious to learn that her mother has wagered her, along with their family properties and a valuable violin, in a card game and then lost, Grace Banbury turns the tables on the winner, Daniel Throckmorten, by making a bet with him instead. He will have two weeks to try to seduce her, in which case she will become his mistress; if he fails, she will win the violin. As their plans unfold, Grace learns that Daniel is not the disreputable rake she'd thought him and he learns that she has character as well as beauty in this passionate romance that has a fair share of secrets, as well.

Other books by the same author:
The Viscount in Her Bedroom, 2007
The Duke in Disguise, 2006
The Lord Next Door, 2005
No Ordinary Groom, 2003
His Scandal, 2002

Other books you might like:
Victoria Alexander, *A Little Bit Wicked*, 2007
Celeste Bradley, *The Duke Next Door*, 2008
Samantha James, *The Seduction of an Unknown Lady*, 2008
Sabrina Jeffries, *Never Seduce a Scoundrel*, 2006
Nicole Jordan, *To Bed a Beauty*, 2008
    Courtship Wars. Book 2

237

CANDACE CAMP

The Bridal Quest

(Don Mills, Ontario: HQN, 2008)

Story type: Historical/Regency; Humor
Series: Matchmakers. Book 2
Subject(s): Aunts and Uncles; Women's Rights; Humor
Major character(s): Irene Wyngate, Noblewoman, Spinster; Widen Banks, Nobleman, Wealthy
Time period(s): 1800s; 1810s (1807-1816)
Locale(s): London, England

Summary: Widen Banks, heir to the estates and title of the Earl of Radbourne, is handsome, rich, and not acceptable to Society. Kidnapped as a child, he grew up on the mean streets of London, a fact that makes him a pariah to the upper classes. His aunt, Lady Odelia Radbourne, determined that her nephew will marry well, hires a matchmaker to find Widen a suitable wife. Lady Irene Wingate fills the ticket. Unfortunately, Irene is determined to remain a spinster to protect her rights, and she has the sharp tongue and sarcastic wit to drive men away.

Where it's reviewed:
Booklist, February 15, 2008, page 42
Publishers Weekly, January 21, 2008, page 160
Romantic Times, March 2008, page 49

Other books by the same author:
A Dangerous Man, 2007
The Marriage Wager, 2007 (Matchmakers. Book 1)
An Independent Woman, 2006
Swept Away, 2005
Mesmerized, 2003

Other books you might like:
Pamela Britton, *Tempted*, 2004
Christina Dodd, *The Barefoot Princess*, 2006
Suzanne Enoch, *Reforming a Rake*, 2000
Eloisa James, *Your Wicked Ways*, 2004
Barbara Metzger, *The Duel*, 2005

238

KATHRYN CASKIE

How to Propose to a Prince

(New York: Avon, 2008)

Story type: Historical/Regency
Series: Royle Sisters. Book 3
Subject(s): Identity, Concealed; Kings, Queens, Rulers, etc.; Secrets
Major character(s): Elizabeth Royle, Gentlewoman; Sumner Lansdowne, Nobleman (Marquess of Whitevale)
Time period(s): 1810s
Locale(s): England

Summary: Elizabeth Royle knows she is going to marry a prince. After all, she dreamt it, and almost all of Elizabeth's dreams come true. The only problem is that the man Elizabeth seems destined to marry, Prince Leopold of Saxe-Coburg Saalfield, is already engaged to Princess Charlotte of England. What Elizabeth doesn't know is that Sumner Lansdowne, the Marquess of Whitevale, has been impersonating his cousin, and since Sumner isn't engaged to anyone, there is still a chance Elizabeth's dream may come true.

Where it's reviewed:
Romantic Times, March 2008, page 40

Other books by the same author:
How to Engage an Earl, 2007
How to Seduce a Duke, 2006
Love Is in the Heir, 2006
A Ladies Guide to Rakes, 2005
Lady in Waiting, 2005

Other books you might like:
Elizabeth Boyle, *This Rake of Mine*, 2005
Christina Dodd, *Some Enchanted Evening*, 2004
Shana Galen, *Blackthorn's Bride*, 2007
Candice Hern, *Just One of Those Flings*, 2006
Julia London, *The Dangers of Deceiving a Viscount*, 2007

Romance

239

DAKOTA CASSIDY (Pseudonym of Connie A. Alberts)

The Accidental Werewolf

(New York: Berkley Sensation, 2008)

Story type: Contemporary; Werewolf Story
Subject(s): Werewolves; Humor; Paranormal
Major character(s): Marty Andrews, Saleswoman (cosmetics representative), Werewolf (reluctant); Keegan Flaherty, Werewolf, Leader (pack alpha male)
Time period(s): 2000s
Locale(s): New York

Summary: Reaching the top Sky Blue level (complete with sky blue convertible) of the Bobbie-Sue color-oriented cosmetics organization is Marty Andrews' career goal until she is accidentally bitten by a large dog and her life suddenly hits the skids. Her coloring changes (she is no longer a Spring), her legs are suddenly hairier, her language becomes saltier, and her temper is out of control. It doesn't help when Keegan Flaherty tells her that he's the "dog" that accidentally bit her and she is now a werewolf, just like he is. Of course, she doesn't believe him, which makes his job of convincing and protecting her even harder—especially when she's kidnapped. Funny, sexy, and irreverent, this lively paranormal twists intriguingly and sparkles with chicklit sass.

Where it's reviewed:
Romantic Times, February 2008, page 98

Other books by the same author:
Accidentally Dead, 2008
Sexylips66, 2006
Whose Bride Is She Anyway?, 2006
Wolf Mates, 2006

Other books you might like:
MaryJanice Davidson, *Undead and Unemployed*, 2004
Lori Handeland, *Blue Moon*, 2004
Katie MacAlister, *Sex and the Single Vampire*, 2004
Lynsay Sands, *Love Bites*, 2004
Lynsay Sands, *Single White Vampire*, 2003

240

KENDRA LEIGH CASTLE

Call of the Highland Moon

(Naperville, Illinois: Sourcebooks Casablanca, 2008)

Story type: Contemporary/Fantasy; Werewolf Story
Subject(s): Werewolves; Family Life; Feuds
Major character(s): Carly Silver, Store Owner (romance book store); Gideon MacInnes, Werewolf, Guardian
Time period(s): 2000s
Locale(s): Kinnik's Harbor, New York (on Lake Ontario)

Summary: Exploring the rest of the world before returning to Scotland and reluctantly assuming the responsibilities of Pack Alpha and Guardian of the Stone, werewolf Gideon MacInnes is attacked in upstate New York by rogue wolves sent by his jealous cousin. Wounded, Gideon is taken in by Carly Silver, the animal loving owner of a romance book store, who is appalled when the next morning she finds a man in her bed instead of the wolf-dog she'd brought home with her the night before. Isolated by a blizzard, they are unable to fight their growing attraction for each other. Deadly danger still lurks as they try to come to terms with the realities of their situation in this sexy, riveting story that sets up a world that Castle seems certain to revisit.

Where it's reviewed:
Romantic Times, May 2008, page 96

Other books by the same author:
Dark Highland Fire, 2008

Other books you might like:
Lori Handeland, *Blue Moon*, 2004
Lori Handeland, *Dark Moon*, 2005
Susan Krinard, *Prince of Shadows*, 1996
Nora Roberts, *Moon Shadows*, 2004 anthology
Ronda Thompson, *Call of the Moon*, 2002

241

TONI MCGEE CAUSEY

Bobbie Faye's (kinda, sorta, not-exactly) Family Jewels

(New York: St. Martin's Griffin, 2008)

Story type: Contemporary; Romantic Suspense
Series: Bobbie Faye. Book 2
Subject(s): Humor; Family Relations; Crime and Criminals
Major character(s): Bobbie Faye Sumrall, Saleswoman (gun counter), Crime Victim (kidnapping, murder attempt); Trevor Cormier, FBI Agent; Cameron Moreau, Detective—Police
Time period(s): 2000s
Locale(s): Lake Charles, Louisiana

Summary: The Irish mob wants her. Her gangster uncle wants her. Both the FBI and Homeland Security want her. Why? Because all of them believe that Bobbie Faye Sumrall has a priceless cache of diamonds. FBI agent Trevor Cormier and Detective Sergeant Cameron Moreau are trying their best to protect her, but where Bobbie Faye goes, trouble races in.

Where it's reviewed:
Publishers Weekly, April 21, 2008, page 35
Romantic Times, June 2008, page 91

Other books by the same author:
Bobbie Faye and the Very (very, very, very) Bad Day, 2007 (Bobbie Faye Sumrall. Book 1)

Other books you might like:
Kathleen Bacus, *Calamity Jayne Goes to College*, 2006
Tressa Jayne Turner. Book 4
Janet Evanovich, *Fearless Fourteen*, 2008
Stephanie Plum. Book 14
Sandra Hill, *Wild Jinx*, 2008
Jinx. Book 3
Leslie Langtry, *Guns Will Keep Us Together*, 2008

Greatest Hits. Book 2
Lisa Lutz, *The Spellman Files*, 2007
Spellman. Book 1

242

LORETTA CHASE   (Pseudonym of Loretta Chekani)

Your Scandalous Ways

(New York: Avon, 2008)

Story type: Historical/Regency
Subject(s): Identity, Concealed; Letters; Secrets
Major character(s): Francesca Bonnard, Prostitute
    (courtesan); James Cordier, Gentleman, Spy
Time period(s): 1820s (1820)
Locale(s): Venice, Italy

Summary: After divorcing her husband Lord Elphick, Francesca Bonnard has created a new life for herself as one of Europe's most celebrated and expensive courtesans. British spy James Cordier's latest—and last if he has anything to say about the matter—assignment is to steal a potentially politically dangerous cache of letters from her ex-husband Francesca keeps as insurance. James thinks the mission couldn't be easier until he meets Francesca and discovers he isn't quite as immune to her charms as he would like to believe.

Where it's reviewed:
Library Journal, April 15, 2008, page 68
Publishers Weekly, April 21, 2008, page 30
Romantic Times, June 2008, page 50

Other books by the same author:
Not Quite a Lady, 2007
Lord Perfect, 2006
Mr. Impossible, 2005
Miss Wonderful, 2004
The Last Hellion, 1998

Other books you might like:
Elizabeth Boyle, *One Night of Passion*, 2002
Liz Carlyle, *Never Lie to a Lady*, 2007
Suzanne Enoch, *Reforming a Rake*, 2000
Eloisa James, *The Taming of the Duke*, 2006
Sophia Nash, *A Dangerous Beauty*, 2007

243

MAUREEN CHILD

A Fiend in Need

(New York: Signet Eclipse, 2008)

Story type: Contemporary; Paranormal
Subject(s): Paranormal; Demons
Major character(s): Cassidy Burke, Hunter (demon killer),
    Single Parent; Brady, Mythical Creature (faery),
    Slave
Time period(s): 2000s
Locale(s): United States

Summary: Demon Duster Cassidy Burke's life becomes even more complicated than normal when her teenage daughter notices that there's a reward out for Cassidy's murder on the web and Brady, an escaped sex slave of the Demon Queen, arrives at her house to claim Sanctuary. This is a funny, sassy urban fantasy romance that is filled with action and plenty of passion.

Where it's reviewed:
Romantic Times, March 2008, page 112

Other books by the same author:
Bargaining for King's Baby, 2008
Falling for King's Fortune, 2008
Marrying for King's Millions, 2008
Captured by the Billionaire, 2007
More than Fiends, 2007

Other books you might like:
Amanda Ashley, *Dead Perfect*, 2008
Dakota Cassidy, *The Accidental Werewolf*, 2008
MaryJanice Davidson, *Undead and Unemployed*, 2004
Kim Harrison, *Dates from Hell*, 2006
    anthology
Angela Knight, *Shifter*, 2008
    anthology

244

PAMELA CLARE

Unlawful Contact

(New York: Berkley Sensation, 2008)

Story type: Contemporary; Romantic Suspense
Subject(s): Crime and Criminals; Drugs; Secrets
Major character(s): Sophie Alton, Journalist, Captive
    (hostage); Marc Hunter, Convict (escaped), Police
    Officer (former DEA agent)
Time period(s): 2000s
Locale(s): Colorado

Summary: In an effort to locate Megan, a young woman on parole and her baby who've suddenly disappeared, journalist Sophie Alton agrees to talk to Megan's incarcerated brother, Marc Hunter, who is doing time for killing a fellow DEA agent. When her visit turns into a prison break, with Marc taking Sophie along as a hostage, it isn't until they are well on their way that Sophie realizes that Marc is the person she knew as Hunt and adored in high school. This fast-paced, passionate tale of suspense and deception, takes Sophie and Marc on a twisted journey as they race to find Megan and dodge dangers from cops and criminals alike in this thriller that features drugs, secrets, and coverups.

Other books by the same author:
Hard Evidence, 2006
Surrender, 2006
Extreme Exposure, 2005
Ride the Fire, 2005
Carnal Gift, 2004

Other books you might like:
Lynn Erickson, *The Eleventh Hour*, 1998
Ginna Gray, *The Witness*, 2001
Kathleen Nance, *Jigsaw*, 2005
Brenda Novak, *Taking the Heat*, 2003
Meryl Sawyer, *Half Past Dead*, 2006

245

KRESLEY COLE

Dark Deeds at Night's Edge

(New York: Pocket, 2008)

Story type: Contemporary/Fantasy
Series: Immortals After Dark. Book 4
Subject(s): Ghosts; Murder; Vampires
Major character(s): Neomi Laress, Dancer, Spirit; Conrad Wroth, Vampire
Time period(s): 1920s (1927); 2000s
Locale(s): New Orleans, Louisiana

Summary: After being murdered by her jealous ex-fiance, ballerina Neomi Laress is doomed to haunt her New Orleans home invisible to everyone. Driven to madness, vampire warrior Conrad Wroth is locked up by his brothers in Neomi's old mansion nearly a century later. Conrad really thinks he is going mad when he begins seeing a woman in his new prison, until Conrad discovers the reason he is the only one who can see Neomi is because he is the only one who can help her.

Where it's reviewed:
Romantic Times, May 2008, page 99

Other books by the same author:
If You Deceive, 2007
Wicked Deeds on a Winter's Night, 2007
If You Desire, 2007
A Hunger Like No Other, 2006
No Rest for the Wicked, 2006

Other books you might like:
Lara Adrian, *Kiss of Midnight*, 2007
Christine Feehan, *The Twilight Before Christmas*, 2003
Sherrilyn Kenyon, *Dance with the Devil*, 2003
Katie MacAlister, *Sex, Lies and Vampires*, 2005
Gena Showalter, *The Pleasure Slave*, 2005

246

CATHERINE COULTER

Wizard's Daughter

(New York: Jove, 2008)

Story type: Historical/Victorian
Series: Sherbrooke Bride. Book 10
Subject(s): Magic; Mystery; Quest
Major character(s): Rosalind de la Fontaine, Orphan (Sherbrooke ward), Singer; Nicholas Vail, Nobleman (Earl of Mountjoy)
Time period(s): 1830s (1835)
Locale(s): England; The Pale, Mythical Place

Summary: Paranormal and mystery elements add excitement to this romance that takes a mysterious orphan with a mesmerizing voice and a threatened nobleman whose dreams have been haunted by the same girl, gives them an ancient mystery to unravel, and lets the adventure begin. Sexy and fast-paced, this tale is another featuring Coulter's renowned Sherbrooke family.

Where it's reviewed:
Publishers Weekly, November 19, 2007, page 44
Romantic Times, January 2008, page 44

Other books by the same author:
Lyon's Gate, 2005 (Sherbrooke Bride. Book 9)
The Sherbrooke Twins, 2004 (Sherbrooke Bride. Book 8)
Pendragon, 2002 (Sherbrooke Bride. Book 7)
The Scottish Bride, 2001 (Sherbrooke Bride. Book 6)
The Courtship, 2000 (Sherbrooke Bride. Book 5)

Other books you might like:
Jo Beverley, *Irresistible Forces*, 2004 anthology
Susan Spencer Paul, *Touch of Night*, 2005
Mary Jo Putney, *A Distant Magic*, 2006
Mary Jo Putney, *A Kiss of Fate*, 2004
Mary Jo Putney, *Stolen Magic*, 2005

247

CHRISTIE CRAIG

Weddings Can Be Murder

(New York: Love Spell, 2008)

Story type: Contemporary; Romantic Suspense
Subject(s): Weddings; Murder; Missing Persons
Major character(s): Katie Ray, Businesswoman (art gallery manager), Artist; Carl Hades, Detective—Private
Time period(s): 2000s
Locale(s): Houston, Texas

Summary: Although she truly likes her intended bridegroom, Katie Ray gets sick every time she thinks about marrying him. All this changes, however, when Katie becomes a murder witness and ends up locked in a room with hunky Carl Hades, a PI investigating some missing brides, and they have a hard time resisting the feelings that sizzle between them. A psychotic serial killer who's targeted Katie as his next bride keeps the tension high in this lively murder mystery that is funny, sassy, and refreshing and finally sorts out two pairs of mismatched couples to everyone's relief.

Where it's reviewed:
Library Journal, April 15, 2008, page 66
Romantic Times, June 2008, page 81

Other books by the same author:
Divorced, Desperate, and Delicious, 2007

Other books you might like:
Kathleen Bacus, *Calamity Jayne Rides Again*, 2006
Stephanie Bond, *Body Movers: 2 Bodies for the Price of 1*, 2007
Stephanie Bond, *Finding Your Mojo*, 2006
Janet Evanovich, *Eleven on Top*, 2005
Harley Jane Kozak, *Dating Is Murder*, 2005

248

SUSAN CRANDALL

Pitch Black

(New York: Forever, 2008)

Story type: Contemporary; Romantic Suspense
Subject(s): Mystery; Small Town Life; Murder
Major character(s): Madison Wade, Journalist, Editor
   (*Buckeye Daily Herald*); Gabriel Wyatt, Police Of-
   ficer (sheriff)
Time period(s): 2000s
Locale(s): Buckeye, Tennessee

Summary: Hoping to give her adopted teenage son a better life, journalist Madison Wade moves from Philadelphia to tiny Buckeye, Tennessee, to become the editor of
the local paper. However, outsiders sometimes have a
hard time in small towns, and when someone is killed on
a camping trip, Maddie's son, Ethan, ends up under
suspicion. Romance blooms between Maddie and Sheriff
Gabe Wyatt, although the investigation doesn't make
things easy. Southern charm and small town atmosphere
(complete with gossip and meddling, well-meant and
otherwise) provide a deceptively innocent backdrop for
the realities of this complex mystery.

Where it's reviewed:
Romantic Times, June 2008, page 82

Other books by the same author:
A Kiss in Winter, 2007
On Blue Falls Pond, 2006
Promises to Keep, 2005
The Road Home, 2004
Back Roads, 2003

Other books you might like:
Helen R. Myers, *Come Sundown*, 1998
Karen Robards, *One Summer*, 1993
Karen Robards, *Whispers at Midnight*, 2003
Karen Rose, *Have You Seen Her?*, 2004
Alicia Scott, *The Quiet One*, 1996

249

CLAUDIA DAIN

The Courtesan's Secret

(New York: Berkley Sensation, 2008)

Story type: Historical/Regency; Humor
Series: Courtesan. Book 2
Subject(s): Humor; Pearls; Interpersonal Relations
Major character(s): Louisa Kirkland, Noblewoman; Henry
   Blakesley, Nobleman
Time period(s): 1800s (1802)
Locale(s): London, England

Summary: Former courtesan Lady Sophia Dalbey is back
to her favorite pastime—matchmaking. Her targets this
time are Lord Henry Blakesley and Lady Louisa
Kirkland. Henry loves Louisa, all right, but there may be
a problem—Louisa loves the Marquis of Dutton instead.

Where it's reviewed:
Romantic Times, May 2008, page 44

Other books by the same author:
The Courtesan's Daughter, 2007
The Fall, 2004
The Temptation, 2003
To Burn, 2002
The Holding, 2001

Other books you might like:
Victoria Alexander, *Secrets of a Proper Lady*, 2007
Christina Dodd, *The Prince Kidnaps a Bride*, 2006
   Lost Princess. Book 6
Sabrina Jeffries, *Never Seduce a Scoundrel*, 2006
Nicole Jordan, *To Seduce a Bride*, 2008
   Regency. Book 3
Lisa Kleypas, *Suddenly You*, 2001

250

JACQUIE D'ALESSANDRO

Confessions at Midnight

(New York: Avon, 2008)

Story type: Historical/Regency
Series: Mayhem in Mayfair. Book 2
Subject(s): Books and Reading; Seduction
Major character(s): Carolyn Turner, Noblewoman
   (Viscountess Wingate), Widow(er); Daniel Sutton,
   Nobleman (Earl Surbrooke)
Time period(s): 1810s
Locale(s): London, England

Summary: When the Ladies Literary Society of London
decides to read *Memoirs of a Mistress* as their next book,
Carolyn Turner has no idea the scandalous novel will
change her life. After reading the book, the widowed
Carolyn realizes even though she loved her husband
Edward, their marriage was not quite as passionate as it
could have been. The ladies' new book club choice
proves to be exactly the key Daniel Sutton, Earl Surbrooke, needs to convince Carolyn to indulge in a
romantic liaison with him, but once he gets to know her
better, Daniel realizes he wants more from Carolyn than
simply a sexy affair.

Where it's reviewed:
Booklist, February 1, 2008, page 34
Romantic Times, January 2008, page 44

Other books by the same author:
Sleepless at Midnight, 2007
Just Trust Me, 2006
Never a Lady, 2006
Not Quite a Gentleman, 2005
Why Not Tonight, 2005

Other books you might like:
Mary Balogh, *Slightly Tempted*, 2004
Liz Carlyle, *A Deal with the Devil*, 2004
Candice Hern, *In the Thrill of the Night*, 2006
Eloisa James, *Much Ado about You*, 2005
Stephanie Laurens, *The Perfect Lover*, 2003

251

CAROLYN DAVIDSON

The Bride

(Don Mills, Ontario: HQN, 2008)

Story type: Historical/American West
Subject(s): American West; Marriage; Jealousy
Major character(s): Isabella Montgomery, Gentlewoman; Rafael McKenzie, Rancher
Time period(s): 1890s
Locale(s): New Mexico (New Mexico Territory)

Summary: Confined to a convent from the age of 14 until she is ready to marry Juan Garcia, an older man of her late father's choice, Isabella Montgomery dreads her future. However, when Rafael McKenzie, a brash rancher who wants her as a bride, kidnaps her, she's not sure that's what she wants either. An escape, another kidnapping, and a bit of treachery add to the confusion in this sexy Western adventure where the heroine wants some say in her own destiny.

Where it's reviewed:
Romantic Times, February 2008, page 49

Other books by the same author:
Haven, 2007
Nightsong, 2007
Lone Star Bride, 2006
Redemption, 2006
The Bachelor Tax, 2000

Other books you might like:
Rebecca Brandewyine, *Desperado*, 1993
Christina Dodd, *Treasure of the Sun*, 1991
Kat Martin, *Midnight Rider*, 1996
Maggie Osborne, *The Bride of Willow Creek*, 2001
Nan Ryan, *Because You're Mine*, 1995

252

MARYJANICE DAVIDSON (Pseudonym of MaryJanice Alongi)

Dead over Heels

(New York: Berkley Sensation, 2008)

Story type: Contemporary; Paranormal
Subject(s): Werewolves; Vampires; Mermaids
Time period(s): 2000s
Locale(s): United States

Summary: This collection of three novellas features stories that are related to earlier books and series by Davidson and are typically offbeat, quirky, and sexy. "Undead and Wed: A Honeymoon Story" takes Vampire Queen Betsy and King Sinclair on a New York honeymoon with unexpected results, naturally; "Survivors" puts a survival TV star in real danger and then sends in a mermaid to help; and "Speed Dating, Werewolf Style—or Ow, I Think You Broke the Bone" ramps up the best-friend-becomes-best-beloved plot with funny, sizzling results.

Where it's reviewed:
Romantic Times, March 2008, page 104

Other books by the same author:
Undead and Unworthy, 2008
Undead and Uneasy, 2007
Sleeping with the Fishes, 2006
Undead and Unpopular, 2006
Undead and Unreturnable, 2005

Other books you might like:
Michele Bardsley, *Because Your Vampire Said So*, 2008
Michele Bardsley, *Don't Talk Back to Your Vampire*, 2007
Katie MacAlister, *Even Vampires Get the Blues*, 2006
Katie MacAlister, *Just One Sip*, 2006
  anthology
Lynsay Sands, *Bite Me If You Can*, 2007

253

SYLVIA DAY

Don't Tempt Me

(New York: Brava, 2008)

Story type: Historical/Georgian
Subject(s): Twins; Secrets; Espionage
Major character(s): Lynette Baillon, Gentlewoman, Twin; Simon Quinn, Mercenary; Lysette Rousseau, Twin, Murderer (assassin)
Time period(s): 1750s (1757); 1780s
Locale(s): France

Summary: Thinking her twin sister is dead, Lynette Baillon is shocked when Simon Quinn, a mysterious Irish mercenary, mistakes her for Lysette. However, Lysette is alive and, through a strange set of circumstances, has become one of the most feared assassins in Europe. Lynette is determined to find her sister; and, even as the danger to her mounts, Lynette and Simon race to untangle a web of old lies and deception before a villain succeeds in covering up his crimes by murder. Sexy and fast-paced.

Where it's reviewed:
Library Journal, February 15, 2008, page 87
Romantic Times, April 2008, page 42

Other books by the same author:
Heat of the Night, 2008
A Passion for Him, 2007
The Stranger I Married, 2007
Passion for the Game, 2007
Bad Boys Ahoy!, 2006

Other books you might like:
Jane Feather, *The Diamond Slipper*, 1997
Cheryl Holt, *Double Fantasy*, 2008
Susan Johnson, *At Her Service*, 2008
Susan Johnson, *Rough around the Edges*, 1998
  anthology
Bertrice Small, *Intrigued*, 2001

254

HELENKAY DIMON

Right Here, Right Now

(New York: Brava, 2008)

Story type: Contemporary; Romantic Suspense
Subject(s): Espionage; Seduction
Major character(s): Gabby Pearson, Accountant; Reed Larkin, Computer Expert, Spy
Time period(s): 2000s
Locale(s): Washington, District of Columbia

Summary: When Reed Larkin tries to break up with Gabby Pearson in a restaurant by telling her she just isn't "exciting" enough for him, Gabby not only dumps Reed but dumps a glass of wine on him, too. Reed thought he was doing Gabby a favor by keeping her from becoming entangled in his danger-filled life as a secret spy for the U.S. government. Instead, Reed discovers that Gabby is the key to cracking his latest assignment, and now Reed must figure out some way to seduce Gabby into giving him another chance.

Where it's reviewed:
Romantic Times, March 2008, page 94

Other books by the same author:
Your Mouth Drives Me Crazy, 2007
Viva Las Bad Boys, 2006

Other books you might like:
Cherry Adair, *Hot Ice*, 2005
Suzanne Brockmann, *Bodyguard*, 1999
Linda Howard, *All the Queen's Men*, 1999
Sydney Ryan, *High-Heeled Alibi*, 2006

255

CHRISTINA DODD

Thigh High

(New York: Signet, 2008)

Story type: Contemporary; Romantic Suspense
Subject(s): Business; Crime and Criminals; Family
Major character(s): Ionessa "Nessa" Dahl, Banker; Jeremiah MacNaught, Businessman, Banker (bank president)
Time period(s): 2000s
Locale(s): Philadelphia, Pennsylvania; New Orleans, Louisiana

Summary: When Nessa Dahl is called into her witch of a supervisor's office, she expects it was because she is finally going to get her long deserved promotion to branch manager. Instead, Nessa is given a new job duty: working with Jeremiah MacNaught, who had been sent by the bank's president to investigate the "Beaded Bandit" robberies. What Nessa doesn't know is that Mac thinks he knows exactly who is responsible for the robberies and his chief suspect is Nessa!

Where it's reviewed:
Booklist, March 15, 2008, page 35
Romantic Times, March 2008, page 93

Other books by the same author:
Scent of Darkness, 2007
Tongue in Chic, 2007
Touch of Darkness, 2007
The Prince Kidnaps a Bride, 2006
Trouble in High Heels, 2006

Other books you might like:
Michele Albert, *One Way Out*, 2005
Jennifer Crusie, *Tell Me Lies*, 1998
Rachel Gibson, *True Confessions*, 2001
Linda Howard, *Open Season*, 2001

256

LAURA DREWRY

The Devil's Daughter

(New York: Leisure, 2008)

Story type: Paranormal; Humor
Subject(s): Devil; Fathers and Daughters; Humor
Major character(s): Lucy Firr, Mythical Creature (Satan's daughter); Jed Caine, Rancher
Time period(s): 1880s (1881)
Locale(s): Redemption, Texas

Summary: Lucy Firr, daughter of the Prince of Darkness, is out to get rancher Jed Caine's soul. If she succeeds, her father will let her leave his kingdom of fire and brimstone for a nicer place. Jed, however, isn't as easily seduced as she'd thought, and now she's looking for his heart as well as his soul.

Where it's reviewed:
Romantic Times, April 2008, page 44

Other books by the same author:
Charming Jo, 2006
Here Comes the Bride, 2005

Other books you might like:
Kathleen Kane, *Just West of Texas*, 2001
Kathleen Kane, *Wish upon a Cowboy*, 2000
Judi McCoy, *Almost a Goddess*, 2006
Stephanie Rowe, *He Loves Me, He Loves Me Hot*, 2007
    Immortally Sexy. Book 3
Vicki Lewis Thompson, *Wild and Hexy*, 2008
    Big Knob. Book 2

257

NELL DUVALL (Pseudonym of M. Jacob)

Train to Yesterday

(Waterville, Maine: Five Star, 2008)

Story type: Time Travel; Historical/Victorian America
Subject(s): Railroads; Time Travel
Major character(s): Penelope Barton, Businesswoman (vice president of marketing); Fletcher Dawe, Businessman (railroad owner), Store Owner (dry goods)
Time period(s): 2000s; 1850s (1855)
Locale(s): Ohio

Romance

Summary: When Penny Barton meets Fletcher Dawe aboard a vintage steam train on an expedition she had arranged for railroad buffs who might be interested in investing in the high-speed rail company she works for, she assumes he's an actor hired to add atmosphere. When she can't locate him later and eventually sees him in a 1851 picture, although she still thinks the man she met was an actor, she begins to research the time period and learns how violent the rivalry was between the canal boats and the fledgling railroads. Transported back to 1855 and into the middle of the controversy, Penny finally understands what has happened, however, she can't convince Fletcher she's really from the future until it's almost too late. There's plenty of interesting history in this romance that will appeal to train lovers and romance fans, alike.

Other books you might like:
Rosanne Bittner, *Thunder on the Plains*, 1992
    mainstream railroad saga
Tracy Cozzens, *A 5th Avenue Christmas*, 2003
    railroads with a holiday touch
Bridget Kraft, *Fields of Gold*, 2005
Betina Krahn, *The Soft Touch*, 1999
Janet Wellington, *Forever Rose*, 2000
    time travel elements

258

KATHLEEN EAGLE

Mystic Horseman

(Don Mills, Ontario: Mira, 2008)

Story type: Contemporary
Subject(s): Television Programs; Animals/Horses; Heritage
Major character(s): Ella Champion, Producer (television), Indian (half Santee); Dillon "Bear" Black, Rancher, Indian (Lakota)
Time period(s): 2000s
Locale(s): South Dakota; Minneapolis, Minnesota

Summary: When high profile television producer Ella Champion approaches Dillon Black with a proposal that his fledgling horse camp for at-risk Lakota youth become the subject of her "make-over" reality show, his first reaction is to turn her down. However, he needs the money in order to make his dream project a reality, so he reluctantly agrees, not thinking that his ex-wife, who gave Ella the idea for the project, has an agenda of her own. Family, self-acceptance, and cultural heritage are at the heart of this poignant,engaging romance that follows *Ride a Painted Pony* and provides abundant cultural detail.

Where it's reviewed:
Library Journal, February 15, 2008, page 88
Romantic Times, March 2008, page 98

Other books by the same author:
Ride a Painted Pony, 2006
A View of the River, 2005
Night Falls Like Silk, 2003
Once upon a Wedding, 2002
You Never Can Tell, 2001

Other books you might like:
Barbara Freethy, *Just the Way You Are*, 2000
Debbie Macomber, *Return to Promise*, 2000
Dinah McCall, *The Return*, 2000
Nora Roberts, *Montana Sky*, 1996
Ruth Wind, *Last Chance Ranch*, 1996

259

SARAH ELLIOTT (Pseudonym of Sarah Lindsey)

The Wayward Debutante

(Toronto: Harlequin, 2008)

Story type: Historical/Regency
Series: Sinclair Siblings. Book 3
Subject(s): Deception; Identity, Concealed; Courtship
Major character(s): Eleanor Sinclair, Gentlewoman; James Bentley, Nobleman ("Honorable James Stanton"), Businessman (theatre owner)
Time period(s): 1810s (1818)
Locale(s): London, England

Summary: Bored with the endless round of insipid parties and small talk that are part of the London Season, Eleanor Sinclair daringly puts her reputation on the line by disguising herself and going to the theatre without an escort—twice. She attracts the attention of theatre investor and reluctant nobleman James Bentley, who ends up thinking she is a governess. They develop a clandestine arrangement and agree to attend the theatre together; however, their deceptions eventually catch up with them when they begin to fall in love and realize that the truth may ruin everything.

Where it's reviewed:
Romantic Times, February 2008, page 51

Other books by the same author:
The Rake's Proposal, 2006 (Sinclair Siblings. Book 2)
Reforming the Rake, 2005 (Sinclair Siblings. Book 1)

Other books you might like:
Victoria Alexander, *Secrets of a Proper Lady*, 2007
Louise Bergin, *The Winter Duke*, 2005
    traditional Regency
Allison Lane, *A Bird in Hand*, 1999
    traditional Regency
Julia London, *The Dangers of Deceiving a Viscount*, 2007
Lisa Manuel, *Mostly a Lady*, 2005

260

LESLIE ESDAILE

Better Than

(New York: Dafina, 2008)

Story type: Contemporary; Multicultural
Subject(s): African Americans; Change; Self-Awareness
Major character(s): Deborah Lee Jackson, Divorced Person, Student; Jason Hastings, Artist (painter), Teacher (temporary)

Time period(s): 2000s
Locale(s): Philadelphia, Pennsylvania

Summary: Divorced and back in Philadelphia to pick up the pieces of her life, the last thing Deborah Jackson needs messing her up is another man. Painter Jason Hastings isn't looking for love either; he has his career to think about and a woman wouldn't be good for him at all. Then Jason and Deborah cross paths and things begin to change. Well-rounded characters drive the simple, but satisfying, plot of this heartwarming romance about a woman trying to reinvent herself and a man who loves her the way she is.

Where it's reviewed:
Romantic Times, June 2008, page 98

Other books by the same author:
No Trust, 2007
Take Me There, 2006
Sister Got Game, 2004
Love Potions, 2002
Through the Storm, 2002

Other books you might like:
Rochelle Alers, *Long Time Coming*, 2008
Sandra Kitt, *For All We Know*, 2008
Kayla Perrin, *If You Want Me*, 2001
Candice Poarch, *Bargain of the Heart*, 2002
Candice Poarch, *Long, Hot Nights*, 2008

261

JANE FEATHER

To Wed a Wicked Prince

(New York: Pocket Star, 2008)

Story type: Historical/Regency; Historical/Georgian
Series: Cavendish Square. Book 2
Subject(s): Spies; Secrets; Politics
Major character(s): Livia Lacey, Noblewoman; Alexander Prokov, Royalty (Russian prince), Spy
Time period(s): 1800s (1807)
Locale(s): England

Summary: Puzzled but thoroughly charmed when handsome Prince Alexander Prokov, new to the London social scene, pursues her with "honorable" intent, Lady Livia Lacey eventually accepts the arrogant half Russian prince's proposal. Once wed the sparks fly as Livia's independence wars with Alex's autocratic behavior and she begins to have questions about who and what he really is. Old secrets, political intrigue, and plenty of sizzling passion add to this lively romance that is the second of Feather's Cavendish Square novels.

Where it's reviewed:
Romantic Times, April 2008, page 39

Other books by the same author:
A Wicked Gentleman, 2007 (Cavendish Square. Book 1)
Almost a Bride, 2005
Almost a Lady, 2005
The Bride Hunt, 2004 (Matchmaker. Book 2)
The Wedding Game, 2004 (Matchmaker. Book 3)

Other books you might like:
Jo Beverley, *A Lady's Secret*, 2008
Elizabeth Hoyt, *To Taste Temptation*, 2008
Madeline Hunter, *Secrets of Surrender*, 2008
Brenda Joyce, *Splendor*, 1997
Johanna Lindsey, *No Choice but Seduction*, 2008

262

CHRISTINE FEEHAN

Predatory Game

(New York: Jove, 2008)

Story type: Contemporary; Paranormal
Series: GhostWalker. Book 6
Subject(s): Psychic Powers; Identity, Concealed; Secrets
Major character(s): Saber Wynter, Psychic (GhostWalker), Radio Personality (Night Siren); Jesse Calhoun, Psychic (GhostWalker), Military Personnel (ex-Navy SEAL)
Time period(s): 2000s
Locale(s): Sheridan, Wyoming

Summary: When waif-like Saber Wynter shows up on his Sheridan, Wyoming, doorstep wanting a job at his radio station, wheelchair-bound Jesse Calhoun takes her in and hires her. Although they guard their secrets carefully, both are GhostWalkers, victims of a brilliant, but unbalanced scientist, whose experiments gave them supernatural psychic and physical powers, and both are being hunted, even as they fight their attraction for each other. Riveting action and well-developed characters keep this GhostWalker adventure on target.

Where it's reviewed:
Romantic Times, March 2008, page 103

Other books by the same author:
Deadly Game, 2007 (GhostWalker. Book 5)
Conspiracy Game, 2006 (GhostWalker. Book 4)
Night Game, 2005 (GhostWalker. Book 3)
Mind Game, 2004 (GhostWalker. Book 2)
Shadow Game, 2003 (GhostWalker. Book 1)

Other books you might like:
Eve Kenin, *Driven*, 2007
Eve Kennin, *Hidden*, 2008
Jayne Ann Krentz, *Sizzle and Burn*, 2008
Jayne Ann Krentz, *White Lies*, 2007
Marjorie M. Liu, *Shadow Touch*, 2006

263

LIZ FIELDING

The Bride's Baby

(Toronto: Harlequin, 2008)

Story type: Contemporary
Series: Bride for All Seasons. Book 1
Subject(s): Weddings
Major character(s): Sylvie Smith, Businesswoman (events

planner); Tom McFarlane, Wealthy (self-made), Businessman
Time period(s): 2000s
Locale(s): England

Summary: When a brief passionate encounter with the wealthy jilted groom of a wedding she'd been in charge of leaves wedding planner Sylvie Smith pregnant, she bravely gets on with her life. However, Tom McFarlane has no idea she's carrying his child, so when he returns, events become even more complicated than before. Misunderstandings and miscommunications are all part of this sweet romance that is the spring story in Harlequin's A Bride for All Seasons quartet.

Where it's reviewed:
Romantic Times, April 2008, page 115

Other books by the same author:
The Sheikh's Unsuitable Bride, 2008
Reunited, 2007

Other books you might like:
Beverly Barton, *Having His Baby*, 1999
   3 Babies for 3 Brothers. Book 3
Fiona Harper, *Saying Yes to the Millionaire*, 2008
   Bride for All Seasons. Book 2. Summer
Shirley Jump, *Marry-Me Christmas*, 2008
   Bride for All Seasons. Book 4. Winter
Shirley Jump, *Sweetheart Lost and Found*, 2008
Trish Wylie, *The Millionaire's Proposal*, 2008
   Bride for All Seasons. Book 3. Autumn

264

DONNA FLETCHER

Return of the Rogue

(New York: Avon, 2008)

Story type: Historical/Medieval
Subject(s): Politics; Marriage
Major character(s): Honora Tannach, Noblewoman; Cavan Sinclare, Nobleman, Warrior
Time period(s): 16th century
Locale(s): Scotland

Summary: Thrilled when she is about to wed Artair Sinclare and thus escape the cruel household in which she was raised, Honora Tannoch is shocked when her wedding is interrupted by the return of Artair's older brother, Cavan, and she is summarily wed to that fierce warrior, instead! A wary relationship soon becomes one of passion in this lively historical as Honora and Cavan discover the depths of love and the importance of loyalty.

Where it's reviewed:
Romantic Times, March 2008, page 47

Other books by the same author:
The Highlander's Bride, 2007
Irish Hope, 2006
Taken by Storm, 2006
The Bewitching Twin, 2006
The Wedding Spell, 1999

Other books you might like:
Julie Garwood, *The Bride*, 1989
Hannah Howell, *Highland Wolf*, 2008
Sophia Nash, *The Kiss*, 2008
Amanda Scott, *Border Wedding*, 2008
Amanda Scott, *Lady's Choice*, 2006

265

BARBARA FREETHY

Silent Fall

(New York: Onyx, 2008)

Story type: Contemporary; Romantic Suspense
Subject(s): Murder; Psychic Powers; Mystery
Major character(s): Catherine Hilliard, Psychic, Artist; Dylan Sanders, Journalist (investigative reporter)
Time period(s): 2000s
Locale(s): Lake Tahoe, California; San Francisco, California

Summary: Lured into the woods and then drugged by a former informant, investigative reporter Dylan Sanders suddenly finds himself the main suspect in the informant's disappearance. At a loss, he turns to psychic Catherine Hilliard for help, hoping her premonitions and visions will help solve the mystery, a mystery which increasingly seems aimed at destroying Dylan and everything he holds dear. Past events play important roles in this intricately plotted suspenseful adventure that is the sequel to *Silent Run*.

Where it's reviewed:
Library Journal, April 15, 2008, page 66
Romantic Times, April 2008, page 80

Other books by the same author:
Silent Run, 2008
Played, 2006
Taken, 2006
Don't Say a Word, 2005
All She Ever Wanted, 2004

Other books you might like:
Christiane Heggan, *Enemy Within*, 2000
Jayne Ann Krentz, *Sizzle and Burn*, 2008
   paranormal elements
Patricia Potter, *Catch a Shadow*, 2008
Patricia Potter, *Twisted Shadows*, 2003
Mariah Stewart, *Dark Truth*, 2005

266

BARBARA FREETHY

Silent Run

(New York: Onyx, 2008)

Story type: Contemporary; Romantic Suspense
Subject(s): Memory Loss; Secrets; Deception
Major character(s): Sarah Tucker, Amnesiac, Parent; Jake Tucker, Architect, Parent
Time period(s): 2000s

Locale(s): California

Summary: With no memory of who she is after she is injured in a car crash, Sarah Tucker is shocked to be confronted in her hospital room by a furious man who wants to know what she has done with their daughter, Caitlyn. At first, no one trusts anyone, but as Sarah's memory begins to return in confusing snatches and it becomes clear that someone is out to kill her, Jake and Sarah are forced to work together if they are ever going to find their little girl and keep Sarah alive. A complex tale filled with twists and turns, this story will keep readers enthralled and is followed by *Silent Fall*.

Where it's reviewed:
Romantic Times, March 2008, page 75

Other books by the same author:
Silent Fall, 2008
Played, 2006
Taken, 2006
Don't Say a Word, 2005
All She Ever Wanted, 2004

Other books you might like:
Lynn Erickson, *Searching for Sarah*, 1999
Linda Howard, *Mr. Perfect*, 2000
Cait London, *With Her Last Breath*, 2003
Dinah McCall, *Tallchief*, 1997
Patricia Potter, *Twisted Shadows*, 2003

267

JENNY GARDINER

Sleeping with Ward Cleaver

(New York: Love Spell, 2008)

Story type: Contemporary
Subject(s): Infidelity; Marriage; Relationships
Major character(s): Claire Doolittle, Spouse, Parent (of five); Jack Doolittle, Spouse, Parent (of five)
Time period(s): 2000s
Locale(s): Washington, District of Columbia

Summary: Claire Doolittle's once passionate sex life has turned into a regularly scheduled chore on Saturday nights. Jack, her handsome, full-of-fun husband is now as staid as "Leave it to Beaver"'s Ward Cleaver. Claire is about to die from boredom. Then her old boyfriend, "Todd the Bod," who's still a hottie, gets in touch with her. Does she want excitement and a sizzling love life badly enough to dump dull but devoted Jack?

Where it's reviewed:
Booklist, January 1, 2008, page 50

Other books you might like:
Patricia Gaffney, *Flight Lessons*, 2002
Cassandra King, *The Sunday Wife*, 2002
Mary Alice Monroe, *Sweetgrass*, 2005
Judith Raxten, *The Secret Dreams of Emily Porter*, 2007
Susan Wiggs, *The Ocean between Us*, 2004

268

AMY GARVEY

Hot Date

(New York: Brava, 2008)

Story type: Contemporary; Humor
Subject(s): Organized Crime; Small Town Life; Humor
Major character(s): Grace Lamb, Divorced Person; Nick Griffin, Police Officer
Time period(s): 2000s
Locale(s): Wrightsville, Pennsylvania

Summary: Grace Lamb has moved back from New York to Wrightsville, Pennsylvania. The first person she runs into—literally—is police officer Nick Griffin, her brother Tommy's forever friend, and her childhood crush. She's as stunned by how handsome he is as he is by her beauty. Sparks fly, and they become a couple. Unfortunately, Grace has a little problem with the mob over some antique sex toys, and Nick, whose typical busts are for things like stealing books from the library, has to deal with organized crime.

Other books by the same author:
Room Service, 2007
I Love You to Death, 2006

Other books you might like:
Sue Civil-Brown, *Next Stop, Paradise*, 2001
Rachel Gibson, *The Trouble with Valentine's Day*, 2005
Cathie Linz, *Big Girls Don't Cry*, 2007
Lisa Plumley, *Josie Day Is Coming Home*, 2005
Deborah Shelley, *Talk about Love*, 1999

269

DIANE GASTON

The Vanishing Viscountess

(Toronto: Harlequin, 2008)

Story type: Historical/Regency
Subject(s): Identity, Concealed; Murder; Shipwrecks
Major character(s): Marlena Parronley, Noblewoman, Widow(er); Adam Vickery, Nobleman (Marquess of Tannerton)
Time period(s): 1810s (1818)
Locale(s): Scotland

Summary: After the ship on which they are both traveling is shipwrecked off the coast of Scotland, Adam Vickery, the Marquess of Tannerton, manages to save himself and one other passenger: a mysterious woman prisoner. Adam has no idea that the woman is Marlena Parronley, the notorious "Vanishing Viscountess." Wrongly accused of murdering her husband, Marlena's only hope of escaping is to give Adam a false name; however, the more time they spend together, the more Marlena begins to think she can trust Adam with the truth.

Where it's reviewed:
Romantic Times, January 2008, page 51

Romance

Other books by the same author:
Innocence and Impropriety, 2007
A Reputable Rake, 2006
The Wagering Widow, 2006
The Mysterious Miss M, 2005

Other books you might like:
Jo Beverley, *The Rogue's Return*, 2006
Christina Dodd, *Lost in Your Arms*, 2002
Gaelen Foley, *The Duke*, 2000
Sabrina Jeffries, *Beware a Scot's Revenge*, 2007
Edith Layton, *The Devil's Bargain*, 2002

270

GEORGINA GENTRY (Pseudonym of Lynne Murphy)

To Wed a Texan

(New York: Zebra, 2008)

Story type: Historical/American West; Humor
Subject(s): Sports/Boxing; Women's Rights; Social Issues
Major character(s): Bonnie O'Neal Schwartz Purdy, Librarian, Activist; Cash McCalley, Rogue, Public Relations (boxing promoter)
Time period(s): 1890s (1895)
Locale(s): Dallas, Texas

Summary: Promoter Cash McCalley has come to Dallas to set up a boxing match between "Gentleman Jim" Corbett and Bob Fitzsimmons. Librarian Bonnie O'Neal Schwartz Purdy, president of the Lone Star Ladies for Decency and Decorum, has other ideas. Her march on city hall only makes Cash more determined than ever to have the fight. A sidesplitting battle of the sexes.

Where it's reviewed:
Booklist, March 15, 2008, page 35
Romantic Times, March 2008, page 42

Other books by the same author:
To Love a Texan, 2007
To Tease a Texan, 2006
To Tempt a Texan, 2005
To Tame a Rebel, 2004
To Tame a Texan, 2003

Other books you might like:
Geralyn Dawson, *Simmer All Night*, 1999
Betina Krahn, *Sweet Talking Man*, 2000
Pamela Nowak, *Chances*, 2008
Maggie Osborne, *I Do! I Do! I Do!*, 2000
Nancy J. Parra, *A Wanted Man*, 2002

271

BLYTHE GIFFORD

Innocence Unveiled

(Toronto: Harlequin, 2008)

Story type: Historical/Medieval
Subject(s): Business; Espionage; War
Major character(s): Katrine de Gravere, Artisan (weaver), Noblewoman; Renard, Smuggler, Spy

Time period(s): 14th century (1337)
Locale(s): Ghent, Netherlands

Summary: Katrine de Gravere desperately needs wool, but with France and England battling for control over Flanders, no wool can be had in Ghent. Without wool to spin, Katrine will soon have to close her father's shop. So when a mysterious smuggler named "Renard" turns up late one night promising Katrine all the wool she needs, she is willing to pay whatever price he names.

Where it's reviewed:
Romantic Times, June 2008, page 56

Other books by the same author:
The Harlot's Daughter, 2007
The Knave and the Maiden, 2004

Other books you might like:
Terri Brisbin, *The King's Mistress*, 2005
Madeline Hunter, *By Arrangement*, 2000
Mary Reed McCall, *Beyond Temptation*, 2005
Joanne Rock, *My Lady's Favor*, 2005
Tina St. John, *Lord of Vengeance*, 1999

272

COLLEEN GLEASON (Pseudonym of Colleen Gleason Schulte)

The Bleeding Dusk

(New York: Signet Eclipse, 2008)

Story type: Historical/Fantasy; Historical/Regency
Series: Gardella Vampire Chronicles. Book 3
Subject(s): Alchemy; Seduction; Vampires
Major character(s): Victoria Gardella Grantworth de Lacy, Noblewoman, Vampire Hunter; Sebastian Vioget, Gentleman; Maximilian Pesaro, Vampire Hunter
Time period(s): 1810s
Locale(s): Rome, Italy

Summary: When a group of Roman vampires begin searching for the key that will unlock an ancient alchemist's long-locked laboratory door, Victoria Gardella Grantworth de Lacy, finds herself forced into an alliance with both Sebastian Vioget and Maximilian Pesaro. While Victoria knows she can't let the vampires gain control of the secrets contained within the laboratory, she also isn't exactly sure just how much she can trust her new "partners."

Where it's reviewed:
Romantic Times, February 2008, page 42

Other books by the same author:
Rises the Night, 2007
The Rest Falls Away, 2007
A Whisper of Rosemary, 2002

Other books you might like:
Naomi Bellis, *Step into Darkness*, 2006
Susan Carroll, *The Bride Finder*, 1998
Teresa Medeiros, *After Midnight*, 2005
Amanda Quick, *Deception*, 1993
Susan Squires, *Sacrament*, 2002

273

SUSAN GRANT (Pseudonym of Susan Grant Gunning)

Moonstruck

(Don Mills, Ontario: HQN, 2008)

Story type: Futuristic; Science Fiction
Series: Borderlands. Book 1
Subject(s): Peace; Space Travel; Politics
Major character(s): Brit Bandar, Spaceship Captain, Military Personnel (admiral); Finnar Rorkken, Military Personnel (warleader), Pirate (former)
Time period(s): Indeterminate Future
Locale(s): *Unity*, Spaceship; Triad Alliance, Interstellar Empire/Federation (Borderlands planets)

Summary: Although the bitter war between the Coalition and the Drakken Horde is over, Admiral Brit Bandar still hates the Drakken with a passion. Now, forced to accept Warleader Finn Rorkken, once known as the pirate Scourge of the Badlands, as her second in command, they head out to patrol the dangerous Borderlands area with an integrated crew just waiting to explode. The situation is complicated by Brit and Finn's unexpected attraction to each other in spite of their lack of trust. Violence, treachery, and muted flashes of humor are part of this lively, somewhat intense story that launches Grant's darker, more serious Borderlands series which a spin-off of her lighter Otherworldly Men trilogy.

Where it's reviewed:
Library Journal, June 15, 2008, page 51
Romantic Times, June 2008, page 104

Other books by the same author:
How to Lose an Extraterrestrial in 10 Days, 2007 (Otherworldly Men. Book 3)
My Favorite Earthling, 2007 (Otherworldly Men. Book 2)
Your Planet or Mine?, 2006 (Otherworldly Men. Book 1)
The Legend of Banzai Maguire, 2004 (2176. Book 1)
The Star Princess, 2003 (Star. Book 3)

Other books you might like:
Lois McMaster Bujold, *Shards of Honor*, 1986
Justine Davis, *The Sky Pirate*, 1995
Amanda Glass, *Shield's Lady*, 1989
    pseud. for Jayne Ann Krentz
Susan Krinard, *Kinsman's Oath*, 2004
Robin D. Owens, *Heart Fate*, 2008

274

JANE GRAVES

Tall Tales and Wedding Veils

(New York: Forever, 2008)

Story type: Contemporary; Humor
Subject(s): Marriage; Weddings; Deception
Major character(s): Heather Montgomery, Accountant (CPA); Tony McCaffrey, Businessman (would-be bar owner)

Time period(s): 2000s
Locale(s): Las Vegas, Nevada; Plano, Texas

Summary: When CPA Heather Montgomery helps bad-boy Tony McCaffrey win enough money in Vegas to buy the bar in Plano, Texas, he's always wanted, their champagne celebration turns into a wedding that neither had planned. An annulment seems to be the answer, except for the fact that Heather's family is ecstatic that she has finally found someone! Agreeing to stay married for a month and then get a divorce, Heather and Tony move in together. Love, passion, and a real marriage are the result, of course. A funny and fast-paced read.

Where it's reviewed:
Library Journal, April 15, 2008, page 66
Romantic Times, June 2008, page 96

Other books by the same author:
Hot Wheels and High Heels, 2007
Light My Fire, 2004
Flirting with Disaster, 2003
Wild at Heart, 2002
I Got You, Babe, 2001

Other books you might like:
Christie Craig, *Weddings Can Be Murder*, 2008
Fiona Harper, *Saying Yes to the Millionaire*, 2008
Shirley Jump, *Sweetheart Lost and Found*, 2008
Wendy Markham, *That's Amore*, 2008
Stephanie Tyler, *Coming Undone*, 2007

275

KAYLA GRAY

Rogue

(New York: Zebra, 2008)

Story type: Historical/Colonial America
Subject(s): Revenge; Kidnapping
Major character(s): Bailey Spencer, Captive; Cole Leighton, Pirate, Sea Captain
Time period(s): 1710s (1713; 1717)
Locale(s): England; North Carolina, American Colonies

Summary: Kidnapped during a pirate raid on her North Carolina home, Bailey Spencer wakes to find herself aboard ship and in the cabin of Captain Cole Leighton, a man on a mission to avenge his father's murder and who plans to use her to achieve it. Sparks fly as the inevitable romance blossoms between the pair in this lively adventure with a relatively uncommon setting and a few interesting twists. First novel.

Where it's reviewed:
Romantic Times, January 2008, page 52

Other books you might like:
Shannon Drake, *Bride of the Wind*, 1992
Gaelen Foley, *The Pirate Prince*, 1998
Kinley MacGregor, *Master of Seduction*, 2000
Kinley MacGregor, *A Pirate of Her Own*, 1999
Laura Renken, *My Lord Pirate*, 2001

276

JENNIFER GREENE   (Pseudonym of Alison Hart)

Blame It on Paris

(Don Mills, Ontario: HQN, 2008)

Story type: Contemporary
Subject(s): Business; Family
Major character(s): Kelly Rochard, Accountant; Will Maguire, Businessman
Time period(s): 2000s
Locale(s): Paris, France; South Bend, Indiana

Summary: Kelly Rochard's once-in-a-lifetime trip to Paris is a dream come true until she is robbed at the Louvre. Fortunately, Will Maguire, a transplanted American, not only helps Kelly deal with the police, but he also offers to let Kelly stay with him until she can replace her money. Caught up in the magic of Paris, Kelly finds herself falling in love with Will, but she is certain their affair will only last as long as she is in France. When Will suddenly turns up in South Bend, though, Kelly has to decide whether to stay with her fiance or take a chance on a future with Will.

Where it's reviewed:
Booklist, April 15, 2008, page 28
Romantic Times, April 2008, page 96

Other books by the same author:
Blame It on Cupid, 2007
Blame It on Chocolate, 2006
Sparkle, 2006
The Soon-to-be-Disinherited Wife, 2006
Hot to the Touch, 2005

Other books you might like:
Judith Arnold, *Love In Bloom's*, 2002
Rachel Gibson, *The Trouble with Valentine's Day*, 2005
Cindy Kirk, *When She Was Bad*, 2007
Kirsten Lobe, *Paris Hangover*, 2006
Susan Elizabeth Phillips, *Match Me If You Can*, 2005

277

LEIGH GREENWOOD   (Pseudonym of Harold Lowry)

Texas Loving

(New York: Leisure, 2008)

Story type: Historical/American West
Series: Cowboys. Book 13
Subject(s): American West; Cattle Drives; Gender Roles
Major character(s): Eden Maxwell, Rancher, Cowboy (cowgirl); Edward Davenport, Nobleman
Time period(s): 1880s (1889)
Locale(s): Texas; London, England

Summary: East meets west when rough-and-tough cowgirl Eden Maxwell falls for Edward Davenport, a refined British nobleman in this lively historical set in the Texas Hill Country.

Where it's reviewed:
Romantic Times, April 2008, page 50

Other books by the same author:
A Texan's Honor, 2006
Bret, 2006
The Mavericks, 2005
The Reluctant Bride, 2005
The Independent Bride, 2004

Other books you might like:
Ruth Ryan Langan, *Heart's Delight*, 2007
Ana Leigh, *His Boots under Her Bed*, 2006
Maureen McKade, *A Reason to Live*, 2006
Linda Lael Miller, *McKettrick's Luck*, 2007
    McKettrick Men. Book 1
Jodi Thomas, *Texas Rain*, 2006

278

LAURA LEE GUHRKE

The Wicked Ways of a Duke

(New York: Avon, 2008)

Story type: Historical/Victorian
Subject(s): Inheritance; Secrets; Seduction
Major character(s): Prudence Bosworth, Heiress, Seamstress; Rhys de Winter, Nobleman (Duke of St. Cyres)
Time period(s): 1890s (1894)
Locale(s): England

Summary: After seamstress Prudence Bosworth inherits a fortune from her long lost and long gone father, she has to marry within a year or she will lose everything. Prudence is determined to marry for true love only, but fortunately for her, she seems to have found the perfect candidate: Rhys de Winter, the Duke of St. Cyres. When Prudence discovers Rhys is really a cynical rake in desperate need of a fortune, she is more than ready to cancel their wedding. However, much to his surprise, Rhys discovers he is falling for his new fiancee, Prudence, and now he must find a way to win her love all over again.

Where it's reviewed:
Romantic Times, January 2008, page 45

Other books by the same author:
And Then He Kissed Her, 2007
She's No Princess, 2006
The Marriage Bed, 2005
Guilty Pleasures, 2004
His Every Kiss, 2004

Other books you might like:
Adele Ashworth, *Duke of Sin*, 2004
Robyn DeHart, *Deliciously Wicked*, 2006
Susan King, *Taming the Heiress*, 2003
Julianne MacLean, *Surrender to a Scoundrel*, 2007
Melody Thomas, *A Match Made in Scandal*, 2005

279

NANCY HADDOCK

La Vida Vampire

(New York: Berkley, 2008)

Story type: Contemporary; Vampire Story
Subject(s): Vampires; Suspense
Major character(s): Francesca Marinelli, Vampire, Guide (ghost tour guide); Deke Saber, Paranormal Investigator (preternatural crimes)
Time period(s): 2000s
Locale(s): St. Augustine, Florida

Summary: Newly resurrected after being underground for more than two centuries, Francesca Marinelli, both a vampire and a psychic, has "gone straight" and is enjoying life as a ghost tour guide in St. Augustine. However, when a member of a recent tour turns up dead, she's a prime suspect, even though she didn't do it. Sexy preternatural crimes investigator Deke Saber adds romance to her life while a group of crazy vampire hunters add suspense in this funny, sassy paranormal debut.

Where it's reviewed:
Romantic Times, April 2008, page 107

Other books you might like:
MaryJanice Davidson, *Undead and Unwed*, 2004
Katie MacAlister, *Sex and the Single Vampire*, 2004
Lynsay Sands, *Bite Me If You Can*, 2007
Lynsay Sands, *Love Bites*, 2004
Kassandra Sims, *The Midnight Work*, 2005

280

SHIRLEY HAILSTOCK

On My Terms

(New York: Dafina, 2008)

Story type: Contemporary; Ethnic
Subject(s): Small Town Life; Healing; Movie Industry
Major character(s): Theresa Ramsey, Guardian; Dean Clayton, Filmmaker; Chelsea, Child
Time period(s): 2000s
Locale(s): Royce, New York

Summary: Returning to her upstate New York family estate after the death of her cousin, Theresa Ramsey is shocked to find a movie crew still on her property. She'd thought they'd be gone by now and she's furious that she and her cousin's young daughter, Chelsea, don't have the peace and quiet they need to heal from the last few months. However, filmmaker Dean Clayton needs to finish this film that will either make or break his career, and somehow he needs to convince Theresa to let him finish his project. This heartwarming, romantic story deals nicely with issues of loss, grief, and healing.

Other books by the same author:
Wrong Dress, Right Guy, 2008
The Secret, 2006
You Made Me Love You, 2005
More than Gold, 2000
Mirror Image, 1998

Other books you might like:
Rochelle Alers, *My Love's Keeper*, 2001
Sandra Kitt, *She's the One*, 2001
Francis Ray, *Only You*, 2007
Janice Sims, *Three Wishes*, 2008
Annie Smith, *Home Again*, 2002

281

TRACI E. HALL

Love's Magic

(Naperville, Illinois: Medallion, 2008)

Story type: Historical/Medieval; Fantasy
Subject(s): Magic; Healing; Legends
Major character(s): Celestia Montehue, Noblewoman, Healer; Nicholas Le Blanc, Knight, Nobleman
Time period(s): 12th century (1192)
Locale(s): England

Summary: Forced into an arranged marriage neither of them want, Celestia Montehue, a magical healer from a gifted family, and Nicholas Le Blanc, a tormented, guilt-ridden knight, agree not to consummate their marriage so they can get an annulment later on. Naturally, this causes a bit of tension, something they don't need as they deal with a castle in shambles, a ghost that haunts the tower, wary townsfolk, and enemies, known and unknown. Magic infuses this complex story that has more than its share of characters.

Other books you might like:
Kimberly Cates, *Briar Rose*, 1999
Juliana Garnett, *The Knight*, 2001
Jennifer Roberson, *Lady of the Forest*, 1992
Maura Seger, *Veil of Secrets*, 1996
Lisa Ann Verge, *The Faery Bride*, 1996

282

GEMMA HALLIDAY

Alibi in High Heels

(New York: Making It, 2008)

Story type: Contemporary; Romantic Suspense
Series: Maddie Springer. Book 4
Subject(s): Fashion Design; Murder
Major character(s): Maddie Springer, Designer (shoe designer); Jack Ramirez, Detective—Police
Time period(s): 2000s
Locale(s): California; Paris, France; London, England

Summary: For Maddie Springer it was the opportunity of a lifetime: the chance to design all the shoes for France's hottest fashion designer Jean Luc LeCroix's show. When Jean Luc's top model is found murdered with one of Maddie's designer shoes, Maddie is not only gifted with the nickname the Couture Killer, she also becomes the police's prime suspect. Now in order to find out exactly who is trying to frame her, Maddie must do a bit of detective work to discover the real murderer.

Where it's reviewed:
Romantic Times, March 2008, page 57

Other books by the same author:
Killer in High Heels, 2007
Undercover in High Heels, 2007
Spying in High Heels, 2006

Other books you might like:
Stephanie Bond, *Kill the Competition*, 2004
Jennifer Crusie, *Fast Women*, 2001
Linda Howard, *To Die For*, 2005
Michelle Jerott, *Her Bodyguard*, 2001
Vicki Lewis Thompson, *Nerd In Shining Armor*, 2003

283

LORI HANDELAND
REBECCA WINTERS , Co-Author
ANNA DESTEFANO , Co-Author

Mothers of the Year

(Toronto: Harlequin, 2008)

Story type: Contemporary; Holiday Themes
Subject(s): Mothers; Family
Time period(s): 2000s
Locale(s): United States

Summary: Moms and their issues, hopes, and concerns are the focus of this Mothers' Day trilogy that has something for everyone. Included are: "Mommy for Rent" by Lori Handeland, the heartwarming story of a girl who hires a mother and ends up with one in fact; "Along Came a Daughter" by Rebecca Winters, in which a matchmaking teen gets what she wants; and "Baby Steps" by Anna DeStefano, the tale of a woman who learns the true meaning of motherhood. This is a well-written, rewarding collection.

Where it's reviewed:
Library Journal, April 15, 2008, page 66
Romantic Times, April 2008, page 115

Other books you might like:
Mary Blayney, *A Husband for Mama*, 2003
  Regency anthology
Lisa Cach, *A Mother's Way*, 2002
  anthology
Bette Ford, *A Mother's Love*, 1996
  anthology
Alice Holden, *A Courtship for Mama*, 2004
  Regency anthology
Emilie Richards, *A Mother's Day*, 2002
  anthology

284

FIONA HARPER

Saying Yes to the Millionaire

(Toronto: Harlequin, 2008)

Story type: Contemporary
Series: Bride for All Seasons. Book 2

Subject(s): Weddings; Adventure and Adventurers; Reunions
Major character(s): Fern Chambers, Insurance Investigator (risk analyst); Josh Adams, Tour Guide, Wealthy
Time period(s): 2000s
Locale(s): England

Summary: When her roommate agrees to donate a considerable sum to her favorite charity if she says "yes" to every question asked her for a week, conservative, wary risk analyst Fern Chambers agrees. However, when josh Adams, a wealthy old friend (and her long-time secret love), asks her to be his partner on an adventurous treasure hunt for charity, she begins to question the wisdom of her bargain. Love and adventure quickly follow in this sweet, heartwarming marriage-oriented romance that has more than its share of thrills.

Where it's reviewed:
Library Journal, April 15, 2008, page 66
Romantic Times, June 2008, page 121

Other books by the same author:
English Lord, Ordinary Lady, 2008
Break Up to Make Up, 2007
Blind-Date Marriage, 2006

Other books you might like:
Georgia Bockoven, *Another Summer*, 2001
Liz Fielding, *The Bride's Baby*, 2008
  Bride for All Seasons. Book 1. Spring
Shirley Jump, *Marry-Me Christmas*, 2008
  Bride for All Seasons. Book 4. Winter
Shirley Jump, *Sweetheart Lost and Found*, 2008
Trish Wylie, *The Millionaire's Proposal*, 2008
  Bride for All Seasons. Book 3. Autumn

285

JULIA HARPER (Pseudonym of Nancy M. Finney)

Hot

(New York: Forever, 2008)

Story type: Contemporary
Subject(s): Animals/Dogs; Crime and Criminals; Money
Major character(s): Turner Hastings, Banker, Librarian; John MacKinnon, FBI Agent
Time period(s): 2000s
Locale(s): Wisconsin

Summary: When two less-than-experienced robbers hold up the First Wisconsin Bank of Winosha, part-time teller Turner Hastings sees a once-in-a-lifetime opportunity to help herself to some of the bank's cash. Once Special Agent John MacKinnon realizes exactly who the real thief is, he finds himself chasing Turner, who seems to have taken the money as part of her own unique plan to avenge an old wrong. At first John is determined to bring Turner in, but when he realizes someone else seems determined to silence Turner permanently, John decides Turner is the one who needs help.

Other books you might like:
Jennifer Crusie, *Fast Women*, 2001
Christina Dodd, *Tongue in Chic*, 2007
Linda Howard, *To Die For*, 2005
Michelle Jerott, *One Way Out*, 2005
Julie Kenner, *Nobody but You*, 2003

286

KAREN HARPER

Below the Surface

(Don Mills, Ontario: Mira, 2008)

Story type: Contemporary; Romantic Suspense
Subject(s): Missing Persons; Sports/Scuba Diving; Mystery
Major character(s): Briana Devon, Diver (salvage expert), Twin; Cole DeRoca, Carpenter
Time period(s): 2000s
Locale(s): Florida

Summary: Stunned to discover her twin sister missing, along with their boat, when she resurfaces after a dive in the Gulf of Mexico, Briana Devon is caught in a fierce storm and rescued by Cole DeRoca who has also been caught in the storm. Confused, Bree tries to piece together the fateful afternoon before the storm to come up with answers to her sister's disappearance, but the answers lie just out of reach—below the surface of the water—and are more dangerous and troubling than she knows. Politics, pollution, and unexpected relationships are all part of this suspenseful romance.

Where it's reviewed:
Romantic Times, February 2008, page 75

Other books by the same author:
Hurricane, 2006
The Falls, 2006
Dark Angel, 2005
Dark Harvest, 2004
Dark Road Home, 2004

Other books you might like:
Heather Graham, *Eyes of Fire*, 1995
Jayne Ann Krentz, *Sharp Edges*, 1998
Alisa Kwitney, *The Dominant Blonde*, 2002
    more humorous
Nora Roberts, *The Reef*, 1998
Suzanne Simmons, *The Paradise Man*, 1997

287

JILLIAN HART
KATE BRIDGES , Co-Author
CHARLENE SANDS , Co-Author

Western Weddings

(Toronto: Harlequin 2008)

Story type: Historical/American West; Historical/Canadian West
Subject(s): Weddings; American West
Time period(s): 19th Century (1880-1899)
Locale(s): United States; Canada

Summary: This trio of charmingly diverse, generally sweet novellas captures the flavor of the North American Old West. Included are: "Rocky Mountain Bride" by Jillian Hart, the tale of a woman who arrives to be married but finds the groom isn't expecting her; "Shotgun Vows" by Kate Bridges, the engaging Klondike Gold Rush story of

a woman whose romantic plans go awry and result in an unexpected marriage; and "Springville Wife" by Charlene Sands, the heartwarming story of two childhood adversaries who meet again with very different results.

Where it's reviewed:
Library Journal, April 15, 2008, page 66
Romantic Times, May 2008, page 48

Other books you might like:
Millie Criswell, *A Western Family Christmas*, 2001
    anthology
Julie Garwood, *One Red Rose*, 1997
Jill Marie Landis, *Come Spring*, 1992
Cathy Maxwell, *Wild West Brides*, 2002
Linda Lael Miller, *Springwater*, 1999

288

AMANDA HARTE (Pseudonym of Christine B. Tayntor)

Stargazer

(New York: Avalon, 2008)

Story type: Contemporary
Series: Hidden Falls. Book 4
Subject(s): Romance; Healing; Small Town Life
Major character(s): Julie Unger, Artisan (restores carousel ponies), Divorced Person; Rick Swanson, Architect, Widow(er); Josh Swanson, Child
Time period(s): 2000s
Locale(s): Hidden Falls, New York

Summary: Hired to restore the animals on an antique carousel, divorcee Julie Unger leaves Texas and heads for upstate New York hoping for a fresh start and a little peace. What she finds, however, is resentment, a divided town, a little boy in need of healing, and a love, in the person of architect and father Rick Swanson, she never expected. A slight mystery adds a bit of tension to this sweet, heartwarming romance in the Hidden Falls series that includes both contemporary and historical romances.

Other books by the same author:
The Golden Thread, 2008 (Hidden Falls. Book 5)
Dream Weaver, 2007 (Hidden Falls. Book 3)
The Brass Ring, 2007 (Hidden Falls. Book 2)
Painted Ponies, 2006 (Hidden Falls. Book 1)
Dancing in the Rain, 2003

Other books you might like:
Kimberly Cates, *Lighthouse Cove*, 2000
Marcia Evanick, *A Berry Merry Christmas*, 2004
Marcia Evanick, *A Misty Harbor Wedding*, 2006
Holly O'Dell, *Spin Control*, 2006
Sherryl Woods, *Ask Anyone*, 2002
    a funnier take on carousels

289

KAREN HAWKINS

To Catch a Highlander

(New York: Pocket, 2008)

Story type: Historical/Regency
Series: MacLean Curse. Book 3

Subject(s): Gambling; Heritage
Major character(s): Sophia MacFarlane, Gentlewoman, Gambler; Dougal MacLean, Nobleman
Time period(s): 1800s
Locale(s): Scotland

Summary: Appalled that her father gambled their home and estate away, Sophia MacFarlane sets out to make sure the notorious Lord Dougal MacLean doesn't keep his winnings. There is nothing she won't do, even trash the home she has worked hard to improve, hoping Dougal won't want it. However, Dougal has other ideas, and they include laying claim to the lady as well as the house. Funny, sexy, and lively, this romance features well-matched protagonists who learn that there's more to winning than they had first thought.

Where it's reviewed:
Romantic Times, January 2008, page 44

Other books by the same author:
How to Abduct a Highland Lord, 2007 (MacLean Curse. Book 1)
To Scotland, with Love, 2007 (MacLean Curse. Book 2)
Her Master and Commander, 2006 (Ask Reeves. Book 1)
Her Officer and Gentleman, 2006 (Ask Reeves. Book 2)
Lady in Red, 2005 (Talisman Ring. Book 5)

Other books you might like:
Nicola Cornick, *Lady Allerton's Wager*, 2003
Eloisa James, *Kiss Me, Annabel*, 2005
Nicole Jordan, *To Pleasure a Lady*, 2008
Stephanie Laurens, *A Rogue's Proposal*, 1999
Julia Ross, *The Seduction*, 2002

290

SHIRL HENKE
JIM HENKE , Co-Author

The River Nymph

(New York: Leisure, 2008)

Story type: Historical/Post-American Civil War
Subject(s): Gambling; Boats and Boating; Rivers
Major character(s): Delilah Mathers Raymond, Gambler, Widow(er); Clint Daniels, Gambler, Businessman (brothel owner)
Time period(s): 19th century (post-Civil War)
Locale(s): St. Louis, Missouri; Missouri River (on *The River Nymph*)

Summary: Gambler Clint Daniels literally loses his shirt as well as his boat, *The River Nymph*, to Delilah Mathers during a poker game. The problem is, Delilah's angered a mob boss, and no one will work for her. Swallowing her pride, she signs on Clint as a partner, but she gets more than she expected in the bargain. This is the Henkes' first collaboration.

Where it's reviewed:
Romantic Times, February 2008, page 51

Other books you might like:
Georgina Gentry, *To Love a Texan*, 2007
Gail Link, *Luck of the Draw*, 2006
Maggie Osborne, *The Seduction of Samantha Kincade*, 1995
Nan Ryan, *A Lifetime of Heaven*, 1993
LaVyrle Spencer, *The Gamble*, 1984

291

PATTI CALLAHAN HENRY

The Art of Keeping Secrets

(New York: NAL, 2008)

Story type: Contemporary
Subject(s): Secrets; Grief; Animals/Dolphins
Major character(s): Annabelle Murphy, Widow(er), Single Parent; Shawn, Divorced Person
Time period(s): 2000s
Locale(s): Marsh Cove, South Carolina; Newboro, North Carolina; Rocky Mountains, Colorado

Summary: Advice columnist Annabelle Murphy's world is shattered for the second time when hikers find the plane her husband crashed two years earlier. His body isn't the only one in the wreckage—there's also a female's. Now, as Annabelle has to face her husband's infidelity, as well as his death, she begins the search for the identity of the other woman.

Where it's reviewed:
Romantic Times, June 2008, page 60

Other books by the same author:
Between the Tides, 2007
When Light Breaks, 2006
Where the River Runs, 2005
Losing the Moon, 2004

Other books you might like:
Kathleen McCleary, *House and Home*, 2008
Mary Alice Monroe, *Time Is a River*, 2008
Barbara Samuel, *A Piece of Heaven*, 2004
Anne Rivers Siddons, *Sweetwater Creek*, 2005
Susan Wiggs, *The Ocean between Us*, 2005

292

SANDRA HILL

Wild Jinx

(New York: Forever, 2008)

Story type: Humor; Contemporary
Series: Jinx Inc. Book 3
Subject(s): Humor; Treasure, Buried; Organized Crime
Major character(s): Celine Arseneux, Journalist, Single Parent; John LeDeux, Detective—Police
Time period(s): 2000s
Locale(s): Baton Rouge, Louisiana; Bayou Black, Louisiana

Summary: Reporter Celine Arseneux and Detective John LeDeux, outed in a sting operation against the Dixie

mob, lie low in Bayou Black until things calm down. Tante Lulu, a 92-year-old swamp granny, uses her super skills as a matchmaker—and lots of help from her good buddy, St. Jude—to see to it that John finds the type of girl she thinks he should have, and Celine fits the bill.

Where it's reviewed:
Booklist, March 15, 2008, page 34
Romantic Times, March 2008, page 99

Other books by the same author:
Pearl Jinx, 2007 (Jinx Inc. Book 2)
Tall, Dark and Cajun, 2007
The Cajun Cowboy, 2007
Pink Jinx, 2006 (Jinx Inc. Book 1)
The Red-Hot Cajun, 2005

Other books you might like:
Jane Blackwood, *A Hard Man Is Good to Find*, 2004
Stephanie Bond, *Finding Your Mojo*, 2006
Gemma Bruce, *Who Loves You, Baby?*, 2005
Suzanne Enoch, *Don't Look Down*, 2005
Dixie Kane, *Chasing Lily*, 2003

293

JEN HOLLING

My Immortal Protector

(New York: Pocket, 2008)

Story type: Historical/Seventeenth Century; Paranormal
Subject(s): Witches and Witchcraft; Vampires; Magic
Major character(s): Deidra MacKay, Healer, Witch (animal whisperer); Stephen Ross, Recluse, Handicapped (crippled)
Time period(s): 17th century (1609)
Locale(s): Scotland

Summary: Descended from an ancient line of healers and blood witches, Deidra MacKay is searching for the vampire who first made the blood pact with her ancestors that granted them the source of their magic. Deidra wants to rid herself of her magical abilities, so she seeks out Stephen Ross, a recluse she believes might have the answers. Together Stephen and Deidra set out on their quest, but witch hunter Luthias Forsyth, who has long been Deidra's nemesis, is hot on their trail and he's not going to rest until he destroys her.

Where it's reviewed:
Romantic Times, March 2008, page 39

Other books by the same author:
My Immortal Promise, 2008
My Devilish Scotsman, 2005
My Shadow Warrior, 2005
My Wicked Highlander, 2004
Tamed by Your Desire, 2002

Other books you might like:
Katherine Deauville, *Eyes of Love*, 1996
Rosemary Edghill, *Met by Moonlight*, 1998
Karyn Monk, *The Witch and the Warrior*, 1998
Marliss Moon, *By Starlight*, 2003
Patricia Rice, *Merely Magic*, 2000
    lighter

294

EMMA HOLLY

Demon's Fire

(New York: Berkley Sensation, 2008)

Story type: Paranormal; Historical/Victorian
Series: Demon World
Subject(s): Demons; Sexual Behavior; Erotica
Major character(s): Beth, Archaeologist; Pahndir, Royalty (prince), Demon (Yama); Charles, Archaeologist
Time period(s): Indeterminate Past
Locale(s): Alternate Earth (Victorian England); Bhamjran, Fictional City

Summary: In the desert community of Bhamjran, adventurers Beth and Charles meet Prince Pahndir, a banished Yamish demon who now runs a pleasure house, and together they explore their passionate fantasies in exotic ways. Past issues impact the present and must be dealt with in this erotic, sexually explicit story that is part of Holly's Demon World series.

Where it's reviewed:
Romantic Times, April 2008, page 120

Other books by the same author:
Prince of Ice, 2006 (Demon World. Book 2)
The Demon Princess, 2004 (Demon World. Book 1)
Catching Midnight, 2003
Hunting Midnight, 2003
Beyond Seduction, 2002

Other books you might like:
Suzanne Forster, *Tease*, 2006
Jade Lee, *Seduced by Crimson*, 2006
Cheyenne McCray, *Forbidden Magic*, 2005
Cheyenne McCray, *Shadow Magic*, 2008
Robin Schone, *Scandalous Lovers*, 2007

295

CHERYL HOLT

Double Fantasy

(New York: St. Martin's Paperbacks, 2008)

Story type: Historical/Regency
Subject(s): Twins; Inheritance; Revenge
Major character(s): Anne Carstairs, Gentlewoman, Orphan; Jamieson Merrick, Nobleman (Earl of Gladstone)
Time period(s): 1810s (1813)
Locale(s): England

Summary: Amazed when the outrageous, attractive man she'd met while walking turns out to the be Jamie Merrick, the long-lost heir to the Earldom of Gladstone and the man who is now in charge of the estate where she and her sister have been living, Anne Carstairs soon finds herself the object of Jamie's matrimonial intentions, and she's not sure she approves. She's wise to be skeptical, however, because all is not as it seems in this sexy story of betrayal and revenge that has not one, but two romantic entanglements to sort out.

Romance

Where it's reviewed:
Romantic Times, March 2008, page 40

Other books by the same author:
Forbidden Fantasy, 2007
Secret Fantasy, 2007
My Only Love, 2006
Too Wicked to Wed, 2006
Too Tempting to Touch, 2006

Other books you might like:
Christina Dodd, *A Well-Pleasured Lady*, 1997
Emma Holly, *Beyond Innocence*, 2001
Emma Holly, *Beyond Seduction*, 2002
Susan Johnson, *Rough around the Edges*, 1998
Stephanie Laurens, *All about Passion*, 2001

296

HANNAH HOWELL

Highland Wolf

(New York: Zebra, 2008)

Story type: Historical/Medieval
Subject(s): Identity, Concealed; Mystery; Revenge
Major character(s): Annora MacKay, Noblewoman, Child-
Care Giver; James Drummond, Laird (former),
Impostor (master carver)
Time period(s): 15th century (1477)

Summary: Determined to prove his innocence and wrest
Dunncraig Keep from Donnell MacKay, the man who'd
killed his wife and branded him a murderer, James
Drummond disguises himself as a master carver and
goes to work at Dunncraig. Annora MacKay is also at
Dunncraig to look after Meggie, James' young daughter;
and when she realizes who Donnell is, she joins with
him to outwit Donnell. Violence and danger follow in
this sensual Scottish adventure.

Where it's reviewed:
Romantic Times, January 28, 2008, page 45

Other books by the same author:
Highland Wedding, 2007
Highland Destiny, 2006
Highland Promise, 2006
My Immortal Highlander, 2006 (anthology)
Highland Conqueror, 2005

Other books you might like:
Julie Garwood, *The Ransom*, 1999
Arnette Lamb, *The Chieftain*, 1996
Ruth Ryan Langan, *The Highlander*, 1994
Jaclyn Reding, *White Heather*, 1997
Amanda Scott, *The Hidden Heiress*, 2002

297

ELIZABETH HOYT (Pseudonym of Nancy M. Finney)

To Taste Temptation

(New York: Forever, 2008)

Story type: Historical/Georgian
Series: Legend of the Four Soldiers. Book 1

Subject(s): Revenge; Romance; Secrets
Major character(s): Lady Emeline Gordon, Noblewoman;
Samuel Hartley, Importer/Exporter, Military Person-
nel (former scout)
Time period(s): 1760s (1764)
Locale(s): England

Summary: In England ostensibly on business but really to
find the man who betrayed him and his men during the
French and Indian War, wealthy American importer Samuel Hartley convinces Lady Emeline Gordon to introduce
his 19-year-old sister to society during their brief stay.
Curious about the brash, unsophisticated American,
especially when he says he knew her brother who was
killed in battle, Emeline knows there's more to Samuel
than meets the eye, and she's determined to figure out
what his motives are. Secrets and passion are the
underpinnings of this sexy tale that is first of a quartet of
stories focusing on four men out for revenge on the man
who betrayed them.

Where it's reviewed:
Romantic Times, May 2008, page 40

Other books by the same author:
To Seduce a Sinner, 2008 (Legend of the Four Soldiers.
Book 2)
The Leopard Prince, 2007 (Prince. Book 2)
The Serpent Prince, 2007 (Prince. Book 3)
The Raven Prince, 2006 (Prince. Book 1)

Other books you might like:
Mary Balogh, *Irresistible*, 1998
Mary Balogh, *Thief of Dreams*, 1998
Jo Beverley, *Hazard*, 2002
Jo Beverley, *A Lady's Secret*, 2008
Celeste Bradley, *The Spy*, 2004

298

MADELINE HUNTER

Secrets of Surrender

(New York: Dell, 2008)

Story type: Historical/Regency
Subject(s): Family; Marriage; Secrets
Major character(s): Roselyn Longworth, Gentlewoman;
Kyle Bradwell, Architect, Businessman
Time period(s): 1820s
Locale(s): England

Summary: After her brother Timothy embezzles money
from a number of investors and then flees the country,
an impoverished Roselyn Longworth has no choice but
to accept Lord Norbury's offer to become his mistress.
That arrangement ends the night Norbury tries to auction
Roselyn off at one of his infamous house parties and
Roselyn is "bought" by Kyle Bradwell. Roselyn never
expected that Kyle would later ask her to marry him, but
marrying Kyle would help restore her ruined reputation.
Once Roselyn discovers the real reason why Kyle
proposed, though, it threatens to destroy their new
marriage.

Where it's reviewed:
Booklist, May 1, 2008, page 74
Romantic Times, June 2008, page 48

Other books by the same author:
Lessons of Desire, 2007
Lady of Sin, 2006
The Rules of Seduction, 2006
Lord of Sin, 2005
The Romantic, 2004

Other books you might like:
Jo Beverley, *The Rogue's Return*, 2006
Liz Carlyle, *A Deal with the Devil*, 2004
Sabrina Jeffries, *Never Seduce a Scoundrel*, 2006
Stephanie Laurens, *The Perfect Lover*, 2003
Julia London, *The Hazards of Hunting a Duke*, 2006

299

JESSICA INCLAN (Pseudonym of Jessica Inclan Barksdale)

Being with Him

(New York: Zebra, 2008)

Story type: Contemporary; Paranormal
Subject(s): Psychic Powers; Time Travel
Major character(s): Mila Adams, Artist, Psychic; Garrick McClellan, Financier (company owner), Psychic
Time period(s): 2000s
Locale(s): San Francisco, California

Summary: Artist Mila Adams and financier Garrick Mc-Clellan resent being set up by well-meaning relatives; but it doesn't take long for them to realize that they have much more in common that anyone had thought. Gifted with the ability to read thoughts and shift time, Mila and Garrick had thought they were alone and had kept their talents secret. Now, as they join forces to discover what it all means, they are drawn to each other romantically, as well. First in a projected trilogy.

Where it's reviewed:
Romantic Times, February 2008, page 102

Other books by the same author:
Believe in Me, 2007
Reason to Believe, 2006
When You Believe, 2006

Other books you might like:
Jennifer Ashley, *Immortals: The Calling*, 2007
Allyson James, *Dragon Heat*, 2007
Katie MacAlister, *Light My Fire*, 2006
    funny paranormal
Pamela Palmer, *The Dark Gate*, 2007
Mary Jo Putney, *A Kiss of Fate*, 2004
    historical

300

LINDA INGMANSON

Promise Me Tomorrow

(Waterville, Maine: Five Star, 2008)

Story type: Contemporary
Subject(s): Reunions; Forgiveness; Love
Major character(s): Abby McGuire, Store Owner (family

deli); Ashton Wheeler, Businessman (security company)
Time period(s): 2000s
Locale(s): Cranberry, Connecticut

Summary: After a difficult stint as a police officer in Los Angeles, Ash Wheeler returns to his New England hometown for a brief visit before he heads for Miami and a new security business venture. However, when he reconnects with his old sweetheart, Abby McGuire, he finds it harder to leave than he'd expected. A light mystery adds interest to this heartwarming romance.

Other books you might like:
Jeanette Baker, *Chesapeake Tide*, 2004
Colleen Faulkner, *Taming Ben*, 2000
Lorraine Heath, *Hard Lovin' Man*, 2003
Deb Stover, *A Matter of Trust*, 2000
Gina Wilkins, *Seductively Yours*, 2000

301

ELIZABETH JEFFREY

Rookhurst Hall

(Sutton, Surrey, England: Severn House, 2008)

Story type: Contemporary; Historical/World War I
Subject(s): Heritage; Social Classes; Family Relations
Major character(s): Lucy Armitage, Secretary, Saleswoman (antiques store); Ben Manton, Antiques Dealer
Time period(s): 20th century (1900-1960)
Locale(s): England

Summary: The discovery of pictures of a manor house and three young girls in Edwardian dress in an antique bureau that belonged to her grandmother sets Lucy Armitage on a quest for her past. What she finds, however, is not at all what she expects. Ben Manton adds the romantic interest in this sweet romance that is strong on historical detail and alternates between the realities of British life during World War I and the influenza epidemic that followed, and the more modern Sixties.

Other books by the same author:
Travellers' Inn, 2006
The Weaver's Daughter, 2003
Cast a Long Shadow, 2001
The Buttercup Fields, 1993
Cassie Jordan, 1990

Other books you might like:
Tessa Barclay, *A True Likeness*, 2002
Amanda Harte, *Whistling in the Dark*, 2004
    World War I setting
Anna Jacobs, *An Independent Woman*, 2005
    World War I setting
Gwen Kirkwood, *The Laird of Lochandee*, 2002
Gwen Kirkwood, *A Tangled Web*, 2003

302

BEVERLY JENKINS

Jewel

(New York: Avon, 2008)

Story type: Historical/Victorian America; Ethnic
Subject(s): Marriage; African Americans; Small Town Life
Major character(s): Jewel Crowley, Spinster, Gardner (rose expert); Eli Grayson, Editor (town newspaper), Journalist
Time period(s): 1880s (1881)
Locale(s): Grayson Grove, Michigan

Summary: Needing a wife in order to meet the requirements of the newspaper publisher who wants to add his failing *Gazette* to his syndicate, bachelor Eli Grayson convinces Jewel Crowley to pose as his wife for the evening. All goes well until the town finds out, and then, with gossip threatening Jewel's reputation, Eli and Jewel wed. Although Jewel considers this a marriage in name only, Eli has other ideas, and eventually they discover a passion that surprises them both. Their happiness is threatened when an evil woman from the past returns to town and their love is put to the test. The story contains links to *Vivid*.

Where it's reviewed:
Romantic Times, May 2008, page 42

Other books by the same author:
Deadly Sexy, 2007
Wild Sweet Love, 2007
Winds of the Storm, 2006
Before the Dawn, 2001
Vivid, 1995 (reprinted in 2001)

Other books you might like:
Rochelle Alers, *Best Kept Secrets*, 2006
Anita Richmond Bunkley, *Starlight Passage*, 1996
Francine Craft, *The Black Pearl*, 1996
Shirley Hailstock, *Clara's Promise*, 1995

303

JOAN JOHNSTON

A Stranger's Game

(New York: Pocket, 2008)

Story type: Contemporary
Series: Bitter Creek. Book 7
Subject(s): Murder; Crime and Criminals; Serial Killers
Major character(s): Grace Smith, Impostor (Merle Raye Finkel), Fugitive; Breed Grayhawk, FBI Agent
Time period(s): 2000s
Locale(s): Texas

Summary: An incredible one night stand suddenly takes on new meaning when FBI Agent Breed Grayhawk learns that the sexy Grace Smith is really an ex-con, convicted of murder as a juvenile, and is now the object of a fake terrorist manhunt. However, Grace has been looking for the real killers of her father and stepmother ever since she broke her parole, and when the killer realizes she's getting close, he sets her up as a terrorist threat and Breed ends up assigned to the job. Things come to a head when he finds her and realizes she's telling the truth; suddenly, they are running from both the killer and the law.

Where it's reviewed:
Romantic Times, March 2008, page 76

Other books by the same author:
The Next Mrs. Blackthorne, 2005 (Bitter Creek. Book 6)
The Rivals, 2004 (Bitter Creek. Book 5)
The Price, 2003 (Bitter Creek. Book 4)
The Loner, 2002 (Bitter Creek. Book 3)
The Texan, 2001 (Bitter Creek. Book 2)

Other books you might like:
Catherine Coulter, *The Cove*, 1996
Lisa Jackson, *The Morning After*, 2004
Dinah McCall, *Storm Warning*, 2001
Karen Robards, *Bait*, 2005
Karen Robards, *To Trust a Stranger*, 2001

304

NICOLE JORDAN (Pseudonym of Anne Bushyhead)

To Bed a Beauty

(New York: Ballantine, 2008)

Story type: Historical/Regency
Series: Courtship Wars. Book 2
Subject(s): Marriage; Courtship; Seduction
Major character(s): Roslyn Loring, Gentlewoman; Andrew Moncrief, Nobleman (Duke of Arden), Rake
Time period(s): 1810s (1817)
Locale(s): London, England

Summary: Hoping for a love match with a neighboring earl, Roslyn Loring decides she needs to learn the seductive ways of mistresses if she wants to keep him from straying. However, she needs instruction, so when the notorious Duke of Arden offers to teach her what she needs to know, she accepts. The results are passionate and expected in this installment of Jordan's trilogy about the Loring sisters.

Where it's reviewed:
Romantic Times, March 2008, page 42

Other books by the same author:
To Seduce a Bride, 2008 (The Courtship Wars. Book 3)
To Pleasure a Lady, 2007 (The Courtship Wars. Book 1)
Fever Dreams, 2006
Wicked Fantasy, 2005
Lord of Seduction, 2004

Other books you might like:
Celeste Bradley, *Duke Most Wanted*, 2008
   The Heiress Brides. Book 3
Connie Brockway, *Promise Me Heaven*, 1994
Patricia Cabot, *Educating Caroline*, 2001
   more humorous
Eloisa James, *The Taming of the Duke*, 2006

Essex Sisters. Book 3
Robin Schone, *The Lady's Tutor*, 1999
erotic

305

NICOLE JORDAN   (Also writes as: Anne Bushyhead)

To Pleasure a Lady

(New York: Ballantine, 2008)

Story type: Historical/Regency
Series: Courtship Wars. Book 1
Subject(s): Seduction
Major character(s): Arabella Loring, Gentlewoman; Marcus Pierce, Nobleman (Baron Danvers)
Time period(s): 1810s (1817)
Locale(s): London, England

Summary: Arabella Loring certainly doesn't need any man to tell her how to run her life, but convincing Marcus Pierce of that fact is not going to be easy. After a spirited debate with Arabella, Marcus proposes a wager: if after two weeks, Arabella can still refuse Marcus' proposal of a marriage of convenience, he will grant her and her two sisters their financial freedom. Arabella, a dedicated spinster, is certain this is one bet she can easily win, but she never counted on exactly how irresistible Marcus would prove to be.

Where it's reviewed:
Romantic Times, February 2008, page 42

Other books by the same author:
Fever Dreams, 2006
Wicked Fantasy, 2005
Lord of Seduction, 2004
Master of Temptation, 2004
The Prince of Pleasure, 2003

Other books you might like:
Kathryn Caskie, *How to Seduce a Duke*, 2006
Suzanne Enoch, *Reforming a Rake*, 2000
Candice Hern, *Her Scandalous Affair*, 2004
Eloisa James, *The Taming of the Duke*, 2006
Stephanie Laurens, *A Rogue's Proposal*, 1999

306

BRENDA JOYCE

A Dangerous Love

(Don Mills, Ontario: HQN, 2008)

Story type: Historical/Victorian
Series: de Warenne Dynasty
Subject(s): Prejudice; Gypsies; Social Issues
Major character(s): Ariella de Warenne, Noblewoman; Emilian St. Xavier, Nobleman (viscount), Gypsy
Time period(s): 1830s (1838)
Locale(s): England

Summary: A free-thinking noblewoman and an embittered half-Gypsy viscount find love and understanding in spite of their differences in this sexy story that is part of

Joyce's popular de Warenne dynasty series. Note: This series follows the fortunes of the de Warenne family from the Middle Ages to the present. Some have links to Joyce's other series, as well.

Where it's reviewed:
Romantic Times, April 2008, page 39

Other books by the same author:
The Perfect Bride, 2007 (de Warenne Dynasty)
A Lady at Last, 2006 (de Warenne Dynasty)
The Stolen Bride, 2006 (de Warenne Dynasty)
The Masquerade, 2005 (de Warenne Dynasty)
The Prize, 2004 (de Warenne Dynasty)

Other books you might like:
Phoebe Conn, *Desire*, 1993
Janet Lane, *Emerald Silk*, 2008
Stephanie Laurens, *All about Love*, 2001
Kat Martin, *Gypsy Lord*, 1992
Connie Mason, *A Breath of Scandal*, 2001

307

LYDIA JOYCE

Shadows of the Night

(New York: Signet Eclipse, 2008)

Story type: Historical/Victorian
Subject(s): Marriage; Secrets; Seduction
Major character(s): Fern Ashcroft, Gentlewoman; Colin Radcliffe, Gentleman
Time period(s): 19th century
Locale(s): England

Summary: Immediately after their wedding, Fern Ashcroft begins to wonder if marrying Colin Radcliffe might not have been a serious mistake. Not only does Colin cut short their honeymoon in Brighton, but he insists on taking Fern to his estate in the country so that they can spend some quiet time alone. Once they arrive in Wrexmere, Fern discovers Colin's estate is badly in need of repair, and that the estate holds secrets from the past that threaten to destroy Fern's new marriage.

Where it's reviewed:
Booklist, March 15, 2008, page 36
Romantic Times, March 2008, page 44

Other books by the same author:
Voices of the Night, 2007
Whispers of the Night, 2006
Music of the Night, 2005
The Veil of Night, 2005

Other books you might like:
Adele Ashworth, *Duke of Sin*, 2004
Jane Goodger, *The Perfect Wife*, 2003
Amanda Quick, *Wait until Midnight*, 2005
Eve Silver, *Dark Desires*, 2005

308

SHIRLEY JUMP

Sweetheart Lost and Found

(Toronto: Harlequin, 2008)

Story type: Contemporary; Humor
Series: Wedding Planners. Book 1
Subject(s): Weddings; Reunions
Major character(s): Callie Phillips, Businesswoman (florist), Designer (wedding flowers); Jared Townsend, Researcher (for Wiley Games), Statistician
Time period(s): 2000s
Locale(s): Boston, Massachusetts

Summary: Wedding florist Callie Phillips has given up on finding Mr. Right after her divorce, but when she unexpectedly meets an old flame who's doing research on love and sex for a game company, she may be forced to reassess her views. A returning ex-husband complicates things, but maybe this time, Callie will make the right choice. This sweet, funny, heartwarming romance nicely launches the Wedding Planners mini-series.

Where it's reviewed:
Library Journal, April 15, 2008, page 67
Romantic Times, April 2008, page 115

Other books by the same author:
Pretty Bad, 2007
Rescued by Mr. Right, 2006
The Angel Craved Lobster, 2005
The Devil Served Tortellini, 2005
The Bride Wore Chocolate, 2004

Other books you might like:
Linda Goodnight, *Winning the Single Mom's Heart*, 2008
    Wedding Planners. Book 4
Melissa James, *The Bridegroom's Secret*, 2008
    Wedding Planners. Book 6
Myrna Mackenzie, *The Heir's Convenient Wife*, 2008
    Wedding Planners. Book 2
Melissa McClone, *SOS Marry Me!*, 2008
    Wedding Planners. Book 3
Susan Meier, *Millionaire Dad, Nanny Needed!*, 2008
    Wedding Planners. Book 5

309

KAREN KAY (Pseudonym of Karen Kay Elstner-Bailey)

The Last Warrior

(New York: Berkley Sensation, 2008)

Story type: Historical/American West; Multicultural
Series: Lost Clan
Subject(s): Legends
Major character(s): Suzette Joselyn, Gentlewoman, Singer; Black Lion, Warrior, Indian
Time period(s): 1890s (1890; 1892)
Locale(s): Colorado (Colorado Territory); London, England

Summary: Sent to find a magical sacred song that will melt the heart of the Thunder God and save his lost people, Black Lion goes to England as part of Buffalo Bill's Wild West show. He is attracted to singer Suzette Joselyn, but since she is engaged to an earl, the relationship fizzles momentarily. Suzette and Black Lion meet again when she, pregnant and jilted, comes to the United States. They marry and then are faced with the challenge of his quest, a quest that involves Suzette in a way she can't imagine. This mystical tale is the concluding volume in Kay's Lost Clan series.

Where it's reviewed:
Romantic Times, Marcy 2008, page 42

Other books by the same author:
Red Hawk's Woman, 2007 (Lost Clan)
The Spirit of the Wolf, 2006 (Lost Clan)
The Angel and the Warrior, 2005 (Lost Clan)
Soaring Eagle's Embrace, 2003
Lone Arrow's Pride, 2002

Other books you might like:
Madeline Baker, *The Spirit Path*, 1993
Cassie Edwards, *Silver Feather*, 2005
Susan Edwards, *White Dawn*, 2002
Kathleen Harrington, *Cherish the Dream*, 1990
Rachel Lee, *Thunder Mountain*, 1994
    contemporary mysticism

310

KAREN KENDALL (Pseudonym of Karen Moser)

Take Me If You Can

(New York: Signet Eclipse, 2008)

Story type: Contemporary; Romantic Suspense
Subject(s): Mystery; Art; Treasure
Major character(s): Ava Brigitte Hunt, Thief (art recovery expert), Businesswoman (partner); Sir Liam James, Thief, Nobleman
Time period(s): 2000s
Locale(s): United States; England; Europe

Summary: On a quest to recover the stolen Sword of Alexander, art recovery expert Avy Hunt zeroes in on British art thief Liam James. However, when it turns out that he's been tracking her as well, they join forces in a lively, sexy chase across Europe that has a few unexpected twists.

Where it's reviewed:
Romantic Times, April 2008, page 96

Other books by the same author:
An Affair to Remember, 2007
Fit to Be Tied, 2007
Midnight Oil, 2006
Midnight Touch, 2006
Who's on Top?, 2005

Other books you might like:
Tori Carrington, *Red-Hot and Reckless*, 2003
Christina Dodd, *Thigh High*, 2008
Suzanne Enoch, *Don't Look Down*, 2006

Samantha Jellicoe. Book 2
Suzanne Enoch, *A Touch of Minx*, 2007
  Samantha Jellicoe. Book 4
Julie Kenner, *Stolen Kisses*, 2004

311

KATHRYNE KENNEDY

Enchanting the Lady

(New York: Love Spell, 2008)

Story type: Historical/Fantasy; Historical/Victorian
Series: Relics of Merlin. Book 1
Subject(s): Magic
Major character(s): Felicity Seymour, Noblewoman; Terence Blackwell, Gentleman
Time period(s): 1880s (1882)
Locale(s): London, England

Summary: Because she has no magical skills, Felicity Seymour has lost her family's title; and with no dowry of her own, Felicity doubts she will ever marry. Terence Blackwell, a shapeshifter working for the British government, believes there is something magical about Felicity. Now, in order to find out more information about the source of her magical powers, Terence begins a romantic relationship with Felicity, never expecting that he would fall under her spell.

Where it's reviewed:
Romantic Times, February 2008, page 46

Other books you might like:
Susan Carroll, *The Night Drifter*, 1999
Tracy Fobes, *My Enchanted Enemy*, 2002
Susan King, *Taming the Heiress*, 2002
Laura Kinsale, *Uncertain Magic*, 1987
Mary Jo Putney, *A Kiss of Fate*, 2004

312

JULIE KENNER
JADE LEE , Co-Author
MARIANNE MANCUSI , Co-Author

These Boots Were Made for Stomping

(New York: Love Spell, 2008)

Story type: Anthology; Contemporary/Fantasy
Subject(s): Change; Magic
Time period(s): 2000s
Locale(s): United States

Summary: Magic shoes from Highheelia.com are the key ingredient in this trio of novellas. When Lydia Carmichael buys a new pair of shoes, she not only gets the courage to change her boring life, but also the chance to team up with the superhero of her dreams in Kenner's "A Step in the Right Direction." Teacher Michaela Becker's new shoes give her the chance to work closely, professionally, and personally, with school cop Joe De-Luce in Lee's "Kung Fu Shoes!" Comic book writer

Hailey Hill's new shoes not only give her the superpowers of her own creation, Karma Kitty, but give her another chance with her old fiance and the first artist she ever worked with, Collin Robinson in Mancusi's "Karma Kitty Goes to Comic Con."

Where it's reviewed:
Romantic Times, April 2008, page 100

Other books you might like:
Elizabeth Bevarly, *Write It Up!*, 2006
Janelle Denison, *Sinfully Sweet*, 2006
Whitney Lyles, *Catch of the Day*, 2006
Deirdre Martin, *Hot Ticket*, 2006
Vicki Lewis Thompson, *A Fare to Remember*, 2006

313

SHERRILYN KENYON

Dream Chaser

(New York: St. Martin's Paperbacks, 2008)

Story type: Contemporary/Fantasy; Paranormal
Series: Dream-Hunter. Book 3
Subject(s): Dreams and Nightmares; Revenge; Atlantis
Major character(s): Simone Dubois, Doctor (medical examiner & professor), Psychic (sees ghosts); Xypher, Deity (demi-god dream-hunter), Demon (half)
Time period(s): 2000s
Locale(s): New Orleans, Louisiana; Mythical Place (Atlantean realms)

Summary: Freed from hell on Tantalus and granted one month to redeem himself and avoid eternal torment, Dream-Hunter Xypher goes to Earth thinking of only one thing—avenging himself on the woman who betrayed him. This, however, is easier said than done, and when he ends up magically bound to human Simone Dubois and they learn that they must both stay alive and together or they both die, his quest becomes much more urgent and a lot more dangerous. Filled with sassy repartee, plenty of action, and steamy sex.

Where it's reviewed:
Romantic Times, February 2008, page 96

Other books by the same author:
Acheron, 2008
Devil May Cry, 2007
The Dream-Hunter, 2007 (Dream-Hunter. Book 1)
Upon the Midnight Clear, 2007 (Dream-Hunter. Book 2)
Unleash the Night, 2006

Other books you might like:
Meljean Brook, *Demon Moon*, 2007
  Guardians. Book 4
Alexandra Ivy, *When Darkness Comes*, 2007
  Guardians of Eternity. Book 1
Jade Lee, *Seduced by Crimson*, 2006
  Crimson City. Book 5
Liz Maverick, *Shards of Crimson*, 2007
  anthology
Cheyenne McCray, *Forbidden Magic*, 2005

314

CINDY KIRK

One Night Stand

(New York: Avon, 2008)

Story type: Contemporary
Subject(s): Teen Relationships; Small Town Life; Family Relations
Major character(s): Marcee Robbens, Accountant (CPA); Sam McKelvey, Widow(er), Police Officer (sheriff)
Time period(s): 2000s
Locale(s): Chicago, Illinois; Ellwood, Illinois

Summary: After an impulsive one night stand following a friend's wedding, Marcee Robbens and Sam McKelvey go their separate ways although still unable to forget each other. Months later, Marcee leaves Chicago to return to her quiet hometown to stay with her youngest brother while he finishes his last year of high school and learns that Sam, now Ellwood's new sheriff, and his teenage daughter have bought the house next door. Wary, but attracted protagonists, a pair of well-drawn teenagers, local gossips, other interfering folks, and plenty of small town atmosphere add to the appeal of this sexy, heartwarming romp.

Where it's reviewed:
Romantic Times, May 2008, page 88

Other books by the same author:
Romancing the Nanny, 2007
The Tycoon's Son, 2007
When She Was Bad, 2007

Other books you might like:
Kate Angell, *Strike Zone*, 2008
Jeanette Baker, *Chesapeake Tide*, 2004
Lorraine Heath, *Hard Lovin' Man*, 2003
Deb Stover, *A Matter of Trust*, 2000
Gina Wilkins, *Seductively Yours*, 2000

315

LISA KLEYPAS

Blue-Eyed Devil

(New York: St. Martin's Press, 2008)

Story type: Contemporary
Subject(s): Abuse; Reunions; Healing
Major character(s): Haven Travis, Wealthy, Abuse Victim; Hardy Cates, Wealthy, Businessman (oil)
Time period(s): 2000s
Locale(s): Texas

Summary: The first time socialite Haven Travis met Hardy Cates was when she mistook him for her boyfriend, Nick, in a wine cellar and they exchanged a passionate, potentially life-changing kiss. Several years later, after an abusive marriage to Nick and subsequent divorce, Haven runs into Hardy, her family's nemesis; this time things take a different turn. Passion, violence, and heart wrenching emotion flavor the plot of this gripping contemporary romance from a popular writer of historicals.

Where it's reviewed:
Booklist, March 15, 2008, page 35
Publishers Weekly, January 28, 2008, page 41
Romantic Times, March 2008, page 97

Other books by the same author:
Mine Till Midnight, 2007
Sugar Daddy, 2007
It Happened One Autumn, 2006
The Devil in Winter, 2006
Scandal in Spring, 2006

Other books you might like:
Catherine Anderson, *Only by Your Touch*, 2003
Paula McKinley, *Silver Threads, Golden Needles*, 2000
Mary Jo Putney, *The Burning Point*, 2000
Karen Robards, *Maggy's Child*, 1994
Ruth Wind, *Last Chance Ranch*, 1995

316

ANGELA KNIGHT
LORA LEIGH , Co-Author
ALYSSA DAY , Co-Author
VIRGINIA KANTRA , Co-Author

Shifter

(New York: Berkley Sensation, 2008)

Story type: Paranormal; Anthology
Subject(s): Paranormal; Supernatural

Summary: This widely varied collection focuses on shape-shifters of all types and includes stories set in the future, past, and present and sweeps its characters across the world and beyond. Included are: "Mad Dog Love" by Angela Knight, a werewolf futuristic; "A Jaguar's Kiss" by Lora Leigh, a romance filled with Cajun lore; "Shifter's Lady" by Alyssa Day, a magical tale of an Atlantean Nereid; and "Sea Crossing" by Virginia Kantra, a historical that makes good use of the Selkie legend. This super-sexy anthology is exceptionally diverse.

Where it's reviewed:
Romantic Times, March 2008, page 106

Other books you might like:
Alyssa Day, *Atlantis Awakening*, 2007
Sherrilyn Kenyon, *Stroke of Midnight*, 2004
   anthology
Lora Leigh, *Harmony's Way*, 2006
Maggie Shayne, *Demon's Kiss*, 2007
Rebecca York, *Unleashed*, 2006
   anthology

317

SHARIE KOHLER

Marked by Moonlight

(New York: Pocket, 2008)

Story type: Contemporary; Werewolf Story
Subject(s): Werewolves

Major character(s): Claire Morgan, Teacher, Werewolf;
  Gideon March, Hunter (werewolf hunter)
Time period(s): 2000s
Locale(s): United States

Summary: When English teacher Claire Morgan is bitten
by one of her students-turned-werewolf, she has no idea
what has happened to her until werewolf hunter Gideon
March shows up in her apartment and gives her the facts.
The problem is that he is part of an organization
dedicated to the elimination of all lycans, which means
that she is going to be one of his targets, unless he can
figure out how to save her before she turns. Passion and
adventure infuse this unusual werewolf story.

Other books by the same author:
Kiss of a Dark Moon, 2008

Other books you might like:
Kresley Cole, *Dark Desires After Dusk*, 2008
Kresley Cole, *A Hunger Like No Other*, 2006
Lori Handeland, *Blue Moon*, 2004
Susan Krinard, *To Catch a Wolf*, 2003
Ronda Thompson, *Call of the Moon*, 2002

318

KATHLEEN KORBEL (Pseudonym of Eileen Dreyer)

Dark Seduction

(New York: Silhouette, 2008)

Story type: Contemporary/Fantasy
Series: Daughters of Myth. Book 2
Subject(s): Fairies; Family; Magic
Major character(s): Sorcha, Mythical Creature (fairy);
  Harold Wyatt, Nobleman (Earl of Harley)
Time period(s): 2000s
Locale(s): Yorkshire, England; Faerie Realm, Mythical
  Place

Summary: If Sorcha, daughter of Mab, Queen of the Faeries, doesn't find the Dearann Stone, the Faerie realm
will be forever trapped under winter's spell. Fortunately,
Sorcha is able to quickly find the stone in England, at
the estate of Harold Wyatt, the Earl of Harley. Unfortunately, Sorcha isn't the only one searching for the stone;
the dark faeries are also on its trail. Now Sorcha's only
hope of saving her world is to convince Harold, an annoyingly practical Englishman, to believe in magic and
love.

Where it's reviewed:
Romantic Times, February 2008, page 111

Other books by the same author:
Dangerous Temptation, 2006
Some Men's Dreams, 2003
Sail Away, 1999
Don't Fence Me In, 1996
A Soldier's Heart, 1994

Other books you might like:
Annette Blair, *The Kitchen Witch*, 2004
Kristine Grayson, *Simply Irresistible*, 2003
Lynn Kurland, *A Garden in the Rain*, 2003
Karen Marie Moning, *Darkfever*, 2006
Evelyn Vaughn, *A.K.A. Goddess*, 2004

319

SUSAN KRINARD

Dark of the Moon

(Don Mills, Ontario: HQN, 2008)

Story type: Historical/Roaring Twenties; Vampire Story
Subject(s): Vampires; Suspense; Redemption
Major character(s): Gwen Murphy, Journalist (newspaper
  reporter); Dorian Black, Vampire
Time period(s): 1920s (1926)
Locale(s): New York, New York

Summary: When outcast vampire Dorian Black rescues
reporter Gwen Murphy from certain death in New York's
East River, he soon becomes involved in her investigation into gang warfare, which she thinks is being caused
by vampires. Exciting, adventurous, and romantic, this
lively paranormal is set during a particularly intriguing
historical period.

Where it's reviewed:
Romantic Times, March 2008, page 44

Other books by the same author:
Chasing Midnight, 2007
Lord of the Beasts, 2006
To Tame a Wolf, 2005
Kinsman's Oath, 2004
The Forest Lord, 2002

Other books you might like:
Amanda Ashley, *After Sundown*, 2003
Kresley Cole, *A Hunger Like No Other*, 2006
Kathy Love, *Fangs for the Memories*, 2005
Caridad Pineiro, *Death Calls*, 2006
Caridad Pineiro, *Devotion Calls*, 2007

320

LYNN KURLAND (Pseudonym of Lynn Curland)

With Every Breath

(New York: Jove, 2008)

Story type: Time Travel
Subject(s): Healing; Time Travel; Magic
Major character(s): Sunshine Phillips, Healer, Witch (clan
  healer); Robert Cameron, Laird, Time Traveler
Time period(s): 2000s; 14th century (1375)
Locale(s): Scotland

Summary: Thrilled at finally being able to come to
Scotland, Sunshine Phillips moves into the witch's cottage she has inherited on the MacLeod estate. However,
she never expects to find medieval Laird Robert Cameron on her doorstep demanding she help heal his
brother, nor does she expect to be transported back to
the 14th century! Romance flourishes, but the time differences cause problems that are eventually resolved in
this light, romantic time travel that is another in
Kurland's series involving the MacLeods.

Where it's reviewed:
Romantic Times, June 2008, page 108

Other books by the same author:
The Mage's Daughter, 2008 (Nine Kingdoms. Book 2)
Much Ado in the Moonlight, 2006
Star of the Morning, 2006 (Nine Kingdoms. Book 1)
A Garden in the Rain, 2003
The More I See You, 1999

Other books you might like:
Diana Gabaldon, *Outlander*, 1991
    classic time travel
Karen Marie Moning, *The Dark Highlander*, 2002
Karen Marie Moning, *Kiss of the Highlander*, 2001
Maura Seger, *The Lady and the Laird*, 1992
Christina Skye, *Bride of the Mist*, 1996

321

JANET LANE

Emerald Silk

(Waterville, Maine: Five Star, 2008)

Story type: Historical/Medieval
Series: Coin Forest. Part 2
Subject(s): Social Classes; Gypsies; Prejudice
Major character(s): Kadriya, Gypsy (half), Gentlewoman; John Wynter, Knight; Teraf, Gypsy, Ruler (king of the gypsies)
Time period(s): 15th Century (1448)
Locale(s): England

Summary: Although gently raised, half-Gypsy Kadriya decides to claim her Roma heritage by linking her life with Teraf, the dashing Gypsy king. However, her plans are shattered when Teraf is accused of stealing a valuable chalice from the local monastery and in the ensuing fight, he is captured and taken away. At the same time, Sir John Wynter, a knight with a violent prejudice against the Gypsies, is wounded and ends up in Kadriya's care. John and Kadriya team up to find the chalice, and in the process they learn something about the healing, eye-opening power of love. There's plenty of adventure in this lively story that follows *Tabor's Trinket*.

Where it's reviewed:
Romantic Times, May 2008, page 47

Other books by the same author:
Tabor's Trinket, 2006 (Coin Forest. Part 1)

Other books you might like:
Alexandra Benedict, *A Forbidden Love*, 2006
    later time period
Mary Daheim, *Gypsy Baron*, 1992
    later time period
Lois Greiman, *Highland Hawk*, 2000
Susan King, *Heather Moon*, 1999
Kat Martin, *Gypsy Lord*, 1992

322

LESLIE LANGTRY

Guns Will Keep Us Together

(New York: Making It, 2008)

Story type: Humor; Romantic Suspense
Series: Greatest Hits. Book 2
Subject(s): Murder; Single Parent Families; Family Relations
Major character(s): Leonie Doubtfire, Criminal (assassin), Undertaker; Dakota Bombay, Criminal (assassin), Single Parent
Time period(s): 2000s
Locale(s): Las Vegas, Nevada; Santa Muerta, Tropical Island (family-owned island)

Summary: Dakota Bombay comes from a long line of assassins. He can kill a person using practically anything. However, Dakota's happy life as a criminal and playboy is rudely interrupted when he's delivered a genius six-year-old son he didn't know he had. To top it off, Dakota falls hard for Leonie Doubtfire, an undertaker who isn't quite what she seems.

Where it's reviewed:
Romantic Times, February 2008, page 82

Other books by the same author:
'Scuse Me While I Kill This Guy, 2007 (Greatest Hits. Book 1)

Other books you might like:
Toni McGee Causey, *Bobbie Faye's (kinda, sorta, not-exactly) Family Jewels*, 2008
    Bobbie Faye Sumrall. Book 2
Richard Condon, *Prizzi's Honor*, 1986
Harley Jane Kozak, *Dating Dead Men*, 2005
Connie Lane, *Guilty Little Secrets*, 2003
Lisa Lutz, *The Spellman Curse*, 2007

323

STEPHANIE LAURENS

Where the Heart Lies

(New York: William Morrow, 2008)

Story type: Historical/Victorian; Romantic Suspense
Series: Cynster. Book 15
Subject(s): Missing Persons; Mystery; Crime and Criminals
Major character(s): Penelope Ashford, Noblewoman (daughter of a viscount), Administrator (orphanage); Barnaby Adair, Nobleman (son of an earl), Detective
Time period(s): 1830s (1835)
Locale(s): England

Summary: Concerned that a number of young orphaned boys have been kidnapped in London's East End before they can be taken to the safety of her Foundling House, unconventional Penelope Ashford comes to Barnaby Adair for help. As they work together to find the answers, Penelope and Barnaby uncover a villainous plot and find a romance they never expected. A secondary romance between Scotland Yard Inspector Basil Stokes and milliner Griselda Martin, who grew up in the East End, adds interest and charm to this sexy, romantic mystery that continues the adventures of the expanding Cynster clan.

Where it's reviewed:
Publishers Weekly, October 15, 2007, page 36
Romantic Times, February 2008, page 44

Romance

Other books by the same author:
The Taste of Innocence, 2007 (Cynster. Book 14)
What Price Love?, 2006 (Cynster. Book 13)
The Truth about Love, 2005 (Cynster. Book 12)
The Ideal Bride, 2004 (Cynster. Book 11)
The Perfect Lover, 2003 (Cynster. Book 10)

Other books you might like:
Connie Brockway, *As You Desire*, 1997
Lisa Kleypas, *Worth Any Price*, 2003
Amanda Quick, *Lie by Moonlight*, 2005
Amanda Quick, *The River Knows*, 2007
Amanda Quick, *Slightly Shady*, 2001

324

SUSAN KAY LAW
The Paper Marriage
(New York: Berkley Books, 2008)

Story type: Contemporary
Subject(s): Marriage; Illness; Courage
Major character(s): Ann McCrary, Architect; Tom Nash, Sports Figure (former baseball star), Single Parent; Mercedes Nash, Teenager
Time period(s): 2000s
Locale(s): Minnesota

Summary: Married to a man who has been in a coma for 12 years, architect Ann McCrary's life has devolved into a placid existence of work and nursing home visits. That all changes, however, when former baseball star Tom Nash moves in next door and his teenage daughter comes to visit. Dogs, an aging hippie mother, a teenager worth the trouble, and still-grieving parents are part of the supporting cast in this poignant, often hilarious, heartwarming romance that deftly tackles the issues of love, loss, and moving on.

Where it's reviewed:
Library Journal, February 15, 2008, page 88

Other books by the same author:
Just Sex, 2007
A Wedding Story, 2003 (Marrying Miss Bright. Book 3)
Marry Me, 2002 (Marrying Miss Bright. Book 2)
The Bad Man's Bride, 2001 (Marrying Miss Bright. Book 1)
The Most Wanted Bachelor, 2000

Other books you might like:
Patti Henry Callahan, *Where the River Runs*, 2005
Mary Alice Monroe, *Skyward*, 2003
Annie Smith, *Home Again*, 2002
Tina Wainscot, *Back in Baby's Arms*, 2001
Susan Wiggs, *Table for Five*, 2005

325

EDITH LAYTON (Pseudonym of Edith Felber)
His Dark and Dangerous Ways
(New York: Avon, 2008)

Story type: Historical/Regency
Subject(s): Spies; Healing; Secrets

Major character(s): Jane Chatham, Teacher (dance); Simon Atwood, Nobleman (Lord Granger), Spy
Time period(s): 1810s
Locale(s): England

Summary: Asked to quietly keep track of how often the younger brother of a fellow agent visits the home of the well-known, rather notorious widow, Lady Stanton, Simon Atwood enlists the aid of financially strapped dance teacher Jane Chatham to help him keep watch. However, there is more to this situation than either of them dreams, and as their feelings for each other grow, so does the danger to them both; and it comes from an unexpected source.

Where it's reviewed:
Romantic Times, June 2008, page 52

Other books by the same author:
For the Love of a Pirate, 2006
How to Seduce a Bride, 2006
The Return of the Earl, 2004
To Tempt a Bride, 2003
To Wed a Stranger, 2003

Other books you might like:
Elizabeth Boyle, *Stealing the Bride*, 2003
Celeste Bradley, *The Pretender*, 2003
Mary Jo Putney, *River of Fire*, 1996
Gayle Wilson, *The Heart's Desire*, 1994
Gayle Wilson, *My Lady's Dare*, 2000

326

DAY LECLAIRE (Pseudonym of Day Totton Smith)
Dante's Stolen Wife
(New York: Silhouette, 2008)

Story type: Contemporary
Series: Dante Legacy. Book 2
Subject(s): Marriage; Family; Identity, Concealed
Major character(s): Caitlyn Vaughn, Businesswoman, Manager (head of finance); Marco Dante, Businessman (family jewelry business), Twin
Time period(s): 2000s
Locale(s): San Francisco, California

Summary: There was a legend in the Dante family that when the Dante men met their true mates, they would know it by an incendiary, compelling reaction known as "The Inferno." Marco, a scandal-causing playboy, has never experienced it. Then he meets Caitlyn Vaughn in the lobby of his office building and the sparks sizzle. Unfortunately, Caitlyn, their company's new head of national finance, thinks he's Marco's twin brother Lazzaro, and the results are nearly disastrous. Deception, interfamily strife, and a dash of mysticism are part of this sexy, highly charged romance, that is second in Leclaire's Dante Legacy quartet.

Where it's reviewed:
Romantic Times, May 2008, page 115

Other books by the same author:

Dante's Blackmailed Bride, 2008 (Dante Legacy. Book 1)

Dante's Contract Marriage, 2008 (Dante Legacy. Book 4)

Dante's Wedding Deception, 2008 (Dante Legacy. Book 3)

The Billionaire's Baby Negotiation, 2007

The Royal Wedding Night, 2007 (Royals. Book 3)

Other books you might like:

Leanne Banks, *Bedded by the Billionaire*, 2008

Maureen Child, *Marrying for King's Millions*, 2008
  Kings of California. Book 2

Brenda Jackson, *Taming Clint Westmoreland*, 2008

Myrna Mackenzie, *Simon Says |PO Marry Me!*, 2000

Paula Roe, *Boardrooms & a Billionaire Heir*, 2008

327

LINDA FRANCIS LEE

The Ex-Debutante

(New York: St. Martin's Press, 2008)

Story type: Contemporary; Humor
Subject(s): Social Classes; Family Relations; Secrets
Major character(s): Carlisle Wainwright Cushing, Wealthy, Lawyer; Jack Blair, Lawyer
Time period(s): 2000s
Locale(s): Willow Creek, Texas

Summary: Carlisle Wainwright Cushing, descendant of a duke and part of one of Texas' first families, becomes a lawyer and moves to Boston, where she enjoys anonymity. Everything goes swimmingly until her mother calls Carlisle to represent her for her divorce, the fifth one. There's another problem—Carlisle hasn't told her family that she's engaged, and she hasn't told her fiance that she's rich. As icing on the cake, opposing counsel on the divorce is Carlisle's hunky ex-boyfriend, Jack Blair.

Where it's reviewed:
Booklist, March 1, 2008, page 55
Romantic Times, April 2008, page 61

Other books by the same author:
The Devil in Junior League, 2007
Ladies Who Lunch, 2006
Simply Sexy, 2004 (Sexy. Book 3)
Sinfully Sexy, 2004 (Sexy. Book 2)
Suddenly Sexy, 2004 (Sexy. Book 1)

Other books you might like:
Mary Kay Andrews, *Hissy Fit*, 2005
Shirley Jump, *The Bride Wore Chocolate*, 2004
Sophie Kinsella, *Shopaholic Takes Manhattan*, 2004
Jane Porter, *The Frog Prince*, 2005
Lauren Weisberger, *The Devil Wears Prada*, 2004

328

ALLISON LEIGH

The Bride and the Bargain

(New York: Silhouette, 2008)

Story type: Contemporary
Subject(s): Marriage; Inheritance
Major character(s): Amelia White, Librarian; Grayson Hunt, Businessman (CEO of family company), Wealthy
Time period(s): 2000s
Locale(s): Seattle, Washington

Summary: When his grandfather announces that he and his brothers must be married and fathers within the year if they want to inherit his considerable wealth, Grayson Hunt is the last one to wed. Although he has no prospects, when librarian Amelia White comes on the scene with the accusation that Gray has fathered her sister's child, this sparks an idea that results in a marriage of convenience that eventually becomes one of love.

Where it's reviewed:
Romantic Times, February 2008, page 112

Other books by the same author:
A Cowboy under Her Tree, 2007
Sarah and the Sheriff, 2007
Wed in Wyoming, 2007
The Tycoon's Marriage Bid, 2005
Mother in a Moment, 2004

Other books you might like:
Dixie Browning, *The Millionaire's Pregnant Bride*, 2001
Charlotte Douglas, *Surprise Inheritance*, 2003
Dallas Schulze, *The Way Home*, 1995
Sharon Swan, *Four-Karat Fiancee*, 2003
Robin Wells, *The Babe Magnet*, 2004

329

JOHANNA LINDSEY

No Choice but Seduction

(New York: Pocket, 2008)

Story type: Historical/Regency
Series: Malory. Book 9
Subject(s): Seduction; Romance; Family
Major character(s): Katey Tyler, Gentlewoman, Orphan; Boyd Anderson, Sea Captain, Businessman (shipping company)
Time period(s): 19th century
Locale(s): Connecticut; England

Summary: On her way to Europe and a long-awaited adventurous grand tour, American Katey Tyler rescues a young girl in a kidnapping scheme and suddenly finds herself embraced by the powerful Malory family in England. At the same time, she attracts the attention of Captain Boyd Anderson, a man with marriage connections to the Malorys, but he botches his relationship with

Katey so badly that the only choice left to him is seduction. Funny, sexy, and lively, this story has a few secrets that fans of the series will enjoy.

Where it's reviewed:
Library Journal, June 15, 2008, page 51

Other books by the same author:
The Devil Who Tamed Her, 2007
Captive of My Desires, 2006 (Malory. Book 8)
A Loving Scoundrel, 2004 (Malory. Book 7)
The Present, 1998 (Malory. Book 6)
Say You Love Me, 1996 (Malory. Book 5)

Other books you might like:
Jo Beverley, *A Lady's Secret*, 2008
Jo Beverley, *Tempting Fortune*, 1995
     Malloren. Book 2
Catherine Coulter, *The Sherbrooke Twins*, 2004
     Sherbrooke. Book 8
Catherine Coulter, *The Valentine Legacy*, 1995
Sabrina Jeffries, *Never Seduce a Scoundrel*, 2006

330

KIMBERLY LOGAN   (Pseudonym of Kimberly Snoke)

Seduced by Sin

(New York: Avon, 2008)

Story type: Historical/Regency; Romantic Suspense
Series: Daventry Sisters. Book 3
Subject(s): Murder; Memory Loss; Healing
Major character(s): Lady Aimee Daventry, Noblewoman, Amnesiac; Royce Grenville, Nobleman (Viscount Stonehurst), Military Personnel (former cavalry officer)
Time period(s): 1820s (1823)
Locale(s): England

Summary: Although she witnessed her mother's murder when she was nine, for years Lady Aimee Daventry had no memory of the details. Now 19, her dreams are beginning to yield small clues, but as she begins to remember, she is in growing danger from the killer who was never caught. At the same time, the love of her life, Royce Grenville, has sworn to protect her. However, Royce needs healing and a bit of protecting of his own, and Aimee is just the person to help. This romantic tale of two wounded people who finally allow themselves to fall in love nicely ties up the mystery in Logan's trilogy.

Where it's reviewed:
Romantic Times, April 2008, page 42

Other books by the same author:
The Devil's Temptation, 2007
Sins of Midnight, 2006
A Kiss Before Dawn, 2005
A Kiss in the Dark, 2005
The Ghost and the Dead Deb, 2005

Other books you might like:
Mary Balogh, *More than a Mistress*, 2000
Jo Beverley, *To Rescue a Rogue*, 2006
Marjorie Farrell, *Red, Red Rose*, 1999
Ann Gracie, *Gallant Waif*, 2001
Gayle Wilson, *My Lady's Dare*, 2000

331

CAIT LONDON   (Pseudonym of Lois Kleinsasser)

A Stranger's Touch

(New York: Avon, 2008)

Story type: Paranormal; Romantic Suspense
Series: Psychic Sisters. Book 2
Subject(s): Psychic Powers; Murder; Triplets
Major character(s): Tempest Storm, Psychic, Artist (sculptor); Marcus Greystone, Businessman
Time period(s): 2000s
Locale(s): New Mexico (near Santa Fe)

Summary: Cursed with the psychometric ability to feel the past of any object she touches, sculptor Tempest Storm is on the trail of an ancient Viking brooch that is connected in some way to her psychic family. Marcus Greystone, the current owner of the brooch and a man with whom she once had a one-night fling, needs her to help him solve a cold case murder for very personal reasons. Reluctantly, they strike a bargain that proves more dangerous than either had expected, and more romantic, as well. *OTL At the Edge

Where it's reviewed:
Romantic Times, April 2008, page 81

Other books by the same author:
Flashback, 2005
Hidden Secrets, 2005
With Her Last Breath, 2003
When Night Falls, 2002

Other books you might like:
Christine Feehan, *Oceans of Fire*, 2005
Jayne Ann Krentz, *Sizzle and Burn*, 2008
Mary Jo Putney, *A Kiss of Fate*, 2004
     historical
Nora Roberts, *Dance upon the Air*, 2001
     Three Sisters Island Trilogy. Book 1
Nora Roberts, *Heaven and Earth*, 2001
     Three Sisters Island Trilogy. Book 2

332

SASHA LORD   (Pseudonym of Rebecca Saria)

Wild Angel

(New York: Signet Eclipse, 2008)

Story type: Historical/Medieval
Series: Wild. Book 6
Subject(s): Quest; Politics; Revenge
Major character(s): Ashleigh, Gypsy, Magician (illusionist); Mangan O'Bannon, Nobleman (warrior son of an earl), Religious (novice monk)
Time period(s): 11th century
Locale(s): Scotland

Summary: After witnessing her parents' deaths at the hands of a brutal Scottish nobleman when he, his soldiers, and some villagers came across their gypsy caravan, Ashleigh, distraught and half-crazed with grief, is swept away by a stream. Mangan, a holy man on a

Romance

quest for both a relic and absolution for his former life as a warrior, pulls her to safety, but is dismayed by his attraction to her. Determined to avenge her parents' deaths, Ashleigh uses her illusionist skills to frighten the guilty villagers, but when Mangan discovers her and learns the truth, he agrees to help her achieve justice. Political intrigue and fast-paced action add to this steamy adventure that adds another to the popular Wild series.

Where it's reviewed:
Romantic Times, February 2008, page 43

Other books by the same author:
In My Wild Dream, 2007 (Wild. Book 5)
Beyond the Wild Wind, 2006 (Wild. Book 4)
Across a Wild Sea, 2005 (Wild. Book 3)
In a Wild Wood, 2004 (Wild. Book 2)
Under a Wild Sky, 2004 (Wild. Book 1)

Other books you might like:
Claire Delacroix, *The Beauty*, 2001
Emma Holly, *Hunting Midnight*, 2003
Lisa Jackson, *Wild and Wicked*, 2002
Karyn Monk, *The Rose and the Warrior*, 2000
Susan Squires, *Danelaw*, 2003

333

KATIE MACALISTER (Pseudonym of Marthe Arends)

Playing with Fire
(New York: Signet, 2008)

Story type: Contemporary/Fantasy; Paranormal
Series: Silver Dragons. Book 1
Subject(s): Dragons; Magic; Humor
Major character(s): May Northcott, Mythical Creature (naiad doppleganger), Twin (magically created); Gabriel Tauhou, Mythical Creature (dragon)
Time period(s): 2000s
Locale(s): Earth

Summary: Created as a doppleganger shadow twin by the naiad Cyrene and gifted with the ability to move unseen by literally becoming one with the shadows, May Northcott is bound to the demon lord Magoth and serves him rather unwillingly by stealing valuable objects. She meets Wyvern (dragon leader) Gabriel during a "visit" to his estate, and when he realizes she is his mate (Silver Dragons are not supposed to have a mate born.), he is determined to claim her as his own, whatever the cost. Sexy, funny, and lively, this new series is an outgrowth of MacAlister's popular Aisling Grey series about the Otherworld and the landscape and characters will be familiar to fans.

Where it's reviewed:
Romantic Times, May 2008, page 93

Other books by the same author:
Holy Smokes, 2007 (Aisling Grey, Guardian. Book 4)
The Last of the Red-Hot Vampires, 2007
Light My Fire, 2006 (Aisling Grey, Guardian. Book 3)
Fire Me Up, 2005 (Aisling Grey, Guardian. Book 2)
You Slay Me, 2004 (Aisling Grey, Guardian. Book 1)

Other books you might like:
Jennifer Ashley, *Immortals: The Calling*, 2007
Allyson James, *The Black Dragon*, 2007
  Dragon. Book 2
Allyson James, *Dragon Heat*, 2007
  Dragon. Book 1
Angela Knight, *Master of Dragons*, 2007
  Mageverse. Book 8
Mary Jo Putney, *A Kiss of Fate*, 2004

334

SALLY MACKENZIE

The Naked Gentleman
(New York: Zebra, 2008)

Story type: Historical/Regency; Humor
Series: Naked. Book 4
Subject(s): Humor; Courtship; Gardens and Gardening
Major character(s): Margaret Peterson, Gentlewoman; John Parker-Roth, Scientist (horticulturist), Gardener
Time period(s): 1800s
Locale(s): London, England

Summary: John Parker-Roth lives for horticulture. His plants are his world. He figures that if he were to marry, it would be to someone who loves horticulture as much as he does. Then Margaret Peterson literally lands in his lap. Not only is Meg in a state of undress, she also asks him to kiss her. John, however, is wary of women, and rightfully so. He's already been stood up at the altar by a fiancee who wanted a titled bridegroom.

Where it's reviewed:
Romantic Times, April 2008, page 48

Other books by the same author:
The Naked Earl, 2007 (Naked. Book 3)
The Naked Marquis, 2006 (Naked. Book 2)
The Naked Duke, 2005 (Naked. Book 1)

Other books you might like:
Liz Carlyle, *Never Lie to a Lady*, 2007
Claudia Dain, *The Courtesan's Daughter*, 2007
Christina Dodd, *Rules of Engagement*, 2000
  Governess Brides. Book 2
Suzanne Enoch, *Sins of a Duke*, 2007
Karen Robards, *Irresistible*, 2002

335

DAWN MACTAVISH (Pseudonym of Dawn Thompson)

The Privateer
(New York: Leisure, 2008)

Story type: Historical/Regency
Subject(s): Family Relations; Revenge; Poverty
Major character(s): Lark Eddington, Noblewoman (impoverished); Basil Kingston, Nobleman (Earl of Greyshire), Privateer
Time period(s): 1800s (1812)
Locale(s): London, England; Cornwall, England

Summary: After her father, the Earl of Roxburgh, runs up such large debts that the only way out is suicide, Lady Lark Eddington finds herself in the infamous Marshalsea Debtors Prison. Basil "King" Kingston, Earl of Greyshire, goes to Marshalsea at the request of his philanthropic mother to find a suitable companion for her, one they could save from the horrors faced by an impoverished woman. King soon finds himself attracted to the spirited Lark, even though he's almost betrothed to someone much more complacent and agreeable. To further add to his already complicated life, the Admiralty wants King to come out of retirement and resume his life as a privateer.

Where it's reviewed:
Romantic Times, January 2008, page 50

Other books by the same author:
The Marsh Hawk, 2007

Other books you might like:
Jennifer Ashley, *The Pirate Next Door*, 2003
Emily Bryant, *Distracting the Duchess*, 2008
Candace Camp, *A Dangerous Man*, 2007
Kinley MacGregor, *A Pirate of Her Own*, 1999
Barbara Metzger, *The Scandalous Life of a True Lady*, 2008

336

ANNETTE MAHON

The Secret Correspondence
(New York: Avalon, 2008)

Story type: Contemporary; Multicultural
Series: Malino, Hawaii
Subject(s): Secrets; Letters; Computers
Major character(s): Julie Wong, Health Care Professional; Ned Smith, Accountant (CPA)
Time period(s): 2000s
Locale(s): Syracuse, New York; Malino, Hawaii

Summary: When her neighbor breaks her leg but doesn't want to notify her CPA son because this is his busy season and she doesn't want him coming all the way from New York to Hawaii, Julie Wong e-mails him just to alert him and let him know he shouldn't worry. What starts as a neighborly gesture, however, turns into something more, and by the time Ned comes to Hawaii, the pair have practically fallen in love already—all via e-mail. A sweet addition to Mahon's Malino, Hawaii series.

Where it's reviewed:
Library Journal, June 15, 2008, page 51

Other books by the same author:
Dolphin Dreams, 2007
An Ominous Death, 2006
The Secret Wish, 2006 (Secret. Book 5)
The Secret Beau, 2004 (Secret. Book 4)
The Secret Wedding, 2002 (Secret. Book 2)

Other books you might like:
Geraldine Burrows, *Stranger in Paradise*, 2003
Marjorie Everitt, *Somewhere Near Paradise*, 1992
Jill Marie Landis, *Glass Beach*, 1998

historical & more intense
Curtiss Ann Matlock, *Cold Tea on a Hot Day*, 2001
Deborah Shelley, *Talk about Love*, 1999

337

SUSAN MALLERY (Pseudonym of Susan Macias Redmond)

Sweet Talk
(Don Mills, Ontario: HQN, 2008)

Story type: Contemporary
Series: Bakery Girls. Book 1
Subject(s): Sisters; Healing; Family Relations
Major character(s): Claire Keyes, Musician (concert pianist), Twin; Wyatt Knight, Baker, Single Parent (of a deaf daughter)
Time period(s): 2000s
Locale(s): Seattle, Washington

Summary: After a long estrangement, concert pianist Claire Keyes returns home to care for her twin sister, Nicole, who's recuperating from major surgery. Nicole's partner and best friend, Wyatt Knight, has heard only terrible things about Claire, the selfish child prodigy. Much to his surprise, Claire is a sensitive, loving person. As Wyatt begins to care for Claire, he wonders if she'll be a good mother to his hearing-impaired daughter, his highest priority.

Other books by the same author:
Accidentally Yours, 2008
Sweet Trouble, 2008 (Bakery Girls. Book 3)
Sweet Spot, 2008 (Bakery Girls. Book 2)
Sizzling, 2007 (Buchanans. Book 3)
Tempting, 2007 (Buchanans. Book 4)

Other books you might like:
Debbie Macomber, *Twenty Wishes*, 2008
    Blossom Street. Book 4
Emilie Richards, *Sister's Choice*, 2008
Nora Roberts, *Chesapeake Blue*, 2004
    Chesapeake Bay. Book 4
Kathryn Shay, *Trust in Me*, 2003
Susan Wiggs, *Table for Five*, 2006

338

ANNE MALLORY (Pseudonym of Anne Hearn)

Three Nights of Sin
(New York: Avon, 2008)

Story type: Historical/Regency
Subject(s): Family; Murder
Major character(s): Marietta Winters, Gentlewoman; Gabriel Noble, Businessman
Time period(s): 1820s (1825)
Locale(s): London, England

Summary: Marietta Winters has no other choice but to agree to Gabriel Noble's terms. After her brother Kenny is charged with murders he didn't commit, the only person who can help Marietta save Kenny from being executed is the mysterious Gabriel. In exchange for his

help, Noble asks for three "favors" from Marietta. Marietta never expected that after only three nights with him, she would fall in love with Gabriel.

Where it's reviewed:
Romantic Times, May 2008, page 40

Other books by the same author:
What Isabella Desires, 2007
The Earl of Her Dreams, 2006
The Viscount's Wicked Ways, 2006
Daring the Duke, 2005
Masquerading the Marquess, 2004

Other books you might like:
Elizabeth Boyle, *One Night of Passion*, 2002
Gaelen Foley, *The Duke*, 2000
Lynn Kerstan, *The Silver Lion*, 2003
Stephanie Laurens, *What Price Love?*, 2006
Julia Ross, *Clandestine*, 2006

339

DEB MARLOWE

Scandalous Lord, Rebellious Miss

(Toronto: Harlequin, 2008)

Story type: Historical/Regency
Subject(s): Courtship; Politics
Major character(s): Sophie Westby, Gentlewoman, Interior Decorator; Charles Alden, Nobleman (Viscount Dayle), Political Figure
Time period(s): 1810s (1817)
Locale(s): England

Summary: Charles Alden, Viscount Dayle, spent months building a new reputation for himself as a respected politician, but all that work is threatened by an anonymous article in one of London's newspapers about Charles' rakish past. Deciding that marriage is the best way to counter the scandal, Charles sets out to find a suitable wife, and he seems to have found the perfect candidate: the ever proper Corrine Ashford. The only problem with Charles' plan is that after he meets Sophie Westby, who has been hired by his mother to redecorate his home, the only woman Charles wants to wed is the slightly scandalous and totally unconventional Sophie.

Where it's reviewed:
Romantic Times, February 2008, page 51

Other books you might like:
Mary Balogh, *Slightly Tempted*, 2004
Christina Dodd, *That Scandalous Evening*, 1998
Diane Farr, *Under a Lucky Star*, 2004
Candice Hern, *Her Scandalous Affair*, 2004
Barbara Metzger, *The Duel*, 2005

340

DEIRDRE MARTIN

Just a Taste

(New York: Berkley Sensation, 2008)

Story type: Contemporary; Humor
Subject(s): Grief; Cooks and Cooking; Restaurants

Major character(s): Vivi Robitaille, Restaurateur; Anthony Dante, Widow(er), Restaurateur
Time period(s): 2000s
Locale(s): New York, New York (Brooklyn)

Summary: Anthony Dante has settled into a life of grieving, which consists of cooking in his restaurant, Dante's, and visiting the cemetery for graveside chats with his deceased wife. Then, Vivi Robitaille, a spunky Frenchwoman, opens a bistro, Vivi's, right by Dante's. As the gauntlet is thrown down, Anthony begins to feel again, even if it is the fires of competition.

Where it's reviewed:
Booklist, December 15, 2007, page 31
Romantic Times, January 2008, page 85

Other books by the same author:
Chasing Stanley, 2007
The Penalty Box, 2006
Total Rush, 2005
Fair Play, 2004
Body Check, 2003

Other books you might like:
Mary Kay Andrews, *Deep Dish*, 2008
Millie Criswell, *The Trouble with Mary*, 2001
Susan Mallery, *Delicious*, 2006
Nora Roberts, *Waiting for Nick*, 1997
Deborah Shelley, *My Favorite Flavor*, 2000

341

J.D. MASON

You Gotta Sin to Get Saved

(New York: St. Martin's Press, 2008)

Story type: Ethnic; Multicultural
Subject(s): African Americans; Adoption; Violence
Major character(s): Reesy Braxton, Parent, Adoptee; Justin Braxton, Spouse
Time period(s): 2000s
Locale(s): Murphy, Kansas; Denver, Colorado

Summary: Reesy Braxton devotes most of her time trying to find her birth mother. This leaves her husband, Justin, feeling so neglected he turns to lap dancers for attention. When her mother does not turn out to be what Reesy expected, she has to dedicate herself to her family before she loses it.

Where it's reviewed:
Romantic Times, April 2008, page 58

Other books by the same author:
This Fire Down in My Soul, 2008
Don't Want No Sugar, 2005
One Day I Saw a Black King, 2004
And on the Eighth Day She Rested, 2003

Other books you might like:
Pearl Cleage, *Seen It All and Done the Rest*, 2008
Eric Jerome Dickey, *Waking with Enemies*, 2007
E. Harris, *Just Too Good to Be True*, 2008
Terry McMillan, *Interruption of Everything*, 2006
Kayla Perrin, *Midnight Dreams*, 2007

342

CATHY MAXWELL

In the Highlander's Bed

(New York: Avon, 2008)

Story type: Historical/Regency
Subject(s): Kidnapping; Politics
Major character(s): Constance Cameron, Gentlewoman, Captive; Gordon Lachlan, Laird
Time period(s): 1800s (1808)
Locale(s): Scotland

Summary: All Constance Cameron wants to do is get out of Scotland and go back to Ohio. So when her plans to run away are foiled by a brawny Scotsman who kidnaps her in order to force her noble brother-in-law to return the Sword of MacKenna, she doesn't take it kindly. A fiery, fearless American miss goes head to head with a fascinated Scot in this lively romance that nicely wraps up Maxwell's series about the Cameron sisters.

Where it's reviewed:
Romantic Times, February 2008, page 42

Other books by the same author:
Bedding the Heiress, 2007
In the Bed of a Duke, 2006
The Price of Indiscretion, 2005
The Temptation of a Proper Governess, 2004
The Adventures of a Scottish Heiress, 2003

Other books you might like:
Mary Balogh, *Slightly Scandalous*, 2003
Karen Hawkins, *To Catch a Highlander*, 2008
Eloisa James, *Kiss Me, Annabel*, 2005
Sabrina Jeffries, *Let Sleeping Rogues Lie*, 2008
Nicole Jordan, *To Pleasure a Lady*, 2008

343

AMANDA MCCABE

A Sinful Alliance

(Toronto: Harlequin, 2008)

Story type: Historical/Tudor Period
Subject(s): Espionage; Identity, Concealed; Politics
Major character(s): Marguerite Dumas, Criminal (assassin); Nicolai Ostrovsky, Actor
Time period(s): 16th century (1525; 1527)
Locale(s): Venice, Italy; France; England

Summary: In her entire career as the Emerald Lily, Marguerite Dumas, France's most skilled assassin, has only failed to kill one man: Nicolai Ostrovsky. Now it seems fate has given Marguerite one more chance when Nicolai turns up at the same political summit being given by Henry VIII that Marguerite is attending. When it turns out that someone else at the gathering wants Marguerite out of the way, the only person she can trust is Nicolai, the man she plans on eliminating.

Where it's reviewed:
Romantic Times, April 2008, page 44

Other books by the same author:
A Notorious Woman, 2007
A Tangled Web, 2006
Lady Midnight, 2005
Star of India, 2004
The Rules of Love, 2004

Other books you might like:
Gayle Callen, *His Scandal*, 2002
Denise Domning, *Lady in Waiting*, 1998
Lauren Royal, *Amber*, 2001
Jeanne Westin, *Lady Merry's Dashing Champion*, 2007

344

KATHLEEN MCCLEARY

House and Home

(New York: Hyperion, 2008)

Story type: Contemporary
Subject(s): Marriage; Divorce; Family Relations
Major character(s): Ellen Flanagan, Businesswoman, Spouse; Sam Flanagan, Inventor, Spouse
Time period(s): 2000s
Locale(s): Portland, Oregon; Cannon Beach, Oregon

Summary: Ellen Flanagan's husband, Sam, is oblivious to reality, his focus on his inventions and magic tricks. Forced to live on the modest income Ellen makes from her antiques store/coffee shop, Coffehome, the family loses their beloved home. Ellen and Sam separate, but her immediate reaction is mourning for the home she spent years decorating inch-by-inch. This sometimes not-so-gentle book begs the question: What makes a house a home? Ellen's journey to find the answer leads her into some surprising situations.

Where it's reviewed:
Publishers Weekly, April 14, 2008, page 35

Other books you might like:
Patti Callahan Henry, *Losing the Moon*, 2004
Mary Alice Monroe, *Sweetgrass*, 2005
Karen White, *Pieces of the Heart*, 2006
Susan Wiggs, *Lakeside Cottage*, 2005
Monica Wood, *My Only Story*, 2001

345

JUDI MCCOY

Making Over Mr. Right

(New York: Avon, 2008)

Story type: Contemporary/Fantasy
Subject(s): Business; Change; Mythology
Major character(s): Zoe Degodessa, Deity (Muse of Beauty); Theodore Maragos, Computer Expert
Time period(s): 2000s
Locale(s): New York, New York; Mount Olympus, Greece

Summary: Zoe, the Muse of Beauty, has been given one last chance to fulfill her destiny by spending a year on

Earth bringing beauty to mortals. While on Earth, Zoe can indulge in as many affairs with mortals as she might wish, but if she should fall in love, she will lose her place on Mount Olympus. Zoe's last project before she returns home is to transform Theo Maragos from geeky computer nerd into successful business CEO. However, once Zoe gets to know the "new" Theo better, she is tempted to risk everything for a chance at love with him.

Where it's reviewed:
Romantic Times, March 2008, page 106

Other books by the same author:
One Night with a Goddess, 2007
Almost a Goddess, 2006
Wanted: One Sexy Night, 2005
Match Made in Heaven, 2004
Wanted: One Special Kiss, 2004

Other books you might like:
Annette Blair, *The Kitchen Witch*, 2004
P.C. Cast, *Goddess of Spring*, 2004
Kristine Grayson, *Utterly Charming*, 2000
Sherrilyn Kenyon, *Fantasy Lover*, 2002
Jenna McKnight, *A Greek God at the Ladies Club*, 2003

346

CHEYENNE MCCRAY (Pseudonym of Debbie Federici)

Moving Target

(New York: St. Martin's Paperbacks, 2008)

Story type: Contemporary; Romantic Suspense
Subject(s): Federal Witness Security Program; Russians; Organized Crime
Major character(s): Anistana King, Antiques Dealer, Impostor (protected witness); Daniel Parker, Police Officer (U.S. Marshal)
Time period(s): 2000s
Locale(s): United States

Summary: Disappearing into the Federal Witness Protection Program after the Russian Mafia killed her family and wounded her, Anistana King, now Ani Carter, has been safely hidden for two years. Now, two weeks away from testifying at the trial that will convict the killers, she tries to help a young burn victim by contacting one of her former clients, and suddenly the Russians are hot on her trail once again. Her only protection is U.S. Deputy Marshal Daniel Parker, and he will do anything to keep her, the woman he also loves, safe. Action-packed and tense, this super-sexy thriller takes its characters on a rousing chase that keeps them just inches ahead of the assassins.

Where it's reviewed:
Romantic Times, January 2008, page 74

Other books by the same author:
Forbidden Magic, 2005
Bewitched, 2004 (The Seraphine Chronicles series)
Wonderland: King of Spades, 2004
Wonderland: King of Diamonds, 2004
Wonderland: King of Hearts, 2003

Other books you might like:
Ginna Gray, *The Witness*, 2001
Shirley Hailstock, *You Made Me Love You*, 2005
Iris Johansen, *The Ugly Duckling*, 1996
Dinah McCall, *Tallchief*, 1997
Sharon Sala, *Dark Water*, 2002

347

CHEYENNE MCCRAY

Shadow Magic

(New York: St. Martin's Paperbacks, 2008)

Story type: Paranormal
Series: Magic. Book 4
Subject(s): Witches and Witchcraft; Good and Evil; War
Major character(s): Hannah Wentworth, Witch (D'Anu); Garran, Royalty (king of the Dark Elves), Mythical Creature (elf)
Time period(s): 2000s
Locale(s): Otherworld, Mythical Place

Summary: D'Anu witch Hannah Wentworth, who is also a practitioner of gray magic, flees San Francisco and goes to Otherworld to seek the help of Garran, the King of the Drow (Dark Elves). She is no more prepared for the instant attraction between them than he is. However, she and the other D'Anu witches need the Drow's help in their battle against Ceithlenn and the evil Fomorii demons who are destroying her world. Even though she has good reason not to trust him, she accepts his help, setting the stage for a dangerous and treacherous battle, as well as a hotly erotic love relationship. Sexually explicit.

Where it's reviewed:
Romantic Times, May 2008, page 97

Other books by the same author:
Moving Target, 2008
Chosen Prey, 2007
Wicked Magic, 2007 (Magic. Book 3)
Seduced by Magic, 2006 (Magic. Book 2)
Forbidden Magic, 2005 (Magic. Book 1)

Other books you might like:
Anya Bast, *Witch Blood*, 2008
Emma Holly, *Hot Spell*, 2005
   anthology
Emma Holly, *Prince of Ice*, 2006
Gena Showalter, *The Darkest Night*, 2008
J.R. Ward, *Lover Unbound*, 2007

348

SHANNON MCKENNA
E.C. SHEEDY , Co-Author
CATE NOBLE , Co-Author

Baddest Bad Boys

(New York: Brava, 2008)

Story type: Contemporary; Romantic Suspense
Subject(s): Sexual Behavior; Romance; Crime and Criminals

Time period(s): 2000s
Locale(s): United States

Summary: Infused with graphic sex and spine-tingling danger, this trio of contemporary novellas features isolated settings and fast-paced adventure. A young woman tracks her long-time crush to a remote cabin and becomes the target of a crazed killer in "Anytime, Anywhere" by Shannon McKenna; a businesswoman flees a murderous thief and takes refuge at the Vancouver Island fishing lodge of the brother of a high school friend in "After the Lovin" by E.C. Sheedy; and a week of passion on a private island results in love and a corporate agreement in Cate Noble's "Deal with the Devil."

Where it's reviewed:
Romantic Times, May 2008, page 78

Other books you might like:
Jaid Black, *One Dark Night*, 2004
MaryJanice Davidson, *Wicked Women Whodunit*, 2005
Tina Donahue, *Wicked Women on Top*, 2004
Amy Garvey, *I Love You to Death*, 2006
Nancy Warren, *Drive Me Crazy*, 2004

349

SARAH MCKERRIGAN (Pseudonym of Glynnis Campbell)

Danger's Kiss

(New York: Forever, 2008)

Story type: Historical/Medieval
Subject(s): Revenge; Middle Ages; Murder
Major character(s): Desiree, Thief, Ward; Nicholas Grimshaw, Government Official (shire-reeve), Guardian
Time period(s): 13th century (1250)
Locale(s): Canterbury, England

Summary: When her grandfather is executed for a murder he didn't commit, Desiree is stunned learn that the shire-reeve, the man who ordered the execution, is now her guardian. After their first violent meeting (she tries to stab him as he sleeps), they begin to work together to discover who framed her grandfather, and why. Love grows between the oddly matched pair in this romance that is filled with rich historical detail and plenty of action and danger.

Where it's reviewed:
Romantic Times, May 2008, page 40

Other books by the same author:
Knight's Prize, 2007
Captive Heart, 2006
Lady Danger, 2006

Other books you might like:
Suzanne Barclay, *The Champion*, 1999
Marsha Canham, *In the Shadow of Midnight*, 1994
Denise Domning, *A Love for All Seasons*, 1996
Juliana Garnett, *The Baron*, 1999
Lisa Jackson, *Wild and Wicked*, 2002

350

CHARLOTTE MEDE

Explosive

(New York: Kensington, 2008)

Story type: Historical/Regency
Subject(s): Espionage; Music and Musicians; Seduction
Major character(s): Devon Caravelle, Musician; Gray Dalton, Nobleman (Marquess of Blackburn)
Time period(s): 1810s (1818)
Locale(s): England; France

Summary: When the formula for a new type of explosive is encoded in the score of Beethoven's Third Symphony, it becomes a weapon that can help Napoleon escape exile and return to power. English spy Gray Dalton is determined to stop the French from finding the score, but he needs the help of Devon Caravelle, an accomplished musician and the daughter of the mathematician who devised the code. Gray is certain he can seduce Devon into going along with his plans, but what he doesn't know is that Devon has plans of her own for the score.

Where it's reviewed:
Booklist, December 15, 2007, page 31
Romantic Times, January 2008, page 44

Other books you might like:
Jacquie D'Alessandro, *The Bride Thief*, 2002
Gaelen Foley, *Devil Takes a Bride*, 2004
Sabrina Jeffries, *Never Seduce a Scoundrel*, 2006
Lynn Kerstan, *Dangerous Deceptions*, 2004
Amanda Quick, *Deception*, 1993

351

MARY ALICE MONROE (Pseudonym of Mary Alice Kruesi)

Time Is a River

(New York: Pocket, 2008)

Story type: Contemporary
Subject(s): Fishing; Cancer; Healing
Major character(s): Mia Landon, Fisherman, Divorced Person; Stuart MacDougal, Fisherman, Businessman
Time period(s): 2000s
Locale(s): Asheville, North Carolina

Summary: Mia Landon, a breast cancer survivor, comes home from Casting for Recovery, a fly-fishing retreat, and finds her husband cheating on her. Mia retreats to an isolated cabin, where she discovers the old journal of Katie Watkins, a wrongly scandalized woman who also loved to fly-fish. Mia's recovery is further helped by fellow fisherman Stuart MacDougal, who loves her just the way she is. A beautifully written novel of self-discovery.

Where it's reviewed:
Publishers Weekly, March 3, 2008, page 25

Other books by the same author:
Swimming Lessons, 2007
Sweetgrass, 2005
Skyward, 2003
The Beach House, 2002
The Four Seasons, 2001

Other books you might like:
Judith Arnold, *Barefoot in the Grass*, 1996
Cara Colter, *9 out of 10 Women Can't Be Wrong*, 2002
Angela Hunt, *A Time to Mend*, 2006
    inspirational fiction
Judith Raxten, *The Secret Dreams of Emily Porter*, 2007
Kay Stockham, *His Perfect Woman*, 2007

352

CINDI MYERS

A Soldier Comes Home

(Toronto: Harlequin, 2008)

Story type: Contemporary
Subject(s): Single Parent Families; Military Life
Major character(s): Christine "Chrissie" Evans, Widow(er) (former military wife), Manager (dentist's office); Ray Hughes, Military Personnel (U.S. Army captain), Single Parent; T.J. Evans, Child
Time period(s): 2000s
Locale(s): Colorado Springs, Colorado

Summary: Chrissie Evans, a young army widow, vows never to fall for another soldier, even though she is surrounded by them in her military home town, Colorado Springs. However, Captain Ray Hughes, returning from Iraq to a broken marriage and single parenthood, lives next door and needs her help, Love soon follows, but it will take a lot for Chrissie to risk loving another man who could so easily end up dead. A charming toddler, plenty of friends and family with their own complications, and military life details round out this Harlequin Superromance.

Where it's reviewed:
Romantic Times, June 2008, page 122

Other books by the same author:
At Her Pleasure, 2008
Her Secret Treasure, 2008
The Right Mr. Wrong, 2008
Wild Child, 2007
Fear of Falling, 2006

Other books you might like:
Leanne Banks, *Bride of Fortune*, 2000
Pamela Britton, *On the Edge*, 2008
Roz Fox Denny, *Hot Chocolate on a Cold Day*, 2006
Merline Lovelace, *The Officer's Bride*, 2001
    historical anthology
Sherryl Woods, *Seaview Inn*, 2008

353

SOPHIA NASH

The Kiss

(New York: Avon, 2008)

Story type: Historical/Regency
Subject(s): Friendship; Marriage
Major character(s): Georgiana Wilde, Noblewoman, Widow(er); Quinn Fortesque, Nobleman (Marquis of Ellesmere)
Time period(s): 1810s
Locale(s): Cornwall, England

Summary: Since Georgiana's husband, Anthony, the Marquis of Ellesmere, died on their wedding night, many, including the dowager marchioness, had questioned if the marriage was truly valid. Now Quinn Fortesque, the new Marquis of Ellesmere, has been given the task of traveling to the family's estate in Cornwall to get rid of Georgiana. When Quinn arrives at Penrose, instead of finding a gold-digging upstart trying to cheat his family, he discovers a woman whose love he thought he had lost forever.

Where it's reviewed:
Library Journal, February 15, 2008, page 87
Romantic Times, March 2008, page 40

Other books by the same author:
A Dangerous Beauty, 2007
Lord Will and Her Grace, 2005
A Passionate Endeavor, 2004
A Secret Passion, 2004

Other books you might like:
Elizabeth Boyle, *Something about Emmaline*, 2005
Loretta Chase, *Miss Wonderful*, 2004
Candice Hern, *The Bride Sale*, 2002
Julia London, *The Dangers of Deceiving a Viscount*, 2007
Barbara Metzger, *The Duel*, 2005

354

CARLA NEGGERS

The Angel

(Don Mills, Ontario: MIRA, 2008)

Story type: Contemporary; Romantic Suspense
Subject(s): Folklore; Murder
Major character(s): Keira Sullivan, Artist (illustrator); Simon Cahill, FBI Agent
Time period(s): 2000s
Locale(s): Boston, Massachusetts; Ireland

Summary: While researching an Irish folktale involving an angel, American illustrator Keira Sullivan becomes trapped in an old ruin. Sent by Keira's family to find her, Simon Cahill, an expert at search and rescue techniques, arrives just as Keira is about to free herself. Keira insists she found a stone angel in the ruins just before they collapsed, but now the mythic angel seems to have vanished. At first Simon believes Keira was just imagining her angel until a series of mysterious events convinces him that Keira may have discovered something really dangerous.

Where it's reviewed:
Booklist, April 15, 2008, page 27
Publishers Weekly, March 20, 2008, page 59
Romantic Times, May 2008, page 74

Other books by the same author:
Abandon, 2007
Breakwater, 2006
The Widow, 2006
Dark Sky, 2005
The Rapids, 2004

Other books you might like:
Cherry Adair, *White Heat*, 2007
Jayne Ann Krentz, *Midnight Jewels*, 1987
Karen Marie Moning, *Darkfever*, 2006
Nora Roberts, *Three Fates*, 2002
Evelyn Vaughn, *A.K.A. Goddess*, 2004

355

KATE NOBLE

Compromised

(New York: Berkley Sensation, 2008)

Story type: Historical/Regency
Subject(s): Family; Sisters
Major character(s): Abigail "Gail" Alton, Gentlewoman; Maximillian, Nobleman (Viscount Fontaine)
Time period(s): 1820s (1829)
Locale(s): London, England

Summary: Bookish Gail Alton has no desire to spend her time in London attending balls and soirees, but somehow she finds herself reluctantly taking part in the season along with her beautiful sister Evangeline. When Gail crosses paths with Maximillian, Viscount Fontaine, she never expects him to fall for her, but fall Max does because Gail's horse knocks his into a lake. Gail shouldn't be jealous when Max and Evangeline are found in a compromising situation, but even so, Gail still can't help but think that she should be the one marrying the annoyingly sexy Max instead.

Where it's reviewed:
Booklist, March 15, 2008, page 34
Romantic Times, March 2008, page 47

Other books you might like:
Elizabeth Boyle, *Love Letters from a Duke*, 2007
Kathryn Caskie, *Rules of Engagement*, 2004
Karen Hawkins, *How to Treat a Lady*, 2003
Eloisa James, *Duchess in Love*, 2002
Julia London, *The Hazards of Hunting a Duke*, 2006

356

PAMELA NOWAK

Chances

(Waterville, Maine: Five Star, 2008)

Story type: Historical/Victorian America; Americana
Subject(s): Women's Rights; Gender Roles; Social Issues
Major character(s): Sarah Donovan, Suffragette, Feminist; Daniel Petterman, Undertaker, Single Parent
Time period(s): 1870s (1876)
Locale(s): Denver, Colorado

Summary: Suffragist Sarah Donovan, on a quest to prove to the world that women can do anything men can, becomes a telegraph operator. Daniel Petterman, the town undertaker, doesn't understand Sarah. She doesn't act the way he thinks a woman should, but then again, she's been awfully good to his motherless girls. Historically accurate, and a good read.

Where it's reviewed:
Booklist, December 15, 2007, page 32
Publisher's Weekly, November 5, 2007, page 43

Other books you might like:
Georgina Gentry, *To Tame a Texan*, 2003
Robin Lee Hatcher, *Kiss Me Katie*, 1996
Shirl Henke, *Night Flower*, 1990
Betina Krahn, *Sweet Talking Man*, 2000
Susan Wiggs, *The Firebrand*, 2003

357

PATTI O'SHEA (Pseudonym of Patti J. Olszoski)

In Twilight's Shadow

(New York: Tor, 2008)

Story type: Contemporary/Fantasy
Series: Light Warriors. Book 2
Subject(s): Magic; Sisters
Major character(s): Maia Frasier, Office Worker; Creed Blackwood, Bounty Hunter, Troubleshooter
Time period(s): 2000s
Locale(s): Minneapolis, Minnesota

Summary: When wounded troubleshooter Creed Blackwood turns up in her home in Minneapolis, Maia Frasier finds herself reluctantly becoming involved in his search for a demon using black magic. With his own magic powers becoming increasingly unreliable, Creed knows he needs Maia, but he never expected that the demon he is searching for would turn out to be Maia's old lover, Seth.

Where it's reviewed:
Publishers Weekly, April 7, 2008, page 47
Romantic Times, June 2008, page 108

Other books by the same author:
In the Midnight Hour, 2007
Eternal Nights, 2006
Through a Crimson Veil, 2005
The Power of Two, 2004
Ravyn's Flight, 2002

Other books you might like:
Lara Adrian, *Kiss of Midnight*, 2007
Nina Bangs, *Wicked Nights*, 2005
Christine Feehan, *Shadow Game*, 2003
Sherrilyn Kenyon, *Dance with the Devil*, 2003
Katie MacAlister, *You Slay Me*, 2004

358

OLIVIA PARKER

At the Bride Hunt Ball

(New York: Avon, 2008)

Story type: Historical/Regency
Subject(s): Competition; Courtship
Major character(s): Madelyn Haywood, Gentlewoman; Gabriel Thurston Devine, Nobleman (Duke of Wolverest)
Time period(s): 1810s
Locale(s): London, England; Yorkshire, England
Summary: When Gabriel Thurston Devine, Duke of Wolverest, decides it is time his brother Tristan weds, he puts together a list of eligible candidates. Now every eligible lady in London wants nothing more than to be one of the finalists to become the next Duchess of Wolverest; every lady, that is, except Madelyn Hunter. Intrigued by the unconventional Madelyn, Gabriel adds her to his list, never expecting that after getting to know Madelyn, he would want to marry her himself!

Where it's reviewed:
Romantic Times, June 2008, page 53

Other books you might like:
Elizabeth Boyle, *Stealing the Bride*, 2003
Kathryn Caskie, *Rules of Engagement*, 2004
Shana Galen, *When Dashing Met Danger*, 2005
Karen Hawkins, *A Belated Bride*, 2001
Eloisa James, *Much Ado about You*, 2005

359

ANDREA PICKENS (Pseudonym of Andrea DaRif)

Seduced by a Spy

(New York: Forever, 2007)

Story type: Historical/Regency
Series: Merlin's Maidens. Book 2
Subject(s): Espionage; Seduction
Major character(s): Shannon, Spy, Orphan; Alexandr Orlov, Spy
Time period(s): 1810s
Locale(s): Ireland; England; Scotland
Summary: Shannon, one of Merlin's Maidens, knew her latest assignment would have some unique challenges, but she never expected that one of them would be her new partner, Russian spy Alexandr Orlov. The last time the two crossed paths, Shannon nearly killed Alexandr while on a mission in Ireland. Now, they must find some way of working together if they want to successfully stop a ruthless French assassin known as D'Etienne.

Where it's reviewed:
Booklist, February 1, 2008, page 34
Romantic Times, March 2008, page 40

Other books by the same author:
The Spy Wore Silk, 2007
A Stroke of Luck, 2003
The Banished Bride, 2002
The Storybook Hero, 2002
Diamond in the Rough, 2001

Other books you might like:
Celeste Bradley, *The Spy*, 2004
Shana Galen, *Pride and Petticoats*, 2006
Karen Hawkins, *To Scotland, with Love*, 2007
Jenna Petersen, *Seduction Is Forever*, 2007
Sari Robins, *When Seducing a Spy*, 2007

360

CANDICE POARCH (Pseudonym of Candice Poarch Baines)

Long, Hot Nights

(New York: Dafina, 2008)

Story type: Contemporary; Romantic Suspense
Series: Quest for the Golden Bowl. Book 2
Subject(s): Murder; Mystery; Small Town Life
Major character(s): Alyssa Claxton, Detective—Police; Jordan Ellis, Businessman (business club owner)
Time period(s): 2000s
Locale(s): Paradise Island, Virginia
Summary: When Alyssa Claxton's cousin's husband and another woman are found murdered, lying naked in the middle of the road on sleepy Paradise Island, Alyssa, as the only detective on the island, is drawn into the investigation. At the same time she is being pursued by handsome, sexy Jordan Ellis, whose attentions both annoy and attract her. Unexpected danger stalks them both in this fast-paced book that is second in a romantic suspense trilogy focusing on an old legend about the people who settled Paradise Island in the 17th century.

Where it's reviewed:
Romantic Suspense, May 2008, page 78

Other books by the same author:
Golden Night, 2007 (Quest for the Golden Bowl. Book 1)
His Tempest, 2007
Then Comes Love, 2007
Bittersweet, 2006
Sweet Southern Comfort, 2006

Other books you might like:
Rochelle Alers, *No Compromise*, 2002
Rochelle Alers, *Stranger in My Arms*, 2007
Leslie Esdaile, *Through the Storm*, 2002
Mildred Riley, *Bad to the Bone*, 2003
Janelle Taylor, *Night Moves*, 2002

361

PATRICIA POTTER

Catch a Shadow

(New York: Berkley Sensation, 2008)

Story type: Contemporary; Romantic Suspense
Subject(s): Mystery; Murder; Suspense
Major character(s): Kirke Palmer, Health Care Professional (paramedic); Jake Kelly, Convict (former), Military Personnel (special forces)
Time period(s): 2000s

Locale(s): Atlanta, Georgia

Summary: When Atlanta paramedic Kirke Palmer agrees to deliver a letter for the dying victim of a hit-and-run accident, she has no idea that this good deed will come back to haunt her in an unexpectedly deadly way. Jake Kelly, a former special ops agent who just finished serving time for a theft he didn't commit, is drawn to Atlanta by a mysterious phone call and arrives just in time to see the accident, recognize the victim as a supposedly dead former CIA agent, and see him give the letter to Kirke. The pieces fall into place as Jake realizes that someone out there doesn't want the past revived, and that both he and Kirke have suddenly become the targets of a cold-blooded killer.

Where it's reviewed:
Romantic Times, March 2008, page 75

Other books by the same author:
Behind the Shadows, 2008
Beloved Warrior, 2007
Beloved Stranger, 2006
Tempting the Devil, 2006
Beloved Impostor, 2004

Other books you might like:
Cherry Adair, *Hide and Seek*, 2001
Suzanne Brockmann, *Gone Too Far*, 2003
Barbara Freethy, *Silent Fall*, 2008
Barbara Freethy, *Silent Run*, 2008
Karen Rose, *Nothing to Fear*, 2005

362

AMANDA QUICK (Pseudonym of Jayne Ann Krentz)

The Third Circle

(New York: Putnam, 2008)

Story type: Historical/Victorian; Romantic Suspense
Series: Arcane Society. Book 4
Subject(s): Psychic Powers; Mystery; Paranormal
Major character(s): Leona Hewitt, Psychic (crystal reader); Thaddeus Ware, Psychic (mesmerist)
Time period(s): 19th century (late)
Locale(s): London, England

Summary: On the trail of the same legendary artifact, Leona Hewitt and Thaddeus Ware become wary allies after Leona uses her abilities with the aurora stone to save Thaddeus from the effects of the villain's diabolically-induced hallucinations, even though they each have their own ideas about what should be the stone's fate. A superhuman sociopath with a love of killing, a shadowy group of power-mad psychics, a creative cast of likable characters, psychically enhanced sex, and Quick's quirky sense of humor are highlights of this lively romance with plenty of paranormal elements. This book is fourth in the series that contains books written as both Jayne Ann Krentz (contemporary) and under the pseudonym Amanda Quick (historical).

Where it's reviewed:
Library Journal, April 15, 2008, page 68

Other books by the same author:
The River Knows, 2007
Second Sight, 2006 (Arcane Society. Book 1)
Lie by Moonlight, 2005
Wait until Midnight, 2005
The Paid Companion, 2004

Other books you might like:
Connie Brockway, *All through the Night*, 1997
Liz Carlyle, *No True Gentleman*, 2002
Jane Feather, *Virtue*, 1993
Elizabeth Kary, *Midnight Lace*, 1990
Carla Simpson, *Seductive Caress*, 1992

363

JULIA QUINN (Pseudonym of Julie Cotler Pottinger)

The Lost Duke of Wyndham

(New York: Avon, 2008)

Story type: Historical/Regency
Subject(s): Identity; Inheritance; Family Life
Major character(s): Grace Eversleigh, Companion, Gentlewoman; Jack Audley, Highwayman, Heir—Lost (possible Duke of Wyndham)
Time period(s): 1810s
Locale(s): England

Summary: When the dowager Duchess of Wyndham identifies highwayman Jack Audley as the long-lost heir to her late husband's title, he reluctantly thinks it might be possible and agrees to go to Belgrave Castle to learn the truth. His arrival causes problems for everyone, especially for his cousin, Thomas, who is currently the acting duke, and his fiancee, Amelia, whose father insists his daughter will marry the true duke. In the meantime, Jack is attracted to Grace Eversleigh, the dowager's companion. Lively fun and plenty of complications are part of this romance that is first of the Two Dukes of Wyndham pair; *Mr. Cavendish, I Presume* is the companion novel.

Where it's reviewed:
Library Journal, June 15, 2008, page 51
Romantic Times, June 2008, page 48

Other books by the same author:
Mr. Cavendish, I Presume, 2008
The Secret Diaries of Miss Miranda Cheever, 2007
On the Way to the Wedding, 2006
The Further Observations of Lady Whistledown, 2003
Romancing Mr. Bridgerton, 2002

Other books you might like:
Jo Beverley, *A Lady's Secret*, 2008
Jo Beverley, *A Most Unsuitable Man*, 2005
Eloisa James, *Kiss Me, Annabel*, 2005
Sabrina Jeffries, *A Dangerous Love*, 2000
Johanna Lindsey, *No Choice but Seduction*, 2008

364

TARA TAYLOR QUINN
JEAN BRASHEAR , Co-Author

Romance

LINDA CARDILLO , Co-Author

The Valentine Gift

(Toronto: Harlequin, 2008)

Story type: Anthology; Holiday Themes
Subject(s): Courtship; Holidays; Marriage
Locale(s): United States

Summary: This trio of poignant, heartwarming stories explores the depths of family and romance and will provide readers with intriguing new insights. In "Valentine's Daughter" by Tara Taylor Quinn, a woman finds advice for her decaying marriage in her mother's new-found diary; in "Our Day" by Jean Brashear, a gifted surgeon discovers he's more married to his job than he is to his wife; and in "The Hand That Gives the Rose" by Linda Cardillo, a wine maker is separated from her true love by the Berlin Wall.

Other books you might like:
Jill Barnett, *Sentimental Journey*, 2001
Jean Brashear, *Forgiveness*, 2005
Linda Cardillo, *Dancing on Sunday Afternoons*, 2007
Mary Alice Monroe, *The Four Seasons*, 2001
Mary Alice Monroe, *The Secrets We Keep*, 2006

365

TESSA RADLEY

Pride & a Pregnancy Secret

(New York: Silhouette, 2008)

Story type: Contemporary
Series: Diamonds Down Under. Book 2
Subject(s): Secrets; Pregnancy; Interpersonal Relations
Major character(s): Jessica Cotter, Businesswoman (jewelry store manager); Ryan Blackstone, Business-man (gem dealer), Wealthy
Time period(s): 2000s
Locale(s): Sydney, Australia

Summary: Jessica Cotter knew the rules of the game when she began a secret affair with diamond mogul Ryan Blackstone. He was a confirmed bachelor and that meant no kids and no commitment. When Jessica finds herself pregnant, she knows she needs to break off the relationship before Ryan finds out. However, Ryan is furious when she walks out and eventually realizes that he will do anything not to lose her. Pride, family feuds, mystery, and old wounds and secrets are part of this romance that puts a slightly new spin on the old secret baby plot. Part of the six book Diamonds Down Under mini-series that involves the fortunes of the Blackstone and Hammond families.

Where it's reviewed:
Romantic Times, February 2008, page 111

Other books by the same author:
Black Widow Bride, 2007
Rich Man's Revenge, 2007
The Apollonides Mistress Scandal, 2007
The Desert Bride of Al Zayed, 2007
The Kyriakos Virgin Bride, 2007

Other books you might like:
Jan Colley, *Satin & a Scandalous Affair*, 2007
  Diamonds Down Under. Book 4
Bronwyn Jameson, *Vows & a Vengeful Groom*, 2007
  Diamonds Down Under. Book 1
Yvonne Lindsay, *Jealousy & a Jeweled Proposition*, 2007
  Diamonds Down Under. Book 6
Paula Roe, *Boardrooms & a Billionaire Heir*, 2007
  Diamonds Down Under. Book 5
Maxine Sullivan, *Mistress & a Million Dollars*, 2007
  Diamonds Down Under. Book 3

366

DEBORAH RALEIGH

Bedding the Baron

(New York: Zebra, 2008)

Story type: Historical/Regency
Subject(s): Inheritance; Secrets
Major character(s): Frederick Smith, Engineer, Bastard Son; Portia Walker, Widow(er), Innkeeper
Time period(s): 1810s
Locale(s): England

Summary: When their former teacher and surrogate father dies and leaves each of them a large sum of money, three men, all well-born bastards and closer than broth-ers, are shocked to learn that their windfalls are the result of extortion and are linked, in some way, to their natural fathers. Frederick Smith, the youngest and most serious of the lot, sets out for his father's country estate, determined to learn the truth. However, a stop at a nearby country inn and a meeting with the beautiful, independent widow who runs the establishment, adds a new, romantic direction to his plans. Secrets abound in this romantic adventure that is first in a projected trilogy.

Where it's reviewed:
Romantic Times, March 2008, page 48

Other books by the same author:
Some Like It Brazen, 2007
Some Like It Sinful, 2006
Some Like It Wicked, 2005

Other books you might like:
Victoria Alexander, *A Little Bit Wicked*, 2007
Mary Balogh, *Simply Perfect*, 2008
Sabrina Jeffries, *To Pleasure a Prince*, 2005
Lisa Kleypas, *Secrets of a Summer Night*, 2004
Lisa Kleypas, *Where Dreams Begin*, 2000

367

KAREN ROBARDS

Guilty

(New York: Putnam, 2008)

Story type: Contemporary; Romantic Suspense
Subject(s): Murder; Kidnapping; Secrets

Major character(s): Kate White, Lawyer, Single Parent;
Tom Braga, Detective—Homicide
Time period(s): 2000s
Locale(s): Philadelphia, Pennsylvania

Summary: When fledgling prosecutor Kate White is taken
hostage after a courtroom bloodbath in which the presid-
ing judge is killed, she is shocked to find that one of her
captors, Mario, is someone from her wild teenage past.
Threatening her with exposure if she doesn't help get
him out of prison, Kate, a single parent with a young
son, has no choice but to agree. Detective Tom Braga
thinks there's something about her supposed killing of
her captor that doesn't ring true, especially when Mario
ends up dead in her garage. However, he finds himself
attracted to her and wanting to protect her, if only she
will trust him with the truth. This romantic thriller is
taut, suspenseful, and filled with well-developed
characters.

Where it's reviewed:
Booklist, March 15, 2008, page 34
Publishers Weekly, February 11, 2008, page 49
Romantic Times, April 2008, page 84

Other books by the same author:
Vanished, 2006
Superstition, 2005
Bait, 2004
Beachcomber, 2003
Whispers at Midnight, 2003

Other books you might like:
Sandra Brown, *French Silk*, 1992
Metsy Hingle, *Flash Point*, 2003
Karen Rose, *Scream for Me*, 2008
Mariah Stewart, *Dark Truth*, 2005
Karen Young, *Someone Knows*, 2002

368

NORA ROBERTS

The Hollow

(New York: Jove, 2008)

Story type: Contemporary; Paranormal
Series: Sign of the Seven Trilogy. Book 2
Subject(s): Demons; Good and Evil; Small Town Life
Major character(s): Layla Darnell, Psychic, Office Worker
(law office); Fox O'Dell, Lawyer, Psychic
Time period(s): 2000s
Locale(s): Hawkins Hollow, Maryland

Summary: Ever since three boys, Fox, Caleb, and Gage,
bonded as blood brothers over the Pagan Stone on their
10th birthday and awoke a demon, every seven years
havoc, increasingly violent, has been visited on the quiet
town of Hawkins Hollow. Now 21 years later, things are
coming to a head, and with the arrival of three women
who are also connected to the demon, the six are preparing to do battle. This time it is Fox and Layla, linked by
their abilities to read people's thoughts who have their
part to play in this race against time to learn more about
how to defeat the demon and save the town.

Where it's reviewed:
Romantic Times, May 2008, page 102

Other books by the same author:
The Pagan Stone, 2008 (Sign of the Seven Trilogy .
Book 3)
Blood Brothers, 2007 (Sign of the Seven Trilogy. Book
1)
Dance of the Gods, 2006 (Circle Trilogy . Book 2)
Morrigan's Cross, 2006 (Circle Trilogy . Book 1)
Valley of Silence, 2006 (Circle Trilogy . Book 3)

Other books you might like:
Tracy Fobes, *The Forbidden Garden*, 2000
Jill Jones, *Circle of the Lily*, 1998
Cait London, *At the Edge*, 2007
Psychic Sisters. Book 1
Carin Rafferty, *A Touch of Magic*, 1995
Patricia Simpson, *The Dark Lord*, 2004
Forbidden Tarot. Book 1

369

SARI ROBINS (Pseudonym of Sari Earl)

The Governess Wears Scarlet

(New York: Avon, 2008)

Story type: Historical/Regency
Subject(s): Family; Identity, Concealed
Major character(s): Abigail West, Governess; Jason Steele,
Lawyer, Nobleman
Time period(s): 1810s (1812)
Locale(s): London, England

Summary: Abigail West spends her nights searching
London's dangerous streets for her missing brother and
her days desperately searching for a job. When Abigail
finally secures a position as a governess working for
Viscount Jason Steele, she has no idea that her new
employer is the same masked man who rescued her one
dark night. By the same token, Jason, who spends his
nights dispensing justice on London's streets, has no
clue that his new employee is the same veiled widow
with whom he has begun a sizzling affair.

Where it's reviewed:
Romantic Times, February 2008, page 48

Other books by the same author:
When Seducing a Spy, 2007
What to Wear to a Seduction, 2006
More than a Scandal, 2005
One Wicked Night, 2004
All Men are Rogues, 2003

Other books you might like:
Elizabeth Boyle, *One Night of Passion*, 2002
Suzanne Enoch, *Sin and Sensibility*, 2005
Karen Hawkins, *Confessions of a Scoundrel*, 2003
Jenna Petersen, *Scandalous*, 2005
Kathryn Smith, *A Game of Scandal*, 2002

370

KAREN ROSE (Pseudonym of Karen Rose Hafer)

Scream for Me

(New York: Grand Central, 2008)

Story type: Contemporary; Romantic Suspense
Subject(s): Murder; Twins; Serial Killers
Major character(s): Alexandra Tremaine Fallon, Nurse (emergency room), Twin; Daniel Vartanian, Detective—Police (special agent, GBI)
Time period(s): 2000s
Locale(s): Dutton, Georgia

Summary: Thirteen years after her twin sister was murdered and her mother committed suicide, Alex Fallon returns to Dutton, Georgia, to take custody of her four-year-old niece when her stepsister, Bailey, goes missing. However, a revenge-driven killer has returned to the area, as well, bringing Georgia Bureau of Investigation Special Agent Daniel Vartanian back to a town he'd just as soon forget. Similarities between her twin's murder and the current one send Alex straight to Daniel to see if the victim is her stepsister. It's not Bailey, but where is she? Is there a connection between her disappearance and the murders that are beginning to crop up in sleepy Dutton? A chilling thriller with enough romance to make it appeal to romance fans, this story also uses the killer's point of view to ramp up the suspense.

Where it's reviewed:
Romantic Times, May 2008, page 81

Other books by the same author:
Count to Ten, 2007
Die for Me, 2007
You Can't Hide, 2006
Nothing to Fear, 2005
Have You Seen Her?, 2004

Other books you might like:
Beverly Barton, *The Fifth Victim*, 2003
Beverly Barton, *What She Doesn't Know*, 2002
Lisa Jackson, *The Night Before*, 2003
Hunter Morgan, *The Other Twin*, 2003
Mariah Stewart, *Dark Truth*, 2005

371

SHARON SALA

The Healer

(Don Mills, Ontario: Mira, 2008)

Story type: Contemporary; Paranormal
Subject(s): Healing; Psychic Powers; Animals
Major character(s): Lucia Maria "Luce" Andahar, Waiter/Waitress; Jonah Gray Wolf, Healer, Psychic (animal communicator)
Time period(s): 2000s
Locale(s): Alaska; Little Top, West Virginia

Summary: Gifted with an uncanny ability to communicate with animals and to heal, Jonah Gray Wolf is on the run from a ruthless man he once healed and who now wants to use his abilities for his own purposes. Jonah arrives in a small town in the mountains of West Virginia and ends up healing a dog for Lucia Andahar, a woman who is as much a loner as he is and who is being stalked by an unknown predator. Passion sizzles between them from the first; and as their bond becomes permanent, their feelings for each other just increase their vulnerability to the growing danger that threatens them on all fronts. This magical, mystical romance adds another to Sala's long list of emotionally involving romances.

Where it's reviewed:
Publishers Weekly, January 1, 2008, page 47

Other books by the same author:
Cut Throat, 2007
Nine Lives, 2006
Missing, 2004
Whippoorwill, 2003
Dark Water, 2002

Other books you might like:
Jessica Inclan, *Reason to Believe*, 2006
Susan Krinard, *Prince of Shadows*, 1996
Susan Krinard, *To Tame a Wolf*, 2008
Rachel Lee, *Thunder Mountain*, 1994
Dinah McCall, *Legend*, 1998

372

LYNSAY SANDS

The Accidental Vampire

(New York: Avon, 2008)

Story type: Vampire Story; Humor
Series: Argeneau. Book 7
Subject(s): Vampires; Humor; Learning
Major character(s): Elvi Black, Vampire (newbie); Victor Argeneau, Vampire, Teacher (mentor)
Time period(s): 2000s
Locale(s): Port Henry, Ontario, Canada

Summary: Newbie vampire Elvi Black needs to learn the ropes about being one of the undead. Elvi's mortal friends are obviously no help, and the old Dracula movies aren't exactly brimming with the information she needs. Enter experienced vampire Victor Argeneau, her new mentor. Victor has to act as her protector, too, because someone wants to see Elvi destroyed.

Where it's reviewed:
Romantic Times, January 2008, page 91

Other books by the same author:
Vampire, Interrupted, 2008 (Argeneau. Book 9)
Vampires Are Forever, 2008 (Argeneau. Book 8)
Bite Me If You Can, 2007 (Argeneau. Book 6)
A Bite to Remember, 2006 (Argeneau. Book 5)
Tall, Dark and Hungry, 2004 (Argeneau. Book 4)

Other books you might like:
Amanda Ashley, *Dead Perfect*, 2008
Gerry Bartlett, *Real Vampires Get Lucky*, 2008

Real Vampires. Book 3
Simon R. Green, *Daemons Are Forever*, 2008
Jennifer Rardin, *Another One Bites the Dust*, 2008
Linda Winston, *50 Ways to Hex Your Lover*, 2008

373

LYNSAY SANDS

Vampire, Interrupted

(New York: Avon, 2008)

Story type: Contemporary; Vampire Story
Series: Argeneau. Book 9
Subject(s): Vampires; Courtship; Humor
Major character(s): Marguerite Argeneau, Detective—
    Private, Vampire; Julius Notte, Vampire
Time period(s): 2000s
Locale(s): England

Summary: Seven-hundred-year-old vampire Marguerite
Argeneau decides it's about time she had a career, so she
gets a job as a private investigator. Her first assignment,
finding a missing mother, almost gets her beheaded. Fellow vampire Julius Notte is determined to protect
Marguerite. He thinks she's hot, and he'd love to get
closer to her. However, he's been out of the dating game
for 500 years, and his wooing skills are a little rusty.

Where it's reviewed:
Romantic Times, March 2008, page 104

Other books by the same author:
Vampires Are Forever, 2008 (Argeneau. Book 8)
Bite Me If You Can, 2007 (Argeneau. Book 6)
The Accidental Vampire, 2007 (Argeneau. Book 7)
A Bite to Remember, 2006 (Argeneau. Book 5)
Tall, Dark and Hungry, 2004 (Argeneau. Book 4)

Other books you might like:
Liz Jasper, *Underdead*, 2008
Katie MacAlister, *Sex, Lies and Vampires*, 2005
    Dark Ones. Book 3
Michelle Rowen, *Lady and the Vamp*, 2008
Minda Webber, *The Remarkable Miss Frankenstein*,
    2005
Linda Wisdom, *50 Ways to Hex Your Lover*, 2008

374

KIRSTEN SAWYER

Not Quite a Mom

(New York: Kensington, 2008)

Story type: Contemporary
Subject(s): Parenthood; Interpersonal Relations;
    Responsibility
Major character(s): Elizabeth Castle, Journalist (aspiring
    TV reporter), Guardian (of a teenager); Buck Planter,
    Lawyer
Time period(s): 2000s
Locale(s): California

Summary: When TV journalist Elizabeth Castle learns she

is the guardian of the teenage daughter of her late high
school best friend, it changes everything, including her
engagement to a man who has no intention of having
children. The fact that the lawyer who is handling the
guardianship situation was also Lizzie's senior prom
date adds a new element to this lively, funny romance
that follows *Not Quite a Bride*.

Where it's reviewed:
Booklist, December 1, 2007, page 29
Romantic Times, February 2008, page 59

Other books by the same author:
Not Quite a Bride, 2007

Other books you might like:
Roz Denny Fox, *Someone to Watch over Me*, 2002
Whitney Gaskell, *Mommy Tracked*, 2008
Sandra Kitt, *She's the One*, 2001
Annie Smith, *Home Again*, 2002
Susan Wiggs, *Table for Five*, 2005

375

ANNA SCHMIDT (Pseudonym of Jo Schmidt)

This Side of Heaven

(Toronto: Harlequin, 2008)

Story type: Contemporary
Subject(s): Marriage; Cancer; Death
Major character(s): Zoe Wingfield, Patient (cancer),
    Spouse; Spencer Andersen, Doctor (psychiatrist),
    Spouse
Time period(s): 2000s
Locale(s): Madison, Wisconsin

Summary: Breast cancer survivor Zoe Wingfield is sick
again. This time, it's lung cancer, and her chances of
survival are almost non-existent. Even though her long-
time husband, Spencer, is a psychiatrist, he has trouble
dealing with the finality of the diagnosis. This is the
moving story of a loving relationship that approaches an
inevitable end, and its effect on all involved.

Where it's reviewed:
Romantic Times, January 2008, page 109

Other books by the same author:
Seaside Cinderella, 2008
Slingshot Moves, 2008
A Mother for Amanda, 2007
Lasso Her Heart, 2006
Love Next Door, 2005

Other books you might like:
Roz Denny Fox, *Someone to Watch over Me*, 2003
Amy Garvey, *Pictures of Us*, 2008
Merline Lovelace, *The Hello Girl*, 2008
Stella MacLean, *Heart of My Heart*, 2008
Rebecca Winters, *The Vow*, 2008

376

AMANDA SCOTT (Pseudonym of Lynne Scott-Drennan)

Border Wedding

(New York: Forever, 2008)

Story type: Historical/Medieval
Subject(s): Marriage; Politics; Loyalty
Major character(s): Lady Margaret Murray, Noblewoman;
    Sir Walter Scott, Nobleman
Time period(s): 14th century (1388)
Locale(s): Scotland

Summary: Faced with the gallows or marriage to the plain
daughter of the man who'd stolen his cattle, Sir Walter
Scott opts to wed Lady Margaret Murray and eventually
realizes it is the best decision he could have ever made.
Treachery, violence, and political intrigue are part of this
engrossing tale that features memorable protagonists
engaged in clandestine activities along the Scottish/
English border during a time of simmering conflict.

Where it's reviewed:
Romantic Times, March 2008, page 39

Other books by the same author:
Knight's Treasure, 2007
Lady's Choice, 2006
Lord of the Isles, 2005
Prince of Danger, 2005
Highland Princess, 2004

Other books you might like:
Julie Garwood, *Saving Grace*, 1993
Hannah Howell, *Highland Barbarian*, 2006
Hannah Howell, *Highland Wolf*, 2008
Susan King, *Laird of the Wind*, 1998
Lyn Stone, *The Highland Wife*, 2001

377

JILL SHALVIS

Strong and Sexy

(New York: Brava, 2008)

Story type: Contemporary; Romantic Suspense
Series: Sky High Air. Book 2
Subject(s): Murder; Suspense
Major character(s): Dani Peterson, Scientist (zoologist);
    Shayne Mahoney, Pilot (charter airline), Businessman
    (charter airline owner)
Time period(s): 2000s
Locale(s): Los Angeles, California

Summary: Reluctantly attending Sky High Air's posh
holiday party at the request of her wealthy mother, zoologist and mammal keeper Dani Peterson suddenly finds
herself in a closet exchanging hot kisses with company
partner Shayne Mahoney. Shocked at herself, she rushes
from the party, witnesses a murder, but has a hard time
convincing anyone it happened because the body disappears before she can show anyone. However, Dani has
become a target, and as Shayne decides to help her, passion flares hot and sexy between them.

Where it's reviewed:
Romantic Times, January 2008, page 74

Other books by the same author:
Superb and Sexy, 2008 (Sky High Air. Book 3)
Out of This World, 2007
Smart and Sexy, 2007 (Sky High Air. Book 1)
Aussie Rules, 2006
Her Sexiest Mistake, 2005

Other books you might like:
Shannon K. Butcher, *No Control*, 2008
Janelle Denison, *Born to Be Wilde*, 2007
Janelle Denison, *The Wilde Side*, 2005
Lora Leigh, *Killer Secrets*, 2008
Shannon McKenna, *Extreme Danger*, 2008

378

MAGGIE SHAYNE (Pseudonym of Margaret Benson)

Lover's Bite

(Don Mills, Ontario: Mira, 2008)

Story type: Paranormal; Vampire Story
Series: Wings in the Night
Subject(s): Vampires; Murder; Trust
Major character(s): Topaz, Vampire; Jack Heart, Vampire
Time period(s): 2000s
Locale(s): California

Summary: Vampire Topaz is determined to solve the
mystery of her movie star mother's murder just months
after her birth. However, she's not happy about the sudden appearance of Jack Heart, the vampire who conned
her out of half a million dollars and stole her heart at the
same time, at the California mansion where her mother
was shot. She is sure he has an agenda of his own and
isn't just here to help her discover her mother's killer.
She's right, of course, but she's also curious and she
does need his help. Their search uncovers startling truths
as well as deadly dangers as Jack and Topaz learn what
their true feelings are for each other, as well, in this
sexy, lightly humorous, paranormal that is the second
book of a new trilogy in Shayne's ever-popular Wings in
the Night series. Follows *Demon's Kiss*.

Where it's reviewed:
Romantic Times, May 2008, page 100

Other books by the same author:
Demon's Kiss, 2007
Blue Twilight, 2005
Darker than Midnight, 2005
Edge of Twilight, 2004
Embrace the Twilight, 2003

Other books you might like:
Christine Feehan, *Hot Blooded*, 2004
    anthology
Christine Feehan, *Lover Beware*, 2003
    anthology
Savannah Russe, *Beyond the Pale*, 2005
Lynsay Sands, *Love Bites*, 2004
Christine Warren, *Walk on the Wild Side*, 2008

379

GENA SHOWALTER

The Darkest Night

(Don Mills, Ontario: HQN, 2008)

Story type: Paranormal
Series: Lords of the Underworld. Book 1
Subject(s): Demons; Mythology
Major character(s): Ashlyn Darrow, Psychic; Maddox, Immortal, Warrior
Time period(s): 2000s
Locale(s): Budapest, Hungary

Summary: When resentment and pique lead Maddox and his fellow immortal warriors to release the demons in Pandora's box, they are condemned to hold the demons within themselves. Living in an isolated ancient fortress in Budapest, each Lord of the Underworld struggles with his individual demons; Maddox is the Keeper of Violence, a demon that brings with it nightly violent death. Ashley Darrow, a psychic who hears voices that eventually lead her to the fortress, encounters Maddox and is amazed when his touch quiets the voices in her head. It's what she had been hoping for; now if she can only stay and learn to quiet them herself. Suspicion and distrust abound with good reason in this dark, tortured tale of violence, pain, and ultimate redeeming love that takes the tormented warriors a little closer to their ultimate goal.

Where it's reviewed:
Romantic Times, May 2008, page 97

Other books by the same author:
The Darkest Fire, 2008 (Lords of the Underworld. E-book prequel)
The Darkest Kiss, 2008 (Lords of the Underworld. Book 2)
The Darkest Pleasure, 2008 (Lords of the Underworld. Book 3)
Catch a Mate, 2007
The Nymph King, 2007

Other books you might like:
Sherrilyn Kenyon, *The Dream-Hunter*, 2007 Dream-Hunter. Book 1
Sherrilyn Kenyon, *Unleash the Night*, 2004
J.R. Ward, *Dark Lover*, 2005 Black Dagger Brotherhood. Book 1
J.R. Ward, *Lover Awakened*, 2006 Black Dagger Brotherhood. Book 3
J.R. Ward, *Lover Eternal*, 2006 Black Dagger Brotherhood. Book 2

380

KASSANDRA SIMS

Hellbent & Heartfirst

(New York: Tor Romance, 2008)

Story type: Contemporary; Paranormal
Subject(s): Disasters; Hurricanes; Supernatural

Major character(s): Jacyn Boaz, Volunteer, Professor (anthropology); Jimmy Wayne Broadus, Singer, Cowboy
Time period(s): 2000s
Locale(s): Biloxi, Mississippi

Summary: A woman trying to make a difference by helping people after the Hurricane Katrina disaster connects with a singer who is on a hunt for a demon in this sexy, creative paranormal romance.

Where it's reviewed:
Romantic Times, April 2008, page 100

Other books by the same author:
Falling Upwards, 2007
The Midnight Work, 2005

Other books you might like:
Maureen Child, *Eternally*, 2006
Christine Feehan, *Fantasy*, 2002 anthology
Sherrilyn Kenyon, *Dream Chaser*, 2008
Cheyenne McCray, *Forbidden Magic*, 2005
Pamela Palmer, *The Dark Gate*, 2007

381

ELIZABETH SINCLAIR

Into the Mist

(St. Charles, Illinois: Medallion, 2008)

Story type: Contemporary/Fantasy; Fantasy
Subject(s): Magic; Memory Loss; Healing
Major character(s): Carrie Henderson, Amnesiac, Artist; Frank Donovan, Doctor (pediatric cardiologist)
Time period(s): 2000s; Indeterminate Past
Locale(s): Tarrytown, New York; Renaissance, Mythical Place

Summary: Bloodstained and without memory, Carrie Henderson seeks refuge in the Tarrytown Public Library and finds unexpected help. Led through the mist to the magical town of Renaissance, Carrie gradually sorts through her past, emerging as the strong woman she was meant to be. Frank Donovan, a doctor emotionally frozen and guilt-ridden over the death of his wife and unborn child, has been guided to Renaissance, as well. As Carrie and Frank begin to heal, they find love with each other as Renaissance works its magic once more in this story that is a sequel to *Miracle in the Mist*. Although not an inspirational romance per se, this sweet romance does have religious overtones.

Where it's reviewed:
Romantic Times, February 2008, page 69

Other books by the same author:
Touch by Fire, 2007
Baptism in Fire, 2006
Eye of the Dream, 2006
Miracle in the Mist, 2005
A Question of Love, 2002

Romance

Other books you might like:
Sarah Addison Allen, *Garden Spells*, 2007
Kristin Hannah, *Waiting for the Moon*, 1995
Marilyn Pappano, *Cabin Fever*, 2003
Marilyn Pappano, *Some Enchanted Season*, 1998
Christy Yorke, *Magic Spells*, 1999

382

NATALE STENZEL

Pandora's Box

(New York: Love Spell, 2008)

Story type: Humor; Paranormal
Subject(s): Humor; Inheritance; Magic
Major character(s): Pandemina Dorothy Avery, Heiress; Jonathan Teague, Contractor
Time period(s): 2000s
Locale(s): Mason County

Summary: It's bad enough that Pandemina Dorothy Avery only inherits a rock when her Aunt Gladys dies, but the rock is inhabited by a puca. Unlike Harvey, the cinematic puca, this one, Riordan, can take on any shape, including human form. Since pucas are designed to make mischief, no one is safe, including Jonathan Teague, the contractor who's trying to clean up the puca's plethora of messes.

Where it's reviewed:
Romantic Times, February 2008, page 101

Other books by the same author:
The Druid Made Me Do It, 2008

Other books you might like:
Maureen Child, *More than Fiends*, 2007
MaryJanice Davidson, *Undead and Unpopular*, 2007
    Undead. Book 5
Stephanie Rowe, *Date Me Baby, One More Time*, 2006
    Immortally Sexy. Book 1
Kerrelyn Sparks, *Vamps and the City*, 2006
    Love at Stake. Book 2
Vicki Lewis Thompson, *Wild and Hexy*, 2008
    Big Knob. Book 2

383

CARA SUMMERS (Pseudonym of Carolyn Hanlon)

A Sexy Time of It

(Toronto: Harlequin, 2008)

Story type: Romantic Suspense; Time Travel
Subject(s): Murder; Crime and Criminals
Major character(s): Neely Rafferty, Time Traveler, Businesswoman (bookseller); Max Gale, Police Officer
Time period(s): 1880s (1888); 2000s (2008)
Locale(s): London, England; New York, New York; San Diego, California

Summary: At first Neely Rafferty thinks she is dreaming when she finds herself transported back to London during the time of Jack the Ripper. Then Neely discovers she really is traveling back in time, and she is not the only one. After finishing his killing spree in 19th-century London, Jack the Ripper moves on to New York in the year 2008. Twenty-second century cop Max Gale has been sent to New York to stop Jack before he time travels again, but Max can't change anything in the past, and that means Neely is still in danger of becoming Jack's last victim.

Where it's reviewed:
Romantic Times, May 2008, page 110

Other books by the same author:
The Cop, 2007
The Defender, 2007
The P.I., 2007
Tell Me Your Secrets, 2006
Two Hot!, 2006

Other books you might like:
Terri Brisbin, *The Queen's Man*, 2000
Lynn Kurland, *A Garden in the Rain*, 2003
Karen Marie Moning, *Spell of the Highlander*, 2005
Hope Tarr, *The Haunting*, 2007
Evelyn Vaughn, *Something Wicked*, 2006

384

KATHLEEN TESSARO

The Flirt

(London: Harper, 2008)

Story type: Contemporary
Subject(s): Courtship; Social Classes; Jealousy
Major character(s): Leticia Vane, Store Owner (lingerie shop); Hughie Armstrong Venables-Smythe, Actor (out-of-work), Companion (professional flirt)
Time period(s): 2000s
Locale(s): London, England

Summary: Charming, out-of-work actor Hughie Armstrong Venables-Smythe is hired to be a professional flirt. Unfortunately, his lover, Leticia Vane, who owns an exclusive lingerie shop, doesn't react to Hughie's new skills as expected.

Where it's reviewed:
Publishers Weekly, May 5, 2008, page 45

Other books by the same author:
Innocence, 2006
Elegance, 2004

Other books you might like:
Helen Fielding, *Olivia Joules and the Overactive Imagination*, 2005
Jane Green, *The Beach House*, 2008
Sophie Kinsella, *Remember Me?*, 2008
Alisa Kwitney, *Does She or Doesn't She?*, 2003
Mary E. Mitchell, *Starting Out Sideways*, 2007

385

JODI THOMAS (Pseudonym of Jodi Koumalats)

Twisted Creek

(New York: Berkley, 2008)

Story type: Contemporary
Subject(s): Inheritance; Small Town Life; Mystery
Major character(s): Allie Daniels, Heiress, Store Owner; Luke Morgan, Government Official (ATF agent), Investigator (undercover)
Time period(s): 2000s
Locale(s): Twisted Creek, Texas

Summary: When Allie Daniels learns that she has inherited her Uncle Jefferson's Texas lakeside property, she and the grandmother who raised her head for Texas, almost afraid to believe in their good luck. The problem is that Allie doesn't have an Uncle Jefferson, or at least she doesn't think she has. A mystery surrounds her "uncle's" death and that is part of the reason that Luke Morgan, an Agent for the Bureau of Alcohol, Tobacco, and Firearms, has decided to vacation undercover in Twisted Creek. A quirky, heartwarming community of appealing misfits add charm to this gentle, poignant romance that has more to offer than the normal love story.

Where it's reviewed:
Romantic Times, April 2008, page 63

Other books by the same author:
Texas Princess, 2007 (Whispering Mountain. Book 2)
Texas Rain, 2006 (Whispering Mountain. Book 1)
The Secrets of Rosa Lee, 2005
The Texan's Reward, 2005 (Wife Lottery. Book 4)
A Texan's Luck, 2004 (Wife Lottery. Book 3)

Other books you might like:
Catherine Anderson, *Bright Eyes*, 2004
   Coulter Family. Book 4
Susan Elizabeth Phillips, *Natural Born Charmer*, 2007
   more humorous
Deborah Smith, *The Crossroads Cafe*, 2006
Deborah Smith, *A Gentle Rain*, 2007
Ruth Wind, *In the Midnight Rain*, 2000

386

VICKI LEWIS THOMPSON

Wild and Hexy

(New York: Onyx, 2008)

Story type: Humor; Paranormal
Series: Big Knob. Book 2
Subject(s): Small Town Life; Monsters
Major character(s): Annie Winston, Beauty Pageant Contestant (winner); Jeremy Dunstan, Computer Expert
Time period(s): 2000s
Locale(s): Big Knob, Indiana

Summary: Disciplined for screwing up an assignment in the paranormal world, Dorcas and Ambrose Lowell, former matchmakers to wizards and witches, are banished to Big Knob, Indiana, and given the task of watching over a dragon named George. With lots of time on their hands, the supernatural pair work as matchmakers for humans. Geeky Jeremy Dunstan has loved beauty queen Annie Winston since high school, and now Dorcas and Ambrose are working their magic to help him court the lady of his dreams, even if it does mean cheating a little. A fun read.

Other books by the same author:
My Nerdy Valentine, 2007
Overhexed, 2007 (Big Knob. Book 1)
Gone with the Nerd, 2006
Nerds Like It Hot, 2006
The Nerd Who Loved Me, 2006

Other books you might like:
Annette Blair, *Sex and the Psychic Witch*, 2007
Mary Castillo, *Switchcraft*, 2007
Katie MacAlister, *Fire Me Up*, 2005
Kimberly Raye, *Your Coffin or Mine?*, 2007
Minda Webber, *The Reinvented Miss Bluebeard*, 2007

387

ELIZABETH VAUGHAN

Dagger-Star

(New York: Berkley Sensation, 2008)

Story type: Futuristic; Fantasy
Subject(s): Magic; War; Prophecy
Major character(s): Red Gloves, Warrior, Mercenary; Josiah, Nobleman (former Baron of Athelbryght), Sorcerer (mage)
Time period(s): Indeterminate
Locale(s): Palins, Fictional Country

Summary: Roaming the countryside in search of work, warrior women Red Gloves and Bethral enter the bleak, destroyed lands of the Palins, and encounter Josiah, a noble mage they think is simply a goatherd. When Josiah sees the dagger-star birthmark on Red Gloves, he tells her she is the Chosen who is prophesied to claim the throne and bring peace and justice to the Palins. Unbelieving, Red Gloves and Bethral continue on their way, but eventually Red Gloves reconsiders and the battles begin. There's plenty of action, magic, and passion in this adventurous story that features a strong, action-oriented heroine, a gentler, but no less powerful hero, and a cast of well-drawn secondary characters.

Where it's reviewed:
Romantic Times, April 2008, page 74

Other books by the same author:
Warlord, 2007 (Chronicles of the Warlands. Book 3)
Warsworn, 2006 (Chronicles of the Warlands. Book 2)
Warprize, 2005 (Chronicles of the Warlands. Book 1)

Other books you might like:
Michele Hauf, *Seraphim*, 2004
Lynn Kurland, *The Mage's Daughter*, 2008
   Nine Kingdoms
Lynn Kurland, *Star of the Morning*, 2006
   Nine Kingdoms
Nora Roberts, *Morrigan's Cross*, 2006

Circle Trilogy. Book 1
Nora Roberts, *Valley of Silence*, 2006
  Circle Trilogy. Book 3

388

J.R. WARD (Pseudonym of Jessica Bird)

Lover Enshrined

(New York: Signet, 2008)

Story type: Contemporary/Fantasy; Paranormal
Series: Black Dagger Brotherhood. Book 6
Subject(s): Vampires; War; Responsibility
Major character(s): Cormia, Spouse (First Mate); Phury, Vampire (Primale)
Time period(s): 2000s
Locale(s): New York

Summary: Secretly troubled by drug addiction and inner self-defeating turmoil, Phury has a hard time accepting his responsibility as the Primale of the Chosen and his duty to mate with his harem and produce children to ensure the continuation of the vampire race. His lack of communication causes First Mate Cormia to agonize over this, thinking it is her fault. Meanwhile Omega and the lessers are on the move and they are determined to destroy the Black Dagger Brotherhood. Secrets, action, and a number of unexpected treacherous and shocking revelations make this an intriguing book that sets this series off in a new, less romantic, urban fantasy direction.

Where it's reviewed:
Romantic Times, June 2008, page 108

Other books by the same author:
Lover Revealed, 2007 (Black Dagger Brotherhood. Book 4)
Lover Unbound, 2007 (Black Dagger Brotherhood. Book 5)
Lover Awakened, 2006 (Black Dagger Brotherhood. Book 3)
Lover Eternal, 2006 (Black Dagger Brotherhood. Book 2)
Dark Lover, 2005 (Black Dagger Brotherhood. Book 1)

Other books you might like:
Jennifer Ashley, *Immortals: The Calling*, 2007
Christine Feehan, *Dark Guardian*, 2002
Sherrilyn Kenyon, *Unleash the Night*, 2007
Cheyenne McCray, *Forbidden Magic*, 2005
Pamela Palmer, *The Dark Gate*, 2007

389

CHRISTINE WARREN

Walk on the Wild Side

(New York: St. Martin's Paperbacks, 2008)

Story type: Contemporary/Fantasy; Paranormal
Series: Others. Book 5
Subject(s): Paranormal; Change; Family Life
Major character(s): Kitty Jane Sugarman, Mythical

Creature (werecat); Marcus Stewart, Mythical Creature (werecat), Parent; Martin Lowe, Mythical Creature (werecat)
Time period(s): 2000s
Locale(s): Tennessee; Las Vegas, Nevada

Summary: Learning that her father is a werelion shapechanger after the stress of a car accident initiates her change into her lioness form, Kitty Sugarman answers a summons from her dying father and heads from rural Tennessee to the dazzle of Las Vegas. However, there are members of the Red Rocks pride (her father is the head) who don't welcome her arrival, something she quickly learns when she is violently attacked in the airport restroom. Family politics, danger, and romance are part of her new life in this installment of Warren's The Others series focusing on supernatural beings of various types who secretly live among humans.

Where it's reviewed:
Romantic Times, June 2008, page 104

Other books by the same author:
One Bite with a Stranger, 2008 (Others. Book 6)
Howl at the Moon, 2007 (Others. Book 4)
The Demon You Know, 2007 (Others. Book 3)
She's No Faerie Princess, 2006 (Others. Book 2)
Wolf at the Door, 2006 (Others. Book 1)

Other books you might like:
Christine Feehan, *Dark Demon*, 2006
Christine Feehan, *Wild Rain*, 2004
Sherrilyn Kenyon, *Stroke of Midnight*, 2004 anthology
Sherrilyn Kenyon, *Unleash the Night*, 2006
Rachel Vincent, *Stray*, 2007

390

ROBIN WELLS

Between the Sheets

(New York: Forever, 2008)

Story type: Contemporary
Subject(s): Scandal; Conduct of Life; Small Town Life
Major character(s): Emma Jamison, Servant (professional butler), Manager (retirement home); Max Duval, Political Figure (mayoral candidate), Lawyer (district attorney)
Time period(s): 2000s
Locale(s): Chartreuse, Louisiana

Summary: Mistakenly "credited" with being the call girl who caused the president-elect's heart attack death, professional butler Emma Jamison goes to ground in Chartreuse, Louisiana, determined to get her life back on track. Mayoral candidate Max Duval comes to her rescue one evening, and as their relationship develops, Emma's notoriety begins to threaten his bid for mayor. Delightful secondary characters, especially those in the retirement home where Emma is the housekeeping manager, entertain as well as educate in this funny, heartwarming romp.

Where it's reviewed:
Library Journal, December 2007, page 96
Romantic Times, February 2008, page 92

Other books by the same author:
The Babe Magnet, 2004
Wild about You, 2003
Ooh, La La!, 2002
Baby, Oh Baby!, 2001
Prince Charming, 1999

Other books you might like:
Luanne Jones, *Sweethearts of the Twilight Lanes*, 2001
Cindy Kirk, *One Night Stand*, 2008
Suzanne MacPherson, *Talk of the Town*, 2003
Susan Elizabeth Phillips, *Ain't She Sweet*, 2004

391

DIANE WHITESIDE

Bond of Fire

(New York: Berkley, 2008)

Story type: Paranormal; Erotic Horror
Series: Texas Vampires. Book 2
Subject(s): Vampires; Family Relations; Revenge
Major character(s): Helene d'Agelet, Vampire (fire starter), Spy (British secret agent); Jean-Marie St. Just, Vampire, Spy
Time period(s): 2000s; 1780s (1787)
Locale(s): London, England; France

Summary: British secret agent Helene d'Agelet is not only a spy, she's also a vampire. Her sister, Madame Celeste, is the evil Vampire Queen of New Orleans. Jean-Marie St. Just, also a spy and a vampire, has loved Helene for hundreds of years, but now, in order to protect his family, he has to kill Celeste.

Where it's reviewed:
Booklist, January 1, 2008, page 50
Romantic Times, January 2008, page 98

Other books by the same author:
The Irish Devil, 2007
The Northern Devil, 2007
Bond of Blood, 2006 (Texas Vampires. Book 1)
The Switch, 2006
The Southern Devil, 2006

Other books you might like:
Delilah Devlin, *Into the Darkness*, 2007
Christine Feehan, *Predatory Game*, 2008
Sherrilyn Kenyon, *Devil May Cry*, 2008
Stephenie Meyer, *Eclipse*, 2007
Susan Squires, *The Companion*, 2005

392

SUSAN WIGGS

Snowfall at Willow Lake

(Don Mills, Ontario: Mira, 2008)

Story type: Contemporary
Series: Lakeshore Chronicles. Book 4

Subject(s): Family Relations; Healing; Country Life
Major character(s): Sophie Bellamy, Lawyer; Noah Shepherd, Veterinarian
Time period(s): 2000s
Locale(s): Avalon, New York

Summary: High-powered international criminal attorney Sophie Bellamy has sacrificed everything for her career, including her marriage and her relationship with her two children. However, when she barely survives a terrorist kidnapping in the Netherlands, the resulting epiphany sends her to tiny Avalon, New York, to try to reconnect with her children where they live with their remarried father. Thanks to a lake effect snowstorm and a wayward deer, Sophie ends up in a ditch on her way to Avalon and is rescued by gorgeous veterinarian Noah Shepherd, a man who just might be important in her life—until she learns she's older than he is. This heartwarming story takes a thoughtful look at what is important in life and makes good use of the older woman/younger man plot device.

Where it's reviewed:
Booklist, March 15, 2008, page 35
Publishers Weekly, January 21, 2008, page 160
Romantic Times, February 2008, page 56

Other books by the same author:
Dockside, 2007 (Lakeshore Chronicles. Book 3)
The Winter Lodge, 2007 (Lakeshore Chronicles. Book 2)
Summer at Willow Lake, 2006 (Lakeshore Chronicles. Book 1)
Lakeside Cottage, 2005
Table for Five, 2005

Other books you might like:
Barbara Bretton, *Just Desserts*, 2008
    more humorous
Kristin Hannah, *On Mystic Lake*, 1999
Kristin Hannah, *Summer Island*, 2001
Barbara Samuel, *A Piece of Heaven*, 2003
Kathleen Gilles Seidel, *Summer's End*, 1999

393

LORI WILDE   (Pseudonym of Laurie Vanzura)

Once Smitten, Twice Shy

(New York: Forever, 2008)

Story type: Contemporary
Series: Wedding Veil Wishes. Book 2
Subject(s): Weddings; Magic
Major character(s): Tish Gallagher, Photographer (wedding videographer); Shane Tremont, Government Official (secret service agent); Elysee Benedict, Young Woman (president's daughter)
Time period(s): 2000s
Locale(s): Texas

Summary: Filming the First Daughter's wedding is the job of a lifetime for Tish Gallagher, who's struggling to make a go of her wedding videographing business. The only problem is that the groom is her ex, a secret service

agent who was injured protecting first daughter Elysee Benedict, who has developed a serious case of hero worship and thinks it is love. Confusion reigns, although by the end of this romp the lovers are all properly aligned. This is part of Wilde's series featuring a magical wedding veil that grants wishes.

Where it's reviewed:
Romantic Times, January 2008, page 84

Other books by the same author:
There Goes the Bride, 2007 (Wedding Veil Wishes. Book 1)
Some Like It Hot, 2006
You Only Love Twice, 2006
Charmed and Dangerous, 2004
License to Thrill, 2004

Other books you might like:
Catherine Anderson, *The True Love Wedding Dress*, 2005
    anthology
Karen Kendall, *First Dance*, 2005
    Bridesmaid Chronicles. Book 3
Karen Kendall, *First Date*, 2005
    Bridesmaid Chronicles. Book 1
Julie Kenner, *First Love*, 2005
    Bridesmaid Chronicles. Book 4
Kasey Michaels, *This Can't Be Love*, 2004

394

SANDRA WILKINS

Ada's Heart

(New York: Avalon, 2008)

Story type: Historical/Edwardian; Historical/American West
Subject(s): Small Town Life; Actors and Actresses; Change
Major character(s): Ada Marsh, Actress; Luke Logan, Farmer
Time period(s): 1900s (1905)
Locale(s): Shawnee, Oklahoma (Oklahoma Territory)

Summary: When a famous actress and her company arrive in Shawnee, Oklahoma, she becomes attracted to both the town and a local farmer, Luke Logan. There's lots of Oklahoma historical detail in this sweet romance that is the author's first novel.

Other books you might like:
Carolyn Brown, *Emma's Folly*, 2002
    Land Rush. Book 1
Carolyn Brown, *Maggie's Mistake*, 2003
    Land Rush. Book 3
Carolyn Brown, *Violet's Wish*, 2002
    Land Rush. Book 2
Susan Kay Law, *A Wedding Story*, 2003
Pamela Morsi, *No Ordinary Princess*, 1997

395

EILEEN WILKS

Night Season

(New York: Berkley Sensation, 2008)

Story type: Paranormal; Fantasy
Series: World of the Lupi. Book 4
Subject(s): Magic; Psychic Powers; Fantasy
Major character(s): Cynna Weaver, FBI Agent (magical crimes division); Cullen Seabourne, Sorcerer, Werewolf
Time period(s): 2000s
Locale(s): Washington, District of Columbia; Edge, Mythical Place

Summary: Three ambassadors from the magical world, Edge, come to Earth to bring Cynna Weaver back with them in order to use her special "finding" talent to help them locate a missing medallion. They succeed, but several others, including sorcerer Cullen Seabourne, are pulled though the portal as well. Magic, adventure, and humor are all part of this tale that reprises characters from Wilks' earlier books and adds another layer to her delightfully magical world.

Where it's reviewed:
Romantic Times, January 2008, page 93

Other books by the same author:
Blood Lines, 2007 (World of the Lupi. Book 3)
Entangled, 2005
Mortal Danger, 2005 (World of the Lupi. Book 2)
Meeting at Midnight, 2004
Tempting Danger, 2004 (World of the Lupi. Book 1)

Other books you might like:
Amanda Ashley, *Midnight Pleasures*, 2003
    anthology
Patricia Briggs, *On the Prowl*, 2007
    anthology
Kim Harrison, *Dates from Hell*, 2000
    anthology
Nora Roberts, *Moon Shadows*, 2004
    anthology
Rebecca York, *Edge of the Moon*, 2003

396

REBECCA WINTERS

The Vow

(Toronto: Harlequin, 2008)

Story type: Contemporary
Subject(s): Memory; Marriage; Airplane Accidents
Major character(s): Stefanie Marsden, Spouse, Businesswoman (flying service); Nick Marsden, Pilot, Businessman (flying service)
Time period(s): Multiple Time Periods; 2000s
Locale(s): Mackenzie, Montana; Pacific Northwest

Summary: Nick and Stefanie have been together since high school, more than 40 years. Their marriage has had its ups and downs, but now the worst thing imaginable

has happened—Nick's small plane has crashed in the mountain wilderness. As an injured Nick struggles to stay alive in subzero conditions, Stefanie clings to the hope that her beloved husband has survived.

Where it's reviewed:
Romantic Times, January 2008, page 109

Other books by the same author:
The Italian Tycoon and the Nanny, 2008
The Duke's Baby, 2007
The Lazaridis Marriage, 2007
The Bride of Montefalco, 2006
The Daughter's Return, 2005

Other books you might like:
Roz Denny Fox, *Looking for Sophie*, 2007
Amy Garvey, *Pictures of Us*, 2008
Merline Lovelace, *The Hello Girl*, 2008
Stella MacLean, *Heart of My Heart*, 2008
Debbie Macomber, *Back on Blossom Street*, 2008

397

LINDA WISDOM

50 Ways to Hex Your Lover

(Naperville, Illinois: Sourcebooks, 2008)

Story type: Contemporary; Paranormal
Subject(s): Paranormal; Murder
Major character(s): Jasmine "Jazz" Tremaine, Witch; Nikolai Gregorivich, Vampire, Detective
Time period(s): 2000s
Locale(s): California

Summary: Whenever Jazz Tremaine and vampire cop Nikolai get together, sparks fly—literally; so when she spots Nickolai in a bar and he follows her outside, she knows there's going to be trouble. Nikolai needs her to help him find out why vampires have been disappearing. Although Jazz resists at first—after all she and Nickolai have loved and hated each other for centuries and she doesn't need the turmoil—she eventually gives in, realizing that she is the only one who can help Nikolai track down the villain. This is a sexy, funny, modern urban fantasy filled with a host of offbeat characters and creatures. Wisdom writes series romances as Linda Randall Wisdom

Where it's reviewed:
Romantic Times, March 2008, page 112

Other books you might like:
Theresa Alan, *Sex and the Single Witch*, 2005 anthology
Annette Blair, *My Favorite Witch*, 2006
Annette Blair, *The Scot, the Witch and the Wardrobe*, 2006
Annette Blair, *Sex and the Psychic Witch*, 2007
Jaclyn Reding, *Spellstruck*, 2007

398

VERONICA WOLFF

Master of the Highlands

(New York: Berkley Sensation, 2008)

Story type: Time Travel; Historical/Seventeenth Century
Subject(s): War; Time Travel; Feuds
Major character(s): Lily Hamlin, Time Traveler, Vacationer; Ewen Cameron, Laird
Time period(s): 2000s; 17th century (1654)
Locale(s): Scotland

Summary: In the Scottish Highlands to discover her roots and get her bearings after a volatile dot com career, artist Lily Hamlin stumbles across an old, eerie maze and a strange stone carving and is suddenly thrown back to the 17th century and into the life of Ewen Cameron, a powerful laird with a clan to protect and no time for a woman. Although he is attracted to her, Lily's arrival makes Ewen uneasy; it's the second arrival of a stranger that has been predicted by Gormshuil, an ancient seer, and he's not sure what it means. Magic, legend, and plenty of action are part of this passionate romance with a good sense of time and place. First novel.

Where it's reviewed:
Romantic Times, February 2008, page 46

Other books you might like:
Dee Davis, *Everything in Its Time*, 2000
Diana Gabaldon, *Dragonfly in Amber*, 1992
Diana Gabaldon, *Outlander*, 1991
Jill Jones, *The Scottish Rose*, 1997
Lynn Kurland, *A Dance through Time*, 1996

399

SHERRYL WOODS

Seaview Inn

(Don Mills, Ontario: Mira, 2008)

Story type: Contemporary
Subject(s): Small Town Life; Family Life; Healing
Major character(s): Hannah Matthews, Public Relations (executive); Luke Stevens, Doctor, Military Personnel (former); Kelsey Matthews, Student—College
Time period(s): 2000s
Locale(s): Seaview Key, Florida (island)

Summary: Returning home to Seaview Key after the death of her mother in order to convince her grandmother to sell their family's old Seaview Inn and retire to a senior center, successful, high-powered executive and cancer survivor Hannah Matthews finds herself dealing with a determined woman who expects Hannah to help renovate the B&B and then run the place. A pregnant college-age daughter who wants to drop out of Stanford and a high school friend, Dr. Luke Stevens, newly returned from Iraq and back in town to heal from war wounds and a broken marriage, add unexpected stressful and romantic complications. This heartwarming story of healing, love, and second chances deals with serious issues, but is lightened by humor and wit.

Where it's reviewed:
Romantic Times, March 2008, page 98

Other books by the same author:
A Slice of Heaven, 2007 (Sweet Magnolias. Book 2)
Feels Like Family, 2007 (Sweet Magnolias. Book 3)
Stealing Home, 2007 (Sweet Magnolias. Book 1)
Waking Up in Charleston, 2006
Flirting with Disaster, 2005

Other books you might like:
Rexanne Becnel, *Old Boyfriends*, 2005
Georgia Bockoven, *Things Remembered*, 1998
Kathleen Eagle, *The Last Good Man*, 2000
Sharon Sala, *Missing*, 2004
    a dash of mystery and suspense
Pat Warren, *Come Morning*, 1998

Backtrailing to the Future; or, The Hunt for a New Frontier: The Western 2008
by
Clay Reynolds

The relatively large number of new titles that lead off this volume's list of books representing new westerns in 2008 is somewhat misleading. Although nearly sixty works are represented here, a good fourth of them are actually books with 2007 copyright dates, as they were issued too late in the calendar year to make the previous 2008 Volume's list, or they actually were not issued until early 2008, even though they carry last year's publication date. This should have the effect, of course, of brightening the somewhat dismal outlook offered by the list of western fiction at the end of 2007. However, when one considers the number of reprints and continuing series in the total list—more than a third—little positive news can be gleaned insofar as the future of the western's return as a major fiction category is concerned, or at least as a category with a familiar and recognizable series of books that can be readily classified as "western."

Continuing speculation as to why the western continues to languish at or near the bottom of publishing categories is probably as useless as it is endless. This year's Western Writers of America meeting in Scottsdale, Arizona reportedly saw more than one major session descend into acrimonious and, to be frank, pointless debate over the issue. Stalwart writers such as Loren D. Estleman, Paul Hutton, Johnny D. Boggs, and others steadfastly continue to declare that the entire argument is moot, that the category is as healthy as it's ever been. Others privately opine that self-publishing, e-publishing, and other questionable publishing practices, including the broadening of the definition of "western," have eroded the integrity of the category overall, thus diminishing its potential to stage a comeback as a major player in popular fiction. In between are the steady producers of the series westerns, who continue to generate title after title, several series running into double digits, with no indication of slowing down, as well as newcomer writers, who stand bewildered to find that they have finally "broken into" a category of publishing that well may be disappearing more rapidly than did the buffalo or Longhorn cow. And standing more or less

"outside" the corral, as it were, are literary writers who pay utterly no attention to WWA or any other outfit, including the more scholarly Western Literature Association—that celebrates or typifies any category.

Where the truth lies is hard to discern. Significant on the last several lists is the growing number of what might be called "contemporary westerns," or novels and stories that are set in a western geography but which have little to do with the traditional elements of the traditional western novel. These would include a healthy number of romance and inspirational novels, as well as a fair representation of fantasy and science fiction pieces, and post-apocalyptic books. The greatest number of books, however, continue to come either from traditional western or romance publishers who specialize in category fiction (Leisure, Forge, etc.) or from small, private and often obscure publishing houses scattered about the country. Not insignificantly, Five-Star, which was practically leading the field a few years ago and gleaned several major awards, is sparsely represented on this newest list; and university presses, about the last bastion for the literary western, also are very few in number. Offerings from the more "literary" presses such as Viking, Dutton, Harper's, etc. are actually more numerous.

Some accoutrements of the old-fashioned oater are present in this list's dozen or so books set in more or less modern times and concerning more or less modern issues, but for the most part, such familiar devices appear in an ironic guise or as "flavor" for a more modern fiction structure. The twenty or so stand-alone historical pieces, also, seem to represent a departure from the standard formula of the old-fashioned western, tending to use the historical American West more as background rather than as an essential element of plot and character development, or certainly as part of an extended allegory with the themes of the American West providing substance as well as moral lesson. But the majority of the works on the list offer pretty much the same old writers producing the same old books with the same old characters doing the same old things in the same old settings. There's a staleness that suggests stagnation

here, and the slight rise in total numbers is betrayed by a decline in originality or vision.

Once again, it's hard not to try to find a reason for this, since other genre categories continue to maintain a healthy presence and even to grow a bit, not only in numbers but in expanding themes and formulaic perimeters. Yet such a query abut the western may be a fool's errand, since it is probably a reflection of a cultural sea-change throughout the American reading public's taste and imagination, something that may extend through the remainder of this year and into next, as the public's attention is more distracted by a different kind of historical prerogative than is characterized by the typical western. A casual observation of the nonfiction lists suggests that interest in the factual, historical West is also down, or at least the number of offerings in history and other fields of inquiry seems to be reduced.

It may well be that the American consumer's love-affair with the frontier as both myth and foundation is over; country and western music is gradually shifting more and more toward a generic soft-rock sound and away from the "cowboy hayride" twangs of the past, and modes of dress and tastes in popular food is reflecting a far more urban—if not urbane—trend than was reflected in the national embracing of buffalo wings, chickenfried steak, and barbeque a decade or so ago. Even the theater and cinema seem to have lost all representation of western themes, especially the cinema.

There has always been a kind of symbiotic relationship between film and print westerns. Certainly the heyday of both began in the late thirties and extended into the seventies, when the slow decline in the film western presaged the sharper decline of the print western ten or twelve years later. A resurgence of western films in the late eighties and early nineties was paralleled by resurgence in the same trend in western fiction, and many long-time western writers anticipate that a similar Hollywood phenomenon might have the same impact, should it recur. To a great extent, of course, this is wishful thinking on the part of western writers. Watching the meteoric success of Larry McMurtry's *Lonesome Dove* or even Elmer Kelton's more modest but still winning novel adaptations, as well as Cormac McCarthy's stunning triumph with *No Country for Old Men* provides an undying dream that at some point Hollywood will once more embrace the western film as a mainstay and start snapping up properties left and right.

Significantly, though, no new western motion pictures or television series are on the horizon (a single offering on a cable network this summer excited only the smallest notice). Even contemporarily set films seem to be avoiding western climes in spite of the Cohen brothers' adaptation of the McCarthy vehicle and the sensational success of the Annie Proulx story, "Brokeback Mountain." But hope dies hard on the frontier of western writing. This past spring, The American Film Institute sponsored an internet poll (one imitated by the WWA) asking members to name the "top ten" westerns. The response was as predictable as it was enthusiastic,

indicating a sharp interest in the topic. The AFI list was as follows:

1. *The Searchers*
2. *High Noon*
3. *Shane*
4. *Unforgiven*
5. *Red River*
6. *The Wild Bunch*
7. *Butch Cassidy & the Sundance Kid*
8. *McCabe & Mrs. Miller*
9. *Stagecoach* (1939)
10. *Cat Ballou*

The WWA list voted on by members was quite similar:

1. *Shane*
2. *High Noon*
3. *The Searchers*
4. *Butch Cassidy and the Sundance Kid*
5. *Dances with Wolves*
6. *The Wild Bunch*
7. *Red River*
8. *Tombstone*
9. *The Magnificent Seven*
10. *Open Range*

Of far more interest than the lists themselves was a series of somewhat fractious debates over the subject—mostly conducted on the internet and mostly centering on questions of historical accuracy—and especially at the WWA, what actually constitutes a western in the first place. And, naturally, there're always questions about cinematic quality and the inevitable argument over individual taste.

Of even greater curiosity, though, was how many of these films were based on original screenplays, not on previously published western novels or stories. On the AFI list, only three original screenplays are represented (surprising from an outfit that counts among its members only a comparative few writers who are not also producers, directors, or actors); on the WWA list, five of the ten selected films had no literary source. Even more curious, both lists have at least one parody or send-up of older forms, and only two or three films on either list might be seen as iconoclastic. This may be the most important point of all when either of the lists is considered.

Making much ado about films or even arguments about the "best films" does not go to the heart of the question of what has happened to the western novel anymore than does speculative debate about changing audience priorities and reading sophistication or the

seemingly endless argument over what constitutes an actual western in the greater scheme of publishing. Ultimately, it comes down to the point that no matter how it's defined, the traditional western is continuing to lag in popularity, and it seems unable to change itself to meet a more contemporary audience's taste.

One might argue that such an argument is the wrong-side-around, that the audience's taste is responsive to whatever the publishing houses have to offer; in other words, if they would print it, the audience would come. But this may beg the question. Large houses, in particular, spend millions of dollars in surveying demographics, polling readerships, and evaluating sales figures of various categories. If there was a potential profit to be made in publishing more western fiction, it's an easy bet they would do so. Certainly, even a casual observation of WWA or like organizations will reveal that there's no shortage of manuscripts being proffered—and rejected. The point is that what is being written just isn't addressing readers' interests; and it may well be that the western author is facing the prospect of either converting what he or she is doing to a more contemporary demand and sensibility, or to watch the whole category die as a recognizable entity.

In a sense, this sort of thing has happened before; but then, the authors (and especially the publishers) of western fiction responded and virtually created a whole new category of fiction. In fairness, though, they had a whole new frontier and, thus, a whole new body of material to work with. About a hundred fifty years ago, the American appetite for western fiction was as great or greater than at any time in the more recent past; but the offerings being produced were losing ground against other stories (tales of the sea, i.e.; or romances set in the plantation South or even in urban environments; or antique historical melodramas set in antique times). Tales of wilderness adventure, Indian-fighting, and exploration of the frontier were still in demand, rejuvenated by a sudden realization that the United States now owned vast amounts of territory west of the Mississippi, lands that were simply here for the taking. The excitement about the new frontier was so great that an entirely new form of fiction publishing was created to answer it. Produced on cheap paper and sold for about twelve cents apiece, these "shilling shockers" (some sold for as much as a quarter) first emerged in the late 1830s. Primarily, the writers relied on stories that mostly followed the same format, heroic portrayal, and plot as could be directly derived from the prototypical hero and familiar plots created by James Fenimore Cooper in his highly popular "Leatherstocking Tales" that featured his creation, Natty Bumppo. Cooper's highly prolific output was overshadowed by these stories of Bumppo as he evolved from Hawekeye to the Pathfinder to the Deerslayer in the five novels of the series published from the mid-1820s through the early 1840s (and which, in their chronological settings, actually worked backwards in time). The clear influence of the romances of Sir Walter Scott may be seen throughout these stories, and few are original in their makeup. Primarily chase/revenge quests, they often featured—in addition to the intrepid hero who embodied both the sensibilities of the civilized, educated easterner as well as the woodcraft-savvy, wise frontiersman—a more rustic character, unlettered and sometimes crudely primitive, whose background generally led him to foil the more genteel protagonist by presenting a rough-and-ready comrade or what would later be called a "side-kick," a kind of reverse of Cervantes model that had been followed more or less consistently up to that point. Cooper would reflect this shift in the final novel of the Natty Bumppo books, *The Deerslayer; or, The First Warpath* (1841).

Such a heroic model morphed slightly throughout the 1830s by the introduction of a Jacksonian image that was more warrior-like and more devoted to purely democratic principles. Ultimately, the late 1830s western writer, such as Robert Montgomery Bird in his *Old Nick of the Woods*, tended to combine the two types into single heroes from time to time, a no-nonsense character who represented both the genteel Eastern sensibility and the rustic frontiersman in one entity. These novels thrived, even so, drawing more and more power from the reported (and wildly exaggerated) exploits of such actual figures as David Crockett and Daniel Boone and finding even more material in the Mexican War and "Gold Rush," until *Malaeska; or, The Indian Wife of the White Hunter* was published by the firm of Beadle and Adams in 1860. Written by Sophia Winterbotham Stephens, a celebrated literary figure and editor of *The Ladies' Companion* and *Ladies' World*, this slim, cheaply produced "novelette," imperfectly bound with a garish paper cover and decorated by elaborate woodcuts, sold for ten cents. It is regarded as the first "dime novel" and began a trend in western publishing that would last for nearly a century and represents possibly the most successful innovation in book publishing that would be seen until the advent of the mass-market paperback. Although Stephens did little to alter or advance the stereotypes and formula previously established, the book itself was so popular that it established a pattern for the western novel that would evolve and develop into the more recognizable forms of the twentieth century.

Beadle and Adams would continue publishing western fiction for nearly fifty years, and they created the industry standard for this inexpensive and highly popular fictional form. Derisively called "yellow backs" (although the covers were more of an orange hue) by "highbrow readers" who despaired of them (but somehow were also very familiar with them), they not only offered the reader a single original story, dime novels also provided a catalogue of the publisher's other offerings and sometimes carried advertising to fill blank space. At one point, more than 250 writers were generating them for Beadle and Adams, each producing "novelettes" that averaged around 60,000 words and sold between 35,000 and 80,000 copies per title. By 1865, over 4,000,000 copies had been published, and the number would continue to grow through the end of the century. During the Civil

War and even after, the booklets were sold literally by the pound, bundled into bales and shipped to soldiers in the field, sailors aboard ships, railroad workers, miners, farmers, and loggers—anywhere people (mostly male) were gathered, isolated, and hungry for reading matter. There, they were devoured, traded, and resold until they quite actually were "read to pieces," the pulpy paper succumbing to over-handling. At a time when the literacy rate among the United States' adult population was less than about twenty percent, it was a true literary happening.

Working parallel to the Beadle and Adams efforts also were "story papers," or serial fiction, published on newsprint. Although some newspaper concerns—most notably *The New York Herald*—produced them, the unqualified leader in that industry was the house of Street and Smith, whose *New York Weekly* was closely watched for new installments by such writers as Ned Buntline and Prentiss Ingraham, among dozens of others. After each tale was brought to a conclusion in between five and ten weekly episodes, they were bound and sold as individual "novelettes," also for ten cents, as part of "library" collections such as the Log Cabin Library or the People's Library or the Lakeside Library. Again, they were collected, traded, resold, and worn out. Street and Smith would continue to produce what would ultimately be called "pulp fiction" until the mid-twentieth century.

Through such media, however, the western actually came into its own. Some scholars estimate that by the end of the 1860s, as many as half of the dime novels printed centered on stories of the frontier, a market share that would steadily grow to a point where more than seventy-five percent of dime novel production was set west of the Mississippi River. This was particularly true after the publication by Street and Smith of *Buffalo Bill: The King of the Border Men*; *The Wildest and Truest Story I Ever Wrote*, by Ned Buntline, in 1869. According to the story, Ned Buntline, en route from Sacramento to New York via the Transcontinental Railroad, de-trained at North Platte, Nebraska, where he found William Cody asleep and probably drunk under a wagon. He was referred to Cody by the local military commandant, who rebuffed Ned Buntline in his offer to write a novelette based on a recent Indian battle in which the commander had figured heroically. The officer told the intrepid dime novelist that he didn't think it was dignified to participate and sent him instead to find a sometimes-scout named William F. Cody, who played a minor role in the fracas and, the commander figured, needed the money.

Ned Buntline did indeed find Cody. He dragged him out into the sunlight, made friends with him, and soon recreated him as "Buffalo Bill," a common sobriquet applied to any number of foragers or scouts for the frontier army. Ned Buntline then packaged and sold Cody, buckskins, sombrero, Shaps rifle and Colt's pistols, white horse, flowing golden locks and all to the American reading public. Since Daniel Boone and David Crockett, no frontiersman other than Kit Carson (About seventy titles

were devoted to Carson between 1860 and 1890, as compared to more than 1,000 featuring Buffalo Bill in one way or another.) has ever captured so much of the American imagination or so closely embodied the western hero; but Carson's life, real or imagined, was never so dramatic as Cody's, and Carson never had the fortune to be discovered by a genuine western fiction writer, one who already had a national reputation as a successful and wildly popular author, one who was an expert at penning rapid, sensational popular fiction.

There's no question that these mass produced tales of derring-do shaped the American vision of the West, promoted the concept of Manifest Destiny, and formed the mythology of the American frontier in the popular imagination. Some scholars suggest that George Armstrong Custer's fondness for fringed buckskin and a broad plainsman's headgear was inspired by his reading of Ned Buntline's tale. So it's fair to ask whether the West created the dime novel and its hero, or whether the dime novel created the West as we came to know it and as it came to know itself.

As a western hero, Buffalo Bill was the apotheosis, in flesh and blood, on stage and in an arena, of both the genteel characteristics of a Natty Bumppo or Daniel Boone and the frontier warrior leader characteristics of an Andy Jackson or Davy Crockett. An expert horseman, a crack shot, he was civil and well-mannered, solicitous of females, only ferocious in the cause of justice, and, as an expert hunter and scout, a good steward of the utopian ideals that the West seemed to offer in abundance. As an international star, he came to represent both the archetype and inspiration of the westerner. But the singular genius behind that icon's creation was Ned Buntline, not William F. Cody, whose principal talents lay in his mastery of showmanship and cunning ability to surround himself with outstanding and fascinating people such as Sitting Bull, Annie Oakley, and others. Ned Buntline's combination of Cody's dramatized adventures with those of the notorious frontier gunfighter James Butler "Wild Bill" Hickok made the complete story—adventure and action, certainly, but more importantly, a reinforcement of all that was good and right in civilization as it marched steadily onto the virgin land of the frontier. This formula moved the whole idea of the western story onto a new literary dimension.

The popularity of such fiction cannot be overstated, and there is no contemporary parallel. In time, the number of western dime novel titles being produced annually would be almost uncountable. Giants in the field such as Prentiss Ingraham (who would seize the Buffalo Bill franchise and make it his own, including ghost writing many of Cody's supposed "autobiographies") was credited with more than five hundred titles (although he probably wrote no more than two hundred, if that many) and Ned Buntline (actually, E.Z.C. Judson, who is credited with more than four hundred volumes, although he may have written more, although only a comparative handful were westerns) were joined or followed by writers such as Edward L. Wheeler who created "Deadwood

Dick," a model for such anti-heroic types as Zorro, Red Rider, and the Lone Ranger and countless "cast-out" heroes (unjustly ruined lawmen or soldiers, unfairly dispossessed ranchers or farmers, the misunderstood, maligned, and mishandled who refuse to forsake their basic values and commitments to goodness) struggle for justice from outside the law. Taken together, the frontiersman (or plainsman, more properly, in the post-war West), the outlaw, and the cowboy (a creation, again, of Prentiss Ingraham, who offered a volume based on the exploits of Buck Taylor, a cowboy in Buffalo Bill's Wild West Show and set up the heroic model for Owen Wister's *The Virginian*), would come to form a literary trinity that would dominate western fiction for more than a century. In time, Calamity Jane, Belle Starr, Jesse James, Billy the Kid, Wyatt Earp, Bat Masterson, Texas Jack, Johnny Ringo, Black Bart, and dozens of other actual western figures would form the foundation for thousands of western tales ranging from the fanciful to the entirely fabricated; the basis for the twentieth-century western would be firmly established by the time the western motion picture arrived.

It's not an accident, then, that probably the first sensational and widely distributed movie was a twelve-minute western, *The Great Train Robbery* (1903). Although it was shot in New Jersey, mostly, and relied heavily on a previously made British film, this "flicker" was the harbinger of a Hollywood staple that would dominate the industry within only few years. Borrowing heavily from the popular literary tradition, the American western movie of the thirties and forties and fifties and even into the sixties reinforced the same stereotypes established by Ned Buntline, Prentiss Ingraham, and Edward L. Wheeler a half-century before, refined as they were by Owen Wister, Zane Grey, Louis L'Amour, Elmore Leonard, and other more "literary minded" authors, including Laura Ingalls Wilder; and they exploited virtually the same formulaic plot lines. For more than seventy years, the film and the novel and western story worked side-by-side to complement one another, and all along the way, pulp writers (including the venerable Elmer Kelton) were grinding out more and more of the cheaply produced tales of the west, always expanding and developing more and more audience, eager, it seemed, for more and more of the same. By the mid-1960s, the television western had emerged to add to the momentum with its wildly successful series such as *Gunsmoke* and *Bonanza*, as well as several others; for the next twenty or twenty-five years, the western could claim its place next to the romance or crime or mystery novel as a major part if not the unquestioned primary thread of the American literary fabric.

So, what happened? Why has that fabric faded or, as some would aver, unraveled? Again, speculation is easier than probity on the issue, but one possibility is that the values and structures of those antique forms, however morphed and evolved and changed, have, like the dime novels themselves, simply worn out. A close look at the more celebrated western forms of the past quarter

century, roughly, indicate that many are spoofs (*Little Big Man*, by Thomas Berger, i.e.) or that the western setting only offers a backdrop for a different kind of philosophical or literary inquiry (*Blood Meridian*, by Cormac McCarthy, i.e., or even the darkly cynical *Power in the Blood*, by Greg Matthews). At the very least, the impact of historical revisionism and a demand for more factual accuracy, foiled as it's been by a national squeamishness when it comes to matters that are not politically correct (extirpation of the Indian, subjugation of women, exploitation and destruction of the environment), has created an antipathy toward the celebration of the conquest of the frontier that turns people away from fictional heroics that may or may not have developed in the process.

Or it may be that there's a sense of triumph evident in traditional western fiction that rings hollow today. As the nation struggles with globalization and the realization that history may well be moving past our own culture without respect for all we have done or planned yet to do, that looking backward into a period of time when all eyes were on the future may be a depressing prospect. It becomes hard to appreciate the zeal of the western pioneer who discovers the enormous potential in the virgin wilderness, in its unspoiled prairies, forests, and mountains and rivers when we sense that those resources may soon be as gone as the American bison, ruined or used up in less time than it took to find them. In a time when international affairs seem to be on our doorstep and limiting our dreams, it's difficult to sympathize with a time when the contemplation of unknown wonders beyond a distant horizon seemed to be too much to imagine. In our present times when discouraging words have become a social litany, it's just not possible to revel in consideration of a past land and a time where they were never heard.

In a way, such a phenomenon recalls the way the American reader turned away from the idealized heroics of Natty Bumppo or Old Ned and embraced the new heroic forms of the dime novel. Then, it was time for a new way of looking at things, time to put away the past with its colonialism, monarchies, and aristocratic structures and to stride confidently forward—into the sunset, as it were—into a realm of social utopia, armed with simply defined moral principles and firmly established democratic values that brooked no question and extolled the virtues of the common man and woman, the courage of the pioneer facing an unspoiled land. The western film has, for better or worse, responded to the modern sensibility and its changes, but the western novel, generally, has not. For the most part, it wallows in antique perspectives that, for many people, are just no longer relevant.

Those writers who continue to exploit the stereotypes and formulaic plots of the past are, I think, contributing to this general malaise in western publishing. They literarily are beating a dead horse, rather than considering the advantages of more modern transport. Like the romance writers who never seem to run out of an audi-

ence for palpitating bosoms and flexing muscles, for beautiful and virginal heroines and handsome and virtuous heroes, regardless of the era, but who have gradually relaxed the restrictions on sexual content and explicit language, the westerners have continued to cater to those who would prefer to believe that Buffalo Bill was truly the "king of the border men," or that Wild Bill actually was the "fastest gun in the West" and that neither was as vulgar and sometimes vile as he truly was. They don't want to think of Calamity Jane or Bell Starr as prostitutes or Billy the Kid and Jesse James as stone killers. They want their myths reinforced, not clarified. But that audience is shrinking—or perhaps dying off—and the clamor for a more realistic and pragmatic approach to the study of who we are and who we might become seems to grow louder, at least among the literate population. We no longer are so ready to believe in white-hatted heroes or virtuous ranchers' daughters, in the unimpeachable integrity of institutions such as churches, schools, governments, or justice systems. And we are, perhaps, no longer willing to accept that the answers to our problems, now and in the future, lie in the dreamy contemplation of some unknown frontier and the leadership of synthetic heroes.

It may well be, though, that the western, as a category, has "bottomed out." If the last two lists for this volume are an indication, the apparent free-fall for the past several years may have slowed, perhaps stopped. It's probably too early to say that it's "bounced," that the western is making a comeback. Indeed, it may never do that, at least not in present readers' lifetimes, but it may be that with the efforts of many of the writers who continue to try to broaden the scope of the genre, using the West less as metaphor and more as a real place with real lessons that can be valuable, that the audience for such fiction will gradually rejuvenate itself and demand more and higher quality writing from those who produce it.

Recommended Titles

Black Rock Canon by Les Savage

The Canyon of Bones by Richard S. Wheeler

The German Bride by Joanna Hershon

Grub Line Rider by Louis L'Amour

Lost Trails by Louis L'Amour, Elmer Kelton, Loren D. Estleman, et al.

Luck by Max Brand

Names on a Map by Bejamin Alire Saenz

Plague of Doves by Louise Erdrich

Pursuit by Vere Athanas

Shavetail by Thomas Cobb

Sun Going Down by Jack Todd

El Tigre by John H. Manhold

Trail of the Red Butterfly by Karl H. Schlesier

The Treasure of Nugget Mountain by Karl May

Winnetou the Apache Knight by Karl May

Western Titles

400

SHERMAN ALEXIE

Flight

(Manitoba, Canada: Black Cat, 2007)

Story type: Science Fantasy; Literary
Subject(s): Adolescence; Time Travel; Fantasy
Major character(s): Justice, Teenager, Time Traveler; Zits, Teenager
Time period(s): Multiple Time Periods
Locale(s): West; Indian Territory

Summary: Having lived the life of a half Indian, half Irish orphan, suffering abuse and running through twenty foster homes in fifteen years, Zits decides to take on a new role as a killer. With the help of Justice, a boy he meets in a juvenile detention center, Zits discovers an ancient ritual called the ghost dance, which will eliminate all the white people. In his chosen location, a bank lobby, Zits prays, dances and wields two guns. When the security guard reacts, Zits finds himself transported through time into the bodies of a pilot who trains a terrorist to fly, an FBI agent confronting Indian activists, a young Indian boy who cannot speak due to injuries inflicted by a white man. and others. He learns as he goes that everyone has both good and evil within them.

Where it's reviewed:
Booklist, March 1, 2007, page 37
Library Journal, April 1, 2007, page 78
Publishers Weekly, February 26, 207, page 54
School Library Journal, August 2007, page 143
Voice of Youth Advocates, August 2007, page 251

Other books by the same author:
The Absolutely True Diary of a Part-Time Indian, 2007 (young adult)
Dangerous Astronomy, 2005 (poetry)
Ten Little Indians, 2003 (stories)
Indian Killer, 1996
Reservation Blues, 1995

Other books you might like:
Mark Z. Danielewski, *Only Revolutions*, 2006
E.R. Frank, *America*, 2002
Ian Frazier, *On the Rez*, 2000
Marita Golden, *And Do Remember Me*, 1992
Steve Hamilton, *Winter of the Wolf Moon*, 2000

401

VERNE ATHANAS

Pursuit

(New York: Leisure Books, 2000)

Story type: Historical/American West
Subject(s): American West
Time period(s): Indeterminate Past

Summary: This collection contains six stories previous published in the 1950s, including "Day of Saint Andrew," "Ointment for Mangas," "A Woman to Be Whipped" "Red Fury," "The Pioneers," and the title story "Pursuit" along with the addition of one previously unpublished work, "Killer at Large."

Other books by the same author:
Maverick, 1957
Rogue Valley, 1954
The Proud Ones, 1953

Other books you might like:
Sanora Babb, *Cry of the Tinamou*, 1997
Cliff Farrell, *Desperate Journey*, 1999
Michael Moorcock, *Tales from the Texas Woods*, 1997
Richard S. Wheeler, *Tales of the American West*, 2000

402

S.M. BALLARD

Borrowed Time

(Sierra Vista, Arizona: Treble Heart Books, 2007)

Story type: Historical/American West; Action/Adventure
Subject(s): American West; Gambling; Adventure and Adventurers
Major character(s): John Henry "Doc" Holliday, Gunfighter, Historical Figure; Wyatt Earp, Gunfighter, Historical Figure
Time period(s): 19th century
Locale(s): Georgia; West

Summary: In this first book of a trilogy, Doc and Wyatt join forces to hunt down the murderers of a local woman. As they travel together pursing the killers, they form a strong and lasting friendship.

Other books you might like:
Jane Candia Coleman, *Doc Holliday's Woman*, 1995
Preston Lewis, *The Mix-Up at the O.K. Corral*, 1996
Karen Holliday Tanner, *Doc Holliday: A Family Portrait*, 2001
Paul West, *O.K.: The Corral, the Earps, and Doc Holliday*, 2000
Romain Wilhelmsen, *Buckskin and Satin*, 1999

403

V.E. BIXENSTINE

Marshal Sands and Mrs. Molly

(Philadelphia: Xlibris Books, 2007)

Story type: Historical/American West; Coming-of-Age
Series: Purgatory Sands. Book 2
Subject(s): Wealth; American West; Family Saga
Major character(s): Justin "Purgatory Sands" Simms, Outlaw (former), Lawman (U.S. Marshal); Molly Dandridge, Young Woman
Time period(s): 1800s (1880)
Locale(s): West; Green River City, Wyoming

Summary: In this sequel to *Pergatory Sands*, Justin Simms is given the opportunity to turn his life around after a judge offers him the chance to become a U.S. Marshal. Striving to leave his outlaw life behind and grow in his new career, he meets the intriguing though deeply despairing Molly Dandridge. Recently disinherited by her wealthy father and then abandoned by her greedy new husband, Molly is trying to move forward while grieving the loss of the life she hoped he would live. Together Molly and Justin change and grow as they work to put the pieces of their new lives together.

Other books by the same author:
Purgatory Sands, 2006

Other books you might like:
Patti Berg, *Something Wild*, 2002
Rosanne Bittner, *In the Shadow of the Mountains*, 1991
David Anthony Durham, *Gabriel's Story*, 2001

404

MARY CLEARMAN BLEW

Jackalope Dreams

(Lincoln: University of Nebraska Press, 2008)

Story type: Family Saga; Literary
Subject(s): Teachers; Family Problems
Major character(s): Corey Henry, Teacher; Ariel Doggett, Teenager
Time period(s): 1950s; 1960s
Locale(s): Montana

Summary: After being fired for slapping disruptive student Ariel Doggett, the daughter of a family who moved to Montana to escape their past, Corey Henry's life takes a dramatic turn. First Corey's father commits suicide, then she's sued by Ariel's father, and finally Ariel comes looking for Corey who takes her in and helps her deal with her past.

Where it's reviewed:
Publishers Weekly, December 3, 2007, page 47

Other books by the same author:
Sister Coyote, 2000
Balsamroot, 1994
All but the Waltz, 1991
Runaway, 1990

Other books you might like:
Liza Fosburgh, *Cruise Control*, 1988
Sally John, *Surrender of the Heart*, 1999
Jane Roberts Wood, *Dance a Little Longer*, 1993

405

C.J. BOX

Free Fire

(New York: G.P. Putnam's Sons, 2007)

Story type: Contemporary; Literary
Series: Joe Pickett. Book 7
Subject(s): Wilderness; Murder; Law
Major character(s): Joe Pickett, Rancher (foreman); Clay McCann, Lawyer, Murderer
Time period(s): 2000s
Locale(s): Wyoming

Summary: Although fired from his previous job as a game warden and adjusting to life as a foreman on his father-in-law's ranch, Joe Pickett is called back to the wilderness, but this time he's mandated to investigate a murder in Yellowstone National Park. The murder itself isn't much of a mystery. Lawyer Clay McCann admits to shooting four campers who harassed him, but a technicality in the law means that McCann cannot be tried for the crime. The story quickly progresses as more murders are discovered over a mining rights debate in the hot springs, and Pickett tries to preserve the natural beauty of Yellowstone and bring justice to those who have chosen to take advantage of the legal loopholes.

Where it's reviewed:
Booklist, January 1, 2007, page 23
Kirkus Reviews, March 15, 2007, page NA
Publishers Weekly, March 12, 2007, age 37

Other books by the same author:
Blue Heaven, 2008
In Plain Sight, 2007
Winter Kill, 2004
Savage Run, 2003
Open Season, 2002

Other books you might like:
Jeremiah F. Healy, *Uncommon Justice*, 2001
John Lescroart, *Guilt*, 1997

Western

406

Luck

(New York: Leisure Books, 2008)

Story type: Historical/American West; Action/Adventure
Subject(s): Jesuits; Frontier and Pioneer Life; Revenge
Major character(s): Pierre Ryder, Religious (Jesuit),
  Adventurer; Jacqueline "Jack" Boone, Young Woman
Time period(s): Indeterminate Past
Locale(s): West

Summary: Exceptionally strong and gentle Pierre is on his way to becoming a Jesuit priest when he receives a letter that changes his path forever. Reading the letter from his father, who is dying from gunshot wound, Pierre's shifts his mission from the priesthood toward revenge. Along the way he meets Jacqueline who further changes his life. Originally published in 1926.

Other books by the same author:
The Silvertip Series, 1942-1994
The Dr. Kildare Series, 1937-1994
The White Wolf, 1926
Children of the Night, 1923

Other books you might like:
J. Lee Butts, *A Bad Day to Die*, 2004
Robert Fate, *Baby Shark*, 2006

407

LYLE BRANDT

Slade's Law

(New York: Berkley, 2008)

Story type: Series; Historical/American West
Series: The Lawman. Book 2
Subject(s): Small Town Life; American West; Mystery
  and Detective Stories
Major character(s): Jack Slade, Lawman (U.S. Marshal)
Time period(s): 19th century
Locale(s): West (Oklahoma territory)

Summary: Jack Slade travels to the small town of Serenity to investigate a mysterious death. Although the marshal of Serenity says the man died as the result of a snake bite, the farmer who discovered the body claims he saw bullet wounds. When Slade has the body exhumed, it seems nearly everyone in Serenity is trying to keep justice from being served.

Other books by the same author:
Cat and Mouse, 1995
China White, 1991
Korea Kill, 1990
The Executioner Series, 1982-
The Lawman Series, 1981-1982

Other books you might like:
Matt Braun, *Jury of Six*, 1990
William W. Johnstone, *Power of the Mountain Man*,
  1995
F.M. Parker, *The Shanghaiers*, 1987
Ben Rehder, *Gun Shy*,

408

MATT BRAUN

Tombstone/The Spoilers

(New York: St. Martin's Paperbacks, 2008)

Story type: Historical/American West; Mystery
Series: Luke Starbuck Westerns
Subject(s): American West; Adventure and Adventurers;
  Crime and Criminals
Major character(s): Luke Starbuck, Detective—Private
Time period(s): 19th century

Summary: Private detective Luke Starbuck features in these two novels. In *Tombstone*, Starbuck is sent to Tombstone, Arizona to investigate a series of robberies. In *The Spoilers*, Starbuck goes undercover as an outlaw to find the man behind a series to train robberies.

Other books by the same author:
Dodge City, 2006
The Wild Ones, 2002
Hickok and Cody, 2001
Deathwalk, 2000
Kinch Riley, 2000

Other books you might like:
John Michael Champlin, *Raiders of the Western and
  Atlantic*, 2002
Loren D. Estleman, *The Adventures of Johnny
  Vermillion*, 2006
Robert J. Randisi, *Backshooter*, 2005

409

CAROLYN BROWN

To Trust

(New York: Avalon, 208)

Story type: Romance; Family Saga
Series: Broken Road. Book 1
Subject(s): Family; Small Town Life; Romance
Major character(s): Dee Hooper, Young Woman; Jack,
  Young Man
Time period(s): 2000s
Locale(s): Buckhorn Corner, Oklahoma

Summary: In this first story of the Broken Road series, Dee Hooper returns home following the annulment of her marriage to a wealthy Pennsylvanian man. While living under the same roof with her grandmother, mother, sister, and niece, she tries to forge a new life for herself. She is then reunited with Jack, a childhood friend with a long-standing crush on her. Although Dee becomes interested, Jack must find a way to move beyond the past and open himself up to her again.

Where it's reviewed:
Booklist, December 15, 2007, page 31
Publishers Weekly, November 19, 2007, page 35

Other books by the same author:
Morning Glory, 2007
The PMS Club, 2006
Trouble in Paradise, 2005
The Wager, 2004
That Way Again, 2003

Other books you might like:
Megan Chance, *A Heart Divided*, 1996
Penelope Williamson, *Heart of the West*, 1995

410

J. LEE BUTTS

Nate Coffin's Revenge

(New York: Berkley Westerns, 1997)

Story type: Historical/American West; Adventure
Series: Lucius Dodge Series. Book 3
Subject(s): Robbers and Outlaws; Revenge; American West
Major character(s): Lucius Dodge, Gunfighter
Time period(s): P
Locale(s): Texas

Summary: There's a price on Lucius Dodge's head, and he has to find the bounty hunter before the bounty hunter finds him.

Other books by the same author:
The Lucius Dodge Series, 2004-
Texas Bad Boys, 2001
The Hayden Tilden Series, 2001-
Texas Bad Girls, 2000

Other books you might like:
Johnny D. Boggs, *Spark on the Prairie*, 2003
Tim McGuire, *Texas Pride*, 2005

411

THOMAS COBB

Shavetail

(New York: Scribner, 2008)

Story type: Historical/American West; Mystery
Subject(s): Frontier and Pioneer Life; Native Americans; Kidnapping
Major character(s): Ned Thorne, Military Personnel
Time period(s): 1870s (1871)
Locale(s): Tucson, Arizona

Summary: Although it was an accident, Ned Thorne takes responsibility for the death of his brother, which torments him at his post in Arizona. His life takes a turn however when he's given the diary of a woman kidnapped by the Apaches. He finds himself drawn to her story and desperate to save her.

Where it's reviewed:
Booklist, February 15, 2008, page 36
Kirkus Reviews, January 15, 2008, page NA
Library Journal, December 1, 2007, page 97
Publishers Weekly, November 26, 2007, page 27

Other books by the same author:
Acts of Contrition, 2003
Crazy Heart, 1987

Other books you might like:
Sallie Bissell, *Call the Devil by His Oldest Name*, 2004

412

BILL CRIDER

Of All Sad Words

(New York: St. Martin's Minotaur, 2008)

Story type: Mystery; Series
Series: Dan Rhodes Mystery Series. Book 16
Subject(s): Drugs; Murder; Small Town Life
Major character(s): Dan Rhodes, Lawman (sheriff); Terry Crawford, Crime Victim, Twin; Larry Crawford, Crime Suspect, Twin
Time period(s): 2000s
Locale(s): Clearview, Texas (Blacklin County)

Summary: When a couple of authors base their latest hero on Sheriff Dan Rhodes, Rhodes finds himself balancing his new celebrity status with investigating a crime wave in small-town Texas. Although Larry Crawford's twin Terry is murdered and their shared home set on fire, Larry doesn't seem too upset. The suspect list grows as does an investigation into a drug ring and bootlegging operation.

Where it's reviewed:
Booklist, January 1, 2008, page 29
Kirkus Reviews, January 15, 2008, page NA
Publishers Weekly, December 3, 2007, page 53

Other books by the same author:
The Texas Capitol Murders, 1992
Blood Marks, 1991
The Truman Smith Series, 1991-
The Carl Burns Series, 1988-

Other books you might like:
A.B Guthrie, Jr., *No Second Wind*, 1980
Jamie Harrison, *Blue Deer Thaw*, 2000
J.A. Jance, *Shoot/Don't Shoot*, 1995
Penny Warner, *Blind Side*, 2001

413

PHIL DUNLAP

Blood on the Rimrock

(New York: Avalon, 2008)

Story type: Historical/American West; Mystery
Subject(s): American West; Murder; Indians of North America
Major character(s): George Alvord, Wanderer; Piedmont Kelly, Lawman (U.S. Marshal); Drago, Lawman (Sheriff); Spotted Dog, Indian (Apache), Crime Suspect
Time period(s): 19th century
Locale(s): Arizona

Summary: When a wanderer who trespasses on Deputy U.S. Marshal Piedmont Kelly's camp is robbed and murdered while being held during the night, Kelly begins a search for the culprit. The trail leads to Spotted Dog who shows off a bullet wound and claims to be a crime victim, but Sheriff Drago knows better. Spotted Dog is guilty of a larger crime, and there is still some informa-

tion they need to get from him.

Where it's reviewed:
Publishers Weekly, November 5, 2007, page 42

Other books by the same author:
The Death of Desert Belle, 2004

Other books you might like:
Eileen Charbonneau, *The Ghosts of Stony Clove*, 1988
Dane Coolidge, *The Wild Bunch*, 2003
Les Roberts, *The Indian Sign*, 2000

414

KATHLEEN EAGLE

Mystic Horseman

(Toronto: Mira, 2008)

Story type: Romance; Ranch Life
Subject(s): Native Americans; Romance; Television
Major character(s): Monica Wilson-Black, Television (host), Spouse (former); Dillon "Bear" Black, Rancher, Indian (Lakota); Ella Champion, Producer (television), Indian (half Santee)
Time period(s): 2000s
Locale(s): South Dakota

Summary: Desperate to save the summer program for at-risk Native-American youth at his ranch, Bear agrees to his ex-wife Monica's plan to have the ranch featured on a reality television makeover show.

Where it's reviewed:
Publishers Weekly, January 7, 2008, page 41

Other books by the same author:
Ride a Painted Pony, 2006
Once upon a Wedding, 2002
You Never Can Tell, 2001
The Last True Cowboy, 1998
What the Heart Knows, 1998

Other books you might like:
Emily Carmichael, *A New Leash on Life*, 2005
Carol Higgins Clark, *Popped*, 2003
Andrea White, *Surviving Antarctica: Reality TV 2083*, 2005

415

LEIF ENGER

So Brave, Young and Handsome

(New York: Atlantic Monthly Press, 2008)

Story type: Adventure; Literary
Subject(s): Adventure and Adventurers; Identity, Concealed; Self-Confidence
Major character(s): Monte Becket, Companion, Writer; Glendon Hale, Outlaw, Aged Person
Time period(s): 2000s
Locale(s): Minnesota; West

Summary: Monte Becket is finding it impossible to follow the astounding success of his debut novel with another

work worthy to release in its wake. He then meets the mysterious Glendon Hale who invites Becket along on a trip west. Amidst adventures and a cast of colorful characters, both men are changed by the journey.

Where it's reviewed:
Booklist, March 15, 2008, page 29
Entertainment Weekly, April 25, 2008, page 121
Kirkus Reviews, February 15, 2008, page NA
Publishers Weekly, January 18, 2008, page 38

Other books by the same author:
Peace Like a River, 2001

Other books you might like:
Donald E. Westlake, *The Hook*, 2000

416

LOUISE ERDRICH

The Plague of Doves

(New York: Harper, 2008)

Story type: Historical/American West; Indian Culture
Subject(s): Indians of North America; Murder; Racial Conflict
Major character(s): Evelina Harp, Young Woman, Indian; Mooshum Milk, Grandparent, Indian
Time period(s): 1960s; 1970s
Locale(s): Pluto, North Dakota

Summary: Young narrator Evelina Harp tells the story of lives intertwined—both stories she experienced and those told to her by her grandfather. Her Ojibwe grandfather Mooshum saved an infant child after the child's family war murdered in the town bordering the reservation. He was subsequently and inexplicably spared by a lynch mob seeking revenge for the crime. Both those descended from the Ojibwe men and those responsible for their hanging engage in complex relationships. There are numerous revelations on every level until the true killer is made known.

Where it's reviewed:
Booklist, January 1, 2008, page 21
Kirkus Reviews, February 1, 2008, page NA
Library Journal, February 15, 2008, page 90
Publishers Weekly, January 14, 2008, page 36

Other books by the same author:
Four Souls, 2004
The Master Butchers Singing Club, 2003
The Last Report on the Miracles at Little No Horse, 2001
The Antelope Wife, 1998
Tales of Burning Love, 1996

Other books you might like:
Benjamin Capps, *A Woman of the People*, 1966
Donald Charles Coldsmith, *Fort De Chastaigne*, 1990

Western

417

MARCUS GALLOWAY

Bucking the Tiger

(New York: Berkley, 2008)

Story type: Historical/American West; Action/Adventure
Series: The Accomplice. Book 2
Subject(s): American West; Gambling; Adventure and Adventurers
Major character(s): Caleb Wayfinder, Gunfighter; John Henry "Doc" Holliday, Gunfighter, Historical Figure
Time period(s): Indeterminate Past
Locale(s): West

Summary: Doc Holliday and Caleb Wayfinder join forces and try to make a fortune gambling, but The Tiger, an organization that wants a cut of the profits, makes life difficult for the duo.

Other books by the same author:
The Accomplice, 2007 (book 1 in the Accomplice series)
The Man from Boot Hill Series, 2004-

Other books you might like:
Henry Wilson Allen, *Who Rides with Wyatt*, 1955
Matt Braun, *Doc Holliday*, 1997
Jane Candia Coleman, *Doc Holliday's Gone*, 2000
Robert B. Parker, *Appaloosa*, 2005
Robert B. Parker, *Gunman's Rhapsody*, 2001

418

DAGOBERTO GILB

The Flowers

(New York: Grove, 2008)

Story type: Contemporary; Literary
Subject(s): Race Relations; Adolescence; City and Town Life
Major character(s): Sonny Bravo, Teenager; Cloyd, Step-Parent, Landlord
Time period(s): 1990s
Locale(s): United States

Summary: Sonny Bravo moves with his mother into Las Flores, an apartment building owned by his new step-dad Cloyd. There, taking on a series of odd jobs given him by Cloyd, Sonny learns about the harsh situations of the other tenants' lives and navigates the racial tensions of his new neighborhood.

Where it's reviewed:
Booklist, Febrary 1, 2008, page 26
Kirkus Reviews, November 15, 2007, page NA
Library Journal, January 1, 2008, page 82
Publishers Weekly, November 19, 2007, page 33

Other books by the same author:
Gritos, 2003
The Last Known Residence of Mickey Acuna, 1995
The Magic of Blood, 1994
Winners on the Pass Line, 1985

Other books you might like:
A.E.E. Cannon, *Amazing Gracie*, 1991
Linda Oatman High, *Maizie*, 1995
David Lubar, *Dunk*, 2002

419

DEEANNE GIST

Courting Trouble

(Grand Rapids, Michigan: Bethany House, 2007)

Story type: Inspirational; Romance
Subject(s): Christian Life; Marriage; Romance
Major character(s): Essie Spreckelmeyer, Young Woman
Time period(s): 1890s (1894)
Locale(s): Corsicana, Texas

Summary: When Essie Spreckelmeyer has something on her mind, it's hard to deter her. In this first of a two-volume set, Essie is on the search for a husband. Her unconventional, tomboyish ways make it difficult to find a match, and in the end she has to decide if finding a husband is really the most important thing.

Other books by the same author:
Deep in the Heart of Trouble, 2008
The Measure of a Lady, 2006
A Bride Most Begrudging, 2005

Other books you might like:
Catherine Leilani Cummings Palmer, *The Bachelor's Bargain*, 2006
Lenora Worth, *The Carpenter's Wife*, 2003

420

JAMES J. GRIFFIN

Big Bend Death Trap

(Lincoln, MI: Condor Publishing, 1997)

Story type: Historical/American West; Mystery
Subject(s): Murder; Faith; Crime and Criminals
Major character(s): Cody Havlicek, Lawman
Time period(s): Indeterminate Past
Locale(s): Texas

Summary: Texas Ranger Cody Havlicek is assigned to track down the men responsible for a series of murders. His faith and his stamina are tested while he untangles the mystery that ultimately leaves him fighting for his life.

Other books by the same author:
The Texas Ranger Jim Blawcyzk Series, 2005-

Other books you might like:
Bill Crider, *Medicine Show*, 1990
Matthew S. Hart, *Border Showdown*, 1991

421

NYLA GRIFFITH

Lucky Strike

(Deadwood, South Dakota: TDG Communications, 2007)

Story type: Mystery; Historical/American West
Subject(s): Murder; Gold Discoveries; Detection
Major character(s): Gretchen Mitchell, Detective—Amateur
Time period(s): 1870s; 2000s
Locale(s): Deadwood, South Dakota

Summary: Following the murder of her close friend, Gretchen Mitchell begins a search for the killer through Deadwood. The search leads her to question a series of men, each with gold on their minds, and she doesn't know who, if anyone, she can trust. First novel.

Other books you might like:
Stephen Bly, *Friends and Enemies*, 2002
Bill Brooks, *The Badmen*, 1992
Robert Kammen, *Bloody Dakota Summer*, 1992

422

MARTHA GRIMES

Dakota

(New York: Viking, 2008)

Story type: Literary; Saga
Subject(s): American West; Animals, Treatment of; Memory
Major character(s): Andi Oliver, Amnesiac
Time period(s): 2000s
Locale(s): Kingdom, North Dakota

Summary: The woman who calls herself Andi Oliver, she suffers from amnesia and doesn't remember her given name, brings unwelcome light to abuses of the Humane Slaughter Act in the small town of Kingdom, North Dakota.

Where it's reviewed:
Booklist, December 15, 2007, page 4
Publishers Weekly, December 17, 2007, page 32

Other books by the same author:
Foul Matter, 2003
Biting the Moon, 1999
The Emma Graham Series, 1996-
Send Bygraves, 1989 (poetry)
The Richard Jury Series, 1981-

Other books you might like:
Kathleen Wendy Peyton, *Poor Badger*, 1990

423

JOANNA HERSHON

The German Bride

(New York: Ballantine, 2008)

Story type: Family Saga; Historical/American West
Subject(s): Guilt; American West; German Americans

Major character(s): Eva Frank, Spouse; Abraham Shein, Spouse (of Eva), Businessman (mercantile)
Time period(s): 1860s
Locale(s): Santa Fe, New Mexico

Summary: Eva Frank is paralyzed with guilt over the death of her sister. Although her sister died from complications during childbirth, Eva believes her death was the result of an affair Eva had with an anti-Semitic painter commissioned to paint the sisters' portraits. With the promise of a new life away from Germany, Eva marries Abraham Shein and travels to Santa Fe. There she finds that life isn't what she had hoped for and suffers from a series of failed pregnancies, a confining house, and a difficult marriage.

Where it's reviewed:
Kirkus Reviews, February 1, 2008, page NA
Library Journal, November 15, 2007, page 49
Publishers Weekly, October 15, 2007, page 35

Other books by the same author:
The Outside of August, 2003
Swimming, 2001

Other books you might like:
Ginna Gray, *Quiet Fires*, 1991
Jill Marie Landis, *Sunflower*, 1988
Alexandra Thorne, *Boundless*,

424

STEVE HOCKENSMITH

On the Wrong Track

(New York: St. Martin's Minotaur)

Story type: Amateur Detective; Historical/American West
Series: A Holmes on the Range Mystery. Book 2
Subject(s): Adventure and Adventurers; Railroads; Mystery and Detective Stories
Major character(s): Gustav "Old Red" Amlingmeyer, Detective—Amateur, Frontiersman; Otto "Big Red" Amlingmeyer, Detective—Amateur, Frontiersman; Burl Lockhart, Lawman
Time period(s): 1890s (1893)
Locale(s): West (Utah Territory)

Summary: Dreaming of being like Sherlock Holmes and Watson but desperate for income, the Amlingmeyer brothers accept work as security guards on the Pacific Express railway. When one of the passengers is decapitated and then the prime suspect is murdered, they finally get their chance to try out their detective skills.

Where it's reviewed:
Booklist, January 1, 2007, page 63
Kirkus Reviews, November 15, 2006, page 1155
Library Journal, November 15, 206, page 64
Publishers Weekly, December 18, 2006, page 56

Other books by the same author:
Holmes on the Range, 2006

Other books you might like:
Kerry Greenwood, *Murder on the Ballarat Train*, 2006
Joe R. Lansdale, *Blood Dance*, 2000
Keith Miles, *Excursion Train*, 2005
Keith Miles, *The Railway Detective*, 2004
Stuart Palmer, *The Puzzle of the Blue Banderilla*, 2004

Western

425

L.P. HOLMES

River Range

(New York: Leisure Books, 2008)

Story type: Historical/American West; Action/Adventure
Subject(s): American West; Ranch Life; Cowboys/
   Cowgirls
Major character(s): Boone Logan, Rancher
Time period(s): Indeterminate Past
Locale(s): West

Summary: In this title story from this trio, a rival rancher crosses the wrong guy when he interferes with Boone Logan's mission to move 200 cattle across the Colorado River.

Other books by the same author:
Black Sage, 1997
Catch and Saddle, 1986
Somewhere They Die, 1976
The Buzzards of Rocky Pass; Side Me at Sundown, 1963
Gunman's Greed, 1957

Other books you might like:
Peter Carter, *Borderlands*, 1990
Jim Miller, *The 600-Mile Stretch*, 1992
Cotton Smith, *Behold a Red Horse*, 2001

426

W.C. JAMESON

Beating the Devil

(Alburquerque: University of New Mexico Press, 2007)

Story type: Historical/American West; Action/Adventure
Subject(s): Revenge; Mexicans
Major character(s): Carlos, Vigilante; Chavez, Vigilante;
   Mueller, Leader (of bandits)
Time period(s): Indeterminate Past
Locale(s): Texas; Mexico

Summary: Carlos leaves the Texas land he never loved and crosses into Mexico searching for meaning but haunted by his traumatic childhood. There he is moved by the story of Chavez, whose family was gruesomely murdered, and Carlos decides to help Chavez exact justice on Mueller and his band of men responsible who were responsible for the crime. When Carlos tires of the journey and attempts to find solace in a beautiful woman, Mueller comes looking for him and revenge becomes a more personal mission for Carlos.

Other books by the same author:
Legend and Lore of the Guadalupe Mountains, 2007
Buried Treasures of Texas, 2006
Lost Treasures of American History, 2006
Colorado Treasure Tales, 2001

Other books you might like:
Louis L'Amour, *Lando*, 1984
Giles Tippette, *The Horse Thieves*, 1993
Dodge Tyler, *Apache Revenge*, 1997

427

JOAN JOHNSTON

A Stranger's Game

(New York: Pocket, 2008)

Story type: Amateur Detective; Romance
Series: Bitter Creek. Book 7
Subject(s): Murder; Mystery; Drama
Major character(s): Breed Grayhawk, FBI Agent; Grace
   "Merle Raye Finkel" Caldwell, Murderer (Innocent),
   Young Woman; Vincent Harkness, FBI Agent
Time period(s): 2000s
Locale(s): Austin, Texas

Summary: Grace Caldwell served eight years in a juvenile detention facility for the crime of murdering her parents—a crime she didn't commit. Upon release, she is determined to find the true killer, and her searching leads her to suspect FBI Agent Vincent Harkness. She seeks the help of Breed Grayhawk, an FBI Agent working under Harkness. When Caldwell uncovers a disturbing diary of from Harkness's wife while Harkness is planning security for a visit from the U.S. President, Grace is accused to planning to assassinate the president.

Where it's reviewed:
Booklist, March 15, 2008, page 35
Publishers Weekly, January 28, 2008

Other books by the same author:
Sisters Found, 2002
Never Tease a Wolf, 2001
Heartbeat, 1997
Marriage by the Book, 1997
I Promise, 1996

Other books you might like:
Elizabeth Lowell, *Innocent as Sin*, 2007
Yvonne Montgomery, *Obstacle Course*, 1990
Karen Robards, *One Summer*, 1993
John Herman Mulso Sherwood, *A Bouquet of Thorns*,
   1989
Robin LeAnne Wiete, *Fortune's Lady*, 1990

428

WILLIAM W. JOHNSTONE

Out of the Ashes

(New York: Pinnacle, 2008)

Story type: Action/Adventure; Futuristic
Series: Ashes. Book 1
Subject(s): War; Nuclear Warfare; Survival
Major character(s): Ben Raines, Survivor
Time period(s): Indeterminate Future
Locale(s): West

Summary: Having survived a nuclear attack on United States' soil, former soldier Ben Raines searches throughout the west for his family. Meanwhile, he recruits an army to rebuild the country that finds itself the recipients of an attack at the hands of the remaining government. This is a reprint of the original 1983 title.

Other books by the same author:
Brotherhood of the Gun, 2006
The Last Gunfighter: Savage Country, 2006
Revenge of the Eagles, 2005
Honor of the Mountain Man, 1998
Blackfoot Messiah, 1996

Other books you might like:
Pat Frank, *Alas, Babylon: A Novel*, 1959
Tolstaya Tatyana, *The Slynx*, 2003

429

WILLIAM W. JOHNSTONE , Co-Author
J.A. JOHNSTONE , Co-Author

Preacher's Showdown

(New York: Kensington Pinnacle, 2008)

Story type: Historical/American West; Action/Adventure
Series: First Mountain Man. Book 13
Subject(s): American West; Adventure and Adventurers
Major character(s): The Preacher, Mountain Man
Time period(s): 19th century
Locale(s): Missouri; West

Summary: Two cousins turn to a man they know as The Preacher to lead them west with a wagon train filled with supplies they hope to sell. The Preacher agrees, but on the trail some unexpected fellow travelers and other surprises have The Preacher fighting for his life.

Other books by the same author:
The Last Gunfighter Series, 2000-
The Eagle Series, 1993-
The Blood Bond Series, 1989-
The Ashes Series, 1983-
The Devil's Series, 1980-1987

Other books you might like:
Clint Hawkins, *Gunpowder Trail*, 1992
Don Johnson, *Brasada*, 1999
Judith R. Parker, *Cato Wahl*, 2003
Alan Riefe, *Against All Odds*, 1996
Richard S. Wheeler, *Bannack*, 1989

430

MIKE KEARBY

Ambush at Mustang Canyon

(Winthrop, Washington: Trail's End Books, 2007)

Story type: Historical/American West; Action/Adventure
Series: Parks Scott Trilogy. Book 3
Subject(s): American West; War; Slavery
Major character(s): George "Free" Anderson, Slave (former), Military Personnel; Parks Scott, Friend
Time period(s): 1870s
Locale(s): Texas

Summary: In this final book of the Parks Scott trilogy, Texas is about to be at war. Free Anderson finds himself with an internal conflict just as the tensions escalate

between the Native Americans and the military. Along with Parks Scott, Free has to assist the military as they move in to kill the herds and force the Native Americans into reservations. After Free witnesses the destruction of one of the Native American camps during the winter, he's torn between his desire to protect his family and his desire to see the Native Americans maintain their freedom.

Other books by the same author:
Ride the Desperate Trail, 2008
The Road to a Hanging, 2008
The 13th Baktun, 2008

431

MIKE KEARBY

The Road to a Hanging

(New York: Leisure Books, 2006)

Story type: Historical/American West; Historical/Post-American Civil War
Series: Parks Scott Trilogy. Book 1
Subject(s): American West; Slavery; Survival
Major character(s): George "Free" Anderson, Slave (former), Military Personnel (Union Army); Clara Mason, Slave (former); Parks Scott, Friend; Jubal Thompson, Lawman (sheriff), Outlaw
Time period(s): 19th century
Locale(s): Texas

Summary: Framed by Sheriff Jubal Thompson and awaiting execution for stealing cattle, former slave Free Anderson is rescued by friends Clara Mason and Parks Scott. With Sheriff Thompson on his trail and fending off dangerous rustlers, Free tries to prove his innocence.

Other books by the same author:
Ambush at Mustang Canyon, 2007
Ride the Desperate Trail, 2007

Other books you might like:
Frederic Bean, *Murder at the Spirit Cave*, 1999
Jay Brandon, *Grudge Match*, 2004
Frederick Faust, *The Masterman: A North-Western Story*, 2000
Steven Mark Krauzer, *God's Country*, 1993
Jake McMasters, *Quick Killer*, 1994

432

ELMER KELTON

Hard Trail to Follow

(New York: Forge Books, 2008)

Story type: Action/Adventure; Historical/American West
Series: Texas Ranger. 7
Subject(s): American West; Revenge; Crime and Criminals
Major character(s): Luther Cordell, Outlaw; Andy Pickard, Lawman (Texas Ranger), Farmer; Tom Blessing, Lawman (Sheriff), Crime Victim
Time period(s): 1870s

Locale(s): West

Summary: Luther Cordell, filled with regret for the crimes of his past, is on the run. He's being pursued by Andy Pickard who is attempting to avenge the death of his friend, Sheriff Tom Blessing. Along the way Pickard is confounded to hear Cordell repeatedly praised for being a good person.

Where it's reviewed:
Booklist, February 15, 2008, page 43
Library Journal, February 1, 2008, page 63
Publishers Weekly, December 17, 2007, page 32

Other books by the same author:
Six Bits a Day, 2005
Texas Vendetta, 2004
The Way of the Coyote, 2001
Frank McCarthy, 1981
The Buckalew Series, 1965-1976

Other books you might like:
John D. Armstrong, *The Return of Jericho Pike*, 1992
Elizabeth Fackler, *Badlands*, 1996
Jake Foster, *Hell-for-Leather Rider*, 1991
Gary Clifton Wisler, *Baron of the Brazos*, 1991

433

KENNETH L. KIESER

Ride the Trail of Death

(Cheyenne, WY: La Frontera Publishing, 1997)

Story type: Historical/American West; Revenge
Subject(s): Revenge; Coming-of-Age; Redemption
Major character(s): Birch Rose, Young Man, Lawman (deputy); Seth Bullock, Lawman (sheriff)
Time period(s): 1870s
Locale(s): West (Dakota Territory)

Summary: Orphaned after his father was killed in an Indian war and his mother was murdered during a robbery, Birch Rose is obsessed with seeking revenge. After Sheriff Seth Bullock takes Birch under his wing, discovers his talent as a shooter, and makes him a deputy, Birch gets the chance to settle the score with those who made him an orphan. Faced with the opportunity to finally get revenge, he has to make decision about the path he wants his life to take. First novel.

Other books you might like:
Peter Brandvold, *Once a Marshal*, 1999
Bill Brooks, *The Last Law There Was*, 1995
Shiff Davis, *The Young Gun*, 1989

434

ALLAN C. KIMBALL

Rainbows Wait for the Sun

(Wimberley, Texas: Sun Country, 2007)

Story type: Historical/American West; Action/Adventure
Subject(s): American West; Historical; Romance
Major character(s): Billy the Kid, Gunfighter, Historical

Figure; Wyatt Earp, Gunfighter, Historical Figure; Joaquin Jaxon, Lawman (Texas Ranger)
Time period(s): 19th century
Locale(s): Texas (Big Bend region)

Summary: This edition collects all three books of the trilogy, *Calamity Creek*, *Woman Hollering Creek*, and *Second Coffee Creek* into one action-packed volume. The stories paint a complete picture of the Big Bend area of Texas in the late 1800s through the lives of historical figures such as Billy the Kid and Wyatt Earp as well as fictional characters born in the rich imagination of the author.

Other books you might like:
Jack Ballas, *Gun Boss*,
Howard Pelham, *A Posse of Outlaws*, 1992
George W. Proctor, *Before Honor*, 1996
Jim Sanderson, *El Camino Del Rio*, 1998

435

R. JOE KING

Shadows in the Rain: A Tale of Old Klamath, California

(Tumacacori, AZ: Blue Traveler Press, 2008)

Story type: Contemporary
Subject(s): American West; Floods; Identity
Major character(s): Vince Jennings, Survivor
Time period(s): 1960s (1964)
Locale(s): California

Summary: Vince Jennings is restless and travels north to Klamath, California with only a few possessions. While Vince learns new trades to earn a living and grapples with his part-Mexican identity, a series of interesting characters color the narrative. When a flood overtakes the region, neither Klamath or Vince will ever be the same.

Other books you might like:
Gloria Skurzynski, *Trapped in Slickrock Canyon*, 1984
John Steinbeck, *Cannery Row*, 1945

436

LOUIS L'AMOUR

Grub Line Rider

(New York: Leisure Books, 2008)

Story type: Historical/American West; Action/Adventure
Subject(s): Frontier and Pioneer Life; Feuds; American West
Major character(s): Kim Sartain, Wanderer, Mountain Man; Jim Targ, Rancher
Time period(s): Indeterminate Past
Locale(s): West

Summary: A collection of seven of L'Amour's best stories, including "Grub Line Rider." In the title story, Kim Sartain wasn't looking for trouble but he found it when he tried to cross an unoccupied bit of land under the watchful eye of Jim Targ. Sartain makes a dangerous, maybe

even deadly, mistake when he decides to homestead the land just to irk Targ.

Other books by the same author:
The Haunted Mesa, 1987
A Trail to the West, 1986
Last of the Breed, 1986
West of the Pilot Range, 1986
The Shadow Riders, 1982

Other books you might like:
Robert Walter Broomall, *Bad Blood*, 1992
Frederick Faust, *Bad Man's Gulch*, 2005
David Thompson, *Blood Feud*, 1999

437

LOUIS L'AMOUR , Co-Author
ELMER KELTON , Co-Author
LOREN D. ESTLEMAN , Co-Author

Lost Trails

(New York: Pinnacle, 2007)

Story type: Collection; Historical/American West
Subject(s): Historical; American West
Time period(s): Multiple Time Periods
Locale(s): West

Summary: This collection of 14 stories from some of the biggest Western authors focuses on famous people from history, including Billy the Kid, Buffalo Bill Cody, Mark Twain, and others.

Other books you might like:
James B. Garry, *This Ol' Drought Ain't Broke Us Yet*, 1992
Robert Ray Hogan, *Legend of a Badman*, 1997
Richard S. Wheeler, *The Honorable Cody*, 2006

438

JOHN H. MANHOLD

El Tigre

(Boise, Idaho: Shoot Magazine Corporation)

Story type: Historical/American West; Action/Adventure
Subject(s): American West; Gold Discoveries; Adventure and Adventurers
Major character(s): Johann "El Tigre" Heinrich von Manfred, Lawman (Texas Ranger)
Time period(s): 19th century
Locale(s): Florida; Texas; California

Summary: In a story unique to the tales of other European immigrants, the adventures of El Tigre, otherwise known as Johann Heinrich von Manfred, take him to the Americas from Prussia, eventually landing him in California during the Gold Rush.

Other books you might like:
Gary McCarthy, *The American River*, 1992
Alan Riefe, *Against All Odds*, 1996
Philip Duffield Strong, *The Adventure of "Horse" Barnsby*, 1956

439

KARL MAY

The Treasure of Nugget Mountain

(Cornwall, UK: Diggory Press, 2008)

Story type: Historical/American West
Series: Winnetou
Subject(s): Native Americans; American West; Friendship
Major character(s): Winnetou, Indian (Apache Chief); Old Shatterhand, Gunfighter
Time period(s): 19th century
Locale(s): West

Summary: A new translation into English of a work from the most-popular German writer of the American West. Old Shatterhand tells the story of his friend Winnetou, an Apache Indian Chief whose tribe is threatened as the railroad comes through his land.

Other books by the same author:
In the Desert, 1980

Other books you might like:
Noel Bertram Gerson, *Apache*, 1987
Virginia Driving Hawk Sneve, *Betrayed*, 1974
Ted Stenhouse, *Across the Steel River*, 2001

440

KARL MAY

Winnetou the Apache Knight

(Cornwall, UK: Diggory Press, 2008)

Story type: Historical/American West
Subject(s): Native Americans; American West; Friendship
Major character(s): Winnetou, Indian (Apache chief); Old Shatterhand, Gunfighter
Time period(s): 19th century
Locale(s): West

Summary: A new translation into English of a work from the most-popular German writer of the American West. Winnetou, an Apache Indian Chief, proves himself a friend to the talented, German-American Old Shatterhand.

Other books by the same author:
In the Desert, 1980

Other books you might like:
Vella Munn, *Blackfeet Season*, 1999
Nasdijj, *The Blood Runs Like a River through My Dreams*, 2000
David William Ross, *Beyond the Stars*, 1990

441

MICHAEL MCGARRITY

Death Song

(Dutton, 1997)

Story type: Mystery
Subject(s): Family Saga; Mystery and Detective Stories; Murder

Western

Major character(s): Kevin Kerney, Police Officer (chief); Clayton Istee, Police Officer (sergeant detective); Tim Riley, Police Officer
Time period(s): 2000s
Locale(s): Santa Fe, New Mexico

Summary: Shortly after Tim Riley, a new member of the Lincoln County sheriff's office, is murdered, his widow is also discovered fatally wounded. Police Chief Kevin Kerney was on his way to enjoying retirement when he was pulled back to investigate the murder alongside his son, Sergeant Clayton Istee. When an autopsy reveals Riley's widow was pregnant at the time of her death and additional information reveals that Riley couldn't have been the father, the investigation takes a drastic turn.

Where it's reviewed:
Booklist, October 15, 2007, page 35
Publishers Weekly, November 26, 2007, page 30

Other books by the same author:
Nothing But Trouble, 2006
Hermit's Peak, 2000
Serpent Gate, 1999
Mexican Hat, 1998
Tularosa, 1997

Other books you might like:
Eleanor Taylor Bland, *Done Wrong*, 1995
Michael Connelly, *The Narrows*, 2004
John Lutz, *Spark*, 1993

442

MARSHA MOYER

Return of the Stardust Cowgirl

(New York: Three Rivers, 2008)

Story type: Family Saga; Contemporary
Series: Lucy Hatch. Book 4
Subject(s): Family Problems; Music and Musicians; Stepmothers
Major character(s): Lucy Hatch, Spouse (Cowboy); Ash Farrell, Spouse, Singer; Denny Culpepper, Young Woman, Singer
Time period(s): 2000s
Locale(s): Mooney, Texas

Summary: Ash Farrell returned home to his reluctant wife Lucy and their son after losing a recording contract. Meanwhile, Ash's pregnant daughter Denny discovers that her husband cheated on her, and she has arrived at Lucy and Ash's house to recover her senses as well. As the story progresses and each character deals with his or her own issues, the bond between Lucy and Denny grows.

Where it's reviewed:
Booklist, February 1, 2008, page 28
Publishers Weekly, December 3, 2007, page 48

Other books by the same author:
Heartbreak Town, 2007 (Book 3)
The Last of the Honky-tonk Angels, 2004 (Book 2)
The Second Coming of Lucy Hatch, 2003 (Book 1)

Other books you might like:
Reynolds Price, *The Source of Light*, 1981
Karen Robards, *Ghost Moon*, 2000
Rhea Beth Ross, *Hillbilly Choir*, 1991

443

MARCIA MULLER , Co-Author
BILL PRONZINI , Co-Author

Crucifixion River

(Detroit: Five Star, 2007)

Story type: Collection; Historical/American West
Subject(s): American West; Short Stories
Time period(s): Indeterminate Past
Locale(s): California; West

Summary: A collection of short stories by a husband and wife team. The title story, "Crucifixion River" is the first Western collaboration by Marcia Muller and Bill Pronzini, and takes place in a town where the Crucifixion River cult was once active. Also includes "The Carville Ghost," "Wrong Place, Wrong Time," and "Irrefutable Evidence."

444

LAURAN PAINE

Man from Durango

(Detroit: Five Star, 2007)

Story type: Historical/American West
Subject(s): American West; Ranch Life
Time period(s): Indeterminate Past
Locale(s): West

Summary: A compilation of two Western tales. In the first, "Prairie Guns," Colton Miller is trying to protect land he uses for his cattle from being taken over by homesteaders. When he frames the homesteaders for stealing cattle and has their building leveled, they fight back to regain what it rightfully theirs. In the second, "Man from Durango," Bent Ander has returned from hiding out in Mexico where he fled after a gunfight. Although he's just looking for work and trying to start his life fresh, he finds himself quickly caught up in a conflict and has to make a big decision about the future path of his life.

Other books by the same author:
The Quiet Gun, 2008
The Plains of Laramie, 2006
Winchester Pass, 2002
The Horseman, 1989
The Marshall, 1989

445

CATHY PICKENS

Hush My Mouth

(New York: St. Martin's Minotaur, 2008)

Story type: Mystery; Ghost Story
Series: A Southern Fried Mystery
Subject(s): Paranormal; Missing Persons; Television
Major character(s): Avery Andrews, Lawyer; Fran French, Wealthy; Neanna Lyles, Young Woman
Time period(s): 2000s
Locale(s): Dacus, South Carolina

Summary: When Neanna disappears following a concert near her sister Fran's hometown, Fran seeks the assistance of lawyer Avery Andreas to help find her troubled sister. Fran and Neanna's aunt was murdered in the town 20 years prior and when when Neanna is also found dead, a group of ghost-hunters hoping to star in a reality TV show mettle in the investigation.

Where it's reviewed:
Booklist, January 1, 2008, page 48
Kirkus Reviews, December 1, 2007, page NA
Publishers Weekly, November 26, 2007, page 32

Other books by the same author:
Hog Wild, 2007
Done Gone Wrong, 2005
Southern Fried, 2004

Other books you might like:
Elizabeth Dearl, *Diamondback*, 2000
Michael McGarrity, *Serpent Gate*, 1998

446

ROBERT J. RANDISI

Texas Iron

(New York: Leisure, 2008)

Story type: Historical/American West; Mystery
Subject(s): American West; Murder; Revenge
Major character(s): Sam McCall, Avenger
Time period(s): 19th century
Locale(s): Vengeance Creek, Texas

Summary: Returning to their hometown to find the truth following the suspicious death of their father, the McCall brothers find themselves fighting for their lives as they attempt to find the truth and avenge their father's death.

Other books by the same author:
The Sons of Daniel Shaye Series, 2004-
Invitation to a Hanging, 2004
Turnback Creek, 2004

Other books you might like:
J. Lee Butts, *A Bad Day to Die*, 2004
Robert Fate, *Baby Shark*,
Douglas Hirt, *Able Gate*,

447

JANA RICHMAN

The Last Cowgirl

(New York: Morrow, 2008)

Story type: Family Saga; Literary
Subject(s): Child Abuse; Family Problems; Military Life
Major character(s): Darlene "Dickie" Sinfield, Journalist, Cowboy
Time period(s): 2000s
Locale(s): Clayton, Utah

Summary: A journalist working in Salt Lake City for 30 years, Dickie hasn't had to deal with day-to-day life back at her childhood home with her abusive parents. When her brother is killed in a military accident and she returns home for the funeral, she is forced to face both a difficult past as well as the present.

Where it's reviewed:
Booklist, November 15, 2007, page 29
Kirkus Reviews, October 1, 2007, page NA
Library Journal, November 15, 2007, page 51
Pubishers Weekly, September 24, 2007, page 43

Other books by the same author:
Riding in the Shadows of Saints, 2005

Other books you might like:
Donna Ball, *Amber Skies*, 1987
Dana Ransom, *Texas Destiny*, 1994

448

BENJAMIN ALIRE SAENZ

Names on a Map

(New York: Harper, 2008)

Story type: Family Saga
Subject(s): Vietnam War; Family Relations; Politics
Major character(s): Gustavo "Gus" Espejo, Twin; Xochil Espejo, Twin; Rosario, Grandparent
Time period(s): 1960s (1967)
Locale(s): El Paso, Texas

Summary: The effect of the Vietnam War on an immigrant family is told through multiple narrators of the Espejo family. The oldest boy, Gus, is against the war and has to decide what he's going to do after receiving a draft notice, while his twin sister, Espejo, dates a young man who voluntarily enlists.

Where it's reviewed:
Booklist, December 15, 2007, page 25
Kirkus Reviews, January 15, 2008, page NA
Library Journal, January 1, 2008, page 87
Publishers Weekly, November 12, 2007, page 34

Other books by the same author:
In Perfect Light, 2005
Sammy and Julia in Hollywood, 2004
The House of Forgetting, 1997
Carry Me Like Water, 1995
Flowers for the Broken, 1992 (short stories)

Other books you might like:
Jennifer Armstrong, *Shattered*, 2002
Marsha Qualey, *Hometown*, 1995

449

LES SAVAGE

Black Rock Canon

(New York: Leisure Books, 2008)

Story type: Historical/American West; Action/Adventure
Subject(s): Animals/Horses; Cowboys/Cowgirls; Ranch Life
Major character(s): Del, Cowboy; Tie, Cowboy
Time period(s): 1940s
Locale(s): Montana

Summary: Originally published in 1949, this classic follows the adventures of Del and Tie as they journey to Montana to rope wild horses.

Where it's reviewed:
Booklist, August 1, 2006, page 62

Other books by the same author:
Trail of the Silver Saddle, 2005
The Devil's Corral, 2004
Table Rock, 1993
Doniphan's Ride, 1959
Beyond Wind River, 1958

Other books you might like:
Louis L'Amour, *May There Be a Road*, 2001
B.M. Bower, *Law on the Flying U*, 2005
Scott Waldie, *Return to Travers Corners*, 2002

450

KARL H. SCHLESIER

Trail of the Red Butterfly

(Lubbock: Texas Tech University Press, 1997)

Story type: Historical/American West
Subject(s): Discovery and Exploration; Indians of North America
Major character(s): Jean Valle, Trader, Historical Figure; Meriwether Lewis, Explorer; William Clark, Explorer
Time period(s): 1800s (1804-1807)
Locale(s): West

Summary: This historical novel recounts the life of Jean Valle, a trader who lived in the Black Hills among the Cheyenne. Valle recountes stories of horse-raiding and other events during his time with the Cheyenne to Lewis and Clark.

Where it's reviewed:
Internet Bookwatch, March 2008, page NA

Other books by the same author:
Aurora Crossing, 2008
Josanie's War, 1998
The Wolves of Heaven, 1993

Other books you might like:
John Killdeer, *Fire on the Prairie*, 1995
Vella Munn, *Cheyenne Summer*, 2001
Richard S. Wheeler, *The Deliverance*, 2003

451

MICHAEL SENUTA

The Vengeance Brand

(New York: Avalon, 2007)

Story type: Historical/American Civil War; Historical/American West
Subject(s): War; American West; Revenge
Major character(s): John Waverly, Military Personnel (captain); Traxler, Military Personnel (lieutenant)
Time period(s): 19th century
Locale(s): West

Summary: At the end of the American Civil War, Captain John Waverly and his men find themselves being tortured as prisoners of war at the hand of Lieutenant Traxler. After being rehabilitated and on their way to California, Waverly and his men find themselves face to face with Traxler once more.

Other books by the same author:
Incident at Copper Creek, 2003

452

JON SHARPE

Missouri Manhunt

(New York: Signet, 2008)

Story type: Historical/American West; Action/Adventure
Series: The Trailsman. Book 315
Subject(s): Kidnapping; American West; Adventure and Adventurers
Major character(s): Skye Fargo, Frontiersman, Gunfighter; Lucille Sparks, Frontierswoman, Captive; Mad Dog Terrell, Gunfighter, Outlaw
Time period(s): 19th century
Locale(s): Springfield, Missouri

Summary: When beautiful frontierswoman Lucille Sparks is kidnapped by Mad Dog Terrell and his gang, Skye Fargo follows in quick pursuit seeking the ultimate revenge.

Other books by the same author:
Shoshoni Spirits, 1990
Sierra Shoot-Out, 1990
Call of the White Wolf, 1988
Utah Slaughter, 1988
Dead Man's Forest, 1988

Other books you might like:
M.R. James, *The Cattle Baron*, 1990
Hank Mitchum, *Grand Teton*, 1989
David Thompson, *People of the Forest*, 2006

453

JORY SHERMAN

The Sundown Man

(New York: Berkley Books, 2007)

Story type: Historical/American West; Adventure
Subject(s): Kidnapping; Family
Major character(s): Jared Sunnedon, Young Man (brother of Kate); Kate Sunnedon, Young Woman (sister of Jared)
Time period(s): Indeterminate Past
Locale(s): West

Summary: While being held captive by the Arapahos who murdered their parents, brother and sister Jared and Kate make a pact. They agree that no matter what happens they will always find one another. After Kate is separated from Jared, Jared risks everything to keep his promise and find his sister.

Other books by the same author:
The Baron Series, 1997-
Grass Kingdom, 1993
Eagles of Destiny, 1990
The Rivers West Series, 1988-
Wyoming Wanton, 1983

Other books you might like:
George Brandsberg, *Afoot*, 2006
Dick Clason, *The Ranger and the Green Derby*, 2004
Sid Fleischman, *Bandit's Moon*, 1998
Joseph A. West, *Me and Johnny Blue*, 2000

454

COTTON SMITH

Blood of Bass Tillman

(New York: Leisure, 2007)

Story type: Historical/American West; Action/Adventure
Subject(s): Revenge; Murder; American West
Major character(s): Bass Tillman, Lawyer, Gunfighter
Time period(s): 1870s (1879)
Locale(s): Colorado

Summary: After trying to leave his violent past behind him, Bill Bass finds himself on the hunt with only revenge on his mind after making a promise at the gravesite of his murdered son and daughter-in-law.

Other books by the same author:
Return of the Spirit Rider, 2007
Blood Brothers, 2006
Death Rides a Red Horse, 2005
Thirteenth Bullet, 2004
Winter Kill, 2004

Other books you might like:
Ralph Cotton, *Border Dogs*, 1999
W.W. Lee, *Cannon's Revenge*, 1995
Thom Nicholson, *Ride the Red Sun Down*, 2005
Charles G. West, *Hangman's Song*, 2005

455

RICK STEBER

Forty Candles on a Cowboy Cake

(Prineville, OR: Bonanza Books, 2007)

Story type: Contemporary
Subject(s): American West; Cowboys/Cowgirls; Romance
Major character(s): Waddy Wilder, Cowboy
Time period(s): 2000s
Locale(s): Oregon; Alaska

Summary: In the middle of his life, Waddy Wilder is contemplating settling down with a divorced woman and her children on her Oregon ranch. Instead, he finds himself on an Alaskan adventure with a woman who soon loses his interest.

Other books by the same author:
Buy the Chief a Cadillac, 2005
Buckaroo Heart, 2002
Gunfighters, 1998
New York to Nome, 1996
Oregon Trail, 1987

Other books you might like:
Lorraine Heath, *Never Marry a Cowboy*, 2001

456

R.W. STONE

Trail Hand

(New York: Leisure Books, 2008)

Story type: Action/Adventure; Historical/American West
Subject(s): Cowboys/Cowgirls; Ranch Life; Romance
Major character(s): Owen Burke, Cowboy; Enrique Allende, Rancher; Rosa Maria Allende, Young Woman (daughter of Enrique); Chavez, Cowboy
Time period(s): Indeterminate Past
Locale(s): West

Summary: Owen Burke finds work at Enrique Allende's horse ranch and is given the task of driving a herd of horses to California, but he quickly makes an enemy after Chavez sees Burke talking with Rosa Maria, the boss's daughter. When the horses are stolen before reaching their destination, Chavez blames the crime on Burke. Burke, now on the run, has to solve the crime before he is caught.

Where it's reviewed:
Booklist, December 1, 2006

Other books you might like:
Janet Dailey, *Calder Storm*, 2006
Linda Lael Miller, *A Wanted Man*, 2007

457

JACK TODD

Sun Going Down

(New York: Touchstone, 2008)

Story type: Family Saga; Historical/American West
Subject(s): Frontier and Pioneer Life; Ranch Life; Family Saga

Western

Major character(s): Ebenezar Paint, Parent, Pioneer; Eli Paint, Twin, Rancher; Ezra Paint, Twin, Cowboy
Time period(s): 19th century; 20th century (1863-1933)
Locale(s): West

Summary: The story weaves together 70 years of the western transition from frontier to modern life through four generations of the Paint family. The focus is on twins Eli and Ezra Paint, the children of pioneers. Eli and Ezra establish wealth through the dangerous trade of horse stealing. After Eli settles down on a ranch, marries and has six children, the story follows Eli's daughter through a series of tumultuous relationships.

Where it's reviewed:
Library Journal, February 15, 2008, page 98
Publishers Weekly, January 7, 2008, page 33

Other books by the same author:
The Taste of Metal, 2001 (memoir)

Other books you might like:
Jim Harrison, *Dalva*, 1988
Thomas McGuane, *Gallatin Canyon*, 2006

458

RICHARD S. WHEELER

The Canyon of Bones

(New York: Forge Books, 2008)

Story type: Action/Adventure; Indian Culture
Series: Skye's West. Book 15
Subject(s): Native Americans; Mountain Life; Journalism
Major character(s): Barnaby Skye, Mountain Man; Graves Duplessis Mercer, Journalist; Victoria Skye, Spouse (of Barnaby), Indian (Crow)
Time period(s): 19th century
Locale(s): West

Summary: Mountain man Barnaby Skye needs work and agrees to take journalist Graves Duplessis Mercer on an adventure to an ancient graveyard for Mercer's latest story. Their journal is filled with perils as Mercer searches for the perfect sensationalist story to fulfill the expectations of his tabloid audience. When, against the warnings of Skye's wife Victoria, Mercer removes a bone to bring back as a souvenir, the group finds themselves fighting for their lives.

Where it's reviewed:
Booklist, April 1, 2007, page 37

Other books by the same author:
The Bounty Trail, 2004
Trouble in Tombstone, 2004
Vengeance Valley, 2004
The Exile, 2003
The Sam Flint Series, 1997-1998

Other books you might like:
Archie Fred Binns, *Mighty Mountain*, 1940
Bill Brooks, *The Badmen*, 1992
Clyde Edgerton, *Redeye*, 1995
Max Evans, *Bluefeather Fellini in the Sacred Realm*, 1994
Nelson Coral Nye, *Gunfight at the O.K. Corral*, 2003

459

RICHARD S. WHEELER

Virgin River

(New York: Forge, 2008)

Story type: Historical/American West; Wagon Train
Series: Skye's West. Book 16
Subject(s): Mormons; Tuberculosis; American West
Major character(s): Barnaby Skye, Mountain Man; Victoria Skye, Spouse, Indian; Mary Skye, Spouse, Indian
Time period(s): 1850s (1857)
Locale(s): Utah

Summary: Barnaby Skye is a new dad and wants to provide for his family. He takes a job leading a group of youngsters afflicted with tuberculosis to Virgin River, thought to have healing properties, in hope that it will ease their symptoms. Barnaby, along with his wives, finds himself facing a series of challenges, including others who fear catching TB, landscape and weather hazards, and trouble with the local indians and governments.

Where it's reviewed:
Booklist, March 15, 2008, page 38
Publishers Weekly, January 14, 2008, page 41

Other books by the same author:
Obituary for Major Reno, 2004
The Bounty Trail, 2004
Trouble in Tombstone, 2004
The Exile, 2003
The Sam Flint Series, 1997-1998

Other books you might like:
Stephen Bly, *My Foot's in the Stirrup—My Pony Won't Stand*, 1996
Mary Ramstetter, *Down in the Valley of the Shadow*, 2001

460

H.R. WILLIAMS

Harris: The Return of the Gunfighter

(Sierra Vista, Arizona: Treble Heart Books, 2007)

Story type: Historical/American West; Action/Adventure
Subject(s): American West; Sheriffs
Major character(s): Henry Harris, Farmer, Gunfighter; Wilkie, Lawman (Sheriff)
Time period(s): 19th century
Locale(s): Medford, Missouri

Summary: Henry Harris is trying put his gunfighting days behind him and enjoy his life as a farmer. When Sheriff Wilkie needs Henry's help to confront a group of brothers seeking revenge on his town, however, Henry can't say no. Sides are taken and a showdown ensues.

Other books you might like:
Will Cade, *The Gallowsman*,
James Reno, *Creed's Law*, 1988
Greg Tobin, *Big Horn*, 1989

The Present State of Fantasy Fiction
by
Don D'Ammassa

The popularity of fantasy fiction has grown so dramatically during the past few years that it has become very difficult to keep track of its development. Originally marketed as a subset of science fiction, it is now a much larger segment of the market and has spilled over into other genres. The most obvious of these hybrids is romance fiction, which has become increasingly dominated by paranormal story lines. These usually involve supernatural creatures either in our own world or in a version of it where magical beings are an accepted part of life. Laurell K. Hamilton's Anita Blake series was the first to explore this interface successfully, but there are now literally dozens of series that make use of the same basic plot elements. These stories also borrow heavily from horror fiction, primarily by using vampires and werewolves as characters, and have turned what were once considered to be frightening monsters into merely another kind of human being, often the object of a romantic affair. Among the more successful authors working in this form of fantasy are Yasmine Galethorn, Patricia Briggs, Rob Thurman, Anton Strout, Mark Del Franco, Karen Chance, Kat Richardson, and Talia Gryphon.

The intermingling of fantasy and romance fiction has been particularly fruitful, with authors from each genre crossing over into the other. Harlequin Books has even established a separate imprint for fantasy romance, Luna Books, and other publishers have very active paranormal romance lines including Tor, Berkley, Jove, Love Spell, and Mira. Fantasy has also crept into mystery and detective fiction, and there has been a resurgence of stories about psychic detectives, benevolent ghosts, and magically talented detectives or villains. In turn, there has been a mild decline in high fantasy—traditional stories of castles, kings, dragons and sorcerers—although that facet of the genre remains strong. Sword and sorcery continues to be only a peripheral part of fantasy, confined primarily to game related novels such as Warhammer, Dragonlance, and Forgotten Realms. Short fantasy fiction is also a relatively minor part of the genre despite a large number of theme anthologies, although there have been some small signs of increased reader interest in more general collections. Single author fantasy collections are still confined almost entirely to the small press.

A very heartening development in recent months has been a number of new novels and new authors whose work is not set in cookie cutter fantasy worlds but actually involves an original, sometimes extraordinary setting, such as the world of bridges in Gregory Frost's *Shadowbridge*. China Mieville, Jeffrey Ford, and Mary Gentle have all consistently avoided standard settings in their fantasy fiction, but very few other writers were willing, or perhaps capable of creating an entirely new world in which to place their characters and stories. Several writers, most of them newcomers, have taken up that challenge over the course of recent months and many of them quite successfully.

Not all of the notable books were by new writers, however. Peter David, much of whose early work consisted of media tie-ins, has proven to be far more interesting when working with worlds entirely of his own making. But his latest, *Tigerheart*, is an excellent re-imagining of J.M. Barrie's *Peter Pan*, comparable to *Peter and the Star Catchers* (2004) by Dave Barry and Ridley Pearson. British writer Adam Roberts also draws on classic work in *Swiftly*, which recounts a war between England and France at the time of Gulliver. The diminutive Lilliputians have become unwilling allies of the English, while the French employ the giants of Brobdingnab to help destroy the enemy fleet. Simon R. Green's *The Unnatural Inquirer*, the eighth title in his Nightside series, is one of his best novels, this one involving a search for a man who may have proof that the afterlife is real. The husband and wife team of Barb and Jay Hendee extended their dark, sword and sorcery series, the Noble Dead, with *Child of a Dead God*, a quest story in which the two increasingly well delineated protagonists seek to prevent a powerful magical artifact from falling into the wrong hands.

Daniel Abraham is one of the more impressive newer writers and the third installment in his debut series, the Long Price Quartet, proves that an outwardly familiar plot can conceal new and interesting qualities. *An*

Autumn War continues the history of a magical alternate world in which a single aggressive kingdom sets out to conquer its neighbors, armed with a magical method of neutralizing defensive spells just prior to an attack. Their quarry in this case appears unlikely to present any difficulty, a city state which has dedicated itself to the arts rather than the art of war. The conquest proves to be a greater challenge than expected due to the unconventional tactics of the defenders and the brilliance of their quirky leader. Abraham's prose is particularly satisfying and he appears likely to break into the top rank of fantasy writers very quickly.

Naomi Novik may already have done so, based on five novels published in just two years, all part of the still unfinished Temeraire series. Alternate history has become increasingly popular in science fiction and has begun to emerge as a significant theme in fantasy as well. Novik's setting is the Napoleonic Wars, but with a difference. There is genuine magic in the world, as well as intelligent flying dragons, some of whom are fighting on each side. Her two protagonists are Temeraire, one of the British dragons, and the human who is bonded to him but whose sometimes unorthodox tactics have led to his disgrace and imprisonment. When Napoleon's magically enhanced armies invade the British Isles, extraordinary measures must be taken to repel the invaders.

One of the most interesting new writers to appear this year is S.M. Peters, whose first novel, *Whitechapel Gods*, is set in a part of London which has somehow become isolated from the rest of the city during the Victorian era and which is ruled by two mechanical gods. Although the human inhabitants are not happy with this arrangement, the gods have various ways of enforcing their wishes. The story of their rebellion is almost overshadowed by the bizarrely imagined and intricately described society in which it takes place. This marriage of magic and the mechanical can also be found in Jay Lake's *Escapement*, sequel to last year's *Mainspring*, set in an alternate version of our reality in which the solar system is quite literally operated by a gigantic clockwork mechanism. *Escapement* introduces a new protagonist and conducts the reader on a marvelous tour of a very unique and fascinating landscape. There's also a mechanistic feel to *Iron Angel* by Alan Campbell, his follow up to *Scar Night*. The city of Deepgate is suspended by chains over a bottomless deep and it's a city where the gods and ghosts are both real. The protagonist discovers that forces are in motion which could undermine Deepgate and send it into the abyss.

Poison Sleep by T.A. Pratt is also a second novel, sequel to *Blood Engines*. Although humorous fantasy has not fared well in the United States in recent years, serious fantasy with comedic elements has been more successful. Pratt's setting is the magical city of Felport where Marla Mason functions as its head magician. Her responsibilities include making sure that bad magic doesn't get out of hand in the city. Mason's challenge this time is the escape of a mentally ill magician from confinement. The escapee is particularly dangerous because she can spread her delusions through the dreams of people in close proximity. The serious theme of detection is balanced by the often quite clever banter between the two protagonists.

Robert Redick is a British author who made a promising debut with *The Red Wolf Conspiracy*, which is technically set in a fairly standard magical alternate world, but alters the rules slightly by having most of the novel take place aboard ship which becomes lost on a vast ocean. Another novel which makes clever use of an old idea is *Waking Brigid* by Francis Clark, who unfortunately passed away before his first novel appeared in print. The story takes place in post Civil War Savannah and is borderline horror as well as fantasy. The city is troubled by the actions of a secretive group of Satanists, who are in turn opposed by an organization of benevolent magicians.

Short fantasy fiction of note continues to be sporadic and spread across a wide array of publications. The best fantasy anthology of early 2008 is *Tales Before Narnia* edited by Douglas Anderson, which samples short fantasy fiction which may have influenced the Narnia novels by C.S. Lewis. *Realms of Fantasy* remains the only professional magazine devoted exclusively to short fantasy fiction, although *The Magazine of Fantasy and Science Fiction* publishes a great deal of it. The majority of the most interesting short fantasy continues to originate in small press magazines and collections, and occasionally online. An excellent sampling can be found in the annual year's best anthology of fantasy and horror fiction edited by Ellen Datlow, Kelly Link, and Gavin Grant.

At present, the fantasy market appears to be largely unaffected by ongoing changes in the publishing world. The overlap with other genres continues to expand although there will certainly be some loss of ground when the market becomes saturated. Fantasy for younger readers has been particularly healthy, ranging from very light adventure to more serious work. The Harry Potter phenomenon is undoubtedly responsible for much of this, but with the end of that series it is unclear whether attention will shift to another genre. Recent films based on the Spiderwick Chronicles, the Narnia books, and Philip Pullman's *The Golden Compass* have not generated the same level of interest. Almost all young adult fantasy fiction consists of open ended series reflecting the trend in adult fantasy.

A few subgenres of fantasy have virtually disappeared. Contemporary novels of fantasy are overwhelmingly blends of romance and adventure. The light fantasy, magic realism, and satiric fantasy have largely disappeared. The interest in fantasies about animals, particularly cats, appears to have peaked and is now in a sharp decline. The number of new Arthurian romances and historical novels with fantastic themes have also dropped off sharply, including stories based on Norse, Roman, or Greek mythology. The one exception is Elizabethan and Victorian England, which continue to provide the background for several new novels each

year. Perhaps the most dramatic change is the near complete absence of time travel fantasies, which were once so common that some book stores placed them in a separate section.

Because fantasy draws its readership from a much broader base than science fiction or most other genres, it is subject to more dramatic fluctuations in both the size of the audience and the themes which interest them. 2008 opened with a clear, strong interest in urban fantasy with strong, female protagonists, but it is impossible to predict how long that interest will last given the very large number of derivative series being published. Fantasy as a whole, however, appears to be a thriving genre and its domination on the bookshelves is not likely to change in the near future.

Recommended Titles

The first half of 2008 has brought a healthy number of excellent fantasy novels, most of them innovative as well as literate. More than half of these are by authors whose first book was published within the last two years, which suggests a promising near term future for those fantasy readers who have grown tired of standard plots and themes.

An Autumn War by Daniel Abraham

Child of a Dead God by Barb & Jay Hendee

Escapement by Jay Lake

Iron Angel by Alan Campbell

Poison Sleep by T.A. Pratt

The Red Wolf Conspiracy by Robert Redick

Swiftly by Adam Roberts

Tales Before Narnia edited by Douglas Anderson

Tigerheart by Peter David

The Unnatural Inquirer by Simon R. Green

Victory of Eagles by Naomi Novik

Waking Brigid by Francis Clark

Whitechapel Gods by S.M. Peters

Fantasy Titles

461

JOE ABERCROMBIE

Last Argument of Kings

(London: Gollancz, 2008)

Story type: Sword and Sorcery; Magic Conflict
Series: First Law. Book 3
Subject(s): Magic; War
Major character(s): Logen Ninefingers, Warrior; Jezal dan Luthar, Warrior; Glokta, Criminal
Time period(s): Indeterminate
Locale(s): Alternate Universe

Summary: All seems to be lost for Logen Ninefingers and his people. They are beset by their enemies on every side and the people have grown weary of war. The king is dying and the people are in open revolt. The story unfolds from the point of view of several characters including a soldier who has decided not to fight any more battles, a brilliant but haunted man who manipulates people through blackmail and threats, and a loyal soldier determined to protect his country.

Where it's reviewed:
Locus, March 2008, page 20

Other books by the same author:
Before They Are Hanged, 2007
The Blade Itself, 2006

Other books you might like:
James Barclay, *Cry of the Newborn*, 2005
David Gemmell, *Ravenheart*, 2001
Paul Kearney, *The Heretic Kings*, 2006
Juliet E. McKenna, *Southern Fire*, 2005
R.A. Salvatore, *The Demon Awakens*, 1996

462

DANIEL ABRAHAM

An Autumn War

(New York: Tor, 2008)

Story type: Magic Conflict; Sword and Sorcery
Series: Long Price. Book 3
Subject(s): Secrets; Magic
Major character(s): Balasar Gice, Military Personnel; Otah

Machi, Ruler; Sinja, Warrior
Time period(s): Indeterminate
Locale(s): Alternate Universe

Summary: The Galt empire has been overcoming one city after another thanks to their secret weapon which makes defensive magic ineffective. When the army sets its sights on Machi, a city known for its poets, it appears to be an easy conquest, but the ruler of Machi has a few secrets up his sleeve.

Other books by the same author:
A Betrayal in Winter, 2007
A Shadow in Summer, 2006

Other books you might like:
Dave Duncan, *Impossible Odds*, 2003
George R.R. Martin, *A Game of Thrones*, 1996
China Mieville, *The Scar*, 2002
Lawrence Watt-Evans, *Touched by the Gods*, 1997
Tad Williams, *Shadowmarch*, 2004

463

DOUGLAS A. ANDERSON , Editor

Tales Before Narnia

(New York: Del Rey, 2007)

Story type: Anthology
Subject(s): Short Stories

Summary: The editor has brought together short stories and excerpts of classic fantasy, some familiar, some very rare, all of which could potentially have been an influence on C.S. Lewis, author of the popular Narnia series for children. Among the authors represented here are William Morris, George MacDonald, Charles Williams, and Rudyard Kipling.

Other books by the same author:
Seekers of Dreams, 2005
Tales Before Tolkien, 2003

Other books you might like:
Roger Lancelyn Green, *From the World's End*, 1948
Rudyard Kipling, *Kipling's Fantasy Stories*, 1992
George MacDonald, *Lilith*, 1895
William Morris, *Early Romances*, 2004
Charles Williams, *Many Dimensions*, 1932

464

ILONA ANDREWS

Magic Burns

(New York: Ace, 2008)

Story type: Urban; Contemporary
Series: Kate Daniels. Book 2
Subject(s): Magic; Secrets
Major character(s): Kate Daniels, Mercenary, Detective—
   Private; Julie Olsen, Witch; Curran, Leader, Were-
   wolf
Time period(s): 2000s
Locale(s): Atlanta, Georgia

Summary: Kate Daniels is a combination of mercenary
and private detective, working the paranormal side of
things in Atlanta. She agrees to attempt to retrieve some
documents for a pack of werewolves, but is also involved
in the search for a young woman's missing mother, both
of which cases eventually intersect. Eventually she
discovers that the documents are connected to an attempt
by superhuman creatures to return to the world of
humankind.

Other books by the same author:
Magic Bites, 2007

Other books you might like:
Patricia Briggs, *Blood Bound*, 2007
Karen Chance, *Embrace the Night*, 2008
Talia Gryphon, *Key to Conflict*, 2007
Kat Richardson, *Underground*, 2008
Rob Thurman, *Madhouse*, 2008

465

ALEX ARCHER

Provenance

(Don Mills, Ontario: Gold Eagle, 2008)

Story type: Contemporary; Magic Conflict
Series: Rogue Angel. Book 11
Subject(s): Magic; Secrets
Major character(s): Annja Creed, Archaeologist; Eddie
   Cao Cao, Pirate; Hevelin, Religious
Time period(s): 2000s
Locale(s): Panama; Pacific Ocean

Summary: Annja Creed is on the trail of another magical
artifact. This one has been seized by a group of modern
day pirates operating in the South China Seas. She is assisted by an ancient secret order who have served as
custodian for the object, and opposed by a government
official who has his own reason for wanting the object
destroyed.

Other books by the same author:
The Soul Stealer, 2008
Secret of the Slaves, 2007
The Chosen, 2007
Solomon's Jar, 2006
The Spider Stone, 2006

Other books you might like:
Christopher Golden, *The Bones of Giants*, 2004
E.E. Knight, *The Lost Cult*, 2004
Marjorie M. Liu, *The Iron Hunt*, 2008
Mike Resnick, *The Amulet of Power*, 2003
James Rollins, *Black Order*, 2006

466

SARAH ASH

Tracing the Shadow

(New York: Bantam, 2008)

Story type: Magic Conflict; Coming-of-Age
Series: Alchymist's Legacy. Book 1
Subject(s): Secrets; Magic
Major character(s): Alois Visant, Government Official;
   Linnaius, Magician (alchemist); Rieuk Mordiern,
   Apprentice
Time period(s): Indeterminate
Locale(s): Alternate Universe

Summary: In a fantasy world where magicians have been
outlawed and executed, the rescue of a young girl found
wandering in the streets begins a cycle of dark revenge.
A magical spirit hovers around the waif, dedicated to the
destruction of the man responsible, and her connection
with a talented apprentice alchemist will have terrible
repercussions.

Where it's reviewed:
Library Jounral, February 15, 2008, page 96

Other books by the same author:
Children of the Serpent Gate, 2005
Prisoner of the Iron Tower, 2004
Lord of Snow and Shadows, 2003
The Lost Child, 1998
Songspinners, 1996

Other books you might like:
Sara Douglass, *Beyond the Hanging Wall*, 2003
Dave Duncan, *The Alchemist's Apprentice*, 2007
Lisa Goldstein, *The Alchemist's Door*, 2002
Elizabeth Haydon, *Rhapsody*, 1999
China Mieville, *King Rat*, 1999

467

ROBERT ASPRIN

Dragons Wild

(New York: Ace, 2008)

Story type: Humor; Contemporary
Series: Griffen McCandless. Book 1
Subject(s): Humor; Dragons
Major character(s): Griffen McCandless, Mythical
   Creature (shapechanger); Valerie McCandless, Mythi-
   cal Creature (shapechanger); Jason Stoner, Govern-
   ment Official
Time period(s): 2000s
Locale(s): New Orleans, Louisiana

Summary: Griffen McCandless has survived as a card shark and small time con artist but his life is about to take a very different turn. His uncle Malcolm tells him that Griffen and his cousin Valerie are both shapechangers who can assume the form of dragons. Although Malcolm suggests that they need to be carefully trained, the two young people decide to strike out on their own and travel to New Orleans, where they run into trouble with a crime ring.

Where it's reviewed:
Publishers Weekly, February 18, 2008, page 140

Other books by the same author:
Class Dis-Mythed, 2007
Myth-Gotten Gains, 2007
Myth-Told Tales, 2007
Something M.Y.T.H. Inc, 2003
Another Fine Myth, 1978

Other books you might like:
Piers Anthony, *Isle of View*, 1990
Joanne Bertin, *The Last Dragonlord*, 1998
Gordon R. Dickson, *The Dragon and the Djinn*, 1996
Ed Greenwood, *The Dragon's Doom*, 2003
Richard A. Knaak, *Firedrake*, 1985

468

CAM BANKS

The Sellsword

(Renton, Washington: Wizards of the Coast, 2008)

Story type: Magic Conflict; Sword and Sorcery
Series: Dragonlance
Subject(s): Quest; Magic
Major character(s): Vanderjack, Mercenary; Gredchen, Mercenary; Rivven Cairn, Military Personnel
Time period(s): Indeterminate
Locale(s): Alternate Universe

Summary: A small group of mercenaries find themselves in a realm governed by the minions of an evil wizard, even though his kind were supposedly defeated in a recent war. Among their number is a man with a haunted sword, a hidden past, and a habit of getting himself into trouble. First novel.

Other books you might like:
Ed Gentry, *Neversfall*, 2007
Richard A. Knaak, *The Citadel*, 2000
Mel Odom, *The Jewel of Turmish*, 2002
Chris Pierson, *Blades of the Tiger*, 2005
Jean Rabe, *Redemption*, 2002

469

ELIZABETH BEAR

Ink and Steel

(New York: Roc, 2008)

Story type: Historical/Elizabethan; Magic Conflict
Series: Promethean Age. Book 4

Subject(s): Magic; Fairies
Major character(s): William Shakespeare, Writer, Historical Figure; Mab, Ruler, Mythical Creature (fairy); Elizabeth I, Ruler, Historical
Time period(s): 16th century
Locale(s): England; Mythical Place

Summary: Christopher Marley, a secret agent of Queen Elizabeth, is murdered but restored to life in the land of the fairies. William Shakespeare is enlisted to take his place and help protect the magical bond that links the two worlds and preserves the power of Elizabeth as well as Queen Mab. His efforts are undermined by the presence of a traitor within the highest councils of government.

Other books by the same author:
Hell and Earth, 2008
New Amsterdam, 2007
The Chains That You Refuse, 2007
Whiskey and Water, 2007
Blood and Iron, 2006

Other books you might like:
Lynn Abbey, *Unicorn and Dragon*, 1987
Sara Douglass, *Darkwitch Rising*, 2005
Sarah A. Hoyt, *Any Man So Daring*, 2003
Mercedes Lackey, *Ill Met by Moonlight*, 2005
     Roberta Gellis co-author
Judith Tarr, *House of War*, 2003

470

ALEX BELL

The Ninth Circle

(London: Gollancz, 2008)

Story type: Mystery; Mystical
Subject(s): Magic; Secrets
Major character(s): Gabriel Antaeus, Amnesiac; Stephomi, Scholar; Casey March, Worker
Time period(s): 2000s
Locale(s): Budapest, Hungary

Summary: Gabriel Antaeus can remember almost nothing of his past but he discovers that he has unusual talents. He is fluent in various languages and has remarkable endurance. He makes friends with a young woman who tries to help, but someone is also sending him hints about his past, hints that suggest that he is more than human. First novel.

Other books you might like:
Steven Brust, *To Reign in Hell*, 1984
Storm Constantine, *Stalking Tender Prey*, 1995
Sara Douglass, *The Crippled Angel*, 2005
Sherrilyn Kenyon, *Daemon's Angel*, 1995
John Shirley, *Demons*, 2002

471

CAROL BERG

Breath and Bone

(New York: Roc, 2008)

Story type: Sword and Sorcery; Magic Conflict
Subject(s): Politics; Magic
Major character(s): Valen, Nobleman; Voushanti, Nobleman; Gram, Warrior
Time period(s): Indeterminate
Locale(s): Alternate Universe

Summary: As his country descends into civil war, Valen wrestles with the predictions of his own doom that haunt his waking moments. He is also physically addicted to a twisted form of magic, and the working out of his own personal destiny might effect the entire world. This is the second half of the story begun in *Flesh and Spirit*.

Where it's reviewed:
Library Journal, December 1, 2007, page 104
Publishers Weekly, October 15, 2007, page 46

Other books by the same author:
Flesh and Spirit, 2007
Daughter of Ancients, 2005
The Soul Weaver, 2005
Guardians of the Keep, 2004
Restoration, 2002

Other books you might like:
Anne Bishop, *Belladonna*, 2007
Jennifer Fallon, *Lord of the Shadows*, 2003
Raymond E. Feist, *Exile's Return*, 2004
Barbara Hambly, *Icefalcon's Quest*, 1998
Mercedes Lackey, *Magic's Price*, 1990

472

DAVID BILSBOROUGH

A Fire in the North

(New York: Tor, 2008)

Story type: Sword and Sorcery; Magic Conflict
Series: Annals of Lindormyn. Book 2
Subject(s): Magic; Quest
Major character(s): Bolldhe, Warrior; Nibulus, Warrior; Appa, Religious
Time period(s): Indeterminate
Locale(s): Alternate Universe

Summary: An evil sorcerer was defeated generations ago, but he was not destroyed and now he's back. A group of warriors and others gather together on a quest to rid the world of this dark presence once and for all. After a long journey and many adventures, they finally reach the remote land where they hope to win the final confrontation.

Where it's reviewed:
Publishers Weekly, April 21, 2008, page 40

Other books by the same author:
The Wanderer's Tale, 2007

Other books you might like:
R. Scott Bakker, *The Darkness That Comes Before*, 2004
Terry Brooks, *The Sword of Shannara*, 1977
Stephen R. Donaldson, *Lord Foul's Bane*, 1977
Robert Newcomb, *The Fifth Sorceress*, 2002
J.R.R. Tolkien, *The Fellowship of the Ring*, 1954

473

ANNE BISHOP

Tangled Webs

(New York: Roc, 2008)

Story type: Mystery; Magic Conflict
Series: Black Jewels. Book 6
Subject(s): Magic; Prisoners and Prisons
Major character(s): Surreal SaDiablo, Criminal (assassin); Jaenelle Angelline, Witch, Noblewoman; Rainier, Royalty (prince)
Time period(s): Indeterminate
Locale(s): Alternate Universe

Summary: Several people are invited to a special entertainment at a mysterious location, each invitation signed by Jaenelle Angelline, although she is unaware of this fact. The guests find themselves magically imprisoned in a dangerous death trap and they struggle to stay alive while those outside attempt to find a way to breach the magical barriers.

Where it's reviewed:
Publishers Weekly, December 17, 2007, page 38

Other books by the same author:
Belladonna, 2007
Sebastian, 2006
Dreams Made Flesh, 2005
Shadows and Light, 2002
Heir to the Shadows, 1999

Other books you might like:
Lorna Freeman, *The King's Own*, 2005
Michael Kurland, *Ten Little Wizards*, 1988
Mercedes Lackey, *Four and Twenty Blackbirds*, 1997
Michelle Sagara, *Cast in Shadow*, 2005
Melissa Scott, *Point of Dreams*, 2001
   Lisa A. Barnett, co-author

474

TOBY BISHOP

Airs and Graces

(New York: Ace, 2008)

Story type: Magic Conflict; Coming-of-Age
Series: Horsemistress Saga. Book 2
Subject(s): Magic; Animals/Horses
Major character(s): Larkyn Hamley, Student; Philippa Winter, Noblewoman; William, Nobleman (duke)
Time period(s): Indeterminate
Locale(s): Alternate Universe

Summary: A young woman has mastered the bonding of herself with a flying horse, a talent limited to only a few. Duke William is not one of those so gifted and he resents this girl in particular. His obsession begins to affect his judgment and his inattention has left the country vulnerable to foreign attacks.

Other books by the same author:
Airs Beneath the Moon, 2007

Other books you might like:
Constance Ash, *The Horse Girl*, 1988
Mary L. Herbert, *Winged Magic*, 1996
Mercedes Lackey, *The River's Gift*, 1999
Jean Rabe, *The Finest Challenge*, 2006
Mary Stanton, *The Piper at the Gate*, 1989

475

PATRICIA BRAY

The Final Sacrifice

(New York: Bantam, 2008)

Story type: Sword and Sorcery; Magic Conflict
Series: Josan. Book 3
Subject(s): Quest; Magic
Major character(s): Josan, Religious; Lucius, Ruler; Ysobel, Noblewoman
Time period(s): Indeterminate
Locale(s): Alternate Universe

Summary: The personality of the monk Josan has been magically relocated into the body of the emperor. Both personalities are aware of one another and the tensions between them threaten to drive both insane. The secret of how to reverse the spell is held in a distant land so the two men, in one body, set out on a quest to find it.

Other books by the same author:
The Sea Change, 2007
The First Betrayal, 2006
Devlin's Justice, 2004
Devlin's Honor, 2003
Devlin's Luck, 2002

Other books you might like:
Sara Douglass, *Beyond the Hanging Wall*, 2003
Dave Duncan, *The Cutting Edge*, 1992
Lynn Flewelling, *The Bone Doll's Twin*, 2001
Barbara Hambly, *The Silicon Mage*, 1988
Dennis L. McKiernan, *Into the Forge*, 1997

476

PATRICIA BRIGGS

Iron Kissed

(New York: Ace, 2008)

Story type: Urban; Mystery
Series: Mercy Thompson. Book 3
Subject(s): Secrets; Magic
Major character(s): Mercy Thompson, Mythical Creature (shapechanger); Adam Hauptman, Werewolf; Siebold Adelbertsmiter, Mechanic
Time period(s): 2000s
Locale(s): United States

Summary: Mercy Thompson is a skinwalker, able to magically change her shape under the right circumstances. When her former boss is arrested for a murder he didn't commit, she decides to find out the truth and clear his name. Her efforts are complicated by pressure from the two men in her life to decide which of them she loves.

Where it's reviewed:
Booklist, February 1, 2008, page 36
Locus, December 2007, page 27
Publishers Weekly, November 5, 2007, page 49

Other books by the same author:
Blood Bound, 2007
Moon Called, 2006
Raven's Strike, 2005
Dragon Blood, 2003
Dragon Bones, 2002

Other books you might like:
Karen Chance, *Touch the Dark*, 2006
Nancy Collins, *Sunglasses After Dark*, 1989
Yasmine Galenorn, *Darkling*, 2007
Laurell K. Hamilton, *Blood Noir*, 2008
Rob Thurman, *Madhouse*, 2008

477

STEVEN BRUST

Jhegaala

(New York: Tor, 2008)

Story type: Sword and Sorcery; Quest
Series: Vlad Taltos. Book 11
Subject(s): Quest; Secrets
Major character(s): Vlad Taltos, Fugitive; Loiosh, Animal (bird); Saekeresh Veodric, Nobleman
Time period(s): Indeterminate
Locale(s): Alternate Universe

Summary: Vlad Taltos has made so many enemies that he decides it might be time to look up a distant branch of the family and spend some time in a faraway land. When he arrives, no one admits to knowing the family name and he has to unravel a mystery in order to discover the truth, and avoid losing his life in the process.

Where it's reviewed:
Publishers Weekly, May 5, 2008, page 50

Other books by the same author:
Dzur, 2006
Sethra Lavode, 2004
The Lord of Castle Black, 2003
The Paths of the Dead, 2002
Issola, 2001

Other books you might like:
Robin Wayne Bailey, *Swords Against the Shadowland*, 1998
Dave Duncan, *Faery Lands Forlorn*, 1991
David Eddings, *The Redemption of Althalus*, 2000

Fantasy

Leigh Eddings, co-author
Jennifer Roberson, *Sword-Born*, 1998
Lawrence Watt-Evans, *The Wizard Lord*, 2006

478

KATHLEEN BRYAN

The Golden Rose

(New York: Tor, 2008)

Story type: Sword and Sorcery; Magic Conflict
Series: Rose. Book 2
Subject(s): Magic; Quest
Major character(s): Averil, Sorceress; Gereint, Knight; Peredur, Wizard
Time period(s): Indeterminate
Locale(s): Alternate Universe

Summary: Averil made an agreement with the King of Lys to marry the man of his choosing. This would give him a political advantage while protecting her people from his wrath, but Averil is in love with Gereint, a knight, who returns her affection. When she discovers that the king is planning another war of aggression, she reneges on her agreement and helps oppose his plans.

Where it's reviewed:
Publishers Weekly, January 7, 2008, page 40

Other books by the same author:
The Serpent and the Rose, 2007
Rite of Conquest, 2004 (as Judith Tarr)
House of War, 2003 (as Judith Tarr)
Daughter of Lir, 2001 (as Judith Tarr)
Kingdom of the Grail, 2000 (as Judith Tarr)

Other books you might like:
Lynn Abbey, *Rifkind's Challenge*, 2006
Jennifer Fallon, *Eye of the Labyrinth*, 2002
Mercedes Lackey, *Arrows of the Queen*, 1987
Juliet Marillier, *Blade of Fortriu*, 2006
Andre Norton, *Three Hands for Scorpio*, 2005

479

ELIZABETH C. BUNCE

A Curse Dark as Gold

(New York: Arthur A. Levine, 2008)

Story type: Young Adult; Legend
Subject(s): Fairy Tales
Major character(s): Charlotte Miller, Teenager; Jack Springer, Salesman; Eben Fuller, Businessman
Time period(s): Indeterminate
Locale(s): Alternate Universe

Summary: When Charlotte Miller's father dies, the family's finances take a turn for the worse and it appears that they may even have to close the mill that is their livelihood. Then the mysterious Jack Springer shows up with magical thread and an offer that Charlotte wants to refuse, but which could save the family fortunes. This is

a retelling of the classic fairy tale "Rumpelstiltskin." First novel.

Other books you might like:
Pamela Dean, *Tam Lin*, 1992
Robin McKinley, *Rose Daughter*, 1997
Sheri S. Tepper, *Beauty*, 1991
Patricia Wrede, *Snow White and Rose Red*, 1989
Jane Yolen, *Briar Rose*, 1992

480

JIM BUTCHER

Small Favor

(New York: Roc, 2007)

Story type: Contemporary; Magic Conflict
Series: Dresden Files. Book 10
Subject(s): Magic; Fairies
Major character(s): Harry Dresden, Wizard; Mab, Ruler, Mythical Creature (fairy); Molly Carpenter, Apprentice
Time period(s): 2000s
Locale(s): Chicago, Illinois

Summary: Harry Dresden is a mildly disreputable but always formidable wizard who is enjoying a relatively peaceful rest from his usual exertions when Queen Mab of the fairies calls in a favor. Her request involves a powerful evil force that doesn't like being investigated, and if that weren't bad enough, even Harry's friends seem determined to get him killed.

Where it's reviewed:
Publishers Weekly, February 18, 2008, page 140

Other books by the same author:
Captain's Fury, 2007
White Night, 2007
Cursor's Fury, 2006
Proven Guilty, 2006
Dead Beat, 2005

Other books you might like:
Glen Cook, *Angry Lead Skies*, 2002
Simon Hawke, *The Wizard of Lovecraft's Cafe*, 1993
Tanya Huff, *Blood Debt*, 1997
Karen Marie Moning, *Bloodfever*, 2006
Rob Thurman, *Madhouse*, 2008

481

ALAN CAMPBELL

Iron Angel

(New York: Bantam, 2008)

Story type: Mystical; Magic Conflict
Series: Deepgate Codex. Book 2
Subject(s): Magic; Legends
Major character(s): Dill, Angel; Rachel Hael, Traitor; Jack Caulker, Criminal
Time period(s): Indeterminate
Locale(s): Deepgate, Alternate Universe

Summary: The city of Deepgate is suspended by chains over a mysterious abyss into which the bodies of the dead are thrown. Dill is an angel who is not in sympathy with the Spine, the new government of Deepgate which has established a strict rule, but he is imprisoned. Meanwhile, outside the walls, the spirits of the dead have become restless.

Where it's reviewed:
Publishers Weekly, March 3, 2008, page 33

Other books by the same author:
Lye Street, 2007
Scar Night, 2006

Other books you might like:
Storm Constantine, *Scenting Hallowed Blood*, 1996
Mary Gentle, *Rats and Gargoyles*, 1990
Scott Lynch, *Red Seas under Red Skies*, 2007
Ian R. MacLeod, *The House of Storms*, 2005
China Mieville, *Perdido Street Station*, 2001

482

JACQUELINE CAREY
Kushiel's Mercy
(New York: Grand Central, 2008)

Story type: Sword and Sorcery; Magic Conflict
Series: Kushiel. Book 6
Subject(s): Magic; Religious Conflict
Major character(s): Imriel de la Courcel, Nobleman; Sidonie de la Courcel, Noblewoman; Ysandre, Ruler
Time period(s): Indeterminate
Locale(s): Alternate Universe

Summary: Two lovers are the focus of great discord in their kingdom. The queen places them under certain restrictions which can only be lifted if Imriel locates his missing mother and brings her back to face charges of treason against the throne. They face a prolonged separation, but events alter course when a magical danger threatens the entire land. This is the final volume in the series.

Other books by the same author:
Kushiel's Justice, 2007
Kushiel's Scion, 2006
Godslayer, 2005
Banewreaker, 2004
Kushiel's Chosen, 2002

Other books you might like:
Sara Douglass, *Enchanter*, 2001
Maggie Furey, *Harp of Winds*, 1994
Elizabeth Haydon, *Requiem for the Sun*, 2003
Juliet Marillier, *Daughter of the Forest*, 2000
L.E. Modesitt Jr., *Shadowsinger*, 2002

483

KAREN CHANCE
Embrace the Night
(New York: Roc, 2008)

Story type: Contemporary; Urban
Series: Cassandra Palmer. Book 3

Subject(s): Magic; Vampires
Major character(s): Cassandra Palmer, Psychic; Mircea, Vampire; John Pritkin, Investigator
Time period(s): 2000s
Locale(s): United States

Summary: Cassie Palmer might be the world's foremost clairvoyant, but she is still tied by a magical bond to the vampire master Mircea, which limits her freedom. To break that link, she and her partner are searching for a mystical book of ancient lore, but as she grows closer to her objective, she begins to realize that the book itself might be an even greater threat.

Other books by the same author:
Claimed by Shadow, 2007
Touch the Dark, 2006

Other books you might like:
Patricia Briggs, *Moon Called*, 2006
Yasmine Galenorn, *Dragon Wytch*, 2008
Laurell K. Hamilton, *Blue Moon*, 1998
C.E. Murphy, *Coyote Dreams*, 2007
Kat Richardson, *Greywalker*, 2006

484

GLEN COOK
Cruel Zinc Melodies
(New York: Roc, 2008)

Story type: Mystery; Magic Conflict
Series: Garrett. Book 12
Subject(s): Magic; Secrets
Major character(s): Garrett, Detective—Private; Max Weider, Businessman; John Stretch, Businessman
Time period(s): Indeterminate
Locale(s): Alternate Universe

Summary: Garrett is a Chandleresque private detective operating in a fantasy world that vaguely resembles this one. His latest case involves problems associated with the construction of a new theater. The project has been hampered by the appearance of various groups of beings including ghosts and oversized insects. What seems at first a relatively straightforward case will have a profound effect on Garrett's future.

Other books by the same author:
Lord of the Silent Kingdom, 2007
Sung in Blood, 2006
Angry Lead Skies, 2002
Soldiers Live, 2000
Faded Steel Heat, 1999

Other books you might like:
P.N. Elrod, *Bloodlist*, 1990
Simon R. Green, *Paths Not Taken*, 2005
J. Michael Reaves, *Darkworld Detective*, 1982
Mike Resnick, *Stalking the Unicorn*, 1987
Anton Strout, *Dead to Me*, 2008

Fantasy

485

BRUCE COVILLE

The One Right Thing

(Framingham, Massachusetts: NESFA, 2008)

Story type: Collection; Young Adult
Subject(s): Short Stories

Summary: This is a collection of previously published stories and poems, all involving fantasy themes, each written for a young adult audience. The stories involve a variety of unlikely heroes, many of whom readers would not ordinarily expect to be cast in that role. Each performs a heroic deed of unusual nature.

Other books by the same author:
Thor's Wedding Day, 2005
Juliet Dove, Queen of Love, 2003
Song of the Wanderer, 2001
Odder than Ever, 1999
Sarah's Unicorn, 1997

Other books you might like:
Joan Aiken, *A Necklace of Raindrops*, 1968
Alan Garner, *A Bag of Moonshine*, 1986
Robin McKinley, *The Door in the Hedge*, 1981
Vivian Van Velde, *Curses Inc. and Other Stories*, 1997
Jane Yolen, *The Faery Flag*, 1989

486

BRIAN CULLEN

Seekers of the Chalice

(New York: Tor, 2008)

Story type: Magic Conflict; Quest
Subject(s): Quest; Magic
Major character(s): Bern, Mythical Creature (elf); Lorgas, Mythical Creature (elf); Cumac, Warrior
Time period(s): Indeterminate Past
Locale(s): Ireland

Summary: A magical artifact that helps maintain peace in ancient Ireland is stolen by villains. A mixed group of human and elvish warriors, plus a wizard, set out to find the Chalice of Fire and recover it before disaster strikes. They find themselves opposed by a veritable army of the creatures of darkness who seek to subjugate the world. First novel.

Where it's reviewed:
Library Journal, December 1, 2007, page 104
Publishers Weekly, December 3, 2007, page 54

Other books you might like:
S.L. Farrell, *Holder of Lightnings*, 2003
Kenneth Flint, *Isle of Destiny*, 1988
Gregory Frost, *Remscela*, 1988
Morgan Llywelyn, *Druids*, 1991
Juliet Marillier, *Daughter of the Forest*, 2000

487

JULIE E. CZERNEDA , Editor

Misspellings

(New York: DAW, 2008)

Story type: Anthology
Subject(s): Short Stories; Magic

Summary: All 17 stories in this anthology appear here for the first time. The common theme is the practice of magic and what happens when a spell goes wrong. The stories are set in this world and in a variety of fantasy realms. The contributors include Kristen Britain, Doranna Durgin, Jim C. Hines, Kristine Smith, and others.

Other books by the same author:
Regeneration, 2006
Migration, 2005
Hidden in Sight, 2003
In the Company of Others, 2001
Changing Vision, 2000

Other books you might like:
Kristen Britain, *The High King's Tomb*, 2007
Doranna Durgin, *Changespell*, 1997
Fritz Leiber, *Conjure Wife*, 1952
Christopher Stasheff, *The Warlock in Spite of Himself*, 1969
Lawrence Watt-Evans, *Ithanalin's Restoration*, 2002

488

PETER DAVID

Tigerheart

(New York: Del Rey, 2008)

Story type: Young Adult; Quest
Subject(s): Magic
Major character(s): Paul Dear, Child; The Boy, Immortal; Captain Slash, Pirate
Time period(s): 2000s
Locale(s): Mythical Place

Summary: Paul is an unusual young boy living in London who secretly communicates with fairies and other magical creatures. When a tragedy strikes his family, he decides to do something about it by traveling to a far world where anything is possible. The Anyplace is clearly meant to be a variation of Neverland and its most colorful figure, The Boy, is a re-imagining of Peter Pan.

Where it's reviewed:
Library Journal, March 15, 2008, page 67
School Library Journal, April 2008, page 172

Other books by the same author:
The Darkness of the Light, 2007
Fall of Knight, 2006
One Knight Only, 2003
The Wood to Wuin, 2002
Sir Apropos of Nothing, 2001

Other books you might like:
J.M. Barrie, *Peter Pan*, 1904
Pamela Dean, *The Secret Country*, 1985
Edward Eager, *Half Magic*, 1954
Alan Garner, *Elidor*, 1965
Norton Juster, *The Phantom Tollbooth*, 1961

489

MELISSA DE LA CRUZ

Masquerade
(New York: Hyperion, 2008)

Story type: Young Adult; Vampire Story
Series: Blue Bloods. Book 2
Subject(s): Vampires
Major character(s): Schuyler Van Alen, Vampire, Teenager; Mimi Force, Vampire; Oliver Hazard-Perry, Vampire, Teenager
Time period(s): 2000s
Locale(s): New York, New York; Italy

Summary: Someone is murdering young vampires and Schuyler Van Alen, a vampire herself, is determined to discover the identity of the killer. Her investigation brings her into the orbit of socialite Mimi Force, an undead mastermind who is involved with a plot that could alter the future of humanity and vampire alike.

Other books by the same author:
Angels of Sunset Boulevard, 2008
Revelations, 2008
Crazy Hot, 2008
Lip Gloss Jungle, 2008
Blue Bloods, 2006

Other books you might like:
Carmen Adams, *The Band*, 1994
Amelia Atwater-Rhodes, *Midnight Predator*, 2002
Rachel Caine, *Glass Houses*, 2006
P.C. Cast, *Betrayed*, 2007
    Kristin Cast, co-author
Vivian Vande Velde, *Companions of the Night*, 1992

490

MARK DEL FRANCO

Unquiet Dreams
(New York: Ace, 2008)

Story type: Urban; Magic Conflict
Series: Connor Grey. Book 2
Subject(s): Magic; Secrets
Major character(s): Connor Grey, Consultant, Wizard; Leonard Murdock, Police Officer; Stinkwort, Mythical Creature (fairy)
Time period(s): 2000s
Locale(s): Boston, Massachusetts

Summary: In a version of Boston where various mythical creatures interact with humans, a war is brewing between the elves and the fairies with innocent humans caught in between. Connor Grey is a druid and a consultant to the police, but he has lost most of his magical talents and hardly seems up to the task of heading off a magical bloodbath.

Where it's reviewed:
Locus, February 2008, page 25

Other books by the same author:
Unshapely Things, 2007

Other books you might like:
Jim Butcher, *Small Favor*, 2008
Glen Cook, *Faded Steel Heat*, 1999
Kim Harrison, *Dead Witch Walking*, 2004
Kat Richardson, *Underground*, 2008
Rob Thurman, *Moonshine*, 2007

491

MARISSA DOYLE

Bewitching Season
(New York: Henry Holt, 2008)

Story type: Historical/Victorian; Political
Subject(s): Historical; Magic
Major character(s): Persephone Leland, Student; Penelope Leland, Student; Lochinvar Seton, Nobleman
Time period(s): 1830s (1837)
Locale(s): London, England

Summary: Persephone and her sister Penelope are studying magic in a variant of early Victorian England. As the day approaches when Victoria will be formally crowned, their governess and teacher is kidnapped, part of a sinister plot to secretly assert control over the throne. They decide to rescue the woman, and find romance along the way. First novel.

Where it's reviewed:
Booklist, January 1, 2008, page 78
Kliatt, March 2008, page 10
School Library Journal, March 2008, page 197

Other books you might like:
Jonathan Barnes, *The Somnambulist*, 2007
James P. Blaylock, *Lord Kelvin's Machine*, 1992
Gordon Dahlquist, *The Glass Books of the Dream Eaters*, 2006
Barbara Hambly, *Bride of the Rat God*, 1994
S.M. Peters, *Whitechapel Gods*, 2008

492

WILLIAM H. DRINKARD

Elom
(New York: Tor, 2008)

Story type: Historical/Pre-history; Mystical
Subject(s): Pre-Columbian History; Magic
Major character(s): Berkana, Religious; Kalmar, Hunter; Dera, Young Woman
Time period(s): Indeterminate
Locale(s): Alternate Universe

Summary: Generations have passed since Geerna taught her people the wisdom of the gods and then disappeared, apparently taken by them. Now the gods—or entities claiming to be gods—have reappeared and the arrangement between them and the people is about to change in unexpected ways. First novel.

Where it's reviewed:
Publishers Weekly, January 21, 2008, page 159

Other books you might like:
Jean Auel, *The Mammoth Hunters*, 1985
John R. Dann, *Song of the Axe*, 2001
W. Michael Gear, *People of the Nightland*, 2007
    Kathleen O'Neal Gear, co-author
Jack London, *Before Adam*, 2006
William Sarabande, *Walkers of the Wind*, 1990

493

DAVE DUNCAN

The Alchemist's Code

(New York: Ace, 2008)

Story type: Historical/Medieval; Mystery
Series: Nostradamus. Book 2
Subject(s): Historical; Secrets
Major character(s): Michel Nostradamus, Astrologer, Doctor; Alfeo Zeno, Apprentice; Danese Dolfin, Nobleman
Time period(s): 16th century
Locale(s): Venice, Italy

Summary: The rulers of Venice approach Nostradamus with an unusual request. They have intercepted messages that prove there is a spy operating somewhere in the city, but they have no other clues about his identity. With his apprentice, Alfeo, Nostradamus tries to track the infiltrator down, but becomes involved with murder and other intrigue before solving the case.

Where it's reviewed:
Publishers Weekly, January 28, 2008, page 45

Other books by the same author:
The Alchemist's Apprentice, 2007
Children of Chaos, 2006
The Jaguar Knights, 2004
Impossible Odds, 2003
The Crooked House, 2000

Other books you might like:
John Dickson Carr, *The Devil in Velvet*, 1951
Esther Friesner, *Druid's Blood*, 1988
Daniel Hood, *Beggar's Banquet*, 1987
Tamara Siler Jones, *Valley of the Soul*, 2006
Phyllis Ann Karr, *The Idylls of the Queen*, 2983

494

ROBERT EARL

Ancient Blood

(Nottingham, United Kingdom: Black Library, 2008)

Story type: Sword and Sorcery; Magic Conflict
Series: Warhammer

Subject(s): Magic; War
Major character(s): Domnu Brock, Gypsy; Mihai Brock, Gypsy; Stirland, Nobleman
Time period(s): Indeterminate
Locale(s): Alternate Universe

Summary: Mysterious disappearances and illnesses have been troubling a remote part of the empire and two local nobles decide that the nomadic Strigany might be responsible. Even if they are innocent, they should serve as a suitable scapegoat. When the nobles mobilize their forces to wipe out the transients, they discover that their prey is allied with magical forces.

Other books by the same author:
The Corrupted, 2006
The Burning Shore, 2004
Wild Kingdoms, 2004

Other books you might like:
Glen Cook, *Soldiers Live*, 2000
Ben Counter, *Soul Drinker*, 2002
Nick Kyme, *Oathbreaker*, 2008
Sandy Mitchell, *Death's City*, 2005
Stan Nicholls, *Legion of Thunder*, 1999

495

KATE ELLIOTT

Shadow Gate

(New York: Tor, 2008)

Story type: Sword and Sorcery; Magic Conflict
Series: Crossroads. Book 2
Subject(s): Magic; Secrets
Major character(s): Marit, Deity; Anji, Warrior; Lirya, Warrior, Slave
Time period(s): Indeterminate
Locale(s): Alternate Universe

Summary: A war-torn land finds its various peoples making unexpected alliances in an effort to restore stability. The story follows the adventures of several characters, including a slave, a professional soldier, and a woman who has died and been recreated as a minor deity. The chaos seems to have been created by a mysterious corruption affecting the very gods who watch over the world.

Where it's reviewed:
Publishers Weekly, February 4, 2008, page 43

Other books by the same author:
Spirit Gate, 2007
Crown of Stars, 2006
In the Ruins, 2005
The Gathering Storm, 2003
Child of Flame, 2000

Other books you might like:
Sara Douglass, *Threshold*, 2003
Dave Duncan, *Children of Chaos*, 2006
Raymond E. Feist, *The King's Buccaneer*, 1992
R.A. Salvatore, *Promise of the Witch-King*, 2005
Patricia Wrede, *Shadow Magic*, 1982

496

STEVEN ERIKSON

Reaper's Gale

(New York: Tor, 2008)

Story type: Sword and Sorcery; Magic Conflict
Series: Malazan Book of the Fallen. Book 7
Subject(s): Magic; Secrets
Major character(s): Rhulad Sengar, Ruler; Karsa Orlong, Warrior; Icarium Lifestealer, Warrior
Time period(s): Indeterminate
Locale(s): Alternate Universe

Summary: The political situation in a magical kingdom is deteriorating. The emperor is insane, the local god has lost much of his power, and various factions are battling for influence on the shape of the future. A large cast of characters interact, some fleeing the chaos, others intending to impose their will on the future.

Other books by the same author:
Midnight Tides, 2007
The Bonehunters, 2007
House of Chains, 2006
Deadhouse Gates, 2005
Gardens of the Moon, 2004

Other books you might like:
Sarah Ash, *Tracing the Shadow*, 2008
S.L. Farrell, *A Magic of Twilight*, 2008
Raymond E. Feist, *Exile's Return*, 2004
Mercedes Lackey, *Storm Rising*, 1996
R.A. MacAvoy, *The Belly of the Wolf*, 1994

497

JENNIFER FALLON

The Immortal Prince

(New York: Tor, 2008)

Story type: Sword and Sorcery; Mystical
Series: Tide Lords. Book 1
Subject(s): Magic; Secrets
Major character(s): Arkady Desean, Scholar; Cayal, Criminal, Religious; Declan Hawkes, Government Official
Time period(s): Indeterminate
Locale(s): Alternate Universe

Summary: When a murderer miraculously survives his own execution, he declares himself to be a reincarnation of a long dead hero, returned and made immortal. Arkady Desean is a scholar who is given the job of interviewing him, presumably to prove that he is a fraud, but she begins to suspect that he may be telling the truth after all.

Other books by the same author:
Warlord, 2007
Warrior, 2006
Medalon, 2004
Treason Keep, 2004
Eye of the Labyrinth, 2002

Other books you might like:
Richard Cowper, *The Road to Corlay*, 1978
David Gemmell, *Ghost King*, 1988
L.E. Modesitt Jr., *The Spellsong War*, 1998
R.A. Salvatore, *The Highwayman*, 2004
Lawrence Watt-Evans, *Touched by the Gods*, 1997

498

S.L. FARRELL

A Magic of Twilight

(New York: DAW, 2008)

Story type: Sword and Sorcery; Magic Conflict
Series: Nessantico Cycle. Book 1
Subject(s): Magic; Politics
Major character(s): Kraljica Marguerite ca'Ludovici, Ruler; Archigos Dhosti ca'Millac, Mythical Creature (dwarf); Ana cu'Seranta, Witch
Time period(s): Indeterminate
Locale(s): Alternate Universe

Summary: Nessantico is the capital of a vast empire whose ruler is nearing the end of her life. The perceived weakness of the throne encourages various political factions, not all of them loyal, to begin maneuvering for power. A dwarf is head of the most powerful religious faction and he hopes to preserve stability through the aid of a young woman with magical powers, but she is as yet not completely committed and others attempt to manipulate her for their own purposes.

Where it's reviewed:
Library Journal, January 1, 2008, page 88

Other books by the same author:
Heir of Stone, 2005
Mage of Clouds, 2004
Holder of Lightnings, 2003

Other books you might like:
Jennifer Fallon, *The Lion of Senet*, 2002
Raymond E. Feist, *Talon of the Silver Hawk*, 2003
Barbara Hambly, *Mother of Winter*, 1996
Mercedes Lackey, *Joust*, 2003
George R.R. Martin, *A Game of Thrones*, 1996

499

ERIC FLINT , Editor
MIKE RESNICK , Co-Editor

The Dragon Done It

(New York: Baen, 2008)

Story type: Anthology; Mystery
Subject(s): Short Stories; Mystery and Detective Stories

Summary: Most of the 19 stories in this anthology have been previously published. Each is cast in the form of a detective story but with elements of magic, either in this world or in one entirely imaginary. The contributors include Mike Resnick, Tanya Huff, Harry Turtledove, Gene Wolfe, and many others.

Other books by the same author:
1633, 2002
Forward the Mage, 2002 (Richard Roach, co-author)
The Philosophical Strangler, 2001
1632, 2000
Mother of Demons, 1997

Other books you might like:
Jim Butcher, *Fool Moon*, 2001
Esther Friesner, *Druid's Blood*, 1988
Daniel Hood, *Beggar's Banquet*, 1997
Mike Resnick, *Stalking the Unicorn*, 1987
Michelle Sagara, *Cast in Shadow*, 2005

500

YASMINE GALENORN

Darkling

(New York: Berkley, 2008)

Story type: Urban; Contemporary
Series: D'Artigo Sisters. Book 3
Subject(s): Magic; Secrets
Major character(s): Camille D'Artigo, Witch; Delilah D'Artigo, Mythical Creature (shapechanger); Menolly D'Artigo, Entertainer, Vampire
Time period(s): 2000s
Locale(s): Seattle, Washington

Summary: Three sisters with varying magical abilities investigate when someone begins preying on humans in Seattle, turning them into vampires. Clearly there is a rogue vampire abroad who doesn't conform to the rules regarding human victims, and it's up to them to find him and stop him. To do that, they will have to visit the Otherworld where magic rules.

Where it's reviewed:
Booklist, December 15, 2007, page 31

Other books by the same author:
Dragon Wytch, 2008
Changeling, 2007
Witchling, 2006
A Harvest of Bones, 2005
Ghost of a Chance, 2003

Other books you might like:
Marie Brennan, *Warrior and Witch*, 2006
Glen Cook, *Whispering Nickel Idols*, 2005
Laurell K. Hamilton, *Bloody Bones*, 1995
Karen Marie Moning, *Darkfever*, 2006
Anton Strout, *Dead to Me*, 2008

501

PAUL GENESSE

The Golden Cord

(Waterville, Maine: Five Star, 2008)

Story type: Magic Conflict; Quest
Subject(s): Magic; Secrets
Major character(s): Drake Bloodstone, Warrior; Bolak

Blackhammer, Warrior; Bellor Fardelver, Religious
Time period(s): Indeterminate
Locale(s): Alternate Universe

Summary: Drake is a Guardian, charged with protecting his village from the soldiers of the Drobin Empire. When two of those soldiers appear, however, they claim not to be a threat and eventually talk Drake into acting as their guide. Only later does he discover the true purpose of their mission and the reason why they are being pursued. First novel.

Other books you might like:
Kristen Britain, *First Rider's Call*, 2003
Mercedes Lackey, *Aerie*, 2006
Anne McCaffrey, *The Skies of Pern*, 2001
L.E. Modesitt Jr., *Legacies*, 2002
Judith Tarr, *Spear of Heaven*, 1994

502

LAURA ANNE GILMAN

Free Fall

(Don Mills, Ontario: Luna, 2008)

Story type: Contemporary; Magic Conflict
Series: Wren Valere. Book 5
Subject(s): Magic
Major character(s): Wren Valere, Detective—Private; Sergei Didier, Detective—Private; Duncan, Leader
Time period(s): 2000s
Locale(s): New York, New York

Summary: Manhattan's surface life conceals a darker mystery, the existence of magical forces and supernatural creatures who lurk just out of sight of ordinary humans. Wren Valere and her partner are placed squarely in the middle of a new battle between rival factions and have to chart their own course to achieve their goals and stay alive. This time they're determined to go on the offensive against their enemies rather than simply react to their presence.

Other books by the same author:
Burning Bridges, 2007
Bring It On, 2006
Morgaine's Revenge, 2006
Curse the Dark, 2005
Staying Dead, 2004

Other books you might like:
Ilona Andrews, *Magic Burns*, 2008
Jim Butcher, *Dead Beat*, 2005
Glen Cook, *Cruel Zinc Melodies*, 2008
Talia Gryphon, *Key to Conspiracy*, 2008
C.E. Murphy, *Urban Shaman*, 2005

503

CHRISTOPHER GOLDEN
TIM LEBBON, Co-Author

Mind the Gap

(New York: Bantam, 2008)

Story type: Contemporary; Magic Conflict
Series: Hidden Cities. Book 1

Subject(s): Legends; Magic
Major character(s): Jasmine Towne, Fugitive; Harry, Orphan; Cadge, Orphan
Time period(s): 2000s
Locale(s): London, England

Summary: When her mother is murdered under mysterious circumstances, Jasmine Towne receives a message from the dead woman's spirit urging her to hide. She manages to disappear into an obscure part of London and finds that the band of orphans who take her in are in touch with a world of spirits hidden from the rest of the world.

Other books by the same author:
Borderkind, 2007
The Bones of Giants, 2004
The Boys Are Back in Town, 2004
The Gathering Dark, 2003
Dark Times, 2001

Other books you might like:
Christopher Fowler, *Darkest Day*, 1993
Simon R. Green, *The Man with the Golden Torc*, 2007
Tappan King, *Down Town*, 1985
    Viido Polikarpus, co-author
Graham Masterton, *The Doorkeepers*, 2001
China Mieville, *King Rat*, 1999

504

SIMON R. GREEN

Daemons Are Forever

(New York: Ace, 2008)

Story type: Contemporary; Magic Conflict
Series: Eddie Drood. Book 2
Subject(s): Secrets; Magic
Major character(s): Eddie Drood, Wizard; Molly Metcalf, Witch; Roger Morningstar, Mythical Creature
Time period(s): 2000s
Locale(s): London, England

Summary: Eddie Drood is a member of a family that has secretly been protecting the human race from the Loathly Ones, a kind of demon race who were invoked during World War II and refused to return to their own reality once the deal was complete. Eddie has recently been promoted to head of the family, but that doesn't mean that he isn't above criticism when the latest battle seems to be going awry.

Other books by the same author:
The Unnatural Inquirer, 2008
The Man with the Golden Torc, 2007
Sharper than a Serpent's Tooth, 2006
Paths Not Taken, 2005
Nightingale's Lament, 2004

Other books you might like:
Rachel Caine, *Ill Wind*, 2003
Katherine Kurtz, *St. Patrick's Gargoyle*, 2001
S.M. Peters, *Whitechapel Gods*, 2008
Irene Radford, *Guardian of the Balance*, 1999
F. Paul Wilson, *Nightworld*, 1992

505

SIMON R. GREEN

The Unnatural Inquirer

(New York: Ace, 2008)

Story type: Urban; Contemporary
Series: Nightside. Book 8
Subject(s): Magic; Secrets
Major character(s): John Taylor, Detective—Private; Pen Donavon, Spy; Bettie Devine, Journalist
Time period(s): 2000s
Locale(s): London, England

Summary: John Taylor is a private investigator whose turf is the Nightside, a hidden part of London where magic works and mythical creatures are real. His latest case is to track down a missing man who claims to have found absolute proof of an afterlife. Someone else is also looking for the missing man, and the other someone is powerful and nasty.

Where it's reviewed:
Booklist, February 1, 2008, page 36
Publishers Weekly, October 22, 2007, page 40

Other books by the same author:
Daemons Are Forever, 2008
Hell to Pay, 2007
Hex and the City, 2005
Nightingale's Lament, 2004
Agents of Light and Darkness, 2003

Other books you might like:
Jim Butcher, *White Night*, 2007
Glen Cook, *Old Tin Sorrows*, 1987
Mark Del Franco, *Unshapely Things*, 2007
Mike Resnick, *Stalking the Unicorn*, 1987
Anton Strout, *Dead to Me*, 2008

506

MARTIN H. GREENBERG , Editor
KERRIE HUGHES , Co-Editor

Fellowship Fantastic

(New York: DAW, 2008)

Story type: Anthology
Subject(s): Short Stories

Summary: Drawing on the popularity of J.R.R. Tolkien, this anthology of 13 original stories takes as its theme the creation of fellowships, groups of individuals who join together for some common purpose. Most stories are primarily adventure. The contributors include Jody Lynn Nye, Alan Dean Foster, Nina Kiriki Hoffman, Alexander Potter, S. Andrew Swann, Donald Bingle, and others.

Other books by the same author:
Apprentice Fantastic, 2002
Battle Magic, 1998 (Larry Segriff, co-editor)
Elf Magic, 1997
Wizard Fantastic, 1997
After the King, 1992

Other books you might like:
Alan Dean Foster, *Chorus Skating*, 1994
Nina Kiriki Hoffman, *A Fistful of Sky*, 2002
Jody Lynn Nye, *The Grand Tour*, 2000
Clifford D. Simak, *The Fellowship of the Talisman*, 1978
S. Andrew Swann, *The Dwarves of Whiskey Island*, 2005

507

MARTIN H. GREENBERG , Editor
SARAH A. HOYT , Co-Editor

Something Magic This Way Comes
(New York: DAW, 2008)

Story type: Anthology
Subject(s): Short Stories; Magic

Summary: The various possibilities that would exist if magic were real are examined in the 20 all original stories in this anthology. The tone varies from humor to suspense and the settings range from realistic to fantastic. The contributors include Kristine Kathryn Rusch, Dave Freer, Irene Radford, Harry Turtledove, Esther Friesner, and others.

Other books by the same author:
Assassin Fantastic, 2001 (Alexander Potter, co-editor)
The Further Adventures of Xena, 2001
Merlin, 1999
Elf Fantastic, 1997
Excalibur, 1995 (Edward E. Kramer, co-editor)

Other books you might like:
Dave Freer, *A Mankind Witch*, 2005
Esther Friesner, *Child of the Eagle*, 1996
Irene Radford, *Guardian of the Freedom*, 2005
Kristine Kathryn Rusch, *Fantasy Life*, 2003
Harry Turtledove, *Advance and Retreat*, 2002

508

TALIA GRYPHON

Key to Conspiracy
(New York: Ace, 2008)

Story type: Urban; Contemporary
Series: Gillian Key. Book 2
Subject(s): Magic; Vampires
Major character(s): Gillian Key, Psychologist, Military Personnel; Dracula, Vampire; Aleksei Rachlav, Vampire
Time period(s): 2000s
Locale(s): Russia; London, England

Summary: Gillian Key is a Marine and a psychologist, the latter discipline specializing in treating nonhumans, like vampires. Her unit is mobilized and sent to Russia to help in the aftermath of an earthquake and her investigation of a child-trafficking ring lands her right in the middle of a turf war between Count Aleksei Rachlav, a

well-respected vampire, and the legendary Count Dracula.

Other books by the same author:
Key to Conflict, 2007

Other books you might like:
Marie Brennan, *Doppelganger*, 2006
Patricia Briggs, *Iron Kissed*, 2008
Mark Del Franco, *Unshapely Things*, 2007
Yasmine Galenorn, *Darkling*, 2007
Karen Marie Moning, *Darkfever*, 2006

509

DAVID GUNN

The Hidden World
(New York: Tor, 2008)

Story type: Alternate Universe; Political
Series: Miranda Popescu. Book 3
Subject(s): Alternate History
Major character(s): Miranda Popescu, Royalty (princess); Peter Gross, Nobleman; Andromeda Bailey, Mythical Creature (shapeshifter)
Time period(s): Indeterminate
Locale(s): Alternate Universe

Summary: Miranda has apparently defeated many of her enemies and has learned that she is a member of the royal family of Roumania. Unfortunately, disembodied spirits plague her and she is briefly possessed by the spirit of a megalomaniacal woman. Fortunately she still has two loyal and talented friends.

Where it's reviewed:
Locus, March 2008, page 17

Other books by the same author:
The White Tyger, 2007
The Tourmaline, 2006
A Princess of Roumania, 2005
Celestis, 1995
The Cult of Loving Kindness, 1991

Other books you might like:
Jeffrey Barlough, *Strange Cargo*, 2004
Kenneth Bulmer, *The Key to Venudine*, 1968
Alexander C. Irvine, *The Narrows*, 2005
Andre Norton, *Leopard in Exile*, 2001
    Rosemary Edghill, co-author
Roger Zelazny, *Nine Princes in Amber*, 1970

510

BARB HENDEE
J.C. HENDEE , Co-Author

Child of a Dead God
(New York: Roc, 2008)

Story type: Sword and Sorcery; Magic Conflict
Series: Noble Dead. Book 6
Subject(s): Magic; Quest

Major character(s): Leesil, Warrior, Mythical Creature (elf); Magiere, Traveler; Chap, Animal (dog)
Time period(s): Indeterminate
Locale(s): Alternate Universe

Summary: Three companions continue their quest to find a magical artifact and ensure it doesn't fall into the hands of someone who will misuse it. A prescient dream suggests it may be found in an icebound castle but there is also a hint that their troubles will become even worse once they have found what they're looking for because others, not all of them human, are searching as well.

Where it's reviewed:
Publishers Weekly, November 12, 2007, page 41

Other books by the same author:
Rebel Fay, 2007
Traitor to the Blood, 2006
Sister of the Dead, 2005
Thief of Lives, 2004
Dhampir, 2003

Other books you might like:
Steven Brust, *Dragon*, 1998
Robert E. Howard, *Conan the Conqueror*, 1950
Richard A. Knaak, *Ruby Flames*, 1999
Andrew J. Offutt, *Conan the Sorcerer*, 1978
David C. Smith, *Sorrowing Vengeance*, 1983

511

JIM C. HINES

Goblin War

(New York: Ace, 2008)

Story type: Humor; Legend
Series: Goblins. Book 3
Subject(s): Humor; Magic
Major character(s): Jig Dragonslayer, Mythical Creature (goblin); Tymalous Shadowstar, Deity; Relka, Mythical Creature (goblin)
Time period(s): Indeterminate
Locale(s): Alternate Universe

Summary: Jig the goblin has had more than his share of adventures and just wants some peace and quiet, but such is not to be. For one thing, there is a small army of humans that have invaded the land of the goblins searching for a magical artifact. For another, there's the small matter of a forgotten god who wants to be remembered.

Where it's reviewed:
Publishers Weekly, January 7, 2008, page 41

Other books by the same author:
Goblin Hero, 2007
Goblin Quest, 2004

Other books you might like:
Piers Anthony, *Ogre, Ogre*, 1982
John DeChancie, *Castle Spellbound*, 1992
Andrew Harman, *The Sorcerer's Appendix*, 1993
Carl Miller, *The Goblin Plain War*, 1991
Stan Nicholls, *Bodyguard of Lightning*, 1998

512

SARAH A. HOYT

The Heart of Light

(New York: Bantam, 2008)

Story type: Historical/Exotic; Alternate World
Subject(s): Historical; Magic
Major character(s): Nigel Oldhall, Spy; Emily Oldhall, Tourist; Nassira, Rebel
Time period(s): 1880s (1889)
Locale(s): Egypt; Alternate Universe

Summary: The Oldhalls are spending their honeymoon in Cairo, but for Nigel there is a deeper purpose. He is searching for a magical artifact that could determine whether or not North Africa remains part of the British Empire. His clash with rebels seeking the same object puts his wife in jeopardy, as well as the future of British rule.

Where it's reviewed:
Locus, February 2008, page 25

Other books by the same author:
Draw One in the Dark, 2006
Any Man So Daring, 2003
All Night Awake, 2002
Crawling between Heaven and Earth, 2002
Ill Met by Moonlight, 2001

Other books you might like:
Jonathan Barnes, *The Somnambulist*, 2007
Gordon Dahlquist, *The Glass Books of the Dream Eaters*, 2006
Esther Friesner, *Druid's Blood*, 1988
Jane Lindskold, *The Buried Pyramid*, 2004
Ian R. MacLeod, *The Light Ages*, 2003

513

JAIDA JONES
DANIELLE BENNETT , Co-Author

Havemercy

(New York: Bantam, 2008)

Story type: Sword and Sorcery; Magic Conflict
Subject(s): Magic; Quest
Major character(s): Margrave Royston, Magician; Thom, Student; Rook, Teenager
Time period(s): Indeterminate
Locale(s): Alternate Universe

Summary: Two nations are engaged in a war fought by means of magic and gigantic mechanical dragons. Just as it appears that Volstov is about to defeat its enemy, a scandal threatens to undermine their efforts. Four unlikely heroes must work together to prevent a disaster and restore the honor of a disgraced magician. First novel.

Other books you might like:
Ian R. MacLeod, *The Light Ages*, 2003
China Mieville, *Iron Council*, 2004
Naomi Novik, *Victory of Eagles*, 2008
Michael Swanwick, *The Dragons of Babel*, 2008
Harry Turtledove, *Into the Darkness*, 1999

Fantasy

514

DAVID KECK

In a Time of Treason
(New York: Tor, 2008)

Story type: Sword and Sorcery; Magic Conflict
Series: Durand Col. Book 2
Subject(s): Magic; War
Major character(s): Durand Col, Military Personnel; Lamoric, Nobleman; Deorwen, Noblewoman
Time period(s): Indeterminate
Locale(s): Alternate Universe

Summary: Durand Col has fought in the war but now that it appears to be over, he finds himself at loose ends and with little money in his pocket. He is also romantically drawn to his liege lord's wife. The peace doesn't last, however, as factions among the nobles rebel and outsiders invade, hoping to find disorganized resistance and an easy victory.

Where it's reviewed:
Booklist, February 1, 2008, page 36
Publishers Weekly, December 3, 2007, page 54

Other books by the same author:
In the Eye of Heaven, 2006

Other books you might like:
Jacqueline Carey, *Kushiel's Justice*, 2007
David B. Coe, *Bonds of Vengeance*, 2004
Steven Erikson, *The Bonehunters*, 2007
David Gemmell, *Ghost King*, 1988
R.A. Salvatore, *Ascendance*, 2001

515

KATHARINE KERR

The Shadow Isle
(New York: DAW, 2008)

Story type: Sword and Sorcery; Magic Conflict
Series: Silver Wyrm. Book 3
Subject(s): Secrets; Magic
Major character(s): Dallandra, Sorceress; Laz, Fugitive; Angmar, Healer
Time period(s): Indeterminate
Locale(s): Alternate Universe

Summary: The northern regions of the world are in danger of falling to a barbaric conqueror. The dwarves attempt to maintain control but their reign seems doomed to fail unless two powerful magicians and a pair of dragons can be induced to intercede on their behalf. Even if they do, the outcome remains uncertain and will not be resolved until the next and concluding volume in the series.

Other books by the same author:
The Spirit Stone, 2007
The Gold Falcon, 2006
The Fire Dragon, 2001
The Black Raven, 1998
Daggerspell, 1986

Other books you might like:
Kate Elliott, *Prince of Dogs*, 1998
Jennifer Fallon, *Warlord*, 2007
David Gemmell, *Ravenheart*, 2001
Ed Greenwood, *The Kingless Land*, 2000
Mercedes Lackey, *Magic's Price*, 1990

516

GREG KEYES

The Born Queen
(New York: Del Rey, 2008)

Story type: Sword and Sorcery; Magic Conflict
Series: Kingdoms of Thorn and Bone. Book 4
Subject(s): Magic; Secrets
Major character(s): Aspar White, Warrior; Anne Dare, Ruler; Marche Hespero, Leader
Time period(s): Indeterminate
Locale(s): Alternate Universe

Summary: The death of the Briar King has led to a general decline in the world. Although the rightful queen is now on the throne, the church has been subverted by a corrupt man who initiates a holy war to remove her. At the same time, an alliance of evil wizards plots to seize power for themselves. Concluding volume in the series.

Other books by the same author:
The Blood Knight, 2006
The Charnel Prince, 2004
The Briar King, 2003
The Shadows of God, 2001
Empire of Unreason, 2000

Other books you might like:
Jennifer Fallon, *The Immortal Prince*, 2008
Elizabeth Haydon, *The Assassin King*, 2006
Dennis L. McKiernan, *The Dark Tide*, 1984
Jennifer Roberson, *Karavans*, 2006
Tad Williams, *The Dragonbone Chair*, 1988

517

NICK KYME

Oathbreaker
(Nottingham, United Kingdom: Black Library, 2008)

Story type: Sword and Sorcery; Magic Conflict
Series: Warhammer
Subject(s): Quest; Magic
Major character(s): Thane Uthor, Mythical Creature (dwarf), Warrior; Gromrund, Mythical Creature (dwarf), Warrior; Halgar, Mythical Creature (dwarf), Warrior
Time period(s): Indeterminate
Locale(s): Alternate Universe

Summary: One of the strongholds of the dwarves has been overrun by their enemies, the rat men. A dwarvish warrior vows to retake the keep, which proves to be even more difficult than expected. He recruits a number of heroic allies, but they are divided in their opinion of

how to set about their quest.

Other books by the same author:
Back from the Dead, 2006

Other books you might like:
Ben Counter, *Crimson Tears*, 2005
Nathan Long, *Manslayer*, 2007
Sandy Mitchell, *Death's Legacy*, 2006
Aaron Rosenberg, *Night of the Daemon*, 2007
Steven Savile, *Dominion*, 2006

518

JAY LAKE

Escapement

(New York: Tor, 2008)

Story type: Alternate World; Coming-of-Age
Series: Clockwork Earth. Book 2
Subject(s): Magic; Coming-of-Age
Major character(s): Paolina Barthes, Genius; Threadgill Angus al-Wazir, Sailor; Childress, Librarian
Time period(s): Indeterminate
Locale(s): Alternate Universe

Summary: The world in this sequel to *Mainspring* strongly resembles the Earth in Victorian times, but the world is actually run by a gigantic clockwork mechanism. Paolina is a young genius who leaves the remote island where she has been raised to explore the greater world beyond. Her magical talents, however, make her the focus of a dangerous power struggle.

Where it's reviewed:
Publishers Weekly, April 28, 2008, page 117

Other books by the same author:
Mainspring, 2007
Rocket Science, 2005
Dogs in the Moonlight, 2004

Other books you might like:
James P. Blaylock, *Lord Kelvin's Machine*, 1992
Paul Di Filippo, *The Steampunk Trilogy*, 1994
Mary Gentle, *Rats and Gargoyles*, 1990
China Mieville, *Perdido Street Station*, 2001
S.M. Peters, *Whitechapel Gods*, 2008

519

TIM LEBBON

Fallen

(New York: Bantam, 2008)

Story type: Sword and Sorcery; Magic Conflict
Series: Noreela. Book 3
Subject(s): Magic; Secrets
Major character(s): Nomi Hyden, Traveler; Ramus Rheel, Traveler; Beko Havison, Military Personnel
Time period(s): Indeterminate
Locale(s): Alternate Universe

Summary: The borders of a fantasy world are defined by magnificent cliffs believed to be the edge of the world because no one who has climbed them has ever returned. Then someone does return, bearing knowledge that will send two people on an arduous quest to avoid an unprecedented change that will affect every living being.

Other books by the same author:
Dawn, 2007
Dusk, 2006
Unnatural Selection, 2006
Berserk, 2004
Desolation, 2004

Other books you might like:
James Barclay, *Dawnthief*, 1999
David Gemmell, *Legend*, 1984
China Mieville, *The Scar*, 2002
Andre Norton, *The Warding of Witch World*, 1996
Tad Williams, *The Dragonbone Chair*, 1988

520

JESS LEBOW

Obsidian Ridge

(Renton, Washington: Wizards of the Coast, 2008)

Story type: Sword and Sorcery; Quest
Series: Forgotten Realms
Subject(s): Magic; Quest
Major character(s): Jallal Tasca, Wizard; Xeries, Wizard; Korox, Ruler
Time period(s): Indeterminate
Locale(s): Alternate Universe

Summary: The wizard Xeries was thwarted once when he sought the hand of a local princess. Now he is the master of a mystical, floating mountain, and upon returning he demands the surrender of the kingdom. The local wizards and soldiers must find a way to defeat an enemy who is literally out of their reach.

Other books by the same author:
Master of Chains, 2005
Darksteel Eye, 2004
Wind of War, 2002

Other books you might like:
Richard Lee Byers, *Unclean*, 2007
Douglas Clark, *Saving Solace*, 2006
Jeff Crook, *Dark Thane*, 2003
Richard A. Knaak, *The Black Talon*, 2008
Douglas Niles, *Winterheim*, 2003

521

HOLLY LISLE

Hawkspar

(New York: Tor, 2008)

Story type: Sword and Sorcery; Magic Conflict
Series: Korre. Book 2
Subject(s): Magic; Slavery
Major character(s): Hawkspar, Psychic; Aaran, Slave; Redbird, Slave

Time period(s): Indeterminate
Locale(s): Alternate Universe

Summary: Several women are taken as slaves to a group administering an oracle, the most powerful member of whom is Hawkspar, a woman who can separate the strands of the future and make accurate predictions. As Hawkspar nears the end of her reign, one of the other slaves is chosen as her most likely successor, but Hawkspar's visions have shown her things about the people who run the oracle, and she is determined to bring an end to their evil.

Where it's reviewed:
Publishers Weekly, April 14, 2008, page 42

Other books by the same author:
The Ruby Key, 2008
Talyn, 2005
Gods Old and Dark, 2004
The Wreck of Heaven, 2003
Memory of Fire, 2002

Other books you might like:
Lynn Abbey, *The Black Flame*, 1980
Hugh Cook, *The Oracle*, 1989
Troy Denning, *The Obsidian Oracle*, 1993
Lynn Flewelling, *The Oracle's Queen*, 2006
Lawrence Watt-Evans, *Dragon Weather*, 1999

522

HOLLY LISLE

The Ruby Key

(New York: Orchard, 2008)

Story type: Young Adult; Magic Conflict
Series: Moon and Sun. Book 1
Subject(s): Magic
Major character(s): Gennadara Yihannisdattar, Child; Danrith Caerrson, Child; Letrin, Ruler
Time period(s): Indeterminate
Locale(s): Alternate Universe

Summary: Genna and Dan are brother and sister, two children in a village in another reality where the forest is home to a mysterious race known as the nightlings. One day they encounter a slave of the nightlings who warns them that the leader of their village has made a secret deal with the nightling ruler. The opening volume of the series ends with their embarkation on a quest to find the secret to defeat King Letrin.

Other books by the same author:
Hawkstar, 2008
Talyn, 2005
Gods Old and Dark, 2004
Memory of Fire, 2002
Courage of Falcons, 2000

Other books you might like:
Craig Shaw Gardner, *Dragon Sleeping*, 1994
Alan Garner, *The Moon of Gomrath*, 1963
William Nicholson, *Noman*, 2008
Garth Nix, *Sabriel*, 1995
Andre Norton, *Warlock of the Witch World*, 1967

523

DENISE LITTLE , Editor

Mystery Date

(New York: DAW, 2008)

Story type: Anthology
Subject(s): Short Stories; Dating (Social Customs)

Summary: Fantasy and romance are blended in this anthology of 17 all new stories about humans who choose to accept a date with creatures that aren't quite human, like fairies and other mythological creatures. The contributors include Kristine Kathryn Rusch, Jean Rabe, Laura Resnick, Diane Duane, Nancy Springer, and others.

Other books by the same author:
The Magic Shop, 2004
Familiars, 2002
A Constellation of Cats, 2001
Creature Fantastic, 2001
Dangerous Magic, 1999

Other books you might like:
Diane Duane, *Stealing the Elf-King's Roses*, 2002
Jean Rabe, *The Finest Challenge*, 2006
Laura Resnick, *Disappearing Nightly*, 2005
Kristine Kathryn Rusch, *The Black Queen*, 1999
Nancy Springer, *Larque on the Wing*, 1994

524

GEORGE MANN , Editor

The Solaris Book of New Fantasy

(Nottingham, United Kingdom: Solaris, 2008)

Story type: Anthology
Subject(s): Short Stories

Summary: This is the first in a projected series of all original anthologies, collecting 16 stories of the fantastic. There is no unifying theme, so the stories vary widely in setting, tone, and subject matter. The contributors include Janny Wurts, T.A. Pratt, Lucius Shepard, Chris Roberson, Jay Lake, and others.

Where it's reviewed:
The Guardian, January 12, 2008, page 17

Other books by the same author:
Child of Time, 2007
The Solaris Book of New Science Fiction, 2007
The Human Abstract, 2004
The Severed Man, 2004

Other books you might like:
Jay Lake, *Dogs in the Moonlight*, 2004
T.A. Pratt, *Blood Engines*, 2007
Chris Roberson, *Set the Seas on Fire*, 2007
Lucius Shepard, *Softspoken*, 2007
Janny Wurts, *To Ride Hell's Chasm*, 2002

525

GAIL Z. MARTIN

The Blood King

(Nottingham, United Kingdom: Solaris, 2008)

Story type: Sword and Sorcery; Magic Conflict
Series: Chronicles of the Necromancer. Book 2
Subject(s): Magic; Secrets
Major character(s): Martris Drayke, Nobleman; Jared Drayke, Nobleman; Foor Arontala, Wizard
Time period(s): Indeterminate
Locale(s): Alternate Universe

Summary: The rightful heir to the throne has been driven into hiding, barely escaping with his life. In order to drive off the usurper, he attempts to raise an army of the dead. There is also a third party confusing matters, an evil sorcerer who hopes to take advantage of the conflict to improve his own position.

Other books by the same author:
The Summoner, 2007

Other books you might like:
Jennifer Fallon, *Harshini*, 2005
Barbara Hambly, *The Armies of Daylight*, 1983
George R.R. Martin, *A Game of Thrones*, 1996
R.A. Salvatore, *The Ancient*, 2008
Sarah Zettel, *Sword of the Deceiver*, 2006

526

MISTY MASSEY

Mad Kestrel

(New York: Tor, 2008)

Story type: Magic Conflict; Coming-of-Age
Subject(s): Magic; Coming-of-Age
Major character(s): Kestrel, Sailor; Artemus Binns, Sea Captain; Jeremie, Royalty (prince)
Time period(s): Indeterminate
Locale(s): Alternate Universe

Summary: Kestrel is born in a land where infants with magical powers are taken from their family and raised by a group of sorcerers. She escapes this fate and works as a sailor, concealing the fact that she can magically control the wind until the day that her captain is falsely arrested as a pirate. She sets out to rescue him, and learns how powerful her talent really is. First novel.

Where it's reviewed:
Booklist, March 1, 2008, page 57
Publishers Weekly, January 14, 2008, page 44

Other books you might like:
Lynn Abbey, *The Forge of Virtue*, 1991
Allan Cole, *The Far Kingdoms*, 1993
    Chris Bunch, co-author
Robin Hobb, *Mad Ship*, 1999
China Mieville, *The Scar*, 2002
Robert V.S. Redick, *The Red Wolf Conspiracy*, 2008

527

KELLY MCCULLOUGH

CodeSpell

(New York: Ace, 2008)

Story type: Contemporary; Magic Conflict
Series: Ravirn. Book 3
Subject(s): Magic; Humor
Major character(s): Ravirn, Sorcerer, Computer Expert; Melchior, Mythical Creature; Zeus, Deity
Time period(s): 21st century
Locale(s): Alternate Universe

Summary: Ravirn is a sorcerer and computer programmer whose previous adventures have gotten him an introduction to Zeus and other creatures of the multiverse, a magical version of reality in which an intelligent computer operates everything. When a virus infects the computer, it's up to Ravirn to straighten things out before all of the magical universe crashes.

Other books by the same author:
Cybermancy, 2007
WebMage, 2006

Other books you might like:
Piers Anthony, *Blue Adept*, 1981
Jim Butcher, *Small Favor*, 2008
John DeChancie, *MagicNet*, 1993
Esther Friesner, *New York by Knight*, 1986
Christopher Stasheff, *The Warlock Enraged*, 1985

528

SEAN MCMULLEN

The Time Engine

(New York: Tor, 2008)

Story type: Sword and Sorcery; Time Travel
Series: Moonworlds Saga. Book 4
Subject(s): Time Travel
Major character(s): Danolarian, Police Officer, Time Traveler; Wallas, Time Traveler, Mythical Creature (shapeshifter); Riellen, Police Officer
Time period(s): Indeterminate Future; Indeterminate Past
Locale(s): Earth

Summary: Danolarian's predictable life is altered when he is abducted into the distant future along with a fellow inspector who has been magically changed into a cat. He finds a way to travel back in time but through a defect in the time machine, he ends up marooned in pre-historic times, and further attempts lead him to believe that it is not time travel he is experiencing after all.

Other books by the same author:
Voidfarer, 2005
Glass Dragons, 2004
Voyage of the Shadowmoon, 2002
Eye of the Calculor, 2001
The Miocene Arrow, 2000

Fantasy

Other books you might like:
Poul Anderson, *A Midsummer Tempest*, 1974
Piers Anthony, *Bearing an Hourglass*, 1984
Louise Cooper, *The Initiate*, 1985
Andre Norton, *Wraiths of Time*, 1976
Richard Powers, *The Anubis Gates*, 1983

529

L.E. MODESITT JR.

Mage-Guard of Honor

(New York: Tor, 2008)

Story type: Sword and Sorcery; Magic Conflict
Series: Recluce. Book 15
Subject(s): Magic; Coming-of-Age
Major character(s): Rahl, Apprentice, Sorcerer; Taryl, Diplomat; Drakeyt, Military Personnel
Time period(s): Indeterminate
Locale(s): Alternate Universe

Summary: Rahl was sent away to Hamor after he got into too much trouble serving as an apprentice sorcerer. Although he is potentially very powerful, he has a tendency to get himself into trouble and as his abilities grow stronger, so does his habit of getting into difficulties, in this case a mission to a foreign country and associated intrigues.

Other books by the same author:
Viewpoints Critical, 2008
Natural Ordermage, 2007
Soarer's Choice, 2006
Ordermaster, 2005
Wellsprings of Chaos, 2004

Other books you might like:
Dave Duncan, *The Cutting Edge*, 1992
Jennifer Fallon, *Lord of the Shadows*, 2002
John Marco, *The Devil's Armor*, 2003
Midori Snyder, *New Moon*, 1989
Lawrence Watt-Evans, *The Wizard Lord*, 2006

530

MICHAEL MOORCOCK

Elric: The Stealer of Souls

(New York: Del Rey, 2008)

Story type: Sword and Sorcery; Collection
Subject(s): Short Stories
Major character(s): Elric, Warrior

Summary: This is the first volume in a new compilation of the stories of Elric of Melnibone, an albino warrior with a magical sword that drinks the souls of those it kills and at times dominates Elric, These are the earliest of his adventures including classics like the title story and "The Dreaming City."

Other books by the same author:
The Skrayling Tree, 2003
The Dreamthief's Daughter, 2001
Count Brass, 1998
Fabulous Harbors, 1995
Blood, 1994

Other books you might like:
David Gemmell, *Bloodstone*, 1994
Fritz Leiber, *The Second Book of Lankhmar*, 2001
Andrew J. Offutt, *Deathknight*, 1990
David C. Smith, *The Ghost Army*, 1983
Karl Edward Wagner, *The Road of Kings*, 1979

531

MOIRA J. MOORE

Heroes Adrift

(New York: Ace, 2008)

Story type: Sword and Sorcery; Magic Conflict
Series: Source and Shield. Book 3
Subject(s): Magic; Quest
Major character(s): Lee Mallorough, Spy; Shintaro Karish, Spy; Aryne, Noblewoman
Time period(s): Indeterminate
Locale(s): Alternate Universe

Summary: Two adventurers are sent on a mission by their ruler into a distant land to track down a missing branch of the family, one of whom might be the heir to the throne. They have various adventures before finally discovering a young woman who appears to be the one they are seeking, but getting her back to their homeland is another matter altogether.

Other books by the same author:
Resenting the Hero, 2006
The Hero Strikes Back, 2006

Other books you might like:
Dave Duncan, *Impossible Odds*, 2003
Simon R. Green, *Blue Moon Rising*, 1991
Gayle Greeno, *Sunderlies Seeking*, 1998
Fritz Leiber, *Swords Against Wizardry*, 1968
Jennifer Roberson, *Karavans*, 2006

532

C.E. MURPHY

The Queen's Bastard

(New York: Del Rey, 2008)

Story type: Historical/Elizabethan; Magic Conflict
Subject(s): Historical; Magic
Major character(s): Belinda Primrose, Bastard Daughter, Spy; Lorraine, Ruler (queen); Javier, Royalty (prince)
Time period(s): 16th century
Locale(s): Alternate Earth

Summary: The setting is an alternate version of Elizabethan Europe. Queen Lorraine rules Aulun but her grip is not always a firm one. She manipulates things behind

the scenes by means of her illegitimate daughter, Belinda, a talented spy and assassin. Belinda discovers that she has a talent for magic, and an attraction for the charming but mysterious Prince Javier.

Where it's reviewed:
Publishers Weekly, February 25, 2008, page 57

Other books by the same author:
Hands of Flame, 2008
House of Cards, 2008
Coyote Dreams, 2007
Heart of Stone, 2007
Thunderbird Falls, 2006

Other books you might like:
Lynn Abbey, *Unicorn and Dragon*, 1987
Gael Baudino, *The Dove Looked In*, 1996
Sara Douglass, *Gods' Concubine*, 2004
Mercedes Lackey, *This Scepter'd Isle*, 2004
    Roberta Gellis, co-author
Judith Tarr, *Pride of Kings*, 2001

533

WILLIAM NICHOLSON

Noman

(New York: Harcourt, 2008)

Story type: Quest
Series: Noble Warriors. Book 3
Subject(s): Magic
Major character(s): Seeker After Truth, Teenager, Student; Morning Star, Teenager; Wildman, Teenager
Time period(s): Indeterminate
Locale(s): Alternate Universe

Summary: Seeker After Truth and his two companions are at loose ends when their training school for Noble Warriors is closed and the students dispersed. Then a new figure appears preaching a different philosophy, and old friendships and loyalties are called into question. Is the newcomer trustworthy, or is everything they have been taught a lie?

Other books by the same author:
Jango, 2007
Seeker, 2006
Firesong, 2003
Slaves of the Mastery, 2001
The Wind Singer, 2000

Other books you might like:
Diana Wynne Jones, *The Crown of Dalemark*, 2003
Ursula K. Le Guin, *Gifts*, 2004
Andre Norton, *Sorceress of the Witch World*, 1968
Lawrence Watt-Evans, *Dragon Weather*, 1999
Mary Frances Zambreno, *A Plague of Sorcerers*, 1991

534

ANDRE NORTON
JEAN RABE , Co-Author

Dragon Mage

(New York: Tor, 2008)

Story type: Young Adult; Time Travel
Subject(s): Magic
Major character(s): Shiloh, Teenager, Time Traveler; Nid-intulugal, Traveler; Arshaka, Magician
Time period(s): Indeterminate Past
Locale(s): Babylon

Summary: Shiloh is a teenager who hears a strange voice calling from the attic. Her investigation results in her being transported back through time to ancient Babylon, a Babylon where magic works and demons are real. There she discovers that she has been cast in the role of heroic savior of the world, destined to battle an evil sorcerer. This is a sequel to Andre Norton's *Dragon Magic*.

Where it's reviewed:
Library Journal, January 1, 2008, page 98

Other books by the same author:
Three Hands for Scorpio, 2005
Scent of Magic, 1998
The Warding of Witch World, 1996
The Hands of Llyr, 1994
Quag Keep, 1978

Other books you might like:
Lloyd Alexander, *The Book of Three*, 1964
Susan Cooper, *Over Sea, Under Stone*, 1965
Alan Garner, *The Weirdstone of Brisingamen*, 1960
William Nicholson, *Seeker*, 2006
Jane Yolen, *The Wild Hunt*, 1995

535

NAOMI NOVIK

Victory of Eagles

(New York: Del Rey, 2008)

Story type: Historical/Napoleonic Wars; Magic Conflict
Series: Temeraire. Book 5
Subject(s): Historical; Magic; Dragons
Major character(s): Temeraire, Mythical Creature (dragon); Will Laurence, Military Personnel; Napoleon Bonaparte, Ruler, Historical Figure
Time period(s): 19th century
Locale(s): England

Summary: In a magical version of the Napoleonic Wars, the French army has invaded the British Isles. Will Laurence has been disgraced and imprisoned, but happenstance leads to his freedom and an attempt to reunite with his dragon partner, Temeraire, so that they can rally the resistance.

Other books by the same author:
Empire of Ivory, 2007
Black Powder War, 2006
Throne of Jade, 2006
His Majesty's Dragon, 2006

Other books you might like:
Sara Douglass, *Druid's Sword*, 2006
Alexander C. Irvine, *The Narrows*, 2005
J. Gregory Keyes, *A Calculus of Angels*, 1999
Mercedes Lackey, *This Scepter'd Isle*, 2004
    Roberta Gellis, co-author
Dean Wesley Smith, *All Eve's Hallows*, 2005

536

ROBIN D. OWENS

Keepers of the Flame

(Don Mills, Ontario: Luna, 2008)

Story type: Romance
Series: Lladrana. Book 4
Subject(s): Romance
Major character(s): Brigid Drystan, Healer; Elizabeth
    Drystan, Doctor; Sevair Masif, Nobleman
Time period(s): 2000s
Locale(s): Alternate Universe

Summary: The sorcerers of a magical other world summon two sisters from this world to help them in their
battle against a magical evil force that threatens their
world. Both sisters have the power to heal, but while
one acknowledges that it is an innate ability, the other
has rationalized it and become a doctor. Together they
overcome a plague sent to weaken the defenders, and
find romance with the mysterious men of this other
reality.

Where it's reviewed:
Publishers Weekly, November 26, 2007, page 34

Other books by the same author:
Heart Dance, 2007
Protector of the Flight, 2007
Heart Quest, 2006
Sorceress of Faith, 2006
Guardian of Honor, 2005

Other books you might like:
Robin Wayne Bailey, *Brothers of the Dragon*, 1992
Caitlin Brennan, *Shattered Dance*, 2006
Craig Shaw Gardner, *Dragon Sleeping*, 1994
Michele Hauf, *Rhiana*, 2006
Mickey Zucker Reichert, *The Beasts of Barakhai*, 2001

537

JOSHUA PALMATIER

The Vacant Throne

(New York: DAW, 2008)

Story type: Sword and Sorcery; Magic Conflict
Series: Throne of Amenkor. Book 3
Subject(s): Magic; Disasters
Major character(s): Varis, Ruler; Eryn, Noblewoman; Sor-
    renti, Nobleman
Time period(s): Indeterminate
Locale(s): Amenkor, Alternate Universe

Summary: The city of Amenkor has survived a number of
tribulations, but its economy is suffering and the political
situation is deteriorating. The new ruler, an untrained
girl who is appointed against her will, has visions of an
even greater disaster to come. She and her mentor must
discover how to defend the city against an invasion force
despite the growing unrest among their own people.

Where it's reviewed:
Library Journal, January 1, 2008, page 89
Publishers Weekly, October 29, 2007, page 34

Other books by the same author:
The Cracked Throne, 2006
The Skewed Throne, 2006

Other books you might like:
Sara Douglass, *The Wayfarer Redemption*, 1998
Dave Duncan, *Paragon Lost*, 2002
Raymond E. Feist, *Krondor: Tear of the Gods*, 2000
David Gemmell, *Ghost King*, 1988
Paula Volsky, *The Grand Ellipse*, 2000

538

S.M. PETERS

Whitechapel Gods

(New York: Roc, 2007)

Story type: Historical/Victorian; Magic Conflict
Subject(s): Magic; Historical
Major character(s): Aaron, Rebel; Oliver, Rebel; Mama
    Engine, Deity
Time period(s): 1880s
Locale(s): London, England

Summary: A portion of London was separated from the
rest of the world in 1877 and is now ruled by two
clockwork deities. Humans have become a subject race
but many of them are organized into a resistance
movement. When conflicting loyalties arise, the stage is
set for a confrontation that could free the populace, or
destroy them utterly. First novel.

Where it's reviewed:
Library Journal, January 1, 2008, page 89

Other books you might like:
James P. Blaylock, *Homunculus*, 1986
Paul Di Filippo, *The Steampunk Trilogy*, 1994
Esther Friesner, *Druid's Blood*, 1988
K.W. Jeter, *Infernal Devices*, 1987
Michael Moorcock, *The Warlord of the Air*, 1971

539

T.A. PRATT

Poison Sleep

(New York: Bantam, 2008)

Story type: Urban; Magic Conflict
Series: Marla Mason. Book 2
Subject(s): Magic; Dreams and Nightmares
Major character(s): Marla Mason, Sorceress, Government

Official; Genevieve Kelley, Sorceress, Mentally Ill Person; Rondeau, Servant
Time period(s): Indeterminate
Locale(s): Felport, Alternate Universe

Summary: Marla Mason is the official magician of the city of Felport, and it is her job to make sure that magic is kept under control and only used in appropriate ways. When an insane sorceress escapes from an institution that specializes in treating insane magicians, Mason has an unusual and urgent challenge because the escapee's insanity begins to affect the dreams of ordinary citizens.

Where it's reviewed:
Publishers Weekly, February 4, 2008, page 43

Other books by the same author:
Blood Engines, 2007

Other books you might like:
Steven Bowkett, *Dreamcatcher*, 2000
Jonathan Carroll, *Bones of the Moon*, 1987
Charles De Lint, *Yarrow*, 1986
Andre Norton, *Perilous Dreams*, 1976
Jody Lynn Nye, *The Grand Tour*, 2000

540

KEN RAND

Pax Dakota

(Waterville, Maine: Five Star, 2008)

Story type: Alternate History; Magic Conflict
Subject(s): Magic; Alternate History
Major character(s): Etta Mae Dooley, Prostitute; Joseph Thorn, Indian; Watcher, Mythical Creature
Time period(s): 1890s (1893-1899)
Locale(s): Alternate Earth (North America)

Summary: In this alternate world fantasy, the Dakotas and their allies were able to defeat the encroachment from the east and establish their own nation in the western part of North America. The Dakota have imprisoned Old Enemy, an evil spirit, but he escapes. A troubled young man and a prostitute are caught up in the battle between Old Enemy and Watcher, a good spirit.

Other books by the same author:
Where Angels Fear, 2008
Fairy BrewHaHa at the Lucky Nickel Saloon, 2005

Other books you might like:
Charles De Lint, *The Dreaming Place*, 1990
Tom Deitz, *The Demons in the Green*, 1996
Graham Masterton, *Manitou Blood*, 2005
Martin Cruz Smith, *The Indians Won*, 1970
Craig Strete, *Death in the Spirit House*, 1988

541

ROBERT V.S. REDICK

The Red Wolf Conspiracy

(London: Gollancz, 2008)

Story type: Mystery; Magic Conflict
Subject(s): Magic; Sea Stories

Major character(s): Pazel Pathkendle, Teenager; Nilus Rose, Sea Captain; Sandor Ott, Spy
Time period(s): Indeterminate
Locale(s): Alternate Universe; At Sea

Summary: In a magical alternate world, a great ship sets sail and is never heard from again, much to the chagrin of the emperor and his court. The solution involves the very varied group of passengers aboard the ship, including a spy master, a domineering captain, a young boy laboring under a curse, and some mysterious stowaways no one quite expected. First novel.

Other books you might like:
Hannes Bok, *The Sorcerer's Ship*, 1969
Chris Bunch, *Corsair*, 2001
Allan Cole, *The Far Kingdoms*, 1993
    Chris Bunch, co-author
China Mieville, *The Scar*, 2002
Tim Powers, *On Stranger Tides*, 1987

542

JENNA RHODES

The Dark Ferryman

(New York: DAW, 2008)

Story type: Sword and Sorcery; Magic Conflict
Series: Elven Ways. Book 2
Subject(s): Magic
Major character(s): Rivergrace, Fugitive; Sevryn, Fugitive
Time period(s): Indeterminate
Locale(s): Alternate Universe

Summary: In the aftermath of a war that left the world without most of its former magic, two lovers are accused of committing treason and forced to travel separately. As each has a variety of adventures, a mysterious figure— the Dark Ferryman—intersects with both their lives, quietly promising them rewards but at an unknown price.

Where it's reviewed:
Publishers Weekly, April 28, 2008, page 116

Other books by the same author:
The Four Forges, 2006
Night of Dragons, 1990 (as R.A.V. Salsitz)
Daughter of Destiny, 1988 (as R.A.V. Salsitz)
The Unicorn Dancer, 1986 (as R.A.V. Salsitz)
Where Dragons Rule, 1986 (as R.A.V. Salsitz)

Other books you might like:
Sara Douglass, *Threshold*, 2003
Jennifer Fallon, *Treason Keep*, 2004
Barbara Hambly, *The Dark Hand of Magic*, 1990
Andre Norton, *Three Hands for Scorpio*, 2005
Jennifer Roberson, *Deepwood*, 2007

543

ADAM ROBERTS

Swiftly

(London: Gollancz, 2008)

Story type: Historical/Victorian; Light Fantasy
Subject(s): Historical; Slavery

Fantasy

Major character(s): Abraham Bates, Rebel, Businessman; Eleanor Burton, Housewife; Jonathan Burton, Businessman
Time period(s): 1840s (1848)
Locale(s): Alternate Earth (England)

Summary: In an alternate world where the travels of Lemuel Gulliver were real, a war has broken out between England and France. The French are allied with the giants of Brobdingnab and the British have enslaved the Lilliputians. The protagonist is determined to see the latter freed, but his life is complicated by his love for a married woman.

Other books by the same author:
Gradisil, 2006
The Snow, 2004
Polystom, 2003
On, 2001
Salt, 2000

Other books you might like:
James P. Blaylock, *The Digging Leviathan*, 1984
Michael Moorcock, *The Steel Tsar*, 1981
Naomi Novik, *Empire of Ivory*, 2007
Jonathan Swift, *Gulliver's Travels*, 1726
T.H. White, *Mistress Masham's Repose*, 1947

544

EMILY RODDA

The Key to Rondo

(New York: Scholastic, 2008)

Story type: Young Adult; Contemporary
Subject(s): Magic
Major character(s): Leo Zifkak, Teenager; Mimi Langlander, Teenager; Blue Queen, Sorceress
Time period(s): 2000s
Locale(s): United States

Summary: Leo inherits a magical music box from his aunt, which comes with a set of rules about how it can be used. When Mimi Langlander comes to visit Leo's family, a chain of circumstances leads to a violation of the rules and the discovery that the music box is a prison holding a sorceress known as the Blue Queen. Can they ensure that she doesn't get free to wreak havoc in the world?

Where it's reviewed:
Booklist, December 15, 2007, page 47
Bulletin of the Center for Children's Books, January 2008, page 224
Kliatt, January 28, 2008, page 12
Publishers Weekly, February 25, 2008, page 79

Other books by the same author:
The Water Sprites, 2008
Rowan and the Keeper of the Crystal, 2002
City of the Rats, 2001
Dread Mountain, 2001
The Forests of Silence, 2001

Other books you might like:
Suzy McKee Charnas, *The Bronze King*, 1985
Bruce Coville, *Jennifer Murdley's Toad*, 1992
Andre Norton, *Dragon Magic*, 1972
Vivian Vande Velde, *Now You See It*, 2004
Jane Yolen, *The Wizard of Washington Square*, 1969

545

R.A. SALVATORE

The Ancient

(New York: Tor, 2008)

Story type: Sword and Sorcery; Magic Conflict
Series: Saga of the First King. Book 1
Subject(s): Magic; Quest
Major character(s): Bransen Garibond, Warrior; Ancient Badden, Leader; Brother Cormack, Religious
Time period(s): Indeterminate
Locale(s): Alternate Universe

Summary: Bransen Garimond is searching for his missing father when he is forced to join an army battling an enemy dominated by a religious dictatorship. Much to his surprise, he finds himself in possession of information that could change the outcome of the war, and prevent a brutal tyrant from enslaving much of the world.

Where it's reviewed:
Publishers Weekly, January 28, 2008, page 46

Other books by the same author:
The Highwayman, 2007
Road of the Patriarch, 2006
The Crimson Shadow, 2006
Promise of the Witch-King, 2005
Mortalis, 2001

Other books you might like:
Steven Erikson, *Reaper's Gale*, 2008
Jennifer Fallon, *Warlord*, 2007
Maggie Furey, *Aurian*, 1994
David Gemmell, *Ironhand's Daughter*, 1995
David Zindell, *Lord of Lies*, 2008

546

MANDA SCOTT

The Crystal Skull

(New York: Delacorte, 2008)

Story type: Contemporary; Mystery
Subject(s): Secrets; Magic
Major character(s): Stella Cody, Scientist; Cedric Owen, Scholar, Doctor; Tony Bookless, Scholar
Time period(s): 16th century; 2000s (2007)
Locale(s): England

Summary: Two cave explorers discover an artifact that once belonged to Cedric Owen, a 16th century scholar. It is believed to be part of a set of items that which need to be reunited at some point in order to save the world. Their search for the others, and efforts by unknown par-

ties to interfere, alternate with flashbacks to the lifetime of Owen.

Where it's reviewed:
Library Journal, March 13, 2008, page 61
Publishers Weekly, February 25, 2008, page 52

Other books by the same author:
Dreaming the Hound, 2007
Dreaming the Serpent Spear, 2007
Boudica, 2004
Stronger than Death, 2000
Hen's Teeth, 1999

Other books you might like:
Alex Archer, *Destiny*, 2006
Clive Cussler, *Black Wind*, 2006
Douglas Preston, *The Cabinet of Curiosities*, 2002
    Lincoln Child, co-author
Mike Resnick, *The Amulet of Power*, 2004
James Rollins, *Excavation*, 2000

547

LISA SHEARIN

Armed & Magical

(New York: Ace, 2008)

Story type: Magic Conflict; Quest
Series: Raine Benares. Book 2
Subject(s): Quest; Magic
Major character(s): Raine Benares, Psychic; Mychael Eiliesor, Guard; Banan Ryce, Criminal
Time period(s): Indeterminate
Locale(s): Alternate Universe

Summary: Raine Benares just wants to learn to use magic constructively, but unfortunately her fate has become linked to that of a mystical artifact which absorbs human souls. In an attempt to regain her old life, she decides to visit a remote school of sorcery and enlist their help, but several groups want her dead for various reasons and a series of mysterious disappearances is apparently her responsibility as well.

Other books by the same author:
Magic Lost, Trouble Found, 2007

Other books you might like:
Randall Garrett, *Too Many Magicians*, 1966
Tamara Siler Jones, *Threads of Malice*, 2005
Mindy L. Klasky, *Season of Sacrifice*, 2002
Holly Lisle, *Minerva Wakes*, 1994
Martin Scott, *Thraxas and the Elvish Isles*, 2000

548

MELINDA SNODGRASS

The Edge of Reason

(New York: Tor, 2008)

Story type: Contemporary; Magic Conflict
Subject(s): Magic; Secrets

Major character(s): Richard Oort, Police Officer; Rhiana Davinovitch, Sorceress, Teenager; Kenntnis, Philanthropist
Time period(s): 2000s
Locale(s): Albuquerque, New Mexico

Summary: Police officer Richard Oort comes to the aid of a young girl when she is attacked, but is shocked to discover that her assailants are magical constructs, not human beings. She tells him that she is a sorceress and that he has just been enlisted as a soldier in a generations-long fight between organizations who use magic for good and evil purposes.

Other books by the same author:
Queen's Gambit Declined, 1989
Circuit Breaker, 1987
Final Circuit, 1987
Circuit, 1986
The Tears of the Singers, 1984

Other books you might like:
Emma Bull, *War for the Oaks*, 1987
Nancy Collins, *Sunglasses After Dark*, 1989
Graham Masterton, *Night Wars*, 2006
Garfield Reeves-Stevens, *Bloodshift*, 1981
    Judith Reeves-Stevens, co-author
Robert Shea, *The Eye in the Pyramid*, 1981
    Robert Anton Wilson, co-author

549

MARIA V. SNYDER

Fire Study

(Don Mills, Ontario: Luna, 2008)

Story type: Sword and Sorcery; Mystical
Series: Yelena. Book 3
Subject(s): Magic; Romance
Major character(s): Yelena Zaltana, Sorceress; Leif Zaltana, Warrior; Valek, Spy
Time period(s): Indeterminate
Locale(s): Alternate Universe

Summary: Yelena is already the subject of considerable debate because of the magical abilities she displayed during her previous adventures. When further information reveals that she can capture and release souls, her reputation grows more menacing despite her benevolent intentions. She hopes to retreat from public view, but an impending war makes that impossible.

Where it's reviewed:
Publishers Weekly, January 14, 2008, page 44

Other books by the same author:
Magic Study, 2006
Poison Study, 2005

Other books you might like:
Lynn Abbey, *Rifkind's Challenge*, 2006
Barbara Hambly, *The Ladies of Mandrigyn*, 1984
Mindy L. Klasky, *The Glasswright's Apprentice*, 2001
Naomi Kritzer, *Freedom's Gate*, 2004
Glenda Larke, *The Aware*, 2005

Fantasy

550

ADAM STEMPLE

Steward of Song

(New York: Tor, 2008)

Story type: Contemporary; Magic Conflict
Subject(s): Fairies; Magic
Major character(s): Douglas Stewart, Musician; Martes, Mythical Creature (fairy); Scott Stewart, Addict
Time period(s): 2000s
Locale(s): Massachusetts; Alternate Universe

Summary: Douglas Stewart went to Ireland and found a gateway to the world of fairies, where he seized power and still rules. Scott Stewart is a recovering addict who is about to discover that the world is a much stranger place than he ever suspected. This is the sequel to the author's first solo novel, *Singer of Souls*.

Where it's reviewed:
Booklist, February 15, 2008, page 32
Publishers Weekly, January 21, 2008, page 159

Other books by the same author:
Singer of Souls, 2005

Other books you might like:
Greg Bear, *The Infinity Concerto*, 1984
Emma Bull, *War for the Oaks*, 1987
Charles De Lint, *Into the Green*, 1993
Karen Marie Moning, *Darkfever*, 2006
Sarban, *Ringstones*, 1961

551

ANTON STROUT

Dead to Me

(New York: Ace, 2008)

Story type: Urban; Contemporary
Subject(s): Psychic Powers; Magic
Major character(s): Simon Canderous, Psychic; Connor Christos, Psychic; Irene, Spirit
Time period(s): 2000s
Locale(s): New York, New York

Summary: Simon Canderous used his magical talents for criminal purposes for a while, but he reformed and now works for the city. When he runs into a ghost who doesn't realize that she's dead, he decides to talk his mentor into helping him track down the people who killed her. First novel.

Other books you might like:
Karen Chance, *Claimed by Shadow*, 2007
Mark Del Franco, *Unquiet Dreams*, 2008
Yasmine Galenorn, *Darkling*, 2008
Kat Richardson, *Greywalker*, 2006
Rob Thurman, *Nightlife*, 2006

552

JUDITH TARR

Bring Down the Sun

(New York: Tor, 2008)

Story type: Historical/Ancient Greece; Magic Conflict
Subject(s): Historical; Magic
Major character(s): Olympias, Religious, Historical Figure; Nikandra, Worker; Myrtale, Noblewoman
Time period(s): 3rd century B.C.
Locale(s): Greece; Macedonia

Summary: This is a story of the mother of Alexander the Great, in the time before she met Philip of Macedon. Olympias is a priestess and a practitioner of magic, a person who can speak to the gods and receive replies. Her powers make her both respected and feared by the people of ancient Greece.

Where it's reviewed:
Publishers Weekly, April 7, 2008, page 46

Other books by the same author:
King's Blood, 2005
Avaryan Resplendent, 2003
House of War, 2003
Devil's Bargain, 2002
Daughter of Lir, 2001

Other books you might like:
Michael Ayrton, *The Maze Maker*, 1967
Roberta Cray, *The Sword and the Lion*, 1993
Rebecca Gellis, *Bull God*, 2000
David Gemmell, *Lord of the Silver Bow*, 2005
Thomas Harlan, *The Shadow of Ararat*, 1999

553

G.P. TAYLOR

Mariah Mundi: The Midas Box

(New York: Putnam, 2008)

Story type: Young Adult; Mystery
Subject(s): Magic
Major character(s): Mariah Mundi, Teenager, Assistant; Monica Luger, Entertainer; Isambard Black, Magician
Time period(s): Indeterminate
Locale(s): England

Summary: Mariah Mundi travels to the Prince Regent hotel to work as an assistant to a magician. He learns almost immediately that all of the previous assistants disappeared under mysterious circumstances, and he is determined not to follow in their paths. Something strange is happening at the hotel, something that twists time itself.

Other books by the same author:
The Curse of Salamander Street, 2007
The Tizzle Sisters & Erik, 2007
Sin, Salvation, and Shadowmancer, 2006
Wormwood, 2005
Shadowmancer, 2004

Other books you might like:
John Bellairs, *House with a Clock in Its Walls*, 1973
Diana Wynne Jones, *Archer's Goon*, 1984
Kai Meyer, *The Water Mirror*, 2005
Brad Strickland, *The Doom of the Haunted Opera*, 1995
    John Bellairs, co-author
Jane Yolen, *The Wizard's Map*, 1999

554

ROB THURMAN

Madhouse

(New York: Roc, 2008)

Story type: Urban; Mystery
Series: Cal Leandros. Book 3
Subject(s): Magic; Secrets
Major character(s): Cal Leandros, Detective—Private;
    Niko Leandros, Detective—Private; Rob Fellows,
    Salesman
Time period(s): 2000s
Locale(s): New York, New York

Summary: Cal and Niko Leandros run a detective agency
in New York City that specializes in paranormal and
supernatural cases. Unfortunately, their business has been
down and they are getting desperate for a job when a
new player enters the game. An ancient evil creature has
come to the city and humans are dying on every side.
Will they foil the villain's plot, or become its next
victims?

Other books by the same author:
Moonshine, 2007
Nightlife, 2006

Other books you might like:
Marie Brennan, *Doppelganger*, 2006
Mark Del Franco, *Unquiet Dreams*, 2008
Yasmine Galenorn, *Changeling*, 2007
Simon R. Green, *Hell to Pay*, 2007
Kat Richardson, *Poltergeist*, 2007

555

EDO VAN BELKOM

Battle Dragon

(Waterville, Maine: Five Star, 2008)

Story type: Historical/World War II; Military
Subject(s): Historical; Magic
Major character(s): Sheridan Ballard, Military Personnel;
    Tibalt, Mythical Creature (dragon); Asvald, Wizard
Time period(s): 1940s (1940)
Locale(s): England

Summary: In ancient times, a wizard saved a village by
sending a dragon forward through time. It reappears in
1940 during the German blitz and begins preying on
British aircraft. Although the authorities don't understand
what's happening, they think it is a German
superweapon. Fortunately, the wizard remains alive and
perhaps can exile the dragon once again.

Other books by the same author:
Scream Queen, 2003
Martyrs, 2001
Teeth, 2001
Death Drives a Semi, 2000
Lord Soth, 1996

Other books you might like:
David Bishop, *Twilight of the Dead*, 2006
Kim Newman, *The Bloody Red Baron*, 1995
Naomi Novik, *His Majesty's Dragon*, 2006
Adam Roberts, *Swiftly*, 2008
Harry Turtledove, *Into the Darkness*, 1999

556

ELIZABETH VAUGHAN

Dagger-Star

(New York: Berkley, 2008)

Story type: Sword and Sorcery; Magic Conflict
Subject(s): Magic; Romance
Major character(s): Red Gloves, Warrior, Mercenary; Jo-
    siah, Warrior; Gloriana, Noblewoman
Time period(s): Indeterminate
Locale(s): Alternate Universe

Summary: The woman known only as Red Gloves works
as a mercenary in a barbaric land where magic works
and where a usurper sits on the throne. The disillusioned
warrior Josiah gets fresh hope when he recognizes a
peculiar birthmark on her body that suggests she has
come to fulfill a prophecy and restore the rightful ruler
to the throne.

Other books by the same author:
Warlord, 2007
Warsworn, 2006
Warprize, 2005

Other books you might like:
Lynn Abbey, *Rifkind's Challenge*, 2006
Sara Douglass, *Enchanter*, 2001
Jennifer Fallon, *Medalon*, 2004
David Gemmell, *The King Beyond the Gate*, 1985
Juliet Marillier, *Blade of Fortriu*, 2006

557

LAWRENCE WATT-EVANS

The Summer Palace

(New York: Tor, 2008)

Story type: Sword and Sorcery; Magic Conflict
Series: Annals of the Chosen. Book 3
Subject(s): Magic
Major character(s): Sword, Warrior; Artil im Salthir,
    Wizard; Whistler, Hunter
Time period(s): Indeterminate
Locale(s): Alternate Universe

Summary: A warrior known as Sword knows that it is his
duty to slay the popular wizard who currently reigns, but

without allies he is forced to hide in a remote part of the world, awaiting a chance. After surviving a grueling winter in a deserted palace, he plans a suicidal mission to end the man's quiet tyranny.

Where it's reviewed:
Publishers Weekly, March 24, 2008, page 57

Other books by the same author:
The Ninth Talisman, 2007
The Spriggan Mirror, 2007
The Wizard Lord, 2006
Dragon Venom, 2003
Ithanalin's Restoration, 2001

Other books you might like:
Glen Cook, *Dreams of Steel*, 1990
Dave Duncan, *The Gilded Chain*, 1998
Simon R. Green, *Blue Moon Rising*, 1991
Fritz Leiber, *The Swords of Lankhmar*, 1968
Michael Shea, *A Quest for Simbilis*, 1974

558

MICHELLE WEST

The Hidden City

(New York: DAW, 2008)

Story type: Sword and Sorcery; Magic Conflict
Series: House War. Book 1
Subject(s): Magic; Coming-of-Age
Major character(s): Jewel Markess, Orphan; Rath, Businessman; Dusty, Orphan
Time period(s): Indeterminate
Locale(s): Alternate Universe

Summary: Jewel Markess is left homeless and without protection when her father dies, and she is finally driven to thievery. When she steals from Rath, a powerful but mysterious man, he catches her but rather than turn her over to the authorities, he provides her with food and shelter. As she grows more sure of herself, she begins to discover the truth about a demonic force that menaced the city once before, and perhaps will do so again.

Other books by the same author:
The Sun Sword, 2004
The Riven Shield, 2003
Sea of Sorrows, 2001
The Uncrowned King, 1998
Broken Crown, 1997

Other books you might like:
Kate Elliott, *Spirit Gate*, 2006
Elizabeth Haydon, *The Assassin King*, 2006
Dennis L. McKiernan, *Silver Wolf, Black Falcon*, 2000
Diana L. Paxson, *The Earthstone*, 1987
Tad Williams, *Shadowplay*, 2007

559

CHRIS WRAIGHT

Masters of Magic

(Nottingham, United Kingdom: Black Library, 2008)

Story type: Sword and Sorcery; Magic Conflict
Series: Warhammer
Major character(s): Lothar Auerbach, Wizard; Marius Joachim, Wizard; Reiner Starke, Administrator
Time period(s): Indeterminate
Locale(s): Alternate Universe

Summary: The human empire maintains a powerful army with which to defend itself from human and inhuman enemies. When a large force of orcs attacks, the army is mobilized, including a group of wizards whose power can change the course of the battle. Unfortunately, the wizards are distracted by divisions among themselves. First novel.

Other books you might like:
Robert Earl, *The Corrupted*, 2006
Graham McNeill, *Heldenhammer*, 2008
Anthony Reynolds, *Empire in Chaos*, 2008
Gav Thorpe, *The Heart of Chaos*, 2004
C.L. Werner, *Runefang*, 2008

560

DAVID ZINDELL

Lord of Lies

(New York: Tor, 2008)

Story type: Sword and Sorcery; Quest
Series: Lightstone. Book 3
Subject(s): Quest; Magic
Major character(s): Valashu Elahad, Warrior, Nobleman; Morjin, Mythical Creature; Kasandra, Noblewoman
Time period(s): Indeterminate
Locale(s): Alternate Universe

Summary: A nobleman has been engaged on a lengthy quest to find the Lightstone, a magical artifact that provides the power to defeat the dark angel Morjin, who seeks to rule the world. By acquiring it, however, he precipitates a battle for which he is unprepared because Morjin knows the Lightstone is the key to victory for the one who possesses it.

Where it's reviewed:
Publishers Weekly, February 18, 2008, page 141

Other books by the same author:
The Silver Sword, 2007
The Lighstone, 2006
Black Jade, 2005
Neverness, 1998
The Wild, 1997

Other books you might like:
Jacqueline Carey, *Banewreaker*, 2004
Steven Erikson, *Gardens of the Moon*, 2004
Ricardo Pinto, *The Chosen*, 2000
R.A. Salvatore, *The Demon Spirit*, 1998
Tad Williams, *Shadowplay*, 2008

The Many Faces of Horror Fiction
by
Don D'Ammassa

The first horror stories were probably told by primitive hunters around campfires, either to explain or exaggerate a frightening experience or just to awe the listeners. The attraction of horror stories has never been completely explained but probably has something to do with our universal fear of death and the unknown, and the sometimes perverse pleasure that often accompanies extreme emotional reactions. It is fun to be scared when we know that we're safe, sitting in a movie theater, riding through a carnival fun house, or curled up in a chair with a good book. We can flirt with death without risking its actual consequences. Ghost stories were particularly popular in Victorian England, notably in the Penny Dreadfuls, which featured lurid serials filled with monsters and bloodletting and eerie landscapes. The term "ghost story" came to mean any story of the supernatural, although today we define the term more narrowly as a subset of horror or supernatural literature.

Horror fiction historically has been primarily a literature for adults and until comparatively recently there was very little supernatural fiction written for a younger audience. It was also long considered a perfectly acceptable form for "serious" authors and such literary luminaries as Henry James could write "The Turn of the Screw," or Oscar Wilde "The Portrait of Dorian Gray," without fear of disapprobation. Other writers, including H.G. Wells, Edith Wharton, Sir Arthur Conan Doyle, and Rudyard Kipling, each turned out notable examples of short horror fiction in addition to their other work. American writers followed suit, including Edgar Allan Poe, Mark Twain, and more recently Shirley Jackson, Joyce Carol Oates, and others.

For most of the 1950s and 1960s, horror fiction in the United States tended to look backward to the authors who wrote for *Weird Tales* magazine and its various imitators. The best known of these was Howard Phillips Lovecraft, most of whose best stories were written within the context of the Cthulhu Mythos, which suggested that our world was once the property of a race of beings so powerful that they were almost godlike, that these beings were expelled from our universe by rival powers but plotted their return, sometimes affecting human events.

Lovecraft welcomed stories by other authors set in this context and writers continue to draw upon the power of his original concept even today. Other well-known horror writers from this period include Clark Ashton Smith and Robert E. Howard, both of whom are probably better known for their fantasy fiction, and William Hope Hodgson. Since the pulp magazines were not well-regarded in literary circles, the work by these authors remained relatively obscure except to collectors until the latter half of the 20th century, when academics finally began examining them more closely, particularly Lovecraft's influential work.

Despite its relative respectability—as contrasted with science fiction or fantasy, for example—horror fiction was not considered a separate genre until the late 1970s. This development followed a series of remarkable successes starting with the publication of Ira Levin's *Rosemary's Baby* in 1967. Levin's very understated novel suggested the possibility that Satan might return to Earth by impregnating a human woman, who would be driven by her maternal instincts to protect the infant even if she understood its true nature. The best-selling novel was turned into a successful movie the following year. The second event that contributed to the birth of modern horror was the publication of *The Exorcist* by William Peter Blatty in 1971. Blatty's novel, supposedly based on true events, chronicles the efforts of two priests to exorcise a female child who has been possessed by a demonic force. The novel also led to a successful, somewhat controversial horror film in 1973. Both authors would later write far less well known sequels to their seminal works.

The popularity of these two works whetted the appetite of publishers who were almost immediately rewarded by the arrival of Stephen King. *Carrie* (1974), *Salem's Lot* (1975), and *The Shining* (1977) were just the first three of a continuing string of best-selling horror novels, so popular that it could easily be argued that King has become a category by himself. King's accomplishments attracted other talented writers, and many not nearly as talented, some of whom wrote in the same general manner, others of whom explored other elements of horror. Among the best of these were Peter Straub,

Robert McCammon, Dean R. Koontz, and Rick Hautala. Toward the end of the 1970s and through much of the 1980s, there was a boom in horror fiction which proved ultimately to be counter-productive. Many of the writers who jumped on the supernatural bandwagon brought nothing new to the table and turned out inferior imitations of more popular works in rapid succession, diluting the quality of the genre. Publishers began packaging horror similarly and the covers became just as indistinguishable as the contents. Inevitably there was a contraction of the market, and just as inevitably it was disproportionate, ending the careers of many good writers while the inferior ones simply switched to the next literary fad.

Part of the difficulty facing horror writers was a lack of markets for their short fiction. Perhaps more than any other genre, horror depends on the short story because it is very difficult to sustain a sense of terror or supernatural awe over the length of an entire novel, particularly as publishers insisted upon longer and longer books. There have been intermittent and largely unsuccessful attempts to create a viable professional quality horror magazine, mostly by the small press. *Weird Tales* has been revived but has not always appeared regularly. *Cemetery Dance* survived a collapse that wiped out a number of excellent small press magazines including *2AM*, *After Hours*, *Deathrealm*, *Terminal Fright*, and *The Tome*. *Twilight Zone Magazine* was a professional market, but was not a commercial success and soon disappeared despite its first rate contents.

The book publishers who had active horror programs reduced or eliminated them, and some horror novels were packaged as mysteries or thrillers or given a new label, "dark fantasy". By the end of the 1990s and increasingly since then, horror fiction has become fragmented and readers of one subgenre may well be unaware of as well as uninterested in the others. The largest and most visible of these is the nebulous one that overlaps with romance novels and fantasy fiction. These books are called variously "urban fantasy," "dark fantasy," "paranormal romance," or left completely unlabeled. The most commonly used elements are a strong female character who usually has some supernatural ability herself—the ability to communicate with the dead, clairvoyance, the ability to change her physical shape—or may even be a supernatural entity, usually a vampire or half vampire, or a werewolf or other shapechanger. There is usually a strong romantic element, consummated but never leading to marriage to allow for sexual tension in sequels, and there are almost always sequels. In most cases, the supernatural beings live in our world but without our knowledge, although there are an increasing number set in a kind of alternate reality where the existence of vampires, werewolves, etc. is an accepted part of life. Writers working in this area include Laurell K. Hamilton, Charlaine Harris, Kat Richardson, Yasmine Galenorn, Karen Chance, Rob Thurston, Marie Brennan, Patricia Briggs, and many, many others.

Overlapping with the urban fantasies described above are the overt vampire romances made popular by writers like Maggie Shayne, Susan Sizemore, and young adult authors like Rachel Caine, Amelia Atwater-Rhodes, P.C. Cast, and L.J. Smith. This romanticized version of the vampire—which is supposed to be an unclean, animated dead thing accompanied by disease and death—seems almost to have moved the vampire outside the horror genre entirely. There are, in fact, very few new horror novels with evil vampires as characters; they are either troubled, reformed, misunderstood, or in a few cases unstable rogues who are hunted down by the rest of their kind.

Other traditional horror themes have receded as well. The traditional ghost story has become a rarity despite excellent work by Peter Straub and Rick Hautala to continue that tradition. Science fiction horror—alien invasions, mutant creatures—virtually disappeared from the written form decades ago and exists only in the occasional movie. There are signs that the zombie story is making a comeback, although that is perhaps the wrong term because it is not the traditional zombie—transformed through voodoo to become an undead servant of its master—but instead variations of the zombie plague movies that followed in the wake of George Romero's *The Night of the Living Dead* (1968) and its many sequels and imitators. Newer writers like Del Stone Jr. and Brian Keene have explored the possibilities of this theme, and there is even a small press dedicated to publishing zombie stories exclusively. This trend is likely to be reinforced by a forthcoming miniflood of zombie movies and computer games.

Much of this could be considered pop culture horror, but literary horror still exists, though it does not flourish. Most writers in this category are more active elsewhere, but one would have to include Lucius Shepard, Peter Straub, Joyce Carol Oates, Elizabeth Hand, and Thomas Ligotti. The last few years have seen the emergence of several new writers who have produced works with notable imagery and originality and who may well dominate the genre as their talents mature. Among these are Christopher Golden, Tim Lebbon, Brian Keene, Cherie Priest, Gary Braunbeck, Laird Barron, Jonathan Maberry, Greg F. Gifune, Stephen Mark Rainey, and Joe Hill. Tragically, two promising new writers had debut novels appear in 2008, but both authors died before they appeared—Nicholas Pekearo and Francis Clark. A few writers who emerged during the horror boom have maintained their popularity, including Ramsey Campbell, Graham Masterton, Stephen Gallagher, Simon Clark, F. Paul Wilson, and Edward Lee. Young adult horror has been given a recent boost by Stephenie Meyer, Tonya Hurley, and Daniel Waters, and even the Goosebumps series by R.L. Stine seems to have been successfully revived.

The prognosis for horror is, however, an uncertain one. There seems little likelihood that it will re-emerge as a separate genre in the foreseeable future. On the other hand, it appears to be doing quite well distributed over a variety of forms, which is a hopeful sign since it suggests that when one area declines in popularity, it

will have a minimal impact on horror as a whole. The explosion of the paranormal urban supernatural adventure series—several dozen strong as of this writing—seems almost certain to eventually implode, but the best of the authors in this area will simply follow the sales trends into fantasy or romance or wherever else it might lead. The small press is still a viable choice for horror writers—albeit with low pay rates—and has not contracted as violently as it did for science fiction and fantasy. Several specialty imprints—Dark Regions, Permuted Press, Black Death Books, and others—appear to be doing very well and have a significant number of titles in print.

The major publishers have not, however, found new writers of the stature of Stephen King, Peter Straub, and Dean R. Koontz, all of whom have been less prolific in recent years. It is not clear whether this is because the horror field is no longer attracting authors capable of writing best-selling novels or whether there are other causes at work. Public taste will eventually make itself known, but there is no way of predicting trends which have not yet begun to emerge.

Recommended Titles

The first half of 2008 was marked by the welcome return to print of many classic short stories in the genre. The overlap between horror, fantasy, and romance continues to be a major factor, with publishers labeling these books as paranormal romance, dark fantasy, etc. Particularly notable is the best Stephen King novel in several years, *Duma Key*, which is certainly the best single novel in the genre to appear thus far in 2008. Thanks to the prejudice against single author short story collections among major publishers, the small press has been responsible for producing most of the better collections this year, a trend which is likely to continue. A few titles stand out well above the others.

By the Sword by F. Paul Wilson

Coffin County by Gary Braunbeck

Duma Key by Stephen King

The 5th Witch by Graham Masterton

Generation Dead by Daniel Waters

The Ghost Quartet edited by Marvin Kaye

The Horror Fiction of Robert E. Howard by Robert E. Howard

Inferno edited by Ellen Datlow

The Necronomicon by H.P. Lovecraft

The New Weird edited by Ann & Jeff VanderMeer

Odd Hours by Dean R. Koontz

Other Gods by Stephen Mark Rainey

Horror Titles

561

MARIO ACEVEDO

The Undead Kama Sutra

(New York: Eos, 2008)

Story type: Vampire Story
Series: Felix Gomez. Book 3
Subject(s): Horror; Aliens; Vampires
Major character(s): Felix Gomez, Detective—Private, Vampire; Carmen Arellano, Scholar; Goodman, Military Personnel
Time period(s): 2000s
Locale(s): Key West, Florida

Summary: Felix Gomez is a private detective vampirized while serving in Iraq. While trying to recover pages from the Vampire Kama Sutra, which supposedly instructs how a vampire can increase his supernatural powers through sex, Gomez stumbles upon a plot, vaguely connected to the military, to help space aliens abduct earth women for scientific experiments.

Other books by the same author:
X-Rated Bloodsuckers, 2007
The Nymphos of Rocky Flats, 2006

Other books you might like:
P.N. Elrod, *Bloodlist*, 1990
Charlie Huston, *Already Dead*, 2005
Lee Killough, *Blood Hunt*, 1988

562

JOHN JOSEPH ADAMS , Editor

The Living Dead

(San Francisco: Night Shade, 2008)

Story type: Anthology; Reanimated Dead
Subject(s): Horror; Short Stories; Supernatural

Summary: Most of these 34 tales of zombies and the living dead, take their inspiration from George Romero's film *The Night of the Living Dead,* in which the newly dead are resurrected as flesh-eating zombies as the result of a plague from outer space. Authors include Poppy Z. Brite, Stephen King, Dan Simmons, Jeffrey Ford, Clive Barker, Joe Hill, Neil Gaiman, and a collaboration between Harlan Ellison and Robert Silverberg.

Other books by the same author:
Wastelands, 2007

Other books you might like:
Stephen Jones, *The Mammoth Book of Zombies*, 1993
    editor
John Skipp, *Book of the Dead*, 1989
    Craig Spector, co-editor
John Skipp, *Mondo Zombie*, 2006
    editor
John Skipp, *Still Dead*, 1991
    Craig Spector, co-editor

563

MARIA ALEXANDER
CHRISTA FAUST , Co-Author
LOREN RHOADS , Co-Author
MEHITOBEL WILSON , Co-Author

Sins of the Sirens

(Naperville, Illinois: Dark Arts Books, 2008)

Story type: Anthology
Subject(s): Horror; Short Stories; Supernatural

Summary: Each of the four authors represented in this volume contributes 20,000 words of horror fiction. Maria Alexander's contributions include "Pinned," an unnerving foray into the dominatrix-sadomasochism subculture. Christa Faust's contributes include "Firebird," set in a frightening drug-fueled near future. Loren Rhoads' works include "Still Life with Broken Glass," about a photographer whose themes reflect her pathological death obsession. Mehitobel Wilson offers "Close," about the terrifying surprise that awaits a voyeuristic hotel clerk who hides under the bed of a couple having sex.

Other books you might like:
Anonymous, *Five Strokes to Midnight*, 2007
    editor
Bill Breadlove, *Candy on the Dumpster*, 2006
    editor
Bill Breadlove, *Like a Chinese Tattoo*, 2008
    editor
Bill Breadlove, *Waiting for October*, 2007

editor
Thomas Tessier, *Night Visions 9*, 1991
  James Kisner, Rick Hautala, co-authors

564

KELLEY ARMSTRONG

Personal Demons

(New York: Bantam, 2008)

Story type: Occult
Series: Women of the Otherworld. Book 8
Subject(s): Occult; Horror; Supernatural
Major character(s): Hope Adams, Journalist; Lucas Cortez, Sorcerer; Karl, Werewolf
Time period(s): 2000s
Locale(s): Miami, Florida

Summary: To repay a debt of gratitude Hope, who is half-human/half-demon, agrees to infiltrate a gang of jaded supernatural youths who are causing problems for the Cortez business cabal. When Hope becomes too deeply involved with the gang, murder ensues and Hope must rely upon her supernatural resources to bail herself out and possibly even save her life.

Other books by the same author:
No Humans Involved, 2007
Broken, 2006
Haunted, 2005
Industrial Magic, 2004
Dime Store Magic, 2003

Other books you might like:
Nancy Collins, *Dead Roses for a Blue Lady*, 2002
Laurell K. Hamilton, *Blood Noir*, 2008
Charlaine Harris, *From Dead to Worse*, 2008
Kim Harrison, *The Outlaw Demon Wails*, 2008
Sherrilyn Kenyon, *One Silent Night*, 2008

565

R. SCOTT BAKKER

Neuropath

(London: Orion, 2008)

Story type: Serial Killer; Science Fiction
Subject(s): Serial Killers; Secrets
Major character(s): Thomas Bible, Professor; Nora Bible, Housewife; Neil Cassidy, Criminal
Time period(s): 2000s
Locale(s): United States

Summary: A scientist working for the government becomes unhinged during a series of experiments on altering the human brain. He begins killing people at random and in horrible ways and the government seems powerless to apprehend him. They turn to his best friend, a college professor and psychologist whose personal life is also unraveling.

Other books by the same author:
The Thousandfold Thought, 2005
The Warrior-Prophet, 2005
The Darkness That Comes Before, 2004

Other books you might like:
Michael Crichton, *The Terminal Man*, 1972
Thomas Harris, *Red Dragon*, 1988
Dean R. Koontz, *The Bad Place*, 1990
Robert J. Sawyer, *The Terminal Experiment*, 1995
Michael Slade, *Kamikaze*, 2006

566

L.A. BANKS (Pseudonym of Leslie Esdaile Banks)

Bad Blood

(New York: St. Martin's, 2008)

Story type: Werewolf Story
Series: Crimson Moon
Subject(s): Horror; Supernatural; Werewolves
Major character(s): Sasha Trudeau, Military Personnel (special ops agent), Werewolf (shadow wolf); Max Hunter, Werewolf
Time period(s): 2000s
Locale(s): New Orleans, Louisiana

Summary: Newly returned from a covert operation, Sasha Trudeau must discover why all the members of her team, all survivors of werewolf attacks, seem to have disappeared without a trace. First novel in a series.

Other books by the same author:
Bite the Bullet, 2008
The Darkness, 2008
The Shadows, 2008
The Cursed, 2007
The Wicked, 2007

Other books you might like:
Edward Lee, *Operator B*, 1999
Brian Lumley, *Necroscope III: The Source*, 1989
Bob Mayer, *Synbat*, 1994
Patricia Rosemoor, *The Last Vampire*, 2008
  Marc Paoletti, co-author

567

TOBY BARLOW

Sharp Teeth

(New York: Harper, 2008)

Story type: Werewolf Story
Subject(s): Horror; Supernatural; Werewolves
Major character(s): Lark, Lawyer, Supernatural Being; Anthony Silvo, Hunter (dogcatcher); Peabody, Detective—Police
Time period(s): 2000s
Locale(s): Los Angeles, California

Summary: Written in free verse, this novel chronicles the exploits of a pack of white-collar werewolves who nightly roam the streets of East Los Angeles, seeking to

take control of the city from its human residents. First novel.

Other books you might like:
Geoffrey Caine, *Wake of the Werewolf*, 1991
Whitley Strieber, *The Wild*, 1991
Whitley Strieber, *The Wolfen*, 1978
Melanie Tem, *Wilding*, 1992

568

CHRISTOPHER BIVINS , Editor
LANE ADAMSON , Co-Editor

The Undead: Headshot Quartet

(Kennett, Missouri: Permuted Press, 2008)

Story type: Anthology
Subject(s): Short Stories

Summary: All four of the long stories in this anthology include zombies, ranging from the traditional story involving a small number of the undead to wholesale rising of the dead to prey on the living. The authors are D.L. Snell, John Sunseri, Ryan C. Thomas, and David Dunwoody. All stories are original in this edition.

Other books you might like:
Ray Garton, *Zombie Love*, 2003
Brian Keene, *Dead Sea*, 2007
Joe R. Lansdale, *Dead in the West*, 1986
Kim Paffenroth, *Dying to Live*, 2007
Del Stone Jr., *Black Tide*, 2007

569

JENNA BLACK

Hungers of the Heart

(New York: Tor, 2008)

Story type: Vampire Story; Erotic Horror
Series: Guardians of the Night. Book 4
Subject(s): Vampires; Romance
Major character(s): Jonathan Drake, Vampire, Leader; Gabriel, Vampire, Leader; Brigitte, Vampire
Time period(s): 2000s
Locale(s): Baltimore, Maryland

Summary: A delegation of European vampires comes to Baltimore just as the latest round in an interminable power struggle is underway between the two strains of vampires, those who kill humans and those who don't. When some of the visitors are murdered, the leader of an American faction appears to be the most likely suspect.

Other books by the same author:
The Devil You Know, 2008
Secrets in the Shadows, 2007
Shadows on the Soul, 2007
Watchers in the Night, 2006

Other books you might like:
Elaine Bergstrom, *Shattered Glass*, 1989
Nancy Gideon, *Midnight Kiss*, 1994
Lori Herter, *Confession*, 1992
Maggie Shayne, *Lover's Bite*, 2008
Susan Sizemore, *I Burn for You*, 2003

570

GARY A. BRAUNBECK

Coffin County

(New York: Leisure, 2008)

Story type: Collection
Subject(s): Horror; Short Stories; Supernatural

Summary: These three stories are set in Cedar Hill, Ohio, a town where the supernatural easily insinuates itself into everyday events. The title story tells of a detective's efforts to solve a string of gruesome murders that follow the same pattern as a series of murders that occurred two centuries before. In "Union Dues," the citizens of the town are increasingly transformed into zombies enslaved to the local industry.

Other books by the same author:
Destinations Unknown, 2006
Home Before Dark, 2005
Graveyard People, 2003
From beneath These Fields of Blood, 2002
Things Left Behind, 1997

Other books you might like:
Douglas Clegg, *The Nightmare Chronicles*, 1999
Jeffrey Conlon, *Thundershowers at Dusk*, 2007
Joe Hill, *Twentieth-Century Ghosts*, 2005
Glen Hirshberg, *American Morons*, 2006
David Niall Wilson, *The Fall of the House of Usher and Other Illusions*, 1995

571

KEALAN PATRICK BURKE

The Number 121 to Pennsylvania and Others

(Baltimore, Maryland: Cemetery Dance, 2008)

Story type: Collection
Subject(s): Horror; Supernatural; Short Stories

Summary: Burke's collection contains 13 stories of dark fantasy and horror. Selections include "Empathy," in which a journalist's witnessing of a gruesome execution prompts nightmares that begin erupting horrifyingly into reality. In "Mr. Goodnight," a young boy's fear of an imaginary monster taints his relationship with his family whose members he distrust as manifestations of the supernatural. In "The Grief Frequency," a young man is haunted by the ghost of his unborn child who died in a car accident for which he was responsible.

Other books by the same author:
Currency of Souls, 2007
Vessels, 2006
The Hides, 2005
Turtle Boy, 2005
Ravenous Ghosts, 2003

Horror

Other books you might like:
Gary A. Braunbeck, *Things Left Behind*, 1997
Peter Crowther, *The Space between the Lines*, 2007
Charles L. Grant, *Tales from the Nightside*, 1981
Alan Ryan, *The Bones Wizard and Other Stories*, 1985

572

JIM BUTCHER

Small Favor

(New York: Roc, 2008)

Story type: Occult
Series: The Dresden Files
Subject(s): Horror
Major character(s): Harry Dresden, Wizard; Karrin Murphy, Detective—Police; Johnny Marcone, Gangster
Time period(s): 2000s
Locale(s): Chicago, Illinois

Summary: In his tenth adventure Wizard PI Harry Dresden, in debt to Mab, the Queen of Air and Darkness, accedes to her demand that he rescue Johnny Marcone, a Chicago gangster. Unfortunately, Mab's sister Titania, has different ideas about Johnny's usefulness, which causes Harry no amount of supernatural complications.

Other books by the same author:
Turn Coat, 2009
White Night, 2007
Proven Guilty, 2006
Dead Beat, 2005
Blood Rites, 2004

Other books you might like:
Kelley Armstrong, *Dime Store Magic*, 1993
Nancy Collins, *Wild Blood*, 1994
P.N. Elrod, *Bloodlist*, 1990
Laurell K. Hamilton, *Blood Noir*, 2008
Tanya Huff, *Smoke and Shadows*, 2004

573

RACHEL CAINE

Feast of Fools

(New York: Jam, 2008)

Story type: Vampire Story; Young Adult
Series: Morganville Vampires. Book 4
Subject(s): Vampires
Major character(s): Claire Danvers, Teenager, Student; Michael Glass, Vampire, Teenager; Eve Rosser, Teenager, Student
Time period(s): 2000s
Locale(s): Morganville, Texas

Summary: Claire Danvers has adjusted to the fact that the residents of the town of Morganville are not all human. Some are vampires, although the majority of the undead are perfectly nice people. That balance is upset when a new vampire comes to town, a predator convinced that he is superior to ordinary humanity.

Other books by the same author:
Gale Force, 2008
Dead Girls' Dance, 2007
Midnight Eve, 2007
Devil's Due, 2006
Glass Houses, 2006

Other books you might like:
Carmen Adams, *Song of the Vampire*, 1996
Amelia Atwater-Rhodes, *Demon in My View*, 2000
Elaine Bergstrom, *Blood Rites*, 1991
P.C. Cast, *Chosen*, 2008
  Kristin Cast, co-author
Debra Doyle, *Hunter's Moon*, 1994
  James Macdonald, co-author

574

RAMSEY CAMPBELL

The Grin of the Dark

(New York: Tor, 2008)

Story type: Contemporary; Mystery
Subject(s): Secrets; Magic
Major character(s): Simon Lester, Critic; Tubby Thackeray, Entertainer; Warren Halloran, Businessman
Time period(s): 2000s
Locale(s): England

Summary: Critic Simon Lester has been having trouble finding work, so he jumps at the chance to do a piece on the late Tubby Thackeray, a comedian turned actor, whose work is mysteriously forgotten. What he uncovers suggests that the man's success was due at least in part to supernatural forces interceding on his behalf.

Other books by the same author:
The Overnight, 2005
The Darkest Part of the Woods, 2002
Meddling with Ghosts, 2001
Pact of the Fathers, 2001
Ghosts and Grisly Things, 2000

Other books you might like:
Rick Hautala, *Dead Voices*, 1990
Stephen King, *Bag of Bones*, 1998
Dean R. Koontz, *Whispers*, 1980
Bentley Little, *The Association*, 2001
Thomas F. Monteleone, *The Resurrectionist*, 1995

575

RAMSEY CAMPBELL

Inconsequential Tales

(New York: Hippocampus Press, 2008)

Story type: Collection
Subject(s): Horror; Short Stories; Supernatural

Summary: These 25 oblique, subtle, richly atmospheric tales of horror and science fiction include "The Reshaping of Rossiter," in which a man's malignant doppel-

ganger takes over his identity; "The Sunshine Club," about a man who specializes in psychoanalyzing vampires; and "The Shadows in the Barn," in which an illusionist's hand-shadows accidentally bring ghastly forms to life.

Other books by the same author:
Told By the Dead, 2003
Ghosts and Grisly Things, 1997
Alone with the Horrors, 1993
Strange Things and Stranger Places, 1993
Dark Companions, 1982

Other books you might like:
Robert Aickman, *The Wine-Dark Sea*, 1988
Dennis Etchison, *Dark Country*, 1982
Thomas Ligotti, *Songs of a Dead Dreamer*, 1990
Nicholas Royle, *Mortality*, 2006
Conrad Williams, *Use Once, Then Destroy*, 2004

576

RAMSEY CAMPBELL

Thieving Fear

(Hornsea, England: PS Publishinhg, 2008)

Story type: Occult
Subject(s): Horror; Occult; Supernatural
Major character(s): Charlotte Nolan, Businesswoman, Publisher; Ellen Lomax, Writer; Rory Lucas, Artist
Time period(s): 2000s
Locale(s): Yorkshire, England

Summary: When their lives begin to go badly off-kilter in their adult years, four cousins—Charlotte, Ellen, Hugh, and Rory—trace the start of their misfortunes to a night they once spent in their youth on Thursaston Common, a place linked to the activities of Arthur Pendemon, a Victorian occultist whose malignant influence is still very much active.

Other books by the same author:
The Grin of the Dark, 2007
Secret Story, 2005
The Overnight, 2004
The Darkest Part of the Woods, 2002
Pact of the Fathers, 2001

Other books you might like:
Jonathan Carroll, *From the Teeth of Angels*, 1994
Matthew J. Costello, *Darkborn*, 1992
Stephen King, *It*, 1987
Steve Rasnic Tem, *Excavation*, 1987

577

MIKE CAREY

Vicious Circle

(New York: Grand Central, 2008)

Story type: Contemporary; Black Magic
Series: Felix Castor. Book 2
Subject(s): Magic; Secrets

Major character(s): Felix Castor, Magician; Ajulutsikael, Mythical Creature; Abigail Torrington, Spirit
Time period(s): 2000s
Locale(s): London, England

Summary: In an alternate London where the dead walk among the living, Felix Castor uses his paranormal powers as a kind of preternatural private detective. His latest case is to track down the kidnapped ghost of a couple's daughter, while avoiding the personal distractions in his life.

Other books by the same author:
The Devil You Know, 2007

Other books you might like:
Jim Butcher, *Dead Beat*, 2005
Simon R. Green, *Hell to Pay*, 2007
Simon Hawke, *The Wizard of Lovecraft's Cafe*, 1993
Tanya Huff, *Blood Debt*, 1997
F. Paul Wilson, *The Haunted Air*, 2002

578

KAREN CHANCE

Midnight's Daughter

(New York: Onyx, 2008)

Story type: Vampire Story; Romance
Subject(s): Vampires; Quest
Major character(s): Dorina Basarab, Mythical Creature (Dhampir); Vlad Dracula, Vampire; Louis-Cesare, Vampire
Time period(s): 2000s
Locale(s): United States

Summary: Dorina Basarab is half vampire and half human, a precarious state which makes her subject to outbursts of murderous rage. She channels this anger into fighting those vampires who prey openly on humans and risk exposing the existence of their kind, so she is recruited into the effort to track down the most famous vampire of them all, because Count Dracula has escaped imprisonment.

Other books by the same author:
Embrace the Night, 2008
Claimed by Shadow, 2007
Touch the Dark, 2006

Other books you might like:
Nancy Collins, *Sunglasses After Dark*, 1989
Susan Krinard, *Prince of Dreams*, 1996
Maggie Shayne, *Devil's Kiss*, 2007
Jeanne C. Stein, *The Becoming*, 2006
Whitley Strieber, *The Hunger*, 1981

579

FRANCIS CLARK

Waking Brigid

(New York: Tor, 2008)

Story type: Occult
Subject(s): Demons; Irish Americans; Supernatural

Major character(s): Brigid Rourke, Religious; Benito, Religious; Jakob Streng, Businessman
Time period(s): 1870s
Locale(s): Savannah, Georgia

Summary: When it is discovered that a cabal of businessman have been sacrificing victims for centuries to the god Belial to further their own interests, the clergy of Savannah, Georgia, descend upon the city and draw upon the gods of their pagan ancestors to fight the ancient evil. A first novel.

Other books you might like:
Robert R. McCammon, *Speaks the Nightbird*, 2006
Michael Mcdowell, *Gilded Needles*, 1980
Rodman Philbrick, *Coffins*, 2002
Cherie Priest, *Dreadful Skin*, 2007

580

PETER CROWTHER

The Land at the End of the Working Day

(London, England: Humdrumming Press, 2008)

Story type: Collection
Subject(s): Saloons; Short Stories; Supernatural

Summary: All of these four novellas are set in a barroom where patrons discuss their collective supernatural experiences over spirits. "Gandolph Cohen and the Land at the End of the Working Day" tells of a supernatural being who shows up at the bar to project futures for many of the patrons. In "Bernard Boyce Bennington and the American Dream," two men share their memories of the same supernatural entity whose love has irrevocably changed their lives. "Front-Page McGuffin and the Greatest Story Never Told" tells of a dead patron whose body continues to show up at the bar, even though his soul has left. In "Cliff Rhodes and the Most Important Journey," two non-regulars are welcomed into the bar's fraternity and its uncanny atmosphere.

Other books by the same author:
The Space between the Lines, 2007
Lonesome Roads, 1999
The Longest Single Note, 1999

Other books you might like:
Gary A. Braunbeck, *Things Left Behind*, 1997
Kealan Patrick Burke, *Brimstone Turnpike*, 2008
Simon Clark, *Hotel Midnight*, 2005
Graham Joyce, *Partial Eclipse and Other Stories*, 2002

581

ELLEN DATLOW , Editor

Inferno

(New York: Tor, 2008)

Story type: Anthology
Subject(s): Short Stories

Summary: This is a collection of twenty short stories ap-

pearing in print for the first time. They tend toward the literary side of the genre without sacrificing strong story lines. The contributors include Joyce Carol Oates, K.W. Jeter, P.D. Cacek, Pat Cadigan, Christopher Fowler, Jeffrey Ford, Stephen Gallagher, Lucius Shepard, and others.

Other books by the same author:
The Dark, 2003
Lethal Kisses, 1996
Twists of the Tale, 1996
Little Deaths, 1995
Blood Is Not Enough, 1989

Other books you might like:
P.D. Cacek, *Leavings*, 1997
Christopher Fowler, *City Jitters*, 1986
Stephen Gallagher, *The Kingdom of Bones*, 2007
Joyce Carol Oates, *The Collector of Hearts*, 2000
Lucius Shepard, *The Golden*, 1993

582

ELLEN DATLOW , Editor

A Whisper of Blood

(New York: Barnes & Noble, 2007)

Story type: Anthology; Vampire Story
Subject(s): Short Stories; Supernatural; Vampires

Summary: This edition combines the anthologies *Blood Is Not Enough* (1989) and *A Whisper of Blood* (1991), both anthologies of uncommon vampire stories that realize the fundamental vampire/victim relationship in ingenious new ways. The 35 stories include Dan Simmons' "Carrion Comfort," about vampires who feed off human misery; Fritz Leiber's "The Girl with the Hungry Eyes," about an advertising model who feeds off the desires and interests of consumer culture; and Thomas Ligotti's "Mrs. Rinaldi's Angel," in which nightmares are a parasitic drain on the resources of the individual.

Other books by the same author:
Inferno, 2008
The Dark, 2003
Lethal Kisses, 1996
Twists of the Tale, 1996
Little Deaths, 1994

Other books you might like:
Poppy Z. Brite, *Love in Vein*, 1994
Stephen Jones, *The Mammoth Book of Vampires*, 1992
Alan Ryan, *Vampires*, 1987
Leonard Wolf, *Blood Thirst*, 1997

583

STEFAN DZIEMIANOWICZ , Editor

Horror: The Best of the Year 2008

(Holicong, Pennsylvania: Prime, 2008)

Story type: Anthology
Series: Horror: The Best of the Year

Subject(s): Horror; Short Stories; Supernatural

Summary: These 15 stories were chosen by the editor as the best short horror stories of 2007. Selections include Caitlin Kiernan's "The Wolf Who Cried Girl," about a female werewolf trapped in her human form; Fredric S. Durbin's "The Bone Man," about a dark legendary folk figure who has inspired a small town's annual Halloween celebration; Glen Hirshberg's "The Janus Tree," which is concerned with an ancient supernatural entity's influence over a teenage boy; and Nancy Etchemendy's "Honey in the Wound," about the tragic consequences of a family's efforts to revive their deceased son by supernatural means.

Other books you might like:

Ellen Datlow, *Inferno*, 2007
  editor
Ellen Datlow, *The Year's Best Fantasy and Horror: 21st Annual Collection*, 2008
  Kelly Link and Gavin Grant, co-editors
Del Howison, *Dark Delicacies II*, 2007
  Jeff Gelb, co-editor
Stephen Jones, *The Mammoth Book of Best New Horror: Volume 19*, 2008
  editor
Barbara Roden, *At Ease with the Dead*, 2007
  Christopher Roden, co-editor

584

P.N. ELROD , Editor

My Big Fat Supernatural Honeymoon

(New York: Ace, 2008)

Story type: Anthology
Subject(s): Horror; Short Stories; Supernatural

Summary: In this follow-up to *My Big Fat Supernatural Wedding*, nine authors renowned for their urban fantasy and paranormal romances series contribute previously unpublished stories on the theme of honeymoons involving, or interrupted by, supernatural events. In Kelley Armstrong's "Stalked," two werewolves from the same wolf pack are stalked by a non-pack "mutt" on their honeymoon. In Jim Butcher's "Heorot," sorcerer detective Harry Dresden rescues a bride abducted by supernatural entities on her honeymoon. Lilith Saintcrow's "Half of Being Married" tells of a werewolf and vampire hunter whose honeymoon itinerary accidentally takes them into a vampire-ridden town.

Other books by the same author:
My Big Fat Supernatural Wedding, 2007
Dracula in London, 2001

Other books you might like:
Anonymous, *Bite*, 2005
  editor
Charlaine Harris, *Many Bloody Returns*, 2007
  Toni P. Kelner, co-editor
Charlaine Harris, *Wolfsbane and Mistletoe*, 2008
  Toni P. Kelner, co-editor

585

TOM ENGLISH , Editor

Bound for Evil

(Modesto, California: Bloodletting Press, 2008)

Story type: Anthology
Subject(s): Horror; Short Stories; Supernatural

Summary: Sixty-six stories by sixty-one authors concerned with forbidden or corrupt books of occult lore. Reprint stories include H.P. Lovecraft's "The Dunwich Horror," in which the nefarious Necronomicon plays a crucial role in disposing of a world-shattering horror; Fred Chappell's "The Adder," in which the Necronomicon exerts its malignant influence by corrupting the text of any book put in its proximity; and Ramsey Campbell's "Worse than Bones," in which marginal notes in a book are an index to its malignant supernatural power over the reader.

Other books you might like:
Paul McAuley, *In Dreams*, 1993
  Kim Newman, co-editor
Robert M. Price, *The Necronomicon*, 1996
  editor
David J. Schow, *Silver Scream*, 1988
  editor
Shane Ryan Staley, *I'll Be Damned*, 2001
  Editor

586

ELIZABETH ENGSTROM

The Northwoods Chronicles

(Waterville, Maine: Five Star, 2008)

Story type: Collection
Subject(s): Short Stories

Summary: This is a collection of short stories which share a common setting: a remote town whose residents all harbor terrifying secrets. Individual episodes are wrapped around a unifying story about the mysterious disappearance of a young boy.

Other books by the same author:
Suspicions, 2002
Nightmare Flower, 1992
Black Ambrosia, 1988
When Darkness Loves Us, 1985

Other books you might like:
Charles G. Finney, *The Circus of Dr. Lao*, 1935
Charles L. Grant, *Nightmare Seasons*, 1982
Rick Hautala, *Cold Whispers*, 1991
Stephen King, *Salems' Lot*, 1975
Thomas F. Monteleone, *The Magnificent Gallery*, 1987

587

JOHN FARRIS

Avenging Fury

(New York: Tor, 2008)

Story type: Wild Talents
Series: Fury. Book 4
Subject(s): Horror; Psychic Powers; Supernatural
Major character(s): Eden Waring, Psychic; Cody Olds, Gambler; Lincoln Grayle, Sorcerer
Time period(s): 2000s
Locale(s): Las Vegas, Nevada

Summary: Having narrowly escaped death at the hands of psychic Avatar Eden Waring, Lincoln Grayle recalls Delilah, the time traveling feminine side of his dark persona, to battle with Eden and her dark doppelganger, Gwen, for control of the world.

Other books by the same author:
You Don't Scare Me, 2007
Phantom Nights, 2005
The Fury and the Power, 2003
The Fury and the Terror, 1999
The Fury, 1996

Other books you might like:
Beth Amos, *Cold White Fury*, 1996
Douglas Clegg, *Eye of the Needle*, 1994
Stephen King, *Firestarter*, 1980
Jack Martin, *Scanners*, 1981
Bari Wood, *The Killing Gift*, 1975

588

JEANIENE FROST

One Foot in the Grave

(New York: Avon, 2008)

Story type: Contemporary; Vampire Story
Series: Night Huntress. Book 2
Subject(s): Vampires; Romance
Major character(s): Cat Crawfield, Mythical Creature, Government Official; Bones, Vampire; Danny Milton, Prisoner
Time period(s): 2000s
Locale(s): United States

Summary: Cat Crawfield is half human and half vampire, which gives her special skills that attract the interest of the government. Now employed as a special agent to deal with paranormal problems, she is reunited with her vampire lover in an effort to uncover a conspiracy that could lead to her permanent death.

Other books by the same author:
At Grave's End, 2008
Halfway to the Grave, 2007

Other books you might like:
Marie Brennan, *Doppelganger*, 2006
Karen Chance, *Midnight's Daughter*, 2008
Yasmine Galenorn, *Darkling*, 2007
Kat Richardson, *Underground*, 2008
Jeanne C. Stein, *Blood Drive*, 2006

589

TERRI GAREY

A Match Made in Hell

(New York: Avon, 2008)

Story type: Psychic Powers
Series: Nicki Styx. Book 2
Subject(s): Romance; Supernatural
Major character(s): Nicki Styx, Store Owner; Joe Bascombe, Doctor; Kelly Bascombe, Spouse
Time period(s): 2000s
Locale(s): Little Five Points, Georgia

Summary: Nicki, a young woman sensitized to paranormal manifestations after a near-death experience, is shocked to discover that she has a twin sister, Kelly, who is not only evidence of the family she never knew, but also her boyfriend's ex-wife. Nicki's relationship with Kelly leads her to her family's creepy house, and precipitates an encounter with the Devil himself.

Other books by the same author:
Dead Girls Are Easy, 2007

Other books you might like:
Maryjanice Davidson, *Undead and Unwed*, 2002
Laurell K. Hamilton, *Guilty Pleasures*, 1993
Charlaine Harris, *Dead Until Dark*, 2001
Kathryn Harrison, *Dead Witch Walking*, 2004

590

RAY GARTON

The Folks 2

(Baltimore, Maryland: Cemetery Dance, 2008)

Story type: Gothic Family Chronicle
Subject(s): Family Life; Horror; Suspense
Major character(s): Andy Sayer, Young Man; Roxanne Shaw, Waiter/Waitress; Matthew Bollinger, Businessman
Time period(s): 2000s
Locale(s): Mount Crag

Summary: Newly rehabilitated after a plastic surgeon has repaired the scars that long deformed him and made him a welcome ward of the grotesquely inbred Bollinger family, Andy sets his sights on moving on in the world and starting a romance with a young woman. The Bollingers, however, exert their claim over Andy and will stop at nothing to keep him a part of their insular family. Sequel to *The Folks*.

Other books by the same author:
Ravenous, 2008
Serpent Girl, 2008
Pieces of Hate, 1995
Methods of Madness, 1990 (OTL The Loveliest Dead)

Other books you might like:
Angela Carter, *Nights at the Circus*, 1985
Deborah Churchman, *Cross a Dark Bridge*, 1996
Warren Murphy, *Destiny's Carnival*, 1992
Tom Piccirilli, *A Choir of Ill Children*, 2003
Brooke Stevens, *The Circus of Earth and Air*, 1984

591

RAY GARTON

Ravenous

(New York: Leisure, 2008)

Story type: Werewolf Story
Subject(s): Horror; Sexuality; Werewolves
Major character(s): Arlin Hurley, Police Officer; Daniel Fargo, Hunter; Jason Sutherland, Clerk
Time period(s): 2000s
Locale(s): Big Rock, California

Summary: An outbreak of lycanthropy overwhelms the small town of Big Rock, and local Sheriff Arlin Hurley is beside himself when he discovers that the werewolf scourge is passed through intimate contact like a sexually transmitted disease

Other books by the same author:
Serpent Girl, 2008
Night Life, 2005
The Loveliest Dead, 2005
Scissors, 2004
Zombie Love, 2003

Other books you might like:
Kelley Armstrong, *Bitten*, 2001
Nancy Collins, *Wild Blood*, 1994
John Skipp, *Animals*, 1993
    Craig Spector, co-author
Whitley Strieber, *The Wild*, 1991

592

RAY GARTON

Slivers of Bone

(Baltimore, Maryland: Cemetery Dance, 2008)

Story type: Collection
Subject(s): Horror; Short Stories; Supernatural

Summary: Thirteen tales of horror and dark suspense include "The Guy Down the Street," about the vigilante justice a town deals out to a sexual predator who pursues the local teenagers; "Second Opinion," about an unfinished story that drives everyone who reads it to murder; and "The Homeless Couple," about a supernaturally endowed telephone booth that communicates with the dead.

Other books by the same author:
Ravenous, 2008
Serpent Girl, 2008
Pieces of Hate, 1995
Methods of Madness, 1990 (OTL The Loveliest Dead)

Other books you might like:
Ed Gorman, *Different Kinds of Dead and Other Tales*, 2005
Jack Ketchum, *Closing Time and Other Stories*, 2007
David J. Schow, *Havoc Swims Jaded*, 2006
John Shirley, *Living Shadows*, 2007

593

CHRISTOPHER GOLDEN , Editor
TIM LEBBON , Co-Editor
JAMES A. MOORE , Co-Editor

British Invasion

(Baltimore, Maryland: Cemetery Dance, 2008)

Story type: Anthology
Subject(s): Horror; Short Stories; Supernatural

Summary: The editors gather 21 previously unpublished tales of horror and the supernatural by British writers who have achieved renown in American markets. Mark Morris' "Puppies for Sale" tells of a distraught man who is convinced that the terrible misfortunes that befall his family are caused by a demonically possessed dog bought as a pet for his child. In Nicholas Royle's "Goldfinch," a man is pursued by the physical incarnation of his cancer. Philip Nutman's "The Misadventure of Fatman and Little Gorge, or How I Made a Monster" is the adventure of a horror film producer who finds his grisly screen fantasy converging with daily reality. Afterword by Kim Newman.

Other books you might like:
Peter Crowther, *Narrow Houses*, 1992
    editor
Stephen Jones, *Dark Voices*, 1990
    Clarence Paget, co-editor
Chris Morgan, *Dark Fantasies*, 1989
    editor
Nicholas Royle, *Darklands*, 1991
    editor

594

J.F. GONZALEZ

Shapeshifter

(New York: Leisure, 2008)

Story type: Werewolf Story
Subject(s): Blackmail; Business; Werewolves
Major character(s): Mark Wiseman, Office Worker, Werewolf; Bernard Roberts, Businessman; Carol Emrich, Office Worker
Time period(s): 2000s
Locale(s): Costa Mesa, California

Summary: When insurance company CEO Bernard Roberts discovers that Mark Wiseman, one of his menial employees, is a werewolf who may have killed his own parents, he blackmails the young man into slaughtering his business rivals. Published as a specialty press hardcover in 2003.

Other books by the same author:
Bully, 2006
When the Darkness Falls, 2006
Fetish, 2005
The Beloved, 2005
Survivor, 2004

Other books you might like:
Kelley Armstrong, *Bitten*, 2001
Henry Garfield, *Moondog*, 1995
Ronald Kelly, *Moon of the Werewolf*, 2001
Whitley Strieber, *The Wolfen*, 1978

595

CHRIS MARIE GREEN

Midnight Reign

(New York: Ace, 2008)

Story type: Vampire Story
Series: Vampire Babylon. Book 2
Subject(s): Horror; Supernatural; Vampires
Major character(s): Dawn Madison, Actress; Jonah Limpet, Wealthy; Kiko Daniels, Psychic
Time period(s): 2000s
Locale(s): Hollywood, California

Summary: Dawn's continuing efforts to discover the fate of her missinf father are complicated by a murder that bears all the hallmarks of a vampire slaying and increasingly unsettling revelations about the role her father and late mother may play in Hollywood's vampire underground.

Other books by the same author:
Break of Dawn, 2008
Night Rising, 2007

Other books you might like:
Nancy Collins, *Dead Roses for a Blue Lady*, 2002
Laurell K. Hamilton, *Blood Noir*, 2008
Charlaine Harris, *From Dead to Worse*, 2008
Sherrilyn Kenyon, *One Silent Night*, 2008

596

LELAND HALL
FRANCIS BRETT YOUNG , Co-Author

Sinister House/Cold Harbour

(New York: Hippocampus Press, 2008)

Story type: Anthology
Series: Lovecraft's Library
Subject(s): Horror; Short Stories; Supernatural

Summary: Both of these early 20th century novels of the macabre were written about by American horror master H.P. Lovecraft in his seminal essay "Supernatural Horror in Literature." Leland Hall's *Sinister House*, first published in 1919, tells of a house haunted by ghosts of the previous owners who are sapping the vitality of the current resident. Francis Brett Young's *Cold Harbour*, first published in 1924, tells of an estate in the English countryside pervaded by malignant ancient occult forces. Each novel features an introduction by series editor S.T. Joshi.

Other books you might like:
Algernon Blackwood, *Incredible Adventures*, 2004
Herbert Gorman, *The Place Called Dagon*, 1927
A. Merritt, *The Metal Monster*, 2002
Barry Pain, *An Exchange of Souls/Lazarus*, 2007

Henri Braud, co-author
M.P. Shiel, *The House of Sounds and Others*, 2005

597

LAURELL K. HAMILTON

Blood Noir

(New York: Ace, 2008)

Story type: Anthology
Series: Anita Blake-Vampire Hunter
Subject(s): Horror; Supernatural; Vampires
Major character(s): Anita Blake, Vampire Hunter, Vampire; Jean-Claude, Vampire; Jason Schuyler, Supernatural Being (Werewolf)
Time period(s): 2000s
Locale(s): St. Louis, Missouri

Summary: In her sixteenth adventure Anita Blake-Vampire Hunter finds herself conflicted over her vampire-hunting profession and the vampirism with which she has been infected, trying to help her vampire boyfriend who is losing face as the vampire leader of St. Louis, and posing as the girlfriend of her buddy Schuyler who is trying to pass as a non-gay werewolf with his family. Set in an alternate St. Louis where humans and supernatural beings mingle and co-exist uneasily.

Other books by the same author:
The Harlequin, 2007
Danse Macabre, 2006
Micah, 2006
Incubus, 2004
Cerulean Sins, 2003

Other books you might like:
L.A. Banks, *The Shadows*, 2008
Poppy Z. Brite, *Lost Souls*, 1992
Nancy Collins, *Tempter*, 1990
MaryJanice Davidson, *Undead and Unwed*, 2002
Laurell K. Hamilton, *Blood Noir*, 2008
Kim Harrison, *The Outlaw Demon Wails*, 2008

598

CHARLAINE HARRIS

From Dead to Worse

(New York: Ace, 2008)

Series: Southern Vampire Mysteries
Subject(s): Fantasy; Supernatural; Vampires
Major character(s): Sookie Stackhouse, Waiter/Waitress; Niall Brigant, Elderly; Sophie-Anne Leclerq, Vampire
Time period(s): 2000s
Locale(s): Bon Temps, Louisiana

Summary: Back in her home town of Bon Temps, Sookie, a ditzy psychic barmaid, finds herself caught up in a power struggle for the state of Louisiana between vampires from Las Vegas and the vampire queen of Louisiana. Eighth novel set in an alternate reality where

human beings and supernatural creatures co-exist uneasily.

Other books by the same author:
Altogether Dead, 2007
Definitely Dead, 2006
Dead as a Doornail, 2005
Dead to the World, 2004
Club Dead, 2003

Other books you might like:
L.A. Banks, *The Shadows*, 2008
Poppy Z. Brite, *Lost Souls*, 1992
Nancy Collins, *Tempter*, 1990
MaryJanice Davidson, *Undead and Unwed*, 2002
Kim Harrison, *The Outlaw Demon Wails*, 2008

599

KIM HARRISON

The Outlaw Demon Wails

(New York: Eos, 2008)

Story type: Occult
Series: Rachel Morgan. Book 6
Subject(s): Demons; Supernatural; Vampires
Major character(s): Rachel Morgan, Witch, Detective—
    Private; Trent Kalamack, Political Figure; Rynn
    Cormel, Vampire
Time period(s): 2000s
Locale(s): Cincinnati, Ohio

Summary: On a mission to retrieve ancient elven DNA to help her newly pregnant demonic familiar witch private eye Rachel Morgan learns some secrets hitherto unknown to her about her own supernatural pedigree. Ultimately, these self-revelations will have an impact on her intimate encounter with a vampire and the hybrid offspring she may be bearing.

Other books by the same author:
For a Few Demons More, 2007
A Fistful of Charms, 2006
Every Which Way but Dead, 2005
The Good, the Bad, and the Undead, 2004
Dead Witch Walking, 2003

Other books you might like:
MaryJanice Davidson, *Undead and Unworthy*, 2008
Laurell K. Hamilton, *Blood Noir*, 2008
Charlaine Harris, *From Dead to Worse*, 2008
Karen Taylor, *Blood of My Blood*, 2000

600

C.J. HENDERSON

Degrees of Fear and Others

(Colusa, California: Dark Regions, 2008)

Story type: Collection
Subject(s): Short Stories

Summary: Two of the twenty stories in this collection are original, while the others are reprints. They cover a wide range of subject matters and themes including a sequel to "Herbert West—Reanimator" by H.P. Lovecraft. Some of the stories share settings or characters and many involve the investigation of some form of mysterious event.

Other books by the same author:
The Tales of Inspector Legrasse, 2005 (H.P. Lovecraft,
    co-author)
The Occult Detectives of C.J. Henderson, 2003

Other books you might like:
William Hope Hodgson, *Carnacki, the Ghost Finder*,
    1910
Seabury Quinn, *The Adventures of Jules de Grandin*,
    1976
Jory Sherman, *Chill*, 1978
Manly Wade Wellman, *Who Fears the Devil?*, 1963
F. Paul Wilson, *The Haunted Air*, 2002

601

SUSAN HILL

The Man in the Picture

(New York: Overlook Press, 2007)

Story type: Ghost Story
Subject(s): Art; Supernatural; Universities and Colleges
Major character(s): Theo Parmitter, Professor; Oliver,
    Scholar; Lady Hawdon, Aged Person
Time period(s): 2000s
Locale(s): Cambridge, England

Summary: On a visit to his old college professor, Oliver learns the secret history of a sinister picture that hangs on the man's wall: an 18th-century drawing of a Venice carnival scene that has the power to absorb the soul of anyone who spends too much time pondering it.

Other books by the same author:
The Beacon, 2008
The Service of Clouds, 2007
Mrs. De Winter, 1993
The Mist in the Mirror, 1992
Air and Angels, 1991

Other books you might like:
Robert Girardi, *Vaporetto 13*, 1997
Stephen King, *Duma Key*, 2008
Charles Palliser, *The Quincunx*, 1989
Rod Serling, *The Season to Be Wary*, 1967

602

E.T.A. HOFFMANN

The Sand-Man and Other Night Pieces

(North Yorkshire, England: Tartarus Press, 2008)

Story type: Collection
Subject(s): Horror; Short Stories; Supernatural

Horror

Summary: These 15 stories of horror and the supernatural are by a German writer who worked in the Gothic tradition of the early 19th century. Included are "The Sand-Man," about a young man haunted since childhood by the legend of a being who steals the eyes of people while they sleep; "The Mines of Falun," about a gem with supernatural powers; and "Automatons," about simulacra with psychic powers. Introduction by James Rockhill.

Other books by the same author:
The Golden Pot, 1992
Tales of E.T.A. Hoffmann, 1972
Selected Writings of E.T.A. Hoffmann, 1969
The Best Tales of Hoffmann, 1963
Tales of Hoffmann, 1932

Other books you might like:
Henry Ferris, *A Night with Mephistopheles*, 1997
Theophile Gautier, *One of the Cleopatra's Nights*, 1882
Edgar Allan Poe, *Fiction and Poetry*, 2006
I.U. Tarchetti, *Fantastic Tales*, 1992

603

ROBERT E. HOWARD

The Horror Stories of Robert E. Howard

(New York: Del Rey, 2008)

Story type: Collection
Subject(s): Short Stories

Summary: Although best known for his fantasy, Robert E. Howard wrote a considerable body of short horror fiction, which is collected in this volume. Included are classics like "Pigeons from Hell," "The Hills of the Dead," "The Cairn on the Headland," and "The Dead Remember," as well as many of his most obscure stories in the genre.

Other books by the same author:
Graveyard Rats and Others, 2003
Nameless Cults, 2001
Black Canaan, 1978
Wolfshead, 1968
The Dark Man and Others, 1963

Other books you might like:
William Hope Hodgson, *Adrift on a Haunted Sea*, 2005
M.R. James, *Count Magnus and Other Ghost Stories*, 2005
H.P. Lovecraft, *Necronomicon*, 2008
Oliver Onions, *Ghost Stories*, 2001
Karl Edward Wagner, *In a Lonely Place*, 1983

604

SUSAN HUBBARD

The Year of Disappearances

(New York: Simon & Schuster, 2008)

Story type: Vampire Story
Subject(s): Adolescence; Supernatural; Vampires

Major character(s): Ariella Montero, Teenager; Autumn Springer, Teenager; Mae Montero, Beekeeper
Time period(s): 2000s
Locale(s): Homosassa Springs, Florida

Summary: When her friend Mysty disappears, Ariella, who is half-human and half-vampire, falls under suspicion by the authorities who are aware of her family's previous association with a string of unresolved deaths. Ariella believes Mysty's disappearance and the suspicious spate of deaths that follow are the work of a group of zombifed human beings, who perhaps not coincidentally begin appearing shortly after the disappearance of her chemist vampire father. Sequel to *The Society of S*.

Other books by the same author:
The Society of S, 2007
Lisa Maria Takes Off, 2005
Lisa Maria's Guide for the Perplexed, 2004

Other books you might like:
Scott Ciencin, *The Vampire Odyssey*, 1992
Pat Graversen, *Sweet Blood*, 1992
Stephenie Meyer, *Twilight*, 2005
L.J. Smith, *The Awakening*, 1991
Karen E. Taylor, *Blood Ties*, 1995

605

TANYA HUFF

Blood Bank

(New York: DAW, 2008)

Story type: Collection
Subject(s): Horror; Short Stories; Supernatural

Summary: This collection of nine stories featuring effete vampire Henry Fitzroy with his scrappy mortal sidekick Vicki Nelson and their adventures investigating paranormal phenomena that sometimes threaten the secret vampire subculture. Included is the screenplay for "Stone Cold," which was adapted for television.

Other books by the same author:
Blood Debt, 1997
Blood Pact, 1993
Blood Lines, 1992
Blood Trail, 1992
Blood Price, 1991

Other books you might like:
Elizabeth Bear, *New Amsterdam*, 2008
Brian Hodge, *Shrines and Desecrations*, 1994
Nancy Kilpatrick, *The Vampire Stories of Nancy Kilpatrick*, 2000
Chelsea Quinn Yarbro, *The Vampire Stories of Chelsea Quinn Yarbro*, 1994

Subject(s): Romance; Demons
Major character(s): Tayla Mancuso, Hunter; Eidolon,
Demon; Shade, Mythical Creature
Time period(s): 2000s
Locale(s): United States

Summary: Eidolon is a demon, but a comparatively benevolent one who doesn't prey on human beings. Tayla is a demon hunter, sworn to protect the human race from the secret monsters that live among us. When the two meet, each is forced to change his or her preconceptions as they find themselves romantically attracted to one another.

Other books by the same author:
Snowbound, 2008

Other books you might like:
Nancy Collins, *Angels on Fire*, 1998
Yasmine Galenorn, *Dragon Wytch*, 2008
Laurell K. Hamilton, *Danse Macabre*, 2006
Marjorie M. Liu, *The Iron Hunt*, 2008
Maggie Shayne, *Wings in the Night*, 2001

609

JEROME K. JEROME

City of the Sea and Other Ghost Stories

(Ashcroft, British Columbia: Ash Tree Press, 2008)

Story type: Collection; Ghost Story
Subject(s): Ghosts; Short Stories; Supernatural

Summary: Jerome was a 19th century British writer better known as a humorist. His complete macabre fiction collected here, inclides "The Faithful Ghost," about a spirit that searches endlessly for the grave of its deceased lover; "The Ruined Home," about a ghost whose mysterious antics in its manifestations are a clue to its status in its past life; and "The Ghost of the Blue Chamber," in which a ghost's disorienting appearances at different times each day are tied to irregularities of the cockcrow. Edited and with an introduction by Jessica Amanda Salmonson.

Other books by the same author:
The Angel and the Author and Others, 1904
The Observations of Henry, 1901
Sketches in Lavender, Blue and Green, 1895
John Ingerfield, 1894
Told After Supper, 1891

Other books you might like:
John Kendrick Bangs, *Ghosts I Have Met*, 1898
Rudyard Kipling, *Kipling's Fantasy*, 1992
Robert Louis Stevenson, *The Supernatural Short Stories of Robert Louis Stevenson*, 1976
Frank R. Stockton, *Spirited Yarns*, 1996

606

TONYA HURLEY

Ghostgirl

(New York: Little, Brown, 2008)

Story type: Young Adult; Humor
Subject(s): Humor
Major character(s): Charlotte Usher, Teenager; Damen Dylan, Teenager; Wendy Anderson, Teenager
Time period(s): 2000s
Locale(s): United States

Summary: Charlotte has always felt isolated from the other students at the school, and the situation gets worse when she dies and is forced to haunt the building, more invisible than ever. A humorous but sentimental look at how loneliness can affect us even when we're in a crowd. First novel.

Other books you might like:
MaryJanice Davidson, *Dead and Loving It*, 2006
Lionel Fenn, *Kent Montana and the Moderately Vicious Vampire*, 1992
Nancy Holder, *Carnival of Souls*, 2006
Mel Odom, *Pirate Pandemonium*, 2001
Daniel Waters, *Generation Dead*, 2008

607

INGULPHUS (Pseudonym of Arthur Gray)

Tedious Brief Tales of Granta and Gramarye

(Ashcroft, British Columbia: Ash Tree Press, 2008)

Story type: Collection
Subject(s): Horror; Short Stories; Supernatural

Summary: Eleven antiquarian ghost stories are all set at Jesus College where the author served as Don for the first two decades of the 20th century. Included are "The Everlasting Club," about a men's club whose members promise to meet annually every All Souls Day, be they dead or alive; "Thankful Thomas," the tale of a necromancer; and "The Palladium," about an alchemist who learns how to transfer his soul into the body of a young student. Edited and with an introduction by Mark Valentine and Rosemary Pardoe.

Other books you might like:
M.R. James, *Ghost Stories of an Antiquary*, 1904
R.H. Malden, *Nine Ghosts*, 1943
A.N.L. Munby, *The Alabaster Hand*, 1949
L.T.C. Rolt, *Sleep No More*, 1948
E.G. Swain, *The Stoneground Ghost Tales*, 1912

608

LARISSA IONE

Pleasure Unbound

(New York: Forever, 2008)

Story type: Contemporary; Erotic Horror
Series: Demonica. Book 1

610

MARVIN KAYE , Editor

The Ghost Quartet

(New York: Tor, 2008)

Story type: Anthology; Ghost Story
Subject(s): Ghosts; Short Stories; Supernatural

Summary: All of these four novella-length ghost stories are original to the volume. In Brian Lumley's "A Place of Waiting," an artist is haunted by a specter on a distant mountain that only he can see. Orson Scott Card's "Hamlet's Father" is a spirited riff on William Shakespeare's famous drama. In "The Haunted Single Malt," Marvin Kaye writes of an unusual liquor with a ghostly pedigree. Tanith Lee, in "Strindberg's Ghost," tells of a man who discovers he has been chosen to be the sacrifice in a ghostly ritual.

Other books by the same author:
The Fair Folk, 2007
Forbidden Planets, 2006
The Dragon Quintet, 2004
Incisions, 2002
The Ultimate Halloween, 2001

Other books you might like:
Ellen Datlow, *The Dark*, 2005
   editor
Charles L. Grant, *Gothic Ghosts*, 1997
   Wendy Webb, co-editor
Claudia O'Keefe, *Ghosttide*, 1993
   editor
Paul F. Olson, *Post Mortem*, 1989
   David Silva, co-editor
Peter Straub, *Ghosts*, 1995

611

BRIAN KEENE

Ghost Walk

(New York: Leisure, 2008)

Story type: Occult
Subject(s): Horror; Small Town Life; Supernatural
Major character(s): Ken Ripple, Businessman; Maria Nasr, Writer; Levi Stoltzfus, Religious
Time period(s): 2000s
Locale(s): Lehorn Hollow, Pennsylvania

Summary: Ken Ripple's plans to turn the forest around Lehorn Hollow into a natural Halloween funhouse are undone by the discovery that Nodens, an ancient demonic entity, has recently been unleashed and is turning those foolish enough to venture into the woods after nightfall into conscripts for his zombie army.

Other books by the same author:
Castaways, 2009
Dead Sea, 2007
Ghoul, 2007
The Conqueror Worms, 2006
The Rutting Season, 2006

Other books you might like:
Douglas Clegg, *Goat Dance*, 1989
Morgan Fields, *Shaman Woods*, 1990
James A. Moore, *The Haunted Forest Tour*, 2007
   James Strand, co-author
Tom Piccirilli, *November Mourns*, 2005
Chet Williamson, *Dreamthorp*, 1989

612

BRIAN KEENE

Kill Whitey

(Baltimore, Maryland: Cemetery Dance, 2008)

Story type: Black Magic
Subject(s): Organized Crime; Russian Americans; Supernatural
Major character(s): Larry Gibson, Worker; Sandra Belov, Prostitute; Zakhar "Whitey" Putin, Organized Crime Figure, Sorcerer
Time period(s): 2000s
Locale(s): York, Pennsylvania

Summary: Larry Gibson's troubles have just begun when he rescues Sondra, a prostitute and exotic dancer from the local strip club. Sondra is coveted by the local Russian mafia and club owner Zakhar Putin, who pursues Larry and Sondra relentlessly. Putin is a member in a cabal of sorcerers who are impervious to death.

Other books by the same author:
Ghost Walk, 2008
Dead Sea, 2007
Ghoul, 2007
The Hollow, 2006
The Rutting Season, 2006

Other books you might like:
Simon Clark, *Lucifer's Ark*, 2007
Ray Garton, *Live Girls*, 1987
Graham Masterton, *The 5th Witch*, 2008
Karen Taylor, *Blood Secrets*, 1994

613

BRIAN KEENE

The Rising: Selected Scenes from the End of the World

(North Werbster, Indiana: Delirium, 2008)

Story type: Collection
Subject(s): Short Stories

Summary: All of the more than two dozen original stories in this collection involve zombies, and collectively they chronicle a plague of the undead which escalates from isolated incidents to a worldwide catastrophe. The collection is a companion book to the author's novel *The Rising*.

Other books by the same author:
Ghost Walk, 2008
Dead Sea, 2007
Ghoul, 2007
The Conqueror Worms, 2006
The Rising, 2003

Other books you might like:
Geoffrey Caine, *Legion of the Dead*, 1992
Andrew Neiderman, *After Life*, 1993
Steve Rasnic Tem, *The Excavation*, 1987
Peter Tremayne, *Zombie!*, 1981
David Wellington, *Monster Island*, 2006

614

JACK KETCHUM (Pseudonym of Dallas Mayr)

Old Flames

(New York: Leisure, 2008)

Story type: Collection
Subject(s): Horror; Short Stories; Supernatural

Summary: This volume collects two novellas of dark suspense by Ketchum. In the title story, a woman psychologically unbalanced by a failed romance seeks out an old high school flame and determines to make a romance with him work at any cost. "Right to Life" is the story of a young pregnant woman's desperate attempts to escape after being abducted by a fanatical band of anti-abortionists.

Other books by the same author:
Closing Time and Other Stories, 2007
Broken on the Wheel of Sex, 2006
Peaceable Kingdom, 2002
The Exit at Toledo Blade Boulevard, 1998

Other books you might like:
Ed Gorman, *Different Kinds of Dead and Other Tales*, 2005
Joe R. Lansdale, *The Shadows Kith and Kin*, 2007
David Morrell, *Nightscape*, 2004
F. Paul Wilson, *Soft and Others*, 1989

615

STEPHEN KING

Duma Key

(New York: Scribner, 2007)

Story type: Occult
Subject(s): Art; Horror; Supernatural
Major character(s): Edgar Freemantle, Contractor; Elizabeth Eastlake, Aged Person; Jerome Wireman, Lawyer
Time period(s): 2000s
Locale(s): Duma Key, Florida

Summary: Following a devastating job-related accident in which he loses an arm and sustains a head injury, Edgar Freemantle moves from Minnesota to Florida seeking a change in life. When Edgar develops a talent for paint-

ing pictures whose images seem to prefigure or cause fatal events, he realizes his injuries have sensitized him to a malignant supernatural force that is using him increasingly to make forays into the world.

Other books by the same author:
Cell, 2006
Lisey's Story, 2006
From a Buick 8, 2002
Dreamcatcher, 2001
Bag of Bones, 1998

Other books you might like:
Giles Blunt, *Cold Eye*, 1990
Ramsey Campbell, *Ancient Images*, 1989
Jonathan Carroll, *After Silence*, 1993
Rod Serling, *The Season to Be Wary*, 1967

616

DEAN R. KOONTZ

Odd Hours

(New York: Bantam, 2008)

Story type: Wild Talents
Series: Odd Thomas
Subject(s): Horror; Suspense; Terrorism
Major character(s): Odd Thomas, Cook; Annamaria, Young Woman; Reverend Moran, Religious
Time period(s): 2000s
Locale(s): Magic Beach, California

Summary: In his fourth adventure, Odd Thomas, a simple fry cook gifted with the ability to converse with the dead, finds himself drawing on his supernatural resources to prevent terrorists from smuggling weapons of mass destruction into a small California town.

Other books by the same author:
Your Heart Belongs to Me, 2008
The Good Guy, 2007
Brother Odd, 2006
Forever Odd, 2005
Odd Thomas, 2003

Other books you might like:
Mark Burnell, *Freak*, 1994
Tananarive Due, *The Between*, 1995
Jack Ellis, *Seeing Eye*, 1995
Stephen King, *The Dead Zone*, 1979

617

MICHAEL LAIMO

Fires Rising

(New York: Leisure, 2008)

Story type: Occult
Subject(s): Catholicism; Homeless People; Supernatural
Major character(s): Anthony Pilazzo, Religious; Jerry Roberts, Vagrant; Timothy, Young Man
Time period(s): 2000s
Locale(s): New York, New York

Horror

Summary: When the Church of St. Peter is renovated, workmen discover a strange crate that has been buried under its floor for decades. Something evil lives within that box, and once unearthed it exerts a malevolent influence on those in its vicinity, recruiting them as foot soldiers in what will ultimately prove a cataclysmic showdown between ultimate Good and Evil.

Other books by the same author:
Dead Souls, 2007
The Demonologist, 2005
Deep in the Darkness, 2004
Sleepwalker, 2004
Atmosphere, 2002

Other books you might like:
James Herbert, *Shrine*, 1983
Sarah Pinborough, *Tower Hill*, 2008
David Seltzer, *The Omen*, 1976
Whitley Strieber, *Unholy Fire*, 1992
David Niall Wilson, *Ancient Eyes*, 2007

618

ALEXANDER LAING

The Cadaver of Gideon Wyck

(Lakewood, Colorado: Millipede Press, 2008)

Story type: Mystery
Subject(s): Scientific Experiments
Major character(s): Gideon Wyck, Doctor; David Saunders, Doctor; Prexy Alling, Doctor
Time period(s): 1930s
Locale(s): Altonville, Maine

Summary: A gruesome murder reveals the bizarre scientific preoccupations of Gideon Wyck, a controversial physician who incarcerates victims of his experiments in teratology and genetic engineering in the local insane asylum. First published in 1934. Introduction by William Hjortsberg.

Other books by the same author:
The Motives of Nicholas Holtz, 1936

Other books you might like:
Mark Hansom, *The Shadow on the House*, 1935
Jack Mann, *The Kleinert Case*, 1938
John Marsh, *Body Made Alive*, 1936
William Sloane, *The Edge of Running Water*, 1939

619

GUSTAVE LE ROUGE

The Vampires of Mars

(Encino, California: Black Coat Press, 2008)

Story type: Collection
Subject(s): Horror; Science Fiction; Vampires

Summary: Repackaging of two novels published originally in France in 1908 and 1909. In *The Prisoner of the Planet Mars*, engineer Robert Darvel runs afoul of bat-winged vampires on his mission to the planet Mars. In *The War of the Vampires*, earth is bedeviled when Darvel returns to his home planet followed by several of the vampire monsters.

Other books you might like:
Jack Butler, *Nightshade*, 1989
Alan Hyder, *Vampires Overhead*, 1935
Christopher Pike, *The Season of Passage*, 1992
Colin Wilson, *The Space Vampires*, 1976

620

EDWARD LEE

Minotauress

(Orlando, Florida: Necro Press, 2008)

Story type: Collection
Subject(s): Horror; Short Stories; Supernatural

Summary: This compilation includes two sexually provocative tales of horror. The previously unpublished title novel is the story of the grim fate that awaits a pair of rednecks who break into a traveling occultist's household and get their comeuppance from a sexually voracious monster that the owner has summoned. Also included is the supernatural murder mystery "The Horn Cranker."

Other books by the same author:
Haunted House and Other Presidential Horrors, 2006
Slither, 2006
Flesh Gothic, 2004
The Ushers, 1999

Other books you might like:
Ray Garton, *Methods of Madness*, 1990
Jack Ketchum, *Broken on the Wheel of Sex*, 2006
Roberta Lannes, *The Mirror of Night*, 1997
Richard Sutphen, *Sexpunks and Savage Sagas*, 1992
Lucy Taylor, *Unnatural Acts*, 1994

621

H.P. LOVECRAFT

The Fiction

(New York: Barnes & Noble, 2008)

Story type: Collection
Subject(s): Horror; Short Stories; Supernatural

Summary: This is the first one-volume collection to gather all the fiction of H.P. Lovecraft, an author who flourished during the pulp magazine era and whose stories of horror and the supernatural have been lauded as the most important contributions to American weird fiction since the stories of Edgar Allan Poe. Lovecraft specialized in a type of cosmic horror fiction that expressed the total insignificance of human endeavor in an indifferent universe through a variety of extraterrestrial monsters and incomprehensible terrors elaborated in "The Call of Cthulhu," "At the Mountains of Madness," "The Shadow over Innsmouth," "The Shadow out of Time," "The Colour out of Space," and other stories. In addition to all of his mature fiction, this volume includes Lovecraft's ju-

venilia and his seminal essay "Supernatural Horror in Literature."

Other books by the same author:

The Dreams in the Witch House and Other Weird Stories, 2004

The Ancient Track, 2001

The Thing on the Doorstep and Other Weird Stories, 2001

The Call of Cthulhu and Other Weird Stories, 1999

Tales of H.P. Lovecraft, 1997

Other books you might like:

Algernon Blackwood, *The Best Ghost Stories of Algernon Blackwood*, 1973

Jorge Luis Borges, *Labyrinths*, 1962

Thomas Ligotti, *The Nightmare Factory*, 1996

Frank Belknap Long, *The Hounds of Tindalos*, 1946

Edgar Allan Poe, *Poetry and Fiction*, 2006

622

H.P. LOVECRAFT

Necronomicon

(London, England: Gollancz, 2008)

Story type: Collection
Subject(s): Horror; Short Stories; Supernatural

Summary: H.P. Lovecraft was a pulp-era writer whose fusions of gothic horror and visionary science fiction distinguished him as the most important American writer of weird fiction after Edgar Allan Poe. Selections include "At the Mountains of Madness," which speculates the colonization of the earth by an extraterrestrial race eons before mankind; "The Shadow over Innsmouth," about a race of half-human and half-amphibious monsters living off the coast of New England; and "The Shadow out of Time," in which an earth man's personality is displaced into the body of an extraterrestrial creature living uncounted eons in the past. Introduction by Stephen Jones.

Other books by the same author:

H.P. Lovecraft: The Fiction, 2008

The Dreams in the Witch House and Other Weird Stories, 2004

The Thing on the Doorstep and Other Weird Stories, 2001

The Call of Cthulhu and Other Weird Stories, 1999

Other books you might like:

Robert Bloch, *Mysteries of the Worm*, 1981

Ramsey Campbell, *Cold Print*, 1985

August Derleth, *The Cthulhu Mythos*, 1997

Henry Kuttner, *The Book of Iod*, 1995

Thomas Ligotti, *The Nightmare Factory*, 1996

623

BRIAN LUMLEY

Hagoppian and Other Stories

(San Francisco: Night Shade, 2008)

Story type: Collection
Subject(s): Horror; Short Stories; Supernatural

Summary: Twenty-four stories comprise the majority of short fiction this British author wrote in emulation of the works of H.P. Lovecraft. In addition to the title story, which concerns a peculiar man who is half-human and half-amphibious, the selections include "The Night the Sea-Maid Went Down," about an oil tanker's run in with an otherworldly monster, and the high fantasy "The House of Cthulhu."

Other books by the same author:

The Taint and Other Novellas, 2007

Screaming Science Fiction, 2006

Brian Lumley's Freaks, 2004

Beneath the Moors and Darker Places, 2002

The Whisperer and Others, 2001

Other books you might like:

Edward P. Berglund, *Shards of Darkness*, 2000

Lin Carter, *The Xothic Legend Cycle*,

Walter C. Debill Jr., *The Black Sutra*, 2007

August Derleth, *The Cthulhu Mythos*, 1997

Stanley Sargent, *Ancient Exhumations*, 1999

624

GRAHAM MASTERTON

The 5th Witch

(New York: Leisure, 2008)

Story type: Witchcraft
Subject(s): Crime and Criminals; Supernatural; Witches and Witchcraft
Major character(s): Dan Fisher, Detective—Police; Annie, Witch; Orestes Vasquez, Organized Crime Figure
Time period(s): 2000s
Locale(s): Los Angeles, California

Summary: When a trio of mobsters begin using witchcraft to kill their enemies in an effort to take control of the city of Los Angeles, police detective Dan Fisher avails himself of the services of his next door neighbor Annie, a white witch, to fight them.

Other books by the same author:

Chaos Theory, 2007

Descendant, 2006

Edgewise, 2006

Innocent Blood, 2005

Unspeakable, 2005

Other books you might like:

Thomas A. Disch, *The Businessman*, 1984

Christopher Fowler, *Rune*, 1991

Andrew Neiderman, *The Devil's Advocate*, 1990

Kim Newman, *The Quorum*, 1994

Horror

PATRICK McGRATH

Trauma

(New York: Knopf, 2008)

Story type: Psychological Suspense
Subject(s): Doctors; Psychological Thriller; Suspense
Major character(s): Charlie Weir, Doctor (psychiatrist);
 Agnes Weir, Teacher; Nora Chiara, Writer
Time period(s): 1970s
Locale(s): New York, New York

Summary: Years after his brother-in-law committed suicide, psychiatrist Charlie Weir, who was his physician, still feels guilt and responsibility. Now that his ex-wife and a new girlfriend have become romantically involved with him, Charlie finds himself examining his motives at the time and slowly uncovering the truth about a forgotten traumatic incident that may have shaped his behavior and perverted his judgment with regard to treatment.

Other books by the same author:
Port Mungo, 2004
Martha Peake, 2000
Asylum, 1996
Dr. Haggard's Disease, 1993
Spider, 1990

Other books you might like:
William Peter Blatty, *The Ninth Configuration*, 1978
Michael Cadnum, *Skyscape*, 1994
Kathe Koja, *Strange Angels*, 1994
Richard Lortz, *Bereavement*, 2002
F. Paul Wilson, *Sibs*, 1992

SARAH MONETTE

The Bone Key

(Holicong, Pennsylvania: Prime Book, 2008)

Story type: Collection
Subject(s): Horror; Short Stories; Supernatural
Major character(s): Charles Murchison Booth, Museum
 Curator

Summary: Monette presents ten variations on the traditional English ghost story, all featuring the exploits of Charles Murchison Booth, a museum archivist whose work bring him frequently into contact with antiquarian horrors. In "Elegy for a Demon Lover," Booth is seduced by an otherworldly demon. In "Bringing Helena Back," Booth helps a friend to resurrect his dead wife and inadvertently opens a door on a variety of supernatural horrors.

Other books by the same author:
Summerdown, 2008
The Mirador, 2007
The Virtu, 2006
Melusine, 2005

Other books you might like:
Elizabeth Bear, *New Amsterdam*, 2007
Steve Duffy, *Five Quarters*, 2002
 Ian Rodwell, co-author
A.F. Kidd, *Summoning Knells*, 2000
Reggie Oliver, *Masques of Satan*, 2007

FITZ-JAMES O'BRIEN

The Wondersmith and Others

(Ashcroft, British Columbia: Ash Tree Press, 2008)

Story type: Collection
Subject(s): Horror; Short Stories; Supernatural

Summary: This volume of the complete poetry and short fiction of a Civil War-era American fantasist, includes "The Lost Room," in which a man experiences bizarre poltergeist phenomena from an invisible invader of his dwelling; the title story, about a gypsy scheme to launch an army of animated dolls equipped with poison-tipped swords; and "The Diamond Lens," in which a scientist discovers a microscopic world in a drop of water he views with his microscope. Edited and with an introduction by Jessica Amanda Salmonson.

Other books by the same author:
The Poems and Stories of Fitz-James O'Brien, 1881

Other books you might like:
Ambrose Bierce, *Can Such Things Be?*, 1893
Robert W. Chambers, *The King in Yellow*, 1895
W.C. Morrow, *The Ape, The Idiot and Others*, 1897
Edgar Allan Poe, *Fiction and Poetry*, 2006

NICHOLAS PEKEARO

The Wolfman

(New York: Tor, 2008)

Story type: Werewolf Story; Mystery
Subject(s): Quest; Werewolves
Major character(s): Marlowe Higgins, Werewolf; Daniel
 Pearce, Police Officer; Anthony Mannuzza,
 Photographer
Time period(s): 2000s
Locale(s): United States

Summary: Marlowe Higgins is a werewolf, and he has hidden himself away in a small town where he can manage to avoid killing anyone when the moon is full. At first he seems to have found peace, but then a serial killer begins to claim victims in the area, and Higgins discovers that he isn't the worst monster around. First novel.

Other books you might like:
Gary Brandner, *The Howling*, 1977
Dennis Danvers, *Wilderness*, 1992
Tanya Huff, *Blood Lines*, 1991
Robert R. McCammon, *The Wolf's Hour*, 1989
Leslie H. Whitten, *Moon of the Wolf*, 1967

629

SARAH PINBOROUGH

Tower Hill

(New York: Leisure, 2008)

Story type: Occult; Ancient Evil Unleashed
Subject(s): Occult; Horror; Supernatural
Major character(s): Peter O'Brien, Religious; Steve Wharton, Student; Jack Kenyon, Professor
Time period(s): 2000s
Locale(s): Tower Hill, Maine

Summary: When ancient artifacts at a small church in Tower Hill are unearthed, a rash of gruesome deaths ensues, suggesting that they are related to an ancient evil newly unleashed.

Other books by the same author:
The Taken, 2007
Breeding Ground, 2006
The Reckoning, 2005
The Hidden, 2004

Other books you might like:
James Herbert, *Shrine*, 1983
Michael Laimo, *Fires Rising*, 2008
Simon Maginn, *Virgins and Martyrs*, 1995
David Seltzer, *The Omen*, 1976
Whitley Strieber, *Unholy Fire*, 1992

630

STEPHEN MARK RAINEY

Other Gods

(Colusa, California: Dark Regions, 2008)

Story type: Collection
Subject(s): Short Stories

Summary: All sixteen short horror stories in this collection were previously published between 1988 and 2007, primarily in the small press. They encompass a wide range of themes and provide an overview of the author's entire professional career. Most achieve their effect through understatement and implication rather than overt action.

Other books by the same author:
The Lebo Coven, 2004
Balak, 2000
The Last Trumpet, 2000
Dreams of the Dark, 1999 (Elizabeth Massie, co-author)
Fugue Devil and Other Weird Horrors, 1993

Other books you might like:
Ramsey Campbell, *Ghosts and Grisly Things*, 2000
Charles L. Grant, *Tales of the Nightside*, 1981
Brian Keene, *The Rising: Selected Scenes from the End of the World*, 2008
Joyce Carol Oates, *Tales of the Grotesque*, 1992
Jeffrey Thomas, *Doomsdays*, 2007

631

JAMES REESE

The Dracula Dossier

(New York: Morrow, 2008)

Story type: Occult; Serial Killer
Subject(s): Horror; Occult; Supernatural
Major character(s): Bram Stoker, Writer, Historical Figure; Francis Tumblety, Doctor; Hall Caine, Writer
Time period(s): 19th century
Locale(s): London, England

Summary: Presented as a lost journal of Bram Stoker, the author of *Dracula*, this novel recounts Stoker's attendance at an indoctrination meeting of the Order of the Gold Dawn at which a susceptible companion, quack physician Francis Tumblety, accidentally becomes a vessel for the malignant Egyptian god Set. Under Set's influence, Tumblety becomes the serial killer whose exploits would be attributed to Jack the Ripper, and challenges Stoker to stop his killing.

Other books by the same author:
The Witchery, 2006
The Book of Spirits, 2005
The Book of Sorrows, 2002

Other books you might like:
Peter Ackroyd, *Hawksmoor*, 1985
Brian Aldiss, *Dracula Unbound*, 1991
Emmanuel Carrere, *Gothic Romance*, 1990
Fred Saberhagen, *Dracula Tape*, 1975

632

PATRICIA ROSEMOOR
MARC PAOLETTI , Co-Author

The Last Vampire

(New York: Del Rey, 2008)

Story type: Vampire Story
Series: Annals of Alchemy and Blood. Book 1
Subject(s): Horror; Vampires; Voodoo
Major character(s): Scott Boulder, Military Personnel; Leah Maguire, Scientist; Rebecca Dumas, Witch
Time period(s): 2000s
Locale(s): New Orleans, Louisiana

Summary: The discovery of a mummified vampire corpse in a Texas cave gives the military an unusual opportunity to extract the creature's DNA and endow normal humans with its superhuman powers. When a *houngan* decides to resurrect the vampire through her voodoo powers, Black Ops leader Scott Boulder quickly discovers that the formidable monster has plans to create its own unvanquishable army of the undead.

Other books by the same author:
The Vampire Agent, 2008

Other books you might like:
Brian Lumley, *Deadspawn*, 1991
Yvonne Navarro, *Species*, 1995
John Steakley, *Vampire$*, 1990
David Wellington, *99 Coffins*, 2007

633

SAKI (Pseudonym of Hector Hugh Munro)

Sredni Vashtar: Sardonic Tales

(North Yorkshire, England: Tartarus Press, 2008)

Story type: Collection
Subject(s): Horror; Short Stories; Supernatural
Summary: Saki (1870-1916) was a British writer whose witty fiction of the supernatural and the Macabre was laced with black humor. Among these 30 stories are "Sredni Vashtar," about a boy who revenges himself supernaturally against adults who do not believe in his imaginary friend; "Laura," a tale of reincarnation; and "Gabriel Ernest," a tale of lycanthropy.

Other books by the same author:
The Complete Works of Saki, 1976
The Square Egg and Other Sketches, 1929
The Toys of Peace, 1919
Reginald in Russia, and Other Sketches, 1910
Reginald, 1904

Other books you might like:
Ambrose Bierce, *Can Such Things Be?*, 1893
L.P. Hartley, *The Traveling Grave and Other Stories*, 1948
Rudyard Kipling, *Kipling's Fantasy Stories*, 2004
Oscar Wilde, *Collected Works*, 2006

634

LYNSAY SANDS

Vampire, Interrupted

(New York: Avon, 2008)

Story type: Vampire Story
Series: Argeneau. Book 9
Subject(s): Romance; Supernatural; Vampires
Major character(s): Marguerite Argeneau, Detective—Private, Vampire; Julius Notte, Vampire; Christian Notte, Vampire
Time period(s): 2000s
Locale(s): London, England

Summary: Vampire Marguerite Argeneau's new assignment as a private detective proves complicated: Christian, a 500-year-old immortal, has hired her to find out the identity and whereabouts of his mother. Then Christian's father Julian, who has told his son since birth that his mother is dead, recognizes Marguerite as his lifemate.

Other books by the same author:
Vampires Are Forever, 2008
The Accidental Vampire, 2007
A Bite to Remember, 2006
Bite Me If You Can, 2006
A Quick Bite, 2005

Other books you might like:
P.N. Elrod, *Bloodlist*, 1990
Charlie Huston, *Already Dead*, 2005
Sherrilyn Kenyon, *Acheron*, 2008
Lee Killough, *Blood Hunt*, 1988

635

LYNSAY SANDS

Vampires Are Forever

(New York: Avon, 2008)

Story type: Vampire Story
Series: Argeneau. Book 8
Subject(s): Romance; Supernatural; Vampires
Major character(s): Inez Urso, Detective—Private; Thomas Argeneau, Vampire; Bastien Argeneau, Vampire
Time period(s): 2000s
Locale(s): London, England

Summary: Vampire Thomas Argeneau's search for his missing Aunt Marguerite is complicated by his need to oversee and protect his partner, Inez, a mortal whom he discovers is his life partner and whom he therefore must vampirize if they are to share immortality.

Other books by the same author:
Vampire, Interrupted, 2008
The Accidental Vampire, 2007
A Bite to Remember, 2006
Bite Me If You Can, 2006
A Quick Bite, 2005

Other books you might like:
P.N. Elrod, *Bloodlist*, 1990
Charlie Huston, *Already Dead*, 2005
Sherrilyn Kenyon, *Acheron*, 2008
Lee Killough, *Blood Hunt*, 1988

636

DARREN SHAN

Demon Apocalypse

(New York: Little, Brown, 2008)

Story type: Young Adult; End of the World
Series: Demonata. Book 6
Subject(s): Demons
Major character(s): Grubbs Grady, Teenager, Werewolf; Lord Loss, Mythical Creature; Beranabus, Wizard
Time period(s): Indeterminate Future
Locale(s): United States

Summary: Lord Loss and his army of demons have invaded and conquered much of the world. Grubbs Grady, a young werewolf, has to find a way to save the human race, which he eventually accomplishes by magically traveling back in time.

Other books by the same author:
Demon Thief, 2006
Lord of the Shadows, 2006
Slawter, 2006
Lord Loss, 2005
The Vampire Prince, 2003

Other books you might like:
Joan Aiken, *The Cockatrice Boys*, 1996
James Blish, *The Day After Judgment*, 1971
Madeline Robins, *The Stone War*, 1999
John Shirley, *Demons*, 2002
F. Paul Wilson, *Nightworld*, 1992

637

MICHAEL SHEA

The Autopsy and Other Tales

(Lakewood, Colorado: Centipede Press, 2008)

Story type: Collection
Subject(s): Horror; Short Stories; Supernatural

Summary: The complete horror, fantasy, and science fiction stories of an author strongly influenced by the writings of H.P. Lovecraft are gathered here. In addition to the title story, a blend of science fiction and visceral horror, the contents include the heroic fantasy "The Angel of Death"; the story of a bug-like race masquerading as humans, "The Horror on the 33"; and the Lovecraftian horror stories "Fat Face" and "The Colour out of Time." Introduction by Laird Barron.

Other books by the same author:
The Incompleat Nifft, 2000
In Yana, the Touch of Undying, 1995
Polyphemus, 1979
A Quest for Simbilis, 1974

Other books you might like:
Michael Bishop, *Blooded on Arachne*, 1982
Michael Blumlein, *The Brains of Rats*, 1986
Lucius Shepard, *Dagger Key and Other Stories*, 2007
John Shirley, *Living Shadows*, 2007

638

BRIAN J. SHOWERS

The Bleeding Horse and Other Ghost Stories

(Cork, Ireland: Mercier Press, 2008)

Story type: Collection; Ghost Story
Subject(s): Ghosts; Short Stories; Supernatural
Locale(s): Ireland

Summary: These seven traditional ghost stories are based on the folklore and legends of Rathmines, a suburban Dublin town where the author, an American expatriate in Ireland, lives. Contents include the title story, about the ghost of a fallen soldier that haunts the pub where it was killed; "Oil on Canvas," in which the ghost of a painter haunts the hotel where he left his last undiscovered canvases; and "Favourite No. 7 Omnibus," about the fates of several several survivors of a tragic carriage accident and its ghostly aftermath. Introduction by James A. Rockhill.

Other books you might like:
Augustus Jessop, *The Phantom Coach and Other Ghost Stories of an Antiquary*, 1998
J. Sheridan Le Fanu, *The Purcell Papers*, 1975
Jessica Amanda Salmonson, *The Mysterious Doom and Other Ghostly Tales of the Pacific Northwest*, 1992
John Manchip White, *Echoes and Shadows*, 2003

639

BRYAN SMITH

Queen of Blood

(New York: Leisure, 2008)

Story type: Occult
Subject(s): Horror; Occult; Supernatural
Major character(s): Dream Weaver, Fugitive; Chad Robbins, Fugitive; Mrs. Wickman, Supernatural Being
Time period(s): 2000s
Locale(s): Chattanooga, Tennessee

Summary: Supernaturally reconstructed from its ruins, the House of Blood—a portal to an occult world where victims are offered in bloody sacrifice to the Death Gods—dispatches emissaries to round up survivors who escaped from it before it was destroyed. Sequel to *House of Blood*.

Other books by the same author:
The Freakshow, 2007
House of Blood, 2004
Deathbringer, 2003

Other books you might like:
Ken Eulo, *The Brownstone*, 1980
Bentley Little, *The House*, 1997
Graham Masterton, *Walkers*, 1989
Al Sarrantonio, *House Haunted*, 1991

640

CLARK ASHTON SMITH

The Last Hieroglyph

(San Francisco: Night Shade, 2008)

Story type: Collection
Series: Collected Fantasies
Subject(s): Horror; Short Stories; Supernatural

Summary: This volume collects 19 stories of horror, fantasy and science fiction by a pulp-era writer and contemporary of H.P. Lovecraft. Selections include the werewolf story "The Beast of Averoigne"; "The Disinterment of Venus," about the seemingly supernatural effect that a sexually provocative statue has on a seminary of monks who dig it out of their grounds; and the Lovecraftian horror tale "Genius Loci."

Other books by the same author:
A Vintage from Atlantis, 2008
The Door to Saturn, 2007
The End of the Story, 2006
The Last Oblivion, 2002

Horror

Other books you might like:
H.P. Lovecraft, *The Fiction*, 2008
Brian McNaughton, *The Throne of Bones*, 1997
Michael Shea, *The Autopsy and Other Stories*, 2008
Jack Vance, *The Jack Vance Treasury*, 2007
Donald Wandrei, *The Eye and the Finger*, 1944

641

CLARK ASHTON SMITH

A Vintage from Atlantis

(San Francisco: Night Shade, 2008)

Story type: Collection
Series: Collected Fantasies. Book 3
Subject(s): Horror; Short Stories; Supernatural

Summary: Smith was a pulp-era writer known for his imaginary world fantasies and florid vocabulary. These 21 tales of horror, fantasy, and science fiction include the extra-dimensional fantasy "Beyond the Singing Flame," the science fiction-horror story "The Vaults of Yoh-Vombis," and the Lovecraftian horror tale "Ubbo Sathla."

Other books by the same author:
The Last Hieroglyph, 2008
The Maze of the Enchanter, 2008
The Door to Saturn, 2007
The End of the Story, 2006
The Last Oblivion, 2002

Other books you might like:
H.P. Lovecraft, *The Fiction*, 2008
Brian McNaughton, *The Throne of Bones*, 1997
Michael Shea, *The Autopsy and Other Tales*, 2008
Jack Vance, *The Jack Vance Treasury*, 2007
Donald Wandrei, *The Eye and the Finger*, 1944

642

KATHRYN SMITH

Let the Night Begin

(New York: Avon, 2008)

Story type: Vampire Story
Series: Brotherhood of Blood
Subject(s): Romance; Supernatural; Vampires
Major character(s): Reign, Vampire; Olivia Gavin, Vampire, Spouse; William Dashbrooke, Vampire
Time period(s): 19th century
Locale(s): Clovelly, England

Summary: Olivia pleads with her estranged vampire husband, Reign, to help find her kidnapped nephew, James. Reign agrees, unaware that James's kidnappers, all of whom belong to the Order of the Silver Palm, are hoping to trap Reign, whom they believe possesses the Blood Grail. The series chronicles the adventures of five Knights Templar who were vampirized when they drank from the Blood Grail centuries before.

Other books by the same author:
Night after Night, 2009
Taken by the Night, 2007
Be Mine Tonight, 2006
Night of the Huntress, 2006

Other books you might like:
Kresley Cole, *Dark Desires After Dusk*, 2008
Jacquelyn Frank, *Damien*, 2008
Sherrilyn Kenyon, *Acheron*, 2008
Lynsay Sands, *Vampire, Interrupted*, 2008
J.R. Ward, *Lover Enshrined*, 2008

643

JEFFREY THOMAS

Voices from Hades

(Colusa, California: Dark Regions, 2008)

Story type: Collection
Subject(s): Short Stories

Summary: The eight stories in this collection all appeared previously and share a common setting but are otherwise unrelated. Each takes place in Hell and involves a demon, an angel, or a condemned soul. The author's version of Hell is a complex creation in itself. *Letters from Hades* is a very similar collection.

Other books by the same author:
The Dream Dealers, 2006
Letters from Hades, 2003
Terra Incognita, 2000
Avatars of the Old Ones, 1997
Black Walls, Red Glass, 1997

Other books you might like:
Wayne Barlowe, *God's Demon*, 2007
Steven Brust, *To Reign in Hell*, 1984
C.J. Cherryh, *The Legions of Hell*, 1987
Tom Holt, *Faust Among Equals*, 1994
Holly Lisle, *Sympathy for the Devil*, 1996

644

THOMAS TRYON

The Other

(Lakewood, Colorado: Millipede Press, 2008)

Story type: Psychological Suspense
Subject(s): Death; Family Life; Twins
Major character(s): Niles Perry, Child; Holland Perry, Child; Alexandra Perry, Housewife
Time period(s): 20th century
Locale(s): Pequot Landing, Connecticut

Summary: Originally published in 1971, this landmark of modern horror tells the story of twin brothers, Niles and his malicious brother Holland whom Niles is always covering up for until the day that Holland's behavior becomes too outrageous and reveals the shocking truth of the unusual bond they share. Introduction by Ramsey Campbell.

Other books by the same author:
Night Magic, 1995
Wings of the Morning, 1990
Night of the Moonbow, 1989
Lady, 1974
Harvest Home, 1973

Other books you might like:
William March, *The Bad Seed*, 1955
Andrew Neiderman, *Perfect Little Angels*, 1989
F. Paul Wilson, *Sibs*, 1991
Bari Wood, *Twins*, 1974
    Jack Geasland, co-author

645

ANN VANDERMEER , Editor
JEFF VANDERMEER , Co-Editor

The New Weird

(San Francisco: Tachyon Publications, 2008)

Story type: Anthology
Subject(s): Fantasy; Horror; Short Stories

Summary: A collection of sixteen stories and essays charting an approach to the weird tale redolent of science fiction's "new wave" movement of the 1960s. Included are Clive Barker's "In the Hills, the Cities," a blend of fantasy and horror; Michael Moorcock's "Crossing into Cambodia," a story of the horrors of nuclear war; and "Festival Lives," a seven part round-robin story written especially for the anthology.

Other books by the same author:
Steampunk, 2008

Other books you might like:
Harlan Ellison, *Dangerous Visions*, 1967
    editor
Dennis Etchison, *Cutting Edge*, 1983
    editor
Kirby McCauley, *Dark Forces*, 1981
    editor
Nicholas Royle, *Darklands*, 1991
    editor
Bruce Sterling, *Mirrorshades*, 1986
    editor

646

RACHEL VINCENT

Rogue

(Don Mills, Ontario: Mira, 2008)

Story type: Romance; Femme Fatale
Series: Cat People. Book 2
Subject(s): Animals/Cats; Secrets
Major character(s): Faythe Sanders, Mythical Creature; Ryan, Mythical Creature; Marc, Mythical Creature
Time period(s): 2000s
Locale(s): Texas

Summary: Faythe is a member of a secret society of shape-shifters that live within human civilization. Her job is to make sure that rogues among her kind don't prey on humans and betray the secret of their existence, but a series of mysterious murders suggests that something even more disastrous may be looming.

Other books by the same author:
Stray, 2007

Other books you might like:
Kelley Armstrong, *Bitten*, 2001
Patricia Briggs, *Blood Bound*, 2007
Nancy Collins, *Walking Wolf*, 1995
Charlaine Harris, *All Together Dead*, 2007
Melanie Tem, *Wilding*, 1992

647

DONALD WANDREI
HOWARD WANDREI , Illustrator

Sanctity and Sin

(New York: Hippocampus Press, 2008)

Story type: Collection
Subject(s): Horror; Poetry; Supernatural

Summary: A colleague and contemporary of H.P. Lovecraft shares his vision of cosmic horror in over 100 exercises in macbre verse. This volume includes the complete contents of the volumes *Ecstasy and Other Poems* (1928), *Dark Odyssey* (1931), and *Poems for Midnight* (1964), as well as a grouping of uncollected poems and poems in prose drawn from Wandrei's other books. Illustrations by the author's brother.

Other books by the same author:
A Donald Wandrei Miscellany, 2001
Don't Dream, 1997
Colossus, 1989
Strange Harvest, 1965
The Eye and the Finger, 1944

Other books you might like:
Leah Bodine Drake, *A Hornbook for Witches*, 1950
Frank Belknap Long, *In Mayan Splendor*, 1977
H.P. Lovecraft, *The Ancient Track*, 2001
Clark Ashton Smith, *Selected Poems*, 1971

648

DANIEL WATERS

Generation Dead

(New York: Hyperion, 2008)

Story type: Young Adult; Humor
Subject(s): Humor
Major character(s): Phoebe Kendall, Teenager, Student; Tommy Williams, Teenager, Student; Pete Martinsburg, Teenager, Student
Time period(s): 2000s
Locale(s): United States

Summary: All over the country, dead teenagers are com-

ing back to life and returning to school. Now known as the "living impaired", they form a separate caste system. The status quo is challenged when one of the most popular girls in the school begins dating one of the dead boys, to the consternation of friends and family. First novel.

Other books you might like:
Mario Acevedo, *The Nymphos of Rocky Flats*, 2006
MaryJanice Davidson, *Undead and Unappreciated*, 2005
Andrew Fox, *Fat White Vampire Blues*, 2003
Tonya Hurley, *Ghostgirl*, 2008
Richard Laymon, *Resurrection Days*, 1988

649

EDITH WHARTON

The Triumph of the Night and Other Tales

(North Yorkshire, England: Tartarus Press, 2008)

Story type: Collection
Subject(s): Horror; Short Stories; Supernatural

Summary: In these 15 tales of ghosts and hauntings, Wharton, a mainstream writer, used the supernatural to crystallize emotions and psychological states. The title tale tells of a man whose spectral doppelganger reveals his true intentions toward his ailing uncle. "Afterward" is the story of an inconspicuous haunting. In "The Lady Maid's Bell," the ghost of a devoted maid thwarts efforts of her mistress's husband to discover her lover.

Other books by the same author:
The Ghost Stories Edith Wharton, 1975
Ghosts, 1937
Here and Beyond, 1926
Xingu and Other Stories, 1916
Tales of Men and Ghosts, 1910

Other books you might like:
Emma Fancis Dawson, *An Itinerant House and Other Stories*, 1897
Olivia Dunbar, *The Shell of Sense*, 1997
Ellen Glasgow, *The Shadowy Third and Other Stories*, 1923
May Sinclair, *Uncanny Tales*, 1923
Mary E. Wilkins-Freeman, *The Wind in the Rosebush*, 1903

650

AUSTIN WILLIAMS

Crimson Orgy

(Fallston, Maryland: Borderlands Press, 2008)

Story type: Mystery
Subject(s): Horror; Movies; Suspense
Major character(s): Sheldon Meyer, Director; Vance Cogburn, Actor; Barbara Cheston, Actress
Time period(s): 2000s

Locale(s): Hillsboro Beach, Florida
Summary: Sheldon Meyer brings his film crew to an out-of-the way location in South Florida under the pretense of filming the ultimate horror B-movie. What Meyer's actors don't know—and what becomes abundantly and bloodily clear—is that their director plans to turn the movie into a genuine snuff film. First novel.

Other books you might like:
John Douglas, *The Late Show*, 1994
Ray Garton, *Sex and Violence in Hollywood*, 2001
Stephen Graham Jones, *Demon Theory*, 2007
Joe R. Lansdale, *The Drive-In*, 1988

651

F. PAUL WILSON

By the Sword

(New York: Forge, 2008)

Story type: Occult
Series: Repairman Jack. Book 11
Subject(s): Horror; Cults; Supernatural
Major character(s): Jack, Mercenary; Hank Thompson, Cult Member; Hideo Takita, Businessman
Time period(s): 2000s
Locale(s): New York, New York

Summary: As Rasolom's plans for earthly Armageddon begin to cohere, Jack, an urban mercenary reluctantly cast in the role of Rasolom's adversary, finds himself besieged on many fronts: by a group of sociopathic cultists who are holding hostage a pregnant woman whose unborn child may help bring about the end of the world; by a Japanese businessman leading a group of gangsters who seek an ancient Japanese sword with magical powers; and by a secret Japanese religious sect who also hope to find the sword and use it to summon the Black Wind, a devastating supernatural force.

Other books by the same author:
Bloodline, 2007
Harbingers, 2006
Infernal, 2005
Crisscross, 2004
Gateways, 2003

Other books you might like:
James Herbert, *The Spear*, 1978
Gordon Linzner, *The Oni*, 1986
Charles Sheffield, *The Judas Cross*, 1994
   David Bischoff, co-author
Robert Weinberg, *The Armageddon Box*, 1991
Dennis Wheatley, *They Used Dark Forces*, 1964

652

T.M. WRIGHT

Bone Soup

(Baltimore, Maryland: Cemetery Dance, 2008)

Story type: Collection
Subject(s): Horror; Supernatural; Short Stories

Summary: This miscellaneous collection of 33 stories, poems, and pieces of incidental prose is by a writer known for his obscure and often surrealistic forays into the macabre. "The House under the Street" tells of a man's obsessive fascination with an entire house found during a subterranean excavation in his neighborhood. "Rainy Day People" is the story of an insular man's vision of people on rainy days who may be phantasms or figments of his imagination. "Cold House" is an uncommon ghost story.

Other books by the same author:
I Am the Bird, 2006
Visiting the Edge, 2004
Cold House, 2003
The House on Orchid Street, 2003
Erthmun, 1995

Other books you might like:
George Clayton Johnson, *All of Us Are Dying and Other Stories*, 1999
Stephen King, *Skeleton Crew*, 1985
William F. Nolan, *Nightshadows*, 2007
Dan Simmons, *Prayers to Broken Stones*, 1990

653

CHELSEA QUINN YARBRO

A Dangerous Climate

(New York: Tor, 2008)

Story type: Vampire Story
Series: Chronicles of Saint-Germain. Book 21
Subject(s): Russian Empire; Supernatural; Vampires
Major character(s): Comte de Saint-Germain, Vampire; Ludmilla Svariskaya, Doctor; Hroger, Monster (ghoul)
Time period(s): 18th century
Locale(s): St. Petersburg, Russia

Summary: In his 21st adventure, the benevolent vampire Count Saint-Germain—here living under the assumed identity Hercegek Gyor for diplomatic purposes—finds his work overseeing the efforts of Peter the Great to build the metropolis of Sankt Pitersburg (St. Petersburg) besieged on several fronts: by persistent sickness and ignorance among humans that thwart his best efforts to treat them medically, by bands of hoodlum gangs sent by some unnamed nemesis to try and kill him, and by an impostor who claims to be his legitimate nephew and heir.

Other books by the same author:
Borne in Blood, 2007
Roman Dusk, 2006
States of Grace, 2005
Dark of the Sun, 2004
Midnight Harvest, 2003

Other books you might like:
Les Daniels, *Citizen Vampire*, 1981
Barbara Hambly, *Traveling with the Dead*, 1995
Pierre Kast, *The Vampires of Alfama*, 1976
Anne Rice, *Queen of the Damned*, 1988
Fred Saberhagen, *A Sharpness on the Neck*, 1996

654

CHELSEA QUINN YARBRO

Lost Prince

(Fallston, Maryland: Borderlands Press, 2008)

Story type: Werewolf Story
Subject(s): Horror; Supernatural; Werewolves
Major character(s): Alteza Rolon, Werewolf; Lugantes, Courtier; Don Alonzo, Werewolf
Time period(s): 16th century
Locale(s): El Morro, Spain

Summary: Don Alonzo grapples with his werewolf nature and his need to feed on human flesh during the height of the Spanish Inquisition, but his supernatural depredations seem minor compared to the atrocities committed by humans in the name of God. A retitling of the author's 1983 novel *The Godforsaken*.

Other books by the same author:
Magnificat, 2000
Monet's Ghost, 1997
Charity, Colorado, 1993
Spider Glass, 1991
Beastnights, 1989

Other books you might like:
Les Daniels, *The Silver Skull*, 1979
Pierre Kast, *The Vampires of Alfama*, 1976
H. Warner Munn, *The Werewolf of Ponkert*, 1958
Anne Rice, *The Vampire Lestat*, 1985

655

ZORAN ZIVKOVIC

The Last Book

(Hornsea, England: PS Publishing, 2008)

Story type: Mystery
Subject(s): Horror; Psychic Powers; Supernatural
Major character(s): Dejan Lukic, Detective—Police; Vera Gavrilovic, Businesswoman; Olga Bogdanovic, Businesswoman
Time period(s): 2000s

Summary: After a series of deaths at the Papyrus Bookstore, inspector Dejan Lukic is called to investigate. Lukic discovers that all of those who died came into contact with a certain book and he must divine what it is about the book's powers that is so fatal.

Other books by the same author:
Impossible Encounters, 2008
Steps through the Mist, 2007
Seven Touches of Music, 2006
Twelve Collections and the Tea Shop, 2006
Hidden Camera, 2005

Other books you might like:
Ray Bradbury, *Death Is a Lonely Business*, 1992
Ramsey Campbell, *Ancient Images*, 1989
Susan Hill, *The Man in the Picture*, 2007
Peter Straub, *The Hellfire Club*, 1996

The Latest Trends in Science Fiction
by
Don D'Ammassa

Even during its earliest days, science fiction tended to split into two main categories—exotic, fast paced and often crudely written adventure stories or more serious extrapolations either of present trends in the world or speculation about the possible impact of extraordinary new discoveries. This is often characterized as the difference between the influence of Jules Verne and H.G. Wells. Then as now, there were well written and literate adventure stories as well as badly written but more ambitious fiction. Trends in the world at large, within the publishing industry, and among the reading public inevitably meant that the focus of speculative fiction would gradually shift over time. As early as the 1940s, the field began a slow but inevitable shift toward the adoption of more mainstream values in writing. This was partly because an increasing number of non-genre writers were discovering the advantages inherent in speculative fiction, partly because the shift from pulp magazines to paperback and then hardcover meant that publishers sought a wider and more discerning audience, and partly because readers themselves became more sophisticated and demanded more careful and skillful writing.

As the decades passed, themes which had at one time dominated the field began to grow less popular and were gradually replaced by new ones. Traditional space adventures, time travel, stories of aliens invading the Earth, tales of marvelous inventions, mutations, telepathy and other psychic powers, nuclear wars and their aftermath, all have waxed and waned in popularity. They have in recent years been largely displaced by more serious cautionary tales, accounts of ecological disaster, overpopulation, the erosion of personal rights, and other contemporary concerns. Darkly humorous satire gave way to more realistic, even grim dystopian fiction. Space adventure has in large part been supplanted by military science fiction and instead of visiting other planets, protagonists are more likely to conduct the reader on tours of alternate histories or radically altered near future societies. Another significant factor has been the rise of fantasy fiction, which has eroded the readership of science fiction, particularly those interested in high adventure. Even hard science fiction has seen a decline.

At one time there was a constant stream of novels and stories about space travel as it might be conducted in the near future. Today such tales are rarities.

The first half of 2008 suggests the possibility that writers and readers have become nostalgic for old style SF. A number of classic works have reappeared in print after long periods of neglect, including novels by Keith Laumer, A.E. van Vogt, and others. Perhaps more significantly, some authors are emulating the kind of story telling that was once so popular. An extreme example is *Space Vulture* by Gary K. Wolf and Archbishop John J. Myers, which recreates the archaic style popularized in pulp magazines like *Planet Stories*. Their novel of the battle between a two fisted, space traveling policeman and a larger than life villain is an admitted homage to the Space Hawk series by Anthony Gilmore, which appeared in the pulp magazines during the 1930s. John C. Wright extended the Gilbert Gosseyn series by A.E. van Vogt in his latest novel, *The Null A Continuum*, just as in 2007 Kevin J. Anderson provided a sequel to the same author's classic *Slan* from 1946.

Similarly, Larry Niven returned to his own Known Space series, immensely popular during the 1960s and 1970s, for *Juggler of Worlds*, written in collaboration with Edward Lerner. Karl Schroeder's *Pirate Sun* and Allen Steele's *Galaxy Blues* are both classic space operas, though with modern twists. S.M. Stirling's *In the Courts of the Crimson Kings* continues his new series set in an alternate version of our universe where Mars and Venus are home to intelligent alien species, a device popular in the works of classic writers like Edgar Rice Burroughs, Leigh Brackett, Ray Bradbury, and others. Roger MacBride Allen's *Final Inquiries*, a blend of science fiction and the detective story, is a traditional other worlds adventure wrapped in a murder mystery. Ben Bova's *Mars Life* expands his very realistic, hard science fiction series about the exploration of our solar system in the near future, this time chronicling the discovery of an intelligent species still surviving on dying Mars.

Mike Brotherton's second novel, *Spider Star*, is a classic space opera about a human colony that discovers

a cache of alien technology, unwisely tinkers with it, and sets off a chain reaction that could destroy their entire planet. Space opera has proven to be particularly fertile ground for British writers, several of whom had new novels this year. Peter Hamilton has written a number of panoramic space adventures full of exotic settings and unusual speculations and *The Dreaming Void* is another one. In this case an anomalous region of space begins to expand and its advance triggers psychological changes in races in close proximity. The mystery must be solved to avoid a terrible disaster.

Alastair Reynolds at least temporarily moved away from his Revelation Space series to present a new vision of the universe, one in which a single human woman has cloned herself and sent nearly immortal copies of her personality out into space in a multitude of bodies, forming a kind of family that periodically meets to compare notes. When someone sabotages the currently scheduled meeting, nearly wiping out the entire membership, the handful of survivors have to discover who was responsible and why before they are also eliminated.

Chris Roberson, a comparatively new author, combines two science fiction themes in his latest novel, *The Dragon's Nine Sons*. Although the setting is in outer space, the future is of a world whose history did not follow the same course as ours. The two major powers are China and Mexico and their conflict on Earth has been extended beyond the atmosphere. Greg Egan also explores an unusual scenario in *Incandescence*. In his vision of the distant future, the galaxy is divided between two great civilizations, one of which refuses to allow any visitors from the other until a mysterious artifact triggers a crisis.

Three of the best science fiction novels during this period came from writers who are not ordinarily associated with the field. *Resistance* by Owen Sheers, whose previous work has been primarily poetry, marked his debut as a novelist with one of the better alternate histories of World War II. In this case, the German army did manage to invade and occupy a portion of the British Isles. The story, told primarily from the point of view of several British women whose husbands have dropped out of sight, is intelligent and moving. James Braziel's *Birmingham, 35 Miles* assumes that global warming is both real and imminent. He suggests that much of the middle portions of North America would become effectively a blasted landscape where only a handful of stubborn people can wrest a living from the land. His observations about the effective change in the size of the world—since automobile travel has become virtually impossible in that area—is particularly striking. Douglas Preston, who most frequently writes marginally fantastic thrillers in collaboration with Lincoln Child, provided a fascinating if somewhat deceptive suspense story about a scientific project which appears to have established communication with an entity analogous to God. Although the closing chapters invalidate the main thesis, the possibilities suggested by the initial story line are fascinating and thought-provoking.

Cyberpunk fiction, which explores the interface between humans and machines, has experienced a recent drop in popularity, but newcomer David Louis Edelman has kept its spirit alive in *Infoquake* and this year's sequel, *Multireal*. Nanotechnology has made it possible to implant microscopic machines into the human body, and the consequences of that technology form the battleground between those who want to make it freely available to the world and those who wish to monopolize it for their own purposes. John Varley, whose reputation was originally established by a series of quirky, out of the ordinary stories and novels, has become much more traditional in recent years. *Rolling Thunder* is very much in the style of the young adult adventures by Robert A. Heinlein. In fact, its protagonist is named Poddy, a reference to *Podkayne of Mars*. She is an equally feisty young woman whose participation in a cultural visit to Europa leads to intrigue and adventure.

Two publishers from the United Kingdom announced changes which are likely to have some impact on the availability of science fiction in the United States. Orbit Books will now be publishing and distributing directly in both countries. BL Publishing, which has a very active line of game related tie-in novels under the Black Library label, has added a new imprint, Solaris, which will publish generic science fiction and fantasy. Wizards of the Coast, an American publisher which has also specialized in game related fantasy, is also planning a separate imprint of non-media fantasy and science fiction novels.

One aspect of the evolution of the field remains unchanged this year. Single author short story collections and reprint anthologies were at one time a major part of the science fiction publishing scheme, but today collections are rarities and most anthologies consist of original stories that are focused on a narrow theme, though there are still a few unthemed original collections. Much of the best of short science fiction still appears in the magazines where it fails to reach as wide an audience as was once the case. The neglect of short fiction in book form is probably the result of the need to attract readers who are not necessarily loyal to the genre. The general reading public has long favored novels over collections. Although the small press has filled the gap in some cases, the future of short science fiction remains uncertain. The most notable example of this is *The Baum Plan for Financial Independence and Other Stories* by John Kessel, a first rate collection which found a home in the small press. Other authors whose short fiction has similarly been published in limited editions include Paul Melko, Ken Rand, Paul Di Filippo, Jeffrey Thomas, Jay Lake, and Kelly Link. Science fiction magazines have maintained their audience but show no signs of returning to their previous popularity.

The publishing field in general is undergoing considerable change. Several small press operations have recently gone out of business or merged, and there has been transition within the major publishing houses as well. The Science Fiction Book Club changed editors

abruptly and with as yet undetermined consequences. The advent of print on demand publishing and ebooks has not yet had a major effect on publishing, but both technologies are in their infancy. Online fiction has continued to increase in quantity, although the quality remains erratic. Jim Baen's Universe remains one of the most reliable sites for science fiction. The novella, once a very popular length in science fiction, has become virtually extinct because there is no longer a healthy market for it.

A review of titles scheduled for release in the latter half of 2008 suggests that these same trends will continue for the foreseeable future. Space opera and hard science fiction are due from Jeffrey Carver, Joe Haldeman, Michael Flynn, Edward Lerner, Kevin J. Anderson, and others. There has been a slight decline in series novels in science fiction even as they becomes more common in fantasy. The prospects in the short term look promising but continuing changes in publishing make the outlook uncertain a year from now.

Recommended Titles

The first half of 2008 has provided a rather diverse range of new science fiction novels, although there have been no notable single author collections or anthologies other than the reliable retrospective of the year edited annually by Gardner Dozois.

The Baum Plan for Financial Independence and Other Stories by John Kessel

Birmingham, 35 Miles by James Braziel

The Dragon's Nine Sons by Chris Roberson

The Dreaming Void by Peter Hamilton

Final Inquiries by Roger MacBride Allen

House of Suns by Alastair Reynolds

In the Courts of the Crimson King by S.M. Stirling

Incandescence by Greg Egan

Mars Life by Ben Bova

Multireal by David Louis Edelman

Resistance by Owen Sheers

Rolling Thunder by John Varley

Spider Star by Mike Brotherton

The Year's Best Science Fiction: Twenty-Fifth Annual edited by Gardner Dozois

Science Fiction Titles

656

DAN ABNETT

Legion

(Nottingham, United Kingdom: Black Library, 2008)

Story type: Space Opera; Military
Series: Warhammer
Subject(s): Aliens; War
Major character(s): Hurtado Bronzi, Military Personnel; John Grammaticus, Military Personnel; Soneka, Military Personnel
Time period(s): Indeterminate Future
Locale(s): Outer Space; Planet—Imaginary

Summary: An officer of a great interstellar empire is suspicious of the motives of one of the legions that serve the emperor. They have been sent to a remote world to suppress what at first appears to be a minor insurrection, but there are indications that this is just the tip of the iceberg, that alien powers are involved, and that the legion itself might be disloyal.

Other books by the same author:
Only in Death, 2007
The Founding, 2007
Horus Rising, 2006
His Last Command, 2005
Ravenor Returned, 2005

Other books you might like:
Bruce Balfour, *Star Crusader*, 1995
Robert Charrette, *Initiation to War*, 2001
William C. Dietz, *The Final Battle*, 1995
Lee Lightner, *Wolf's Honour*, 2008
David Weber, *Ashes of Victory*, 2000

657

JOHN JOSEPH ADAMS , Editor

Wastelands

(San Francisco: Night Shade, 2008)

Story type: Anthology
Subject(s): Short Stories; Apocalypse

Summary: This is an anthology collection of 22 previously published stories each of which deals with some form of apocalypse. Although there is a strong religious theme in several of the stories, they are predominantly science fiction. The contributors include Stephen King, Gene Wolfe, Jonathan Lethem, George R.R. Martin, Nancy Kress, and others.

Where it's reviewed:
Booklist, February 1, 2008, page 35
Library Journal, January 1, 2008, page 89
Publishers Weekly, November 26, 2007, page 32

Other books you might like:
Stephen King, *The Stand*, 1978
Jonathan Lethem, *Amnesia Moon*, 1995
George R.R. Martin, *The Armageddon Rag*, 1983
James Van Pelt, *Summer of the Apocalypse*, 2006
Gene Wolfe, *The Fifth Head of Cerberus*, 1972

658

ANN AGUIRRE

Grimspace

(New York: Ace, 2008)

Story type: Space Opera; Mystery
Subject(s): Psychic Powers; Space Travel
Major character(s): Sirantha Jax, Spacewoman, Mutant; March, Spy; Hon-Durren, Criminal
Time period(s): Indeterminate Future
Locale(s): Planet—Imaginary; Outer Space

Summary: Sirantha Jax possesses the mutant gene that allows her to navigate starships through interstellar space. When her ship crashes and she is the only survivor, there are claims that she was responsible for the deaths of the rest of the crew, but she is suffering memory loss and can't defend herself. Then a mysterious man appears and tells her she is facing a slow but inevitable death unless she comes with him. First novel.

Other books you might like:
C.J. Cherryh, *Finity's End*, 1997
Julie E. Czerneda, *Hidden in Sight*, 2003
Melissa Scott, *Dreamships*, 1992
Alison Sinclair, *Legacies*, 1995
S.L. Viehl, *Blade Dancer*, 2003

659

ROGER MACBRIDE ALLEN

Final Inquiries

(New York: Bantam, 2008)

Story type: Mystery; Space Opera
Series: BSI. Book 3
Subject(s): Aliens; Mystery
Major character(s): Jamie Mendez, Police Officer; Hannah Wolfson, Police Officer; Brox 231, Alien, Police Officer
Time period(s): Indeterminate Future
Locale(s): Planet—Imaginary

Summary: Two human police officers find themselves aboard a highly advanced starship of one of the Elder races, which takes them to one of their worlds where a Kendari diplomat has been murdered, apparently at the hands of a human. They are compelled to cooperate with a Kendari investigator in order to advert a major interstellar confrontation.

Other books by the same author:
Death Sentence, 2007
The Cause of Death, 2006
The Shores of Tomorrow, 2004
The Ocean of Years, 2002
The Depths of Time, 2000

Other books you might like:
Alan Dean Foster, *Greenthieves*, 1994
Lynn Hightower, *Alien Rites*, 1995
Frank A. Javor, *The Rim-World Legacy*, 1967
Lee Killough, *Deadly Silents*, 1981
Katherine Kurtz, *The Legacy of Lehr*, 1986

660

LOU ANDERS , Editor

Sideways in Crime

(Nottingham, United Kingdom: Solaris, 2008)

Story type: Anthology; Alternate World
Subject(s): Short Stories; Mystery and Detective Stories

Summary: Each of the 15 original stories in this anthology makes use of two themes, the commission of some sort of crime and the existence of alternate versions of our reality. The contributors include Stephen Baxter, Paul Di Filippo, Eric Flint, Mike Resnick, S.M. Stirling, and others. The treatment varies from serious to farcical.

Other books by the same author:
Fast Forward 1, 2007
Futureshocks, 2006
Live without a Net, 2003

Other books you might like:
David Brin, *The Practice Effect*, 1984
John Brunner, *The Infinitive of Go*, 1980
Joe Haldeman, *The Hemingway Hoax*, 1990
Ward Hawkins, *Blaze of Wrath*, 1983
Robert J. Sawyer, *Hominids*, 2002

661

TAYLOR ANDERSON

Into the Storm

(New York: Roc, 2008)

Story type: Military; Alternate Universe
Series: Destroyermen. Book 1
Subject(s): War; Aliens
Major character(s): Matthew Patrick Reddy, Military Personnel, Sea Captain; Ben Mallory, Military Personnel; Greg Garrett, Military Personnel
Time period(s): 1940s (1942)
Locale(s): At Sea; Alternate Earth

Summary: During the early months of World War II, an elderly destroyer escapes the enemy by driving into a storm and finds itself transported to an alternate Earth. The dinosaurs have not died out and two intelligent species have arisen, neither of them human, and the visitors find themselves caught in a war between them. First novel.

Other books you might like:
John Birmingham, *Weapons of Choice*, 2004
Martin Caidin, *The Final Countdown*, 1980
William R. Forstchen, *Rally Cry*, 1990
Harry Harrison, *West of Eden*, 1984
John Ringo, *Vorpal Blade*, 2007
Travis S. Taylor, co-author

662

CATHERINE ASARO

The Ruby Dice

(New York: Baen, 2008)

Story type: Space Opera; Psychic Powers
Series: Skolian Empire. Book 12
Subject(s): Psychic Powers; Space Travel
Major character(s): Kelrickson Garlin, Ruler; Jaibriol Qox, Ruler; Sauscony Lahaylia, Noblewoman
Time period(s): Indeterminate Future
Locale(s): Planet—Imaginary; Outer Space

Summary: The two human empires are at peace although they are still recovering from a devastating war. Each of the two rulers has a secret to conceal. One has discovered that he possesses psychic powers, the other is hiding an incident from his past. Revelation of either secret could result in destabilization and a renewal of the old conflict neither desires.

Other books by the same author:
Alpha, 2006
Schism, 2004
Sunrise Alley, 2004
Skyfall, 2003
Ascendant Sun, 2000

Other books you might like:
Poul Anderson, *The Day of Their Return*, 1973
C.J. Cherryh, *The Kif Strike Back*, 1985
Frank Herbert, *Dune Messiah*, 1969
Melissa Scott, *The Game Beyond*, 1984
Robert Silverberg, *Star of Gypsies*, 1986

663

PAUL L. BATES

Dreamer

(Waterville, Maine: Five Star, 2008)

Story type: Dystopian; Psychic Powers
Subject(s): Immortality
Major character(s): Jennie Height, Psychic; Walter Vellum, Businessman; Carpathia Coyle, Psychic, Empath
Time period(s): Indeterminate Future
Locale(s): Earth

Summary: A far future society is slipping rapidly into decay, repression, and chaos. Several psychic talents have begun to manifest themselves, including empaths and prescient dreamers. There is a resistance movement, but somehow the government seems to anticipate their every move, and it is only the psychic dreams of a young woman that prevent them from being completely wiped out. This is related to the author's first novel *Imprint*, but is not a sequel.

Other books by the same author:
Imprint, 2006

Other books you might like:
Chester Aaron, *Out of Sight, Out of Mind*, 1985
Jeff Bredenberg, *The Dream Compass*, 1991
Philip K. Dick, *The World Jones Made*, 1956
Leo F. Kelley, *Brother John*, 1971
Bruce McAllister, *Dream Baby*, 1989

664

STEPHEN BAXTER

Flood

(London: Gollancz, 2008)

Story type: Disaster; End of the World
Subject(s): Floods; Disasters
Major character(s): Piers Michaelmas, Military Personnel; Lily Brooke, Pilot, Military Personnel; Gary Boyle, Scientist
Time period(s): 21st century (2016-2041)
Locale(s): England

Summary: A group of people who have been held captive by fanatics in Spain for several years finally free themselves. They are taken to England where they discover that the sea level has been rising steadily while they were out of touch and that floods now threaten to wash away many of the most famous cities in the world.

Other books by the same author:
The H-Bomb Girl, 2007
Conqueror, 2006
Exultant, 2004
Coalescent, 2003
Evolution, 2003

Other books you might like:
Piers Anthony, *Rings of Ice*, 1974
J.G. Ballard, *The Drowned World*, 1962
John Bowen, *After the Rain*, 1958
Steven Gould, *Blind Waves*, 2000
Kim Stanley Robinson, *Forty Signs of Rain*, 2004

665

STEPHEN BAXTER

Weaver

(London: Gollancz, 2008)

Story type: Alternate History; Military
Series: Time's Tapestry. Book 4
Subject(s): Alternate History; World War II
Major character(s): Ben Kamen, Historian; Julia Fiveash, Zealot; Gary Wooler, Military Personnel
Time period(s): 1940s (1941-1945)
Locale(s): England

Summary: In an alternate version of World War II, the Germans manage to invade the British Isles, forcing the Nazi creed on the population. The story follows the adventures of several people caught up in the struggle, as well as giving glimpses of the Weaver, a mysterious figure that manipulates the course of history.

Other books by the same author:
Flood, 2008
Emperor, 2006
Exultant, 2004
Coalescent, 2003
Evolution, 2003

Other books you might like:
Ben Bova, *Triumph*, 1993
Len Deighton, *S.S. GB*, 1978
Philip K. Dick, *The Man in the High Castle*, 1962
James P. Hogan, *The Proteus Operation*, 1985
Brad Linaweaver, *Moon of Ice*, 1988

666

GREG BEAR

City at the End of Time

(New York: Del Rey, 2008)

Story type: Time Travel; Mystical
Subject(s): Time Travel; Utopia/Dystopia
Major character(s): Jack Rohmer, Time Traveler; Max Glaucous, Time Traveler; Daniel Iremonk, Time Traveler
Time period(s): 2000s; Indeterminate Future
Locale(s): Earth; Seattle, Washington

Summary: Three people in contemporary Seattle experience similar visions of the future, a world where a dying city might mean the end of time. They each respond to a mysterious newspaper advertisement and find themselves responsible for saving the future of the universe.

Other books by the same author:
Quantico, 2007
Darwin's Children, 2003
The Collected Stories of Greg Bear, 2002
Darwin's Radio, 1999
Dinosaur Summer, 1998

Other books you might like:
Gregory Benford, *Timescape*, 1980
Paul Cook, *The Alejandra Variations*, 1984
Philip Jose Farmer, *Dark Is the Sun*, 1979
Joe Haldeman, *The Accidental Time Machine*, 2007
Charles Eric Maine, *Timeliner*, 1955

667

BEN BOVA

Mars Life

(New York: Tor, 2008)

Story type: Hard Science Fiction; Religious
Series: Mars. Book 3
Subject(s): Space Exploration; Aliens
Major character(s): Carter Carleton, Scientist; Jamie Waterman, Professor; Doreen McManus, Scientist
Time period(s): 21st century
Locale(s): Mars; Albuquerque, New Mexico

Summary: Scientists on Mars discover the fossil of a being which suggests that at one time in the distant past, the planet had intelligent inhabitants. This causes repercussions back on Earth where a college professor discovers that the increasingly influential religious fanatics dominating the world's politics are not happy with the possibility that intelligent life arose elsewhere than on Earth.

Other books by the same author:
The Aftermath, 2007
The Green Trap, 2006
Rock Rats, 2002
Return to Mars, 1999
Mars, 1992

Other books you might like:
Greg Bear, *Moving Mars*, 1993
Geoffrey A. Landis, *Mars Crossing*, 2000
Paul J. McAuley, *Red Dust*, 1993
Frederik Pohl, *Man Plus*, 1976
Kim Stanley Robinson, *The Martians*, 1998

668

JAMES BRAZIEL

Birmingham, 35 Miles

(New York: Bantam, 2008)

Story type: Disaster; Dystopian
Subject(s): Ecology; Disasters
Major character(s): Mathew Harrison, Farmer; Bossey, Farmer; Jennifer Phillips, Refugee
Time period(s): 2040s (2044)
Locale(s): Alabama

Summary: The ozone layer opens over North America, turning much of the southern half of the continent into a dangerous, near desert. Mathew Harrison is a young man whose ties to the land are so strong that he is reluctant to leave, even when the woman he loves gives up and moves into the relatively safer areas to the north. The

disaster shatters the world into a much more fragmented place.

Where it's reviewed:
Entertainment Weekly, February 29, 2008, page 64
Publishers Weekly, December 17, 2007, page 31

Other books you might like:
Steven Gould, *Blind Waves*, 2000
Susan Palwick, *Shelter*, 2007
Kim Stanley Robinson, *Sixty Days and Counting*, 2007
Norman Spinrad, *Greenhouse Summer*, 1999
Philip Wylie, *The End of the Dream*, 1972

669

MIKE BROTHERTON

Spider Star

(New York: Tor, 2008)

Story type: Mystery; Space Opera
Subject(s): Aliens; Secrets
Major character(s): Mike Rusk, Archaeologist; Frank Klingston, Explorer; Sloan Griffin, Scientist
Time period(s): 25th century
Locale(s): Outer Space

Summary: A human colony world has been experimenting with the artifacts left behind by a now extinct alien race when one of the objects becomes active and refuses to be shut down. Projections indicate that it will eventually destroy the entire planet unless it can be switched off, so an expedition is launched to find clues about its origin.

Where it's reviewed:
Locus, February 2008, page 21
Publishers Weekly, January 7, 2008, page 40

Other books by the same author:
Star Dragon, 2003

Other books you might like:
Roger MacBride Allen, *The Shattered Sphere*, 1994
Stephen Baxter, *Ring*, 1994
Jack McDevitt, *The Engines of God*, 1994
Richard Paul Russo, *Ship of Fools*, 2001
Karl Schroeder, *Permanence*, 2002

670

ERIC BROWN

Kethani

(Nottingham, United Kingdom: Solaris, 2008)

Story type: First Contact; Immortality
Subject(s): Aliens; Immortality
Major character(s): Khalid Azzam, Doctor, Immortal; Zara Azzam, Immortal; Jeff Morrow, Teacher, Immortal
Time period(s): Indeterminate Future
Locale(s): England

Summary: The Kethani are an alien race who appear simultaneously in various locations on Earth. They make a gift of immortality to the human race, but many suspect that their motives aren't entirely altruistic. Eventually

the world discovers that the gift will make even more fundamental changes in humanity than suspected, but it may be too late to reverse course.

Where it's reviewed:
Publishers Weekly, March 3, 2008, page 33

Other books by the same author:
Helix, 2007
Approaching Omega, 2005
The Fall of Tartarus, 2005
Bengal Station, 2004
New York Dreams, 2004

Other books you might like:
Arthur C. Clarke, *Childhood's End*, 1953
James L. Halperin, *The First Immortal*, 1998
Murray Leinster, *The Greks Bring Gifts*, 1964
Marta Randall, *Islands*, 1976
John Wyndham, *Trouble with Lichen*, 1960

671

JACK CAMPBELL

Courageous

(New York: Ace, 2008)

Story type: Space Opera; Military
Series: Lost Fleet. Book 3
Subject(s): Military Life; Space Travel
Major character(s): John Geary, Military Personnel; Tanya Desjani, Military Personnel; Victoria Rione, Political Figure
Time period(s): Indeterminate Future
Locale(s): Outer Space

Summary: An interstellar war has broken out and the aggressor has been steadily winning. The defenders bring back a legendary military hero from suspended animation and give him command of their outnumbered fleet. There are also indications that an alien race is about to enter the war with the secret agenda of destroying the human race.

Other books by the same author:
Valiant, 2008
Fearless, 2007
Against All Enemies, 2006
Dauntless, 2006
Rules of Evidence, 2005

Other books you might like:
Roger MacBride Allen, *Allies and Aliens*, 1995
Chris Bunch, *The Last Legion*, 1999
William R. Forstchen, *Action Stations*, 1998
Rick Shelley, *Deep Strike*, 2002
David Weber, *At All Costs*, 2005

672

JACK CAMPBELL

Valiant

(New York: Ace, 2008)

Story type: Space Opera; Military
Series: Lost Fleet. Book 4

Subject(s): Space Travel; Military Life
Major character(s): John Geary, Spaceship Captain, Military Personnel; Tanya Desjani, Spaceship Captain, Military Personnel; Victoria Rione, Government Official
Time period(s): Indeterminate Future
Locale(s): Outer Space

Summary: Despite the fact that John Geary has managed to keep his outnumbered fleet of starships functioning, with only minor losses, some of the officers under his command want to see him replaced. They become more active in that pursuit when he gives a controversial order to move the fleet to a star system where they were nearly destroyed not long before.

Other books by the same author:
Courageous, 2008
Fearless, 2007
Dauntless, 2006

Other books you might like:
Bruce Balfour, *Star Crusader*, 1995
William C. Dietz, *The Final Battle*, 1995
David Feintuch, *Challenger's Hope*, 1995
Roland Green, *Squadron Alert*, 1989
S.N. Lewitt, *Angel at Apogee*, 1987

673

ORSON SCOTT CARD

Keeper of Dreams

(New York: Tor, 2008)

Story type: Collection
Subject(s): Short Stories

Summary: This is a large collection of more than 20 stories, not all of which are science fiction, and consists almost entirely of work first published during the last six years. Included are two of the author's better novelettes, "Atlantis" and "Space Boy," and four stories involving the Mormon religion.

Where it's reviewed:
Publishers Weekly, February 18, 2008, page 140

Other books by the same author:
Empire, 2006
Shadow of the Hegemon, 2001
Children of the Mind, 1996
Pastwatch, 1996
Ender's Game, 1985

Other books you might like:
Poul Anderson, *Alight in the Void*, 1991
Ben Bova, *Future Crime*, 1990
Gordon R. Dickson, *The Stranger*, 1987
James P. Hogan, *Catastrophes, Chaos, and Convolutions*, 2005
Jack Williamson, *People Machines*, 1971

Science Fiction

674

BRENDA COOPER

Reading the Wind
(New York: Tor, 2008)

Story type: Space Colony; Genetic Manipulation
Series: Silver Ship. Book 2
Subject(s): Genetic Engineering; Space Colonies
Major character(s): Chelo Lee, Genetically Altered Being, Teenager; Joseph Lee, Genetically Altered Being, Teenager; Kayleen, Teenager
Time period(s): Indeterminate Future
Locale(s): Fremont, Planet—Imaginary; Earth

Summary: The planet Fremont is violently opposed to any variation of genetic engineering, so when four teenagers are stranded there, the reception is anything but welcoming. All but one escape, but Chelo Lee remains behind with the boy she loves. The others discover that authorities on Earth, believing the teens were all executed, are planning to wipe out the colony.

Other books by the same author:
The Silver Ship and the Sea, 2007

Other books you might like:
Ben Bova, *Flight of Exiles*, 1972
Sheila Finch, *The Garden of the Shaped*, 1987
Laura J. Mixon, *Burning the Ice*, 2002
Pamela Sargent, *Cloned Lives*, 1976
Allen Steele, *Coyote*, 2002

675

MATTHEW J. COSTELLO

Worlds on Fire
(New York: Pocket Star, 2008)

Story type: Horror; Invasion of Earth
Series: Doom
Subject(s): Aliens; Secrets
Major character(s): John Kane, Military Personnel; Jack Campbell, Security Officer; Ian Kelliher, Administrator
Time period(s): 22nd century (2145)
Locale(s): Mars

Summary: An Earth devastated by local wars and economic disaster has established a base on Mars where scientists are investigating a trove of alien artifacts. Their investigation opens a gateway through which murderous, alien creatures emerge, killing everyone they encounter and turning their victims into animated slaves.

Other books by the same author:
Wurm, 2001
Fire Below, 1994
Day of the Snake, 1992
Hour of the Scorpion, 1991
Time of the Fox, 1990

Other books you might like:
Daffyd ab Hugh, *Kneedeep in the Dead*, 1995

Brad Linaweaver, co-author
Ray Garton, *Invaders from Mars*, 1986
Dean R. Koontz, *Winter Moon*, 1994
Murray Leinster, *Creatures of the Abyss*, 1961
John Lymington, *The Night Spiders*, 1965

676

MAURICE G. DANTEC

Cosmos Incorporated
(New York: Del Rey, 2008)

Story type: Dystopian; Space Colony
Subject(s): Space Travel; Secrets
Major character(s): Sergei Diego Plotkin, Amnesiac, Criminal (assassin); Cheyenne Hawkwind, Criminal; Clovis Drummond, Businessman
Time period(s): 22nd century
Locale(s): Space Station

Summary: Most of Sergei Plotkin's memories have been erased so that he can pass through the security systems in a future world where plague and war have radically reduced the Earth's population. He has been programmed to travel to an orbiting habitat to murder a man he doesn't know, but the mission has other implications, which are only slowly revealed to him. This novel originally appeared in French.

Other books by the same author:
Babylon Babies, 2008

Other books you might like:
Jeff Bredenberg, *The Man in the Moon Must Die*, 1993
John Brunner, *Stand on Zanzibar*, 1968
Algis Budrys, *Who?*, 1958
Barney Cohen, *Blood on the Moon*, 1984
Larry Niven, *The Long Arm of Gil Hamilton*, 1976

677

ELLEN DATLOW, Editor

The Del Rey Book of Science Fiction and Fantasy
(New York: Del Rey, 2008)

Story type: Anthology
Subject(s): Short Stories

Summary: The 16 original stories in this anthology are split evenly between science fiction and fantasy. The science fiction is mostly set in the near future and on Earth. All of the stories tend toward the literary end of the spectrum. Included are contributions by Pat Cadigan, Carol Emshwiller, Jeffrey Ford, Margo Lanagan, Barry N. Malzberg, and others.

Other books by the same author:
Inferno, 2007
The Dark, 2003
Vanishing Acts, 2000
Off Limits, 1996
Alien Sex, 1992

Other books you might like:
Pat Cadigan, *Dirty Work*, 1993
Carol Emshwiller, *I Live With You*, 2005
Jeffrey Ford, *The Fantasy Writer's Assistant*, 2002
Margo Lanagan, *Black Juice*, 2005
Barry N. Malzberg, *In the Stone House*, 2000

678

KEITH R.A. DECANDIDO

A Burning House

(New York: Pocket, 2008)

Story type: Space Opera; Mystery
Series: Star Trek: Klingon Empire
Subject(s): Aliens; Secrets
Major character(s): Worf, Military Personnel, Alien (Klingon); B'Oraq, Politician, Alien (Klingon); Wol, Military Personnel, Alien (Klingon)
Time period(s): Indeterminate Future
Locale(s): Outer Space; Klingon Empire, Interstellar Empire/Federation

Summary: This story is peripheral to the Star Trek series, set within the Klingon Empire and with virtually no human characters. The code of behavior and emphasis on assertiveness creates a society and a government that is prone to sudden, dramatic changes in orientation. The story relates a number of these changes as seen from the points of view of a large cast of characters.

Other books by the same author:
Command & Conquer, 2007
Down These Mean Streets, 2006
Articles of the Federation, 2005
Destruction of Illusions, 2003
The Art of the Impossible, 2003

Other books you might like:
Greg Cox, *To Reign in Hell*, 2006
Gene De Weese, *Engines of Destiny*, 2005
Michael Jan Friedman, *Her Klingon Soul*, 1997
David Mack, *Harbinger*, 2005
Kevin Ryan, *Killing Blow*, 2002

679

GARDNER DOZOIS , Editor

The Year's Best Science Fiction: Twenty-Fifth Annual Collection

(New York: St Martin's, 2008)

Story type: Anthology
Subject(s): Short Stories

Summary: This is a selection of the best science fiction stories published in 2007, more than 30 tales drawn from the professional magazines, online publications, original collections, and a few from sources where many might not expect to find fiction. The editor also includes an exhaustive summary of developments in the field during that year and a lengthy list of honorable mentions.

Other books by the same author:
Strange Days, 2001
Geodesic Dreams, 1992
Slow Dancing through Time, 1990
Strangers, 1978
The Visible Man, 1977

Other books you might like:
Paul Di Filippo, *Neutrino Drag*, 2004
Greg Egan, *Luminous*, 1998
John Kessel, *The Baum Plan for Financial Independence and Other Stories*, 2008
Kim Stanley Robinson, *The Martians*, 1998
Michael Swanwick, *The Dog Said Bow-Wow*, 2007

680

DAVID DRAKE

When the Tide Rises

(New York: Baen, 2008)

Story type: Military; Space Opera
Series: Lieutenant Leary. Book 6
Subject(s): Space Travel
Major character(s): Daniel Leary, Military Personnel; Adele Mundy, Military Personnel, Spy; Rene Cazelet, Military Personnel
Time period(s): Indeterminate Future
Locale(s): Outer Space; Bagaria, Planet—Imaginary

Summary: Daniel Leary is in disfavor when the command of the navy of Cinnabar changes hands. He is reassigned to an outlying system that is currently under siege by hostile forces, but equipped with inadequate resources to turn the tide conventionally. Fortunately, he has a talented spy with him who is able to change the rules of engagement.

Where it's reviewed:
Publishers Weekly, January 28, 2008, page 47

Other books by the same author:
Other Times than Peace, 2006
Some Golden Harbor, 2006
Grimmer than Hell, 2003
The Far Side of the Stars, 2003
Lieutenant Leary Commanding, 2000

Other books you might like:
Lois McMaster Bujold, *Diplomatic Immunity*, 2002
R.M. Meluch, *The Queen's Squadron*, 1992
Mike Resnick, *Starship Mutiny*, 2006
Mike Shepherd, *Mutineer*, 2004
David Weber, *The Armageddon Inheritance*, 193

681

L. TIMMEL DUCHAMP

Stretto

(Seattle: Aqueduct, 2008)

Story type: Dystopian; Political
Series: Marq'ssan. Book 5

Science Fiction

Subject(s): Utopia/Dystopia; Espionage
Major character(s): Anne Hawthorne, Security Officer; Hazel Bell, Political Figure; Alexandra Sedgewick, Prisoner
Time period(s): 2090s (2096)
Locale(s): North America

Summary: North America has splintered into multiple countries although the remnants of the United States remain the single most powerful. A group of women within the administration of that country are quietly working to undermine the repressive methods in use and replace them with more liberal rules, while various other characters react to the rapid rate of change in the world and the presence of alien observers. This is the concluding volume in the series.

Other books by the same author:
Blood in the Fruit, 2007
Tsunami, 2007
Renegade, 2006
Alanya to Alanya, 2005

Other books you might like:
Ron Goulart, *After Things Fell Apart*, 1977
Kim Stanley Robinson, *The Pacific Edge*, 1990
Pamela Sargent, *The Shore of Women*, 1986
Joan Slonczewski, *A Door into Ocean*, 1986
Sheri S. Tepper, *The Gate to Women's Country*, 1988

682

DAVID LOUIS EDELMAN

Multireal

(Amherst, New York: Pyr, 2008)

Story type: Dystopian; Techno-Thriller
Series: Jump 225. Book 2
Subject(s): Computers; Secrets
Major character(s): Natch, Businessman, Computer Expert; Len Borda, Government Official; Magan Kai Lee, Military Personnel
Time period(s): Indeterminate Future
Locale(s): India; Australia

Summary: Natch has developed a new form of information technology that threatens to break the stranglehold of the current global government establishment. The fight to avoid being absorbed into their system takes a new turn as efforts are made to subvert some of his former allies and employees.

Other books by the same author:
Infoquake, 2006

Other books you might like:
John Brunner, *Shockwave Rider*, 1975
William Gibson, *Count Zero*, 1986
Christopher Hodder-Williams, *A Fistful of Digits*, 1968
Pierre Oulette, *The Deus Machine*, 1993
Neal Stephenson, *Snow Crash*, 1992

683

GREG EGAN

Incandescence

(London: Gollancz, 2008)

Story type: Space Opera; Hard Science Fiction
Subject(s): Secrets; Space Exploration
Major character(s): Rakesh, Investigator; Roi, Worker; Zak, Worker
Time period(s): Indeterminate Future
Locale(s): Outer Space

Summary: In the distant future, the galaxy is divided between two great civilizations, the Amalgam and the Aloof. The Aloof don't allow visitors, but they will accept people who wish to be digitized and pass through their realm. One day an inquisitive man encounters someone who says she was embodied for a brief time en route but doesn't know why.

Other books by the same author:
Schild's Ladder, 2002
Teranesia, 1999
Luminous, 1998
Diaspora, 1997
Axiomatic, 1995

Other books you might like:
Iain Banks, *Excession*, 1996
Gregory Benford, *Great Sky River*, 1987
Peter F. Hamilton, *The Dreaming Void*, 2008
Alastair Reynolds, *House of Suns*, 2008
Vernor Vinge, *A Deepness in the Sky*, 1999

684

SAM ENTHOVEN

Tim, Defender of the Earth

(New York: RazorBill, 2008)

Story type: Young Adult; Humor
Subject(s): Humor; Dinosaurs
Major character(s): Tim, Animal (dinosaur); Chris Pitman, Teenager; Anna Mallahide, Teenager
Time period(s): 2000s (2008)
Locale(s): England

Summary: The British government has secretly created an intelligent, high powered tyrannosaurus as a weapon, but they decide the project was a wasted effort. Tim, the dinosaur, discovers that funding for his maintenance is going to be cut, so he escapes from the laboratory because he fears that they will kill him to save money. He and two teenagers team up and eventually help save the world from a mad scientist.

Where it's reviewed:
Booklist, January 1, 2008, page 84

Other books by the same author:
The Black Tattoo, 2006

Other books you might like:
Clyde Ames, *Gorgonzola, Won't You Please Come Home?*, 1967
Robert Bakker, *Raptor Red*, 1995
Eleanor Cameron, *The Terrible Churnadryne*, 1959
Eric Garcia, *Anonymous Rex*, 1999
Geoffrey Household, *The Spanish Cave*, 1936

685

JAINE FENN

Principles of Angels
(London: Gollancz, 2008)

Story type: Dystopian; Mystery
Subject(s): Utopia/Dystopia; Espionage
Major character(s): Taro, Fugitive, Spy; Naul, Criminal (assassin); Federin, Spy
Time period(s): Indeterminate Future
Locale(s): Earth

Summary: In a far future megalopolis, the government is a form of democratic anarchy enforced by assassination. Taro is in love with one of the Angels, those licensed to kill legally, but someone kills her and he becomes a fugitive until he is recruited to spy on Nual, another Angel who appears to have a hidden agenda. First novel.

Other books you might like:
Brian Aldiss, *Enemies of the System*, 1978
T.J. Bass, *Half Past Human*, 1971
John Brunner, *Shockwave Rider*, 1975
James Patrick Kelly, *Burn*, 2005
Mack Reynolds, *The Cosmic Eye*, 1969

686

ERIC FLINT , Editor

Ring of Fire II
(New York: Baen, 2008)

Story type: Anthology
Subject(s): Short Stories

Summary: The nine short stories in this anthology all appear for the first time and were written by fans of editor Flint's series of alternate history novels which began with *1632*. The premise is that a town from the present is mysteriously sent back through time to the 17th century where its advanced technology and democratic views alter the course of history.

Where it's reviewed:
Publishers Weekly, December 24, 2007, page 34

Other books by the same author:
1635: The Cannon Law, 2006 (Andrew Dennis, co-author)
1824: The Arkansas War, 2006
1812: The Rivers of War, 2005
1633, 2002
1632, 2000

Other books you might like:
Poul Anderson, *Time Patrol*, 2006
Leo Frankowski, *Conrad's Time Machine*, 2002
Edmond Hamilton, *City at World's End*, 1951
H. Beam Piper, *Lord Kalvan of Otherwhen*, 1965
S.M. Stirling, *Island in the Sea of Time*, 1998

687

VICTOR GISCHLER

Go-Go Girls of the Apocalypse
(New York: Touchstone, 2008)

Story type: Humor; Satire
Subject(s): Humor; Disasters
Major character(s): Mortimer Tate, Salesman; Joey Armageddon, Businessman; Buffalo Bill, Cowboy
Time period(s): 21st century
Locale(s): Tennessee; Georgia

Summary: Mortimer Tate spends ten years in a bomb shelter, then emerges to find a post-apocalyptic world in which America has become fragmented. Accompanied by a cowboy and two exotic dancers, he sets out on a journey from Tennessee to Georgia, having various humorous adventures along the way as the author satirizes various aspects of contemporary life. First novel.

Other books by the same author:
Suicide Squeeze, 2004
Gun Monkeys, 2002

Other books you might like:
William Anderson, *Pandemonium on the Potomac*, 1966
Michael Armstrong, *After the Zap*, 1987
Ron Goulart, *After Things Fell Apart*, 1970
Jake Saunders, *The Texas-Israeli War*, 1974
    Howard Waldrop, co-author
Robert Lewis Taylor, *Adrift in a Boneyard*, 1947

688

MARTIN H. GREENBERG , Editor
KERRIE HUGHES , Co-Editor

The Dimension Next Door
(New York: DAW, 2008)

Story type: Anthology; Alternate World
Subject(s): Short Stories

Summary: All 13 stories in this anthology appear here for the first time. Each deals with worlds not quite ours, either parallel universes, other dimensions, or just other realities. The contributors include Jody Lynn Nye, Irene Radford, Brenda Cooper, and Chris Pierson and the stories are generally light adventure.

Other books by the same author:
Alien Abductions, 1999 (John Helfers, co-editor)
Dinosaurs, 1996
Animal Brigade 3000, 1994 (Charles G. Waugh, co-editor)
Christmas on Ganymede, 1990
Cosmic Critiques, 1990 (Isaac Asimov, co-editor)

Other books you might like:
Taylor Anderson, *Into the Storm*, 2008
Joe Haldeman, *The Hemingway Hoax*, 1990
James P. Hogan, *Entoverse*, 1991
S.M. Stirling, *Conquistador*, 2003
Roger Zelazny, *Roadmarks*, 1980

689

DAVID GUNN

Maximum Offense

(New York: Del Rey, 2008)

Story type: Military; Space Opera
Series: Death's Head. Book 2
Subject(s): Aliens
Major character(s): Sven Tveskoeg, Military Personnel;
   OctoV, Ruler; Paper Osamu, Diplomat
Time period(s): Indeterminate Future
Locale(s): Outer Space

Summary: Sven Tveskoeg is a man of many talents, most of them deadly. He serves in the armed forces of an interstellar empire, where he carries a sentient gun and kills almost indiscriminately. An assignment involving an ambassador is just the beginning of a series of wild adventures. Although this is military science fiction in format, the author satirizes many of the conventions of that genre through exaggeration.

Other books by the same author:
Death's Head, 2007

Other books you might like:
Robert Asprin, *Phule's Company*, 1990
Karl Hansen, *War Games*, 1981
Harry Harrison, *Bill, the Galactic Hero*, 1965
Mike McQuay, *The Deadliest Game in Town*, 1982
Richard K. Morgan, *Altered Carbon*, 2002

690

PETER F. HAMILTON

The Dreaming Void

(New York: Del Rey, 2008)

Story type: Space Opera; Mystery
Series: Void. Book 1
Subject(s): Aliens; Secrets
Major character(s): Araminta, Waiter/Waitress; Edeard,
   Telepath; Inigo, Religious
Time period(s): 36th century (3589)
Locale(s): Outer Space; Planet—Imaginary

Summary: In the distant future, a part of colonized space is the Void, an area dominated by the technology left behind by a now extinct alien race. A human claims to have communicated with the devices in his dreams, and he begins to attract a large body of followers. Others are less certain of his visions, but many are convinced it is a sign the alien constructs are about to become active.

Where it's reviewed:
Booklist, November 15, 2007, page 25
Library Journal, December 1, 2007, page 104
Locus, January 2008, page 27
Publishers Weekly, February 4, 2008, page 42

Other books by the same author:
Judas Unchained, 2006
Misspent Youth, 2006
Pandora's Star, 2004
Fallen Dragon, 2002
The Naked God, 1999

Other books you might like:
Iain Banks, *Inversions*, 1998
Gregory Benford, *Furious Gulf*, 1994
Alastair Reynolds, *House of Suns*, 2008
Dan Simmons, *Hyperion*, 1989
Vernor Vinge, *A Deepness in the Sky*, 1999

691

JOHN HELFERS , Editor
MARTIN H. GREENBERG , Co-Editor

Future Americas

(New York: DAW, 2008)

Story type: Anthology
Subject(s): Short Stories
Locale(s): United States

Summary: All 16 stories in this antholohy appear here in print for the first time. Each involves a different vision of the future of America, from near future scenarios in which technology changes to others in a more distant future when the United States no longer exists as a single country. The contributors include Brendan DuBois, Pamela Sargent, George Zebrowski, Brian Stableford, Kristine Kathryn Rusch, and others.

Other books you might like:
David Brin, *The Postman*, 1985
L. Timmel Duchamp, *Alanya to Alanya*, 2005
Ron Goulart, *After Things Fell Apart*, 1970
Kim Stanley Robinson, *Forty Signs of Rain*, 2004
Michael Swanwick, *In the Drift*, 1985

692

JAMES P. HOGAN

Moon Flower

(New York: Baen, 2008)

Story type: Space Colony; Mystery
Subject(s): Aliens; Space Colonies
Major character(s): Myles Callen, Investigator; Marc
   Shearer, Scientist; Evan Wade, Scientist
Time period(s): Indeterminate Future
Locale(s): Cyrene, Planet—Imaginary

Summary: A human corporation has been developing the planet Cyrene as a colony but recently there have been problems with the project, specifically the disappearance

of several people. A tough-minded investigator and a scientist are sent to look into matters, but what they eventually discover affects not only the future of Cyrene but life on Earth as well.

Other books by the same author:
Echoes of an Alien Sky, 2007
Mission to Minerva, 2005
The Anguished Dawn, 2003
Martian Knightlife, 2001
The Legend That Was Earth, 2000

Other books you might like:
Gordon R. Dickson, *Mission to Universe*, 1965
Alan Dean Foster, *Sentenced to Prism*, 1985
Kenneth F. Gantz, *Not in Solitude*, 1959
Harry Harrison, *Deathworld*, 1960
Larry Niven, *The Legacy of Heorot*, 1987
    Jerry Pournelle, Steven Barnes, co-authors

693

TANYA HUFF

Valor's Trial

(New York: DAW, 2008)

Story type: Military; Space Opera
Series: Confederation. Book 4
Subject(s): Aliens; Secrets
Major character(s): Torin Kerr, Military Personnel; Craig Ryder, Businessman; Ressk, Alien
Time period(s): Indeterminate Future
Locale(s): Planet—Imaginary

Summary: Torin Kerr is a seasoned soldier who is assigned the job of leading a unit to a new area of space where the conflict with the alien Others has just begun. She and her forces are quickly overwhelmed by a massive attack force and she is believed to be dead. Her father and a friend still believe she's alive and they're right. She's loose in an underground enemy installation where she has a chance to materially affect the outcome of the war.

Where it's reviewed:
Publishers Weekly, April 28, 2008, page 117

Other books by the same author:
Finding Magic, 2007
The Heart of Valor, 2007
The Better Part of Valor, 2002
Valor's Choice, 2000
Blood Debt, 1997

Other books you might like:
John Blair, *A Landscape of Darkness*, 1990
Richard Fawkes, *Face of the Enemy*, 1999
Barry B. Longyear, *Enemy Mine*, 1985
    David Gerrold, co-author
Joel Rosenberg, *Hero*, 1990
Timothy Zahn, *Conqueror's Pride*, 1994

694

MICHAEL JASPER

The Wannoshay Cycle

(Waterville, Maine: Five Star, 2008)

Story type: First Contact; Mystery
Subject(s): Aliens; Secrets
Major character(s): Joshua McDowell, Religious; Ally Trang, Addict; Tim Blair, Worker
Time period(s): Indeterminate Future
Locale(s): North America

Summary: A large alien spaceship crashlands in North America and its crew and passengers become the objects of fear and suspicion when a series of mysterious explosions occur following their evacuation from the wreckage. A priest and several unlikely characters become involved in an effort to understand the aliens' culture and integrate them into human society. First novel.

Where it's reviewed:
Booklist, December 15, 2007, page 33
Library Journal, December 1, 2007, page 105

Other books you might like:
Algis Budrys, *Hard Landing*, 1993
Arthur C. Clarke, *Rendezvous with Rama*, 1973
K.W. Jeter, *Dark Horizon*, 1993
Barry B. Longyear, *The Change*, 1994
Robert J. Sawyer, *Illegal Alien*, 1997

695

THEODORE JUDSON

The Martian General's Daughter

(Amherst, New York: Pyr, 2008)

Story type: Political; Post-Disaster
Subject(s): Politics; Futuristic Fiction
Major character(s): Peter Black, Military Personnel; Luke Anthony, Ruler; Justa, Bastard Daughter
Time period(s): Indeterminate Future
Locale(s): Earth

Summary: Human civilization has disintegrated into a new culture that strongly resembles the ancient world. General Peter Black is a soldier of an empire that mimics Rome, and, like Rome, it is suffering from a succession of weak rulers, leading to corruption and internal disorder.

Where it's reviewed:
Publishers Weekly, February 11, 2008, page 55

Other books by the same author:
Fitzpatrick's War, 2004

Other books you might like:
Poul Anderson, *Maurai and Kith*, 1982
Piers Anthony, *SOS the Rope*, 1968
Kirk Mitchell, *Cry Republic*, 1989
Edgar Pangborn, *Davy*, 1964
Eric Vinicoff, *Maiden Flight*, 1988

696

DANIEL KALLA

Cold Plague

(New York: Forge, 2008)

Story type: Medical; Mystery
Subject(s): Secrets; Medical Thriller; Conspiracies
Major character(s): Noah Haldane, Doctor; Duncan McLeod, Worker; Elise Renard, Diplomat
Time period(s): 2000s
Locale(s): France; United States

Summary: The discovery of a body of unpolluted water in Antarctica provides access to microscopic life forms which have otherwise become extinct. When a strange variant of mad cow disease appears in France, the investigating medical team comes to the conclusion that this was an intentional outbreak created by an international conspiracy.

Where it's reviewed:
Library Journal, March 15, 2008, page 59
Publishers Weekly, February 4, 2008, page 37

Other books by the same author:
Blood Lies, 2007
Rage Therapy, 2007
Pandemic, 2005
Resistance, 2005

Other books you might like:
Michael Crichton, *The Andromeda Strain*, 1969
Jeff Long, *Year Zero*, 2002
Alan Scott, *The Anthrax Mutation*, 1971
Graham Watkins, *Virus*, 1995
Chelsea Quinn Yarbro, *Time of the Fourth Horseman*, 1977

697

DREW KARPYSHYN

Rule of Two

(New York: Del Rey, 2008)

Story type: Space Opera; Psychic Powers
Series: Star Wars
Subject(s): Space Travel; Coming-of-Age
Major character(s): Darth Bane, Psychic, Teacher; Zannah, Psychic, Student; Johun Othone, Apprentice, Warrior
Time period(s): Indeterminate Past
Locale(s): Outer Space

Summary: Darth Bane rose to dominate the Sith, a group plotting to seize control of the galaxy, but he destroyed his own organization in order to rebuild it as his weapon. His apprentice is Zannah, who shows great potential, but his secret plans are put in jeopardy when a young apprentice Jedi warrior suspects that he has survived.

Other books by the same author:
Revelation, 2007
Path of Destruction, 2006
Temple Hill, 2001
Throne of Bhaal, 2001

Other books you might like:
Steven Barnes, *The Cestus Deception*, 2004
James Luceno, *Labyrinth of Evil*, 2005
Michael Reaves, *Shadow Hunter*, 2001
Matthew Stover, *Shatterpoint*, 2003
Karen Traviss, *Bloodlines*, 2006

698

SUSAN KEARNEY

Solar Heat

(New York: Tor, 2008)

Story type: Space Opera; Romance
Subject(s): Espionage; Space Travel
Major character(s): Derrek Archer, Businessman; Azsla, Spy, Psychic
Time period(s): Indeterminate Future
Locale(s): Planet—Imaginary; Outer Space

Summary: A businessman who hopes to make his fortune mining in the asteroid belt becomes involved with a mysterious woman whom he meets while on an inspection trip. What he doesn't realize is that she is a psychically gifted spy from an enemy power. What she doesn't realize is that her attraction to him will become more important than her political loyalties.

Other books by the same author:
Island Heat, 2007
The Quest, 2006
The Ultimatum, 2006
The Challenge, 2005
The Dare, 2005

Other books you might like:
Kathryne Kennedy, *Beneath the Thirteen Moons*, 2003
Sherrilyn Kenyon, *Born of the Night*, 1996
Liz Maverick, *The Shadow Runners*, 2004
Gena Showalter, *Awaken Me Darkly*, 2005
Catherine Spangler, *Shamara*, 2001

699

KAY KENYON

A World Too Near

(Amherst, New York: Pyr, 2008)

Story type: Hard Science Fiction; Quest
Series: Entire and Rose. Book 2
Subject(s): Quest; Secrets
Major character(s): Titus Quinn, Spaceman; Johanna Quinn, Prisoner; SuMing, Servant
Time period(s): Indeterminate Future
Locale(s): Alternate Universe

Summary: In a parallel universe where stars and planets don't exist, Titus Quinn seeks to destroy a fortress even though by doing so he may risk destroying much more because the alternative is the destruction of this reality. Using nanotechnology and other devices, he presses toward his destination, determined to persevere even

though his wife is a prisoner whose life will be forfeit if he succeeds.

Where it's reviewed:
Publishers Weekly, January 7, 2008, page 40

Other books by the same author:
Bright of the Sky, 2007
The Braided World, 2003
Maximum Ice, 2002
Tropic of Creation, 2000
Rift, 1999

Other books you might like:
Stephen Baxter, *Raft*, 1991
Philip Jose Farmer, *The Maker of Universes*, 1965
Christopher Priest, *The Inverted World*, 1974
Adam Roberts, *Polystom*, 2003
Bob Shaw, *The Fugitive Worlds*, 1990

700

JOHN KESSEL

The Baum Plan for Financial Independence and Other Stories

(Easthampton, Massachusetts: Small Beer, 2008)

Story type: Collection
Subject(s): Short Stories

Summary: John Kessel is not a prolific writer and these 14 stories represent most of his short fiction published between 1998 and 2007. His work is generally set in the present or near future and employs dark humor. Included is a short sequence of stories about life on the moon and others that include allusions to Jane Austen, L. Frank Baum, and other writers.

Where it's reviewed:
Locus, March 2008, page 25

Other books by the same author:
Corrupting Dr. Nice, 1997
The Pure Product, 1997
Meeting in Infinity, 1992
Another Orphan, 1989
Good News from Outer Space, 1989

Other books you might like:
Paul Di Filippo, *Fuzzy Dice*, 2003
Greg Egan, *Luminous*, 1998
James Patrick Kelly, *Think Like a Dinosaur*, 1997
Nancy Kress, *Baker's Dozen*, 1998
Robert Sheckley, *Is That What People Do?*, 1984

701

E.E. KNIGHT

Fall with Honor

(New York: Roc, 2008)

Story type: Invasion of Earth; Military
Series: Vampire Earth. Book 7

Subject(s): Aliens; Military Life
Major character(s): David Valentine, Military Personnel; Ahn-Kha, Alien; Brother Mark, Religious
Time period(s): Indeterminate Future
Locale(s): North America

Summary: More battles ensue between human forces and the vampiric alien invaders who conquered much of the Earth. This time the campaign is to establish a major base on the East Coast of North America to gain a strategic advantage over the enemy. The expedition to do so runs into an unexpected surprise when they reach their destination.

Other books by the same author:
Valentine's Resolve, 2007
Valentine's Exile, 2006
Tale of the Thunderbolt, 2005
Valentine's Rising, 2005
Choice of the Cat, 2004

Other books you might like:
Brian Aldiss, *Dracula Unbound*, 1991
Gordon Eklund, *The Twilight River*, 1979
Tanith Lee, *Sabella*, 1980
Larry Niven, *The Ringworld Throne*, 1996
Colin Wilson, *The Space Vampires*, 1976

702

CONOR KOSTICK

Saga

(New York: Viking, 2008)

Story type: Young Adult; Fantasy
Subject(s): Virtual Reality
Major character(s): Ghost, Teenager; Cindella, Teenager; Dark Queen, Video Game Player
Time period(s): Indeterminate Future
Locale(s): Cyberspace

Summary: All of the characters in this novel, sequel to *Epic*, are virtual persons existing in a vast and elaborate role playing game. There have always been strict rules but suddenly people are appearing and disappearing as if by magic and it is clear that someone is undermining the basic programming of the setting. A group of teenaged players try to find out who and why.

Other books by the same author:
Epic, 2007

Other books you might like:
James Bassett, *Living Real*, 1997
Graham Joyce, *Spiderbite*, 1997
Richard Peck, *Lost in Cyberspace*, 1997
Neal Stephenson, *Snow Crash*, 1992
Vivian Vande Velde, *User Unfriendly*, 1991

703

TOM KRATMAN

Caliphate

(New York: Baen, 2008)

Story type: Dystopian; Religious
Subject(s): Slavery; Religious Conflict

Science Fiction

Major character(s): Petra Minden, Slave; Hans Minden, Slave; John Hamilton, Student
Time period(s): 22nd century (2103-2113)
Locale(s): Europe

Summary: The influx of Muslims into Europe results in a change in the structure of society. Christians are marginalized and slavery is reintroduced. A young German girl is sold by her family and yearns to escape to America. The novel covers the future of Europe as it affects a large cast of characters.

Other books by the same author:
A Desert Called Peace, 2007
Carnifex, 2007
A State of Disobedience, 2003

Other books you might like:
George Alec Effinger, *When Gravity Fails*, 1986
Jon Courtenay Grimwood, *Arabesk*, 2007
Maureen McHugh, *Nekropolis*, 2001
Donald Moffitt, *Crescent in the Sky*, 1990
Kim Stanley Robinson, *The Years of Rice and Salt*, 2002

704

KEITH LAUMER
ROSEL GEORGE BROWN , Co-Author

Earthblood & Other Stories

(New York: Baen, 2008)

Story type: Collection
Subject(s): Short Stories

Summary: This collection gathers together a representative selection of short stories by each of the two authors individually, plus the complete text of their collaborative novel, *Earthblood*, which was first published in 1966. Laumer's stories tend to emphasize adventure and the wonders of the universe, while Brown's are more concerned with characters and personal situations.

Other books by the same author:
Imperium, 2005
Legions of Space, 2004
Future Imperfect, 2003
The Lighter Side, 2002
Back to the Time Trap, 1992

Other books you might like:
Rosel George Brown, *Sibyl Sue Blue*, 1968
Harry Harrison, *Fifty in Fifty*, 2001
Damon Knight, *One Side Laughing*, 1991
Murray Leinster, *First Contacts*, 1998
Robert Sheckley, *Store of Infinity*, 1960

705

LEE LIGHTNER

Wolf's Honour

(Nottingham, United Kingdom: Black Library, 2008)

Story type: Space Opera; Military
Series: Warhammer

Subject(s): War; Space Travel
Major character(s): Ragnar Blackmane, Military Personnel; Berek Thunderfist, Military Personnel; Mikal Sternmark, Military Personnel
Time period(s): Indeterminate Future
Locale(s): Outer Space

Summary: A series of battles between two heavily armed forces has resulted in very little change in their relative positions. Determined to bring the stalemate to an end, Ragnar Blackmane conceives a daring plan, a strike at their enemy's stronghold on a well-defended planet. Success could end the war but failure could be disastrous.

Other books by the same author:
Sons of Fenris, 2007

Other books you might like:
Dan Abnett, *Legion*, 2008
Loren L. Coleman, *A Call to Arms*, 2003
Ben Counter, *Battle for the Abyss*, 2008
Andy Hoare, *Star of Damocles*, 2007
Robert Thurston, *Falcon Rising*, 1999

706

DENISE LITTLE , Editor

Front Lines

(New York: DAW, 2008)

Story type: Anthology
Subject(s): Short Stories

Summary: The editor has gathered together 21 stories that involve future wars but has avoided most of the trappings of military science fiction, concentrating instead on the effect of war on noncombatants. All of the stories appear here for the first time. The contributors include Jean Rabe, Laura Resnick, Josepha Sherman, Dave Freer, and others.

Other books by the same author:
Cosmic Cocktails, 2006
Time After Time, 2005
A Constellation of Cats, 2001
Creature Fantastic, 2001
Alien Pets, 1998

Other books you might like:
John Blair, *A Landscape of Darkness*, 1990
Gordon R. Dickson, *Naked to the Stars*, 1961
W. Michael Gear, *Relic of Empire*, 1992
Joe Haldeman, *The Forever War*, 1974
John Scalzi, *Old Man's War*, 2005

707

SALLIE LOWENSTEIN

In the Company of Whispers

(Kensington, Maryland: Lion Stone, 2008)

Story type: Dystopian; Family Saga
Subject(s): Utopia/Dystopia
Major character(s): Zeyya, Teenager; Granna, Aged

Person; Jonah, Mentally Ill Person
Time period(s): 2040s (2047)
Locale(s): United States; Burma

Summary: A young girl takes refuge with her grandmother when her parents are taken into quarantine by the government in 2047. There she becomes involved with Jonah, an odd young man who may or may not be insane. The problems of their present are contrasted with her grandmother's memories of the past. First novel.

Other books you might like:
Brian Aldiss, *Earthworks*, 1965
Anthony Burgess, *The Wanting Seed*, 1962
Octavia Butler, *Dawn*, 1987
Norman Spinrad, *Greenhouse Summer*, 1999
George Turner, *Drowning Towers*, 1996

708

SCOTT MACKAY

Omega Sol

(New York: Roc, 2008)

Story type: First Contact; Disaster
Subject(s): Aliens; Scientific Experiments
Major character(s): Cameron Conrad, Scientist; Timothy Pittman, Military Personnel; Lesha Weeks, Scientist
Time period(s): Indeterminate Future
Locale(s): Earth; Moon (Earth's)

Summary: Scientists on the moon discover an elaborate alien artifact, by means of which they are able to open communication with an alien intelligence. After a short while the aliens stop responding and the scientists discover that the artifact is altering the sun in such a way that it will lead to the extinction of the human race.

Other books by the same author:
Phytosphere, 2007
Omnifix, 2004
Orbis, 2002
The Meek, 2001
Outpost, 1998

Other books you might like:
Roger MacBride Allen, *The Ring of Charon*, 1990
Greg Bear, *Eon*, 1985
Gregory Benford, *Cosm*, 1998
Arthur C. Clarke, *Rendezvous with Rama*, 1973
Alastair Reynolds, *Pushing Ice*, 2005

709

GEORGE MANN , Editor

The Solaris Book of New Science Fiction II

(Nottingham, United Kingdom: Solaris, 2008)

Story type: Anthology
Subject(s): Short Stories

Summary: The second volume in this series of unthemed,

all original stories contains predominantly adventure oriented fiction, mixed with some mild satire and a dose of humor. The contributors include Karl Schroeder, Peter Watts, Robert Reed, Michael Moorcock, Paul Di Filippo, Neal Asher, and others.

Where it's reviewed:
Locus, February 2008, page 70

Other books by the same author:
Child of Time, 2007
The Solaris Book of New Science Fiction, 2007
The Solaris Book of New Fantasy, 2007
The Human Abstract, 2004
The Severed Man, 2004

Other books you might like:
Paul Di Filippo, *Shuteye for the Timebroker*, 2006
Michael Moorcock, *The Black Corridor*, 1969
Robert Reed, *The Dragons of Springplace*, 1999
Karl Schroeder, *Sun of Suns*, 2006
Peter Watts, *Ten Monkeys, Ten Minutes*, 2000

710

GEORGE R.R. MARTIN , Editor

Inside Straight

(New York: Tor, 2008)

Story type: Anthology
Series: Wild Cards
Subject(s): Short Stories

Summary: The stories in this anthology are all interwoven into a story about a group of people with extraordinary powers who are arranged in teams to compete against one another in a reality television show. The separate segments concentrate on subsets of the characters, exploring the potential of their power and the interactions among them. The contributors include Melinda Snodgrass, Carrie Vaughn, Daniel Abraham, and others.

Where it's reviewed:
Booklist, February 1, 2008, page 36
Library Journal, January 1, 2008, page 88
Publishers Weekly, November 19, 2007, page 43

Other books by the same author:
Dreamsongs, 2006
A Feast for Crows, 2005
A Storm of Swords, 2000
A Clash of Kings, 1997
A Game of Thrones, 1996

Other books you might like:
Michael Bishop, *Count Geiger's Blues*, 1992
Arthur Byron Cover, *Born in Fire*, 2002
Tom De Haven, *Freaks' Amour*, 1979
Victor Milan, *Turn of the Cards*, 1993
John J. Miller, *Death Draws Five*, 2006

Science Fiction

711

A. LEE MARTINEZ

The Automatic Detective

(New York: Tor, 2008)

Story type: Robot Fiction; Mystery
Subject(s): Humor; Robots
Major character(s): Mack Megaton, Robot; Alfred
  Sanchez, Police Officer; Tony Ringo, Criminal
Time period(s): Indeterminate Future
Locale(s): Earth

Summary: In a distant future when robots have human
rights, Mack Megaton is trying to find a way to earn his
citizenship. When his neighbors are kidnapped and the
police seem unable to track them down, Mack decides to
try his hand at detection and see if he can rescue them
from a band of criminals.

Where it's reviewed:
Booklist, December 15, 2007, page 28
Entertainment Weekly, February 29, 2008, page 63
Publishers Weekly, November 19, 2007, page 42

Other books by the same author:
A Nameless Witch, 2007
In the Company of Ogres, 2006
Gil's All Fright Diner, 2005

Other books you might like:
Roger MacBride Allen, *The Modular Man*, 1992
Isaac Asimov, *The Caves of Steel*, 1954
Ron Goulart, *The Robot in the Closet*, 1981
Henry Kuttner, *Robots Have No Tails*, 1952
Clifford D. Simak, *Special Deliverance*, 1982

712

ANNE MCCAFFREY
ELIZABETH ANN SCARBOROUGH , Co-Author

Deluge

(New York: Del Rey, 2008)

Story type: Adventure; Space Opera
Series: Twins of Petaybee. Book 3
Subject(s): Twins; Scientific Experiments
Major character(s): Ronan, Mutant, Twin; Muriel, Mutant,
  Twin; Marmion de Revers Algemeine, Prisoner
Time period(s): Indeterminate Future
Locale(s): Petaybee, Planet—Imaginary; Outer Space

Summary: The two mutant shapechanging twins from the
planet Petaybee, Ronan and Muriel, travel off world on a
rescue mission and find themselves taken prisoner by
scientists who want to study their abilities. Elsewhere,
the company that has designs on the planet Petaybee,
whose ecosystem is one vast intelligent being, seek to
gain total power over that world.

Where it's reviewed:
Booklist, February 1, 2008, page 36
Publishers Weekly, January 7, 2008, page 40

Other books by the same author:
Freedom's Ransom, 2003
A Gift of Dragons, 2002
The Skies of Pern, 2001
Pegasus in Space, 2000
Acorna, 1997

Other books you might like:
Jo Clayton, *Skeen's Leap*, 1986
Sheila Finch, *Shaper's Legacy*, 1989
Howard V. Hendrix, *Empty Cities of the Full Moon*,
  2001
Scott Westerfeld, *Polymorph*, 1997
Gene Wolfe, *The Fifth Head of Cerberus*, 1972

713

SANDRA MCDONALD

The Stars Down Under

(New York: Tor, 2008)

Story type: Military; Space Opera
Series: Jodenny Scott. Book 2
Subject(s): Space Travel; Scientific Experiments
Major character(s): Jodenny Scott, Military Personnel;
  Terry Myell, Military Personnel; Nam, Military
  Personnel
Time period(s): Indeterminate Future
Locale(s): Outer Space; Planet—Imaginary

Summary: The Earth is polluted but colonies are being
established on other worlds. Travel by spaceship is time
-onsuming, expensive, and inadequate for the number of
people wishing to emigrate so experimentation is
underway with some alien technology that makes matter
transmission possible. Two members of the interplanetary
military find their own futures connected to the future of
the program.

Where it's reviewed:
Publishers Weekly, January 21, 2008, page 159

Other books by the same author:
The Outback Stars, 2007

Other books you might like:
Neal Asher, *Gridlinked*, 2003
Greg Bear, *Eternity*, 1988
C.J. Cherryh, *Gate of Ivrel*, 1976
Jack McDevitt, *Ancient Shores*, 1996
Frederik Pohl, *Gateway*, 1977

714

GRAHAM MCNEILL

Storm of Iron

(Nottingham, United Kingdom: Black Library, 2008)

Story type: Space Opera; Military
Series: Warhammer
Subject(s): Military Life; Space Travel
Major character(s): Honsou, Military Personnel; Laran

Utorian, Military Personnel; Leonid, Military Personnel

Time period(s): Indeterminate Future
Locale(s): Hydra Cordatus, Planet—Imaginary

Summary: A relatively small contingent of marines has been assigned to garrison the planet Hydra Cordatus. To their complete surprise, a massive invasion force arrives, overwhelms the initial resistance, and lays siege to the capital city. The defenders are uncertain whether they can hold out until help is sent, and even less certain about the reasons why this particular planet is deemed so valuable.

Other books by the same author:
The Killing Ground, 2008
False Gods, 2006
Dead Sky, Black Sun, 2004
Warriors of Ultramar, 2003
Nightbringer, 2002

Other books you might like:
Bill Baldwin, *The Defenders*, 1992
Robert Buettner, *Orphanage*, 2004
John Dalmas, *The Kalif's War*, 1991
John Ringo, *Hell's Faire*, 2003
Timothy Zahn, *Blackcollar*, 2006

715

PAUL MELKO

Singularity's Ring

(New York: Tor, 2008)

Story type: Hard Science Fiction; Mystery
Subject(s): Futuristic Fiction; Space Exploration
Major character(s): Apollo Papadopulos, Spaceship Captain, Mutant; Strom, Mutant; Moira, Mutant
Time period(s): Indeterminate Future
Locale(s): Outer Space

Summary: In the far distant future, most of the human race mysteriously disappears when a singularity leaves the Earth with an artificial ring. Mutations are common as well, including one in which several people are effectively joined mentally as one individual. The unusual protagonist of this story is a spaceship captain who consists of five separate but linked personalities, all of whom contribute to the investigation of the singularity. First novel.

Where it's reviewed:
Booklist, February 1, 2008, page 35
Locus, February 2008, page 17
Publishers Weekly, December 10, 2007, page 39

Other books you might like:
Roger MacBride Allen, *The Ring of Charon*, 1990
William Barton, *The Transmigration of Souls*, 1996
Robert Reed, *Beyond the Veil of Stars*, 1994
Alastair Reynolds, *Century Rain*, 2004
Robert J. Sawyer, *Flashforward*, 1999

716

PAUL MELKO

Ten Sigmas & Other Unlikelihoods

(Bonney Lake, Washington: Fairwood, 2008)

Story type: Collection
Subject(s): Short Stories

Summary: The 12 stories in this collection were all originally published in 2004 or later. There is a mixture of serious and comic stories, and a wide range of subject matter including alternate worlds, aliens, and superheroes. Two of the stories are related to the author's novel *Singularity's Ring*.

Other books by the same author:
Singularity's Ring, 2008

Other books you might like:
Lester Del Rey, *The Early Del Rey*, 1975
Alan Dean Foster, *Impossible Places*, 2002
Nancy Kress, *The Aliens of Earth*, 1993
Murray Leinster, *First Contacts*, 1998
Frederik Pohl, *The Platinum Pohl*, 2005

717

SANDY MITCHELL

Scourge the Heretic

(Nottingham, United Kingdom: Black Library, 2008)

Story type: Space Opera; Military
Series: Warhammer
Subject(s): Aliens; Space Travel
Major character(s): Vos Kyrlock, Military Personnel; Carolus Finurbi, Government Official; Drake, Military Personnel
Time period(s): Indeterminate Future
Locale(s): Outer Space

Summary: The Inquisitors are a combination of religious and political agents who search for heretics and criminals within the human empire, which is engaged in an endless war with aliens. When they learn of what appears to be a simple interplanetary slavery ring, they send marines to crack down on the operation, but an even greater secret lies concealed beneath the surface.

Other books by the same author:
Ciaphas Cain: Hero of the Imperium, 2007
Duty Calls, 2007
Death's City, 2005
Caves of Ice, 2004
For the Emperor, 2003

Other books you might like:
Robert Buettner, *Orphanage*, 2004
John Dalmas, *The Regiment*, 1987
Richard Fawkes, *Nature of the Beast*, 2004
Gordon Kendall, *White Wing*, 1985
Elizabeth Moon, *Victory Conditions*, 2008

718

L.E. MODESITT JR.

Viewpoints Critical

(New York: Tor, 2008)

Story type: Collection
Subject(s): Short Stories

Summary: This volume collects selected stories from throughout the author's career, ranging from 1973 to 2007. There is a broad range of subject matter including military science fiction, space travel, satire, and two fantasies. Included is the author's first published story, "The Great American Economy," an early tale of computer crime.

Where it's reviewed:
Booklist, February 1, 2008, page 38
Publishers Weekly, January 28, 2008, page 44

Other books by the same author:
The Elysium Commission, 2006
The Eternity Artifact, 2005
Flash, 2004
Archform: Beauty, 2002
Adiamonte, 1996

Other books you might like:
Lester Del Rey, *Gods and Golems*, 1973
Harry Harrison, *One Step from Earth*, 1970
Robert A. Heinlein, *Off the Main Sequence*, 2005
Keith Laumer, *Legions of Space*, 2004
Mack Reynolds, *Compounded Interest*, 1983

719

ELIZABETH MOON

Victory Conditions

(New York: Del Rey, 2008)

Story type: Space Opera; Military
Series: Ty Vatta. Book 5
Subject(s): Space Travel; Quest
Major character(s): Ty Vatta, Spaceship Captain, Military Personnel; Stella Vatta, Businesswoman; Gammis Turek, Criminal (space pirate)
Time period(s): Indeterminate Future
Locale(s): Outer Space

Summary: Ty Vatta has taken control of her family's interstellar trading company and added a military component as well. The depredations of a daring space pirate who has gathered a virtual army in space threaten the stability of every planet, and she is determined to end the reign of terror and avenge the wrongs done to her own family. This is the final novel in the series.

Where it's reviewed:
Booklist, February 1, 2008, page 36
Publishers Weekly, December 17, 2007, page 38

Other books by the same author:
Command Decision, 2007
Engaging the Enemy, 2006
The Speed of Dark, 2003
Trading in Danger, 2003
Against the Odds, 2000

Other books you might like:
C.J. Cherryh, *The Chanur Saga*, 2005
Julie E. Czerneda, *A Thousand Words for Stranger*, 1997
S.N. Lewitt, *Angel at Apogee*, 1987
Melisa Michaels, *Skirmish*, 1985
S.L. Viehl, *Afterburn*, 2005

720

JAMIL NASIR

The Houses of Time

(New York: Tor, 2008)

Story type: Mystical; Literary
Subject(s): Scientific Experiments; Dreams and Nightmares
Major character(s): David Grant, Psychic, Lawyer; P. Thotmoses, Administrator; Katerina Hatshep, Psychic
Time period(s): 2000s (2008)
Locale(s): United States

Summary: David Grant has been experiencing particularly realistic lucid dreams, in several of which he imagines himself married to a woman he has never met. Then he does meet her, although she has a different name, and he becomes more interested in delving into the nature of his dreams at an establishment run by the mysterious Dr. Thotmoses, who has a hidden agenda.

Where it's reviewed:
Locus, March 2008, page 63
Publishers Weekly, January 14, 2008, page 43

Other books by the same author:
Distance Haze, 2000
Tower of Dreams, 1999
Higher Space, 1996
Quasar, 1995

Other books you might like:
D.G. Compton, *Synthajoy*, 1968
Raymond Harris, *The Schizogenic Man*, 1990
K.W. Jeter, *The Dreamfields*, 1976
Christopher Priest, *The Affirmation*, 1981
Elisabeth Vonarburg, *Dreams of the Sea*, 2004

721

LARRY NIVEN
EDWARD M. LERNER , Co-Author

Juggler of Worlds

(New York: Tor, 2008)

Story type: Hard Science Fiction; Mystery
Series: Known Space

Subject(s): Aliens; Secrets
Major character(s): Sigmund Ausfaller, Mentally Ill Person (paranoid), Spy; Nessus, Alien, Government Official; Beowulf Shaeffer, Spaceman
Time period(s): 27th century
Locale(s): Outer Space; Planet—Imaginary

Summary: The human race has assigned a paranoid man to act as a secret agent to investigate the actions of the Puppeteers, a race that has quietly been manipulating the rest of the galaxy for purposes of their own. Since the aliens as a race are paranoid themselves, he is much more successful than his predecessors and discovers that the fate of worlds is in the balance.

Other books by the same author:
The Draco Tavern, 2006
Ringworld's Children, 2004
Scatterbrain, 2003
Rainbow Mars, 1999
Tales of Known Space, 1975

Other books you might like:
Poul Anderson, *The People of the Wind*, 1973
John Brunner, *A Maze of Stars*, 1991
Keith Laumer, *Retief and the Warlords*, 1968
Murray Leinster, *The Greks Bring Gifts*, 1964
Jack Vance, *Night Lamp*, 1996

722

MARY E. PEARSON

The Adoration of Jenna Fox

(New York: Henry Holt, 2008)

Story type: Young Adult; Genetic Manipulation
Subject(s): Scientific Experiments
Major character(s): Jenna Fox, Teenager, Android; Matthew Fox, Scientist; Lily, Servant
Time period(s): Indeterminate Future
Locale(s): United States

Summary: Jenna Fox wakens from a coma with nearly complete amnesia. She subsequently discovers that she is an artificially created person with sophisticated electronic biochips and other advances that will enable her to live much longer than ordinary humans, an experiment designed to improve the species.

Other books by the same author:
A Room on Lorelei Street, 2005
Scribbler of Dreams, 2002

Other books you might like:
Richard Bowker, *Replica*, 1987
L.P. Davies, *The Artificial Man*, 1965
Stephen Fine, *Molly Dear*, 1988
K.W. Jeter, *The Edge of Human*, 1995
Pamela Sargent, *Cloned Lives*, 1976

723

S.D. PERRY
BRITTA DENNISON , Co-Author

Night of the Wolves

(New York: Pocket, 2008)

Story type: Space Opera; Military
Series: Star Trek
Subject(s): Aliens
Major character(s): Skrain Dukat, Military Personnel, Alien; Mora Pol, Scientist, Alien; Ro Laren, Rebel, Alien
Time period(s): Indeterminate Future
Locale(s): Bajor, Planet—Imaginary

Summary: The Cardassian military has defeated and occupied the planet Bajor, but they have been unable to stifle an active resistance movement. When the Cardassians erect a new symbol of their domination, it leads to an unprecedented outbreak of sabotage and straightforward battles between the two races.

Other books by the same author:
State of War, 2003
Avatar, 2001
Cloak, 2001
Berserker, 1998
Caliban Cove, 1998

Other books you might like:
Diane Carey, *What You Leave Behind*, 1999
Heather Jarman, *This Gray Spirit*, 2002
J. Noah Kym, *Bajor*, 2005
David Mack, *Warpath*, 2006
James Swallow, *Day of the Vipers*, 2008

724

STEVE PERRY

Turnabout

(Milwaukee, Oregon: Dark Horse, 2008)

Story type: Invasion of Earth; First Contact
Series: Predator
Subject(s): Aliens; Hunting
Major character(s): Sloane, Game Warden; Mary Collins, Tourist; Jack Regal, Criminal
Time period(s): 2000s (2008)
Locale(s): Alaska

Summary: A game warden in Alaska is concerned when a woman arrives, searching for the place where her brother died. Her efforts place her in danger because of the activities of a poacher operating in the area. The greatest threat, however, is not human at all, but the presence of an alien visitor who likes to hunt prey, including human beings.

Other books by the same author:
CyberNation, 2001
Breaking Point, 2000
Target Earth, 1997
The Digital Effect, 1997
Brother Death, 1992

Other books you might like:
Nathan Archer, *Cold War*, 1997
David Bischoff, *Genocide*, 1994
Diane Carey, *DNA War*, 2006
Michael Jan Friedman, *Original Sin*, 2005
John Shirley, *Steel Egg*, 2007

725

SUSAN BETH PFEFFER

The Dead & the Gone

(New York: Harcourt, 2008)

Story type: Young Adult; Post-Disaster
Subject(s): Disasters
Major character(s): Alex Morales, Teenager; Briana
    Morales, Teenager; Father Franco, Religious
Time period(s): Indeterminate Future
Locale(s): New York, New York

Summary: An asteroid glances off the moon and alters its orbit, resulting in disastrous tides and earthquakes all over the Earth. A handful of teenagers in New York City follow the news and try to deal with the radically altered future that faces them. This is a companion to the author's *Life As We Knew It*, but is not a sequel.

Other books by the same author:
Life As We Knew It, 2006

Other books you might like:
Arthur C. Clarke, *The Hammer of God*, 1993
Elizabeth Hand, *Icarus Descending*, 1993
Fritz Leiber, *The Wanderer*, 1964
Yvonne Navarro, *Final Impact*, 1997
Charles Sheffield, *Aftermath*, 1998

726

DOUGLAS PRESTON

Blasphemy

(New York: Forge, 2008)

Story type: Religious; Techno-Thriller
Subject(s): Religious Conflict; Scientific Experiments
Major character(s): Wyman Ford, Investigator; Gregory
    Hazelius, Scientist, Religious (televangelist); Don T.
    Spates, Television Personality
Time period(s): 2000s (2008)
Locale(s): New Mexico

Summary: The largest supercollider in the world has been built in New Mexico, but the scientists running the operation have run into an unusual problem. Whenever they apply full power, they begin receiving messages from an intelligence that claims to be God. This leads to a violent reaction when news begins to leak to a prominent televangelist.

Where it's reviewed:
Booklist, November 15, 2007, page 5
Entertainment Weekly, January 18, 2008, page 87
Library Journal, November 15, 2007, page 50
Publishers Weekly, October 22, 2007, page 33

Other books by the same author:
Book of the Dead, 2006 (Lincoln Child, co-author)
Tyrannosaur Canyon, 2005
Brimstone, 2004 (Lincoln Child, co-author)
The Cabinet of Curiosities, 2002 (Lincoln Child,
    co-author)
Thunderhead, 1999 (Lincoln Child, co-author)

Other books you might like:
William Barton, *The Transmigration of Souls*, 1996
Karel Capek, *The Absolute at Large*, 1927
Dean R. Koontz, *Fear That Man*, 1969
Michael Moorcock, *Behold the Man*, 1968
Gore Vidal, *Messiah*, 1954

727

KEN RAND

Where Angels Fear

(Bonney Lake, Washington: Fairwood, 2008)

Story type: Collection
Subject(s): Short Stories

Summary: This collection of 35 short stories includes 13 which have never been previously published. Although there are some fantasy stories as well, they are predominantly science fiction. The author is fond of sudden reversals in his stories, and surprise endings are quite common. The subject matter includes thought control, insect attacks, and aliens.

Other books by the same author:
Pax Dakota, 2008
Fairy BrewHaHa at the Lucky Nickel Saloon, 2005

Other books you might like:
James Patrick Kelly, *Heroines*, 1990
Nancy Kress, *Beaker's Dozen*, 1998
Keith Laumer, *Future Imperfect*, 2003
Murray Leinster, *First Contacts*, 1998
Robert Sheckley, *Uncanny Tales*, 2003

728

MIKE RESNICK

Starship Mercenary

(Amherst, New York: Pyr, 2008)

Story type: Space Opera; Military
Series: Starship. Book 3
Subject(s): Space Travel; Military Life
Major character(s): Wilson Cole, Spaceship Captain;
    Valkyrie, Spaceship Captain, Military Personnel; For-
    rice, Alien, Military Personnel
Time period(s): Indeterminate Future
Locale(s): Outer Space

Summary: After rebelling against a military hierarchy that is shortsighted and repressive, Wilson Cole and his crew decide to make a living by hiring themselves out as mercenaries. They are remarkably successful and soon staff additional ships, but eventually their wide-ranging

activities pit them against some of their former friends and allies.

Other books by the same author:
Starship Mutiny, 2006
Starship Pirate, 2006
The Return of Santiago, 2003
With a Little Help from My Friends, 2002
The Widowmaker Unleashed, 1998

Other books you might like:
Chris Bunch, *The Last Legion*, 1999
William C. Dietz, *By Blood Alone*, 1999
R.M. Meluch, *The Sagittarius Command*, 2007
John Scalzi, *The Last Colony*, 2007
Mike Shepherd, *Audacious*, 2007

729

ALASTAIR REYNOLDS

House of Chains

(London: Gollancz, 2008)

Story type: Space Opera; Hard Science Fiction
Subject(s): Space Travel; Secrets
Major character(s): Campion, Clone, Spaceship Captain; Purslane, Clone, Spaceship Captain; Hesperus, Robot
Time period(s): Indeterminate Future
Locale(s): Outer Space

Summary: Campion and Purslane are two of 1,000 clones of Abigail Gentry, each of whom has lived tens of thousands of years and explored countless star systems. Periodically the clones reunite but this time the reunion is a trap that results in the death of the vast majority of them. The survivors must determine who was responsible and why.

Other books by the same author:
The Prefect, 2007
Galactic North, 2006
Pushing Ice, 2005
Century Rain, 2004
Chasm City, 2000

Other books you might like:
Iain Banks, *The Algebraist*, 2004
Peter F. Hamilton, *The Dreaming Void*, 2008
Jack McDevitt, *Polaris*, 2004
Dan Simmons, *Olympos*, 2004
Vernor Vinge, *A Fire upon the Deep*, 1992

730

JOHN RINGO
TRAVIS S. TAYLOR , Co-Author

Manxome Foe

(New York: Baen, 2008)

Story type: Space Opera; Military
Series: Vorpal Blade. Book 3
Subject(s): Space Travel; Aliens
Major character(s): William Weaver, Scientist, Military

Personnel; Eric Bergstresser, Military Personnel; Miriam Moon, Linguist
Time period(s): Indeterminate Future
Locale(s): Outer Space

Summary: Mysterious portals to the stars have opened up within humanity's reach, but the initial efforts to explore lead to contact with hostile aliens. The crew of the *Vorpal Blade* is just recovering from one attacl when a fresh one causes them to return to action and find allies in their battle against the malevolent Dreen.

Other books by the same author:
East of the Sun, West of the Moon, 2006
Ghost, 2005
Emerald Sea, 2004
Hell's Faire, 2003
Gust Front, 2001

Other books you might like:
Chris Bunch, *Firemask*, 2000
William C. Dietz, *For Those Who Fell*, 2004
William R. Forstchen, *Down to the Sea*, 2000
William King, *Space Wolf*, 2000
Mike Resnick, *Starship Pirate*, 2008

731

J.D. ROBB   (Pseudonym of Nora Roberts)

Strangers in Death

(New York: Putnam, 2008)

Story type: Mystery; Futuristic
Series: Eve Dallas. Book 28
Subject(s): Secrets; Murder; Police Procedural
Major character(s): Eve Dallas, Detective—Homicide; Roarke, Businessman, Spouse (Eve's husband); Ava Anders, Widow(er)
Time period(s): 2060s (2060)
Locale(s): New York, New York

Summary: Eve Dallas and her crew investigate a bizarre murder in which the victim was doped, then arranged to look as though he had been involved in an elaborate sex game at the time of his death. The various suspects all seem to have alibis, but there are hidden motives and connections that are only revealed under pressure.

Where it's reviewed:
Publishers Weekly, January 7, 2008, page 38

Other books by the same author:
Creation in Death, 2007
Innocent in Death, 2007
Born in Death, 2006
Memory in Death, 2006
Origin in Death, 2005

Other books you might like:
Wilhelmina Baird, *Clipjoint*, 1994
Alfred Bester, *The Demolished Man*, 1953
Lynn Hightower, *Alien Rites*, 1995
Mel Odom, *Lethal Interface*, 1992
Mark Tiedemann, *Remains*, 2005

732

CHRIS ROBERSON

The Dragon's Nine Sons

(Nottingham, United Kingdom: Solaris, 2008)

Story type: Space Opera; Military
Subject(s): Space Travel; War
Major character(s): Zhuan Jie, Military Personnel; Yao Guanzhong, Military Personnel; Fukudu Uyeda
Time period(s): 2050s (2052)
Locale(s): Outer Space

Summary: In an alternate universe, the two major world powers are China and Mexico, both of which have a strong presence in space. The two empires are at war and a small crew of disgraced Chinese officers are enlisted in a suicide mission to destroy a secret base in the asteroid belt. They discover that the base contains a large number of Chinese prisoners, and choose to disobey their orders once again.

Where it's reviewed:
Locus, February 2008, page 21
Publishers Weekly, December 10, 2007, page 40

Other books by the same author:
Set the Seas on Fire, 2007
Paragaea, 2006
The Voyage of Night Shining White, 2006
Here, There, and Everywhere, 2005
Voices of Thunder, 2001

Other books you might like:
Colin Greenland, *Harm's Way*, 1993
Donald Moffitt, *Crescent in the Sky*, 1990
Alan E. Nourse, *Raiders from the Rings*, 1962
S.M. Stirling, *In the Courts of the Crimson Kings*, 2008
John Wyndham, *The Outward Urge*, 1959

733

KARL SCHROEDER

Pirate Sun

(New York: Tor, 2008)

Story type: Alternate Universe; Space Opera
Series: Virga. Book 3
Subject(s): Space Travel; Space Exploration
Major character(s): Chaison Fanning, Military Personnel; Venera Fanning, Noblewoman; Richard Reiss, Military Personnel
Time period(s): Indeterminate Future
Locale(s): Alternate Universe

Summary: Virga is a miniature universe constructed by humans in the distant past. Within it exist a number of planets amongst which travel is practical, and each has its own distinct culture. Chaison Fanning is an admiral in the navy of one of these worlds, but he is betrayed into captivity and his wife disappears on a mission of her own.

Other books by the same author:
The Queen of Candesce, 2007
Sun of Suns, 2006
Lady of Mazes, 2005
Permanence, 2002
Ventus, 2000

Other books you might like:
Stephen Baxter, *Raft*, 1991
Philip Jose Farmer, *The Gates of Creation*, 1966
Christopher Priest, *The Inverted World*, 1974
Alastair Reynolds, *Century Rain*, 2004
Bob Shaw, *The Ragged Astronauts*, 1986

734

EDMUND R. SCHUBERT , Editor
ORSON SCOTT CARD , Co-Editor

Orson Scott Card's Intergalactic Medicine Show

(New York: Tor, 2008)

Story type: Anthology
Subject(s): Short Stories

Summary: These 18 stories originally appeared in an on-line magazine and appear here in book form for the first time. There is no central theme or focus. Included are stories by Card set in the Ender's Universe series, and other work by David Farland, Tim Pratt, Richard Lubar, and others. Most of the writers are relatively new to the field.

Other books you might like:
Isaac Asimov, *The Early Asimov*, 1972
Orson Scott Card, *Ender's Game*, 1985
Arthur C. Clarke, *The Collected Stories of Arthur C. Clarke*, 2000
Richard Lubar, *True Talents*, 2007
Tim Pratt, *Little Gods*, 2003

735

OWEN SHEERS

Resistance

(New York: Doubleday, 2008)

Story type: Alternate History; Military
Subject(s): Alternate History; Secrets
Major character(s): Maggie Jones, Farmer; Sarah Lewis, Housewife, Young Woman; Albrecht Wolfram, Military Personnel
Time period(s): 1940s
Locale(s): England

Summary: This is an alternate history novel in which the Germans successfully invade and occupy the British Isles during World War II. Most of the able-bodied civilian men become part of a hidden resistance movement. The story is told mostly through the eyes of their wives and lovers. First novel.

Where it's reviewed:
Booklist, February 1, 2008, page 28
Entertainment Weekly, February 22, 2008, page 100
Library Journal, February 1, 2008, page 65
New York Times Book Review, March 2, 2008, page 24

Other books you might like:
Brian Aldiss, *The Year Before Yesterday*, 1987
Ben Bova, *Triumph*, 1993
Len Deighton, *SS-GB*, 1978
James P. Hogan, *The Proteus Operation*, 1985
Brad Linaweaver, *Moon of Ice*, 1988

736

SCOTT SIGLER

Infected

(New York: Crown, 2008)

Story type: Medical
Subject(s): Medical Thriller
Major character(s): Dew Phillips, Investigator; Margaret
    Montoya, Scientist; Perry Dawsey, Worker
Time period(s): 2000s
Locale(s): United States

Summary: A strange new disease begins to spread across
the world. Those infected exhibit extreme changes in
behavior, eventually becoming homicidally violent. An
epidemiologist and a CIA investigator are the two key
players in a race against time to discover what is causing
the disease and how to reverse its effects before it
consumes the human race.

Where it's reviewed:
Library Journal, March 15, 2008, page 67
Publishers Weekly, February 25, 2008, page 51

Other books by the same author:
Earthcore, 2005

Other books you might like:
Martin Caidin, *Four Came Back*, 1968
Jack Haldeman, *Vector Analysis*, 1978
Harry Harrison, *Plague from Space*, 1965
Martin Cruz Smith, *Nightwing*, 1978
Norman Spinrad, *Journal of the Plague Years*, 1995

737

ALLEN STEELE

Galaxy Blues

(New York: Ace, 2008)

Story type: Space Opera; Hard Science Fiction
Series: Coyote. Book 5
Subject(s): Space Colonies; Aliens
Major character(s): Jules Truffaut, Spaceman; Morgan
    Goldstein, Businessman; Rain Thompson, Space-
    woman
Time period(s): Indeterminate Future
Locale(s): *Price of Cucamonga*, Spaceship; Outer Space

Summary: Jules Truffaut stows away to Coyote but is

soon in more trouble and imprisoned. His chance at
redemption comes when he is offered a job as star pilot
and informal ambassador to an alien race. When things
go awry, he has to undertake an even more perilous mission in order to square things with both humans and
aliens.

Where it's reviewed:
Publisher's Weekly, February 25, 2008, page 58

Other books by the same author:
Spindrift, 2007
The River Horses, 2007
Coyote Frontier, 2005
Coyote Rising, 2004
Coyote, 2002

Other books you might like:
John Brunner, *The Wrong End of Time*, 1971
Jack McDevitt, *Odyssey*, 2006
Robert J. Sawyer, *Starplex*, 1996
Peter Watts, *Blindsight*, 2006
James White, *Federation World*, 1988

738

S.M. STIRLING

In the Courts of the Crimson Kings

(New York: Tor, 2008)

Story type: Alternate World; Space Colony
Series: Universe Next Door. Book 2
Subject(s): Space Colonies; Aliens
Major character(s): Jeremy Wainman, Archaeologist;
    Teyud za-Zhalt, Alien, Mercenary; Heltaw sa-
    Veynau, Alien, Nobleman
Time period(s): 2000s (2000)
Locale(s): Mars

Summary: In an alternate version of our world where Mars
and Venus were made habitable millions of years in the
past, expeditions to those planets discovered that they
are in fact inhabited. An expedition on Mars runs into
trouble when the local guide proves to be someone with
concealed knowledge of a secret that could change the
future of all three races.

Where it's reviewed:
Publishers Weekly, December 17, 2007, page 38

Other books by the same author:
A Meeting at Corvallis, 2006
Dies the Fire, 2004
Conquistador, 2003
The Future War, 2003
Against the Tide of Years, 1999

Other books you might like:
Leigh Brackett, *The Ginger Star*, 1974
Lin Carter, *The Man Who Loved Mars*, 1973
A. Bertram Chandler, *The Alternate Martians*, 1965
Colin Greenland, *Take Back Plenty*, 1990
Michael Moorcock, *Blades of Mars*, 1965

Science Fiction

739

CHARLES STROSS

Saturn's Children

(New York: Ace, 2008)

Story type: Hard Science Fiction; Robot Fiction
Subject(s): Secrets; Robots
Major character(s): Freya Nakamichi 47, Android, Messenger; Katherine Sorico, Android, Aristocrat; Daks, Android
Time period(s): Indeterminate Future
Locale(s): Earth; Mars

Summary: In a far future, humanity has become extinct but sentient androids that were created as property have continued human civilization, exploring outer space and functioning in much the same fashion as did the human race. Freya is an android who takes a job as an interplanetary messenger and who becomes the focus of a deadly battle for control of the package she is carrying.

Other books by the same author:
Halting State, 2007
Glasshouse, 2006
Iron Sunrise, 2004
The Atrocity Archives, 2004
Singularity Sky, 2003

Other books you might like:
Edmund Cooper, *Deadly Image*, 1958
Robert A. Heinlein, *Friday*, 1982
Andre Norton, *Android at Arms*, 1971
Robert Silverberg, *Tower of Glass*, 1970
Clifford D. Simak, *City*, 1952

740

JAMES SWALLOW

Day of the Vipers

(New York: Pocket, 2008)

Story type: Space Opera; Political
Series: Star Trek: Terok Nor. Book 1
Subject(s): Aliens; Secrets
Major character(s): Skrain Dukat, Military Personnel, Alien; Darrah Mace, Military Personnel, Alien; Gar Osen, Religious, Alien
Time period(s): Indeterminate Future
Locale(s): Bajor, Planet—Imaginary

Summary: This is the first in a series recounting the initial contact and eventual war between Cardassia and Bajor in the Star Trek universe. A military mission arrives to negotiate contact but there are political and social conflicts between the two races that lead to increasingly violent hostilities and eventually to an open break. The conflict is seen through the eyes of representatives of both races.

Other books by the same author:
Faith and Fire, 2006
Jade Dragon, 2006
Blood Relative, 2005
Deus Encarmine, 2004
Eclipse, 2004

Other books you might like:
Kevin J. Anderson, *Blindfold*, 1995
Poul Anderson, *The Day of Their Return*, 1973
Greg Bear, *Corona*, 1984
Gordon R. Dickson, *Naked to the Stars*, 1961
Keith Laumer, *The Glory Game*, 1972

741

SHERI S. TEPPER

The Margarets

(London: Gollancz, 2008)

Story type: Dystopian; Mystical
Subject(s): Space Colonies; Aliens
Major character(s): Margaret Bain, Psychic; David Mackey, Scientist; Ongamar, Slave
Time period(s): Indeterminate Future
Locale(s): Earth; Mars; Outer Space

Summary: As a child, Margaret Bain lived with her parents on one of the moons of Mars during an abortive effort to make that planet habitable. In some fashion never completely explained, her subsequent choices split her personality into a variety of distinct individuals, about each of whom a story is told.

Other books by the same author:
The Companions, 2003
The Visitor, 2002
The Fresco, 2000
Singer from the Sea, 1999
Shadow's End, 1995

Other books you might like:
Barrington J. Bayley, *Empire of Two Worlds*, 1972
Richard A. Lupoff, *The Triune Man*, 1977
Pamela Reynolds, *Earth Times Two*, 1970
Bob Shaw, *The Two-Timers*, 1968
Lisa Tuttle, *Lost Futures*, 1992

742

JEFFREY THOMAS

Blue War

(Nottingham, United Kingdom: Solaris, 2008)

Story type: Alternate Universe; Mystery
Series: Punktown
Subject(s): Cloning; Aliens
Major character(s): Jeremy Stake, Detective—Private; Rick Henderson, Military Personnel; Ami Pattaya, Scientist
Time period(s): Indeterminate Future
Locale(s): Planet—Imaginary

Summary: Punktown is a decadent city set on a human colony world. Among its denizens is Jeremy Stake, an ex-soldier and private investigator who possesses the strange and now always controlled ability to alter his face to resemble others. His latest case suggests the possibility that the peace between humans and aliens may be on the verge of ending.

Where it's reviewed:
Locus, February 2008, page 20

Other books by the same author:
Deadstock, 2007
Doomsdays, 2007
Everybody Scream, 2005
Monstrocity, 2003
Punktown, 1999

Other books you might like:
Gregory Benford, *Find the Changeling*, 1980
    Gordon Eklund, co-author
Arthur Byron Cover, *Autumn Angels*, 1975
Howard V. Hendrix, *Empty Cities of the Full Moon*,
    2001
Robert Reed, *Beneath the Gated Sky*, 1997
Scott Westerfeld, *Polymorph*, 1997

743

KAREN TRAVISS

Revelation

(New York: Del Rey, 2008)

Story type: Space Opera; Military
Series: Star Wars
Subject(s): Space Travel; Secrets
Major character(s): Ben Skywalker, Military Personnel;
    Jacen Solo, Ruler; Luke Skywalker, Warrior
Time period(s): Indeterminate Past
Locale(s): Outer Space; Planet—Imaginary

Summary: Jacen Solo has solidified his tyrannical rule of
the Galactic Alliance. Opposed to him is his only family
plus the Skywalkers, one of whom believes him responsible for a long-concealed murder. The opposition
reluctantly accepts the fact that he can only be dethroned
through a massive military effort.

Other books by the same author:
Sacrifice, 2007
Matriarch, 2006
Triple Zero, 2006
The World Before, 2005
City of Pearl, 2004

Other books you might like:
Elaine Cunningham, *Dark Journey*, 2002
Troy Denning, *Tattooine Ghost*, 2003
Greg Keyes, *Conquest*, 2001
James Luceno, *The Unifying Force*, 2003
Kathy Tyers, *Balance Point*, 2000

744

HARRY TURTLEDOVE

The Valley-Westside War

(New York: Tor, 2008)

Story type: Young Adult; Alternate World
Series: Crosstime Traffic. Book 5

Subject(s): Secrets
Major character(s): Liz Mendoza, Teenager; Zev, Ruler;
    Dan, Teenager
Time period(s): Indeterminate Future
Locale(s): Los Angeles, California; Alternate Earth

Summary: Crosstime agents travel from one version of
history to another, exploring and trading without revealing their origins. In some of these worlds, a nuclear war
destroyed civilization and a teenager gets involved in an
investigation to find out why it happened.

Other books by the same author:
The Gladiator, 2007
In High Places, 2006
The Disunited States of America, 2006
Drive to the East, 2005
Days of Infamy, 2004

Other books you might like:
John Brunner, *The Infinitive of Go*, 1980
John Dalmas, *The Reality Matrix*, 1986
Philip Jose Farmer, *The Gate of Time*, 1966
Steven Gould, *Wildside*, 1996
Ted White, *The Jewels of Elsewhen*, 1967

745

MARK L. VAN NAME , Editor
T.K.F. WEISSKOPT , Co-Editor

Transhuman

(New York: Baen, 2008)

Story type: Anthology
Subject(s): Short Stories

Summary: This is an anthology of 11 original stories about
the possibilities connected to the development of
superhuman entities. These include robots, cyborgs,
genetically altered humans, and artificial intelligences.
The contributors include Esther Friesner, Wil McCarthy,
Wen Spencer, and James P. Hogan, and are predominantly
hard science fiction.

Other books by the same author:
One Jump Ahead, 2007
Intersections, 1996 (Richard Butner, co-editor)

Other books you might like:
Steve Alten, *Goliath*, 2002
Philip K. Dick, *Do Androids Dream of Electric Sheep?*,
    1968
Frederik Pohl, *Man Plus*, 1976
John Scalzi, *The Android's Dream*, 2006
Jack Vance, *The Dragon Masters*, 1962

746

JOHN VARLEY

Rolling Thunder

(New York: Ace, 2008)

Story type: Hard Science Fiction; Space Colony
Subject(s): Space Travel; Space Colonies

Major character(s): Patricia "Podkayne" Strickland-Garcia-Redmund, Military Personnel, Entertainer; Quinn, Entertainer; Slomo, Entertainer
Time period(s): Indeterminate Future
Locale(s): Europa, Jupiter

Summary: Podkayne is a Martian colonist who joins the military but who is also a talented musician. She is sent on a cultural mission to Europa, one of Jupiter's moons, with a group of other talented people, but her supposedly routine mission takes a dangerous new turn after she arrives.

Where it's reviewed:
Publishers Weekly, January 28, 2008, page 46

Other books by the same author:
Red Lightning, 2006
Mammoth, 2005
Red Thunder, 2003
The Golden Globe, 1998
Steel Beach, 1992

Other books you might like:
Poul Anderson, *Three Worlds to Conquer*, 1964
Gregory Benford, *Jupiter Project*, 1975
Ben Bova, *Jupiter*, 2000
Robert A. Heinlein, *Podkayne of Mars*, 1963
Timothy Zahn, *Manta's Gift*, 2002

747

DAVID WEBER

By Schism Rent Asunder

(New York: Tor, 2008)

Story type: Military; Religious
Series: Safehold. Book 2
Subject(s): Space Colonies; Religion
Major character(s): Merlin Athrawes, Military Personnel; Caleb Ahrmahk, Ruler; Rahzhyr Mahklyn, Scholar
Time period(s): Indeterminate Future
Locale(s): Safehold, Planet—Imaginary

Summary: The planet Safehold is a theocracy whose religious leaders rule with an iron hand. When the ruler of one island kingdom rebels, they attempt to make an example of him to discourage further unrest, but the Charisians refuse to be defeated easily. One of the king's advisers is imprinted with the personality of a woman from lost Earth.

Other books by the same author:
Off Armageddon Reef, 2006
At All Costs, 2005
Old Soldiers, 2005
The Shadow of Saganami, 2004
War of Honor, 2002

Other books you might like:
Poul Anderson, *The Day of Their Return*, 1973
David Drake, *Justice*, 1992
Keith Laumer, *Star Colony*, 1981
Andre Norton, *Star Born*, 1958
Allen Steele, *Coyote*, 2002

748

EDWARD WILLETT

Marseguro

(New York: DAW, 2008)

Story type: Space Opera; Space Colony
Subject(s): Space Colonies; Genetic Engineering
Major character(s): Chris Keating, Settler; Emily Wood, Genetically Altered Being; Richard Hansen, Military Personnel
Time period(s): Indeterminate Future
Locale(s): Marseguro, Planet—Imaginary

Summary: The planet Marseguro has two separate populations, one a group of normal humans seeking freedom from the laws of a repressive Earth, the other a genetically altered race is capable of living in the ocean. When an angry man activates a distress beacon and announces the planet's location to the authorities, a military expedition is sent to destroy the altered humans.

Other books by the same author:
Soulworm, 2007
Lost in Translation, 2005
Spirit Singer, 2003

Other books you might like:
Poul Anderson, *The Day of Their Return*, 1973
Michael Bishop, *Stolen Faces*, 1977
David Brin, *Brightness Reef*, 1996
Max Allan Collins, *Waterworld*, 1995
Stephen Leigh, *Dark Water's Embrace*, 1998

749

DAVID J. WILLIAMS

Mirrored Heaven

(New York: Bantam, 2008)

Story type: Political; Post-Disaster
Subject(s): Political Thriller; Heroes and Heroines
Major character(s): Claire Haskell, Spy; Jason Marlowe, Spy; Sarmax, Criminal
Time period(s): 22nd century (2110)
Locale(s): Outer Space; Earth

Summary: The major powers on Earth cooperated in creating the space elevator, designed to help in the exploration of the solar system, but the elevator is sabotaged and destroyed by a mysterious group of subversives. Two intelligence agents who were once romantically involved are enlisted in a desperate search to discover the truth before the ensuing tensions destabilize the international community. First novel.

Other books you might like:
John Barnes, *Orbital Resonance*, 1991
Ben Bova, *Powersat*, 2005
Howard V. Hendrix, *Lightpaths*, 1997
Syne Mitchell, *End in Fire*, 2005
Allen Steele, *Orbital Decay*, 1989

750

RICHARD WILLIAMS

Relentless

(Nottingham, United Kingdom: Black Library, 2008)

Story type: Space Opera; Military
Series: Warhammer
Subject(s): Space Travel; Secrets
Major character(s): Becket, Spaceship Captain, Military Personnel Ward, Spaceman, Military Personnel; Vickers, Spaceman, Military Personnel
Time period(s): Indeterminate Future
Locale(s): *Relentless*, Spaceship

Summary: When Captain Becket is assigned to command of the *Relentless*, Commander Ward is incensed that he was overlooked. He responds by arranging for the captain's murder, but with limited success. Although Ward believes Becket dead, the injured captain still lives and plots to regain control of his ship. First novel.

Other books you might like:
Avram Davidson, *Mutiny in Space*, 1964
David Feintuch, *Midshipman's Hope*, 1994
John G. Hemry, *Burden of Proof*, 2004
Mike Resnick, *Starship: Mutiny*, 2006
Mike Shepherd, *Mutineer*, 2004

751

SEAN WILLIAMS

Earth Ascendant

(New York: Ace, 2008)

Story type: Immortality; Space Opera
Series: Astropolis. Book 2
Subject(s): Immortality; Space and Time
Major character(s): Imre Bergamasc, Ruler; Emlee Copas, Government Official; Gravaman Zerah, Diplomat
Time period(s): Indeterminate Future
Locale(s): Earth; Planet—Imaginary

Summary: Imre Bergamasc has ruled much of the galaxy for hundreds of thousands of years, imposing stability although his methods are sometimes questionable. He is briefly waylaid by a mysterious entity who warns him that the Earth faces a hidden and imminent danger. When he returns to Earth, he barely avoids assassination and discovers that the warning is valid.

Other books by the same author:
Saturn Returns, 2007
Geodesica Ascendant, 2004 (Shane Dix, co-author)
Heirs of Earth, 2004 (Shane Dix, co-author)
Metal Fatigue, 1999
The Resurrected Man, 1999

Other books you might like:
Kevin J. Anderson, *Hidden Empire*, 2002
Poul Anderson, *The Day of Their Return*, 1973
Iain Banks, *Against a Dark Background*, 1992
Peter F. Hamilton, *Fallen Dragon*, 2002
Alastair Reynolds, *The Prefect*, 2007

752

GARY K. WOLF
JOHN J. MYERS , Co-Author

Space Vulture

(New York: Tor, 2008)

Story type: Space Opera; Space Colony
Subject(s): Space Travel; Space and Time
Major character(s): Victor Corsaire, Police Officer, Spaceman; Gil Terry, Criminal; Space Vulture, Criminal, Spaceman
Time period(s): Indeterminate Future
Locale(s): Outer Space

Summary: The authors wrote this novel as an homage to the early days of science fiction when space rangers roamed the stars battling villains who were only known by their nicknames. Their hero is in pursuit of a particularly infamous pirate and thief known as the Space Vulture, a quest which takes him across the galaxy and to a variety of planets.

Where it's reviewed:
Publishers Weekly, January 14, 2008, page 44

Other books by the same author:
Who P-P-P-Plugged Roger Rabbit?, 1991
Who Censored Roger Rabbit?, 1982
The Resurrectionist, 1979
A Generation Removed, 1977
Killerbowl, 1976

Other books you might like:
Anthony Gilmore, *Space Hawk*, 1952
Edmond Hamilton, *Planets in Peril*, 1967
Mike Resnick, *A Gathering of Widowmakers*, 2005
Edward E. Smith, *Spacehounds of IPC*, 1947
Jack Williamson, *The Legion of Space*, 1947

753

PHOEBE WRAY

Jemma7729

(Calgary, Alberta: Edge, 2008)

Story type: Dystopian; Political
Subject(s): Utopia/Dystopia; Feminism
Major character(s): Jemma7729, Fugitive; Erol7734, Government Official; Annie, Rebel
Time period(s): Indeterminate Future
Locale(s): North America

Summary: In a distant future, women have become subordinated to men and have virtually no rights. Jemma7729 conforms to her society until one day when she reacts to a male in a manner proscribed by the government. She becomes a fugitive and eventually links up with a small revolutionary movement. First novel.

Other books you might like:
Margaret Atwood, *The Handmaid's Tale*, 1985
Suzy McKee Charnas, *Motherlines*, 1978
Candas Jane Dorsey, *Black Wine*, 1997
Esther Friesner, *The Sword of Mary*, 1996
Sheri S. Tepper, *The Gate to Women's Country*, 1988

754

JOHN C. WRIGHT

Null-A Continuum
(New York: Tor, 2008)

Story type: Space Opera; Futuristic
Subject(s): Space and Time; Scientific Experiments
Major character(s): Gilbert Gosseyn, Mutant; Patricia Hardie, Political Figure; Peter Clayton, Investigator
Time period(s): 26th century
Locale(s): Earth; Outer Space

Summary: Gilbert Gosseyn is a man whose mental powers enable him to travel through both space and time. His extraordinary insights allow him to sense a danger that threatens the entire known universe and his abilities make him the only one who can avert the disaster. This is a sequel to the Null-A books by A.E. van Vogt and are deliberately written in an archaic style popular in the pulp magazines of the 1940s.

Other books by the same author:
Fugitives of Chaos, 2006
Mists of Everness, 2005
The Golden Transcendance, 2003
The Phoenix Exultant, 2003
The Golden Age, 2002

Other books you might like:
John W. Campbell Jr., *The Mightiest Machine*, 1947
Edmond Hamilton, *Doomstar*, 1966
Clifford D. Simak, *The Cosmic Engineers*, 1950
Edward E. Smith, *Children of the Lens*, 1954
A.E. van Vogt, *The World of Null-A*, 1948

755

TIMOTHY ZAHN

Dragon and Liberator
(New York: Tor, 2008)

Story type: Young Adult; Space Opera
Series: Dragonback. Book 6
Subject(s): Aliens
Major character(s): Jack Morgan, Teenager, Spaceman; Draycos, Alien; Alison Kayna, Teenager
Time period(s): Indeterminate Future
Locale(s): Outer Space

Summary: The man responsible for the deaths of many people, including Jack Morgan's family, is about to launch another strike. Standing in his way is teenaged Jack and his alien companion, Draycos, who can disguise himself by appearing as a tattoo on Jack's body. This is the final volume in the series.

Other books by the same author:
Dragon and Judge, 2007
The Third Lynx, 2007
Dragon and Herdsman, 2006
Night Rain to Rigel, 2005
The Green and the Gray, 2004

Other books you might like:
John Barnes, *Sin of Origin*, 1986
Hal Clement, *Needle*, 1957
Robert A. Heinlein, *The Star Beast*, 1954
Raymond F. Jones, *Son of the Stars*, 1952
Milton Lesser, *Star Seekers*, 1953

The Year in Historical Fiction
by
Daniel S. Burt

I n a quote that can serve as the *modus operandi* of the historical novelist, Oscar Wilde observed, "The one duty we have to history is to rewrite it." Who has not fantasized about a "do over" in one's life? What might have been and the road not taken continually beckon, and if the temptation to rewrite one's life story is irresistible, what about revisiting and redrafting the historical past? It is not surprising that the historical novel has proven to be such a durable and popular form of fiction, offering reader and writer access to the past and new possibilities in the seemingly dead facts of history. "What is history but a fable agreed upon," Napoleon famously declared. If history is a narrative in search of meaning, then historical novelists, as well as professional historians, are key guides in that search. If the historian is confined to the known, the historical novelist is privileged to add the resources of the imagination to deepen and broaden our understanding. Like Dorothy's arrival in Oz, history, in the hands of the skilled historical novelist, can be transformed from the black-and-white world of dates, dynasties, and shadowy events to the technicolor world of living individuals and vivid representation. Accordingly, the historical novel remains our only effective time machine to bridge the gap between our era and the recent or distant past. Certainly that is why the form still commands a wide audience and attracts some of the best fiction writers.

The historical novels collected here from the first half of 2008 all share the common enterprise of rewriting a particular portion of the historical past. Drawing on what is known, these novels extend and expand our knowledge of eras, cultures, and individuals in intriguing and compelling ways. Some re-introduce us to the familiar or provide new contexts and contours for what we thought we already knew. Others shock us with the strange and offer us new acquaintances or events that alter our sense of the past and our understanding of the world. Each re-write offers us the means of re-visioning history, or what novelist Toni Morrison has called the act of "remembering": reassembling the past into a living present.

Selection Criteria

More so than any other fictional genre, it is essential to define exactly what constitutes a historical novel. All novels deal with the past, except science fiction that is set in the future, or fantasy novels set in an imagined, alternative world outside historical time. Yet not all novels are truly historical. Central to any workable definition of historical fiction is the degree to which the writer attempts not to recall the past but to recreate it. In some cases the time frame, setting, and customs of a novel's era are merely incidental to its action and characterization. In other cases, period details function as little more than a colorful backdrop for characters and situations that could as easily be played out in a different era with little alteration. So-called historical "costume dramas" could to a greater or lesser degree work as well with a change of costume in a different place and time. The novels that we can identify as truly historical, however, attempt much more than incidental period surface details or interchangeable historical eras. What justifies a designation as a historical novel is the writer's efforts at providing an accurate and believable representation of a particular historical era. The writer of historical fiction shares with the historian a verifiable depiction of past events, lives, and customs. In historical fiction, the past itself becomes as much a subject for the novelist as the characters and action.

Most of us use the phrase "historical novel" casually, never really needing an exact definition to make ourselves understood. We just know it when we see it. This listing, however, requires a set of criteria to determine what's in and what's out. Otherwise the list has no boundaries. If the working definition of historical fiction is too loose, every novel set in a period before the present qualifies, and nearly every novel becomes a historical novel immediately upon publication. If the definition is so strict that only books set in a time before the author's birth, for example, make the cut, then countless works that critics, readers, librarians, and the authors

themselves think of as historical novels would be excluded.

My challenge here, therefore, has been to fashion a definition or set of criteria flexible enough to include novels that pass what can be regarded as the litmus test for historical fiction: Did the author use his or her imagination—and often quite a bit of research—to evoke another and earlier time than the author's own? Walter Scott, who is credited with "inventing" the historical novel in English during the early nineteenth century provides a useful criterion in the subtitle of *Waverley*, his initial historical novel, the story of Scottish life at the time of the Jacobite Rebellion of 1745: "'Tis Sixty Years Since." This supplies a possible formula for separating the created past from the remembered past. What is unique and distinctive about the so-called historical novel is its attempt to imagine a distant period of time before the novelist's lifetime. Scott's sixty-year span between a novel's composition and its imagined era offers an arbitrary but useful means to distinguish between the personal and the historical past. The distance of two generations or nearly a lifetime provides a necessary span for the past to emerge as history and forces the writer to rely on more than recollection to uncover the patterns and textures of the past. I have, therefore, adopted Scott's formula but adjusted it to fifty years, including those books in which the significant portion of their plots is set in a period fifty years or more before the novel was written.

Because a rigid application of this fifty-year rule might disqualify quite a few books intended by their authors and regarded by their readers to be historical novels, another test has been applied to books written about more recent eras: did the author use actual historical figures and events while setting out to recreate a specific, rather than a general or incidental, historical period? Although it is, of course, risky to speculate about a writer's intention, it is possible by looking at the book's approach, its use of actual historical figures, and its emphasis on a distinctive time and place that enhances the reader's knowledge of past lives, events, and customs to detect when a book conforms to what most would consider a central preoccupation of the historical novel.

I have tried to apply these criteria for the historical novel thoughtfully, and have allowed some exceptions when warranted by special circumstances. I hope I have been able to anticipate what most readers would consider historical novels, but I recognize that I may have overlooked some worthy representations of the past in the interest of dealing with a manageable list of titles. Finally, not every title in the Western, historical mystery, or historical romance genres has been included to avoid unnecessary duplication with the other sections of this book. I have included those novels that share characteristics with another genre-whether fantasy, Western, mystery, or romance-that seem to put the strongest emphasis on historical interest, detail, and accuracy.

Historical Fiction Highlights in the First Half of 2008

Recent trends in the genre remain in play. Series have retained their hold on the way many historical novels are packaged and marketed. Long a fixture of the historical mystery and adventure novel, series increasingly serve all kinds of historical fiction. Collected here are installments of several well-regarded and popular series, including Bernard Cornwell's *Sword Song*, David Donachie's *A Flag of Truce*, Conn Iggulden's *Genghis: Lords of the Bow*, Kathleen and W. Michael Gear's *People of the Weeping Eye*, and Jeff Shaara's *The Steel Wave*. Morgan Llwelyn in *1999* brings to a close her fascinating series on Irish history during the twentieth century. There are also several intriguing sequels: Tony Earley's *The Blue Star*, book two in Anne Rice's life of Jesus, *Christ the Lord*, and Robert Alexander's account of the Romanov's, *The Romanov Bride*. Also present is an interesting prequel. In honor of the 100th anniversary of the publication of *Anne of Green Gables*, Budge Wilson's *Before Green Gables* offers an account of Anne Shirley's orphan years before her arrival in Avonlea.

Wilson's take on an established literary classic suggests another trend, at least based on several of the novels collected here: using existing works of literature as launching points. Examples include Lenore Hart's *Becky*, a retelling and expansion of Mark Twain's *Tom Sawyer* from the perspective of Tom's girlfriend Becky Thatcher, Edward Chupack's *Silver* that provides a back story and continuation of Robert Louis Stevenson's *Treasure Island* from the vantage point of Long John Silver, Susan Fraser King's *Lady Macbeth* that reflects Shakespeare's play from the distaff side, Chitra Banerjee Divakaruni's *The Palace of Illusions* that retells the great Indian epic the *Mahabharata*, and Ursula Le Guin's *Lavinia* that offers a different viewpoint on Virgil's *Aeneid*.

Le Guin is not the only well-known writer with historical novels represented here. Others include Pat Barker, who returns to the consequences of the Great War in *Life Class*, and Richard Bausch who explores combat during World War II in *Peace*. Joyce Carol Oates's *Wild Nights!* provides the last days (and in one case the afterlife) of five American literary icons from Poe to Hemingway; while Salman Rushdie's *The Enchantress of Florence* explores the connection between Renaissance Italy and the Mughal Court of Akbar the Great. Historical novels have attracted others of non-literary fame: Newt Gingrich provides another chapter of his alternative history series with *Days of Infamy*, Gene Hackman co-writes a rousing Civil War adventure tale with *Escape from Andersonville*, and Gene Wilder's second novel, *The Woman Who Wouldn't* is set in a sanitarium in 1903 and features an appearance by Russian writer Anton Chekhov.

Besides attracting the well known, historical fiction is the preferred genre for several first-time writers, such as Eric Lerner (*Pinkerton's Secret*), Jennifer Cody Epstein (*The Painter from Shanghai*), Karl Iagnemma (*The Expe-*

dition), Nick Taylor (*The Disagreement*), and Sara Young (*My Enemy's Cradle*).

The list includes one significant last novel as well: George Macdonald Fraser's *The Reavers*. Fraser is the author of multiple historical novels but is best known for his inventive Flashman series in which the bully from *Tom Brown's Schooldays* is shown misbehaving and blundering across the nineteenth century at some of the milestone moments and alongside the era's most famous individuals. The one characteristic missing aspect of the historical is humor, and Fraser countered this deficit with some of the wittiest and amusing historical fiction in the canon. He will be missed.

Historical Mysteries

The largest sub-category of the novels collected here continues to be historical mysteries. Like the form as a whole, there is a wide range of historical periods and a diversity of approaches. Series continue to be the preferred format for the historical mystery writer, and there are new installments of several popular and acclaimed serials, including Boris Akunin's *Special Assignment* and *Sister Pelagia and the Black Monk*, David Dickinson's *Death on the Holy Mountain*, Rhys Bowen's *Tell Me, Pretty Maiden*, Alan Gordon's *The Moneylender of Toulouse*, Anne Perry's *Buckingham Palace Gardens*, and Jacqueline Winspear's *An Incomplete Revenge*. Several popular serial mystery writers have launched new serials, or at least prospective new serials: Ian Morson changes his scene from the middle ages to thirteenth-century Venice in *City of the Dead*; Stephanie Barron, the author of a Regency era series featuring Jane Austen as sleuth, moves into the Victorian period in *A Flaw in the Blood*; Sharan Newman shifts from medieval France to Portland, Oregon, during the 1860s in *The Shanghai Tunnel*, and Laura Joh Rowland takes a break from medieval Japan to create a mystery also set during the Victorian period featuring novelist Charlotte Bronte as sleuth in *The Secret Adventures of Charlotte Bronte*.

Among the other unusual sleuths detecting in the novels collected here are Oscar Wilde, who joins forces with Arthur Conan Doyle in Gyles Brandreth's *Oscar Wilde and a Death of No Importance*, Leonardo da Vinci in Diane A.S. Stuckart's *The Queen's Gambit*, and real-life detective novelist Josephine Tey in Nicola Upson's *Expert in Murder*. Among the historical figures who are featured as characters, there are French painter Paul Cezanne in Barbara Pope's *Cezanne's Quarry*, Eleanor of Aquitaine in Ariana Franklin's *The Serpent's Tale*, and Julius Caesar in Steven Saylor's *The Triumph of Caesar*.

Fictional Biographies

Another mainstay sub-genre of the historical novel is fictional biography in which a historical figure's life is presented in full or in part. Among the well-known figures treated, there are American poet Robert Frost in Brian Hall's *Fall of Frost*, Genghis Khan in Conn Iggulden's *Genghis: Lords of the Bow*, Elizabeth Tudor in

Alison Weir's *The Lady Elizabeth*, and the Kennedy clan in Laurie Graham's *The Importance of Being Kennedy*. Several novels take on Biblical figures, including Deborah (Eva Etzioni-Halevy's *The Triumph of Deborah*), Solomon and Sheba (Doreen Virtue's *Solomon's Angel*), the apostle John (Niall Williams's *John*), Mary (Marek Halter's *Mary of Nazareth*), and her son Jesus in Anne Rice's *Christ the Lord* and Kathleen and W. Michael Gear's *The Betrayal: The Lost Life of Jesus*.

Several novels introduce readers to lesser known but fascinating figures (or less well known incidents in the lives of famous individuals). May I introduce you to: Benjamin Thompson, colonial America's most renowned inventor (Nicholas Delbanco's *The Count of Concord*), Louise de la Valliere, mistress of Louis IV (Sandra Gulland's *Mistress of the Sun*), sixteenth-century Zionist David Reubeni (Marek Halter's *The Messiah*), poet Gerard Manley Hopkins (*Exiles*), or the father of American medicine William Osler (Lawrence Goldstone's *The Anatomy of Deception*)? What about one of the leaders of the Jacobite Rebellion of 1745, Anne Farquharson (Janet Paisley's *White Rose Rebel*) or Chinese painter Pan Yuliang (Jennifer Cody Epstein's *The Painter from Shanghai*)? Consider scenes from novelist George Eliot's marriage (Deborah Weisgall's *The World Before Her*) or the relationship between American writers Catherine Fenimore Woolson and Henry James (Elizabeth Maquire's *The Open Door*). How about a round of golf with the great Ben Hogan (John Coyne's *The Caddie Who Played with Hickory*)? What about experiencing the great scandal of the nineteenth century involving preacher Henry Ward Beecher from the perspective of his sisters-suffragette Isabella Hooker and writer Harriet Beecher Stowe (Patricia O'Brien's *Harriet and Isabella*)?

Several biographically-based novels take considerable liberties with the facts, placing historical figures in interesting invented situations or relationships. Samantha Hunt looks at the end of the life of famous inventor Nikola Tesla in the Bronx during World War II (*The Invention of Everything Else*). Jay Neugeboren imagines Hitler's childhood physician, Eduard Bloch, in the same city during the same period (*1940*). Perhaps the most amusing twisting of biographical facts is the linking of writer and scholar Henry and William James with their long-lost brothers, the outlaws Jessie and Frank James in Richard Liebmann-Smith's *The James Boys*. Who wouldn't want to attend that family reunion?

Historical Fantasy

Violating the known with the supernatural and disrupting the space/time continuum have created another increasingly popular sub-genre of historical fiction: historical fantasy. Here, history gets either a complete re-write or a mind-blowing make-over. Collected here are several alternate histories. Besides Gingrich and Forstchen's what-if in the aftermath of Pearl Harbor and the Gears's alternative biography of Jesus, Owen Sheers presents a story of occupied Britain during World War II in *Resistance*, while Peter Schilling offers a decidedly

different history of baseball during the war as Bill Veck integrates the game long before the arrival of Jackie Robinson in *The End of Baseball*.

Other novels combine the real and the surreal or supernatural in intriguing ways. Francis Clark locates Satan's minions in Savannah, Georgia, in the 1870s in *Waking Brigid*; Jonathan Barnes teams up a magician and a mute giant as detective partners in *The Somnambulist*; and Lauren Groff uses the discovery of a sea monster to launch an exploration of a family and a community in upstate New York in *The Monsters of Templeton*.

Unusual Eras, Events, and Oddities

What finally sustains the historical novel as such a popular fictional form year after year is the resourcefulness of its writers to transport readers to the by-ways and back alleys of history, introducing them either to the unknown or finding new slants on the familiar. There are several examples of such original excavation of the past on display here. Aleksandar Hemon's *The Lazarus Project* takes an actual 1908 murder case of a Jewish immigrant in Chicago to launch a globe-spanning exploration with contemporary relevance. Ellen Feldman explores another actual crime and trial in *Scottsboro*. Mary Doria Russell's *Dreamers of the Day* injects an ordinary Midwestern matron into the Cairo Peace Conference of 1921 and association with the likes of Winston Churchill and T.E. Lawrence. Karen Essex's *Stealing Athena* presents the story behind the famous Elgin Marbles of Athens' Parthenon: when they were first created and why they came to be called the Elgin Marbles and wound up in the British Museum. Geraldine Brooks's *People of the Book* follows another great work of art, the Sarajevo Haggadah, one of the earliest illuminated Jewish texts from its creation in Seville in 1480 to its discovery in 1889. Sara Young's *My Enemy's Cradle* takes readers inside the Nazi's Lebensborn birthing center; while Jeffrey Hanover transports readers to sixteenth-century Burma in *The Jewel Trader of Pegu*.

These novels and the others collected from the first half of 2008 suggest that the historical novel is still going strong after nearly two centuries, and that readers still have much to learn and enjoy from these multiple rewrites of history.

Recommended Titles

Here finally are my selections of the 30 most accomplished and interesting historical novels for the first half of 2008:

The Blue Star by Tony Earley

Cathedral of the Sea by Ildefonso Falcones

The Count of Concord by Nicholas Delbanco

The Enchantress of Florence by Salman Rushdie

Exiles by Ron Hansen

Fall of Frost by Brian Hall

The Fire Walker by Ben Pastor

Harriet and Isabella by Patricia O'Brien

Johnny One-Eye by Jerome Charyn

An Incomplete Revenge by Jacqueline Winspear

The Lady Elizabeth by Alison Weir

Lavinia by Ursula Le Guin

The Lazarus Project by Aleksandar Hemon

Life Class by Pat Barker

The Moneylender of Toulouse by Alan Gordon

The Painter from Shanghai by Jennifer Cody Epstein

Peace by Richard Bausch

People of the Book by Geraldine Brooks

The Reavers by George Macdonald Fraser

The Reserve by Russell Banks

The Romanov Bride by Robert Alexander

Scottsboro by Ellen Feldman

The Somnambulist by Jonathan Barnes

Song Yet Sung by James McBride

The Spies of Warsaw by Alan Furst

Stealing Athena by Karen Essex

Sword Song by Bernard Cornwell

The Steel Wave by Jeff Shaara

Wild Nights! by Joyce Carol Oates

The World Before Her by Deborah Weisgall

For More Information about Historical Fiction

Printed Sources

Lynda G. Adamson, *American Historical Fiction: An Annotated Guide to Novels for Adults and Young Adults*. Phoenix: Oryx Press, 1999.

Lynda G. Adamson, *World Historical Fiction: An Annotated Guide to Novels for Adults and Young Adults*. Phoenix: Oryx Press, 1999.

Daniel S. Burt, *What Historical Fiction Do I Read Next?*. Detroit: Gale, Vols. 1-3, 1997-2003.

Daniel S. Burt, *The Biography Book*. Westport: Oryx/ Greenwood Press, 2001.

Mark C. Carnes, *Novel History: Historians and Novelists Confront America's Past (and Each Other)*. New York: Simon & Schuster, 2001.

Donald K Hartman, *Historical Figures in Fiction*. Phoenix: Oryx Press, 1994.

Electronic Sources

The Historical Novel Society (http//www.historicalnovel
society.org). Includes articles, interviews, and reviews
of historical novels.

*Of Ages Past: The Online Magazine of Historical Fic-
tion* (http://www.angelfire.com/il/ofagespast/). Includes novel excerpts, short stories, articles, author
profiles, and reviews.

Soon's Historical Fiction Site (http://uts.cc.utexas.edu/~
soon/histfiction/). A rich source of information on the
historical novel genre, including links to more specialized sites on particular authors and types of historical
fiction.

Historical Titles

756

GIL ADAMSON

The Outlander

(New York: Ecco Press, 2008)

Story type: Historical/American West
Subject(s): American West; Travel
Major character(s): Mary Boulton, Widow(er); William Moreland, Frontiersman
Time period(s): 1900s (1903)
Locale(s): Idaho; Montana

Summary: This western tale tells the story of young Mary Boulton who kills her husband and becomes a fugitive who is tracked by her two vicious brothers-in-law. On her journey she encounters frontiersman William Moreland, who eventually abandons her. Saved by a Crow Indian woman, Mary recovers in a mining town, the site of the novel's climax as the brothers-in-law and a repentant Moreland converge over the fate of Mary.

Where it's reviewed:
Booklist, March 15, 2008, page 28
Kirkus Reviews, February 1, 2008, page 103
Library Journal, April 1, 2008, page 72
Publishers Weekly, February 11, 2008, page 50

Other books by the same author:
Ashland, 2003
Help Me, Jacques Cousteau, 1995
Primitive, 1991
Thud, 1989
We Need a Modern Galileo, 1988

Other books you might like:
Ruth Glover, *A Place Called Bliss*, 2001
Jean Little, *The Belonging Place*, 1997
Sarah Neilan, *Paradise*, 1982
Stef Penney, *The Tenderness of Wolves*, 2007
Patricia Roy, *The Wedding Knot*, 1999

757

BORIS AKUNIN (Pseudonym of Grigory Chkhartishvili)

Sister Pelagia and the Black Monk

(New York: Random House, 2008)

Story type: Mystery; Historical/Victorian
Series: Sister Pelagia. Book 2
Subject(s): Mystery and Detective Stories; Russians; Religious Life
Major character(s): Sister Pelagia, Religious (nun); Bishop Mishenka Mitrofanii, Religious (bishop of Zavolzhsk)
Time period(s): 19th century
Locale(s): Russia

Summary: Word reaches Bishop Mitrofanii of Zavolzhsk that something is amiss at the Hermitage, an ancient monastery. After several emissaries sent to investigate wind up dead, Mitrofanii agrees to send Sister Pelagia. Because of the prohibition on women entering the monastery, Sister Pelagia must go undercover to see who or what is causing the violence.

Where it's reviewed:
Booklist, May 1, 2008, page 42
Publishers Weekly, March 24, 2008, page 57

Other books by the same author:
Sister Pelagia and the White Bulldog, 2007
The Death of Achilles, 2006
The Turkish Gambit, 2005
Murder on the Leviathan, 2004
The Winter Queen, 2003

Other books you might like:
Helen Dunmore, *The Siege*, 2002
Andrew Miller, *Ingenious Pain*, 1997
Jody Shields, *The Fig Eater*, 2000
Paullina Simons, *The Bronze Horseman*, 2001
Joan Spicci, *Beyond the Limit*, 2002

758

BORIS AKUNIN (Pseudonym of Grigory Chkhartishvili)

Special Assignments

(New York: Random House, 2008)

Story type: Mystery; Historical/Victorian
Series: Erast Fandorin. Book 5

Subject(s): Mystery and Detective Stories; Russians; Espionage
Major character(s): Erast Fandorin, Detective—Police, Diplomat
Time period(s): 1880s
Locale(s): Moscow, Russia
Summary: Akunin supplies two novella-length cases for 19th-century Moscow diplomat and detective Erast Fandorin. In the first, Fandorin pursues a master of disguise and swindler. In the second, evidence suggests that Jack the Ripper has left London to stalk the streets of Moscow, and Fandorin sets out to end his career as the body count mounts.

Where it's reviewed:
Kirkus Reviews, December 15, 2007, page 1266
Library Journal, January 1, 2008, page 68
Publishers Weekly, December 3, 2007, page 52

Other books by the same author:
Sister Pelagia and the Black Monk, 2008
The Death of Achilles, 2006
The Turkish Gambit, 2005
Murder on the Leviathan, 2004
The Winter Queen, 2003

Other books you might like:
Robert Cormier, *The Rag and Bone Shop*, 2001
Helen Dunmore, *The Siege*, 2002
Andrew Miller, *Ingenious Pain*, 1997
Jody Shields, *The Fig Eater*, 2000
Daniel Silva, *The English Assassin*, 2001
Paullina Simons, *The Bronze Horseman*, 2001

759

ROBERT ALEXANDER

The Romanov Bride

(New York: Viking Press, 2008)

Story type: Historical/World War I
Subject(s): Kings, Queens, Rulers, etc.; Russian Empire; Revolutions
Major character(s): Elisavyeta, Historical Figure, Royalty; Pavel, Worker; Sergei, Historical Figure, Royalty
Time period(s): 1900s; 1910s
Locale(s): Russia
Summary: Alexander's third volume documenting the fall of the Romanovs focuses on the life of the Grand Duchess Elisavyeta, sister of Alexandra, the wife of Czar Nicholas II. Elixavyeta marries the uncle of Nicholas, Grand Duke Sergei, and is caught up in the collapse of the Romanov dynasty. Her story alternates with that of Pavel, a peasant who becomes a dedicated revolutionary and whose path crosses that of Elixavyeta.

Where it's reviewed:
Booklist, March 1, 2008, page 49
Kirkus Reviews, March 1, 2008, page 207
Library Journal, March 1, 2008, page 73
Publishers Weekly, March 3, 2008, page 29

Other books by the same author:
Rasputin's Daughter, 2006
The Kitchen Boy, 2003

Other books you might like:
John Elliot, *Brood on the Snow*, 1977
Catherine Gavin, *The Snow Mountain*, 1974
William M. Green, *The Romanov Connection*, 1986
Alexsandr Solzhenitsyn, *November 1916*, 1999
Charles Whiting, *Passage to Petrograd*, 1995

760

TASHA ALEXANDER

A Fatal Waltz

(New York: William Morrow, 2008)

Story type: Historical/Victorian; Mystery
Series: Lady Emily Ashton. Book 3
Subject(s): Mystery and Detective Stories; Victorian Period
Major character(s): Lady Emily Ashton, Noblewoman, Detective—Amateur; Kristiana von Lange, Noblewoman; Lord Fortescue, Nobleman
Time period(s): 1890s
Locale(s): England
Summary: Aristocratic sleauth Lady Emily Ashton attends a party at the country estate of Lord Forescue. Also in attendance is Kristiana von Lange, an Austrian countess once romantically linked with Emily's fiance. When Lord Fortescue is found murdered, Emily takes up the investigation to clear the man arrested for the crime. Emily is forced to place her fiance in harm's way, and to save him she must negotiate with her rival, the Countess von Lange.

Where it's reviewed:
Booklist, May 1, 2008, page 33
Kirkus Reviews, May 1, 2008, page 447
Library Journal, April 1, 2008, page 63
Publishers Weekly, April 7, 2008, page 42

Other books by the same author:
A Poisoned Season, 2007
Elizabeth: The Golden Age, 2007
And Only to Deceive, 2005

Other books you might like:
Jonathan Barnes, *The Somnambulist*, 2008
David Dickinson, *Death of an Old Master*, 2004
Michel Faber, *The Crimson Petal and the White*, 2002
Will Thomas, *To Kingdom Come*, 2005
Barbara Vine, *The Blood Doctor*, 2002

761

SUZANNE ARRUDA

The Serpent's Daughter

(New York: Obsidian, 2008)

Story type: Mystery; Historical/Roaring Twenties
Series: Jade del Cameron. Book 3
Subject(s): Mystery and Detective Stories; Crime and Criminals
Major character(s): Jade del Cameron, Detective,

Photojournalist; Inez del Cameron, Crime Victim
Time period(s): 1920s (1920)
Locale(s): Tangier, Morocco; Marrakech, Morocco; Atlas Mountains, Morocco

Summary: Jade del Cameron, Arruda's intrepid photojournalist, adventuress, and detective, journeys to Morrocco in 1920 for a rendezvous with her mother, Inez, to patch up their contentious relationship. When Inez is kidnapped, Jade searches for her mother in Marrakech and then in a Berber village in the Atlas Mountains. Along the way she must contends with drug smugglers, slave traders, and an old nemesis.

Where it's reviewed:
Booklist, November 15, 2007, page 22
Kirkus Reviews, November 1, 2007, page 1137
Library Journal, November 1, 2007, page 46
Publishers Weekly, October 29, 2007, page 34

Other books by the same author:
Stalking Ivory, 2007
Mark of the Lion, 2006

Other books you might like:
Rennie Airth, *The Blood-Dimmed Tide*, 2005
Carola Dunn, *The Gunpowder Plot*, 2006
Gillian Linscott, *The Nell Bray Series*, 1991-
Alexander McCall Smith, *The No. 1 Ladies' Detective Agency Series*, 1998
Jacqueline Winspear, *An Incomplete Revenge*, 2008

762

HOWARD BAHR

Pelican Road

(San Francisco: MacAdam Cage, 2008)

Story type: Historical/World War II
Subject(s): Railroads
Major character(s): A.P. Dunn, Engineer, Railroad Worker; Artemus Kane, Railroad Worker (brakeman)
Time period(s): 1940s (1940)
Locale(s): Mississippi; Louisiana

Summary: After multiple novels set during the Civil War, Bahr turns to the 1940s in Mississippi and the perspective of railroad men A.P. Dunn and Artemus Kane, who in a freak winter storm, find themselves on different trains on a collision course. As they come together, both men's past lives and their railroad world are brought to vivid life.

Where it's reviewed:
Booklist, May 15, 2008, page 23

Other books by the same author:
The Judas Field, 2006
The Year of Jubilo, 2000
The Black Flower, 1997

Other books you might like:
Ellen Feldman, *Scottsboro*, 2008
Molly Gloss, *Wild Life*, 2000
Cecelia Holland, *Railroad Schemes*, 1997
Stephen Hunter, *Pale Horse Coming*, 2001
Brad Kessler, *Lick Creek*, 2001

763

RUSSELL BANKS

The Reserve

(New York: HarperCollins, 2008)

Story type: Historical/Depression Era
Subject(s): Family Relations; Social Classes
Major character(s): Jordan Groves, Artist; Vanessa Cole, Socialite
Time period(s): 1930s (1936)
Locale(s): New York (Adirondacks)

Summary: Artist Jordan Groves visits the well-to-do Coles to examine some of their paintings. He comes into contact with the Coles' deeply disturbed adopted daughter, Vanessa. Multiple family secrets are revealed, and the family and all who become connected to them spin toward self-destruction. Class tension is a focus here as well in this period domestic tragedy.

Where it's reviewed:
Booklist, January 1, 2008, page 16
Publishers Weekly, November 26, 2007, page 26

Other books by the same author:
The Darling, 2004
Cloudsplitter, 1998
Rule of the Bone, 1995
The Sweet Hereafter, 1991
Continental Drift, 1985

Other books you might like:
Andrea Barrett, *The Air We Breathe*, 2007
E.L. Doctorow, *Loon Lake*, 1980
Thomas Perry, *Vanishing Act*, 1995
Roxana Robinson, *Sweetwater*, 2003
Julia Spencer-Fleming, *To Darkness and to Death*, 2005

764

TESSA BARCLAY

A Tissue of Lies

(Sutton, England: Severn House, 2008)

Story type: Historical/Victorian
Subject(s): Victorian Period; Factories; Marriage
Major character(s): Jenny Corvill, Spouse (of Ronald), Businesswoman; Ronald Armstrong, Spouse (of Jenny)
Time period(s): 19th century
Locale(s): Scotland; London, England; Australia

Summary: In the sequel to Barclay's *A Web of Dreams*, Jenny Corvill runs her family's wool-weaving mill and marries the mill's master dyer, Ronald Armstrong. Their marriage is troubled, and Ronald departs to find himself, while Jenny's sister-in-law runs off with a dashing playboy and Jenny and Ronald's daughter, sending Jenny on a frantic search that takes her from her Scottish home to London and then on to Australia to save her marriage and her family.

Historical

Where it's reviewed:
Booklist, March 1, 2008, page 50
Publishers Weekly, February 11, 2008, page 53

Other books by the same author:
To Die For, 2007
A Web of Dreams, 2006
A Final Discord, 2005
The Dallancy Bequest, 2005
Her Father's Child, 1994

Other books you might like:
Malcolm Archibald, *Pryde's Rock*, 2007
George Macdonald Fraser, *The Reavers*, 2008
Jane Gardam, *The Flight of the Maidens*, 2001
Janice Graham, *The Tailor's Daughter*, 2006
Alice Hoffman, *The Ice Queen*, 2005

765

PAT BARKER

Life Class

(New York: Doubleday, 2008)

Story type: Historical/World War I
Subject(s): World War I; Artists and Art
Major character(s): Paul Tarrant, Artist; Elinor Brooke, Artist; Kit Neville, Artist
Time period(s): 1910s
Locale(s): London, England; France

Summary: Barker returns to her central subject—the impact of the Great War on individuals and society—in this novel that focuses on artists Paul Tarrant, Elinor Brooke, and Kit Neville. As looms, begins, Paul begins an affair with a troubled artist's model, while Kit and Elinor become lovers. When hostilities commence, the men rush off to the front to tend to the wounded. Their experiences dramatize the horrors of the war and its consequences on both art and love.

Where it's reviewed:
Booklist, October 1, 2007, page 5
Library Journal, November 15, 2007, page 48
New York Times Book Review, January 27, 2008, page 17
Publishers Weekly, October 22, 2007, page 34

Other books by the same author:
Double Vision, 2003
Border Crossing, 2001
The Ghost Road, 1996
The Eye in the Door, 1994
Regeneration, 1991

Other books you might like:
Rennie Airth, *River of Darkness*, 1999
Philippa Gregory, *Fallen Skies*, 1995
Doris Lessing, *Alfred and Emily*, 2008
Christine Schwarz, *Drowning Ruth*, 2000
Jody Shields, *The Crimson Portrait*, 2007

766

JONATHAN BARNES

The Somnambulist

(New York: William Morrow, 2008)

Story type: Historical/Victorian; Mystery
Subject(s): Mystery and Detective Stories; Victorian Period; Magic
Major character(s): Edward Moon, Magician, Detective—Private; Somnambulist, Assistant, Sidekick
Time period(s): 19th century
Locale(s): London, England

Summary: This odd Victorian thriller employs two unorthodox detectives: magician Edward Moon and a mute giant called the Somnambulist. This odd couple sets out to solve a series of murders but quickly uncovers a massive conspiracy by an underground cult determined to topple the powerful and establish a pantisocracy—based on a utopian ideology created by poets Samuel Coleridge and Robert Southey. Extremely imaginative, if often bizarre, this is an ingenious mystery and impressive debut.

Where it's reviewed:
Booklist, November 15, 2007, page 31
Kirkus Reviews, November 1, 2007, page 1115
Library Journal, February 1, 2008, page 59
New York Times Book Review, February 24, 2008, page 30
Publishers Weekly, November 19, 2007, page 34

Other books you might like:
Tracy Chevalier, *Burning Bright*, 2007
Jason Goodwin, *The Snake Stone*, 2007
Amy Myers, *Tom Wasp and the Murdered Stunner*, 2008
Will Thomas, *The Limehouse Text*, 2006
Janet A. Warner, *Other Sorrows, Other Joys*, 2003

767

STEPHANIE BARRON (Pseudonym of Francine Mathews)

A Flaw in the Blood

(New York: Bantam Books, 2008)

Story type: Historical/Victorian; Mystery
Subject(s): Victorian Period; Mystery and Detective Stories; Kings, Queens, Rulers, etc.
Major character(s): Victoria, Historical Figure, Ruler (Queen of England); Patrick Fitzgerald, Lawyer
Time period(s): 1860s (1861)
Locale(s): England

Summary: Barron sets aside her Jane Austen Regency-era mystery series to venture into the Victorian period and a mystery surrounding the death of Prince Albert in 1861. Irish barrister Patrick Fitzgerald has been summoned by the queen, and after the royal coach is overturned, nearly killing him and his ward, more and more evidence points to an elaborate intrigue and a world-shaking royal secret.

Where it's reviewed:
Booklist, February 1, 2008, page 31
Kirkus Reviews, January 1, 2008, page 14
Publishers Weekly, January 21, 2008, page 158

Other books by the same author:
Jane and the Barque of Frailty, 2006
Jane and His Lordship's Legacy, 2005

Other books you might like:
Marjorie Eccles, *Shadows and Lies*, 2007
Sara Fraser, *The Reluctant Constable*, 2007
David Holland, *The Devil in Bellminster*, 2002
Anne Perry, *A Christmas Secret*, 2006
Gerard Williams, *Dr. Mortimer and the Aldgate Mystery*, 2001

768

LLUIS-ANTON BAULENAS

For a Sack of Bones

(Orlando, Florida: Harcourt, 2008)

Story type: Historical/World War II
Subject(s): War; Civil War/Spanish; Family Relations
Major character(s): Genis Aleu, Military Personnel (Spanish Foreign Legion); Joan Aleu, Prisoner
Time period(s): 1940s (1949); 1930s
Locale(s): Barcelona, Spain

Summary: Franco's Spain is the subject of this novel that has Sergeant Genis Aleu, a member of the Spanish Foreign Legion, returning to Barcelona to avenge his father, Joan, who died in a prisoner of war camp as a participant in the Spanish Civil War. Present action is interwoven with details about Joan's activities during the Civil War. The novel offers a gritty and at times bitter portrait of Spain under Franco's repressive regime.

Where it's reviewed:
Booklist, April 15, 2008, page 31
Kirkus Reviews, May 1, 2008, page 448
Publishers Weekly, February 25, 2008, page 45

Other books you might like:
Juan Eslava Galan, *The Mule*, 2008
Ildefonso Falcones, *Cathedral of the Sea*, 2008
Jose Maria Girondella, *One Million Dead*, 1963
Jose Maria Girondella, *Peace After War*, 1969
Rosie Thomas, *The White Dove*, 1986

769

RICHARD BAUSCH

Peace

(New York: Knopf, 2008)

Story type: Historical/World War II
Subject(s): World War II; Military Life; War
Major character(s): Robert Marson, Military Personnel (U.S. army corporal); Saul Asch, Military Personnel (U.S. army private); Benny Joyner, Military Personnel (U.S. army private)

Time period(s): 1940s (1944)
Locale(s): Italy

Summary: In Bausch's anatomy of battlefield reality, three American soldiers—Robert Marson, Saul Asch, and Benny Joyner—are given a reconnaissance mission, guided by a 70-year-old Italian man who may or not be trustworthy. Facing sniper fire and an unforgiving winter landscape, the men demonstrate differing reactions to the pressures and consequences of war.

Where it's reviewed:
Booklist, April 15, 2008, page 32
Kirkus Reviews, March 15, 2008, page 259
Library Journal, March 15, 2008, page 56
Publishers Weekly, February 25, 2008, page 50

Other books by the same author:
Thanksgiving, 2006
Hello to the Cannibals, 2002
In the Night Season, 1998
Good Evening Mr. & Mrs. America, and All the Ships at Sea, 1996
Rebel Powers, 1993

Other books you might like:
Louis De Bernieres, *Corelli's Mandolin*, 1994
Matthew Eck, *The Farther Shore*, 2007
William R. Forstchen, *We Look Like Men of War*, 2001
Guy Johnson, *Standing at the Scratch Line*, 1998
James McBride, *Miracle at St. Anna*, 2002

770

RHYS BOWEN

Tell Me, Pretty Maiden

(New York: St. Martin's Minotaur, 2008)

Story type: Historical/Victorian America; Mystery
Series: Molly Murphy. Book 7
Subject(s): Mystery and Detective Stories; Irish Americans; Actors and Actresses
Major character(s): Molly Murphy, Immigrant (Irish), Detective—Private; Daniel Sullivan, Detective—Police (suspended); Blanche Lovejoy, Actor
Time period(s): 1900s (1902)
Locale(s): New York, New York

Summary: Irish immigrant detective Molly Murphy and her beau, suspended New York police captain Daniel Sullivan, discover a near-dead young woman in a Central Park snowdrift. Molly sets out to discover the identity of the traumatized woman and whoever was responsible for casting her into the snow. Meanwhile, actress Blanche Lovejoy hires Molly to find out what is afflicting the production of her new play, and a wealthy society matron hires Molly to find out if her missing nephew is guilty of murder.

Where it's reviewed:
Booklist, March 1, 2008, page 55
Kirkus Reviews, January 1, 2008, page 67
Publishers Weekly, January 21, 2008, page 158

Historical

Other books by the same author:
In Dublin's Fair City, 2007
Oh Danny Boy, 2006
For the Love of Mike, 2003
Death of Riley, 2002
Murphy's Law, 2001

Other books you might like:
Richard E. Crabbe, *The Empire of Shadows*, 2003
Carole Nelson Douglas, *Femme Fatale*, 2003
Thomas J. Fleming, *A Passionate Girl*, 2004
Myla Goldberg, *Wickett's Remedy*, 2005
Christine Shea, *Moira's Crossing*, 2000

771

JOHN BOYNE

Next of Kin

(New York: St. Martin's Press, 2008)

Story type: Mystery
Subject(s): Mystery and Detective Stories; Kings, Queens, Rulers, etc.
Major character(s): Owen Montignac, Nobleman; Gareth Bentley, Gentleman
Time period(s): 1930s (1936)
Locale(s): London, England

Summary: Set in 1936 as rumors swirl surrounding Edward VIII's relationship with Wallace Simpson, Boyne's thriller concerns aristocrat Owen Montignac who is counting on an inheritance to pay off a huge gambling debt to a vindictive casino boss. Meanwhile, the feckless Gareth Bentley is framed for murder. Their stories serve to illustrate the lifestyles of the rich and famous between the wars.

Where it's reviewed:
Publishers Weekly, December 24, 2007, page 29

Other books by the same author:
The Thief of Time, 2007
Crippen, 2006

Other books you might like:
Barbara Cleverly, *The Bee's Kiss*, 2006
Julian Fellowes, *Snobs*, 2005
Anne Perry, *A Christmas Journey*, 2003
David Roberts, *Hollow Crown*, 2002
Jacqueline Winspear, *An Incomplete Revenge*, 2008

772

GYLES BRANDRETH

Oscar Wilde and a Death of No Importance

(New York: Simon & Schuster, 2008)

Story type: Mystery; Historical/Victorian
Subject(s): Mystery and Detective Stories; Authors and Writers
Major character(s): Oscar Wilde, Writer, Historical Figure;

Arthur Conan Doyle, Historical Figure, Writer; Robert Sherard, Historical Figure, Writer
Time period(s): 1880s (1889)
Locale(s): London, England

Summary: In this inventive Victorian mystery, Oscar Wilde joins forces with Arthur Conan Doyle to solve the mystery behind the murder and disappearance of an artist's model. Narrated by Wilde's friend and biographer, Robert Sherard, the novel records the meeting in 1889 between Wilde and Doyle, fresh from his first literary success with Sherlock Holmes. The novel shows the deductive powers of Doyle and the inspiration for Wilde's *The Picture of Dorian Gray*.

Where it's reviewed:
Library Journal, November 1, 2007, page 46

Other books you might like:
Peter Ackroyd, *The Last Testament of Oscar Wilde*, 1983
Louis Edwards, *Oscar Wilde Discovers America*, 2003
Blossom Effman, *The Case of the Pederast's Wife*, 2000
Desmond Hall, *I Give You Oscar Wilde*, 1965
Robert Reilly, *The God of Mirrors*, 1986

773

GERRI BRIGHTWELL

The Dark Lantern

(New York: Crown, 2008)

Story type: Historical/Victorian; Mystery
Subject(s): Mystery and Detective Stories; Victorian Period
Major character(s): Jane Wilbred, Servant
Time period(s): 1890s (1893)
Locale(s): London, England

Summary: The secrets in a respectable Victorian home are the subjects of this novel in which Devon-born housemaid Jane Wilbred comes to work for the Bentley family with a reference she has forged, omitting any mention that her mother was a notorious murderer. Jane is drawn into other secrets, both upstairs and downstairs, in this dark and brooding Victorian thriller.

Where it's reviewed:
Booklist, February 1, 2008, page 26
Kirkus Reviews, January 1, 2008, page 4
Publishers Weekly, December 17, 2007, page 29

Other books you might like:
Stephanie Barron, *Jane and the Stillroom Maid*, 2000
Clare Clark, *The Nature of Monsters*, 2007
Margaret Forster, *Lady's Maid*, 1991
Valerie Martin, *Mary Reilly*, 1990
Betsy Tobin, *Bone House*, 2000

774

GERALDINE BROOKS

People of the Book

(New York: Viking Press, 2008)

Story type: Saga
Subject(s): Books and Reading; Jews; Religious Life

Major character(s): Hanna Heath, Researcher, Antiquarian
Time period(s): Multiple Time Periods
Locale(s): Sarajevo, Serbia; Europe
Summary: Brooks' inventive novel dramatizes the story of the famous Sarajevo Haggadah, one of the earliest illuminated Jewish religious texts. Rare-book researcher Hanna Heath comes to Sarajevo where the book has been found, and the novel proceeds in two directions, following Hanna's experiences in the present and back in time showing how the book was found, lost, and made, stretching from the Serbian conflict in the 1990s and World War II to Seville in 1480. Using the fate of the book, Brooks is able to provide a moving history of anti-Semitism and Jewish beliefs over the centuries.

Where it's reviewed:
Booklist, October 1, 2007, page 5
Kirkus Reviews, November 1, 2007, page 1116
Library Journal, November 1, 2007, page 58
New York Book Review, January 27, 2008, page 18
Publishers Weekly, October 1, 2007, page 34

Other books by the same author:
March, 2005
Year of Wonders, 2001

Other books you might like:
Lisa Goldstein, *The Alchemist's Door*, 2002
Kanan Makiya, *The Rock*, 2001
Andre Schwarz-Bart, *The Last of the Just*, 1960
Frances Sherwood, *The Book of Splendor*, 2002
Bodie Thoene, *The Jerusalem Scrolls*, 2001
  Brock Thoene, co-author

775

BRIAN CALLISON

Trapp's Secret War

(Sutton, England: Severn House, 2008)

Story type: Historical/World War II
Series: Edward Trapp. Book 5
Subject(s): World War II; Sea Stories
Major character(s): Captain Edward Trapp, Sea Captain
Time period(s): 1940s (1943)
Locale(s): *Charon II*, At Sea
Summary: Sea Captain Edward Trapp, has joined a British and American convoy heading to Murmansk. His real destination, however, is a remote location near the Arctic Circle where he hopes to find a ship filled with gold that has been trapped in the ice. Trapp is an intriguing anti-hero, and the novel is suffused with nautical and period details for those who relish documented naval adventure tales.

Where it's reviewed:
Booklist, March 1, 2008, page 55
Publishers Weekly, February 2, 2008, page 39

Other books by the same author:
Tramp's Peace, 1980
The Judas Ship, 1978
An Act of War, 1977
A Ship Is Dying, 1976
A Flock of Ships, 1970

Other books you might like:
Max Allan Collins, *U-571*, 2000
C.S. Forester, *The Ship*, 1954
Gunter Grass, *Crabwalk*, 2003
Dudley Pope, *Convoy*, 1987
Ken Wales, *Sea of Glory*, 2001

776

JEROME CHARYN

Johnny One-Eye

(New York: W.W. Norton, 2008)

Story type: Historical/American Revolution; Adventure
Subject(s): Revolutionary War; Adventure and Adventurers; Espionage
Major character(s): John Stocking, Spy; George Washington, Historical Figure, Military Personnel; William Howe, Historical Figure, Military Personnel
Time period(s): 1770s
Locale(s): New York, New York, American Colonies
Summary: Charyn's account of the Revolutionary War follows the picaresque adventures of John Stocking in colonial Manhattan. A double agent, Stocking works on behalf of the struggling Revolutionary Army, as well as for the British Army's Howe brothers—General William and Lord Admiral Richard—as they mount their assault on the rebels. Along the way, Charyn offers offbeat and provocative portraits of George Washington, Alexander Hamilton, Benedict Arnold, and others.

Where it's reviewed:
Booklist, January 1, 2008, page 42
Library Journal, January 1, 2008, page 81
New York Times Book Review, February 24, 2008, page 15
Publishers Weekly, November 12, 2007, page 32

Other books by the same author:
Citizen Sidel, 1999
Elsinore, 1991
The Good Policeman, 1990
Paradise Man, 1987
Darlin' Bill, 1980

Other books you might like:
Rita Cleary, *Spies and Tories*, 1999
William Eastlake, *The Long Naked Descent into Boston*, 1977
Paul Lussier, *The Last Refuge of Scoundrels*, 2001
Catherine Rae, *Marike's World*, 2000
William Safire, *Scandalmonger*, 2000

777

EDWARD CHUPACK

Silver

(New York: St. Martin's Press, 2008)

Story type: Historical/Georgian
Subject(s): Sea Stories; Pirates; Autobiography

Historical

Major character(s): Long John Silver, Pirate
Time period(s): 18th century
Locale(s): England; At Sea; Caribbean

Summary: Long John Silver of *Treasure Island* fame offers his own account of his life of piracy in this colorful first novel. Captured and bound for England to be hanged, Silver narrates his early days as a pickpocket in Bristol, through his first voyages and adventures, including what really happened on Treasure Island. Familiar faces make appearances, including Ben Gunn, Pew, and Jim Hawkins. This is an impressive exercise in re-animation of a famous literary figure as well as a believable depiction of his pirate ways.

Where it's reviewed:
Kirkus Reviews, November 1, 2007, page 1117
New York Times Book Review, March 16, 2008, page 26
Publishers Weekly, December 3, 2007, page 51

Other books you might like:
Francis Bryan, *The Curse of Treasure Island*, 2002
Denis Judd, *The Adventures of Long John Silver*, 1977
Wilbur A. Smith, *Birds of Prey*, 1997
Neal Stephenson, *The Confession*, 2004
Robert Louis Stevenson, *Treasure Island*, 1883

778

ALYS CLARE

The Enchanter's Forest

(London: Hodder & Stoughton, 2008)

Story type: Mystery; Historical/Medieval
Series: Helewise of Hawkenlye
Subject(s): Mystery and Detective Stories; Middle Ages; Religious Life
Major character(s): Helewise, Religious; Josse d'Acquin, Mercenary (soldier of fortune)
Time period(s): 12th century
Locale(s): England; France

Summary: This addition to the author's medieval mystery series has Abbess Helewise of Hawkenlye and Sir Josse d'Acquin investigate a claim that the bones of Merlin have been discovered in a mystical forest. In France, Sir Josse is stalked by a murderer; in England Helewise investigates the death of the man who claims to have discovered Merlin's remains.

Where it's reviewed:
Booklist, May 1, 2008, page 39
Kirkus Reviews, April 1, 2008, page 330

Other books by the same author:
Heart of Ice, 2006
The Faithful Dead, 2003
The Tavern in the Morning, 2002
Ashes of the Elements, 2001
Fortune Like the Moon, 2000

Other books you might like:
P.C. Doherty, *The Matthew Jankyn Series*, 1988-
Margaret Frazer, *The Prioress' Tale*, 1997
Ian Morson, *The William Falconer Series*, 1994-
Ellis Peters, *The Brother Cadfael Series*, 1977-1994
Kate Sedley, *The Midsummer Rose*, 2004

779

FRANCIS CLARK

Waking Brigid

(New York: Tor, 2008)

Story type: Historical/Fantasy; Historical/Post-American Civil War
Subject(s): Religious Life; Magic
Major character(s): Brigid Rourke, Religious (nun)
Time period(s): 1870s (1874)
Locale(s): Savannah, Georgia

Summary: Savannah, Georgia, in 1874 is the setting for this historical fantasy pitting a group of magicians working secretly within the Catholic Church against Satanists who have been ritually sacrificing women around the town. The novel focuses on Brigid Rourke, a nun who is drawn into the circle of magicians summoned to combat the evil that is stalking Savannah.

Where it's reviewed:
Booklist, January 1, 2008, page 51
Library Journal, December 1, 2007, page 104
Publishers Weekly, December 17, 2007, page 38

Other books you might like:
Thomas Fleming, *The Spoils of War*, 1985
William Charles Harris, *Delirium of the Brave*, 1999
Donald McCaig, *Canaan*, 2007
Alison McLeay, *Sea Change*, 1992
Eugenia Price, *Savannah*, 1983

780

THOMAS COBB

Shavetail

(New York: Scribner, 2008)

Story type: Historical/American West; Historical/Post-American Civil War
Subject(s): Military Life; Indians of North America
Major character(s): Ned Thorne, Teenager, Military Personnel; Robert Franklin, Military Personnel
Time period(s): 1870s (1871)
Locale(s): Tucson, Arizona

Summary: This western tale narrates the adventures of Connecticut runaway Ned Thorne who joins the cavalry and serves at Camp Grant, along the edge of Arizona's Chiricahua mountains under Capt. Robert Franklin. An Apache attack on a rancher's family and the abduction of the wife leads to a harrowing and bloody rescue attempt.

Where it's reviewed:
Booklist, February 1, 2008, page 36
Kirkus Reviews, January 1, 2008, page 56
Library Journal, December 1, 2007, page 97
Publishers Weekly, November 26, 2007, page 27

Other books by the same author:
Acts of Contrition, 2003
Crazy Heart, 1987

Other books you might like:
Emma Bull, *Territory*, 2007
Will Henry, *Chiricahua*, 1972
Karl Iagnemma, *The Expeditions*, 2008
Nancy E. Turner, *These Is My Words*, 1999
Richard S. Wheeler, *Flint's Honor*, 1999

781

ELLEN COONEY

Lambrusco

(New York: Pantheon, 2008)

Story type: Historical/World War II
Subject(s): World War II; Family Life; Restaurants
Major character(s): Lucia Fantini, Widow(er), Singer
  (opera); Beppi Fantini, Resistance Fighter
Time period(s): 1940s (1943)
Locale(s): Italy

Summary: Cooney's novel follows the attempts of widow
Lucia Fantini to find her son, Beppi, who has gone into
hiding after blowing up a Nazi tank. Lucia, an amateur
opera singer who used to entertain the customers at the
family's trattoria, must contend with the Nazis and Mus-
solini's Blackshirts as well as her bittersweet recollections of her now-dead husband and their life together
before the war.

Where it's reviewed:
Booklist, February 15, 2008, page 35
Kirkus Reviews, February 1, 2008, page 104
Publishers Weekly, February 11, 2008, page 50

Other books by the same author:
A Private Hotel for Gentle Ladies, 2005
Gun Ball Hill, 2004
The White Palazzo, 2002
All the Way Home, 1984
Small-Town Girl, 1983

Other books you might like:
Louis De Bernieres, *Corelli's Mandolin*, 1994
Sebastian Faulk, *Charlotte Gray*, 1998
Ken Follett, *Jackdaws*, 2001
James McBride, *Miracle at St. Anna*, 2002
Mary Doria Russell, *A Thread of Grace*, 2005

782

BERNARD CORNWELL

Sword Song

(New York: Harper, 2008)

Story type: Historical/Medieval
Series: Saxon Tales. Book 4
Subject(s): Middle Ages; Vikings; Kings, Queens, Rulers,
  etc.
Major character(s): Uhtred of Bebbanburg, Warrior; Al-
  fred, Historical Figure, Ruler (King of the Wessex)
Time period(s): 9th century (885)
Locale(s): London, England

Summary: Uhtred of Bebbanburg, the Saxon warlord
raised by Vikings who is pledged to serve King Alfred
of Wessex, is given the responsibility of ousting the
Vikings from London. Uhtred's conflict, between his
distrust of Alfred and his former allegiance to his Viking
brothers, provides an interesting angle to view the
combat and its implications. Cornwell excels in depicting period battle action, and this installment of Uhtred's
adventures is filled with the elements that have made
Cornwell one of the reigning masters of period action
and adventure.

Where it's reviewed:
Booklist, November 15, 2007, page 6
Kirkus Reviews, December 1, 2007, page 1213
Library Journal, December 1, 2007, page 97
Publishers Weekly, November 13, 2007, page 37

Other books by the same author:
Lords of the North, 2007
The Pale Horseman, 2006
The Last Kingdom, 2004
Vagabond, 2002
The Archer's Tale, 2001

Other books you might like:
Peter Ackroyd, *The Clerkenwell Tales*, 2003
Alfred Duggan, *The Right Line of Cerdric*, 1961
Jeffrey Farnol, *The King Liveth*, 1944
Geoffrey Trease, *Escape to King Alfred*, 1958
Joan Wolf, *The Edge of Light*, 1990

783

JOHN COYNE

*The Caddie Who Played with
Hickory*

(New York: St. Martin's Press, 2008)

Story type: Historical/World War II
Subject(s): Sports/Golf
Major character(s): Jack Handley, Teenager; Matt Richard-
  son, Sports Figure (golfer); Ben Hogan, Historical
  Figure, Sports Figure (golfer)
Time period(s): 1940s (1946)
Locale(s): Illinois

Summary: This atmospheric golfing novel follows the
adventures of 14-year-old Jack Handley, a caddie at a
club outside Chicago. He is befriended by the club's assistant pro, Matt Richardson, who is romancing Sarah
DuPree, daughter of the club president. When Ben Hogan
comes to the club for a practice round before the U.S.
Open, he goes up against Matt, and Jack gets to caddie
for one of the game's greatest players while facing a test
of divided loyalties.

Where it's reviewed:
Booklist, April 15, 2008, page 36
Kirkus Reviews, March 15, 2008, page 250
Publishers Weekly, March 24, 2008, page 53

Historical

Other books by the same author:
The Caddie Who Knew Ben Hogan, 2007
The Shroud, 1983
The Scoring, 1980
The Legacy, 1979
The Piercing, 1978

Other books you might like:
William Bernhardt, *Final Round*, 2002
Bob Cupp, *The Edict*, 2007
Roland Merulio, *Golfing with God*, 2005
Bob Mitchell, *Once upon a Fastball*, 2008
Steven Pressfield, *The Legend of Bagger Vance*, 1995

784

NICHOLAS DELBANCO

The Count of Concord

(Champaign, Illinois: Dalkey Press, 2008)

Story type: Historical/Colonial America; Historical/
American Revolution
Subject(s): Biography; Science; Inventors and Inventions
Major character(s): Benjamin Thompson, Historical
Figure, Scientist
Time period(s): 18th century; 19th century
Locale(s): New Hampshire, American Colonies; England;
Europe

Summary: Delbanco offers a fictional biographical portrait
of an American contemporary and peer of Benjamin
Franklin and Thomas Jefferson, Benjamin Thompson
(1753-1814). Growing up in colonial New Hampshire,
Thompson becomes one of America's greatest scientists
and inventors whose reputation is compromised when he
sides with the British during the Revolutionary War. The
novel, told from the perspective of one of Thompson's
descendants, traces his scientific, military, and romantic
affairs, providing a valuable portrait of an unsung 18th-
century American.

Where it's reviewed:
Library Journal, March 15, 2008, page 56
Publishers Weekly, February 18, 2008, page 134

Other books by the same author:
Spring and Fall, 2006
The Vagabonds, 2004
What Remains, 2000
Old Scores, 1997
Stillness and Shadows, 1986

Other books you might like:
Max Byrd, *Jefferson*, 1993
Barbara Hambly, *Patriot Hearts*, 2007
William Martin, *Citizen Washington*, 1999
William Safire, *Scandalmonger*, 2000
Gore Vidal, *Burr*, 1973

785

CATHERINE DELORS

Mistress of the Revolution

(New York: Dutton, 2008)

Story type: Historical/French Revolution
Subject(s): Revolutions; Marriage
Major character(s): Gabrielle de Montserrat, Spouse (of
Baron de Peyre), Widow(er); Baron de Peyre, Noble-
man, Spouse (of Gabrielle); Pierre-Andre Coffinhal,
Lawyer
Time period(s): 1780s
Locale(s): France

Summary: Set against a background of the French Revolution, Delors' novel treats the career of Gabrielle de Mon-
serrat who is forced into an advantageous marriage with
the Baron de Peyre, who is abusive and cruel. When he
dies, Gabrielle goes to Paris and the court world of Louis
XVI and Marie-Antoinette. As events move toward the
Revolution, Gabrielle manages to reunite with her first
love, Pierre-Andre Coffinhal. The novel offers a glimpse
of several historical figures here, including Thomas Jefferson and Robespierre.

Where it's reviewed:
Booklist, February 1, 2008, page 28
Kirkus Reviews, January 1, 2008, page 5
Publishers Weekly, November 26, 2007, page 24

Other books you might like:
Carolly Erickson, *The Hidden Diary of Marie
Antoinette*, 2005
Jane Feather, *The Diamond Slipper*, 1997
Sheila Kohler, *Bluebird, or, The Invention of Happiness*,
2007
Rosalind Laker, *The Sugar Pavilion*, 1994
Frances Sherwood, *Vindication*, 1993

786

DAVID DICKINSON

Death on the Holy Mountain

(New York: Soho Constable, 2008)

Story type: Historical/Edwardian; Mystery
Series: Lord Francis Powerscourt. Book 7
Subject(s): Mystery and Detective Stories
Major character(s): Lord Francis Powerscourt, Nobleman,
Detective—Private; Lucy Powerscourt, Spouse,
Noblewoman
Time period(s): 1900s (1905)
Locale(s): Ireland

Summary: Lord Francis and his lady journey to Ireland to
investigate the theft of paintings at an Ascendency Big
House. Things escalate when some of the wives of the
local gentry disappear. As Lord Powerscourt investigates,
threats to his life increase. The novel offers a convincing
depiction of the unrest in Ireland at the time.

Where it's reviewed:
Booklist, March 1, 2008, page 52
Kirkus Reviews, February 1, 2008, page 117
Publishers Weekly, January 28, 2008, page 43

Other books by the same author:
Death of a Chancellor, 2005
Death of an Old Master, 2004
Death on the Nevskii Prospekt, 2004
Death and the Jubilee, 2003
Goodnight Sweet Prince, 2002

Other books you might like:
Carole Nelson Douglas, *Castle Rouge*, 2002
Robert Lee Hall, *The King Edward Plot*, 1980
Peter Lovesey, *The Bertie, Prince of Wales Series*, 1987-
Francis Selwyn, *Sergeant Verity and the Blood Royal*, 1979
Barbara Vine, *The Blood Doctor*, 2002

787

WILLIAM DIETRICH

The Rosetta Key

(New York: HarperCollins, 2008)

Story type: Historical/Napoleonic Wars; Adventure
Subject(s): Adventure and Adventurers
Major character(s): Ethan Gage, Adventurer; Napoleon Bonaparte, Historical Figure, Military Personnel
Time period(s): 1790s (1798)
Locale(s): Egypt; Jerusalem, Palestine

Summary: In this sequel to Dietrich's *Napoleon's Pyramids*, an adventure tale set during Napoleon's invasion of Egypt in 1798, Ethan Gage goes from Napoleon's trusted protege to his implacable enemy. Accused of treason, Gage flees to Jerusalem where he searches for his former lover and the fabled book of Toth, an ancient text purportedly containing the secrets of the universe. The action here is non-stop with an attractive scamp of a protagonist.

Where it's reviewed:
Booklist, February 1, 2008, page 5
Library Journal, February 15, 2008, page 90
Publishers Weekly, February 18, 2008, page 136

Other books by the same author:
Napoleon's Pyramids, 2007
The Scourge of God, 2005
Hadrian's Wall, 2004
Dark Winter, 2001
Getting Back, 2000

Other books you might like:
Jane Lindskold, *The Buried Pyramid*, 2004
Jeanne Mackin, *Dream of Empire*, 1996
Ruth McKenney, *Mirage*, 1956
Arthur Phillips, *The Egyptologist*, 2004
Paul Sussman, *The Last Secret of the Temple*, 2005

788

ANNABEL DILKE

A Perfect Revenge

(New York: St. Martin's Press, 2008)

Story type: Family Saga
Subject(s): Family Relations; Secrets; Feuds
Major character(s): Laura Delancey, Young Woman; Stanley Trafford, Gardener (former)
Time period(s): 20th century
Locale(s): England

Summary: A multi-generational family feud drives this novel dramatizing the conflict between the Delanceys, English landowners, and the Traffords, their former gardener's family who eventually manage to gain the Delanceys' ancestral home. The truth about the past to explain the feud is investigated when Laura Delancey returns home. She attempts to learn what occurred in 1947 with Stanley Trafford, the Delancey's former gardener, that altered both families' history.

Where it's reviewed:
Publishers Weekly, January 28, 2008, page 40

Other books by the same author:
Secret Relations, 2007
The Inheritance, 2005
Rule Three, 1965

Other books you might like:
Tessa Barclay, *A Tissue of Lies*, 2008
Adele Geras, *Hester's Story*, 2004
Anne Herries, *Love Is Not Enough*, 2008
Frances McNeil, *Sisters of Fortune*, 2008
Nicholas Rhea, *Some Assured*, 2004

789

CHITRA BANERJEE DIVAKARUNI

The Palace of Illusions

(New York: Doubleday, 2008)

Story type: Historical/Fantasy; Historical/Exotic
Subject(s): Mythology; Legends
Major character(s): Panchaali, Royalty; Yudhisthir, Royalty
Time period(s): Indeterminate Past
Locale(s): India

Summary: This retelling of the famous Indian epic poem, *The Mahabharata* treats the story of Princess Panchaali, who is born from fire and marries all five of the Pandava brothers. Becoming queen, she builds the Palace of Illusions, the most magnificent dwelling on earth. When her husband, Yudhisthir, loses their kingdom gambling, they are forced into exile, only to return to begin a war that pits all the kings of India against one another.

Where it's reviewed:
Booklist, January 1, 2008, page 46
Kirkus Reviews, December 15, 2007, page 1257
Library Journal, January 1, 2008, page 81
Publishers Weekly, November 26, 2007, page 27

Historical

Other books by the same author:
Queen of Dreams, 2004
The Vine of Desire, 2002
The Unknown Errors of Our Lines, 2001
Sister of My Heart, 1999
The Mistress of Spices, 1997

Other books you might like:
Jonathan Fast, *Golden Fire*, 1986
Thomas Hoover, *The Moghul*, 1983
John Shors, *Beneath a Marble Sky*, 2004
John Speed, *Tiger Claws*, 2007
Indu Sundaresan, *The Twentieth Wife*, 2002

790

DAVID DONACHIE

A Flag of Truce

(London: Allison & Busby, 2008)

Story type: Historical/French Revolution
Series: John Pearce
Subject(s): Military Life
Major character(s): John Pearce, Military Personnel
Time period(s): 1780s
Locale(s): Toulon, France; At Sea

Summary: In this installment of Donachie's nautical adventure series, John Pearce, who has been unlawfully pressed into naval service pursues legal redress against the British officer responsible. Meanwhile, the siege of Toulon is taking place, and Pearce is sent to serve with other disgruntled sailors while facing challenges on land and sea, particularly in the form of the French revolutionary forces led by a young Napoleon Bonaparte.

Other books by the same author:
An Awkward Commission, 2007
A Shot Rolling Ship, 2005
By the Mast Divided, 2005
An Element of Chance, 2002
The Devil's Own Luck, 2001

Other books you might like:
Tom Connery, *Honor Redeemed*, 2000
Dewey Lambdin, *Troubled Waters*, 2008
Allan Mallinson, *A Close Run Thing*, 1999
Patrick O'Brian, *The Aubrey/Maturin Series*, 1968-2004
Julian Stockwin, *Quarterdeck*, 2005

791

JENNIFER DONNELLY

The White Rose

(New York: Hyperion, 2008)

Story type: Historical/Victorian
Subject(s): Victorian Period; Crime and Criminals; Doctors
Major character(s): India Selwyn Jones, Doctor; Sid Malone, Criminal; Freddie Lytton, Fiance(e) (of)
Time period(s): 1900s

Locale(s): London, England

Summary: Idealist and recent medical school graduate India Selwyn Jones sets up her practice in the mean streets of London's East End. There she meets underworld crime boss Sid Malone who turns out to be the brother of a tea heiress. India's relationship with Sid provokes her fiance, Freddie Lytton, into drastic measures as ruthless as any Sid is accused of committing. This is a fast-paced, action-packed period thriller that offers a colorful tour of London in the 1900s.

Where it's reviewed:
Booklist, October 15, 2007, page 34
Kirkus Reviews, November 15, 2007, page 1169
Library Journal, October 15, 2007, page 51
Publishers Weekly, November 12, 2007, page 36

Other books by the same author:
The Tea Rose, 2002

Other books you might like:
Barbara Cleverly, *The Bee's Kiss*, 2005
Patricia Hall, *Dead on Arrival*, 2001
Gillian Linscott, *Dance in Blood*, 1998
Jem Poster, *Courting Shadows*, 2008
Gerard Williams, *Dr. Mortimer and the Barking Man Mystery*, 2001

792

ANNE DOUGHTY

A Girl Called Rosie

(New York: Severn House, 2008)

Story type: Historical/Roaring Twenties; Family Saga
Series: Hamiltons of Ballydown
Subject(s): Family Life
Major character(s): Rosie Hamilton, Teenager
Time period(s): 1920s (1924)
Locale(s): Kerry, Ireland

Summary: Doughty continues the story of the Hamiltons of Ballydown. It is 1924 following the Irish War of Independence and Civil War, and the novel focuses on 16-year-old Rosie Hamilton who escapes her grim family life on a trip to Kerry to stay with her grandparents. There she experiences a different side of Irish life and entry into adulthood.

Where it's reviewed:
Booklist, March 1, 2008, page 47

Other books by the same author:
The Hawthorns Bloom in May, 2005
The Hamiltons of Ballydown, 2004
The Woman from Kerry, 2003
Beyond the Green Hills, 2002
On a Clear Day, 2001

Other books you might like:
Susan Howatch, *Cashelmara*, 1974
Julia O'Faolain, *No Country for Young Men*, 1986
Cathy Cash Spellman, *An Excess of Love*, 1985
William Trevor, *The Silence in the Garden*, 1988
Niall Williams, *The Fall of Light*, 2002

793

ANNE DOUGLAS

The Girl from Wish Lane

(Sutton, England: Severn House, 2008)

Story type: Historical/Roaring Twenties
Subject(s): City and Town Life
Major character(s): Eva Masson, Young Woman; Nicholas
  North, Gentleman
Time period(s): 1920s
Locale(s): Dundee, Scotland

Summary: Eva Masson is raised in poverty in Dundee,
Scotland, during the 1920s. She falls in love with the
son of the local mill owner, Nicholas North, and the
novel follows the various obstacles the lovers face.

Other books by the same author:
Ginger Street, 2002
The Butterfly Girls, 2001
Bridge of Hope, 2000
As the Years Go By, 1999
Catherine's Land, 1997

Other books you might like:
Tessa Barclay, *A Tissue of Lies*, 2008
Diane Cosgrove, *That Monroe Girl*, 2003
Anne Doughty, *A Girl Called Rosie*, 2008
Elizabeth Gill, *Silver Street*, 2008
Cathy Cash Spellman, *An Excess of Love*, 1985

794

RUTH DOWNIE

Terra Incognita

(New York: Bloomsbury, 2008)

Story type: Historical/Ancient Rome; Mystery
Series: Roman Empire. Book 2
Subject(s): Roman Empire; Medicine; Mystery and Detec-
  tive Stories
Major character(s): Gaius Petreius Ruso, Doctor, Military
  Personnel; Thessalus, Doctor
Time period(s): 2nd century (118)
Locale(s): England

Summary: Downie's sequel to *Medicus*, her Roman
Empire-era mystery, brings back doctor Gaius Petreius
Ruso, attached to the 10th Batavians of the Roman army,
who are dispatched to the northernmost edge of the Roman Empire in Britannia. When a soldier is found
beheaded, Ruso is asked to investigate, despite the fact
that the retiring medic, Thessalus, has confessed to the
killing. Ruso discovers that many others had a motive
for murder.

Where it's reviewed:
Kirkus Reviews, January 1, 2008, page 58
Library Journal, January 1, 2008, page 81
Publishers Weekly, January 7, 2008, page 37

Other books by the same author:
Medicus, 2007

Other books you might like:
Albert Noyer, *The Saint's Day Deaths*, 2000
John Maddox Roberts, *The SPQR Series*, 1990-
Steven Saylor, *The Roma Sub Rosa Series*, 1991-
David Wishart, *Parthian Shot*, 2004
Marguerite Yourcenar, *Memoir of Hadrian*, 1954

795

DAVID DOWNING

Silesian Station

(New York: Soho, 2008)

Story type: Historical/World War II; Espionage Thriller
Subject(s): Nazis; Espionage
Major character(s): John Russell, Journalist; Effi Koenen,
  Actress; Miriam Rosenfeld, Young Woman
Time period(s): 1930s (1939)
Locale(s): Berlin, Germany

Summary: On the eve of World War II British journalist
John Russell is forced to become a triple agent, working
for the Americans, the Nazis, and the Soviets in order to
free his girlfriend, actress Effi Koenen. As events move
toward war, Russell searches for a vanished Jewish girl,
Miriam Rosenfeld, a woman from his past who was sent
by her family from their farm in Silesia to the presumed
safety of Berlin.

Where it's reviewed:
Booklist, March 1, 2008, page 54
Kirkus Reviews, March 15, 2008, page 259
Publishers Weekly, January 1, 2008, page 28

Other books by the same author:
Zoo Station, 2007
The Red Eagles, 1987

Other books you might like:
Jeffery Deaver, *Garden of Beasts*, 2004
Pierre Frei, *Berlin*, 2006
Joseph Kanon, *The Good German*, 2001
Philip Kerr, *The One from the Other*, 2006
Daniel Silva, *A Death in Vienna*, 2004

796

TONY EARLEY

The Blue Door

(New York: Little, Brown, 2008)

Story type: Historical/World War II; Coming-of-Age
Subject(s): World War II; Love; Adolescence
Major character(s): Jim Glass, Teenager, Orphan; Chrissie
  Steppe, Teenager
Time period(s): 1940s (1941)
Locale(s): North Carolina

Summary: Earley returns with a sequel to his critically acclaimed *Jim the Boy*, his evocative rendering of small
town life in North Carolina during the Depression. Here,
it is the eve of World War II and Jim Glass is now a
high school senior. Jim has fallen for Chrissie Steppe

Historical

who lives on the property of the influential Bucklaws. Their son, Bucky, has joined the Navy and expects Chrissie to wait for him, leaving Jim with a major challenge. As in his first novel, Earley excels at creating lifelike and believable characters and settings.

Where it's reviewed:
Booklist, February 1, 2008, page 24
Library Journal, January 1, 2008, page 82
New York Times Book Review, March 9, 2008, page 1
Publishers Weekly, December 3, 2007, page 47

Other books by the same author:
Jim the Boy, 2000

Other books you might like:
Alice Adams, *Southern Exposure*, 1995
Virginia Chase, *One Crow, Two Crows*, 1971
Lonnie Coleman, *Orphan Jim*, 1975
Cormac McCarthy, *The Crossing*, 1994
Nicholas Sparks, *A Walk to Remember*, 1999

797

KATHY LYNN EMERSON

Lethal Legend

(Corona del Mar, California: Pemberley Press, 2008)

Story type: Mystery
Series: Diana Spaulding. Book 4
Subject(s): Mystery and Detective Stories
Major character(s): Diana Spaulding, Journalist; Ben Northcote, Doctor
Time period(s): 1880s (1888)
Locale(s): Maine

Summary: Emerson brings to a close her mystery series set in Maine in the 1880s. As reporter Diana Spaulding prepares for her wedding to Dr. Ben Northcote, three men working on an archaeological dig on a Maine island have been poisoned. Diana and Ben investigate as suspicion falls on their friend Graham Somener. They uncover a complex tangle of fraud, professional jealousy, and revenge.

Where it's reviewed:
Kirkus Reviews, February 1, 2008, page 118
Publishers Weekly, January 14, 2008, page 42

Other books by the same author:
No Mortal Reason, 2007
Face Down Beside St. Anne's Well, 2006
Face Down O'er the Border, 2006
Fatal as a Fallen Woman, 2005
Face Down Beneath the Eleanor Cross, 2001

Other books you might like:
C.R. Corwin, *Dig*, 2008
Mary Anna Evans, *Relics*, 2006
Jason Goodwin, *The Snake Stone*, 2007
Van Reid, *Cordelia Underwood*, 1998
Anne Stuart, *Cameron's Landing*, 1977

798

LEIF ENGER

So Brave, Young and Handsome

(New York: Atlantic Monthly Press, 2008)

Story type: Historical/American West
Subject(s): American West; Crime and Criminals
Major character(s): Glendon Hale, Outlaw, Aged Person; Monte Becket, Companion, Writer
Time period(s): 1900s
Locale(s): Minnesota; West

Summary: Enger's second novel is a Western tale in which outlaw Glendon Hale sets out to make restitution for his past. He encounters struggling novelist Monte Becket in Minnesota, and the pair sets out for Mexico so Hale can find his estranged wife. Their journey is fraught with various dangers and rousing encounters with a colorful cast of western characters.

Where it's reviewed:
Booklist, March 15, 2008, page 29
Kirkus Reviews, February 15, 2008, page 163
Library Journal, April 1, 2008, page 73
Publishers Weekly, January 28, 2008, page 38

Other books by the same author:
Peace Like a River, 2001

Other books you might like:
Andrew Huebner, *American by Blood*, 2000
Brad Leithauser, *Darlington's Fall*, 2002
Eric Lerner, *Pinkerton's Secret*, 2008
Larry McMurtry, *Boone's Lick*, 2000
Robert B. Parker, *Resolution*, 2008

799

JENNIFER CODY EPSTEIN

The Painter from Shanghai

(New York: W.W. Norton, 2008)

Story type: Historical/Roaring Twenties
Subject(s): Biography; Artists and Art; China
Major character(s): Pan Yuliang, Historical Figure, Artist
Time period(s): 20th century
Locale(s): Shanghai, China; Paris, France

Summary: Epstein offers a fictional biography of Chinese painter Pan Yuliang. Orphaned and sold into prostitution by her uncle, she eventually becomes the concubine of a customs inspector in Shanghai where she begins to study art. Winning a scholarship to study in Paris, Pan Yuliang absorbs the styles and methods infusing Paris in the 1920s, but her evolving Western style, particularly in the nudes she creates, produces a charge of pornography when she returns to China. The novel believably portrays details from Pan Yuliang's life and times.

Where it's reviewed:
Booklist, February 1, 2008, page 28
Kirkus Reviews, December 15, 2007, page 1257
New York Times Book Review, March 23, 2008, page 18
Publishers Weekly, November 26, 2007, page 24

Other books you might like:
Lisa Huang Fleischman, *Dream of the Walled City*, 2000
Anthony Gray, *Peking*, 1988
Anchee Min, *Becoming Madame Mao*, 2000
Lydia Y. Minatoya, *The Strangeness of Beauty*, 1999
Alyson Richman, *The Mask Carver's Son*, 2000

800

KAREN ESSEX

Stealing Athena
(New York: Doubleday, 2008)

Story type: Historical/Ancient Greece; Historical/ Napoleonic Wars
Subject(s): Sculptors and Sculpting; Women
Major character(s): Mary Nisbet, Noblewoman, Historical Figure; Aspasia, Noblewoman, Historical Figure
Time period(s): 1790s (1799); 5th century B.C.
Locale(s): Greece; England

Summary: Essex inventively documents the famous Elgin Marbles that decorated the Parthenon in Athens from the perspective of two women millennia apart. Mary Nisbet is the wife of the Earl of Elgin, the British ambassador who arranges for the priceless statues to be sent back to England; Aspasia, is the mistress of Pericles who commissioned the statues during Athens' Golden Age. Both women's stories, connected by a shared theme of the role of women in the lives of powerful men, are intertwined with the fate of the marbles themselves.

Where it's reviewed:
Booklist, April 15, 2008, page 34
Kirkus Reviews, April 1, 2008, page 321
Publishers Weekly, March 3, 2008, page 26

Other books by the same author:
Leonardo's Swans, 2006
Pharaoh, 2002
Kleopatra, 2001

Other books you might like:
Peter Ackroyd, *The Fall of Troy*, 2007
Sally Emerson, *Broken Bodies*, 2001
Paul Muller, *Flight of the Marbles*, 2004
Irving Stone, *The Greek Treasure*, 1975
Theodore Vrettos, *Lord Elgin's Lady*, 1982

801

EVA ETZIONI-HALEVY

The Triumph of Deborah
(New York: Plume, 2008)

Story type: Legend; Biblical Fiction
Subject(s): Ancient History; Biblical Fiction; Women
Major character(s): Deborah, Biblical Figure; Barak, Biblical Figure, Warrior
Time period(s): Indeterminate Past
Locale(s): Israel

Summary: In the third of the author's fictional lives of women of the Old Testament, the subject here is the prophetess Deborah who convinces the warrior Barak to go to war against the neighboring Canaanites. After he succeeds, a love triangle develops between Barak and his two female prisoners. Deborah, recently cast off by her husband, struggles to mediate the crisis that develops. Filled with period details, the novel offers a believable portrait of a strong woman leader.

Where it's reviewed:
Booklist, May 1, 2008, page 73
Library Journal, February 1, 2008, page 60

Other books by the same author:
The Garden of Ruth, 2007
The Song of Hannah, 2005

Other books you might like:
Ann Burton, *Deborah's Story*, 2005
Anita Diamant, *The Red Tent*, 1997
India Edghill, *Queenmaker*, 2002
Rebecca Kohn, *The Gilded Chamber*, 2004
Bette M. Ross, *Song of Deborah*, 1981

802

ILDEFONSO FALCONES

Cathedral of the Sea
(New York: Dutton, 2008)

Story type: Historical/Medieval
Subject(s): Middle Ages
Major character(s): Arnau Estanyol, Artisan (stone mason); Joan Estanyol, Religious; Mar, Young Woman
Time period(s): 14th century
Locale(s): Barcelona, Spain

Summary: Falcones's Spanish bestseller treats the construction of Barcelona's Santa Maria de la Mar Cathedral from the perspective of the Estanyol family. Arnau is a stonemason who helps build the church; his adopted brother, Joan, studies to become a priest. Arnau's relationship with a Jewish woman named Mar puts him on a collision course with the Inquisition and a confrontation with his brother. Despite its melodramatic elements, the novel offers a page-turning and authentic animation of the city and its era.

Where it's reviewed:
Kirkus Reviews, February 15, 2008, page 163
Library Journal, February 1, 2008, page 60
Publishers Weekly, March 24, 2008, page 55

Other books you might like:
Ken Follett, *Pillars of the Earth*, 1989
William Golding, *The Spire*, 1963
Susan Howatch, *Absolute Truths*, 1995
Mike Jahn, *City of God*, 1992
Arturo Perez-Reverte, *The Fencing Master*, 1999

Historical

803

ELLEN FELDMAN

Scottsboro

(New York: W.W. Norton, 2008)

Story type: Historical/Depression Era
Subject(s): Racial Conflict; Trials; African Americans
Major character(s): Alice Whittier, Journalist; Ruby Bates, Prostitute
Time period(s): 1930s (1931)
Locale(s): Scottsboro, Alabama

Summary: Feldman dramatizes the infamous Scottsboro case in which nine young African American men were charged with the rape of two white prostitutes. The novel follows their trial and the repercussions when eight of the men are sentenced to death from the perspective of journalist Alice Whittier and one of the men's accusers, Ruby Bates. The novel offers a telling account of life in the Jim Crow South of the period and one of its most notorious miscarriages of justice.

Where it's reviewed:
Booklist, April 15, 2008, page 34
Library Journal, April 1, 2008, page 73
Publishers Weekly, January 21, 2008, page 148

Other books by the same author:
Lucy, 2003
The Boy Who Loved Anne Frank, 2003
God Bless the Child, 1998
Too Close for Comfort, 1994
Looking for Love, 1990

Other books you might like:
Kelly Covin, *Hear That Train Blow*, 1970
Joy Fielding, *Tell Me No Secrets*, 1993
Lee Gruenfeld, *The Halls of Justice*, 1996
Barbara Hall, *A Summons to New Orleans*, 2000
Harper Lee, *To Kill a Mockingbird*, 1960

804

ARIANA FRANKLIN (Pseudonym of Diana Norman)

The Serpent's Tale

(New York: G.P. Putnam's Sons, 2008)

Story type: Historical/Medieval; Mystery
Subject(s): Mystery and Detective Stories; Middle Ages; Kings, Queens, Rulers, etc.
Major character(s): Adelia Aguilar, Doctor; Eleanor of Aquitaine, Historical Figure, Royalty; Henry II, Historical Figure, Ruler (King of England)
Time period(s): 12th century
Locale(s): England

Summary: When King Henry III's mistress is poisoned, doctor Adelia Aquilar sets out to uncover the killer. The prime suspect is Henry's estranged wife, Eleanor of Aquitaine. Adelia and the king's trusted lieutenant, Rowley Picot, the Bishop of St. Albans, are taken prisoner by Eleanor and her band of mercenaries who bide their time before mounting a rebellion.

Where it's reviewed:
Library Journal, February 15, 2008, page 145
New York Times Book Review, February 10, 2008, page 34
Publishers Weekly, November 12, 2007, page 37

Other books by the same author:
Mistress of the Art of Death, 2007
City of Shadows, 2005

Other books you might like:
Susanna Gregory, *The Matthew Bartholomew Series*, 1996-
Edward Marston, *The Domesday Book Series*, 1994-
Ian Morson, *The William Falconer Series*, 1994-
Ellis Peters, *The Brother Cadfael Series*, 1977-1994
Candace Robb, *The Owen Archer Series*, 1993-

805

GEORGE MACDONALD FRASER

The Reavers

(New York: Knopf, 2008)

Story type: Historical/Elizabethan; Adventure
Subject(s): Espionage; Adventure and Adventurers
Major character(s): Archie Noble, Spy; Lady Godiva Dacre, Gentlewoman; Gilderoy, Highwayman
Time period(s): 16th century
Locale(s): Scotland

Summary: The late George Macdonald Fraser's farewell is, fittingly, a rollicking comic adventure set in Elizabethan-era Scotland. A trio of unlikely companions—English spy Archie Noble, Gilderoy, a Scottish highwayman, and the voluptuous Lady Godiva Dacre—stumble upon a Spanish plot to put an imposter James IV on the throne. All is a bit over-the-top with anachronisms abounding but with the patented Fraser brio and derring-do. The master of the comic historical will be missed.

Where it's reviewed:
Booklist, March 1, 2008, page 30
Kirkus Reviews, March 1, 2008, page 209
Library Journal, April 1, 2008, page 74

Other books by the same author:
Flashman on the March, 2005
Black Ajax, 1998
The Candlemass Road, 1993
The Steel Bonnets, 1971
Flashman, 1969

Other books you might like:
P.F. Chisholm, *A Famine of Horses*, 1995
Catherine Creel, *The Reiver's Woman*, 1997
Virginia Henley, *The Border Hostage*, 2001
Elisabeth McNeill, *Unforgettable*, 2001
Nigel G. Tranter, *The Marchman*, 1997

806

MARGARET FRAZER

The Apostate's Tale

(New York: Berkley Prime Crime, 2008)

Story type: Historical/Medieval; Mystery
Series: Dame Frevisse. Book 17
Subject(s): Mystery and Detective Stories; Religious Life
Major character(s): Dame Frevisse, Religious (nun);
    Cecely, Religious (nun)
Time period(s): 15th century
Locale(s): England

Summary: The return of the long-vanished Sister Cecely plunges the convent of St. Frideswide into chaos. Having run off with a man nine years before, Cecely now has returned, penitent, with her illegitimate son. Events, however, prove to contradict the apostate nun's assertions, and threat escalates, forcing Dame Frevisse to get to the bottom of Cecely's story.

Other books by the same author:
The Traitor's Tale, 2007
The Sempster's Tale, 2006
The Widow's Tale, 2005
The Hunter's Tale, 2004
The Bastard's Tale, 2003

Other books you might like:
Bernard Knight, *Figure of Hate*, 2005
Edward Marston, *The Domesday Book Series*, 1994-
Ian Morson, *The William Falconer Series*, 1994-
Ellis Peters, *The Brother Cadfael Series*, 1977-1994
Peter Tremayne, *The Sister Fidelma Series*, 1995-

807

ALAN FURST

The Spies of Warsaw

(New York: Random House, 2008)

Story type: Espionage Thriller; Historical/World War II
Subject(s): Espionage
Major character(s): Jean-Francois Mercier, Military
    Personnel, Spy; Edvard Uhl, Engineer, Spy
Time period(s): 1930s (1937)
Locale(s): Warsaw, Poland

Summary: Col. Jean-Francois Mercier, a French military attache who runs a spy network, matches wits with his Nazi counterparts to save the life of one of his agents, engineer Edvard Uhl. When Mercier discovers that the German army is conducting maneuvers near the Polish border, he tries to learn what exactly is Germany's intention toward Poland. Furst is the reigning master of the World War II espionage thriller, and this novel shows him at the top of his game.

Where it's reviewed:
Booklist, March 15, 2008, page 6
Kirkus Reviews, April 15, 2008, page 383
Library Journal, April 1, 2008, page 75
Publishers Weekly, April 15, 2008, page 35

Other books by the same author:
The Foreign Correspondent, 2006
Dark Voyage, 2004
Blood of Victory, 2002
Kingdom of Shadows, 2001
Red Gold, 1999

Other books you might like:
Philip Kerr, *Berlin Noir*, 1994
Robert J. Mrasek, *The Deadly Embrace*, 2006
Christopher Reich, *The Runner*, 2000
Sarah Waters, *The Night Watch*, 2006
Robert Wilson, *The Company of Strangers*, 2001

808

JUAN ESLAVA GALAN

The Mule

(New York: Bantam Books, 2008)

Story type: Historical/Depression Era
Subject(s): War; Animals/Mules; Civil War/Spanish
Major character(s): Juan Castro Perez, Military Personnel
    (muleteer); Valentina, Animal (mule)
Time period(s): 1930s
Locale(s): Spain

Summary: Set during the Spanish Civil War, this picaresque tale follows the misadventures of a muleteer, Juan Castro Perez, who finds a stray mule that he names Valentina. He smuggles her into his army regiment, planning to bring her to his family when the war is over. His plan faces considerable challenges, and along the way the novel takes the reader on a tour of the battlefields and the contending sides during the Spanish Civil War.

Where it's reviewed:
Kirkus Reviews, December 15, 2007, page 1258
Library Journal, January 1, 2008, page 62
Publishers Weekly, December 24, 2007, page 30

Other books you might like:
Jose Maria Girondella, *One Million Dead*, 1963
Ernest Hemingway, *For Whom the Bell Tolls*, 1940
David Leavitt, *While England Sleeps*, 1993
Andre Malraux, *Man's Hope*, 1938
Rosie Thomas, *The White Dove*, 1986

809

NICOLE GALLAND

Crossed

(New York: Harper, 2008)

Story type: Historical/Medieval
Subject(s): Middle Ages; Crusades; Knights and Knighthood
Major character(s): The Briton, Musician; Gregor of
    Mainz, Knight; Jamila of Alexandria, Royalty
    (princess)
Time period(s): 13th century (1202)

Historical

Locale(s): Venice, Italy; Mediterranean; Constantinople, Ottoman Empire

Summary: Set during the Fourth Crusade, Galland's novel follows the adventures of an itinerant musician known as the Briton who joins German knight Gregor of Mainz, and a mysterious Arab princess, Jamila of Alexandria, on the mission to liberate Jerusalem. Along the way, they are diverted to Constantinople where they take part in the siege of the city. There Jamila is revealed as a Jewish woman who is enlisted in the cause of the city's Jewish community. This is a rousing adventure in the classic mode of a big, thick historical that recreates a believable world.

Where it's reviewed:
Kirkus Reviews, December 15, 2007, page 1258
Publishers Weekly, December 24, 2007, page 30

Other books by the same author:
Revenge of the Rose, 2006
The Fool's Tale, 2005

Other books you might like:
Alan Gordon, *A Death in the Venetian Quarter*, 2001
Tom Harper, *Siege of Heaven*, 2007
Russell Hoban, *Pilgermann*, 1983
Stephen J. Rivele, *A Book of Days*, 1997
Judith Tarr, *Pride of Kings*, 2001

810

KIP GAYDEN

Miscarriage of Justice

(New York: Center Street, 2008)

Story type: Historical/Victorian America
Subject(s): Marriage; Murder; Trials
Major character(s): Anna Dennis, Spouse (of Walter); Walter Dotson, Doctor; Charlie Cobb, Businessman
Time period(s): 1890s; 1900s
Locale(s): Tennessee

Summary: Nashville Circuit Court judge Gayden's debut dramatizes a tragic love story that begins in 1896 as a pastor's daughter, Anna Dennis, falls for medical student Walter Dotson. They marry and after a stint in Vienna, return with their children to Tennessee where Anna's relationship with another man, Charlie Cobb, leads to murder and scandal and a trial, based on real events.

Where it's reviewed:
Publishers Weekly, September 10, 2007, page 36

Other books you might like:
Lisa Alther, *Original Sins*, 1981
Charlaine Harris, *Grave Surprise*, 2006
Robert Hicks, *The Widow of the South*, 2005
Jonathan Kellerman, *Capital Crimes*, 2006
Phillip Margolin, *The Burning Man*, 1996

811

W. MICHAEL GEAR , Co-Author

The Betrayal: The Lost Life of Jesus Christ

(New York: Forge, 2008)

Story type: Biblical Fiction; Alternate History
Subject(s): Biography; Roman Empire; Bible
Major character(s): Jesus Christ, Historical Figure, Biblical Figure; Brother Barnabas, Religious
Time period(s): 1st century; 4th century (325)
Locale(s): Judea

Summary: Archaeologist authors the Gears offer an alternate version of the life of Jesus. Based on historical and archaeological research, this novel suggests that details about the historical life of Jesus were suppressed by the early Church. The novel shuttles between the end of Jesus' life and the Council of Nicea in 325 where a renegade monk, Brother Barnabas, is able to piece together the suppressed details glimpsed in alternate scenes from Jesus' life. Archaeologist authors the Gears offer an alternate version of the life of Jesus. Based on historical and archaeological research, this novel suggests that details about the historical life of Jesus were suppressed by the early Church. The novel shuttles between the end of Jesus' life and the Council of Nicea in 325 where a renegade monk, Brother Barnabas, is able to piece together the suppressed details glimpsed in alternate scenes from Jesus' life.

Where it's reviewed:
Booklist, April 15, 2008, page 6

Other books by the same author:
Raising Abel, 2002
Raising Abel, 2002
Dark Inheritance, 2001
Dark Inheritance, 2001
The Summoning God, 2000
The Summoning God, 2000
The Visitant, 1999
The Visitant, 1999

Other books you might like:
Anthony Burgess, *Man of Nazareth*, 1970
Anthony Burgess, *Man of Nazareth*, 1970
Norman Mailer, *The Gospel According to the Son*, 1997
Norman Mailer, *The Gospel According to the Son*, 1997
Anne Rice, *Christ the Lord: The Road to Cana*, 2008
Anne Rice, *Christ the Lord: The Road to Cana*, 2008
Jose Saramago, *The Gospel According to Jesus Christ*, 1994
Jose Saramago, *The Gospel According to Jesus Christ*, 1994
Walter Wangerin, *Jesus*, 2005
Walter Wangerin, *Jesus*, 2005

812

W. MICHAEL GEAR
KATHLEEN O'NEAL GEAR , Co-Author

People of the Weeping Eye

(New York: Forge, 2008)

Story type: Historical/Pre-history
Series: First North Americans. Book 15
Subject(s): Indians of North America; Pre-Columbian History; Cultures and Customs
Major character(s): Old White, Wanderer; Trader, Trader; Two Petals, Young Woman
Time period(s): 13th century
Locale(s): North America

Summary: This installment of the authors' First North Americans series treats the cultural and tribal life of the Mississippi region in the 13th century. The area is ruled by the Sky Hand tribe. When one clan resists, however, retribution threatens to destroy the entire region. Its fate begins to depend on three unlikely persons: a wanderer named Old White, a loner named Trader, and Two Petals, a young woman with magical powers. This entry, like all in the series, is believably based on archaeological and anthropological research.

Where it's reviewed:
Booklist, March 1, 2008, page 29
Publishers Weekly, February 25, 2008, page 49

Other books by the same author:
Dark Inheritance, 2001
The Summoning God, 2000
The Visitant, 1999
The First North American Series, 1990-

Other books you might like:
Jim Crace, *The Gift of Stones*, 1988
Sue Harrison, *Song of the River*, 1997
Cecelia Holland, *Pillar of the Sky*, 1985
William Sarabande, *The First Americans Series*, 1987-
Linda Lay Shuler, *Let the Drum Speak*, 1996

813

ELIZABETH GILL

Silver Street

(Sutton, England: Severn House, 2008)

Story type: Historical/World War II; Historical/Depression Era
Subject(s): World War II; Family Relations; Marriage
Major character(s): Iris Black, Nurse; Johnny Fenwick, Spouse (of Nan); Nan Fielding, Spouse (of Johnny)
Time period(s): 1930s
Locale(s): England

Summary: This World War II-era tale treats the consequence of Iris Black's falling in love with Johnny Fenwick. When Iris learns the truth about Johnny's family, she leaves him to train as a nurse. Johnny, in despair, marries another, Nan Fielding, not knowing that Iris is pregnant with his child. The novel dramatizes this triangle with the war as a further complication.

Other books by the same author:
Swan Island, 2007
The Secret, 2007
Home to the High Fells, 2006
The Foxglove Tree, 2006
The Preacher's Son, 2005

Other books you might like:
Gil Adamson, *The Outlander*, 2008
Tessa Barclay, *A Tissue of Lies*, 2008
Anne Douglas, *The Girl from Wish Lane*, 2008
Andrew Sean Greer, *The Story of a Marriage*, 2008
Una-Mary Parker, *Alexia's Secrets*, 2008

814

NEWT GINGRICH
WILLIAM R. FORSTCHEN , Co-Author

Days of Infamy

(New York: St. Martin's Press, 2008)

Story type: Historical/World War II; Alternate History
Series: Pacific War. Book 2
Subject(s): World War II; War; Alternate History
Major character(s): Isoroku Yamamoto, Historical Figure, Military Personnel (Japanese naval commander); William Frederick "Bull" Halsey, Historical Figure, Military Personnel (U.S. naval commander); Franklin Delano Roosevelt, Historical Figure, Political Figure
Time period(s): 1940s
Locale(s): United States; Japan; Pacific Ocean

Summary: The authors' second installment of their alternate history of World War II considers what might have happened had Admiral Yamamoto personally directed the attack on Pearl Harbor instead of remaining in Japan. Yamamoto launches a "third-wave attack" and then uses his fleet to hunt down and destroy the surviving American aircraft carriers. Yamamoto's adversary is William "Bull" Halsey, and the novel offers plausible scenarios and portraits of leading figures such as Franklin Delano Roosevelt.

Where it's reviewed:
Library Journal, May 1, 2008, page 55

Other books by the same author:
Pearl Harbor, 2007
Never Call Retreat, 2005
Grant Comes East, 2004
Gettysburg, 2003
1945, 1995

Other books you might like:
Robert Conroy, *1945*, 2007
Thomas Fleming, *Time and Tide*, 1987
John Hamamura, *Color of the Sea*, 2006
Martin Cruz Smith, *December 6*, 2002
Harry Turtledove, *Days of Infamy*, 2004

Historical

815

LAUREN GROFF

The Monsters of Templeton

(New York: Voice/Hyperion, 2008)

Story type: Historical/Fantasy
Subject(s): Small Town Life; Identity
Major character(s): Willie Upton, Student—Graduate
Time period(s): Multiple Time Periods
Locale(s): New York

Summary: In this inventive first novel, graduate student Willie Upton returns home to Templeton, New York, where the 50-foot-long body of a monster is discovered floating in the town's lake. This discovery leads to others about the mysterious identity of Willie's father and the secrets of the town, which cover several centuries of American history. Borrowing setting and characters from James Fenimore Cooper's *The Pioneers*, this is a richly imagined treatment of the American past.

Where it's reviewed:
Booklist, November 1, 2007, page 27
Library Journal, January 1, 2008, page 83
Publishers Weekly, November 26, 2007, page 27

Other books you might like:
Steve Allen, *Meg*, 1997
David Angsten, *Dark Gold*, 2006
John R. Hayes, *Catskill*, 2001
Vonde N. McIntyre, *The Moon and the Sun*, 1997
Dan Simmons, *The Terror*, 2007

816

LAWRENCE GOLDSTONE

The Anatomy of Deception

(New York: Delacorte Press, 2008)

Story type: Historical/Victorian America; Medical
Subject(s): Medical Thriller; Mystery and Detective Stories
Major character(s): Ephraim Carroll, Doctor; William Osler, Historical Figure, Doctor
Time period(s): 1880s (1889)
Locale(s): Philadelphia, Pennsylvania

Summary: Historian Goldstone makes his fiction debut with this medical thriller. Ephraim Carroll is a young, idealistic doctor working beside the real-life William Osler, often described as the father of modern medicine. When Osler fails to order an autopsy on a woman, Carroll's suspicions are raised. They increase when a colleague, who has upset Osler, is found dead with traces of arsenic in his system. Carroll's investigation is set against a solidly detailed background drawn from the life and works of historical physicians such as Osler and William Stewart Halsted.

Where it's reviewed:
Booklist, December 15, 2007, page 27
New York Times Book Review, March 9, 2008, page 23
Publishers Weekly, November 12, 2007, page 33

Other books by the same author:
Off-Line, 1998
Rights, 1992

Other books you might like:
Nicholas Griffin, *The House of Sight and Shadow*, 2001
Andrew Miller, *Ingenious Pain*, 1997
David Pirie, *The Patient's Eyes*, 2002
Beverly Swerling, *City of Dreams*, 2001
Barbara Vine, *The Blood Doctor*, 2002

817

ALAN GORDON

The Moneylender of Toulouse

(New York: St. Martin's Minotaur, 2008)

Story type: Historical/Medieval; Mystery
Series: Fools' Guild. Book 7
Subject(s): Mystery and Detective Stories; Middle Ages
Major character(s): Theophilos, Entertainer (jester), Spy; Claudia, Entertainer (jester), Spouse
Time period(s): 13th century (1204)
Locale(s): Toulouse, France

Summary: In this entry in Gordon's popular and entertaining Fools' Guild mystery series, as one of the guild's most trusted agents, Theophilos, tries to affect the selection of a new bishop. When the body of a local moneylender is discovered in a tanner's pit, Theophilos and his trusted wife Claudia investigate, convinced that there is a connection with this murder and the controversy surrounding the new bishop.

Where it's reviewed:
Booklist, May 1, 2008, page 37
Publishers Weekly, March 24, 2008, page 56

Other books by the same author:
The Lark's Lament, 2007
An Antic Disposition, 2004
The Widow of Jerusalem, 2003
A Death in the Venetian Quarter, 2002
Thirteenth Night, 1999

Other books you might like:
Michael Jecks, *The Templar's Penance*, 2003
Edward Marston, *The Domesday Book Series*, 1994-
Ian Morson, *The William Falconer Series*, 1994-
James Patterson, *The Jester*, 2003
Mary Reed, *Seven for a Secret*, 2008
    Eric Mayer, co-author

818

LAURIE GRAHAM

The Importance of Being Kennedy

(New York: Harper, 2008)

Story type: Historical/Roaring Twenties; Historical/Depression Era
Subject(s): Family Life; Biography; Servants
Major character(s): Nora Brennan, Child-Care Giver

(nanny); Rose Kennedy, Historical Figure, Spouse (of Joseph); Joseph Kennedy, Historical Figure, Spouse (of Rose)

Time period(s): 20th century (1910s-1940s)
Locale(s): Massachusetts; England

Summary: Graham tells the story of the Kennedy clan in the years between the world wars from the perspective of an Irish immigrant nanny, Nora Brennan. This is an intimate family portrait of Rose Kennedy's troubled marriage to the philandering Joseph Kennedy, including his stint as a Hollywood mogul and ambassador to Britain, and the childhood of the overachieving and competitive children, including the disabled Rosie, and the wartime careers of young Joe and Jack.

Where it's reviewed:
Booklist, January 1, 2008, page 42
Kirkus Reviews, January 15, 2008, page 60
Publishers Weekly, October 15, 2007, page 34

Other books by the same author:
Gone with the Windsors, 2006
Mr. Starlight, 2004
The Great Husband Hunt, 2003
The Future Homemakers of America, 2002
The Ten O'Clock Horses, 1996

Other books you might like:
Robert Mayer, *I, J.F.K.*, 1989
Caroline Preston, *Jackie by Josie*, 1997
Mario Puzo, *The Fourth K*, 1990
Mike Resnick, *Alternate Kennedys*, 1992
Caryl Rivers, *Camelot*, 1998

819

ANDREW SEAN GREER

The Story of a Marriage

(New York: Farrar, Straus and Giroux, 2008)

Story type: Family Saga
Subject(s): Marriage; Family Life; Family Relations
Major character(s): Pearlie Cook, Spouse (of Holland); Holland Cook, Spouse (of Pearlie)
Time period(s): 1950s (1953)
Locale(s): San Francisco, California

Summary: In this imaginative novel, Greer explores the married life of Pearlie and Holland Cook. The couple is tested when a stranger arrives and puts into question everything Pearlie assumed about her husband. This domestic tale is set firmly, and believably, in the social and political context of the period.

Where it's reviewed:
Booklist, May 1, 2008, page 73
Kirkus Reviews, March 1, 2008, page 210
Publishers Weekly, January 28, 2008, page 38

Other books by the same author:
The Confessions of Max Tivoli, 2004
The Path of Minor Planets, 2001
How It Was for Me, 2000

Other books you might like:
David Ebershoff, *Pasedena*, 2002
Robert Gatewood, *The Sound of the Trees*, 2002
Brad Leithauser, *Darlington's Fall*, 2002
Amy Tan, *The Joy Luck Club*, 1989
Robert Vaughan, *Cold War*, 1994

820

SANDRA GULLAND

Mistress of the Sun

(New York: Simon & Schuster, 2008)

Story type: Historical/Seventeenth Century
Subject(s): Biography; Kings, Queens, Rulers, etc.
Major character(s): Louise de la Valliere, Historical Figure (aka Petite), Noblewoman; Louis XIV, Historical Figure, Ruler
Time period(s): 17th century
Locale(s): France

Summary: Gulland offers a biographical portrait of Louise de la Valliere, nicknamed "Petite," who, though born to lower nobility, attracts the attention of Louis XIV, the Sun King, and becomes one of his most favored mistresses. To maintain her privileged place at court, Petite must contend with bitter rivalries and attempts to topple her from her position. In telling Petite's story, Gulland manages a nuanced and colorful dramatization of French court life in the 17th century.

Where it's reviewed:
Booklist, April 15, 2008, page 32
Kirkus Reviews, April 15, 2008, page 384
Library Journal, March 1, 2008, page 57
Publishers Weekly, March 3, 2008, page 27

Other books by the same author:
The Last Great Dance on Earth, 2000
Tales of Passion, Tales of Woe, 1999
The Many Lives & Secret Sorrows of Josephine B., 1999

Other books you might like:
Louis Auchincloss, *The Cat and the King*, 1981
Francoise Chandernagor, *The King's Way*, 1984
Sylvia Pell, *The Shadow of the Sun*, 1978
Frederic Richaud, *Gardener to the King*, 2000
Jean Christophe Rufin, *The Abyssinian*, 2000

821

SALLY GUNNING

Bound

(New York: William Morrow, 2008)

Story type: Historical/Colonial America
Subject(s): American Colonies; Servants
Major character(s): Alice Cole, Servant (indentured); Nabby Morton, Young Woman
Time period(s): 1750s; 1760s
Locale(s): Dedham, Massachusetts, American Colonies;

Historical

Cape Cod, Massachusetts, American Colonies

Summary: In 1756, Alice Cole travels with her family from England to America to start a new life. On the voyage her mother and brothers die, and to pay his debts, Alice's father indentures her for 11 years. First doing housework for a family in Dedham, Massachusetts, Alice is befriended by Nabby Morton and accompanies her when she marries. Nabby's husband rapes and mistreats Alice who escapes to Cape Cod and further travails when she learns she is pregnant. Often grim and horrifying, this is a powerful look at the conventions of indentured servitude in colonial America.

Where it's reviewed:
Kirkus Reviews, February 1, 2008, page 107
Publishers Weekly, January 21, 2008, page 149

Other books by the same author:
The Widow's War, 2006
Fire Water, 1999
Dirty Water, 1998
Muddy Water, 1997
Ice Water, 1993

Other books you might like:
Robert J. Begiebling, *The Strange Death of Mistress Coffin*, 1991
Cynthia Lamb, *Brigid's Charge*, 1997
William Martin, *Cape Cod*, 1991
Kate McCafferty, *Testimony of an Irish Slave Girl*, 2002
Marcy Witnesses, *1980,*

822

GENE HACKMAN
DANIEL LENIHAN , Co-Author

Escape from Andersonville

(New York: St. Martin's Press, 2008)

Story type: Historical/American Civil War
Subject(s): Civil War; Prisoners and Prisons; Prisoners of War
Major character(s): Nathan Parker, Military Personnel (Union officer), Prisoner; Marcel LaFarge, Military Personnel (former Confederate soldier); Ulysses S. Grant, Historical Figure, Military Personnel (Union commander)
Time period(s): 1860s (1864)
Locale(s): Andersonville, Georgia

Summary: The authors' third effort is a Civil War-era tale in which Union officer Nathan Parker manages to escape from the infamous Georgia prison, Andersonville. Determined to return to help free his comrades, Parker is unable to convince Ulysses S. Grant or other Union commanders to help, and he mounts his own rescue mission with a band of cutthroats, assisted by a former Confederate soldier, Marcel LaFarge.

Where it's reviewed:
Library Journal, April 15, 2008, page 72
Publishers Weekly, March 24, 2008, page 53

Other books by the same author:
Justice for None, 2004 (Daniel Lenihan, co-author)
Wake of the Perdido Star, 1999 (Daniel Lenihan, co-author)

Other books you might like:
James Follett, *A Forest of Eagles*, 2004
Charles Frazier, *Cold Mountain*, 1997
MacKinlay Kantor, *Andersonville*, 1955
Richard Parry, *That Fateful Lightning*, 2000
John Wray, *Canaan's Tongue*, 2005

823

DIANE HAEGER

The Secret Bride

(New York: New American Library, 2008)

Story type: Historical/Tudor Period
Subject(s): Kings, Queens, Rulers, etc.; Princes and Princesses; Politics
Major character(s): Mary Tudor, Historical Figure, Royalty; Henry VIII, Historical Figure, Ruler; Charles Brandon, Gentleman
Time period(s): 16th century
Locale(s): England

Summary: Haeger offers a biographical portrait of Mary Tudor, the younger sister of King Henry VIII. Mary is consigned to an arranged marriage to an old ruler, but she falls in love with Charles Brandon, Henry's best friend. The novel traces the repercussions of Mary's insistence that she be allowed to marry for love rather than for the good of the state.

Where it's reviewed:
Booklist, April 15, 2008, page 34

Other books by the same author:
The Perfect Royal Mistress, 2007
The Ruby Ring, 2005
My Dearest Cecelia, 2003
The Secret Wife of King George IV, 2000
Pieces of April, 1997

Other books you might like:
Jane Feather, *The Widow's Kiss*, 2001
Philippa Gregory, *The Boleyn Inheritance*, 2006
Molly Costain Haycraft, *The Reluctant Queen*, 1962
Norah Lofts, *The King's Pleasure*, 1969
Jean Plaidy, *Mary, Queen of France*, 1964

824

KATHRYN MILLER HAINES

The Winter of Her Discontent

(New York: HarperCollins, 2008)

Story type: Historical/World War II; Mystery
Series: Rosie Winter. Book 2
Subject(s): Mystery and Detective Stories; World War II; Actors and Actresses
Major character(s): Rosie Winter, Actress

Time period(s): 1940s (1943)
Locale(s): New York, New York

Summary: During World War II, aspiring Broadway actress Rosie Winter investigates a murder charge against her shady gangster friend Al. A backstage drama ensues in which Rosie, while dancing in the chorus of a musical bound to flop, contends with jealous fellow actresses, the advances of soldiers, and the underworld. This is an atmospheric recreation of wartime New York City.

Where it's reviewed:
Booklist, May 1, 2008, page 45
Kirkus Reviews, April 1, 2008, page 331
Publishers Weekly, April 7, 2008, page 45

Other books by the same author:
The War Against Miss Winter, 2007

Other books you might like:
James R. Benn, *The First Wave*, 2007
John Dunning, *Two O'Clock, Eastern Wartime*, 2000
Mark Frost, *Second Objective*, 2007
David L. Robbins, *The Assassins Gallery*, 2006
Daniel Silva, *The Secret Servant*, 2007

825

BRIAN HALL

Fall of Frost

(New York: Viking Press, 2008)

Story type: Literary
Subject(s): Biography; Authors and Writers
Major character(s): Robert Frost, Historical Figure, Writer
Time period(s): 20th century; 19th century
Locale(s): United States; England; Russia

Summary: Hall offers a fictionalized version of the life of poet Robert Frost in a non-chronological arrangement of vignettes from his life. Dramatized are scenes from Frost's troubled childhood in San Francisco, his initial literary successes in England at the onset of World War II, and his family life, including the early deaths of four of Frost's six children. Hall's approach offers an immediacy to the biographical details as well as a penetrating inner view of the poet's temperament and sensibility.

Where it's reviewed:
Kirkus Reviews, April 1, 2007, page 322
Publishers Weekly, January 14, 2007, page 40

Other books by the same author:
I Should Be Extremely Happy in Your Company, 2003
The Saskiad, 1997
The Dreamers, 1989

Other books you might like:
Jamie Fuller, *The Diary of Emily Dickinson*, 1996
Joyce Carol Oates, *Wild Nights!*, 2008
Colm Toibin, *The Master*, 2004
John Vernon, *Peter Doyle*, 1991
Vernor Vinge, *Rainbows End*, 2007

826

MAREK HALTER

Mary of Nazareth

(New York: Crown, 2008)

Story type: Historical/Ancient Rome; Biblical Fiction
Subject(s): Biography; Bible; Jews
Major character(s): Mary, Historical Figure, Biblical Figure; Joseph of Arimathea, Historical Figure, Biblical Figure; Barabbas, Biblical Figure, Historical Figure
Time period(s): 1st century
Locale(s): Nazareth, Judea

Summary: Halter imagines a vivid backstory for the Biblical Mary. Here, Miriam (Mary) participates in the resistance to Roman rule with Barabbas and Joseph of Arimathea. An independent thinker and early feminist, Mary here is shown against a complex historical and political background. Biblical purists may object to the many liberties taken and the speculation that predominates here, but others will find the New Testament story told from an energizing and vital perspective.

Where it's reviewed:
Kirkus Reviews, February 1, 2008, page 108
Library Journal, March 15, 2008, page 57

Other books by the same author:
The Messiah, 2008
Lilah, 2006
Zipporah, Wife of Moses, 2005
Sarah, 2004
The Winds of the Khazars, 2003

Other books you might like:
Nikki Grimes, *Portrait of Mary*, 1994
Marjorie Holmes, *Two from Galilee*, 1973
Norah Lofts, *How Far to Bethlehem?*, 1965
Brian Moore, *Cold Heaven*, 1983
Anne Rice, *Christ the Lord: The Road to Cana*, 2008

827

MAREK HALTER

The Messiah

(New Milford, Connecticut: Toby Press, 2008)

Story type: Historical/Renaissance
Subject(s): Jews; Religious Conflict; Biography
Major character(s): David Reubeni, Historical Figure, Nobleman; Pope Clement VII, Historical Figure, Religious
Time period(s): 16th century
Locale(s): Venice, Italy; Rome, Italy

Summary: Halter's intriguing novel sheds light on a little-known historical figure: David Reubeni, a charismatic leader and Jewish nobleman who arrives in 16th century Italy to arrange an alliance between Christians and Jews to retake Jerusalem from the Ottoman Empire and create a Jewish state. Reubeni is shown arriving in Venice where he is greeted as the long-awaited messiah by the

Historical

persecuted European Jews. He negotiates with Pope Clement VII and others to achieve a Jewish homeland. Impressively imagined, the novel offers an interesting look at its era and a fascinating historical figure.

Where it's reviewed:
Kirkus Reviews, March 1, 2008, page 210
Library Journal, March 15, 2008, page 57
Publishers Weekly, February 18, 2008, page 137

Other books by the same author:
Mary of Nazareth, 2008
Lilah, 2006
Zipporah, Wife of Moses, 2005
Sarah, 2004
The Book of Abraham, 1986

Other books you might like:
Michael Chabon, *Gentlemen of the Road*, 2007
Frances Kazan, *Halide's Gift*, 2001
Kanan Makiya, *The Rock*, 2001
David R. Slavitt, *The Killing of the King*, 1974
Leonard Wolf, *The False Messiah*, 1982

828

CHRIS HANNAN

Missy

(New York: Farrar, Straus and Giroux, 2008)

Story type: Historical/American West
Subject(s): American West; Women; Drugs
Major character(s): Dol McQueen, Prostitute, Addict (opium)
Time period(s): 19th century
Locale(s): Virginia City, Nevada

Summary: "Missy" refers to liquid opium, the source of many complications in this western-era novel that tells the story of 19-year-old prostitute Dol McQueen who comes into possession of a crate of the drug. A brutal gang is enlisted by the rightful owners of the opium and dispatched to recover it, forcing Dol, her mother, and a pimp named Pontius to flee into the desert where they must contend with the elements, Indians, their pursuers, and Dol's addiction.

Where it's reviewed:
Kirkus Reviews, April 1, 2008, page 322
Library Journal, April 1, 2008, page 75
Publishers Weekly, February 4, 2008, page 34

Other books you might like:
Gil Adamson, *The Outlander*, 2008
Kurt Andersen, *Heyday*, 2007
Larry McMurtry, *Boone's Lick*, 2000
Joseph O'Connor, *Redemption Falls*, 2007
Susan Sontag, *In America*, 2000

829

RON HANSEN

The Exiles

(New York: Farrar, Straus and Giroux, 2008)

Story type: Historical/Victorian
Subject(s): Shipwrecks; Authors and Writers; Religious Life
Major character(s): Gerard Manley Hopkins, Historical Figure, Writer
Time period(s): 1870s (1875)
Locale(s): Wales; At Sea

Summary: In 1875, the steamship *Deutschland* is sailing from Bremen to England and then on to America. On board are five young nuns exiled from Germany by Bismarck's laws against Catholic religious orders. The ship runs aground in the Thames and more than 60 die, including the sisters. Poet and Jesuit seminarian Gerard Manley Hopkins is inspired by the disaster to break his poetic silence and to produce a masterwork, "The Wreck of the *Deutschland*." The novel imagines both the shipwreck and Hopkins' poetic process.

Where it's reviewed:
Booklist, April 15, 2008, page 31
Kirkus Reviews, March 15, 2008, page 262
Publishers Weekly, March 3, 2008, page 28

Other books by the same author:
Isn't It Romantic?, 2003
Hitler's Niece, 1999
Atticus, 1996
Marietta in Ecstasy, 1991
The Assassination of Jesse James by the Coward Robert Ford, 1983

Other books you might like:
Poppy Adams, *The Sister*, 2008
Michael Cunningham, *The Hours*, 1998
Gunter Grass, *Crabwalk*, 2002
Ellen Hawkes, *The Shadow of the Moth*, 1983
Colum McCann, *Dancer*, 2002

830

JEFFREY HANTOVER

The Jewel Trader of Pegu

(New York: William Morrow, 2008)

Story type: Historical/Exotic; Historical/Renaissance
Subject(s): Jews; Business Enterprises
Major character(s): Abraham, Businessman (gem trader); Mya, Young Woman
Time period(s): 16th century (1598)
Locale(s): Venice, Italy; Pegu, Burma

Summary: In 1598, Abraham, a Jewish jewel trader, leaves Venice for Pegu, a Burmese kingdom, where he acquires precious gems for his business. In a series of letters home, Abraham reveals his delight in being beyond the restraints of the ghetto and Jewish law. Falling in love with a local woman named Mya, Abraham must discover

what matters most to him as political unrest threatens his relationship and livelihood. This debut offers a fascinating look at its era and its remote and exotic setting.

Where it's reviewed:
Booklist, November 15, 2007, page 19
Kirkus Reviews, November 1, 2007, page 1119
Publishers Weekly, November 5, 2007, page 44

Other books you might like:
Maurice Collis, *She Was a Queen*, 1962
Amitav Ghosh, *The Glass Palace*, 2001
Alexandra Jones, *Mandalay*, 1988
Daniel Mason, *The Piano Tuner*, 2002
Rebecca Ryman, *Shalimar*, 1999

831

LENORE HART

Becky

(New York: St. Martin's Press, 2008)

Story type: Historical/American Civil War; Historical/American West
Subject(s): Civil War; Women
Major character(s): Becky Thatcher, Young Woman; Tom Sawyer, Young Man; Samuel Clemens, Historical Figure (aka Mark Twain), Writer
Time period(s): 19th century
Locale(s): United States

Summary: In this interesting rewriting of a literary classic, the helpless and whiny Becky Thatcher, Tom Sawyer's girlfriend in Mark Twain's *The Adventures of Tom Sawyer*, proves to be far more resourceful and strong than Twain's version. Giving her own perspective on the events in the Twain novel, Becky is shown afterwards as well, as the wife of Tom's cousin Sid, during and after the Civil War. Disguised as a man to find her husband on a battlefield, Becky survives life in a Nevada mining town and eventually finds success as a newspaperwoman in San Francisco.

Where it's reviewed:
Booklist, December 1, 2007, page 21
Publishers Weekly, October 22, 2007, page 34

Other books by the same author:
Ordinary Springs, 2005
Waterwoman, 2003

Other books you might like:
Jennifer Chiaverini, *The Runaway Quilt*, 2002
Jon Clinch, *Finn*, 2007
David Anthony Durham, *Walk through Darkness*, 2002
Josephine Humphreys, *Nowhere Else on Earth*, 2000
Stephen Wright, *The Amalgamation Polka*, 2006

832

ALEKSANDAR HEMON

The Lazarus Project

(New York: Riverhead Books, 2008)

Story type: Historical/Victorian America
Subject(s): Crime and Criminals

Major character(s): Lazarus Averbuch, Historical Figure, Crime Victim; George Shippy, Police Officer, Historical Figure; Vladimir Brik, Writer
Time period(s): 1900s (1908); 2000s
Locale(s): Chicago, Illinois; Europe (eastern)

Summary: Hemon builds his novel out of an actual event: the 1908 killing of Lazarus Averbuch, a young Jewish immigrant, by George Shippy, the Chicago chief of police. What really happened and why are still unsolved, and the novel offers an explanation based on the research of Vladimir Brik, a Bosnian-American writer who travels to Eastern Europe to get to the truth. Brik's research in the present is intercut with the aftermath of Lazarus' death in the past.

Where it's reviewed:
Kirkus Reviews, March 1, 2008, page 211
Library Journal, April 1, 2008, page 76
New York Times Book Review, May 25, 2008, page 13
Publishers Weekly, March 24, 2008, page 53

Other books by the same author:
Nowhere Man, 2002
The Question of Bruno, 2000

Other books you might like:
Michael Chabon, *The Amazing Adventures of Kavalier & Clay*, 2000
Karen Rose, *You Can't Hide*, 2006
Edith Skom, *The Charles Dickens Murders*, 1998
Darin Strauss, *The Real McCoy*, 2002
Paul Theroux, *Chicago Loop*, 1991

833

ANNE HERRIES

Love Is Not Enough

(Sutton: Severn House, 2008)

Story type: Historical/World War I
Subject(s): Family Life; Sisters
Major character(s): Marianne Trenwith, Young Woman; Sarah Trenwith, Young Woman; Troy Pelham, Young Man
Time period(s): 1910s (1913)
Locale(s): England

Summary: Set on the eve of World War I, Herries' novel looks at a rivalry between two sisters over the same man. Marianne Trenwith breaks off her engagement to Troy Pelham only to find her sister, Sarah and Troy falling in love. Marianne and her family are opposed to the match, and as war begins, Sarah finds herself on her own in wartime England with none of the old securities and assurances.

Where it's reviewed:
Booklist, April 15, 2008, page 32

Other books by the same author:
Love Lies Weeping, 2006
The Seeds of Sin, 2006
Lovers and Enemies, 2005
My Lady, My Love, 2005
Milady's Revenge, 2004

Historical

Other books you might like:
Arabella Edge, *The God of Spring*, 2007
Elizabeth Lord, *A Secret Inheritance*, 2008
Caroline Seebohm, *The Innocents*, 2007
Rowena Summers, *Taking Heart*, 2000
Michael Wallner, *April in Paris*, 2007

834

JOANNA HERSHON

The German Bride

(New York: Ballantine Books, 2008)

Story type: Historical/American West; Historical/Post-American Civil War
Subject(s): Marriage; Jews; German Americans
Major character(s): Eva Frank, Spouse (of Abraham); Abraham Shein, Spouse (of Eva), Businessman (mercantile)
Time period(s): 1860s
Locale(s): Berlin, Germany; Santa Fe, New Mexico

Summary: This is an account of life for a German-Jewish young woman in the post-Civil War American Southwest. Eva Frank departs Germany with her new husband, Abraham Shein, for a new life in Santa Fe, New Mexico. There Eva must contend with the strangeness of life in the West and the disappointment with her husband, an abusive philanderer. Dreaming of abandoning him and Santa Fe for a better life in San Francisco, Eva faces considerable challenges in her desire for fulfillment.

Where it's reviewed:
Kirkus Reviews, February 1, 2008, page 108
Library Journal, November 15, 2007, page 49
Publishers Weekly, October 15, 2007, page 35

Other books by the same author:
The Outside of August, 2003
Swimming, 2001

Other books you might like:
March Cost, *I, Rachel*, 1957
Homer H. Hickam, *The Keeper's Son*, 2003
Sena Jeter Naslund, *Ahab's Wife*, 1999
Susan Sontag, *In America*, 2000
Wesley Strick, *Out There in the Dark*, 2006

835

STEVE HOCKENSMITH

The Black Dove

(New York: St. Martin's Minotaur, 2008)

Story type: Mystery; Historical/American West
Series: Holmes on the Range. Book 3
Subject(s): Mystery and Detective Stories; American West; Cowboys/Cowgirls
Major character(s): Gustav "Old Red" Amlingmeyer, Cowboy, Detective—Amateur; Otto "Big Red" Amlingmeyer, Cowboy, Detective—Amateur
Time period(s): 1890s (1893)
Locale(s): San Francisco, California

Summary: In this third mystery featuring cowboy-sleuths Old Red and Big Red Amlingmeyer, the good old boys are in San Francisco investigating the death of their acquaintance, Dr. Chan. The case leads them on a colorful tour of period Frisco. The novel offers rollicking period fun in the company of this Wild West Holmes and Watson.

Where it's reviewed:
Booklist, December 15, 2007, page 28
Kirkus Reviews, January 1, 2008, page 16
Library Journal, October 15, 2007, page 61
Publishers Weekly, November 5, 2007, page 46

Other books by the same author:
On the Wrong Track, 2007
Holmes on the Range, 2006

Other books you might like:
Nicholas Evans, *The Divide*, 2005
Oakley Hall, *The Ambrose Bierce Series*, 1998-
Donald Honig, *The Ghost of Major Pryor*, 1997
Mardi Oakley Medawar, *The Ft. Larned Incident*, 2000
James Welch, *Fools Crow*, 1986

836

SAMANTHA HUNT

The Invention of Everything Else

(Boston: Houghton Mifflin, 2008)

Story type: Historical/World War II
Subject(s): Inventors and Inventions; World War II; Science
Major character(s): Nikola Tesla, Historical Figure, Scientist; Louisa Dewell, Servant (chambermaid)
Time period(s): 1940s (1943)
Locale(s): New York, New York

Summary: In this quirky novel, the aging scientist and inventor Nikola Tesla is living quietly in a city hotel. He forms an unlikely bond with a young chambermaid, Louisa Dewell, and the novel treats both of their stories: Louisa's involvement with Tesla's father's mission to travel back in time and reconnect with Tesla's dead wife, and Tesla's recollections of his career and his relationship with the likes of Thomas Edison and John Muir. The novel offers a fitting tribute to Tesla's genius and achievements while recreating a period New York that is suffused with magic realism.

Where it's reviewed:
Booklist, December 15, 2007, page 25
Kirkus Reviews, November 1, 2007, page 1119
Library Journal, October 1, 2007, page 61
New York Times Book Review, March 12, 2008, page 18
Publishers Weekly, January 7, 2008, page 38

Other books by the same author:
The Seas, 2004

Other books you might like:
Robert G. Barrett, *The Tesla Legacy*, 2006
Joyce Carol Oates, *A Bloodsmoor Romance*, 1982
Mona Simpson, *The Regular Guy*, 1996
Tad Wise, *Tesla*, 1994
Maxim Zohler, *Between Thunder and Lightning*, 1961

837

KARL IAGNEMMA

The Expeditions

(New York: Dial Press, 2008)

Story type: Coming-of-Age
Subject(s): Coming-of-Age; Travel
Major character(s): Elisha Stone, Teenager; William Edward Stone, Religious
Time period(s): 1840s (1844)
Locale(s): Michigan; Massachusetts

Summary: This first novel is a coming-of-age tale in which a budding naturalist, young Elisha Stone, runs away from his Massachusetts home in 1844 to participate in a survey expedition in the unexplored northern Michigan peninsula. Elisha's minister father, after the death of his wife, sets out to find his son to tell him of his mother's death and to seek reconciliation. Both journeys are narrated with convincing period details.

Where it's reviewed:
Booklist, December 1, 2007, page 21
Kirkus Reviews, November 1, 2006, page 1119
Library Journal, January 1, 2008, page 83
Publishers Weekly, October 15, 2007, page 39

Other books by the same author:
Children of Hunger, 2003
On the Nature of Human Interaction, 2003

Other books you might like:
Kurt Andersen, *Heyday*, 2007
Julie Dash, *Daughters of the Dust*, 1997
Tony Earley, *Jim the Boy*, 2000
Alison McLeay, *Passage Home*, 1990
Diane Smith, *Letters from Yellowstone*, 1999

838

CONN IGGULDEN

Genghis: Lords of the Bow

(New York: Delacorte Press, 2008)

Story type: Historical/Exotic
Subject(s): Biography; China
Major character(s): Genghis Khan, Historical Figure, Military Personnel
Time period(s): 12th century
Locale(s): Asia

Summary: In the second volume of Iggulden's treatment of the life and times of Genghis Khan, the warlord is shown consolidating his power over his native tribes while mounting an invasion of China. Leading his force across the Gobi Desert, Genghis moves across China for a climactic showdown with the Chinese Empire outside of the city of Yenking (modern-day Beijing). Well researched, the book balances political and military strategy with insights into Genghis' temperament and domestic life and Mongol culture.

Where it's reviewed:
Library Journal, March 1, 2008, page 74
Publishers Weekly, January 7, 2008, page 34

Other books by the same author:
Genghis: Birth of an Empire, 2007
Emperor: The Field of Swords, 2006
Emperor: The Gods of War, 2006
Emperor: The Death of Kings, 2004
Emperor: The Gates of Rome, 2003

Other books you might like:
Taylor Caldwell, *The Earth Is the Lord's*, 1940
Don Dandrea, *Orlok*, 1986
Pamela Sargent, *Ruler of the Sky*, 1993
R.F. Tapsell, *The Year of the Horsetails*, 1967
Judith Tarr, *Lady of Horses*, 2000

839

MICHAEL JECKS

The Templar, the Queen and Her Lover

(London: Headline, 2008)

Story type: Historical/Medieval; Mystery
Series: Medieval West Country Mystery
Subject(s): Mystery and Detective Stories; Middle Ages; Kings, Queens, Rulers, etc.
Major character(s): Sir Baldwin de Furnshill, Knight, Government Official (keeper of the king's peace); Simon Puttock, Lawman (bailiff); Isabella, Historical Figure, Royalty (consort of Edward II)
Time period(s): 14th century (1325)
Locale(s): England; France

Summary: In this installment of Jecks' popular and accomplished medieval mystery series, there is trouble with the English royal couple. King Edward II is consumed with jealousy and has stripped Queen Isabella of all her privileges. When she is sent to France to negotiate a peace treaty, Sir Baldwin de Furnshill is given the responsibility for her safety. Given the king's disfavor and others opposed to Isabella's mission, this is no easy assignment as murder stalks the royal retinue.

Other books by the same author:
A Friar's Bloodfeud, 2005
The Butcher of St. Peter's, 2005
The Tolls of Death, 2004
The Mad Monk of Gidleigh, 2003
The Templar's Penance, 2003

Other books you might like:
Margaret Frazer, *The Widow's Tale*, 2005
Jules Hardy, *Altered Land*, 2002
Janet Lawrence, *Death at the Table*, 1997
Priscilla Royal, *Tyrant of the Mind*, 2004
Peter Tremayne, *The Leper's Bell*, 2005

Historical

840

JANE JOHNSON

The Tenth Gift

(New York: Crown, 2008)

Story type: Historical/Seventeenth Century
Subject(s): Pirates; Women; Slavery
Major character(s): Julia Lovat, Young Woman; Catherine Ann Tregenna, Young Woman
Time period(s): 17th century; 2000s
Locale(s): London, England; Morocco

Summary: This novel links two women and their adventures 400 years apart. In the present, Julia Lovat receives a gift of a book of 17th-century embroidery patterns belonging to a woman named Catherine Ann Tregenna who was kidnapped from Cornwall in 1625 by Muslim pirates and sold into slavery in Morocco. Fascinated by Catherine's story, Julia travels to Morocco herself to learn more about Catherine's adventure while having an adventure of her own.

Where it's reviewed:
Kirkus Reviews, May 1, 2008, page 453
Publishers Weekly, March 10, 2008, page 58

Other books by the same author:
Crossed Bones, 2008

Other books you might like:
Elizabeth Garrett, *The Sweet Trade*, 2001
Janice Graham, *The Tailor's Daughter*, 2006
Alice Hoffman, *The Ice Queen*, 2005
Pamela Jekel, *Sea Star*, 1983
Alison Macleod, *The Changeling*, 1996

841

DAVID H. JONES

Two Brothers: One North, One South

(Encino, California: Staghorn Press, 2008)

Story type: Historical/American Civil War
Subject(s): War; Brothers; Biography
Major character(s): Walt Whitman, Historical Figure, Writer; William Prentiss, Military Personnel (Confederate soldier); Clifton Prentiss, Military Personnel (Union soldier)
Time period(s): 1860s
Locale(s): Washington, District of Columbia; Baltimore, Maryland

Summary: Based on poet Walt Whitman's experiences as a nurse in a Washington, D.C., hospital during the Civil War, the novel dramatizes the impact of the war on a single family. Two brothers—Confederate soldier William Prentiss and Union soldier Clifton Prentiss—are being treated in the same hospital where Whitman works. The poet becomes the sole link between the brothers, and the novel explores their wartime experiences and the consequences.

Other books you might like:
Chris Adrian, *Gob's Grief*, 2000
Howard Bahr, *The Year of Jubilo*, 2000
Frederick Busch, *The Night Inspector*, 1999
Charles Frazier, *Cold Mountain*, 1997
John Vernon, *Peter Doyle*, 1991

842

SADIE JONES

The Outcast

(New York: Harper, 2008)

Story type: Historical/World War II
Subject(s): Family Life; Childhood
Major character(s): Lewis Aldridge, Teenager
Time period(s): 1940s; 1950s
Locale(s): London, England

Summary: This first novel explores the impact of World War II on a family. Beginning in 1957, 19-year-old Lewis Aldridge returns to his suburban London home from jail ready to begin his life over. What is revealed is a tragedy that occurred ten years before and the challenges that Lewis faces in dealing with his guilt and rage. Through exploring a family's destruction, the novel reveals the consequences of the war on its many survivors.

Where it's reviewed:
Booklist, November 15, 2007, page 30
Kirkus Reviews, December 15, 2007, page 1260
Publishers Weekly, October 29, 2007, page 28

Other books you might like:
Ray Banks, *Saturday's Child*, 2006
Margaret Drabble, *The Sea Lady*, 2006
Ian McEwan, *Atonement*, 2001
Roger Ormerod, *The Second Jeopardy*, 1987
Barbara Vine, *The House of Stairs*, 1989

843

A.L. KENNEDY

Day

(New York: Knopf, 2008)

Story type: Historical/World War II
Subject(s): World War II; Prisoners of War; Movie Industry
Major character(s): Alfred Day, Military Personnel, Prisoner
Time period(s): 1940s
Locale(s): Germany

Summary: In 1949, former Royal Air Force tail gunner Alfred Day signs on as an extra on a war film. The job releases all his repressed experiences as a prisoner of war in a German camp. Flashbacks reveal Alfred's turbulent childhood, wartime experiences, and the traumas that afflicted him as a prisoner. This is a stylish and perceptive psychological study of the impact of war on a survivor.

Where it's reviewed:

Library Journal, December 1, 2007, page 101
Publishers Weekly, October 22, 2007, page 34

Other books by the same author:

Paradise, 2005
Indelible Acts, 2003
Everything You Need, 2001
So I Am Glad, 2000
Original Bliss, 1999

Other books you might like:

Stephen D. Becker, *Dog Tags*, 1973
Melvyn Bragg, *The Soldier's Return*, 1999
John Katzenbach, *Hart's War*, 1999
Milena McGraw, *After Dunkirk*, 1998
Yannick Murphy, *The Sea of Trees*, 1997

844

SUSAN KING

Lady Macbeth

(New York: Crown, 2008)

Story type: Historical/Fantasy; Historical/Medieval
Subject(s): Kings, Queens, Rulers, etc.
Major character(s): Lady Gruadh, Royalty; Macbeth,
Historical Figure, Royalty; Gillecomgan, Warrior
Time period(s): 11th century
Locale(s): Scotland

Summary: Lady Macbeth provides her side of the story in
this inventive novel. Here, Gruadh, the future Lady Macbeth, is the daughter of an 11th-century Scottish prince
and a proud and fierce Celtic woman warrior. She marries the warrior Gillecomgan whom Macbeth kills.
Claiming Gruadh as his prize, Macbeth sets out to challenge the tyranny of King Malcolm. Based on the historical record as well as much speculation, the novel offers
an interesting alternative rendering of Shakespeare's
bloody couple.

Where it's reviewed:

Booklist, February 1, 2008, page 35
Library Journal, January 1, 2008, page 84
Publishers Weekly, December 17, 2007, page 33

Other books by the same author:

Kissing the Countess, 2003
Waking the Princess, 2003
Taming the Heiress, 2003
The Sword March, 2001
The Stone Maiden, 2000

Other books you might like:

Gillian Bradshaw, *The Wolf Hunt*, 2001
Bonnie Copeland, *Lady of Moray*, 1979
Dorothy Dunnett, *King Hereafter*, 1982
Rebecca Reisert, *The Third Witch*, 2001
Nigel G. Tranter, *Macbeth the King*, 1978

845

BERNARD KNIGHT

The Noble Outlaw

(London: Simon & Schuster, 2008)

Story type: Historical/Medieval; Mystery
Series: Crowner John. Book 11
Subject(s): Middle Ages; Crime and Criminals; Knights
and Knighthood
Major character(s): Sir John de Wolf, Nobleman; Nicholas
de Arundell, Knight
Time period(s): 12th century
Locale(s): Exeter, England

Summary: The discovery of a mummified body in Exeter
provides the occasion for the investigation of coroner Sir
John de Wolfe. The case becomes connected with a
disgraced Cornish knight, Nicholas de Arundell, as a
killer is stalks several prominent members of the Exeter
Guild.

Where it's reviewed:

Kirkus Reviews, December 15, 2007, page 1268
Publishers Weekly, December 17, 2007, page 36

Other books by the same author:

The Elixir of Death, 2006
Figure of Hate, 2005
Crowner's Quest, 2004
The Poisoned Chalice, 2003
The Sanctuary Seeker, 2003

Other books you might like:

Susanna Gregory, *A Summer of Discontent*, 2003
Michael Jecks, *The Outlaws of Ennor*, 2004
Sharon Kay Penman, *Time and Chance*, 2002
Priscilla Royal, *Wine of Violence*, 2003
Kate Sedley, *Nine Men Dancing*, 2003

846

DEWEY LAMBDIN

Troubled Waters

(New York: St. Martin's Press, 2008)

Story type: Historical/Napoleonic Wars; Adventure
Series: Alan Lewrie. Book 14
Subject(s): Sea Stories; Military Life; Slavery
Major character(s): Alan Lewrie, Military Personnel (Brit-
ish naval officer)
Time period(s): 1800s (1800)
Locale(s): *HMS Savage*, At Sea; Jamaica; England

Summary: In this installment of Lambdin's period naval
series, Royal Navy Capt. Alan Lewrie has returned a
hero from his exploits in the South Atlantic and been,
given command of the frigate *HMS Savage*. However,
back in Jamaica, Lewrie has been tried in absentia and
sentenced to be hanged for the theft of black slaves to
man his former ship. Seized upon by Sir William Wil-
berforce's abolitionists, Lewrie's case becomes a *cause
celebre*. While awaiting the outcome, Lewrie serves on
blockade duty off southwest France that turns into an

Historical

amphibious raid against a French coastal fortification and an encounter with an old nemesis.

Where it's reviewed:
Kirkus Reviews, November 1, 2007, page 1122
Publishers Weekly, November 5, 2007, page 45

Other books by the same author:
A King's Trade, 2006
The Captain's Vengeance, 2004
Havoc's Sword, 2002
Sea of Grey, 2002
King's Captain, 2000

Other books you might like:
C.S. Forester, *The Horatio Hornblower Series*, 1933-1966
Alexander Kent, *The Richard Bolitho Series*, 1968-1986
Patrick O'Brian, *The Aubrey/Maturin Series*, 1968-2004
Dudley Pope, *The Nicholas Ramage Series*, 1965-
Richard Woodman, *The Nathaniel Drinkwater Series*, 1984-

847

STEPHANIE LAURENS

Where the Heart Leads

(New York: William Morrow, 2008)

Story type: Historical/Regency; Mystery
Series: Cynster
Subject(s): Romance; Mystery and Detective Stories
Major character(s): Penelope Ashford, Gentlewoman; Barnaby Adair, Detective—Private
Time period(s): 1830s
Locale(s): England

Summary: Romance and mystery combine in this installment of Laurens' Cynster series. Socialite Penelope. Ashford enlists the aid of private investigator Barnaby Adair to find four kidnapped orphans. While pursuing leads in the slums of London's East End, the pair discovers a mutual attraction.

Where it's reviewed:
Publishers Weekly, October 15, 2007, page 36

Other books by the same author:
The Taste of Innocence, 2007
What Price Love?, 2006
The Truth about Love, 2005
The Ideal Bride, 2004
The Perfect Lover, 2003

Other books you might like:
Geraldine Burrows, *Miss Sedgewick and the Spy*, 2001
Tracy Grant, *Daughter of the Game*, 2002
Robin Paige, *Death at Epsom Downs*, 2001
Amanda Quick, *Affair*, 1997
Joan Wolf, *The Gamble*, 1998

848

URSULA K. LE GUIN

Lavinia

(Orlando, Florida: Harcourt, 2008)

Story type: Legend
Subject(s): Legends; Marriage; Kings, Queens, Rulers, etc.
Major character(s): Lavinia, Royalty, Spouse (of Aeneas); Aeneas, Warrior, Spouse (of Lavinia); Latinus, Ruler
Time period(s): Indeterminate Past
Locale(s): Latinum, Italy

Summary: Le Guin gives voice to Lavinia, the daughter of King Latinus and Queen Amata, who ruled Latinum before the founding of Rome. In Roman mythology, Lavinia is intended as the wife of Turnus, the king of neighboring Tutuli. However, King Latinus decides, based on an oracle, that she should marry a newly arrived stranger from Troy named Aeneas. The decision prompts a war and paves the way for the creation of Rome. Brilliantly imagined, the novel offers a convincing evocation of this pre-Roman world.

Where it's reviewed:
Booklist, March 1, 2008, page 28
Kirkus Reviews, February 15, 2008, page 166
Publishers Weekly, December 24, 2007, page 24

Other books by the same author:
Gifts, 2004
Changing Planes, 2003
Tales from Earthsea, 2001
The Other Wind, 2001
The Telling, 2000

Other books you might like:
Gertrude Atherton, *Dido, Queen of Hearts*, 1929
Elizabeth Cook, *Achilles*, 2002
Richard Matturo, *Troy*, 1989
Colleen McCullough, *The Song of Troy*, 2001
Mary Renault, *The King Must Die*, 1958

849

ERIC LERNER

Pinkerton's Secret

(New York: Henry Holt, 2008)

Story type: Historical/American Civil War; Historical/Post-American Civil War
Subject(s): Autobiography; Espionage; Detection
Major character(s): Allan Pinkerton, Historical Figure, Detective—Private; Kate Warne, Detective—Private
Time period(s): 19th century
Locale(s): United States

Summary: Allan Pinkerton, founder of America's first detective agency, narrates the story of his career beginning in 1856 Chicago when he opens the Pinkerton National Detective Agency and hires Kate Warne, who becomes history's first recorded female detective. Pinkerton's relationship with Kate is central here as the Pink-

erton agency foils an assassination attempt on Abraham Lincoln, and Pinkerton establishes the nation's first secret service unit during the Civil War.

Where it's reviewed:
Booklist, February 1, 2008, page 28
Kirkus Reviews, December 15, 2007, page 1261
New York Times Book Review, March 9, 2008, page 20
Publishers Weekly, December 17, 2007, page 29

Other books you might like:
Marie Jacober, *Only Call Us Faithful*, 2002
John Jakes, *On Secret Service*, 2000
Richard Moquist, *Eye of the Agency*, 1997
Kerry Newcomb, *Only the Gallant*, 1991
Walter Satterthwait, *Masquerade*, 1998

850

PAUL M. LEVITT

Come With Me to Babylon

(Albuquerque: University of New Mexico Press, 2008)

Story type: Historical/Victorian America
Subject(s): Family Life; Jews
Major character(s): Ben Cohen, Immigrant
Time period(s): 1910s
Locale(s): New York, New York; New Jersey

Summary: Levitt dramatizes the life of an immigrant family—the Cohens—who in 1910 journey from Russia to the United States in pursuit of the American Dream. Focusing on the son, Ben Cohen, the novel dramatizes the family's experiences in New York City and on a farm in New Jersey. Ben is pushed to marry the daughter of a rich Jewish factory owner, but he resists a future as a sweatshop boss and falls in love with a Gentile. Evocative of its time and place, the novel offers a believable portrait of immigrant life in the early 20th century.

Where it's reviewed:
Booklist, February 15, 2008, page 36

Other books you might like:
Amy Bloom, *Away*, 2007
Steven D. Salinger, *White Darkness*, 2001
Susan Fromberg Schaeffer, *Love*, 1980
Josef Skvorecky, *The Bride of Texas*, 1996
Wesley Strick, *Out There in the Dark*, 2006

851

RICHARD LIEBMANN-SMITH

The James Boys

(New York: Random House, 2008)

Story type: Alternate History; Historical/Victorian America
Subject(s): Alternate History; Brothers; Crime and Criminals
Major character(s): Jesse James, Historical Figure, Outlaw; Henry James, Historical Figure, Writer; William James, Historical Figure, Philosopher
Time period(s): 19th century; 20th century (1876-1916)
Locale(s): United States

Summary: Historian Otis Pease once remarked that 19-century American history could be encapsulated in the lives of two sets of James brothers—writers William and Henry James and the outlaws Jesse and Frank James. Here, Liebmann-Smith brings them together as members of the same family. Traveling in Missouri in 1876, Henry James is taken hostage by the James Gang and realizes that Frank and Jesse are his and William's long-lost brothers who disappeared during the Civil War and were presumed dead. The story offers a wild convergence: intellectuals in the world of outlaws and outlaws in the worlds of academia and the arts.

Where it's reviewed:
Kirkus Reviews, April 1, 2008, page 324
Library Journal, April 15, 2008, page 73

Other books by the same author:
Famous, 1979

Other books you might like:
Desmond Barry, *The Chivalry of Crime*, 2000
Susan M. Dodd, *Mamaw*, 1988
Ron Hansen, *The Assassination of Jesse James by the Coward Robert Ford*, 1983
Joyce Carol Oates, *Wild Nights!*, 2008
Colm Toibin, *The Master*, 2004

852

MORGAN LLYWELYN

1999

(New York: Forge, 2008)

Story type: Political
Series: Irish Century. Book 5
Subject(s): Politics; Irish Republican Army
Major character(s): Barry Halloran, Journalist
Time period(s): 20th century (1970s-1990s); 21st century
Locale(s): Ireland

Summary: In the and final installment of Llywelyn's Irish Century series, former IRA soldier and photojournalist Barry Halloran experiences the events following the Bloody Sunday killings in 1972 and the escalation of violence of the Troubles up to the disarmament talks and beginnings of reconciliation between the two sides in the conflict.

Where it's reviewed:
Booklist, February 1, 2008, page 24
Publishers Weekly, December 3, 2007, page 51

Other books by the same author:
1972, 2005
1949, 2003
1921, 2001
1916, 1998
Pride of Lions, 1996

Other books you might like:
Seamus Deane, *Reading in the Dark*, 1997
Pat McCabe, *Call Me the Breeze*, 2003
Bernard McLaverty, *Grace Notes*, 1997
Brian Moore, *Lies of Silence*, 1990
Daniel Silva, *The Marching Season*, 1999

Historical

853

ELIZABETH LORD

A Secret Inheritance

(New York: Severn House, 2008)

Story type: Historical/Victorian
Subject(s): Family Relations; Inheritance
Major character(s): Therese Daurignac, Young Woman
Time period(s): 19th century
Locale(s): Toulouse, France; Paris, France

Summary: Therese Daurignac endeavors to claim her family's rightful due, fueled by the claims of her spendthrift and unreliable father that a secret inheritance lies just beyond their grasp. Therese inherits her father's scheming ways, and through her wiles the family manages to gain some distinction, only to falter under the pressure of change brought in with the 20th century.

Where it's reviewed:
Booklist, January 1, 2008, page 46

Other books by the same author:
To Caste a Stone, 2007
Company of Rebels, 2004
Winter Wine, 2001

Other books you might like:
Arabella Edge, *The God of Spring*, 2007
John Rolfe Gardner, *Somewhere in France*, 1999
Rosalind Laker, *Brilliance*, 2007
Caroline Seebohm, *The Innocents*, 2007
Michael Wallner, *April in Paris*, 2007

854

ELIZABETH MAGUIRE

The Open Door

(New York: Other Press, 2008)

Story type: Historical/Victorian
Subject(s): Authors and Writers; Biography
Major character(s): Constance Fenimore Woolson, Historical Figure, Writer; Henry James, Historical Figure, Writer
Time period(s): 1880s
Locale(s): Florence, Italy

Summary: Maguire's posthumous novel explores the literary and personal relationship between writers Henry James and Constance Fenimore Woolson, grandniece of James Fenimore Cooper. A fictionalized autobiography from Woolson, the novel treats her friendship with James that begins when they meet in Europe. At the time she is the more famous and popular writer, and their relationship suffers from James' harsh critique of his friend's works and from the revelations of his homosexuality. Based on biographical fact, the novel provides an interesting angle to view the Master and his lesser-known fellow writer.

Where it's reviewed:
Booklist, April 15, 2008, page 32
Kirkus Reviews, April 15, 2008, page 386
Publishers Weekly, March 17, 2008, page 44

Other books by the same author:
Thinner, Blonder, Whiter, 2002

Other books you might like:
David Lodge, *Author, Author*, 2004
Joyce Carol Oates, *Wild Nights!*, 2008
Jonathan Tell, *Freud's Alphabet*, 2003
Colm Toibin, *The Master*, 2004
Edmund White, *Fanny*, 2003

855

BERYL MATTHEWS

Diamonds in the Dust

(Sutton, England: Severn House, 2008)

Story type: Historical/Roaring Twenties; Mystery
Subject(s): Mystery and Detective Stories; Brothers and Sisters; Family Life
Major character(s): Dora Bentley, Teenager; Tom Bentley, Child; Lily Bentley, Child
Time period(s): 1920s
Locale(s): London, England

Summary: In this mystery/thriller, the three Bentley children—Dora, Tom, and Lily—investigate the whereabouts of their widowed mother who fails to return home after working the night shift at a factory. When the children inquire at the factory, they are told that no one resembling their mother works there. Desperate to solve the mystery, the children turn to a World War I veteran and former policeman for help.

Where it's reviewed:
Booklist, February 1, 2008, page 31

Other books by the same author:
A Flight of Golden Wings, 2007
The Forgotten Family, 2006
A Time of Peace, 2005
A Change of Fortune, 2004
Wings in the Morning, 2004

Other books you might like:
Charles Bennett, *Noble Lies*, 2007
Ann Granger, *The Companion*, 2007
Marcia Muller, *Vanishing Point*, 2006
James Patterson, *7th Heaven*, 2008
Mariah Stewart, *Last Look*, 2007

856

JAMES MCBRIDE

Song Yet Sung

(New York: Riverhead Books, 2008)

Story type: Historical/Antebellum American South
Subject(s): Slavery
Major character(s): Liz Spocott, Slave; Patty Cannon, Bounty Hunter (slave catcher); Denwood Long, Bounty Hunter (slave catcher)
Time period(s): 1850s
Locale(s): Chesapeake Bay, Maryland

Summary: Liz Spocott, a beautiful young runaway slave, suffers a head injury that leaves her with the ability to see into the future. She uses her knowledge to seek her freedom along the underground railroad. Opposing her plans are slave catchers Patty Cannon and Denwood Long. This is a vivid and exciting narrative featuring kidnappings, gunfights, and chases through woods and swamps as well as a thoughtful meditation on the nature of freedom and race relations with relevance both to America's past and present.

Where it's reviewed:
Booklist, November 1, 2007, page 27
Kirkus Reviews, November 1, 2007, page 1119
Library Journal, December 1, 2007, page 101
New York Times Book Review, March 2, 2008, page 14
Publishers Weekly, September 24, 2007, page 40

Other books by the same author:
Miracle at St. Anna, 2002

Other books you might like:
David Anthony Durham, *Walk through Darkness*, 2002
Toni Morrison, *Beloved*, 1987
Alice Randall, *The Wind Done Gone*, 2001
Lalita Tademy, *Cane River*, 2001
Michael C. White, *Soul Catcher*, 2007

857

FRANCES MCNEIL

Sisters of Fortune

(New York: Severn House, 2008)

Story type: Historical/Depression Era
Subject(s): City and Town Life; Friendship; Suspense
Major character(s): Lydia Bellamy, Young Woman; Sophie Moran, Young Woman
Time period(s): 1930s
Locale(s): Yorkshire, England

Summary: McNeil's novel dramatizes the relationship between two young woman of different backgrounds. Lydia Bellamy is the stepdaughter of the owner of the town's bank; Sophie Moran is the daughter of Irish immigrants living in the slums. Sophie's father works at the bank, and when it is robbed and an employee is killed, he is charged with the crime. Sophie, believing him innocent, appeals to Lydia, and the pair sets out to clear Sophie's father and find the real bank robber and killer.

Where it's reviewed:
Booklist, February 1, 2008, page 29

Other books by the same author:
Sixpence in Her Shoe, 2006
Somewhere Behind the Morning, 2005
Sisters on Bread Street, 2003

Other books you might like:
Tessa Barclay, *A Tissue of Lies*, 2008
Anne Doughty, *A Girl Called Rosie*, 2008
Adele Geras, *Hester's Story*, 2004
Anne Herries, *Love Is Not Enough*, 2008
Nicholas Rhea, *Some Assured*, 2004

858

ELISABETH MCNEILL

Flodden Field

(New York: Severn House, 2008)

Story type: Historical/Renaissance
Subject(s): War; Kings, Queens, Rulers, etc.; Politics
Major character(s): James IV, Historical Figure, Ruler (King of Scotland)
Time period(s): 16th century (1513)
Locale(s): Scotland; England

Summary: McNeill recreates the famous 1513 battle of Flodden Field. With King Henry VIII away in France, King James IV of Scotland decides that the time is ripe for an invasion of England. Issuing a call to arms, the king summons all his feudal lords to his assistance, and the result is one of the bloodiest battles ever fought on the British Isles. The novel captures both the battle and its era with depictions of the highborn and the ordinary.

Where it's reviewed:
Booklist, November 15, 2007, page 18

Other books by the same author:
The Storm, 2006
Turn of the Tide, 2006
The Lady of Cawnpore, 2004
A Bombay Affair, 2000
Money Trouble, 1999

Other books you might like:
Pat McIntosh, *St. Mungo's Robin*, 2007
Jean Plaidy, *The Thistle and the Rose*, 1973
Bertrice Small, *Until You*, 2003
Hunter Steele, *Chasing the Gilded Shadow*, 1986
Nigel G. Tranter, *A Flame for the Fire*, 1998

859

IAN MORSON

City of the Dead

(Sutton, England: Severn House, 2008)

Story type: Mystery; Historical/Medieval
Series: Niccolo Zuliani. Book 1
Subject(s): Mystery and Detective Stories; Middle Ages
Major character(s): Niccolo Zuliani, Businessman; Friar Alberoni, Religious
Time period(s): 13th century (1262)
Locale(s): Venice, Italy; Xanadu, China

Summary: Morson launches a new medieval mystery series featuring down-on-his-luck Venetian businessman Niccolo Zuliani who agrees to accompany Friar Alberoni to Kubla Khan's fabled city of Xanadu. When a friar whom Alberoni is seeking there turns up dead, Zuliani investigates. Atmospheric and colorful, this is a promising launch of a series with an intriguing premise and protagonist.

Where it's reviewed:
Publishers Weekly, March 17, 2008, page 53

Historical

Other books by the same author:
Falconer and the Great Beast, 1999
A Psalm for Falconer, 1997
Falconer's Judgement, 1997
Falconer and the Face of God, 1997
Falconer's Crusade, 1996

Other books you might like:
Margaret Frazer, *The Widow's Tale*, 2005
Tom Harper, *Siege of Heaven*, 2007
Conn Iggulden, *Genghis: Birth of an Empire*, 2007
Michael Jecks, *The Malice of Unnatural Death*, 2007
Priscilla Royal, *Tyrant of the Mind*, 2004

860

KATE MORTON

The House at Riverton

(New York: Atria Books, 2008)

Story type: Historical/World War I; Family Saga
Subject(s): World War I; Family Life
Major character(s): Grace Reeves, Servant; R.S. Hunter, Writer (poet); Hannah Ashbury, Socialite
Time period(s): 1910s; 1920s
Locale(s): England

Summary: Set in the years surrounding World War I, this debut novel explores the family secrets of the Ashburys from the perspective of their servant Grace Reeves who, when interviewed by a filmmaker about the family recalls the circumstances surrounding the presumed suicide death of a famous young poet, R.S. Hunter, and the attempt of young Hannah Ashbury to achieve independence and fulfillment out of the shadow of her family. Told in flashbacks, the novel convincingly evokes the Edwardian era, the war years, and its aftermath.

Where it's reviewed:
Booklist, February 15, 2008, page 34
Kirkus Reviews, February 15, 2008, page 168
Library Journal, February 1, 2008, page 64
Publishers Weekly, December 3, 2007, page 46

Other books by the same author:
The Forgotten Garden, 2008
The Shifting Fog, 2006

Other books you might like:
Neil Bartlett, *The House on Brooke Street*, 1997
Jeannie Johnson, *Where the Wild Thyme Grows*, 2007
David Roberts, *Hollow Crown*, 2002
Linda Sole, *Miscarriage of Justice*, 2007
Rowena Summers, *Taking Heart*, 2000

861

BEVERLE GRAVES MYERS

The Iron Tongue of Midnight

(Scottsdale, Arizona: Poisoned Pen Press, 2008)

Story type: Historical/Georgian; Mystery
Series: Baroque Mystery. Book 4

Subject(s): Mystery and Detective Stories; Opera; Music and Musicians
Major character(s): Tito Amato, Singer (opera)
Time period(s): 1740s (1740)
Locale(s): Rome, Italy

Summary: Eighteenth century Venetian castrato Tito Amato arrives at a country villa to rehearse a new opera. When the body of an unidentified man is discovered and one of the company is found dead in a vat of crushed grapes, Tito attempts to find out who is responsible and what the connection might be between these deaths and his recently discovered sister, Grisella Amato, whom Tito had believed dead.

Where it's reviewed:
Kirkus Reviews, January 1, 2008, page 17
Library Journal, February 1, 2008, page 49
Publishers Weekly, January 1, 2008, page 43

Other books by the same author:
Cruel Music, 2006
Painted Veil, 2005
Interrupted Aria, 2004

Other books you might like:
Lawrence Goldman, *The Castrato*, 1973
Elaine Isaak, *The Singer's Crown*, 2005
Ross King, *Domino*, 1995
Anne Rice, *Cry to Heaven*, 1982
Jim Williams, *Scherzo*, 1999

862

JAY NEUGEBOREN

1940

(Brooklyn, New York: Two Dollar Radio, 2008)

Story type: Historical/World War II
Subject(s): World War II; Biography; Nazis
Major character(s): Eduard Bloch, Historical Figure, Doctor; Elisabeth Rofman, Artist; Adolf Hitler, Historical Figure, Poltical Figure
Time period(s): 1940s
Locale(s): New York, New York (Bronx)

Summary: Neugeboren's novel focuses on the historical figure Dr. Eduard Bloch who served as Adolf Hitler's childhood and family doctor. On the eve of America's entry into the war, Dr. Bloch is living quietly in the Bronx where he comes to the attention of Elisabeth Rofman, a medical illustrator, and gets involved in her troubled relationship with her ex-husband and mentally ill son. Bloch's journal records his relationship with Elisabeth and his recollections of the young Hitler and his guilt over the favors his association afforded him.

Where it's reviewed:
Kirkus Reviews, February 1, 2008, page 111
Publishers Weekly, January 28, 2008, page 30

Other books by the same author:
Before My Life Began, 1985
The Stolen Jew, 1981
An Orphan's Tales, 1976
Sam's Legacy, 1974
Listen, Ruben Fontanez, 1968

Other books you might like:
Beryl Bainbridge, *Young Adolf*, 1979
Ron Hansen, *Hitler's Niece*, 1999
Jacques Levine, *Hitler's Secret Diaries*, 1988
Norman Mailer, *The Castle in the Forest*, 2007
Paul West, *The Dry Danube*, 2000

863

SHARAN NEWMAN

The Shanghai Tunnel

(New York: Forge, 2008)

Story type: Historical/American West Coast; Historical/
  Post-American Civil War
Subject(s): Women; Business Enterprises; China
Major character(s): Emily Stratton, Widow(er)
Time period(s): 1860s (1868)
Locale(s): Portland, Oregon

Summary: Newman, the author of the admired Catherine
LeVendeur medieval mystery series, turns to her
hometown of Portland, Oregon, for the setting of this
novel. Horace Stratton, who has made a fortune in China,
dies on his way home, accompanied by his new wife,
Emily, the daughter of American missionaries in China.
Delving into her husband's affairs, Emily learns that
Horace made his fortune in the opium trade. When she
tries to make amends, the city's elite resist violently,
and, as the body count rises, Emily's safety is threatened.

Where it's reviewed:
Booklist, February 15, 2008, page 41
Library Journal, January 1, 2008, page 66
Publishers Weekly, December 17, 2007, page 37

Other books by the same author:
The Catherine LeVendeur Series, 1994-

Other books you might like:
Jon Boorstin, *The Newsboys' Lodging House*, 2003
Rhys Bowen, *The Molly Murphy Series*, 2002-
Joel Rose, *The Blackest Bird*, 2007
Linda Sole, *Miscarriage of Justice*, 2007
Victoria Thompson, *Murder in Chinatown*, 2007

864

JOYCE CAROL OATES

Wild Nights!

(New York: HarperCollins, 2008)

Story type: Literary
Subject(s): Biography; Authors and Writers; Death
Major character(s): Edgar Allan Poe, Historical Figure,
  Writer; Emily Dickinson, Historical Figure, Writer;
  Henry James, Historical Figure, Writer
Time period(s): 19th century; 20th century
Locale(s): United States; England

Summary: In this inventive volume, Oates imagines the
deaths (or afterlife) of five great American writers—Poe,
Dickinson, Mark Twain, James, and Ernest Hemingway.

Poe's end is treated in diary-fashion recorded after the
writer's death; Dickinson is imagined as a replicant in a
21st-century suburban home; Twain's befriending of
adolescent girls marks his passing; James is shown working in a hospital during World War I, and Hemingway
descends into despair and psychosis. Each version is
intriguing and revealing about both the writer and his or
her work and its impact.

Where it's reviewed:
Booklist, November 1, 2007, page 6
Kirkus Reviews, February 15, 2008, page 169
Library Journal, December 1, 2007, page 107
New York Times Book Review, April 20, 2008, page 9
Publishers Weekly, October 15, 2007, page 34

Other books by the same author:
The Gravedigger's Daughter, 2007
Broke Heart Blues, 2005
Missing Mom, 2005
The Falls, 2004
Middle Age, 2001

Other books you might like:
Clancy Carlile, *The Paris Pilgrims*, 1999
Judith Farr, *I Never Came to You in White*, 1996
Brian Hall, *Fall of Frost*, 2008
Thomas Hauser, *Mark Twain Remembers*, 1999
Colm Toibin, *The Master*, 2004

865

PATRICIA O'BRIEN

Harriet and Isabella

(New York: Touchstone, 2008)

Story type: Historical/Post-American Civil War
Subject(s): Scandal; Religious Life
Major character(s): Henry Ward Beecher, Historical
  Figure, Religious; Isabella Hooker, Historical Figure,
  Suffragette; Harriet Beecher Stowe, Historical Figure,
  Writer
Time period(s): 1880s; 1870s
Locale(s): Brooklyn Heights, New York

Summary: O'Brien dramatizes 19th America's greatest
scandal when the famous preacher, Henry Ward Beecher,
is accused of sexual misconduct with one of his married
parishioners. Told in flashback in 1887, when Beecher is
on his deathbed, the question of his guilt or innocence
divides his famous family, particular his sisters, suffragette Isabella Hooker and Harriet Beecher Stowe,
author of *Uncle Tom's Cabin*.

Where it's reviewed:
Booklist, November 15, 2007, page 19
Library Journal, October 1, 2007, page 64
Publishers Weekly, August 27, 2007, page 58

Other books by the same author:
The Glory Cloak, 2004
Good Intentions, 1997
The Ladies' Lunch, 1994
The Candidate's Wife, 1992

Historical

Other books you might like:
Chris Adrian, *Gob's Grief*, 2000
Dan McCall, *Beecher*, 1979
Jacqueline Sheckan, *Truth*, 2003
Jane Smiley, *The All-True Travels and Adventures of Lidie Newton*, 1998
John Vernon, *Peter Doyle*, 1991

866

PAMELA OLDFIELD

Fateful Voyage

(New York: Severn House, 2008)

Story type: Historical/Edwardian
Subject(s): Ships
Major character(s): Hester Shaw, Young Woman; Alexander Waring, Detective—Police; Charlie Barnes, Servant (ship's steward)
Time period(s): 1900s (1907)
Locale(s): London, England; *Mauretania*, At Sea; New York, New York

Summary: Hester Shaw, the mistress of Scotland Yard detective Alexander Waring, accompanies Waring's aunt on the maiden voyage of the *Mauretania* to New York. While on board, Hester meets Charlie Barnes, one of the ship's stewards. They fall in love, and when Hester returns to London to tell Waring, a series of violent events follows in this atmospheric, period drama.

Where it's reviewed:
Booklist, January 1, 2008, page 40

Other books by the same author:
Jack's Shadow, 2006
Henry's Women, 2005
New Beginnings, 2002
Early One Morning, 2001
Riding the Storm, 2000

Other books you might like:
Conrad Allen, *Murder on the Mauretania*, 2000
John Boyne, *Crippen*, 2006
Marion Chesney, *Hasty Death*, 2004
Tracy Chevalier, *Falling Angels*, 2001
Penny Vicenzi, *No Angel*, 2000

867

JANET PAISLEY

White Rose Rebel

(New York: Overlook Press, 2008)

Story type: Historical/Georgian
Subject(s): Jacobite Rebellion; Kings, Queens, Rulers, etc.; Marriage
Major character(s): Anne Farquharson, Historical Figure, Spouse (of Aeneas); Aeneas Macintosh, Military Personnel, Spouse (of Anne)
Time period(s): 1740s (1745)
Locale(s): Scotland

Summary: Paisley dramatizes the life of Anne Farquharson and events of the Jacobite Rebellion of 1745 that attempted to regain the Stuart throne of Scotland for Bonnie Prince Charlie. Anne is committed to the Jacobite cause, even when her husband, Aeneas Macintosh, joins the opposing British army. She joins the uprising to become its legendary "Colonel Anne." Based on historical fact, the novel is a rousing account of the Jacobite Rebellion and a unique and little-known historical figure.

Where it's reviewed:
Kirkus Reviews, March 15, 2008, page 265
Publishers Weekly, March 17, 2008, page 46

Other books you might like:
George Macdonald Fraser, *The Reavers*, 2008
Diana Gabaldon, *Outlander*, 1991
Heather Graham, *Come the Morning*, 1999
Mollie Hardwick, *Charlie Is My Darling*, 1977
Walter Scott, *Waverley*, 1814

868

ROBERT B. PARKER

Resolution

(New York: G.P. Putnam's Sons, 2008)

Story type: Historical/American West
Subject(s): American West; Cowboys/Cowgirls; Small Town Life
Major character(s): Everett Hitch, Gunfighter; Virgil Cole, Gunfighter; Amos Wolfson, Businessman
Time period(s): 19th century
Locale(s): West

Summary: Parker offers a Western continuing the stories of Everett Hitch and Virgil Cole, introduced in *Appaloosa*. As hired guns they find themselves opposing the efforts of Amos Wolfson who is trying to buy up the whole town of Resolution, provoking a range war with the local farmers and small ranchers.

Where it's reviewed:
Kirkus Reviews, April 1, 2008, page 387
Library Journal, May 1, 2008, page 59
Publishers Weekly, March 31, 2008, page 35

Other books by the same author:
Appaloosa, 2005
Bad Business, 2004
Double Play, 2004
Backstory, 2003
Gunman's Rhapsody, 2001

Other books you might like:
Kurt Andersen, *Heyday*, 2007
Ivan Doig, *The Whistling Season*, 2006
Leif Enger, *So Brave, Young and Handsome*, 2008
Joseph O'Connor, *Redemption Falls*, 2007
Edwin Shrake, *The Borderland*, 2000

869

UNA-MARY PARKER

Alexia's Secrets

(Sutton, England: Severn House, 2008)

Story type: Historical/World War I
Subject(s): Secrets; Family Relations; Marriage
Major character(s): Alexia Erskine, Debutante; Simon
   Seymour, Nobleman
Time period(s): 1910s (1919)
Locale(s): England

Summary: Parker's novel follows the romantic entanglements of Alexia Erskine, whose father gambled away the family fortune. Afforded the opportunity to "come out" as a debutante, Alexia meets and falls in love with Simon Seymour, heir to the Earl of Clifton. When they marry, Alexia's problems only escalate as she comes to understand that aristocratic family life is not all that it seems.

Where it's reviewed:
Booklist, April 15, 2008, page 27

Other books by the same author:
The Granville Affairs, 2006
The Granville Legacy, 2006
The Granville Sisters, 2005
Veil of Secrets, 1990
Scandals, 1988

Other books you might like:
Tessa Barclay, *A Tissue of Lies*, 2008
Chris Gilson, *Crazy for Cornelia*, 2000
Frances McNeil, *Sisters of Fortune*, 2008
Teresa Medeiros, *One Night for Scandal*, 2003
Danielle Steel, *Coming Out*, 2006

870

BEN PASTOR

The Fire Walker

(New York: St. Martin's Minotaur, 2008)

Story type: Historical/Ancient Rome; Mystery
Series: Aelius Spartianus. Book 2
Subject(s): Mystery and Detective Stories; Roman Empire
Major character(s): Aelius Spartianus, Historian; Agnus,
   Healer
Time period(s): 4th century (304)
Locale(s): Trier, Roman Empire

Summary: In the second of Pastor's mysteries set during the reign of Emperor Diocletian, Aelius Spartianus, Diocletian's official historian, is sent to Trier with a message for Emperor Constantius. There he hears of a Christian healer named Agnus, known as the "fire walker," who supposedly resurrected a man from the dead. Aelius sets out to uncover the truth behind this apparent miracle but discovers that the resurrected man has been murdered. To solve the case, Aelius gets to the heart of the corruption that is pulling the Roman Empire apart.

Where it's reviewed:
Publishers Weekly, February 25, 2008, page 57

Other books by the same author:
The Water Thief, 2007
Liar Moon, 2001
Lumen, 1999

Other books you might like:
Kenneth Barton, *Death on the Appian Way*, 1974
Ron Burns, *The Livinius Severus Series*, 1991-
Lindsey Davis, *The Marcus Didius Falco Series*, 1989-
John Maddox Roberts, *The SPQR Series*, 1990-
Steven Saylor, *The Roma Sub Rosa Series*, 1991-

871

MICHAEL PEARCE

Mark of the Pasha

(Scottsdale, Arizona: Poisoned Pen Press, 2008)

Story type: Mystery; Historical/World War I
Series: Mamur Zapt. Book 16
Subject(s): Mystery and Detective Stories; World War I
Major character(s): Gareth Owen, Civil Servant, Police
   Officer; Zeinab, Spouse (of Gareth)
Time period(s): 1910s (1918)

Summary: At the end of World War I, the push for Egyptian independence increases, and Gareth Owen (aka Mamur Zapt or the head of the secret police) faces fresh challenges in this installment of Pearce's period mystery series. Owen searches for the bombers who threaten a government ceremony. Meanwhile, Owen's new wife, Zeinab, asserts her independence and autonomy.

Where it's reviewed:
Booklist, May 1, 2008, page 37
Kirkus Reviews, March 1, 2008, page 222
Publishers Weekly, March 3, 2008, page 32

Other books by the same author:
The Point in the Market, 2005
A Cold Touch of Ice, 2004
A Face in the Cemetery, 2004
A Dead Man in Trieste, 2004
The Fig Tree Murder, 2003

Other books you might like:
Olivia Manning, *The Danger Tree*, 1977
Glenn Meade, *The Sands of Sakkara*, 1999
Elizabeth Peters, *The Amelia Peabody Series*, 1975-
Robert Sole, *The Photographer's Wife*, 1999
David Stevens, *The Waters of Babylon*, 2000

872

ANNE PERRY

Buckingham Palace Gardens

(New York: Ballantine Books, 2008)

Story type: Historical/Victorian; Mystery
Series: Thomas and Charlotte Pitt

Historical

Subject(s): Mystery and Detective Stories
Major character(s): Thomas Pitt, Police Officer (inspector), Spouse (of Charlotte); Charlotte Pitt, Socialite, Spouse (of Thomas); Edward VII, Historical Figure, Royalty
Time period(s): 1890s (1893)
Locale(s): London, England

Summary: Set in 1893, this installment of Perry's popular Victorian mystery series featuring husband-and-wife sleuths Thomas and Charlotte Pitt has the couple investigating the death of a prostitute in Buckingham Palace brought in for the evening entertainment of the Prince of Wales and associates. Called in to ward off a public scandal, Thomas Pitt recruits their Cockney maid, Gracie Phipps, to work undercover in the palace to gather information. The novel offers a convincing look at palace life under Queen Victoria.

Where it's reviewed:
Booklist, February 15, 2008, page 38
New York Times Book Review, March 23, 2008, page 11
Publishers Weekly, January 28, 2008, page 31

Other books by the same author:
Half Moon Street, 2005
Shoulder the Sky, 2004
No Graves as Yet, 2003
Seven Dials, 2003
Southampton Row, 2002
The Whitechapel Conspiracy, 2001

Other books you might like:
John MacLachlan Gray, *The Fiend in Human*, 2003
Laurie R. King, *The Mary Russell/Sherlock Holmes Series*, 1994-
Gillian Linscott, *The Nell Bray Series*, 1991-
Will Thomas, *To Kingdom Come*, 2005
Sarah Waters, *Fingersmith*, 2002

873

BARBARA POPE

Cezanne's Quarry
(New York: W.W. Norton, 2008)

Story type: Mystery; Historical/Victorian
Subject(s): Mystery and Detective Stories; Artists and Art
Major character(s): Bernard Martin, Detective—Police (magistrate); Paul Cezanne, Historical Figure, Artist; Charles Westbury, Scholar
Time period(s): 1880s (1885)
Locale(s): Aix-en-Provence, France

Summary: Pope's inventive and atmospheric period mystery, has a young magistrate, Bernard Martin, investigating the strangling death of a mysterious young woman who has come to Aix with her lover, a Darwinian scholar named Charles Westbury. He and painter Paul Cezanne are the prime suspects in what appears to be a *crime de passion* by the spurned Cezanne or the betrayed Westbury.

Where it's reviewed:
Booklist, May 1, 2008, page 24
Kirkus Reviews, April 15, 2008, page 394
Publishers Weekly, March 17, 2008, page 49

Other books you might like:
Gillian Bray, *The Nell Bray Series*, 1991-
Carola Dunn, *The Daisy Dalrymple Series*, 1994-
Ann Granger, *The Companion*, 2007
Jane Jakeman, *In the City of Dark Water*, 2006
Laurie R. King, *The Mary Russell/Sherlock Holmes Series*, 1994-

---

874

JEM POSTER

Courting Shadows
(Woodstock, New York: Overlook Press, 2008)

Story type: Historical/Victorian
Subject(s): Victorian Period; Small Town Life; Art Restoration
Major character(s): John Stannard, Architect; Ann Rosewell, Young Woman
Time period(s): 1880s (1881)
Locale(s): England

Summary: This atmospheric first novel is set in a small English village in 1881. John Stannard is a young architect engaged in repairing the parish church. Stannard finds the assignment onerous and beneath him until he develops a relationship with a local girl, Ann Rosewell, and he discovers a Doom Painting—a folk mural combining Christian and pagan influences that dates back to the Middle Ages. The novel captures period small town life while considering a number of interesting themes surrounding the restoration work.

Where it's reviewed:
Booklist, November 15, 2007, page 28
Kirkus Reviews, November 1, 2007, page 1119
Publishers Weekly, October 1, 2007, page 35

Other books you might like:
Peter Ackroyd, *Hawksmoor*, 1985
Michel Faber, *The Crimson Petal and the White*, 2002
Esther Freud, *The Sea Press House*, 2004
Anne Perry, *Buckingham Palace Gardens*, 2008
Barbara Vine, *The Blood Doctor*, 2002

875

STEVEN PRESSFIELD

Killing Rommel
(New York: Doubleday, 2008)

Story type: Historical/World War II
Subject(s): World War II
Major character(s): Erwin Rommel, Historical Figure, Military Personnel; Lawrence Chapman, Military Personnel (naval intelligence officer); Rose McCall, Young Woman
Time period(s): 1940s (1942-1943)
Locale(s): Africa; England

Summary: Based on historical fact, this exciting thriller describes the actual British plot to assassinate the "Desert Fox," German field marshal Erwin Rommel in North

Africa. The plot is seen from the perspective of a young naval intelligence officer, Lawrence "Chap" Chapman, whose relationship with a young woman, Rose McCall, leads to his involvement in the assassination attempt.

Where it's reviewed:
Booklist, February 1, 2008, page 27
Kirkus Reviews, February 15, 2008, page 170
Library Journal, November 1, 2007, page 60
Publishers Weekly, February 4, 2008, page 36

Other books by the same author:
The Afghan Campaign, 2006
The Virtues of War, 2004
Last of the Amazons, 2002
Tides of War, 2000
Gates of Fire, 1998

Other books you might like:
Alan Furst, *The World at Night*, 1991
Leo Kessler, *Rommel's Last Battle*, 2006
Jeff Shaara, *The Rising Tide*, 2006
Paul Watkins, *The Forger*, 2000
Lawrence Wells, *Rommel and the Rebel*, 1986

876

BRANT RANDALL

Blood Harvest

(Fort Collins, Colorado: Capital Crime Press, 2008)

Story type: Historical/Roaring Twenties; Mystery
Subject(s): Small Town Life; Mystery and Detective Stories; Prejudice
Major character(s): Jackie Sue McKay, Young Woman; Angus DeCosta, Young Man
Time period(s): 1920s (1929)
Locale(s): New England

Summary: Set in Prohibition-era New England, this suspense novel treats star-crossed lovers and competition between rival moonshiners that escalates into attempted murder and a lynching. The relationship between Jackie Sue McKay and Angus DeCosta sets in motion a family feud that results in the lynching death of a DeCosta. What appears to be the work of the Ku Klux Klan and an incident of ethnic prejudice is actually far more complicated, and the solution to the mystery of the lynching reveals the tensions in a New England community during the period.

Where it's reviewed:
Kirkus Reviews, April 1, 2008, page 334
Library Journal, March 15, 2008, page 60
Publishers Weekly, March 3, 2008, page 32

Other books you might like:
Tom Bailey, *Cotton Song*, 2006
Pete Earley, *The Big Secret*, 2004
David Mamet, *The Old Religion*, 1997
Kate Wilhelm, *Skeletons*, 2002
David Wiltse, *The Hangman's Knot*, 2001

877

MARY REED
ERIC MAYER , Co-Author

Seven for a Secret

(Scottsdale, Arizona: Poisoned Pen Press, 2008)

Story type: Mystery; Historical/Ancient Rome
Series: John the Eunuch. Book 7
Subject(s): Mystery and Detective Stories; Byzantine Empire
Major character(s): John the Eunuch, Government Official (lord chamberlain)
Time period(s): 6th century
Locale(s): Constantinople, Byzantium

Summary: John the Eunuch, the lord chamberlain to Emperor Justinian, investigates the murder of a woman who claims to be the model for a figure in a mosaic on the wall of John's study. Getting to the bottom of the crime and the woman's identity takes readers on a colorful tour of Constantinople during the reign of Justinian.

Where it's reviewed:
Booklist, January 1, 2008, page 50
Kirkus Reviews, February 15, 2008, page 173
Publishers Weekly, January 7, 2008, page 38

Other books by the same author:
Five for Silver, 2004
Four for a Boy, 2003
Three for a Letter, 2001
Two for Joy, 2000
One for Sorrow, 1999

Other books you might like:
Gillian Bradshaw, *The Bearkeeper's Daughter*, 1987
Michael Ennis, *Byzantium*, 1989
Harold Lamb, *Theodora and the Emperor*, 1952
John Maddox Roberts, *The SPQR Series*, 1990-
Steven Saylor, *The Roma Sub Rosa Series*, 1991-

878

ANNE RICE

Christ the Lord: The Road to Cana

(New York: Knopf, 2008)

Story type: Historical/Ancient Rome; Biblical Fiction
Series: Christ the Lord. Book 2
Subject(s): Biography; Bible; Jews
Major character(s): Yeshua, Historical Figure, Biblical Figure; Mary, Historical Figure, Biblical Figure; Joseph, Historical Figure, Biblical Figure
Time period(s): 1st century
Locale(s): Nazareth, Judea

Summary: Rice supplies a second volume of her fictionalized biography of Jesus, bringing the story from boyhood up to the wedding at Cana where Jesus' turning water into wine signals the beginning of his public ministry. Rice depicts the struggles of Yeshua (Jesus) as he realizes what his duty to his "father's business" will entail for both himself and his earthly parents, Mary and

Joseph. Rice's speculation predominates here in the absence of established accounts of Jesus' young adulthood.

Where it's reviewed:
Booklist, December 15, 2007, page 4
Kirkus Reviews, January 15, 2008, page 64
Library Journal, March 15, 2008, page 60
New York Times, March 13, 2008, page E1
Publishers Weekly, February 4, 2008, page 40

Other books by the same author:
Christ the Lord: Out of Egypt, 2005
Blackwood Farm, 2002
Merrick, 2000
Violin, 1997
Servant of the Bones, 1996

Other books you might like:
Anthony Burgess, *Man of Nazareth*, 1970
Marek Halter, *Mary of Nazareth*, 2008
Norman Mailer, *The Gospel According to the Son*, 1997
Jose Saramago, *The Gospel According to Jesus Christ*, 1994
Walter Wangerin, *Jesus*, 2005

879

LINDA L. RICHARDS

Death Was the Other Woman

(New York: St. Martin's Press, 2008)

Story type: Historical/Depression Era; Mystery
Subject(s): Mystery and Detective Stories
Major character(s): Dex Theroux, Detective—Private; Kitty Pangborn, Secretary
Time period(s): 1930s (1931)
Locale(s): Los Angeles, California

Summary: L.A. private detective Dex Theroux is hired by a wealthy woman to tail her married boyfriend. When Dex's quarry turns up dead, it's actually Dex's secretary, Kitty Pangborn, who takes over the investigation that gets complicated when the murder victim turns out to be alive and well. This is a colorful and effective hard-boiled thriller, full of convincing period elements.

Where it's reviewed:
Booklist, January 1, 2008, page 9
Kirkus Reviews, November 15, 2007, page 1181
Library Journal, January 1, 2008, page 66
Publishers Weekly, November 19, 2007, page 42

Other books by the same author:
The Next Ex, 2005
Mad Money, 2004

Other books you might like:
Megan Abbott, *Die a Little*, 2007
Max Allan Collins, *Angel in Black*, 2001
Michael Connelly, *The Narrows*, 2004
Stuart M. Kaminsky, *Mildred Pierced*, 2003
Walter Mosley, *Black Betty*, 1994

880

ELISABETH PAYNE ROSEN

Hallam's War

(Denver: Unbridled Books, 2008)

Story type: Historical/American Civil War; Historical/Antebellum American South
Subject(s): Marriage; Civil War
Major character(s): Serena Hallam, Spouse (of Hugh); Hugh Hallam, Spouse (of Serena), Military Personnel (Confederate officer)
Time period(s): 1860s
Locale(s): Tennessee

Summary: This first novel looks at the impact of the Civil War from the perspective of husband and wife Serena and Hugh Hallam. The couple is living in Tennessee when war breaks out. Although filled with misgivings, Hugh joins the Confederate army. He is wounded and taken prisoner at Shiloh. In his absence, Serena struggles to keep her farm running and hold her family together. Both provide vivid and believable depictions of wartime life both on and off the battlefield.

Where it's reviewed:
Library Journal, April 1, 2008, page 78
Publishers Weekly, February 18, 2008, page 134

Other books you might like:
Howard Bahr, *The Year of Jubilo*, 2000
Octavia Butler, *Kindred*, 1979
Donald McCaig, *Rhett Butler's People*, 2007
Jane Smiley, *The All-True Travels and Adventures of Lidie Newton*, 1998
Stephen Wright, *The Amalgamation Polka*, 2006

881

LAURA JOH ROWLAND

The Secret Adventures of Charlotte Bronte

(New York: Overlook Press, 2008)

Story type: Historical/Victorian; Mystery
Subject(s): Mystery and Detective Stories; Authors and Writers
Major character(s): Charlotte Bronte, Historical Figure, Writer; Anne Bronte, Historical Figure, Writer
Time period(s): 1840s
Locale(s): Haworth, England; London, England

Summary: Rowland takes a break from her popular mystery series set in 17th-century Japan to employ writer Charlotte Bronte as a sleuth. Following her success with *Jane Eyre*, Charlotte travels to London with her sisters Anne to defend herself from a charge of breaching her publishing contract. On the train the sisters meet a mysterious girl who turns up murdered. Charlotte investigates, uncovering a complex intrigue with international implications.

Where it's reviewed:
Kirkus Reviews, February 1, 2008, page 112
Library Journal, November 15, 2007, page 54
Publishers Weekly, December 24, 2007, page 26

Other books by the same author:
Red Chrysanthemum, 2006
The Assassin's Touch, 2005
The Pillow Book of Lady Wisteria, 2002
Black Lotus, 2001
The Samurai's Wife, 2000

Other books you might like:
Lynne Reid Banks, *Path to the Silent Country*, 1977
Stevie Davies, *Four Dreamers and Emily*, 1997
D.M. Thomas, *Charlotte*, 2000
James Tully, *The Crimes of Charlotte Bronte*, 1999
Jane Urquhart, *Changing Heaven*, 1993

882

SALMAN RUSHDIE

The Enchantress of Florence
(New York: Random House, 2008)

Story type: Historical/Renaissance; Historical/Exotic
Subject(s): Princes and Princesses; Indian Empire; Kings, Queens, Rulers, etc.
Major character(s): Qara Koz, Royalty (princess); Niccollo Machiavelli, Historical Figure, Writer; Akbar the Great, Historical Figure, Ruler
Time period(s): 16th century
Locale(s): Sikra, India; Florence, Italy

Summary: Rushdie's novel brings together two worlds: Renaissance Florence and the Mughal court of Akbar the Great. The connection is the story of the beauty Qara Koz, told by a young European traveler to Akbar's court who calls himself "Mogor dell'Amore." Through his relationship with Akbar and the stories he tells, the differences between Renaissance Italy, in which Niccollo Machiavelli plays an important role, and Mughal India are bridged, and the novel offers a brilliant recreation of both places and eras.

Where it's reviewed:
Booklist, April 15, 2008, page 6
Kirkus Reviews, April 1, 2008, page 326
Publishers Weekly, March 24, 2008, page 52

Other books by the same author:
Shalimar the Clown, 2005
Fury, 2001
The Ground Beneath Her Feet, 1999
The Moor's Last Sigh, 1995
Midnight's Children, 1981

Other books you might like:
Amitav Ghosh, *The Glass Palace*, 2001
Jeffrey Hantover, *The Jewel Trader of Pegu*, 2008
Thomas Hoover, *The Moghul*, 1983
Rebecca Ryman, *Shalimar*, 1999
Indu Sundaresan, *The Twentieth Wife*, 2002

883

MARY DORIA RUSSELL

Dreamers of the Day
(New York: Random House, 2008)

Story type: Historical/Roaring Twenties; Political
Subject(s): World War I; Politics; Middle East
Major character(s): Agnes Shanklin, Teacher; Winston Churchill, Historical Figure, Political Figure; T.E. Lawrence, Historical Figure, Writer
Time period(s): 1920s
Locale(s): Ohio; Cairo, Egypt

Summary: Russell's novel sends an Ohio schoolteacher, Agnes Shanklin, to Egypt at the time of the Cairo Peace Conference in 1921 in which the shape of the modern Middle East is to be determined. There she falls in love with a German spy, Karl Weilbacher, and befriends such historical figures as Winston Churchill, T.E. Lawrence (Lawrence of Arabia) and Lady Gertrude Bell. Narrated by Agnes from the grave, the novel offers an intriguing look at the political and diplomatic maneuvering that resulted in the creation of Middle Eastern states and multiple unresolved problems.

Where it's reviewed:
Booklist, February 1, 2008, page 26
Library Journal, January 1, 2008, page 87
Publishers Weekly, November 5, 2007, page 40

Other books by the same author:
A Thread of Grace, 2005
Children of God, 1998
The Sparrow, 1996

Other books you might like:
James Aldridge, *Heroes of the Empty View*, 1954
Michael Blankfort, *Behold the Fire*, 1965
Martin Booth, *Dreaming of Samarkand*, 1989
Glenn Meade, *The Sands of Sakkara*, 1999
David Stevens, *The Waters of Babylon*, 2000

884

STEVEN SAYLOR

The Triumph of Caesar
(New York: St. Martin's Minotaur, 2008)

Story type: Historical/Ancient Rome; Mystery
Series: Roma Sub Rosa. Book 10
Subject(s): Mystery and Detective Stories; Roman Empire; Politics
Major character(s): Gordianus the Finder, Detective—Private; Julius Caesar, Historical Figure, Military Personnel; Calpurnia, Historical Figure, Spouse (of Julius Caesar)
Time period(s): 1st century B.C. (42 B.C.)
Locale(s): Rome, Roman Empire

Summary: Gordianus the Finder is hired by Calpurnia, Julius Caesar's wife, to learn which of her husband's many rivals might be plotting his assassination. To do so, Gordianus must learn who is responsible for the murder of

Historical

an old friend who was first hired by Calpurnia to investigate the threat to Caesar's life. Suspects include such figures as Mark Antony and Cleopatra.

Where it's reviewed:
Booklist, May 1, 2008, page 45
Kirkus Reviews, April 15, 2008, page 388
Publishers Weekly, March 31, 2008, page 42

Other books by the same author:
Roma, 2007
The Judgment of Caesar, 2004
Have You Seen Dawn?, 2003
A Mist of Prophecies, 2002
Rubicon, 1999

Other books you might like:
Ron Burns, *Roman Shadows*, 1992
Lindsey Davis, *The Marcus Didius Falco Series*, 1989-
Conn Iggulden, *Emperor: The Gates of Rome*, 2003
Colleen McCullough, *The Master of Rome Series*, 1990-2002
John Maddox Roberts, *The SPQR Series*, 1990-

885

PETER SCHILLING

The End of Baseball

(Chicago: Ivan R. Dee, 2008)

Story type: Historical/World War II; Alternate History
Subject(s): Sports/Baseball
Major character(s): Bill Veeck, Historical Figure, Businessman; Josh Gibson, Historical Figure, Sports Figure; Satchel Page, Historical Figure, Sports Figure
Time period(s): 1940s
Locale(s): Philadelphia, Pennsylvania

Summary: This entertaining "what if" novel imagines the reality of a rumor that baseball promoter Bill Veeck intended in 1944 to buy the Philadelphia Athletics and to fill the team's roster with stars from the Negro League, integrating baseball well before Jackie Robinson historically broke the color barrier. Here, Veeck delivers on the rumor, and the novel imagines the consequences. The novel provides portraits of such historical figures as Walter Winchell, J. Edgar Hoover, and baseball greats Satchel Paige, Josh Gibson, Martin Dihigo, Cool "Papa" Bell, Willie Wells, Roy Campanella, and Buck Leonard.

Where it's reviewed:
Kirkus Reviews, March 15, 2008, page 266
Publishers Weekly, February 25, 2008, page 47

Other books you might like:
Daryl Brock, *If I Never Get Back*, 1990
Karen Joy Fowler, *The Sweetheart Season*, 1990
Pete Hammil, *Snow in August*, 1997
Howard Frank Mosher, *Waiting for Teddy Williams*, 2004
Michael Shaara, *For Love of the Game*, 1991

886

JEFF SHAARA

The Steel Wave

(New York: Ballantine Books, 2008)

Story type: Historical/World War II
Series: Second World War Trilogy. Book 2
Subject(s): World War II; War; Military Life
Major character(s): Dwight Eisenhower, Historical Figure, Military Personnel; Erwin Rommel, Historical Figure, Military Personnel; Jesse Adams, Military Personnel
Time period(s): 1940s (1944)
Locale(s): England; France; Germany

Summary: The second installment of Shaara's World War II trilogy dramatizes D-Day from the perspective of the Allied military commanders, such as Dwight Eisenhower, Omar Bradley, and Bernard Montgomery, as well as the German commander, Erwin Rommel. The view from the ground is provided in the experiences of Sergeant Jesse Adams of the 82nd Airborne. The careful preparations and strategies leading up to the "great waves of steel" in the greatest amphibian landings in history are believably presented.

Where it's reviewed:
Publishers Weekly, March 31, 2008, page 39

Other books by the same author:
The Rising Tide, 2006
To the Last Man, 2004
The Glorious Cause, 2002
Rise to Rebellion, 2001
Gone for Soldiers, 2000

Other books you might like:
Max Allan Collins, *Saving Private Ryan*, 1998
Duncan Harding, *Ramps Down, Troops Away!*, 2005
William P. Mack, *Normandy*, 1995
Steven Pressfield, *Killing Rommel*, 2008
Elleston Trevor, *The Killing Ground*, 1958

887

DAWN SHAMP

On Account of Conspicuous Women

(New York: St. Martin's Press, 2008)

Story type: Historical/Roaring Twenties
Subject(s): Women
Major character(s): Ina Fitzhugh, Widow(er); Guerine Loftis, Young Woman; Bertie Daye, Suffragette
Time period(s): 1920s
Locale(s): North Carolina

Summary: This first novel portrays four suffragette-era women in rural North Carolina during the 1920s. Women's rights and racial attitudes are explored in the stories of young widow and teacher Ina Fitzhugh, socialite Guerine Loftis, tomboy Doodle Shuford, and Bertie Daye, a women's suffrage advocate. The novel

supplies a believable portrait of a community and its era.

Where it's reviewed:
Booklist, April 15, 2008, page 32
Publishers Weekly, March 17, 2008, page 46

Other books you might like:
Theresa Crane, *Molly*, 1982
Sybil Downing, *The Vote*, 2006
Fannie Flagg, *Fried Green Tomatoes at the Whistle Stop Cafe*, 1987
Diana Palmer, *The Savage Heart*, 1997
Rebecca Wells, *Divine Secrets of the Ya-Ya Sisterhood*, 1996

███ 888 ███

OWEN SHEERS

Resistance

(New York: Doubleday, 2008)

Story type: Historical/World War II; Alternate History
Subject(s): World War II; Alternate History; Resistance Movements
Major character(s): Sarah Lewis, Housewife, Young Woman; Albrecht Wolfram, Military Personnel (German officer)
Time period(s): 1940s (1944)
Locale(s): Wales

Summary: Sheers imagines a successful German invasion of Britain in 1944 in this atmospheric what-if novel. The impact of the German occupation is dramatized as it affects a small Welsh village. Left on their own after all the local men suddenly disappear, Sarah Lewis and the other women villagers must contend with the arrival of Capt. Albrecht Wolfram and his German force who settle in for the duration. During a harsh winter, both sides are forced to rely on one another in order to survive, and the novel ingeniously follows their interactions.

Where it's reviewed:
Booklist, February 1, 2008, page 28
Kirkus Reviews, November 15, 2007, page 1175
Library Journal, February 1, 2007, page 65
Publishers Weekly, October 22, 2007, page 31

Other books you might like:
Peter Ho Davies, *The Welsh Girl*, 2007
Len Deighton, *SS-GB*, 1979
Judith Saxton, *First Love*, 1993
Grace Thompson, *Waiting for Yesterday*, 2001
Jo Walton, *Ha'penny*, 2007

███ 889 ███

DIANE A.S. STUCKART

The Queen's Gambit

(New York: Berkley Prime Crime, 2008)

Story type: Historical/Renaissance; Mystery
Series: Leonardo da Vinci
Subject(s): Mystery and Detective Stories; Middle Ages

Major character(s): Leonardo da Vinci, Historical Figure, Artist; Ludovico Sforza, Ruler (of Milan), Historical Figure; Dino, Servant
Time period(s): 15th century
Locale(s): Milan, Italy

Summary: This Renaissance mystery debut features artist and inventor Leonardo da Vinci as sleuth. Ludovico Sforza, the duke of Milan, asks Leonardo to organize an elaborate live chess match to settle a dispute between the duke and the French ambassador. When the white bishop is found murdered (with the duke's knife), the duke asks Leonardo to investigate. Narrated by Dino, Leonardo's apprentice (a woman disguised as a man), the mystery provides a believable tour of 15th-century Milan and the political intrigues of the period.

Where it's reviewed:
Kirkus Reviews, November 15, 2007, page 1181
Library Journal, January 1, 2008, page 66
Publishers Weekly, November 12, 2007, page 39

Other books you might like:
Jack Dann, *The Memory Cathedral*, 1995
Karen Essex, *Leonardo's Swans*, 2006
David Hewson, *The Sacred Cut*, 2006
Cameron West, *The Medici Dagger*, 2001
Martin Woodhouse, *The Medici Guns*, 1975
    Robert Ross, co-author

███ 890 ███

FRANK TALLIS

Vienna Blood

(New York: Random House, 2008)

Story type: Mystery; Historical/Victorian
Subject(s): Mystery and Detective Stories; Psychology
Major character(s): Max Liebermann, Psychologist; Oskar Rheinhardt, Detective—Police
Time period(s): 1900s (1902)
Locale(s): Vienna, Austria

Summary: Tallis' follow-up to *A Death in Vienna* is a taut murder mystery set in 1902 Vienna in the grip of a serial killer. Viennese Det. Insp. Oskar Rheinhardt asks Freudian disciple Max Liebermann to assist in the investigation of a bizarre ritualistic killing at the Vienna zoo that is followed by the deaths of several prostitutes. It soon becomes apparent that the killer is choosing his victims to correspond with the plot of Mozart's *The Magic Flute*. Tallis, a practicing clinical psychologist, offers an atmospheric account of period Vienna and an early practitioner of his craft.

Where it's reviewed:
Booklist, November 15, 2007, page 23
Kirkus Reviews, December 1, 2007, page 1222
Publishers Weekly, November 19, 2007, page 41

Other books by the same author:
Fatal Lies, 2008
A Death in Vienna, 2005
Mortal Mischief, 2005

Historical

Other books you might like:
Ronan Bennett, *Zugzwang*, 2007
Kathryn Harrison, *Envy*, 2005
Jody Shields, *The Fig Eater*, 2000
Morris L. West, *The World Is Made of Glass*, 1983
Allen Wheelis, *The Doctor of Desire*, 1987

891

NICK TAYLOR

The Disagreement

(New York: Simon & Schuster, 2008)

Story type: Historical/American Civil War; Coming-of-Age

Subject(s): Civil War; Coming-of-Age

Major character(s): John Naro, Student (medical); Lorrie Wigfall, Gentlewoman

Time period(s): 1860s

Locale(s): Lynchburg, Virginia; Charlottesville, Virginia

Summary: This Civil War novel takes a different look at the combat from the perspective of John Naro of Lynchburg, Virginia, who, when war begins, avoids the Confederate draft by enrolling as a medical student at the University of Virginia. There he gains experience in the casualty wards and falls in love with Lorrie Wigfall. As the war proceeds, Naro grows further and further away from his family and closer to the new family he makes in the hospital wards, including his friendship with a Union officer whose life he saves.

Where it's reviewed:
Kirkus Reviews, February 1, 2008, page 114
Publishers Weekly, February 25, 2008, page 52

Other books you might like:
Geraldine Brooks, *March*, 2005
James Lee Burke, *White Doves at Morning*, 2002
Horold Coyle, *Look Away*, 1995
Jeffrey Lent, *In the Fall*, 2000
Robert Penn Warren, *Wilderness*, 1961

892

JACK TODD

Sun Going Down

(New York: Simon & Schuster, 2008)

Story type: Family Saga; Historical/Post-American Civil War

Subject(s): Family Relations; Frontier and Pioneer Life; Ranch Life

Major character(s): Ebenezar Paint, Spouse (of Cora); Cora Paint, Spouse (of Ebenezer); Eli Paint, Twin, Rancher; Ezra Paint, Twin, Cowboy

Time period(s): 19th century; 20th century (1863-1933)

Locale(s): Nebraska; Montana

Summary: This family saga follows three generations of the Paint family on the Western plains from the days of the Civil War through the 1930s. Ebenezar Paint marries the twice-widowed Cora, producing two sons, Ezra, a cowboy-turned-wanderer, and Eli who becomes a successful rancher and father to Velma, whose story carries into the Depression era. Through this generational family story the transformation of the West from frontier to the modern age is chronicled.

Where it's reviewed:
Booklist, April 15, 2008, page 35
Library Journal, February 15, 2008, page 98
Publishers Weekly, January 7, 2008, page 33

Other books you might like:
Nevada Barr, *Bittersweet*, 1984
Harold Burton, *Reservations*, 1999
Thomas Cobb, *Shavetail*, 2008
Robert Laxalt, *Time of the Rabies*, 2000
Diane Smith, *Letters from Yellowstone*, 1999

893

NICOLA UPSON

Expert in Murder

(New York: HarperCollins, 2008)

Story type: Historical/Depression Era; Mystery

Series: Josephine Tey

Subject(s): Authors and Writers; Theater

Major character(s): Josephine Tey, Historical Figure, Writer; Archie Penrose, Detective—Police

Time period(s): 1930s (1934)

Locale(s): Scotland; London, England

Summary: Upson employs the actual British mystery writer Josephine Tey as the sleuth in this period mystery. Traveling from Scotland to London, Tey learns that a young woman she has befriended on the train has been murdered. Detective Inspector Archie Penrose is convinced that the crime is connected with Tey's own play, *Richard of Bordeaux*, the surprise hit of the season. A second murder confirms that someone connected with the production is responsible, and Tey and Penrose search for clues to the killer's identity and motive.

Where it's reviewed:
Booklist, May 1, 2008, page 33
Kirkus Reviews, April 15, 2008, page 394
Publishers Weekly, April 21, 2008, page 39

Other books you might like:
David Dickinson, *Death on the Holy Mountain*, 2008
Gaylord Larsen, *Dorothy and Agatha*, 1990
Sam McCarver, *The Case of Compartment 7*, 2000
Elizabeth Peters, *The Amelia Peabody Series*, 1975-
Kathleen Tynan, *Agatha*, 1978

894

DOREEN VIRTUE

Solomon's Angels

(Carlsbad, Colorado: Hay House, 2008)

Story type: Legend; Biblical Fiction

Subject(s): Biblical Fiction; Kings, Queens, Rulers, etc.; Jews

Major character(s): Solomon, Historical Figure, Biblical
Figure; Makeda, Historical Figure, Biblical Figure
(Queen of Sheba)
Time period(s): 10th century B.C.
Locale(s): Jerusalem, Israel

Summary: This first novel chronicles the relationship
between King Solomon of Israel and Makeda, the Queen
of Sheba. Solomon is shown as a forceful and determined
leader who harnesses both worldly and unworldly powers to construct the great temple in Jerusalem. The one
thing lacking for the king is true love that is to be supplied by the Queen of Sheba.

Other books you might like:
Roberta Kells Dorr, *The Queen of Sheba*, 1996
India Edghill, *Wisdom's Daughter*, 2004
Vardis Fisher, *The Valley of Vision*, 1951
Richard Hubler, *Love and Wisdom*, 1968
Jay Williams, *Solomon and Sheba*, 1959

895

DAN VYLETA

Pavel & I

(New York: Bloomsbury, 2008)

Story type: Historical/World War II
Subject(s): World War II; City and Town Life
Major character(s): Pavel Richter, Military Personnel
(American soldier); Anders, Orphan, Streetperson;
Sonia, Prostitute
Time period(s): 1940s (1946)
Locale(s): Berlin, Germany

Summary: This atmospheric first novel is set in Berlin in
the immediate aftermath of World War II and concerns
an American soldier, Pavel Richter, who remains in
Berlin as the Cold War heats up. He is surprised by a
friend who shows up with a dead German midget. Agreeing to hide the body, Richter and his friend Anders, a
young street urchin, are soon caught up in a complex
espionage tangle as the midget turns out to be a Russian
agent with crucial documents that both sides want. One
of Richter's pursuers is the prostitute Sonia, with whom
Pavel falls in love.

Where it's reviewed:
Booklist, November 15, 2007, page 31
Kirkus Reviews, November 1, 2007, page 126
Library Journal, December 1, 2007, page 103
Publishers Weekly, September 24, 2007, page 40

Other books you might like:
Jeffery Deaver, *Garden of Beasts*, 2004
David Downing, *Zoo Station*, 2007
Pierre Frei, *Berlin*, 2006
Joseph Kanon, *The Good German*, 2001
Philip Kerr, *The One from the Other*, 2006

896

ALISON WEIR

The Lady Elizabeth

(New York: Ballantine Books, 2008)

Story type: Historical/Elizabethan; Historical/Tudor
Period
Subject(s): Kings, Queens, Rulers, etc.; Princes and
Princesses; Politics
Major character(s): Elizabeth I, Historical Figure, Ruler;
Henry VIII, Historical Figure, Ruler; Mary I, Histori-
cal Figure, Ruler
Time period(s): 16th century
Locale(s): England

Summary: Historian Weir offers a fictionalized biographical portrait of Elizabeth Tudor through her childhood
and her perilous route to the throne. Elizabeth must
survive the displeasure of her father, Henry VIII, the
distrust and animosity of her half-sister, Mary, and the
sexual advances of her stepuncle, Thomas Seymour. The
novel is skilled in creating the political intrigue of the
period and the developmental instances that prepare
Elizabeth Tudor to become Elizabeth I.

Where it's reviewed:
Booklist, April 15, 2008, page 32
Library Journal, April 15, 2008, page 77

Other books by the same author:
Innocent Traitor, 2006

Other books you might like:
Joanna Dessau, *The Red-Haired Brat*, 1978
Patricia Finney, *Gloriana's Torch*, 2003
Robin Maxwell, *Virgin: Prelude to the Throne*, 2001
Rosalind Miles, *I, Elizabeth*, 1994
Jean Plaidy, *Queen of This Realm*, 1984

897

DEBORAH WEISGALL

The World Before Her

(Boston: Houghton Mifflin, 2008)

Story type: Historical/Victorian
Subject(s): Authors and Writers; Marriage; Artists and Art
Major character(s): Marian Evans, Historical Figure (aka
George Eliot), Writer; Caroline Spingold, Artist
(sculptor); Johnnie Cross, Historical Figure, Spouse
(of Marian Evans)
Time period(s): 1880s (1880); 1980s (1980)
Locale(s): Venice, Italy

Summary: Weisgall links two marriages separated by a
century. In 1880, Marian Evans, better known as writer
George Eliot, is on her honeymoon in Venice, having
married in the last year of her life Johnnie Cross, a man
20 years her junior. Their relationship is juxtaposed with
that of sculptor Caroline Spingold in 1980, who has also
come to Venice with her older husband Malcolm. Both
stories are linked by themes of art, love, and marriage,
and are united by the magic and appeal of Venice.

Historical

Where it's reviewed:
Booklist, April 15, 2008, page 35
Kirkus Reviews, March 15, 2008, page 268
Publishers Weekly, March 3, 2008, page 29

Other books by the same author:
Still Point, 1990

Other books you might like:
Emma Donoghue, *Life Mask*, 2004
Annie Jameson, *Silhouette of Mary Ann*, 1981
Iris Johansen, *Parody of Love*, 1992
Minette Walters, *The Sculptress*, 1993
Terence DeVere White, *Johnnie Cross*, 1983

898

JENNY WHITE

The Abyssinian Proof
(New York: W.W. Norton, 2008)

Story type: Mystery; Historical/Exotic
Subject(s): Mystery and Detective Stories
Major character(s): Kamil Pasha, Government Official (magistrate), Detective
Time period(s): 19th century
Locale(s): Istanbul, Ottoman Empire

Summary: In late-19th-century Istanbul, the city magistrate, Kamil Pasha, attempts to track down the thieves who are looting Istanbul of its religious relics. Pasha is most concerned with locating one of the stolen items, a reliquary containing a secret message known as the Proof of God, which has the potential to bring about world peace. The search leads the reader on a colorful tour of Istanbul under the Ottoman Empire.

Where it's reviewed:
Booklist, February 1, 2008, page 29
Publishers Weekly, October 1, 2007, page 35

Other books by the same author:
The Sultan's Seal, 2006

Other books you might like:
Jason Goodwin, *The Snake Stone*, 2007
Frances Kazan, *Halide's Gift*, 2001
Susan Moody, *Mosaic*, 1991
Barbara Nadel, *Belshazzar's Daughter*, 2004
Orhan Pamuk, *My Name Is Red*, 2001

899

GENE WILDER

The Woman Who Wouldn't
(New York: St. Martin's Press, 2008)

Story type: Historical/Edwardian
Subject(s): Music and Musicians; Hospitals; Women
Major character(s): Jeremy Spencer Webb, Musician (violinist); Anton Chekhov, Historical Figure, Writer; Clara Mulpas, Patient
Time period(s): 1900s (1903)
Locale(s): Badenweiler, Germany

Summary: Wilder's second novel concerns British concert violinist Jeremy Spencer Webb whose breakdown during a performance sends him to a German health resort to recover. There he meets Russian writer Anton Chekhov and a beautiful but elusive young woman, Clara Mulpas. Webb becomes fascinated with Clara and tries to uncover her background to explain her resistance to his charms.

Where it's reviewed:
Kirkus Reviews, December 15, 2007, page 1265
Publishers Weekly, November 26, 2007, page 24

Other books by the same author:
My French Whore, 2007

Other books you might like:
Andrea Barrett, *The Air We Breathe*, 2007
Myla Goldberg, *Wickett's Remedy*, 2005
Janice Graham, *Firebird*, 1998
Richard Rayner, *The Cloud Sketcher*, 2001
Pamela Thompson, *Every Past Thing We Do*, 2007

900

NIALL WILLIAMS

John
(New York: Bloomsbury, 2008)

Story type: Historical/Ancient Rome; Biblical Fiction
Subject(s): Biblical Fiction; Religious Life; Biography
Major character(s): John, Historical Figure, Biblical Figure
Time period(s): 1st century
Locale(s): Patmos, Greece

Summary: Williams chronicles the last days of the Apostle John, the author of the apocalyptic book of Revelation as well as the Gospel and Epistles of John. Blind and nearly 100 years old, John lives banished on the Greek island of Patmos and recalls his time with Jesus and the years following, including the contested reception of the Christian message.

Where it's reviewed:
Booklist, December 15, 2007, page 25
Publishers Weekly, November 12, 2007, page 36

Other books by the same author:
The Fall of Light, 2002
As It Is in Heaven, 1999
Four Letters of Love, 1997

Other books you might like:
Taylor Caldwell, *Great Lion of God*, 1970
Lloyd Douglas, *The Big Fisherman*, 1948
John Hagee, *Devil's Island*, 2001
Tim LaHaye, *John's Story*, 2006
Ellen G. Traylor, *John, Son of Thunder*, 1979

901

LAUREN WILLIG

The Seduction of the Crimson Rose
(New York: Dutton, 2008)

Story type: Historical/Napoleonic Wars; Espionage Thriller

Series: Pink Carnation. Book 4
Subject(s): Espionage; Adventure and Adventurers
Major character(s): Mary Alsworthy, Spy; Eloise Kelly, Student—Graduate; Lord Vaughan, Nobleman
Time period(s): 1800s

Summary: Graduate student Eloise Kelly continues her research to expose the spy network operated by the Frenchman named the Black Tulip during the Napoleonic era. The focus here is on Mary Alsworthy who accepts the assignment from spymaster Lord Vaughan to try to expose the Black Tulip. In exchange Mary will be given the means to find a husband and recoup her fortune. Amidst the threat from the Black Tulip, romantic sparks begin to fly between Mary and Vaughan.

Where it's reviewed:
Booklist, January 1, 2008, page 46
Kirkus Reviews, November 15, 2007, page 1177
Library Journal, December 1, 2007, page 103
Publishers Weekly, November 26, 2007, page 27

Other books by the same author:
The Deception of the Emerald Ring, 2006
The Masque of the Black Tulip, 2006
The Secret History of the Pink Carnation, 2005

Other books you might like:
Evelyn Anthony, *The Defector*, 1981
T.F. Banks, *The Thief-Taker*, 2002
Dorothy Gilman, *Mrs. Polifax Unveiled*, 2000
Tracy Grant, *Daughter of the Game*, 2002
Neal Stephenson, *The Confusion*, 2004

902

BUDGE WILSON

Before Green Gables

(New York: Putnam, 2008)

Story type: Historical/Victorian; Coming-of-Age
Subject(s): Orphans; Family Life
Major character(s): Anne Shirley, Orphan
Time period(s): 1890s
Locale(s): Canada

Summary: On the 100th anniversary of the publication of L. M. Montgomery's classic *Anne of Green Gables*, Budge offers a prequel depicting plucky Anne Shirley's life as an orphan before arriving at Avonlea and Green Gables. When both of her parents die during an epidemic when Anne is three months old, she becomes a ward of the Thomas family where she must endure poverty, hardship, and occasional violence. Through it all, Anne's characteristic optimism emerges.

Where it's reviewed:
Booklist, March 15, 2008, page 25
Kirkus Reviews, February 15, 2008, page 171

Other books by the same author:
The Long Wait, 1997
Mothers and Other Strangers, 1996
The Leaving and Other Stories, 1992

Other books you might like:
Margaret Wander Bonanno, *Ember Days*, 1980
Wayne Johnston, *The Colony of Unrequited Dreams*, 1999
Robert MacNeil, *Burden of Desire*, 1992
Alison McLeay, *Passage Home*, 1990
L.M. Montgomery, *Anne of Green Gables*, 1908

903

JACQUELINE WINSPEAR

An Incomplete Revenge

(New York: Henry Holt, 2008)

Story type: Mystery; Historical/World War I
Series: Maisie Dobbs. Book 5
Subject(s): Mystery and Detective Stories; World War I
Major character(s): Maisie Dobbs, Detective—Private
Time period(s): 1930s (1931)
Locale(s): Kent, England

Summary: In this installment of Winspear's period mystery series drawing on the consequences of World War I, the psychologist and sleuth Maisie Dobbs investigates strange goings-on in the Kentish hamlet of Heronsdene. Maisie sets out to learn the secret that the villagers are keeping involving a zeppelin raid during the war that killed a local family.

Where it's reviewed:
Booklist, December 1, 2007, page 26
Kirkus Reviews, November 15, 2007, page 1182
Library Journal, January 1, 2008, page 69
Publishers Weekly, November 26, 2007, page 31

Other books by the same author:
Messenger of Truth, 2006
Pardonable Lies, 2005
Birds of a Feather, 2004
Maisie Dobbs, 2003

Other books you might like:
John Boyne, *Next of Kin*, 2008
Laurie R. King, *Touchstone*, 2008
Fidelis Morgan, *Unnatural Fire*, 2000
David Roberts, *The Bones of the Buried*, 2001
Charles Todd, *A Pale Horse*, 2008

904

STUART WOODS

Beverly Hills Dead

(New York: G. P. Putnam's Sons, 2008)

Story type: Mystery
Subject(s): Mystery and Detective Stories; Movie Industry
Major character(s): Rick Barron, Detective—Police (former), Businessman (movie executive); Sid Brook, Writer
Time period(s): 1940s

Historical

Locale(s): Hollywood, California

Summary: This sequel to *The Prince of Beverly Hills* has former L.A. detective Rick Barron working as a movie studio's head of production during the late 1940s. Trouble comes in the form of a threat by the House Un-American Activities Committee who subpoena Rick's friend, screenwriter Sid Brook. A star who disappears adds to Rick's problems, as does evidence that suggests that his wife is a member of the Communist Party. Period Hollywood during the blacklist era is the focus here.

Where it's reviewed:
Booklist, November 1, 2007, page 15
Kirkus Reviews, November 1, 2007, page 1127
Publishers Weekly, November 5, 2007, page 43

Other books by the same author:
Reckless Abandon, 2004
The Prince of Beverly Hills, 2004
Capital Crimes, 2003
Dirty Work, 2003
Blood Orchid, 2002

Other books you might like:
Stephen J. Cannell, *Riding the Snake*, 1998
Jennifer Colt, *The Butcher of Beverly Hills*, 2005
Leslie Epstein, *Pandaemonium*, 1997
Stuart M. Kaminsky, *A Few Minutes Past Midnight*, 2001
C.J. Songer, *Bait*, 1998

905

SARA YOUNG
My Enemy's Cradle
(Orlando, FL: Harcourt, 2008)

Story type: Historical/World War II
Subject(s): World War II; Jews; Hospitals
Major character(s): Cyrla, Young Woman
Time period(s): 1940s
Locale(s): Netherlands

Summary: This adult novel debut by children's book writer Young tells the story of Cyrla, a half-Jewish young woman, who, to survive in World War II-era Europe assumes the identity of a pregnant cousin and enters a *Lebensborn*, a birthing center for Aryan children run by the Nazis. The novel explores this aspect of Nazi policy in which mothers-to-be received proper care until their children were taken from them for adoption by proper Aryan families.

Where it's reviewed:
Booklist, January 1, 2008, page 27
Library Journal, October 1, 2007, page 66
Publishers Weekly, October 1, 2007, page 37

Other books you might like:
A.L Kennedy, *Day*, 2008
Richard A. Lourie, *Hatred of Tulips*, 2007
Harry Mulisch, *The Assault*, 1986
Caryl Phillips, *The Nature of Blood*, 1997
John Updike, *Seek My Face*, 2002

Inspirational Fiction in 2008
by
Melissa Hudak

Inspirational fiction can be a fairly static. Very little that is radical or different ever appears in this genre. Despite this limitation, readers continue to flock to and, well, find inspiration in these titles. As with other genres, the subgenres remain ever constant, including various "lits", historicals, mystery and suspense, along with occasionally more distinctive titles that make the genre a bit more appealing to the average reader.

Several years ago, when chick lit hit the scene, inspirational fiction publishers entered into the fray, but they couldn't stay with the usual chick lit topics of women serially dating and bedding men. Inspirational readers rarely find such topics acceptable and the publishers know that. Instead, the "lits" of inspirational fiction tend to focus on women finding their way towards Christ or finding a Christian man to love. Many inspirational fiction lits also feature older or married women and emphasize female bonding.

Melody Carlson has written a few entries in the chick lit subgenre, and she had two fine titles this year. *A Mile in My Flip-Flops* is cute and a little silly, with an appealing heroine in amateur house-flipper Gretchen Hanover, who may have watched more television than is good for her when she decides that she too can refab a house and make a huge profit like the people on TV. In this title, Carlson roughly sticks to the tried and true of inspirational fiction chick lit, with pretty Gretchen finding her man in the end.

Carlson's other title is a bit more daring, with a culturally diverse cast of characters who care about more than the typical shoes and shopping. In *I Heart Bloomberg* Kendall Weis is pretty much a shoes and shopping sort of gal, but she is also a girl with a mission: to live on her own without having to get a job.

Getting the use of her grandmother's house for free, she comes up with a scheme that will keep her out of the workforce. She gets three roommates, thinking that their rent checks will support her in the style she believes she deserves. Kendall isn't what you would call a likable character. She is shallow, selfish, and not particularly pleasant, but she is certainly real. With many inspirational fiction characters still fairly one-dimensional, it is always nice to come across characters who don't conform to the normal standards of "pretty and perfect." Adding to the interest of *I Heart Bloomberg* is the diversity. In this case, the diversity comes with two of Kendall's roommates, one of whom is Hispanic and the other half Hawaiian.

Diversity is still rare in inspirational fiction. One of the only, if not *the* only, lead Asian character in inspirational fiction was introduced in 2007 by author Camy Tang in her "Sushi" series. While this hasn't led to an influx of other Asian characters, Tang is still writing her highly appealing series. This year's entry is *Single Sashimi*, which features video game developer Venus Chau. If the plot of the book isn't particularly groundbreaking, it is great to see a non-white character in a well-written and entertaining series. Hopefully Tang has a long future as a writer and may open the doors for other Asian writers in this genre.

Because of its special readership, inspirational fiction "lits" go beyond the young, single chick lit protagonist and bring in older characters, or married characters, or sometimes a combination of ages. Such is the case with Beth Pattillo's *The Sweetgum Knit Lit Society*. Librarian Eugenie Pierce isn't going to see twenty again, or even thirty, but she is still the driving force in the book. Determined to help troubled teen Hannah Simmons, she vaguely blackmails the girl (who had been caught vandalizing a library book) into joining her group of knitters/book enthusiasts at their club in a Sweetgum, Tennessee church. The group of women ranges in age, and Pattillo does a fine job of portraying all of her characters in a realistic and often moving way.

Although the lits have proved to be very popular in inspirational fiction, one subgenre that continually struggles for attention is that of the mystery/thriller. Few breakout writers have achieved success in this field, which continues to be an afterthought in the industry.

One writer who has had numerous successes with her mysteries is Colleen Coble, who took a break from her "Rock Harbor" series to write a thriller set in Amish

country. *Anathema* is the story of a young woman named Hannah Schwartz, who returns to her Amish roots to try to find her parents' killer. An anathema is an outcast, and that is exactly what Hannah is. Shunned by her Amish community, she finds it difficult to pursue justice when most of her old friends and family refuse to even speak to her. The book gives a different portrait of Amish life, one that reveals the often harsh cruelty that the religion inflicts on those who have strayed from the path. Since most inspirational fiction titles that portray the Amish tend toward a more gentle view, *Anathema* is intriguing for its startlingly harsh depictions.

Male writers of inspirational thrillers tend to be a little more successful than their female counterparts, although their books often move away from the gentle viewpoints that publishers seem to prefer. Case in point is Ted Dekker, an astoundingly successful writer, and one whose success is well deserved.

His latest book is called *Adam*, and it is an unflinching yet still strangely uplifting book about one man's search for an evil serial killer. Daniel Clark is an FBI behavior psychologist on the track of a brutal serial killer named Eve. Daniel gets a little too close to finding Eve, and ends up almost becoming one of the killer's victims. Dekker never shies away from violence and the often brutal realities of life, and this book is no different. With books closer to mainstream thrillers than cozy mysteries, Ted Dekker is quickly becoming inspirational fiction's answer to James Patterson.

However, cozies do still tend to predominate the inspirational mystery title list. In fact, Barbour Publishing recently launched a new line of titles specifically aimed towards the reader of cozy mysteries. Available mainly through an online/mail book club, the series offers titles that readers should find enjoyable. Barbour is aiming for clean and wholesome, and the titles included in this section certainly reflect that.

Susan Page Davis is a multi-published inspirational fiction writer, and she teamed up with her daughter Megan Elaine Davis to write *Homicide at Blue Heron*, the first in the "Mainely Murder" series. Nancy Mehl chose Kansas as the setting of *In the Dead of Winter*. Both books feature feisty heroines, small towns, and a hint of romance to go along with the mystery. While there is nothing revolutionary in these books, that will certainly be fine with their target audience, who want nothing more than a nice, clean mystery, which these books deliver in spades.

As to revolutionary, it used to be that if you said the phrase "historical fiction" in an inspirational bookstore, that meant the book would be set in the post Civil War years in the American West. There was some variation of course, but the majority of inspirational fiction historicals tended mimic aspects of the Western genre. That has changed drastically over the past few years, and now those titles are the rarities. Taking their place are a wider range of settings and eras.

Showing an intriguing differential are three titles featuring famous women of history. Nancy Moser began a series called the Ladies of History in 2006 with a title about Mozart's lesser known sister. She followed that up with everybody's favorite literary lady Jane Austen in 2007, and returns this year with an uneven portrait of Martha Washington in *Washington's Lady*.

Because Martha Washington is a fairly unknown figure, it would be difficult for a fiction writer to easily pin her down. While Moser rarely has a misfire, Martha doesn't really come alive in this title. However, readers would probably still find the book interesting thanks to Moser's eye for historical detail, and an interesting cast of supporting characters.

Conversely, everybody seems to know all there is to know about Anne Boleyn, but readers might end up going to the non-fiction shelves for a couple of biographies after reading Ginger Garrett's *In the Shadow of Lions*. While Anne Boleyn is usually portrayed as a schemer, often a sexually promiscuous one, in Garrett's book she is shown as a devout woman trying to bring the Bible to all. Readers can decide for themselves which Anne Boleyn they think is the real one, which is the true fun of biographical historical fiction.

One true standout this year in historical fiction is Ann H. Gabhart's *The Outsider*, which depicts a religious sect that was once popular but has now largely disappeared. The Shakers were an intensely devout (and celibate) group that began in the East and spread rapidly to the Midwest. One Shaker colony that can still be visited today, although no Shakers live there any longer, is that of Pleasant Hill in Kentucky. *The Outsider* is set at Pleasant Hill and features young Shaker sister Gabrielle Hope, who is dedicated to her faith, but can't help but wonder what the outside world might offer her. This is a captivating portrait of a woman fighting for her faith, while trying to find an elusive happiness. It is highly recommended.

Also recommended are some oddities that popped up in the inspirational fiction world this year, both written by new authors. Both also present unique points of view and are humorous, albeit in very different ways.

Michael Snyder's *My Name is Russell Fink* is quirky and odd and not your usual male-oriented Christian fiction title. Russell Fink is a copier salesman who doesn't like anything about his life. He might be described as a loser, if he wasn't so sympathetic. When Russell's basset hound, Sonny, dies under mysterious circumstances, Russell decides to find out what happened to his dog. Along the way, he has a few adventures, and manages to straighten his life out a bit.

Most readers would probably enjoy Russell's misadventures, but many readers might find Rob Stennett's *The Almost True Story of Ryan* a little off-putting. It is a satire, and satire is incredibly rare in inspirational fiction. Some readers may, in fact, be offended by the satirical tone of this book.

However, for readers willing to give it a chance, there are rewards at the end. The book follows real estate

agent Ryan Fisher who transforms himself into a Christian via placing a "Jesus fish" in his advertising, and by attending a few church services to pick up clients. Somehow he finds himself starting his own megachurch and becoming a spiritual leader. Thought-provoking and often bitingly humorous, this book isn't for everybody, but it will probably earn Stennett quite a few fans.

Another oddity of a book is Lisa Samson's *Embrace Me*, which is most likely the only inspirational fiction book set in the world of sideshow freaks. Valentine and Lella have deformities that set them apart from the world at large, but that doesn't mean they aren't normal women. Unfortunately, life isn't kind to them, and probably never will be. Samson never takes the easy route, and her books can be a challenge to readers. However, they are usually a challenge worth taking, and this book is no different. It will probably cause more than one reader to flinch at its honesty, but it is a brilliant book with a cast of fascinating characters.

Recommended Titles

Adam by Ted Dekker

The Almost True Story of Ryan Fisher by Rob Stennett

Anathema by Colleen Coble

Blue Hole Back Home by Joy Jordan-Lake

Embrace Me by Lisa Samson

My Name is Russell Fink by Michael Snyder

The Outsider by Ann H. Gabhart

Single Sashimi by Camy Tang

Summer Snow by Nicole Baart

The Sweetgum Knit Lit Society by Beth Pattillo

Tuesday Night at the Blue Moon by Debbie Fuller Thomas

Inspirational Titles

906

GINNY AIKEN

A Cut Above

(Grand Rapids, Michigan: Fleming H. Revell, 2008)

Story type: Contemporary
Series: Shop-Til-U-Drop. Book 3
Subject(s): Shopping; Travel
Major character(s): Andie Adams, Television Personality;
    Max Matthews, Television Personality
Time period(s): 2000s
Locale(s): Colombia

Summary: Gemologist and home shopping network personality Andie Adams is thrilled to receive yet another buying assignment. This time she is to travel to Colombia, and purchase some emeralds for the network. Even better, she is going alone. Thinking her trip will be short and sweet without the hassles of dragging along a crew and her useless co-anchor Max, Andie lands in Colombia, where everything immediately goes awry. Her guide doesn't show up, her Spanish is lackluster at best, and she finds herself at the mercy of a rogue taxi driver. Suddenly America and Max are looking better and better, and when Max shows up, Andie is faced with the realization that he just might mean more to her than she thought.

Other books by the same author:
A Steal of a Deal, 2008
Priced to Move, 2007
Decorating Schemes, 2006
Interior Motives, 2006
Married to the Mob, 2006

Other books you might like:
Kristin Billerbeck, *The Ashley Stockingdale Series*,
    2004-
Colleen Coble, *The Aloha Reef Series*, 2005-
Robin Jones Gunn, *The Sisterchicks Series*, 2003-
Camy Tang, *The Sushi Series*, 2007-
Linda Windsor, *Not Exactly Eden*, 2000

907

TAMERA ALEXANDER

From a Distance

(Minneapolis: Bethany House, 2008)

Story type: Historical
Series: Timber Ridge Reflections. Book 1
Subject(s): Illness; Murder; Photography
Major character(s): Elizabeth Westbrook, Photographer;
    Daniel Ranslett, Military Personnel (former
    sharpshooter)
Time period(s): 1870s
Locale(s): Timber Ridge, Colorado

Summary: Suffering from a mysterious debilitating illness, photographer Elizabeth Westbrook ventures west to document life in the Colorado Territory, and hopefully regain her health at the same time. Though female photographers are rare in the 1870s, Elizabeth is determined to let neither her sex or her bad health keep her from her dreams. When Elizabeth inadvertently takes a picture that ends up as evidence in a murder case, she finds that her life is in danger, and former Confederate sharpshooter Daniel Ranslett feels compelled to put aside his solitary life in order to protect her.

Other books by the same author:
Remembered, 2007
Rekindled, 2006
Revealed, 2006

Other books you might like:
Stephen Bly, *Miss Fontenot*, 1999
Molly Noble Bull, *The Winter Pearl*, 2004
Kristen Heitzmann, *The Rocky Mountain Legacy Series*,
    1998-
Kathleen Morgan, *The Brides of Culdee Creek Series*,
    1999-
Lori Wick, *The Rocky Mountain Memories Series*,
    1996-

908

NICOLE BAART

Summer Snow

(Carol Stream, Illinois: Tyndale House, 2008)

Story type: Contemporary
Subject(s): Grandmothers; Mothers and Daughters; Pregnancy
Major character(s): Julia DeSmit, Worker (grocery store)
Time period(s): 2000s
Locale(s): Mason, South Dakota
Summary: Young Julia DeSmit is just barely out of high school, pregnant, and, except for her beloved grandmother, alone. With her life about to change drastically, Julia gets a minimum wage job at a grocery store and hopes it will be enough to get by. Then her mother, who she hasn't seen for ten years, comes back to town. Julia isn't thrilled to see the woman who abandoned her as a child, and doesn't want a reconciliation. She needs help though, and as her mother seems willing to make amends, Julia begins to soften. Sequel to *After the Leaves Fall*.

Other books by the same author:
After the Leaves Fall, 2007

Other books you might like:
Deborah Bedford, *A Rose by the Door*, 2001
Brandilyn Collins, *Capture the Wind for Me*, 2003
Denise Hunter, *Saving Grace*, 2005
Sally John, *Castles in the Sand*, 2006
Elizabeth Musser, *The Dwelling Place*, 2005
Catherine Palmer, *The Happy Room*, 2002

909

ELAINE BARBIERI

The Redemption of Jake Scully

(New York: Steeple Hill, 2008)

Story type: Historical/American West; Romance
Subject(s): Redemption
Major character(s): Lacey Stewart, Young Woman; Jake Scully, Saloon Keeper/Owner
Time period(s): 1880s
Locale(s): Weaver, Arizona
Summary: Born in a wild western town, Lacey Stewart was sent east by her "Uncle Scully" to go to finishing school, an attempt to save her from the savagery of the west. Now grown, Lacey has decided to return to Arizona and care for her "aged" benefactor. Little does she know that Jake Scully is still a young man, and a very handsome one. He is still determined to keep her from the ways of the west though, and Jake wants her to return to civilization. All Lacey wants is to be with Jake, and she is determined to make that happen.

Other books by the same author:
Cry of the Wolf, 2008
Night of the Wolf, 2007
Sign of the Wolf, 2007
Hawk's Passion, 2006
Hawk's Prize, 2006

Other books you might like:
Rosanne Bittner, *Walk by Faith*, 2005
Lori Copeland, *Yellow Rose Bride*, 2006
Sharon Gillenwater, *Twice Blessed*, 2004
Valerie Hansen, *Frontier Courtship*, 2008
Jillian Hart, *Homespun Bride*, 2008

910

JAMES SCOTT BELL

Try Darkness

(New York: Center Street, 2008)

Story type: Mystery
Series: Ty Buchanan. Book 2
Subject(s): Children; Law; Legal Thriller
Major character(s): Ty Buchanan, Lawyer
Time period(s): 2000s
Locale(s): Los Angeles, California
Summary: Ty Buchanan was once a rising attorney, eager to take on cases involving powerful clients and big money. However, a false accusation of murder and the death of his fiancee have left Ty considering the things that really matter in life. No longer wanting the big money legal cases, Ty now concentrates on providing legal services to the poor and disenfranchised, working out of a makeshift office in a coffee shop. Visited by a young mother who is about to be evicted from a hotel for transients, Ty takes her case, even though it means going up against one of his former colleagues. Then the mother turns up murdered, and Ty is suddenly faced with saving her daughter from a killer.

Other books by the same author:
The Whole Truth, 2008
No Legal Grounds, 2007
Try Dying, 2007
Presumed Guilty, 2006
Sins of the Fathers, 2005

Other books you might like:
T. Davis Bunn, *The Great Divide*, 2000
Joe Hilley, *The Mike Connolly Series*, 2004-
Craig Parshall, *The Chambers of Justice Series*, 2002-
Randy Singer, *Directed Verdict*, 2002
Robert Whitlow, *The Santee Series*, 2003-

911

TERRI BLACKSTOCK

Dawn's Light

(Grand Rapids, Michigan: Zondervan, 2008)

Story type: Futuristic
Series: Restoration. Book 4
Subject(s): Survival
Major character(s): Deni Branning, Survivor; Beth Branning, Teenager
Time period(s): Indeterminate Future
Locale(s): Birmingham, Alabama
Summary: A mysterious blackout affecting the entire world

has made the planet regress to a time before civilization. Without power of any sort, many people reverted to savagery and evil. The Branning family has tried to remain true to their Christian beliefs, but it hasn't been easy. With the end of the electrical outage finally in sight, daughter Deni Branning is facing more questions, this time of a romantic nature, as she tries to decide who she wants to spend her life with.

Other books by the same author:
True Light, 2007
Night Light, 2006
Breaker's Reef, 2005
Last Light, 2005
River's Edge, 2004

Other books you might like:
Larry Burkett, *Solar Flare*, 1997
Ted Dekker, *The Color Trilogy*, 2004-
Alton Gansky, *Dark Moon*, 2002
Jerry B. Jenkins, *The Underground Zealot Series*, 2003-
Jim Kraus, *The Silence*, 2004
James R. Lucas, *A Perfect Persecution*, 2001

912

SIGMUND BROUWER

Broken Angel

(Colorado Springs, Colorado: WaterBrook, 2008)

Story type: Futuristic
Subject(s): Future; Futuristic Fiction
Major character(s): Caitlyn, Fugitive
Time period(s): Indeterminate Future
Locale(s): United States

Summary: In the distant future, the Unites States has become a Christian dystopia, a land where controlling fundamentalists run the country and will allow no dissention. Young Caitlin has been born with severe deformities. Because of this, the fundamentalists demand that she should die. Instead, her father sends her out into the world to try to escape to the "Outside." She finds two friends who help her, and they are aided along their way by a makeshift group of people determined to find freedom at any cost.

Where it's reviewed:
Publishers Weekly, March 24, 2008, page 54

Other books by the same author:
The Lies of Saints, 2003
Crown of Thorns, 2002
The Leper, 2002
Out of the Shadows, 2001
Evening Star, 2000

Other books you might like:
Karen Hancock, *The Legends of the Guardian King Series*, 2003-
Jerry B. Jenkins, *The Underground Zealot Series*, 2003-
Jim Kraus, *The Silence*, 2004
James R. Lucas, *A Perfect Persecution*, 2001
Kathy Tyers, *The Firebird Trilogy*, 1999-

913

DON BROWN

The Black Sea Affair

(Grand Rapids, Michigan: Zondervan, 2008)

Story type: Action/Adventure
Series: Navy Justice. Book 4
Subject(s): Submarines; Terrorism
Major character(s): Zack Brewer, Military Personnel (Lawyer), JAG officer; Pete Miranda, Military Personnel (submarine captain)
Time period(s): 2000s
Locale(s): At Sea; United States; Russia

Summary: An important Russian shipment of plutonium has been waylaid by terrorists. Russia will do anything to get the plutonium back, even declare war on Chechnya. As the tension between Russia and Chechnya builds, the United States learns that the shipment is actually on a Russian freighter somewhere in the Black Sea. Then a submarine accident brings Pete Miranda and his crew into the brewing trouble, as they are taken before a military court in Moscow. JAG officer Zack Brewer goes to Russia to defend Miranda and his crew, and soon finds himself deep in an incident that may lead to war.

Other books by the same author:
Defiance, 2007
Hostage, 2005
Treason, 2005

Other books you might like:
Susan Page Davis, *Frasier Island*, 2007
Alton Gansky, *A Ship Possessed*, 1999
Dee Henderson, *The Uncommon Heroes Series*, 2000-
Paul T. McHenry, *Code Name—Antidote*, 2000
Mel Odom, *The NCIS Series*, 2006-

914

WANDA E. BRUNSTETTER

White Christmas Pie

(Uhrichsville, Ohio: Barbour, 2008)

Story type: Romance
Subject(s): Abuse; Amish; Christmas
Major character(s): Will Henderson, Fiance(e) (Amish), Adoptee; Karen Yoder, Fiance(e) (Amish); Frank Henderson, Parent
Time period(s): 2000s
Locale(s): United States

Summary: Will Henderson and Karen Yoder have become engaged, and should be happy. Unfortunately, Will cannot forget that he was abandoned by his birth father and placed with an Amish couple to be raised. He is bitter about his childhood, and although he was lovingly raised by his adoptive parents, he cannot let go of the past. Karen deeply loves her fiance but isn't certain she can cope with being married to a man with so many insecurities. When Will's birth father Frank shows up, hoping for a reconciliation with his son, Will is distraught and Karen finds herself even more unable to deal with

her fiance's troubles. She turns to her former boyfriend for advice, which only makes the situation more volatile.

Other books by the same author:
A Sister's Hope, 2008
Allison's Journey, 2008
A Sister's Test, 2008
A Sister's Secret, 2007
Going Home, 2007

Other books you might like:
Carrie Bender, *The Dora's Diary Series*, 1999-
Colleen Coble, *Anathema*, 2008
Dudley J. Delffs, *The Father Grif Series*, 1998-
Beverly Lewis, *The Courtship of Nellie Fisher Series*, 2007-
Gayle Roper, *The Document*, 2008

915

DAVIS BUNN

Full Circle

(Nashville: Thomas Nelson, 2008)

Story type: Contemporary
Subject(s): Employment; Illness; Travel
Major character(s): Adam Wright, Financier (financial analyst); Kayla Austin, Religious (missionary)
Time period(s): 2000s
Locale(s): Oxford, England

Summary: With his mother gravely ill, Adam Wright isn't too enthusiastic about accepting a job that will take him away from her, and all the way to Oxford, England. However, Oxford Ventures is a company that desperately needs help, and Adam needs a job, so he agrees to attempt to turn the company around. When he meets Kayla Austin, the missionary daughter of his boss, Adam is intrigued. For her part, Kayla is more interested in getting the funds to keep her African relief project afloat than in romance. Soon though, they begin to realize that they are kindred spirits.

Other books by the same author:
All through the Night, 2008
My Soul to Keep, 2007
Heartland, 2006
Imposter, 2006
The Lazarus Trap, 2005

Other books you might like:
Terri Blackstock, *Emerald Windows*, 2001
David Gregory, *Dinner with a Perfect Stranger*, 2005
Kristen Heitzmann, *The Still of Night*, 2003
Denise Hunter, *Mending Places*, 2004
Maureen Lang, *The Oak Leaves*, 2007
Lisa Samson, *Tiger Lillie*, 2004

916

SANDRA BYRD

Bon Appetit

(Colorado Springs, Colorado: WaterBrook, 2008)

Story type: Contemporary
Series: French Twist. Book 2
Subject(s): Cooks and Cooking; Travel
Major character(s): Lexi Stuart, Student, Baker
Time period(s): 2000s
Locale(s): France

Summary: With her career and life going nowhere in Seattle, Lexi Stuart packs up and moves to France. She hopes to gain some culinary knowledge that will help her transform her love of baking into a career. Settling in isn't all that easy, but once settled, Lexi discovers she loves France and its people. After pursuing her quest for the perfect pastry for awhile, Lexi begins to wonder if she wants to go back to Seattle, or if France may become her new home.

Other books by the same author:
Let Them Eat Cake, 2007

Other books you might like:
Kristin Billerbeck, *The Ashley Stockingdale Series*, 2004-
Melody Carlson, *The 86 Bloomberg Place Series*, 2008-
Robin Jones Gunn, *Sisterchicks Say Ooh La La!*, 2005
Allie Pleiter, *My So-Called Love Life*, 2006
Camy Tang, *The Sushi Series*, 2007-

917

MELODY CARLSON

I Heart Bloomberg

(Colorado Springs, Colorado: David C. Cook, 2008)

Story type: Contemporary
Series: 86 Bloomberg Place. Book 1
Subject(s): Friendship
Major character(s): Kendall Weis, Landlord; Megan Abernathy, Interior Decorator (assistant); Anna Mendez, Editor
Time period(s): 2000s
Locale(s): Portland, Oregon

Summary: Kendall Weis thinks she has found the perfect way to avoid work. Instead of getting a job, she convinces her grandmother to let her live in her Portland, Oregon, house and, to pay the bills, Kendall advertises for roommates. She portrays the house as exclusive and luxurious, but it might be better described as a fixer-upper. Still, she manages to find three roommates, Megan, Anna, and Lelani, all of whom have their own reasons for wanting to get out of their current living arrangements. The girls aren't thrilled at Kendall's optimistic description of the house, however, and are soon threatening to leave unless changes are made.

Other books by the same author:
A Mile in My Flip-Flops, 2008
All I Have to Give, 2008
An Irish Christmas, 2007
These Boots Weren't Made for Walking, 2007
Ready to Wed, 2007

Other books you might like:
Judy Baer, *Norah's Ark*, 2006
Kristin Billerbeck, *The Spa Girls Series*, 2005-
Terri Kraus, *The Renovation*, 2008
Camy Tang, *The Sushi Series*, 2007-
Susan May Warren, *Happily Ever After*, 2003

918

MELODY CARLSON

A Mile in My Flip-Flops

(Colorado Springs, Colorado: WaterBrook, 2008)

Story type: Romance
Subject(s): Construction
Major character(s): Gretchen Hanover, Teacher (kindergarten); Noah Campbell, Carpenter
Time period(s): 2000s
Locale(s): El Ocaso, California

Summary: After kindergarten teacher Gretchen Hanover is dumped by her fiance, less than a month before the wedding, she becomes obsessed with redecorating shows on TV. Deciding that what she needs to fix her shattered life is a huge project, she decides to become a house flipper. After all, it seems so easy on TV. Unfortunately, real life proves to be more challenging than TV life. Her plan had been to buy a fixer-upper, renovate it with her father's help, then resell it at a profit so she can buy a house for herself. Unfortunately, the problems start to pile up quickly. The house she buys needs more work than she can devote to it and her retired father seems more intent on urging Gretchen to work with his carpenter friend Noah Campbell than helping his daughter. As Gretchen begins to work with Noah, though, she suddenly starts to forget about her former fiance.

Other books by the same author:
All I Have to Give, 2008
I Heart Bloomberg, 2008
An Irish Christmas, 2007
These Boots Weren't Made for Walking, 2007
Ready to Wed, 2007

Other books you might like:
Sharon Hinck, *Renovating Becky Miller*, 2007
Diann Hunt, *Hearts under Construction*, 2005
David Ryan Long, *Quinlin's Estate*, 2002
Susan May Warren, *Happily Ever After*, 2003
Linda Windsor, *Fiesta Moon*, 2005

919

JULIE CAROBINI

Truffles by the Sea

(Minneapolis: Bethany House, 2008)

Story type: Contemporary
Subject(s): Beaches; Conduct of Life
Major character(s): Gaby Flores, Store Owner (flower shop owner)
Time period(s): 2000s
Locale(s): California

Summary: When the apartment building Gaby Flores lives in burns down, she decides it is a sign for her to restart her life. Intent on focusing on her business, a small floral shop, and not her love life, Gaby does her best to keep her promise to herself to put men on hold for awhile. However, as often happens, once she has decided that her love life has to take second place to the other aspects of her life, she soon has not one but two men interested in her. Unfortunately, problems continue to plague Gaby. Her business is on shaky ground, she is hit with a lawsuit, and she finds the men in her life as confusing as ever. In the middle of all her troubles, she soon finds herself having to make some romantic decisions, and Gaby is unsure of what path she wants her life to take. Sequel to *Chocolate Beach*.

Other books by the same author:
Chocolate Beach, 2007

Other books you might like:
Judy Baer, *Be My Neat-Heart*, 2006
Kristin Billerbeck, *The Ashley Stockingdale Series*, 2004-
Robin Jones Gunn, *The Sisterchicks Series*, 2003-
Allie Pleiter, *My So-Called Love Life*, 2006
Camy Tang, *The Sushi Series*, 2007-

920

ROBIN CAROLL

Bayou Paradox

(New York: Steeple Hill, 2008)

Story type: Mystery; Romance
Series: Bayou. Book 4
Subject(s): Healing
Major character(s): Tara LeBlanc, Healer; Rene "Bubba" Theriot, Police Officer (sheriff)
Time period(s): 2000s
Locale(s): Lagniappe, Louisiana

Summary: Something strange is going on in Lagniappe, Louisiana. Deep in the bayou, the people should be able to live as they please without cares or worries. Then two elderly women are found unconscious for no apparent reason, and both Sheriff Bubba Theriot and Tara LeBlanc know something is wrong. Tara has studied the old arts of healing, but even she cannot help the victims. All she knows is that she and the sheriff have to find out what is going on before more people are hurt.

Inspirational

Other books by the same author:
Bayou Corruption, 2008
Bayou Judgment, 2008
Danger in a Small Town, 2008
Bayou Justice, 2007

Other books you might like:
Hannah Alexander, *Double Blind*, 2008
Valerie Hansen, *Hidden in the Wall*, 2008
Carol Steward, *Guardian of Justice*, 2008
Cheryl Wolverton, *Shelter from the Storm*, 2003
Lenora Worth, *Deadly Texas Rose*, 2008

921

JACK CAVANAUGH

The Guardians

(Colorado Springs, Colorado: David C. Cook, 2008)

Story type: Mystery
Series: American Family Portrait. Book 9
Subject(s): Family; Murder; Twins
Major character(s): Ethan Morgan, Police Officer;
    Meredith Morgan, Widow(er)
Time period(s): 2000s
Locale(s): San Diego, California

Summary: When Ethan Morgan's twin brother Anthony is killed, he vows to have his revenge. The killing was actually a mistake, and Ethan was the intended victim. The killer wanted to exact his own revenge upon Ethan, and to steal the Morgan family Bible. Anthony's widow Meredith is intent on getting the Bible back. Ethan and Meredith know the killing was somehow wrapped up in the Morgan family history, and they must find the killer before there are more deaths.

Other books by the same author:
Tartarus, 2008
A Hideous Beauty, 2007
Fury, 2006
The Victors, 2006
Dear Enemy, 2005

Other books you might like:
Randy Alcorn, *Deception*, 2007
Karen Ball, *Shattered Justice*, 2005
Dee Henderson, *The Witness*, 2006
F.P. Lione, *The Midtown Blues Series*, 2005-
Kathi Mills-Macias, *The Toni Matthews Series*, 2001-

922

COLLEEN COBLE

Anathema

(Nashville: Thomas Nelson, 2008)

Story type: Contemporary
Subject(s): Amish; Forgiveness; Murder
Major character(s): Hannah Swartz Ericson, Young
    Woman (Amish); Reece Ericson, Spouse
Time period(s): 2000s

Locale(s): Indiana
Summary: As a young woman, Hannah Swartz disobeyed her parents and snuck out of her house one evening to meet her boyfriend Reece. When she came back, she found her parents murdered. The motive for the hideous crime was apparently the theft of some valuable quilts. Hannah was subsequently shunned by her community, and she left town with Reece. After four years of a bad marriage, Hannah has come back to her rural Indiana community to try to find out what really happened the night her parents died.

Other books by the same author:
Abomination, 2007
Lonestar Sanctuary, 2007
Midnight Sea, 2007
Alaska Twilight, 2006
Fire Dancer, 2006

Other books you might like:
Carrie Bender, *The Dora's Diary Series*, 1999-
Wanda E. Brunstetter, *The Daughters of Lancaster
    County Series*, 2005-
Beverly Lewis, *The Anniel's People Series*, 2005-
Gayle Roper, *The Document*, 1998
Cindy Woodsmall, *The Sisters of the Quilt Series*, 2006-

923

ACE COLLINS

Farraday Road

(Grand Rapids, Michigan: Zondervan, 2008)

Story type: Mystery
Subject(s): Conspiracies
Major character(s): Lije Evans, Lawyer; Mikki Stuart,
    Police Officer (deputy)
Time period(s): 2000s
Locale(s): Arkansas

Summary: Deputy Mikki Stuart is on routine patrol when she stumbles across a hideous crime scene. Somebody has murdered Kaitlyn Evans and left her husband Lije fighting for his life. When Lije recovers, he is determined to track down his wife's killers, but he soon finds himself facing a blank wall, which leads him to believe that he and his wife may be the victims not only of a murderer, but of a vicious cover-up and conspiracy as well. First novel.

Other books you might like:
John Bayer, *Necessary Risk*, 1998
Kristen Heitzmann, *Freefall*, 2006
Joseph H. Hilley, *Sober Justice*, 2004
Clay Jacobsen, *Circle of Seven*, 2000
Randy Singer, *Dying Declaration*, 2004

924

LORI COPELAND

Twice Loved

(New York: Avon Inspired, 2008)

Story type: Romance; Historical/Post-American Civil War
Series: Belles of Timber Creek. Book 1

Subject(s): Teachers
Major character(s): Willow Madison, Teacher; Tucker Gray, Businessman (sawmill owner); Silas Sterling, Wealthy
Time period(s): 1860s
Locale(s): Thunder Ridge, Texas

Summary: With the War Between the States finally over, schoolteacher Willow Madison can begin to feel secure again. After the Yankees invaded her town and left behind a trail of destruction, Willow is truly starting over, and is penniless. She finds herself with what she thinks may be a wonderful solution to her problems. Wealthy Silas Sterling wants to marry her and take care of her. Although Silas is 30 years older than she is, Willow is tempted, if only for the security such a match will bring. Unfortunately, there is an obstacle in the form of handsome sawmill owner Tucker Gray. Willow can't get Tucker out of her mind, and in the end she must choose between love and security.

Other books by the same author:
Now and Always, 2008
Bluebonnet Belle, 2007
Simple Gifts, 2007
Unwrapping Christmas, 2007
The Plainsman, 2006

Other books you might like:
Tamera Alexander, *The Timber Ridge Reflections Series*, 2008-
Gary E. Parker, *The Southern Tides Series*, 2004-
Michael Phillips, *The Shenandoah Sisters Series*, 2003-
Allison Pittman, *The Crossroads of Grace Series*, 2006-
Lauraine Snelling, *The Secret Refuge Series*, 2000-

925

SUSAN PAGE DAVIS
MEGAN ELAINE DAVIS , Co-Author

Homicide at Blue Heron

(Uhrichsville, Ohio: Barbour, 2008)

Story type: Mystery
Series: Mainely Murder. Book 1
Subject(s): Secrets; Small Town Life
Major character(s): Emily Grant, Journalist (investigative reporter); Nate Holman, Businessman (marina owner)
Time period(s): 2000s
Locale(s): Baxter, Maine

Summary: Emily Grant wants to sell her family's lakeside cottage, and then leave the little island town in Maine behind for the last time. Then she meets up with her old boyfriend, Nate Holman, and she realizes there are still sparks of a romance there. Unfortunately, Emily and Nate's potential romance is tempered when they discover the body of a neighbor who has been brutally murdered. Why would anybody want to kill an inoffensive senior citizen? As Emily's investigative reporter genes kick in, she teams up with Nate, who had always dreamed of a career in law enforcement, to find out who killed Henry Derbin. This is the first novel from mother-daughter team Susan Page and Megan Elaine Davis, though Susan has written several other inspirational novels.

Other books you might like:
Lynn Bulock, *The Gracie Lee Harris Series*, 2005-
Lori Copeland, *The Morning Shade Series*, 2003-
Peggy Darty, *The Christy Castleman Series*, 2005-
Christine Lynxwiler, *Death on a Deadline*, 2008
Nancy Mehl, *In the Dead of Winter*, 2008

926

TED DEKKER

Adam

(Nashville: Thomas Nelson, 2008)

Story type: Mystery
Subject(s): Death; Serial Killers
Major character(s): Daniel Clark, Psychologist (behavioral psychologist); Eve, Serial Killer
Time period(s): 2000s
Locale(s): Los Angeles, California

Summary: FBI behavioral psychologist Daniel Clark has become obsessed with the thought of capturing a horrifying serial killer known only as "Eve". Eve has killed 16 women, using a bizarre series of religious motifs when doing so. Daniel thinks he is getting close to finding out who Eve is, and he is right, so Eve comes after him. Shot by the killer he is chasing, Daniel is found in time and resuscitated, with a crucial part of his memory gone. He thinks that if he can remember what happened in that lost time, he will finally find Eve. Eve, on the other hand, is determined not to be found, and will try to kill Daniel again, or target those close to him, in order to remain free.

Other books by the same author:
Blink of an Eye, 2007
Skin, 2007
Saint, 2006
Showdown, 2006
Obsessed, 2005

Other books you might like:
Brandilyn Collins, *The Hidden Faces Series*, 2004-
Tim Downs, *The Bug Man Series*, 2003-
T. L. Hines, *Waking Lazarus*, 2006
David Ryan Long, *Ezekiel's Shadow*, 2001
Sharon Carter Rogers, *Unpretty*, 2008
Melanie Wells, *The Day of Evil Series*, 2005-

927

ATHOL DICKSON

Winter Haven

(Minneapolis: Bethany House, 2008)

Story type: Contemporary
Subject(s): Brothers and Sisters
Major character(s): Vera Gamble, Accountant
Time period(s): 2000s
Locale(s): Winter Haven, Maine

Summary: Vera Gamble has always kept her distance from

people. The pain she went through as a child makes her unwilling to undergo more suffering. Most of her problems stem from the disappearance of her autistic brother Siggy, who vanished when he was 15 years old. Vera had always wondered what happened to him, and one day she gets the call she has been dreading her entire adult life. Siggy has been found dead, washed up on the shores of Winter Haven, Maine. Vera goes to Maine to identify her brother and is puzzled to see that Siggy's body is exactly as she remembered. It is as if the past years never happened, and Siggy didn't age a day.

Other books by the same author:
The Cure, 2007
River Rising, 2006
They Shall See God, 2002
Every Hidden Thing, 1998
Whom Shall I Fear?, 1996

Other books you might like:
Terri Blackstock, *Southern Storm*, 2003
Davis Bunn, *Elixir*, 2004
Catherine Palmer, *The Happy Room*, 2002
Patricia H. Rushford, *As Good as Dead*, 2005
Travis Thrasher, *Isolation*, 2007

928

MELANIE DOBSON

The Black Cloister

(Grand Rapids, Michigan: Kregel, 2008)

Story type: Contemporary
Subject(s): Cults; Mothers and Daughters; Secrets
Major character(s): Elise Friedman, Student—College
Time period(s): 2000s
Locale(s): Germany

Summary: When Elise Friedman was eight, her mother committed suicide. As a young college student, Elise begins to reflect more and more on what may have caused her mother to take her own life. Determined to find the truth, no matter what the cost, Elise goes to Germany, where her mother spent her formative years. Elise learns that her mother grew up in the clutches of a cult, and that people from the cult do not want the truth of their group to get out, and will do anything to stop Elise from letting others know their secrets.

Other books by the same author:
Going for Broke, 2007
Together for Good, 2006

Other books you might like:
Shelley Bates, *Grounds to Believe*, 2004
Sigmund Brouwer, *Crown of Thorns*, 2002
Craig Parshall, *The Last Judgment*, 2005
James H. Pence, *Blind Sight*, 2003
Carol D. Slama, *Shroud of Silence*, 1998

929

BRANDT DODSON

White Soul

(Eugene, Oregon: Harvest House, 2008)

Story type: Mystery
Series: To Protect and Serve. Book 1
Subject(s): Gangs
Major character(s): Ron Ortega, Police Officer; Michael Santiago, Drug Dealer
Time period(s): 2000s
Locale(s): Miami, Florida

Summary: Ron Ortega is a dedicated cop, dedicated to the point where he puts his wife and child second to his job. He has infiltrated a notorious gang and, in the middle of a drug deal gone wrong, he gets involved in a shoot-out. Ron saves the life of Michael Santiago, who is linked to one of the biggest drug lords in Miami. Although Ron's wife wants him to give up undercover work, he can't. Now that he has made an important contact, he finds it impossible to give up his dangerous work, knowing that he has to keep close to Santiago so he can bring down the entire drug syndicate.

Other books by the same author:
The Lost Sheep, 2007
The Root of All Evil, 2007
Original Sin, 2006
Seventy Times Seven, 2006

Other books you might like:
Dee Henderson, *Before I Wake*, 2007
Sally John, *Moment of Truth*, 2005
F.P. Lione, *The Midtown Blues Series*, 2005-
Kathi Mills-Macias, *The Toni Matthews Series*, 2001-
Kathryn Springer, *Tested by Fire*, 2004

930

RICHARD DOSTER

Safe at Home

(Colorado Springs, Colorado: David C. Cook, 2008)

Story type: Contemporary
Subject(s): Race Relations; Sports/Baseball
Major character(s): Jack Hall, Sportswriter; Rose Marie Hall, Spouse; Percy Jackson, Sports Figure (baseball player)
Time period(s): 1950s
Locale(s): Whitney, Mississippi

Summary: It is 1953, and sportswriter Jack Hall is eagerly looking forward to opening day of the Whitney Bobcats. Not so the team itself, which is in a slump. Desperate to turn his team around, the owner of the Bobcats signs 17-year-old phenomenon Percy Jackson. Percy is African-American, the first to be signed by the team, and Jack Hall isn't certain his racially divided town is ready for such a step. As the summer progresses, the entire town finds themselves facing questions of race in ways they never had previously. First novel.

Other books you might like:
John Aubrey Anderson, *Black or White*, 2005
Linda Dorrell, *True Believers*, 2001
Ann H. Gabhart, *Orchard of Hope*, 2006
Jerry B. Jenkins, *The Youngest Hero*, 2002
Elizabeth Musser, *The Swan House*, 2001

931

PAMELA BINNINGS EWEN

The Moon in the Mango Tree

(Nashville: B & H Publishing, 2008)

Story type: Historical
Subject(s): Independence; Marriage
Major character(s): Barbara Bond Perkins, Singer (opera);
   Harvey Perkins, Religious (missionary)
Time period(s): 1920s
Locale(s): Thailand; Europe

Summary: Barbara Bond is a beautiful young opera singer who values her independence, and is unwilling to give it up for anybody. Her life in the glamorous capitals of Europe is enviable. However, when Barbara marries a young missionary named Harvey Perkins, she must begin to rethink her life, and attempt to decide if her husband's work should take precedence over her own. Traveling to Siam, she is suddenly confronted by a world that is so unlike her own that she cannot cope. Suffering a nervous breakdown, she leaves Siam, only to return and continue to struggle with questions of faith and love.

Where it's reviewed:
Publishers Weekly, March 17, 2008, page 48

Other books by the same author:
Walk Back the Cat, 2006

Other books you might like:
Linda Chaikin, *The East of the Sun Series*, 2003-
John Dalton, *Heaven Lake*, 2004
C. Hope Flinchbaugh, *Daughter of China*, 2002
Shirlee McCoy, *Even in the Darkness*, 2006
Jane Orcutt, *All the Tea in China*, 2007

932

CHRIS FABRY

Dogwood

(Carol Stream, Illinois: Tyndale House, 2008)

Story type: Contemporary
Subject(s): Secrets
Major character(s): Will Hatfield, Convict (ex-convict);
   Karin, Spouse; Ruthie Bowles, Aged Person
Time period(s): 2000s
Locale(s): Dogwood, West Virginia

Summary: Will Hatfield was living a quietly happy life when he was convicted of killing two young girls in a drunk driving accident. After spending 12 years in prison, Will is scheduled for release. He desperately wants to return home to Dogwood, West Virginia, and see his family again. He hopes he can rekindle his love affair with Karin, not realizing that she has married another man and is the mother of three children. For herself, Karin knows that her marriage is a loveless sham, and that she still loves Will. When Will returns to Dogwood, he soon realizes that people aren't so willing for forgive his past, and that even Karin may not be willing to be his friend. First adult novel.

Where it's reviewed:
Publishers Weekly, May 5, 2008, page 43

Other books you might like:
Kathryn Cushman, *A Promise to Remember*, 2007
Karen Kingsbury, *Waiting for Morning*, 1999
Jane Orcutt, *The Living Stone*, 2000
Travis Thrasher, *The Watermark*, 2001
Jamie Langston Turner, *No Dark Valley*, 2004

933

LINDA FORD

The Road to Love

(New York: Steeple Hill, 2008)

Story type: Historical/Depression Era
Series: Depression. Book 1
Subject(s): Depression (Economic); Farm Life
Major character(s): Kate Bradshaw, Widow(er); Hatcher
   Jones, Drifter
Time period(s): 1930s
Locale(s): South Dakota

Summary: Kate Bradshaw is finding life as a widow incredibly difficult. Being a farm wife was hard enough. Being a farm wife without a farmer is seemingly impossible. Then drifter Hatcher Jones comes into her life. He is a good, quiet man who is more than willing to help the pretty widow and be a surrogate father to her two children, but he has problems that he believes will prevent him from marrying the Widow Bradshaw. Kate, however, soon comes to see that Hatcher would make a wonderful husband for herself, if only she can convince him of that.

Other books by the same author:
Darcy's Inheritance, 2007
Everlasting Love, 2007
The Dreams of Hannah Williams, 2007
Cry of My Heart, 2006
Grace, 2004

Other books you might like:
Patricia Hickman, *The Millwood Hollow Series*, 2003-
Leisha Kelly, *Julia's Hope*, 2002
Bonnie Leon, *The Sowers Trilogy*, 1998-
Gary E. Parker, *The Blue Ridge Legacy Series*, 2001-
Tracie Peterson, *Beneath a Harvest Sky*, 2003

934

TINA ANN FORKNER

Ruby among Us

(Colorado Springs, Colorado: WaterBrook, 2008)

Story type: Contemporary
Subject(s): Grandmothers; Mothers and Daughters

Inspirational

Major character(s): Lucy DiCamillo, Young Woman; Kitty DiCamillo, Grandparent
Time period(s): 2000s
Locale(s): California

Summary: Lucy DiCamillo never quite managed to shake the guilt she felt for not getting her mother's inhaler to her when she was having an asthma attack. Believing she caused her mother Ruby's death, Lucy has remained steadfastly isolated from the world, protected by her grandmother Kitty. As Lucy grows older, however, she begins to wonder about her mother, and her unknown father. As Lucy begins to unearth her family's secrets, she learns a great deal about herself in the process. First novel.

Other books you might like:
Lynn Austin, *All She Ever Wanted*, 2005
Sylvia Bambola, *Return to Appleton*, 2005
Deborah Bedford, *If I Had You*, 2004
Robin Jones Gunn, *Gardenias for Breakfast*, 2005
Delia Parr, *Day by Day*, 2007
Tracie Peterson, *A Slender Thread*, 2000

935

ANN H. GABHART

The Outsider

(Grand Rapids, Michigan: Fleming H. Revell, 2008)

Story type: Historical
Subject(s): Religious Life; Shakers
Major character(s): Gabrielle Hope, Young Woman (Shaker sister), Psychic
Time period(s): 1800s
Locale(s): Pleasant Hill, Kentucky

Summary: Gabrielle Hope has visions during which she can see the future. This "gift" frightens Gabrielle, for the visions can be gentle, or frightening and intense. Even worse, her visions come true, and Gabrielle is burdened with the knowledge of impending death or disaster, with no way of preventing the upcoming events. Gabrielle's visions are much admired by her fellow Shakers in the community of Pleasant Hill, Kentucky, and she is a valued member of their society. When a young doctor is brought to the Shaker village to help a young man, one Gabrielle knew would be injured, Gabrielle is shocked to find herself drawn to the outsider. She must soon face the question of staying in her beloved community, with all she knows, or venturing into the outside world with the man she loves.

Other books by the same author:
Summer of Joy, 2008
Orchard of Hope, 2006
The Scent of Lilacs, 2005

Other books you might like:
Louise M. Gouge, *The Ahab Series*, 2004-
Gilbert Morris, *The Spirit of Appalachia Series*, 1997-
Janette Oke, *The Song of Acadia Series*, 1999-
Delia Parr, *The Trinity Series*, 2002-
Lori Wick, *The Tucker Mills Series*, 2005-

936

GINGER GARRETT

In the Shadow of Lions

(Colorado Springs, Colorado: David C. Cook, 2008)

Story type: Historical/Tudor Period
Subject(s): Kings, Queens, Rulers, etc.
Major character(s): Anne Boleyn, Royalty (queen), Historical Figure; Henry VIII, Ruler (King of England), Historical Figure; Sir Thomas More, Nobleman, Historical Figure
Time period(s): 16th century
Locale(s): England

Summary: Young Anne Boleyn catches the eye of her king, Henry the VIII. Flattered by the attention, Anne soon realizes that she can use the king's infatuation to persuade him to support the translation of the Bible into English. Meanwhile, Sir Thomas More is using his powers to further his own agendas. As the people at the top pummel each other in their attempts to get their own way, young prostitute Rose is encouraged to find her way to God, regardless of what people may think of her.

Other books by the same author:
Dark Hour, 2006
Chosen, 2005

Other books you might like:
Jack Cavanaugh, *The Book of Books Series*, 1999-
Reg Grant, *Storm*, 2001
Joe Musser, *The Infidel*, 2001
Craig Parshall, *The Thistle and the Cross Series*, 2005-
Lori Wick, *The Knight and the Dove*, 1995

937

DEEANNE GIST

Deep in the Heart of Trouble

(Minneapolis: Bethany House, 2008)

Story type: Historical
Series: Essie Spreckelmeyer. Book 2
Subject(s): Bicycles and Bicycling; Courtship
Major character(s): Essie Spreckelmeyer, Spinster; Tony Morgan, Heir—Dispossessed
Time period(s): 1890s
Locale(s): Corsicana, Texas

Summary: Essie Spreckelmeyer has pretty much come to terms with the fact that her independent nature has made her virtually unmarriageable. For most women in 1898, that would have been a fate worse than death, but Essie has more than enough to keep her busy. Her love of bicycling has given her a great deal of fun, and even won her an award. Then Tony Morgan comes to Corsicana, Texas to work for Essie's father. Tony's own father, an oil baron, has disinherited him, and Tony has to make his own way in the world It appears as if Essie may finally have met the man who can handle a free-spirited woman.

Other books by the same author:
Courting Trouble, 2007
The Measure of a Lady, 2006
A Bride Most Begrudging, 2005

Other books you might like:
B.J. Hoff, *The American Anthem Series*, 2002-
Sara Mitchell, *The Sinclair Legacy Series*, 2001-
Kathleen Morgan, *The Brides of Culdee Creek Series*, 1999-
Tracie Peterson, *The Bells of Lowell Series*, 2003-
Lauraine Snelling, *The Dakotah Treasures Series*, 2003-

938

TRICIA GOYER

A Whisper of Freedom
(Chicago: Moody, 2008)

Story type: Historical
Series: Chronicles of the Spanish Civil War. Book 3
Subject(s): Civil War/Spanish
Major character(s): Sophie Grace, Revolutionary; Walt Block, Journalist (newspaper correspondent); Philip Stanford, Military Personnel (volunteer)
Time period(s): 1930s
Locale(s): Spain

Summary: Sophie Grace has been in Spain for over a year, fighting for those on the side of the Republic alongside some of her friends. However, Sophie is learning that nothing is as simple as it seems, and that betrayal can come from anyone and at any time. Her former fiance, and dear friend Michael turned out to be a liar, and now Sophie is uncertain who she can trust. Walt, her partner in a gold heist, or even Philip, her new love? Unable to know whom to trust any longer, Sophie puts her faith in God and prays that she will survive her latest tribulations.

Other books by the same author:
A Shadow of Treason, 2007
Arms of Deliverance, 2006
Dawn of a Thousand Nights, 2005
Night Song, 2004
From Dust and Ashes, 2003

Other books you might like:
Maureen Lang, *Pieces of Silver*, 2006
Bonnie Leon, *A Sacred Place*, 2000
Judith Pella, *The Daughters of Fortune Series*, 2002-
Michael Phillips, *The Secret of the Rose Series*, 1993-
Wilma Wall, *Forbidden*, 2004

939

RENE GUTTERIDGE

Skid
(Colorado Springs, Colorado: WaterBrook, 2008)

Story type: Contemporary; Humor
Series: Occupational Hazards. Book 3
Subject(s): Air Travel; Airplanes; Travel

Major character(s): Hank Hazard, Investigator (airline spy)
Time period(s): 2000s
Locale(s): In the Air

Summary: As Flight 1945 prepares to take off from Atlanta to fly to Amsterdam, nobody aboard realizes just what is in store for them. From a flight crew fraught with difficult personalities to a cabin filled with eccentrics, Hank Hazard has his hands full. Hank is an airline spy, and it is his job to see how the crew reacts to problems, both real and imagined. As he peppers the overworked crew with request after request to see how they respond under pressure, it soon becomes apparent that something is afoot on the plane, something that will test everybody to the limits.

Where it's reviewed:
Publishers Weekly, March 17, 2008, page 47

Other books by the same author:
Boo Humbug, 2007
Snitch, 2007
My Life as a Doormat (in three acts), 2006
Scoop, 2006
Storm Gathering, 2005

Other books you might like:
Charlene Ann Baumbich, *The Dearest Dorothy Series*, 2004-
Ray Blackston, *The Jay Jarvis Series*, 2003-
Lori Copeland, *The Morning Shade Series*, 2003-
Robin Jones Gunn, *The Sisterchicks Series*, 2003-
Camy Tang, *The Sushi Series*, 2007-

940

BETH WEBB HART

The Wedding Machine
(Nashville: Thomas Nelson, 2008)

Story type: Contemporary
Subject(s): Aging; Friendship; Weddings
Major character(s): Elizabeth Mims, Widow(er); Ray Montgomery, Parent; Hilda Prescott, Divorced Person
Time period(s): 2000s
Locale(s): Jasper, South Carolina

Summary: For years the residents of Jasper, South Carolina, have depended on the members of the "wedding machine" to make certain their all-important marriage ceremonies are arranged with the greatest of care. Time is taking a toll on the four members of the machine though. Their own marriages have ended due to death or divorce, their children are looking at other ways of doing things other than the old Southern ways, and middle-age is bringing aches and pains and complaints to the lives of the ladies. As summer approaches and the latest wedding season begins, the ladies begin to wonder if the "wedding machine" has a place in modern society.

Where it's reviewed:
Booklist, February 15, 2008, page 38
Publishers Weekly, December 3, 2007, page 51

Other books by the same author:
Adelaide Piper, 2006
Grace at Low Tide, 2005

Other books you might like:
Ginny Aiken, *The Bellamy's Blossoms Series*, 2000-
Ann H. Gabhart, *Summer of Joy*, 2008
Denise Hildreth, *The Savannah Series*, 2005-
Minnie Lamberth, *Life with Strings Attached*, 2005
Lisa Samson, *The Church Ladies*, 2001

941

ROBIN LEE HATCHER

Wagered Heart

(Grand Rapids, Michigan: Zondervan, 2008)

Story type: Historical/American West
Subject(s): Love
Major character(s): Bethany Silverton, Young Woman;
    Hawk Chandler, Cowboy; Vince Richards, Political
    Figure (gubernatorial candidate)
Time period(s): 1880s
Locale(s): Sweetwater, Montana

Summary: Preacher's daughter Bethany Silverton gradu-
ates from a genteel ladies' academy in Philadelphia and
travels west to join her father. He is the preacher at a
church in rugged Sweetwater, Montana. Bethany's eye is
caught by handsome cowboy Hawk Chandler, and she is
determined to get him to attend her father's church. Bethany's plotting is undermined by ruthless Vince Richards, a man who intends to become governor of Montana
no matter who he hurts in the process. Vince believes
Bethany will make a perfect politician's wife, and is
determined to steal her away from Hawk.

Other books by the same author:
The Perfect Life, 2008
Home to Hart's Crossing, 2007
Trouble in Paradise, 2007
Sweet Dreams Drive, 2007
Return to Me, 2007

Other books you might like:
Stephen Bly, *Miss Fontenot*, 1999
Jillian Hart, *Homespun Bride*, 2008
Al Lacy, *Sincerely Yours*, 2001
Tracie Peterson, *The Heirs of Montana Series*, 2004-
Lori Wick, *Cassidy*, 2007

942

RACHEL HAUCK

Love Starts with Elle

(Nashville: Thomas Nelson, 2008)

Story type: Contemporary
Subject(s): Artists and Art
Major character(s): Elle Garvey, Art Dealer, Artist
Time period(s): 2000s
Locale(s): Beaufort, South Carolina

Summary: Elle Garvey should be thrilled. Her boyfriend
Jeremiah has finally proposed, meaning that she, the last
of six sisters, can get married (much to the relief of her
family). When Jeremiah mentions that the marriage

means leaving South Carolina and moving to Houston,
Elle is suddenly full of doubts. Wedding preparations go
on regardless, but as time passes, Elle begins to realize
that she loves her life in Beaufort, South Carolina. She
loves running her art gallery, and painting, and everything
about her small coastal town. She soon realizes that she
just might not love Jeremiah enough to give it all up.

Other books by the same author:
Diva NashVegas, 2007
Sweet Caroline, 2007
Georgia on Her Mind, 2006
Lambert's Peace, 2006
Lost in NashVegas, 2006

Other books you might like:
Terri Blackstock, *Emerald Windows*, 2001
Mary Carlson, *The Whispering Pines Series*, 1999-
Denise Hildreth, *The Savannah Series*, 2005-
Deborah Raney, *Leaving November*, 2007
Lauraine Snelling, *The Brushstroke Legacy*, 2006

943

RACHEL HAUCK

Sweet Caroline

(Nashville: Thomas Nelson, 2008)

Story type: Romance
Subject(s): Music and Musicians; Restaurants
Major character(s): Caroline Sweeney, Restaurateur; J.D.
    Rand, Police Officer (deputy sheriff); Mitch O'Neal,
    Singer (country singer)
Time period(s): 2000s
Locale(s): South Carolina

Summary: Caroline Sweeney has never been adventurous.
She has always been the person her friends and family
could count on to always be there. When Caroline is offered a dream job in Barcelona, Spain, one of her friends
challenges her to accept it, and for once think of her
own dreams first. Then Caroline inherits the tiny
restaurant where she works, and she is suddenly facing a
dilemma. It was going to be easy enough to give up a
difficult job for a great one, but now she has to give up a
business. Caroline's life is further complicated when an
old boyfriend, now a famous country singer, returns to
South Carolina to try to convince her to take another
shot at love.

Where it's reviewed:
Library Journal, February 1, 2008, page 56

Other books by the same author:
Diva NashVegas, 2007
Georgia on Her Mind, 2006
Lost in NashVegas, 2006
Lambert's Peace, 2006

Other books you might like:
Robin Jones Gunn, *Wildflowers*, 2001
Robin Lee Hatcher, *Return to Me*, 2007
Sharon Hinck, *Symphony of Secrets*, 2008
Mae Nunn, *Amazing Love*, 2006
Cynthia Rutledge, *Judging Sara*, 2001

944

LAURA HAYDEN

America the Beautiful

(Carol Stream, Illinois: Tyndale House, 2008)

Story type: Contemporary
Series: America. Book 1
Subject(s): Campaigns, Political; Politics
Major character(s): Emily Benton, Political Figure (presidential candidate); Kate Rosen, Manager (campaign)
Time period(s): 2000s
Locale(s): United States

Summary: Former governor Emily Benton wants to be the President of the United States. She wants it so badly that she is willing to do whatever it takes to reach her goal. Her campaign manager, Kate Rosen is at first intent on helping Benton reach the White House. However, Kate soon realizes that her one-time best friend is ruthless when it comes to achieving her goals, and will use any methods imaginable to win, even if it means destroying her rival in the process.

Other books by the same author:
Stolen Hearts, 2001
Chance of a Lifetime, 1996
A Margin in Time, 1995

Other books you might like:
James Scott Bell, *Deadlock*, 2002
Alton Gansky, *The Incumbent*, 2004
Neesa Hart, *End of State*, 2003
Clay Jacobsen, *Circle of Seven*, 2000
Josh McDowell, *Vote of Intolerance*, 1997
Joel C. Rosenberg, *The Copper Scroll*, 2006

945

KATHY HERMAN

The Grand Scheme

(Colorado Springs, Colorado: Multnomah, 2008)

Story type: Mystery
Series: Phantom Hollow. Book 3
Subject(s): Stalking; Suspense
Major character(s): Rue Kessler, Construction Worker (supervisor); Ivy Kessler, Spouse
Time period(s): 2000s
Locale(s): Jacob's Ear, Colorado

Summary: Rue Kessler is finally turning his life around after years of drug and alcohol addiction. He has married his long-time love Ivy and is becoming a true father to their son Montana. With a year and a half of sobriety under his belt, Rue is beginning to think he might succeed. When his father-in-law hires him as the supervisor of a condo construction project, Rue is thrilled, thinking that a successful completion of the project will finally end the doubts people around him still retain about his willingness to turn his life around. Things go well at first, but when a series of accidents and acts of vandalism hit his project, Rue begins to doubt himself. When a

man on his work crew turns up dead, Rue begins to think that somebody is serious about not letting him succeed.

Other books by the same author:
Ever Present Danger, 2007
Never Look Back, 2007
All Things Hidden, 2006
Not by Chance, 2006
Eye of the Beholder, 2005

Other books you might like:
Terri Blackstock, *The Cape Refuge Series*, 2002-
Brandilyn Collins, *The Hidden Faces Series*, 2001-
Rene Gutteridge, *The Splitting Storm*, 2004
Dee Henderson, *The O'Malley Series*, 2001-
Melanie Wells, *The Day of Evil Series*, 2005-

946

PATRICIA HICKMAN

Painted Dresses

(Colorado Springs, Colorado: WaterBrook, 2008)

Story type: Contemporary
Subject(s): Family Problems; Secrets; Sisters
Major character(s): Gaylen Syler-Boatwright, Spouse; Delia Syler, Criminal
Time period(s): 2000s
Locale(s): North Carolina

Summary: In the middle of a bad patch in her marriage, Gaylen Syler-Boatwright doesn't feel up to dealing with anything but her own problems. Unfortunately, after her father's death, Gaylen finds herself in the awkward position of having to care for her younger sister Delia. Gaylen had always been the trustworthy sister, the one charged with taking care of the flaky Delia. Now Delia needs help yet again, and Gaylen isn't willing or able to provide it. Unfortunately, Delia has gotten herself into some serious trouble this time, and Gaylen is forced to go on the run with Delia to save both of their lives.

Other books by the same author:
Earthly Vows, 2006
Whisper Town, 2005
Nazareth's Song, 2004
Fallen Angels, 2003
Sandpebbles, 2002

Other books you might like:
Robin Lee Hatcher, *Return to Me*, 2007
Dee Henderson, *The Witness*, 2006
Catherine Palmer, *The Happy Room*, 2002
Tracie Peterson, *Where My Heart Belongs*, 2007
Debra White Smith, *The Seven Sisters Series*, 2000-

947

SHARON HINCK

The Restorer's Journey

(Colorado Springs, Colorado: Nav Press, 2008)

Story type: Fantasy
Series: Sword of Lyric. Book 3

Inspirational

Subject(s): Mothers and Sons
Major character(s): Susan Mitchell, Parent, Spouse; Jake Mitchell, Teenager; Mark Mitchell, Parent, Spouse
Time period(s): Indeterminate
Locale(s): Lyric, Fictional Country; United States

Summary: Suburban mother Susan Mitchell and her teenage son Jake have been drawn into another world, that of Lyric, home to the People of the Verses. Susan and Jake manage to escape to their own world, a typical suburban community in the United States, only to learn they cannot escape that easily. Susan is kidnapped and brought back to Lyric, and Jake and his father Mark prepare to follow in order to save her. Unfortunately, Mark has made too many trips through the portal, and Jake must go on his own, and save his mother.

Other books by the same author:
Symphony of Secrets, 2008
Renovating Becky Miller, 2007
The Restorer, 2007
The Restorer's Son, 2007
The Secret Life of Becky Miller, 2006

Other books you might like:
Shaunti Feldhahn, *The Veritas Conflict*, 2001
Karen Hancock, *The Legends of the Guardian King Series*, 2003-
Kathleen Morgan, *The Guardians of Gadiel Series*, 2005-
Kathy Tyers, *The Firebird Trilogy*, 1999-
Chris Walley, *The Lamb Among the Stars Series*, 2004-

948

BOB HOSTETLER

The Bone Box

(New York: Howard Books, 2008)

Story type: Action/Adventure
Subject(s): Archaeology
Major character(s): Randall Bullock, Archaeologist; Miri Sharon, Government Official (Israeli Antiques Authority); Tracy Bullock, Teenager
Time period(s): 2000s
Locale(s): Israel

Summary: His professional and personal lives both in shambles, archaeologist Randall Bullock travels to Israel hoping to discover something that will recharge his career. To his surprise, with the assistance of Miri Sharon, a member of the Israeli Antiques Authority, he does. They uncover a stone casket that is marked "Joseph, son of Caiaphas." Inside the casket are scrolls said to document the last days on earth of Jesus. When the press hears of the find, which would seemingly confirm the truth of Jesus' crucifixion and resurrection, Randall, Miri, and Randall's estranged daughter Tracy find themselves in the middle of a media circus, with many people desperate to have the find be once again lost forever. First adult novel.

Other books you might like:
T. L. Higley, *Marduk's Tablet*, 2003
C. J. Illinik, *The Tablets of Ararat*, 2002
John Olson, *Fossil Hunter*, 2008
Kel Richards, *Dark Storm*, 2004
Frank Simon, *Walls of Terror*, 1997

949

ANGELA HUNT

She Always Wore Red

(Carol Stream, Illinois: Tyndale House, 2008)

Story type: Contemporary
Series: Fairlawn. Book 2
Subject(s): Friendship
Major character(s): Jennifer Graham, Apprentice (to embalmer), Parent; McLane Larson, Spouse
Time period(s): 2000s
Locale(s): Mt. Dora, Florida

Summary: After inheriting a funeral home, divorced single mother Jennifer Graham is still trying to learn her new trade, and is an embalmer's apprentice. Though she has plenty to keep her busy, Jennifer is anxious to make a female friend. When she meets a pregnant young woman named McLane Larson, a newcomer to town, Jennifer is thrilled to take the woman under her wing. When McLane's military man husband is sent overseas, Jennifer becomes even closer to the woman.

Where it's reviewed:
Publishers Weekly, March 10, 2008, page 59

Other books by the same author:
Doesn't She Look Natural?, 2007
The Elevator, 2007
Magdalene, 2006
Uncharted, 2006
The Novelist, 2006

Other books you might like:
Lori Copeland, *Mother of Prevention*, 2005
Robin Jones Gunn, *The Sisterchicks Series*, 2003-
Neta Jackson, *The Yada Yada Prayer Group Series*, 2003-
Annie Jones, *Mom over Miami*, 2005
Laura Jensen Walker, *The Phoebe Grant Series*, 2005-

950

DENISE HUNTER

The Convenient Groom

(Nashville: Thomas Nelson, 2008)

Story type: Romance
Series: Nantucket Love Stories. Book 2
Subject(s): Weddings
Major character(s): Kate Lawrence, Radio Personality; Lucas Wright, Artisan (furniture maker)
Time period(s): 2000s
Locale(s): Nantucket Island, Massachusetts

Summary: Kate Lawrence has earned a name for herself as an expert in marriage. She doles out advice on the radio, writes newspaper columns on the subject, and is the author-of-an about to be published book on finding the right man. The book's release is to coincide with Kate's own marriage, to be held on the romantic beaches of Nantucket Island. Then Kate's groom bails at the last minute and with her entire career about to crash around her, Kate accepts the proposal of her long-time friend Lucas Wright. A marriage of convenience, they both call it. Lucas though, has always had a secret love for Kate and, soon enough, Kate also wants to make the marriage a real thing.

Other books by the same author:

Surrender Bay, 2007
Finding Faith, 2006
Saving Grace, 2005
Mending Places, 2004

Other books you might like:

Tracey Bateman, *I Love Claire*, 2007
Mary Davis, *Newlywed Games*, 2000
Deb Kastner, *Hart's Harbor*, 2003
Hope Lyda, *Altar Call*, 2006
Marta Perry, *Hunter's Bride*, 2002

951

ARLENE JAMES

His Small-Town Girl

(New York: Steeple Hill, 2008)

Story type: Romance
Subject(s): Small Town Life; Wealth
Major character(s): Charlotte Jefford, Hotel Owner; Tyler Aldrich, Businessman (CEO of grocery store chain)
Time period(s): 2000s
Locale(s): Eden, Oklahoma

Summary: Charlotte Jefford enjoys her life in small town Eden, Oklahoma. Eden may not have the amenities of a large town, but neither does it have a large town's problems. Everybody knows everyone else in Eden, and they all pretty much get along. So Charlotte runs the town's one hotel, and is happy and content. Not so wealthy Texan Tyler Aldrich, who has everything imaginable. As CEO of a chain of grocery stores, he has power, and the wealth that comes with it. He isn't particularly happy though. He may have all the status symbols in the world, but he lacks the one thing he truly needs, the love of a good woman. When his car runs out of gas in Eden, he believes he may have found that missing piece of his life in the person of Charlotte Jefford.

Other books by the same author:

A Mommy in Mind, 2007
When Love Comes Home, 2007
A Family to Share, 2006
A Love So Strong, 2006
Butterfly Summer, 2006

Other books you might like:

Margaret Daley, *Sadie's Hero*, 2002
Linda Goodnight, *A Very Special Delivery*, 2006
Marta Perry, *Tangled Memories*, 2006
Cynthia Rutledge, *Unforgettable Faith*, 2000
Janet Tronstad, *A Rich Man for Dry Creek*, 2002

952

JOY JORDAN-LAKE

Blue Hole Back Home

(Colorado Springs, Colorado: David C. Cook, 2008)

Story type: Contemporary
Subject(s): Race Relations; Racial Conflict; Teen Relationships
Major character(s): Shelby "Turtle" Maynard, Teenager; Farsanna Moulavi, Teenager
Time period(s): 1970s (1979)
Locale(s): North Carolina

Summary: Teenager Turtle Maynard is looking forward to another lazy summer hanging around with her brother and his friends. Turtle has never been one to make friends with girls, since she finds them vapid and backstabbing at best. As school draws to a close, Turtle meets the new girl, and she is not only new but very different. Farsanna Moulavi is nothing like the girls Turtle knows. She is intelligent and serious and polite. She is also not white, and even in 1979, racism is very much alive and well in the small Appalachian town Turtle calls home. Turtle wants to be friends with the new girl from Sri Lanka, but she soon finds that others in town want nothing more than for the new girl and her family to "go back where they came from." First novel.

Other books you might like:

John Aubrey Anderson, *Abiding Darkness*, 2005
Athol Dickson, *River Rising*, 2006
Ann H. Gabhart, *Orchard of Hope*, 2006
Neta Jackson, *The Yada Yada Prayer Group Gets Tough*, 2005
Ann Tatlock, *All the Way Home*, 2002

953

CLINT KELLY

Delicacy

(Grand Rapids, Michigan: Zondervan, 2008)

Story type: Mystery
Series: Sensations. Book 3
Subject(s): Cooks and Cooking; Homeless People
Major character(s): Cassie Dixon, Businesswoman (entrepreneur); Nick Dixon, Businessman (entrepreneur)
Time period(s): 2000s
Locale(s): San Francisco, California

Summary: Perfumers and entrepreneurs Nick and Cassie Dixon are trying to give back to the community. They volunteer with an organization called Taste of Success

that teaches homeless people the skills they will need to work in restaurants. Unfortunately, the building that houses the Taste of Success program sits on a prime piece of San Francisco real estate, and somebody wants the program to fail so they can buy the property. That somebody seems willing to kill to get what they want, and the Dixons soon find their own lives may be in danger.

Other books by the same author:
Echo, 2007
Scent, 2006
The Power and the Glory, 1999
Deliver Us from Evil, 1998
The Aryan, 1995

Other books you might like:
Davis Bunn, *Elixir*, 2004
Brandilyn Collins, *The Kanner Lake Series*, 2006-
David Ryan Long, *Ezekiel's Shadow*, 2001
Catherine Palmer, *Fatal Harvest*, 2003
Randy Singer, *False Witness*, 2007

954

GINGER KOLBABA
CHRISTY SCANNELL , Co-Author

A Matter of Wife and Death

(New York: Howard Books, 2008)

Story type: Contemporary
Series: Secrets From Lulu's Cafe. Book 2
Subject(s): Friendship
Major character(s): Mimi Plaisance, Spouse, Parent; Jennifer Shores, Spouse; Lisa Barton, Spouse, Parent
Time period(s): 2000s
Locale(s): Red River, Ohio

Summary: A group of pastors' wives have bonded together to share their problems, joys, and sorrows. Because they are married to ministers, it is often only in their own small group that they can let their hair down and be themselves, without worrying what others might think. All of the women face problems. Jennifer Shores has been married for ten years, and has yet to become pregnant. She worries that motherhood may never happen for her. Meanwhile, Lisa Barton's daughter is going through her difficult teenage years and Mimi Plaisance's newborn, her fourth child, is going through a crying stage. With nobody else to turn to for help, the women lean on each other to get through the hard times.

Other books by the same author:
Desperate Pastors' Wives, 2007

Other books you might like:
Vonette Z. Bright, *The Sister Circle Series*, 2003-
Robin Jones Gunn, *The Sisterchicks Series*, 2003-
Roxanne Henke, *The Coming Home to Brewster Series*, 2002-
Neta Jackson, *The Yada Yada Prayer Group Series*, 2003-
Lauraine Snelling, *The Way of Women*, 2004

955

HARRY LEE KRAUS

Perfect

(Grand Rapids, Michigan: Zondervan, 2008)

Story type: Contemporary
Subject(s): Accidents; Marriage
Major character(s): Wendi Stratford, Investigator (accident reconstructionist); Henry Stratford, Doctor
Time period(s): 2000s
Locale(s): Charlottesville, Virginia

Summary: Wendi Stratford has the perfect life. She is the adored wife of a brilliant physician, she has a dream job as an accident reconstructionist, her home is admired and envied—and all of it is a sham. Wendi knows that to her husband she is nothing more than a trophy wife, and that her entire life is a lie. Wendi is planning to begin her life again when a terrible accident puts an end to her plans. When she begins to reconstruct the accident, Wendi is horrified to learn that it was not an accident at all, but a deliberate attempt to murder her.

Other books by the same author:
All I'll Ever Need, 2007
For the Rest of My Life, 2003
Could I Have This Dance?, 2002
Serenity, 2002
The Chairman, 1999

Other books you might like:
Karen Ball, *The Breaking Point*, 2003
Terri Blackstock, *The Cape Refuge Series*, 2002-
Kathryn Cushman, *A Promise to Remember*, 2007
Rene Gutteridge, *The Splitting Storm*, 2004
T.D. Jakes, *Not Easily Broken*, 2006
Lorena McCourtney, *The Julesburg Mysteries Series*, 2002-
Melanie Wells, *The Day of Evil Series*, 2005-

956

TERRI KRAUS

The Renovation

(Colorado Springs, Colorado: David C. Cook, 2008)

Story type: Romance
Series: Project Restoration. Book 1
Subject(s): Construction
Major character(s): Ethan Willis, Widow(er); Cameron Dane, Journalist; Chase Willis, Teenager
Time period(s): 2000s
Locale(s): Franklin, Pennsylvania

Summary: Ethan Willis has thrown himself into the renovation project of a lifetime: restoring the great Carter Mansion of Franklin, Pennsylvania, to its former glory. Part of the appeal of the project is that it allows Ethan escape from the grief and guilt he feels over the death of his wife Lynne, who was murdered several years earlier during a carjacking. Ethan doesn't realize that his refusal to deal with Lynne's death is causing even more pain to

their son Chase, who blames himself for his mother's death. When reporter Cameron Dane is given the assignment of writing a story about the Carter Mansion restoration, she soon finds herself involved in the lives of the two Willis men. This is the first solo novel by Terri Kraus, though she has written several novels with her husband Jim.

Where it's reviewed:
Publishers Weekly, January 28, 2008, page 43

Other books you might like:
Melody Carlson, *A Mile in My Flip-Flops*, 2008
Sharon Hinck, *Renovating Becky Miller*, 2007
Diann Hunt, *Hearts under Construction*, 2005
David Ryan Long, *Quinlin's Estate*, 2002
Susan May Warren, *Happily Ever After*, 2003

957

TIM LAHAYE
GREGORY S. DINALLO , Co-Author

Always Grace

(New York: Kensington, 2008)

Story type: Historical
Subject(s): Love; War
Major character(s): Dylan Cooper, Photographer; Grace MacVicar Cooper, Spouse
Time period(s): 1930s
Locale(s): Newbury, Massachusetts

Summary: Photographer Dylan Cooper returns from fighting in World War I to find that his wife Grace has disappeared. She had been told he was killed in action. Unable to find his beloved Grace, Dylan retreats to a small town in Massachusetts, where he continues to take pictures and hope that someday he will find his wife again. Finally, 20 years later, he and Grace are reunited. However, it seems as if the 20 years they were separated is too long a gap for them to overcome. Sequel to *Come Spring*.

Other books by the same author:
Come Spring, 2005
Babylon Rising, 2004

Other books you might like:
Lyn Cote, *The Women of Ivy Manor Series*, 2005-
Clint Kelly, *In the Shadow of the Mountains Series*, 1998-
Charles Martin, *Wrapped in Rain*, 2005
Judith Pella, *The Daughters of Fortune Series*, 2002-
Lance Wubbels, *The Gentle Hills Series*, 1994-

958

JULIE LESSMAN

A Passion Redeemed

(Grand Rapids, Michigan: Fleming H. Revell, 2008)

Story type: Historical/Roaring Twenties; Romance
Series: Daughters of Boston. Book Two

Subject(s): Irish Americans; Sisters
Major character(s): Charity O'Connor, Young Woman; Mitch Dennehy, Editor (newspaper)
Time period(s): 1920s
Locale(s): Boston, Massachusetts

Summary: When Charity O'Connor decides she wants something, she usually gets it. She is simply not a woman people say "no" to easily. When Charity decides she loves her sister's former fiance, she finally runs up against somebody whose will is as strong as her own. Mitch Dennehy is a tough newspaper editor, and he sees nothing appealing about Charity, the woman who broke up his relationship with her sister. Charity refuses to take no for an answer though, and pursues Mitch with a vehemence that astounds him.

Other books by the same author:
A Passion Most Pure, 2008

Other books you might like:
Lawana Blackwell, *The Tales of London Series*, 2001-
B.J. Hoff, *The American Anthem Series*, 2002-
Maureen Lang, *Pieces of Silver*, 2006
Catherine Palmer, *The Victorian Rose Series*, 2002-
Tracie Peterson, *The Bells of Lowell Series*, 2003

959

BEVERLY LEWIS

The Forbidden

(Minneapolis: Bethany House, 2008)

Story type: Romance
Series: Courtship of Nellie Fisher. Book 2
Subject(s): Amish; Family; Religious Conflict
Major character(s): Nellie Mae Fisher, Baker (bakery owner); Caleb Yoder, Farmer
Time period(s): 1960s
Locale(s): Lancaster County, Pennsylvania

Summary: Nellie Mae Fisher has been engaged to handsome Caleb Yoder for some time, and hopes to become his bride in the near future. However, after her father breaks away from the Amish faith, Caleb's father orders him to stop seeing Nellie Mae. Not wanting to go against his father's wishes, which will mean losing his inheritance, Caleb is torn. He desperately loves Nellie Mae, but cannot turn his back on his father either. As Caleb struggles to find a way around his problems, Nellie Mae has her own troubles. Though loyal to the ways of the Amish, she is also intrigued by the beliefs of her father's new church. She is also struggling to come to terms with the drowning death of her sister.

Other books by the same author:
The Parting, 2007
The Brethren, 2006
The Englisher, 2006
The Preacher's Daughter, 2005
The Revelation, 2005

Inspirational

Other books you might like:
Carrie Bender, *The Dora's Diary Series*, 1999-
Wanda E. Brunstetter, *The Daughters of Lancaster
    County Series*, 2005-
Colleen Coble, *Anathema*, 2008
Gayle Roper, *The Document*, 1998
Cindy Woodsmall, *The Sisters of the Quilt Series*, 2006-

960

CHRISTINE LYNXWILER

Along Came a Cowboy

(Uhrichsville, Ohio: Barbour, 2008)

Story type: Romance
Series: Pinky Promise Sisterhood. Book 2
Subject(s): Forgiveness
Major character(s): Rachel Donovan, Doctor (chiroprac-
    tor); Jack Westwood, Cowboy
Time period(s): 2000s
Locale(s): Shady Grove, Arkansas

Summary: When Rachel Donovan was young, she fell
head over heels in love with a cowboy. When that situation didn't work out, Rachel vowed to steer clear of
cowboys in the future. Then handsome Jack Westwood
comes to town, and once again Rachel is smitten with a
cowboy. Can she forget her past hurts to see the man
Jack truly is, or will she let superficialities cost her a
romance?

Other books by the same author:
Forever Christmas, 2007
Arkansas, 2006
Promise Me Always, 2006
Longing for Home, 2005
Through the Fire, 2004

Other books you might like:
Carolyne Aarsen, *The Cowboy's Bride*, 1999
Debra Clopton, *The Cowboy Takes a Bride*, 2008
Valerie Hansen, *Blessings of the Heart*, 2003
Robin Lee Hatcher, *Trouble in Paradise*, 2007
Lenora Worth, *Mountain Sanctuary*, 2008

961

SHARLENE MACLAREN

Courting Emma

(New Kensington, Pennsylvania: Whitaker House, 2008)

Story type: Historical
Series: Little Hickman Creek. Book 3
Subject(s): Boarding Houses
Major character(s): Browning, Landlord (boardinghouse
    owner); Jonathan Atkins, Religious (preacher)
Time period(s): 1890s
Locale(s): Little Hickman, Kentucky

Summary: Emma Browning is none too thrilled when
preacher Jonathan Atkins takes up residence in her
boardinghouse. Emma is used to a more rowdy sort of
man, and she is afraid that Jonathan won't fit in with her
regular boarders. She is also fearful that the preacher
may try to convert her, something she stubbornly refuses
to even consider as a possibility. Then a miracle happens, and Emma's father, whom she had written off as
an unrepentant, abusive drunk, finds God. Facing this
miracle, Emma begins to wonder if a life with religion
in it is indeed a path she might want to follow.

Other books by the same author:
Loving Liza Jane, 2007
Sarah, My Beloved, 2007
Through Every Storm, 2006
Spring's Promise, 2002

Other books you might like:
Ann H. Gabhart, *The Outsider*, 2008
B.J. Hoff, *The Penny Whistle*, 1996
Sara Mitchell, *The Sinclair Legacy Series*, 2001-
Allison Pittman, *The Crossroads of Grace Series*, 2006-
Jan Watson, *Troublesome Creek*, 2005

962

TIA MCCOLLORS

The Truth about Love

(Chicago: Moody, 2008)

Story type: Contemporary
Subject(s): African Americans; Friendship; Relationships
Major character(s): Paula Manns, Spouse, Parent; Darryl
    Manns, Spouse, Parent; Belinda Stokes, Spouse,
    Step-Parent
Time period(s): 2000s
Locale(s): United States

Summary: Four women have come together through their
church's discipleship group, and have bonded into true
friends. This is a truly good thing, since they are all facing problems and need each other's support. Paula Manns
is facing the end of her marriage, and she doesn't know
what, if anything, she can do to keep her husband Darryl
at her side. Belinda Stokes is disconcerted when her
husband's teenage son comes to live with them. She
isn't certain she wants to be a stepmother, and isn't
thrilled at the demands the young man makes on her
marriage. Zora is a newlywed who is stunned to learn
her husband is feeling a call to the ministry. She feels no
matching call to become a minister's wife. Meanwhile,
Monet, the only single woman in the group, is heading
towards marriage, but afraid of commitment. Sequel to
Zora's Cry.

Other books by the same author:
Zora's Cry, 2006
A Heart of Devotion, 2005

Other books you might like:
Angela Benson, *The Genesis House Series*, 2000-
Venise Berry, *Colored Sugar Water*, 2002
Cherie Paris Edwards, *Plenty Good Room*, 2005
Felicia Mason, *Testimony*, 2002
Jacquelin Thomas, *A Change Is Gonna Come*, 2003

963

NANCY MEHL

In the Dead of Winter

(Uhrichsville, Ohio: Barbour, 2008)

Story type: Mystery
Series: Ivy Towers. Book 1
Subject(s): Books and Reading; Inheritance
Major character(s): Samantha "Ivy" Towers, Store Owner (bookstore); Amos Parker, Police Officer (deputy sheriff)
Time period(s): 2000s
Locale(s): Winter Break, Kansas

Summary: When her great-aunt Bitty dies in a fall at her rare book shop in Winter Break, Kansas, Ivy Towers is stunned to learn she has inherited the bookstore. She also feels guilty, since she hasn't seen her aunt in three years. Arriving in Winter Break, Ivy begins to suspect things are not as clear-cut as an "accidental fall." She meets Bitty's friend Amos Parker, a deputy sheriff, and is more than a little perturbed at Amos' unsubtle attempts to get her to leave town quickly. When Ivy receives a note telling her that Bitty was murdered, Ivy decides to stay in Winter Break until she learns the truth.

Other books by the same author:
Sinner's Song, 2006
Malevolence, 2005
Graven Images, 1998

Other books you might like:
Christine Lynxwiler, *Death on a Deadline*, 2008
Lynn Bulock, *The Gracie Lee Harris Series*, 2005-
Lori Copeland, *The Morning Shade Series*, 2003-
Peggy Darty, *The Christy Castleman Series*, 2005-
Susan Page Davis, *Homicide at Blue Heron*, 2008

964

SUSAN MEISSNER

Blue Heart Blessed

(Eugene, Oregon: Harvest House, 2008)

Story type: Romance
Subject(s): Clothes; Fathers and Sons; Weddings
Major character(s): Daisy Murien, Store Owner (secondhand bridal gown store); Ramsey Laurent, Divorced Person, Single Parent; Father Laurent, Religious (Episcopal priest)
Time period(s): 2000s
Locale(s): Minneapolis, Minnesota

Summary: Daisy Murien has opened a secondhand bridal gown store, with only one dress she is unwilling to sell: the one she was going to wear at her own wedding. Daisy's fiance, jilted her, and she is left with nothing but the gown to remind her of what might have been. One of Daisy's best friends is Father Laurent, a retired Episcopal priest who blesses the little blue hearts Daisy sews into each gown for luck. When Father Laurent has a heart attack, his son Ramsey comes to town, intent on taking him away so he can be better cared for. This upsets both Daisy and Father Laurent, and soon sparks are flying between all those involved.

Where it's reviewed:
Publishers Weekly, October 29, 2007, page 30

Other books by the same author:
The Shape of Mercy, 2008
Days & Hours, 2007
Sticks & Stones, 2007
A Seahorse in the Thames, 2006
Widows & Orphans, 2006

Other books you might like:
Rachel Hauck, *Love Starts with Elle*, 2008
Denise Hunter, *The Convenient Groom*, 2008
Terri Kraus, *The Renovation*, 2008
Janette Oke, *The Matchmakers*, 1997
Gary E. Parker, *The Wedding Dress*, 2001

965

SARA MITCHELL

Legacy of Secrets

(New York: Steeple Hill, 2008)

Story type: Historical
Subject(s): Family; Secrets
Major character(s): Neala Shaw, Heiress—Dispossessed; Grayson Faulkner, Detective—Private
Time period(s): 1880s
Locale(s): United States

Summary: After her parents are killed in an accident, Neala Shaw finds herself suddenly bereft. Her father, a respected university professor, left little money to help support his children. When Neala's brother leaves town for better opportunities, Neala finds herself truly alone. She soon learns that her family is the target of a killer, and she may be the next victim. She turns to detective Grayson Faulkner for help. Faulkner is a tough man who has more knowledge of the seedy side of life than Neala ever will. However, he is agreeable to helping protect Neala by pretending to be her suitor. As time passes, he comes to realize that Neala is a charming woman he would love to have a future with, if he could move away from the hurts of his past life.

Other books by the same author:
Virginia Autumn, 2002
Because of You, 2001
Shenandoah Home, 2001
Ransomed Heart, 1999
Shelter of His Arms, 1998

Other books you might like:
Lawana Blackwell, *The Tales of London Series*, 2001-
Cathy Marie Hake, *Letter Perfect*, 2006
Catherine Palmer, *The Victorian Rose Series*, 2002-
Tracie Peterson, *The Broadmoor Legacy Series*, 2008-
Lori Wick, *The English Garden Series*, 2002-

Inspirational

966

STEPHANIE PERRY MOORE

Wearing My Halo Tilted

(New York: Kensington, 2008)

Story type: Contemporary
Subject(s): African Americans; Marriage
Major character(s): Shari Maddox, Writer; Dillon Maddox, Coach (college football team); Bryce McCray, Singer (gospel)
Time period(s): 2000s
Locale(s): United States

Summary: Shari Maddox's marriage to her football coach husband has been on shaky ground for awhile, but with his refusing to admit they are having problems, Shari doesn't know what to do. Then her agent calls with great news. One of Shari's books is being turned into a play, and her agent wants her to tour along with the play and sell copies of her books. Shari jumps at the chance to get away from her toxic marriage, and is soon on the road. The star of the play is handsome gospel singer Bryce McCray, who has some marriage problems of his own. Soon Shari finds herself tempted to stray, and she has to struggle to remember to stay on the right path.

Other books by the same author:
Chasing Faith, 2007
A Lova' Like No Otha', 2003
Flame, 2001

Other books you might like:
ReShonda Tate Billingsley, *The Pastor's Wife*, 2007
Cherie Paris Edwards, *Plenty Good Room*, 2005
Aisha Ford, *Flippin' the Script*, 2004
Jacquelin Thomas, *Singsation*, 2001
Carl Weber, *The First Lady*, 2007

967

RUTH AXTELL MORREN

Hearts in the Highlands

(New York: Steeple Hill, 2008)

Story type: Historical
Subject(s): Archaeology
Major character(s): Maddie Norton, Companion; Reid Gallagher, Archaeologist
Time period(s): 1890s
Locale(s): London, England; Highlands, Scotland

Summary: Maddie Norton has long since accepted the fact that romance has passed her by, and she is fine with that. She has her charity work to keep her busy, and her work as a companion to an old lady. Then Lady Haversham's archaeologist nephew returns from a dig in Egypt. Maddie is enthralled by Reid Gallagher's thrilling stories of adventure and daring-do, and soon becomes attracted to the handsome man. When Reid asks Maddie to accompany the family to the Scottish Highlands, she eagerly agrees, hoping that romance may bloom.

Other books by the same author:
The Making of a Gentleman, 2008
The Rogue's Redemption, 2008
The Healing Season, 2007
Wild Rose, 2007
Dawn in My Heart, 2006

Other books you might like:
Lawana Blackwell, *The Tales of London Series*, 2001-
Liz Curtis Higgs, *Grace in Thine Eyes*, 2006
Grace Johnson, *The Scottish Shores Series*, 1997-
Kathleen Morgan, *Embrace the Dawn*, 2002
Craig Parshall, *The Thistle and the Rose Series*, 2005-

968

GILBERT MORRIS

Dawn of a New Day

(Grand Rapids, Michigan: Fleming H. Revell, 2008)

Story type: Contemporary
Series: American Century. Book 7
Subject(s): Drugs
Major character(s): Bobby Stuart, Actor
Time period(s): 1960s
Locale(s): Los Angeles, California

Summary: In this final book of the Stuart family saga, it is now the 1960s. Boundaries are breaking down, as are many traditional family values. Bobby Stuart finds this out firsthand when his Hollywood career begins to take off. With temptations like sex and drugs all around him, Bobby finds it very hard to stay true to himself, and to his faith.

Other books by the same author:
A Man for Temperance, 2007
What the Cat Dragged In, 2007
The Courtship, 2007
The Miracle, 2007
The White Knight, 2007

Other books you might like:
Jack Cavanaugh, *The American Family Portrait Series*, 1994-
Karen Kingsbury, *Fame*, 2005
Jane Peart, *The Brides of Montclair Series*, 1989-
Tracie Peterson, *A Slender Thread*, 2000
Alison Strobel, *Worlds Collide*, 2005

969

TOM MORRISEY

Wind River

(Minneapolis: Bethany House, 2008)

Story type: Contemporary
Subject(s): Aging; Fishing
Major character(s): Tyler Perkins, Veteran; Soren Andeman, Aged Person
Time period(s): 2000s
Locale(s): Wyoming

Summary: Returning from a tour of duty in Iraq, Tyler Perkins wants to try to forget what he saw overseas. He goes off to Wyoming, where the emptiness of the country gives him time to reflect. It also allows him to meet up with his long-time friend Soren Andeman and do some fly fishing. However, as Tyler and Soren begin their journey to the river to catch trout, they uncover some secrets from the past that others want to keep hidden.

Other books by the same author:
In High Places, 2007
Dark Fathom, 2005
Deep Blue, 2004
Turn 4, 2004

Other books you might like:
Linda Goodnight, *The Heart of Grace*, 2007
Robin Lee Hatcher, *Beyond the Shadows*, 2004
Patricia Hickman, *Sandpebbles*, 2002
Alan Maki, *Written on Her Heart*, 2002
Shirlee McCoy, *Lakeview Protector*, 2008

970

NANCY MOSER

Washington's Lady

(Minneapolis: Bethany House, 2008)

Story type: Historical/American Revolution; Historical/Post-American Revolution
Series: Ladies of History. Book 3
Subject(s): American Colonies; Biography; Revolutionary War
Major character(s): Martha Custis Washington, Spouse, Historical Figure; George Washington, Military Personnel, Political Figure (president)
Time period(s): 18th century
Locale(s): United States

Summary: Young widow Martha Custis feels no compelling need to remarry. Her wealthy husband left her comfortably off, and she is content to be a mother to her children. Then she meets George Washington, and decides to marry again. Their life together is not an easy one. Soon after the wedding, George is called away to lead the newly formed American government through its Revolution. Afterwards, George is elected president. Through it all, Martha stands by with him, doing her best to support her husband.

Where it's reviewed:
Publishers Weekly, April 21, 2008, page 36

Other books by the same author:
John 3:16, 2008
Just Jane, 2007
Solemnly Swear, 2007
Mozart's Sister, 2006
The Good Nearby, 2006

Other books you might like:
Reg Grant, *Storm*, 2001
Joe Musser, *The Infidel*, 2001
Caroline Coleman O'Neill, *Loving Soren*, 2005
Catherine Palmer, *The Treasure of Timbuktu*, 1997
Christine Schaub, *Finding Anna*, 2005

971

CATHERINE PALMER
GARY CHAPMAN , Co-Author

Winter Turns to Spring

(Carol Stream, Illinois: Tyndale House, 2008)

Story type: Contemporary
Series: Four Seasons. Book Four
Subject(s): Marriage
Major character(s): Brad Hanes, Spouse; Ashley Hanes, Spouse
Time period(s): 2000s
Locale(s): Deepwater Cover, Missouri

Summary: Brad and Ashley Hanes thought they had found everlasting bliss when they got married, but newlywed life is proving to be a true challenge. Both are working too hard, but bills are still piling up. Ashley thinks Brad wastes money, and Brad thinks Ashley is too frugal. When betrayals begin to creep into the marriage, both of the newlyweds begin to wonder if they made a huge mistake by getting married.

Other books by the same author:
Falling for You Again, 2007
Summer Breeze, 2007
It Happens Every Spring, 2006

Other books you might like:
Charlene Ann Baumbich, *The Dearest Dorothy Series*, 2004-
Julie Carobini, *Chocolate Beach*, 2007
Thomas Kinkade, *The Cape Light Series*, 2002-
Linda Nichols, *If I Gained the World*, 2003
Debra White Smith, *The Seven Sisters Series*, 2000-

972

DELIA PARR

Where Love Dwells

(Minneapolis: Bethany House, 2008)

Story type: Historical
Series: Candlewood Trilogy. Book Three
Subject(s): Boarding Houses
Major character(s): Emma Garret, Landlord (boardinghouse owner); Zachary Breckenwith, Lawyer
Time period(s): 1840s
Locale(s): Candlewood, New York

Summary: Emma Garret is excited at the prospect of finally introducing her children and grandchildren to her beau, Zachary Breckenwith. With her family due to visit her for her upcoming birthday, Emma hopes they will approve of her courtship. Unfortunately, the family reunion does not go well. Her sons have problems that make them unsympathetic to their mother's concerns. As Zachary begins to press Emma for an answer to his marriage proposal, she begins to wonder if there is any way she can have total happiness.

Other books by the same author:
Day by Day, 2007
Refining Emma, 2007
A Hearth in Candlewood, 2006
Abide with Me, 2006
Home to Trinity, 2003

Other books you might like:
Deeanne Gist, *A Bride Most Begrudging*, 2005
Louise M. Gouge, *The Ahab Series*, 2004-
B.J. Hoff, *The American Anthem Series*, 2002-
Tracie Peterson, *The Bells of Lowell Series*, 2003-
Lori Wick, *The Tucker Mills Series*, 2005-

973

BETH PATTILLO

The Sweetgum Knit Lit Society

(Colorado Springs, Colorado: WaterBrook, 2008)

Story type: Contemporary
Subject(s): Books and Reading; Small Town Life
Major character(s): Eugenie Pierce, Librarian; Hannah Simmons, Teenager
Time period(s): 2000s
Locale(s): Sweetgum, Tennessee

Summary: When librarian Eugenia Pierce runs across troubled teenager Hannah Simmons misbehaving in her library, she ropes the girl into joining her book discussion and knitting group. She even has the group start reading classic novels that she believes Hannah should be introduced to. As the ladies begin to help Hannah, they begin to realize they could use a bit of help with life themselves.

Other books by the same author:
Earth to Betsy, 2006
Heavens to Betsy, 2005
Princess Charming, 2003

Other books you might like:
Linda Dorrell, *True Believers*, 2001
Beth Webb Hart, *The Wedding Machine*, 2007
Susan Meissner, *In All Deep Places*, 2006
Deborah Raney, *Playing by Heart*, 2003
Jamie Langston Turner, *A Garden to Keep*, 2001

974

JUDITH PELLA

Sister's Choice

(Minneapolis: Bethany House, 2008)

Story type: Historical
Series: Patchwork Circle. Book 2
Subject(s): Courtship; Quilts; Trials
Major character(s): Maggie Newcomb, Artisan (aspiring quilter); Colby Stoddard, Farmer; Evan Parker, Lawyer
Time period(s): 1880s
Locale(s): Maintown, Oregon

Summary: Maggie Newcomb is deeply in love with Colby Stoddard and is thrilled when his one-time love falls for another man. Thinking she now is within Colby's sights, Maggie decides to do all she can to win his approval. She decides she is going to become the best quilter in town, something she knows will call Colby's attention to her. Unfortunately, Maggie is inept at quilting, so that plan doesn't bode well. Also making her situation look bad is the arrival of beautiful Tamara Brennan, who immediately catches the eye of nearly every man in town, including that of Colby Stoddard. Maggie, along with her friend Evan, begins to hatch more schemes. Then Maggie takes another look at Evan, and starts to wonder if that is where her heart truly lies.

Other books by the same author:
Bachelor's Puzzle, 2007
Mark of the Cross, 2006
Homeward My Heart, 2004
Toward the Sunrise, 2003
Written on the Wind, 2002

Other books you might like:
Tamera Alexander, *The Fountain Creek Chronicles*, 2006-
Jane Kirkpatrick, *The Kinship and Courage Series*, 2000-
Kathleen Morgan, *The Brides of Culdee Creek Series*, 1999-
Catherine Palmer, *The Victorian Rose Series*, 2002-
Tracie Peterson, *The Heirs of Montana Series*, 2004-

975

TRISH PERRY

Beach Dreams

(Eugene, Oregon: Harvest House, 2008)

Story type: Contemporary
Series: Beach House. Book 3
Subject(s): Beaches; Friendship; Grief
Major character(s): Tiffany LeBoeuf, Vacationer, Unemployed; Jeremy Beckett, Vacationer; Eve, Vacationer
Time period(s): 2000s
Locale(s): San Diego, California

Summary: Tiffany LeBoeuf is drained from the stress of caring for her mother, who has recently died of cancer. Adding to her troubles is her sudden job loss, the result of taking too much time away from work to be with her mom. Needing to get away, Tiffany arranges to stay at a beach cottage in San Diego. A scheduling conflict lands her there at the same time as a young woman named Eve. Tiffany doesn't really mind, until Eve's boyfriend Jeremy shows up. Tiffany and Jeremy have met, and Tiffany doesn't have pleasant memories of the experience. When Jeremy settles in at the beach house next door, Tiffany is forced to get along with him, and she begins to realize that Jeremy may not only be all that bad, but just might be the man of her dreams. This book is a continuation of the Beach House series begun by Sally John, using some of the characters from John's earlier

books, as well as characters from Trish Perry's book *Too Good to Be True*.

Other books by the same author:
Too Good to Be True, 2007
The Guy I'm Not Dating, 2006

Other books you might like:
Terri Blackstock, *Seaside*, 2001
Susan Meissner, *The Remedy for Regret*, 2005
Carole Gift Page, *A Bungalow for Two*, 2001
Jane Peart, *Sandcastles*, 2004
Gayle Roper, *The Seaside Seasons Series*, 2001-

976

TRACIE PETERSON

A Lady of Hidden Intent

(Minneapolis: Bethany House, 2008)

Story type: Historical
Series: Ladies of Liberty. Book 2
Subject(s): Fathers and Daughters; Sewing
Major character(s): Catherine Newbury, Seamstress; Carter Danby, Architect
Time period(s): 1850s
Locale(s): Philadelphia, Pennsylvania

Summary: Catherine Newbury is forced to flee her opulent life in England after her father is falsely imprisoned for slave trading. To her horror, she learns she must make her own living. In Philadelphia, Catherine begins to work as a seamstress, and her fine dresses are soon in high demand by the upper-class ladies of the city. Then Catherine runs into handsome architect Carter Danby, a man she had met (and spurned) while living in England. Hoping he won't remember her, Catherine is shocked to find that she is now attracted to the man she once thought beneath her notice.

Where it's reviewed:
Library Journal, February 1, 2008, page 56

Other books by the same author:
A Lady of Secret Devotion, 2008
A Lady of High Regard, 2007
Where My Heart Belongs, 2007
Summer of the Midnight Sun, 2006
Under the Northern Lights, 2006

Other books you might like:
Lawana Blackwell, *The Tales of London Series*, 2001-
Linda Chaikin, *The Silk House Series*, 2006-
B.J. Hoff, *The American Anthem Series*, 2002-
Catherine Palmer, *The English Ivy Series*, 2002-
Lori Wick, *The Tucker Mills Series*, 2005-

977

MICHAEL PHILLIPS

Dream of Love

(Carol Stream, Illinois: Tyndale House, 2008)

Story type: Historical/American Civil War
Series: American Dreams. Book 3
Subject(s): American South; Civil War; Slavery
Major character(s): Seth Davidson, Photographer; Cherity Waters, Wealthy; Richmond Davidson, Parent, Spouse
Time period(s): 1860s
Locale(s): United States

Summary: Richmond and Carolyn Davidson have done their best to maintain their faith and their beliefs during the trials caused by the American Civil War. With one son serving in the Confederate Army and a second working for the North as a war photographer, they are torn in one respect, but realize that slavery cannot continue. They have worked as conductors on the Underground Railroad for years, and continue to do so, often putting their own lives at risk. The war has taken its toll on the Davidsons' financial state, and they are about to lose their land. Their son Seth's longtime love, Cherity, is willing to help them, until she sees Seth with another woman. She begins to believe that she might be wrong about the integrity of the entire Davidson family, and withdraws her offer of assistance. With time running out, the Davidsons can only pray for a miracle to save their land.

Other books by the same author:
Miss Katie's Rosewood, 2007
Never Too Late, 2007
Dream of Life, 2006
The Soldier's Lady, 2006
A Perilous Proposal, 2005

Other books you might like:
Lynn Austin, *The Refiner's Fire Series*, 2002-
Roger Elwood, *The Plantation Letters Series*, 1997-
Virginia Gaffney, *The Richmond Chronicles*, 1996-
Gary E. Parker, *The Southern Tides Series*, 2004-
Lauraine Snelling, *The Secret Refuge Series*, 2000-

978

ALLIE PLEITER

Masked by Moonlight

(New York: Steeple Hill, 2008)

Story type: Historical/American West Coast; Romance
Subject(s): Crime and Criminals; Identity, Concealed
Major character(s): Georgia Waterhouse, Journalist; Matthew Covington, Wealthy, Adventurer
Time period(s): 1890s
Locale(s): San Francisco, California

Summary: Georgia Waterhouse, like all of San Francisco, is enthralled by the daring deeds of the Black Bandit, a mysterious masked crime fighter. In fact, the Bandit's actions have become public knowledge largely due to Georgia, who writes about him for a newspaper under a nom-de-plume. She wishes that more men were like the Black Bandit, especially wealthy socialite Matthew Covington, who in Georgia's mind has more money than sense. Little does Georgia know that the man she spurns as useless is actually the Black Bandit, and that under both of his guises he finds her a very intriguing woman indeed.

Other books by the same author:
Bluegrass Hero, 2008
The Perfect Blend, 2007
My So-Called Love Life, 2006
Queen Esther and the Second Graders of Doom, 2006
Bad Heiress Day, 2005

Other books you might like:
Victoria Bylin, *The Bounty Hunter's Bride*, 2008
Dorothy Clark, *Beauty for Ashes*, 2004
Deeanne Gist, *The Measure of a Lady*, 2006
Sara Mitchell, *Legacy of Secrets*, 2008
Allison Pittman, *Speak through the Wind*, 2007

979

DEBORAH RANEY

Leaving November

(New York: Howard Books, 2008)

Story type: Contemporary
Series: Clayburn. Book 2
Subject(s): Alcoholism; Small Town Life
Major character(s): Vienne Kenney, Lawyer; Jackson Linder, Art Dealer (art gallery owner)
Time period(s): 2000s
Locale(s): Clayburn, Kansas

Summary: Vienne Kenney left her tiny hometown of Clayburn, Kansas, intending to never come back, but after attending law school in California, Vienne is having trouble passing the bar exam. After two failed attempts, she has no choice but to return to Clayburn and try to put her life together. It isn't easy though, since everybody in town knows her only as the daughter of one of the town's failures. Also coming back to Clayburn is Jackson Linder, who is fighting some demons of his own, but is intent on making a success of his art gallery.

Other books by the same author:
Remember to Forget, 2007
Within This Circle, 2007
A Vow to Cherish, 2006
Over the Waters, 2005
A Nest of Sparrows, 2004

Other books you might like:
Deborah Bedford, *Only You*, 2007
Linda Dorrell, *Face to Face*, 2003
Robin Lee Hatcher, *Beyond the Shadows*, 2004
Karen Kingsbury, *Sunrise*, 2007
Lisa Samson, *Straight Up*, 2006

980

RALPH REED

Dark Horse

(New York: Howard Books, 2008)

Story type: Contemporary
Subject(s): Political Thriller; Politics
Major character(s): Salmon Stanley, Political Figure

(presidential candidate); Bob Long, Political Figure (presidential candidate); David Petty, Political Figure (presidential candidate)
Time period(s): 2000s
Locale(s): United States

Summary: The latest presidential race is shaping up to be like one never seen before. After a fight at the Democratic National convention, a moderate candidate named Bob Long launches an independent run for the presidency against the candidate he believes got the nomination unfairly, Salmon Stanley. As the presidential race gets nasty, Stanley is indicted for perjury and obstruction of justice, but he refuses to give up the nomination. Meanwhile, the Republican candidate seems to be a shoo-in, but after he is killed in a terrorist attack, the Republican nomination is given to David Petty, the first African-American Republican nominee in history. The three-way race gets nastier as time passes, and soon all three men are facing accusations of scandal that can leave none of them blameless. First novel, though Reed has written several nonfiction titles.

Where it's reviewed:
Publishers Weekly, April 21, 2008, page 35

Other books you might like:
Alton Gansky, *The Madison Glenn Series*, 2004-
Laura Hayden, *America the Beautiful*, 2008
Shane Johnson, *A Form of Godliness*, 2004
Oliver North, *Mission Compromised*, 2002
Joel C. Rosenberg, *Dead Heat*, 2008

981

ANNE RICE

Christ the Lord: The Road to Cana

(New York: Alfred A. Knopf, 2008)

Story type: Biblical Fiction
Series: Christ the Lord. Book 2
Subject(s): Jesus
Major character(s): Yeshua, Historical Figure, Biblical Figure
Time period(s): 1st century
Locale(s): Israel

Summary: Yeshua knows that his life is to serve a higher purpose, but he cannot put aside worldly thoughts altogether. Feeling highly attracted to a beautiful young woman, he begins to wonder about his future. However, as time passes, Yeshua's life becomes one of miracles performed and blessings given. When he attends a wedding at Cana, and performs a miracle that will once and for all let people know that he is truly the son of God, Yeshua accepts the path his life must take.

Where it's reviewed:
Booklist, December 15, 2007, page 4
Entertainment Weekly, March 7, 2008, page 95
Publishers Weekly, February 4, 2008, page 40

Other books by the same author:
Christ the Lord: Out of Egypt, 2005
Blood Canticle, 2003
Blackwood Farm, 2002
Blood and Gold, 2001
Merrick, 2000

Other books you might like:
Gene Edwards, *The First Century Diaries Series*, 1998-
Tracy Groot, *The Brother's Keeper*, 2003
Thom Lemmons, *The Daughters of Faith Series*, 1999-
Gilbert Morris, *The Lions of Judah Series*, 2002-
Francine Rivers, *The Lineage of Grace Series*, 2000-

982

PAUL ROBERTSON

Road to Nowhere

(Minneapolis: Bethany House, 2008)

Story type: Mystery
Subject(s): Business
Major character(s): Joe Esterhouse, Political Figure
Time period(s): 2000s
Locale(s): Wardsville, North Carolina

Summary: Joe Esterhouse has served for years on the board of supervisors in the tiny town of Wardsville, North Carolina, and he has never faced a problem like he does now. It is proposed that a highway project, long delayed, be completed, but the proposition has far reaching consequences. Great money can be made out of the deal, but it will change the town forever. The townspeople begin to fight over what is truly best for the town, versus what is best for some. Then it begins to appear as if somebody is willing to kill in order to get their way over the project.

Other books by the same author:
The Heir, 2007

Other books you might like:
Beth Webb Hart, *The Wedding Machine*, 2007
Patricia Hickman, *Sandpebbles*, 2002
Penelope J. Stokes, *The Blue Bottle Club*, 1999
Jamie Langston Turner, *A Garden to Keep*, 2001
Eric Wilson, *The Best of Evil*, 2006

983

SHARON CARTER ROGERS

Unpretty

(New York: Howard Books, 2008)

Story type: Mystery
Subject(s): Cults; Suspense
Major character(s): Hummingbird Collins, Artist; Buck Barnes, Police Officer; Ready Robinson, Religious (priest)
Time period(s): 2000s
Locale(s): Lehigh, West Virginia

Summary: An insidious cult is intent on destroying everything in the world that it considers "unpretty." The cult's latest target is an art exhibition at a gallery in West Virginia. After a bomb goes off, destroying the building and killing eight people, the cult turns its attention to the only eyewitness, an artist named Hummingbird Collins. When Hummingbird begins receiving threatening messages from the cult, she is scared, but

determined not to give in to the threats. Then Hummingbird is kidnapped, and it is up to her brother and a family friend to find her before it is too late.

Other books by the same author:
Sinner, 2007

Other books you might like:
Stephen Arterburn, *The Forsaken*, 2006
James Scott Bell, *The Whole Truth*, 2008
Sigmund Brouwer, *Crown of Thorns*, 2002
Ted Dekker, *Saint*, 2006
Mel Odom, *Blood Evidence*, 2007
Craig Parshall, *The Last Judgment*, 2005

984

GAYLE ROPER

Fatal Deduction

(Colorado Springs, Colorado: Multnomah, 2008)

Story type: Mystery
Subject(s): Secrets; Sisters; Twins
Major character(s): Libby Keating, Heiress, Single Parent; Tori Burton, Heiress; Chloe Burton, Teenager
Time period(s): 2000s
Locale(s): Philadelphia, Pennsylvania

Summary: Libby Burton Keating has inherited her great aunt Stella's Philadelphia home, in a way. The inheritance comes with some strings attached. First off, Libby is to share the inheritance with her twin sister Tori. Both sisters must move into the house and live together for six months. If either leaves, neither inherits. Since Libby and Tori don't get along too well, things don't bode well for them making it to the six-month mark. Neither does the fact that their arrival is seriously marred by a dead body on the porch. Near the body is a crossword puzzle, and Libby soon realizes she must solve the puzzle to identify the killer and save herself, her sister, and her daughter.

Where it's reviewed:
Publishers Weekly, March 10, 2008, page 60

Other books by the same author:
Caught Redhanded, 2007
Caught in the Middle, 2007
Caught in a Bind, 2007
Caught in the Act, 2007
See No Evil, 2007

Other books you might like:
Mindy Starns Clark, *Whispers of the Bayou*, 2008
Sharon Dunn, *The Bargain Hunters Series*, 2007-
Angela Kiesling, *Skizzer*, 2008
Lorena McCourtney, *The Andi McConnell Series*, 2007-
Cyndy Salzmann, *The Crime and Clutter Series*, 2007-

985

JOEL C. ROSENBERG

Dead Heat

(Carol Stream, Illinois: Tyndale House, 2008)

Story type: Action/Adventure
Series: Last Jihad. Book 5

Inspirational

Subject(s): Political Thriller; Terrorism
Major character(s): Jon Bennett, Government Official (former presidential advisor); Erin Bennett, Spy (former CIA agent); James MacPherson, Political Figure (President of the United States)
Time period(s): Indeterminate Future
Locale(s): United States; Middle East

Summary: Over the past few years, Jon and Erin Bennett have seen their world change forever. Now even more terrifying changes are in store for them. North Korea is threatening the west, as is Iraq. With war breaking out in the Middle East, the Bennetts can only hope and pray that their new president is able to guide their country through its troubled times. As James MacPherson's term comes to an end, the presidential race begins, and becomes acrimonious. It becomes clear to the Bennetts that terrorists are planning to assassinate one of the presidential candidates. Unfortunately, they do not know who the target is, so they are powerless to stop the assassins.

Where it's reviewed:
Booklist, May 1, 2008, page 26

Other books by the same author:
Epicenter, 2006
The Copper Scroll, 2006
The Ezekiel Option, 2005
The Last Days, 2005
The Last Jihad, 2002

Other books you might like:
T. Davis Bunn, *Riders of the Pale Horse*, 2002
Ted Dekker, *Thunder of Heaven*, 2002
Kathy Herman, *Eye of the Beholder*, 2005
Phil Little, *The Matt Cooper Series*, 2006-
Mike Yorkey, *The Amber Robbins Series*, 2006-

986

LISA SAMSON

Embrace Me

(Nashville: Thomas Nelson, 2008)

Story type: Contemporary
Subject(s): Circus; Difference; Friendship
Major character(s): Valentine, Entertainer (sideshow performer); Lella, Entertainer (sideshow performer); Drew Parrish, Religious (former minister)
Time period(s): 2000s
Locale(s): Mount Oak, North Carolina

Summary: As part of a circus sideshow, "Lizard Woman" Valentine and "Human Cocoon" Lella know it is their job to shock, mystify, and perhaps frighten the circus patrons. However, beyond their disfigurements, both Valentine and Lella are ordinary women with the hopes and dreams of any other woman. Valentine is hideously scarred, for reasons she keeps secret, and she is often bitter and sad. Lella, though born without arms and legs, is more upbeat and optimistic. As the sideshow settles into a small town in North Carolina for the winter, Lella is disturbed when Valentine catches the attention of a traveling evangelist, who wants Valentine to accompany him on the road. Lella is fearful for her friend's future,

and is also terrified of being left behind.

Where it's reviewed:
Library Journal, February 1, 2008, page 54

Other books by the same author:
Finding Hollywood Nobody, 2008
Romancing Hollywood Nobody, 2008
Goodbye Hollywood Nobody, 2008
Embrace Me, 2007
Quaker Summer, 2007

Other books you might like:
Kathy Herman, *Poor Mrs. Rigsby*, 2004
Angela Hunt, *The Fairlawn Series*, 2007-
Charles Martin, *When Crickets Cry*, 2006
Gilbert Morris, *The Fiery Ring*, 2002
Lauraine Snelling, *The Way of Women*, 2004

987

MARLO SCHALESKY

Beyond the Night

(Colorado Springs, Colorado: Multnomah, 2008)

Story type: Contemporary
Subject(s): Accidents; Blindness; Love
Major character(s): Paul Tilden, Spouse; Maddie Foster Tilden, Spouse, Accident Victim
Time period(s): 20th century; 2000s (1973-2008)
Locale(s): United States

Summary: Maddie Tilden is in a car accident that leaves her in a coma, fighting for her life. At her bedside is her beloved husband Paul. As Paul prays for his wife's recovery, he thinks back over their life together, from their start as good friends, through their romance, and marriage. It hasn't been an easy road. Maddie suffered from a genetic illness that left her knowing she would go blind, and she had difficulty accepting that anybody could love her. Paul did, and does, love her, though, and desperately wants her to survive.

Other books by the same author:
Veil of Fire, 2007
Only the Wind Remembers, 2003
Freedom's Shadow, 2001
Cry Freedom, 2000

Other books you might like:
Angela Benson, *Abiding Hope*, 2001
Melody Carlson, *Angels in the Snow*, 2002
Karen Kingsbury, *A Time to Embrace*, 2002
Beverly Lewis, *The Sunroom*, 1998
Charles Martin, *The Dead Don't Dance*, 2004
Jane Orcutt, *The Living Stone*, 2000

988

NICOLE SEITZ

Trouble the Water

(Nashville: Thomas Nelson, 2008)

Story type: Contemporary
Subject(s): Abuse; Depression; Suicide

Major character(s): Honor Maddox, Unemployed; The Duchess, Care Giver
Time period(s): 2000s
Locale(s): Sea Islands, South Carolina

Summary: Honor Maddox feels she has nothing left to live for. She doesn't have a job, and her history of abuse gives her no reason to hope for better. She goes to an island off the coast of South Carolina, intending to kill herself. Instead, she is saved by some wonderful women who give her hope. Honor moves in with one of the women, named Duchess, and under Duchess' gentle care, even decides to reconnect with her long-estranged sister.

Other books by the same author:
The Spirit of Sweetgrass, 2007

Other books you might like:
Angela Benson, *The Amen Sisters*, 2005
Linda Hall, *Sadie's Song*, 2001
Charles Martin, *Chasing Fireflies*, 2007
Bette Nordberg, *Serenity Bay*, 2000
Deborah Raney, *Remember to Forget*, 2007
Venita Hampton Wright, *Velma Still Cooks in Leeway*, 2000

989

LINDA EVANS SHEPHERD
EVA MARIE EVERSON , Co-Author

The Secret's in the Sauce

(Grand Rapids, Michigan: Fleming H. Revell, 2008)

Story type: Contemporary
Series: Potluck Catering Club. Book 1
Subject(s): Catering Business; Cooks and Cooking; Friendship
Major character(s): Evangeline Benson, Caterer; Lisa Leann Lambert, Caterer; Goldie Dippel, Caterer
Time period(s): 2000s
Locale(s): Summit View, Colorado

Summary: The ladies of the Summit View, Colorado, prayer group The Potluck Club have decided to take their love of cooking and make money at it by opening a catering company. Unfortunately things don't go smoothly for the ladies. Little disagreements become big ones under the pressures of working together, and their personal lives begin to interfere with the business. Especially dangerous is a long-kept secret that threatens one of the ladies' once steadfast marriage.

Other books by the same author:
The Potluck Club Takes the Cake, 2007
Trouble's Brewing, 2006
The Potluck Club, 2005

Other books you might like:
Kristin Billerbeck, *The Spa Girls Series*, 2005-
Sandra Byrd, *The French Twist Series*, 2007-
Melody Carlson, *The 86 Bloomberg Place Series*, 2008-
Robin Jones Gunn, *The Sisterchicks Series*, 2003-
Neta Jackson, *The Yada Yada Prayer Group Series*, 2003-

990

RANDY SINGER

By Reason of Insanity

(Carol Stream, Illinois: Tyndale House, 2008)

Story type: Mystery
Subject(s): Legal Thriller; Trials
Major character(s): Quinn Newberg, Lawyer; Catherine O'Rourke, Journalist, Crime Suspect (serial killer)
Time period(s): 2000s
Locale(s): Virginia Beach, Virginia

Summary: Quinn Newberg is a lawyer used to lost causes, but his latest client is a true challenge. Catherine O'Rourke is accused of being a notorious serial killer known as the Avenger of Blood. Unfortunately, Catherine is of little help to her own defense. She knew far too much about the crimes before even the police did, but can only claim that she witnessed the hideous murders in dreams. With no other options, Quinn decides to use an insanity defense to save Catherine's life, claiming the dreams are the result of a personality disorder. However, it doesn't look as if anything will save Catherine from a guilty verdict.

Other books by the same author:
False Witness, 2007
The Cross Examination of Jesus Christ, 2006
The Cross Examination of Oliver Finney, 2006
Self Incrimination, 2005
The Judge Who Stole Christmas, 2005

Other books you might like:
James Scott Bell, *Blind Justice*, 2000
Brandilyn Collins, *Dread Champion*, 2002
Joe Hilley, *The Mike Connolly Series*, 2004-
Susan Meissner, *The Rachael Flynn Series*, 2006-
Nancy Moser, *Solemnly Swear*, 2007

991

DEBRA WHITE SMITH

Brittan

(Eugene, Oregon: Harvest House, 2008)

Story type: Mystery
Series: Debutantes. Book 3
Subject(s): Crime and Criminals; Trust
Major character(s): Brittan Shay, Debutante, Detective—Amateur; Rob Lightly, Police Officer; Jose Herrera, Young Man
Time period(s): 2000s
Locale(s): Houston, Texas

Summary: Brittan Shay has watched her two best friends, Lorna and Heather, find love, and now it might be her turn. Brittan meets handsome Jose Herrera, and thinks she is in love. The trouble is that a little investigative work turns up the fact that Jose's mother may be involved in a money laundering scheme. Brittan desperately wants to trust Jose, but his mysterious behavior doesn't help her any. Then handsome police chief Rob Lightly gets involved in the case, and Brittan finds

herself more confused than ever.

Other books by the same author:
Lorna, 2008
Heather, 2007
Amanda, 2006
Possibilities, 2006
Central Park, 2005

Other books you might like:
Lynn Bulock, *The Gracie Lee Harris Series*, 2005-
Mindy Starns Clark, *The Million Dollar Mysteries Series*, 2002-
Peggy Darty, *The Christy Castleman Series*, 2005-
Kathi Mills-Macias, *The Toni Matthews Series*, 2001-
Gilbert Morris, *One by One*, 2000

992

DEBRA WHITE SMITH

Lorna

(Eugene, Oregon: Harvest House, 2008)

Story type: Mystery; Amateur Detective
Series: Debutantes. Book 2
Subject(s): Politics; Scandal; Sports/Tennis
Major character(s): Lorna Leigh, Debutante, Detective—Amateur; Michael Hayden, Political Figure (mayor)
Time period(s): 2000s
Locale(s): Houston, Texas

Summary: Lorna Leigh finds the life of a debutante to be a boring one. She would much rather be playing tennis than attending parties. When she sneaks out of a party for the new mayor of Houston to get a breath of fresh air in the garden, she meets handsome Michael Hayden, who is none other than the new mayor himself. Something clicks between the two, and they are soon an item. However, when a local minister is arrested on charges of possessing pornography, Lorna puts her romance aside to investigate the case with her fellow debutante amateur detectives. Unfortunately, they unearth evidence that suggests Michael may somehow be involved with pornography himself, and Lorna is soon beginning to wonder if her new boyfriend is what he seems to be.

Other books by the same author:
Brittan, 2008
Heather, 2007
Amanda, 2006
Possibilities, 2006
Central Park, 2005

Other books you might like:
Nikki Arana, *The Regalo Grande Series*, 2005-
Kristin Billerbeck, *The Spa Girls Series*, 2005-
Mindy Starns Clark, *The Million Dollar Mysteries Series*, 2002-
Camy Tang, *The Sushi Series*, 2007-
Susan May Warren, *Finding Stefanie*, 2008

993

MICHAEL SNYDER

My Name Is Russell Fink

(Grand Rapids, Michigan: Zondervan, 2008)

Story type: Contemporary
Subject(s): Animals/Dogs; Humor; Relationships
Major character(s): Russell Fink, Salesman (copy machines)
Time period(s): 2000s
Locale(s): United States

Summary: Russell Fink is, to put it mildly, messed up. At age 26, he still lives with his parents. He hates his job; He has a fiancee he doesn't like, let alone love; and he is convinced that he somehow caused his twin sister to get cancer when they were both nine. Now Russell is determined to turn his life around. Unfortunately before he can make any progress towards this goal, his beloved basset hound Sonny is found murdered, and Russell once again finds himself on the losing edge of life. First novel.

Where it's reviewed:
Publishers Weekly, January 28, 2008, page 41

Other books you might like:
Judy Baer, *Million Dollar Dilemma*, 2005
Ray Blackston, *The Jay Jarvis Series*, 2003-
Allie Pleiter, *My So-Called Love Life*, 2006
Virginia Smith, *Just as I Am*, 2006
Rob Stennett, *The Almost True Story of Ryan Fisher*, 2008

994

ROB STENNETT

The Almost True Story of Ryan Fisher

(Grand Rapids, Michigan: Zondervan, 2008)

Story type: Contemporary
Subject(s): Christian Life; Real Estate; Satire
Major character(s): Ryan Fisher, Real Estate Agent, Religious (phony pastor)
Time period(s): 2000s
Locale(s): Denver, Colorado

Summary: Ryan Fisher is determined to succeed. As an up-and-coming real estate agent, he is willing to do whatever it takes to make it. With clients hard to come by, Ryan decides to advertise himself as a Christian real estate agent, thinking that devout believers will want to do business with one of their own. To his surprise, his plan works exceedingly well, and he is soon selling homes at an unbelievable rate. Thinking that he might as well expand this method of selling, Ryan starts his own church, and once again proves to be a phenomenal success. The trouble is that Ryan didn't realize that his lies are going to start costing him, once the truth about his lack of beliefs comes out. First novel.

Other books you might like:
Charlene Ann Baumbich, *The Dearest Dorothy Series*,
   2004-
Ray Blackston, *Flabbergasted*, 2003
Hope Lyda, *Hip to Be Square*, 2005
Beth Pattillo, *Heavens to Betsy*, 2005
Michael Snyder, *My Name Is Russell Fink*, 2008

995

KIMBERLY STUART

Act Two

(Colorado Springs, Colorado: David C. Cook, 2008)

Story type: Contemporary
Subject(s): College Life; Singing; Small Town Life
Major character(s): Sadie Maddox, Singer, Professor
Time period(s): 2000s
Locale(s): Maplewood, Iowa

Summary: Classical singer Sadie Maddox is world famous,
but her career could use a boost. Her CDs aren't selling
like they used to, and her reputation as a hard to please
diva is starting to get in the way of her appeal to concert
bookers. So when Sadie's agent suggests she take up a
college professorship, she decides she has nothing to
lose. After all, she's survived pretty much everything in
her long career. Surely she can handle college students.
Then she learns the college is in small town Iowa, and
the appeal diminishes since Sadie is a city girl, through
and through. Once she actually gets to Maplewood,
though, the town starts to grow on her, and she begins to
wonder if she even wants to go back to the city when
her contract is up.

Other books by the same author:
Bottom Line, 2007
Balancing Act, 2006

Other books you might like:
Robin Lee Hatcher, *Return to Me*, 2007
Rachel Hauck, *Diva NashVegas*, 2007
Sharon Hinck, *Symphony of Secrets*, 2008
Felicia Mason, *Sweet Harmony*, 2004
Mae Nunn, *Amazing Love*, 2006

996

CAMY TANG

Single Sashimi

(Grand Rapids, Michigan: Zondervan, 2008)

Story type: Romance
Series: Sushi. Book 3
Subject(s): Asian Americans; Computer Games
Major character(s): Venus Chau, Businesswoman (video
   game developer); Drake Yu, Businessman
Time period(s): 2000s
Locale(s): California

Summary: Venus Chau is a video game developer with
massive plans for the future. Unfortunately, putting those
plans into action will take money, and money is

something Venus doesn't have. To get the start-up fees
she needs, Venus agrees to do something she once
promised herself she would never do: accept the help of
Drake Yu. She hates Drake, but Drake's sister needs help
with her startup, so Venus agrees to the bargain. What
she doesn't realize is that both she and Drake have
changed, and they might just find something to like about
each other, if they give romance a shot.

Other books by the same author:
Only Uni, 2008
Sushi for One?, 2007

Other books you might like:
Judy Baer, *Be My Neat-Heart*, 2006
Kristin Billerbeck, *The Ashley Stockingdale Series*,
   2004-
Sandra Byrd, *The French Twist Series*, 2007-
Melody Carlson, *The 86 Bloomberg Place Series*, 2008-
Laura Jensen Walker, *The Phoebe Grant Series*, 2005-

997

BODIE THOENE
BROCK THOENE , Co-Author

Eighth Shepherd

(Carol Stream, Illinois: Tyndale House, 2008)

Story type: Biblical Fiction
Series: A.D. Chronicles. Book 8
Subject(s): Bible; Biblical Fiction; Jesus
Major character(s): Yeshua, Biblical Figure; Simona,
   Handicapped (leper); Zacchaeus, Government Official
   (tax collector)
Time period(s): 1st century
Locale(s): Israel

Summary: Yeshua's fame as a miracle worker has spread.
His raising of El'azar from the dead is a feat that cannot
be explained away, and people begin to realize he truly
is the son of God. One of Yeshua's followers is a leper
named Simona. Though cured by Yeshua, Simona is still
cut off from the world. Also set apart from the world is a
tax collector named Zacchaeus, who is hated by all
because of his profession. Simona meets Zacchaeus, and
tells him of Yeshua. As Zacchaeus becomes intrigued by
Yeshua, he becomes determined to have Yeshua save
him as he has saved so many others.

Other books by the same author:
Seventh Day, 2007
Sixth Covenant, 2007
Fifth Seal, 2006
Fourth Dawn, 2005
London Refrain, 2005

Other books you might like:
Gene Edwards, *The First Century Diaries Series*, 1998-
Angela Hunt, *The Shadow Woman*, 2002
Thom Lemmons, *The Daughters of Faith Series*, 1999-
Gilbert Morris, *The Lions of Judah Series*, 2002-
Robert L. Wise, *The People of the Covenant Series*,
   1991-

Inspirational

998

DEBBIE FULLER THOMAS

Tuesday Night at the Blue Moon

(Chicago: Moody, 2008)

Story type: Contemporary
Series: Also Rans. Book 1
Subject(s): Children; Death; Mothers and Daughters
Major character(s): Marty Winslow, Single Parent; Andie Lockhart, Child; Deja Winslow, Teenager
Time period(s): 2000s
Locale(s): United States

Summary: Marty Winslow's life is turned upside down when her beloved daughter Ginger dies from Niemann-Pick Disease. Marty's grief is worsened when she learns that the genetic disease cannot have been passed to her daughter from her. It turns out that Ginger was not her biological daughter, and her own birth daughter is actually a young girl named Andi Lockhart. Because Andi is orphaned and her grandparents' senior community won't let her move in with them, the courts grant Marty temporary custody of the confused young girl. Reunited with her birth family, Andi is traumatized and bewildered by all of the changes in her life and Marty, a stressed single mom at the best of times, finds it difficult to cope with her newfound middle daughter. First novel.

Other books you might like:
Robin Lee Hatcher, *Firstborn*, 2002
Kristen Heitzmann, *The Still of Night*, 2003
Denise Hunter, *Finding Faith*, 2006
Nancy Jo Jenkins, *Coldwater Revival*, 2006
Carole Gift Page, *In Search of Her Own*, 1997

999

TRAVIS THRASHER

Isolation

(New York: Faith Words, 2008)

Story type: Mystery
Subject(s): Fathers and Sons; Suspense
Major character(s): James Miller, Writer, Spouse; Stephanie Miller, Spouse
Time period(s): 2000s
Locale(s): North Carolina

Summary: Missionaries James and Stephanie Miller have been through some horrible times, and they want to take some time to unwind and relax. Leaving suburbia behind, they go to a remote cabin in the mountains of North Carolina. James plans to write, while Stephanie just wants to have some family time with her husband and their two children. Things being to go wrong almost immediately for the couple, however. A snowstorm isolates them, and they soon begin to realize they are becoming the targets of spiritual attacks that threaten not only their lives on earth, but their spiritual lives as well.

Where it's reviewed:
Publishers Weekly, June 9, 2008, page 30

Other books by the same author:
Out of the Devil's Mouth, 2008
Sky Blue, 2007
Admission, 2006
Blinded, 2006
Gun Lake, 2004

Other books you might like:
Karen Hancock, *Arena*, 2002
Angela Hunt, *The Truth Teller*, 1999
Gilbert Morris, *Through a Glass Darkly*, 1999
Bill Myers, *The Soul Trackers Series*, 2004-
Lauraine Snelling, *Saturday Morning*, 2005
Eric Wilson, *The Best of Evil*, 2006

1000

TRAVIS THRASHER

Out of the Devil's Mouth

(Chicago: Moody, 2008)

Story type: Historical
Series: Henry Wolfe. Book 1
Subject(s): Missionaries
Major character(s): Henry Wolfe, Journalist, Adventurer; Louis Prescott, Wealthy
Time period(s): 1920s
Locale(s): Venezuela

Summary: In 1928, the wealthy Prescott family asks adventurer and reporter Henry Wolfe to travel to South America to try and find their son. Louis Prescott has disappeared while trying to find evidence of a lost tribe that supposedly held the secret to everlasting life. Traveling through the jungles of Venezuela, Henry Wolfe soon finds himself fighting for his life, while still trying to find traces of Louis Prescott.

Other books by the same author:
Isolation, 2008
Sky Blue, 2007
Admission, 2006
Blinded, 2006
Gun Lake, 2004

Other books you might like:
James Scott Bell, *Glimpses of Paradise*, 2005
Margaret Daley, *Heart of the Amazon*, 2007
Anne De Graaf, *Into the Nevernight*, 2003
Pamela Binnings Ewen, *The Moon in the Mango Tree*, 2008
Angela Hunt, *The Canopy*, 2003

1001

CHRIS WALLEY

The Infinite Day

(Carol Stream, Illinois: Tyndale House, 2008)

Story type: Science Fiction
Series: Lamb Among the Stars. Book 3
Subject(s): Heroes and Heroines; Hostages
Major character(s): Merral D'Avanos, Leader; Nezhuala, Ruler (emperor)

Time period(s): Indeterminate Future
Locale(s): Dominion Worlds, Interstellar Empire/
 Federation

Summary: The Dominion forces have been defeated, but
brave Commander Merral D'Avanos still has a battle on
his hands. He has to rescue some hostages before they
are taken to the Dominion worlds, where they will most
likely not survive. A rescue mission is dangerous, as it
will take D'Avanos' crew into Dominion territory, but he
is determined to rescue the brave fighters. However, as
D'Avanos is planning his rescue mission, the Emperor
Nezhuala will not let this one defeat stand, and he is
determined to launch yet another attack.

Other books by the same author:
The Dark Foundations, 2006
The Shadow and Night, 2006

Other books you might like:
Austin Boyd, *The Mars Hill Classified Series*, 2006-
Karen Hancock, *The Legends of the Guardian King
 Series*, 2003-
Sharon Hinck, *The Sword of Lyric Series*, 2007-
Kathleen Morgan, *The Guardians of Gadiel Series*,
 2005-
Gilbert Morris, *The Far Fields Series*, 1994-
Kathy Tyers, *The Firebird Trilogy*, 1999-

1002

SUSAN MAY WARREN

Finding Stefanie

(Carol Stream, Illinois: Tyndale House, 2008)

Story type: Romance
Series: Noble Legacy. Book 3
Subject(s): Arson; Ranch Life
Major character(s): Stefanie Noble, Wealthy; Lincoln
 Cash, Actor
Time period(s): 2000s
Locale(s): Phillips, Montana

Summary: Stefanie Noble knows that she should be
content. She has a comfortable existence, living on her
family's ranch in Montana. Something is missing though,
and when she runs across some troubled kids, Stefanie
finally finds a purpose in life. As she helps a boy named
Gideon and his two younger sisters, Stefanie starts to
realize that not everybody wants the three to get a new
start. Chief among their detractors is Hollywood hotshot
Lincoln Cash, who has come to Montana to restart his
career. When a fire blamed on arson is seen as Gideon's
work, Lincoln on intent of chasing Gideon out of town,
no matter how staunchly Stefanie defends him.

Other books by the same author:
Chill Out, Josey!, 2007
Taming Rafe, 2007
Everything's Coming Up Josey, 2006
Expect the Sunrise, 2006
Sands of Time, 2006

Other books you might like:
Robin Lee Hatcher, *Whispers From Yesterday*, 1999
Kristen Heitzmann, *A Rush of Wings*, 2003
Elizabeth Musser, *The Swan House*, 2001
Catherine Palmer, *Fatal Harvest*, 2003
Lois Richer, *Heaven's Kiss*, 2004

1003

ELIZABETH WHITE

Controlling Interest

(Grand Rapids, Michigan: Zondervan, 2008)

Story type: Mystery; Humor
Subject(s): Detection; Fathers and Daughters; Missing
 Persons
Major character(s): Natalie Tubberville, Detective—
 Private; Matt Hogan, Detective—Private
Time period(s): 2000s
Locale(s): Memphis, Tennessee

Summary: Private detective Matt Hogan's detective
agency is hanging by a thread. He needs an influx of
cash fast, or he is going to have to fold up his business.
Money comes along in the person of investor Eddie
Tubberville. There is only one catch: Eddie's daughter
Natalie is part of the deal. Matt isn't thrilled at the
thought of working with a spoiled rich girl, and Natalie
isn't so thrilled herself. She has a degree in criminal
justice and has spent two years working in a sheriff's office, so she hates the idea of her father buying her a
position. Soon Matt and Natalie become involved in an
intense rivalry that explodes over the case of Yasmine
Patel. Yasmine is a young woman who is unwillingly
engaged to a man she has never met. Not wanting to
marry a stranger, she disappears, and soon Matt and Natalie realize what should have been a simple case of
finding a missing woman is growing into an international
incident.

Other books by the same author:
Fair Game, 2007
Off the Record, 2007
On Wings of Deliverance, 2006
Fireworks, 2005
Under Cover of Darkness, 2005

Other books you might like:
Christy Barritt, *The Squeaky Clean Mysteries Series*,
 2006-
Ron Benrey, *The Royal Tunbridge Wells Series*, 2004-
Mindy Starns Clark, *The Jo Tulip Series*, 2005-
Lori Copeland, *The Morning Shade Series*, 2003-
Sharon Dunn, *The Bargain Hunters Series*, 2007-

1004

ROBERT WHITLOW

Deeper Water

(Nashville: Thomas Nelson, 2008)

Story type: Mystery
Series: Tides of Truth. Book 1
Subject(s): Legal Thriller

Inspirational

Major character(s): Tami Taylor, Lawyer
Time period(s): 2000s
Locale(s): Savannah, Georgia
Summary: Leaving her small town behind to take a job at a prestigious law firm, Tami Taylor refuses to let the big city corrupt her. Remaining true to her values, she is determined to do her best for her clients, without compromising herself. At first, this seems like an easy goal. However, as time passes, Tami begins to realize that not everybody at her law firm feels the same way she does, and that her fellow lawyers may not only be covering up crimes, but committing them as well.

Other books by the same author:
Mountain Top, 2006
Jimmy, 2005
Life Everlasting, 2004
Life Support, 2003
The Sacrifice, 2002

Other books you might like:
James Scott Bell, *Try Darkness*, 2008
Joe Hilley, *The Mike Connolly Series*, 2004-
Susan Meissner, *The Rachael Flynn Series*, 2006-
Craig Parshall, *The Last Judgment*, 2005
Randy Singer, *By Reason of Insanity*, 2008

1005

LINDA WINDSOR

For Pete's Sake

(New York: Avon Inspire, 2008)

Story type: Romance
Series: Piper Cove Chronicles. Book 2

Subject(s): Fathers and Sons; Neighbors and Neighborhoods
Major character(s): Ellen Brittingham, Landscaper; Adrian Sinclair, Widow(er), Single Parent; Pete Sinclair, Child
Time period(s): 2000s
Locale(s): Piper Cove, Maryland

Summary: Ellen Brittingham has pretty much given up on true love, as has widower Adrian Sinclair. Adrian, however, is about to get married again, to a suitable woman who he thinks will be a good mother to his son Pete. He doesn't think love is as important as compatibility. When Pete meets Ellen, he realizes that she is the perfect woman for his father. As the two bond, Adrian begins to see Ellen in a different light as well.

Other books by the same author:
Wedding Bell Blues, 2007
Blue Moon, 2006
Fiesta Moon, 2005
Paper Moon, 2005
Along Came Jones, 2003

Other books you might like:
Judy Baer, *The Whitney Chronicles*, 2004
Kristin Billerbeck, *The Ashley Stockingdale Series*, 2004-
Penny Culliford, *The Theodora Series*, 2004-
Allie Pleiter, *My So-Called Love Life*, 2006
Camy Tang, *The Sushi Series*, 2007-

Men at Mid-Life
by
Natalie Danford

The coming-of-age story is one of the most common for a novel, especially a first novel. Almost all writers of fiction draw on their own autobiographies to some extent, and everyone who is an adult has experienced coming of age in at least some capacity. It's what makes so many of these books—J.D. Salinger's *The Catcher in the Rye* would be the classic example—perennial favorites. Everyone, writer or not, has experienced coming of age, growing older, transitioning from childhood to adulthood. Any reader can relate in some way to the move from a young point-of-view to a more seasoned one.

But recently a spate of novels has turned to mid-life rather than early life. Writing fiction is a career with a long training period. Many writers spend a decade, even two or three, writing work that then remains unpublished. So while the coming-of-age story is commonly told because everyone has one, the mid-life crisis story may be commonly told because so many writers begin publishing successfully as they reach that stage of life, or at least approach it. Middle age is also a time in a character's life when he has a bit more control and a wider variety of options. This leaves more options open for the writer. The same basic theme, though, is apparent in both coming-of-age and mid-life novels: The question of what a life might mean and how it might be led in order to infuse it with the greatest significance possible.

The category of novels about men's mid-life crises is particularly flourishing at the moment. There are plenty of stories of women's crises at all ages as well, from *Madame Bovary*, Gustave Flaubert's tale of a bored doctor's wife originally published in 1857, to Elizabeth Strout's *Olive Kitteredge*, about a disgruntled former schoolteacher in modern Maine. Indeed, there are so many such stories that they're less of a novelty. Not that male mid-life crisis has never been examined before, but it's approached now with a new openness and often sly humor.

Take, for example, the eccentric protagonist of Tod Wodicka's *All Shall Be Well; And All Shall Be Well; And All Manner of Things Shall Be Well*. Burt Hecker stands at a crossroads at the age of 63. His wife, Kitty, has died, and he sells their upstate New York bed and breakfast (and home) and takes off for Germany. Burt is not without a more specific goal to his travel, however: He is on the road with a musical group that performs Medieval (a different kind of Middle Age) chants, and Burt himself is a reenactor of that period and keeps to the strict rules of the Confraternity of Times Lost Regained, which means he refuses to drive a car or wear modern clothing. (His *nom de histoire* is Eckbert Attquiet.)

Burt is also distanced from his adult children, and he takes the opportunity to meet up with one of them, Tristan, a jazz musician in Prague. Tristan and his sister, June, are strongly connected to their mother's Lemko heritage. Their maternal grandmother, Anna Bibko, is deeply invested—Burt would say obsessed—with the tragedy of the Lemko past. While traveling in Europe, Burt also learns more about the history of the Lemkos.

As he travels, Burt experiences memories that help to explicate his past more completely. While he loved his wife, he doesn't recall much about her death at the start of the novel, due to either depression over her demise or alcoholism induced by over-consuming home-brewed mead or both. Burt is not a likeable character in any traditional sense. Like many of these middle-aged narrators, he is a classic misanthrope. But, there is much poignant humor to be found in Burt's restlessness and his inability to function in the modern world. Unlike a coming-of-age story in which the protagonist is finding his way toward adulthood, Burt is staring down the end of his life. His wife's death has made him cognizant of his own mortality.

Also teetering on the edge of his twilight years is Arthur Camden, the down-on-his-luck protagonist of Michael Dahlie's funny, moving debut novel, *A Gentleman's Guide to Graceful Living*. Nothing goes right for Arthur, who at the start of the novel has learned that his ex-wife is remarrying rather quickly. Arthur has also run his family's import-export business into the ground, and while he's escaped with enough money to live nicely on

Manhattan's tony Upper East Side, he's at loose ends. In the coup de grace, Arthur visits the fly-fishing clubhouse, where he has inherited membership through a long line of Camdens, with a female guest—which is verboten—and the two light a fire in the fireplace and promptly burn down the historic old building, making him an outcast among his fly-fishing companions.

Arthur escapes to his son's ranch in Colorado, but that doesn't do much for his mood. He then tries visiting an old friend in the French countryside, but the friend has not been forthcoming about his own situation in the midst of an ugly divorce. As a result, Arthur has a run-in with the French police and must again skip town, this time to avoid the real or imagined threat of being tossed into a French prison. He tries Nantucket, too, where a cousin with whom he has always competed shows up and makes Arthur feel bad about himself. In Manhattan he's surrounded by people who pity him, at best, and in some cases outright dislike him.

Running through all of this is a vein of dark, poignant humor, most of which derives from Arthur's own relationship with his now-dead father, who was just the competent, get-along-in-the-world type of man Arthur has aspired to be. Recurring in many titles about men in middle age is the realization that they are nowhere near as commanding as their fathers were at their age.

Billy Mernit's *Imagine Me and You* also features a protagonist, Jordan, who has been dumped by his wife. Jordan, however, is driven so mad by his wife's leaving him (Isabella, a native Italian, has returned to Italy) that rather than try to get over her by clumsily seeking female companionship as Arthur Camden does, he decides to invent a fake girlfriend to drive her back into his own arms with jealousy. This is natural for Jordan, who is a screenwriter and also teaches screenwriting, so he's practiced at creating believable characters out of whole cloth. By following his own seven-step system for setting up a romantic comedy, he easily invents a woman who will drive his ex-wife crazy with jealousy.

What he's not accustomed to, however, is having his creations come to actual life. Soon after he invents "Naomi," Jordan begins to see and have conversations with his imaginary perfect girlfriend. Then he can't stop himself from talking to Naomi, and that in itself begins to hinder his attempts to win back Isabelle. Also, no one else can see Naomi—only Jordan can—so he fears for his own sanity.

This plot combines many of the typical tropes of the male mid-life crisis story with classic Hollywood romantic comedy (not to mention movies like *Harvey*, the 1950 film in which James Stewart plays Elwood P. Dowd, who carries on a running conversation with a gigantic rabbit only he can see). Naturally, Jordan begins to fear that in his attempts to make Isabella mad, he's lost his own mind instead. Ultimately, Mernit manages to craft true romance and to satirize it at the same time.

In *The Future of Love*, Shirley Abbott has assembled a whole cast of characters undergoing different types of crises in New York City in the fall of 2001. There's Sam Mendel, a former publishing bigwig cheating on his prim and proper wife with Antonia. He can't bring himself to leave his wife, Edith, however, and so their affair seems doomed from the start. Antonia's daughter, Maggie, is somewhat disappointed in her life with feckless and perpetually unemployed husband Mark (recently laid off from an investment firm) and daughter Sophie. For his part, Mark begins an aimless affair with Sophie's young nursery school teacher. The events of September 11 bring Mark's affair to a head much sooner than it otherwise might have reached that point. He is meant to be in the Twin Towers on that morning for a job interview and, seeing his out, he runs off to Queens with his lover and decides to fake his own death. The disappearance never quite convinces anyone, however, and eventually even his lover tires of him (for much the same reasons his wife had earlier).

Abbott works the situation for poignancy and feeling by not making Mark too much of a creep. Though he's the character with the "classic" mid-life crisis here, all the characters (with the exception of Sophie, perhaps) could be said to be undergoing similar types of crisis, no matter their ages. Sam is facing the fact that he is more dedicated to his material belongings and his station in life than he previously thought; Antonia is acknowledging her loneliness. Going with the flow has backed each of these characters into a different corner.

In *Netherland* by Joseph O'Neill, too, September 11 sets off a male middle-age crisis. Dutch New York City resident Hans van den Broek, a banker, is left solo after his wife decamps to London with their two young children (their marriage is already faltering), and he's forced out of their Tribeca loft and takes up residence at the Hotel Chelsea. Hans fills the gap not with another woman, but with a renewed enthusiasm for cricket, which he played as a child. He becomes involved in a league filled with other expats, mostly from the West Indies and parts of Asia that were once British colonies, who play in the outer boroughs of New York in areas that previously had been unfamiliar to him.

Hans also strikes up a friendship with Chuck, a Trinidadian entrepreneur who longs to construct a cricket stadium as a moneymaking venture and is involved with organized crime. (The book begins a few years in the future with Hans receiving a call telling him that Chuck's body has been found in the Gowanus Canal, so the reader knows that he won't come to a good end.) Without his family to ground him, Hans drifts through the days and revels in memories of other chapters in his life, questioning the very issue of identity. Hans contemplates the idea that every person is a completely different individual at different points in his or her life, and that we tell ourselves ever-changing versions of a life narrative. As he grapples to regain his bearings—in a quest that runs parallel to the city's own struggle to right itself after almost toppling—he also works to reestablish his identity and to get over the hump of his mid-life crisis.

The title *The Story of a Marriage*, Andrew Sean

Greer's new novel (follow-up to the well-received *The Confessions of Max Tivoli*), is slightly misleading. The novel is more the story of a man, who happens to be married. More specifically, it is the story of Holland Cook, as seen through the eyes of Pearlie Ash, who is first his childhood sweetheart in Kentucky and then his wife in San Francisco. The two are out of touch in the 1940s, when Holland is serving overseas. They meet by happenstance shortly after he returns, renew their relationship, and soon wed.

Holland has been injured in the war and suffers from a weak heart, and the couple's son has polio, but to all appearances the pair seem happily married in 1953 when Buzz Drumer, who served with Holland, appears at their door in San Francisco. Buzz is a wealthy man who has made a fortune off of corsets. He identifies himself to Pearlie as Holland's former boss and proceeds to hang around every night for almost six months, but Pearlie senses that there is something more between the two men. For one thing, they dress in a very similar style.

Though the novel is a story of male mid-life crisis, some of the narrative is provided through Pearlie's eyes. Slowly it dawns on her that Buzz is more than a mere acquaintance of her husband's: she realizes that the two have been lovers. Holland's aunts' warnings that she will be forced to take extra-special care of Holland and perhaps shouldn't marry him suddenly take on new meaning. Pearlie is also following the Rosenberg trial closely and spends a great deal of time considering what Ethel Rosenberg's heated defense of her own husband says about the nature of love.

While Holland's particular mask and cover-up may be extreme, most stories of male mid-life crisis seem to rely on the feeling that the mask is being pulled away, or that somehow the path that a protagonist has followed has not led to the expected end point. (Think of the Talking Heads song "Once in a Lifetime," with David Byrne droning, "This is not my beautiful house! This is not my beautiful wife!") In Rivka Galchen's *Atmospheric Disturbances*, that idea takes concrete shape when Leo Liebenstein awakens one morning, looks at his wife, Rema, and decides that the being living with him is not the real Rema, but what he calls a "simulacrum." Much like Arthur Camden, who sets off looking for peace of mind in *A Gentleman's Guide to Graceful Living*, psychiatrist Leo sets off to track down his actual wife. This picaresque journey takes him as far as Patagonia and puts him in touch with a renowned meteorologist who may or may not be involved in controlling the weather. This plays off Leo's strange relationship with a psychiatric patient, Harvey, who goes missing around the same time. Harvey was seeking treatment because he thought he was the target of coded newspaper messages from the Royal Academy of Meteorology that would enable him to control the weather. At Rema's suggestion, Leo's treatment of Harvey consisted in part in revealing that he, too, was part of the same weather-controlling apparatus.

Throughout his search, Leo serves as an unreliable guide to the events surrounding him. Rema, or her simulacrum, accompanies him on his journey, insisting all the while that she is who she says she is. But Leo is too rocked by middle-age self-doubt to believe her and ignores her in favor of the imagined real Rema he seeks.

If coming-of-age stories are popular in part due to the identification factor—surely everybody has one—what about airport horror stories? Jonathan Miles's novel of mid-life crisis, *Dear American Airlines*, takes the form of a long letter to the airline of the title, composed by one very cranky Benjamin Ford, who is in his mid-fifties. Benjamin is stuck in Chicago's O'Hare Airport on his way to his daughter's wedding in California from New York. His connecting flight is cancelled, and in writing to the airline to complain and to request reimbursement, he airs a lifetime of grievances with his friends, his family, and himself. In doing so, he reveals the classic restlessness and lack of fulfillment found in the male mid-life crisis novel.

Benjamin starts off demanding a refund, but before long he has laid out the sad (though humorously told) story of his failed marriage—like most of the characters in these books, Benjamin is a bit of a drinker—and the decline of his mother into mental illness. Benjamin's father survived a Nazi labor camp, and Benjamin himself makes a living translating literature from Polish into English. The job is clearly meant to symbolize the arm's reach distance that Benjamin keeps from everyone and everything. For a person with literary pretensions, working as a translator is the equivalent of serving as bridesmaid rather than standing as bride. It turns out the daughter Benjamin is flying to see wed is none too fond of him, either. Indeed, he has troubled relationships with almost everyone he knows. That's the sad—yet funny—fate of almost all men suffering from mid-life crises, at least as represented in many current novels.

Recommended Titles

All Shall Be Well; And All Shall Be Well; And All Manner of Things Shall Be Well by Tod Wodicka

Atmospheric Disturbances by Rivka Galchen

Dear American Airlines by Jonathan Miles

The Future of Love by Shirley Abbott

A Gentleman's Guide to Graceful Living by Michael Dahlie

Imagine Me and You by Billy Mernit

Netherland by Joseph O'Neill

Olive Kitteredge by Elizabeth Strout

The Story of a Marriage by Andrew Sean Greer

Popular Fiction Titles

1006

SHIRLEY ABBOTT

The Future of Love

(Chapel Hill, North Carolina: Algonquin Books, 2008)

Story type: Literary
Major character(s): Mark Adler, Unemployed; Sam Mendel, Aged Person
Time period(s): 2000s (2001)
Locale(s): New York, New York

Summary: In the fall of 2001, Mark Adler is caring for his young daughter, Sophie, and halfheartedly looking for a new job. He begins an affair with Sophie's teacher, while his wife's mother, Antonia, begins an affair with moneyed and married retired publisher Sam Mendel. On September 11, they all make choices. Mark tries to play dead, unsuccessfully, while Antonia realizes she'll never come first for Sam and leaves him.

Where it's reviewed:
Booklist, February 15, 2008, page 38
New York Times Book Review, March 16, 2008, page 18
Publishers Weekly, December 24, 2007, page 26

Other books by the same author:
The Bookmaker's Daughter, 1991 (memoir)

Other books you might like:
Claire Messud, *The Emperor's Children*, 2006
Helen Schulman, *A Day at the Beach*, 2007

1007

MELANIE ABRAMS

Playing

(New York: Grove Press/Black Cat, 2008)

Story type: Literary
Subject(s): Sexual Behavior
Major character(s): Josie, Student—Graduate, Child-Care Giver; Devesh, Doctor
Time period(s): 2000s
Locale(s): United States

Summary: Josie is a graduate student in anthropology and works as a babysitter to make ends meet, but her true passion is sadomasochistic sex. As she explores this facet of her desires with her lover, Devesh, she comes to terms with her past, which includes a difficult relationship with her mother and a brother who died as an infant.

Where it's reviewed:
Publishers Weekly, January 21, 2008, page 150

Other books you might like:
Heather Lewis, *House Rules*, 1994
Chuck Palahniuk, *Snuff*, 2008

1008

ARAVIND ADIGA

The White Tiger

(New York: Free Press, 2008)

Story type: Literary
Subject(s): Poverty
Major character(s): Balram Halwai, Chauffeur
Time period(s): 2000s
Locale(s): Delhi, India

Summary: A disillusioned chauffeur in India who has pulled himself out of poverty writes a letter to the prime minister of China on the eve of the prime minister's visit to India. Balram Halwai explains to the visiting dignitary how the poor live in India.

Where it's reviewed:
The New Yorker, April 14, 2008, page 75
Publishers Weekly, January 14, 2008, page 37

Other books you might like:
Vikram Seth, *Two Lives*, 2005
Indra Sinha, *Animal's People*, 2008

1009

MARY KAY ANDREWS

Deep Dish

(New York: Harper, 2008)

Story type: Contemporary
Subject(s): Cooks and Cooking; Television
Major character(s): Gina Foxton, Cook; Tate Moody,

Television Personality (cooking show, "Vittles"),
Cook

Time period(s): 2000s
Locale(s): Georgia

Summary: Gina Foxton loses her cooking show, with its focus on healthy food, when her producer is caught canoodling with the sponsor's wife. She and Tate Moody (catchphrase: "kill it and grill it") find themselves competing for a single slot on the Cooking Channel's schedule. Rather than choose one or the other, the channel chooses to stage an ongoing on-air competition between the two of them.

Where it's reviewed:
Publishers Weekly, December 3, 2007, page 49

Other books by the same author:
Blue Christmas, 2006
Savannah Breeze, 2006
Hissy Fit, 2004
Little Bitty Lies, 2003
Savannah Blues, 2002

Other books you might like:
Nancy Verde Barr, *Last Bite*, 2006
Nina Killham, *How to Cook a Tart*, 2002

1010

ELIZABETH ASTON

The Darcy Connection

(New York: Touchstone, 2008)

Story type: Literary; Historical/Regency
Subject(s): Literature; Romance
Major character(s): Charlotte Collins, Young Woman; Eliza Collins, Young Woman
Time period(s): 19th century
Locale(s): London, England

Summary: In a Jane Austen spin-off, Charlotte and Eliza, daughters of the Collins family, head off to London. There, the two sisters grapple with suitors and fall in and out of love.

Where it's reviewed:
Publishers Weekly, January 7, 2008, page 35

Other books by the same author:
The Second Mrs. Darcy, 2007
The True Darcy Spirit, 2006
The Exploits and Adventures of Miss Alethea Darcy, 2005
Mr. Darcy's Daughters, 2003

Other books you might like:
Shannon Hale, *Austenland*, 2007
Jude Morgan, *Indiscretion*, 2006

1011

JO BARRETT

This Is How It Happened (Not a Love Story)

(New York: Avon A, 2008)

Story type: Contemporary
Subject(s): Marriage; Revenge
Major character(s): Madeline Piatro, Businesswoman, Public Relations; Carlton Connors, Businessman
Time period(s): 2000s
Locale(s): Texas

Summary: Madeline and Carlton meet while studying for business degrees, and once they're engaged she shares her brilliant business idea with him. He borrows money from his wealthy father, makes a mint, then dumps her. Naturally, Madeline's thoughts turn to revenge and eventually she hires a hit man.

Where it's reviewed:
Booklist, February 1, 2008, page 33
Publishers Weekly, December 24, 2007, page 29

Other books by the same author:
The Men's Guide to the Women's Bathroom, 2007

Other books you might like:
Elizabeth Buchan, *Revenge of the Middle-Aged Woman*, 2003
Liza Palmer, *Seeing Me Naked*, 2008

1012

ELIZABETH BERG

The Day I Ate Whatever I Wanted

(New York: Random House, 2008)

Story type: Contemporary; Collection
Subject(s): Short Stories; Women

Summary: The stories in this collection focus on women, many of whom are dieting. The protagonist of the title story leaves a Weight Watchers meeting and heads straight to a doughnut shop. Another depicts a woman trying to get over her ex-husband, who has gotten over her.

Where it's reviewed:
Booklist, March 15, 2008, page 26
Entertainment Weekly, April 25, 2008, page 123
People, April 28, 2008, page 53
Publishers Weekly, February 11, 2008, page 51

Other books by the same author:
Dream When You're Feeling Blue, 2007
We Are All Welcome Here, 2006
Open House, 2000
The Pull of the Moon, 1996
Talk Before Sleep, 1994

Other books you might like:
Melissa Bank, *The Girls' Guide to Hunting and Fishing*, 1999
Jennifer Weiner, *The Guy Not Taken*, 2007

1013

SALLIE BINGHAM

Red Car

(Louisville, Kentucky: Sarabande Books, 2008)

Story type: Literary; Collection
Subject(s): Short Stories

Summary: Narrators in the second half of their lives recount 12 stories. One narrator is a woman who has been married four times and whose daughter has become a novelist. Another shows an American vacationing in Normandy as World War II comes to a close. In the title story, a red convertible marks the transitions in a marriage.

Where it's reviewed:
Entertainment Weekly, May 16, 2008, page 70
Publishers Weekly, January 21, 2008, page 150

Other books by the same author:
Nick of Time, 2006 (novel)
Transgressions, 2002
Passion and Prejudice, 1989 (memoir)
The Way It Is Now, 1972
The Touching Hand, 1967

Other books you might like:
Ann Hood, *An Ornithologist's Guide to Life*, 2004
Marilyn Krysl, *Dinner with Osama*, 2008

1014

BENJAMIN BLACK

The Silver Swan

(New York: Holt, 2008)

Story type: Literary
Subject(s): Mystery
Major character(s): Garrett Quirke, Doctor; Billy Hunt, Businessman, Friend
Time period(s): 1950s
Locale(s): Ireland

Summary: Pathologist Garrett Quirke receives a visit from an old acquaintance, who asks him not to perform an autopsy on the body of the man's wife. Garrett is curious and begins investigating the woman's life, including a suspicious business venture in which she became involved.

Where it's reviewed:
Booklist, February 1, 2008, page 32
Christian Science Monitor, March 28, 2008, page 14
Entertainment Weekly, March 7, 2008, page 95
New York Times, April 20, 2008, page 17
Publishers Weekly, January 7, 2008, page 36

Other books by the same author:
Christine Falls, 2007

Other books you might like:
William Boyd, *Restless*, 2006
Denise Mina, *Slip of the Knife*, 2008

1015

FRANCESCA LIA BLOCK

Quakeland

(San Francisco: Manic D Press, 2008)

Story type: Contemporary; Collection
Subject(s): Short Stories
Major character(s): Katrina, Child-Care Giver; Jasper, Teacher
Time period(s): 2000s
Locale(s): Venice, California

Summary: Four short stories and a novella follow depressed Katrina, who runs a California daycare center and dreams of having children of her own. Charming Jasper gets involved with Katrina and several of her friends.

Where it's reviewed:
Publishers Weekly, December 24, 2007, page 24

Other books by the same author:
Blood Roses, 2008
Necklace of Kisses, 2005
Wasteland, 2003
Echo, 2001
Weetzie Bat, 1989 (young adult)

Other books you might like:
Alice Hoffman, *Seventh Heaven*, 1990
Melissa Marr, *Wicked Lovely*, 2007

1016

STEFAN MERRILL BLOCK

The Story of Forgetting

(New York: Random House, 2008)

Story type: Literary
Subject(s): Diseases; Family Relations
Major character(s): Seth Waller, Teenager; Abel Haggard, Aged Person
Time period(s): 2000s
Locale(s): Texas; Isidora, Alternate Universe

Summary: Teenager Seth Waller's mother is succumbing to the early stages of Alzheimer's; Abel Haggard lives a cloistered life and is tormented by memories of a lost love. They share a connection, though: each thinks about a fantastical place known as Isidora.

Where it's reviewed:
Entertainment Weekly, April 4, 2008, page 67
People, April 28, 2008, page 53
Publishers Weekly, February 4, 2008, page 37
USA Today, April 24, 2008, page 7D

Other books you might like:
Debra Dean, *The Madonnas of Leningrad*, 2006
Joshua Furst, *The Sabotage Cafe*, 2007

1017

CHRIS BOHJALIAN

Skeletons at the Feast
(New York: Shaye Areheart Books, 2008)

Story type: Literary
Subject(s): War
Major character(s): Rolf Emmerich, Military Personnel;
   Uri Singer, Prisoner
Time period(s): 1940s
Locale(s): Germany

Summary: While Rolf Emmerich and two of his sons fight
for the Nazi army, Rolf's wife flees across Germany
with their other children. Uri Singer, a Jew who has
escaped from a transport to Auschwitz, helps the Nazi
officer's wife and brood evade the authorities.

Where it's reviewed:
Entertainment Weekly, May 9, 2008, page 67
Publishers Weekly, February 4, 2008, page 35
USA Today, May 22, 2008, page 8D

Other books by the same author:
The Double Bind, 2007
Before You Know Kindness, 2004
Trans-Sister Radio, 2000
Midwives, 1998
Water Witches, 1995

Other books you might like:
Jenna Blum, *Those Who Save Us*, 2004
Michael Lavigne, *Not Me*, 2005

1018

JOHN BRANDON

Arkansas
(San Francisco: McSweeney's, 2008)

Story type: Literary
Subject(s): Drugs; Friendship
Major character(s): Swin Ruiz, Drug Dealer; Kyle Ribb,
   Thief; Ken Hovan, Criminal
Time period(s): 2000s
Locale(s): Arkansas

Summary: In a rundown state park, the various members
of a ragtag criminal organization that sells drugs and
steals small goods face their outcast status. This loosely
bonded band of young male criminals has crisscrossed
the country as they hone their skills.

Where it's reviewed:
Publishers Weekly, January 7, 2008, page 38

Other books you might like:
Harry Crews, *A Feast of Snakes*, 1976
Denis Johnson, *Jesus' Son*, 1992

1019

KEVIN BROCKMEIER

The View from the Seventh Layer
(New York: Pantheon, 2008)

Story type: Literary; Collection
Subject(s): Short Stories

Summary: Thirteen stories limn quirky characters, often
mixing fantasy and reality. Olivia sells souvenirs and
condoms to tourists, but believes she was abducted by
aliens. A woman in Afghanistan believes that God
reaches out only in a very few moments in life.

Where it's reviewed:
Publishers Weekly, January 14, 2008, page 38

Other books by the same author:
The Brief History of the Dead, 2006
The Truth about Celia, 2003
Things That Fall from the Sky, 2002

Other books you might like:
Keith Donohue, *The Stolen Child*, 2006
Andrew Sean Greer, *The Confessions of Max Tivoli*,
   2004

1020

GERALDINE BROOKS

People of the Book
(New York: Viking, 2008)

Story type: Literary
Subject(s): Judaism
Major character(s): Hanna Heath, Researcher, Antiquarian
Time period(s): Multiple Time Periods
Locale(s): 15th century; Sydney, Australia; Sarajevo,
   Bosnia-Hercegovina

Summary: Rare book expert Hanna Heath, living in Sydney, is invited to look at a book that may be the Sarajevo Haggadah, an ancient and valuable Jewish prayer
book that went missing during unrest in Sarajevo in
1992. The story of Hanna in modern times researching
the book and its provenance is interspersed with the
story of the creation of the book itself, stretching back to
1480.

Where it's reviewed:
Chicago Tribune Books, January 26, 2008, page 2
The New Yorker, February 11, 2008, page 153
USA Today, January 17, 2008, page 11D
Washington Post Book World, January 6, 2008, page 1

Other books by the same author:
March, 2005
Year of Wonders, 2001
Foreign Correspondence, 1997 (nonfiction)
Nine Parts of Desire, 1994 (nonfiction)

Other books you might like:
A.S. Byatt, *Possession*, 1990
Susan Vreeland, *Girl in Hyacinth Blue*, 1999

1021

JIMMY BUFFET

Swine Not?

(New York: Little, Brown, 2008)

Story type: Humor
Subject(s): Animals/Pigs
Major character(s): Ellie McBride, Hotel Worker; Rumpy, Animal (pig)
Time period(s): 2000s
Locale(s): New York, New York

Summary: When Ellie McBride uproots her children from Tennessee and moves them to New York City, she can't bear to leave their beloved pet pig, Rumpy, behind. The family is living in the hotel where Ellie works, however, and it takes effort to hide Rumpy's existence.

Where it's reviewed:
Entertainment Weekly, May 23, 2008, page 127

Other books by the same author:
A Salty Piece of Land, 2004
A Pirate Looks at Fifty, 1998 (memoir)
Where Is Joe Merchant?, 1992
Tales from Margaritaville, 1989 (short stories)

Other books you might like:
Mary Kay Andrews, *Deep Dish*, 2008
Jan Karon, *A Common Life*, 2002
Ann B. Ross, *Miss Julia Strikes Back*, 2007

1022

VINCENT LOUIS CARRELLA

Serpent Box

(New York: Harper Perennial, 2008)

Story type: Literary
Subject(s): Family Relations; Religion
Major character(s): Charles Flint, Religious; Rebecca Flint, Spouse; Jacob Flint, Child
Time period(s): 1930s
Locale(s): Leatherwood, Tennessee

Summary: Pentecostal preacher Charles Flint heads to the mountains to commune with God late in his wife's pregnancy. As a result, she gives birth alone in the woods. The resulting child, Jacob, is born deformed. As he grows, his father comes to believe he is a messenger from God.

Where it's reviewed:
Booklist, February 15, 2008, page 36
Publishers Weekly, December 24, 2007, page 29

Other books you might like:
Katherine Dunn, *Geek Love*, 1989
Karl Iagnemma, *The Expeditions*, 2008
Stephen King, *Duma Key*, 2008

1023

LESLIE CARROLL

Choosing Sophie

(New York: Avon A, 2008)

Story type: Contemporary
Subject(s): Adoption; Sports
Major character(s): Olivia deMarley, Entertainer; Augie deMarley, Parent; Sophie, Sports Figure
Time period(s): 2000s
Locale(s): New York, New York

Summary: Olivia deMarley is 40 and engaged to be married for the first time when her estranged father dies. She travels to New York to attend his funeral, and discovers that in his will he has left her ownership of a minor league baseball team, provided she can reunite and form a relationship with the daughter she gave up for adoption. That daughter, Sophie, now 20, is an accomplished softball player.

Where it's reviewed:
Booklist, February 1, 2008, page 24
Publishers Weekly, December 24, 2007, page 31

Other books by the same author:
Herself, 2007
Spin Doctor, 2006
Play Dates, 2005
Temporary Insanity, 2004
Miss Match, 2002

Other books you might like:
Kate Angell, *Strike Zone*, 2008
Sophie Kinsella, *Remember Me?*, 2008

1024

PEARL CLEAGE

Seen It All and Done the Rest

(New York: Ballantine/One World, 2008)

Story type: Contemporary
Subject(s): Actors and Actresses
Major character(s): Josephine Evans, Actress
Time period(s): 2000s
Locale(s): Atlanta, Georgia

Summary: Josephine Evans loses her stage role in Amsterdam and moves back to the United States. More specifically, she moves to Atlanta and into the house of her granddaughter, whose life has been altered by murder.

Where it's reviewed:
Booklist, February 15, 2008, page 36
Ebony, April 2008, page 35
Essence, April 2008, page 79
Publishers Weekly, December 24, 2007, page 27

Other books by the same author:
Baby Brother's Blues, 2006
Babylon Sisters, 2005
Some Things I Never Thought I'd Do, 2003
I Wish I Had a Red Dress, 2001
What Looks Like Crazy on an Ordinary Day, 1997

Other books you might like:
Eric Jerome Dickey, *Sister, Sister*, 1996
Terry McMillan, *A Day Late and a Dollar Short*, 2001

1025

JONATHAN COE

The Rain Before It Falls

(New York: Knopf, 2008)

Story type: Literary
Subject(s): Family Relations
Major character(s): Rosamond, Aged Person; Beatrix, Cousin
Time period(s): 20th century (1930-1980)
Locale(s): England

Summary: From her deathbed, elderly Rosamond recalls her tempestuous relationship with her cousin and sometimes friend, Beatrix. She describes a series of photographs from across five decades and illustrates the vagaries of memory.

Where it's reviewed:
The Atlantic Monthly, May 2008, page 103
The Nation, May 26, 2008, page 25
New York Times Book Review, April 13, 2008, page 8
The New Yorker, April 14, 2008, page 75
People, March 10, 2008, page 59

Other books by the same author:
The Closed Circle, 2005
The Rotters' Club, 2002
The House of Sleep, 1998
The Winshaw Legacy, 1995
The Dwarves of Death, 1990

Other books you might like:
Anne Enright, *The Gathering*, 2007
Susan Minot, *Evening*, 1998

1026

ANNE CUSHMAN

Enlightenment for Idiots

(New York: Shaye Areheart Books, 2008)

Story type: Literary
Subject(s): Pregnancy; Travel
Major character(s): Amanda, Writer; Devi Das, Traveler
Time period(s): 2000s
Locale(s): India

Summary: American writer Amanda is sent to India to write a guidebook for those seeking enlightenment. There she hooks up with Devi Das, who offers a wry perspective on the country. While traveling and taking notes, Amanda discovers that she's pregnant.

Where it's reviewed:
Publishers Weekly, February 11, 2008, page 51

Other books by the same author:
From Here to Nirvana, 1998 (non-fiction)

Other books you might like:
Debra Galant, *Fear and Yoga in New Jersey*, 2008
Natalie Goldberg, *Banana Rose*, 1995

1027

SOPHIE DAHL

Playing with the Grown-Ups

(New York: Nan A. Talese, 2008)

Story type: Literary
Subject(s): Family Relations
Major character(s): Marina, Parent; Kitty, Spouse
Time period(s): 2000s
Locale(s): New York, New York

Summary: When Kitty hears that her mother, Marina, has fallen ill, she begins thinking about her adolescence. Her memories cover the time she was growing up on New York City's Park Avenue with her eccentric artist mother.

Where it's reviewed:
Booklist, March 1, 2008, page 49
New Statesman, December 10, 2007, page 59
Publishers Weekly, December 24, 2007, page 24
USA Today, April 10, 2008, page 7D

Other books you might like:
Esther Freud, *Hideous Kinky*, 1992
Mona Simpson, *Anywhere but Here*, 1986

1028

MICHAEL DAHLIE

A Gentleman's Guide to Graceful Living

(New York: W.W. Norton, 2008)

Story type: Literary
Subject(s): Divorce; Fishing
Major character(s): Arthur Camden, Importer/Exporter
Time period(s): 2000s
Locale(s): New York, New York; Colorado

Summary: Arthur Camden, a member of the lower echelons of New York City's upper crust, is having a mid-life breakdown. His wife leaves him abruptly. He has ruined his family's import-export business. Then he embarrasses himself further by breaking into tears during a heartfelt speech at a meeting of his fly-fishing club. He tries to settle his issues by visiting his son in Colorado, but that doesn't help.

Where it's reviewed:
Booklist, May 1, 2008, page 70
Publishers Weekly, March 10, 2008, page 56

Other books you might like:
Louis Begley, *About Schmidt*, 1996
Rex Pickett, *Sideways*, 2004
John Updike, *Marry Me*, 1996

1029

MICHELLE DE KRETSER

The Lost Dog

(New York: Little, Brown and Company, 2008)

Story type: Literary
Subject(s): Academia; Animals/Dogs
Major character(s): Tom Loxley, Professor; Nelly Zhang, Artist
Time period(s): 2000s (2001)
Locale(s): Australia

Summary: Henry James expert Tom Loxley is looking for his lost dog. As he does, he recalls the troubled love affair he conducted with artist Nelly Zhang after her husband disappeared.

Where it's reviewed:
Booklist, March 15, 2008, page 28
New York Times Book Review, May 4, 2008, page 17
Publishers Weekly, January 21, 2008, page 148

Other books by the same author:
The Hamilton Case, 2004
The Rose Grower, 2000

Other books you might like:
Benjamin Black, *The Silver Swan*, 2008
Peter Carey, *Theft*, 2006

1030

MARISA DE LOS SANTOS

Belong to Me

(New York: Morrow, 2008)

Story type: Contemporary
Subject(s): Friendship
Major character(s): Cornelia Brown, Spouse; Dev Tremain, Teenager; Lake Tremain, Single Parent
Time period(s): 2000s
Locale(s): Pennsylvania

Summary: Shaken by both 9/11 and a miscarriage, Cornelia Brown and her husband, Teo, move to a manicured suburb of Philadelphia, where Cornelia has trouble fitting in. She befriends single mother Lake Tremain, whose genius son, Dev, is trying to figure out who his father was. She is shunned, however, by the prissy Piper Truitt.

Where it's reviewed:
New York Times, April 17, 2008, page E8
People, May 12, 2008, page 61
Publishers Weekly, March 31, 2008, page 38

Other books by the same author:
Love Walked In, 2005
From the Bones Out, 2000 (poetry)

Other books you might like:
Emily Giffin, *Baby Proof*, 2006
Jane Green, *To Have and to Hold*, 2004
Louise Limerick, *Friends and Mothers*, 2007

1031

DEBRA DEAN

Confessions of a Falling Woman and Other Stories

(New York: Harper Perennial, 2008)

Story type: Collection; Literary
Subject(s): Short Stories; Actors and Actresses

Summary: Troubled characters, many of them actors and actresses, humorously deal with problems in this collection of stories. In one, a man makes fun of his neighbors in his comedy act. In another, a bartender auditions for various parts, some intellectually satisfying and some less so.

Where it's reviewed:
Booklist, February 1, 2008, page 24
Publishers Weekly, December 17, 2007, page 33

Other books by the same author:
The Madonnas of Leningrad, 2006

Other books you might like:
Christopher Bram, *Lives of the Circus Animals*, 2003
Enid Shomer, *Tourist Season*, 2007

1032

ANJANETTE DELGADO

The Heartbreak Pill

(New York: Atria, 2008)

Story type: Literary
Subject(s): Relationships
Major character(s): Erika Luna, Researcher; Gilberto, Parent
Time period(s): 2000s
Locale(s): Miami, Florida

Summary: Pharmaceutical researcher Erika Luna has been dumped by her cheating husband. At first she seeks advice from her father, Gilberto, but then she decides to do something about the pain. Erika invents a pill to stop herself from feeling sad.

Where it's reviewed:
Booklist, February 15, 2008, page 34
Publishers Weekly, January 7, 2008, page 35

Other books you might like:
Robert Cohen, *Inspired Sleep*, 2001
James Collins, *Beginner's Greek*, 2008
Pagan Kennedy, *Confessions of a Memory Eater*, 2006

1033

RUTH DOWNIE

Terra Incognita

(New York: Bloomsbury, 2008)

Story type: Literary; Historical/Ancient Rome
Subject(s): Murder

Major character(s): Gaius Petreius Ruso, Doctor, Military Personnel; Thessalus, Doctor
Time period(s): 2nd century (118)
Locale(s): Roman Empire

Summary: Doctor Gaius Petreius Ruso is traveling with troops in the Roman army when a soldier is murdered. Another army medic confesses to the crime, and Ruso must investigate.

Where it's reviewed:
Publishers Weekly, January 7, 2008, page 37

Other books by the same author:
Medicus, 2007

Other books you might like:
Rosemary Rowe, *A Coin for the Ferryman*, 2007
Steven Saylor, *Roma*, 2007

1034

TAN TWAN ENG

The Gift of Rain
(New York: Weinstein Books, 2008)

Story type: Literary
Subject(s): Martial Arts; Historical
Major character(s): Phillip Hutton, Expatriate, Teacher
Time period(s): 1940s
Locale(s): Penang, Malaysia

Summary: Phillip Hutton lives on the island of Penang and teaches akido. The bulk of this debut novel is devoted to a flashback to his own days as a student of akido, when he trained with a Japanese neighbor one summer during the lead-up to World War II. When the war breaks out, he is torn between his loyalties to his Japanese teacher and to his British family.

Where it's reviewed:
Publishers Weekly, January 14, 2008, page 36

Other books you might like:
Jennifer Cody Epstein, *The Painter from Shanghai*, 2008
Julie Otsuka, *When the Emperor Was Divine*, 2002

1035

LEIF ENGER

So Brave, Young and Handsome
(New York: Atlantic Monthly Press, 2008)

Story type: Literary; Historical/American West
Subject(s): American West; Travel
Major character(s): Monte Becket, Companion, Writer; Glendon Hale, Outlaw, Aged Person
Time period(s): 1910s (1915)
Locale(s): West; Mexico

Summary: Monte Becket has written one successful book, but he's now blocked. Glendon Hale shows up on the river near Becket's house in Minnesota and invites him to travel to California. Becket accepts and during the journey discovers that Hale may not have been honest and may even be a criminal. The two make their way to Mexico.

Where it's reviewed:
Booklist, March 15, 2008, page 29
Entertainment Weekly, April 25, 2008, page 121
Publishers Weekly, January 28, 2008, page 38

Other books by the same author:
Peace Like a River, 2001

Other books you might like:
Michael Ondaatje, *Divisadero*, 2007
Per Petterson, *Out Stealing Horses*, 2008

1036

LOUISE ERDRICH

The Plague of Doves
(New York: Harper, 2008)

Story type: Literary
Subject(s): Indians of North America
Major character(s): Mooshum Milk, Indian; Corwin Peace, Criminal
Time period(s): 1910s (1911); 1960s
Locale(s): Pluto, North Dakota

Summary: Events in the early 20th century continue to reverberate in rural North Dakota. In 1911, a family is murdered and three Indians are blamed for the crime. Mooshum Milk survives the ensuing lynching, and both his descendants and the descendants of members of the lynch mob cross paths for generations. Milk's granddaughter develops a crush on Corwin Peace, who goes on to become a criminal.

Where it's reviewed:
Christian Science Monitor, May 6, 2008, page 14
New York Times, April 29, 2008, page E1
New York Times Book Review, May 11, 2008, page 9
Newsweek, May 26, 2008, page 12
USA Today, May 1, 2008, page 6D

Other books by the same author:
The Painted Drum, 2005
The Master Butchers Singing Club, 2003
The Last Report on the Miracles at Little No Horse, 2001
The Birchbark House, 1999
Tracks, 1988

Other books you might like:
Leif Enger, *So Brave, Young and Handsome*, 2008
Thomas King, *Truth and Bright Water*, 2000

1037

ELLEN FELDMAN

Scottsboro
(New York: W.W. Norton, 2008)

Story type: Literary
Subject(s): Historical; Civil Rights

Major character(s): Alice Whittier, Journalist
Time period(s): 1930s (1931)
Locale(s): Scottsboro, Alabama

Summary: Journalist Alice Whittier goes from New York City to Scottsboro to cover the infamous court case in which nine young African-American men were framed for rape. Alice is the only female journalist covering the story, and she scores an interview with one of the two accusers.

Where it's reviewed:
Booklist, April 15, 2008, page 34
Publishers Weekly, January 21, 2008, page 148

Other books by the same author:
The Boy Who Loved Anne Frank, 2005
Lucy, 2003

Other books you might like:
Jenna Blum, *Those Who Save Us*, 2004
Edward P. Jones, *The Known World*, 2003

1038

ZOE FERRARIS

Finding Nouf

(Boston: Houghton Mifflin, 2008)

Story type: Literary; Mystery
Major character(s): Nayir al-Sharqi, Investigator; Katya Hijazi, Health Care Professional
Time period(s): 2000s
Locale(s): Saudi Arabia

Summary: A 16-year-old girl in Saudi Arabia disappears before her arranged marriage, then is found dead and pregnant. Her wealthy family engages Nayir al-Sharqi, a conservative Palestinian, to find out what happened. He works with Katya Hijazi from the medical examiner's office. The point-of-view switches between the two, digging into not only the mystery of the girl's death, but also the different positions of men and women in Saudi society.

Where it's reviewed:
Booklist, March 1, 2008, page 52
Publishers Weekly, January 7, 2008, page 32

Other books you might like:
Hanan Al-Shaykh, *Women of Sand and Myrrh*, 1992
Matt Benyon Rees, *The Collaborator of Bethlehem*, 2007

1039

KATIE FFORDE

Practically Perfect

(New York: St. Martin's Press, 2008)

Story type: Contemporary
Subject(s): Animals/Dogs; Real Estate
Major character(s): Anna, Interior Decorator; Rob Hunter, Rescuer, Inspector; Max Gordon, Professor
Time period(s): 2000s

Locale(s): Cotswolds, England

Summary: Anna must deal with annoying Rob on two fronts: He's both the local greyhound rescuer responsible for seeing that she takes good care of the dog she's adopted and the historical inspector who will pass judgment on the accuracy of her renovation of a cottage. She both likes and hates him. Anna is also interested in Max, an architecture expert with whom she has crossed paths over the years.

Where it's reviewed:
Booklist, February 15, 2008, page 36
Publishers Weekly, January 7, 2008, page 35

Other books by the same author:
Bidding for Love, 2007
Going Dutch, 2007
Restoring Grace, 2006
Living Dangerously, 2003
The Rose Revived, 1996

Other books you might like:
Maeve Binchy, *Whitethorn Woods*, 2007
Fiona Walker, *Well Groomed*, 2003

1040

KAREN JOY FOWLER

Wit's End

(New York: Putnam, 2008)

Story type: Literary
Subject(s): Family Relations; Writing
Major character(s): Rima Lanisell, Teacher; Addison Early, Writer
Time period(s): 2000s
Locale(s): Santa Cruz, California

Summary: Rima Lanisell visits her godmother, mystery writer Addison Early, in California and interrogates Early about her relationship with Rima's father. Early has a quirky habit of mapping out the plots of her books with dollhouse dioramas. Someone breaks into the house and steals a figure from the current diorama, and Rima wants to investigate.

Where it's reviewed:
Christian Science Monitor, April 4, 2008, page 14
Entertainment Weekly, April 4, 2008, page 66
New York Times Book Review, May 18, 2008, page 16
USA Today, April 8, 2008, page 4D

Other books by the same author:
The Jane Austen Book Club, 2004
Sister Noon, 2001
Black Glass, 1998 (short stories)
The Sweetheart Season, 1996
Sarah Canary, 1991

Other books you might like:
Kate Atkinson, *Case Histories*, 2004
William Boyd, *Restless*, 2006

1041

JAMES FREY

Bright Shiny Morning

(New York: HarperCollins, 2008)

Story type: Contemporary
Subject(s): Modern Life
Major character(s): Esperanza, Servant, Immigrant (illegal); Joe, Streetperson; Amberton Parker, Actor, Homosexual
Time period(s): 2000s
Locale(s): Los Angeles, California

Summary: Denizens of Los Angeles live varied lives. Esperanza is an illegal immigrant working as a maid. Joe is homeless. Amberton Parker is a famous actor hiding the fact that he's gay with a sham marriage to a famous actress who is also gay. Reportorial chapters give brief bits of information about the city. The author became infamous when his two first books, which had been published as memoirs, were discovered to be fabrications. This is his first novel.

Where it's reviewed:
Entertainment Weekly, May 16, 2008, page 68
New York Times, May 12, 2008, page E1
Newsweek, May 19, 2008, page 51
USA Today, May 15, 2008, page 7D

Other books by the same author:
My Friend Leonard, 2005 (published as memoir)
A Million Little Pieces, 2003 (published as memoir)

Other books you might like:
Charles Bock, *Beautiful Children*, 2008
Bret Easton Ellis, *Glamorama*, 1998
Mark Winegardner, *Crooked River Burning*, 2000

1042

JUAN ESLAVA GALAN

The Mule

(New York: Bantam, 2008)

Story type: Literary; Historical
Subject(s): Civil War/Spanish; Animals/Mules
Major character(s): Juan Castro Perez, Military Personnel; Valentina, Animal
Time period(s): 1930s
Locale(s): Spain

Summary: Juan Castro Perez is a muleteer in the Spanish Civil War, but his loyalty lies more with his mule, Valentina, than with either side. In fact, he's fought for both sides at different times. The author is well-known in Spain, but this is his first work to appear in English. Translated from the Spanish by Lisa Dillman.

Where it's reviewed:
Publishers Weekly, December 24, 2007, page 30

Other books you might like:
Daniel Alarcon, *Lost City Radio*, 2007
Ernest Hemingway, *For Whom the Bell Tolls*, 1940

1043

RIVKA GALCHEN

Atmospheric Disturbances

(New York: Farrar, Straus and Giroux, 2008)

Story type: Literary
Subject(s): Marriage; Mental Health
Major character(s): Leo Liebenstein, Doctor; Rema, Spouse
Time period(s): 2000s
Locale(s): New York, New York; Buenos Aires, Argentina

Summary: Psychiatrist Leo Liebenstein wakes one day and decides that his beloved wife, Rema, has been replaced by an impostor, whom he refers to as a "simulacrum." Leo then takes off and travels as far as Argentina in search of his wife.

Where it's reviewed:
Booklist, May 1, 2008, page 69
Entertainment Weekly, June 6, 2008, page 121
Publishers Weekly, February 11, 2008, page 47
Time, June 2, 2008, page 62

Other books you might like:
Thomas Pynchon, *The Crying of Lot 49*, 1966
Deborah Schupack, *The Boy on the Bus*, 2003

1044

STEVEN GALLOWAY

The Cellist of Sarajevo

(New York: Riverhead, 2008)

Story type: Literary
Subject(s): War
Major character(s): Arrow, Military Personnel; Unnamed Character, Musician
Time period(s): 1990s
Locale(s): Sarajevo, Bosnia-Hercegovina

Summary: After 22 people are killed in Sarajevo, a cellist is assigned to play on the spot for 22 days as a kind of memorial. Sniper Arrow is assigned to protect the musician. Other characters struggle to survive in a city under siege.

Where it's reviewed:
Entertainment Weekly, May 23, 2008, page 127
Publishers Weekly, February 4, 2008, page 34

Other books by the same author:
Finnie Walsh, 2006
Ascension, 2003

Other books you might like:
Daniel Alarcon, *Lost City Radio*, 2007
Geraldine Brooks, *People of the Book*, 2008

1045

SAGARIKA GHOSE

Blind Faith

(New York: Harper, 2008)

Story type: Literary
Subject(s): Family Relations; Marriage
Major character(s): Mia Bhagat, Journalist; Karna, Religious; Vik Ray, Businessman
Time period(s): 2000s
Locale(s): London, England; New Delhi, India

Summary: Television reporter Mia meets and falls in love with a man while living in England. Her mother arranges a marriage, however, and Mia moves to New Delhi with her husband-to-be. She lives a wealthy existence with him, but still dreams of the man she met first.

Where it's reviewed:
Booklist, February 1, 2008, page 24
Publishers Weekly, January 7, 2008, page 37

Other books by the same author:
The Gin Drinkers, 2000

Other books you might like:
V.V. Ganeshananthan, *Love Marriage*, 2008
Jhumpa Lahiri, *The Namesake*, 2003

1046

EMILY GIFFIN

Love the One You're With

(New York: St. Martin's Press, 2008)

Story type: Contemporary
Subject(s): Marriage
Major character(s): Ellen Dempsey, Spouse; Leo, Writer; Andy, Spouse
Time period(s): 2000s
Locale(s): New York, New York; Atlanta, Georgia

Summary: Ellen Dempsey is still a newlywed when she runs into the one who got away on the street. Leo is a sexy writer who broke her heart eight years earlier. Ellen knows she should be grateful to be married to sweet, stable Andy, but she can't help wondering what might have happened with Leo. Ellen and Andy move to Atlanta to be near his family, and she finds herself uncomfortable in that social milieu.

Where it's reviewed:
USA Today, May 22, 2008, page 7D

Other books by the same author:
Baby Proof, 2006
Something Blue, 2005
Something Borrowed, 2004

Other books you might like:
Megan Crane, *Names My Sisters Call Me*, 2008
Sophie Kinsella, *Remember Me?*, 2008
Jennifer Weiner, *The Guy Not Taken*, 2006
    short stories

1047

ANDREW SEAN GREER

The Story of a Marriage

(New York: Farrar, Straus and Giroux, 2008)

Story type: Literary
Subject(s): Marriage; Homosexuality/Lesbianism
Major character(s): Pearlie Cook, Spouse; Holland Cook, Spouse; Buzz Drumer, Wealthy
Time period(s): 1950s
Locale(s): San Francisco, California

Summary: Pearl and Holland meet as children, then are separated by World War II. Eventually they encounter each other again and marry. Several years later, however, wealthy Buzz Drumer appears, looking for Holland. Slowly, Pearl realizes that her husband and Buzz were lovers during the war, and that they love each other still.

Where it's reviewed:
New York Times, April 23, 2008, page E8
New York Times Book Review, May 11, 2008, page 35
The New Yorker, May 5, 2008, page 78

Other books by the same author:
The Confessions of Max Tivoli, 2004
The Path of Minor Planets, 2001
How It Was for Me, 2000 (short stories)

Other books you might like:
Ian McEwan, *On Chesil Beach*, 2007
Richard Powers, *The Time of Our Singing*, 2003

1048

MARTHA GRIMES

Dakota

(New York: Viking, 2008)

Story type: Contemporary
Subject(s): Animals, Treatment of
Major character(s): Andi Oliver, Amnesiac
Time period(s): 2000s
Locale(s): Kingdom, North Dakota

Summary: Andi Oliver works at different waitress jobs until she lands in Kingdom, North Dakota, where she works on a pig farm and tries to save the animals from being slaughtered. The locals are not happy with her actions.

Where it's reviewed:
Booklist, December 15, 2007, page 4
Publishers Weekly, December 17, 2007, page 32

Other books by the same author:
Dust, 2007
Biting the Moon, 1999
Jerusalem Inn, 1984
The Dirty Duck, 1984
The Man with a Load of Mischief, 1981

Other books you might like:
Barbara Kingsolver, *The Poisonwood Bible*, 1999
Sara Peretsky, *Bleeding Kansas*, 2008

1049

SARAH HALL

Daughters of the North

(New York: Harper Perennial, 2008)

Story type: Literary
Subject(s): War
Major character(s): Sister, Settler
Time period(s): Indeterminate Future
Locale(s): Carhullan, England

Summary: In the near future, England is living under a repressive regime of forced sterilization and constant war. Global warming has reached crisis proportions. A woman named Sister lives on a commune and considers joining the rebel forces.

Where it's reviewed:
Booklist, March 1, 2008, page 47
Publishers Weekly, January 7, 2008, page 35

Other books by the same author:
The Electric Michelangelo, 2005
Haweswater, 2003

Other books you might like:
Jim Crace, *The Pesthouse*, 2007
Cormac McCarthy, *The Road*, 2006

1050

ADENA HALPERN

The Ten Best Days of My Life

(New York: Plume, 2008)

Story type: Contemporary
Subject(s): Heaven
Major character(s): Alex Dorenfield, Spirit; Peaches, Animal (dog)
Time period(s): 2000s
Locale(s): Heaven

Summary: Alex Dorenfield is hit by a car before she turns 30 and ends up in heaven, along with her dog, Peaches. Alex soon discovers that she needs to earn her place in the good part of heaven, or else she will be relegated to the less desirable area.

Where it's reviewed:
Publishers Weekly, January 7, 2008, page 34

Other books by the same author:
Target Underwear and a Vera Wang Gown, 2006 (memoir)

Other books you might like:
Sophie Kinsella, *Remember Me?*, 2008
Lauren Weisberger, *Chasing Harry Winston*, 2008

1051

CHRIS HANNAN

Missy

(New York: Farrar, Straus and Giroux, 2008)

Story type: Literary; Historical/American West
Subject(s): American West

Major character(s): Dol McQueen, Prostitute, Addict; Pontius, Criminal
Time period(s): 19th century
Locale(s): Virginia City, Nevada

Summary: Dol McQueen is a prostitute in the Wild West. A pimp named Pontius makes the mistake of trusting Dol with his "missy," or opium, and she takes off with it, with Pontius in hot pursuit.

Where it's reviewed:
Publishers Weekly, February 4, 2008, page 34

Other books you might like:
Michael Chabon, *The Yiddish Policemen's Union*, 2007
Cormac McCarthy, *No Country for Old Men*, 2005

1052

JOANNE HARRIS

The Girl with No Shadow

(New York: William Morrow, 2008)

Story type: Literary
Subject(s): Family Relations
Major character(s): Yanne Charbonneau, Store Owner; Annie, Child
Time period(s): 2000s
Locale(s): Paris, France

Summary: The characters from *Chocolat* have changed their names and moved to Paris, but soon Yanne (formerly known as Vianne) opens up a new chocolate shop. Trouble arises with her 11-year-old daughter, now called Annie, who seems to be drifting.

Where it's reviewed:
Christian Science Monitor, April 25, 2008, page 14
Entertainment Weekly, April 11, 2008, page 75
Good Housekeeping, May 2008, page 218
Publishers Weekly, January 21, 2008, page 148
USA Today, May 1, 2008, page 4D

Other books by the same author:
Five Quarters of the Orange, 2007
Gentlemen and Players, 2006
Sleep, Pale Sister, 2004
Blackberry Wine, 2000
Chocolat, 1999

Other books you might like:
Alice Hoffman, *The Third Angel*, 2008
Jodi Picoult, *Change of Heart*, 2008

1053

ELLEN HAWLEY

Open Line

(Minneapolis: Coffee House Press, 2008)

Story type: Literary
Subject(s): Conspiracies; War
Major character(s): Annette Majoris, Radio Personality; Walter Bishop, Wealthy; Stan Marlin, Political Figure
Time period(s): 2000s

Locale(s): Minneapolis, Minnesota

Summary: Radio talk-show host Annette Majoris is half-kidding when she proposes that perhaps the Vietnam War never actually happened, but soon she finds herself buoyed by right-wing supporters. Wealthy Republican Walter Bishop begins courting her; right-winger Stan Marlin promotes her.

Where it's reviewed:
Booklist, April 15, 2008, page 26
Entertainment Weekly, May 23, 2008, page 125
Publishers Weekly, January 28, 2008, page 38

Other books by the same author:
Trip Sheets, 1998

Other books you might like:
Tom Perrotta, *Election*, 1998
Theresa Rebeck, *Three Girls and Their Brother*, 2008

1054

ELIZABETH HAY

Late Nights on Air

(New York: Counterpoint, 2008)

Story type: Literary
Subject(s): Small Town Life; Radio Broadcasting
Major character(s): Harry Boyd, Radio Personality; Dido Paris, Radio Personality
Time period(s): 2000s
Locale(s): Yellowknife, Northwest Territories, Canada

Summary: Harry Boyd becomes manager at a radio station in the small northern Canadian town of Yellowknife. He gets involved with local anchor Dido Paris. Most of the inhabitants of the remote town just wish they could have a television station. This novel won the Giller Prize.

Where it's reviewed:
New York Times Book Review, June 1, 2008, page 44
Publishers Weekly, February 18, 2008, page 137

Other books by the same author:
Garbo Laughs, 2003
A Student of Weather, 2001
Small Change, 2001 (short stories)
The Only Snow in Havana, 1996

Other books you might like:
Garrison Keillor, *Pontoon*, 2007
Michael Ondaatje, *Divisadero*, 2007

1055

SAMANTHA HUNT

The Invention of Everything Else

(Boston: Houghton Mifflin, 2008)

Story type: Literary
Subject(s): Historical; Friendship
Major character(s): Nikola Tesla, Historical Figure, Scientist; Louisa Dewell, Servant (chambermaid)
Time period(s): 1940s (1943)

Locale(s): New York, New York

Summary: Elderly Serbian inventor Nikola Tesla, who was involved in the inception of electricity, strikes up a friendship with Louisa Dewell, a maid in the New York City hotel where he is living. Tesla rants about the past and about people who have stabbed him in the back or disrespected his genius; Dewell worries about her father's involvement with a time machine.

Where it's reviewed:
Booklist, December 15, 2007, page 25
Christian Science Monitor, March 4, 2008, page 13
New York Times Book Review, March 23, 2008, page 18
Publishers Weekly, January 7, 2008, page 38

Other books by the same author:
The Seas, 2004

Other books you might like:
Lauren Groff, *The Monsters of Templeton*, 2008
Liz Jensen, *My Dirty Little Book of Stolen Time*, 2006

1056

MORAG JOSS

The Night Following

(New York: Delacorte Press, 2008)

Story type: Literary
Subject(s): Marriage
Major character(s): Unnamed Character, Spouse; Arthur Mitchell, Aged Person, Widow(er)
Time period(s): 2000s
Locale(s): Wiltshire, England

Summary: Finding a condom wrapper in her doctor husband's car distracts the unnamed protagonist so much while driving that she hits and kills a cyclist. Wracked with guilt, she becomes obsessed with the dead woman, an English teacher, and the widowed husband left behind. She reads the manuscript the dead woman was writing.

Where it's reviewed:
Booklist, January 1, 2008, page 49
Entertainment Weekly, February 29, 2008, page 64
Publishers Weekly, January 28, 2008, page 42

Other books by the same author:
Puccini's Ghosts, 2006
Fruitful Bodies, 2005
Half Broken Things, 2005
Fearful Symmetry, 1999
Funeral Music, 1998

Other books you might like:
Elizabeth George, *What Came Before He Shot Her*, 2006
Ruth Rendell, *The Water's Lovely*, 2007

1057

ETGAR KERET

The Girl on the Fridge

(New York: Farrar, Straus and Giroux, 2008)

Story type: Collection
Subject(s): Short Stories

Summary: In 46 short-short stories, the author offers whimsical and imaginative situations. In one story, a man who can bring all action to a halt uses his power to make sexual conquests. In another, an Israeli soldier is punished brutally for objecting to poor treatment of an Arab. Translated from the Hebrew by Miriam Shlesinger and Sondra Silverston.

Where it's reviewed:
New York Times Book Review, May 18, 2008, page 13
Publishers Weekly, January 21, 2008, page 149

Other books by the same author:
Missing Kissinger, 2007
The Nimrod Flipout, 2006
The Bus Driver Who Wanted to Be God, 2001

Other books you might like:
Bernard Cooper, *Guess Again*, 2000
Miranda July, *No One Belongs Here More than You*, 2007

1058

CHIP KIDD

The Learners

(New York: Scribner, 2008)

Story type: Literary; Satire
Subject(s): Work
Major character(s): Happy, Advertising
Time period(s): 1960s
Locale(s): New Haven, Connecticut

Summary: Recent graduate Happy is working for an advertising firm when he's engaged to design an ad looking for participants in a memory experiment at Yale University. Happy loves his own ad so much that he's unable to resist signing up as a subject. The author is a well-known designer of book jackets.

Where it's reviewed:
Entertainment Weekly, February 22, 2008, page 101
I.D., March-April 2008, page 99
New York Times Book Review, March 9, 2008, page 14
Newsweek, March 3, 2008, page 54
USA Today, February 28, 2008, page 5D

Other books by the same author:
The Cheese Monkeys, 2001

Other books you might like:
Jonathan Dee, *Palladio*, 2002
Joshua Ferris, *Then We Came to the End*, 2007

1059

JHUMPA LAHIRI

Unaccustomed Earth

(New York: Knopf, 2008)

Story type: Literary; Collection
Subject(s): Short Stories

Summary: Eight stories consider relatives and their relationship to each other. Several stories feature the children of Indian parents born in the United States and their struggles to deal with each other's expectations. One such daughter can't decide whether to have her elderly father move in with her. Another story focuses on a woman's arranged marriage and her last-minute feelings for another man.

Where it's reviewed:
New York, April 7, 2008, page 67
New York Times, April 4, 2008, page E27
New York Times Book Review, April 6, 2008, page 1
Time, April 7, 2008, page 63
USA Today, April 3, 2008, page 5D

Other books by the same author:
The Namesake, 2003 (novel)
Interpreter of Maladies, 1999 (Pulitzer Prize winner)

Other books you might like:
Nam Le, *The Boat*, 2008
Arundhati Roy, *The God of Small Things*, 1998
Vikram Seth, *A Suitable Boy*, 1993

1060

KAY LANGDALE

If Not Love

(New York: Thomas Dunne Books, 2008)

Story type: Literary
Subject(s): Marriage
Major character(s): Isobel, Parent; Martha, Aged Person; Shelia, Nurse
Time period(s): 2000s
Locale(s): England

Summary: A variety of characters are linked to each other through present relationships or shared pasts. Isobel reveals to her daughter, Kate, that Kate's father had an affair that tested their marriage. The other woman in that relationship, Martha, now lives in a nursing home, where nurse Shelia attends to her. Shelia has an adopted child on whom she dotes, trying to bury the fact that her husband has never been attracted to her. Meanwhile, another woman suffers physical ailments since giving up her biological child for adoption.

Where it's reviewed:
Publishers Weekly, December 24, 2007, page 30

Other books you might like:
Ian McEwan, *On Chesil Beach*, 2007
Penny Vincenzi, *Sheer Abandon*, 2007

1061

WILL LAVENDER

Obedience

(New York: Shaye Areheart Books, 2008)

Story type: Mystery
Subject(s): Murder
Major character(s): Brian House, Student—college; Den-

nis Flaherty, Student—college; Mary Butler, Student—college
Time period(s): 2000s
Locale(s): Midwest

Summary: Three students take a disturbing college class with the mysterious Professor Williams. The first day, the professor discusses a hypothetical murder due to happen in six weeks. As they progress toward the scheduled murder date, the line between reality and academic invention blurs.

Where it's reviewed:
Entertainment Weekly, February 29, 2008, page 65
New York Times Book Review, March 9, 2008, page 23
Publishers Weekly, February 26, 2008, page 22
USA Today, March 6, 2008, page 7D

Other books you might like:
Benjamin Black, *Christine Falls*, 2007
Lauren Groff, *The Monsters of Templeton*, 2008

☐1062

MARGOT LIVESEY

The House on Fortune Street
(New York: Harper, 2008)

Story type: Literary
Subject(s): Relationships
Major character(s): Dara MacLeod, Counselor; Sean Wyman, Professor
Time period(s): 2000s
Locale(s): London, England

Summary: Four separate episodes in the life of London therapist Dara MacLeod connect to famous literary works. In one, Dara's father cultivates an interest in Lewis Carroll. In another, her best friend's boyfriend investigates John Keats. In a third, Dara meets the man who will become her romantic partner, and in the fourth, Dara is in college.

Where it's reviewed:
Booklist, March 1, 2008, page 47
Entertainment Weekly, May 9, 2008, page 68
Publishers Weekly, January 7, 2008, page 32

Other books by the same author:
Banishing Verona, 2004
Eva Moves the Furniture, 2001
The Missing World, 2000
Criminals, 1996
Homework, 1990

Other books you might like:
Michael Cunningham, *The Hours*, 1998
Julia Glass, *Three Junes*, 2002

☐1063

LISA LUTZ

Curse of the Spellmans
(New York: Simon & Schuster, 2008)

Story type: Contemporary
Subject(s): Family Relations

Major character(s): Isabel Spellman, Detective—Private; Rae Spellman, Teenager; Henry Stone, Police Officer
Time period(s): 2000s
Locale(s): San Francisco, California

Summary: Wacky private investigator Isabel Spellman is attracted to her next-door neighbor, though she's meant to be performing surveillance on him. Isabel's kid sister, Rae, has a crush on a police officer who may be helpful to Isabel in her work.

Where it's reviewed:
New York Times Book Review, March 23, 2008, page 11
Publishers Weekly, January 14, 2008, page 39

Other books by the same author:
The Spellman Files, 2007

Other books you might like:
Janet Evanovich, *Fearless Fourteen*, 2008
Laura Lippman, *Another Thing to Fall*, 2008

☐1064

FIONA MAAZEL

Last Last Chance
(New York: Farrar, Straus and Giroux, 2008)

Story type: Literary
Subject(s): Family Relations
Major character(s): Lucy, Addict
Time period(s): 2000s
Locale(s): New York, New York; Texas

Summary: Lucy is a drug addict working in a chicken plant in New York City after several stints in rehab. She hits the road to see her best friend get married and has lots of adventures on the way before heading into a treatment center yet again.

Where it's reviewed:
Booklist, February 1, 2008, page 27
New York Times, March 31, 2007, page E7
Publishers Weekly, December 24, 2007, page 26
USA Today, January 3, 2008, page 5D

Other books you might like:
Charles Bock, *Beautiful Children*, 2008
Denis Johnson, *Jesus' Son*, 1992

☐1065

HEATHER MACDOWELL
ROSE MACDOWELL , Co-Author

Turning Tables
(New York: Dial Press, 2008)

Story type: Contemporary
Subject(s): Restaurants
Major character(s): Erin Edwards, Waiter/Waitress; Cato Poole, Waiter/Waitress; Carl, Cook
Time period(s): 2000s
Locale(s): New York, New York

Summary: Erin Edwards loses her office job and starts waiting tables at a classy restaurant. Her skills aren't up-

to-snuff, however, and she comes to rely on fellow waiter Cato Poole to help her out. Chef Carl, however, keeps a close watch on her.

Where it's reviewed:
Publishers Weekly, January 14, 2008, page 40

Other books you might like:
Claire Cook, *Must Love Dogs*, 2002
Phoebe Damrosch, *Service Included*, 2007
   memoir
Alex Witchel, *The Spare Wife*, 2008

DAVID MAINE

Monster, 1959

(New York: St. Martin's Press, 2008)

Story type: Literary
Subject(s): Monsters
Major character(s): K., Monster; Billy, Businessman; Betty, Actress
Time period(s): 1950s
Locale(s): United States; Pacific Islands

Summary: K. is a monster, a 40-foot-tall apelike animal probably resulting from weapons testing on his South Pacific island. Showman Billy and his fellow explorers bring K. to the United States and tour him around for money.

Where it's reviewed:
New York Times Book Review, April 6, 2008, page 11
The New York Times, February 25, 2008, page B10
O, The Oprah Magazine, March 2008, page 174

Other books by the same author:
The Book of Samson, 2006
Fallen, 2005
The Preservationist, 2004

Other books you might like:
Tana French, *In the Woods*, 2007
Lauren Groff, *The Monsters of Templeton*, 2008

1067

MAMEVE MEDWED

Of Men and Their Mothers

(New York: Morrow, 2008)

Story type: Literary
Subject(s): Family Relations
Major character(s): Maisie, Parent, Divorced Person; Tommy, Teenager; Rex Pollock, Parent, Divorced Person
Time period(s): 2000s
Locale(s): Massachusetts

Summary: Professional organizer Maisie never got along with her mother-in-law when she was married to Rex, and now that they're divorced the relationship isn't any better. Rex's mother is always meddling and trying to tell Maisie how to raise her son, Tommy. Meanwhile,

Maisie may have found drugs in Tommy's backpack, and she's not crazy about Tommy's girlfriend.

Where it's reviewed:
Booklist, April 15, 2008, page 26
Publishers Weekly, February 11, 2008, page 48

Other books by the same author:
How Elizabeth Barrett Browning Saved My Life, 2006
The End of an Error, 2003
Host Family, 2000
Mail, 1997

Other books you might like:
Elinor Lipman, *The Way Men Act*, 1993
Jennifer Weiner, *Certain Girls*, 2008

1068

BILLY MERNIT

Imagine Me and You

(New York: Shaye Areheart Books, 2008)

Story type: Literary
Subject(s): Marriage
Major character(s): Jordan, Writer; Naomi, Student
Time period(s): 2000s
Locale(s): Los Angeles, California

Summary: Dejected Jordan makes up a girlfriend to goad his estranged wife into jealousy. He bases the imaginary young woman on a former student, and soon his fictional creation begins to appear to him and talk to him.

Where it's reviewed:
Publishers Weekly, December 24, 2007, page 24

Other books by the same author:
Writing the Romantic Comedy, 2000 (nonfiction)

Other books you might like:
Emily Giffin, *Love the One You're With*, 2008
Lorrie Moore, *Anagrams*, 1986

1069

JONATHAN MILES

Dear American Airlines

(Boston: Houghton Mifflin, 2008)

Story type: Literary
Subject(s): Family Relations; Air Travel
Major character(s): Benjamin Ford, Writer
Time period(s): 2000s
Locale(s): Chicago, Illinois

Summary: Benjamin Ford is experiencing a long layover in Chicago's O'Hare Airport as he waits to fly out to Los Angeles for his daughter's wedding. As he sits, he composes a long letter to the airline, in which he touches on his marriages, his unsatisfactory parenting, and his relationship with his ill mother and Holocaust survivor father.

Where it's reviewed:
Entertainment Weekly, June 6, 2008, page 121
New York Times Book Review, June 1, 2008, page 1
Publishers Weekly, February 18, 2008, page 133
USA Today, May 29, 2008, page 5D
Wall Street Journal (Eastern Edition), May 24, 2008,
    page A19

Other books you might like:
Louis Begley, *About Schmidt*, 1996
Walter Kirn, *Up in the Air*, 2001

1070

LYDIA MILLET

How the Dead Dream

(New York: Counterpoint, 2008)

Story type: Literary
Subject(s): Family Relations; Animals, Treatment of
Major character(s): T., Businessman
Time period(s): 2000s
Locale(s): Los Angeles, California

Summary: T. has never liked people much. As a child and
as a teenager, his focus was on money, and he remained
distant from others. Now he is a real estate developer in
Los Angeles. He finds—then loses—true love, and his
father leaves his mother, who comes to live with him
and begins to come unglued. In reaction, T. develops a
strong connection with animals. He begins to break into
zoos at night to be close to them, and he grows very
concerned about the fate of the planet.

Where it's reviewed:
Book World, January 6, 2008, page 4
Booklist, September 15, 2007, page 32
New York Times Book Review, March 9, 2008, page 22
Publishers Weekly, October 8, 2007, page 36

Other books by the same author:
Oh Pure and Radiant Heart, 2006
Everyone's Pretty, 2005
My Happy Life, 2002
George Bush, Dark Prince of Love, 2000
Omnivores, 1996

Other books you might like:
Annie Dillard, *The Maytrees*, 2007
Joy Williams, *The Quick and the Dead*, 2000

1071

STEVEN MILLHAUSER

Dangerous Laughter

(New York: Knopf, 2008)

Story type: Literary; Collection
Subject(s): Short Stories

Summary: Thirteen stories look at what people (and others) want and what happens when they get it. One story
reveals the inner lives of cartoon characters. Another

focuses on a painter developing a whole new style. The
title story depicts teenagers who engage in forced
laughter that turns sinister.

Where it's reviewed:
Entertainment Weekly, February 15, 2008, page 69
New York Times Book Review, February 24, 2008, page
    10
Publishers Weekly, December 17, 2007, page 33

Other books by the same author:
The Knife Thrower, 1998
Martin Dressler, 1996 (novel; winner of the Pulitzer
    Prize for fiction)
Little Kingdoms, 1993 (three novellas)
The Barnum Museum, 1990
In the Penny Arcade, 1985

Other books you might like:
Adam Johnson, *Emporium*, 2002
Jim Shepard, *Like You'd Understand Anyway*, 2007

1072

SANTA MONTEFIORE

The Sea of Lost Love

(New York: Touchstone, 2008)

Story type: Literary
Subject(s): Missing Persons; Family Relations
Major character(s): Celestria Montague, Traveler
Time period(s): 1950s (1958)
Locale(s): Cornwall, England; Italy

Summary: In 1958, when spoiled Celestria Montague is
only 21, her father dies in an apparent suicide, leaving
behind a great deal of debt. Celestria sets off for Italy,
where her father had been sending money to someone in
a small town in the region of Puglia. There she discovers
her father's secrets.

Where it's reviewed:
Booklist, March 1, 2008, page 49
Publishers Weekly, January 7, 2008, page 33

Other books by the same author:
The Gypsy Madonna, 2007
Last Voyage of the Valentina, 2005
The Swallow and the Hummingbird, 2004
The Forget-Me-Not Sonata, 2003
The Butterfly Box, 2002

Other books you might like:
Margaret Cezair-Thompson, *The Pirate's Daughter*,
    2007
Penny Vincenzi, *No Angel*, 2003

1073

JACK O'CONNELL

The Resurrectionist

(Chapel Hill, North Carolina: Algonquin Books, 2008)

Story type: Literary
Subject(s): Mental Illness; Cartoons and Comics

Major character(s): Danny Sweeney, Child, Mentally Ill Person; Sweeney, Pharmacist; Micah Peck, Doctor
Time period(s): 2000s
Locale(s): Quinsigamond, Massachusetts

Summary: Danny Sweeney's father, known only as Sweeney, uproots his catatonic son and moves the family from Ohio to Massachusetts to accept a job with a doctor named Micah Peck, who claims to have cured patients with problems similar to Danny's. Part of the attempted cure involves comic books, and Danny becomes absorbed in the world of comics.

Where it's reviewed:
New York Times Book Review, April 27, 2008, page 26
Publishers Weekly, February 4, 2008, page 38

Other books by the same author:
Word Made Flesh, 1999
The Skin Palace, 1996
Wireless, 1993
Box Nine, 1992

Other books you might like:
Michael Chabon, *The Amazing Adventures of Kavalier & Clay*, 2000
Greg Hollingshead, *Bedlam*, 2006

1074

JOSEPH O'NEILL

Netherland

(New York: Pantheon, 2008)

Story type: Literary
Subject(s): Emigration and Immigration; Sports/Cricket
Major character(s): Hans van den Broek, Banker; Chuck Ramkissoon, Businessman
Time period(s): 2000s (2001)
Locale(s): New York, New York

Summary: The terrorist attacks of 9/11 disrupt Dutch banker Hans van den Broek's life. His wife and child go to London, and he has to move out of his apartment. He joins a cricket league and becomes very involved with the sport and with Trinidadian entrepreneur Chuck Ramkissoon, who may or may not be engaged in shady dealings.

Where it's reviewed:
Entertainment Weekly, May 30, 2008, page 93
New York Times Book Review, May 18, 2008, page 1
The New York Times, May 16, 2008, page E25
Newsweek, June 16, 2008, page 10
Vogue, May 2008, page 162

Other books by the same author:
Blood-Dark Track, 2001 (memoir)
The Breezes, 1995
This Is the Life, 1991

Other books you might like:
Don DeLillo, *Falling Man*, 2007
Helen Schulman, *A Day at the Beach*, 2007

1075

CYNTHIA OZICK

Dictation

(Boston: Houghton Mifflin, 2008)

Story type: Literary; Collection
Subject(s): Short Stories

Summary: Four stories involve quirky outsiders. In the title story, the secretaries of the writers Henry James and Joseph Conrad suffer at the hands of their genius bosses. In another, an American intellectual in Fascist Italy falls in love with a peasant.

Where it's reviewed:
Christian Science Monitor, May 6, 2008, page 16
New York Times Book Review, April 20, 2008, page 11
Publishers Weekly, January 14, 2008, page 37

Other books by the same author:
Heir to the Glimmering World, 2004
The Puttermesser Papers, 1997
The Shawl, 1989
The Messiah of Stockholm, 1987
The Pagan Rabbi and Other Stories, 1971

Other books you might like:
Mary Gordon, *The Rest of Life*, 1993
Jhumpa Lahiri, *Unaccustomed Earth*, 2008

1076

CHUCK PALAHNIUK

Snuff

(New York: Doubleday, 2008)

Story type: Contemporary
Subject(s): Sexual Behavior
Major character(s): Cassie Wright, Actress
Time period(s): 2000s
Locale(s): United States

Summary: Aging porn star Cassie Wright wants to break a record and have sex with 600 men on film. Several of the men who have been hired tell their stories: one wants to create a reality television show with Cassie; another believes he is her biological son.

Where it's reviewed:
Booklist, March 1, 2008, page 30
Entertainment Weekly, May 23, 2008, page 127
New York Times Book Review, June 8, 2008, page 27
Publishers Weekly, February 11, 2008, page 47

Other books by the same author:
Rant, 2007
Lullaby, 2002
Choke, 2001
Survivor, 1999
Fight Club, 1996

Other books you might like:
James Frey, *Bright Shiny Morning*, 2008
Walter Mosley, *Killing Johnny Fry*, 2007

1077

DAVID PARK

The Truth Commissioner

(New York: Bloomsbury, 2008)

Story type: Literary
Subject(s): Missing Persons; Irish Republican Army
Major character(s): Henry Stanfield, Lawyer; James Fenton, Police Officer; Frances Gilroy, Political Figure
Time period(s): 2000s
Locale(s): Belfast, Ireland, Northern

Summary: In 1990, a teenager was found to be an IRA informer and disappeared shortly thereafter. Now a government committee has been formed to investigate what happened to Connor Walshe. The head of the committee is a lawyer who calls three major witnesses: former IRA member Francis Gilroy, now a government minister; former cop James Fenton, who recruited the ill-fated teen; and Michael Madden, who drove Connor to his fate and has fled to the United States to try and forget the past.

Where it's reviewed:
Booklist, March 1, 2008, page 51
Publishers Weekly, December 24, 2007, page 26

Other books by the same author:
Swallowing the Sun, 2004

Other books you might like:
Susan Choi, *American Woman*, 2003
Amy Wilentz, *Martyr's Crossing*, 2001

1078

GIN PHILLIPS

The Well and the Mine

(Portland, Oregon: Hawthorne Books, 2008)

Story type: Literary
Subject(s): Family Relations
Major character(s): Albert, Miner; Leta, Spouse
Time period(s): 1930s (1931)
Locale(s): Carbon Hill, Alabama

Summary: Miner Albert, his wife, Leta, and their young children witness horrific accidents at the mine. Even those who escape death and disfigurement live in terribly poor conditions. One daughter sees a woman kill her own child in despair; another hopes to avoid the trap of early marriage.

Where it's reviewed:
Publishers Weekly, December 24, 2007, page 28

Other books you might like:
Dorothy Allison, *Bastard out of Carolina*, 1992
Jim Grimsley, *Winter Birds*, 1994
Elizabeth Strout, *Olive Kitteredge*, 2008

1079

JODI PICOULT

Change of Heart

(New York: Atria, 2008)

Story type: Contemporary
Subject(s): Death; Transplants
Major character(s): Shay Bourne, Prisoner; Claire, Patient
Time period(s): 2000s
Locale(s): New Hampshire

Summary: Claire needs a heart transplant, and death row inmate Shay is willing to donate his heart. Eleven years earlier, Shay was convicted of killing Claire's sister, Elizabeth.

Where it's reviewed:
Booklist, January 1, 2008, page 21
Entertainment Weekly, March 7, 2008, page 95
Publishers Weekly, January 21, 2008, page 151
USA Today, March 4, 2008, page 7D

Other books by the same author:
Nineteen Minutes, 2007
The Tenth Circle, 2006
My Sister's Keeper, 2004
Salem Falls, 2001
The Pact, 1998

Other books you might like:
Barbara Delinsky, *The Secret between Us*, 2008
Anita Shreve, *Body Surfing*, 2007

1080

MARCIA PRESTON

Trudy's Promise

(New York: Mira, 2008)

Story type: Literary
Subject(s): Political Movements
Major character(s): Trudy Hulst, Spouse
Time period(s): 1960s
Locale(s): East Berlin, German Democratic Republic; United States; West Berlin, Germany, West

Summary: One day East Berliner Trudy Hulst's husband simply disappears. When the police come for Trudy, she flees to West Berlin. There she works as a waitress and lives on little money. She tries to get her son and mother out of East Germany as well. Eventually she travels to the United States to talk about the Cold War.

Where it's reviewed:
Publishers Weekly, January 7, 2008, page 38

Other books by the same author:
The Story of Us, 2007
The Piano Man, 2006
The Butterfly House, 2005

Other books you might like:
Susan Isaacs, *Shining Through*, 1988
Nancy Lukens, *Daughters of Eve*, 1993

1081

RICHARD PRICE

Lush Life

(New York: Farrar, Straus and Giroux, 2008)

Story type: Literary
Subject(s): Law Enforcement; Real Estate
Major character(s): Matty Clark, Police Officer; Eric Cash, Restaurateur; Tristan, Teenager
Time period(s): 2000s
Locale(s): New York, New York

Summary: Matty Clark is called to investigate a shooting on Manhattan's Lower East Side, a rapidly gentrifying area where swank bars sit side-by-side with housing projects. Eric Cash claims that local thugs killed his bartender friend in a mugging-gone-bad, but his story doesn't add up. Teenager Tristan, who falls under suspicion, also has his say.

Where it's reviewed:
New York, March 10, 2008, page 144
New York Times Book Review, March 16, 2008, page 1
The New Yorker, April 7, 2008, page 79
Time, March 10, 2008, page 71
USA Today, March 4, 2008, page 7D

Other books by the same author:
Samaritan, 2003
Freedomland, 1998
Bloodbrothers, 1993
Clockers, 1992
The Wanderers, 1974

Other books you might like:
Laura Lippman, *What the Dead Know*, 2007
Nathan McCall, *Them*, 2007

1082

THERESA REBECK

Three Girls and Their Brother

(New York: Shaye Areheart Books, 2008)

Story type: Literary
Subject(s): Family Relations
Major character(s): Daria Heller, Teenager; Polly Heller, Teenager; Amelia Heller, Teenager
Time period(s): 2000s
Locale(s): New York, New York

Summary: The three Heller sisters become famous for nothing more than being attractive, and soon their photos appear in magazines and one is cast in an off-Broadway play. They and their sardonic brother all narrate their ascent into short-lived celebrity.

Where it's reviewed:
Booklist, February 1, 2008, page 29
Entertainment Weekly, April 4, 2008, page 67
New York Times, April 14, 2008, page E7
People, April 28, 2008, page 53
Publishers Weekly, December 24, 2007, page 26

Other books by the same author:
Free Fire Zone, 2007 (nonfiction)

Other books you might like:
Jonathan Franzen, *The Corrections*, 2001
Adam Langer, *Ellington Boulevard*, 2008

1083

ANN B. ROSS

Miss Julia Paints the Town

(New York: Viking, 2008)

Story type: Contemporary
Series: Miss Julia. Book 9
Subject(s): Real Estate
Major character(s): Julia Murdoch, Widow(er); Arthur Kessler, Businessman
Time period(s): 2000s
Locale(s): Abbotsville, North Carolina

Summary: When a developer arrives in her small town to tear down the courthouse, Julia fights back. Arthur Kessler would like to build a big condo development and ruin the town's character. He doesn't account for the feistiness of Southern women.

Where it's reviewed:
Publishers Weekly, January 7, 2008, page 37

Other books by the same author:
Miss Julia Strikes Back, 2007
Miss Julia Hits the Road, 2003
Miss Julia Throws a Wedding, 2002
Miss Julia Takes Over, 2001
Miss Julia Speaks Her Mind, 1999

Other books you might like:
Maeve Binchy, *Whitethorn Woods*, 2007
Debra Galant, *Fear and Yoga in New Jersey*, 2008

1084

LAURA JOH ROWLAND

The Secret Adventures of Charlotte Bronte

(New York: Overlook Press, 2008)

Story type: Literary; Mystery
Subject(s): Murder; Writing; Historical
Major character(s): Charlotte Bronte, Historical Figure, Writer; Emily Bronte, Historical Figure, Writer; Anne Bronte, Historical Figure, Writer
Time period(s): 1840s (1848)
Locale(s): London, England

Summary: When she receives a letter from her publisher charging her with breach of contract, Charlotte Bronte boards a train to London with her writer sister Anne, leaving their third literary sibling, Emily, at home. On the train the two sisters meet a young governess who is soon murdered. The pair investigates.

Where it's reviewed:
Christian Science Monitor, April 11, 2008, page 14
Entertainment Weekly, March 21, 2008, page 63
Kirkus Reviews, February 1, 2008, page NA
Publishers Weekly, December 24, 2007, page 26

Other books by the same author:
The Snow Empress, 2007
Red Chrysanthemum, 2006
The Assassin's Touch, 2005
The Pillow Book of Lady Wisteria, 2002
Shinju, 1994

Other books you might like:
Sarah Dunant, *The Birth of Venus*, 2004
Carolly Erickson, *The Hidden Diary of Marie Antoinette*, 2005
Philippa Gregory, *The Other Boleyn Girl*, 2002

1085

MIKE SAGER

Deviant Behavior
(New York: Grove Press/Black Cat, 2008)

Story type: Literary
Subject(s): Drugs; Fathers
Major character(s): Jonathan Seede, Journalist
Time period(s): 1980s
Locale(s): Washington, District of Columbia

Summary: On the surface, Jonathan Seede seems to have it all: a good job as a reporter, a new baby, an attractive wife. Then, while working on a book on drugs, he gets involved with a drug dealer and other unsavory characters. He also finds that drugs are beginning to appeal to him personally.

Where it's reviewed:
Publishers Weekly, December 24, 2007, page 25

Other books by the same author:
Wounded Warriors, 2008 (nonfiction)
Revenge of the Donut Boys, 2007 (nonfiction)
Scary Monsters and Super Freaks, 2003 (nonfiction)

Other books you might like:
Charles Bock, *Beautiful Children*, 2008
Richard Price, *Lush Life*, 2008

1086

PREETA SAMARASAN

Evening Is the Whole Day
(Boston: Houghton Mifflin, 2008)

Story type: Literary
Subject(s): Family Relations
Major character(s): Raju Rajasekharan, Parent; Vasanthi Rajasekharan, Parent; Uma Rajasekharan, Student
Time period(s): 2000s
Locale(s): Ipoh, Malaysia

Summary: The various members of the Rajasekharan family of Malaysia deal with the death of one family member and the departure of a long-time servant. Father Raju still dreams of a career in politics. Mother Vasanthi wants to see her children cross class boundaries. Their eldest daughter, Uma, has been accepted to Columbia University in the United States and can't wait to escape their clutches.

Where it's reviewed:
Publishers Weekly, February 4, 2008, page 34

Other books you might like:
Aravind Adiga, *The White Tiger*, 2008
V.V. Ganeshananthan, *Love Marriage*, 2008

1087

CHRISTINE SCHUTT

All Souls
(New York: Harcourt, 2008)

Story type: Literary
Subject(s): Teen Relationships; Eating Disorders
Major character(s): Astra Dell, Patient, Teenager; Car, Teenager; Marlene, Teenager
Time period(s): 1990s (1997)
Locale(s): New York, New York

Summary: Astra Dell must take a leave of absence from an all girls Manhattan prep school to be hospitalized for cancer. Her absence has an effect on other students, including anorexic Car and lesbian Lisa, as well as on some teachers in the school.

Where it's reviewed:
Booklist, February 15, 2008, page 34
Publishers Weekly, January 21, 2008, page 149

Other books by the same author:
A Day, a Night, Another Day, Summer, 2005
Florida, 2004
Nightwork, 1996 (short stories)

Other books you might like:
Phil LaMarche, *American Youth*, 2007
Tom Perrotta, *Election*, 1998

1088

NINA SIEGAL

A Little Trouble with the Facts
(New York: Harper, 2008)

Story type: Contemporary
Subject(s): Murder
Major character(s): Valerie Vane, Journalist
Time period(s): 1990s (1999)
Locale(s): New York, New York

Summary: Valerie Vane lands a job as a gossip columnist. Then she develops a drug problem and gets moved to obituaries, where she investigates a murder.

Where it's reviewed:
Publishers Weekly, December 24, 2007, page 30

Other books you might like:
Porter Shreve, *The Obituary Writer*, 2000
Lauren Weisberger, *The Devil Wears Prada*, 2003

1089

KELLY SIMMONS

Standing Still

(New York: Atria, 2008)

Story type: Contemporary
Subject(s): Terror; Family Relations
Major character(s): Claire Cooper, Journalist; Sam, Spouse
Time period(s): 2000s
Locale(s): United States

Summary: Claire Cooper is alone in her suburban home with her children as her husband travels on business. When an intruder threatens to kidnap her eldest child, Claire volunteers herself as a hostage instead. The intruder takes her up on her offer, and the two develop a strange relationship as Claire reflects on her past as a journalist and her flawed marriage.

Where it's reviewed:
Entertainment Weekly, February 8, 2008, page 71
Publishers Weekly, December 24, 2007, page 29

Other books you might like:
Bill Floyd, *The Killer's Wife*, 2008
Kitty Sewell, *Ice Trap*, 2008

1090

INDRA SINHA

Animal's People

(New York: Simon & Schuster, 2008)

Story type: Literary
Subject(s): Poverty
Major character(s): Animal, Accident Victim
Time period(s): 1980s
Locale(s): Bhopal, India

Summary: Animal was once able-bodied, but the infamous Bhopal incident has left him walking on all fours, a twisted wreck. He narrates his ordeal as he waits for someone to be found responsible. Meanwhile, a suspicious doctor opens a clinic and lawyers try to negotiate a settlement.

Where it's reviewed:
Entertainment Weekly, March 7, 2008, page 96
New York Times Book Review, March 9, 2008, page 13
Publishers Weekly, December 24, 2007, page 29

Other books by the same author:
The Death of Mr. Love, 2004
Tantra, 2003
The Cybergypsies, 1999

Other books you might like:
Nicola Barker, *Darkmans*, 2007
Charles Baxter, *First Light*, 1987
Katherine Dunn, *Geek Love*, 1989

1091

SASA STANISIC

How the Soldier Repairs the Gramophone

(New York: Grove Press, 2008)

Story type: Literary
Subject(s): Emigration and Immigration; War
Major character(s): Aleksandar Krsmanovic, Refugee
Time period(s): 1990s (1992)
Locale(s): Germany; Bosnia-Hercegovina

Summary: From safety in Germany, a young Bosnian refugee recalls life in his hometown. Some of his stories are told in letters to a girlfriend; others are related in the voices of friends and relatives. All are an attempt to hold on to the fading memories of a lost place. Translated by Anthea Bell.

Where it's reviewed:
Publishers Weekly, February 4, 2008, page 34

Other books you might like:
Jonathan Safran Foer, *Everything Is Illuminated*, 2002
Aleksandar Hemon, *Nowhere Man*, 2002

1092

DANIELLE STEEL

Honor Thyself

(New York: Delacorte Press, 2008)

Story type: Romance
Subject(s): Actors and Actresses
Major character(s): Carole Barber, Actress
Time period(s): 2000s
Locale(s): Paris, France

Summary: Legendary actress Carole Barber is in Paris writing a novel when she loses her memory in a car accident. She must piece together her life from the beginning to understand herself. In doing so, she ruminates on a destructive affair and her poor relationship with her daughter.

Where it's reviewed:
Booklist, December 1, 2007, page 4
Publishers Weekly, December 24, 2007, page 28

Other books by the same author:
Amazing Grace, 2007
Bungalow 2, 2007
Sisters, 2007
Coming Out, 2006
H.R.H., 2006

Other books you might like:
Barbara Delinsky, *The Secret between Us*, 2008
Elizabeth Dewberry, *His Lovely Wife*, 2006

1093

TOM STONER

The Comfort of Our Kind

(New York: Thomas Dunne Books, 2008)

Story type: Literary
Subject(s): Family Relations; Marriage
Major character(s): Donica Lenore Moffat, Spouse; Wes Moffat, Spouse
Time period(s): 2000s
Locale(s): Franklin Notch, New Hampshire

Summary: As Donica Lenore Moffat, who was once a nun, and Wes Moffat prepare to celebrate their 50th wedding anniversary in the quirky New Hampshire town of Franklin Notch, Wes stirs up trouble by fabricating local history for his small-time television show. Controversy arises about a made-up local tribe.

Where it's reviewed:
Booklist, February 15, 2008, page 34
Publishers Weekly, December 24, 2007, page 27

Other books you might like:
John Irving, *The World According to Garp*, 1978
Matthew Sharpe, *Jamestown*, 2007

1094

DARIN STRAUSS

More Than It Hurts You

(New York: Dutton, 2008)

Story type: Literary
Subject(s): Family Relations
Major character(s): Josh Goldin, Parent; Dori Goldin, Parent; Darlene Stokes, Doctor
Time period(s): 2000s
Locale(s): United States

Summary: Twice while Josh Goldin is out of town, his eight-month-old son falls unconscious for no reason that anyone can discern. Eventually, a doctor suspects Goldin's wife suffers from Munchausen-by-proxy syndrome and is making the child sick on purpose. When lawyers get involved, the conflict between the African-American doctor and the Jewish Goldin family grows ugly.

Where it's reviewed:
Publishers Weekly, January 7, 2008, page 32

Other books by the same author:
The Real McCoy, 2003
Chang and Eng, 2000

Other books you might like:
Gillian Flynn, *Sharp Objects*, 2006
Laura Lippman, *What the Dead Know*, 2007

1095

ALAIN CLAUDE SULZER

A Perfect Waiter

(New York: Bloomsbury, 2008)

Story type: Literary
Subject(s): Coming-of-Age
Major character(s): Erneste, Waiter/Waitress
Time period(s): 1960s (1966)
Locale(s): Switzerland

Summary: Orderly and subdued Erneste has been a waiter in a fancy Swiss restaurant for 16 years when he receives a letter from his lost love of decades earlier. The letter asks Erneste to track down a third man who previously left for the United States but has since returned to Switzerland.

Where it's reviewed:
Booklist, February 1, 2008, page 28
Publishers Weekly, January 7, 2008, page 35

Other books you might like:
Andre Aciman, *Call Me by Your Name*, 2007
Kazuo Ishiguro, *Remains of the Day*, 1989

1096

WILLIAM SUTCLIFFE

Whatever Makes You Happy

(New York: Bloomsbury, 2008)

Story type: Literary
Subject(s): Family Relations
Major character(s): Carol, Parent; Gillian, Parent; Helen, Parent
Time period(s): 2000s
Locale(s): England

Summary: Three women with sons in their thirties decide to force their sons to shape up. They are determined to get them to settle down, so each shows up at her son's home and insists on staying.

Where it's reviewed:
Entertainment Weekly, April 4, 2008, page 66
The New York Times, April 17, 2008, page E8
Publishers Weekly, February 4, 2008, page 36

Other books by the same author:
Bad Influence, 2004
The Love Hexagon, 2000
Are You Experienced?, 1999
New Boy, 1998

Other books you might like:
Lauren Groff, *The Monsters of Templeton*, 2008
Sophie Kinsella, *Remember Me?*, 2008

1097

JACK TODD

Sun Going Down

(New York: Touchstone, 2008)

Story type: Literary; Family Saga
Subject(s): Family Relations; Pioneers
Major character(s): Eli Paint, Twin, Rancher; Ezra Paint, Twin, Cowboy
Time period(s): 19th century; 1920s
Locale(s): West

Summary: This family saga covers seven decades and several generations. The Paint family patriarch is Ebenezer Paint, who sets out from Mississippi for the Dakotas during the Civil War. He marries and has twin boys, Eli and Ezra, who grow up to be cowboys, one stable and wealthy, the other less grounded. Eli's daughter Velma, one of six children, carries the story into the 20th century.

Where it's reviewed:
Publishers Weekly, January 7, 2008, page 33

Other books by the same author:
Desertion, 2001 (memoir)

Other books you might like:
Leif Enger, *Peace Like a River*, 2001
James Michener, *Texas*, 1985

1098

KATE VEITCH

Without a Backward Glance

(New York: Plume, 2008)

Story type: Literary
Subject(s): Family Relations
Major character(s): Rosemarie McDonald, Parent
Time period(s): 1960s (1967); 1990s
Locale(s): Melbourne, Australia

Summary: Rosemarie McDonald abandons her four children when they're still young, marking them for life. Decades later, one of them locates her, and they all must deal with their feelings about being reunited with her, or choose not to be reunited with her.

Where it's reviewed:
Publishers Weekly, January 7, 2008, page 32

Other books you might like:
Louise Limerick, *Friends and Mothers*, 2007
Tom Perrotta, *Little Children*, 2004
Meg Wolitzer, *The Ten-Year Nap*, 2008

1099

CHRISTIAN VON DITFURTH

A Paragon of Virtue

(New Milford: Toby Press, 2008)

Story type: Literary
Subject(s): Mystery
Major character(s): Josef Stachelmann, Professor; Oskar Winter, Police Officer
Time period(s): 1990s
Locale(s): Hamburg, Germany

Summary: Professor Josef Stachelmann helps his friend, the Hamburg police commissioner, make sense of the seemingly disproportionate number of deaths in the family of a local businessman. The two discover that the man was involved in questionable business dealings during the Nazi era. Translated from the German by Helen Atkins.

Where it's reviewed:
Publishers Weekly, January 7, 2008, page 38

Other books you might like:
Jenna Blum, *Those Who Save Us*, 2004
William Boyd, *Restless*, 2006

1100

JESSE WASHINGTON

Black Will Shoot

(New York: Simon Spotlight Entertainment, 2008)

Story type: Contemporary
Subject(s): Music and Musicians
Major character(s): Marquis Wise, Writer; Holliday Watkins, Lawyer; Dontay Wise, Musician
Time period(s): 2000s
Locale(s): New York, New York

Summary: Marquis Wise is a writer for the hip-hop magazine *Fever* and has authored an article on Large, a hip-hop star and actor who was murdered. His brother, Dontay, is a rapper with a drug problem who idolized Large. The two take turns relating Large's story in a journalistic voice and one informed by rap lyrics.

Where it's reviewed:
Ebony, February 2008, page 32
Publishers Weekly, December 17, 2007, page 33

Other books you might like:
Erica Kennedy, *Bling*, 2004
Tia Williams, *The Accidental Diva*, 2004

1101

JENNIFER WEINER

Certain Girls

(New York: Atria, 2008)

Story type: Contemporary
Subject(s): Marriage; Parenthood
Major character(s): Cannie Shapiro, Parent; Peter Krushelevansky, Doctor; Joy Shapiro, Teenager
Time period(s): 2000s
Locale(s): United States

Summary: The star of the author's 2001 novel, *Good in Bed*, returns a little older and wiser. Cannie Shapiro is happily married to a doctor and raising Joy, a daughter from a previous relationship. Cannie has come to terms

with being overweight and not as glamorous as her sister. Her husband wants to have a child with her, however, so they need a surrogate. Also, Joy is worried about her upcoming bat mitzvah and about being popular in school.

Where it's reviewed:
Entertainment Weekly, April 11, 2008, page 74
Good Housekeeping, April 2008, page 218
Harper's Bazaar, April 2008, page 208
USA Today, April 8, 2008, page 4D

Other books by the same author:
The Guy Not Taken, 2007
Goodnight Nobody, 2005
Little Earthquakes, 2004
In Her Shoes, 2002
Good in Bed, 2001

Other books you might like:
Sophie Kinsella, *Remember Me?*, 2008
Elizabeth Noble, *Things I Want My Daughters to Know*, 2008

1102

DEBBIE LEE WESSELMANN

Captivity

(Winston-Salem; North Carolina: John F. Blair, 2008)

Story type: Literary
Subject(s): Animals/Chimpanzees
Major character(s): Dana Armstrong, Scientist
Time period(s): 2000s
Locale(s): South Carolina

Summary: Primatologist Dana Andrews works in a chimpanzee sanctuary, and every day the animals in her care remind her of her own childhood. Dana was raised with a female chimpanzee "sibling," an experiment that ended tragically. When someone begins breaking into the sanctuary and freeing the chimpanzees, Dana must act to save the animals, who are not prepared to live outside of captivity.

Where it's reviewed:
Publishers Weekly, December 17, 2007, page 34

Other books by the same author:
The Earth and the Sky, 1997 (short stories)
Trutor and the Balloonist, 1997

Other books you might like:
Elizabeth Hess, *Nim Chimpsky*, 2008
   nonfiction
Barbara Kingsolver, *The Poisonwood Bible*, 1999
Aryn Kyle, *The God of Animals*, 2007

1103

JEANETTE WINTERSON

The Stone Gods

(New York: Harcourt, 2008)

Story type: Literary
Subject(s): Apocalypse

Major character(s): Billie Crusoe, Explorer; Spike, Robot
Time period(s): Indeterminate Future
Locale(s): Orbus, Planet—Imaginary; Planet Blue, Planet—Imaginary

Summary: Space explorer Billie Crusoe leaves her home planet of Orbus (which may have once been the earth) with her faithful sidekick and romantic partner, a robot named Spike, to explore Planet Blue. The two hope to find a place hospitable to humans.

Where it's reviewed:
Booklist, March 15, 2008, page 29
Publishers Weekly, January 28, 2008, page 39

Other books by the same author:
Lighthousekeeping, 2005
Written on the Body, 1993
Sexing the Cherry, 1990
The Passion, 1988
Oranges Are Not the Only Fruit, 1985

Other books you might like:
David Mitchell, *Cloud Atlas*, 2004
Kurt Vonnegut, *Slaughterhouse-Five*, 1969

1104

MEG WOLITZER

The Ten-Year Nap

(New York: Riverhead, 2008)

Story type: Literary
Subject(s): Parenthood
Major character(s): Amy, Parent; Jill, Parent; Roberta, Parent
Time period(s): 2000s
Locale(s): New York, New York

Summary: Four female friends leave good jobs to stay home with their children in New York City. Though they thought the move would be temporary, a decade later they find themselves questioning what has happened, especially when one of them befriends a woman who still works outside the home and appears fulfilled.

Where it's reviewed:
Booklist, December 15, 2007, page 5
Entertainment Weekly, March 28, 2008, page 69
O, The Oprah Magazine, April 2008, page 186
Publishers Weekly, December 24, 2007, page 25

Other books by the same author:
The Position, 2005
The Wife, 2003
Surrender, Dorothy, 1999
Friends for Life, 1994
Sleepwalking, 1982

Other books you might like:
Louise Limerick, *Friends and Mothers*, 2007
Tom Perrotta, *Little Children*, 2004

Popular Fiction

Series Index

This index alphabetically lists series to which books featured in the entries belong. Beneath each series name, book titles are listed alphabetically with author names and genre codes. The genre codes are as follows: *c* Popular Fiction, *f* Fantasy, *h* Horror, *i* Inspirational, *m* Mystery, *r* Romance, *s* Science Fiction, *t* Historical, and *w* Western. Numbers refer to the entries that feature each title.

Time Period Index

This index chronologically lists the time settings in which the featured books take place. Main headings refer to a century; where no specific time is given, the headings MULTIPLE TIME PERIODS, INDETERMINATE PAST, INDETERMINATE FUTURE, and INDETERMINATE are used. The 18th through 21st centuries are broken down into decades when possible. (Note: 1800s, for example, refers to the first decade of the 19th century.) Featured titles are listed alphabetically beneath time headings, with author names and genre codes. The genre codes are as follows: *c* Popular Fiction, *f* Fantasy, *h* Horror, *i* Inspirational, *m* Mystery, *r* Romance, *s* Science Fiction, *t* Historical, and *w* Western. Numbers refer to the entries that feature each title.

MULTIPLE TIME PERIODS

Flight - Sherman Alexie *w* 400
Lost Trails - Louis L'Amour *w* 437
The Monsters of Templeton - Lauren Goff *t* 815
People of the Book - Geraldine Brooks *c* 1020
People of the Book - Geraldine Brooks *t* 774
The Vow - Rebecca Winters *r* 396

INDETERMINATE PAST

Beating the Devil - W.C. Jameson *w* 426
Big Bend Death Trap - James J. Griffin *w* 420
Bucking the Tiger - Marcus Galloway *w* 417
Crucifixion River - Marcia Muller *w* 443
Demon's Fire - Emma Holly *r* 294
Dragon Mage - Andre Norton *f* 534
Grub Line Rider - Louis L'Amour *w* 436
Into the Mist - Elizabeth Sinclair *r* 381
Lavinia - Ursula K. Le Guin *t* 848
Luck - Max Brand *w* 406
Man from Durango - Lauran Paine *w* 444
Nate Coffin's Revenge - J. Lee Butts *w* 410
The Palace of Illusions - Chitra Banerjee Divakaruni *t* 789
Pursuit - Verne Athanas *w* 401
Revelation - Karen Traviss *s* 743
River Range - L.P. Holmes *w* 425
Rule of Two - Drew Karpyshyn *s* 697
Seekers of the Chalice - Brian Cullen *f* 486
The Sundown Man - Jory Sherman *w* 453
The Time Engine - Sean McMullen *f* 528
Trail Hand - R.W. Stone *w* 456
The Triumph of Deborah - Eva Etzioni-Halevy *t* 801

10th CENTURY B.C.

Solomon's Angels - Doreen Virtue *t* 894

5th CENTURY B.C.

Stealing Athena - Karen Essex *t* 800

3rd CENTURY B.C.

Bring Down the Sun - Judith Tarr *f* 552

1st CENTURY B.C.

The Triumph of Caesar - Steven Saylor *t* 884

1st CENTURY

The Betrayal: The Lost Life of Jesus Christ - W. Michael Gear *t* 811
Buried Too Deep - Jane Finnis *m* 70
Christ the Lord: The Road to Cana - Anne Rice *i* 981
Christ the Lord: The Road to Cana - Anne Rice *t* 878
Eighth Shepherd - Bodie Thoene *i* 997
John - Niall Williams *t* 900
Mary of Nazareth - Marek Halter *t* 826

2nd CENTURY

Terra Incognita - Ruth Downie *t* 794
Terra Incognita - Ruth Downie *c* 1033

4th CENTURY

The Betrayal: The Lost Life of Jesus Christ - W. Michael Gear *t* 811
The Fire Walker - Ben Pastor *t* 870

5th CENTURY

The Abyssinian Proof - Jenny White *m* 192

6th CENTURY

Seven for a Secret - Mary Reed *m* 154
Seven for a Secret - Mary Reed *t* 877

9th CENTURY

Sword Song - Bernard Cornwell *t* 782

11th CENTURY

Lady Macbeth - Susan King *t* 844
Wild Angel - Sasha Lord *r* 332

12th CENTURY

The Enchanter's Forest - Alys Clare *t* 778
Genghis: Lords of the Bow - Conn Iggulden *t* 838

Love's Magic - Traci E. Hall *r* 281
The Noble Outlaw - Bernard Knight *t* 845
The Serpent's Tale - Ariana Franklin *m* 77
The Serpent's Tale - Ariana Franklin *t* 804

13th CENTURY

City of the Dead - Ian Morson *t* 859
Crossed - Nicole Galland *t* 809
Danger's Kiss - Sarah McKerrigan *r* 349
The Moneylender of Toulouse - Alan Gordon *t* 817
The Moneylender of Toulouse - Alan Gordon *m* 87
People of the Weeping Eye - W. Michael Gear *t* 812

14th CENTURY

Border Wedding - Amanda Scott *r* 376
Cathedral of the Sea - Ildefonso Falcones *t* 802
Innocence Unveiled - Blythe Gifford *r* 271
Surrender to the Highlander - Terri Brisbin *r* 231
The Templar, the Queen and Her Lover - Michael Jecks *t* 839
With Every Breath - Lynn Kurland *r* 320

15th CENTURY

The Apostate's Tale - Margaret Frazer *t* 806
Emerald Silk - Janet Lane *r* 321
Highland Wolf - Hannah Howell *r* 296
The Queen's Gambit - Diane A.S. Stuckart *t* 889
The Rough Collier - Pat McIntosh *m* 132

16th CENTURY

The Alchemist's Code - Dave Duncan *f* 493
The Crystal Skull - Manda Scott *f* 546
The Crystal Skull - Manda Scott *m* 167
The Enchantress of Florence - Salman Rushdie *t* 882
Flodden Field - Elisabeth McNeill *t* 858
In the Shadow of Lions - Ginger Garrett *i* 936
Ink and Steel - Elizabeth Bear *f* 469
The Jewel Trader of Pegu - Jeffrey Hantover *t* 830
The Lady Elizabeth - Alison Weir *t* 896

Geographic Index

This index provides access to all featured books by geographic settings—such as countries, continents, oceans, and planets. States and provinces are indicated for the United States and Canada. Also interfiled are headings for fictional place names (Spaceships, Imaginary Planets, etc.). Sections are further broken down by city or the specific name of the imaginary locale. Book titles are listed alphabetically under headings, with author names and genre codes. The genre codes are as follows: *c* Popular Fiction, *f* Fantasy, *h* Horror, *i* Inspirational, *m* Mystery, *r* Romance, *s* Science Fiction, *t* Historical, and *w* Western. Numbers refer to the entries that feature each title.

Cairo

Luxor

Mount Horeb

ENGLAND

Birmingham

Broadstairs

Cambridge

Canterbury

Carhullan

Chichester

Clovelly

Cornwall

Cotswolds

Derbyshire

Exeter

Finch

Flagford

Gipping-on-Plym

Harrington

Haworth

Kelton Bridge

Kent

Kingsmarkham

Liverpool

London

Geographic Index

Joyeuse Island
Findings - Mary Anna Evans   *m*   67

Key West
The Undead Kama Sutra - Mario
   Acevedo   *h*   561

Miami
The Heartbreak Pill - Anjanette
   Delgado   *c*   1032
The Law of Second Chances - James
   Sheehan   *m*   168
Personal Demons - Kelley Armstrong   *h*   564
White Soul - Brandt Dodson   *i*   929
White Soul - Brandt Dodson   *m*   56

Mt. Dora
She Always Wore Red - Angela Hunt   *i*   949

St. Augustine
La Vida Vampire - Nancy Haddock   *r*   279

Sanibel Island
Black Widow - Randy Wayne White   *m*   193

Seaview Key
Seaview Inn - Sherryl Woods   *r*   399

Siesta Key
Even Cat Sitters Get the Blues - Blaize
   Clement   *m*   40

Tampa
Atomic Lobster - Tim Dorsey   *m*   57

GEORGIA
Borrowed Time - S.M. Ballard   *w*   402
Deep Dish - Mary Kay Andrews   *c*   1009
Go-Go Girls of the Apocalypse - Victor
   Gischler   *s*   687

Andersonville
Escape from Andersonville - Gene
   Hackman   *t*   822

Atlanta
Catch a Shadow - Patricia Potter   *r*   361
Deep Dish - Mary Kay Andrews   *r*   202
Love the One You're With - Emily
   Giffin   *c*   1046
Magic Burns - Ilona Andrews   *f*   464
Seen It All and Done the Rest - Pearl
   Cleage   *c*   1024
The Sinai Secret - Gregg Loomis   *m*   125

Dutton
Scream for Me - Karen Rose   *r*   370

Hopemore
What Are You Wearing to Die? - Patricia
   Sprinkle   *m*   174

Little Five Points
A Match Made in Hell - Terri Garey   *h*   589

Savannah
Deeper Water - Robert Whitlow   *i*   1004
Waking Brigid - Francis Clark   *h*   579
Waking Brigid - Francis Clark   *t*   779

HAWAII

Malino
The Secret Correspondence - Annette
   Mahon   *r*   336

IDAHO
The Outlander - Gil Adamson   *t*   756

Kootenai Bay
Blue Heaven - C.J. Box   *m*   26

ILLINOIS
The Caddie Who Played with Hickory - John
   Coyne   *t*   783
Witch Blood - Anya Bast   *r*   215

Chicago
At the City's Edge - Marcus Sakey   *m*   160
Close Call - John McEvoy   *m*   129
Dear American Airlines - Jonathan
   Miles   *c*   1069
Easy Innocence - Libby Fischer
   Hellmann   *m*   96
Fuzzy Navel - J.A. Konrath   *m*   116
In the Wind - Barbara Fister   *m*   71
The Lazarus Project - Aleksandar
   Hemon   *t*   832
One Night Stand - Cindy Kirk   *r*   314
An Ordinary Spy - Joseph Weisberg   *m*   188
Pinkerton's Secret - Eric Lerner   *m*   122
St. Barts Breakdown - Don Bruns   *m*   32
Small Favor - Jim Butcher   *h*   572
Small Favor - Jim Butcher   *f*   480

Ellwood
One Night Stand - Cindy Kirk   *r*   314

Glencoe
Easy Innocence - Libby Fischer
   Hellmann   *m*   96

Scumble River
Murder of a Chocolate-Covered Cherry - Denise
   Swanson   *m*   177

Skokie
Fiddle Game - Richard A. Thompson   *m*   182

Winnetka
Easy Innocence - Libby Fischer
   Hellmann   *m*   96

INDIAN TERRITORY
Flight - Sherman Alexie   *w*   400

INDIANA
Anathema - Colleen Coble   *i*   922
Obedience - Will Lavender   *m*   118

Big Knob
Wild and Hexy - Vicki Lewis
   Thompson   *r*   386

Indianapolis
City of the Sun - David Levien   *m*   123

South Bend
Blame It on Paris - Jennifer Greene   *r*   276

Stony Mill
Hex Marks the Spot - Madelyn Alt   *m*   7

IOWA

Maplewood
Act Two - Kimberly Stuart   *i*   995

KANSAS

Clayburn
Leaving November - Deborah Raney   *i*   979

Murphy
You Gotta Sin to Get Saved - J.D.
   Mason   *r*   341

Winter Break
In the Dead of Winter - Nancy Mehl   *i*   963

KENTUCKY
Fast and Loose - Elizabeth Bevarly   *r*   219

Little Hickman
Courting Emma - Sharlene MacLaren   *i*   961

Pleasant Hill
The Outsider - Ann H. Gabhart   *i*   935

LOUISIANA
Pelican Road - Howard Bahr   *t*   762

Baton Rouge
Wild Jinx - Sandra Hill   *r*   292

Bayou Black
Wild Jinx - Sandra Hill   *r*   292

Belle Ville
Delusion - Peter Abrahams   *m*   2

Bon Temps
From Dead to Worse - Charlaine Harris   *h*   598

Chartreuse
Between the Sheets - Robin Wells   *r*   390

Lagniappe
Bayou Paradox - Robin Caroll   *i*   920

Lake Charles
*Bobbie Faye's (kinda, sorta, not-exactly) Family
   Jewels* - Toni McGee Causey   *r*   241

New Orleans
Bad Blood - L.A. Banks   *h*   566
Collision - Jeff Abbott   *m*   1
Dark Deeds at Night's Edge - Kresley
   Cole   *r*   245
Delusion - Peter Abrahams   *m*   2
Dragons Wild - Robert Asprin   *f*   467
Dream Chaser - Sherrilyn Kenyon   *r*   313
The Last Vampire - Patricia Rosemoor   *h*   632
Thigh High - Christina Dodd   *r*   255

MAINE
Lethal Legend - Kathy Lynn Emerson   *t*   797

Mackenzie
The Vow - Rebecca Winters   *r*   396

Missoula
Dead Silver - Neil McMahon   *m*   134

Phillips
Finding Stefanie - Susan May Warren   *i*   1002

Phosphor
Dead Silver - Neil McMahon   *m*   134

Sweetwater
Wagered Heart - Robin Lee Hatcher   *i*   941

NEBRASKA
Sun Going Down - Jack Todd   *t*   892

NEVADA

Las Vegas
Avenging Fury - John Farris   *h*   587
Guns Will Keep Us Together - Leslie
    Langtry   *r*   322
Luck Be a Lady, Don't Die - Robert J.
    Randisi   *m*   152
Tall Tales and Wedding Veils - Jane
    Graves   *r*   274
Walk on the Wild Side - Christine
    Warren   *r*   389

Virginia City
Missy - Chris Hannan   *c*   1051
Missy - Chris Hannan   *t*   828

NEW ENGLAND
Blood Harvest - Brant Randall   *t*   876

NEW HAMPSHIRE
Change of Heart - Jodi Picoult   *c*   1079
Stalking Death - Kate Flora   *m*   72

Beekridge
An Ordinary Spy - Joseph Weisberg   *m*   188

Franklin Notch
The Comfort of Our Kind - Tom
    Stoner   *c*   1093

Stoneham
Murder Is Binding - Lorna Barrett   *m*   15

NEW JERSEY
Come With Me to Babylon - Paul M.
    Levitt   *t*   850
Just Desserts - Barbara Bretton   *r*   230

Fort Lee
Don't Tell a Soul - David Rosenfelt   *m*   158

Glen Rock
Hold Tight - Harlan Coben   *m*   41

Hoboken
The Murder Notebook - Jonathan
    Santlofer   *m*   162

Jersey City
Of Blood and Sorrow - Valerie Wilson
    Wesley   *m*   190

Newark
Of Blood and Sorrow - Valerie Wilson
    Wesley   *m*   190

Trenton
Fearless Fourteen - Janet Evanovich   *m*   65

NEW MEXICO
Blasphemy - Douglas Preston   *s*   726
The Bride - Carolyn Davidson   *r*   251
A Stranger's Touch - Cait London   *r*   331

Albuquerque
The Edge of Reason - Melinda
    Snodgrass   *f*   548
Mars Life - Ben Bova   *s*   667
The Socorro Blast - Pari Noskin
    Taichert   *m*   180

Fort Sumner
The Guilty - Jason Pinter   *m*   150

San Antonio
The Socorro Blast - Pari Noskin
    Taichert   *m*   180

Santa Fe
Death Song - Michael McGarrity   *m*   131
Death Song - Michael McGarrity   *w*   441
The German Bride - Joanna Hershon   *w*   423
The German Bride - Joanna Hershon   *t*   834

Socorro
The Socorro Blast - Pari Noskin
    Taichert   *m*   180

NEW YORK
The Accidental Werewolf - Dakota
    Cassidy   *r*   239
Big Boned - Meg Cabot   *m*   34
Just Desserts - Barbara Bretton   *r*   230
Lover Enshrined - J.R. Ward   *r*   388
The Monsters of Templeton - Lauren
    Goff   *t*   815
The Reserve - Russell Banks   *t*   763
Twilight - Brendan DuBois   *m*   59

Avalon
Snowfall at Willow Lake - Susan Wiggs   *r*   392

Bridgehampton
Head Wounds - Chris Knopf   *m*   115

Brooklyn
Streets of Fire - Troy Soos   *m*   172

Brooklyn Heights
Harriet and Isabella - Patricia O'Brien   *t*   865

Candlewood
Where Love Dwells - Delia Parr   *i*   972

Crawford
TKO - Tom Schreck   *m*   165

Hidden Falls
Stargazer - Amanda Harte   *r*   288

Hungerford
Head Wounds - Chris Knopf   *m*   115

Kinnik's Harbor
Call of the Highland Moon - Kendra Leigh
    Castle   *r*   240

Long Island
The Shadow Year - Jeffrey Ford   *m*   75

Miller's Kill
I Shall Not Want - Julia
    Spencer-Fleming   *m*   173

New York
1940 - Jay Neugeboren   *t*   862
All Souls - Christine Schutt   *c*   1087
Atmospheric Disturbances - Rivka
    Galchen   *c*   1043
Black Will Shoot - Jesse Washington   *c*   1100
Blood Alley - Tom Coffey   *m*   42
The Broken Window - Jeffery Deaver   *m*   52
By the Sword - F. Paul Wilson   *h*   651
Chocolate Secrets - Zelda Benjamin   *r*   216
Choosing Sophie - Leslie Carroll   *c*   1023
Come With Me to Babylon - Paul M.
    Levitt   *t*   850
Compulsion - Jonathan Kellerman   *m*   111
Dark of the Moon - Susan Krinard   *r*   319
The Dead & the Gone - Susan Beth
    Pfeffer   *s*   725
Dead Time - Stephen White   *m*   194
Dead to Me - Anton Strout   *f*   551
Death Will Get You Sober - Elizabeth
    Zelvin   *m*   199
A Dog Among Diplomats - J.F. Englert   *m*   61
Empty Ever After - Reed Farrel
    Coleman   *m*   44
Fateful Voyage - Pamela Oldfield   *t*   866
Fires Rising - Michael Laimo   *h*   617
Free Fall - Laura Anne Gilman   *f*   502
The Future of Love - Shirley Abbott   *c*   1006
A Gentleman's Guide to Graceful Living -
    Michael Dahlie   *c*   1028
The Ghost and the Femme Fatale - Alice
    Kimberly   *m*   113
The Guilty - Jason Pinter   *m*   150
Hold Tight - Harlan Coben   *m*   41
Homecoming - Bernhard Schlink   *m*   164
The Invention of Everything Else - Samantha
    Hunt   *t*   836
The Invention of Everything Else - Samantha
    Hunt   *c*   1055
Just a Taste - Deirdre Martin   *r*   340
Killer Heat - Linda Fairstein   *m*   68
Last Last Chance - Fiona Maazel   *c*   1064
The Law of Second Chances - James
    Sheehan   *m*   168
A Little Trouble with the Facts - Nina
    Siegal   *c*   1088
Love the One You're With - Emily
    Giffin   *c*   1046
Lush Life - Richard Price   *c*   1081
Madhouse - Rob Thurman   *f*   554
Making Over Mr. Right - Judi McCoy   *r*   345
Masquerade - Melissa de la Cruz   *f*   489
Murder Bay - David Horwitz   *m*   103
The Murder Notebook - Jonathan
    Santlofer   *m*   162
Netherland - Joseph O'Neill   *c*   1074
Playing with the Grown-Ups - Sophie
    Dahl   *c*   1027
Queen of Babble Gets Hitched - Meg
    Cabot   *r*   235

408   **WHAT DO I READ NEXT? 2008 • VOLUME 2**

Deadwood
Lucky Strike - Nyla Griffith   *w*   421

Mason
Summer Snow - Nicole Baart   *i*   908

TENNESSEE
Go-Go Girls of the Apocalypse - Victor
  Gischler   *s*   687
Hallam's War - Elisabeth Payne Rosen   *t*   880
Miscarriage of Justice - Kip Gayden   *t*   810
Walk on the Wild Side - Christine
  Warren   *r*   389

Buckeye
Pitch Black - Susan Crandall   *r*   248

Chattanooga
Queen of Blood - Bryan Smith   *h*   639

Leatherwood
Serpent Box - Vincent Louis Carrella   *c*   1022

Memphis
Controlling Interest - Elizabeth White   *i*   1003

Sweetgum
The Sweetgum Knit Lit Society - Beth
  Pattillo   *i*   973

TEXAS
Ambush at Mustang Canyon - Mike
  Kearby   *w*   430
Beating the Devil - W.C. Jameson   *w*   426
Big Bend Death Trap - James J. Griffin   *w*   420
Blue-Eyed Devil - Lisa Kleypas   *r*   315
El Tigre - John H. Manhold   *w*   438
Last Last Chance - Fiona Maazel   *c*   1064
Nate Coffin's Revenge - J. Lee Butts   *w*   410
Once Smitten, Twice Shy - Lori Wilde   *r*   393
Rainbows Wait for the Sun - Allan C.
  Kimball   *w*   434
The Road to a Hanging - Mike Kearby   *w*   431
Rogue - Rachel Vincent   *h*   646
The Story of Forgetting - Stefan Merrill
  Block   *c*   1016
A Stranger's Game - Joan Johnston   *r*   303
Texas Loving - Leigh Greenwood   *r*   277
This Is How It Happened (Not a Love Story) - Jo
  Barrett   *c*   1011

Austin
Collision - Jeff Abbott   *m*   1
A Stranger's Game - Joan Johnston   *w*   427
This Is How It Happened (Not a Love Story) - Jo
  Barrett   *r*   212

Blanco County
Holy Moly - Ben Rehder   *m*   156

Clearview
Of All Sad Words - Bill Crider   *w*   412

Corsicana
Courting Trouble - Deeanne Gist   *w*   419
Deep in the Heart of Trouble - Deeanne
  Gist   *i*   937

Dallas
To Wed a Texan - Georgina Gentry   *r*   270

El Paso
Names on a Map - Benjamin Alire
  Saenz   *w*   448

Houston
Brittan - Debra White Smith   *i*   991
Lorna - Debra White Smith   *i*   992
Pushing Up Bluebonnets - Leann
  Sweeney   *m*   178
Weddings Can Be Murder - Christie
  Craig   *r*   247

Mooney
Return of the Stardust Cowgirl - Marsha
  Moyer   *w*   442

Morganville
Feast of Fools - Rachel Caine   *h*   573

Plano
Tall Tales and Wedding Veils - Jane
  Graves   *r*   274

Redemption
The Devil's Daughter - Laura Drewry   *r*   256

Thunder Ridge
Twice Loved - Lori Copeland   *i*   924

Twisted Creek
Twisted Creek - Jodi Thomas   *r*   385

Vengeance Creek
Texas Iron - Robert J. Randisi   *w*   446

Willow Creek
The Ex-Debutante - Linda Francis Lee   *r*   327

UTAH
Virgin River - Richard S. Wheeler   *w*   459

Clayton
The Last Cowgirl - Jana Richman   *w*   447

VIRGINIA

Charlottesville
The Disagreement - Nick Taylor   *t*   891
Perfect - Harry Lee Kraus   *i*   955

Crozet
The Purrfect Murder - Rita Mae Brown   *m*   31

Georgetown
Overnight Male - Elizabeth Bevarly   *r*   220

Lynchburg
The Disagreement - Nick Taylor   *t*   891

Manassas
Murder Bay - David Horwitz   *m*   103

Paradise Island
Long, Hot Nights - Candice Poarch   *r*   360

Richmond
Strike Zone - Kate Angell   *r*   203

Virginia Beach
By Reason of Insanity - Randy Singer   *i*   990

WASHINGTON

Alpine
The Alpine Traitor - Mary Daheim   *m*   51

Bellehaven
Index to Murder - Jo Dereske   *m*   54

Seattle
The Anatomy of Deception - Lawrence
  Goldstone   *m*   85
The Bride and the Bargain - Allison
  Leigh   *r*   328
City at the End of Time - Greg Bear   *s*   666
Darkling - Yasmine Galenorn   *f*   500
Sweet Talk - Susan Mallery   *r*   337

WEST
Borrowed Time - S.M. Ballard   *w*   402
Bucking the Tiger - Marcus Galloway   *w*   417
The Canyon of Bones - Richard S.
  Wheeler   *w*   458
Crucifixion River - Marcia Muller   *w*   443
Flight - Sherman Alexie   *w*   400
Grub Line Rider - Louis L'Amour   *w*   436
Hard Trail to Follow - Elmer Kelton   *w*   432
Lost Trails - Louis L'Amour   *w*   437
Luck - Max Brand   *w*   406
Man from Durango - Lauran Paine   *w*   444
Marshal Sands and Mrs. Molly - V.E.
  Bixenstine   *w*   403
On the Wrong Track - Steve
  Hockensmith   *w*   424
Out of the Ashes - William W.
  Johnstone   *w*   428
Preacher's Showdown - William W.
  Johnstone   *w*   429
Resolution - Robert B. Parker   *t*   868
Ride the Trail of Death - Kenneth L.
  Kieser   *w*   433
River Range - L.P. Holmes   *w*   425
Slade's Law - Lyle Brandt   *w*   407
So Brave, Young and Handsome - Leif
  Enger   *c*   1035
So Brave, Young and Handsome - Leif
  Enger   *w*   415
So Brave, Young and Handsome - Leif
  Enger   *t*   798
Sun Going Down - Jack Todd   *c*   1097
Sun Going Down - Jack Todd   *w*   457
The Sundown Man - Jory Sherman   *w*   453
Trail Hand - R.W. Stone   *w*   456
Trail of the Red Butterfly - Karl H.
  Schlesier   *w*   450
The Treasure of Nugget Mountain - Karl
  May   *w*   439
The Vengeance Brand - Michael
  Senuta   *w*   451
Winnetou the Apache Knight - Karl
  May   *w*   440

WEST VIRGINIA

Dogwood
Dogwood - Chris Fabry   *i*   932

Lehigh
Unpretty - Sharon Carter Rogers   *i*   983

Little Top
The Healer - Sharon Sala   *r*   371

Morgantown
Delicate Chaos - Jeff Buick *m* 33

WISCONSIN
Hot - Julia Harper *r* 285

Madison
This Side of Heaven - Anna Schmidt *r* 375

Shepherdstown
Obsessions - Marshall Cook *m* 46

WYOMING
Free Fire - C.J. Box *w* 405
Wind River - Tom Morrisey *i* 969

Durant
Another Man's Moccasins - Craig
  Johnson *m* 109

Green River City
Marshal Sands and Mrs. Molly - V.E.
  Bixenstine *w* 403

Saddlestring
Blood Trail - C.J. Box *m* 25

Sheridan
Predatory Game - Christine Feehan *r* 262

VENEZUELA

Out of the Devil's Mouth - Travis
  Thrasher *i* 1000

VIETNAM

Another Man's Moccasins - Craig
  Johnson *m* 109

Saigon
The Prince of Bagram Prison - Alex
  Carr *m* 37

WALES

The Exiles - Ron Hansen *t* 829
Resistance - Owen Sheers *t* 888

Hay-on-Wye
Assassins at Ospreys - R.T. Raichev *m* 151

Geographic Index

Genre Index

This index lists the books featured as main entries in *What Do I Read Next?* by genre and story type within each genre. Beneath each of the nine genres, the story types appear alphabetically, and titles appear alphabetically under story type headings. The name of the primary author, genre code and the book entry number also appear with each title. The genre codes are as follows: *c* Popular Fiction, *f* Fantasy, *h* Horror, *i* Inspirational, *m* Mystery, *r* Romance, *s* Science Fiction, *t* Historical, and *w* Western. For definitions of the story types, see the "Key to Genre Terms" following the Introduction.

FANTASY

Alternate History

Pax Dakota - Ken Rand *f* 540

Alternate Universe

The Hidden World - David Gunn *f* 509

Alternate World

Escapement - Jay Lake *f* 518
The Heart of Light - Sarah A. Hoyt *f* 512

Anthology

The Dragon Done It - Eric Flint *f* 499
Fellowship Fantastic - Martin H. Greenberg *f* 506
Misspellings - Julie E. Czerneda *f* 487
Mystery Date - Denise Little *f* 523
The Solaris Book of New Fantasy - George Mann *f* 524
Something Magic This Way Comes - Martin H. Greenberg *f* 507
Tales Before Narnia - Douglas A. Anderson *f* 463

Collection

Elric: The Stealer of Souls - Michael Moorcock *f* 530
The One Right Thing - Bruce Coville *f* 485

Coming-of-Age

Airs and Graces - Toby Bishop *f* 474
Escapement - Jay Lake *f* 518
Mad Kestrel - Misty Massey *f* 526
Tracing the Shadow - Sarah Ash *f* 466

Contemporary

CodeSpell - Kelly McCullough *f* 527
The Crystal Skull - Manda Scott *f* 546
Daemons Are Forever - Simon R. Green *f* 504
Darkling - Yasmine Galenorn *f* 500
Dead to Me - Anton Strout *f* 551
Dragons Wild - Robert Asprin *f* 467
The Edge of Reason - Melinda Snodgrass *f* 548

Embrace the Night - Karen Chance *f* 483
Free Fall - Laura Anne Gilman *f* 502
Key to Conspiracy - Talia Gryphon *f* 508
The Key to Rondo - Emily Rodda *f* 544
Magic Burns - Ilona Andrews *f* 464
Mind the Gap - Christopher Golden *f* 503
Provenance - Alex Archer *f* 465
Small Favor - Jim Butcher *f* 480
Steward of Song - Adam Stemple *f* 550
The Unnatural Inquirer - Simon R. Green *f* 505

Historical/Ancient Greece

Bring Down the Sun - Judith Tarr *f* 552

Historical/Elizabethan

Ink and Steel - Elizabeth Bear *f* 469
The Queen's Bastard - C.E. Murphy *f* 532

Historical/Exotic

The Heart of Light - Sarah A. Hoyt *f* 512

Historical/Medieval

The Alchemist's Code - Dave Duncan *f* 493

Historical/Napoleonic Wars

Victory of Eagles - Naomi Novik *f* 535

Historical/Pre-history

Elom - William H. Drinkard *f* 492

Historical/Victorian

Bewitching Season - Marissa Doyle *f* 491
Swiftly - Adam Roberts *f* 543
Whitechapel Gods - S.M. Peters *f* 538

Historical/World War II

Battle Dragon - Edo van Belkom *f* 555

Humor

Dragons Wild - Robert Asprin *f* 467
Goblin War - Jim C. Hines *f* 511

Legend

A Curse Dark as Gold - Elizabeth C. Bunce *f* 479
Goblin War - Jim C. Hines *f* 511

Light Fantasy

Swiftly - Adam Roberts *f* 543

Magic Conflict

Airs and Graces - Toby Bishop *f* 474
The Ancient - R.A. Salvatore *f* 545
Ancient Blood - Robert Earl *f* 494
Armed & Magical - Lisa Shearin *f* 547
An Autumn War - Daniel Abraham *f* 462
The Blood King - Gail Z. Martin *f* 525
The Born Queen - Greg Keyes *f* 516
Breath and Bone - Carol Berg *f* 471
Bring Down the Sun - Judith Tarr *f* 552
Child of a Dead God - Barb Hendee *f* 510
CodeSpell - Kelly McCullough *f* 527
Cruel Zinc Melodies - Glen Cook *f* 484
Daemons Are Forever - Simon R. Green *f* 504
Dagger-Star - Elizabeth Vaughan *f* 556
The Dark Ferryman - Jenna Rhodes *f* 542
The Edge of Reason - Melinda Snodgrass *f* 548
Fallen - Tim Lebbon *f* 519
The Final Sacrifice - Patricia Bray *f* 475
A Fire in the North - David Bilsborough *f* 472
Free Fall - Laura Anne Gilman *f* 502
The Golden Cord - Paul Genesse *f* 501
The Golden Rose - Kathleen Bryan *f* 478
Havemercy - Jaida Jones *f* 513
Hawkspar - Holly Lisle *f* 521
Heroes Adrift - Moira J. Moore *f* 531
The Hidden City - Michelle West *f* 558
In a Time of Treason - David Keck *f* 514
Ink and Steel - Elizabeth Bear *f* 469
Iron Angel - Alan Campbell *f* 481
Kushiel's Mercy - Jacqueline Carey *f* 482
Last Argument of Kings - Joe Abercrombie *f* 461
Mad Kestrel - Misty Massey *f* 526
Mage-Guard of Honor - L. E. Modesitt Jr. *f* 529
A Magic of Twilight - S.L. Farrell *f* 498
Masters of Magic - Chris Wraight *f* 559
Mind the Gap - Christopher Golden *f* 503

HISTORICAL

HORROR

Genre Index

MYSTERY

WESTERN

Genre Index

Subject Index

This index lists subjects which are covered in the featured titles. Beneath each subject heading, titles are arranged alphabetically with the author names, genre codes, and entry numbers also indicated. The genre codes are as follows: *c* Popular Fiction, *f* Fantasy, *h* Horror, *i* Inspirational, *m* Mystery, *r* Romance, *s* Science Fiction, *t* Historical, and *w* Western.

Museums

Music and Musicians

Mystery

Mystery and Detective Stories

Mythology

Native Americans

Nazis

Neighbors and Neighborhoods

Newspapers

Nuclear Warfare

Occult

Opera

Organized Crime

Orphans

Paranormal

Racial Conflict

Blue Hole Back Home - Joy
Jordan-Lake   *i*   952
The Plague of Doves - Louise Erdrich   *w*   416
Scottsboro - Ellen Feldman   *t*   803

Radio Broadcasting

Late Nights on Air - Elizabeth Hay   *c*   1054

Railroads

On the Wrong Track - Steve
Hockensmith   *w*   424
Pelican Road - Howard Bahr   *t*   762
Train to Yesterday - Nell DuVall   *r*   257

Ranch Life

Black Rock Canon - Les Savage   *w*   449
Finding Stefanie - Susan May Warren   *i*   1002
Man from Durango - Lauran Paine   *w*   444
River Range - L.P. Holmes   *w*   425
Sun Going Down - Jack Todd   *w*   457
Sun Going Down - Jack Todd   *t*   892
Trail Hand - R.W. Stone   *w*   456

Real Estate

The Almost True Story of Ryan Fisher - Rob
Stennett   *i*   994
Lush Life - Richard Price   *c*   1081
Miss Julia Paints the Town - Ann B.
Ross   *c*   1083
Murder Is Binding - Lorna Barrett   *m*   15
Practically Perfect - Katie Fforde   *c*   1039
Whiskey and Water - Nina Wright   *m*   198

Redemption

Dark of the Moon - Susan Krinard   *r*   319
The Redemption of Jake Scully - Elaine
Barbieri   *i*   909
Ride the Trail of Death - Kenneth L.
Kieser   *w*   433

Relationships

The Heartbreak Pill - Anjanette
Delgado   *c*   1032
The House on Fortune Street - Margot
Livesey   *c*   1062
My Name Is Russell Fink - Michael
Snyder   *i*   993
Sleeping with Ward Cleaver - Jenny
Gardiner   *r*   267
The Truth about Love - Tia McCollors   *i*   962

Religion

By Schism Rent Asunder - David Weber   *s*   747
The Chorister at the Abbey - Lis
Howell   *m*   105
Serpent Box - Vincent Louis Carrella   *c*   1022
Sister Pelagia and the Black Monk - Boris
Akunin   *m*   4

Religious Conflict

Blasphemy - Douglas Preston   *s*   726
Caliphate - Tom Kratman   *s*   703
The Forbidden - Beverly Lewis   *i*   959
A Grave in Gaza - Matt Beynon Rees   *m*   155
Kushiel's Mercy - Jacqueline Carey   *f*   482

The Messiah - Marek Halter   *t*   827

Religious Life

The Apostate's Tale - Margaret Frazer   *t*   806
The Enchanter's Forest - Alys Clare   *t*   778
The Exiles - Ron Hansen   *t*   829
Harriet and Isabella - Patricia O'Brien   *t*   865
John - Niall Williams   *t*   900
The Moneylender of Toulouse - Alan
Gordon   *m*   87
The Outsider - Ann H. Gabhart   *i*   935
People of the Book - Geraldine Brooks   *t*   774
Sister Pelagia and the Black Monk - Boris
Akunin   *t*   757
Waking Brigid - Francis Clark   *t*   779

Resistance Movements

Resistance - Owen Sheers   *t*   888

Responsibility

Lover Enshrined - J.R. Ward   *r*   388
Not Quite a Mom - Kirsten Sawyer   *r*   374
Skinny Dipping - Connie Brockway   *r*   232

Restaurants

Just a Taste - Deirdre Martin   *r*   340
Lambrusco - Ellen Cooney   *t*   781
Sweet Caroline - Rachel Hauck   *i*   943
Turning Tables - Heather MacDowell   *c*   1065

Reunions

Blue-Eyed Devil - Lisa Kleypas   *r*   315
Carrot Cake Murder - Joanne Fluke   *m*   74
The Martinez Marriage Revenge - Helen
Bianchin   *r*   222
Promise Me Tomorrow - Linda
Ingmanson   *r*   300
Saying Yes to the Millionaire - Fiona
Harper   *r*   284
Sweetheart Lost and Found - Shirley
Jump   *r*   308

Revenge

Beating the Devil - W.C. Jameson   *w*   426
Blood of Bass Tillman - Cotton Smith   *w*   454
Blood Trail - C.J. Box   *m*   25
Bond of Fire - Diane Whiteside   *r*   391
Danger's Kiss - Sarah McKerrigan   *r*   349
Double Fantasy - Cheryl Holt   *r*   295
Dream Chaser - Sherrilyn Kenyon   *r*   313
Fuzzy Navel - J.A. Konrath   *m*   116
Hard Trail to Follow - Elmer Kelton   *w*   432
Highland Wolf - Hannah Howell   *r*   296
Killing Fear - Allison Brennan   *r*   229
Luck - Max Brand   *w*   406
The Martinez Marriage Revenge - Helen
Bianchin   *r*   222
Nate Coffin's Revenge - J. Lee Butts   *w*   410
A Paragon of Virtue - Christian Von
Ditfurth   *m*   185
The Privateer - Dawn MacTavish   *r*   335
Ride the Trail of Death - Kenneth L.
Kieser   *w*   433
Rogue - Kayla Gray   *r*   275
South of Shiloh - Chuck Logan   *m*   124
Stalked - Brian Freeman   *m*   78
Texas Iron - Robert J. Randisi   *w*   446

This Is How It Happened (Not a Love Story) - Jo
Barrett   *r*   212
This Is How It Happened (Not a Love Story) - Jo
Barrett   *c*   1011
To Taste Temptation - Elizabeth Hoyt   *r*   297
The Vengeance Brand - Michael
Senuta   *w*   451
Wild Angel - Sasha Lord   *r*   332

Revolutionary War

Johnny One-Eye - Jerome Charyn   *t*   776
Washington's Lady - Nancy Moser   *i*   970

Revolutions

Mistress of the Revolution - Catherine
Delors   *t*   785
The Romanov Bride - Robert Alexander   *t*   759

Rivers

The River Nymph - Shirl Henke   *r*   290

Robbers and Outlaws

Fearless Fourteen - Janet Evanovich   *m*   65
Murder Talks Turkey - Deb Baker   *m*   12
Nate Coffin's Revenge - J. Lee Butts   *w*   410

Robots

The Automatic Detective - A. Lee
Martinez   *s*   711
Saturn's Children - Charles Stross   *s*   739

Roman Empire

The Betrayal: The Lost Life of Jesus Christ - W.
Michael Gear   *t*   811
Buried Too Deep - Jane Finnis   *m*   70
The Fire Walker - Ben Pastor   *t*   870
Terra Incognita - Ruth Downie   *t*   794
The Triumph of Caesar - Steven Saylor   *t*   884

Romance

Baddest Bad Boys - Shannon McKenna   *r*   348
Courting Trouble - Deeanne Gist   *w*   419
Dagger-Star - Elizabeth Vaughan   *f*   556
The Darcy Connection - Elizabeth
Aston   *c*   1010
Fire Study - Maria V. Snyder   *f*   549
Forty Candles on a Cowboy Cake - Rick
Steber   *w*   455
Hungers of the Heart - Jenna Black   *h*   569
Keepers of the Flame - Robin D.
Owens   *f*   536
Let the Night Begin - Kathryn Smith   *h*   642
A Match Made in Hell - Terri Garey   *h*   589
Mystic Horseman - Kathleen Eagle   *w*   414
No Choice but Seduction - Johanna
Lindsey   *r*   329
One Foot in the Grave - Jeaniene Frost   *h*   588
Pleasure Unbound - Larissa Ione   *h*   608
Rainbows Wait for the Sun - Allan C.
Kimball   *w*   434
Stargazer - Amanda Harte   *r*   288
To Taste Temptation - Elizabeth Hoyt   *r*   297
To Trust - Carolyn Brown   *w*   409
Trail Hand - R.W. Stone   *w*   456
Vampire, Interrupted - Lynsay Sands   *h*   634
Vampires Are Forever - Lynsay Sands   *h*   635
Where the Heart Leads - Stephanie
Laurens   *t*   847

Stepmothers

Return of the Stardust Cowgirl - Marsha
   Moyer *w*   442

Strikes and Lockouts

Streets of Fire - Troy Soos *m*   172

Submarines

The Black Sea Affair - Don Brown *i*   913

Suicide

Hold Tight - Harlan Coben *m*   41
Trouble the Water - Nicole Seitz *i*   988

Supernatural

The 5th Witch - Graham Masterton *h*   624
The Autopsy and Other Tales - Michael
   Shea *h*   637
Avenging Fury - John Farris *h*   587
Bad Blood - L.A. Banks *h*   566
The Bleeding Horse and Other Ghost Stories -
   Brian J. Showers *h*   638
Blood Bank - Tanya Huff *h*   605
Blood Noir - Laurell K. Hamilton *h*   597
The Bone Key - Sarah Monette *h*   626
Bone Soup - T.M. Wright *h*   652
Bound for Evil - Tom English *h*   585
British Invasion - Christopher Golden *h*   593
By the Sword - F. Paul Wilson *h*   651
City of the Sea and Other Ghost Stories - Jerome
   K. Jerome *h*   609
Coffin County - Gary A. Braunbeck *h*   570
A Dangerous Climate - Chelsea Quinn
   Yarbro *h*   653
The Dracula Dossier - James Reese *h*   631
Duma Key - Stephen King *h*   615
The Fiction - H.P. Lovecraft *h*   621
Fires Rising - Michael Laimo *h*   617
From Dead to Worse - Charlaine Harris *h*   598
The Ghost Quartet - Marvin Kaye *h*   610
Ghost Walk - Brian Keene *h*   611
Hagoppian and Other Stories - Brian
   Lumley *h*   623
Hellbent & Heartfirst - Kassandra Sims *r*   380
Horror: The Best of the Year 2008 - Stefan
   Dziemianowicz *h*   583
Inconsequential Tales - Ramsey
   Campbell *h*   575
Kill Whitey - Brian Keene *h*   612
The Land at the End of the Working Day - Peter
   Crowther *h*   580
The Last Book - Zoran Zivkovic *h*   655
The Last Hieroglyph - Clark Ashton
   Smith *h*   640
Let the Night Begin - Kathryn Smith *h*   642
The Living Dead - John Joseph Adams *h*   562
Lost Prince - Chelsea Quinn Yarbro *h*   654
The Man in the Picture - Susan Hill *h*   601
A Match Made in Hell - Terri Garey *h*   589
Midnight Reign - Chris Marie Green *h*   595
Minotauress - Edward Lee *h*   620
My Big Fat Supernatural Honeymoon - P.N.
   Elrod *h*   584
Necronomicon - H.P. Lovecraft *h*   622
The number 121 to Pennsylvania and Others -
   Kealan Patrick Burke *h*   571
Old Flames - Jack Ketchum *h*   614
The Outlaw Demon Wails - Kim
   Harrison *h*   599
Personal Demons - Kelley Armstrong *h*   564

Queen of Blood - Bryan Smith *h*   639
Sanctity and Sin - Donald Wandrei *h*   647
The Sand-Man and Other Night Pieces - E.T.A.
   Hoffmann *h*   602
Sharp Teeth - Toby Barlow *h*   567
Shifter - Angela Knight *r*   316
Sinister House/Cold Harbour - Leland
   Hall *h*   596
Sins of the Sirens - Maria Alexander *h*   563
Slivers of Bone - Ray Garton *h*   592
Sredni Vashtar: Sardonic Tales - Saki *h*   633
Tedious Brief Tales of Granta and Gramarye -
   Ingulphus *h*   607
Thieving Fear - Ramsey Campbell *h*   576
Tower Hill - Sarah Pinborough *h*   629
The Triumph of the Night and Other Tales - Edith
   Wharton *h*   649
Vampire, Interrupted - Lynsay Sands *h*   634
Vampires Are Forever - Lynsay Sands *h*   635
A Vintage from Atlantis - Clark Ashton
   Smith *h*   641
Waking Brigid - Francis Clark *h*   579
A Whisper of Blood - Ellen Datlow *h*   582
The Wondersmith and Others - Fitz-James
   O'Brien *h*   627
The Year of Disappearances - Susan
   Hubbard *h*   604

Surprises

Just Desserts - Barbara Bretton *r*   230

Survival

Dawn's Light - Terri Blackstock *i*   911
Out of the Ashes - William W.
   Johnstone *w*   428
The Road to a Hanging - Mike Kearby *w*   431

Suspense

Catch a Shadow - Patricia Potter *r*   361
Crimson Orgy - Austin Williams *h*   650
The Crystal Skull - Manda Scott *m*   167
Dark of the Moon - Susan Krinard *r*   319
Delicate Chaos - Jeff Buick *m*   33
The Folks 2 - Ray Garton *h*   590
The Grand Scheme - Kathy Herman *i*   945
Isolation - Travis Thrasher *i*   999
La Vida Vampire - Nancy Haddock *r*   279
The Murder Game - Beverly Barton *r*   213
Odd Hours - Dean R. Koontz *h*   616
Sisters of Fortune - Frances McNeil *t*   857
Strong and Sexy - Jill Shalvis *r*   377
Trauma - Patrick McGrath *h*   625
Unpretty - Sharon Carter Rogers *i*   983

Teachers

Jackalope Dreams - Mary Clearman
   Blew *w*   404
Tie Dyed and Dead - Sharon Short *m*   169
Twice Loved - Lori Copeland *i*   924

Technology

Without Warning - Eugenia Lovett
   West *m*   191

Teen Relationships

All Souls - Christine Schutt *c*   1087
Blue Hole Back Home - Joy
   Jordan-Lake *i*   952
One Night Stand - Cindy Kirk *r*   314

Poisoned Tarts - G.A. McKevett *m*   133

Television

Deep Dish - Mary Kay Andrews *c*   1009
Hush My Mouth - Cathy Pickens *w*   445
Mystic Horseman - Kathleen Eagle *w*   414

Television Programs

Deep Dish - Mary Kay Andrews *r*   202
Holy Moly - Ben Rehder *m*   156
Mystic Horseman - Kathleen Eagle *r*   258

Terror

Standing Still - Kelly Simmons *c*   1089

Terrorism

The Black Sea Affair - Don Brown *i*   913
Capitol Conspiracy - William Bernhardt *m*   17
Dead Heat - Joel C. Rosenberg *i*   985
House Rules - Mike Lawson *m*   120
The Invisible - Andrew Britton *m*   29
Murder in the Rue de Paradis - Cara
   Black *m*   19
No Control - Shannon K. Butcher *r*   233
Odd Hours - Dean R. Koontz *h*   616
Twilight - Brendan DuBois *m*   59

Theater

Expert in Murder - Nicola Upson *t*   893

Time Travel

Being with Him - Jessica Inclan *r*   299
City at the End of Time - Greg Bear *s*   666
Flight - Sherman Alexie *w*   400
Master of the Highlands - Veronica
   Wolff *r*   398
The Time Engine - Sean McMullen *f*   528
Train to Yesterday - Nell DuVall *r*   257
With Every Breath - Lynn Kurland *r*   320

Transplants

Change of Heart - Jodi Picoult *c*   1079

Travel

Bon Appetit - Sandra Byrd *i*   916
A Cut Above - Ginny Aiken *i*   906
Enlightenment for Idiots - Anne
   Cushman *c*   1026
The Expeditions - Karl Iagnemma *t*   837
Full Circle - Davis Bunn *i*   915
The Outlander - Gil Adamson *t*   756
Skid - Rene Gutteridge *i*   939
So Brave, Young and Handsome - Leif
   Enger *c*   1035

Treasure

Take Me If You Can - Karen Kendall *r*   310

Treasure, Buried

Wild Jinx - Sandra Hill *r*   292

Trials

By Reason of Insanity - Randy Singer   *i*   990
The Law of Second Chances - James
 Sheehan   *m*   168
Miscarriage of Justice - Kip Gayden   *t*   810
Scottsboro - Ellen Feldman   *t*   803
Sister's Choice - Judith Pella   *i*   974

Triplets

A Stranger's Touch - Cait London   *r*   331

Trust

Brittan - Debra White Smith   *i*   991
Chocolate Secrets - Zelda Benjamin   *r*   216
Lover's Bite - Maggie Shayne   *r*   378

Tuberculosis

Virgin River - Richard S. Wheeler   *w*   459

Twins

Deluge - Anne McCaffrey   *s*   712
Don't Tempt Me - Sylvia Day   *r*   253
Double Fantasy - Cheryl Holt   *r*   295
Fatal Deduction - Gayle Roper   *i*   984
The Guardians - Jack Cavanaugh   *i*   921
Hooked Up - Joyce Lavene   *m*   119
The Other - Thomas Tryon   *h*   644
Scream for Me - Karen Rose   *r*   370

Universities and Colleges

The Man in the Picture - Susan Hill   *h*   601

Utopia/Dystopia

City at the End of Time - Greg Bear   *s*   666
In the Company of Whispers - Sallie
 Lowenstein   *s*   707
Jemma7729 - Phoebe Wray   *s*   753
Principles of Angels - Jaine Fenn   *s*   685
Stretto - L. Timmel Duchamp   *s*   681

Vampires

The Accidental Vampire - Lynsay Sands   *r*   372
Aunt Dimity: Vampire Hunter - Nancy
 Atherton   *m*   10
Because Your Vampire Said So - Michele
 Bardsley   *r*   211
The Bleeding Dusk - Colleen Gleason   *r*   272
Blood Noir - Laurell K. Hamilton   *h*   597
Bond of Fire - Diane Whiteside   *r*   391
A Dangerous Climate - Chelsea Quinn
 Yarbro   *h*   653
Dark Deeds at Night's Edge - Kresley
 Cole   *r*   245
Dark of the Moon - Susan Krinard   *r*   319
Dead over Heels - MaryJanice
 Davidson   *r*   252
Dead Perfect - Amanda Ashley   *r*   204
Embrace the Night - Karen Chance   *f*   483
Feast of Fools - Rachel Caine   *h*   573
From Dead to Worse - Charlaine Harris   *h*   598
Hungers of the Heart - Jenna Black   *r*   569
Hungers of the Heart - Jenna Black   *r*   223
Key to Conspiracy - Talia Gryphon   *f*   508
La Vida Vampire - Nancy Haddock   *r*   279
The Last Vampire - Patricia Rosemoor   *h*   632
Let the Night Begin - Kathryn Smith   *h*   642
Lover Enshrined - J.R. Ward   *r*   388

Lover's Bite - Maggie Shayne   *r*   378
Masquerade - Melissa de la Cruz   *f*   489
Midnight Reign - Chris Marie Green   *h*   595
Midnight's Daughter - Karen Chance   *h*   578
My Immortal Protector - Jen Holling   *r*   293
One Bite Stand - Nina Bangs   *r*   209
One Foot in the Grave - Jeaniene Frost   *h*   588
The Outlaw Demon Wails - Kim
 Harrison   *h*   599
The Undead Kama Sutra - Mario
 Acevedo   *h*   561
Vampire, Interrupted - Lynsay Sands   *h*   634
Vampire, Interrupted - Lynsay Sands   *r*   373
Vampires Are Forever - Lynsay Sands   *h*   635
The Vampires of Mars - Gustave Le
 Rouge   *h*   619
A Whisper of Blood - Ellen Datlow   *h*   582
The Year of Disappearances - Susan
 Hubbard   *h*   604

Veterinarians

Chasing Cans - Laura Crum   *m*   49

Victorian Period

Courting Shadows - Jem Poster   *t*   874
The Dark Lantern - Gerri Brightwell   *t*   773
Fatal Waltz - Tasha Alexander   *t*   760
A Flaw in the Blood - Stephanie Barron   *t*   767
The Somnambulist - Jonathan Barnes   *t*   766
A Tissue of Lies - Tessa Barclay   *t*   764
The White Rose - Jennifer Donnelly   *t*   791

Vietnam War

Another Man's Moccasins - Craig
 Johnson   *m*   109
Names on a Map - Benjamin Alire
 Saenz   *w*   448

Vikings

Sword Song - Bernard Cornwell   *t*   782

Violence

The Chameleon's Shadow - Minette
 Walters   *m*   186
You Gotta Sin to Get Saved - J.D.
 Mason   *r*   341

Virtual Reality

Saga - Conor Kostick   *s*   702

Voodoo

The Last Vampire - Patricia Rosemoor   *h*   632

War

Always Grace - Tim LaHaye   *i*   957
Ambush at Mustang Canyon - Mike
 Kearby   *w*   430
Ancient Blood - Robert Earl   *f*   494
The Cellist of Sarajevo - Steven
 Galloway   *c*   1044
Dagger-Star - Elizabeth Vaughan   *r*   387
Daughters of the North - Sarah Hall   *c*   1049
Days of Infamy - Newt Gingrich   *t*   814
The Dragon's Nine Sons - Chris
 Roberson   *s*   732
Flodden Field - Elisabeth McNeill   *t*   858

For a Sack of Bones - Lluis-Anton
 Baulenas   *t*   768
How the Soldier Repairs the Gramophone - Sasa
 Stanisic   *c*   1091
In a Time of Treason - David Keck   *f*   514
Innocence Unveiled - Blythe Gifford   *r*   271
Into the Storm - Taylor Anderson   *s*   661
Last Argument of Kings - Joe
 Abercrombie   *f*   461
Legion - Dan Abnett   *s*   656
Lover Enshrined - J.R. Ward   *r*   388
Master of the Highlands - Veronica
 Wolff   *r*   398
The Mule - Juan Eslava Galan   *t*   808
Open Line - Ellen Hawley   *c*   1053
Out of the Ashes - William W.
 Johnstone   *w*   428
Peace - Richard Bausch   *t*   769
Shadow Magic - Cheyenne McCray   *r*   347
Skeletons at the Feast - Chris
 Bohjalian   *c*   1017
The Steel Wave - Jeff Shaara   *t*   886
Two Brothers: One North, One South - David H.
 Jones   *t*   841
The Vengeance Brand - Michael
 Senuta   *w*   451
Wolf's Honour - Lee Lightner   *s*   705

Wealth

Buckingham Palace Gardens - Anne
 Perry   *m*   148
His Small-Town Girl - Arlene James   *i*   951
Marshal Sands and Mrs. Molly - V.E.
 Bixenstine   *w*   403

Weddings

Blue Heart Blessed - Susan Meissner   *i*   964
The Bride's Baby - Liz Fielding   *r*   263
The Convenient Groom - Denise Hunter   *i*   950
Once Smitten, Twice Shy - Lori Wilde   *r*   393
Queen of Babble Gets Hitched - Meg
 Cabot   *r*   235
Saying Yes to the Millionaire - Fiona
 Harper   *r*   284
Shadow Waltz - Amy Patricia Meade   *m*   135
Sweetheart Lost and Found - Shirley
 Jump   *r*   308
Tall Tales and Wedding Veils - Jane
 Graves   *r*   274
The Wedding Machine - Beth Webb
 Hart   *i*   940
Weddings Can Be Murder - Christie
 Craig   *r*   247
Western Weddings - Jillian Hart   *r*   287

Werewolves

The Accidental Werewolf - Dakota
 Cassidy   *r*   239
Bad Blood - L.A. Banks   *r*   210
Bad Blood - L.A. Banks   *h*   566
Call of the Highland Moon - Kendra Leigh
 Castle   *r*   240
Dead over Heels - MaryJanice
 Davidson   *r*   252
Lost Prince - Chelsea Quinn Yarbro   *h*   654
Marked by Moonlight - Sharie Kohler   *r*   317
Ravenous - Ray Garton   *h*   591
Shapeshifter - J.F. Gonzalez   *h*   594
Sharp Teeth - Toby Barlow   *h*   567
The Wolfman - Nicholas Pekearo   *h*   628

Character Name Index

This index alphabetically lists the major characters in each featured title. Each character name is followed by a description of the character. Citations also provide titles of the books featuring the character, listed alphabetically if there is more than one title; author names and genre codes. The genre codes are as follows: *c* Popular Fiction, *f* Fantasy, *h* Horror, *i* Inspirational, *m* Mystery, *r* Romance, *s* Science Fiction, *t* Historical, and *w* Western. Numbers refer to the entries that feature each title.

A

Aaran (Slave)
Hawkspar - Holly Lisle *f* 521

Aaron (Rebel)
Whitechapel Gods - S.M. Peters *f* 538

Abernathy, Megan (Interior Decorator)
I Heart Bloomberg - Melody Carlson *i* 917

Abouz, Nadira (Terrorist)
Murder in the Rue de Paradis - Cara Black *m* 19

Abraham (Businessman)
The Jewel Trader of Pegu - Jeffrey Hantover *t* 830

Acland, Charles (Military Personnel)
The Chameleon's Shadow - Minette Walters *m* 186

Acquillo, Sam (Carpenter; Detective—Amateur)
Head Wounds - Chris Knopf *m* 115

Adair, Barnaby (Detective—Private)
Where the Heart Leads - Stephanie Laurens *t* 847

Adair, Barnaby (Nobleman; Detective)
Where the Heart Lies - Stephanie Laurens *r* 323

Adair, Robin (Researcher)
Winter Study - Nevada Barr *m* 14

Adams, Andie (Television Personality)
A Cut Above - Ginny Aiken *i* 906

Adams, Hope (Journalist)
Personal Demons - Kelley Armstrong *h* 564

Adams, Jesse (Military Personnel)
The Steel Wave - Jeff Shaara *t* 886

Adams, Josh (Tour Guide; Wealthy)
Saying Yes to the Millionaire - Fiona Harper *r* 284

Adams, Mila (Artist; Psychic)
Being with Him - Jessica Inclan *r* 299

Adams, Wendy (Police Officer)
Murder Is Binding - Lorna Barrett *m* 15

Adelbertsmiter, Siebold (Mechanic)
Iron Kissed - Patricia Briggs *f* 476

Adler, Mark (Unemployed)
The Future of Love - Shirley Abbott *c* 1006

Aeneas (Warrior; Spouse)
Lavinia - Ursula K. Le Guin *t* 848

Agnus (Healer)
The Fire Walker - Ben Pastor *t* 870

Aguilar, Adelia (Doctor)
The Serpent's Tale - Ariana Franklin *m* 77
The Serpent's Tale - Ariana Franklin *t* 804

Ahn-Kha (Alien)
Fall with Honor - E.E. Knight *s* 701

Ahrmahk, Caleb (Ruler)
By Schism Rent Asunder - David Weber *s* 747

Ajulutsikael (Mythical Creature)
Vicious Circle - Mike Carey *h* 577

Akbar the Great (Historical Figure; Ruler)
The Enchantress of Florence - Salman Rushdie *t* 882

al-Baroody, Omar (Civil Servant)
The Amateur Spy - Dan Fesperman *m* 69

al-Sharqi, Nayir (Investigator)
Finding Nouf - Zoe Ferraris *c* 1038

al-Wazir, Threadgill Angus (Sailor)
Escapement - Jay Lake *f* 518

Alberoni (Religious)
City of the Dead - Ian Morson *t* 859

Albert (Miner)
The Well and the Mine - Gin Phillips *c* 1078

Alden, Charles (Nobleman; Political Figure)
Scandalous Lord, Rebellious Miss - Deb Marlowe *r* 339

Aldrich, Tyler (Businessman)
His Small-Town Girl - Arlene James *i* 951

Aldridge, Lewis (Teenager)
The Outcast - Sadie Jones *t* 842

Aleu, Genis (Military Personnel)
For a Sack of Bones - Lluis-Anton Baulenas *t* 768

Aleu, Joan (Prisoner)
For a Sack of Bones - Lluis-Anton Baulenas *t* 768

Alfred (Historical Figure; Ruler)
Sword Song - Bernard Cornwell *t* 782

Algemeine, Marmion de Revers (Prisoner)
Deluge - Anne McCaffrey *s* 712

Allende, Enrique (Rancher)
Trail Hand - R.W. Stone *w* 456

Allende, Rosa Maria (Young Woman)
Trail Hand - R.W. Stone *w* 456

Alling, Prexy (Doctor)
The Cadaver of Gideon Wyck - Alexander Laing *h* 618

Alonzo, Don (Werewolf)
Lost Prince - Chelsea Quinn Yarbro *h* 654

Alsworthy, Mary (Spy)
The Seduction of the Crimson Rose - Lauren Willig *t* 901

Alton, Abigail "Gail" (Gentlewoman)
Compromised - Kate Noble *r* 355

Alton, Sophie (Journalist; Captive)
Unlawful Contact - Pamela Clare *r* 244

Alvarez, Manuel (Migrant Worker)
The Demon of Dakar - Kjell Eriksson *m* 62

Alvord, George (Wanderer)
Blood on the Rimrock - Phil Dunlap *w* 413

Amanda (Writer)
Enlightenment for Idiots - Anne Cushman *c* 1026

Amato, Tito (Singer)
The Iron Tongue of Midnight - Beverle Graves Myers *m* 140
Iron Tongue of Midnight - Beverle Graves Myers *t* 861

Amlingmeyer, Gustav "Old Red" (Cowboy; Detective—Amateur)
The Black Dove - Steve Hockensmith *t* 835
The Black Dove - Steve Hockensmith *m* 101

Amlingmeyer, Gustav "Old Red" (Detective—Amateur; Frontiersman)
On the Wrong Track - Steve Hockensmith *w* 424

Amlingmeyer, Otto "Big Red" (Cowboy; Detective—Amateur)
The Black Dove - Steve Hockensmith *m* 101
The Black Dove - Steve Hockensmith *t* 835

Amlingmeyer, Otto "Big Red" (Detective—Amateur; Frontiersman)
On the Wrong Track - Steve Hockensmith *w* 424

Amy (Parent)
The Ten-Year Nap - Meg Wolitzer *c* 1104

Anatolius (Lawyer)
Seven for a Secret - Mary Reed *m* 154

Ancient Badden (Leader)
The Ancient - R.A. Salvatore *f* 545

Burton, Jonathan (Businessman)
Swiftly - Adam Roberts   *f*   543

Burton, Tori (Heiress)
Fatal Deduction - Gayle Roper   *i*   984

Butler, Mary (Student—college)
Obedience - Will
  Lavender   *c*   1061,   *m*   118

Butler, Richard (Landowner)
Death on the Holy Mountain - David
  Dickinson   *m*   55

C

Cadge (Orphan)
Mind the Gap - Christopher Golden   *f*   503

Caerrson, Danrith (Child)
The Ruby Key - Holly Lisle   *f*   522

Cahill, Simon (FBI Agent)
The Angel - Carla Neggers   *r*   354

Caine, Hall (Writer)
The Dracula Dossier - James Reese   *h*   631

Caine, Jed (Rancher)
The Devil's Daughter - Laura Drewry   *r*   256

Cairn, Rivven (Military Personnel)
The Sellsword - Cam Banks   *f*   468

Caitlyn (Fugitive)
Broken Angel - Sigmund Brouwer   *i*   912

Caldwell, Grace "Merle Raye Finkel" (Murderer;
  Young Woman)
A Stranger's Game - Joan Johnston   *w*   427

Caldwell, Katherine (Military Personnel; Teacher)
The Prince of Bagram Prison - Alex
  Carr   *m*   37

Calhoun, Jesse (Psychic; Military Personnel)
Predatory Game - Christine Feehan   *r*   262

Calhoun, Ty (Sports Figure)
Game for Anything - Bella Andre   *r*   201

Callen, Myles (Investigator)
Moon Flower - James P. Hogan   *s*   692

Callister, Renee (Scientist; Researcher)
Dead Silver - Neil McMahon   *m*   134

Calpurnia (Historical Figure; Spouse)
The Triumph of Caesar - Steven Saylor   *t*   884

ca'Ludovici, Kraljica Marguerite (Ruler)
A Magic of Twilight - S.L. Farrell   *f*   498

Camden, Arthur (Importer/Exporter)
A Gentleman's Guide to Graceful Living -
  Michael Dahlie   *c*   1028

Cameron, Constance (Gentlewoman; Captive)
In the Highlander's Bed - Cathy
  Maxwell   *r*   342

Cameron, Ewen (Laird)
Master of the Highlands - Veronica
  Wolff   *r*   398

Cameron, Inez del (Crime Victim)
The Serpent's Daughter - Suzanne
  Arruda   *t*   761

Cameron, Jade del (Detective; Photojournalist)
The Serpent's Daughter - Suzanne
  Arruda   *t*   761

Cameron, Robert (Laird; Time Traveler)
With Every Breath - Lynn Kurland   *r*   320

ca'Millac, Archigos Dhosti (Mythical Creature)
A Magic of Twilight - S.L. Farrell   *f*   498

Campbell, Jack (Security Officer)
Worlds on Fire - Matthew J. Costello   *s*   675

Campbell, Margaret (Scientist)
The Killing Room - Peter May   *m*   128

Campbell, Noah (Carpenter)
A Mile in My Flip-Flops - Melody
  Carlson   *i*   918

Campion (Clone; Spaceship Captain)
House of Chains - Alastair Reynolds   *s*   729

Canderous, Simon (Psychic)
Dead to Me - Anton Strout   *f*   551

Cannon, Patty (Bounty Hunter)
Song Yet Sung - James McBride   *t*   856

Cantor, Deirdre (Gentlewoman)
The Duke Next Door - Celeste Bradley   *r*   227

Cao Cao, Eddie (Pirate)
Provenance - Alex Archer   *f*   465

Car (Teenager)
All Souls - Christine Schutt   *c*   1087

Caravelle, Devon (Musician)
Explosive - Charlotte Mede   *r*   350

Carey, Benjamin (Police Officer)
Murder Bay - David Horwitz   *m*   103

Carl (Cook)
Turning Tables - Heather MacDowell   *c*   1065

Carleton, Carter (Scientist)
Mars Life - Ben Bova   *s*   667

Carlos (Vigilante)
Beating the Devil - W.C. Jameson   *w*   426

Carol (Parent)
Whatever Makes You Happy - William
  Sutcliffe   *c*   1096

Carpenter, Molly (Apprentice)
Small Favor - Jim Butcher   *f*   480

Carroll, Ephraim (Doctor)
The Anatomy of Deception - Lawrence
  Goldstone   *t*   816
The Anatomy of Deception - Lawrence
  Goldstone   *m*   85

Carstairs, Aldous (Government Official)
Touchstone - Laurie R. King   *m*   114

Carstairs, Anne (Gentlewoman; Orphan)
Double Fantasy - Cheryl Holt   *r*   295

Carver, Samuel (Criminal)
The Accident Man - Tom Cain   *m*   35

Cash, Eric (Restaurateur)
Lush Life - Richard Price   *c*   1081

Cash, Lincoln (Actor)
Finding Stefanie - Susan May Warren   *i*   1002

Cassidy, Neil (Criminal)
Neuropath - Scott Bakker   *h*   565

Castle, Elizabeth (Journalist; Guardian)
Not Quite a Mom - Kirsten Sawyer   *r*   374

Castor, Felix (Magician)
Vicious Circle - Mike Carey   *h*   577

Cates, Hardy (Wealthy; Businessman)
Blue-Eyed Devil - Lisa Kleypas   *r*   315

Caulker, Jack (Criminal)
Iron Angel - Alan Campbell   *f*   481

Cavanaugh, Lucy (Television Personality)
Pushing Up Daisies - Rosemary Harris   *m*   95

Cavendish, Graham (Nobleman)
Duke Most Wanted - Celeste Bradley   *r*   226

Cayal (Criminal; Religious)
The Immortal Prince - Jennifer Fallon   *f*   497

Cazelet, Rene (Military Personnel)
When the Tide Rises - David Drake   *s*   680

Cecely (Religious)
The Apostate's Tale - Margaret Frazer   *t*   806

Cenni, Alessandro (Detective—Homicide)
A Deadly Paradise - Grace Brophy   *m*   30

Cero, Eddie (Sports Figure)
The Blue Door - David Fulmer   *m*   79

Cezanne, Paul (Historical Figure; Artist)
Cezanne's Quarry - Barbara Pope   *t*   873

Chambers, Fern (Insurance Investigator)
Saying Yes to the Millionaire - Fiona
  Harper   *r*   284

Champion, Ella (Producer; Indian)
Mystic Horseman - Kathleen Eagle   *r*   258
Mystic Horseman - Kathleen Eagle   *w*   414

Chandler, Hawk (Cowboy)
Wagered Heart - Robin Lee Hatcher   *i*   941

Chap (Animal)
Child of a Dead God - Barb Hendee   *f*   510

Chapman, Lawrence (Military Personnel)
Killing Rommel - Steven Pressfield   *t*   875

Chapman, Mike (Detective—Homicide)
Killer Heat - Linda Fairstein   *m*   68

Chappers, Tazio (Architect)
The Purrfect Murder - Rita Mae Brown   *m*   31

Charbonneau, Yanne (Store Owner)
The Girl with No Shadow - Joanne
  Harris   *c*   1052

Charles (Archaeologist)
Demon's Fire - Emma Holly   *r*   294

Chatham, Jane (Teacher)
His Dark and Dangerous Ways - Edith
  Layton   *r*   325

Chau, Venus (Businesswoman)
Single Sashimi - Camy Tang   *i*   996

Chavet, Jean (Psychic)
The Cruelest Month - Louise Penny   *m*   147

Chavez (Vigilante)
Beating the Devil - W.C. Jameson   *w*   426

Chavez (Cowboy)
Trail Hand - R.W. Stone   *w*   456

Chekhov, Anton (Historical Figure; Writer)
The Woman Who Wouldn't - Gene
  Wilder   *t*   899

Chelsea (Child)
On My Terms - Shirley Hailstock   *r*   280

Cheston, Barbara (Actress)
Crimson Orgy - Austin Williams   *h*   650

Chiara, Nora (Writer)
Trauma - Patrick McGrath   *h*   625

Childress (Librarian)
Escapement - Jay Lake   *f*   518

Choate, Randall (Criminal)
Collision - Jeff Abbott   *m*   1

Christos, Connor (Psychic)
Dead to Me - Anton Strout   *f*   551

Churchill, Winston (Historical Figure; Political
  Figure)
Dreamers of the Day - Mary Doria
  Russell   *t*   883

Cindella (Teenager)
Saga - Conor Kostick   *s*   702

Claire (Patient)
Change of Heart - Jodi Picoult   *c*   1079

Cyrla (Young Woman)
My Enemy's Cradle - Sara Young *t* 905

D

d'Acquin, Josse (Mercenary)
The Enchanter's Forest - Alys Clare *t* 778

Dacre, Godiva (Gentlewoman)
The Reavers - George Macdonald Fraser *t* 805

d'Agelet, Helene (Vampire; Spy)
Bond of Fire - Diane Whiteside *r* 391

Dahl, Ionessa "Nessa" (Banker)
Thigh High - Christina Dodd *r* 255

Daisy (Secretary)
An Ordinary Spy - Joseph Weisberg *m* 188

Daks (Android)
Saturn's Children - Charles Stross *s* 739

Dallandra (Sorceress)
The Shadow Isle - Katharine Kerr *f* 515

Dallas, Eve (Detective—Homicide)
Strangers in Death - J.D. Robb *s* 731

Dalton, Gray (Nobleman)
Explosive - Charlotte Mede *r* 350

Dan (Teenager)
The Valley-Westside War - Harry Turtledove *s* 744

dan Luthar, Jezal (Warrior)
Last Argument of Kings - Joe Abercrombie *f* 461

Danby, Carter (Architect)
A Lady of Hidden Intent - Tracie Peterson *i* 976

Dandridge, Molly (Young Woman)
Marshal Sands and Mrs. Molly - V.E. Bixenstine *w* 403

Dane, Cameron (Journalist)
The Renovation - Terri Kraus *i* 956

Daniels, Allie (Heiress; Store Owner)
Twisted Creek - Jodi Thomas *r* 385

Daniels, Boone (Detective—Private)
The Dawn Patrol - Don Winslow *m* 195

Daniels, Clint (Gambler; Businessman)
The River Nymph - Shirl Henke *r* 290

Daniels, Jack (Detective—Police)
Fuzzy Navel - J.A. Konrath *m* 116

Daniels, Kate (Mercenary; Detective—Private)
Magic Burns - Ilona Andrews *f* 464

Daniels, Kiko (Psychic)
Midnight Reign - Chris Marie Green *h* 595

Danolarian (Police Officer; Time Traveler)
The Time Engine - Sean McMullen *f* 528

Dante, Anthony (Widow(er); Restaurateur)
Just a Taste - Deirdre Martin *r* 340

Dante, Marco (Businessman; Twin)
Dante's Stolen Wife - Day Leclaire *r* 326

Dante, Tiffany (Socialite; Heiress)
Poisoned Tarts - G.A. McKevett *m* 133

Danvers, Claire (Teenager; Student)
Feast of Fools - Rachel Caine *h* 573

Darcy, Antonia (Writer; Detective—Amateur)
Assassins at Ospreys - R.T. Raichev *m* 151

Dare, Anne (Ruler)
The Born Queen - Greg Keyes *f* 516

Dare, Madeline (Teacher; Detective—Amateur)
The Crazy School - Cornelia Read *m* 153

Daria (Mythical Creature; Hotel Worker)
One Bite Stand - Nina Bangs *r* 209

Dark, Ronan (Vampire; Writer)
Dead Perfect - Amanda Ashley *r* 204

Dark Queen (Video Game Player)
Saga - Conor Kostick *s* 702

Darnell, Godfrey (Criminal)
The Shadow Year - Jeffrey Ford *m* 75

Darnell, Layla (Psychic; Office Worker)
The Hollow - Nora Roberts *r* 368

Darrow, Ashlyn (Psychic)
The Darkest Night - Gena Showalter *r* 379

D'Artigo, Camille (Witch)
Darkling - Yasmine Galenorn *f* 500

D'Artigo, Delilah (Mythical Creature)
Darkling - Yasmine Galenorn *f* 500

D'Artigo, Menolly (Entertainer; Vampire)
Darkling - Yasmine Galenorn *f* 500

Das, Devi (Traveler)
Enlightenment for Idiots - Anne Cushman *c* 1026

Dashbrooke, William (Vampire)
Let the Night Begin - Kathryn Smith *h* 642

Daurignac, Therese (Young Woman)
A Secret Inheritance - Elizabeth Lord *t* 853

D'Avanos, Merral (Leader)
The Infinite Day - Chris Walley *i* 1001

Davenport, Edward (Nobleman)
Texas Loving - Leigh Greenwood *r* 277

Daventry, Aimee (Noblewoman; Amnesiac)
Seduced by Sin - Kimberly Logan *r* 330

d'Averio, Petra (Gentlewoman)
A Lady's Secret - Jo Beverley *r* 221

Davidson, Richmond (Parent; Spouse)
Dream of Love - Michael Phillips *i* 977

Davidson, Seth (Photographer)
Dream of Love - Michael Phillips *i* 977

Davies, Amanda (Lawyer)
The Guilty - Jason Pinter *m* 150

Davies, Rebecca (Activist)
Streets of Fire - Troy Soos *m* 172

Davinovitch, Rhiana (Sorceress; Teenager)
The Edge of Reason - Melinda Snodgrass *f* 548

Davis, Georgia (Detective—Private)
Easy Innocence - Libby Fischer Hellmann *m* 96

Davis, Peter (Detective—Police)
A Dog Among Diplomats - J.F. Englert *m* 61

Davoren, Hugh (Carpenter; Detective—Amateur)
Dead Silver - Neil McMahon *m* 134

Dawe, Fletcher (Businessman; Store Owner)
Train to Yesterday - Nell DuVall *r* 257

Dawsey, Perry (Worker)
Infected - Scott Sigler *s* 736

Day, Alfred (Military Personnel; Prisoner)
Day - A.L. Kennedy *t* 843

Daye, Bertie (Suffragette)
On Account of Conspicuous Women - Dawn Shamp *t* 887

de Gravere, Katrine (Artisan; Noblewoman)
Innocence Unveiled - Blythe Gifford *r* 271

de la Courcel, Imriel (Nobleman)
Kushiel's Mercy - Jacqueline Carey *f* 482

de la Courcel, Sidonie (Noblewoman)
Kushiel's Mercy - Jacqueline Carey *f* 482

de la Fontaine, Rosalind (Orphan; Singer)
Wizard's Daughter - Catherine Coulter *r* 246

de Peyre (Nobleman; Spouse)
Mistress of the Revolution - Catherine Delors *t* 785

de Vincente, Inez Maria Isabelle
The Serpent's Daughter - Suzanne Arruda *m* 9

de Warenne, Ariella (Noblewoman)
A Dangerous Love - Brenda Joyce *r* 306

de Winter, Rhys (Nobleman)
The Wicked Ways of a Duke - Laura Lee Guhrke *r* 278

Dean (Businessman; Spouse)
They Did It with Love - Kate Morgenroth *m* 137

Dear, Paul (Child)
Tigerheart - Peter David *f* 488

Debauer, Peter (Editor)
Homecoming - Bernhard Schlink *m* 164

Deborah (Biblical Figure)
The Triumph of Deborah - Eva Etzioni-Halevy *t* 801

DeBroux, Jamie (Employer)
Severance Package - Duane Swierczynski *m* 179

DeCosta, Angus (Young Man)
Blood Harvest - Brant Randall *t* 876

Degodessa, Zoe (Deity)
Making Over Mr. Right - Judi McCoy *r* 345

Del (Cowboy)
Black Rock Canon - Les Savage *w* 449

del Cameron, Jade (Photojournalist)
The Serpent's Daughter - Suzanne Arruda *m* 9

Delancey, Laura (Young Woman)
A Perfect Revenge - Annabel Dilke *t* 788

Delaware, Alex (Psychologist)
Compulsion - Jonathan Kellerman *m* 111

Dell, Astra (Patient; Teenager)
All Souls - Christine Schutt *c* 1087

DeMarco, Joe (Lawyer; Troubleshooter)
House Rules - Mike Lawson *m* 120

Demarkian, Gregor (Consultant)
Cheating at Solitaire - Jane Haddam *m* 92

deMarley, Augie (Parent)
Choosing Sophie - Leslie Carroll *c* 1023

deMarley, Olivia (Entertainer)
Choosing Sophie - Leslie Carroll *c* 1023

Demidov, Leo (Detective—Police)
Child 44 - Tom Rob Smith *m* 171

Demidov, Raisa (Teacher; Spouse)
Child 44 - Tom Rob Smith *m* 171

Dempsey, Ellen (Spouse)
Love the One You're With - Emily Giffin *c* 1046

Denison, Skye (Psychologist)
Murder of a Chocolate-Covered Cherry - Denise Swanson *m* 177

Dennehy, Mitch (Editor)
A Passion Redeemed - Julie Lessman *i* 958

E

Early, Cole (Horse Trainer)
Fast and Loose - Elizabeth Bevarly   *r*   219

Earp, Wyatt (Gunfighter; Historical Figure)
Borrowed Time - S.M. Ballard   *w*   402
Rainbows Wait for the Sun - Allan C.
   Kimball   *w*   434

Eastlake, Elizabeth (Aged Person)
Duma Key - Stephen King   *h*   615

Eddington, Lark (Noblewoman)
The Privateer - Dawn MacTavish   *r*   335

Edeard (Telepath)
The Dreaming Void - Peter F. Hamilton   *s*   690

Edward VII (Historical Figure; Royalty)
Buckingham Palace Gardens - Anne
   Perry   *t*   872

Edwards, Erin (Waiter/Waitress)
Turning Tables - Heather MacDowell   *c*   1065

Eidolon (Demon)
Pleasure Unbound - Larissa Ione   *h*   608

Eiliesor, Mychael (Guard)
Armed & Magical - Lisa Shearin   *f*   547

Eisenhower, Dwight (Historical Figure; Military
   Personnel)
The Steel Wave - Jeff Shaara   *t*   886

Elahad, Valashu (Warrior; Nobleman)
Lord of Lies - David Zindell   *f*   560

Eleanor of Aquitaine (Historical Figure; Royalty)
The Serpent's Tale - Ariana Franklin   *t*   804

Eliot, Tom (Religious)
The Shanghai Tunnel - Sharan
   Newman   *m*   143

Elisavyeta (Historical Figure; Royalty)
The Romanov Bride - Robert Alexander   *t*   759

Elizabeth I (Ruler; Historical)
Ink and Steel - Elizabeth Bear   *f*   469

Elizabeth I (Historical Figure; Ruler)
The Lady Elizabeth - Alison Weir   *t*   896

Ellerslie, Portia (Noblewoman; Widow(er))
A Seduction in Scarlet - Sara Bennett   *r*   217

Ellingham, Gwendolyn (Gentlewoman)
How to Enjoy a Scandal - Adrienne
   Basso   *r*   214

Ellis, Jordan (Businessman)
Long, Hot Nights - Candice Poarch   *r*   360

Elric (Warrior)
Elric: The Stealer of Souls - Michael
   Moorcock   *f*   530

Elton, Marcus (Nobleman)
Enticing the Earl - Nicole Byrd   *r*   234

Emmerich, Rolf (Military Personnel)
Skeletons at the Feast - Chris
   Bohjalian   *c*   1017

Emrich, Carol (Office Worker)
Shapeshifter - J.F. Gonzalez   *h*   594

Engine, Mama (Deity)
Whitechapel Gods - S.M. Peters   *f*   538

Epstein, Jerry (Bodyguard)
Luck Be a Lady, Don't Die - Robert J.
   Randisi   *m*   152

Erengislsson, Rurik (Knight)
Surrender to the Highlander - Terri
   Brisbin   *r*   231

Ericson, Hannah Swartz (Young Woman)
Anathema - Colleen Coble   *i*   922

Ericson, Reece (Spouse)
Anathema - Colleen Coble   *i*   922

Erneste (Waiter/Waitress)
A Perfect Waiter - Alain Claude
   Sulzer   *c*   1095

Erol7734 (Government Official)
Jemma7729 - Phoebe Wray   *s*   753

Erskine, Alexia (Debutante)
Alexia's Secrets - Una-Mary Parker   *t*   869

Eryn (Noblewoman)
The Vacant Throne - Joshua Palmatier   *f*   537

Espejo, Gustavo "Gus" (Twin)
Names on a Map - Benjamin Alire
   Saenz   *w*   448

Espejo, Xochil (Twin)
Names on a Map - Benjamin Alire
   Saenz   *w*   448

Esperanza (Servant; Immigrant)
Bright Shiny Morning - James Frey   *c*   1041

Estanyol, Arnau (Artisan)
Cathedral of the Sea - Ildefonso
   Falcones   *t*   802

Estanyol, Joan (Religious)
Cathedral of the Sea - Ildefonso
   Falcones   *t*   802

Esterhouse, Joe (Political Figure)
Road to Nowhere - Paul Robertson   *i*   982

Estevez, Ricardo (Drug Dealer)
White Soul - Brandt Dodson   *m*   56

Evans, Christine "Chrissie" (Widow(er); Manager)
A Soldier Comes Home - Cindi Myers   *r*   352

Evans, Josephine (Actress)
Seen It All and Done the Rest - Pearl
   Cleage   *c*   1024

Evans, Lije (Lawyer)
Farraday Road - Ace Collins   *i*   923

Evans, Marian (Historical Figure; Writer)
The World Before Her - Deborah
   Weisgall   *t*   897

Evans, T.J. (Child)
A Soldier Comes Home - Cindi Myers   *r*   352

Eve (Serial Killer)
Adam - Ted Dekker   *i*   926

Eve (Vacationer)
Beach Dreams - Trish Perry   *i*   975

Eversleigh, Grace (Companion; Gentlewoman)
The Lost Duke of Wyndham - Julia
   Quinn   *r*   363

F

Fairchild, Faith (Caterer; Detective—Amateur)
The Body in the Gallery - Katherine Hall
   Page   *m*   144

Fairchild, Tom (Spouse)
The Body in the Gallery - Katherine Hall
   Page   *m*   144

Faith (Vampire; Prostitute)
Hungers of the Heart - Jenna Black   *r*   223

Fallon, Alexandra Tremaine (Nurse; Twin)
Scream for Me - Karen Rose   *r*   370

Fandorin, Erast (Detective—Police; Diplomat)
Special Assignments - Boris Akunin   *m*   5
Special Assignments - Boris Akunin   *t*   758

Fanning, Chaison (Military Personnel)
Pirate Sun - Karl Schroeder   *s*   733

Fanning, Venera (Noblewoman)
Pirate Sun - Karl Schroeder   *s*   733

Fanta (Student—College)
Frames - Loren D. Estleman   *m*   63

Fantini, Beppi (Resistance Fighter)
Lambrusco - Ellen Cooney   *t*   781

Fantini, Lucia (Widow(er); Singer)
Lambrusco - Ellen Cooney   *t*   781

Faraday, Joel (Spy)
Overnight Male - Elizabeth Bevarly   *r*   220

Fardelver, Bellor (Religious)
The Golden Cord - Paul Genesse   *f*   501

Fargo, Daniel (Hunter)
Ravenous - Ray Garton   *h*   591

Fargo, Skye (Frontiersman; Gunfighter)
Missouri Manhunt - Jon Sharpe   *w*   452

Farquharson, Anne (Historical Figure; Spouse)
White Rose Rebel - Janet Paisley   *t*   867

Farrell, Ash (Spouse; Singer)
Return of the Stardust Cowgirl - Marsha
   Moyer   *w*   442

Faulkner, Grayson (Detective—Private)
Legacy of Secrets - Sara Mitchell   *i*   965

Fawcitt, Joseph (Nobleman)
Simply Perfect - Mary Balogh   *r*   208

Federin (Spy)
Principles of Angels - Jaine Fenn   *s*   685

Felix (Military Personnel)
Seven for a Secret - Mary Reed   *m*   154

Fellows, Rob (Salesman)
Madhouse - Rob Thurman   *f*   554

Felton, Cora (Detective—Amateur)
The Sudoku Puzzle Murders - Parnell
   Hall   *m*   93

Felton, Sherry (Writer)
The Sudoku Puzzle Murders - Parnell
   Hall   *m*   93

Fenton, James (Police Officer)
The Truth Commissioner - David Park   *c*   1077

Fenwick, Johnny (Spouse)
Silver Street - Elizabeth Gill   *t*   813

Fergusson, Clare (Religious; Detective—Amateur)
I Shall Not Want - Julia
   Spencer-Fleming   *m*   173

Fielding, Nan (Spouse)
Silver Street - Elizabeth Gill   *t*   813

Fielding, Tom (Poloce Officer)
Hex Marks the Spot - Madelyn Alt   *m*   7

Fink, Russell (Salesman)
My Name Is Russell Fink - Michael
   Snyder   *i*   993

Finurbi, Carolus (Government Official)
Scourge the Heretic - Sandy Mitchell   *s*   717

Firr, Lucy (Mythical Creature)
The Devil's Daughter - Laura Drewry   *r*   256

Fisher, Dan (Detective—Police)
The 5th Witch - Graham Masterton   *h*   624

Fisher, Nellie Mae (Baker)
The Forbidden - Beverly Lewis   *i*   959

Fisher, Phryne (Detective—Amateur; Socialite)
Queen of the Flowers - Kerry
   Greenwood   *m*   89

Fisher, Ryan (Real Estate Agent; Religious)
The Almost True Story of Ryan Fisher - Rob
   Stennett   *i*   994

G

Glenn, Theodore (Serial Killer; Lawyer)
Killing Fear - Allison Brennan   *r*   229

Glokta (Criminal)
Last Argument of Kings - Joe
  Abercrombie   *f*   461

Gloriana (Noblewoman)
Dagger-Star - Elizabeth Vaughan   *f*   556

Goldin, Dori (Parent)
More than It Hurts You - Darin
  Strauss   *c*   1094

Goldin, Josh (Parent)
More than It Hurts You - Darin
  Strauss   *c*   1094

Goldstein, Bobby (Spy; Teacher)
An Ordinary Spy - Joseph Weisberg   *m*   188

Goldstein, Hayley Maitland (Baker; Store Owner)
Just Desserts - Barbara Bretton   *r*   230

Goldstein, Morgan (Businessman)
Galaxy Blues - Allen Steele   *s*   737

Gomez, Felix (Detective—Private; Vampire)
The Undead Kama Sutra - Mario
  Acevedo   *h*   561

Goodman (Military Personnel)
The Undead Kama Sutra - Mario
  Acevedo   *h*   561

Gordianus the Finder (Detective—Private)
The Triumph of Caesar - Steven Saylor   *t*   884

Gordon, Emeline (Noblewoman)
To Taste Temptation - Elizabeth Hoyt   *r*   297

Gordon, Max (Professor)
Practically Perfect - Katie Fforde   *c*   1039

Gosseyn, Gilbert (Mutant)
Null-A Continuum - John C. Wright   *s*   754

Grace, John (Detective—Police)
Little Criminals - Gene Kerrigan   *m*   112

Grace, Sophie (Revolutionary)
A Whisper of Freedom - Tricia Goyer   *i*   938

Grady, Grubbs (Teenager; Werewolf)
Demon Apocalypse - Darren Shan   *h*   636

Graham, Jennifer (Apprentice; Parent)
She Always Wore Red - Angela Hunt   *i*   949

Gram (Warrior)
Breath and Bone - Carol Berg   *f*   471

Grammaticus, John (Military Personnel)
Legion - Dan Abnett   *s*   656

Granna (Aged Person)
In the Company of Whispers - Sallie
  Lowenstein   *s*   707

Grant, David (Psychic; Lawyer)
The Houses of Time - Jamil Nasir   *s*   720

Grant, Emily (Journalist)
Homicide at Blue Heron - Susan Page
  Davis   *i*   925

Grant, Ulysses S. (Historical Figure; Military
Personnel)
Escape from Andersonville - Gene
  Hackman   *t*   822

Gray, Bennett (Gentleman; Veteran)
Touchstone - Laurie R. King   *m*   114

Gray, Tucker (Businessman)
Twice Loved - Lori Copeland   *i*   924

Gray Wolf, Jonah (Healer; Psychic)
The Healer - Sharon Sala   *r*   371

Grayhawk, Breed (FBI Agent)
A Stranger's Game - Joan Johnston   *r*   303
A Stranger's Game - Joan Johnston   *w*   427

Grayle, Lincoln (Sorcerer)
Avenging Fury - John Farris   *h*   587

Grayson, Eli (Editor; Journalist)
Jewel - Beverly Jenkins   *r*   302

Graziano, Agata (Religious)
The Garden of Evil - David Hewson   *m*   98

Gredchen (Mercenary)
The Sellsword - Cam Banks   *f*   468

Gregor of Mainz (Knight)
Crossed - Nicole Galland   *t*   809

Gregorivich, Nikolai (Vampire; Detective)
50 Ways to Hex Your Lover - Linda
  Wisdom   *r*   397

Gregory, Alan (Psychologist)
Dead Time - Stephen White   *m*   194

Gregory, Merideth (Journalist)
Dead Time - Stephen White   *m*   194

Grenville, Royce (Nobleman; Military Personnel)
Seduced by Sin - Kimberly Logan   *r*   330

Grey, Connor (Consultant; Wizard)
Unquiet Dreams - Mark Del Franco   *f*   490

Grey, Robert (Spy)
The Spymaster's Lady - Joanna Bourne   *r*   224

Greystone, Marcus (Businessman)
A Stranger's Touch - Cait London   *r*   331

Griffin, Nick (Police Officer)
Hot Date - Amy Garvey   *r*   268

Griffin, Sloan (Scientist)
Spider Star - Mike Brotherton   *s*   669

Grimes, Patrick (Journalist; Veteran)
Blood Alley - Tom Coffey   *m*   42

Grimshaw, Nicholas (Government Official; Guardian)
Danger's Kiss - Sarah McKerrigan   *r*   349

Gromrund (Mythical Creature; Warrior)
Oathbreaker - Nick Kyme   *f*   517

Gross, Peter (Nobleman)
The Hidden World - David Gunn   *f*   509

Groves, Jordan (Artist)
The Reserve - Russell Banks   *t*   763

Grovian, Rudolf (Police Officer)
The Sinner - Petra Hammesfahr   *m*   94

Gruadh (Royalty)
Lady Macbeth - Susan King   *t*   844

Guarnaccia, Marshal (Detective—Police)
Vita Nuova - Magdalen Nabb   *m*   141

Gunnarsdottir, Margriet (Noblewoman)
Surrender to the Highlander - Terri
  Brisbin   *r*   231

H

Hades, Carl (Detective—Private)
Weddings Can Be Murder - Christie
  Craig   *r*   247

Hael, Rachel (Traitor)
Iron Angel - Alan Campbell   *f*   481

Haggard, Abel (Aged Person)
The Story of Forgetting - Stefan Merrill
  Block   *c*   1016

Haldane, Noah (Doctor)
Cold Plague - Daniel Kalla   *s*   696

Hale, Glendon (Outlaw; Aged Person)
So Brave, Young and Handsome - Leif
  Enger   *w*   415
So Brave, Young and Handsome - Leif
  Enger   *c*   1035
So Brave, Young and Handsome - Leif
  Enger   *t*   798

Halgar (Mythical Creature; Warrior)
Oathbreaker - Nick Kyme   *f*   517

Hall, Jack (Sportswriter)
Safe at Home - Richard Doster   *i*   930

Hall, Nicole (Teenager; Runaway)
Desert Cut - Betty Webb   *m*   187

Hall, Petra (Lawyer)
The Dawn Patrol - Don Winslow   *m*   195

Hall, Rose Marie (Spouse)
Safe at Home - Richard Doster   *i*   930

Hallam, Hugh (Spouse; Military Personnel)
Hallam's War - Elisabeth Payne Rosen   *t*   880

Hallam, Serena (Spouse)
Hallam's War - Elisabeth Payne Rosen   *t*   880

Halloran, Barry (Journalist)
1999 - Morgan Llywelyn   *t*   852

Halloran, Warren (Businessman)
The Grin of the Dark - Ramsey
  Campbell   *h*   574

Halsey, William Frederick "Bull" (Historical Figure; Military Personnel)
Days of Infamy - Newt Gingrich   *t*   814

Halwai, Balram (Chauffeur)
The White Tiger - Aravind Adiga   *c*   1008

Hamilton, John (Student)
Caliphate - Tom Kratman   *s*   703

Hamilton, Rosie (Teenager)
A Girl Called Rosie - Anne Doughty   *t*   792

Hamley, Larkyn (Student)
Airs and Graces - Toby Bishop   *f*   474

Hamlin, Lily (Time Traveler; Vacationer)
Master of the Highlands - Veronica
  Wolff   *r*   398

Hancock, Lana (Survivor; Activist)
No Control - Shannon K. Butcher   *r*   233

Handley, Jack (Teenager)
The Caddie Who Played with Hickory - John
  Coyne   *t*   783

Hanes, Ashley (Spouse)
Winter Turns to Spring - Catherine
  Palmer   *i*   971

Hanes, Brad (Spouse)
Winter Turns to Spring - Catherine
  Palmer   *i*   971

Hannaford, Bea (Detective—Police)
Careless in Red - Elizabeth George   *m*   83

Hannah, Taylor (Businesswoman; Adventurer)
Strike Zone - Kate Angell   *r*   203

Hanover, Gretchen (Teacher)
A Mile in My Flip-Flops - Melody
  Carlson   *i*   918

Hanratty, Niall (Businessman)
Close Call - John McEvoy   *m*   129

Hansen, Richard (Military Personnel)
Marseguro - Edward Willett   *s*   748

Hanson, Rita (Technician; Murderer)
Chasing Cans - Laura Crum   *m*   49

Happy (Advertising)
The Learners - Chip Kidd   *c*   1058

Hopkins, Gerard Manley (Historical Figure; Writer)
The Exiles - Ron Hansen   *t*   829

Horne, Evan (Musician; Detective—Amateur)
Shades of Blue - Bill Moody   *m*   136

House, Brian (Student—college)
Obedience - Will Lavender   *c*   1061,   *m*   118

Hovan, Ken (Criminal)
Arkansas - John Brandon   *c*   1018

Howe, William (Historical Figure; Military Personnel)
Johnny One-Eye - Jerome Charyn   *t*   776

Hroger (Monster)
A Dangerous Climate - Chelsea Quinn Yarbro   *h*   653

Hughes, Ray (Military Personnel; Single Parent)
A Soldier Comes Home - Cindi Myers   *r*   352

Hulst, Trudy (Spouse)
Trudy's Promise - Marcia Preston   *c*   1080

Hunt, Ava Brigitte (Thief; Businesswoman)
Take Me If You Can - Karen Kendall   *r*   310

Hunt, Billy (Businessman; Friend)
The Silver Swan - Benjamin Black   *c*   1014
The Silver Swan - Benjamin Black   *m*   18

Hunt, Grayson (Businessman; Wealthy)
The Bride and the Bargain - Allison Leigh   *r*   328

Hunter, Marc (Convict; Police Officer)
Unlawful Contact - Pamela Clare   *r*   244

Hunter, Max (Werewolf)
Bad Blood - L.A. Banks   *r*   210
Bad Blood - L.A. Banks   *h*   566

Hunter, R.S. (Writer)
The House at Riverton - Kate Morton   *t*   860

Hunter, Rob (Rescuer; Inspector)
Practically Perfect - Katie Fforde   *c*   1039

Hurley, Arlin (Police Officer)
Ravenous - Ray Garton   *h*   591

Hutton, Phillip (Expatriate; Teacher)
The Gift of Rain - Tan Twan Eng   *c*   1034

Hyden, Nomi (Traveler)
Fallen - Tim Lebbon   *f*   519

I

Inigo (Religious)
The Dreaming Void - Peter F. Hamilton   *s*   690

Iremonk, Daniel (Time Traveler)
City at the End of Time - Greg Bear   *s*   666

Irene (Spirit)
Dead to Me - Anton Strout   *f*   551

Isabella (Historical Figure; Royalty)
The Templar, the Queen and Her Lover - Michael Jecks   *t*   839

Isobel (Parent)
If Not Love - Kay Langdale   *c*   1060

Istee, Clayton (Police Officer)
Death Song - Michael McGarrity   *m*   131
Death Song - Michael McGarrity   *w*   441

J

Jack (Mercenary)
By the Sword - F. Paul Wilson   *h*   651

Jack (Young Man)
To Trust - Carolyn Brown   *w*   409

Jackson (Doctor)
The Chameleon's Shadow - Minette Walters   *m*   186

Jackson, Deborah Lee (Divorced Person; Student)
Better Than - Leslie Esdaile   *r*   260

Jackson, Herman (Bail Bondsman)
Fiddle Game - Richard A. Thompson   *m*   182

Jackson, J.W. (Police Officer)
Vineyard Chill - Philip R. Craig   *m*   48

Jackson, Percy (Sports Figure)
Safe at Home - Richard Doster   *i*   930

Jackson, Zee (Nurse)
Vineyard Chill - Philip R. Craig   *m*   48

Jamal (Fugitive)
The Prince of Bagram Prison - Alex Carr   *m*   37

James, Henry (Historical Figure; Writer)
The James Boys - Richard Liebmann-Smith   *t*   851
The Open Door - Elizabeth Maguire   *t*   854
Wild Nights! - Joyce Carol Oates   *t*   864

James, Jesse (Historical Figure; Outlaw)
The James Boys - Richard Liebmann-Smith   *t*   851

James, Liam (Thief; Nobleman)
Take Me If You Can - Karen Kendall   *r*   310

James, William (Historical Figure; Philosopher)
The James Boys - Richard Liebmann-Smith   *t*   851

James IV (Historical Figure; Ruler)
Flodden Field - Elisabeth McNeill   *t*   858

Jameson, Robert (Detective—Police)
Shadow Waltz - Amy Patricia Meade   *m*   135

Jamila of Alexandria (Royalty)
Crossed - Nicole Galland   *t*   809

Jamison, Emma (Servant; Manager)
Between the Sheets - Robin Wells   *r*   390

Japanangka, Blakie (Sorcerer)
Moonlight Downs - Adrian Hyland   *m*   106

Jarreau, Clay (Police Officer)
Delusion - Peter Abrahams   *m*   2

Jarreau, Nell (Museum Curator; Assistant)
Delusion - Peter Abrahams   *m*   2

Jasper (Teacher)
Quakeland - Francesca Lia Block   *c*   1015

Javier (Royalty)
The Queen's Bastard - C.E. Murphy   *f*   532

Jax, Sirantha (Spacewoman; Mutant)
Grimspace - Ann Aguirre   *s*   658

Jaxon, Joaquin (Lawman)
Rainbows Wait for the Sun - Allan C. Kimball   *w*   434

Jean-Claude (Vampire)
Blood Noir - Laurell K. Hamilton   *h*   597

Jefford, Charlotte (Hotel Owner)
His Small-Town Girl - Arlene James   *i*   951

Jemma7729 (Fugitive)
Jemma7729 - Phoebe Wray   *s*   753

Jenkins, Judy (Police Officer)
Whiskey and Water - Nina Wright   *m*   198

Jennings, Vince (Survivor)
Shadows in the Rain: A Tale of Old Klamath, California - R. Joe King   *w*   435

Jeremie (Royalty)
Mad Kestrel - Misty Massey   *f*   526

Jesus Christ (Historical Figure; Biblical Figure)
The Betrayal: The Lost Life of Jesus Christ - W. Michael Gear   *t*   811

Jill (Parent)
The Ten-Year Nap - Meg Wolitzer   *c*   1104

Jimmy (Computer Expert)
Death Will Get You Sober - Elizabeth Zelvin   *m*   199

Joachim, Marius (Wizard)
Masters of Magic - Chris Wraight   *f*   559

Joe (Streetperson)
Bright Shiny Morning - James Frey   *c*   1041

John (Historical Figure; Biblical Figure)
John - Niall Williams   *t*   900

John the Eunach (Government Official)
Seven for a Secret - Mary Reed   *m*   154,   *t*   877

Johnson, Blaze (Police Officer)
Murder Talks Turkey - Deb Baker   *m*   12

Johnson, Gertie (Aged Person)
Murder Talks Turkey - Deb Baker   *m*   12

Jonah (Mentally Ill Person)
In the Company of Whispers - Sallie Lowenstein   *s*   707

Joner, Helga (Parent)
Black Seconds - Karin Fossum   *m*   76

Joner, Ida (Crime Victim; Child)
Black Seconds - Karin Fossum   *m*   76

Jones, Hatcher (Drifter)
The Road to Love - Linda Ford   *i*   933

Jones, India Selwyn (Doctor)
The White Rose - Jennifer Donnelly   *t*   791

Jones, Jamison (Student—Boarding School)
Stalking Death - Kate Flora   *m*   72

Jones, Lena (Detective—Private)
Desert Cut - Betty Webb   *m*   187

Jones, Maggie (Farmer)
Resistance - Owen Sheers   *s*   735

Jones, Shondra (Student—Boarding School)
Stalking Death - Kate Flora   *m*   72

Jordan (Writer)
Imagine Me and You - Billy Mernit   *c*   1068

Josan (Religious)
The Final Sacrifice - Patricia Bray   *f*   475

Joselyn, Suzette (Gentlewoman; Singer)
The Last Warrior - Karen Kay   *r*   309

Joseph (Historical Figure; Biblical Figure)
Christ the Lord: The Road to Cana - Anne Rice   *t*   878

Joseph of Arimathea (Historical Figure; Biblical Figure)
Mary of Nazareth - Marek Halter   *t*   826

Josiah (Warrior)
Dagger-Star - Elizabeth Vaughan   *f*   556

Josiah (Nobleman; Sorcerer)
Dagger-Star - Elizabeth Vaughan   *r*   387

Josie (Student—Graduate; Child-Care Giver)
Playing - Melanie Abrams   *c*   1007

Jourdain, Michel (Psychic)
The Spiritualist - Megan Chance   *m*   38

Joyner, Benny (Military Personnel)
Peace - Richard Bausch   *t*   769

Character Name Index

Murien, Daisy (Store Owner)
Blue Heart Blessed - Susan Meissner   *i*   964

Murphy, Annabelle (Widow(er); Single Parent)
The Art of Keeping Secrets - Patti Callahan Henry   *r*   291

Murphy, Gwen (Journalist)
Dark of the Moon - Susan Krinard   *r*   319

Murphy, Karrin (Detective—Police)
Small Favor - Jim Butcher   *h*   572

Murphy, Molly (Immigrant; Detective—Private)
Tell Me, Pretty Maiden - Rhys Bowen   *t*   770
Tell Me, Pretty Maiden - Rhys Bowen   *m*   24

Murphy, Rachel (Mechanic; Designer)
Peak Performance - Helen Brenna   *r*   228

Murray, James (Musician)
Queen of the Flowers - Kerry Greenwood   *m*   89

Murray, Margaret (Noblewoman)
Border Wedding - Amanda Scott   *r*   376

Murtz, Danny (Musician; Murderer)
St. Barts Breakdown - Don Bruns   *m*   32

Mya (Young Woman)
The Jewel Trader of Pegu - Jeffrey Hantover   *t*   830

Myell, Terry (Military Personnel)
The Stars Down Under - Sandra McDonald   *s*   713

Myrtale (Noblewoman)
Bring Down the Sun - Judith Tarr   *f*   552

N

Nakamichi 47, Freya (Android; Messenger)
Saturn's Children - Charles Stross   *s*   739

Nam (Military Personnel)
The Stars Down Under - Sandra McDonald   *s*   713

Naomi (Student)
Imagine Me and You - Billy Mernit   *c*   1068

Naro, John (Student)
The Disagreement - Nick Taylor   *t*   891

Narraway, Victor (Government Official)
Buckingham Palace Gardens - Anne Perry   *m*   148

Nash, Mercedes (Teenager)
The Paper Marriage - Susan Kay Law   *r*   324

Nash, Tom (Sports Figure; Single Parent)
The Paper Marriage - Susan Kay Law   *r*   324

Nasr, Maria (Writer)
Ghost Walk - Brian Keene   *h*   611

Nassira (Rebel)
The Heart of Light - Sarah A. Hoyt   *f*   512

Natch (Businessman; Computer Expert)
Multireal - David Louis Edelman   *s*   682

Naul (Criminal)
Principles of Angels - Jaine Fenn   *s*   685

Nessus (Alien; Government Official)
Juggler of Worlds - Larry Niven   *s*   721

Neville, Kit (Artist)
Life Class - Pat Barker   *t*   765

Newberg, Quinn (Lawyer)
By Reason of Insanity - Randy Singer   *i*   990

Newbury, Catherine (Seamstress)
A Lady of Hidden Intent - Tracie Peterson   *i*   976

Newcomb, Maggie (Artisan)
Sister's Choice - Judith Pella   *i*   974

Nezhuala (Ruler)
The Infinite Day - Chris Walley   *i*   1001

Nibulus (Warrior)
A Fire in the North - David Bilsborough   *f*   472

Nicholas de Arundell (Knight)
The Noble Outlaw - Bernard Knight   *t*   845

Nichols, Lizzie (Fiance(e); Designer)
Queen of Babble Gets Hitched - Meg Cabot   *r*   235

Nickels, Mitchell Lee (Radio Personality; Murderer)
South of Shiloh - Chuck Logan   *m*   124

Nicol, Yvette (Detective—Police)
The Cruelest Month - Louise Penny   *m*   147

Nidintulugal (Traveler)
Dragon Mage - Andre Norton   *f*   534

Nikandra (Worker)
Bring Down the Sun - Judith Tarr   *f*   552

Ninefingers, Logen (Warrior)
Last Argument of Kings - Joe Abercrombie   *f*   461

Nisbet, Mary (Noblewoman; Historical Figure)
Stealing Athena - Karen Essex   *t*   800

Noble, Archie (Spy)
The Reavers - George Macdonald Fraser   *t*   805

Noble, Gabriel (Businessman)
Three Nights of Sin - Anne Mallory   *r*   338

Noble, Stefanie (Wealthy)
Finding Stefanie - Susan May Warren   *i*   1002

Nolan, Charlotte (Businesswoman; Publisher)
Thieving Fear - Ramsey Campbell   *h*   576

Normand, Arrow (Actress)
Cheating at Solitaire - Jane Haddam   *m*   92

North, Nicholas (Gentleman)
The Girl from Wish Lane - Anne Douglas   *t*   793

Northcote, Ben (Doctor)
Lethal Legend - Kathy Lynn Emerson   *t*   797

Northcott, May (Mythical Creature; Twin)
Playing with Fire - Katie MacAlister   *r*   333

Norton, Maddie (Companion)
Hearts in the Highlands - Ruth Axtell Morren   *i*   967

Nostradamus, Michel (Astrologer; Doctor)
The Alchemist's Code - Dave Duncan   *f*   493

Notte, Christian (Vampire)
Vampire, Interrupted - Lynsay Sands   *h*   634

Notte, Julius (Vampire)
Vampire, Interrupted - Lynsay Sands   *h*   634
Vampire, Interrupted - Lynsay Sands   *r*   373

Novack, Jonathon (Detective—Police)
Don't Tell a Soul - David Rosenfelt   *m*   158

Novak, Isabelle (Witch)
Witch Blood - Anya Bast   *r*   215

O

O'Bannon, Mangan (Nobleman; Religious)
Wild Angel - Sasha Lord   *r*   332

O'Brien, Peter (Religious)
Tower Hill - Sarah Pinborough   *h*   629

O'Connor, Charity (Young Woman)
A Passion Redeemed - Julie Lessman   *i*   958

O'Connor, Kit (Scientist)
The Crystal Skull - Manda Scott   *m*   167

OctoV (Ruler)
Maximum Offense - David Gunn   *s*   689

Odd Thomas (Cook)
Odd Hours - Dean R. Koontz   *h*   616

O'Dell, Fox (Lawyer; Psychic)
The Hollow - Nora Roberts   *r*   368

Odoms, Lloyd (Mentally Ill Person)
Obsessions - Marshall Cook   *m*   46

Olbricht, Andreas (Artist; Serial Killer)
Vienna Blood - Frank Tallis   *m*   181

Old Shatterhand (Gunfighter)
The Treasure of Nugget Mountain - Karl May   *w*   439
Winnetou the Apache Knight - Karl May   *w*   440

Old White (Wanderer)
People of the Weeping Eye - W. Michael Gear   *t*   812

Oldhall, Emily (Tourist)
The Heart of Light - Sarah A. Hoyt   *f*   512

Oldhall, Nigel (Spy)
The Heart of Light - Sarah A. Hoyt   *f*   512

Olds, Cody (Gambler)
Avenging Fury - John Farris   *h*   587

Oliver (Scholar)
The Man in the Picture - Susan Hill   *h*   601

Oliver (Rebel)
Whitechapel Gods - S.M. Peters   *f*   538

Oliver, Andi (Amnesiac)
Dakota - Martha Grimes   *w*   422
Dakota - Martha Grimes   *c*   1048

Olsen, Julie (Witch)
Magic Burns - Ilona Andrews   *f*   464

Olson, Mignonette "Mimi" (Psychic)
Skinny Dipping - Connie Brockway   *r*   232

Olympias (Religious; Historical Figure)
Bring Down the Sun - Judith Tarr   *f*   552

O'Malley, Mike (Police Officer)
Pushing Up Daisies - Rosemary Harris   *m*   95

O'Mara, Darcy (Nobleman)
A Royal Pain - Rhys Bowen   *m*   23

O'Neal, Mitch (Singer)
Sweet Caroline - Rachel Hauck   *i*   943

O'Neill, Maggie (Empath; Detective—Amateur)
Hex Marks the Spot - Madelyn Alt   *m*   7

Ongamar (Slave)
The Margarets - Sheri S. Tepper   *s*   741

Oort, Richard (Police Officer)
The Edge of Reason - Melinda Snodgrass   *f*   548

Orlong, Karsa (Warrior)
Reaper's Gale - Steven Erikson   *f*   496

Orlov, Alexandr (Spy)
Seduced by a Spy - Andrea Pickens   *r*   359

O'Rourke, Catherine (Journalist; Crime Suspect)
By Reason of Insanity - Randy Singer   *i*   990

Ortega, Libby (Spouse)
White Soul - Brandt Dodson   *m*   56

Ortega, Ron (Police Officer)
White Soul - Brandt Dodson   *m*   56
White Soul - Brandt Dodson   *i*   929

Q

R

Ravirn (Sorcerer; Computer Expert)
CodeSpell - Kelly McCullough *f* 527

Rawlins, Jess (Rancher)
Blue Heaven - C.J. Box *m* 26

Ray, Katie (Businesswoman; Artist)
Weddings Can Be Murder - Christie Craig *r* 247

Ray, Vik (Businessman)
Blind Faith - Sagarika Ghose *c* 1045

Raymond, Delilah Mathers (Gambler; Widow(er))
The River Nymph - Shirl Henke *r* 290

Red Gloves (Warrior; Mercenary)
Dagger-Star - Elizabeth Vaughan *r* 387
Dagger-Star - Elizabeth Vaughan *f* 556

Redbird (Slave)
Hawkspar - Holly Lisle *f* 521

Reddy, Matthew Patrick (Military Personnel; Sea Captain)
Into the Storm - Taylor Anderson *s* 661

Reed, Kerry (Ranger)
Wild Inferno - Sandi Ault *m* 11

Reese, Payton (Journalist; Mountaineer)
Peak Performance - Helen Brenna *r* 228

Reeves, Grace (Servant)
The House at Riverton - Kate Morton *t* 860

Regal, Jack (Criminal)
Turnabout - Steve Perry *s* 724

Reid, Savannah (Detective—Private)
Poisoned Tarts - G.A. McKevett *m* 133

Reign (Vampire)
Let the Night Begin - Kathryn Smith *h* 642

Reilly, Lang (Lawyer; Businessman)
The Sinai Secret - Gregg Loomis *m* 125

Reiss, Richard (Military Personnel)
Pirate Sun - Karl Schroeder *s* 733

Relka (Mythical Creature)
Goblin War - Jim C. Hines *f* 511

Rema (Spouse)
Atmospheric Disturbances - Rivka Galchen *c* 1043

Renard (Smuggler; Spy)
Innocence Unveiled - Blythe Gifford *r* 271

Renard, Elise (Diplomat)
Cold Plague - Daniel Kalla *s* 696

Ressk (Alien)
Valor's Trial - Tanya Huff *s* 693

Reubeni, David (Historical Figure; Nobleman)
The Messiah - Marek Halter *t* 827

Reynolds, Alison (Journalist; Detective—Amateur)
Hand of Evil - J.A. Jance *m* 108

Reynolds, Eve (Gambler; Con Artist)
A Rogue's Game - Renee Bernard *r* 218

Rheel, Ramus (Traveler)
Fallen - Tim Lebbon *f* 519

Rheinhardt, Oskar (Detective—Police)
Vienna Blood - Frank Tallis *t* 890
Vienna Blood - Frank Tallis *m* 181

Rhode, Kendra (Socialite)
Cheating at Solitaire - Jane Haddam *m* 92

Rhodes, Dan (Lawman)
Of All Sad Words - Bill Crider *w* 412

Rhodes, Norman (Dentist)
Carrot Cake Murder - Joanne Fluke *m* 74

Rhyme, Lincoln (Criminologist; Handicapped)
The Broken Window - Jeffery Deaver *m* 52

Ribb, Kyle (Thief)
Arkansas - John Brandon *c* 1018

Richards, Vince (Political Figure)
Wagered Heart - Robin Lee Hatcher *i* 941

Richardson, Matt (Sports Figure)
The Caddie Who Played with Hickory - John Coyne *t* 783

Richter, Pavel (Military Personnel)
Pavel & I - Dan Vyleta *t* 895

Riellen (Police Officer)
The Time Engine - Sean McMullen *f* 528

Riggi, Oscar (Criminal; Businessman)
City of the Sun - David Levien *m* 123

Riley, Brian (Teenager)
Death Song - Michael McGarrity *m* 131

Riley, Tim (Police Officer)
Death Song - Michael McGarrity *w* 441

Ringmar, Rolf (Twin; Murderer)
Mind's Eye - Hakan Nesser *m* 142

Ringo, Tony (Criminal)
The Automatic Detective - A. Lee Martinez *s* 711

Rione, Victoria (Political Figure)
Courageous - Jack Campbell *s* 671

Rione, Victoria (Government Official)
Valiant - Jack Campbell *s* 672

Ripple, Ken (Businessman)
Ghost Walk - Brian Keene *h* 611

Rivergrace (Fugitive)
The Dark Ferryman - Jenna Rhodes *f* 542

Ro Laren (Rebel; Alien)
Night of the Wolves - S.D. Perry *s* 723

Roarke (Businessman; Spouse)
Strangers in Death - J.D. Robb *s* 731

Robbens, Marcee (Accountant)
One Night Stand - Cindy Kirk *r* 314

Robbins, Chad (Fugitive)
Queen of Blood - Bryan Smith *h* 639

Roberta (Parent)
The Ten-Year Nap - Meg Wolitzer *c* 1104

Roberts, Bernard (Businessman)
Shapeshifter - J.F. Gonzalez *h* 594

Roberts, Jerry (Vagrant)
Fires Rising - Michael Laimo *h* 617

Robinson, Ready (Religious)
Unpretty - Sharon Carter Rogers *i* 983

Robitaille, Vivi (Restaurateur)
Just a Taste - Deirdre Martin *r* 340

Rochard, Kelly (Accountant)
Blame It on Paris - Jennifer Greene *r* 276

Rodale, Andrew (Nobleman; Consultant)
Without Warning - Eugenia Lovett West *m* 191

Rodriguez, Nathan (Artist)
The Murder Notebook - Jonathan Santlofer *m* 162

Rofman, Elisabeth (Artist)
1940 - Jay Neugeboren *t* 862

Rohmer, Jack (Time Traveler)
City at the End of Time - Greg Bear *s* 666

Roi (Worker)
Incandescence - Greg Egan *s* 683

Rolon, Alteza (Werewolf)
Lost Prince - Chelsea Quinn Yarbro *h* 654

Romanowski, Nate (Fugitive)
Blood Trail - C.J. Box *m* 25

Rommel, Erwin (Historical Figure; Military Personnel)
Killing Rommel - Steven Pressfield *t* 875
The Steel Wave - Jeff Shaara *t* 886

Ronan (Mutant; Twin)
Deluge - Anne McCaffrey *s* 712

Rondeau (Servant)
Poison Sleep - T.A. Pratt *f* 539

Rook (Teenager)
Havemercy - Jaida Jones *f* 513

Roosevelt, Franklin Delano (Historical Figure; Political Figure)
Days of Infamy - Newt Gingrich *t* 814

Rorkken, Finnar (Military Personnel; Pirate)
Moonstruck - Susan Grant *r* 273

Rosamond (Aged Person)
The Rain Before It Falls - Jonathan Coe *c* 1025

Rosario (Grandparent)
Names on a Map - Benjamin Alire Saenz *w* 448

Rose, Abby (Detective—Private)
Pushing Up Bluebonnets - Leann Sweeney *m* 178

Rose, Birch (Young Man; Lawman)
Ride the Trail of Death - Kenneth L. Kieser *w* 433

Rose, Kate (Psychologist)
Pushing Up Bluebonnets - Leann Sweeney *m* 178

Rose, Nilus (Sea Captain)
The Red Wolf Conspiracy - Robert V.S. Redick *f* 541

Rosen, Kate (Manager)
America the Beautiful - Laura Hayden *i* 944

Rosen, Peter (Police Officer)
Mummy Dearest - Joan Hess *m* 97

Rosenfeld, Miriam (Young Woman)
Silesian Station - David Downing *t* 795

Rosewell, Ann (Young Woman)
Courting Shadows - Jem Poster *t* 874

Rosie (Waiter/Waitress; Gypsy)
Fiddle Game - Richard A. Thompson *m* 182

Ross, Stephen (Recluse; Handicapped)
My Immortal Protector - Jen Holling *r* 293

Rosser, Eve (Teenager; Student)
Feast of Fools - Rachel Caine *h* 573

Rourke, Brigid (Religious)
Waking Brigid - Francis Clark *h* 579
Waking Brigid - Francis Clark *t* 779

Rousseeau, Lysette (Twin; Murderer)
Don't Tempt Me - Sylvia Day *r* 253

Royle, Elizabeth (Gentlewoman)
How to Propose to a Prince - Kathryn Caskie *r* 238

Royston, Margrave (Magician)
Havemercy - Jaida Jones *f* 513

Ruiz, Swin (Drug Dealer)
Arkansas - John Brandon *c* 1018

Rumbolt, Augustus (Artist)
The Iron Tongue of Midnight - Beverle Graves Myers *m* 140

Rumpy (Animal)
Swine Not? - Jimmy Buffet *c* 1021

Rusk, Mike (Archaeologist)
Spider Star - Mike Brotherton   *s*   669

Ruso, Gaius Petreius (Doctor; Military Personnel)
Terra Incognita - Ruth Downie   *c*   1033
Terra Incognita - Ruth Downie   *t*   794

Russell, Francis (Police Officer)
Gas City - Loren D. Estleman   *m*   64

Russell, John (Journalist)
Silesian Station - David Downing   *t*   795

Russo, Terri (Detective—Homicide)
The Murder Notebook - Jonathan
    Santlofer   *m*   162

Rutledge, Ian (Detective—Police)
A Pale Horse - Charles Todd   *m*   183

Ruttenberg, Mark (Spy; Teacher)
An Ordinary Spy - Joseph Weisberg   *m*   188

Ryan (Mythical Creature)
Rogue - Rachel Vincent   *h*   646

Ryce, Banan (Criminal)
Armed & Magical - Lisa Shearin   *f*   547

Ryder, Craig (Businessman)
Valor's Trial - Tanya Huff   *s*   693

Ryder, Pierre (Religious; Adventurer)
Luck - Max Brand   *w*   406

S

sa-Veynau, Heltaw (Alien; Nobleman)
In the Courts of the Crimson Kings - S.M.
    Stirling   *s*   738

Saber, Deke (Paranormal Investigator)
La Vida Vampire - Nancy Haddock   *r*   279

Sachs, Amelia (Detective—Police)
The Broken Window - Jeffery Deaver   *m*   52

SaDiablo, Surreal (Criminal)
Tangled Webs - Anne Bishop   *f*   473

Saint-Germain (Vampire)
A Dangerous Climate - Chelsea Quinn
    Yarbro   *h*   653

St. Just, Jean-Marie (Vampire; Spy)
Bond of Fire - Diane Whiteside   *r*   391

St. Xavier, Emilian (Nobleman; Gypsy)
A Dangerous Love - Brenda Joyce   *r*   306

Sakhnov, Dimitri (Criminal)
Vodka Neat - Anna Blundy   *m*   21

Salthir, Artil im (Wizard)
The Summer Palace - Lawrence
    Watt-Evans   *f*   557

Salvare, Marco (Businessman)
A Rose from the Dead - Kate Collins   *m*   45

Sam (Spouse)
Standing Still - Kelly Simmons   *c*   1089

Sanchez, Alfred (Police Officer)
The Automatic Detective - A. Lee
    Martinez   *s*   711

Sanchez, Vincent (Detective—Police)
The Socorro Blast - Pari Noskin
    Taichert   *m*   180

Sanders, Dylan (Journalist)
Silent Fall - Barbara Freethy   *r*   265

Sanders, Faythe (Mythical Creature)
Rogue - Rachel Vincent   *h*   646

Santiago, Michael (Drug Dealer)
White Soul - Brandt Dodson   *i*   929

Sarmax (Criminal)
Mirrored Heaven - David J. Williams   *s*   749

Sartain, Kim (Wanderer; Mountain Man)
Grub Line Rider - Louis L'Amour   *w*   436

Saunders, David (Doctor)
The Cadaver of Gideon Wyck - Alexander
    Laing   *h*   618

Savvin, Mitenka (Criminal)
Special Assignments - Boris Akunin   *m*   5

Sawyer, Tom (Young Man)
Becky - Lenore Hart   *t*   831

Sayer, Andy (Young Man)
The Folks 2 - Ray Garton   *h*   590

Schreiber, Roberto (Actor)
The Fisher Boy - Stephen Anable   *m*   8

Schuyler, Jason (Supernatural Being)
Blood Noir - Laurell K. Hamilton   *h*   597

Scott, Helen (Girlfriend; Writer)
The Salisbury Manuscript - Philip
    Gooden   *m*   86

Scott, Jodenny (Military Personnel)
The Stars Down Under - Sandra
    McDonald   *s*   713

Scott, Parks (Friend)
Ambush at Mustang Canyon - Mike
    Kearby   *w*   430
The Road to a Hanging - Mike Kearby   *w*   431

Scott, Walter (Nobleman)
Border Wedding - Amanda Scott   *r*   376

Scully, Jake (Saloon Keeper/Owner)
The Redemption of Jake Scully - Elaine
    Barbieri   *i*   909

Seabourne, Cullen (Sorcerer; Werewolf)
Night Season - Eileen Wilks   *r*   395

Sedgewick, Alexandra (Prisoner)
Stretto - L. Timmel Duchamp   *s*   681

Seede, Jonathan (Journalist)
Deviant Behavior - Mike Sager   *c*   1085

Seeker After Truth (Teenager; Student)
Noman - William Nicholson   *f*   533

Sejer, Konrad (Police Officer)
Black Seconds - Karin Fossum   *m*   76

Selby, Eric (Religious)
The Salisbury Manuscript - Philip
    Gooden   *m*   86

Sengar, Rhulad (Ruler)
Reaper's Gale - Steven Erikson   *f*   496

Sergei (Historical Figure; Royalty)
The Romanov Bride - Robert Alexander   *t*   759

Seton, Lochinvar (Nobleman)
Bewitching Season - Marissa Doyle   *f*   491

Sever, Mick (Journalist)
St. Barts Breakdown - Don Bruns   *m*   32

Sevryn (Fugitive)
The Dark Ferryman - Jenna Rhodes   *f*   542

Seymour, Felicity (Noblewoman)
Enchanting the Lady - Kathryne
    Kennedy   *r*   311

Seymour, Simon (Nobleman)
Alexia's Secrets - Una-Mary Parker   *t*   869

Sforza, Ludovico (Ruler; Historical Figure)
The Queen's Gambit - Diane A.S.
    Stuckart   *t*   889

Shade (Mythical Creature)
Pleasure Unbound - Larissa Ione   *h*   608

Shadowstar, Tymalous (Deity)
Goblin War - Jim C. Hines   *f*   511

Shaeffer, Beowulf (Spaceman)
Juggler of Worlds - Larry Niven   *s*   721

Shakespeare, William (Writer; Historical Figure)
Ink and Steel - Elizabeth Bear   *f*   469

Shanklin, Agnes (Teacher)
Dreamers of the Day - Mary Doria
    Russell   *t*   883

Shannah (Impostor; Invalid)
Dead Perfect - Amanda Ashley   *r*   204

Shannon (Spy; Orphan)
Seduced by a Spy - Andrea Pickens   *r*   359

Shapiro, Cannie (Parent)
Certain Girls - Jennifer Weiner   *c*   1101

Shapiro, Joy (Teenager)
Certain Girls - Jennifer Weiner   *c*   1101

Sharon, Miri (Government Official)
The Bone Box - Bob Hostetler   *i*   948

Shaw, Hester (Young Woman)
Fateful Voyage - Pamela Oldfield   *t*   866

Shaw, Neala (Heiress—Dispossessed)
Legacy of Secrets - Sara Mitchell   *i*   965

Shaw, Roxanne (Waiter/Waitress)
The Folks 2 - Ray Garton   *h*   590

Shawn (Divorced Person)
The Art of Keeping Secrets - Patti Callahan
    Henry   *r*   291

Shay, Brittan (Debutante; Detective—Amateur)
Brittan - Debra White Smith   *i*   991

Shearer, Marc (Scientist)
Moon Flower - James P. Hogan   *s*   692

Shein, Abraham (Spouse; Businessman)
The German Bride - Joanna Hershon   *w*   423
The German Bride - Joanna Hershon   *t*   834

Shelia (Nurse)
If Not Love - Kay Langdale   *c*   1060

Shepard, Jack (Spirit; Detective—Private)
The Ghost and the Femme Fatale - Alice
    Kimberly   *m*   113

Shepherd, Lori (Housewife)
Aunt Dimity: Vampire Hunter - Nancy
    Atherton   *m*   10

Shepherd, Noah (Veterinarian)
Snowfall at Willow Lake - Susan Wiggs   *r*   392

Sherard, Robert (Historical Figure; Writer)
Oscar Wilde and a Death of No Importance -
    Gyles Brandreth   *t*   772
Oscar Wilde and a Death of No Importance -
    Gyles Brandreth   *m*   27

Shiloh (Teenager; Time Traveler)
Dragon Mage - Andre Norton   *f*   534

Shippy, George (Police Officer; Historical Figure)
The Lazarus Project - Aleksandar
    Hemon   *t*   832

Shirley, Anne (Orphan)
Before Green Gables - Budge Wilson   *t*   902

Shogun (Werewolf)
Bad Blood - L.A. Banks   *r*   210

Shore, Marla (Hairdresser; Detective—Amateur)
Killer Knots - Nancy J. Cohen   *m*   43

Shores, Jennifer (Spouse)
A Matter of Wife and Death - Ginger
    Kolbaba   *i*   954

Shuler, Lourdes (Crime Suspect)
The Vagabond Virgins - Ken Kuhlken   *m*   117

U

Unnamed Character (Spouse)
The Night Following - Morag Joss *c* 1056
The Night Following - Morag Joss *m* 110

Upton, Willie (Student—Graduate)
The Monsters of Templeton - Lauren Goff *t* 815

Urso, Inez (Detective—Private)
Vampires Are Forever - Lynsay Sands *h* 635

Usher, Charlotte (Teenager)
Ghostgirl - Tonya Hurley *h* 606

Uthor, Thane (Mythical Creature; Warrior)
Oathbreaker - Nick Kyme *f* 517

Utorian, Laran (Military Personnel)
Storm of Iron - Graham McNeill *s* 714

Uyeda, Fukudu
The Dragon's Nine Sons - Chris Roberson *s* 732

V

Vail, Dalton (Detective—Police)
Killer Knots - Nancy J. Cohen *m* 43

Vail, Nicholas (Nobleman)
Wizard's Daughter - Catherine Coulter *r* 246

Valek (Spy)
Fire Study - Maria V. Snyder *f* 549

Valen (Nobleman)
Breath and Bone - Carol Berg *f* 471

Valentina (Animal)
The Mule - Juan Eslava Galan *t* 808
The Mule - Juan Eslava Galan *c* 1042

Valentine (Entertainer)
Embrace Me - Lisa Samson *i* 986

Valentine, David (Military Personnel)
Fall with Honor - E.E. Knight *s* 701

Valentino (Detective—Amateur)
Frames - Loren D. Estleman *m* 63

Valere, Wren (Detective—Private)
Free Fall - Laura Anne Gilman *f* 502

Valkyrie (Spaceship Captain; Military Personnel)
Starship Mercenary - Mike Resnick *s* 728

Valle, Jean (Trader; Historical Figure)
Trail of the Red Butterfly - Karl H. Schlesier *w* 450

Valliere, Louise de la (Historical Figure; Noblewoman)
Mistress of the Sun - Sandra Gulland *t* 820

Van Alen, Schuyler (Vampire; Teenager)
Masquerade - Melissa de la Cruz *f* 489

Van Alstyne, Russ (Police Officer)
I Shall Not Want - Julia Spencer-Fleming *m* 173

van den Broek, Hans (Banker)
Netherland - Joseph O'Neill *c* 1074

van der Pol, Miriam (Doctor)
Twilight - Brendan DuBois *m* 59

Van Tuyen, Tran (Businessman)
Another Man's Moccasins - Craig Johnson *m* 109

Van Veeteren (Detective—Homicide)
Mind's Eye - Hakan Nesser *m* 142

Vanderjack (Mercenary)
The Sellsword - Cam Banks *f* 468

Vane, Leticia (Store Owner)
The Flirt - Kathleen Tessaro *r* 384

Vane, Valerie (Journalist)
A Little Trouble with the Facts - Nina Siegal *c* 1088

Varis (Ruler)
The Vacant Throne - Joshua Palmatier *f* 537

Vartanian, Daniel (Detective—Police)
Scream for Me - Karen Rose *r* 370

Vasquez, Orestes (Organized Crime Figure)
The 5th Witch - Graham Masterton *h* 624

Vatta, Stella (Businesswoman)
Victory Conditions - Elizabeth Moon *s* 719

Vatta, Ty (Spaceship Captain; Military Personnel)
Victory Conditions - Elizabeth Moon *s* 719

Vaughan (Nobleman)
The Seduction of the Crimson Rose - Lauren Willig *t* 901

Vaughn, Caitlyn (Businesswoman; Manager)
Dante's Stolen Wife - Day Leclaire *r* 326

Veeck, Bill (Historical Figure; Businessman)
The End of Baseball - Peter Schilling *t* 885

Vegas, Johnny (Friend)
Atomic Lobster - Tim Dorsey *m* 57

Vellum, Walter (Businessman)
Dreamer - Paul L. Bates *s* 663

Venables-Smythe, Hughie Armstrong (Actor; Companion)
The Flirt - Kathleen Tessaro *r* 384

Veodric, Saekeresh (Nobleman)
Jhegaala - Steven Brust *f* 477

Vickers (Spaceman; Military Personnel)
Relentless - Richard Williams *s* 750

Vickery, Adam (Nobleman)
The Vanishing Viscountess - Diane Gaston *r* 269

Victoria (Historical Figure; Ruler)
A Flaw in the Blood - Stephanie Barron *t* 767

Vik, Johanne (Spouse; Lawyer)
What Never Happens - Anne Holt *m* 102

Villiers, Annique (Spy)
The Spymaster's Lady - Joanna Bourne *r* 224

Vioget, Sebastian (Gentleman)
The Bleeding Dusk - Colleen Gleason *r* 272

Virginsky, Pavel (Government Official)
A Vengeful Longing - R.N. Morris *m* 138

Visant, Alois (Government Official)
Tracing the Shadow - Sarah Ash *f* 466

Vochek, Joanna (Government Official)
Collision - Jeff Abbott *m* 1

von Lange, Kristiana (Spy; Noblewoman)
A Fatal Waltz - Tasha Alexander *m* 6

von Stuhlen, Wolfgang (Nobleman)
A Flaw in the Blood - Stephanie Barron *m* 16

Voss, August (Military Personnel)
The Spies of Warsaw - Alan Furst *m* 80

Voushanti (Nobleman)
Breath and Bone - Carol Berg *f* 471

W

Wade, Evan (Scientist)
Moon Flower - James P. Hogan *s* 692

Wade, Madison (Journalist; Editor)
Pitch Black - Susan Crandall *r* 248

Wahl, Aaron (Professor)
The Socorro Blast - Pari Noskin Taichert *m* 180

Wainman, Jeremy (Archaeologist)
In the Courts of the Crimson Kings - S.M. Stirling *s* 738

Walcher, Lauren (Student—High School; Madam)
Easy Innocence - Libby Fischer Hellmann *m* 96

Walker, Portia (Widow(er); Innkeeper)
Bedding the Baron - Deborah Raleigh *r* 366

Wallace, Tim (Businessman)
Don't Tell a Soul - David Rosenfelt *m* 158

Wallas (Time Traveler; Mythical Creature)
The Time Engine - Sean McMullen *f* 528

Wallender, Magnus (Inspector)
A Grave in Gaza - Matt Beynon Rees *m* 155

Waller, Seth (Teenager)
The Story of Forgetting - Stefan Merrill Block *c* 1016

Ward, Jeri (Detective—Police)
Chasing Cans - Laura Crum *m* 49

Ware, Thaddeus (Psychic)
The Third Circle - Amanda Quick *r* 362

Waring, Alexander (Detective—Police)
Fateful Voyage - Pamela Oldfield *t* 866

Waring, Eden (Psychic)
Avenging Fury - John Farris *h* 587

Warne, Kate (Detective—Private)
Pinkerton's Secret - Eric Lerner *t* 849
Pinkerton's Secret - Eric Lerner *m* 122

Warner, Alicia (Lawyer)
The Sinai Secret - Gregg Loomis *m* 125

Warren, Bill (Detective—Police)
Bring Your Own Poison - Jimmie Ruth Evans *m* 66

Washington, George (Historical Figure; Military Personnel)
Johnny One-Eye - Jerome Charyn *t* 776

Washington, George (Military Personnel; Political Figure)
Washington's Lady - Nancy Moser *i* 970

Washington, Martha Custis (Spouse; Historical Figure)
Washington's Lady - Nancy Moser *i* 970

Watcher (Mythical Creature)
Pax Dakota - Ken Rand *f* 540

Waterhouse, Georgia (Journalist)
Masked by Moonlight - Allie Pleiter *i* 978

Waterman, Jamie (Professor)
Mars Life - Ben Bova *s* 667

Waters, Cherity (Wealthy)
Dream of Love - Michael Phillips *i* 977

Watkins, Holliday (Lawyer)
Black Will Shoot - Jesse Washington *c* 1100

Waverly, John (Military Personnel)
The Vengeance Brand - Michael Senuta *w* 451

Wayfinder, Caleb (Gunfighter)
Bucking the Tiger - Marcus Galloway *w* 417

Weaver, Cynna (FBI Agent)
Night Season - Eileen Wilks *r* 395

Weaver, Dream (Fugitive)
Queen of Blood - Bryan Smith *h* 639

Character Description Index

This index alphabetically lists descriptions of the major characters in featured titles. The descriptions may be occupations (astronaut, lawyer, etc.) or may describe persona (amnesiac, runaway, teenager, etc.). For each description, character names are listed alphabetically. Also provided are book titles, author names, genre codes and entry numbers. The genre codes are as follows: *c* Popular Fiction, *f* Fantasy, *h* Horror, *i* Inspirational, *m* Mystery, *r* Romance, *s* Science Fiction, *t* Historical, and *w* Western.

ABUSE VICTIM

Travis, Haven
Blue-Eyed Devil - Lisa Kleypas *r* 315

ACCIDENT VICTIM

Animal
Animal's People - Indra Sinha *c* 1090

Ardleigh, Beatrice
Assassins at Ospreys - R.T. Raichev *m* 151

Tilden, Maddie Foster
Beyond the Night - Marlo Schalesky *i* 987

ACCOUNTANT

Bender, Cora
The Sinner - Petra Hammesfahr *m* 94

Gamble, Vera
Winter Haven - Athol Dickson *i* 927

Montgomery, Heather
Tall Tales and Wedding Veils - Jane Graves *r* 274

Pearson, Gabby
Right Here, Right Now - HelenKay Dimon *r* 254

Robbens, Marcee
One Night Stand - Cindy Kirk *r* 314

Rochard, Kelly
Blame It on Paris - Jennifer Greene *r* 276

Smith, Ned
The Secret Correspondence - Annette Mahon *r* 336

Stennett, Douglas
Obsessions - Marshall Cook *m* 46

ACTIVIST

Davies, Rebecca
Streets of Fire - Troy Soos *m* 172

Hancock, Lana
No Control - Shannon K. Butcher *r* 233

Moore, Klamath
Blood Trail - C.J. Box *m* 25

Purdy, Bonnie O'Neal Schwartz
To Wed a Texan - Georgina Gentry *r* 270

ACTOR

Cash, Lincoln
Finding Stefanie - Susan May Warren *i* 1002

Cogburn, Vance
Crimson Orgy - Austin Williams *h* 650

Lovejoy, Blanche
Tell Me, Pretty Maiden - Rhys Bowen *t* 770

Ostrovsky, Nicolai
A Sinful Alliance - Amanda McCabe *r* 343

Parker, Amberton
Bright Shiny Morning - James Frey *c* 1041

Schreiber, Roberto
The Fisher Boy - Stephen Anable *m* 8

Stuart, Bobby
Dawn of a New Day - Gilbert Morris *i* 968

Venables-Smythe, Hughie Armstrong
The Flirt - Kathleen Tessaro *r* 384

Winslow, Mark
The Fisher Boy - Stephen Anable *m* 8

ACTRESS

Barber, Carole
Honor Thyself - Danielle Steel *c* 1092

Betty
Monster, 1959 - David Maine *c* 1066

Cheston, Barbara
Crimson Orgy - Austin Williams *h* 650

Evans, Josephine
Seen It All and Done the Rest - Pearl Cleage *c* 1024

Hartford, Emmeline
The House at Riverton - Kate Morton *m* 139

Koenen, Effi
Silesian Station - David Downing *t* 795

Madison, Dawn
Midnight Reign - Chris Marie Green *h* 595

Marsh, Ada
Ada's Heart - Sandra Wilkins *r* 394

Normand, Arrow
Cheating at Solitaire - Jane Haddam *m* 92

Winter, Rosie
The Winter of Her Discontent - Kathryn Miller Haines *t* 824

Wright, Cassie
Snuff - Chuck Palahniuk *c* 1076

ADDICT

Avrile, Benny
The Law of Second Chances - James Sheehan *m* 168

Lucy
Last Last Chance - Fiona Maazel *c* 1064

McQueen, Dol
Missy - Chris Hannan *c* 1051
Missy - Chris Hannan *t* 828

Stewart, Scott
Steward of Song - Adam Stemple *f* 550

Trang, Ally
The Wannoshay Cycle - Michael Jasper *s* 694

White, Leslie
The Silver Swan - Benjamin Black *m* 18

ADMINISTRATOR

Ashford, Penelope
Where the Heart Lies - Stephanie Laurens *r* 323

Kelliher, Ian
Worlds on Fire - Matthew J. Costello *s* 675

Starke, Reiner
Masters of Magic - Chris Wraight *f* 559

Thotmoses, P.
The Houses of Time - Jamil Nasir *s* 720

Wells, Heather
Big Boned - Meg Cabot *m* 34

ADOPTEE

Braxton, Reesy
You Gotta Sin to Get Saved - J.D. Mason *r* 341

Henderson, Will
White Christmas Pie - Wanda E. Brunstetter *i* 914

ADVENTURER

Covington, Matthew
Masked by Moonlight - Allie Pleiter *i* 978

Dunkeld, Cahoon
Buckingham Palace Gardens - Anne Perry *m* 148

Gage, Ethan
The Rosetta Key - William Dietrich *t* 787

Hannah, Taylor
Strike Zone - Kate Angell *r* 203

Ryder, Pierre
Luck - Max Brand *w* 406

Wolfe, Henry
Out of the Devil's Mouth - Travis Thrasher *i* 1000

ADVERTISING

Happy
The Learners - Chip Kidd   *c* 1058

AGED PERSON

Andeman, Soren
Wind River - Tom Morrisey   *i* 969

Bowles, Ruthie
Dogwood - Chris Fabry   *i* 932

Comfort, Harry
The Prince of Bagram Prison - Alex Carr   *m* 37

Eastlake, Elizabeth
Duma Key - Stephen King   *h* 615

Granna
In the Company of Whispers - Sallie
   Lowenstein   *s* 707

Haggard, Abel
The Story of Forgetting - Stefan Merrill
   Block   *c* 1016

Hale, Glendon
So Brave, Young and Handsome - Leif
   Enger   *c* 1035
So Brave, Young and Handsome - Leif
   Enger   *t* 798
So Brave, Young and Handsome - Leif
   Enger   *w* 415

Hawdon
The Man in the Picture - Susan Hill   *h* 601

Johnson, Gertie
Murder Talks Turkey - Deb Baker   *m* 12

Martha
If Not Love - Kay Langdale   *c* 1060

Mendel, Sam
The Future of Love - Shirley Abbott   *c* 1006

Mitchell, Arthur
The Night Following - Morag Joss   *c* 1056
The Night Following - Morag Joss   *m* 110

Rosamond
The Rain Before It Falls - Jonathan Coe   *c* 1025

ALCOHOLIC

Kettleworth, Godfrey R03
Death Will Get You Sober - Elizabeth
   Zelvin   *m* 199

Kohler, Bruce
Death Will Get You Sober - Elizabeth
   Zelvin   *m* 199

ALIEN

Ahn-Kha
Fall with Honor - E.E. Knight   *s* 701

B'Oraq
A Burning House - Keith R.A. DeCandido   *s* 678

Brox 231
Final Inquiries - Roger MacBride Allen   *s* 659

Draycos
Dragon and Liberator - Timothy Zahn   *s* 755

Dukat, Skrain
Day of the Vipers - James Swallow   *s* 740
Night of the Wolves - S.D. Perry   *s* 723

Forrice
Starship Mercenary - Mike Resnick   *s* 728

Mace, Darrah
Day of the Vipers - James Swallow   *s* 740

Nessus
Juggler of Worlds - Larry Niven   *s* 721

Osen, Gar
Day of the Vipers - James Swallow   *s* 740

Pol, Mora
Night of the Wolves - S.D. Perry   *s* 723

Ressk
Valor's Trial - Tanya Huff   *s* 693

Ro Laren
Night of the Wolves - S.D. Perry   *s* 723

sa-Veynau, Heltaw
In the Courts of the Crimson Kings - S.M.
   Stirling   *s* 738

Wol
A Burning House - Keith R.A. DeCandido   *s* 678

Worf
A Burning House - Keith R.A. DeCandido   *s* 678

za-Zhalt, Teyud
In the Courts of the Crimson Kings - S.M.
   Stirling   *s* 738

AMNESIAC

Antaeus, Gabriel
The Ninth Circle - Alex Bell   *f* 470

Daventry, Aimee
Seduced by Sin - Kimberly Logan   *r* 330

Henderson, Carrie
Into the Mist - Elizabeth Sinclair   *r* 381

Oliver, Andi
Dakota - Martha Grimes   *c* 1048
Dakota - Martha Grimes   *w* 422

Plotkin, Sergei Diego
Cosmos Incorporated - Maurice G.
   Dantec   *s* 676

Tucker, Sarah
Silent Run - Barbara Freethy   *r* 266

ANDROID

Daks
Saturn's Children - Charles Stross   *s* 739

Fox, Jenna
The Adoration of Jenna Fox - Mary E.
   Pearson   *s* 722

Nakamichi 47, Freya
Saturn's Children - Charles Stross   *s* 739

Sorico, Katherine
Saturn's Children - Charles Stross   *s* 739

ANGEL

Dill
Iron Angel - Alan Campbell   *f* 481

ANIMAL

Chap
Child of a Dead God - Barb Hendee   *f* 510

Loiosh
Jhegaala - Steven Brust   *f* 477

Peaches
The Ten Best Days of My Life - Adena
   Halpern   *c* 1050

Randolph
A Dog Among Diplomats - J.F. Englert   *m* 61

Rumpy
Swine Not? - Jimmy Buffet   *c* 1021

Tim
Tim, Defender of the Earth - Sam
   Enthoven   *s* 684

Valentina
The Mule - Juan Eslava Galan   *c* 1042
The Mule - Juan Eslava Galan   *t* 808

ANTIQUARIAN

Heath, Hanna
People of the Book - Geraldine Brooks   *t* 774
People of the Book - Geraldine Brooks   *c* 1020

ANTIQUES DEALER

King, Anistana
Moving Target - Cheyenne McCray   *r* 346

Manton, Ben
Rookhurst Hall - Elizabeth Jeffrey   *r* 301

APPRENTICE

Carpenter, Molly
Small Favor - Jim Butcher   *f* 480

Graham, Jennifer
She Always Wore Red - Angela Hunt   *i* 949

Helga
The Moneylender of Toulouse - Alan
   Gordon   *m* 87

Mordiern, Rieuk
Tracing the Shadow - Sarah Ash   *f* 466

Othone, Johun
Rule of Two - Drew Karpyshyn   *s* 697

Rahl
Mage-Guard of Honor - L. E. Modesitt Jr.   *f* 529

Zeno, Alfeo
The Alchemist's Code - Dave Duncan   *f* 493

ARCHAEOLOGIST

Ben Daniel, Danielle
The Secret Scroll - Ronald Cutler   *m* 50

Beth
Demon's Fire - Emma Holly   *r* 294

Bradley, Grace Reeves
The House at Riverton - Kate Morton   *m* 139

Bullock, Randall
The Bone Box - Bob Hostetler   *i* 948

Charles
Demon's Fire - Emma Holly   *r* 294

Cohan, Josh
The Secret Scroll - Ronald Cutler   *m* 50

Creed, Annja
Provenance - Alex Archer   *f* 465

Gallagher, Reid
Hearts in the Highlands - Ruth Axtell
   Morren   *i* 967

Longchamp, Faye
Findings - Mary Anna Evans   *m* 67

Mantooth, Joe Wolf
Findings - Mary Anna Evans   *m* 67

Rusk, Mike
Spider Star - Mike Brotherton   *s* 669

Wainman, Jeremy
In the Courts of the Crimson Kings - S.M.
   Stirling   *s* 738

ARCHITECT

Bradwell, Kyle
Secrets of Surrender - Madeline Hunter   *r* 298

Chappers, Tazio
The Purrfect Murder - Rita Mae Brown   *m* 31

Josie
Playing - Melanie Abrams   *c* 1007

Katrina
Quakeland - Francesca Lia Block   *c* 1015

MacKay, Annora
Highland Wolf - Hannah Howell   *r* 296

CIVIL SERVANT

al-Baroody, Omar
The Amateur Spy - Dan Fesperman   *m* 69

Lockhart, Freeman
The Amateur Spy - Dan Fesperman   *m* 69

Owen, Gareth
Mark of the Pasha - Michael Pearce   *m* 146
Mark of the Pasha - Michael Pearce   *t* 871

Yefimov
A Vengeful Longing - R.N. Morris   *m* 138

CLERK

Sutherland, Jason
Ravenous - Ray Garton   *h* 591

Tulipov, Anisii
Special Assignments - Boris Akunin   *m* 5

CLONE

Campion
House of Chains - Alastair Reynolds   *s* 729

Purslane
House of Chains - Alastair Reynolds   *s* 729

COACH

Maddox, Dillon
Wearing My Halo Tilted - Stephanie Perry Moore   *i* 966

COMPANION

Becket, Monte
So Brave, Young and Handsome - Leif Enger   *t* 798
So Brave, Young and Handsome - Leif Enger   *c* 1035
So Brave, Young and Handsome - Leif Enger   *w* 415

Eversleigh, Grace
The Lost Duke of Wyndham - Julia Quinn   *r* 363

Norton, Maddie
Hearts in the Highlands - Ruth Axtell Morren   *i* 967

Venables-Smythe, Hughie Armstrong
The Flirt - Kathleen Tessaro   *r* 384

COMPUTER EXPERT

Dunstan, Jeremy
Wild and Hexy - Vicki Lewis Thompson   *r* 386

Jimmy
Death Will Get You Sober - Elizabeth Zelvin   *m* 199

Larkin, Reed
Right Here, Right Now - HelenKay Dimon   *r* 254

Maragos, Theodore
Making Over Mr. Right - Judi McCoy   *r* 345

Mosley, Nina
The Killer's Wife - Bill Floyd   *m* 73

Natch
Multireal - David Louis Edelman   *s* 682

Ravirn
CodeSpell - Kelly McCullough   *f* 527

Sterling, Andrew
The Broken Window - Jeffery Deaver   *m* 52

CON ARTIST

Reynolds, Eve
A Rogue's Game - Renee Bernard   *r* 218

CONSTRUCTION WORKER

Kessler, Rue
The Grand Scheme - Kathy Herman   *i* 945

CONSULTANT

Demarkian, Gregor
Cheating at Solitaire - Jane Haddam   *m* 92

Forsberg, Benjamin
Collision - Jeff Abbott   *m* 1

Grey, Connor
Unquiet Dreams - Mark Del Franco   *f* 490

Leffler, Eric
Dead Time - Stephen White   *m* 194

Quirke
The Silver Swan - Benjamin Black   *m* 18

Rodale, Andrew
Without Warning - Eugenia Lovett West   *m* 191

Solomon, Sasha
The Socorro Blast - Pari Noskin Taichert   *m* 180

CONTRACTOR

Freemantle, Edgar
Duma Key - Stephen King   *h* 615

Teague, Jonathan
Pandora's Box - Natale Stenzel   *r* 382

CONVICT

Curran, Jack
Quiver - Peter Leonard   *m* 121

DuPree, Alvin
Delusion - Peter Abrahams   *m* 2

Hatfield, Will
Dogwood - Chris Fabry   *i* 932

Hunter, Marc
Unlawful Contact - Pamela Clare   *r* 244

Kelly, Jake
Catch a Shadow - Patricia Potter   *r* 361

Mitter, Janek
Mind's Eye - Hakan Nesser   *m* 142

Wilson, Henry
The Law of Second Chances - James Sheehan   *m* 168

COOK

Carl
Turning Tables - Heather MacDowell   *c* 1065

Foxton, Gina
Deep Dish - Mary Kay Andrews   *r* 202
Deep Dish - Mary Kay Andrews   *c* 1009

Moody, Tate
Deep Dish - Mary Kay Andrews   *r* 202
Deep Dish - Mary Kay Andrews   *c* 1009

Odd Thomas
Odd Hours - Dean R. Koontz   *h* 616

Paras, Olivia
State of the Onion - Julie Hyzy   *m* 107

COUNSELOR

MacLeod, Dara
The House on Fortune Street - Margot Livesey   *c* 1062

COURTIER

Lugantes
Lost Prince - Chelsea Quinn Yarbro   *h* 654

COUSIN

Beatrix
The Rain Before It Falls - Jonathan Coe   *c* 1025

COWBOY

Amlingmeyer, Gustav "Old Red"
The Black Dove - Steve Hockensmith   *m* 101
The Black Dove - Steve Hockensmith   *t* 835

Amlingmeyer, Otto "Big Red"
The Black Dove - Steve Hockensmith   *t* 835
The Black Dove - Steve Hockensmith   *m* 101

Broadus, Jimmy Wayne
Hellbent & Heartfirst - Kassandra Sims   *r* 380

Buffalo Bill
Go-Go Girls of the Apocalypse - Victor Gischler   *s* 687

Burke, Owen
Trail Hand - R.W. Stone   *w* 456

Chandler, Hawk
Wagered Heart - Robin Lee Hatcher   *i* 941

Chavez
Trail Hand - R.W. Stone   *w* 456

Del
Black Rock Canon - Les Savage   *w* 449

Maxwell, Eden
Texas Loving - Leigh Greenwood   *r* 277

Paint, Ezra
Sun Going Down - Jack Todd   *w* 457
Sun Going Down - Jack Todd   *c* 1097
Sun Going Down - Jack Todd   *t* 892

Sinfield, Darlene "Dickie"
The Last Cowgirl - Jana Richman   *w* 447

Tie
Black Rock Canon - Les Savage   *w* 449

Westwood, Jack
Along Came a Cowboy - Christine Lynxwiler   *i* 960

Wilder, Waddy
Forty Candles on a Cowboy Cake - Rick Steber   *w* 455

CRIME SUSPECT

Crawford, Larry
Of All Sad Words - Bill Crider   *w* 412

O'Rourke, Catherine
By Reason of Insanity - Randy Singer   *i* 990

Shuler, Lourdes
The Vagabond Virgins - Ken Kuhlken   *m* 117

Spotted Dog
Blood on the Rimrock - Phil Dunlap   *w* 413

CRIME VICTIM

Averbuch, Lazarus
The Lazarus Project - Aleksandar Hemon   *t* 832

Beckman, Carson
The Killer's Wife - Bill Floyd   *m* 73

Blessing, Tom
Hard Trail to Follow - Elmer Kelton *w* 432
Cameron, Inez del
The Serpent's Daughter - Suzanne Arruda *t* 761
Crawford, Terry
Of All Sad Words - Bill Crider *w* 412
Joner, Ida
Black Seconds - Karin Fossum *m* 76
Kennedy, Angela
Little Criminals - Gene Kerrigan *m* 112
Sumrall, Bobbie Faye
Bobbie Faye's (kinda, sorta, not-exactly) Family Jewels - Toni McGee Causey *r* 241

CRIMINAL

Bombay, Dakota
Guns Will Keep Us Together - Leslie Langtry *r* 322
Carver, Samuel
The Accident Man - Tom Cain *m* 35
Cassidy, Neil
Neuropath - Scott Bakker *h* 565
Caulker, Jack
Iron Angel - Alan Campbell *f* 481
Cayal
The Immortal Prince - Jennifer Fallon *f* 497
Choate, Randall
Collision - Jeff Abbott *m* 1
Crowe, Frankie
Little Criminals - Gene Kerrigan *m* 112
Darnell, Godfrey
The Shadow Year - Jeffrey Ford *m* 75
Doubtfire, Leonie
Guns Will Keep Us Together - Leslie Langtry *r* 322
Dumas, Marguerite
A Sinful Alliance - Amanda McCabe *r* 343
Glokta
Last Argument of Kings - Joe Abercrombie *f* 461
Hawkwind, Cheyenne
Cosmos Incorporated - Maurice G. Dantec *s* 676
Hobart, Jerry
Fidelity - Thomas Perry *m* 149
Hon-Durren
Grimspace - Ann Aguirre *s* 658
Hovan, Ken
Arkansas - John Brandon *c* 1018
King, Ratcliffe
The Roar of the Butterflies - Reginald Hill *m* 99
Kursk, Grigori
The Accident Man - Tom Cain *m* 35
Malaspina, Franco
The Garden of Evil - David Hewson *m* 98
Malone, Sid
The White Rose - Jennifer Donnelly *t* 791
Naul
Principles of Angels - Jaine Fenn *s* 685
Owen, Magnus
The Abyssinian Proof - Jenny White *m* 192
Peace, Corwin
The Plague of Doves - Louise Erdrich *c* 1036
Petrova, Alexandra
The Accident Man - Tom Cain *m* 35

Plotkin, Sergei Diego
Cosmos Incorporated - Maurice G. Dantec *s* 676
Pontius
Missy - Chris Hannan *c* 1051
Rasheed, Troy
Killer Heat - Linda Fairstein *m* 68
Regal, Jack
Turnabout - Steve Perry *s* 724
Riggi, Oscar
City of the Sun - David Levien *m* 123
Ringo, Tony
The Automatic Detective - A. Lee Martinez *s* 711
Ryce, Banan
Armed & Magical - Lisa Shearin *f* 547
SaDiablo, Surreal
Tangled Webs - Anne Bishop *f* 473
Sakhnov, Dimitri
Vodka Neat - Anna Blundy *m* 21
Sarmax
Mirrored Heaven - David J. Williams *s* 749
Savvin, Mitenka
Special Assignments - Boris Akunin *m* 5
Space Vulture
Space Vulture - Gary K. Wolf *s* 752
Syler, Delia
Painted Dresses - Patricia Hickman *i* 946
Terry, Gil
Space Vulture - Gary K. Wolf *s* 752
Turek, Gammis
Victory Conditions - Elizabeth Moon *s* 719

CRIMINOLOGIST

Rhyme, Lincoln
The Broken Window - Jeffery Deaver *m* 52

CRITIC

Lester, Simon
The Grin of the Dark - Ramsey Campbell *h* 574

CULT MEMBER

Babineaux, Edward
The Fisher Boy - Stephen Anable *m* 8
Thompson, Hank
By the Sword - F. Paul Wilson *h* 651

DANCER

Laress, Neomi
Dark Deeds at Night's Edge - Kresley Cole *r* 245

DEBUTANTE

Erskine, Alexia
Alexia's Secrets - Una-Mary Parker *t* 869
Leigh, Lorna
Lorna - Debra White Smith *i* 992
Shay, Brittan
Brittan - Debra White Smith *i* 991

DEITY

Degodessa, Zoe
Making Over Mr. Right - Judi McCoy *r* 345
Engine, Mama
Whitechapel Gods - S.M. Peters *f* 538

Marit
Shadow Gate - Kate Elliott *f* 495
Shadowstar, Tymalous
Goblin War - Jim C. Hines *f* 511
Xypher
Dream Chaser - Sherrilyn Kenyon *r* 313
Zeus
CodeSpell - Kelly McCullough *f* 527

DEMON

Eidolon
Pleasure Unbound - Larissa Ione *h* 608
Pahndir
Demon's Fire - Emma Holly *r* 294
Xypher
Dream Chaser - Sherrilyn Kenyon *r* 313

DENTIST

Rhodes, Norman
Carrot Cake Murder - Joanne Fluke *m* 74

DESIGNER

Murphy, Rachel
Peak Performance - Helen Brenna *r* 228
Nichols, Lizzie
Queen of Babble Gets Hitched - Meg Cabot *r* 235
Phillips, Callie
Sweetheart Lost and Found - Shirley Jump *r* 308
Springer, Maddie
Alibi in High Heels - Gemma Halliday *r* 282

DETECTIVE

Adair, Barnaby
Where the Heart Lies - Stephanie Laurens *r* 323
Cameron, Jade del
The Serpent's Daughter - Suzanne Arruda *t* 761
Gregorivich, Nikolai
50 Ways to Hex Your Lover - Linda Wisdom *r* 397
Pasha, Kamil
The Abyssinian Proof - Jenny White *m* 192
The Abyssinian Proof - Jenny White *t* 898

DETECTIVE—AMATEUR

Acquillo, Sam
Head Wounds - Chris Knopf *m* 115
Amlingmeyer, Gustav "Old Red"
The Black Dove - Steve Hockensmith *t* 835
The Black Dove - Steve Hockensmith *m* 101
On the Wrong Track - Steve Hockensmith *w* 424
Amlingmeyer, Otto "Big Red"
The Black Dove - Steve Hockensmith *m* 101
The Black Dove - Steve Hockensmith *t* 835
On the Wrong Track - Steve Hockensmith *w* 424
Ashton, Emily
Fatal Waltz - Tasha Alexander *t* 760
Avery, Ellie
Getting Away Is Deadly - Sara Rosett *m* 159
Benjamin, Rachel
The Hunt - Jennifer Sturman *m* 176
Browning, Theodosia
The Silver Needle Murder - Laura Childs *m* 39
Craddock, Billy Don
Holy Moly - Ben Rehder *m* 156

DETECTIVE—HOMICIDE

DETECTIVE—POLICE

DIRECTOR

Meyer, Sheldon
Crimson Orgy - Austin Williams   *h* 650

DISEMBODIED PERSONALITY

Westwood, Dimity
Aunt Dimity: Vampire Hunter - Nancy
Atherton   *m* 10

DIVER

Devon, Briana
Below the Surface - Karen Harper   *r* 286

DIVORCED PERSON

Jackson, Deborah Lee
Better Than - Leslie Esdaile   *r* 260

Lamb, Grace
Hot Date - Amy Garvey   *r* 268

Landon, Mia
Time Is a River - Mary Alice Monroe   *r* 351

Laurent, Ramsey
Blue Heart Blessed - Susan Meissner   *i* 964

Maisie
Of Men and Their Mothers - Mameve
Medwed   *c* 1067

Maloney, Katy
Empty Ever After - Reed Farrel Coleman   *m* 44

Pollock, Rex
Of Men and Their Mothers - Mameve
Medwed   *c* 1067

Prescott, Hilda
The Wedding Machine - Beth Webb Hart   *i* 940

Shawn
The Art of Keeping Secrets - Patti Callahan
Henry   *r* 291

Unger, Julie
Stargazer - Amanda Harte   *r* 288

DOCTOR

Aguilar, Adelia
The Serpent's Tale - Ariana Franklin   *m* 77
The Serpent's Tale - Ariana Franklin   *t* 804

Alling, Prexy
The Cadaver of Gideon Wyck - Alexander
Laing   *h* 618

Andersen, Spencer
This Side of Heaven - Anna Schmidt   *r* 375

Armistead, Georgiana
A Flaw in the Blood - Stephanie Barron   *m* 16

Azzam, Khalid
Kethani - Eric Brown   *s* 670

Bascombe, Joe
A Match Made in Hell - Terri Garey   *h* 589

Baye, Mike
Hold Tight - Harlan Coben   *m* 41

Bloch, Eduard
1940 - Jay Neugeboren   *t* 862

Carroll, Ephraim
The Anatomy of Deception - Lawrence
Goldstone   *t* 816
The Anatomy of Deception - Lawrence
Goldstone   *m* 85

Devesh
Playing - Melanie Abrams   *c* 1007

Donovan, Frank
Into the Mist - Elizabeth Sinclair   *r* 381

Donovan, Rachel
Along Came a Cowboy - Christine
Lynxwiler   *i* 960

Dotson, Walter
Miscarriage of Justice - Kip Gayden   *t* 810

Drystan, Elizabeth
Keepers of the Flame - Robin D. Owens   *f* 536

Dubois, Simone
Dream Chaser - Sherrilyn Kenyon   *r* 313

Frankenberg, Georg
The Sinner - Petra Hammesfahr   *m* 94

Haldane, Noah
Cold Plague - Daniel Kalla   *s* 696

Jackson
The Chameleon's Shadow - Minette
Walters   *m* 186

Jones, India Selwyn
The White Rose - Jennifer Donnelly   *t* 791

Korovin, Donat Savvich
Sister Pelagia and the Black Monk - Boris
Akunin   *m* 4

Krushelevansky, Peter
Certain Girls - Jennifer Weiner   *c* 1101

Liebenstein, Leo
Atmospheric Disturbances - Rivka
Galchen   *c* 1043

Northcote, Ben
Lethal Legend - Kathy Lynn Emerson   *t* 797

Nostradamus, Michel
The Alchemist's Code - Dave Duncan   *f* 493

Osler, William
The Anatomy of Deception - Lawrence
Goldstone   *t* 816
The Anatomy of Deception - Lawrence
Goldstone   *m* 85

Owen, Cedric
The Crystal Skull - Manda Scott   *f* 546
The Crystal Skull - Manda Scott   *m* 167

Peck, Micah
The Resurrectionist - Jack O'Connell   *c* 1073

Quirke
The Silver Swan - Benjamin Black   *m* 18

Quirke, Garrett
The Silver Swan - Benjamin Black   *c* 1014

Rahim, Abbas
The Amateur Spy - Dan Fesperman   *m* 69

Ruso, Gaius Petreius
Terra Incognita - Ruth Downie   *c* 1033
Terra Incognita - Ruth Downie   *t* 794

Saunders, David
The Cadaver of Gideon Wyck - Alexander
Laing   *h* 618

Stevens, Luke
Seaview Inn - Sherryl Woods   *r* 399

Stokes, Darlene
More than It Hurts You - Darin Strauss   *c* 1094

Stratford, Henry
Perfect - Harry Lee Kraus   *i* 955

Svariskaya, Ludmilla
A Dangerous Climate - Chelsea Quinn
Yarbro   *h* 653

Thessalus
Terra Incognita - Ruth Downie   *t* 794
Terra Incognita - Ruth Downie   *c* 1033

Tumblety, Francis
The Dracula Dossier - James Reese   *h* 631

van der Pol, Miriam
Twilight - Brendan DuBois   *m* 59

Weir, Charlie
Trauma - Patrick McGrath   *h* 625

Wyck, Gideon
The Cadaver of Gideon Wyck - Alexander
Laing   *h* 618

DRIFTER

Jones, Hatcher
The Road to Love - Linda Ford   *i* 933

DRIVER

MacArthur
Whiskey and Water - Nina Wright   *m* 198

DRUG DEALER

Estevez, Ricardo
White Soul - Brandt Dodson   *m* 56

MacDonald, Sharon
Everybody Knows This Is Nowhere - John
McFetridge   *m* 130

Ruiz, Swin
Arkansas - John Brandon   *c* 1018

Santiago, Michael
White Soul - Brandt Dodson   *i* 929

EDITOR

Debauer, Peter
Homecoming - Bernhard Schlink   *m* 164

Dennehy, Mitch
A Passion Redeemed - Julie Lessman   *i* 958

Grayson, Eli
Jewel - Beverly Jenkins   *r* 302

McCracken
Blood Alley - Tom Coffey   *m* 42

Mendez, Anna
I Heart Bloomberg - Melody Carlson   *i* 917

Quinn, Monona
Obsessions - Marshall Cook   *m* 46

Wade, Madison
Pitch Black - Susan Crandall   *r* 248

ELDERLY

Brigant, Niall
From Dead to Worse - Charlaine Harris   *h* 598

EMPATH

Coyle, Carpathia
Dreamer - Paul L. Bates   *s* 663

O'Neill, Maggie
Hex Marks the Spot - Madelyn Alt   *m* 7

EMPLOYER

DeBroux, Jamie
Severance Package - Duane
Swierczynski   *m* 179

ENGINEER

Dunn, A.P.
Pelican Road - Howard Bahr   *t* 762

Smith, Frederick
Bedding the Baron - Deborah Raleigh   *r* 366

Uhl, Edvard
The Spies of Warsaw - Alan Furst   *t* 807

ENTERTAINER

Claudia
The Moneylender of Toulouse - Alan
    Gordon *m* 87
The Moneylender of Toulouse - Alan
    Gordon *t* 817

D'Artigo, Menolly
Darkling - Yasmine Galenorn *f* 500

deMarley, Olivia
Choosing Sophie - Leslie Carroll *c* 1023

Lella
Embrace Me - Lisa Samson *i* 986

Luger, Monica
Mariah Mundi: The Midas Box - G.P.
    Taylor *f* 553

Quinn
Rolling Thunder - John Varley *s* 746

Sinatra, Frank
Luck Be a Lady, Don't Die - Robert J.
    Randisi *m* 152

Slomo
Rolling Thunder - John Varley *s* 746

**Strickland-Garcia-Redmund, Patricia "Pod-
kayne"**
Rolling Thunder - John Varley *s* 746

Thackeray, Tubby
The Grin of the Dark - Ramsey Campbell *h* 574

Theophilos
The Moneylender of Toulouse - Alan
    Gordon *m* 87
The Moneylender of Toulouse - Alan
    Gordon *t* 817

Valentine
Embrace Me - Lisa Samson *i* 986

Winslow, Mark
The Fisher Boy - Stephen Anable *m* 8

EQUESTRIAN

Smith, Christopher
Aunt Dimity: Vampire Hunter - Nancy
    Atherton *m* 10

EXPATRIATE

Hutton, Phillip
The Gift of Rain - Tan Twan Eng *c* 1034

EXPLORER

Clark, William
Trail of the Red Butterfly - Karl H.
    Schlesier *w* 450

Crusoe, Billie
The Stone Gods - Jeanette Winterson *c* 1103

Klingston, Frank
Spider Star - Mike Brotherton *s* 669

Lewis, Meriwether
Trail of the Red Butterfly - Karl H.
    Schlesier *w* 450

FARMER

Bossey
Birmingham, 35 Miles - James Braziel *s* 668

Harris, Henry
Harris: The Return of the Gunfighter - H.R.
    Williams *w* 460

Harrison, Mathew
Birmingham, 35 Miles - James Braziel *s* 668

Jones, Maggie
Resistance - Owen Sheers *s* 735

Logan, Luke
Ada's Heart - Sandra Wilkins *r* 394

Pickard, Andy
Hard Trail to Follow - Elmer Kelton *w* 432

Stoddard, Colby
Sister's Choice - Judith Pella *i* 974

Yoder, Caleb
The Forbidden - Beverly Lewis *i* 959

FBI AGENT

Baxter, Nicole
The Murder Game - Beverly Barton *r* 213

Cahill, Simon
The Angel - Carla Neggers *r* 354

Cormier, Trevor
*Bobbie Faye's (kinda, sorta, not-exactly) Family
    Jewels* - Toni McGee Causey *r* 241

Crane, Rob
Wild Inferno - Sandi Ault *m* 11

Grayhawk, Breed
A Stranger's Game - Joan Johnston *r* 303
A Stranger's Game - Joan Johnston *w* 427

Harkness, Vincent
A Stranger's Game - Joan Johnston *w* 427

Lattimer, Ben
The Hunt - Jennifer Sturman *m* 176

Lawrence, Andie
Shades of Blue - Bill Moody *m* 136

MacKinnon, John
Hot - Julia Harper *r* 285

Tilquist, Jim
In the Wind - Barbara Fister *m* 71

Weaver, Cynna
Night Season - Eileen Wilks *r* 395

Zobart, Tony
Getting Away Is Deadly - Sara Rosett *m* 159

FEMINIST

Donovan, Sarah
Chances - Pamela Nowak *r* 356

FIANCE(E)

Forrest, Peter
The Hunt - Jennifer Sturman *m* 176

Henderson, Will
White Christmas Pie - Wanda E.
    Brunstetter *i* 914

Lytton, Freddie
The White Rose - Jennifer Donnelly *t* 791

Nichols, Lizzie
Queen of Babble Gets Hitched - Meg
    Cabot *r* 235

Yoder, Karen
White Christmas Pie - Wanda E.
    Brunstetter *i* 914

FILMMAKER

Clayton, Dean
On My Terms - Shirley Hailstock *r* 280

FINANCIER

McClellan, Garrick
Being with Him - Jessica Inclan *r* 299

Wright, Adam
Full Circle - Davis Bunn *i* 915

FIRE FIGHTER

Simone, Mike
Chocolate Secrets - Zelda Benjamin *r* 216

FISHERMAN

Landon, Mia
Time Is a River - Mary Alice Monroe *r* 351

MacDougal, Stuart
Time Is a River - Mary Alice Monroe *r* 351

FRIEND

Avery, Patsy
The Body in the Gallery - Katherine Hall
    Page *m* 144

Frayne, Trixie
Murder of a Chocolate-Covered Cherry - Denise
    Swanson *m* 177

Hunt, Billy
The Silver Swan - Benjamin Black *c* 1014
The Silver Swan - Benjamin Black *m* 18

May, Theresa
Waterloo Sunset - Martin Edwards *m* 60

Scott, Parks
Ambush at Mustang Canyon - Mike
    Kearby *w* 430
The Road to a Hanging - Mike Kearby *w* 431

Standing Bear, Henry
Another Man's Moccasins - Craig
    Johnson *m* 109

Stockton, Clay
Vineyard Chill - Philip R. Craig *m* 48

Vegas, Johnny
Atomic Lobster - Tim Dorsey *m* 57

FRONTIERSMAN

Amlingmeyer, Gustav "Old Red"
On the Wrong Track - Steve Hockensmith *w* 424

Amlingmeyer, Otto "Big Red"
On the Wrong Track - Steve Hockensmith *w* 424

Fargo, Skye
Missouri Manhunt - Jon Sharpe *w* 452

Moreland, William
The Outlander - Gil Adamson *t* 756

FRONTIERSWOMAN

Sparks, Lucille
Missouri Manhunt - Jon Sharpe *w* 452

FUGITIVE

Caitlyn
Broken Angel - Sigmund Brouwer *i* 912

Jamal
The Prince of Bagram Prison - Alex Carr *m* 37

Jemma7729
Jemma7729 - Phoebe Wray *s* 753

Laz
The Shadow Isle - Katharine Kerr *f* 515

Rivergrace
The Dark Ferryman - Jenna Rhodes *f* 542

Robbins, Chad
Queen of Blood - Bryan Smith *h* 639

Menechinn, Bob
Winter Study - Nevada Barr   *m* 14

Montana, Nick
This Is How It Happened (Not a Love Story) - Jo Barrett   *r* 212

Morgan, Luke
Twisted Creek - Jodi Thomas   *r* 385

Muldoon, Nichole
Capitol Conspiracy - William Bernhardt   *m* 17

Narraway, Victor
Buckingham Palace Gardens - Anne Perry   *m* 148

Nessus
Juggler of Worlds - Larry Niven   *s* 721

Owen, Magnus
The Abyssinian Proof - Jenny White   *m* 192

Pasha, Kamil
The Abyssinian Proof - Jenny White   *m* 192
The Abyssinian Proof - Jenny White   *t* 898

Petrovich, Porfiry
A Vengeful Longing - R.N. Morris   *m* 138

Rione, Victoria
Valiant - Jack Campbell   *s* 672

Sharon, Miri
The Bone Box - Bob Hostetler   *i* 948

Stoner, Jason
Dragons Wild - Robert Asprin   *f* 467

Stuvyesant, Harris
Touchstone - Laurie R. King   *m* 114

Tremont, Shane
Once Smitten, Twice Shy - Lori Wilde   *r* 393

Trevelyan, Paul
Mark of the Pasha - Michael Pearce   *m* 146

Tulipov, Anisii
Special Assignments - Boris Akunin   *m* 5

Virginsky, Pavel
A Vengeful Longing - R.N. Morris   *m* 138

Visant, Alois
Tracing the Shadow - Sarah Ash   *f* 466

Vochek, Joanna
Collision - Jeff Abbott   *m* 1

Zacchaeus
Eighth Shepherd - Bodie Thoene   *i* 997

GRANDPARENT

DiCamillo, Kitty
Ruby among Us - Tina Ann Forkner   *i* 934

Milk, Mooshum
The Plague of Doves - Louise Erdrich   *w* 416

Rosario
Names on a Map - Benjamin Alire Saenz   *w* 448

GUARD

Eiliesor, Mychael
Armed & Magical - Lisa Shearin   *f* 547

GUARDIAN

Castle, Elizabeth
Not Quite a Mom - Kirsten Sawyer   *r* 374

Grimshaw, Nicholas
Danger's Kiss - Sarah McKerrigan   *r* 349

MacInnes, Gideon
Call of the Highland Moon - Kendra Leigh Castle   *r* 240

Ramsey, Theresa
On My Terms - Shirley Hailstock   *r* 280

GUIDE

Marinelli, Francesca
La Vida Vampire - Nancy Haddock   *r* 279

GUNFIGHTER

Billy the Kid
Rainbows Wait for the Sun - Allan C. Kimball   *w* 434

Cole, Virgil
Resolution - Robert B. Parker   *t* 868

Dodge, Lucius
Nate Coffin's Revenge - J. Lee Butts   *w* 410

Earp, Wyatt
Borrowed Time - S.M. Ballard   *w* 402
Rainbows Wait for the Sun - Allan C. Kimball   *w* 434

Fargo, Skye
Missouri Manhunt - Jon Sharpe   *w* 452

Harris, Henry
Harris: The Return of the Gunfighter - H.R. Williams   *w* 460

Hitch, Everett
Resolution - Robert B. Parker   *t* 868

Holliday, John Henry "Doc"
Borrowed Time - S.M. Ballard   *w* 402
Bucking the Tiger - Marcus Galloway   *w* 417

Old Shatterhand
The Treasure of Nugget Mountain - Karl May   *w* 439
Winnetou the Apache Knight - Karl May   *w* 440

Terrell, Mad Dog
Missouri Manhunt - Jon Sharpe   *w* 452

Tillman, Bass
Blood of Bass Tillman - Cotton Smith   *w* 454

Wayfinder, Caleb
Bucking the Tiger - Marcus Galloway   *w* 417

GYPSY

Ashleigh
Wild Angel - Sasha Lord   *r* 332

Brock, Domnu
Ancient Blood - Robert Earl   *f* 494

Brock, Mihai
Ancient Blood - Robert Earl   *f* 494

Kadriya
Emerald Silk - Janet Lane   *r* 321

Rosie
Fiddle Game - Richard A. Thompson   *m* 182

St. Xavier, Emilian
A Dangerous Love - Brenda Joyce   *r* 306

Teraf
Emerald Silk - Janet Lane   *r* 321

Webb
An Incomplete Revenge - Jacqueline Winspear   *m* 196

HAIRDRESSER

Donahue, Patsy
Because Your Vampire Said So - Michele Bardsley   *r* 211

Shore, Marla
Killer Knots - Nancy J. Cohen   *m* 43

HANDICAPPED

Moran, Cadence
The Fault Tree - Louise Ure   *m* 184

Rhyme, Lincoln
The Broken Window - Jeffery Deaver   *m* 52

Ross, Stephen
My Immortal Protector - Jen Holling   *r* 293

Simona
Eighth Shepherd - Bodie Thoene   *i* 997

HEALER

Agnus
The Fire Walker - Ben Pastor   *t* 870

Angmar
The Shadow Isle - Katharine Kerr   *f* 515

Drystan, Brigid
Keepers of the Flame - Robin D. Owens   *f* 536

Gray Wolf, Jonah
The Healer - Sharon Sala   *r* 371

LeBlanc, Tara
Bayou Paradox - Robin Caroll   *i* 920

Lithgo, Beatrice
The Rough Collier - Pat McIntosh   *m* 132

Lively, Hazel Flinders
Moonlight Downs - Adrian Hyland   *m* 106

MacKay, Deidra
My Immortal Protector - Jen Holling   *r* 293

Montehue, Celestia
Love's Magic - Traci E. Hall   *r* 281

Phillips, Sunshine
With Every Breath - Lynn Kurland   *r* 320

HEALTH CARE PROFESSIONAL

Hijazi, Katya
Finding Nouf - Zoe Ferraris   *c* 1038

Palmer, Kirke
Catch a Shadow - Patricia Potter   *r* 361

Wong, Julie
The Secret Correspondence - Annette Mahon   *r* 336

HEIR

Porphyry, Christian
The Roar of the Butterflies - Reginald Hill   *m* 99

HEIR—DISPOSSESSED

Morgan, Tony
Deep in the Heart of Trouble - Deeanne Gist   *i* 937

HEIR—LOST

Audley, Jack
The Lost Duke of Wyndham - Julia Quinn   *r* 363

HEIRESS

Avery, Pandemina Dorothy
Pandora's Box - Natale Stenzel   *r* 382

Benedict, Abigail
The Anatomy of Deception - Lawrence Goldstone   *m* 85

Bosworth, Prudence
The Wicked Ways of a Duke - Laura Lee Guhrke   *r* 278

Burton, Tori
Fatal Deduction - Gayle Roper   *i* 984

Daniels, Allie
Twisted Creek - Jodi Thomas   *r* 385
Dante, Tiffany
Poisoned Tarts - G.A. McKevett   *m* 133
Hofmeyr, Dianna
A Carrion Death - Michael Stanley   *m* 175
Keating, Libby
Fatal Deduction - Gayle Roper   *i* 984
McCann, Celia
Close Call - John McEvoy   *m* 129
Platte, Kelsey Cavanaugh
The Alpine Traitor - Mary Daheim   *m* 51

HEIRESS—DISPOSSESSED

Shaw, Neala
Legacy of Secrets - Sara Mitchell   *i* 965

HIGHWAYMAN

Audley, Jack
The Lost Duke of Wyndham - Julia Quinn   *r* 363
Gilderoy
The Reavers - George Macdonald Fraser   *t* 805

HISTORIAN

Kamen, Ben
Weaver - Stephen Baxter   *s* 665
Spartianus, Aelius
The Fire Walker - Ben Pastor   *t* 870
Stachelmann, Josef
A Paragon of Virtue - Christian Von
   Ditfurth   *m* 185

HISTORICAL

Elizabeth I
Ink and Steel - Elizabeth Bear   *f* 469

HISTORICAL FIGURE

Akbar the Great
The Enchantress of Florence - Salman
   Rushdie   *t* 882
Alfred
Sword Song - Bernard Cornwell   *t* 782
Aspasia
Stealing Athena - Karen Essex   *t* 800
Averbuch, Lazarus
The Lazarus Project - Aleksandar Hemon   *t* 832
Barabbas
Mary of Nazareth - Marek Halter   *t* 826
Beecher, Henry Ward
Harriet and Isabella - Patricia O'Brien   *t* 865
Billy the Kid
Rainbows Wait for the Sun - Allan C.
   Kimball   *w* 434
Bloch, Eduard
1940 - Jay Neugeboren   *t* 862
Boleyn, Anne
In the Shadow of Lions - Ginger Garrett   *i* 936
Bonaparte, Napoleon
The Rosetta Key - William Dietrich   *t* 787
Victory of Eagles - Naomi Novik   *f* 535
Bronte, Anne
The Secret Adventures of Charlotte Bronte - Laura
   Joh Rowland   *t* 881
The Secret Adventures of Charlotte Bronte - Laura
   Joh Rowland   *c* 1084

Bronte, Charlotte
The Secret Adventures of Charlotte Bronte - Laura
   Joh Rowland   *c* 1084
The Secret Adventures of Charlotte Bronte - Laura
   Joh Rowland   *t* 881
Bronte, Emily
The Secret Adventures of Charlotte Bronte - Laura
   Joh Rowland   *c* 1084
Calpurnia
The Triumph of Caesar - Steven Saylor   *t* 884
Cezanne, Paul
Cezanne's Quarry - Barbara Pope   *t* 873
Chekhov, Anton
The Woman Who Wouldn't - Gene Wilder   *t* 899
Churchill, Winston
Dreamers of the Day - Mary Doria
   Russell   *t* 883
Clemens, Samuel
Becky - Lenore Hart   *t* 831
Clement VII
The Messiah - Marek Halter   *t* 827
Cross, Johnnie
The World Before Her - Deborah Weisgall   *t* 897
Dickinson, Emily
Wild Nights! - Joyce Carol Oates   *t* 864
Doyle, Arthur Conan
Oscar Wilde and a Death of No Importance -
   Gyles Brandreth   *t* 772
Earp, Wyatt
Borrowed Time - S.M. Ballard   *w* 402
Rainbows Wait for the Sun - Allan C.
   Kimball   *w* 434
Edward VII
Buckingham Palace Gardens - Anne Perry   *t* 872
Eisenhower, Dwight
The Steel Wave - Jeff Shaara   *t* 886
Eleanor of Aquitaine
The Serpent's Tale - Ariana Franklin   *t* 804
Elisavyeta
The Romanov Bride - Robert Alexander   *t* 759
Elizabeth I
The Lady Elizabeth - Alison Weir   *t* 896
Evans, Marian
The World Before Her - Deborah Weisgall   *t* 897
Farquharson, Anne
White Rose Rebel - Janet Paisley   *t* 867
Frost, Robert
Fall of Frost - Brian Hall   *t* 825
Genghis Khan
Genghis: Lords of the Bow - Conn
   Iggulden   *t* 838
Gibson, Josh
The End of Baseball - Peter Schilling   *t* 885
Grant, Ulysses S.
Escape from Andersonville - Gene
   Hackman   *t* 822
Halsey, William Frederick "Bull"
Days of Infamy - Newt Gingrich   *t* 814
Henry II
The Serpent's Tale - Ariana Franklin   *t* 804
Henry VIII
In the Shadow of Lions - Ginger Garrett   *i* 936
The Lady Elizabeth - Alison Weir   *t* 896
The Secret Bride - Diane Haeger   *t* 823
Hitler, Adolf
1940 - Jay Neugeboren   *t* 862

Hogan, Ben
The Caddie Who Played with Hickory - John
   Coyne   *t* 783
Holliday, John Henry "Doc"
Borrowed Time - S.M. Ballard   *w* 402
Bucking the Tiger - Marcus Galloway   *w* 417
Hooker, Isabella
Harriet and Isabella - Patricia O'Brien   *t* 865
Hopkins, Gerard Manley
The Exiles - Ron Hansen   *t* 829
Howe, William
Johnny One-Eye - Jerome Charyn   *t* 776
Isabella
The Templar, the Queen and Her Lover - Michael
   Jecks   *t* 839
James, Henry
The James Boys - Richard
   Liebmann-Smith   *t* 851
The Open Door - Elizabeth Maguire   *t* 854
Wild Nights! - Joyce Carol Oates   *t* 864
James, Jesse
The James Boys - Richard
   Liebmann-Smith   *t* 851
James, William
The James Boys - Richard
   Liebmann-Smith   *t* 851
James IV
Flodden Field - Elisabeth McNeill   *t* 858
Jesus Christ
The Betrayal: The Lost Life of Jesus Christ - W.
   Michael Gear   *t* 811
John
John - Niall Williams   *t* 900
Joseph
Christ the Lord: The Road to Cana - Anne
   Rice   *t* 878
Joseph of Arimathea
Mary of Nazareth - Marek Halter   *t* 826
Julius Caesar
The Triumph of Caesar - Steven Saylor   *t* 884
Kennedy, Joseph
The Importance of Being Kennedy - Laurie
   Graham   *t* 818
Kennedy, Rose
The Importance of Being Kennedy - Laurie
   Graham   *t* 818
Lawrence, T.E.
Dreamers of the Day - Mary Doria
   Russell   *t* 883
Leonardo da Vinci
The Queen's Gambit - Diane A.S. Stuckart   *t* 889
Louis XIV
Mistress of the Sun - Sandra Gulland   *t* 820
Macbeth
Lady Macbeth - Susan King   *t* 844
Machiavelli, Niccollo
The Enchantress of Florence - Salman
   Rushdie   *t* 882
Makeda
Solomon's Angels - Doreen Virtue   *t* 894
Mary
Christ the Lord: The Road to Cana - Anne
   Rice   *t* 878
Mary of Nazareth - Marek Halter   *t* 826
Mary I
The Lady Elizabeth - Alison Weir   *t* 896

KNIGHT

Baldwin de Furnshill
The Templar, the Queen and Her Lover - Michael Jecks *t* 839

Erengislsson, Rurik
Surrender to the Highlander - Terri Brisbin *r* 231

Gereint
The Golden Rose - Kathleen Bryan *f* 478

Gregor of Mainz
Crossed - Nicole Galland *t* 809

Le Blanc, Nicholas
Love's Magic - Traci E. Hall *r* 281

Nicholas de Arundell
The Noble Outlaw - Bernard Knight *t* 845

Wynter, John
Emerald Silk - Janet Lane *r* 321

LAIRD

Cameron, Ewen
Master of the Highlands - Veronica Wolff *r* 398

Cameron, Robert
With Every Breath - Lynn Kurland *r* 320

Drummond, James
Highland Wolf - Hannah Howell *r* 296

Lachlan, Gordon
In the Highlander's Bed - Cathy Maxwell *r* 342

MacDonald, Egan
Highlander Ever After - Jennifer Ashley *r* 205

LANDLORD

Browning
Courting Emma - Sharlene MacLaren *i* 961

Cloyd
The Flowers - Dagoberto Gilb *w* 418

Colville, Leonard
Assassins at Ospreys - R.T. Raichev *m* 151

Garret, Emma
Where Love Dwells - Delia Parr *i* 972

Tangassi, Anita
A Deadly Paradise - Grace Brophy *m* 30

Weis, Kendall
I Heart Bloomberg - Melody Carlson *i* 917

LANDOWNER

Anselma, Amanda
Head Wounds - Chris Knopf *m* 115

Butler, Richard
Death on the Holy Mountain - David Dickinson *m* 55

Muniz, Orlando
Blood of the Wicked - Leighton Gage *m* 81

LANDSCAPER

Brittingham, Ellen
For Pete's Sake - Linda Windsor *i* 1005

LAWMAN

Blessing, Tom
Hard Trail to Follow - Elmer Kelton *w* 432

Bullock, Seth
Ride the Trail of Death - Kenneth L. Kieser *w* 433

Drago
Blood on the Rimrock - Phil Dunlap *w* 413

Havlicek, Cody
Big Bend Death Trap - James J. Griffin *w* 420

Heinrich von Manfred, Johann "El Tigre"
El Tigre - John H. Manhold *w* 438

Jaxon, Joaquin
Rainbows Wait for the Sun - Allan C. Kimball *w* 434

Kelly, Piedmont
Blood on the Rimrock - Phil Dunlap *w* 413

Lockhart, Burl
On the Wrong Track - Steve Hockensmith *w* 424

Pickard, Andy
Hard Trail to Follow - Elmer Kelton *w* 432

Puttock, Simon
The Templar, the Queen and Her Lover - Michael Jecks *t* 839

Rhodes, Dan
Of All Sad Words - Bill Crider *w* 412

Rose, Birch
Ride the Trail of Death - Kenneth L. Kieser *w* 433

Simms, Justin "Purgatory Sands"
Marshal Sands and Mrs. Molly - V.E. Bixenstine *w* 403

Slade, Jack
Slade's Law - Lyle Brandt *w* 407

Thompson, Jubal
The Road to a Hanging - Mike Kearby *w* 431

Wilkie
Harris: The Return of the Gunfighter - H.R. Williams *w* 460

LAWYER

Anatolius
Seven for a Secret - Mary Reed *m* 154

Andrews, Avery
Hush My Mouth - Cathy Pickens *w* 445

Annueliwitz, Jacob
The Sinai Secret - Gregg Loomis *m* 125

Ansell, Thomas
The Salisbury Manuscript - Philip Gooden *m* 86

Baye, Tia
Hold Tight - Harlan Coben *m* 41

Bellamy, Sophie
Snowfall at Willow Lake - Susan Wiggs *r* 392

Blair, Jack
The Ex-Debutante - Linda Francis Lee *r* 327

Breckenwith, Zachary
Where Love Dwells - Delia Parr *i* 972

Buchanan, Ty
Try Darkness - James Scott Bell *i* 910

Coffinhal, Pierre-Andre
Mistress of the Revolution - Catherine Delors *t* 785

Cooper, Alexandra
Killer Heat - Linda Fairstein *m* 68

Crusoe, Jim
Waterloo Sunset - Martin Edwards *m* 60

Cunningham, Gilbert
The Rough Collier - Pat McIntosh *m* 132

Cushing, Carlisle Wainwright
The Ex-Debutante - Linda Francis Lee *r* 327

Davies, Amanda
The Guilty - Jason Pinter *m* 150

DeMarco, Joe
House Rules - Mike Lawson *m* 120

Devlin, Harry
Waterloo Sunset - Martin Edwards *m* 60

Duval, Max
Between the Sheets - Robin Wells *r* 390

Evans, Lije
Farraday Road - Ace Collins *i* 923

Fitzgerald, Patrick
A Flaw in the Blood - Stephanie Barron *m* 16
A Flaw in the Blood - Stephanie Barron *t* 767

Glenn, Theodore
Killing Fear - Allison Brennan *r* 229

Grant, David
The Houses of Time - Jamil Nasir *s* 720

Hall, Petra
The Dawn Patrol - Don Winslow *m* 195

Kelly, Paul
Easy Innocence - Libby Fischer Hellmann *m* 96

Kenney, Vienne
Leaving November - Deborah Raney *i* 979

Kincaid, Ben
Capitol Conspiracy - William Bernhardt *m* 17

Lark
Sharp Teeth - Toby Barlow *h* 567

Lincoln, Abraham
Pinkerton's Secret - Eric Lerner *m* 122

McCann, Clay
Free Fire - C.J. Box *w* 405

Newberg, Quinn
By Reason of Insanity - Randy Singer *i* 990

O'Dell, Fox
The Hollow - Nora Roberts *r* 368

Parker, Evan
Sister's Choice - Judith Pella *i* 974

Planter, Buck
Not Quite a Mom - Kirsten Sawyer *r* 374

Rafferty, Finn
Just Desserts - Barbara Bretton *r* 230

Rampling, Benjamin
The Spiritualist - Megan Chance *m* 38

Reilly, Lang
The Sinai Secret - Gregg Loomis *m* 125

Stanfield, Henry
The Truth Commissioner - David Park *c* 1077

Steele, Jason
The Governess Wears Scarlet - Sari Robins *r* 369

Swaitkowski, Jackie
Head Wounds - Chris Knopf *m* 115

Szarbek, Anna
The Spies of Warsaw - Alan Furst *m* 80

Taylor, Tami
Deeper Water - Robert Whitlow *i* 1004

Tillman, Bass
Blood of Bass Tillman - Cotton Smith *w* 454

Tobin, Jack
The Law of Second Chances - James Sheehan *m* 168

Vik, Johanne
What Never Happens - Anne Holt *m* 102

Warner, Alicia
The Sinai Secret - Gregg Loomis *m* 125

Watkins, Holliday
Black Will Shoot - Jesse Washington *c* 1100

White, Kate
Guilty - Karen Robards *r* 367

MINER

Albert
The Well and the Mine - Gin Phillips   *c* 1078

MONSTER

Hroger
A Dangerous Climate - Chelsea Quinn
    Yarbro   *h* 653

K.
Monster, 1959 - David Maine   *c* 1066

MOUNTAIN MAN

The Preacher
Preacher's Showdown - William W.
    Johnstone   *w* 429

Sartain, Kim
Grub Line Rider - Louis L'Amour   *w* 436

Skye, Barnaby
The Canyon of Bones - Richard S.
    Wheeler   *w* 458
Virgin River - Richard S. Wheeler   *w* 459

MOUNTAINEER

Reese, Payton
Peak Performance - Helen Brenna   *r* 228

MURDERER

Beckman, Carson
The Killer's Wife - Bill Floyd   *m* 73

Caldwell, Grace "Merle Raye Finkel"
A Stranger's Game - Joan Johnston   *w* 427

Hanson, Rita
Chasing Cans - Laura Crum   *m* 49

Kohn, Leopold
A Paragon of Virtue - Christian Von
    Ditfurth   *m* 185

McCann, Clay
Free Fire - C.J. Box   *w* 405

Murtz, Danny
St. Barts Breakdown - Don Bruns   *m* 32

Nickels, Mitchell Lee
South of Shiloh - Chuck Logan   *m* 124

Ringmar, Rolf
Mind's Eye - Hakan Nesser   *m* 142

Rouseeau, Lysette
Don't Tempt Me - Sylvia Day   *r* 253

Storms, Serge
Atomic Lobster - Tim Dorsey   *m* 57

MUSEUM CURATOR

Booth, Charles Murchison
The Bone Key - Sarah Monette   *h* 626

Jarreau, Nell
Delusion - Peter Abrahams   *m* 2

Smernoff, Oliver
Killer Knots - Nancy J. Cohen   *m* 43

MUSICIAN

Armstrong, Edwin
The Chorister at the Abbey - Lis Howell   *m* 105

Briton
Crossed - Nicole Galland   *t* 809

Caravelle, Devon
Explosive - Charlotte Mede   *r* 350

Horne, Evan
Shades of Blue - Bill Moody   *m* 136

Keyes, Claire
Sweet Talk - Susan Mallery   *r* 337

Konig, Hayden
The Mezzo Wore Mink - Mark Schweizer   *m* 166

Murray, James
Queen of the Flowers - Kerry Greenwood   *m* 89

Murtz, Danny
St. Barts Breakdown - Don Bruns   *m* 32

Stewart, Douglas
Steward of Song - Adam Stemple   *f* 550

Unnamed Character
The Cellist of Sarajevo - Steven
    Galloway   *c* 1044

Webb, Jeremy Spencer
The Woman Who Wouldn't - Gene Wilder   *t* 899

Wise, Dontay
Black Will Shoot - Jesse Washington   *c* 1100

MUTANT

Gosseyn, Gilbert
Null-A Continuum - John C. Wright   *s* 754

Jax, Sirantha
Grimspace - Ann Aguirre   *s* 658

Moira
Singularity's Ring - Paul Melko   *s* 715

Muriel
Deluge - Anne McCaffrey   *s* 712

Papadopulos, Apollo
Singularity's Ring - Paul Melko   *s* 715

Ronan
Deluge - Anne McCaffrey   *s* 712

Strom
Singularity's Ring - Paul Melko   *s* 715

MYTHICAL CREATURE

Ajulutsikael
Vicious Circle - Mike Carey   *h* 577

Bailey, Andromeda
The Hidden World - David Gunn   *f* 509

Basarab, Dorina
Midnight's Daughter - Karen Chance   *h* 578

Bern
Seekers of the Chalice - Brian Cullen   *f* 486

Brady
A Fiend in Need - Maureen Child   *r* 243

ca'Millac, Archigos Dhosti
A Magic of Twilight - S.L. Farrell   *f* 498

Crawfield, Cat
One Foot in the Grave - Jeaniene Frost   *h* 588

Daria
One Bite Stand - Nina Bangs   *r* 209

D'Artigo, Delilah
Darkling - Yasmine Galenorn   *f* 500

Dragonslayer, Jig
Goblin War - Jim C. Hines   *f* 511

Firr, Lucy
The Devil's Daughter - Laura Drewry   *r* 256

Garran
Shadow Magic - Cheyenne McCray   *r* 347

Gromrund
Oathbreaker - Nick Kyme   *f* 517

Halgar
Oathbreaker - Nick Kyme   *f* 517

Langford, Kimber
Queen of Dragons - Shana Abe   *r* 200

Leesil
Child of a Dead God - Barb Hendee   *f* 510

Lorgas
Seekers of the Chalice - Brian Cullen   *f* 486

Loss
Demon Apocalypse - Darren Shan   *h* 636

Lowe, Martin
Walk on the Wild Side - Christine Warren   *r* 389

Mab
Ink and Steel - Elizabeth Bear   *f* 469
Small Favor - Jim Butcher   *f* 480

Marc
Rogue - Rachel Vincent   *h* 646

Maricara
Queen of Dragons - Shana Abe   *r* 200

Martes
Steward of Song - Adam Stemple   *f* 550

McCandless, Griffen
Dragons Wild - Robert Asprin   *f* 467

McCandless, Valerie
Dragons Wild - Robert Asprin   *f* 467

Melchior
CodeSpell - Kelly McCullough   *f* 527

Morjin
Lord of Lies - David Zindell   *f* 560

Morningstar, Roger
Daemons Are Forever - Simon R. Green   *f* 504

Northcott, May
Playing with Fire - Katie MacAlister   *r* 333

Relka
Goblin War - Jim C. Hines   *f* 511

Ryan
Rogue - Rachel Vincent   *h* 646

Sanders, Faythe
Rogue - Rachel Vincent   *h* 646

Shade
Pleasure Unbound - Larissa Ione   *h* 608

Sorcha
Dark Seduction - Kathleen Korbel   *r* 318

Stewart, Marcus
Walk on the Wild Side - Christine Warren   *r* 389

Stinkwort
Unquiet Dreams - Mark Del Franco   *f* 490

Sugarman, Kitty Jane
Walk on the Wild Side - Christine Warren   *r* 389

Tauhou, Gabriel
Playing with Fire - Katie MacAlister   *r* 333

Temeraire
Victory of Eagles - Naomi Novik   *f* 535

Thompson, Mercy
Iron Kissed - Patricia Briggs   *f* 476

Tibalt
Battle Dragon - Edo van Belkom   *f* 555

Uthor, Thane
Oathbreaker - Nick Kyme   *f* 517

Wallas
The Time Engine - Sean McMullen   *f* 528

Watcher
Pax Dakota - Ken Rand   *f* 540

NOBLEMAN

Adair, Barnaby
Where the Heart Lies - Stephanie Laurens   *r* 323

NOBLEWOMAN

Gunnarsdottir, Margriet
Surrender to the Highlander - Terri
    Brisbin   *r* 231

Kasandra
Lord of Lies - David Zindell   *f* 560

Kirkland, Louisa
The Courtesan's Secret - Claudia Dain   *r* 249

Lacey, Livia
To Wed a Wicked Prince - Jane Feather   *r* 261

Lahaylia, Sauscony
The Ruby Dice - Catherine Asaro   *s* 662

Lange, Kristiana von
Fatal Waltz - Tasha Alexander   *t* 760

MacKay, Annora
Highland Wolf - Hannah Howell   *r* 296

Montehue, Celestia
Love's Magic - Traci E. Hall   *r* 281

Murray, Margaret
Border Wedding - Amanda Scott   *r* 376

Myrtale
Bring Down the Sun - Judith Tarr   *f* 552

Nisbet, Mary
Stealing Athena - Karen Essex   *t* 800

Parronley, Marlena
The Vanishing Viscountess - Diane Gaston   *r* 269

Powerscourt, Lucy
Death on the Holy Mountain - David
    Dickinson   *t* 786

Raine, Madeline
The Devil's Web - Mary Balogh   *r* 207

Rannoch, Victoria G. C. Eugenie
A Royal Pain - Rhys Bowen   *m* 23

Seymour, Felicity
Enchanting the Lady - Kathryne Kennedy   *r* 311

Tannach, Honora
Return of the Rogue - Donna Fletcher   *r* 264

Turner, Carolyn
Confessions at Midnight - Jacquie
    D'Alessandro   *r* 250

Valliere, Louise de la
Mistress of the Sun - Sandra Gulland   *t* 820

von Lange, Kristiana
A Fatal Waltz - Tasha Alexander   *m* 6

Wentworth, Ivy
A Notorious Proposition - Adele Ashworth   *r* 206

Wilde, Georgiana
The Kiss - Sophia Nash   *r* 353

Winter, Philippa
Airs and Graces - Toby Bishop   *f* 474

Wyngate, Irene
The Bridal Quest - Candace Camp   *r* 237

Ysobel
The Final Sacrifice - Patricia Bray   *f* 475

NURSE

Black, Iris
Silver Street - Elizabeth Gill   *t* 813

Clare, Barbara
Winter in Madrid - C.J. Sansom   *m* 161

Fallon, Alexandra Tremaine
Scream for Me - Karen Rose   *r* 370

Jackson, Zee
Vineyard Chill - Philip R. Craig   *m* 48

Martinelli, Alex
Chocolate Secrets - Zelda Benjamin   *r* 216

Morrison, Louisa
Murder Bay - David Horwitz   *m* 103

Shelia
If Not Love - Kay Langdale   *c* 1060

OFFICE WORKER

Darnell, Layla
The Hollow - Nora Roberts   *r* 368

Emrich, Carol
Shapeshifter - J.F. Gonzalez   *h* 594

Frasier, Maia
In Twilight's Shadow - Patti O'Shea   *r* 357

Gates, Angie
Murder Talks Turkey - Deb Baker   *m* 12

Owen, Zeinab
Mark of the Pasha - Michael Pearce   *m* 146

Wiseman, Mark
Shapeshifter - J.F. Gonzalez   *h* 594

ORGANIZED CRIME FIGURE

Putin, Zakhar "Whitey"
Kill Whitey - Brian Keene   *h* 612

Vasquez, Orestes
The 5th Witch - Graham Masterton   *h* 624

Zeno, Anthony
Gas City - Loren D. Estleman   *m* 64

ORPHAN

Anders
Pavel & I - Dan Vyleta   *t* 895

Cadge
Mind the Gap - Christopher Golden   *f* 503

Carstairs, Anne
Double Fantasy - Cheryl Holt   *r* 295

de la Fontaine, Rosalind
Wizard's Daughter - Catherine Coulter   *r* 246

Dusty
The Hidden City - Michelle West   *f* 558

Glass, Jim
The Blue Door - Tony Earley   *t* 796

Harry
Mind the Gap - Christopher Golden   *f* 503

Markess, Jewel
The Hidden City - Michelle West   *f* 558

Shannon
Seduced by a Spy - Andrea Pickens   *r* 359

Shirley, Anne
Before Green Gables - Budge Wilson   *t* 902

Tyler, Katey
No Choice but Seduction - Johanna
    Lindsey   *r* 329

OUTLAW

Cordell, Luther
Hard Trail to Follow - Elmer Kelton   *w* 432

Hale, Glendon
So Brave, Young and Handsome - Leif
    Enger   *c* 1035
So Brave, Young and Handsome - Leif
    Enger   *t* 798
So Brave, Young and Handsome - Leif
    Enger   *w* 415

James, Jesse
The James Boys - Richard
    Liebmann-Smith   *t* 851

Simms, Justin "Purgatory Sands"
Marshal Sands and Mrs. Molly - V.E.
    Bixenstine   *w* 403

Terrell, Mad Dog
Missouri Manhunt - Jon Sharpe   *w* 452

Thompson, Jubal
The Road to a Hanging - Mike Kearby   *w* 431

PARANORMAL INVESTIGATOR

Saber, Deke
La Vida Vampire - Nancy Haddock   *r* 279

PARENT

Amy
The Ten-Year Nap - Meg Wolitzer   *c* 1104

Barton, Lisa
A Matter of Wife and Death - Ginger
    Kolbaba   *i* 954

Baye, Mike
Hold Tight - Harlan Coben   *m* 41

Baye, Tia
Hold Tight - Harlan Coben   *m* 41

Braxton, Reesy
You Gotta Sin to Get Saved - J.D. Mason   *r* 341

Carol
Whatever Makes You Happy - William
    Sutcliffe   *c* 1096

Davidson, Richmond
Dream of Love - Michael Phillips   *i* 977

deMarley, Augie
Choosing Sophie - Leslie Carroll   *c* 1023

Doolittle, Claire
Sleeping with Ward Cleaver - Jenny
    Gardiner   *r* 267

Doolittle, Jack
Sleeping with Ward Cleaver - Jenny
    Gardiner   *r* 267

Gabriel, Paul
City of the Sun - David Levien   *m* 123

Gilberto
The Heartbreak Pill - Anjanette Delgado   *c* 1032

Gillian
Whatever Makes You Happy - William
    Sutcliffe   *c* 1096

Goldin, Dori
More than It Hurts You - Darin Strauss   *c* 1094

Goldin, Josh
More than It Hurts You - Darin Strauss   *c* 1094

Graham, Jennifer
She Always Wore Red - Angela Hunt   *i* 949

Helen
Whatever Makes You Happy - William
    Sutcliffe   *c* 1096

Henderson, Frank
White Christmas Pie - Wanda E.
    Brunstetter   *i* 914

Isobel
If Not Love - Kay Langdale   *c* 1060

Jill
The Ten-Year Nap - Meg Wolitzer   *c* 1104

Joner, Helga
Black Seconds - Karin Fossum   *m* 76

Maisie
Of Men and Their Mothers - Mameve
    Medwed   *c* 1067

McIntire, John
The Kingdom Where Nobody Dies - Kathleen
  Hills   *m* 100

McKelvey, Sam
One Night Stand - Cindy Kirk   *r* 314

McKenzie, Mike
Findings - Mary Anna Evans   *m* 67

Mendez, Jamie
Final Inquiries - Roger MacBride Allen   *s* 659

Morgan, Ethan
The Guardians - Jack Cavanaugh   *i* 921

Murdock, Leonard
Unquiet Dreams - Mark Del Franco   *f* 490

O'Malley, Mike
Pushing Up Daisies - Rosemary Harris   *m* 95

Oort, Richard
The Edge of Reason - Melinda Snodgrass   *f* 548

Ortega, Ron
White Soul - Brandt Dodson   *i* 929
White Soul - Brandt Dodson   *m* 56

Ottaviani, Elena
A Deadly Paradise - Grace Brophy   *m* 30

Owen, Gareth
Mark of the Pasha - Michael Pearce   *m* 146
Mark of the Pasha - Michael Pearce   *t* 871

Parker, Amos
In the Dead of Winter - Nancy Mehl   *i* 963

Parker, Daniel
Moving Target - Cheyenne McCray   *r* 346

Pearce, Daniel
The Wolfman - Nicholas Pekearo   *h* 628

Pitt, Thomas
Buckingham Palace Gardens - Anne
  Perry   *m* 148
Buckingham Palace Gardens - Anne Perry   *t* 872

Rand, J.D.
Sweet Caroline - Rachel Hauck   *i* 943

Riellen
The Time Engine - Sean McMullen   *f* 528

Riley, Tim
Death Song - Michael McGarrity   *w* 441

Rosen, Peter
Mummy Dearest - Joan Hess   *m* 97

Russell, Francis
Gas City - Loren D. Estleman   *m* 64

Sanchez, Alfred
The Automatic Detective - A. Lee
  Martinez   *s* 711

Sejer, Konrad
Black Seconds - Karin Fossum   *m* 76

Shippy, George
The Lazarus Project - Aleksandar Hemon   *t* 832

Stone, Henry
Curse of the Spellmans - Lisa Lutz   *m* 127
Curse of the Spellmans - Lisa Lutz   *c* 1063

Stride, Jonathan
Stalked - Brian Freeman   *m* 78

Stuart, Mikki
Farraday Road - Ace Collins   *i* 923

Theriot, Rene "Bubba"
Bayou Paradox - Robin Caroll   *i* 920

Van Alstyne, Russ
I Shall Not Want - Julia Spencer-Fleming   *m* 173

Winter, Oskar
A Paragon of Virtue - Christian Von
  Ditfurth   *c* 1099

A Paragon of Virtue - Christian Von
  Ditfurth   *m* 185

Wolfson, Hannah
Final Inquiries - Roger MacBride Allen   *s* 659

Wyatt, Gabriel
Pitch Black - Susan Crandall   *r* 248

POLITICAL FIGURE

Alden, Charles
Scandalous Lord, Rebellious Miss - Deb
  Marlowe   *r* 339

Bell, Hazel
Stretto - L. Timmel Duchamp   *s* 681

Benton, Emily
America the Beautiful - Laura Hayden   *i* 944

Churchill, Winston
Dreamers of the Day - Mary Doria
  Russell   *t* 883

Duval, Max
Between the Sheets - Robin Wells   *r* 390

Esterhouse, Joe
Road to Nowhere - Paul Robertson   *i* 982

Gilroy, Frances
The Truth Commissioner - David Park   *c* 1077

Hardie, Patricia
Null-A Continuum - John C. Wright   *s* 754

Hayden, Michael
Lorna - Debra White Smith   *i* 992

Kalamack, Trent
The Outlaw Demon Wails - Kim Harrison   *h* 599

Kincaid, Ben
Capitol Conspiracy - William Bernhardt   *m* 17

Leffler, Eric
Dead Time - Stephen White   *m* 194

Lincoln, Abraham
Pinkerton's Secret - Eric Lerner   *m* 122

Long, Bob
Dark Horse - Ralph Reed   *i* 980

MacPherson, James
Dead Heat - Joel C. Rosenberg   *i* 985

Mahoney, John
House Rules - Mike Lawson   *m* 120

Marlin, Stan
Open Line - Ellen Hawley   *c* 1053

Petty, David
Dark Horse - Ralph Reed   *i* 980

Richards, Vince
Wagered Heart - Robin Lee Hatcher   *i* 941

Rione, Victoria
Courageous - Jack Campbell   *s* 671

Roosevelt, Franklin Delano
Days of Infamy - Newt Gingrich   *t* 814

Stanley, Salmon
Dark Horse - Ralph Reed   *i* 980

Washington, George
Washington's Lady - Nancy Moser   *i* 970

POLITICIAN

B'Oraq
A Burning House - Keith R.A. DeCandido   *s* 678

POLOCE OFFICER

Fielding, Tom
Hex Marks the Spot - Madelyn Alt   *m* 7

POLTICAL FIGURE

Hitler, Adolf
1940 - Jay Neugeboren   *t* 862

POSTAL WORKER

Haristeen, Mary Minor
The Purrfect Murder - Rita Mae Brown   *m* 31

PRINCIPAL

Battle
Goodbye, Ms. Chips - Dorothy Cannell   *m* 36

PRISONER

Aleu, Joan
For a Sack of Bones - Lluis-Anton
  Baulenas   *t* 768

Algemeine, Marmion de Revers
Deluge - Anne McCaffrey   *s* 712

Bourne, Shay
Change of Heart - Jodi Picoult   *c* 1079

Day, Alfred
Day - A.L. Kennedy   *t* 843

McCallum, Duncan
Bone Rattler - Eliot Pattison   *m* 145

Milton, Danny
One Foot in the Grave - Jeaniene Frost   *h* 588

Parker, Nathan
Escape from Andersonville - Gene
  Hackman   *t* 822

Quinn, Johanna
A World Too Near - Kay Kenyon   *s* 699

Sedgewick, Alexandra
Stretto - L. Timmel Duchamp   *s* 681

Singer, Uri
Skeletons at the Feast - Chris Bohjalian   *c* 1017

PRIVATEER

Kingston, Basil
The Privateer - Dawn MacTavish   *r* 335

PRODUCER

Champion, Ella
Mystic Horseman - Kathleen Eagle   *r* 258
Mystic Horseman - Kathleen Eagle   *w* 414

Spencer, Suzy
The Chorister at the Abbey - Lis Howell   *m* 105

PROFESSOR

Bible, Thomas
Neuropath - Scott Bakker   *h* 565

Boaz, Jacyn
Hellbent & Heartfirst - Kassandra Sims   *r* 380

Broadhead, Kyle
Frames - Loren D. Estleman   *m* 63

Cohan, Josh
The Secret Scroll - Ronald Cutler   *m* 50

Gordon, Max
Practically Perfect - Katie Fforde   *c* 1039

Kenyon, Jack
Tower Hill - Sarah Pinborough   *h* 629

Loxley, Tom
The Lost Dog - Michelle de Kretser   *c* 1029

Maddox, Sadie
Act Two - Kimberly Stuart   *i* 995

Parmitter, Theo
The Man in the Picture - Susan Hill *h* 601

Sibisi, Bongani
A Carrion Death - Michael Stanley *m* 175

Stachelmann, Josef
A Paragon of Virtue - Christian Von
Ditfurth *c* 1099

A Paragon of Virtue - Christian Von
Ditfurth *m* 185

Wahl, Aaron
The Socorro Blast - Pari Noskin Taichert *m* 180

Waterman, Jamie
Mars Life - Ben Bova *s* 667

Williams, Leonard
Obedience - Will Lavender *m* 118

Wyman, Sean
The House on Fortune Street - Margot
Livesey *c* 1062

PROSTITUTE

Bates, Ruby
Scottsboro - Ellen Feldman *t* 803

Belov, Sandra
Kill Whitey - Brian Keene *h* 612

Bonnard, Francesca
Your Scandalous Ways - Loretta Chase *r* 242

Dooley, Etta Mae
Pax Dakota - Ken Rand *f* 540

Faith
Hungers of the Heart - Jenna Black *r* 223

McQueen, Dol
Missy - Chris Hannan *c* 1051
Missy - Chris Hannan *t* 828

Morley, Jen
The Chameleon's Shadow - Minette
Walters *m* 186

Sonia
Pavel & I - Dan Vyleta *t* 895

PSYCHIC

Adams, Mila
Being with Him - Jessica Inclan *r* 299

Azsla
Solar Heat - Susan Kearney *s* 698

Bain, Margaret
The Margarets - Sheri S. Tepper *s* 741

Bane, Darth
Rule of Two - Drew Karpyshyn *s* 697

Benares, Raine
Armed & Magical - Lisa Shearin *f* 547

Calhoun, Jesse
Predatory Game - Christine Feehan *r* 262

Canderous, Simon
Dead to Me - Anton Strout *f* 551

Chavet, Jean
The Cruelest Month - Louise Penny *m* 147

Christos, Connor
Dead to Me - Anton Strout *f* 551

Coyle, Carpathia
Dreamer - Paul L. Bates *s* 663

Daniels, Kiko
Midnight Reign - Chris Marie Green *h* 595

Darnell, Layla
The Hollow - Nora Roberts *r* 368

Darrow, Ashlyn
The Darkest Night - Gena Showalter *r* 379

Dubois, Simone
Dream Chaser - Sherrilyn Kenyon *r* 313

Grant, David
The Houses of Time - Jamil Nasir *s* 720

Gray Wolf, Jonah
The Healer - Sharon Sala *r* 371

Hatshep, Katerina
The Houses of Time - Jamil Nasir *s* 720

Hawkspar
Hawkspar - Holly Lisle *f* 521

Height, Jennie
Dreamer - Paul L. Bates *s* 663

Hewitt, Leona
The Third Circle - Amanda Quick *r* 362

Hilliard, Catherine
Silent Fall - Barbara Freethy *r* 265

Hope, Gabrielle
The Outsider - Ann H. Gabhart *i* 935

Jourdain, Michel
The Spiritualist - Megan Chance *m* 38

McClellan, Garrick
Being with Him - Jessica Inclan *r* 299

O'Dell, Fox
The Hollow - Nora Roberts *r* 368

Olson, Mignonette "Mimi"
Skinny Dipping - Connie Brockway *r* 232

Palmer, Cassandra
Embrace the Night - Karen Chance *f* 483

Storm, Tempest
A Stranger's Touch - Cait London *r* 331

Ware, Thaddeus
The Third Circle - Amanda Quick *r* 362

Waring, Eden
Avenging Fury - John Farris *h* 587

Wynter, Saber
Predatory Game - Christine Feehan *r* 262

Zannah
Rule of Two - Drew Karpyshyn *s* 697

PSYCHOLOGIST

Clark, Daniel
Adam - Ted Dekker *i* 926

Delaware, Alex
Compulsion - Jonathan Kellerman *m* 111

Denison, Skye
Murder of a Chocolate-Covered Cherry - Denise
Swanson *m* 177

Gregory, Alan
Dead Time - Stephen White *m* 194

Key, Gillian
Key to Conspiracy - Talia Gryphon *f* 508

Liebermann, Max
Vienna Blood - Frank Tallis *t* 890
Vienna Blood - Frank Tallis *m* 181

Rose, Kate
Pushing Up Bluebonnets - Leann
Sweeney *m* 178

PUBLIC RELATIONS

Doyle, Jack
Close Call - John McEvoy *m* 129

Matthews, Hannah
Seaview Inn - Sherryl Woods *r* 399

McCalley, Cash
To Wed a Texan - Georgina Gentry *r* 270

Piatro, Madeline
This Is How It Happened (Not a Love Story) - Jo
Barrett *r* 212

This Is How It Happened (Not a Love Story) - Jo
Barrett *c* 1011

Solomon, Sasha
The Socorro Blast - Pari Noskin Taichert *m* 180

PUBLISHER

Lord, Emma
The Alpine Traitor - Mary Daheim *m* 51

Nolan, Charlotte
Thieving Fear - Ramsey Campbell *h* 576

RADIO PERSONALITY

Boyd, Harry
Late Nights on Air - Elizabeth Hay *c* 1054

Lawrence, Kate
The Convenient Groom - Denise Hunter *i* 950

Majoris, Annette
Open Line - Ellen Hawley *c* 1053

Nickels, Mitchell Lee
South of Shiloh - Chuck Logan *m* 124

Paris, Dido
Late Nights on Air - Elizabeth Hay *c* 1054

Wynter, Saber
Predatory Game - Christine Feehan *r* 262

RAILROAD WORKER

Dunn, A.P.
Pelican Road - Howard Bahr *t* 762

Kane, Artemus
Pelican Road - Howard Bahr *t* 762

RAKE

Moncrief, Andrew
To Bed a Beauty - Nicole Jordan *r* 304

RANCHER

Allende, Enrique
Trail Hand - R.W. Stone *w* 456

Black, Dillon "Bear"
Mystic Horseman - Kathleen Eagle *r* 258
Mystic Horseman - Kathleen Eagle *w* 414

Caine, Jed
The Devil's Daughter - Laura Drewry *r* 256

Logan, Boone
River Range - L.P. Holmes *w* 425

Maxwell, Eden
Texas Loving - Leigh Greenwood *r* 277

McKenzie, Rafael
The Bride - Carolyn Davidson *r* 251

Paint, Eli
Sun Going Down - Jack Todd *c* 1097
Sun Going Down - Jack Todd *w* 457
Sun Going Down - Jack Todd *t* 892

Pickett, Joe
Free Fire - C.J. Box *w* 405

Rawlins, Jess
Blue Heaven - C.J. Box *m* 26

Targ, Jim
Grub Line Rider - Louis L'Amour *w* 436

RANGER

Pigeon, Anna
Winter Study - Nevada Barr   *m* 14

Reed, Kerry
Wild Inferno - Sandi Ault   *m* 11

Wild, Jamaica
Wild Inferno - Sandi Ault   *m* 11

REAL ESTATE AGENT

Fisher, Ryan
The Almost True Story of Ryan Fisher - Rob
   Stennett   *i* 994

Friedman, Karen
The Dark Tide - Andrew Gross   *m* 91

MacArthur
Whiskey and Water - Nina Wright   *m* 198

Mattimoe, Whiskey
Whiskey and Water - Nina Wright   *m* 198

REBEL

Aaron
Whitechapel Gods - S.M. Peters   *f* 538

Annie
Jemma7729 - Phoebe Wray   *s* 753

Bates, Abraham
Swiftly - Adam Roberts   *f* 543

Nassira
The Heart of Light - Sarah A. Hoyt   *f* 512

Oliver
Whitechapel Gods - S.M. Peters   *f* 538

Ro Laren
Night of the Wolves - S.D. Perry   *s* 723

RECLUSE

Ross, Stephen
My Immortal Protector - Jen Holling   *r* 293

REFUGEE

Krsmanovic, Aleksandar
How the Soldier Repairs the Gramophone - Sasa
   Stanisic   *c* 1091

Phillips, Jennifer
Birmingham, 35 Miles - James Braziel   *s* 668

RELATIVE

Paoletti, Silvana
Vita Nuova - Magdalen Nabb   *m* 141

Prescott, Angelica
Murder Is Binding - Lorna Barrett   *m* 15

Sweets, Edna
Of Blood and Sorrow - Valerie Wilson
   Wesley   *m* 190

RELIGIOUS

Alberoni
City of the Dead - Ian Morson   *t* 859

Appa
A Fire in the North - David Bilsborough   *f* 472

Atkins, Jonathan
Courting Emma - Sharlene MacLaren   *i* 961

Austin, Kayla
Full Circle - Davis Bunn   *i* 915

Barnabas
The Betrayal: The Lost Life of Jesus Christ - W.
   Michael Gear   *t* 811

Beecher, Henry Ward
Harriet and Isabella - Patricia O'Brien   *t* 865

Benito
Waking Brigid - Francis Clark   *h* 579

Berkana
Elom - William H. Drinkard   *f* 492

Cayal
The Immortal Prince - Jennifer Fallon   *f* 497

Cecely
The Apostate's Tale - Margaret Frazer   *t* 806

Clement VII
The Messiah - Marek Halter   *t* 827

Cormack
The Ancient - R.A. Salvatore   *f* 545

Eliot, Tom
The Shanghai Tunnel - Sharan Newman   *m* 143

Estanyol, Joan
Cathedral of the Sea - Ildefonso Falcones   *t* 802

Fardelver, Bellor
The Golden Cord - Paul Genesse   *f* 501

Fergusson, Clare
I Shall Not Want - Julia Spencer-Fleming   *m* 173

Fisher, Ryan
The Almost True Story of Ryan Fisher - Rob
   Stennett   *i* 994

Flint, Charles
Serpent Box - Vincent Louis Carrella   *c* 1022

Franco
The Dead & the Gone - Susan Beth
   Pfeffer   *s* 725

Frevisse
The Apostate's Tale - Margaret Frazer   *t* 806

Graziano, Agata
The Garden of Evil - David Hewson   *m* 98

Hazelius, Gregory
Blasphemy - Douglas Preston   *s* 726

Helewise
The Enchanter's Forest - Alys Clare   *t* 778

Hevelin
Provenance - Alex Archer   *f* 465

Inigo
The Dreaming Void - Peter F. Hamilton   *s* 690

Josan
The Final Sacrifice - Patricia Bray   *f* 475

Karna
Blind Faith - Sagarika Ghose   *c* 1045

Laurent
Blue Heart Blessed - Susan Meissner   *i* 964

Mark
Fall with Honor - E.E. Knight   *s* 701

McDowell, Joshua
The Wannoshay Cycle - Michael Jasper   *s* 694

Mitrofanii, Mishenka
Sister Pelagia and the Black Monk - Boris
   Akunin   *m* 4
Sister Pelagia and the Black Monk - Boris
   Akunin   *t* 757

Moran
Odd Hours - Dean R. Koontz   *h* 616

O'Bannon, Mangan
Wild Angel - Sasha Lord   *r* 332

O'Brien, Peter
Tower Hill - Sarah Pinborough   *h* 629

Olympias
Bring Down the Sun - Judith Tarr   *f* 552

Osen, Gar
Day of the Vipers - James Swallow   *s* 740

Parrish, Drew
Embrace Me - Lisa Samson   *i* 986

Pelagia
Sister Pelagia and the Black Monk - Boris
   Akunin   *m* 4
Sister Pelagia and the Black Monk - Boris
   Akunin   *t* 757

Perkins, Harvey
The Moon in the Mango Tree - Pamela Binnings
   Ewen   *i* 931

Picot, Rowley
The Serpent's Tale - Ariana Franklin   *m* 77

Pilazzo, Anthony
Fires Rising - Michael Laimo   *h* 617

Robinson, Ready
Unpretty - Sharon Carter Rogers   *i* 983

Rourke, Brigid
Waking Brigid - Francis Clark   *h* 579
Waking Brigid - Francis Clark   *t* 779

Ryder, Pierre
Luck - Max Brand   *w* 406

Selby, Eric
The Salisbury Manuscript - Philip Gooden   *m* 86

Stoltzfus, Levi
Ghost Walk - Brian Keene   *h* 611

Stone, William Edward
The Expeditions - Karl Iagnemma   *t* 837

RESCUER

Hunter, Rob
Practically Perfect - Katie Fforde   *c* 1039

RESEARCHER

Adair, Robin
Winter Study - Nevada Barr   *m* 14

Callister, Renee
Dead Silver - Neil McMahon   *m* 134

Heath, Hanna
People of the Book - Geraldine Brooks   *c* 1020
People of the Book - Geraldine Brooks   *t* 774

Levy, Rebecca
Skate Crime - Alina Adams   *m* 3

Luna, Erika
The Heartbreak Pill - Anjanette Delgado   *c* 1032

Townsend, Jared
Sweetheart Lost and Found - Shirley
   Jump   *r* 308

RESISTANCE FIGHTER

Fantini, Beppi
Lambrusco - Ellen Cooney   *t* 781

RESTAURATEUR

Andersson, Slobodan
The Demon of Dakar - Kjell Eriksson   *m* 62

Cash, Eric
Lush Life - Richard Price   *c* 1081

Dante, Anthony
Just a Taste - Deirdre Martin   *r* 340

Hewitt, Leona
Delicate Chaos - Jeff Buick   *m* 33

Robitaille, Vivi
Just a Taste - Deirdre Martin   *r* 340

Sweeney, Caroline
Sweet Caroline - Rachel Hauck   *i* 943

REVOLUTIONARY

Grace, Sophie
A Whisper of Freedom - Tricia Goyer   *i* 938

ROBOT

Hesperus
House of Chains - Alastair Reynolds   *s* 729

Megaton, Mack
The Automatic Detective - A. Lee
   Martinez   *s* 711

Spike
The Stone Gods - Jeanette Winterson   *c* 1103

ROGUE

McCalley, Cash
To Wed a Texan - Georgina Gentry   *r* 270

ROYALTY

Boleyn, Anne
In the Shadow of Lions - Ginger Garrett   *i* 936

Edward VII
Buckingham Palace Gardens - Anne Perry   *t* 872

Eleanor of Aquitaine
The Serpent's Tale - Ariana Franklin   *t* 804

Elisavyeta
The Romanov Bride - Robert Alexander   *t* 759

Garran
Shadow Magic - Cheyenne McCray   *r* 347

Gruadh
Lady Macbeth - Susan King   *t* 844

Isabella
The Templar, the Queen and Her Lover - Michael
   Jecks   *t* 839

Jamila of Alexandria
Crossed - Nicole Galland   *t* 809

Javier
The Queen's Bastard - C.E. Murphy   *f* 532

Jeremie
Mad Kestrel - Misty Massey   *f* 526

Koz, Qara
The Enchantress of Florence - Salman
   Rushdie   *t* 882

Lavinia
Lavinia - Ursula K. Le Guin   *t* 848

Macbeth
Lady Macbeth - Susan King   *t* 844

Maricara
Queen of Dragons - Shana Abe   *r* 200

Pahndir
Demon's Fire - Emma Holly   *r* 294

Panchaali
The Palace of Illusions - Chitra Banerjee
   Divakaruni   *t* 789

Popescu, Miranda
The Hidden World - David Gunn   *f* 509

Prokov, Alexander
To Wed a Wicked Prince - Jane Feather   *r* 261

Rainier
Tangled Webs - Anne Bishop   *f* 473

Sergei
The Romanov Bride - Robert Alexander   *t* 759

Tudor, Mary
The Secret Bride - Diane Haeger   *t* 823

Yudhisthir
The Palace of Illusions - Chitra Banerjee
   Divakaruni   *t* 789

Zarabeth
Highlander Ever After - Jennifer Ashley   *r* 205

RULER

Ahrmahk, Caleb
By Schism Rent Asunder - David Weber   *s* 747

Akbar the Great
The Enchantress of Florence - Salman
   Rushdie   *t* 882

Alfred
Sword Song - Bernard Cornwell   *t* 782

Anthony, Luke
The Martian General's Daughter - Theodore
   Judson   *s* 695

Bergamasc, Imre
Earth Ascendant - Sean Williams   *s* 751

Bonaparte, Napoleon
Victory of Eagles - Naomi Novik   *f* 535

ca'Ludovici, Kraljica Marguerite
A Magic of Twilight - S.L. Farrell   *f* 498

Dare, Anne
The Born Queen - Greg Keyes   *f* 516

Elizabeth I
Ink and Steel - Elizabeth Bear   *f* 469
The Lady Elizabeth - Alison Weir   *t* 896

Garlin, Kelrickson
The Ruby Dice - Catherine Asaro   *s* 662

Henry II
The Serpent's Tale - Ariana Franklin   *t* 804

Henry VIII
In the Shadow of Lions - Ginger Garrett   *i* 936
The Lady Elizabeth - Alison Weir   *t* 896
The Secret Bride - Diane Haeger   *t* 823

James IV
Flodden Field - Elisabeth McNeill   *t* 858

Korox
Obsidian Ridge - Jess Lebow   *f* 520

Latinus
Lavinia - Ursula K. Le Guin   *t* 848

Letrin
The Ruby Key - Holly Lisle   *f* 522

Lorraine
The Queen's Bastard - C.E. Murphy   *f* 532

Louis XIV
Mistress of the Sun - Sandra Gulland   *t* 820

Lucius
The Final Sacrifice - Patricia Bray   *f* 475

Mab
Ink and Steel - Elizabeth Bear   *f* 469
Small Favor - Jim Butcher   *f* 480

Machi, Otah
An Autumn War - Daniel Abraham   *f* 462

Mary I
The Lady Elizabeth - Alison Weir   *t* 896

Nezhuala
The Infinite Day - Chris Walley   *i* 1001

OctoV
Maximum Offense - David Gunn   *s* 689

Qox, Jaibriol
The Ruby Dice - Catherine Asaro   *s* 662

Sengar, Rhulad
Reaper's Gale - Steven Erikson   *f* 496

Sforza, Ludovico
The Queen's Gambit - Diane A.S. Stuckart   *t* 889

Solo, Jacen
Revelation - Karen Traviss   *s* 743

Teraf
Emerald Silk - Janet Lane   *r* 321

Varis
The Vacant Throne - Joshua Palmatier   *f* 537

Victoria
A Flaw in the Blood - Stephanie Barron   *t* 767

Ysandre
Kushiel's Mercy - Jacqueline Carey   *f* 482

Zev
The Valley-Westside War - Harry
   Turtledove   *s* 744

RUNAWAY

Hall, Nicole
Desert Cut - Betty Webb   *m* 187

SAILOR

al-Wazir, Threadgill Angus
Escapement - Jay Lake   *f* 518

Kestrel
Mad Kestrel - Misty Massey   *f* 526

SALESMAN

Fellows, Rob
Madhouse - Rob Thurman   *f* 554

Fink, Russell
My Name Is Russell Fink - Michael
   Snyder   *i* 993

Springer, Jack
A Curse Dark as Gold - Elizabeth C.
   Bunce   *f* 479

Tate, Mortimer
Go-Go Girls of the Apocalypse - Victor
   Gischler   *s* 687

SALESWOMAN

Andrews, Marty
The Accidental Werewolf - Dakota Cassidy   *r* 239

Armitage, Lucy
Rookhurst Hall - Elizabeth Jeffrey   *r* 301

Sumrall, Bobbie Faye
*Bobbie Faye's (kinda, sorta, not-exactly) Family
   Jewels* - Toni McGee Causey   *r* 241

SALOON KEEPER/OWNER

Scully, Jake
The Redemption of Jake Scully - Elaine
   Barbieri   *i* 909

SCHOLAR

Arellano, Carmen
The Undead Kama Sutra - Mario
   Acevedo   *h* 561

Blake, Sophie
Duke Most Wanted - Celeste Bradley   *r* 226

Bookless, Tony
The Crystal Skull - Manda Scott   *f* 546

Desean, Arkady
The Immortal Prince - Jennifer Fallon   *f* 497

Mahklyn, Rahzhyr
By Schism Rent Asunder - David Weber   *s* 747
Oliver
The Man in the Picture - Susan Hill   *h* 601
Owen, Cedric
The Crystal Skull - Manda Scott   *f* 546
The Crystal Skull - Manda Scott   *m* 167
Stephomi
The Ninth Circle - Alex Bell   *f* 470
Westbury, Charles
Cezanne's Quarry - Barbara Pope   *t* 873

SCIENTIST

Armstrong, Dana
Captivity - Debbie Lee Wesselmann   *c* 1102
Bentley, Robert
The Dark Lantern - Gerri Brightwell   *m* 28
Boyle, Gary
Flood - Stephen Baxter   *s* 664
Callister, Renee
Dead Silver - Neil McMahon   *m* 134
Campbell, Margaret
The Killing Room - Peter May   *m* 128
Carleton, Carter
Mars Life - Ben Bova   *s* 667
Cody, Stella
The Crystal Skull - Manda Scott   *m* 167
The Crystal Skull - Manda Scott   *f* 546
Conrad, Cameron
Omega Sol - Scott Mackay   *s* 708
Ford, Marion "Doc"
Black Widow - Randy Wayne White   *m* 193
Fox, Matthew
The Adoration of Jenna Fox - Mary E.
   Pearson   *s* 722
Griffin, Sloan
Spider Star - Mike Brotherton   *s* 669
Hazelius, Gregory
Blasphemy - Douglas Preston   *s* 726
Kurtz, Ken
Even Cat Sitters Get the Blues - Blaize
   Clement   *m* 40
Mackey, David
The Margarets - Sheri S. Tepper   *s* 741
Maguire, Leah
The Last Vampire - Patricia Rosemoor   *h* 632
McManus, Doreen
Mars Life - Ben Bova   *s* 667
Montoya, Margaret
Infected - Scott Sigler   *s* 736
O'Connor, Kit
The Crystal Skull - Manda Scott   *m* 167
Parker-Roth, John
The Naked Gentleman - Sally MacKenzie   *r* 334
Pattaya, Ami
Blue War - Jeffrey Thomas   *s* 742
Peterson, Dani
Strong and Sexy - Jill Shalvis   *r* 377
Pol, Mora
Night of the Wolves - S.D. Perry   *s* 723
Shearer, Marc
Moon Flower - James P. Hogan   *s* 692
Tesla, Nikola
The Invention of Everything Else - Samantha
   Hunt   *c* 1055

The Invention of Everything Else - Samantha
   Hunt   *t* 836
Thompson, Benjamin
The Count of Concord - Nicholas
   Delbanco   *t* 784
Wade, Evan
Moon Flower - James P. Hogan   *s* 692
Weaver, William
Manxome Foe - John Ringo   *s* 730
Weeks, Lesha
Omega Sol - Scott Mackay   *s* 708

SEA CAPTAIN

Anderson, Boyd
No Choice but Seduction - Johanna
   Lindsey   *r* 329
Binns, Artemus
Mad Kestrel - Misty Massey   *f* 526
Leighton, Cole
Rogue - Kayla Gray   *r* 275
Reddy, Matthew Patrick
Into the Storm - Taylor Anderson   *s* 661
Rose, Nilus
The Red Wolf Conspiracy - Robert V.S.
   Redick   *f* 541
Trapp, Edward
Trapp's Secret War - Brian Callison   *t* 775

SEAMSTRESS

Bosworth, Prudence
The Wicked Ways of a Duke - Laura Lee
   Guhrke   *r* 278
Newbury, Catherine
A Lady of Hidden Intent - Tracie Peterson   *i* 976

SECRETARY

Armitage, Lucy
Rookhurst Hall - Elizabeth Jeffrey   *r* 301
Daisy
An Ordinary Spy - Joseph Weisberg   *m* 188
Gibson, Alex
The Chorister at the Abbey - Lis Howell   *m* 105
Pangborn, Kitty
Death Was the Other Woman - Linda L.
   Richards   *t* 879

SECURITY OFFICER

Campbell, Jack
Worlds on Fire - Matthew J. Costello   *s* 675
Hawthorne, Anne
Stretto - L. Timmel Duchamp   *s* 681

SERIAL KILLER

Berger, Wencke
What Never Happens - Anne Holt   *m* 102
Eve
Adam - Ted Dekker   *i* 926
Glenn, Theodore
Killing Fear - Allison Brennan   *r* 229
Mallick, Simon
The Calling - Inger Wolfe   *m* 197
Mosley, Randall
The Killer's Wife - Bill Floyd   *m* 73
Olbricht, Andreas
Vienna Blood - Frank Tallis   *m* 181

Pudge
The Murder Game - Beverly Barton   *r* 213

SERVANT

Barnes, Charlie
Fateful Voyage - Pamela Oldfield   *t* 866
Bradley, Grace Reeves
The House at Riverton - Kate Morton   *m* 139
Cole, Alice
Bound - Sally Gunning   *t* 821
Dewell, Louisa
The Invention of Everything Else - Samantha
   Hunt   *t* 836
The Invention of Everything Else - Samantha
   Hunt   *c* 1055
Dino
The Queen's Gambit - Diane A.S. Stuckart   *t* 889
Esperanza
Bright Shiny Morning - James Frey   *c* 1041
Jamison, Emma
Between the Sheets - Robin Wells   *r* 390
Lily
The Adoration of Jenna Fox - Mary E.
   Pearson   *s* 722
Reeves, Grace
The House at Riverton - Kate Morton   *t* 860
Rondeau
Poison Sleep - T.A. Pratt   *f* 539
SuMing
A World Too Near - Kay Kenyon   *s* 699
Wilbred, Jane
The Dark Lantern - Gerri Brightwell   *t* 773
The Dark Lantern - Gerri Brightwell   *m* 28

SETTLER

Keating, Chris
Marseguro - Edward Willett   *s* 748
Sister
Daughters of the North - Sarah Hall   *c* 1049

SIDEKICK

Coleman
Atomic Lobster - Tim Dorsey   *m* 57
Lula
Fearless Fourteen - Janet Evanovich   *m* 65
Somnambulist
The Somnambulist - Jonathan Barnes   *t* 766
The Somnambulist - Jonathan Barnes   *m* 13

SINGER

Amato, Tito
Iron Tongue of Midnight - Beverle Graves
   Myers   *t* 861
The Iron Tongue of Midnight - Beverle Graves
   Myers   *m* 140
Broadus, Jimmy Wayne
Hellbent & Heartfirst - Kassandra Sims   *r* 380
Culpepper, Denny
Return of the Stardust Cowgirl - Marsha
   Moyer   *w* 442
de la Fontaine, Rosalind
Wizard's Daughter - Catherine Coulter   *r* 246
Fantini, Lucia
Lambrusco - Ellen Cooney   *t* 781

Farrell, Ash
Return of the Stardust Cowgirl - Marsha Moyer *w* 442

Fouquet, Gabrielle
The Iron Tongue of Midnight - Beverle Graves Myers *m* 140

Joselyn, Suzette
The Last Warrior - Karen Kay *r* 309

Maddox, Sadie
Act Two - Kimberly Stuart *i* 995

McCray, Bryce
Wearing My Halo Tilted - Stephanie Perry Moore *i* 966

O'Neal, Mitch
Sweet Caroline - Rachel Hauck *i* 943

Perkins, Barbara Bond
The Moon in the Mango Tree - Pamela Binnings Ewen *i* 931

Pope, Valerie
The Blue Door - David Fulmer *m* 79

SINGLE PARENT

Arseneux, Celine
Wild Jinx - Sandra Hill *r* 292

Bombay, Dakota
Guns Will Keep Us Together - Leslie Langtry *r* 322

Burke, Cassidy
A Fiend in Need - Maureen Child *r* 243

Culpepper, Miranda
Bring Your Own Poison - Jimmie Ruth Evans *m* 66

Hughes, Ray
A Soldier Comes Home - Cindi Myers *r* 352

Keating, Libby
Fatal Deduction - Gayle Roper *i* 984

Knight, Wyatt
Sweet Talk - Susan Mallery *r* 337

Laurent, Ramsey
Blue Heart Blessed - Susan Meissner *i* 964

Murphy, Annabelle
The Art of Keeping Secrets - Patti Callahan Henry *r* 291

Nash, Tom
The Paper Marriage - Susan Kay Law *r* 324

Paoletti, Daniela
Vita Nuova - Magdalen Nabb *m* 141

Petterman, Daniel
Chances - Pamela Nowak *r* 356

Sinclair, Adrian
For Pete's Sake - Linda Windsor *i* 1005

Tremain, Lake
Belong to Me - Marisa de los Santos *c* 1030

White, Kate
Guilty - Karen Robards *r* 367

Winslow, Marty
Tuesday Night at the Blue Moon - Debbie Fuller Thomas *i* 998

SLAVE

Aaran
Hawkspar - Holly Lisle *f* 521

Anderson, George "Free"
Ambush at Mustang Canyon - Mike Kearby *w* 430
The Road to a Hanging - Mike Kearby *w* 431

Brady
A Fiend in Need - Maureen Child *r* 243

Lirya
Shadow Gate - Kate Elliott *f* 495

Mason, Clara
The Road to a Hanging - Mike Kearby *w* 431

Minden, Hans
Caliphate - Tom Kratman *s* 703

Minden, Petra
Caliphate - Tom Kratman *s* 703

Ongamar
The Margarets - Sheri S. Tepper *s* 741

Redbird
Hawkspar - Holly Lisle *f* 521

Spocott, Liz
Song Yet Sung - James McBride *t* 856

SMUGGLER

Renard
Innocence Unveiled - Blythe Gifford *r* 271

SOCIAL WORKER

Dombrowski, Duffy
TKO - Tom Schreck *m* 165

SOCIALITE

Ashbury, Hannah
The House at Riverton - Kate Morton *t* 860

Cole, Vanessa
The Reserve - Russell Banks *t* 763

Dante, Tiffany
Poisoned Tarts - G.A. McKevett *m* 133

Fisher, Phryne
Queen of the Flowers - Kerry Greenwood *m* 89

Hartford, Emmeline
The House at Riverton - Kate Morton *m* 139

Pitt, Charlotte
Buckingham Palace Gardens - Anne Perry *t* 872

Price, Sylvia
Blood Alley - Tom Coffey *m* 42

Rhode, Kendra
Cheating at Solitaire - Jane Haddam *m* 92

SORCERER

Cortez, Lucas
Personal Demons - Kelley Armstrong *h* 564

Grayle, Lincoln
Avenging Fury - John Farris *h* 587

Japanangka, Blakie
Moonlight Downs - Adrian Hyland *m* 106

Josiah
Dagger-Star - Elizabeth Vaughan *r* 387

Putin, Zakhar "Whitey"
Kill Whitey - Brian Keene *h* 612

Rahl
Mage-Guard of Honor - L. E. Modesitt Jr. *f* 529

Ravirn
CodeSpell - Kelly McCullough *f* 527

Seabourne, Cullen
Night Season - Eileen Wilks *r* 395

SORCERESS

Averil
The Golden Rose - Kathleen Bryan *f* 478

Blue Queen
The Key to Rondo - Emily Rodda *f* 544

Dallandra
The Shadow Isle - Katharine Kerr *f* 515

Davinovitch, Rhiana
The Edge of Reason - Melinda Snodgrass *f* 548

Kelley, Genevieve
Poison Sleep - T.A. Pratt *f* 539

Mason, Marla
Poison Sleep - T.A. Pratt *f* 539

Zaltana, Yelena
Fire Study - Maria V. Snyder *f* 549

SPACEMAN

Corsaire, Victor
Space Vulture - Gary K. Wolf *s* 752

Morgan, Jack
Dragon and Liberator - Timothy Zahn *s* 755

Quinn, Titus
A World Too Near - Kay Kenyon *s* 699

Shaeffer, Beowulf
Juggler of Worlds - Larry Niven *s* 721

Space Vulture
Space Vulture - Gary K. Wolf *s* 752

Truffaut, Jules
Galaxy Blues - Allen Steele *s* 737

Vickers
Relentless - Richard Williams *s* 750

SPACESHIP CAPTAIN

Bandar, Brit
Moonstruck - Susan Grant *r* 273

Becket
Relentless - Richard Williams *s* 750

Campion
House of Chains - Alastair Reynolds *s* 729

Cole, Wilson
Starship Mercenary - Mike Resnick *s* 728

Desjani, Tanya
Valiant - Jack Campbell *s* 672

Geary, John
Valiant - Jack Campbell *s* 672

Papadopulos, Apollo
Singularity's Ring - Paul Melko *s* 715

Purslane
House of Chains - Alastair Reynolds *s* 729

Valkyrie
Starship Mercenary - Mike Resnick *s* 728

Vatta, Ty
Victory Conditions - Elizabeth Moon *s* 719

SPACEWOMAN

Jax, Sirantha
Grimspace - Ann Aguirre *s* 658

Thompson, Rain
Galaxy Blues - Allen Steele *s* 737

SPINSTER

Crowley, Jewel
Jewel - Beverly Jenkins *r* 302

Spreckelmeyer, Essie
Deep in the Heart of Trouble - Deeanne Gist *i* 937

Wyngate, Irene
The Bridal Quest - Candace Camp *r* 237

SPIRIT

Dorenfield, Alex
The Ten Best Days of My Life - Adena Halpern *c* 1050

Irene
Dead to Me - Anton Strout *f* 551

Laress, Neomi
Dark Deeds at Night's Edge - Kresley Cole *r* 245

Shepard, Jack
The Ghost and the Femme Fatale - Alice Kimberly *m* 113

Torrington, Abigail
Vicious Circle - Mike Carey *h* 577

Westwood, Dimity
Aunt Dimity: Vampire Hunter - Nancy Atherton *m* 10

SPORTS FIGURE

Calhoun, Ty
Game for Anything - Bella Andre *r* 201

Cero, Eddie
The Blue Door - David Fulmer *m* 79

Dombrowski, Duffy
TKO - Tom Schreck *m* 165

Gibson, Josh
The End of Baseball - Peter Schilling *t* 885

Hogan, Ben
The Caddie Who Played with Hickory - John Coyne *t* 783

Jackson, Percy
Safe at Home - Richard Doster *i* 930

Nash, Tom
The Paper Marriage - Susan Kay Law *r* 324

Page, Satchel
The End of Baseball - Peter Schilling *t* 885

Richardson, Matt
The Caddie Who Played with Hickory - John Coyne *t* 783

Sophie
Choosing Sophie - Leslie Carroll *c* 1023

Stryker, Brek
Strike Zone - Kate Angell *r* 203

SPORTSWRITER

Hall, Jack
Safe at Home - Richard Doster *i* 930

SPOUSE

Aeneas
Lavinia - Ursula K. Le Guin *t* 848

Andersen, Spencer
This Side of Heaven - Anna Schmidt *r* 375

Andy
Love the One You're With - Emily Giffin *c* 1046

Armstrong, Ronald
A Tissue of Lies - Tessa Barclay *t* 764

Barton, Lisa
A Matter of Wife and Death - Ginger Kolbaba *i* 954

Bascombe, Kelly
A Match Made in Hell - Terri Garey *h* 589

Bentley, Mina
The Dark Lantern - Gerri Brightwell *m* 28

Braxton, Justin
You Gotta Sin to Get Saved - J.D. Mason *r* 341

Brown, Cornelia
Belong to Me - Marisa de los Santos *c* 1030

Calpurnia
The Triumph of Caesar - Steven Saylor *t* 884

Claudia
The Moneylender of Toulouse - Alan Gordon *m* 87
The Moneylender of Toulouse - Alan Gordon *t* 817

Cook, Holland
The Story of a Marriage - Andrew Sean Greer *c* 1047
The Story of a Marriage - Andrew Sean Greer *t* 819

Cook, Pearlie
The Story of a Marriage - Andrew Sean Greer *t* 819
The Story of a Marriage - Andrew Sean Greer *c* 1047

Cooper, Grace MacVicar
Always Grace - Tim LaHaye *i* 957

Cormia
Lover Enshrined - J.R. Ward *r* 388

Corvill, Jenny
A Tissue of Lies - Tessa Barclay *t* 764

Cross, Johnnie
The World Before Her - Deborah Weisgall *t* 897

Cunningham, Alys Mason
The Rough Collier - Pat McIntosh *m* 132

Davidson, Richmond
Dream of Love - Michael Phillips *i* 977

de Peyre
Mistress of the Revolution - Catherine Delors *t* 785

Dean
They Did It with Love - Kate Morgenroth *m* 137

Demidov, Raisa
Child 44 - Tom Rob Smith *m* 171

Dempsey, Ellen
Love the One You're With - Emily Giffin *c* 1046

Dennis, Anna
Miscarriage of Justice - Kip Gayden *t* 810

Doolittle, Claire
Sleeping with Ward Cleaver - Jenny Gardiner *r* 267

Doolittle, Jack
Sleeping with Ward Cleaver - Jenny Gardiner *r* 267

Ericson, Reece
Anathema - Colleen Coble *i* 922

Fairchild, Tom
The Body in the Gallery - Katherine Hall Page *m* 144

Farquharson, Anne
White Rose Rebel - Janet Paisley *t* 867

Farrell, Ash
Return of the Stardust Cowgirl - Marsha Moyer *w* 442

Fenwick, Johnny
Silver Street - Elizabeth Gill *t* 813

Fielding, Nan
Silver Street - Elizabeth Gill *t* 813

Flanagan, Ellen
House and Home - Kathleen McCleary *r* 344

Flanagan, Sam
House and Home - Kathleen McCleary *r* 344

Flint, Rebecca
Serpent Box - Vincent Louis Carrella *c* 1022

Frank, Eva
The German Bride - Joanna Hershon *w* 423
The German Bride - Joanna Hershon *t* 834

Gavin, Olivia
Let the Night Begin - Kathryn Smith *h* 642

Hall, Rose Marie
Safe at Home - Richard Doster *i* 930

Hallam, Hugh
Hallam's War - Elisabeth Payne Rosen *t* 880

Hallam, Serena
Hallam's War - Elisabeth Payne Rosen *t* 880

Hanes, Ashley
Winter Turns to Spring - Catherine Palmer *i* 971

Hanes, Brad
Winter Turns to Spring - Catherine Palmer *i* 971

Haristeen, Pharamond
The Purrfect Murder - Rita Mae Brown *m* 31

Hatch, Lucy
Return of the Stardust Cowgirl - Marsha Moyer *w* 442

Hulst, Trudy
Trudy's Promise - Marcia Preston *c* 1080

Karin
Dogwood - Chris Fabry *i* 932

Kennedy, Joseph
The Importance of Being Kennedy - Laurie Graham *t* 818

Kennedy, Rose
The Importance of Being Kennedy - Laurie Graham *t* 818

Kessler, Ivy
The Grand Scheme - Kathy Herman *i* 945

Kitty
Playing with the Grown-Ups - Sophie Dahl *c* 1027

Larson, McLane
She Always Wore Red - Angela Hunt *i* 949

Lavinia
Lavinia - Ursula K. Le Guin *t* 848

Leta
The Well and the Mine - Gin Phillips *c* 1078

Luxton, Hannah Hartford
The House at Riverton - Kate Morton *m* 139

Macintosh, Aeneas
White Rose Rebel - Janet Paisley *t* 867

Manns, Darryl
The Truth about Love - Tia McCollors *i* 962

Manns, Paula
The Truth about Love - Tia McCollors *i* 962

Marsden, Stefanie
The Vow - Rebecca Winters *r* 396

McCall, Christina
Capitol Conspiracy - William Bernhardt *m* 17

Miller, James
Isolation - Travis Thrasher *i* 999

Miller, Stephanie
Isolation - Travis Thrasher *i* 999

Mitchell, Mark
The Restorer's Journey - Sharon Hinck *i* 947

Mitchell, Ruth
The Night Following - Morag Joss *m* 110

Mitchell, Susan
The Restorer's Journey - Sharon Hinck *i* 947

Moffat, Donica Lenore
The Comfort of Our Kind - Tom Stoner *c* 1093

Moffat, Wes
The Comfort of Our Kind - Tom Stoner *c* 1093

Montserrat, Gabrielle de
Mistress of the Revolution - Catherine
    Delors *t* 785

Mullen, Brian
Scared to Live - Stephen Booth *m* 22

Ortega, Libby
White Soul - Brandt Dodson *m* 56

Owen, Zeinab
Mark of the Pasha - Michael Pearce *m* 146

Paint, Cora
Sun Going Down - Jack Todd *t* 892

Paint, Ebenezar
Sun Going Down - Jack Todd *t* 892

Pitt, Charlotte
Buckingham Palace Gardens - Anne Perry *t* 872

Pitt, Thomas
Buckingham Palace Gardens - Anne Perry *t* 872
Buckingham Palace Gardens - Anne
    Perry *m* 148

Plaisance, Mimi
A Matter of Wife and Death - Ginger
    Kolbaba *i* 954

Powerscourt, Lucy
Death on the Holy Mountain - David
    Dickinson *t* 786

Rema
Atmospheric Disturbances - Rivka
    Galchen *c* 1043

Roarke
Strangers in Death - J.D. Robb *s* 731

Sam
Standing Still - Kelly Simmons *c* 1089

Shein, Abraham
The German Bride - Joanna Hershon *w* 423
The German Bride - Joanna Hershon *t* 834

Shores, Jennifer
A Matter of Wife and Death - Ginger
    Kolbaba *i* 954

Skye, Mary
Virgin River - Richard S. Wheeler *w* 459

Skye, Victoria
The Canyon of Bones - Richard S.
    Wheeler *w* 458
Virgin River - Richard S. Wheeler *w* 459

Stiffeniis, Helena
Days of Atonement - Michael Gregorio *m* 90

Stokes, Belinda
The Truth about Love - Tia McCollors *i* 962

Syler-Boatwright, Gaylen
Painted Dresses - Patricia Hickman *i* 946

Tilden, Maddie Foster
Beyond the Night - Marlo Schalesky *i* 987

Tilden, Paul
Beyond the Night - Marlo Schalesky *i* 987

Unnamed Character
The Night Following - Morag Joss *m* 110
The Night Following - Morag Joss *c* 1056

Vik, Johanne
What Never Happens - Anne Holt *m* 102

Washington, Martha Custis
Washington's Lady - Nancy Moser *i* 970

Wilson-Black, Monica
Mystic Horseman - Kathleen Eagle *w* 414

Wingfield, Zoe
This Side of Heaven - Anna Schmidt *r* 375

Wycznewski, Ruby
Hooked Up - Joyce Lavene *m* 119

Zeinab
Mark of the Pasha - Michael Pearce *t* 871

SPY

Alsworthy, Mary
The Seduction of the Crimson Rose - Lauren
    Willig *t* 901

Atwood, Simon
His Dark and Dangerous Ways - Edith
    Layton *r* 325

Ausfaller, Sigmund
Juggler of Worlds - Larry Niven *s* 721

Azsla
Solar Heat - Susan Kearney *s* 698

Bennett, Erin
Dead Heat - Joel C. Rosenberg *i* 985

Brett, Harry
Winter in Madrid - C.J. Sansom *m* 161

Burke, Garrett
A Notorious Proposition - Adele Ashworth *r* 206

Comfort, Harry
The Prince of Bagram Prison - Alex Carr *m* 37

Cordier, James
Your Scandalous Ways - Loretta Chase *r* 242

d'Agelet, Helene
Bond of Fire - Diane Whiteside *r* 391

Donavon, Pen
The Unnatural Inquirer - Simon R. Green *f* 505

Faraday, Joel
Overnight Male - Elizabeth Bevarly *r* 220

Federin
Principles of Angels - Jaine Fenn *s* 685

Goldstein, Bobby
An Ordinary Spy - Joseph Weisberg *m* 188

Grey, Robert
The Spymaster's Lady - Joanna Bourne *r* 224

Hargreaves, Colin
A Fatal Waltz - Tasha Alexander *m* 6

Harper, Jonathan
The Invisible - Andrew Britton *m* 29

Haskell, Claire
Mirrored Heaven - David J. Williams *s* 749

Karish, Shintaro
Heroes Adrift - Moira J. Moore *f* 531

Kealey, Ryan
The Invisible - Andrew Britton *m* 29

Kharmai, Naomi
The Invisible - Andrew Britton *m* 29

Larkin, Reed
Right Here, Right Now - HelenKay Dimon *r* 254

Lewis, Molly
Severance Package - Duane
    Swierczynski *m* 179

Mallorough, Lee
Heroes Adrift - Moira J. Moore *f* 531

Marcellus, Lucius Aurelius
Buried Too Deep - Jane Finnis *m* 70

March
Grimspace - Ann Aguirre *s* 658

Marlowe, Jason
Mirrored Heaven - David J. Williams *s* 749

Mercier, Jean-Francois
The Spies of Warsaw - Alan Furst *t* 807
The Spies of Warsaw - Alan Furst *m* 80

Moreau, Lila
Overnight Male - Elizabeth Bevarly *r* 220

Mundy, Adele
When the Tide Rises - David Drake *s* 680

Noble, Archie
The Reavers - George Macdonald Fraser *t* 805

Oldhall, Nigel
The Heart of Light - Sarah A. Hoyt *f* 512

Orlov, Alexandr
Seduced by a Spy - Andrea Pickens *r* 359

Ott, Sandor
The Red Wolf Conspiracy - Robert V.S.
    Redick *f* 541

Petrova, Alexandra
The Accident Man - Tom Cain *m* 35

Primrose, Belinda
The Queen's Bastard - C.E. Murphy *f* 532

Prokov, Alexander
To Wed a Wicked Prince - Jane Feather *r* 261

Renard
Innocence Unveiled - Blythe Gifford *r* 271

Ruttenberg, Mark
An Ordinary Spy - Joseph Weisberg *m* 188

St. Just, Jean-Marie
Bond of Fire - Diane Whiteside *r* 391

Shannon
Seduced by a Spy - Andrea Pickens *r* 359

Stocking, John
Johnny One-Eye - Jerome Charyn *t* 776

Stone, Caleb
No Control - Shannon K. Butcher *r* 233

Taro
Principles of Angels - Jaine Fenn *s* 685

Theophilos
The Moneylender of Toulouse - Alan
    Gordon *m* 87
The Moneylender of Toulouse - Alan
    Gordon *t* 817

Uhl, Edvard
The Spies of Warsaw - Alan Furst *t* 807

Valek
Fire Study - Maria V. Snyder *f* 549

Villiers, Annique
The Spymaster's Lady - Joanna Bourne *r* 224

von Lange, Kristiana
A Fatal Waltz - Tasha Alexander *m* 6

Wentworth, Ivy
A Notorious Proposition - Adele Ashworth *r* 206

STATISTICIAN

Townsend, Jared
Sweetheart Lost and Found - Shirley
    Jump *r* 308

STEP-PARENT

Cloyd
The Flowers - Dagoberto Gilb *w* 418

Stokes, Belinda
The Truth about Love - Tia McCollors *i* 962

STORE OWNER

Charbonneau, Yanne
The Girl with No Shadow - Joanne Harris   *c* 1052

Daniels, Allie
Twisted Creek - Jodi Thomas   *r* 385

Dawe, Fletcher
Train to Yesterday - Nell DuVall   *r* 257

Flores, Gaby
Truffles by the Sea - Julie Carobini   *i* 919

Goldstein, Hayley Maitland
Just Desserts - Barbara Bretton   *r* 230

Knight, Abby
A Rose from the Dead - Kate Collins   *m* 45

Malloy, Claire
Mummy Dearest - Joan Hess   *m* 97

McGuire, Abby
Promise Me Tomorrow - Linda Ingmanson   *r* 300

Miles, Tricia
Murder Is Binding - Lorna Barrett   *m* 15

Murien, Daisy
Blue Heart Blessed - Susan Meissner   *i* 964

Silver, Carly
Call of the Highland Moon - Kendra Leigh Castle   *r* 240

Styx, Nicki
A Match Made in Hell - Terri Garey   *h* 589

Thornton-McClure, Penelope
The Ghost and the Femme Fatale - Alice Kimberly   *m* 113

Towers, Samantha "Ivy"
In the Dead of Winter - Nancy Mehl   *i* 963

Vane, Leticia
The Flirt - Kathleen Tessaro   *r* 384

STREETPERSON

Anders
Pavel & I - Dan Vyleta   *t* 895

Joe
Bright Shiny Morning - James Frey   *c* 1041

STRIPPER

McKenna, Robin
Killing Fear - Allison Brennan   *r* 229

STUDENT

Danvers, Claire
Feast of Fools - Rachel Caine   *h* 573

Hamilton, John
Caliphate - Tom Kratman   *s* 703

Hamley, Larkyn
Airs and Graces - Toby Bishop   *f* 474

Jackson, Deborah Lee
Better Than - Leslie Esdaile   *r* 260

Kendall, Phoebe
Generation Dead - Daniel Waters   *h* 648

Leland, Penelope
Bewitching Season - Marissa Doyle   *f* 491

Leland, Persephone
Bewitching Season - Marissa Doyle   *f* 491

Martinsburg, Pete
Generation Dead - Daniel Waters   *h* 648

Naomi
Imagine Me and You - Billy Mernit   *c* 1068

Naro, John
The Disagreement - Nick Taylor   *t* 891

Rajasekharan, Uma
Evening Is the Whole Day - Preeta Samarasan   *c* 1086

Rosser, Eve
Feast of Fools - Rachel Caine   *h* 573

Seeker After Truth
Noman - William Nicholson   *f* 533

Stuart, Lexi
Bon Appetit - Sandra Byrd   *i* 916

Thom
Havemercy - Jaida Jones   *f* 513

Wharton, Steve
Tower Hill - Sarah Pinborough   *h* 629

Williams, Tommy
Generation Dead - Daniel Waters   *h* 648

Zannah
Rule of Two - Drew Karpyshyn   *s* 697

STUDENT—BOARDING SCHOOL

Jones, Jamison
Stalking Death - Kate Flora   *m* 72

Jones, Shondra
Stalking Death - Kate Flora   *m* 72

STUDENT—COLLEGE

Avery, Summer
Getting Away Is Deadly - Sara Rosett   *m* 159

Butler, Mary
Obedience - Will Lavender   *c* 1061
Obedience - Will Lavender   *m* 118

Fanta
Frames - Loren D. Estleman   *m* 63

Flaherty, Dennis
Obedience - Will Lavender   *c* 1061

Friedman, Elise
The Black Cloister - Melanie Dobson   *i* 928

House, Brian
Obedience - Will Lavender   *c* 1061
Obedience - Will Lavender   *m* 118

Matthews, Kelsey
Seaview Inn - Sherryl Woods   *r* 399

STUDENT—GRADUATE

Josie
Playing - Melanie Abrams   *c* 1007

Kelly, Eloise
The Seduction of the Crimson Rose - Lauren Willig   *t* 901

Paoletti, Daniela
Vita Nuova - Magdalen Nabb   *m* 141

Upton, Willie
The Monsters of Templeton - Lauren Goff   *t* 815

STUDENT—HIGH SCHOOL

Miller, Eddie
Master of the Delta - Thomas H. Cook   *m* 47

Walcher, Lauren
Easy Innocence - Libby Fischer Hellmann   *m* 96

SUFFRAGETTE

Daye, Bertie
On Account of Conspicuous Women - Dawn Shamp   *t* 887

Donovan, Sarah
Chances - Pamela Nowak   *r* 356

Hooker, Isabella
Harriet and Isabella - Patricia O'Brien   *t* 865

SUPERNATURAL BEING

Lark
Sharp Teeth - Toby Barlow   *h* 567

Schuyler, Jason
Blood Noir - Laurell K. Hamilton   *h* 597

Wickman
Queen of Blood - Bryan Smith   *h* 639

SURVIVOR

Branning, Deni
Dawn's Light - Terri Blackstock   *i* 911

Hancock, Lana
No Control - Shannon K. Butcher   *r* 233

Jennings, Vince
Shadows in the Rain: A Tale of Old Klamath, California - R. Joe King   *w* 435

Mullen, Brian
Scared to Live - Stephen Booth   *m* 22

Raines, Ben
Out of the Ashes - William W. Johnstone   *w* 428

TEACHER

Argeneau, Victor
The Accidental Vampire - Lynsay Sands   *r* 372

Bane, Darth
Rule of Two - Drew Karpyshyn   *s* 697

Branch, Jack
Master of the Delta - Thomas H. Cook   *m* 47

Caldwell, Katherine
The Prince of Bagram Prison - Alex Carr   *m* 37

Chatham, Jane
His Dark and Dangerous Ways - Edith Layton   *r* 325

Critchley, Dorcas
Goodbye, Ms. Chips - Dorothy Cannell   *m* 36

Dare, Madeline
The Crazy School - Cornelia Read   *m* 153

Demidov, Raisa
Child 44 - Tom Rob Smith   *m* 171

Goldstein, Bobby
An Ordinary Spy - Joseph Weisberg   *m* 188

Hanover, Gretchen
A Mile in My Flip-Flops - Melody Carlson   *i* 918

Hastings, Jason
Better Than - Leslie Esdaile   *r* 260

Henry, Corey
Jackalope Dreams - Mary Clearman Blew   *w* 404

Hutton, Phillip
The Gift of Rain - Tan Twan Eng   *c* 1034

Jasper
Quakeland - Francesca Lia Block   *c* 1015

Lanisell, Rima
Wit's End - Karen Joy Fowler   *c* 1040

Lord, Donna
A Darker Side - Shirley Wells   *m* 189

Madison, Willow
Twice Loved - Lori Copeland   *i* 924

Martin, Claudia
Simply Perfect - Mary Balogh   *r* 208

Mitter, Janek
Mind's Eye - Hakan Nesser   *m* 142

Morgan, Claire
Marked by Moonlight - Sharie Kohler   *r* 317

Morrow, Jeff
Kethani - Eric Brown   *s* 670

Ruttenberg, Mark
An Ordinary Spy - Joseph Weisberg   *m* 188

Shanklin, Agnes
Dreamers of the Day - Mary Doria
    Russell   *t* 883

Weir, Agnes
Trauma - Patrick McGrath   *h* 625

Yussef, Omar
A Grave in Gaza - Matt Beynon Rees   *m* 155

TECHNICIAN

Descanso, Grace
The Timer Game - Susan Arnout Smith   *m* 170

Hanson, Rita
Chasing Cans - Laura Crum   *m* 49

TEENAGER

Aldridge, Lewis
The Outcast - Sadie Jones   *t* 842

Anderson, Wendy
Ghostgirl - Tonya Hurley   *h* 606

Baye, Adam
Hold Tight - Harlan Coben   *m* 41

Bentley, Dora
Diamonds in the Dust - Beryl Matthews   *t* 855

Branning, Beth
Dawn's Light - Terri Blackstock   *i* 911

Bravo, Sonny
The Flowers - Dagoberto Gilb   *w* 418

Bullock, Tracy
The Bone Box - Bob Hostetler   *i* 948

Burton, Chloe
Fatal Deduction - Gayle Roper   *i* 984

Car
All Souls - Christine Schutt   *c* 1087

Cindella
Saga - Conor Kostick   *s* 702

Dan
The Valley-Westside War - Harry
    Turtledove   *s* 744

Danvers, Claire
Feast of Fools - Rachel Caine   *h* 573

Davinovitch, Rhiana
The Edge of Reason - Melinda Snodgrass   *f* 548

Dell, Astra
All Souls - Christine Schutt   *c* 1087

Doggett, Ariel
Jackalope Dreams - Mary Clearman
    Blew   *w* 404

Dylan, Damen
Ghostgirl - Tonya Hurley   *h* 606

Fox, Jenna
The Adoration of Jenna Fox - Mary E.
    Pearson   *s* 722

Ghost
Saga - Conor Kostick   *s* 702

Glass, Jim
The Blue Door - Tony Earley   *t* 796

Glass, Michael
Feast of Fools - Rachel Caine   *h* 573

Grady, Grubbs
Demon Apocalypse - Darren Shan   *h* 636

Hall, Nicole
Desert Cut - Betty Webb   *m* 187

Hamilton, Rosie
A Girl Called Rosie - Anne Doughty   *t* 792

Handley, Jack
The Caddie Who Played with Hickory - John
    Coyne   *t* 783

Hazard-Perry, Oliver
Masquerade - Melissa de la Cruz   *f* 489

Heller, Amelia
Three Girls and Their Brother - Theresa
    Rebeck   *c* 1082

Heller, Daria
Three Girls and Their Brother - Theresa
    Rebeck   *c* 1082

Heller, Polly
Three Girls and Their Brother - Theresa
    Rebeck   *c* 1082

Justice
Flight - Sherman Alexie   *w* 400

Kayleen
Reading the Wind - Brenda Cooper   *s* 674

Kayna, Alison
Dragon and Liberator - Timothy Zahn   *s* 755

Kendall, Phoebe
Generation Dead - Daniel Waters   *h* 648

Langlander, Mimi
The Key to Rondo - Emily Rodda   *f* 544

Lee, Chelo
Reading the Wind - Brenda Cooper   *s* 674

Lee, Joseph
Reading the Wind - Brenda Cooper   *s* 674

Mallahide, Anna
Tim, Defender of the Earth - Sam
    Enthoven   *s* 684

Marlene
All Souls - Christine Schutt   *c* 1087

Martinsburg, Pete
Generation Dead - Daniel Waters   *h* 648

Maynard, Shelby "Turtle"
Blue Hole Back Home - Joy Jordan-Lake   *i* 952

Mendoza, Liz
The Valley-Westside War - Harry
    Turtledove   *s* 744

Miller, Charlotte
A Curse Dark as Gold - Elizabeth C.
    Bunce   *f* 479

Mitchell, Jake
The Restorer's Journey - Sharon Hinck   *i* 947

Montero, Ariella
The Year of Disappearances - Susan
    Hubbard   *h* 604

Morales, Alex
The Dead & the Gone - Susan Beth
    Pfeffer   *s* 725

Morales, Briana
The Dead & the Gone - Susan Beth
    Pfeffer   *s* 725

Morgan, Jack
Dragon and Liberator - Timothy Zahn   *s* 755

Morning Star
Noman - William Nicholson   *f* 533

Moulavi, Farsanna
Blue Hole Back Home - Joy Jordan-Lake   *i* 952

Mundi, Mariah
Mariah Mundi: The Midas Box - G.P.
    Taylor   *f* 553

Nash, Mercedes
The Paper Marriage - Susan Kay Law   *r* 324

Pathkendle, Pazel
The Red Wolf Conspiracy - Robert V.S.
    Redick   *f* 541

Pitman, Chris
Tim, Defender of the Earth - Sam
    Enthoven   *s* 684

Riley, Brian
Death Song - Michael McGarrity   *m* 131

Rook
Havemercy - Jaida Jones   *f* 513

Rosser, Eve
Feast of Fools - Rachel Caine   *h* 573

Seeker After Truth
Noman - William Nicholson   *f* 533

Shapiro, Joy
Certain Girls - Jennifer Weiner   *c* 1101

Shiloh
Dragon Mage - Andre Norton   *f* 534

Simmons, Hannah
The Sweetgum Knit Lit Society - Beth
    Pattillo   *i* 973

Spellman, Rae
Curse of the Spellmans - Lisa Lutz   *m* 127
Curse of the Spellmans - Lisa Lutz   *c* 1063

Springer, Autumn
The Year of Disappearances - Susan
    Hubbard   *h* 604

Steppe, Chrissie
The Blue Door - Tony Earley   *t* 796

Stone, Elisha
The Expeditions - Karl Iagnemma   *t* 837

Stratton, Robert
The Shanghai Tunnel - Sharan Newman   *m* 143

Sweets, Thelma Lee
Of Blood and Sorrow - Valerie Wilson
    Wesley   *m* 190

Thorne, Ned
Shavetail - Thomas Cobb   *t* 780

Tierney, Prescott
Skinny Dipping - Connie Brockway   *r* 232

Tommy
Of Men and Their Mothers - Mameve
    Medwed   *c* 1067

Tremain, Dev
Belong to Me - Marisa de los Santos   *c* 1030

Tristan
Lush Life - Richard Price   *c* 1081

Usher, Charlotte
Ghostgirl - Tonya Hurley   *h* 606

Van Alen, Schuyler
Masquerade - Melissa de la Cruz   *f* 489

Waller, Seth
The Story of Forgetting - Stefan Merrill
    Block   *c* 1016

Wildman
Noman - William Nicholson   *f* 533

Williams, Tommy
Generation Dead - Daniel Waters   *h* 648

VAMPIRE

Argeneau, Bastien
Vampires Are Forever - Lynsay Sands   h 635

Argeneau, Marguerite
Vampire, Interrupted - Lynsay Sands   h 634
Vampire, Interrupted - Lynsay Sands   r 373

Argeneau, Thomas
Vampires Are Forever - Lynsay Sands   h 635

Argeneau, Victor
The Accidental Vampire - Lynsay Sands   r 372

Black, Dorian
Dark of the Moon - Susan Krinard   r 319

Black, Elvi
The Accidental Vampire - Lynsay Sands   r 372

Blake, Anita
Blood Noir - Laurell K. Hamilton   h 597

Bones
One Foot in the Grave - Jeaniene Frost   h 588

Brigitte
Hungers of the Heart - Jenna Black   h 569

Cormel, Rynn
The Outlaw Demon Wails - Kim Harrison   h 599

d'Agelet, Helene
Bond of Fire - Diane Whiteside   r 391

Dark, Ronan
Dead Perfect - Amanda Ashley   r 204

D'Artigo, Menolly
Darkling - Yasmine Galenorn   f 500

Dashbrooke, William
Let the Night Begin - Kathryn Smith   h 642

Donahue, Patsy
Because Your Vampire Said So - Michele
   Bardsley   r 211

Dracula
Key to Conspiracy - Talia Gryphon   f 508

Dracula, Vlad
Midnight's Daughter - Karen Chance   h 578

Drake
Hungers of the Heart - Jenna Black   r 223

Drake, Jonathan
Hungers of the Heart - Jenna Black   h 569

Faith
Hungers of the Heart - Jenna Black   r 223

Force, Mimi
Masquerade - Melissa de la Cruz   f 489

Gabriel
Hungers of the Heart - Jenna Black   h 569

Gavin, Olivia
Let the Night Begin - Kathryn Smith   h 642

Glass, Michael
Feast of Fools - Rachel Caine   h 573

Gomez, Felix
The Undead Kama Sutra - Mario
   Acevedo   h 561

Gregorivich, Nikolai
50 Ways to Hex Your Lover - Linda
   Wisdom   r 397

Hazard-Perry, Oliver
Masquerade - Melissa de la Cruz   f 489

Heart, Jack
Lover's Bite - Maggie Shayne   r 378

Jean-Claude
Blood Noir - Laurell K. Hamilton   h 597

Leclerq, Sophie-Anne
From Dead to Worse - Charlaine Harris   h 598

Louis-Cesare
Midnight's Daughter - Karen Chance   h 578

MacKenzie, Declan
One Bite Stand - Nina Bangs   r 209

Marinelli, Francesca
La Vida Vampire - Nancy Haddock   r 279

Mircea
Embrace the Night - Karen Chance   f 483

Notte, Christian
Vampire, Interrupted - Lynsay Sands   h 634

Notte, Julius
Vampire, Interrupted - Lynsay Sands   h 634
Vampire, Interrupted - Lynsay Sands   r 373

Phury
Lover Enshrined - J.R. Ward   r 388

Rachlav, Aleksei
Key to Conspiracy - Talia Gryphon   f 508

Reign
Let the Night Begin - Kathryn Smith   h 642

Saint-Germain
A Dangerous Climate - Chelsea Quinn
   Yarbro   h 653

St. Just, Jean-Marie
Bond of Fire - Diane Whiteside   r 391

Topaz
Lover's Bite - Maggie Shayne   r 378

Van Alen, Schuyler
Masquerade - Melissa de la Cruz   f 489

Wroth, Conrad
Dark Deeds at Night's Edge - Kresley
   Cole   r 245

VAMPIRE HUNTER

Blake, Anita
Blood Noir - Laurell K. Hamilton   h 597

Gardella Grantworth de Lacy, Victoria
The Bleeding Dusk - Colleen Gleason   r 272

Pesaro, Maximilian
The Bleeding Dusk - Colleen Gleason   r 272

VETERAN

Gray, Bennett
Touchstone - Laurie R. King   m 114

Grimes, Patrick
Blood Alley - Tom Coffey   m 42

Palmer, Jason
At the City's Edge - Marcus Sakey   m 160

Perkins, Tyler
Wind River - Tom Morrisey   i 969

VETERINARIAN

Haristeen, Pharamond
The Purrfect Murder - Rita Mae Brown   m 31

McCarthy, Gail
Chasing Cans - Laura Crum   m 49

Shepherd, Noah
Snowfall at Willow Lake - Susan Wiggs   r 392

VIDEO GAME PLAYER

Dark Queen
Saga - Conor Kostick   s 702

VIGILANTE

Carlos
Beating the Devil - W.C. Jameson   w 426

Chavez
Beating the Devil - W.C. Jameson   w 426

VOLUNTEER

Boaz, Jacyn
Hellbent & Heartfirst - Kassandra Sims   r 380

WAITER/WAITRESS

Andahar, Lucia Maria "Luce"
The Healer - Sharon Sala   r 371

Araminta
The Dreaming Void - Peter F. Hamilton   s 690

Culpepper, Wanda Nell
Bring Your Own Poison - Jimmie Ruth
   Evans   m 66

Edwards, Erin
Turning Tables - Heather MacDowell   c 1065

Erneste
A Perfect Waiter - Alain Claude Sulzer   c 1095

Poole, Cato
Turning Tables - Heather MacDowell   c 1065

Rosie
Fiddle Game - Richard A. Thompson   m 182

Shaw, Roxanne
The Folks 2 - Ray Garton   h 590

Stackhouse, Sookie
From Dead to Worse - Charlaine Harris   h 598

Williams, Eva
The Demon of Dakar - Kjell Eriksson   m 62

WANDERER

Alvord, George
Blood on the Rimrock - Phil Dunlap   w 413

Old White
People of the Weeping Eye - W. Michael
   Gear   t 812

Sartain, Kim
Grub Line Rider - Louis L'Amour   w 436

WARD

Armistead, Georgiana
A Flaw in the Blood - Stephanie Barron   m 16

Desiree
Danger's Kiss - Sarah McKerrigan   r 349

WARRIOR

Aeneas
Lavinia - Ursula K. Le Guin   t 848

Anji
Shadow Gate - Kate Elliott   f 495

Barak
The Triumph of Deborah - Eva
   Etzioni-Halevy   t 801

Black Lion
The Last Warrior - Karen Kay   r 309

Blackhammer, Bolak
The Golden Cord - Paul Genesse   f 501

Bloodstone, Drake
The Golden Cord - Paul Genesse   f 501

Bolldhe
A Fire in the North - David Bilsborough   f 472

Cumac
Seekers of the Chalice - Brian Cullen   f 486

dan Luthar, Jezal
Last Argument of Kings - Joe Abercrombie   f 461

Morgan, Meredith
The Guardians - Jack Cavanaugh *i* 921

Murdoch, Julia
Miss Julia Paints the Town - Ann B. Ross *c* 1083

Murphy, Annabelle
The Art of Keeping Secrets - Patti Callahan Henry *r* 291

Parronley, Marlena
The Vanishing Viscountess - Diane Gaston *r* 269

Raymond, Delilah Mathers
The River Nymph - Shirl Henke *r* 290

Sinclair, Adrian
For Pete's Sake - Linda Windsor *i* 1005

Stratton, Emily
The Shanghai Tunnel - Sharan Newman *t* 863
The Shanghai Tunnel - Sharan Newman *m* 143

Swanson, Rick
Stargazer - Amanda Harte *r* 288

Turner, Carolyn
Confessions at Midnight - Jacquie D'Alessandro *r* 250

Twigg, Jane
Mighty Old Bones - Mary Saums *m* 163

Twistle, Phoebe
Mighty Old Bones - Mary Saums *m* 163

Walker, Portia
Bedding the Baron - Deborah Raleigh *r* 366

Wilde, Georgiana
The Kiss - Sophia Nash *r* 353

Willis, Ethan
The Renovation - Terri Kraus *i* 956

WITCH

Angelline, Jaenelle
Tangled Webs - Anne Bishop *f* 473

Annie
The 5th Witch - Graham Masterton *h* 624

cu'Seranta, Ana
A Magic of Twilight - S.L. Farrell *f* 498

D'Artigo, Camille
Darkling - Yasmine Galenorn *f* 500

Dumas, Rebecca
The Last Vampire - Patricia Rosemoor *h* 632

MacKay, Deidra
My Immortal Protector - Jen Holling *r* 293

Metcalf, Molly
Daemons Are Forever - Simon R. Green *f* 504

Monahan, Thomas
Witch Blood - Anya Bast *r* 215

Morgan, Rachel
The Outlaw Demon Wails - Kim Harrison *h* 599

Novak, Isabelle
Witch Blood - Anya Bast *r* 215

Olsen, Julie
Magic Burns - Ilona Andrews *f* 464

Phillips, Sunshine
With Every Breath - Lynn Kurland *r* 320

Tremaine, Jasmine "Jazz"
50 Ways to Hex Your Lover - Linda Wisdom *r* 397

Wentworth, Hannah
Shadow Magic - Cheyenne McCray *r* 347

WIZARD

Arontala, Foor
The Blood King - Gail Z. Martin *f* 525

Asvald
Battle Dragon - Edo van Belkom *f* 555

Auerbach, Lothar
Masters of Magic - Chris Wraight *f* 559

Beranabus
Demon Apocalypse - Darren Shan *h* 636

Dresden, Harry
Small Favor - Jim Butcher *h* 572
Small Favor - Jim Butcher *f* 480

Drood, Eddie
Daemons Are Forever - Simon R. Green *f* 504

Grey, Connor
Unquiet Dreams - Mark Del Franco *f* 490

Joachim, Marius
Masters of Magic - Chris Wraight *f* 559

Peredur
The Golden Rose - Kathleen Bryan *f* 478

Salthir, Artil im
The Summer Palace - Lawrence Watt-Evans *f* 557

Tasca, Jallal
Obsidian Ridge - Jess Lebow *f* 520

Xeries
Obsidian Ridge - Jess Lebow *f* 520

WORKER

Blair, Tim
The Wannoshay Cycle - Michael Jasper *s* 694

Dawsey, Perry
Infected - Scott Sigler *s* 736

DeSmit, Julia
Summer Snow - Nicole Baart *i* 908

Gibson, Larry
Kill Whitey - Brian Keene *h* 612

March, Casey
The Ninth Circle - Alex Bell *f* 470

McLeod, Duncan
Cold Plague - Daniel Kalla *s* 696

Nikandra
Bring Down the Sun - Judith Tarr *f* 552

Pavel
The Romanov Bride - Robert Alexander *t* 759

Roi
Incandescence - Greg Egan *s* 683

Zak
Incandescence - Greg Egan *s* 683

WRITER

Amanda
Enlightenment for Idiots - Anne Cushman *c* 1026

Becket, Monte
So Brave, Young and Handsome - Leif Enger *c* 1035
So Brave, Young and Handsome - Leif Enger *t* 798
So Brave, Young and Handsome - Leif Enger *w* 415

Berger, Wencke
What Never Happens - Anne Holt *m* 102

Brik, Vladimir
The Lazarus Project - Aleksandar Hemon *t* 832

Bronte, Anne
The Secret Adventures of Charlotte Bronte - Laura Joh Rowland *t* 881
The Secret Adventures of Charlotte Bronte - Laura Joh Rowland *c* 1084

Bronte, Charlotte
The Secret Adventures of Charlotte Bronte - Laura Joh Rowland *c* 1084
The Secret Adventures of Charlotte Bronte - Laura Joh Rowland *t* 881

Bronte, Emily
The Secret Adventures of Charlotte Bronte - Laura Joh Rowland *c* 1084

Brook, Sid
Beverly Hills Dead - Stuart Woods *t* 904

Caine, Hall
The Dracula Dossier - James Reese *h* 631

Chekhov, Anton
The Woman Who Wouldn't - Gene Wilder *t* 899

Chiara, Nora
Trauma - Patrick McGrath *h* 625

Clemens, Samuel
Becky - Lenore Hart *t* 831

Darcy, Antonia
Assassins at Ospreys - R.T. Raichev *m* 151

Dark, Ronan
Dead Perfect - Amanda Ashley *r* 204

Dickinson, Emily
Wild Nights! - Joyce Carol Oates *t* 864

Doyle, Arthur Conan
Oscar Wilde and a Death of No Importance - Gyles Brandreth *t* 772

Early, Addison
Wit's End - Karen Joy Fowler *c* 1040

Evans, Marian
The World Before Her - Deborah Weisgall *t* 897

Felton, Sherry
The Sudoku Puzzle Murders - Parnell Hall *m* 93

Fitzgerald, Johnny
Death on the Holy Mountain - David Dickinson *m* 55

Ford, Benjamin
Dear American Airlines - Jonathan Miles *c* 1069

Frost, Robert
Fall of Frost - Brian Hall *t* 825

Gibson, Alex
The Chorister at the Abbey - Lis Howell *m* 105

Hopkins, Gerard Manley
The Exiles - Ron Hansen *t* 829

Hunter, R.S.
The House at Riverton - Kate Morton *t* 860

James, Henry
The James Boys - Richard Liebmann-Smith *t* 851
The Open Door - Elizabeth Maguire *t* 854
Wild Nights! - Joyce Carol Oates *t* 864

Jordan
Imagine Me and You - Billy Mernit *c* 1068

Kennedy, Jill
A Darker Side - Shirley Wells *m* 189

Kline, Maggie
The Ghost and the Femme Fatale - Alice Kimberly *m* 113

Lawrence, T.E.
Dreamers of the Day - Mary Doria Russell *t* 883

Leo
Love the One You're With - Emily Giffin *c* 1046

Lomax, Ellen
Thieving Fear - Ramsey Campbell *h* 576

Machiavelli, Niccollo
The Enchantress of Florence - Salman Rushdie *t* 882

Maddox, Shari
Wearing My Halo Tilted - Stephanie Perry Moore *i* 966

McClelland, Marjorie
Shadow Waltz - Amy Patricia Meade *m* 135

Miller, James
Isolation - Travis Thrasher *i* 999

Nasr, Maria
Ghost Walk - Brian Keene *h* 611

Poe, Edgar Allan
Wild Nights! - Joyce Carol Oates *t* 864

Rane, John
South of Shiloh - Chuck Logan *m* 124

Scott, Helen
The Salisbury Manuscript - Philip Gooden *m* 86

Shakespeare, William
Ink and Steel - Elizabeth Bear *f* 469

Sherard, Robert
Oscar Wilde and a Death of No Importance - Gyles Brandreth *m* 27
Oscar Wilde and a Death of No Importance - Gyles Brandreth *t* 772

Stoker, Bram
The Dracula Dossier - James Reese *h* 631

Stowe, Harriet Beecher
Harriet and Isabella - Patricia O'Brien *t* 865

Tey, Josephine
Expert in Murder - Nicola Upson *t* 893

Tredown, Owen
Not in The Flesh - Ruth Rendell *m* 157

Webb, Marshall
Streets of Fire - Troy Soos *m* 172

Whitman, Walt
Two Brothers: One North, One South - David H. Jones *t* 841

Wilde, Oscar
Oscar Wilde and a Death of No Importance - Gyles Brandreth *m* 27
Oscar Wilde and a Death of No Importance - Gyles Brandreth *t* 772

Wise, Marquis
Black Will Shoot - Jesse Washington *c* 1100

Woolson, Constance Fenimore
The Open Door - Elizabeth Maguire *t* 854

YOUNG MAN

DeCosta, Angus
Blood Harvest - Brant Randall *t* 876

Herrera, Jose
Brittan - Debra White Smith *i* 991

Jack
To Trust - Carolyn Brown *w* 409

Pelham, Troy
Love Is Not Enough - Anne Herries *t* 833

Rose, Birch
Ride the Trail of Death - Kenneth L. Kieser *w* 433

Sawyer, Tom
Becky - Lenore Hart *t* 831

Sayer, Andy
The Folks 2 - Ray Garton *h* 590

Sunnedon, Jared
The Sundown Man - Jory Sherman *w* 453

Timothy
Fires Rising - Michael Laimo *h* 617

YOUNG WOMAN

Allende, Rosa Maria
Trail Hand - R.W. Stone *w* 456

Annamaria
Odd Hours - Dean R. Koontz *h* 616

Bellamy, Lydia
Sisters of Fortune - Frances McNeil *t* 857

Benedict, Elysee
Once Smitten, Twice Shy - Lori Wilde *r* 393

Boone, Jacqueline "Jack"
Luck - Max Brand *w* 406

Caldwell, Grace "Merle Raye Finkel"
A Stranger's Game - Joan Johnston *w* 427

Collins, Charlotte
The Darcy Connection - Elizabeth Aston *c* 1010

Collins, Eliza
The Darcy Connection - Elizabeth Aston *c* 1010

Culpepper, Denny
Return of the Stardust Cowgirl - Marsha Moyer *w* 442

Cyrla
My Enemy's Cradle - Sara Young *t* 905

Dandridge, Molly
Marshal Sands and Mrs. Molly - V.E. Bixenstine *w* 403

Daurignac, Therese
A Secret Inheritance - Elizabeth Lord *t* 853

Delancey, Laura
A Perfect Revenge - Annabel Dilke *t* 788

Dera
Elom - William H. Drinkard *f* 492

DiCamillo, Lucy
Ruby among Us - Tina Ann Forkner *i* 934

Ericson, Hannah Swartz
Anathema - Colleen Coble *i* 922

Harp, Evelina
The Plague of Doves - Louise Erdrich *w* 416

Hooper, Dee
To Trust - Carolyn Brown *w* 409

Hope, Gabrielle
The Outsider - Ann H. Gabhart *i* 935

Lewis, Sarah
Resistance - Owen Sheers *t* 888
Resistance - Owen Sheers *s* 735

Loftis, Guerine
On Account of Conspicuous Women - Dawn Shamp *t* 887

Lovat, Julia
The Tenth Gift - Jane Johnson *t* 840

Lyles, Neanna
Hush My Mouth - Cathy Pickens *w* 445

Mar
Cathedral of the Sea - Ildefonso Falcones *t* 802

Masson, Eva
The Girl from Wish Lane - Anne Douglas *t* 793

McCall, Rose
Killing Rommel - Steven Pressfield *t* 875

McKay, Jackie Sue
Blood Harvest - Brant Randall *t* 876

Moran, Sophie
Sisters of Fortune - Frances McNeil *t* 857

Morton, Nabby
Bound - Sally Gunning *t* 821

Mya
The Jewel Trader of Pegu - Jeffrey Hantover *t* 830

O'Connor, Charity
A Passion Redeemed - Julie Lessman *i* 958

Rosenfeld, Miriam
Silesian Station - David Downing *t* 795

Rosewell, Ann
Courting Shadows - Jem Poster *t* 874

Shaw, Hester
Fateful Voyage - Pamela Oldfield *t* 866

Silverton, Bethany
Wagered Heart - Robin Lee Hatcher *i* 941

Spreckelmeyer, Essie
Courting Trouble - Deeanne Gist *w* 419

Stewart, Lacey
The Redemption of Jake Scully - Elaine Barbieri *i* 909

Sunnedon, Kate
The Sundown Man - Jory Sherman *w* 453

Thatcher, Becky
Becky - Lenore Hart *t* 831

Tregenna, Catherine Ann
The Tenth Gift - Jane Johnson *t* 840

Trenwith, Marianne
Love Is Not Enough - Anne Herries *t* 833

Trenwith, Sarah
Love Is Not Enough - Anne Herries *t* 833

Two Petals
People of the Weeping Eye - W. Michael Gear *t* 812

ZEALOT

Fiveash, Julia
Weaver - Stephen Baxter *s* 665

Rahim, Abbas
The Amateur Spy - Dan Fesperman *m* 69

Author Index

This index is an alphabetical listing of the authors of books featured in entries and those listed within entries under the rubrics "Other books by the same author" and "Other books you might like." For each author, the titles of books described or listed in this edition and their entry numbers appear. Bold numbers indicate a featured main entry; light-face numbers refer to books recommended for further reading.

Author Index

Author Index

Author Index

Author Index

Author Index

Title Index

This index alphabetically lists all titles featured in entries and those listed within entries under "Other books by the same author" and "Other books you might like." Each title is followed by the author's name and the number of the entry where the book is described or listed. Bold numbers indicate featured main entries; light-face numbers refer to books recommended for further reading.

Title Index

Title Index

Title Index

Title Index

Title Index

Title Index

Title Index

Title Index

G

Title Index

Title Index

Title Index

Title Index

Title Index

Title Index

Title Index

Title Index

Title Index

Title Index

Title Index

Title Index

Title Index